ENCYCLOPEDIA OF
WORLD BIOGRAPHY
SUPPLEMENT

22

ENCYCLOPEDIA OF
WORLD BIOGRAPHY

SUPPLEMENT

$$\dfrac{A}{Z} \quad \mathbf{22}$$

GALE®

THOMSON
™
GALE

Detroit • New York • San Diego • San Francisco • Cleveland • New Haven, Conn. • Waterville, Maine • London • Munich

Encyclopedia of World Biography Supplement, Volume 22

Project Editor
Andrea Kovacs Henderson

Editorial
Laura Avery, Luann Brennan, Leigh Ann DeRemer, Jennifer Mossman, Tracie Ratiner

Editorial Support Services
Andrea Lopeman

Permissions
Margaret Chamberlain

Imaging and Multimedia
Robert Duncan, Leitha Etheridge-Sims, Lezlie Light, Dan Newell, David G. Oblender, Robyn V. Young

Manufacturing
Stacey Melson

ISBN 0-7876-5284-9
ISSN 1099-7326

Printed in the United States of America
10 9 8 7 6 5 4 3 2 1

CONTENTS

The study of biography has always held an important, if not explicitly stated, place in school curricula. The absence in schools of a class specifically devoted to studying the lives of the giants of human history belies the focus most courses have always had on people. From ancient times to the present, the world has been shaped by the decisions, philosophies, inventions, discoveries, artistic creations, medical breakthroughs, and written works of its myriad personalities. Librarians, teachers, and students alike recognize that our lives are immensely enriched when we learn about those individuals who have made their mark on the world we live in today.

Encyclopedia of World Biography Supplement, Volume 22, provides biographical information on 200 individuals not covered in the 17-volume second edition of *Encyclopedia of World Biography (EWB)* and its supplements, Volumes 18, 19, 20, and 21. Like other volumes in the *EWB* series, this supplement represents a unique, comprehensive source for biographical information on those people who, for their contributions to human culture and society, have reputations that stand the test of time. Each original article ends with a bibliographic section. There is also an index to names and subjects, which cumulates all persons appearing as main entries in the *EWB* second edition, the Volume 18, 19, 20, and 21 supplements, and this supplement—nearly 8,000 people!

Articles. Arranged alphabetically following the letter-by-letter convention (spaces and hyphens have been ignored), articles begin with the full name of the person profiled in large, bold type. Next is a boldfaced, descriptive paragraph that includes birth and death years in parentheses. It provides a capsule identification and a statement of the person's significance. The essay that follows is approximately 2000 words in length and offers a substantial treatment of the person's life. Some of the essays proceed chronologically while others confine biographical data to a paragraph or two and move on to a consideration and evaluation of the subject's work. Where very few biographical facts are known, the article is necessarily devoted to an analysis of the subject's contribution.

Following the essay is a bibliographic section arranged by source type. Citations include books, periodicals, and online Internet addresses for World Wide Web pages, where current information can be found.

Portraits accompany many of the articles and provide either an authentic likeness, contemporaneous with the subject, or a later representation of artistic merit. For artists, occasionally self-portraits have been included. Of the ancient figures, there are depictions from coins, engravings, and sculptures; of the moderns, there are many portrait photographs.

Index. The *EWB Supplement* index is a useful key to the encyclopedia. Persons, places, battles, treaties, institutions, buildings, inventions, books, works of art, ideas, philosophies, styles, movements—all are indexed for quick reference just as in a general encyclopedia. The index entry for a person includes a brief identification with birth and death dates *and* is cumulative so that any person for whom an article was written who appears in the second edition of *EWB* (volumes 1-16) and its supplements (volumes 18-22) can be located. The subject terms within the index, however, apply only to volume 22. Every index reference includes the title of the article to which the reader is being directed as well as the volume and page numbers.

Because *EWB Supplement,* Volume 22, is an encyclopedia of biography, its index differs in important ways from the indexes to other encyclopedias. Basically, this is an index of people, and that fact has several interesting consequences. First, the information to which the index refers the reader on a particular topic is always about people associated with that topic. Thus the entry 'Quantum theory (physics)' lists articles on people associated with quantum theory. Each article may discuss a person's contribution to quantum theory, but no single article or group of articles is intended to provide a comprehensive treatment of quantum theory as such. Second, the index is rich in classified entries. All persons who are subjects of articles in the encyclopedia, for example, are listed in one or more classifications in the index—abolitionists, astronomers, engineers, philosophers, zoologists, etc.

The index, together with the biographical articles, make *EWB Supplement* an enduring and valuable source for biographical information. As school course work changes to reflect advances in technology and fur-

ther revelations about the universe, the life stories of the people who have risen above the ordinary and earned a place in the annals of human history will continue to fascinate students of all ages.

We Welcome Your Suggestions. Mail your comments and suggestions for enhancing and improving the *Encyclopedia of World Biography Supplement* to:

The Editors
Encyclopedia of World Biography Supplement
Gale Group
27500 Drake Road
Farmington Hills, MI 48331-3535
Phone: (800) 347-4253

ADVISORY BOARD

ACKNOWLEDGMENTS

Photographs and illustrations appearing in the *Encyclopedia of World Biography* Supplement, Volume 22, have been used with the permission of the following sources:

AP/WIDE WORLD PHOTOS: Abdullah II, Mortimer Adler, Steve Allen, Chet Atkins, Burt Bacharach, Leonard Baskin, Alan Bean, Charles William Beebe, Osama bin Laden, Leonardo Boff, Bennett Cerf, Eugene Cernan, Jewel Plummer Cobb, Charles "Pete" Conrad, Colin Davis, Elmer Holmes Davis, Fats Domino, Thomas A. Dorsey, Dale Earnhardt, Marriner Stoddard Eccles, Judah Folkman, John Frederick Fuller, Casimir Funk, Robert Gallo, Erle Stanley Gardner, Dan George, Edith Hamilton, Lionel Hampton, Howard Hawks, Chester Himes, John Huston, John Irving, James Irwin, Garrison Keillor, Patrick Kelly, Walt Kelly, Jack Lemmon, Miriam Makeba, Walter Matthau, Edgar Dean Mitchell, Ashley Montagu, Willard Motley, Pervez Musharraf, Youssou N'Dour, Carroll O'Connor, John Joseph O'Connor, Grace Paley, Jean-Pierre Rampal, Nicholas Ray, Judith A. Resnik, Allan Rex Sandage, Harrison "Jack" Schmitt, Menachem Mendel Schneerson, William Schuman, George C. Scott, Eric Sevareid, Ravi Shankar, George Stevens, Roger Vadim, Richie Valens, Edward Bennett Williams, Mohammad Zahir Shah

JERRY BAUER: Andre Brink, Stanley Kunitz

CALIFORNIA ACADEMY OF SCIENCES/SPECIAL COLLECTIONS LIBRARY: Alice Eastwood

CATHOLIC NEWS SERVICE: Basil Cardinal Hume

BEVERLY CLEARY: Beverly Cleary

CORBIS: Claudio Abbado, Sofonisba Anguissola, Helena Petrovna Blavatsky, Louise Boyd, John Cabell Breckinridge, Thomas Alexander Browne, Edward Bulwer-Lytton, Emma Perry Carr, Joseph H. Choate, Rufus Choate, James Couzens, Tilly Edinger, John Arbuthnot Fisher, John Frankenheimer, Alfred Mossman Landon, Tom Landry, Marie Lavoisier, Jacques Loeb, Reinhold Messner, Dhan Gopal Mukerji, Christabel Pankhurst, Mary E. Pennington, Jean Renoir, John Ross, Joan Sutherland, Gustavus Franklin Swift, Pinchas Zukerman

DOVER PUBLICATIONS: David Einhorn, Robert Henri

FISK UNIVERSITY LIBRARY: Juliette Derricotte, Robert Hayden

MARK GERSON: Dan Jacobson

GETTY IMAGES: Vladimir Ashkenazy, Sidney Bechet, Harrison Birtwistle, Isabel Bishop, Edward William Bok, Henry Brougham, Jose Carreras, Alfred Denning, Thomas Erskine, James Harper, Buddy Holly, William Johnson, Montezuma I, F. W. Murnau, William Pinkney, Thomas Alexander Scott, Thomas Sully, Lawrence Welk

THE GRANGER COLLECTION: Gabrielle-Emilie du Chatelet, Thomas McIntyre Cooley, Anna J. Cooper, Ellen Craft, Grenville Mellen Dodge, Artemisia Gentileschi, Henry Osborne Havemeyer, Elwood Haynes, Hildegard von Bingen, Sofya Kovalevskaya, Biddy Mason

THE KOBAL COLLECTION: John Cassavetes, Carl Dreyer, Max Fleischer, Juzo Itami, Sidney Lumet, Jason Robards, Jacques Tati, William Wyler, Loretta Young

THE LIBRARY OF CONGRESS: Gracie Allen, Gertrude Bell, John Shaw Billings, Joseph P. Bradley, Henry Wager Halleck, William Stewart Halsted, James Longstreet, John Rollin Ridge

ROBERT P. MATTHEWS: John Nash

MT. HOLYOKE COLLEGE ARCHIVE: Helen Sawyer Hogg

NATIONAL ARCHIVES AND RECORDS ADMINISTRATION: William J. Donovan, Charles Lee

NATIONAL BASEBALL LIBRARY AND ARCHIVE: Kenesaw Mountain Landis

PUBLIC DOMAIN: Aspasia, Ishi

JOHN REEVES: Mordecai Richler

THE SOPHIA SMITH COLLECTION: Florence Bascom

The following people, appearing in volumes 1-21 of the *Encyclopedia of World Biography,* have died since the publication of the second edition and its supplements. Each entry lists the volume where the full biography can be found.

BARNARD, CHRISTIAAN N. (born 1922), South African surgeon, died in Paphos, Cyprus, on September 2, 2001 (Vol. 2).

BERLE, MILTON (born 1908), American entertainer and actor, died in Los Angeles, California, on March 27, 2002 (Vol. 18).

BIRENDRA (born 1945), Nepalese king, died on June 1, 2001 (Vol. 2).

BLOCK, HERBERT (born 1909), American newspaper cartoonist, died of pneumonia in Washington, D.C. on October 7, 2001 (Vol. 2).

CAMPOS, ROBERTO OLIVEIRA (born 1917), Brazilian economist and diplomat, died of heart failure in Rio de Janeiro, Brazil, on October 9, 2001 (Vol. 18).

ELIZABETH BOWES-LYON (born 1900), queen and queen mother of Great Britain, died in Windsor, England, on March 30, 2002 (Vol. 5).

GRAHAM, KATHARINE MEYER (born 1917), American publisher, died in Boise, Idaho, on July 17, 2001 (Vol. 6).

HUSSEINI, FAISAL (born 1940), Palestinian political leader, died of heart failure in Kuwait on May 31, 2001 (Vol. 19).

KYPRIANOU, SPYROS (born 1932), Republic of Cyprus president, died of cancer in Nicosia, Cyprus, on March 12, 2002 (Vol. 9).

ONG TENG CHEONG (born 1936), Singaporean president, died of lymphoma on February 8, 2002 (Vol. 11).

PAZ ESTENSSORO, VICTOR (born 1907), Bolivian statesman, died of complications of a severe blood clot in Tarija, Bolivia, on June 7, 2001 (Vol. 12).

PEREZ JIMENEZ, MARCOS (born 1914), Venezuelan dictator, died in Madrid, Spain, on September 20, 2001 (Vol. 12).

SAVIMBI, JONAS MALHEIROS (born 1934), Angolan leader, died in eastern Angola on February 22, 2002 (Vol. 13).

SULLIVAN, LEON HOWARD (born 1922), African American civil rights leader and minister, died of leukemia in Scottsdale, Arizona, on April 24, 2001 (Vol. 15).

THIEU, NGUYEN VAN (born 1923), South Vietnamese president, died in Boston, Massachusetts, on September 29, 2001 (Vol. 15).

THOMAS, DAVE (born 1932), American businessman, died of liver cancer in Ft. Lauderdale, Florida, on January 8, 2002 (Vol. 18).

WARMERDAM, DUTCH (born 1915), American pole vaulter, died in Fresno, California, on November 13, 2001 (Vol. 21).

Claudio Abbado

Italian-born conductor Claudio Abbado (born 1933) established a reputation for musical excellence on the fine edge between scholar and performing genius. A meticulous reader of scores, he mastered symphonic detail to such a degree that his conducting has often overshadowed the lead singers. Devoted to artistry, he has ventured beyond the safe German favorites—Johann Brahms, Wolfgang Amadeus Mozart, Robert Schumann, Richard Wagner—to modern opera by Luciano Berio, Pierre Boulez, Krzysztof Penderecki, Alfred Schnittke, and Karlheinz Stockhausen.

Born on June 26, 1933, in Milan, Abbado began training under his father, Michelangelo Abbado, before entering Milan's Giuseppe Verdi Conservatory to study piano. After graduation in 1955, he continued piano classes with Austrian concertist Friedrich Gulda and began learning conducting from Antonio Votto, a specialist in Italian symphonic music. Over the next three years, Abbado pursued conducting with Hans Swarowsky, conductor of the Vienna State Opera Orchestra. In class at the Vienna Academy of Music, Abbado sometimes sang in the Singverein choir under Herbert von Karajan, his mentor and role model. Abbado further refined his orchestral skills at the Accademia Chigiana in Siena under Alceo Galliera, conductor of the Philharmonia Orchestra, and Carlo Zecchi, leader of the Czech Philharmonic.

Attained a Balance

Abbado first took the baton at the Teatro Communale in Trieste, conducting Sergei Prokofiev's *Love for Three Oranges* at the age of 25. Still unpolished and uncertain of his own identity as an orchestral interpreter, Abbado displayed a mature regard for the markings of the composer's original score. Strong of arm, he forced both instrumentalists and singers to stay within the bounds of a precise, balanced presentation that was both historically correct and artistically pleasing.

Abbado's debut prefaced a noteworthy entrance into a profession that quickly introduced his promise to the world. At Tanglewood, home of the Boston Symphony Orchestra, he earned the Koussevitzky conducting prize in 1958. He first encountered American music lovers that April at a concert with the New York Philharmonic.

Broadened His Perspective

For Abbado's early mastery of a wide repertory of classical and romantic music, he won the Mitropoulos Prize for conducting in 1963, shared with Pedro Calderon and Zdenek Kosler, both older and more experienced artists. At the time, critical opinion had not reached a firm consensus on Abbado, but critics soon acknowledged that he possessed the talent of another Arturo Toscanini. In 1965, von Karajan signaled formal acceptance among the music community by introducing Abbado at the Salzburg Easter Festival conducting Mahler's *Second Symphony*. Abbado valued the older musician's guidance and compared him to a sage, compassionate father. After twelve years at the Teatro alla Scala, Abbado made a significant career move by leaving his country in 1965 to lead the Vienna Philharmonic. He returned in triumph in 1968 to become opera conductor of Milan's La Scala, the mecca of Italian opera.

Up the orchestral ladder, Abbado retained the respect of his peers by guest conducting for the London Symphony in 1972 and for a tour of China and Japan with the Vienna Philharmonic in 1972 and 1973. That same year, he won the Mozart Medal of the Mozart Gemeinde of Vienna. Entering his peak years, he took the La Scala company to the Soviet Union in 1974 and led the Vienna Philharmonic and the La Scala company in the United States in 1976.

Master of Self

The main attraction at an Abbado concert is leadership, a character trait he claims to have derived from Wilhelm Furtwangler, one of Germany's most beloved maestros. Unlike the prima donnas of an earlier generation, Abbado throws no tantrums, yet manages to elicit from orchestra, choir, and soloists a high quality of sound and delivery. With the caution of a true connoisseur of the arts, he subdues his urge to venture into individual interpretation by consistent reproduction of the original music.

Remaining at the head of La Scala until 1980, Abbado strove for new challenges. For programs such as the 1976 presentation of Verdi's *Simon Boccanegra* at London's Covent Garden, he earned praise for achievements that boosted the cast's reputation and elevated classical opera itself. Dissatisfied with seasons that polished old gems he insisted on breaking new ground with at least one new contemporary title each year. For his final production at La Scala, Abbado chose an original score of Peter Mussorgsky's *Boris Godunov,* which was repeated after his promotion to direc-

tor of the 1994 Salzburg Easter Festival. For the second performance, he arranged post-modern staging that echoed the demoralization of Russia in the mid-1990s.

International Star

Abbado's globe-trotting schedule has placed him before the world's major symphonies to direct a variety of demanding music. For all his promotion of a broad range of works, he has exhibited an affinity for Italy's beloved Giuseppe Verdi, whose works he interpreted before adoring fans at Covent Garden. Equally at home among opera lovers at the Kennedy Center in Washington, D.C., Abbado has developed style and performance capabilities that suit most opera houses. In Austria in the late 1980s, he led the Vienna State Opera in a virtuoso performance of Alban Berg's grimly atonal *Wozzeck,* the basis of a CD that collectors immediately ranked a classic.

Built Opera's Future

Energetic and visionary, Abbado began leaving his mark on the musical scene by establishing the European Community Youth Orchestra in 1978 and by conducting the Chamber Orchestra of Europe three years later. After serving as principal conductor of the London Symphony Orchestra in 1979, he earned the Golden Nicolai Medal of the Vienna Philharmonic the next year. In 1982, he established Milan's La Filarmonica della Scala. Returned to the United States, he was principal guest conductor of the Chicago Symphony from 1982 to 1986.

Late in the 1980s, Abbado kept up the pace of fine music by serving from 1983 to 1988 as the London Symphony Orchestra music director. He won the Gran Croce in 1984 and the Mahler Medal of Vienna the next year. Concurrently with his other projects, he assumed the baton of the Vienna State Opera in 1986, the year that he founded Vienna's Gustav Mahler Youth Orchestra. At his height, he received France's Legion d'Honneur in 1986. The following year, Abbado produced a masterful *Le Nozze di Figaro*, one of Mozart's most beloved works. In 1988, he established *Wien Modern*, an annual festival showcasing the contemporary arts.

A World-Class Conductor

In 1989, Abbado succeeded his friend and mentor Herbert von Karajan as the first Italian-born artistic director of the Berlin Philharmonic and inaugurated a twelve-year career marked by variety and flexibility unknown under past masters. Of his qualifications, a music critic at the *Economist* called him "reserved and outwardly unassuming but also intensely ambitious," perhaps in reference to his recording contracts with competitors Deutsche Grammophon and CBS/Sony. Instrumentalists under his direction discovered a taskmaster devoted to removing even a hint of imperfection or uncertainty with long hours of rehearsal and refinement. To ready the next generation of attentive musicians, in 1992, he collaborated with cellist Natalia Gutman in initiating the "Berlin Movement," an annual chamber music festival combining the talents of adult professionals with young and untried instrumentalists.

Left His Mark

Still perfecting his art, Abbado lent a professional touch to a delicately atmospheric 1993 performance of Claude Debussy's *Pelleas et Melisande;* a textured, intimate dramatization of Richard Strauss's *Elektra;* and a melodic 1995 performance of Robert Schumann's *Scenes from Goethe's Faust.* Abbado energized the 1996 Salzburg Easter Festival with a dynamic dramatization of Verdi's *Otello,* an operatic version of a moving Shakespearean tragedy. In 1998, Abbado continued to refresh musical favorites with a conscientiously lyric suite of Verdi arias, an energetic presentation of Felix Mendelssohn's *A Midsummer Night's Dream,* and a dramatic, unified rendering of Mozart's *Don Giovanni,* which Abbado enhanced with graceful embellishments to balance the terror of the protagonist's descent into Hell.

Retirement

As conductor of the Berlin Philharmonic, which most Europeans consider the height of orchestral attainment, Abbado astounded arm-chair critics by departing from the paths of his predecessors, Furtwangler and von Karajan. The fifth of five Berlin conductors, Abbado had made a smooth transition and promised ticket-holders a succession of inspired seasons. In 1998, he chose not to renew his contract. His resignation, effective in 2002, dismayed the German musical elite, who expected their maestros to die in office. To public consternation, he insisted on reserving more time for books, sailboats, and vacations on the ski slopes. Murmurs that he had grown slack sounded more like sour grapes than honest critiques of the man who had broadened the orchestra's horizons, hired younger instrumentalists, invited a higher percentage of female vocalists to perform, and occasionally lent his baton to star conductors as well as newcomers to the podium.

Maintained High Standards

In 1999, Abbado showed no sign of slowing down. He continued a demanding schedule of the best in symphonic music. He refined Wagner's *Tristan und Isolde* for the Salzburg Easter Festival and added to a growing canon of recordings an expert performance of Mahler's *Des Knaben Wunderhorn.* The new millennium brought additional treasures from Abbado, who performed Richard Strauss's works with superb emotional clarity, from languorous to passionate. In August, a public squabble with director Gerard Mortier caused the disbanding of a fine cast and prevented further staging of Verdi's *Simon Boccanegra.* Still very much in control, at the age of 68, Abbado again challenged his musicians to perform a spirited version of Verdi's *Falstaff,* which unsettled the audience with its rapid-fire phrasing.

Books

Almanac of Famous People, 7th ed. Gale Group, 2001.
Complete Marquis Who's Who, Marquis Who's Who, 2001.
Debrett's People of Today, Debrett's Peerage Ltd., 2001.
International Dictionary of Opera, 2 vols. St. James Press, 1993.

Periodicals

Christian Science Monitor, July 25, 1984.

The Economist, October 21, 1989; March 14, 1998.
The Independent (London), August 29, 1998.
National Review, July 14, 1989; July 9, 1990.
New York Times, March 1, 1987; October 9, 1989; November 8, 1989; February 28, 1991; October 11, 1991; May 8, 1992; May 12, 1992; May 24, 1992; January 17, 1993; October 24, 1993; October 30, 1993; November 2, 1993; April 9, 1994; June 26, 1994; March 14, 1996; March 15, 1996; October 4, 1996; October 5, 1996; October 9, 1996; December 29, 1996; August 2, 1998; October 1998; June 20, 1999; September 15, 1999; October 27, 1999.
Notes, December 1993.
Opera News, February 13, 1993; August 1993; September 1994; December 24, 1994; September 1995; October 1995; August 1996; January 11, 1997; August 1997; January 17, 1998; May 1998; December 1998; August 1999; October 1999; February 2000; August 2000; August 2001.
Wall Street Journal, December 13, 1989; March 13, 1996; October 9, 1996; November 10, 1999.

Online

"Claudio Abbado," *The Alden Theatre,* http://www.wgms.com/conductor_abbado.shtm (October 22, 2001).
"Claudio Abbado," *The Artistic Director,* http://berlin-philharmonic.com/engl/2orch/b20201c_.htm (October 22, 2001). □

Abdul-Baha

One in a series of four founders and shapers of a Muslim sect known as the Baha'is, Persian-born religious leader Abdul-Baha (1844-1921) perpetuated the teachings of his father, the Baha'u'llah, by becoming the community's third religious leader. Essential to Abdul-Baha's work as superintendent of the faith was the dissemination of the Baha'i message of world peace, justice, racial and gender equality, and the unity of all people. He composed a history of Baha'ism and spread its tenets throughout the Middle East, India, Burma, western Europe, the Americas, South Africa, and the Pacific rim.

Named Abbas Effendi in infancy, Abdul-Baha was marked from the beginning for a religious career. He was born on May 23, 1844, in Tehran, Persia (now Iran) on the day that Mirza Ali Muhammed of Shiraz, Persia, the self-proclaimed Bab (The Gate) and successor to Muhammed, launched the Baha'i faith. As the eldest son of Navvab and Mirza Husayn Ali, Abdul-Baha was prepared for leadership. He received a suitable education and encouragement to advance Baha'ism and to carry its beliefs to people beyond the Middle East.

After the Bab's execution in 1850 and the murder of some 20,000 followers, Abdul-Baha, then six years old, witnessed social instability and the persecution of his father and other religious leaders by Shi'ite Muslims. A mob overran and pillaged the family home, forcing them into poverty.

He cringed to see his father bound hand, foot, and neck in irons and imprisoned in Tehran's infamous Black Hole. During Baha'u'llah's absence, Abdul-Baha recognized himself as the messiah prophesied in the Bab's covenant book. To prepare himself for a religious life, Abdul-Baha meditated daily, memorized the Bab's writings, and visited the village mosque to discuss theology with experts.

Exile in Baghdad

After the liberation of the Baha'u'llah, nine-year-old Abdul-Baha accompanied his father and seventy other devout Baha'ists into exile in Baghdad, Arabia, where they initiated a thriving Babi community. As he matured and grew strong, he became his father's aide and protector against the threats of detractors and the demands of visitors and pilgrims. After the sect's forced removal to Constantinople (now Istanbul, Turkey), the boy's support of the family left the father free to develop a comprehensive teaching based on social and moral ethics. Tall, erect, and blessed with a sharp profile, piercing eyes, and shoulder-length black hair, Abdul-Baha dressed simply in robe and white turban, yet made a memorable impression on others. According to Edward Granville Browne, an English physician and orientalist from Gloucestershire: "One more eloquent of speech, more ready of argument, more apt of illustration, more intimately acquainted with the sacred books of the Jews, the Christians, the Muhammadans, could, I should think, scarcely be found."

Began a Holy Life

At the age of 22, Abdul-Baha formally proclaimed himself the third religious leader of the Baha'is as well as the slave of Baha, interpreter of divine revelation, and the promised successor described in the Bab's covenant. To demonstrate the correct lifestyle of his sect, Abdul-Baha limited his diet to two meals per day and shared his food and belongings with the needy. In 1867, political shifts forced him and other Baha'is out of the Middle East. He left Constantinople and traveled northwest to Adrianople (modern Edirne, Turkey).

As modern Europe destabilized power bases along the eastern Mediterranean, the Ottoman Turks imprisoned Abdul-Baha and his holy band at Acca (now Akko, Israel) in Ottoman Syria on the northern horn of the Bay of Haifa. To curtail the expansion of Baha'ism, his captors restricted inmate communication with the outside world and spied on them in fear of the movement's political intent. The prisoners—men, women, and children—suffered malaria, typhoid and dysentery. Lacking medicines, Abdul-Baha nursed the sick with broth before he too fell ill with dysentery, which kept him from comforting his followers for a month.

Spokesman for Baha'i

Abdul-Baha expanded his ministry from one-on-one teaching and counseling to administering religious affairs and formulating the sect's philosophy. In 1886, he compiled the first history of the Baha'i movement, later published with his collected papers. After the Baha'u'llah's death in May

1892, just as the Bab planned, the succession passed to Abdul-Baha. As characterized by his biographer, Isabel Fraser Chamberlain, author of *Abdul Baha on Baha'i Philosophy,* he continued the work of Baha'i's first two patriarchs by reviving his father's teachings, exemplifying divine law, and establishing a new kingdom on earth. A half-brother, Mirza Mohammad Ali, and other kin stirred a revolt against Abdul-Baha. To justify his ouster, they accused him of overreaching the Bab's covenant and Baha'u'llah's intent for him.

Prison and Release

In 1904 and 1907, as power struggles shook the established order in the eastern Mediterranean, government commissioners grew suspicious of organized groups and inquired into the source and nature of Abdul-Baha's influence. Hostile agents jailed him at a Turkish prison, where he continued to receive representatives of all faiths and races. During his imprisonment, he married Munirih Khanum, mother of their four daughters. Fluent in Persian, Arabic, and Turkish, he carried on an enormous correspondence of some 27,000 letters to philosophers, religious leaders, and pilgrims from all parts of the globe. Despite his personal plight and the danger to his family, he spread faith, cheer, and hope to the hopeless.

Risking execution by the sultan, Abdul-Baha refused to plead his innocence before a corrupt investigating committee or to attempt escape by an Italian ship that his sympathizers arranged for him in the harbor. In September 1908, the Turkish revolution resulted in the overthrow of the Ottoman Empire and the freeing of political and religious prisoners. Immediately, Abdul-Baha left his cell and made a formal gesture to the demoralized Baha'is. He finished building the shrine of the Bab above Haifa on Mount Carmel and buried the remains of the founder in hallowed ground.

A Mission to the World

At the newly established Baha'i headquarters in Acre, Palestine, Abdul-Baha continued composing sacred writings, now collected in two compendia, *Baha'i Scriptures* and *Baha'i World Faith.* When his daughters matured, they interpreted and transcribed his writings to free him for more important community missions to the oppressed, sick, and poor. As sect leader, he promoted the unity of world religions and the universalism of Baha'i. He summarized ten principles of the faith: (1) the independent search for truth; (2) the unity of all people; (3) the harmony of religion and science; (4) the equality of female and male; (5) the compulsory education for all; (6) the establishment of one global language; (7) the creation of a world court; (8) harmonious relations of all people in work and love; (9) the condemnation of prejudice; and (10) the abolition of poverty and extreme wealth.

Resettled in Alexandria, Egypt, Abdul-Baha received all comers to his center and, in August 1911, visited France and England. He dispatched reformers to the United States, which he toured in April 1912. In Wilmette, Illinois, he dedicated the site of a Baha'i temple, the first such structure in the Western Hemisphere. He next championed peace, women's rights, racial equality, and social justice in Great Britain, France, Germany, Austria, and Hungary.

A Life Dedicated to Peace

In the last years of his service to Baha'i, Abdul-Baha returned to Palestine and resumed control of his headquarters at Haifa. During World War I, he nurtured the sick and helped to avert famine by stockpiling adequate stores of wheat. Because travel was hampered by warships in sea lanes, he remained at his office to outline future goals for the Baha'i community in *Tablets of the Divine Plan Revealed by Abdul-Baha to the North American Baha'is.* After the British army liberated Palestine, in April 1920, an agent of the King of England knighted him for promoting peace in the Middle East.

Still visiting the aged and struggling underclass to the last, Abdul-Baha died peacefully in his sleep on November 28, 1921. Amid a throng of mourners, his body was interred in the northern rooms of the Bab's tomb on Mount Carmel. The mission begun by the Bab and the Baha'u'llah passed from Abdul-Baha to his eldest grandson, Shoghi Effendi Rabbani, the next guardian of the Baha'i faith. By 1995, with five million members in 232 countries, Baha'i had become the world's second most widely spread religion.

Books

Almanac of Famous People, 7th ed. Gale Group, 2001.
Chamberlain, Isabel Fraser, *Abdul Baha on Divine Philosophy,* Tudor Press, 1918.
The Oxford Dictionary of World Religions, edited by John Bowker, Oxford University Press, 1997.
Religious Leaders of America, 2nd ed. Gale Group, 1999.
A Sourcebook for Earth's Community of Religions, edited by Joel Beversluis, CoNexus Press, 1995.

Periodicals

Journal for the Scientific Study of Religion, June 1998.

Online

"Abdul-Baha," http://www.bahai.lu/Neue%20Seiten/abdbaha.html (October 23, 2001).
"Abdul-Baha," *The Baha'i World,* http://www.bahai.org/article-1-2-0-7.html.
"Abdul-Baha," http://www.dornochbahaigroup.freeserve.co.uk/abdulbaha.htm.
"Abdul-Baha," *The History of the Baha'i Faith,* http://www.northill.demon.co.uk/bahai/intro8.htm#abd.
"Abdul-Baha, Baha'i Faith," http://www.bahainyc.org/abdul.html.
"The Baha'i Faith, http://www.bahai.cc/Introduction/introduction.html.
Biography Resource Center, http://galenet.galegroup.com/servlet/BioRC (October 22, 2001). □

Abdullah II

Abdullah II (born 1962) succeeded his father, the late King Hussein, as king of the Hashemite Kingdom of Jordan on February 7, 1999. Little known outside

Jordan before becoming king, Abdullah has surprised many observers by displaying a natural flair for a job many said he could never handle.

Abdullah's ascension to the throne was a surprise to almost everyone. In the final months of King Hussein's life, he had entrusted power to his brother, Crown Prince Hassan, heir apparent to the Jordanian throne. Less than two weeks before his death, some feuding within the royal family angered Hussein and caused him to announce that Abdullah was now next in line for the throne. It was an announcement that shocked and worried many in Jordan. Abdullah, Hussein's eldest son by his second wife, Princess Mona, was known as a competent military leader, serving as a major general in charge of Jordan's elite Special Forces. However, he had no experience in handling affairs of state, particularly worrisome in a country that requires delicate diplomatic maneuvering just to maintain a fragile state of peace with its neighbors.

State of Shock

Typical of the reactions to Abdullah's sudden elevation to the highest levels of power in Jordan was this comment made to *Maclean's* magazine by K. Aburish, a London-based Palestinian writer who was born in Jordan: "I think everybody in the country is still in a state of shock." Abdullah's military background served him well in Jordan where the military is one of two centers of power, the second being the Islamic movement.

Had Hussein lived longer, he was widely expected to have passed the mantle of power to Prince Hamzah, the oldest son of Hussein's third wife, American-born Queen Noor. However, since Hamzah was only 19 years of age at the time of his father's death, he was considered too young and not adequately prepared to lead the country. Critics decried Hussein's choice of Abdullah as his successor, charging that Abdullah was a superficial playboy, patently unsuitable for a job of such immense responsibility. However, almost from the moment he ascended to the throne, Abdullah has confounded his most vocal critics with his ability to handle the job. In the first months following his father's death, Abdullah moved quickly to try to mend frayed diplomatic ties with Syria and Saudi Arabia. His grasp of political issues and pro-Western leanings quickly endeared him to diplomats in Washington, London, and other Western capitals.

Although many political observers focused on the contrasts between Hussein and his eldest son, Roscoe Suddath, president of the Middle East Institute, in a February 1999 interview with ABC News, chose to spotlight the similarities between father and son. "He's a lot like the king," Suddath told ABC. "He's got that wonderful charismatic and winning personality, winning smile. He's personally very physical, very vigorous. He loves to jump out of airplanes, drive fast cars, just like his father." Suddath went on to give his feelings about how Abdullah would fare as king. "I think he's capable of becoming king, yes. I think he will rely more on the institutions, on the prime ministry, on the royal advisers, on the parliament."

Married Since 1993

Abdullah has been married since June 1993 to the former Rania al-Yasin, the daughter of Palestinian parents living in Kuwait. The couple has two children, Prince Hussein, born in 1994, and Princess Iman, born in 1996. Abdullah and Queen Rania have gone to great lengths to maintain close ties to the Jordanian people, choosing to live outside the royal compound and rubbing elbows now and again when they dine out at the Howard Johnson's restaurant in Amman.

Abdullah, the eldest son of Hussein, is a product of his father's marriage to British-born Queen Mona. He was born Prince Abdullah bin al-Hussein on January 30, 1962, and is one of 11 children of Hussein. Abdullah began his education at the Islamic Educational College in Jordan. He later studied at St. Edmund's School in Surrey, England, and Eaglebrook School and Deerfield Academy in Deerfield, Massachusetts. After completing his secondary education, Abdullah enrolled in 1980 at the Royal Military Academy at Sandhurst, where he received his military education. In 1984, the prince enrolled at Oxford University to take a one-year course in international politics and foreign affairs.

After studying at Oxford, Abdullah returned to active duty in Jordan's military service. He quickly rose to the rank of captain and won command of a tank company in the 91st Armored Brigade. From 1986 to 1987, he was attached to the Helicopter Anti-Tank Wing of the Royal Jordanian Air Force as a tactics instructor. During this period, Abdullah was qualified as a Cobra attack helicopter pilot.

Studied International Affairs

Late in 1987, Abdullah traveled to Washington, D.C., to attend Georgetown University's School of Foreign Service. He undertook advanced study in international affairs. After completing his studies in Washington, Abdullah returned to Jordan to resume his military career. He was first assigned to the 17th Tank Battalion, 2nd Royal Guards Brigade. In the summer of 1989, he was elevated to major and named second in command of the 17th Tank Battalion. Two years later, in 1991, he was named armor representative in the Office of the Inspector General. Late that year, Abdullah was promoted to the rank of lieutenant colonel and given command of the 2nd Armored Car Regiment in the 10th Brigade. In January 1993, Abdullah became a full colonel and named deputy commander of Jordan's Special Forces. In June 1994 he was advanced to brigadier general and given command of Special Forces, in which capacity he continued until October 1997 when he was named commander of the Special Operations Command. In May of 1998, he was promoted to the rank of major general.

Somehow lost in the shuffle following the death of King Hussein was his widow, Queen Noor, the former Lisa Halaby who was married to Hussein for 21 years. Although her oldest son, Hamzah, had long been considered the most likely candidate to succeed Hussein, his father's sudden decline came at a time when Hamzah was not considered old enough to shoulder such a responsibility. In any case, the sudden elevation of Abdullah to power, and the appearance on the scene of a new, younger queen, has pretty much left Noor in the shadows. In compliance with his father's dying wish, Abdullah has named Hamzah crown prince. Whether he will continue as heir apparent, however, remains to be seen. Abdullah has a young son, and in time he may choose to take the title of crown prince away from his half-brother and confer it instead on his own child.

Doubts about Abdullah's ability to hold his own in the international arena have gradually been dispelled, as the king has demonstrated a remarkable facility for dealing with national leaders the world over. It was evident from the start of Adbullah's reign that he would carry on his father's campaign to bring a lasting peace to the embattled Middle East. Speaking to the World Economic Forum in Davos, Switzerland, in January of 2000, Abdullah said: "It is the task of the new generation of leaders in the Middle East to transform peace settlements into a permanent reality of economic hope and opportunity for the peoples of the region. These leaders are the ones who can closely associate with the hopes and dreams of the people of the Middle East who long to be able to live and work like so many others around the world with the promise of hope and fulfillment."

Pledged Support to the U.S.

Even more telling was the king's reaction to the terrorist attacks on the United States on September 11, 2001. Abdullah swiftly pledged Jordan's "full, unequivocal support" in the American war on terrorism. In a meeting with President George W. Bush only weeks after the attacks on the World Trade Center and Pentagon, Abdullah told the American president "we will stand by you in these very difficult times." When asked if he thought it might be difficult to unite Middle Eastern countries against Saudi-born Osama bin Laden and his band of al Quieda terrorists, the king said: "I think it will be very, very easy for people to stand together. As the president said, this is a fight against evil, and the majority of Arabs and Muslims will band together with our colleagues all over the world to be able to put an end to this horrible scourge of international terrorism, and you'll see a united front." In a later meeting with European Union officials on the U.S. terrorist attack, the king left no doubt about what he felt it would take to bring peace to the Middle East. "Israel's recognizing of the legitimate rights of the Palestinians, which is recognized by international resolutions, is the only route to defuse the tensions in the region," he said.

Some of Abdullah's own countrymen have expressed unhappiness with the king's close ties to the United States and its allies. As Abdullah met in Washington with President Bush, a comedy troupe in Amman drew riotous laughter from its audience when members suggested that Jordan's leaders say "no" to their own people but "only know how to say OK" to the United States.

A solution to the Palestinian problem is crucial for Jordan and King Abdullah, because nearly two-thirds of all Jordanians are of Palestinian extraction. The kingdom and its ruler have experienced problems in the past with civil unrest fomented by extremist Palestinian groups. In a meeting with British Prime Minister Tony Blair in October of 2001, Abdullah said the establishment of a Palestinian state was "inevitable" and the only sure way to guarantee stability in the region. The king added that "it is in everybody's interest to bring" such a state into reality.

Before succeeding his father as king, Abdullah had acted as regent in the absence of his father and frequently traveled with Hussein on state visits to other countries. In addition, Abdullah had often represented his country and King Hussein on a variety of visits to countries around the Middle East, developing close relationships with a number of Arab leaders in the process.

Although the citizens of Jordan enjoy as wide a range of personal freedoms as can be found in the Arab world, the country's political system still falls well short of Western-style democracy. Its parliament has limited powers, and even Muslim clerics must submit the text of their sermons for government approval. Freedom of the press is likewise constrained by complicated licensing requirements for newspapers and vague statutes that prohibit any threats to national security. A recent survey taken by the Jordanian Center for Strategic Studies found that more than three-quarters of respondents believed they would face government punishment if they attempted to demonstrate peacefully in public.

Abdullah has earned a reputation as a daredevil, counting among his favorite pastimes car racing and free-fall parachuting. He is also a qualified frogman, pilot, and scuba diver. Abdullah is an avid collector of ancient weapons and other armaments.

Periodicals

Jerusalem Post, September 30, 2001.
Maclean's, February 15, 1999.
Newsweek International, June 28, 1999.
Palm Beach Post, September 29, 2001.
Reuters, October 16, 2001.
United Press International, August 28, 2001; September 28, 2001.
Xinhua News Agency, October 25, 2001.

Online

"Biography of His Majesty King Abdullah bin al-Hussein," http://www.kingAbdullah.net/biography.html (November 1, 2001). □

Mohammad Abdullah

Sheikh Mohammad Abdullah (1905-1982) earned the peasants' trust during a transitional period that raised hopes for an independent nation of Kashmir. Despite being imprisoned nine times, his fight for human rights helped win partial autonomy from India. He risked family, political position, and reputation by continued peaceful negotiations with Indian and Pakistani leaders in an attempt to gain freedom for Kashmir.

Born to a merchant family in Soura a few miles outside the capital city of Srinagar, Kashmir, on December 5, 1905, Abdullah was orphaned in childhood. He graduated from Jammu's Prince of Wales College and Islamia College in Lahore, Pakistan. It was at this time that he first developed an interest in political reform. Working his way through school, he completed a graduate degree in physics from Aligarh Muslim University at age 25 and became a high school science teacher. In 1933, he married Begum Akbar Jehan, daughter of a wealthy European businessman in Gulmarj. Abdullah and his wife would later raise two daughters and three sons.

Defended Freedom

To preserve Muslim rights, Abdullah first came to the political fore by defying the autocratic Maharaja of Kashmir, spokesman for India's Hindu majority. In 1931, Abdullah joined with high priest Mirwaiz Maulvi Yusuf Shah against the tyrannical Maharaja, but abandoned the Maulvi upon learning that he regularly accepted bribes from India. The disclosure of corruption caused Abdullah to reject the communal politics of the Muslim Conference. From that point on, he supported the rights of all people over the rule of a single religious group.

As punishment for advocating a secular state, Abdullah was transferred to a teaching post at Muzzafarabad. He resigned his classroom position and, on May 19, 1946, received the first of nine prison sentences. His family left a comfortable home to live in meager rented rooms in Srinagar while Begum Jehan led her husband's party. Upon completion of a nine-year sentence, he established the All Jammu and Kashmir Muslim Conference, later called the National Conference of Kashmir to acknowledge a coalition of Hindus, Muslims, and Sikhs. This group pressed for home rule and the creation of a democracy in Kashmir.

Negotiated for the People

When Great Britain restored Indian home rule, Abdullah supported Prime Minister Jawaharlal Nehru and pacifist Mohandas K. Gandhi of the Indian National Congress. During the partitioning of India and Pakistan into separate Hindu and Muslim states, Abdullah gained control of Kashmir in a 1947 coup. However, he opposed siding with Muslim Pakistan in favor of secular autonomy. Initially, Kashmiris received economic safeguards and recognition as a unique nation and culture while avoiding the bloodshed of territorial wars that raged around them.

Abdullah summarized much of the passion and intrigue of this period of unrest in his autobiography, *Aatish-e-Chinar* [The Fire of Chinar Trees]. He recounted the failed attempts of Mohammed Ali Jinnah, the founder of Pakistan, to win Kashmir to Pakistan's pro-Muslim cause. The distancing of the two men was largely a result of character flaws in Jinnah. He ruined his chances for a coalition with Abdullah by maligning Maulvi Mirwaiz Yusuf Shah and by discounting the will of the Kashmiri people.

As Kashmir's prime minister and delegate to the United Nations in 1948, Abdullah stirred citizens and outsiders alike with patriotic oratory. Concerning the nation's constitution, enacted in 1944, he reminded Kashmiris that their assembly was "the fountain-head of basic laws laying the foundation of a just social order and safeguarding the democratic rights of all the citizens of the State." He championed free speech, a free press, and a higher standard of living for the poor. At the core of his speech lay his belief in "equality of rights of all citizens irrespective of their religion, color, caste, and class."

Prison and Violence

Placing three choices before the nation—yield to India, yield to Pakistan, or remain independent—Abdullah superintended moderation until 1953, when India accused him of sedition and formally charged him with illegally seeking Kashmir's independence. Stripped of power and imprisoned once more by the Maharaja for demanding the national rights that India guaranteed in 1947, Abdullah remained adamantly opposed to an alliance with India during 11 years of house arrest. His family was turned out into the streets and refused shelter even by relatives. Abdullah's enemies twice assaulted his wife, who, in her husband's absence, took charge of the party mascot and flag.

Against raids on Kashmir by the Pakistani army, Abdullah organized a home guard of mostly unarmed volunteers to defend the area from rape, arson, and pillage.

This militia had to remain vigilant to threats of sabotage to bridges and intervention in supplies of gasoline, salt, and currency, which had to pass through Pakistan from India. While the nation was in grave danger, Abdullah dispatched Farooq, his son and political heir, to safety in London.

Courage and Compromise

Caught between two hostile nations, Abdullah had little choice but accept the Maharaja's demand that Kashmir yield to India, which was ostensibly a more tolerant state than Pakistan. On October 27, Lord Louis Mountbatten, governor-general of India, accepted the nation's capitulation and dispatched troops from the Indian Army to halt Pakistani insurgents. Allama Iqbal, Pakistan's philosopher-poet, praised Abdullah for "[wiping] the fear of the tyrant from the hearts of the people of Kashmir." Of his courage, Ayub Khan, president of Pakistan, declared, "Sheikh Abdullah is a lion-hearted leader." The phrase popularized his nickname, "Lion of Kashmir."

In 1964, Nehru granted Abdullah's freedom. He returned to solid public support and a more positive atmosphere for guaranteeing Kashmiri autonomy constitutionally under Article 370 of Indian law. In 1968, he won the hearts of devout Muslims by remodeling the Hazratbal Mosque, the seventeenth-century repository of the Moi-e-Muqqadus, a sacred hair of the prophet Mohammed, for display on holy days. The nation's prime Muslim shrine on Dal Lake in Srinagar, it took shape in marble under the leadership of the Muslim Auqaf Trust, chaired by Abdullah, and reached completion in 1979.

Developed Statecraft

To shore up international goodwill, Abdullah toured Algeria and Pakistan. His position shifted once more as the public began doubting his loyalty during the uncertainty of the political climate on the Indian subcontinent. In 1953, the deterioration of relations with India caused him to demand an end to Kashmir's subservience. He returned to a benign house arrest until 1968, when he headed the Plebiscite Front, a political movement seeking a nationwide vote on independence. After the party failed to gain enough popular support to override the Congress Party in 1972, he moderated his stance on self-determination for Kashmir.

After Syed Mir Qasim and the Congress Party relinquished power on February 24, 1975, Abdullah became Kashmir's chief minister. He gained support of the State Congress Legislative Party for the formation of a new government led by deputy chief minister Mirza Afzel Beg and under-ministers Sonam Narboo and D. D. Thakur. In talks with India's pime minister Indira Gandhi, Abdullah moved beyond their differences of opinion to negotiate more independence for Kashmir. On March 13, 1975, Parliament approved the Indira-Abdullah Accord, granting partial autonomy to Kashmir. To implement the transition to a new constitutional status, he appointed a four-member coordination committee on October 13.

Abdullah's political position seemed certain after his election as president of the National Conference on April 13, 1976, and the first cabinet session at Doda on December 8. He initiated a youth wing of the ruling National Conference, led by his son Farooq. By the following March 25, Abdullah's followers lost sympathy during investigations of corruption and the dissolution of the state assembly. Under a local governor, on July 8, Abdullah once more rebuilt the machinery of home rule. Refusing confrontational politics, he maintained his popularity as a critic of the dynastic control of Kashmir. In a show of honest dealings with the people, in September 25, 1978, he demanded the resignation of his former deputy chief minister Mirza Afzal Beg and oversaw his expulsion from the National Conference.

Relinquished Power

In 1981, when the Begum Jehan refused to replace her ailing husband, Abdullah engineered the rise of surgeon Farooq Abdullah, the son whom he had educated in diplomacy by taking him along in boyhood during state missions to Pakistan. Abdullah publicly declared Farooq's succession to leadership of moderate Kashmiris. Still highly visible after Dr. Farooq Abdullah was elected head of the National Conference on March 1, Mohammad Abdullah dedicated the Tawi Bridge on August 26, only three weeks before his death from an acute illness in Srinagar on September 8, 1982. At his funeral, over a million mourners paid their respects to the loyal statesman. His son replaced him as chief minister and pledged to continue the fight for religious tolerance and an independent Kashmir.

Books

Almanac of Famous People, 7th ed. Gale Group, 2001.

Periodicals

Washington Post, July 24, 2000.

Online

"Abdullah, Sheikh Mohammed (nickname The Lion of Kashmir)," *Biography.com*, http://search.biography.com/cgi-bin/frameit.cgi?p+http% 3A//search.biography.com/print_record.pl%3FidA%3D6950.

Biography Resource Center, http://galenet.galegroup.com/servlet/BioRC (October 22, 2001).

Kotru, M. L., "Jammu and Kashmir," *The Kashmir Story*, http://kashmir-information.com/KashmirStory/chapter2.html.

Meraj, Zafar, "The Survivor," *News on Sunday*, http://www.jang-group.com/thenews/aug2000-weekly/nos-13-08-2000/spr.htm.

"An Outline of the History of Kashmir," http://www.kashmir.s5.com/history.htm.

"Pilgrim Tourism in Kashmirk," *Holy Places*, http://www.tradwingstravel.com/jkholyplaces.html.

"Profile," *Jammu & Kashmir*, http://jammukashmir.nic.in/welcome.html.

Rais, Rasul Bakhsh, "A Card in the Power Game," *The International News*, http://www.jang.com.pk/thenews/jul2000-daily/08-07-2000/oped/o5.htm.

"Speech of Sheikh Mohammad Abdullah in the Constituent Assembly," http://www.kashmir-information.ocm/LegalDocs/Sheikh_Speech.html. □

Mortimer Jerome Adler

American philosopher-educator Mortimer J. Adler (1902-2001) raised a stir in public schools, colleges, and universities over the place of classic works in the curriculum. For more than sixty years, his writings exposed to public scrutiny radical ideas about how to enlighten and educate the well-rounded individual. Whether admired, ridiculed, or detested for encouraging self-directed reading, he encouraged a healthy debate on learning and values.

B orn to teacher Clarissa Manheim and Ignatz Adler, a jewelry salesman, in New York City on December 28, 1902, Adler emerged from an unassuming background. In his early teens, he considered becoming a journalist and worked as copyboy and secretary to the editor of the *New York Sun*. After reading the autobiography of nineteenth-century English philosopher John Stuart Mill, Adler quit high school to direct his own education. He began by reading Plato. On scholarship, he earned an undergraduate degree in philosophy at Columbia University in three years, but left without a diploma because he refused to complete the swimming requirement. In 1983, the university relented and awarded him the long-delayed Bachelor of Arts degree.

The Rise of Genius

Skipping intermediate graduate work altogether, Adler wrote a dissertation on how to measure music appreciation and earned a doctorate in psychology from Columbia by the age of 26. His research became the impetus for a book, *Music Appreciation: An Experimental Approach to Its Measurement* (1929). During his last year at the university, he married Helen Leavenworth Boyton, mother of their two sons, Mark Arthur and Michael Boyton. After a divorce, a subsequent marriage in 1963 to Caroline Sage Pring produced two more sons, Douglas Robert and Philip Pring.

Adler began teaching psychology at the University of Chicago in 1930. Central to his classroom philosophy was a rebuttal of the prevailing notions of educational philosopher John Dewey, who had taught him at Columbia. Opposed to Dewey's focus on experimentation and the free selection of values that are applicable to the times, Adler published articles and books charging that such a belief system produced shoddy, poorly prepared thinkers and precipitated social unrest. Based on his understanding of Aristotle and St. Thomas Aquinas, he argued that students need to learn a set of fixed truths and values that have lasting and universal significance. His most famous and best-selling work, *How to Read a Book: The Art of Getting a Liberal Education* (1940), brought to public attention the gist of his educational plan.

Education Through Great Books

In 1946, Adler expanded his book into a full-scale revamping of learning. He established an alternative to undergraduate educational methods that centered on text-

books and lectures permeated with academic jargon and shallow academic trends, which students reiterated on subjective essay exams. In their place, he outlined a systematized reading schedule paired with discussion of great books. He surmised that, by mastering one worthy book per week, as proposed by Columbia University professor John Erskine, the average learner would acquire a suitable command of logic and of the major topics that impinge on human choices, such as honesty and goodness.

After convincing Robert M. Hutchins, president of the University of Chicago, of the efficacy of a book-based curriculum, Adler overturned standard college courses and superintended the implementation of his program at off-campus sites. Under the leadership of a coordinator, readers of all ages from across the spectrum of educational and socio-economic backgrounds gathered for seminars and coursework on moral and intellectual issues. Although Catholic scholars applauded Adler's uncompromising absolutism, his Great Books curriculum never rose above the level of a passing fad.

Critics challenged the dogmatic selection of classics of Western civilization and proposed numerous worthy authors whom Adler omitted, notably non-white and female writers. Nonetheless, in 1954, he convinced *Encyclopaedia Britannica* publishers to issue a bound set of Great Books, a 54-volume collection of 443 works that presented no commentary or direction to readers. Adler's only challenge to students beyond their own discussion was the two-volume *The Great Ideas: A Synopticon of Great Books of the West-*

ern World (1952), a 2,000-page index to the set that provided the location within individual titles of 102 subjects, including deity, peace, work, justice, equality, and citizenship.

A Man of Ideas

Despite rejection by his generation's noted scholars and educational leaders, Adler fought the skepticism, subjectivism, and relativism that he believed sapped human interaction of meaning and substance. He issued an astonishing list of works intended to restore philosophy to a central place in public education, including *How to Think about War and Peace* (1944) and *How to Think about God* (1980). The topics of his writings ranged from capitalism, industry, racism, politics, jurisprudence, and criminology to the arts, science, theology, and scholasticism. To encourage humanistic thinking as the cornerstone of a satisfying life, he furthered the ordinary reader's understanding of Homer, Plato, St. Augustine, David Hume, and Sigmund Freud. At the same time, he ignored or refuted modern thinking by such philosophers as Jean-Paul Sartre, Martin Heidegger, and Friedrich Nietzsche.

Packaged Basic Principles

Adler pursued a variety of modes to express his concepts. He served as consultant to the Ford Foundation and wrote an autobiography, *Philosopher At Large: An Intellectual Autobiography* (1977). To clarify misconceptions, he refined his original Great Books program in 1990. Despite these efforts, he produced only unsubstantiated success contained in individual testimonials from satisfied pupils and teachers. Overall, his insistence on self-directed education never achieved the level of student enlightenment that he had originally envisioned.

Late in his career, Adler published *The Paideia Proposal: An Educational Manifesto* (1982), which offered to public educators "a unique concept of teaching great works to children. He joined commentator Bill Moyers for a PBS-TV series entitled *Six Great Ideas* (1982). In 1990, he founded the Center for the Study of Great Ideas and lectured at the University of North Carolina at Chapel Hill. Still highly respected for his wisdom and enthusiasm for learning, he directed Chicago's Institute for Philosophical Research and chaired the editorial board of *Encyclopaedia Britannica* until 1995. At the age of 93, he issued an overview, *Adler's Philosophical Dictionary* (1995). His insistence on quality and depth of learning for all students earned him an Aquinas Medal, an alumni award from Columbia University, and the Wilma and Roswell Messing Award from St. Louis University Libraries.

Assessing Genius at Work

At the time of Adler's death on June 29, 2001, in San Mateo, California, his belief that "Philosophy is everybody's business" was still influencing educators. Analysts of the twentieth century accorded him guarded praise for denouncing wasteful, destructive educational trends, including student-centered elective programs and vocational training. Others were more critical of his influence, particularly his dismissal of female and non-white authors from lists of recommended readings that he based entirely on "dead white males." For his whites-only choices, African-American author Henry Louis Gates accused him of "profound disrespect for the intellectual capacities of people of color."

In Adler's defense, proponents of Paideia and of Great Books curricula have found useful advice for turning unproductive classrooms into opportunities for in-depth reading. His followers have advocated Socratic learning over textbooks and homework and have supported charter and magnet schools and home schooling, the emerging educational trends of the late twentieth century. Without endorsing or defaming Adler's revolutionary educational philosophies, critic William F. Buckley, Jr. summarized his unique intellectual gifts: "Phenomena like Mortimer Adler don't happen very often."

Books

American Decades, Gale Research, 1998.

Periodicals

America, September 18, 1982; July 23, 1988.
American Education, July 1983.
American Heritage, February 1989.
American Scientist, March-April 1992.
Booklist, June 1, 1993; March 15, 1995; July 1995; October 15, 1996; May 1, 2000.
Chicago Tribune, January 5, 1983; March 25, 1987; November 27, 1988; March 20, 1989.
The Christian Century, January 28, 1981; June 3, 1981; May 12, 1982; April 22, 1992; April 22, 1992.
Christianity Today, November 21, 1980; November 19, 1990.
Library Journal, June 1, 1980; April 15, 1981; April 1, 1982; August 1982; April 15, 1983; November 1, 1983; March 15, 1984; October 15, 1984; April 1, 1985; March 1, 1986; May 1, 1987; April 15, 1989; February 15, 1990; February 15, 1990; October 1, 1990; April 1, 1991; October 15, 1991; August 1992; May 15, 1993; June 1, 1994; November 1, 1994; June 15, 1995.
National Review, February 6, 1981; May 27, 1983; November 19, 1990; July 23, 2001; August 6, 2001; October 1, 2001.
Publishers Weekly, January 11, 1980; March 6, 1981; January 29, 1981; July 23, 1982; March 4, 1983; July 29, 1983; August 24, 1992; May 24, 1993; April 17, 2000.
Saturday Review, January 1982; February 8, 1985; March 8, 1985; January 17, 1986; January 27, 1989; February 23, 1990; August 17, 1990; February 8, 1991; September 27, 1991.
Time, September 29, 1980; June 22, 1981; September 6, 1982; May 6, 1985; May 4, 1987; July 9, 2001.
U. S. Catholic, August 1980; October 1980; August 1981.

Online

Biography Resource Center, http://galenet.galegroup.com/servlet/BioRC (October 22, 2001).
"Center for the Study of Great Ideas," http://www.thegreatideas.org/
Contemporary Authors Online, The Gale Group, 2001. □

Adalet Agaoglu

Beginning a writing career under Turkey's more liberal constitution of 1960, Adalet Agaoglu (born 1929), a playwright, author, and human rights activist, became Turkey's most prized female novelist. A revered intellectual and a co-founder of the Arena Theatre Company, she got her start in drama while directing Turkish national radio. In her sixties, she lent her support to human rights causes and to liberals protesting the suffering of Kurdish political prisoners.

Adalet Agaoglu was born in 1929 in Nallihan in the Ankara Province of west central Turkey. After completing a degree in French literature from the University of Ankara, she began graduate work in Paris. On return to Turkey, she assisted with cultural programming for the state radio and co-founded the Arena Theatre Company. At the start of her writing career, she pursued free expression of controversial subject matter during a period of intellectual and ethical ferment and published essays and drama reviews in *Ulus,* an Ankara daily newspaper and verse in *Kaynak,* a literary journal. Later, under the nation's liberalized 1960 constitution, she exploited the writer's freedom to examine complex issues.

From Radio to Print

When Agaoglu initiated a career as playwright, she focused on drama, beginning with *Let's Write a Play* (1953). While preparing literary programming and directing plays for Ankara Radio Theatre, she produced an original work, *Yasamak* (Doing It) (1955), which was presented on French and German stations. She broached serious issues of sexual repression in 1964 with *Evcilik Oyunu* (Playing House). Her stage works appeared in a collection of eight titles covering 1964 to 1971. In 1974, she received a drama award from the Turkish Language Society.

In addition to stage works. Agaoglu produced award-winning short fiction and novels in the 1970s and 1980s. These included the anthology *Yuksek Gerilim* (High Voltage) (1974), winner of the 1975 Sait Faik short fiction award, and two subsequent collections, *Sessizligin ilk Sesi* (The First Sound of Silence) (1978) and *Hadi Gidelim* (Come On, Let's Go) (1982). Longer fiction included *Olmeye Yatmak* (Lie Down to Die) (1974), *Fikrimin Ince Gulu* (The Delicate Rose of My Mind) (1976), and *The Wedding Night* (1979), which received the Sedat Simavi prize, the Orhan Kemal award, and the 1980 Madarali award. She followed with *Yazsonu* (The End of Summer) (1980) and the autobiographical *Goc Temizligi* (Clean-up before Moving) (1985), an anthology of memoirs. In addition to plays, she issued *Gecerken* (In Passing) (1986), a collection of literary commentaries and essays. Her published titles include translations of the works of classic French dramatists Jean Anouilh and Bertolt Brecht and fiction writer Jean-Paul Sartre.

Fiction with a Personal Touch

After nearly being sideswiped by a careless driver at a seaside bench, Agaoglu composed *Hayati Savunma Bicimleri* (Ways of Defending Life), a collection of eight stories. Focused on the theme of self-protection from a variety of threats—violence, want, madness, insensitivity, corruption, tyranny, annihilation, and brutality—the stories characterize the acts of survivalists combatting physical and emotional attack. In "Cinlama" (Ringing), the character Seyfi Bey battles an internal demon, a Jekyll-and-Hyde motif that results in his slaughtering a neighbor's child who threatens the beauty of his yard. In "Sehrin Gozyaslari" (The Tears of the City), Agaoglu describes a sociologist who collects quirky human behaviors, including outmoded dress and deportment and a pattern of dining each night at the same restaurant. The last of the eight stories, "Tanrinin Sonuncu Tebligi" (God's Last Declaration), satirizes the perversion of religion by insensitive practitioners.

One popular title written in 1984, *Uc Bes Kisi (Curfew)*, translated into English by John Goulden, Britain's ambassador to Turkey, studies the country during a revolutionary period, when the government fought terrorism by banning political parties and arresting party leaders and militants. Against a backdrop of suspicion, military coups, and martial law, seven characters in Ankara, Istanbul, and the Anatolian town of Eskisehir reflect before making critical life decisions prior to the evening's mandated 2:00 A. M. curfew. Along with four familiar character types, she spotlights three emerging figures—the young idealist, the liberated housewife, and the cutthroat capitalist. Through their seven dramatic scenarios, Agaoglu symbolizes the dilemmas of the nation as a whole from the foundation of the republic through the Cold War and its hopes for a more promising future.

Recreated Turkish Themes

At the heart of Agaoglu's thoughtful, tightly constructed prose is a balance between a realistic milieu of the Turkey she knows firsthand and the broader, more humanistic elements of gender prejudice, social pressure, and personal action. The social texture of her writings expresses the influence of Ottoman Turkish history on a people exiting an agrarian past. As the nation wrote its own script for the future, her themes illuminated hidden social and economic problems, particularly those faced by peasant families and villagers living far from cities. In an unfamiliar urban world, her fictional newcomers to modernity struggle with age-old issues complicated by perplexing political, religious, economic, and social forces.

For her perception of subtle and overt changes in modern Turkish society, in December 1998, Agaoglu journeyed to Columbus, Ohio, to receive an honorary Ph.D. in literature from Ohio State University. The faculty acknowledged her work with a ceremony before an audience of Turkish students and officials at the Turkish Consulate General in Chicago. The occasion concluded with a two-day symposium on her writing and social activism entitled "Modernism and Social Change." The event earned media attention as the first time the award recognized a Turkish writer.

Agaoglu the Activist

In August 1998, Agaoglu joined hundreds of artists, leftists, and citizen protesters in Istanbul's Ortakoy District Square to demand attention to the plight of some 24,708 inmates jailed since the 1970s as terrorists and subversives. Calling for a general amnesty prior to the Turkish Republic's 75th anniversary, the gathering stressed the innocence of Kurds seeking self-determination for their ancestral homeland in southeastern Turkey. Agaoglu risked jailing as an illegal separatist. Nonetheless, she joined 500 signers of a petition demanding action to free political prisoners. The signing paralleled a previous collection of signatures in October 1996, when Agaoglu joined one million to press the Turkish Grand National Assembly for peace amid the nation's ongoing internal conflicts.

During Human Rights Week in December 2000, Agaoglu took part in human rights demonstrations on behalf of Kurdish political prisoners participating in hunger strikes. Sympathizers demanded the closure of F-type prison cells, which isolated inmates, some of whom suffered torture. A petition stated: "We hereby declare that the Minister of Justice and the government will be responsible for any deaths, impairments and any and all sad results with no return." Additional demands called for a revocation of unjust sentences and stringent anti-terrorist statutes, closure of state security courts, and monitoring of prisons to prevent human rights violations. Agaoglu and other respected Turkish journalists, artists, and writers offered their services to negotiate with the Ministry of Justice the rights and needs of striking prisoners.

In August 2001, Agaoglu joined 65 intellectuals in pressing for greater freedom of speech and action. Along with artists, attorneys, musicians, politicians, and other writers, she endorsed a pamphlet, "Freedom of Thought-For Everyone." As a result of the action, she and the other signers were threatened with eight years' imprisonment.

Books

The Reader's Encyclopedia of World Drama, edited by John Gassner and Edward Quinn, Thomas Y. Crowell Co., 1969.
Who's Who in Contemporary Women's Literature, edited by Jane E. Miller, Routledge, 1999.

Periodicals

Anadolu Agency, December 10, 1998.
IMK Weekly Information Service, December 21, 2000.
Inter Press Service, August 11, 1998; August 12, 1998.
Journal of Social History, October 1, 2001.
Kurdish Observer, November 11, 2000.
Middle East Studies Association Bulletin, Summer 2001
Turkish Daily News, October 26, 1996.
Turkish Press Review, August 12, 1998; October 22, 1999.
UNESCO Courier, November 1981.
World Literature Today, Spring 1998.

Online

Agaoglu, Adalet, "Yerli Yersiz," http://www.anaserve.com/~dersaadet/ykmz0246.htm (October 25, 2001).

"Biographical Notes," *Women Writers,* http://www.contrib.andrew.cmu.edu/usr/pk2c/women/writer/writer_bio.htm (October 25, 2001).

"Contemporary Understanding in Turkish Theatre: Republican Period," http://artel.net.az/grupd/theatre7.htm (October 25, 2001).

"Curfew," *UT Press,* http://web1.cc.utexas.edu/utpress/books/agacup.html (October 25, 2001).

"Human Rights Yesterday and Today," http://sskt.nu/nw0806.htm (October 25, 2001)

Sener, Sevda, "Turkish Drama," http://interactive.m2.org/Theather/SSener.html (October 25, 2001) ☐

Ryunosuke Akutagawa

The first Japanese author popularized in the West, Ryunosuke Akutagawa (1892-1927) restated old legends and medieval history in modernist psychological terms. A prolific writer of naturalistic "slice of life" short fiction, he produced 150 stories and novellas that address human dilemmas and struggles of conscience tinged with gothic darkness. Contributing to his mystique was his rapid mental decline and suicide at age the age of 35.

A Tokyo native, Akutagawa was born in the historic, multicultural Irifunecho district on March 1, 1892, to Fuku Niihara and Binzo Shinhara, a dairy merchant. He was named Niihara Ryunosuke in infancy to honor the family of his mother, the scion of an ancient samurai clan. After her mental deterioration when he was nine months old, he passed from the custody of his father, who was unable to care for him. His maternal uncle, Michiaki Akutagawa, adopted him, giving him the surname Akutagawa. Shaken by what he perceived to be parental abandonment, he grew up friendless. In place of human peer relationships, he absorbed fictional characters from Japanese storybooks. In adolescence, he advanced to translations of Anatole France and Heinrich Ibsen.

An Early Literary Master

At the age of 21, Akutagawa entered the Imperial University of Tokyo and majored in English literature with a concentration in the works of British poet-artist William Morris. Two years before graduating, Akutagawa joined Kikuchi Kan and Kume Masao in founding a literary journal, *Shin Shicho* (New Thought), in which he published his translations of Anatole France and John Keats. In his early twenties, Akutagawa produced "Rashomon" (The Rasho Gate) (1915), a novella set on a barren, war-torn landscape in twelfth-century Kyoto. It is the tale of an encounter between a grasping Japanese servant and an old woman who weaves wigs from the hair she salvages from corpses. The action, which depicts post-war survivalism, derives its

power from widespread poverty and a short-term morality suited to the demands of self-preservation. In the estimation of critic Richard P. Benton, the story "suggests that people have the morality they can afford."

After reading "Rashomon," novelist Natsume Soseki, the literary editor of Asahi, a national Japanese newspaper, became Akutagawa's mentor and encouraged his efforts. "Rashomon" remained his masterwork and became his most dissected title following director Akira Kurosawa's screen version in 1951, which won an Academy Award for best foreign film.

A brilliant student and reader of world literature, Akutagawa taught English for one year at the Naval Engineering College in Yokosuka, Honshu. At age 26, he married Tsukamoto Fumi and sired three sons. To support his family, in 1919, he edited the newspaper *Osaka Mainichi,* which sent him on assignment to China and Korea. Because of poor mental and physical health, he left the post. Rejecting teaching posts at the universities of Kyoto and Tokyo, he devoted the rest of his life to writing short stories, essays, and haiku.

Literature from Classic Sources

Akutagawa filled his works with allusions to classic literature, including early Christian writing and the fiction of China and Russia, both of which he visited in 1921. Among his publications were critical essays and translations of works by William Butler Yeats. A major contributor to Japanese prose, Akutagawa expressed to a wide reading public a vivid imagination, stylistic perfectionism, and psychological probing. For "The Nose" (1916), the story of a holy man obsessed by his ungainly nose, he invested the Cyrano-like tale with deep personal dissatisfaction not unlike the feelings of discontent and alienation that plagued the writer himself.

As described by literary historian Shuichi Kato in Volume 3 of *A History of Japanese Literature* (1983), Akutagawa developed literary tastes from the shogunate period of late sixteenth-century Japan. Kato states: "From this tradition came his taste in clothes, disdain for boorishness, a certain respect for punctilio and, more important, his wide knowledge of Chinese and Japanese literature and delicate sensitivity to language." As a means of viewing his own country with fresh insight, he cultivated a keen interest in European fiction by August Strindberg, Friedrich Nietzsche, Fyodor Dostoevsky, Nicholai Gogol, Charles Baudelaire, Leo Tolstoy, and Jonathan Swift. In particular, he studied Franz Kafka and American poet Edgar Allan Poe, masters of the grotesque.

Retreated into Self

Writing in earnest at the age of 25, Akutagawa produced memorable short fiction in the Japanese "I" novel tradition of *shishosetsu,* which is both confessional and self-revealing. At the height of his creativity, he began examining deeply personal attitudes toward art and life in such symbolic writings as "Niwa" (The Garden), the story of a failed family and the tuberculosis-wracked son who restores a magnificent garden. As the author began expressing more of his own neuroses, delicate physical condition and drug addiction, the tone and atmosphere of his fiction darkened with hints of madness and a will to die.

One dramatically grim story, "Hell Screen" (1918), depicts the artist Yoshihide who pleases a feudal lord by painting a Buddhist hell. For source material, the lord agrees to set fire to a cart, in which a beautiful woman rides, but tricks the artist by selecting Yoshihide's beloved daughter Yuzuki as the victim. For the sake of art, Yoshihide watches her torment and paints the screen with bright flames devouring her hair. His work complete, he becomes a martyr to art by hanging himself at his studio.

Suicide at 35

In his last two years, Akutagawa suffered visual hallucinations, alienation, and increasing self-absorption as he searched himself for signs of his mother's insanity. As macabre thoughts and exaggerated self-doubts marred his perspective, he pondered the future of his art in a prophetic essay, "What is Proletarian Literature" (1927). Morbidly introspective and burdened by his uncle's debts, he considered himself a failure and his writings negligible. Two of his most effective fictions, "Cogwheels" and "A Fool's Life," recount his terror of madness as it gradually consumed his mind and art.

Following months of brooding and a detailed study of the mechanics of dying, Akutagawa carefully chose death at home by a drug overdose as the least disturbing to his family. He left a letter, entitled "A Note to a Certain Old Friend," describing his detachment from life, the product of "diseased nerves, lucid as ice." In death, he anticipated peace and contentment.

Much of Akutagawa's most intriguing writing—"Hell Screen," "The Garden," "In the Grove," "Kappa," "A Fool's Life," and the nightmarish "Cogwheels"—reached the reading public over a half century after his death. Largely through increased interest in Asian literature in translation and through cinema versions, these titles bolstered the value of Japanese short fiction. To honor Akutagawa's genius, in 1935, Kikuchi Kan, his friend from their university days, and the Bungei Shunju publishing house established the Akutagawa Award for Fiction, a prestigious biennial Japanese literary prize. The Nihon Bungaku Shinkokai (Society for the Promotion of Japanese Literature) selects the best short story from a beginning author to receive the prize as well as publication in the literary magazine *Bungei Shunju*.

Books

Almanac of Famous People, 7th ed. Gale Group, 2001.
Columbia Encyclopedia, Edition 6, 2000.
World Literature, edited by Donna Rosenberg, National Textbook Company, 1992.

Periodicals

Criticism, Winter 2000.
English Journal, November 1986.
Journal of Asian Studies, February 2, 1999.
Library Journal, May 15, 1988.

New York, April 18, 1988.
New York Review of Books, December 22, 1988.
Publishers Weekly, January 29, 1988.

Online

"Akutagawa Award for Fiction," http://www.csua.net/~raytrace/lit/awards/Akutagawa.html (October 27, 2001).
"Akutagawa Ryunosuke, http://www.kalin.lm.com/akut.html (October 27, 2001).
"Akutagawa Ryunosuke (1892-1927)," *Books and Writers,* http://kirjasto.sci.fi/akuta.htm (October 27, 2001).
"Akutagawa Ryunosuke (1892-1927)," http://macareo.pucp.edu.pe/~elejalde/ensayo/akutagawa.html (October 27, 2001).
Biography Resource Center, http://galenet.galegroup.com/servlet/BioRC (October 27, 2001).
Contemporary Authors Online, The Gale Group, 2000 (October 27, 2001). □

Al-Farabi

During the tenth-century, philosopher, scholar, and alchemist Al-Farabi (c. 870-c. 950) popularized the philosophical systems of Greek philosophers Aristotle and Plato. He integrated their views into his Islam-based metaphysical, psychological, and political theories. Al-Farabi was among the first philosophical theologians of the Islamic faith.

Historians classify Al-Farabi as a member of the eastern group of Moslem philosophers who were influenced by the Arabic translations of Greek philosophers by Nestorian Christians in Syria and Baghdad. During his life, he placed a heavy emphasis on logic and believed that each human individual possesses the ability to discern between good and evil, which he considered the basis for all morality. He is credited by historians for preserving the works of Aristotle that otherwise might have been forgotten and subsequently destroyed during the Dark Ages. He earned the nickname Mallim-e-Sani, which often is translated as "second master" or "second teacher" after Aristotle, who was considered the first master.

By 832, Baghdad contained a group of translators dedicated to converting Greek texts by Plato, Aristotle, Themistius, Porphyry, and Ammonius into Arabic. These efforts resulted in the progenitors of Islamic philosophy adopting a Neo-platonic approach to religious thought, of whom Al-Farabi is considered the first. Influenced by Islamic Sufism and his reading of Plato, Al-Farabi also explored mysticism and metaphysics and placed contemplation above action. In his interpretations of Islamic religious suppositions based upon his readings of Plato and Aristotle, Al-Farabi attempted to provide rational explications of such metaphysical concepts as prophecy, heaven, predestination, and God. Al-Farabi also believed that prophets developed their gift by adhering to a rigidly moral lifestyle, rather than simply being born with divine inspiration. In addition to his philosophical theology, Al-

Farabi is considered a preeminent musical theorist. Among his works on musical theory are *Kitab Mausiqi al-Kabir (Grand Book of Music)*, *Styles in Music,* and *On the Classification of Rhythms* in which he identified and provided detailed descriptions of musical instruments and discussed acoustics. Among the many works attributed to him, including such scientific examinations as *The Classification of the Sciences* and *The Origin of Sciences,* Al-Farabi also wrote respected works on mathematics, political science, astronomy, and sociology.

Al-Farabi was born in Faral in Asia Minor, in what is known now as Othrar, Turkistan. His father is reported to have been either a Turkistan general or a bodyguard for the Turkish Caliph, and Al-Farabi's parents raised him in the mystical Sufi tradition of Islam. He was schooled in the towns of Farab and Bukhara, before continuing his studies of Greek philosophy in Hanan and Baghdad. He spoke seventy languages and traveled widely throughout the Arabian kingdoms of Persia, Egypt, and Asia Minor. Al-Farabi studied with the Nestorian Christian physician Yuhanna ibn-Haylan, a noted logician, and Abu-Bishr Matta ibn-Yunus, a Christian scholar of Aristotle.

Al-Farabi relied on the writings of Aristotle and Plato in what is considered to be his major work of political science and religion, *On the Principles of the Views of the Inhabitants of the Excellent State,* also titled *The Ideal City.* In this work, he borrows freely from Plato's *Republic* and *Laws* to construct a treatise on his idea of a utopian society. In such a society, Al-Farabi reasoned that a political system could be made to adhere to Islamic beliefs through the combined study of philosophy, hard sciences, mathematics, and religion. Such a political theology would result in an ordered society that recognizes the need for community and a hierarchal structure that revolves around the received knowledge of divine law by the community's prophets and lawgivers. Divided into three sections, *The Ideal City* begins with a section on metaphysics, in which he elaborated upon his concepts of philosophy and religion. The second section is a discussion of psychology, and, in the third section, Al-Farabi presented his views on the qualities he believed identify the perfectly governed and populated state.

Al-Farabi divided his studies into two distinct categories, which he labeled physics and metaphysics. Physics applied to the physical sciences and phenomenology, and metaphysics applied to ethics, philosophy, and theology. Al-Farabi also divided the study of logic into two categories, which he labeled imagination and proof. He believed religious faith was an example of the former and that philosophy represented the latter. Al-Farabi ultimately believed that philosophy was purer than religion because philosophy represented the study of verifiable truths by an intellectual elite. The truths that have been identified by the philosophers are subsequently converted into religious symbols that can be easily interpreted by the imaginations of the general populous. Al-Farabi explained that a religion's validity lay in its ability to accurately convey philosophical concepts into readily identifiable religious symbolism. He further noted that each culture employed its own symbols to interpret the same philosophical truths. Although he believed that phi-losophy was superior over religion, he also contended that religion was necessary in order to make philosophical concepts understandable to the uneducated.

Al-Farabi inverted previous theological methodology by insisting on the study of philosophy before attempting religious understanding, whereas philosophers previously had developed philosophical systems to support preexisting religious dogma. Applying Aristotelian notions of logic to the Muslim faith, Al-Farabi concerned himself with such theological issues as proving the existence of God; God's omnipotence and infinite capacity for justice in meting out punishment or rewards in the afterlife; and the responsibilities of the individual in a moral and social context. Al-Farabi believed that a thorough grounding in logic was a necessary introduction for the continued study of philosophy, and he was instrumental in separating the study of philosophy as an inherently theological enterprise. Employing Aristotle's notion that a passive force moves everything in the world, Al-Farabi concluded that the First Movement emanates from a primary source, God, which aligns Greek philosophy with the Islamic belief that God imbues all things with existence. If all existence emanates from God, Al-Farabi argued, then all human intelligence proceeds directly from God in the form of inspiration, illumination, or prophecy as it did when the angel Gabriel imparted cosmic wisdom to the prophet Mohammed.

Predisposed to mysticism through his Sufi upbringing, Al-Farabi also integrated Platonic thought into his cosmology by asserting that the highest goal of humankind should be the attainment of the knowledge of God. If all worldly material emanates from God, Al-Farabi reasoned, then enlightened humans should aspire to a return to God through the study of religious texts and moral acts. Al-Farabi's writings since have influenced a wide range of subsequent religious, philosophical, and sociological thought. The Moslem philosopher Avicenna (980-1037) credits Al-Farabi's analysis of Aristotle's *Metaphysics* with his own understanding. Avicenna claimed he had read the Greek philosopher's work forty times but was unable to comprehend the work's meaning until he read Al-Farabi's explication. By asserting the metaphysical concept that a higher being contributes knowledge to the intellectual pursuits of humankind, Al-Farabi anticipated Henri Bergson's theory of philosophical intuition. Al-Farabi's theory that individuals make the conscious decision to group together according to their beliefs and needs anticipated the social contract of Henri Rousseau. In his *History of Philosophy,* Frederick Copleston noted that Al-Farabi's concept of God as the First Mover of all physical essence has been appropriated also by the Jewish philosopher Maimonides and such Roman Catholics writers as St. Thomas Aquinas and Dante Alighieri. Al-Farabi believed that the distinction between essence and existence proved that existence is an accidental byproduct of essence. His adherence to philosophical rationalism has been detected also in the works of Immanuel Kant.

Al-Farabi is also considered by many historians and critics to be the most important musical theorist of the Muslim world. He claimed to have written *Kitab Musiqi al-Kabir (Grand Book of Music)* to dispel what he felt was the erroneous assumptions of Pythagoras's music of the spheres. Instead, Al-Farabi asserted that sound emanates from atmospheric vibrations. Other works of music theory include *Styles in Music.* Several of his scientific works, including *The Classification of the Sciences* and *The Origin of the Sciences,* contain essays focused on the physical and physiological principles of sound, including harmonics and acoustical vibrations. He is credited also for inventing the musical instruments rabab and quanun.

Later in life, during a pilgrimage to Mecca, Al-Farabi arrived at Aleppo, in modern-day Syria, where he encountered the country's ruler, Saifuddawlah. When Saifuddawlah offered him a seat, Al-Farabi broke Aleppo custom by taking Saifuddawlah's seat. Speaking in an obscure dialect, Saifuddawlah told his servant that Al-Farabi should be dealt with severely. Speaking in the same dialect, Al-Farabi responded, "Sire, he who acts hastily, in haste repents." Impressed with Al-Farabi, Saifuddawlah allowed him to speak freely on many subjects. When Al-Farabi finished speaking, the ruler offered him food and drink, which Al-Farabi refused. Instead he played a lute masterfully, reputedly moving his audience from tears to laughter depending on the music. Saifuddawlah invited Al-Farabi to stay at his court, where he remained for the rest of his life. Despite the fact that Saifuddawlah belonged to the Suni sect of Islam, Al-Farabi retained his Sufi affiliation.

Reports on Al-Farabi's death are unclear but often note he died around 950. Some historians believe that Al-Farabi died in Damascus, where he was traveling with Saifuddawlah's court. Others write that he was killed by robbers while searching for the philosopher's stone. The philosopher's stone was a legendary substance sought by alchemists, which was believed to possess the properties to transform base metals into gold or silver. Regardless, he is believed to have written more than one-hundred books on a wide-range of scientific, musical, religious, and philosophical topics during his lifetime. Of these works, only one-fifth are believed to have survived.

Books

Ahmad, K. J., *Hundred Great Muslims,* Library of Islam, 1987.
Copleston, Frederick, S. J., *A History of Philosophy, Volume II: Medieval Philosophy from Augustine to Duns Scotus,* Doubleday, 1993.
Edwards, Paul, editor, *The Encyclopedia of Philosophy, Volume 3,* Macmillan and the Free Press, 1967.
Eliade, Mircea, editor, *The Encyclopedia of Religion, Volume 5,* Macmillan Publishing Company, 1987.
Melton, J. Gordon, editor, *Encyclopedia of Occultism and Parapsychology, Fifth Edition, Volume 1, A-L,* Gale Group, 2001.
□

Ahmed Ali

Scholar, poet, teacher, and diplomat Ahmed Ali (1908-1998) holds an honored place as novelist and chronicler of India's shift from an English colony to a free state. In addition to being a prolific author of poems and world-class novels, translator of the Koran and the ghazals of Ghalib, and critic of poet T. S. Eliot, Ali lived a double life in business and politics. He worked as a public relations director and was a foreign spokesman for Pakistan. While serving in the diplomatic corps, he traveled the world.

The son of Ahmad Kaniz Begum and Syed Shujauddin, a civil servant, Ali was born in Delhi, India, on July 1, 1908. He grew up during the emergence of Indian nationalism and the Muslim League, the impetus behind the creation of a separate state of Pakistan. After his father's death, he passed into the care of conservative relatives who lived under a medieval set of standards. According to their orthodox views, Ali could not read poetry or fiction in Urdu, even the classic fable collection *The Arabian Nights,* which they denounced as immoral.

Escape Through Reading

To flee intellectual isolation, Ali read a volume of children's fables—Charles Kingsley's *The Water-Babies: A Fairy Tale for a Land-Baby* (1863)—and began writing his own fiction around the age of eleven. For material, he adapted adventure stories and tales he heard from his aunts and from storytellers. In his teens, he expanded his reading experience to European novelists James Joyce, D. H. Lawrence, and Marcel Proust and the verse of revolutionary English poet T. S. Eliot.

An Intellectual in the Making

During Ali's youth, the era was gloomy with upheaval as India struggled to free itself from British colonialism. At this momentous time in the nation's transformation, from 1925 to 1927, he attended Aligarh Muslim University in southeast Delhi. After transferring to Lucknow University, where he completed a B.A. and M.A. with honors, he thrived in an academic community and enjoyed the atmosphere of the King's Garden and the River Gomti. He was influenced by socialist and communist doctrines and gained the camaraderie of British and Indian professors, who admired his candor.

Ali channeled his idealism into political activism. The rise of the freedom movement that followed the Simon Commission Report on Indian Reforms stressed the nation's need for total change. He recognized that Indians lived a shallow existence that perpetuated failed ideals adopted from their British overlords. He realized that the people's reliance on religion and fatalism worsened slavery, hunger, and other remnants of imperialism.

After graduating in 1931, Ali earned his living by lecturing in English at Lucknow, Allahabad, and Agra universities. Choosing Urdu, the language of the Progressive Writers' Movement, he simultaneously began writing short fiction. He collaborated with three friends to publish a first pro-revolution anthology, *Angaray* (Burning Coals), which earned the scorn of conservatives and Islamic fanatics. In addition to ridiculing the authors, his critics threatened them with death by stoning. Three months later, agitators caused the British government to ban the book. In response to censorship, Ali maintained hope for the future through literature. To advance Indian reform, he helped to found the Progressive Writers' League and dedicated himself to a literary life.

Finding a Voice

For the next twelve years, Ali wrote short stories, some of which reached English and American readers in translation. His experiments with symbolism, realism, and introspection helped to direct the modern Urdu short story. He followed the joint fiction collection with his own anthology, *Sholay* (Flames) (1932) and two plays, *Break the Chains* (1932) and the one-act *The Land of Twilight* (1937). In 1936, he co-founded the All-India Progressive Writers Association, the preface to a new era in Urdu literature. The league's internal squabbles over progressivism caused a break with orthodox members. Opposed to stodgy conservative proponents of the working class, he chose a more inclusive, humanistic world view.

To reach more readers, Ali abandoned Urdu in favor of English. In 1939, he produced his masterwork, *Twilight in Delhi,* the saga of an upper-class Muslim merchant and his family during and after the 1857 mutiny, India's first war of independence. In an act of personal and ethnic introspection, Ali locked himself in his apartment and composed fiction that exposed his homeland's social problems. He believed that India was trapped in an inescapable low, an historic ebb that was part of a universal cycle of rise and fall, birth and decay. He stressed the powerlessness of human actors caught up in events orchestrated by invisible forces.

At the beginning of World War II, Ali carried his novel manuscript to London and sold it to Hogarth Press. After editorial clashes over themes the staff considered subversive, the company issued his book in 1940. It found immediate favor with critics Bonamy Dobree, E. M. Forster, and Edwin Muir. When a later edition reached American audiences in 1994, *Publishers Weekly* called it a fascinating history and cultural record of India.

A Taste of Success

When Ali returned home, he had become a legend. His novel was a popular favorite that All-India Radio broadcast to listeners. Still much in demand, it has become a classic of world literature. He turned to scholarly writing and published *Mr. Eliot's Penny World of Dreams: An Essay in the Interpretation of T. S. Eliot's Poetry* (1941).

During World War II, Ali worked for the British Broadcasting Corporation in Delhi as representative and listener research director. He continued writing short stories and issued three Urdu collections: *Hamari Gali* (1944), *Maut se Pahle* (1945), and *Qaid Khana* (1945). In the late 1940s, he headed the English department at Presidency College in Calcutta and was visiting professor for the British Council in Nanking at the National Central University of China. The next year, he resided in Karachi and directed foreign publicity for the government of Pakistan.

Restored Initial Aims

Ali discovered that his academic and civic work was not conducive to the demands of writing. Retreating to the solitude of the Kulu Valley in the Himalayas, he followed his first novel with *Ocean of Night,* a sequel set between the world wars and depicting the 1947 split of the Indian state into India and Pakistan. Sensitive to the hardships that reform placed on individual citizens, the text focused on India's loss of traditions and the new and uncharted direction that his fellow Indians faced.

During a reflective period, Ali worked for twelve years as counselor and deputy ambassador in the diplomatic service and resided in China, England, Morocco, and the United States. In traveling over four continents, he encountered new mindsets and attitudes. He composed *Muslim China* (1949) for the Pakistan Institute of International Affairs and translated *The Flaming Earth: An Anthology of Indonesian Poetry* (1949) and *The Falcon and the Hunted Bird* (1950). These translations introduced the English-speaking world to classic Urdu verse.

Family life also competed for Ali's attention. In 1950, he married Bilqees Jehan Rant, mother of their sons Eram, Orooj, and Deed and a daughter, Shehana. In 1960, he began supporting his family by directing public relations for business and industry. On the side, he collected verse for *Purple Gold Mountain: Poems from China* (1960) and translated and edited *The Bulbul and the Rose: An Anthology of Urdu Poetry* (1960). In 1964, he returned to his second novel and published it.

When Ali again scheduled time for intensive writing, he edited *Under the Green Canopy: Selections from Contemporary Creative Writings from Pakistan* (1966). He also produced bilingual Italian-Urdu short fiction entitled *Prima della Morte* (1966) and composed *The Failure of an Intellect* (1968) and *Problems of Style and Technique in Ghalib* (1969). In addition, he translated *Ghalib: Selected Poems* (1969), the ghazals of early 19th-century poet Mirza Asadullah Khan Ghalib of Agra. As India's socio-political obsessions shifted from secular to religious, Ali found an absorbing set of problems to ponder. These challenges formed the plot of a third novel, *Rats and Diplomats,* a fictional canvas stripped of old themes and motifs. He completed it in 1969, but withheld it from publication until 1985.

Balanced Work and Art

In this second waiting period, Ali worked as deputy director for the United Kingdom Immigrants Advisory Service and chairman of Lomen Fabrics, Ltd., until 1978. He also translated *The Golden Tradition: An Anthology of Urdu Poetry* (1973) and published a critical volume, *The Shadow and the Substance: Principles of Reality, Art and Literature* (1977). Retired from business, he lectured at Michigan State and Karachi University and served Western Kentucky and Southern Illinois universities as Fulbright visiting professor.

Still driven to write fiction that illuminated India's growth pangs, Ali pursued his career for internal reasons rather than for royalties. Working twelve-hour days at his home in Karachi, he created stories that expressed his joy in national advances and that taught the new generation about the forces that brought India into the modern age. In 1980, he received Pakistan's Sitara-e-Imtiaz (Star of Distinction), his most treasured award.

In his 70s, Ali issued a contemporary bilingual edition of the Koran, which critic Edwin Muir applauded for its pictorial elegance, rhythm, and spiritual power. He continued to produce short stories and verse and published *The Prison-House* (1985) and *Selected Poems* (1988). His collection of antiques, Gandhara art, and Chinese porcelain allowed him moments of relaxation. The University of Karachi presented him an honorary degree in 1993. Ali died on March 19, 1998, in Stockport, England.

Books

Almanac of Famous People, 7th ed. Gale Group, 2001.
Larousse Dictionary of Writers, edited by Rosemary Goring, Larousse, 1994.
The Complete Marquis Who's Who, Marquis Who's Who, 2001.

Periodicals

Booklist, June 1, 1994.
Journal of Modern Literature, Summer 1990.
Publishers Weekly, May 9, 1994.

Online

Biography Resource Center, http://galenet.galegroup.com/servlet/BioRC (October 28, 2001).
Contemporary Authors Online, The Gale Group, 2000 (October 27, 2001). □

Gracie Allen

Gracie Allen (1906-1964), wife of comedian and actor George Burns, was half of one of America's most popular comedy couples. They began their careers on the vaudeville stage, then transitioned to radio, movies, and television. Allen was known as a "dizzy dame," whose "illogical logic" and high nasal voice entertained the public for more than four decades.

Although her comedy routines and publicity stunts, such as running for president on the Surprise Party ticket, made her a household word and the symbol of female silliness, in reality Allen was not much like the character she played. She was a private person who enjoyed a quiet family life when she was not meeting the demands of her highly successful show business career.

A Performer From the Start

Grace Ethel Cecile Rosalie Allen was born on July 26, 1906, in San Francisco, California, to George and Margaret "Pidgie" Allen. George Allen was a song and dance man who abandoned his family when Gracie was about five

years old. Her mother later married Edward Pidgeon, a police captain.

Allen first performed at the age of three, doing an Irish dance at a church social. Her mother sewed dresses for Allen and her sisters Bessie, Pearl and Hazel to wear while performing Irish and Scottish dances. The family taught dancing in the basement of their house. From the start, Allen was determined to get into show business. Almost every day after coming home from the Star of the Sea Catholic School, Allen would walk from theater to theater dreaming of a time when her picture would be posted in one. She loved the film star Charlie Chaplin and, for her sixth birthday, her stepfather arranged for her to meet him.

Allen began working professionally as a singer while she was still a child. During school vacations she sang in local movie houses. After graduating, she and her sisters performed a song and dance act as The Four Colleens. When they broke up, Allen became part of a vaudeville act, for which she was paid $22 a week. (Vaudeville was a type of entertainment popular in the early 20th century, consisting of a variety of acts, such as song-and-dance, juggling and comedy routines.) At about age 18, Allen quit that act and found herself alone and unemployed in New York City. After six months of searching for a partner, she enrolled in stenography school to learn to be a secretary.

Partnership with Burns

In 1923, Allen's roommate took her to see an act performed by Billy Lorraine and George Burns, whose real name was Nathan Birnbaum, son of immigrant Orthodox Jewish parents. Burns and Allen decided to work together, first performing in Newark, New Jersey, for $5 a day. At first, Burns played the comedian and Allen the "straight man," feeding Burns the straight lines, to which he would respond with the punch lines. Allen, however, got all the laughs. Eventually the act was changed so that Burns was the straight man and Allen the comedian. Allen played a type of character known as a "Dumb Dora," or "dizzy dame." According to Burns, in his book, *Gracie: A Love Story,* "What made Gracie different was her sincerity. She didn't try to be funny. Gracie never told a joke in her life, she simply answered the questions I asked her as best she could, and seemed genuinely surprised when the audience found her answers funny. Onstage, Gracie was totally honest. . . . The character was simply the dizziest dame in the world, but what made her different from all the other 'Dumb Doras' was that Gracie played her as if she were totally sane, as if her answers actually made sense. We called it illogical-logic."

In 1924, the team began working as a "disappointment act," which substituted on short notice if a regularly scheduled act could not perform. For two years, Burns and Allen traveled, filling in for other acts.

Burns fell in love with Allen, although she was planning to marry an entertainer named Benny Ryan. In 1925, she almost married Ryan, but a last minute booking for a tour of the Orpheum circuit theaters took her out of town. On that trip, Burns proposed to Allen; but she said no. Finally she chose Burns over Ryan, and the two were married in Cleveland, Ohio. Six weeks after the wedding, the team signed a five-year contract, which paid between $450 and $600 a week. They had hit the big time. In 1930, they played on Broadway for 17 weeks, a vaudeville record.

From Vaudeville to Movies and Radio

In 1929, the couple performed on radio for the first time. Also that year, they appeared in their first film, a nine-minute short, for which they were paid $1,800. Paramount was so pleased with the result that the firm signed the pair to a contract for four more shorts at a rate of $3,500 each. Over the next two years, they made a total of 14 short films. Their first of 12 full-length feature films was *The Big Broadcast of 1932* and their last film was *Two Girls and a Sailor,* made in 1944.

In 1932, the pair joined bandleader Guy Lombardo's radio show. CBS gave them their own radio program called "The George Burns and Gracie Allen Show" in 1933, which featured comedy routines and songs. A publicity stunt turned the pair into major radio stars: Allen suddenly appeared on other radio shows asking if people had seen her missing brother. This gimmick lasted quite a while and brought the couple much attention. Other stunts included Allen's mock run for president in 1940 and her exhibit of surrealist paintings. Their radio show lasted 17 years.

In 1934, the couple adopted a baby girl, Sandra Jean, and bought a home in Beverly Hills, California. In 1935, they adopted Ronald John.

From Radio to Television

The first episode of the television program "The Burns and Allen Show" aired on October 12, 1950. For a while, the couple did both their radio and television programs, until they were sure that television, a new medium, would succeed. Many of the shows that changed over from a radio format to television failed, but "The Burns and Allen Show" was a big hit. The TV show ran for eight years—299 episodes. Allen and Burns played themselves as television actors, and the show took place in their "home." The plots often involved their neighbors, with whom they socialized by going out to movies or playing cards. Burns moved in and out of character, sometimes addressing the audience directly and sometimes participating in the action of the show. The early shows combined sitcom and vaudeville, with guest singers and dancers. Commercials were worked in as part of the show. The program ended with Burns saying, "Say good night, Gracie." She would bow and say, "Good night."

Allen's acting ability came from the fact that she did not "act"—she simply "did." Noted Allen, as quoted in *Say Good Night, Gracie,* "I really don't act. I just live what George and I are doing. It has to make some sort of sense to me or it won't ring true. No matter what the script says there's no audience and no footlights and no camera for me. There's no make-believe. It's for real."

For the first two years, the show was performed live, every other week. After that it became a weekly, but was filmed. Theirs was one of the first shows to use cue cards. It was also one of the first television programs to be filmed in color, the first color episode airing on October 4, 1954. In 1955, the couple's son joined the show playing their son, another innovation. Daughter Sandy appeared on the show 30 times.

Allen at Home

Allen suffered from intense migraine headaches but rarely missed work because of them. For relaxation, she loved to shop and had a special fondness for furs. She was always perfectly groomed and wore beautiful clothes, always with three-quarter length sleeves to hide scars from a childhood accident caused when she pulled a boiling pot off the stove, burning her arm and shoulder. Allen's name was often on the list of the ten best dressed women. She was petite, weighing 103 pounds and wearing a 4 1/2 shoe size.

Allen had her first heart attack in the early 1950s and suffered heart problems over the next several years. She did not enjoy the intense pace of a weekly TV program, and on June 4,1958, the couple filmed their last show. In eight years, the show received 12 Emmy Award nominations but never won. Allen received six nominations as best actress/comedienne, and the show received four nominations for best comedy series.

Allen spent her retirement years shopping, playing cards, reading, visiting friends and redecorating her home. She loved going out at night, especially to the theater, but after suffering a serious heart attack in 1961, she no longer had the energy to do so. Allen lived six years after her retirement, dying on August 27, 1964, in Los Angeles. She was buried in Forest Lawn Memorial Park in Hollywood.

Burns noted in his book, *Gracie: A Love Story* "I go to Forest Lawn Cemetery once a month to see her and I tell her everything that's going on. I told her I was writing this book about her. Evidently she approves—she didn't say anything. I don't know if she hears me, but I do know that every time I talk to her, I feel better."

In 1975, the Annual Gracie Allen Awards were established for broadcasting that demonstrates superior quality and stellar portrayal of the changing roles and concerns of women. The Awards seek to promote positive and realistic portrayals of women in all broadcasting mediums.

Burns died in 1996, a few weeks after his 100th birthday. He worked until he was 99 years old, performing in nightclubs and making television commercials. A good friend, actress Ann Miller, noted in an interview with CNN that Burns looked forward to being reunited with Allen. After his death, Miller said, "He has finally joined Gracie. That was his love. I know he missed her so terribly and now he will be with her."

Books

Blythe, Cheryl and Susan Sackett, *Say Goodnight, Gracie: The Story of Burns and Allen,* E.P. Dutton, 1986.
Burns, George, *Gracie: A Love Story,* G.P. Putnam's Sons, 1988.

Online

"Clinton, Others Pay Tribute to Burns," *CNN,* http://www10.cnn.com (October 23, 2001). □

Steve Allen

A true Renaissance man, Steve Allen (1921-2000) accomplished more in one lifetime than most men could in ten. Author of more than 50 books, composer of thousands of songs, and a comic genius, Allen will undoubtedly be remembered best as a pioneer of the late-night television talk show.

Allen's stint as the first host of the *Tonight Show,* a late-night TV institution, paved the way for his well-known successors, including Jack Paar, Johnny Carson, and Jay Leno. But Allen was far more than just a witty, wise cracking television personality. For decades he captivated radio and television audiences with his unique blend of humor—sometimes sophisticated and subtle and other times bordering on the slapstick. However, this somewhat superficial comic facade masked a complex man of many parts. He was an accomplished pianist who loved jazz, a composer of note, an activist who championed many causes, an actor, and a thoughtful author. Steven Allen was a true fount of creativity, driven by a force that he admitted as bigger than he. "I don't seem to have much control over it," he told *People* Magazine not long before his death.

"There's always a certain excitement that accompanies the creative impulse, and that energy always gets me going."

Born into Vaudeville

Born Stephen Valentine Patrick William Allen in New York City on December 21, 1921, he was the son of vaudeville comedians Billy Allen and Belle Montrose. When Allen was only 18 months old, his father died suddenly. Because she needed to continue performing to earn a living, his mother left young Allen in the care of her family—the Donohues—in Chicago while she traveled the vaudeville circuit. His boyhood was unsettled at best, and he attended 18 different schools before finally graduating from high school. Of Belle, Allen later observed that "she had an innate wit" but "was really not ideally cast for the role of mother."

Despite the turbulence of his childhood, Allen credits his years with the Donohues with ingraining in him a sense of comedy and comic timing that, in the years to come, would serve him well. The Donohues created for Allen a world of laughter, bantering and bickering constantly but never without at least a touch of humor. In 1989 he told the *Boston Globe*: "The reason I don't have ego problems is that I'm clear about one thing. My gifts are in the same category as the color of my eyes: genetic. It's just a roll of the dice."

After finishing high school in Chicago, Allen headed to Drake University in Des Moines, Iowa, and later transferred to Arizona State Teachers College (now Arizona State University) in Tempe. Even the change in location failed to jump-start Allen's interest in formal higher education, and he dropped out of college in 1942. Alone in Arizona after leaving school, he managed to land a job as a disk jockey at Phoenix radio station KOY, where he produced his own show. Outside of work, he developed a comedy act that he showcased in local clubs. In 1943, Allen wed Dorothy Goodman, his college sweetheart, with whom he had three sons, Steve Jr., Brian, and David. The couple was divorced in 1952.

Before long, with World War II raging in Europe and the Pacific, Allen was drafted into the Army, but he was released from his military service obligation after only a few months because of his frequent asthma attacks. In his 1960 autobiography, *Mark It and Strike It,* Allen described himself in the early 1940s as "a pampered, sickly bean-pole, too weak for athletics and too asthmatic for the Army."

A Job in Hollywood

After his release from the Army, Allen headed west to Hollywood, where he landed a job with radio station KNX in 1948. It was at KNX that Allen developed his now-familiar routine of blending relaxed banter, tickling the ivories, discussing his mail, and spur-of-the-moment improvisations—a blend that clearly appealed to his radio audience. So popular was Allen's radio show that two years later he decided to take it to television. On Christmas Day 1950, the *Steve Allen Show* made its television debut. Before long, Allen was invited to join the panel of the popular television quiz show, *What's My Line?*

In 1953, Allen's big break came when he was asked to host a late-night talk show on NBC television. It was an untried format at a time of night—11:30 p.m. to 1 a.m.—that usually attracted few viewers, and most knowledgeable observers held out little hope for its success. But they hadn't reckoned on the magic that Allen could conjure up on very short notice. And conjure it, he did. Building on a base made up of the same blend of music, banter, and zany sketches that had so charmed his radio audiences, Allen added the allure of high-profile guest stars. The combination proved irresistible to television viewers who suddenly started pushing back their bedtimes so they wouldn't miss the *Tonight Show.* Not only did Allen fashion a roaring success out of a format most thought held little promise, but he laid the groundwork for some of the skits his successors would be performing on the *Tonight Show* years later. Johnny Carson's Carnac owes much to Allen's Question Man, first showcased on the late-night show in the mid-1950s. In 1954, Allen married Jayne Meadows, a film and television actress he had met at a dinner party. Meadows, born of missionary parents in Wu Chang, China, was the sister of Audrey Meadows, who was best known for her portrayal of Jackie Gleason's wife in the "Honeymooners" sketches. Two years later, Allen played the title role in *The Benny Goodman Story,* a feature motion picture.

Head to Head with Sullivan

Encouraged by the success of the *Tonight Show,* a success built largely on the charisma and creativity of Allen, NBC, in 1956, asked the comedian to put together a variety/ comedy show the network could air opposite the wildly popular *Ed Sullivan Show* on CBS Sunday nights. For a while, Allen juggled the responsibilities for both shows. By 1957, however, he left the *Tonight Show* to focus solely on his Sunday night *Steve Allen Show.* Allen's show proved to be stiff competition for Ed Sullivan, running neck and neck in the ratings for the four years it was on the air. In 1960, after winning the Peabody Award for the best comedy show, Allen decided to leave the show after seven years with NBC.

However, Allen was hardly through with television. He took his many talents to ABC, which hosted Allen's weekly comedy hour during the 1961-62 season. This was followed by a show patterned closely after his very successful *Tonight Show* format. That show, sponsored by Westinghouse, ran for three years, after which Allen jumped to CBS to host for three seasons that network's popular game show *I've Got a Secret.* Allen and his wife hosted a weekly comedy show for CBS during the summer of 1967. He followed up the summer show with a daily TV series that was syndicated by Filmways and Golden West Broadcasters and ran from 1968 through 1972.

Throughout his years in television, Allen introduced to American audiences some of the most gifted comedians in the land. Among his finds were Jonathan Winters, Don Knotts, Bill Dana, Louis Nye, Tom Poston, Foster Brooks, Gabe Dell, and Tim Conway. Many of these comics worked on Allen's next major television project, a weekly 90-minute program entitled *Laughback,* which featured a mixture of live comic routines and filmed highlights from past Allen shows.

In a 1989 interview with a reporter for the *Boston Globe,* Allen offered his views on humor: "Jokes are always about sexual frustrations, about being too fat or too skinny. We laugh at our tragedies in order to prevent our suffering . . . If we think about the tragedies on our planet, we could spend all day in bed crying. So we laugh to survive, to continue our lives."

Developed Comedy Specials

Allen earned a reputation as a man who could successfully juggle a vast number of projects. In addition to his long-running TV projects, he developed a number of successful comedy specials. Among these was ABC's annual spoof of the beauty pageant phenomenon. Entitled the *Unofficial Miss Las Vegas Showgirl Beauty Queen Pageant,* the show's premiere outing in 1974 was hailed by Johnny Carson as "the funniest show of the year."

A prolific author and songwriter, Allen turned out more than 50 books and literally thousands of songs, earning a place in the Guinness Book of World Records as the modern era's most productive composer of songs. Perhaps his best-known song is "This Could Be the Start of Something Big," which became his theme. His books ran the gamut from humor to social protest. Shortly before his death, he was putting the finishing touches on *Vulgarians at the Gate,* a protest against what Allen saw as excessive sex and violence on television. One of Allen's earlier books, *Beloved Son,* drew its theme from a painful family experience. In the mid-1970s, his son Brian joined a commune, operated by what many believed was a cult, and changed his name to Logic Israel. His son's sudden distancing of himself from his father and the rest of his family "hurt and stunned" Allen at first, but in time he came to better understand and appreciate Brian's beliefs. It was this gradual process of acceptance that he recounted in *Beloved Son.*

Throughout his career, Allen was outspoken on a number of sensitive issues close to his heart. A lifelong Democrat, he once considered running for Congress. In the 1960s he campaigned hard for migrant workers' rights. He held strong opinions about a variety of topics, including capital punishment, nuclear policy, and freedom of expression. Although he remained committed to the importance of freedom of speech, he was deeply offended by the growing sexual content on television, particularly from the tabloid TV shows in the late 1990s. He lashed out at those responsible for such programming, contending that they were "taking television to the garbage dump."

Remained Humble

Despite his success, Allen remained a humble man, marveling at being able to achieve all that he had. On that subject, Allen said in an interview with Associated Press: "The world has already let me do about 28 times more than I thought I was gonna be able to do at the age of 217—so, thanks, to the universe." Worried that he might not accomplish all of his goals, Allen in 1979 told *People* Magazine: "It kills me that someday I'll have to die. I don't see how I'll ever get it all done."

The end came for Allen on October 30, 2000. He showed up that evening at the Encino, California, home of his son Bill, bearing a Halloween cake. He clucked over the Halloween costume granddaughter Amanda, 6, was planning to wear the next night and played with his grandchildren for awhile. Later, he complained of feeling tired and asked if could rest in the guest bedroom. When son Bill went to check on him later, he discovered that his father was no longer breathing. He had died of a massive heart attack.

His death was felt keenly among Allen's friends in the entertainment business. Milton Berle told *People* Magazine: "We've lost a heavyweight. He was one of the most talented and kindest men we had in the industry." Jay Leno, who recalled fondly watching Allen on TV as a boy, wrote in *Time*: "He never played dumb. Rather, he played to his intellect. And he was as comfortable talking to the man on the street as with world leaders. The highest compliment my mom could give anyone was that he was a nice man. Steve Allen was truly a nice man." Bill Maher of ABC-TV's *Politically Incorrect* told *People* Magazine that Allen was "the Beatles of talk shows. Anybody could get his comedy, and he touched audiences in a powerful way. Everything that came after was just a variation."

Periodicals

Entertainment Weekly, November 10, 2000.
People, November 13, 2000.
Time, November 13, 2000.

Online

"Entertainer Steve Allen Dead at 78," CNN.com, http://www .cnn.com/2000/SHOWBIZ/TV/10/31/steve.allen.02/ (November 11, 2001).
"Steve Allen," http://www.uoregon.edu/~splat/Steve_Allen .html (November 11, 2001).
"Steve Allen," Friars Club of California, http://www.friarsclub-ca .org/biosteve.html (November 11, 2001). □

Sofonisba Anguissola

An internationally respected Renaissance portrait and genre artist, Sofonisba Anguissola (1535?-1625) thrived as a professional painter in a male-dominated milieu. As court painter to Philip II of Spain and art instructor to Queen Isabella of Valois, Anguissola took seriously her pursuit of the liberal arts. On numerous canvases, she demonstrated the development of realistic domestic scenarios, original studies that did not emulate the concepts of contemporary male painters.

S ofonisba was the daughter of Blanca Ponzone and Amilcare Anguissola, a minor noble and land owner in partnership with his father-in-law as a dealer in books, leather, silk, and art supplies. She was born around 1535 or a little earlier in Cremona, Lombardy, a north-central Italian province then under Spanish control. She and her five younger sisters and one brother lived in a comfortable palazzo on the Via Tibaldi two blocks from the city center and enjoyed an inherited family estate to the west at Bonzanaria on the Po River near Piacenza. At the height of the Italian Renaissance, when the gentry educated women only in courtesy, refined living, religion, and needlework, Anguissola had his girls trained in piano and painting. With Sofonisba as mentor, four of her sisters—Lucia, Europa, Elena, and Anna Maria—honed their talents well enough to interest the art community in Mantua, Urbino, Ferrara, Parma, and Rome.

Established International Reputation

A contemporary of Titian and Leonardo da Vinci, Anguissola studied under frescoist Bernardino Campi around 1546 and, upon his departure from Cremona, with draftsman and frescoist Bernardino Gatti, a former apprentice of Antonio Correggio. According to an article in *Renaissance Quarterly* by historian Mary D. Gerrard, Anguissola painted into the poses of her subjects numerous clues to her success in a patriarchal society and to her position among male artists. A double view of the painter and her first teacher earned fame for its lifelike imagery. She dated the canvas 1554 and added "Sophonisba Anguissola Virgo Se Ipsam Fecit" [Miss Sofonisba Anguissola herself made this]. The paired intensive pronouns, "Se Ipsam," indicate her pride in accomplishment. The choice of "virgo," which denotes that she is unmarried, also suggests

self-possession and independence as well as the unquestioned moral reputation of an upper-class gentlewoman.

To promote his daughter's prowess to an elite audience outside of Cremona, Amilcare sent her self-portraits to Pope Julius III and to the Este court in Ferrara. The paintings earned the praise of critic Giorgio Vasari and sculptor-painter Michelangelo, who admired her depiction of a laughing girl. Michelangelo challenged her to paint the opposite emotion. Instead of choosing a weeping Madonna, she produced for him "Boy Pinched by a Crayfish" (1555?), a glimpse of a tearful boy protesting a wounded finger after he plunged his hand into a tray of fresh shellfish held by a smiling girl. Michelangelo's emissary, Tomasso Cavaliere, delivered the second work, along with Michelangelo's portrait of Cleopatra, to Florentine philanthropist and art collector Cosimo I de Medici, Duke of Florence.

Captured Spirit of the Age

In addition to commissioned portraits and a minor amount of allegorical religious art, Anguissola produced luminous, energetic paintings of family groupings, including a much admired portrait of her sister Minerva in courtly dress and resplendent gold jewelry. A boon to historians, the depictions Sofonsiba painted of home life to hang in their Cremona palazzo preserve minute autobiographical details of furnishings, hairstyles, dress, art objects, and activities. Social scientists study her domestic pictures to learn the family's economic status as well as the nature of the Anguissolas' private behavior, gender expectations, and re-

lations among her parents and siblings, especially her brother, who was Amilcare's heir.

Anguissola's masterwork, an intimate conversation piece entitled "Three of the Artist's Sisters Playing Chess" (1555), introduced naturalism to the traditionally stiff, sometimes pompous home scenarios produced by her contemporaries. The painting glimpses the novelty of girls in competitive mode playing a board game popular among nobles since the early Renaissance. Because it requires logic and strategy, it characterizes the players as well educated and exposed to pastimes usually reserved for boys. Anguissola obviously admired her sisters for their spirit and displayed them as active, amiable, and intellectually curious.

Public acclaim for Anguissola's work tended to discount her innate gifts and hard work. Florentine artist Francesco Salviati wrote Campi in praise of his pupil and gave sole credit for her accomplishments to the teacher. In 1558, author Annibale Caro congratulated Anguissola's father on her skills as though they were a father-to-daughter gift. Other viewers of her art marveled that a mere woman could possess such talent. Poet Angelo Grillo praised Anguissola herself, but implied there was something freakish about her outstanding painting career by calling her a "miracle of nature."

Contribution to Art History

In her self-portraits, a genre in demand during the period, Anguissola pictures her wide-eyed likeness in austere braided hairstyle, no jewelry, and dignified black dress. Unlike the frivolous curls, gold baubles, ornate laces, and brocades fashionable among her female peers, this representation stresses a serious side to her personality as well as high self-esteem, decorum, nobility, and maturity. Her backdrops feature art paraphernalia, books, a chess set, and musical instruments, all elements of privilege and wealth and of her life as a serious student of high culture.

One of Anguissola's assets was her kinship with other females venturing into the arts. A valuable painting to art historians is her portrait of Croat illuminator and miniature painter Giulio Clovio, completed around 1557. He poses holding a treasured miniature of the Flemish artist Lavinia Terlincks (or Teerlinc), that Anguissola's painting preserves. She also fostered Bolognese painter Lavinia Fontana and Roman artist Artemisia Gentileschi and encouraged the instruction of other girls in the arts.

Court of Philip II

In 1559, Anguissola received an invitation to the court of Philip II of Spain, Europe's most powerful Hapsburg king, who learned of her talent from the Duke of Alba. Under the escort of the Duke of Sessa, she arrived in Madrid to take her place among mostly male courtiers and artists. During her 14-year residence, she guided the artistic development of his new French queen, Isabella (or Elizabeth) of Valois, and influenced the artwork of her two daughters, Isabella Clara Eugenia and Caterina Michaela. Anguissola painted a portrait of the king's sister, Marguerite of Spain, for Pope Pius IV in 1561 and, after Queen Isabella's death in childbirth in

1568, painted the likeness of Anne of Austria, Philip's third wife. For the royal family, Anguissola produced detailed scenes of their lives that now hang in the Prado Museum. With the gifts and a dowry of 12,000 scudi she earned along with her salary as court painter and lady-in-waiting to the queen, she amassed an admirable return from her craft.

In her late 30s, Anguissola entered an arranged marriage to Fabrizio de Moncada, a Sicilian nobleman chosen for her by the Spanish court. She lived with him in Palermo from 1571 to 1579 and received a royal pension of 100 ducats that enabled her to continue working and tutoring would-be painters. Her private fortune also supported her family and brother Asdrubale following Amilcare Anguissola's financial decline and death. Fabrizio died in 1579. Two years later, while traveling to Genoa by sea, she fell in love with the ship's captain, sea merchant Orazio Lomellini. Against the wishes of her brother, they married and lived in Genoa until 1620. She had no children, but maintained cordial relationships with her nieces and her husband's son Giulio.

Still productive into her 80s, Anguissola painted less often as her eyesight dimmed. In an atmosphere of collegiality, she welcomed art fanciers to her home and salon. In 1623, she befriended the young Flemish painter Sir Anthony Van Dyck, whom she advised on technique. In token of his regard, he painted her portrait.

Anguissola's adoring second husband described her as small of frame, yet "great among mortals." At her death around age 90, he buried her with honor in Palermo at the Church of San Giorgio dei Genovese. In 1632, the dedication of her tombstone celebrated her life. A Cremonese school bears the name Liceo Statale Sofonisba Anguissola. Reclaimed to art history during the rise of feminism, in 1995, 20 of her 50 paintings toured Europe and appeared at an exhibition at the National Museum of Women in the Arts in Washington, D. C., entitled "Sofonisba Anguissola: A Renaissance Woman."

Books

The Concise Oxford Dicitonary of Art and Artists, edited by Ian Chilvers, Oxford University Press, 1996.

History of Art, fifth edition, edited by H. W. Janson and Anthony F. Janson, Harry N. Abrams, Inc., 1997.

Perlingieri, Ilya Sandra, *Sofonisba Anguissola: The First Great Woman of the Renaissance,* Rizzoli, 1992.

Periodicals

ARTnews, September 1995.
Ms. Magazine, September 1988.
The Nation, July 31, 1995.
Renaissance Quarterly, Spring 1994; Autumn 1994.
Smithsonian, May 1995.

Online

"Anguissola, Sofonisba," *Encarta,* http://encarta.msn.com/index/conciseindex/AD/OAD95000.htm. (October 28, 2001).

"Sofonisba Anguissola (1532-1625)," *Women in Art,* http://mystudios.com/women/abcde/s_anguissola.html (October 28, 2001).

"Women Artists, Sixteenth-Seventeenth Centuries," *California State University at Pomona,* http://www.csupomona.edu/~plin/women/16_17century.html (October 28, 2001). □

Vladimir Ashkenazy

An internationally recognized solo pianist, chamber music performer, and concert conductor, Vladimir Ashkenazy (born 1937) has made music with some of the most prestigious orchestras and soloists. In addition, he has recorded a large storehouse of classical and romantic works. His virtuoso recordings have earned him five Grammy awards plus Iceland's Order of the Falcon.

Born to Evstolia Plotnova and David Ashkenazy in Gorky (now Nizhni Novgorod), Russia, on July 6, 1937, Vladimir Davidovich Ashkenazy showed talent early in his childhood. He attended Moscow's Central Music School and the Moscow Conservatory, where he studied with Anaida Sumbatyan and Lev Oborin. In his late teens, he won second place in an international Chopin piano competition in Warsaw, Poland. In 1956, he won first prize in the Queen Elizabeth International Piano Competition in Brussels, Belgium. At the age of 23, Ashkenazy married Icelandic pianist and fellow student Thorunn Johannsdottir, who became his travel manager and the mother of their five children—Vladimir Stefan, Nadia Liza, Dmitri Thor, Sonia Edda, and Alexandra Inga.

From Russia to the World

Beginning his musical career at the keyboard, Ashkenazy clenched his place as a master musician by winning the 1962 Tchaikovsky international piano competition. According to his KGB [Soviet secret police] companion, travel ignited Ashkenazy's enthusiasm for freedom in the West. He debuted in concert with the London Symphony Orchestra and performed a recital at London's Festival Hall in 1963, the year he parted permanently with his homeland.

The break was not without trauma. In an interview with John Stratford and John Riley in October 1991, Ashkenazy reflected on the miseries of living under Communist mind control. He spoke of the constant brainwashing, which forced people into madness. Under a nightmarish regime, he recalled how easily some citizens became disoriented and retreated into psychotic states.

Ashkenazy left all that behind, settled in Iceland in 1973, and refused to teach his children Russian. It was in the 1970s that he began directing his efforts away from piano toward conducting. He performed with the best—the Berlin Philharmonic, Boston Symphony, Los Angeles Philharmonic, Philadelphia Orchestra, San Francisco Symphony, and Concertgebouw Orchestra—and toured the United States, South America, China, Japan, and Australia.

Recalled the Past

In 1985, with the aid of Jasper Parrott, his British manager and close friend, Ashkenazy published a straightforward autobiography, *Ashkenazy: Beyond Frontiers.* The text covers his childhood and musical training at special schools, where the talented children of Russia's elite were prepared for competition against foreign musicians. He describes the privileges that the top performers earned for themselves by winning contests and denounces state suppression of individuality, spirituality, and self-knowledge. Critic Peter G. Davis of the *New York Times Book Review* compared Ashkenazy's revelations to similarly painful memories expressed by other artists fleeing to the West from Soviet regimentation.

In a distinguished, post-Russian musical career, Ashkenazy has earned a reputation for accuracy, dynamism, and silken phrasing. He has teamed with such star performers as Itzhak Perlman, Pinchas Zukerman, Lynn Harrell, Elisabeth Soederstroem, Barbara Bonney, and Matthias Goerne. In 1987, Ashkenazy began a long and profitable alliance as conductor of the Royal Philharmonic Orchestra. He has served as guest conductor for the Cleveland Orchestra, and, since 1989, as chief conductor of the Berlin Radio Orchestra.

Of Ashkenazy's lengthy discography and excellent public performances, reviewers tend to choose lavish descriptives—natural, poetic, opulent, tonally rich, energetic, and virtuoso. Later critiques noted that the competent, passionate young pianist gave place to a serious conductor who

slacks when he returns to the keyboard for a solo concert. In September 2000, *American Record Guide* critic John Beversluis hesitantly suggested that Ashkenazy has lost interest in piano and charged that his lackluster performances sound routine, detached, and mechanical.

Absorbed in Music

While serving as music director of the European Union Youth Orchestra, conductor laureate of the Philharmonia Orchestra, and honorary chairman of the Greater Princeton Steinway Society, Ashkenazy makes his home in Meggan, Switzerland. His residence is separate from the studio, which he can reach in bad weather by a ten-meter tunnel. He owns two pianos—a Steinway and a Bosendorfer—and a library containing thousands of CDs. For performances, his wife buys polo shirts in London, which he wears with custom-made suits from Switzerland. His wooden batons come from Amsterdam. He remains attuned to his work and considers conducting and piano practice a strenuous form of physical exercise.

In his mid-sixties, Ashkenazy credited his wife Thorunn with simplifying his life by traveling with him and helping with minor difficulties, like removing a splinter when he jabbed a baton into his hand. During air travel, he uses quiet time for studying scores rather than reading novels. He depends on dinner after a late concert and sometimes stays up after midnight for post-performance receptions with fans, foreign dignitaries, and royalty. At night, he hears music in his dreams. When he has time alone with his family, he enjoys reading nonfiction about the Cold War era, watching the news, and eating simple meals cooked by his wife and her sister, who is the family housekeeper. On vacation in Greece or Turkey, he follows a daily regimen of swimming, boating, or walking.

In speaking of his career, Ashkenazy hesitates to explain why he chose music or why music so consumes his life. In a June 2000 interview with journalist Michael Green of *Swiss News,* Ashkenazy described his interests as just music rather than solo piano, chamber music, or orchestral conducting. Modestly, he explained, "Naturally, I understand what it means to play an instrument, what it takes to produce the sound, but I'm not exceptional."

Ashkenazy characterized the approach of the instrumentalist-conductor as different from that of the conductor who has never performed, either solo or with a symphony. He surmised that the conductor who is also an instrumentalist has more empathy for symphony members. He supplied examples of his patient efforts to make individual players feel comfortable and relaxed. In estimating the future of music, however, he warned that there are more talented young musicians than the market demands.

In a critique for *American Record Guide* of Ashkenazy's 2001 recording of Mozart's piano concertos, music analyst Thomas McClain characterized the man in multiple disciplines: "Ashkenazy relishes the roles of pianist and conductor, and to his credit he fills both roles quite well." Comparing him to Bruno Walter, Jose Iturbi, and Mozart himself, McClain added that "Ashkenazy has the excellent musicians of the Philharmonia to work with, so he has a built-in advantage'' for producing a sound that is ''big, bold, and lively.''

Books

Almanac of Famous People, 7th ed., Gale Group, 2001.
Debrett's People of Today, Debrett's Peerage Ltd., 2001.

Periodicals

American Record Guide, March 1981; July-Aug 1981; September 1981; February-March 1982; July-August 1982; January-February 1995; May-June 1995; July-August 1995; July-August 1996; September-October 1996; September-October 1997; January 2000; July 2000; September 2000; July 2001.
Atlantic, July 1981.
Audio, January 1984; March 1984.
Billboard, May 2, 1981.
High Fidelity, June 1980; July 1980; September 1981; November 1981; December 1981.
Library Journal, January 1998.
Los Angeles Magazine, August 1981.
Los Angeles Times, January 16, 1985.
New Statesman, December 17, 1982.
New Yorker, April 20, 1981; October 19, 1981.
New York Times, December 27, 1981; October 4, 1996; March 12, 1997; November 24, 1997; March 26, 2000; March 29, 2000.
People Weekly, June 15, 1981; March 29, 1982.
Progressive, January 1984.
San Francisco, May 1981; March 1984.
Stereo Review, June 1980; November 1980; July 1981; October 1981; October 1982; January 1983; February 1983; April 1983; December 1983; January 1984; January 1995; April 1995; May 1995; July 1996.
Swiss News, June 2000.
The Washington Post, January 23, 1985; March 10, 1997; November 25, 1997.
Yale Review, Winter 1981; Spring 1981; October 1982; Autumn 1983; Spring 1984.

Online

''Ashkenazy, Vladimir,'' *Biography.Com,* http://search.biography.com/cgi-bin/frameit.cgi?p=http%3A//search.biography.com/print_record.pl%3Fid%3D3955 (October 29, 2001).
Biography Resource Center, http://galenet.galegroup.com/servlet/BioRC (October 28, 2001).
Contemporary Authors Online, The Gale Group, 2000 (October 28, 2001).
''Shostakovich and the Soviet State,'' *Shostakovichiana,* http://www.siue.edu/~aho/musov/ash/ash.html (October 29, 2001).
''Vladimir Ashkenazy,'' http://tms.hkcampus.net/~tms95225/ashkenazy.htm (October 29, 2001).
''Vladimir Ashkenazy,'' http://www.koningin-elisabethwedstrijd.be/bots/archives/bio/ashkenazycv.html (October 29, 2001).
''Vladimir Ashkenazy,'' *The Greater Princeton Steinway Society,* http://www.princetonol.com/groups/steinway/Ashkenazy.htm (October 29, 2001). □

Aspasia

A contributor to learning in Athens, Aspasia of Miletus (c. 470-410 BC) boldly surpassed the limited expectations for women by establishing a renowned girl's school and a popular salon. She lived free of female seclusion and conducted herself like a male intellectual while expounding on current events, philosophy, and rhetoric. Her fans included the philosopher Socrates and his followers, the teacher Plato, the orator Cicero, the historian Xenophon, the writer Athenaeus, and the statesman and general Pericles, her adoring common-law husband.

R enowned for talent, brilliant accomplishments, and beauty, Aspasia, daughter of Axiochus, was born to a literate Anatolian household around 470 BC in Miletus, the southernmost Ionian city and the greatest Greek metropolis of Asia Minor. Although there is no history of her early life, she obtained an education and developed interests in high culture. Her attainments were unusual for a woman living in the male-dominated societies of the eastern Mediterranean.

A New Life in Athens

Aspasia may have left home because she was orphaned about the time she reached marriageable age. As a member of the household of her sister, wife of the Athenian military leader Alcibiades, she emigrated northwest to Greece around 445 BC. For a livelihood, she developed a reputation as a fascinating, vivacious *hetaira,* one of many refined, educated courtesans or companions to learned male aristocrats. In the spite-tinged words of the comic playwright Aristophanes, she first opened a brothel at Megara. Along with some of her prostitutes, she traveled east to Athens to seek her fortune.

According to the biographer Plutarch's "Life of Pericles," Aspasia studied the flirtations of the courtesan Thargelia of Ionia and openly courted powerful men. Aspasia's "rare political wisdom" attracted the top male, Pericles, the Greek statesman and general who was then governor of Athens. Escaping a faltering marriage of many years, he divorced his wife, who took up with another man, and pursued Aspasia.

The alliance benefited both parties. Pericles established a loving relationship with Aspasia, whom some describe as his second wife. He drew criticism for becoming a homebody and the love slave of the Milesian outsider, whom malicious gossips privately accused of procuring women for the Athenian elite. In truth, Aspasia's brilliance may have had a greater appeal than her charm or sexual skills. As his mistress and intellectual equal, she maintained a stimulating open house that drew scholars, artists, scientists, statesmen, and intellectuals to discussions of current events, literature, and philosophy.

Advanced Education for Women

Because Aspasia was a Milesian, she lacked the protections of Athenian citizenship, including the right to marry. However, she turned her unique social position into an advantage. Living outside the traditional obstacles to education and the arts that Greek males imposed on women, she wrote and taught rhetoric at a home school she established for upper-class Athenian girls. She audaciously encouraged female students to seek more education than mere home tutoring in sewing, weaving, dance, and flute playing. The quality of her instruction also attracted interested men and their wives and mistresses. Famous Athenians participating in her salon include Socrates, his disciples Aeschines and Antisthenes, and perhaps the sculptor Pheidias and tragedian Euripides.

Aspasia's excellence at conversation, logic, and eloquent speech influenced Athenian philosophy and oratory. Socrates quoted her advice on establishing a lasting marriage by selecting a truthful matchmaker. Ironically, he held up Aspasia as a model mate. Distinguishing herself from the average Athenian housewife, she was an equal marriage partner to Pericles and the wise steward of their household goods.

Numerous accounts depict Aspasia's behind-the-scenes influence on political affairs. Socrates's dialogue "Menexenus" praises Aspasia for composing speeches for Pericles. One example, the classic funeral oration that he delivered over the casualties of the Peloponnesian War, Plato credits entirely to Aspasia. The comic playwright Aristophanes implied that her influence on the great statesman was so powerful that, in 432 BC, she persuaded him to issue a restrictive Megarian trade accord in retaliation against citizens of Megara who kidnapped girls from her brothel. Historically, his charge remains unsubstantiated.

The Price of Influence

Although highly regarded by the wise men of Athens and valued by Pericles for her counsel, Aspasia was charged with engineering wars on Samos and Sparta. Greek satirists ridiculed Pericles by calling his mistress unflattering names—Omphale, Dejanira, Juno, and harlot. In the stage comedy *Demes,* Eupolis openly denigrated Pericles by labelling his domestic companion a common courtesan. In 431 BC, on the eve of the Peloponnesian War, Pericles successfully defended her before 1,500 jurors from the Athenian comic poet Hermippus's unfounded charges that she procured freeborn women for Pericles and that she also maligned Greek gods. Despite these public humiliations, she remained with Pericles for about 16 years, until his political decline and death in 429 BC, during the outbreak of plague that killed a third of the city's population.

According to the historian Thucydides, for political reasons, Pericles sponsored a law in 451 BC that declared as aliens all people born of non-Athenian parentage. The statute not only denied Athenian citizenship to Aspasia, but also to her son, the younger Pericles, the statesman's only surviving son and heir after Xanthippus and Paralus, two sons born to his first marriage, died of plague. Because so many leaders perished during the epidemic, under a special dispensation requested by the elder Pericles, Aspasia's son became a citizen. He distinguished himself during the Peloponnesian War as a general at the battle of Arginusae in 406 BC and afterward was executed along with other captured Athenian war strategists.

Aspasia's last years are largely unchronicled. She took up with Lysicles, a minor leader and sheep dealer who fathered her second son. Until Lysicles's death in 428 BC, he profited politically from associating with Pericles's former common-law wife. Although many references to her appear in ancient writings, her words survive only through quotations from contemporaries. In the first century BC, the Roman orator Cicero adapted her lesson in inductive logic into a chapter on debate. In 1836, the English poet Walter Savage Landor wrote a series of imaginary letters that pass between Pericles and Aspasia.

Books

Biographical Dictionary of Ancient Greek and Roman Women, edited by Marjorie Lightman and Benjamin Lightman, Facts on File, 2000.
Durant, Will, *The Life of Greece,* Simon and Schuster, 1939.
Henry, Madeleine M., *Prisoner of History: Aspasia of Miletus and Her Biographical Tradition,* Oxford University Press, 1995.
Lefkowitz, Mary R., and Maureen B. Fant, *Women's Life in Greece and Rome,* Johns Hopkins University Press, 1992.
Miles, Christopher, and John Julius Norwich, *Love in the Ancient World,* St. Martin's Press, 1997.
The Oxford Classical Dictionary, edited by N. G. L. Hammond and H. H. Scullard, Oxford Press, 1992.

Radice, Betty, *Who's Who in the Ancient World,* Penguin Books, 1973.
Who Was Who in the Greek World, edited by Diana Bowder, Washington Square Press, 1982.

Periodicals

College English, January 2000.
Criticism, Winter, 1999.

Online

''Aspasia,'' http://itsa.ucsf.edu/~snlrc/encyclopaedia_romana/greece/hetairai/aspasia.html (October 30, 2001).
''Aspasia,'' *Biography.Com,* http://search.biography.com/cgi-bin/frameit.cgi?p=http%3A//search.biography.com/print_record.pl%3Fid%3D7292 (October 30, 2001).
''Aspasia,'' *The Woman Behind the Great Men of 5th Century B. C.,* http://students.ou.edu/L/Lisa.A.Lewis-1/ (October 30, 2001).
''Aspasia of Miletus,'' http://sangha.net/messengers/aspasia.htm (October 30, 2001).
''Democracy as Introduced by Athens,'' http://www.iamoconf.xroads.net/globetrotter/greece/grdemocracy.htm (October 30, 2001).
''The Plague in Athens during the Peloponnesian War,'' http://www.indiana.edu/~ancmed/plague.htm (October 30, 2001). □

Chet Atkins

With his unique guitar-picking style, Chet Atkins (1924-2001) produced music from country to jazz in a career spanning over 50 years, making him the most recorded solo instrumentalist in country music history. His talent for finding and nurturing new recording stars and introducing new sounds earned him a second career as a record company producer and executive.

Chet Atkins was born Chester Burton Atkins on a farm near Luttrell, Tennessee, a small town about 20 miles north of Knoxville, on June 20, 1924. His parents, James Arly Atkins and Ida Sharp Atkins, each had children from a previous marriage. The family was large and poor. With a father who was a music teacher, piano tuner, and evangelist singer, a mother who played piano and sang, and siblings who played instruments, Atkins was surrounded by music from birth. At the age of six he played his first instrument, a ukulele, replacing broken strings with wire pulled from a screen door. Three years later he began playing a Sears Silvertone guitar and a fiddle along with his siblings and their stepfather, Willie Strevel. He and a brother played at local gatherings, throwing a hat on the ground into which listeners were encouraged to toss spare change. They were quite successful with this during the Depression years of the 1930s. Atkins idolized his talented half-brother, Jim, who was 13 years older. Jim Atkins was a guitar player on network radio and later performed with guitarist Les Paul. The younger, budding musician was influenced by what he heard on radio and records, including the songs of country music pioneer Jimmie Rodgers.

However, despite the music and large family, Atkins had a difficult childhood. He was an extremely shy and asthmatic child. Music became a way for him to express himself in those early years. He referred to his childhood in eastern Tennessee in a letter to friend Garrison Keillor, writing, ''Those were some of the worst years of the old man's life, don't you know. But even the bad ones are good now that I think about it.'' James and Ida Atkins divorced in 1932. In hopes that a different climate would improve Atkins' asthma, he was sent to live with his father in Columbus, Georgia, in 1936.

Developed a Unique Style

Atkins' move to Georgia widened his musical sphere, bringing him radio programs from Knoxville and Atlanta, Cincinnati and New York City. As a boy he listened to guitarists on a crystal radio set he had assembled by himself and tried to imitate them. Cincinnati's station WLW is where he first heard and tried to copy Merle Travis playing guitar. In doing so, Atkins developed his own style. Because he could not observe Travis, only listen to him on the radio, Atkins couldn't see that Travis played the guitar with his thumb and just one finger. So, as Atkins told Bill Milkowski in *Down Beat* magazine, ''I started fooling around with three fingers and a thumb, which turned out to be this pseudo-classical style that I stuck with.'' His admiration for his hero never waned. Atkins named his daughter Merle.

When he signed an autograph for Travis years later, he wrote, "My claim to fame is bragging that we're friends. People just don't pick any better." This signature thumb and finger guitar-picking style Atkins created not only influenced future musicians, but led Atkins to design guitar models, collaborating with the Gretsch Guitar Company, and later with Gibson.

Began Performing

While still in school, Atkins began performing on radio stations. At the age of 17 he quit high school to enter the music field. Atkins returned to Tennessee and landed his first job at radio station WNOX in Knoxville, fiddling for the duo of Archie Campbell and Bill Carlisle. He later played on the daily barn dance show. Atkins was also moonlighting as a jazz guitarist. Though management and other artists recognized his talent, this tendency to mix jazz with country, along with absences due to asthma, got him fired often from radio stations during the 1940s. Restless by nature, Atkins moved to Cincinnati's WLW and then to Chicago's WLS "National Barn Dance." He was there just a short time before country star and host Red Foley whisked him off for a stint at the Grand Ole Opry in Nashville. That same year, 1946, Atkins made his first recording, "Guitar Blues," for Bullet Records.

Atkins left Nashville again, this time for station KWTO in Springfield, Missouri, where Si Siman nicknamed him "Chet" and promoted his artistry to record companies. The station eventually fired him, thinking his sound too polished for country music audiences, but Atkins was attracting fans. About this time, a woman saw him perform in a roadhouse. She wrote: "He sat hunched in the spotlight and played and the whole room suddenly got quiet. It was a drinking and dancing crowd, but there was something about Chet Atkins that could take your breath away." While in Cincinnati, he met Leona Pearl Johnson, a singer, who with her twin sister Lois, performed on station WLW. Atkins and Leona married a year later, July 3, 1946, when Atkins was 22 years old. They would remain together for the next 50 years, until the guitarist's death in 2001.

Hired by RCA

Impressed by Atkins' talent, RCA Victor recording executive Steve Shoal set off in search of the guitarist. He finally tracked him down in Colorado and offered him a contract. From his early RCA recording sessions came attention-getting numbers like "Canned Heat," Bug Dance," and "Main Street Brakedown." He sang on some of these recordings, many of which Atkins later tried to destroy. In 1949, along with performers Homer and Jethro, Henry Haynes and Kenneth Burns, he recorded "Galloping Guitar," which became Atkins' first big success. It was this year, too, that the industry dropped the derogatory term "hillbilly" in reference to country music. Not confident about a career in recording, Atkins continued performing on radio and stage.

The 1950s brought more exposure and a big career boost when the Carter family and Homer and Jethro invited Atkins back to the Opry stage. Country music publisher Fred Rose also befriended Atkins and involved him as a session player on some of the '50s top hits. He played with country music's great singer-songwriter, Hank Williams, on such big hits as "Cold, Cold Heart," Kaw-liga," and "Jambalaya," and on "Release Me" by "the first lady of country music," Kitty Wells. After years of listening to different styles of music and experimenting with his own, Atkins helped pioneer the era of rock and roll, playing on early rock records like Elvis Presley's "Heartbreak Hotel" and "Wake Up Little Susie" by the Everly Brothers.

RCA management's decision to not only feature Atkins as a solo performer but to use his talent as a session player proved lucrative for him and the company. Recording executives noticed how Atkins' suggestions helped other performers succeed, and they put him in charge of recruiting new talent. He found and nurtured talents who became top-of-the-chart country singers, including Don Gibson, Waylon Jennings, Bobbie Bare and Dottie West. His own stardom increased with the release of two albums in 1951. His hit version of "Mr. Sandman" in 1955 showed his knack for interpreting music written by others.

Increased Country Music's Audience

Atkins played a major role in popularizing country music by finding talent and producing hits for many great names, including Don Gibson, Skeeter Davis, Jim Reeves, Roy Orbison, Charley Pride, Jerry Reed, Eddy Arnold, and many others. RCA made Atkins manager of their new Nashville recording studio that opened in 1957. As a producer with an eye for talent, Atkins succeeded in signing future stars, including singer-songwriter-musicians Dolly Parton and Willie Nelson, who both became diversified entertainers with crossover record hits and starring movie roles. Just as Atkins continued to adapt his own style to changing trends, the country music industry now needed to do the same to compete with the popularity of rock and roll. RCA named Atkins as their division vice president for country music in 1968. He helped to attract a wider audience by producing a more modern sound, using string arrangements instead of the traditional fiddles and steel guitars. He and Owen Bradley of Decca Records are credited with this style of orchestration, later called the "Nashville Sound."

During the 1960s, Atkins signed on singer-songwriter Bobby Bare and encouraged Bare's flair for "recitation" songs, which mixed singing and speaking. Results included "Detroit City" and "500 Miles Away From Home," both of which hit not only the top of country charts, but also pop music's top-ten lists. As radio, television, and Opry host Ralph Emery relates in his book, *50 Years Down a Country Road,* Atkins trusted Bare's musical and recording know-how "to such an extent that Chet did the unthinkable in those days. He allowed Bare to produce his own records. That was the beginning of the so-called Outlaw Movement of the 1970s." Along with the growth of 'outlaw' music, the gap between country and pop music narrowed in the 1970s. Performers were using more electric guitars, and country music gained more urban audiences.

Career Continued to Flourish

At the age of 49 in 1973, Atkins became the youngest artist ever inducted into the Country Music Hall of Fame. He had already performed at the White House for President Kennedy and the Newport Jazz Festival in the previous decade, and went on to perform in diverse fields when he played classical music with Arthur Fiedler and the Boston Pops Orchestra and recorded with Paul McCartney. He played with legendary guitarists Doc Watson, Les Paul, and his lifetime idol, Merle Travis; with British rock star, Mark Knopfler; and with contemporary country singer-guitarist, Suzy Bogguss. Compact discs containing Atkins' older numbers still pleased music critics, while some of his recordings aired on progressive and new age music radio stations. Appropriately dubbed ''Mr. Guitar,'' the title of his 1960 album release, Atkins earned recognition as Country Music Association's instrumentalist of the year nine times between 1967 and 1988, and as *Cash Box* magazine's top guitarist many times throughout the 1960's and 1970's. Atkins remarked to *Rolling Stone* magazine, '' . . . 'world's greatest guitar player' is a misnomer. I think I'm one of the best-*known* guitar players in the world, I'll admit to that.'' If a title was used, he preferred:''c.g.p'' for certified guitar player.

In 1982, after more than 30 years with RCA, Atkins left the label and joined Columbia Records. He released his first album with Columbia the same year, ''Work It Out With Chet Atkins.'' He continued recording and releasing albums during the 1980s and 1990s, touring the United States, Africa, and Europe with his music. At age 72, Atkins started doing club dates, performing with bass, drums, and even a little singing. In an interview at Caffe Milano, he said. ''That's my favorite thing, I guess, to play for an audience, because it's such a challenge. . . . You got to get out there and do it right . . . I think I'm a better musician than ever because my taste has improved.''

While managing to promote both country music and rock and roll, Atkins' own recordings, ranging across the musical spectrum, garnered 14 Grammy awards. The Lifetime Achievement Award presented to Atkins in 1993 by the organization that presents the Grammy awards cited his ''peerless finger-style guitar technique, his extensive creative legacy documented on more than 100 albums, and his influential work on both sides of the recording console as a primary architect of the Nashville sound.'' A street in Music Row in Nashville is named after him, and a downtown statue of Atkins with his guitar was erected in the year 2000.

A Farewell in Nashville

Twenty years after being treated for colon cancer, Atkins underwent surgery in 1997 for a benign brain tumor and to repair damage caused by a stroke. He continued working, releasing an album of contemporary artists singing country classics the following year. However, complications from his cancer led to Atkins death at his home in Nashville on June 30, 2001. Atkins was buried at Harpeth Hills Cemetery in Nashville, leaving his wife Leona, daughter Merle, two grandchildren and a sister. His life is described in two Atkins' books, one put out near the end of his

life, *Just Me and My Guitars*, and his 1974 autobiography, *Country Gentleman*.

At a memorial service held at Ryman Auditorium in Nashville, original site of the Grand Ole Opry, radio host, author, and longtime friend Garrison Keillor delivered a heartfelt eulogy. To an audience of over a thousand, he described Atkins as a man who loved doing shows but liked to be alone backstage to enjoy the quiet and calm; a restless man; a musician with a mind of his own; and a great storyteller. He was an inspiration to others, but also admired other performers' works and went out of his way to tell them so. ''He was the guitar player of the 20th century,'' Keillor continued, describing Atkins as the perfect model of a guitarist: ''You could tell it whenever he picked up a guitar, the way it fit him. His upper body was shaped to it, from a lifetime of playing: his back was slightly hunched, his shoulders rounded. . . .''

Keillor's tribute and the picture he painted of the legendary guitarist seemed an altogether fitting image to leave with Atkins' legions of fans and for the generations of fans yet to come.

Books

Contemporary Musicians, Gale Research, 1991.
Emery, Ralph, *50 Years Down a Country Road,* William Morrow, 2000.

Online

''Chet Atkins,'' World Music Portal, http://www .worldmusicportal.com/Artists/USA_artists/chet_atkins.htm (October 31, 2001).
Contemporary Authors Online, ''Chester Burton Atkins,'' The Gale Group, http://www.galenet.com/servlet/BioRC.
Flippo, Chet, ''Nashville Music Legend Chet Atkins Dead at 77,'' Country.com, ysiwyg://10/http://www.country.com/news/ feat/catkins.obit2.063001.jhtml (October 30, 2001).
Detroit News staff, ''Chet Atkins, 77, dies of cancer,'' Detroit News, wysiwyg://47/http://detnews.com/2001/obituaries/ 0107/02/a02-242409.html (October 31, 2001).
Kar, Paromita, ''Legendary guitarist Chet Atkins dies,'' britannicaindia, wysiwyg://27/http://www.britannicaindia.com (October 31, 2001).
Keillor, Garrison, ''Eulogy to Chet at his funeral,'' MisterGuitar, wysiwyg://6/http://www.misterguitar.com/news/eulogy.html.
Orr, Jay, ''Chet Atkins Remembered as 'A Great Giant','' wysiwyg://8/http://www.halloffame.org/news/archibe/hof-chet-atkins-funeral-0701.html (October 31, 2001).
Patterson, Jim, ''No rust on Atkins,'' http://www.canoe.ca/ JamMusicArtistsA/atkins_chet.html (October 31, 2001). □

Louisa Atkinson

Caroline Louisa Waring Atkinson (1834-1872), known as Louisa Atkinson, was an Australian writer, botanist, and illustrator; she is best known for her natural history journalism.

Atkinson was born on February 25, 1834, the fourth child of James and Charlotte Barton Atkinson. James, a successful farmer, was also a magistrate; Charlotte was well-educated and artistically gifted. Atkinson was born at her parents' estate, Oldbury Farm, in the lower Southern Highlands of New South Wales. She was born less than fifty years after the first British fleet arrived in Australia, carrying convicts to colonize Australia. At the time of her birth, she was one of only 12,000 people of European descent who were Australian-born. In the Australia of her time, convicts sent from England, Scotland, and Ireland were a common part of society. They labored on farms and in towns, and when they escaped, became "bushrangers," or outlaw bandits. Aboriginal people and the white settlers often had bloody clashes, and the Aborigines began to be pushed off their old territories by force and through attrition brought on by European diseases. Atkinson eventually wrote about all of these topics, as well as the gold rushes of the 1850s, the advent of large-scale sheep and cattle farming, and the native plants, animals, and birds of Australia.

As a child, Atkinson was greatly interested in nature, an interest encouraged by her mother. Charlotte, who was an artist and the author of the first children's book both written and published in Australia. The book was titled *A Mother's Offering to Her Children* (1841). Her father also set an example. He wrote *An Account of the State of Agriculture and Grazing in New South Wales,* a handbook for English people who wanted to emigrate to Australia.

Childhood

Atkinson's father died just two months after she was born, and her mother took over the management of the family estate. This job was made more difficult by the lack of law and order in the district. Once, while riding to a remote sheep station, she and George Bruce Barton, the estate's superintendent, were held up by bushrangers. Charlotte evidently decided that the situation was too difficult for a woman alone, and in 1836 she married Barton. Barton, however, turned out to be mentally unstable and dangerous. In 1839, when Atkinson was five years old, her mother fled with her and her siblings to the Atkinsons' cattle station at Budgong. They spent the next six months in a rough shack in remote country. Later, Atkinson and her mother both said that despite the primitive accommodations, the time they spent there was a welcome refuge. While in the shack, Charlotte told her children stories and taught them to observe and draw native plants, animals, and birds.

Eventually, they were forced to move to Sydney and seek financial support from the Atkinson estate. A six-year court battle ensued with the estate's executors. At the time, mothers were not automatically considered their children's guardians, and Charlotte did not win custody of her children at first. The court used her actions in fleeing from her husband as proof of her unstable nature and her unfitness to keep her children. Eventually Charlotte did win custody of her children. The long legal battle left a mark on Atkinson, who included critical commentary on lawyers in several of her novels. Her novel *Tom Hellicar's Children* (1871) is semi-autobiographical.

When Atkinson was twelve, the family returned to the estate at Oldbury, where she lived for the next seven or eight years. Her older siblings were sent to a private school, where they won honors, but Atkinson, who had suffered from tuberculosis since childhood, was taught at home. Although there was no cure for the disease at that time, patients sometimes had spontaneous remissions of their symptoms. Atkinson used these healthier times to do her reading and nature exploring. She was noted for her cheerful, kind manner, which made her attractive to many people, especially children.

At Oldbury, Atkinson studied birds, animals, and plants and learned to study nature systematically. She eventually trained herself to be a natural historian; a collector of botanical specimens, animals, and birds; and an illustrator. She observed animals and birds in the wild, dissected them, and taught herself taxidermy. In a notebook, she recorded changes in the seasons, animal behavior, and plants and illustrated her observations with her own sketches. During this time, she also continued to read widely. Her interests included poetry and prose as well as works of natural history such as Samuel Griswold Goodrich's *Peter Parley's Cyclopedia of Botany, Including Familiar Descriptions of Trees, Shrubs, and Plants* (1838). She had similar reference books on geology and zoology.

Work Published

In 1853, when she was nineteen, Atkinson wrote and illustrated an article of nature notes, and offered it to the editor of the new *Illustrated Sydney News*. It appeared in the second issue of the paper on October 15, 1853. This began her career as a writer. Between 1853 and her death in 1872, she wrote many popular articles on natural history, for which she was known only by the initials "LA." These articles were published in the *Illustrated Sydney News, Sydney Morning Herald, Sydney Mail,* and the *Horticultural Magazine.* She also wrote about Aboriginal life and customs. In 1855 she began to draw a small income from her father's estate, which allowed her to have a small measure of financial independence.

Atkinson wrote six novels, using the pseudonym, "An Australian Lady." These novels, according to Elizabeth Lawson in the *Oxford Companion to Australian Literature,* are notable for "their close observation of colonial life from a domestic point of view." Her first novel, *Gertrude the Emigrant: A Tale of Colonial Life* was published when she was twenty-three and was the first Australian novel written by a native born Australian woman, as well as the first to be illustrated by its author. The novel, set at an estate similar to Oldbury, stars Gertrude, a young immigrant woman who is "making a life in a colony which is itself in the making," according to the publisher of the modern edition. Drawing on her own experiences as well as family stories, Atkinson set her novel in the convict and immigrant culture of Sutton Forest, Sydney, and the Shoalhaven in the late 1830s and 1840s. The novel is both a traditional romance and a murder mystery, and according to the publisher, Atkinson as journalist and writer "cannot avoid a wandering mode of picaresque which allows her recording eye free play."

Readers of the time enjoyed the novel because it was one of the first that depicted their own Australian colonial society. It was sympathetically written by a woman who was born and raised in that society. The novel was first published in serial format: twenty-four sections, each eight pages long. Each section sold for threepence. It took six months to release the entire serial. The story appeared in novel form in 1857 and was published by J. R. Clarke of Sydney. The book included over twenty woodcut illustrations by Atkinson.

According to the publisher, the novel's value for modern readers lies in its detailed description of Australian life of the time, as well as its description of forests and ecologies that are now lost to development. In addition, the novel presents Australian life as a culture in and of itself, not simply an example of transplanted European culture. It is also an example of early feminism: most of the important characters are women who are independent, strong, and capable.

Atkinson followed *Gertrude the Emigrant* with *Cowanda, the Veteran's Grant: An Australian Story* (1859). Also published by J. R. Clarke, it was set in a different part of New South Wales, based on Atkinson's new home at Kurrajong Heights in the Blue Mountains west of Sydney. Atkinson and her mother had moved there hoping that the fresh mountain air would improve her health. The book is set on the estate of an old veteran, Captain Dell, but some scenes feature the gold fields west of Sydney, Dell's outback sheep station, and offices in Sydney. The novel follows the lives of Dell's grandchildren: Rachel, who is strong and courageous and Gilbert, who is ruined when he gives up his job and joins the gold rush. Beginning during the gold rush, the novel later depicts their romantic relationships with others.

Like *Gertrude the Emigrant,* the novel was attractive to contemporary readers, most of whom knew someone who had gone to the gold fields and who enjoyed seeing their own communities and experiences in fictional form. Both novels shared flaws in structure, character development, and had intrusive authorial commentary on religion, but many readers were willing to overlook these for the sake of reading about contemporary Australia.

Became Expert Botantist

While living at Kurrajong Heights, Atkinson's tuberculosis went into remission, and she spent a great deal of time exploring the outdoors and collecting plants and animals. Beginning in 1860, she wrote a series of articles, titled "A Voice from the Country," for the *Sydney Morning Herald.* Although she was untrained and a woman, she became an expert botanist in a time when the unusual flora and fauna of Australia was a topic of great fascination for natural scientists all over the world. She often took two days to explore, riding and walking and collecting plant specimens in a pouch that she had designed herself. On returning home, she wrote articles about what she had seen. She also spent much of her free time visiting sick people and teaching Sunday school in her home.

A local schoolmaster, William Woolls, introduced Atkinson to some of the well-known scientists of her time, including Ferdinand von Mueller, who was director of the Melbourne Botanic Gardens; naturalist William Sharp Macleay; and geologist/clergyman William Branwhite Clark. She sent von Mueller three hundred specimens of plants she had found in Kurrajong. Von Mueller realized that Atkinson had discovered plants that were unknown to European science, as well as plants that were so rare that they had been seen only once or twice before. One orchid that she found had not been seen by anyone since the early days of the nineteenth century. When von Mueller published his twelve-volume compendium of Australian plants, *Fragmentia Phytographiae Australiae,* between 1858 and 1882, he named several plants after her. These include the Loranthaceous genus *Atkinsonia,* as well as the plants *Erechtites atkinsoniae* and *Epacris calvertiana.* When British botanist George Bentham published his seven-volume work on the plants of Australia, *Flora Australiaensis,* he mentioned Atkinson's work 116 times. In addition, a fern, *Doodia atkinsonii,* was named in her honor.

Atkinson's four subsequent novels, including *Debatable Ground, or the Carillawarra Claimants* (1861), *Myra* (1864), *Tom Hellicar's Children* (1871), and *Tressa's Resolve* (1872) were published as serials in the *Sydney Mail* and the *Sydney Morning Herald.* All of these except *Tressa's Resolve* were reprinted in the 1980s and 1990s by Mulimi Press and Books on Demand. Mulimi Press has also published two collections of Atkinson's natural history journalism, *A Voice From the Country* (1978) and *Louisa Atkinson, Excursions from Berrima and a Trip to Manaro and Molonglo in the 1870s* (1980).

Marriage and Death

In the mid-1860s, Atkinson's health deteriorated. At the same time, her mother fell and broke her arm in several places, dislocated her elbow, and suffered a spinal injury. Atkinson spent all her meager energy tending to her mother, with great strain on her own health. In the meantime, however, she had met James Snowden Calvert. Calvert had been injured in an Aboriginal attack while exploring with an expedition in northeast Australia. When he returned from the expedition after being given up for dead, he became a farmer and engaged in botanical research. Although Atkinson wanted to marry him, her mother objected, partly because she did not want her daughter to leave her and partly because she was worried about Atkinson's health.

In October of 1867, Atkinson's mother died, leaving her free to marry Calvert. More than a year later, on March 11, 1869, the couple married and moved to Calvert's property, named Cavan, on the Murrumbudgee River. She took up writing nature columns again and continued writing when they moved to Oldbury and then to Winstead, near Berrima. Atkinson's brother James and his wife lived in the main house on this property, and Atkinson and her husband lived in a small cottage. Their marriage was happy, and Atkinson's health and creative energy improved. She wrote her nature columns and continued to collect plants.

When Atkinson was thirty-seven, she became pregnant. Because of her age and her precarious health, this was a matter of some concern to her and her husband. She gave up her botanical excursions to rest and worked on her last novel, *Tressa's Resolve*. On April 10, 1872, her daughter, Louise Snowden Annie Calvert, was born. Eighteen days later, however, Atkinson suffered a shock when she saw her husband's horse gallop into the yard without a rider. Fearing that he had fallen from the horse and been killed, she had a heart attack and died. Some time later, her husband, who had fallen but was not hurt, came home to find her dead. She was buried in the Atkinson family vault at All Saints' Anglican Church in Sutton Forest. *Tressa's Resolve* was published in the *Sydney Mail* after her death.

During the last year of her life, Atkinson wrote and illustrated a major work on Australian plants and animals. She sent it to von Mueller, who passed it on to other scientists. Unfortunately, due to the turmoil of the Franco-Prussian war, most of the manuscript was lost. In the *Dictionary of Literary Biography*, Patricia Clarke wrote, "If she had lived to see this project through to publication, possibly it would have gained for her an international reputation as a naturalist and illustrator."

Books

Jones, Joseph, and Johanna Jones, *Australian Fiction,* Twayne Publishers, 1983.

Lawson, Elizabeth, "Atkinson, Louisa," in *Oxford Companion to Australian Literature,* edited by William H. Wilde, Joy Hooton, and Barry Andrews, Oxford University Press, 1994.

Pierre, Peter, editor, *Oxford Literary Guide to Australia,* Oxford University Press, 1993.

Samuels, Selina, *Dictionary of Literary Biography, Volume 230: Australian Literature, 1788-1914,* Gale Research, 2001.

Online

"Atkinson, C. Louisa W. (1834-1872)," in *Australian National Botanic Gardens: Biography,* http://www.anbg.gov.au/biography/Atkinson-louisa.html (February 1, 2002).

"Atkinson, Caroline Louisa Waring (1834-1872)," in *Bright Sparcs, University of Melbourne* http://www.asap.unimelb.edu.au/bsparcs/biogs/P000072b.htm (January 21, 2002).

"The Gentle Arts: Australia's Women Pioneers in the Fields of Literature, Music and Fine Art," *National Pioneer Women's Hall of Fame,* http://www.pioneerwomen.com.au/gentlearts.htm (January 31, 2002).

"Gertrude the Emigrant," Australian Defence Force Academy University College Web Site, http://idun.itsc.adfa.edu.au/ASEC/CTS_books/gertrude.html (January 30, 2002). □

John Austin

British legal philosopher John Austin (1790-1859) is noted for providing the terminology necessary to analyze the interrelationship between ethics and proper law that has evolved into the modern field of jurisprudence.

A friend of noted nineteenth-century Utilitarian thinkers Jeremy Bentham and John Stuart Mill, British attorney and educator John Austin became well-known for his attempt to provide an easily understandable ethical framework that could establish the rule of law as distinct from the rule of "God" and Christian morality. Although they were little discussed during his own lifetime, Austin's writings, such as his 1832 work *The Province of Jurisprudence Determined,* paved the way for the more recent development of the school of analytical jurisprudence. As one of the foremost promoters of legal positivism, Austin argued that law, as opposed to moral imperatives, should be viewed simply as a form of command, made by an acknowledged and legitimate ruler, that gains adherence solely by means of an effective punishment.

Lackluster Career in Court

Austin was born in Creeting Mill, Suffolk, England, in 1790, to parents of average means. His father, a merchant, provided sufficiently for his family to enable his son to gain a commission in the military, where Austin remained from 1807 to 1812. Studying the law upon his release, he was called to the Bar in 1818. Disliking appearing in public and uncomfortable with his rhetorical skills, the bookish Austin practiced infrequently in England's chancery court and within only a few years had developed a rather lackluster reputation as an attorney due to his small caseload, his limited public-speaking skills, and his disposition toward illness and depression. In 1820 he had married Sarah Taylor, who as Sarah Taylor Austin became a successful editor and translator. Her works included the 1840 publication of *A History of the Popes* by German author Leopold von Ranke and French historian Francois Guizot's 1850 *The English Revolution.* Bolstered by his wife's emotional support and ability to earn enough money to support the couple's needs, Austin quit the practice of law in 1825.

Despite his less than stellar performance as a practicing attorney, Austin's obvious intelligence and his interest in the analytical aspects of legal theory drew the attention of Jeremy Bentham, an attorney and ethicist who had developed a following—its members known as Benthamites—to promote his philosophical views. Bentham's support resulted in Austin's 1826 appointment as the first professor of jurisprudence at the University of London, then just newly established (the University of London would eventually become University College, London) with Bentham as a founder. Austin's wife, who also shared her husband's utilitarian leanings and interest in legal reform, enjoyed the opportunity to frequent intellectual circles, and the couple eventually met such noteworthy individuals as Thomas Carlyle and John Mill. Throughout Austin's life she worked tirelessly to promote her husband's career despite his frequent bouts of melancholy.

Prior to beginning his teaching assignment at the university, Austin spent two years in Bonn, Germany, where he undertook the study of the law of ancient Rome. He also became fascinated with the classification systems and methods of analysis developed by German scholars to organize civil laws then on the books in the continent. A perfectionist, he wanted to devise a context in which to discuss his subject that would make it easily understood by the average student. Influenced by seventeenth-century English political philosopher Thomas Hobbes and his attempt to extend deductive reasoning to the study of man and society in his *Leviathan* (1651), Austin also looked to mathematical theory to develop a clear framework for his subject.

Returning to University College in 1828 to begin his classroom teaching, Austin made an early friend of John Stuart Mill, a Scottish-born ethicist fourteen years Austin's junior who would go on to become the most famous proponent of Utilitarianism—the ethical theory that maintains that one should always act to maximize the welfare of the greatest number. Along with his wife, Austin became close friends with Mill, as well as Bentham, who would die in 1832. While he shared his friends' Utilitarian bent, he did not share their ambition and their ability to get along well in social settings. As had been the case while attempting a career as a practicing attorney, Austin found himself still plagued by a frequent melancholy which prevented him from energetically opposing setbacks to his career.

Creates Foundational Framework for Philosophical Study

Jurisprudence—the philosophy of law as it relates to the restrictions imposed on the structure and actions of the court—was a relatively new area of legal study when Austin undertook his teaching post in London in 1828. Indeed, its roots can be found in the relatively new ideas of Utilitarian thinkers such as Mill and Bentham, particularly its concern over how to best determine the rule of law that will result in the greatest advantage to the greatest number in the community affected by the litigation in question. It is through the science of jurisprudence that courts formulate rules that determine the appropriate rules under which new cases or administrative matters with no established legal precedent should be handled.

In addition to being a "new" science, Jurisprudence was not a required part of the law curriculum in the early 1800s, and its theoretical element made it less than appealing to students more in need of strong oratory skills than theoretical understanding. Although he lectured in the subject for several years and drew many notable scholars of his day to his first lectures, Austin soon saw attendance at his lectures fall. Insufficient registration in his classes prompted him to resign his chair at University College, London in the spring of 1832.

Revolutionary Publication Initially Ignored

The publication of Austin's most notable contribution to British law, his *The Province of Jurisprudence Determined,* was concurrent with its author's departure from academic life. The volume included excerpts from his lectures on the subject, and in it he attempted to clarify the difference between proper law—the law that has its basis in the desire of the governmental authority—and moral law. According to Austin, laws can best be interpreted as a type of command: an expressed desire that another party perform or refrain from performing a specific action, this expression accompanied by the threat of a clearly defined sanction or punishment if not obeyed. To qualify as laws rather than other forms of commands, laws must outline a prescribed course of conduct rather than a specific act and must be set by a "sovereign" body: a supreme ruler or governing body to whom an independent society habitually looks for leadership. Sanctions can be positive or negative, and can include reward or punishment by state agencies; natural consequences or the dictate of one's conscience are not, in this case, legitimate sanctions. In this manner, "positive law" is distinguished from the laws of God that take their shape in moral principles and precepts and such things as social etiquette and international laws such as the unwritten laws of warfare, which have no source in a sovereign body.

In his work Austin outlines the basic theory, originated by Bentham, underlying what has since come to be called legal positivism due to its implicit argument that the law is based on no higher authority than the will of the sovereign power. Austin's utilitarian beliefs also inform his argument, for he further maintains that a law's "utility" is based on its general application rather than application to a specific instance or action. While a procedural matter may result in one guilty man being set free, it is nonetheless a just law if by its continued application it results in most guilty men being convicted.

Although not widely read by members of the legal profession immediately after its publication, Austin's book eventually gained influence over both English and American law by revolutionizing concepts of ethics as they relate to the legal system. By introducing terminology appropriate to the consideration of ethical matters within the legal realm, Austin's book facilitated the discussion that culminated in the establishment of the English analytical school of jurists.

The discussion of jurisprudence set forth in *The Providence of Jurisprudence Determined* was prefatory to an understanding of Austin's subsequent collection of lectures, compiled in Lectures of Jurisprudence, and published posthumously by Sarah Taylor Austin in 1863. Although unfinished at the time of his death, these lectures expand upon concepts relevant to the study of jurisprudence, such as "pervading notions" of duty, liberty, injury, punishment, right, status, and sources of laws. Austin viewed such institutional analysis as separate from a discussion of the institutions themselves, but maintained that a grounding in jurisprudence would facilitate the consideration of other aspects of the legal process.

Life Ended in Relative Seclusion

In 1834 Austin attempted to make a living by lecturing on jurisprudence in the Inner Temple, but was unsuccessful in this attempt and abandoned teaching altogether. Austin was appointed to the Criminal Law Commission in 1838 and participated in that body's first two reports. However, his frustration at not having his ideas incorporated in the commission's decisions prompted Austin to once more resign. An appointment by the British Crown as commissioner on the affairs of Malta, a group of three islands in the

Mediterranean off the south coast of Sicily, took the Austins abroad once more, and after retiring from his commission the couple moved to Paris. While attempting to revise his *Province* several times due to his own increasingly conservative views on politics and morality, Austin was unable to complete the task, likely due to the depression that haunted him throughout his life and the incapacity of the perfectionist. During the 1850s Sarah Austin provided for both she and her husband through her work as a translator and reviewer for English periodicals. In 1848 Austin and his wife returned to England and purchased a home in Weybridge, Surrey, where he lived until his death in December of 1859 at the age of sixty-nine. His wife survived him by eight years, dying in 1867.

Although Austin's life was noteworthy as much for its string of defeats, his analysis of proper law served as the basis for continued study in his field. Later jurists of his own century, such as the Americans Oliver Wendell Holmes and J. C. Grey, acknowledged Austin's contributions to legal theory, particularly his ability to draw a distinction between the law and morality. While his views have been more recently condemned by twentieth-century scholars such as H. L. A. Hart due to their inflexibility in the wake of changing social priorities, the structure and continuity of his analytical framework remains a respected standard.

Books

Campbell, E. M., *John Austin and Jurisprudence in Nineteenth-Century England,* 1959.

George, Robert P., editor, *The Autonomy of Law: Essays on Legal Positivism,* Oxford University Press, 1999.

Hamburger, Lotte, and Joseph Hamburger, *Troubled Lives: John and Sarah Austin,* University of Toronto Press, 1985.

Hart, H. L. A., *Of Laws in General,* Althone Press, 1970.

Mill, John Stuart, "Austin on Jurisprudence," *Dissertations and Discussions,* Vol. 4, 1874.

Rumble, Wilfred E., *The Thought of John Austin: Jurisprudence, Colonial Reform, and the British Constitution,* Althone Press, 1985.

Online

"John Austin," *Stanford Encyclopedia of Philosophy,* http://plato .stanford.edu (February 2, 2002). □

B

Irving Babbitt

Irving Babbitt (1865-1933) and Paul Elmer More were the two chief proponents of the New Humanist movement in the first half of the twentieth century.

Babbitt and the New Humanists perceived that Western culture had been negatively impacted by the naturalism of eighteenth-century French philosopher Jean-Jacques Rousseau, which was, in turn, perpetuated by the reliance on intuition and emotion in the works of the nineteenth-century Romantic era. Instead, Babbitt prescribed a thorough background in the literature that he believed instilled classical ethics, morality, and disciplined reason divorced from contemporaneous political and materialistic ideology and focused on universal conservative values. This conservatism in an era increasingly concerned with modernism made Babbitt and the New Humanists lightning rods for derision from the prevailing cultural critics, including Sinclair Lewis, who allegedly named the repressed title character of his 1922 novel *Babbitt* after him, and openly denounced the New Humanists in his Nobel Prize acceptance address. As a result of the popular novel, the name Babbitt became synonymous for a type of philistine individual who is mired in the past and rejects anything new out of fear. Babbitt had many supporters, however, including his former student T. S. Eliot, who adopted many of Babbitt's views on classical literature and the decline of cultural values, as well as his teachings on the Oriental belief systems Confucianism and Buddhism in his poem *The Waste Land.* Eliot and Babbitt remained lifelong friends but differed on Babbitt's belief in humankind's possession of an internal ethical will, an "inner check" with which Eliot disagreed on the grounds that it did not allow for the consideration of the existence of a higher spiritual power. Chief among his cultural concerns, Babbitt identified the notion of individuality as advanced by democratic approaches to education: "One is inclined, indeed, to ask, in certain moods, whether the net result of the [commercialism] movement that has been sweeping the Occident for several generations may not be a huge mass of standardized mediocrity; and whether in this country in particular we are not in danger of producing in the name of democracy one of the most trifling brands of the human species that the world has yet seen." Babbitt is credited also with creating a national forum to discuss literature as a means to shape and influence political and moral thought. In his book *The Conservative Mind,* Russell Kirk wrote that Babbitt "joined the broken links between politics and morals, and that is a work of genius. He knew that the conservation of the old things we love must be founded upon valid ideas of the highest order, if conservatism is to withstand naturalism and its political progeny."

From Ohio to Harvard

Babbitt was born in Dayton, Ohio, to Edwin Dwight and Augusta Darling Babbitt. His mother died when he was eleven years old. His father, a physician and businessman father, was engaged in several get-rich-quick schemes, including founding the New York College of Magnetics and publishing several health manuals with such titles as "Vital Magnetism: The Life Fountain." Historians conjecture that Babbitt's father's socialist politics and outlandish schemes served to encourage Babbitt's later outspoken conservatism. As a young man, Babbitt sold newspapers in New York City; lived for a time with relatives in Ohio; worked as farmhand; worked on a ranch in Wyoming; and was a police reporter in Cincinnati, Ohio. With financial assistance from his uncles, he attended Harvard College in 1885, where he earned a four-year degree in classics. Upon graduation, he accepted a position as a classics instructor at the College of Montana, earning enough money to enroll in Sanskrit and Pali classes held in Paris, France. He returned to Harvard, earning a graduate degree in 1893. He was appointed professor of Romance languages at Williams College, but returned to Harvard to teach French and comparative literature until his death in 1933. In his writings and lectures, Babbitt disparaged sentimentality, materialism, and a disregard for the past, while advocating self-restraint and personal discipline. He married one of his former students, Dora May Drew, in 1900, and the couple produced two children. In 1926, he was named a corresponding member of the Institute of France. In 1930, he was elected to the American Academy of Arts and Sciences, and received an honorary degree from Bowdoin College in 1932.

Babbitt was among the first literary critics to gain a wide audience by publishing essays in such mass-circulation periodicals as the *Atlantic Monthly* and the *Nation.* Several of these essays are included in his first book, *Literature and the American College: Essays in Defense of the Humanities,* which was published in 1908. In such essays as "The College and the Democratic Spirit" and "Literature and the Doctor's Degree," Babbitt negatively criticized the academic policies of Harvard president Charles William Eliot that allowed students to establish their own courses of study rather than enforce a rigid academic regimen emphasizing self-discipline. Babbitt argued that allowing students to elect their own course of study reduces the universal authority of the academy in favor of the individual. Among the chief culprits against a wide-ranging cultural education, Babbitt believed, was the influence of the French philosopher Jean-Jacques Rousseau. According to Babbitt, the wide acceptance of Rousseau's theories in Western culture resulted in the blurring of lines between natural laws for humans and laws for things. Agreeing with Ralph Waldo Emerson that the two laws remain separate, Babbitt believed that Rousseau and the Romantics endangered classical intellectual and rationalist humanist standards by replacing them with a sentimental and emotional attachment with nature. Such was his vehement attacks on Rousseau that his Harvard students joked that Babbitt checked under his bed for Rousseau each night before going to sleep.

Laokoon and the Inner Check

In his second book, *The New Laokoon: An Essay on the Confusion of the Arts,* published in 1910, Babbitt attacked the nineteenth-century Romantic movement, believing it to be a logical extension of Rousseau's philosophy of naturalism. By emphasizing powerful emotion, Babbitt believed, the Romantics negated form as a restraining mechanism necessary to raise art from the temporal to the universal. Borrowing the phrase "inner check" from Emerson—who had borrowed it from Eastern philosophy—Babbitt believed that a degree of self-discipline was necessary to temper what he perceived to be the excessive emotional and individualistic nature of nineteenth-century literature. According to Russell Kirk: "Those checks are supplied by reason—

not the private rationality of the Enlightenment, but by the higher reason that grows out of a respect for the wisdom of one's ancestors and out of the endeavor to apprehend the character of good and evil." In his next volume, *The Masters of Modern French Criticism,* published in 1912, Babbitt establishes a lineage of like-minded critics to support his belief that literature since Rousseau had been in steady decline. One critical measure of a literary work's merit, he wrote, was its historical perspective.

Following World War I, Babbitt widened his attacks on modernism, romanticism, and democracy, which he perceived to expediting the decadence of Western culture through materialism and unlimited growth. The resulting democratic aims of equality he believed resulted in the anarchy of proletarian art in place of high art. In *Democracy and Leadership,* he furthered his attacks on the democratization of literature and, by extension, society. Russell Kirk wrote: *Democracy and Leadership* is perhaps the most penetrating work on politics ever written by an American—and this precisely because it is not properly a political treatise, but really a work of moral philosophy." Among the philosophers and social critics Babbitt interpreted in this work was Edmund Burke, who advocated an adherence to the permanence of traditional values, which Babbitt called "imaginative conservatism." Babbitt's views were controversial, coming under attack for his authoritarian refusal by writers in such publications as *The New Republic* and the *Hound and Horn.* These writers faulted Babbitt's refusal to consider literature from the previous century, and his authoritarian approach to political and social beliefs. Babbitt argued his points to an audience of more than three thousand at New York City's Carnegie Hall, as well as in the pages of *The Bookman* and *The Forum,* as well as receiving support from T. S. Eliot in the *Criterion.* Eliot, however, rejected the secular nature of the humanist "inner check" because he felt it advocated ethics without religion. Paul Elmer More, perhaps the most ardent supporter of Babbitt's beliefs, also rejected the secular nature of the inner check.

Books

Adams, Hazard, *Critical Theory since Plato,* Harcourt Brace Jovanovich, Inc., New York, 1971.

Dictionary of Literary Biography, Vol. 63: Modern American Critics, 1920-1955, Gale Group, Detroit, Michigan, 1988.

Eliot, T. S., "The Humanism of Irving Babbitt," in *Selected Prose of T. S. Eliot,* Harcourt Brace Jovanovich, Publishers, Farrar, Straus and Giroux, New York, 1975.

Kirk, Russell, "Critical Conservatism: Babbitt, More, Santayana," in *The Conservative Mind: From Burke to Eliot,* Regenery Publishing, Inc., Washington, D. C., 1985.

Kirk, Russell, *Eliot and His Age: T. S. Eliot's Moral Imagination in the Twentieth Century,* Sherwood, Sugden & Company Publishers, Peru, Illinois, 1984.

Nevin, Thomas, *Irving Babbitt: An Intellectual Study,* University of North Carolina Press, Chapel Hill, North Carolina, 1984.

Periodicals

The New Republic, June 17, 1985, p. 36.

Online

Contemporary Authors Online, The Gale Group, 2000. □

Burt Bacharach

Composer/arranger Burt Bacharach (born 1928) established himself in the 1960s as one of America's premier pop songwriters. After achieving considerable success with recordings by Dionne Warwick and B.J. Thomas, among many others, he found his style of music out of fashion during the 1970s and 1980s. In the late 1990s, he returned to active composing as a new generation discovered his music.

The sophisticated melodies of Burt Bacharach were among the defining sounds of American popular music in the 1960s and early 1970s. In an era when rock gained ascendancy, his elegant compositions echoed the heyday of the great Broadway and Tin Pan Alley songwriters. In tandem with lyricist Hal David, Bacharach created songs graced with complex rhythms and fresh harmonic patterns that were rich in color and mood. The Bacharach/David team produced a remarkable body of work for the stage and screen as well as for the record-buying market. The Carpenters, Tom Jones, B.J. Thomas, Dusty Springfield and, most of all, Dionne Warwick were among the artists who popularized Bacharach's songs. The start of the 21st century found him increasingly productive, working with new collaborators and releasing retrospectives of his best work.

Early Years

Burt Bacharach was born in Kansas City, Missouri, on May 12, 1928. His father, Bert Bacharach, was a syndicated columnist and men's fashion journalist. His mother, Irma, was an amateur singer and pianist who encouraged her son to study music. Moving with his family to Forest Hills, New York, Bacharach studied cello, drums and piano as a child. His first strong interest was in sports. However, by the time he reached high school his piano playing abilities began to make him popular at school functions and local dances. Beyond his classical training, Bacharach found inspiration by sneaking into Manhattan jazz clubs and absorbing the sounds of such bebop innovators as Charlie Parker and Dizzy Gillespie. After high school, he studied music at McGill University in Montreal and at New York's Mannes School of Music. It was at the latter school that he came under the influence of composer Darius Milhaud, who encouraged his young student to develop his melodic talents.

During a stint in the armed services from 1950 through 1952, Bacharach was kept busy performing at army bases as part of a dance band. Back in civilian life, he became a New York nightclub pianist and arranger, working with such singers as Vic Damone, Steve Lawrence and the Ames Brothers. In 1953, he married vocalist Paula Stewart and began to find work in Las Vegas. His horizons broadened further when he signed on as actress/singer Marlene Dietrich's musical director in 1958. Bacharach began to become more serious about songwriting during this time. Exposure to the music of Brazilian bossa nova composers

Antonio Carlos Jobim and Dori Caymmi helped him develop his style further.

First Recordings

Bachrach's first hit recordings included Marty Robbins' "The Story of My Life" (1957) and Perry Como's "Magic Moments" (1958). Undoubtedly his oddest early tune was "The Blob" (1958), the novelty theme song from the horror film of the same title. His songwriting partnership with lyricist Hal David was beginning to solidify, paving the way for the exceptional songs that would come out of them a few years later. David and Bacharach worked together in New York's legendary Brill Building, a haven for hardworking songwriters. Increasingly, Bacharach was taking chances with his music. Some of his more unusual melodic and harmonic ideas met resistance from record companies. "All those so-called abnormalities seemed perfectly normal to me," he commented in the liner notes to *The Look of Love: The Burt Bacharach Collection*, a CD retrospective released by Rhino Records in 1998. "In the beginning, the A and R [Artist and Repertoire] guys, who were like first lieutenants, would say, 'You can't dance to it' or 'That bar of three needs to be changed to a bar of four,' and because I wanted to get the stuff recorded, I listened and ended up ruining some good songs. I've always believed if it's a good tune people will find a way to move to it." His unorthodox but appealing work began to reach a wider audience with such tunes as "Baby It's You" (recorded by the Shirelles and, later, by the Beatles) and "(The Man Who Shot) Liberty Valance" (a 1962 hit for Gene Pitney).

The elements that would define the Bacharach sound began to fall into place in the early 1960s. "Make It Easy On Yourself," released as a single by pop/rhythm and blues singer Jerry Butler in 1962, displayed the melodic grandeur and bittersweet lyric sentiments that would become the hallmarks of later hits. An even more significant release that same year was "Don't Make Me Over," the first Bachrach/David song recorded by Dionne Warwick. Her delicate phrasing and ability to convey both strength and vulnerability made her the ideal interpreter of the duo's songs. Warwick was able to handle the intricacies of Bacharach's demanding music with ease. The result was a series of enduring hit singles, among them "Anyone Who Had A Heart" (1963), "Walk On By" (1964), "I Say A Little Prayer" (1967) and "Do You Know The Way To San Jose" (1968). Bacharach arranged and co-produced his hits with Warwick, surrounding her voice with elegant strings, muted trumpets, tastefully-used background singers and other touches that became his trademarks.

Numerous other artists in both America and Britain found success with Bacharach/David songs, including Jackie DeShannon ("What the World Needs Now is Love"), Dusty Springfield ("Wishin' and Hopin'"), Herb Alpert ("This Guy's in Love With You"), and Sandie Shaw ("(There's) Always Something There to Remind Me"). Such films as What's New, Pussycat? Alfie, and Casino Royale featured the duo's material on their soundtracks. Bacharach and David made yet another leap when they wrote the score for the 1969 stage musical Promises, Promises, which enjoyed a long Broadway run and earned both a Tony and a Grammy Award.

In an era when songwriter/performers became the norm, Bacharach remained largely behind the scenes. His limited singing abilities were not seen as the best vehicles for his music. That being said, he did release a series of albums on his own, among them 1965's Hit Maker and 1967's Reach Out. These and subsequent efforts emphasized his arranging abilities as much or more than his vocal talents. The 1970s began on a high note for Bacharach when his score for the film Butch Cassidy and the Sundance Kid won an Academy Award, with the Bacharach/David song "Raindrops Keep Fallin' on My Head" chosen as best theme song as well. The success of "One Less Bell to Answer" by the 5th Dimension" and "(They Long to Be) Close to You" by the Carpenters (both 1970) continued the songwriting team's winning streak into the new decade.

Collaboration with David Ended

Unfortunately, the chemistry between Bacharach and David began to sour after their music for the 1973 film Lost Horizon proved to be a critical and commercial failure. The songwriters sued each other over a publishing dispute and their years of collaboration ended. Bacharach's career went into decline and he was largely absent from the record charts for the remainder of the 1970s. He remained a familiar enough figure to appear in television advertisements for Martini and Rossi vermouth with his then wife, actress Angie Dickinson.

It wasn't until the early 1980s that Bacharach began to emerge from his career doldrums. A working relationship with lyricist Carole Bayer Sager led to the pair's marriage in 1982. Among the Bacharach/Sager songs of note from this period was "Arthur's Theme (The Best that You Can Do)," recorded by Christopher Cross for the 1981 film Arthur. Another tune of theirs, "That's What Friends Are For," was released as an AIDS research benefit recording in 1986 and featured vocals by Dionne Warwick and Elton John, among others. The song became a hit and led to further recordings with Warwick in the early 1990s.

Revival in 1990s

Remarkably, a Bacharach revival began in the mid-1990s, when a younger generation discovered the so-called "easy listening" music of the 1960s. Such notable young rock acts as Oasis and Stereolab began to perform Bacharach songs, reworking his classic melodies in a modern context. The composer was the subject of a British television documentary and his recordings were reissued in several CD anthologies. British singer/songwriter Elvis Costello, a long-time fan, collaborated with Bacharach on a song for the 1996 film Grace of My Heart, which led to an album's worth of songs together, Painted From Memory two years later. Bacharach and Costello went on a concert tour in 1998 as well. Enjoying his renewed celebrity, Bacharach shared the stage with Oasis at a 1996 London concert and made a cameo appearance in the 1997 film comedy Austin Powers.

Bacharach continued to remain active into the new century, performing occasional shows with symphony orchestras and working on stage musicals. In May 2001, he accepted the Royal Academy of Music award, presented by King Carl Gustav XVI in Stockholm. Such recognition confirmed Bacharach's stature as one of popular music's most distinctive and enduring songwriting talents.

Books

Contemporary Musicians, Gale, 1997.

Gammon, Peter. Oxford Companion to Popular Music, Oxford University Press, 1991.

Stambler, Irwin, Encyclopedia of Pop, Rock and Soul, St. Martin's Press, 1977.

Online

"Burt Bacharach Biography," Rolling Stone.com, http:www .rollingstone.com (November 15, 2001). □

George Frederick Baer

George Frederick Baer (1842-1914) worked closely with legendary financier J. P. Morgan during American industry's most expansionary era. He headed the Philadelphia and Reading Railway Co., which carried coal from Morgan-owned coal mines in Pennsylvania to the cities of the East Coast. Baer is perhaps most remembered for his opposition to labor unions.

Baer was born on September 26, 1842, in Pennsylvania's Somerset County near a town called Lavansville. The family of his father, Major Solomon Baer, had emigrated from Germany and settled in the area in the 18th century. Baer was educated at the local Somerset Institute and the Somerset Academy, and began an apprenticeship at the local newspaper, the Somerset *Democrat,* as a teen. At the age of 15, he enrolled at Franklin and Marshall College in Lancaster, Pennsylvania. However, Baer left in 1861, when hostilities erupted between the North and South and first shots were fired in the U.S. Civil War. That same year, he purchased the Somerset *Democrat* with his brother Henry. Its coverage sometimes angered citizens in the area, and its offices were once besieged by a group of protesters determined to destroy its presses. When Henry Baer enlisted in the military, Baer was left to run the paper alone, writing its content and typesetting its pages; in his spare time, he studied to become a lawyer.

In the summer of 1862 Baer organized a company for the 133rd Pennsylvania Volunteers, and the men elected him captain. His unit joined the Army of the Potomac. Over the next year Baer led his men in several charges, including one during the second Battle of Bull Run. They also participated in the Antietam, Fredericksburg and Chancellorsville campaigns. He rose to the rank of adjutant general during his year of service, and then returned to Somerset and his law books. Admitted to the bar in April of 1864, Baer had established himself in a private practice in Reading, Pennsylvania by 1868. He argued one damage suit against the Philadelphia and Reading Railway Company so successfully that his opponent hired him as corporate counsel in 1870. This began Baer's long, and sometimes controversial, tenure with Philadelphia and Reading companies.

Morgan's Pennsylvania Agent

Baer became an investor in various manufacturing enterprises in the region, and was named to their board of directors. Through these activities he came to know legendary Wall Street financier J. P. Morgan, who made him the House of Morgan's representative in Pennsylvania. Baer helped Morgan secure a terminal in Pittsburgh for one of his railroads. When Morgan acquired and reorganized the Philadelphia and Reading Railroad in 1901, he named Baer as president of three Reading companies: Philadelphia and Reading Railway Co., the Philadelphia and Reading Coal and Iron Co., and the Central Railroad Co. of New Jersey.

It was a prosperous time in American business history for men such as Morgan and Baer, for there were few federal regulations regarding how they operated their businesses, taxes were almost nonexistent, and enormous profits were reaped. Wages and working conditions for the rank and file, however, were often abysmal. There was a growing trade union movement in the country—a development that executives like Baer and Morgan bitterly opposed. In May of 1902, the United Mine Workers of America led 147,000 employees of Pennsylvania's anthracite mining region off the job in protest. The workers petitioned the mine owners and operators for an eight-hour day, instead of a ten-hour one, and complained that they had not had a wage increase

in twenty years. The leaders of the union steered clear of the violence that had marked other labor actions in the recent past, which won them some sympathy from newspapers and politicians. Morgan, however, refused to become involved in the public battle in the nation's newspapers. Much of the task was then passed to Baer, who became the focal point for the consortium of mine owners and executives vehemently opposed to the strike. Initially, they were adamant in refusing to negotiate with the union. "We will give no consideration," Baer declared in a statement released to the press, according to the *Dictionary of American Biography,* "to any plan of arbitration or mediation or to any interference on the part of any outside party."

Controversial Letter

Baer's prominence in leading the opposition to the strike brought letters from ordinary citizens to his desk. Some supported his hard-line approach to the strikers— whom more conservative elements in American derided as anarchists, communists, or simple malcontents—while others pleaded with him to consider the side of the miners. In the latter camp was a minister from Wilkes-Barre, Pennsylvania, who urged Baer to end the strike. In a letter dated July 17, 1902, Baer responded to it in terms that were construed by many as arrogant and even blasphemous. "The rights and interests of the laboring man," Baer's response allegedly stated, "will be protected and cared for— not by the labor agitators, but by the Christian men to whom God in his infinite wisdom has given the control of the property interests of the country, and upon the successful management of which so much depends."

Baer's letter was reprinted in newspapers across the United States, and caused a minor stir. Editorial cartoons mocked him as a blasphemer, for his statement amounted to the declaration that God had placed men like himself in charge of the mines. Politicians, members of the clergy, and ordinary citizens were outraged; the controversy was seen to mark a turning point in American labor history, helping win more public sympathy for the passage of laws allowing workers the right to organize and to strike. Famed attorney Clarence Darrow dubbed Baer "George the Last," and writer Jack London mentioned it in a footnote in his 1907 science-fiction novel, *The Iron Heel.* The novel posited that capitalism would evolve into fascism. In one passage, London took American business leaders to task for their greed. "When they want to do a thing, in business of course, they must wait till there arises in their brains, somehow, a religious, or ethical, or scientific, or philosophic concept that the thing is right. . . . One of the pleasant and axiomatic fictions they have created is that they are superior to the rest of mankind in wisdom and efficiency," London continued. "Therefrom comes their sanction to manage the bread and butter of the rest of mankind. They have even resurrected the theory of the divine right of kings—commercial kings in their case."

Baer later denied the letter's authenticity, asserting that the quotes taken from it were not his words. The anthracite strike still dragged on, however, and there was talk of nationalizing the mines. As the autumn of 1902 approached,

East Coast coal supplies dwindled. The obstinacy of executives finally exasperated President Theodore Roosevelt, who intervened and demanded that both sides appear at the conference table. Baer initially stated that he refused to "waste time negotiating with the fomenters of this anarchy," and wanted Roosevelt to call in federal troops to end the strike; but Roosevelt had already stationed troops in the area and was considering using them to take over the mines. Faced with this potentially ruinous loss, Baer complied. A provisional agreement was struck that found the miners back at work on October 23.

Mired in Anti-Trust Controversy

Baer was called before the Interstate Commerce Commission in 1903. The *American* newspaper, owned by William Randolph Hearst, claimed that the Reading and other railroads were actively trying to restrict the output of coal and set the commodity's market price. This placed the companies in violation of a Pennsylvania law, dating from 1874, which stated that no railroad company could engage in mining, nor any coal company own a railroad that exceeded fifty miles in length. Baer claimed that the Philadelphia and Reading Railway Co., the Reading Co., and the Philadelphia and Reading Coal and Iron Co. were each distinct companies and had not violated the letter of the law.

Baer was an avid reader, and sometimes spoke at public dinners. He was known for a quiet demeanor. He was well liked by those close to him, but could be a tenacious and determined negotiator in the business world. His 1866 marriage to Emily Kimmel resulted in five daughters. When he died in April of 1914, his personal fortune was estimated at $15 million.

Books

Dictionary of American Biography Base Set, American Council of Learned Societies, 1928-1936.
National Cyclopedia of American Biography, James T. White and Co., 1910.
Strouse, Jean, *Morgan: American Financier,* Random House, 1999. □

Lakshmi Bai

Lakshmi Bai (c. 1835-1858), the Rani of Jhansi, is a national hero in India for her fight against the injustices of the British Raj.

As the reigning queen (Rani) of the Jhansi province of India, Bai was killed in a battle during the Indian First War of Independence provoked by the reigning British invocation of lapse, a policy by which the British claimed the lands of Indian kings (Rajas) without male heirs. She has since become emblematic of Indian rebellion against the encroachment of British imperialism and is celebrated by her country people as a woman who lived contrary to the perceived notions of nineteenth-century Indian feminine decorum. Many contradictory stories have been

written about Bai that depict her as either an honorable head of state or as a ruthless, deceitful, and cunning warrior. Likewise physical descriptions of Bai vary; some describing her as possessing beautiful facial features, and others describing her as badly scarred by smallpox. Nevertheless, she is considered an Indian national hero for leading the Jahnsi army against the British, resulting in many embellished stories and legends relating her attributes and accomplishments.

Rani of Jhansi

Bai was the daughter of Moropant Tabme, a court advisor, and his wife, Bhagirathi, who was reportedly a very learned woman. Born in Poona, her birth date is believed to be November 19, 1835. Named Maninkarnika and nicknamed Manu at birth, Bai moved with her high-caste Hindu parents to Varanasi in the northern portion of India from Poona in Western India at an early age. Her mother died when she was still very young, and her father inexplicably raised his daughter in the manner more customarily associated with sons. Two of her childhood friends were Nana Sahib and Tatya Tope, both of whom were active participants in the Great Rebellion. She learned to ride elephants and horses as well as how to handle weapons. While still a child, probably seven-years-old, she was promised in marriage to Raja Gangadhar Rao of Jhansi, a recently widowed king between the ages of forty and fifty. Upon her wedding, she took the name Lakshmibai or, alternately, Lakshmi Bai. When she was fourteen-years-old in 1849, Bai and Rao consummated their marriage, and Bai subsequently gave birth to a son who died three months later. Rao refused to allow Bai to continue her military studies with male students, and, undeterred, she assembled a regiment of female soldiers from her maidservants. Her husband's grief over the death of his heir was said to be so great that he took ill and died in 1853, making Bai the ruler of Jhansi when she was eighteen-years-old. Before his death, Rao named a male relative, Damodar Rao, his successor. Following her husband's death, Bai resumed her military training and recruited more women for her all-female militia.

In the nineteenth-century, the British government was intent on expanding and protecting its political and economic presence in India, which often resulted in it forcefully taking over entire states. Governor-General (later Lord) James Dalhousie also implemented the rule of lapse, which allowed the British to seize control of all land holdings by deceased Rajas without male heirs. In the case of Jhansi following the death of Rao, Dalhousie chose not to accept the adoption of Damodar Rao and proceeded to annex the kingdom in February 1854. The insult was furthered on religious grounds; according to Hindu law, a father's heir is responsible for performing specific rites ensuring that the father's soul is saved from punishment. By denying the legitimacy of Damodar's adoption, Dalhousie jeopardized the fate of Rao's soul. Bai is credited with drafting several letters to Dalhousie that are noted for their sound and reasoned arguments against annexing, including reminding him that a British official had been present when Rao adopted Damodar. When Dalhousie refused her requests anyway, she wrote him: "It is notorious, my Lord, that the more powerful a state . . . the less disposed it is to acknowledge an error or an act of arbitrary character." She later appealed to the Court of Directors of London, writing that the lapse represented a "gross violation and negation of the Treaties of the Government of India." She continued that if the actions were "persisted in they must involve a gross violation and negation of British faith and honor." In May 1854, Jahnsi lapsed to the British, and Bai was allowed to keep her palace and a pension of 60,000 rupees. She was forced to abdicate rule and abandon the fort in Jahnsi. Damodar Rao was allowed to inherit Rao's estate. Shortly thereafter, Bai was notified that the British expected her to repay her husband's debts out of her pension.

Insurrection and Revolution

During the next three years, Indian resentment and hostility grew toward the British. The Great Rebellion, or the First War for Independence, began in May 1857 in Upper India. Indian soldiers working for the British Raj rebelled violently, massacring British soldiers and their families. Within a month, the Indian soldiers had rebelled at the fort in Jhansi. History at this point relies on conjecture to accurately portray the true nature of what happened. Some sources note that Bai was cooperative with the British and offered to protect them in her palace although her authority could not, in the end, protect them from the essential massacre. Others say she was motivated by revenge and invited the families to her palace in order that they would be ambushed and killed en route. One of her defenders, Major W. C. Erskine, Commissioner of the Sagar Division, defended her as a ruler caught in an untenable situation. He wrote that Bai regretted her inability to help the British, and that the Indian mutineers had threatened to blow up her palace if she did not comply with their monetary requests. Erskine eventually changed his position, however, writing that Bai had instigated the mutiny.

Bai had reestablished herself as ruler of the state, enlisted and trained fourteen-thousand troops, and prepared for war by moving back into the fort at Jahnsi. In retaliation for the mutiny, the British sent an army to Jahnsi led by Major-General Sir Hugh Rose and laid siege upon the fort. After battling for more than two weeks, the British overran the fort. Total casualties for both sides were estimated at five thousand. Bai escaped and was tracked to Banda, where Rose's forces reported that "her escort made a hard fight of it, and though the fellows did their utmost and killed every man she got away. . . . She is a wonderful woman, very brave and determined. It is fortunate for us that the men are not all like her." Bai joined forces with her childhood friend Tatya Tope and they retreated to Kalpi, which also fell to Rose's forces in May 1858. The Indian rebels mounted an attack on the Rose's forces outside Gwalior in June 1958, and Bai was killed in battle in Gwalior on June 17, 1858. Reports of her death vary, with some stating that she was knocked from her horse by a bayonet or sword and shot at her assailant but missed. He, in turn, allegedly shot her, failing to realize who she was because she was dressed in men's clothing. Some reports say that Bai was not killed instantly, but was removed to a mango grove where she reportedly distributed her jewels to her subordinates. Her servants cremated her body according to Hindu custom. Rose wrote about his foe: "The Ranee was remarkable for her bravery, cleverness and perseverance; her generocity to her Subordinates was unbounded. These qualities, combined with her rank, rendered her the most dangerous of all the rebel leaders."

Books

Commire, Anne, editor, "Lakshmibai," in *Women in World History: A Biographical Encyclopedia, Vol. 9: Laa-Lydu,* Yorkin Publications and The Gale Group, 2001.

Hibbert, Christopher, *The Great Mutiny: India 1857,* The Viking Press, 1978.

James, Lawrence, *Raj: The Making and Unmaking of British India,* St. Martin's Press, 1997.

Online

"Lakshmi Bai," *Distinguised Women,* http:www .distinguishedwomen.com/biographies/bai.html, (January 29, 2002). □

Florence Bascom

Florence Bascom (1862-1945) was a pioneer in expanding career opportunities for women in the sciences. She was the first woman to receive a Ph.D. in geology from an American university, the first female to receive a Ph.D. of any kind from the Johns Hopkins University (1893), and the first woman to join the United States Geological Survey (1896). Bascom was a widely known and respected geologist whose work mapping the crystalline rock formations in Pennsylvania, New Jersey, and Maryland became the basis for many later studies of the area.

B ascom was born on July 14, 1862, in Williamstown, Massachusetts. This town was the home of prestigious Williams College, where her father, Dr. John Bascom was professor of oratory and rhetoric. Both Professor Bascom and his wife Emma (Curtiss) Bascom actively supported women's rights and had strong interests in the natural sciences. In 1874, John Bascom accepted the presidency of the University of Wisconsin, and his family left Williamstown. Florence Bascom was less than fifteen years old when she graduated from high school in Madison, Wisconsin. She then obtained, in 1882, two degrees—Bachelor of Arts and Bachelor of Letters degrees—from the University of Wisconsin. Two years later she earned a Bachelor of Science degree, and in 1887 completed a Master's degree in geology.

Roland D. Irving and Charles R. Van Hise were Bascom's mentors at Wisconsin. Both were eminent geologists, and it was under their tutelage that Bascom learned the techniques of an emerging field of geology—the analysis of thin, translucent rock sections using microscopes and polarized light. These methods had only recently been devel-

oped in Germany, and there existed no textbook from which to learn them. Instead, Bascom studied directly from the original research papers, written in German.

Attended Johns Hopkins University

As president of the University of Wisconsin, John Bascom was instrumental in instituting coeducation. Conversely, his daughter faced immense obstacles in applying for a doctoral program. She hoped to study with George H. Williams, a professor at the Johns Hopkins University renowned for his use of microscopic geological techniques. The Johns Hopkins, however, had not yet allowed a woman to officially complete a degree program. Bascom applied for admission to the Geology Department in September of 1890. Seven months later, the executive committee concluded that Bascom could attend without being officially enrolled as a student, and charged only for her laboratory fees. During classes, Bascom's seat was located in the corner of the classroom—and hidden behind a screen. Undaunted, Bascom applied formally to the doctoral program in 1892. She was accepted secretly. By intrepidly completing difficult and often solitary field work, Bascom produced a dissertation that a writer in *American Mineralogist* later described as "brilliant." For this, Bascom earned in 1893 the first Ph.D. in geology ever awarded to a woman by an American university.

After receiving her Ph.D., Bascom taught for two years at Ohio State University. In 1895, she accepted an invitation to join the faculty of Bryn Mawr College in Pennsylvania as

a Reader in Geology. She was hired to teach a single course, and the college had no plans to create a new department of geology. Because of her success, however, within a few years the single course grew into an entire major. Bascom was granted a full professorship in 1906. Bascom's specialty was petrology, the study of how present-day rocks were formed. Much of her research focused on the mid-Atlantic Piedmont region, and she wrote approximately 40 publications.

An Important Legacy

Bascom retired from Bryn Mawr in 1928. She had been editor of *The American Geologist,* a Fellow of the Geological Society of America (1894), and vice-president of that organization (1930). Through her research and teaching, Bascom left an important scientific legacy. In 1937, a total of eleven women were Fellows of the Geological Society of America; eight of them were Bryn Mawr College graduates. Never married, Bascom lived after retirement in her farmhouse atop Hoosac Mountain in northwestern Massachusetts. For several winters, she traveled to Washington, D.C., to complete work for the United States Geological Survey. Despite being shy, concise, and serious-minded, Bascom maintained close ties to her academic family of students and colleagues. She died of cerebral hemorrhage in Williamstown, Massachusetts, on June 18, 1945, and was buried next to her family in a small Williams College cemetery. According to former student Eleanora Bliss Knopf writing in *American Mineralogist,* Bascom's death left "to her colleagues, her students, and her friends the inspiring memory of a scholarly and brilliant mind combined with a forceful and vigorous personality."

Books

Arnold, Lois Barber, *Four Lives in Sciences,* Schocken Books, 1984.
Smith, Isabel F., *The Stone Lady: A Memoir of Florence Bascom,* Bryn Mawr College, 1981.

Periodicals

American Mineralogist, Volume 31, 1946.
Bryn Mawr Alumnae Bulletin, November, 1945; spring, 1965.
Science, September, 1945.
University of Wisconsin Department of Geology and Geophysics Alumni Newsletter, 1991. □

Leonard Baskin

Leonard Baskin (1922-2000) was one of the twentieth century's greatest sculptors and printmakers. Railing against the trends of the time, he maintained a focus on figurative art. Strongly influenced by classical forms, his work reflected his interests in Greek mythology and Jewish tradition and culture. Baskin is also known for having founded one of the longest-running arts presses in the United States.

Leonard Baskin was born in New Brunswick, New
Jersey, on August 15, 1922, to Samuel and May
(Guss) Baskin. His father was an orthodox rabbi, and
his brother became a rabbi, too. The family moved to New
York when he was seven, and he attended what he later
called a "dark, medieval" yeshiva in Brooklyn. When he
was a young man he worked in a synagogue for extra
money. This strong Jewish upbringing would eventually
form the foundation, or context, for his artistic vision. By age
15, he was interested in becoming a sculptor. He studied
sculpting as an apprentice to Maurice Glickman from 1937
to 1939 at the Educational Alliance in New York City.

In 1939, at the age of 17, he held his first one-man
exhibition of sculptures at the Glickman Studio Gallery. The
Prix de Rome awarded his work an honorable mention. This
was the first of 40 exhibitions in which his woodcuts, prints,
sculptures, and paintings would appear.

Inspired to Print His Own Books

From 1939 to 1941, Baskin attended the New York
University School of Architecture and Applied Arts. In 1941,
he won a scholarship to Yale, where he studied for two
years. At the Yale library he discovered William Blake's
illustrated books. He was so impressed by Blake that he
decided to learn to print and make his own books.

Baskin founded his own press, called Gehenna Press,
in 1942 (the name came from a line in *Paradise Lost,* "and
black Gehenna call'd, the type of hell"), while attending
Yale. One of the nation's first fine art presses, the Gehenna

Press printed over 100 books and became one of this country's longest running private presses. It ran until his death in
2000.

The first book from the Press was Baskin's book of
poems, *On a Pyre of Withered Roses.* Baskin illustrated
books by other authors as well, such as *Crow* by Ted
Hughes, *Seven Deadly Sins* by Anthony Hecht, and *Seven
Sybils* by Ruth Fainlight. He also published great works of
literature such as Blake's *Auguries of Innocence* and
Euripides's *Hippolytos,* and children's books, like *Hosie's
Alphabet,* which won the 1974 Caldecot Medal. Another
children's book, written and illustrated by Baskin, was
1984's *Imps, Demons, Hobgoblins, Witches, Fairies and
Elves.* The characters that populate the book were taken
from timeless stories by the Brothers Grimm, Shakespeare,
and folk traditions.

Baskin served in U.S. Navy in the Pacific at the end of
World War II, followed by a brief stint in the Merchant
Marines. He returned to the States and attended The New
School for Social Research in New York, where he gradu-
ated with a Bachelor of Arts in 1949. In 1946, he married
Esther Tane, with whom he had one son. Esther died in
1967.

In 1949, he made his first limited edition prints. The
following year, he spent in Paris at the Academie de la
Grande Chaumiere. In 1951, he attended the Accademia di
Belle Arti in Florence. He won a Guggenheim Fellowship in
1953. That year, he also had a show at the Grace Borgenicht
Gallery in New York City that spread interest in his art.
Customers, dealers, and artists started to visit him in his
studio in Leeds, Massachusetts. In the 1950s, he was the first
artist to create oversized woodblock prints. Indeed, he has
been referred to as a pioneer in large-scale printmaking. His
work was always figurative, whether mythical or common-
place in subject matter.

Themes and Influences

Birds appear frequently in his work, often as harbingers
or representatives from another plane. For example,
"Artist's Nightmare," (1995) shows a bird wearing a red
robe standing on a naked man who is lying flat. Baskin was
also interested in Greek mythology, philosophy and history
and used the sibyl, a prophetic female from Greek mythology, as a central figure in many sculptures and paintings.

He was also influenced by his Jewish upbringing. His
religious art such as illustrations of the Haggadah and of the
Biblical Five Scrolls was informed by his knowledge of
Jewish tradition. This influence carried over into later works,
such as the "Angels to the Jews" series, as well.

Baskin served as Professor at Smith College in Northampton, Massachusetts, from 1953 to 1974, where he
taught sculpture and printmaking. Albert H. Friedlander,
writing for the *Independent in London,* reported years later
in Baskin's obituary, "(He) taught with caustic wit joined
with deep concern and affection for his students, from
whom he demanded the utmost diligence. He applied the
same standards to himself, even in the most difficult times."

Collaborative Work at Gehenna Press

In Britain, Baskin was best known for his collaborations with poets Ted Hughes and Anthony Hecht. He illustrated (with wood engravings) and published Hecht's *Seven Deadly Sins* in 1958 in a limited edition of 300 copies. Later, in 1995, they again collaborated on a book, *The Presumptions of Death*. Baskin illustrated Hughes's words at the Gehenna Press for over three decades. Baskin and Hughes became friends and starting in the mid-70s, Baskin and his second wife, Lisa (Unger), lived near Hughes in Tiverton, Devon.

One of the best-known collaborations of Baskin and Hughes was *Crow* in 1970. The work was a result of Baskin's suggestion that Hughes write an entire book of poems about the bird. The book was followed by three more limited editions on the same theme. They also collaborated in 1981 on a *Primer of Birds,* which the Press released in a limited edition of 250.

The *Portland Press Herald,* reporting on a 2001 show at the June Fitzpatrick Gallery at MECA called "Woodcuts for 'The Oresteia' by Leonard Baskin," wrote: "Baskin's images—heavy, consequential, confronting mortality but granting a social transcendence of the spirit—and Hughes' words—at least equally monumental—nourished one another, although Baskin as an emblem of that admiration, credited the weight to Hughes."

Baskin returned to the United States in 1984 to teach at Hampshire College in Amherst, Massachusetts. Baskin also survived a stroke that year. In 1992, The Gehenna Press had a 50-year retrospective, called "Caprices, Grotesques and Homages: Leonard Baskin and the Gehenna Press," which toured museums throughout the country, including the Library of Congress.

The works of William Blake continued to influence Baskin's work in later life as well. "Angels to the Jews," a series of large-scale gouaches, was inspired both by Blake and by the Gulf War. The series, first shown in 1991 at the Midtown Payson Gallery in New York, inaugurated the Fine Arts Galleries of the Elsie K. Rudin Judaica Museum of Temple Beth-el in Great Neck, New York, in May 1992. The series portrays the angels wearing ceremonial robes, each one representing a human behavior through gesture and colors.

Vehemently Preferred Traditional Art

Baskin created figurative art during an era of abstract expressionism and pop art. He despised those trends and did not make a secret of it. He was quoted in *Publisher's Weekly,* as saying that "Pop art is the inedible raised to the unspeakable." Baskin preferred art that was representative; some called it old fashioned. In the *Times of London* he was quoted as having said, "Human beings have not changed. No matter how fast we go we still function as physical beings. That is of overwhelming importance to my art—the continuum of human life—that is what makes art sublime."

His work was shown in more than 40 exhibition during his lifetime. Currently, Baskin's work is displayed in The Art Institute of Chicago, the Library of Congress, National Gallery of Art in Washington, the Smithsonian Institute, The Vatican Museum, and the British Museum, to name a few. His work varied in size from a small Abraham Lincoln stamp he produced for the U.S. Mint, to large monuments like the Woodrow Wilson Memorial in Washington and the Holocaust Memorial in Ann Arbor, Michigan.

Sculpted National Memorials

Baskin's Holocaust Memorial resides at the First Jewish Cemetery in Ann Arbor, Michigan. The Memorial, unveiled in 1994, is a sculpture of a robed, seated man, seven feet high. With one fist over its face, and its other hand stretched toward the sky, the figure is a dramatic reminder of the anguish of the victims of the Holocaust.

Baskin created a series of woodcuts about the Holocaust during the mid-1990s. One, more than five feet in length, portrayed a skeleton rising, surrounded by crows and owls. Printed on the work is a Yiddish proverb written by the artist: "The resurrection of the dead; we don't believe in it. In any case, the owls and the crows will represent us."

Baskin was one of five artists who worked on the Roosevelt Memorial in Washington. Designer and landscape architect Lawrence Halprin planned the memorial for Roosevelt that would have four galleries representing the 32nd President's four terms in office. Baskin's work is on the fourth panel, a 30-foot long bas-relief of Roosevelt's funeral procession. "He was the first president I ever voted for," Baskin told the *Jewish Bulletin* in May 1997. "He was a paragon, a mighty man with the most wondrous common touch ever perceived." The Roosevelt Memorial is a series of open-air galleries spread out over seven and a half acres near the Potomac River. It was dedicated in May 1997 by President Clinton. In April 1997, Baskin told Susan Stamberg, of NPR's "All Things Considered:" "When I had the task to deal with this funeral cortege, I of course replaced all of those cars with weeping and mourning people. That's the essential difference, but I think it's a difference in which art is providing a reality which perhaps the true reality would deny."

A Lifetime of Artistic Achievement

Richard Michelson, an art dealer from Northhampton, Massachussets, has represented Baskin since 1985. He told *The Omaha World-Herald* in June 2000, "I've felt all along that Leonard is one of the last great renaissance men. He's somebody who worked in many different fields and in a sense had a career in different fields that was equal to people who only concentrated in one."

Among Baskin's lifetime of Honors are six honorary doctorates, a Gold Medal for Graphic Arts from the National Institute and Academy of Arts and Letters in 1969, and a Special Medal of Merit of the American Institute of Graphic Arts and the Gold Medal of the National Academy of Design. Baskin was a member of various national and royal academies in Belgium, Italy, and U.S. The National Foundation of Jewish Culture in the U.S. presented him with its "Jewish Cultural Achievement Award in Visual Arts" in 2000.

Baskin died on June 3, 2000, at the age of 77. He never quit working, organizing his last show, a collection of his woodcuts, from his deathbed. The show ran through August 27, 2000, at the M.H. de Young Museum in San Francisco. In a June 6, 2000, obituary, the *Washington Post* quoted Baskin, "My sculptures are memorials to ordinary human beings, gigantic monuments to the unnoticed dead: the exhausted factory worker, the forgotten tailor, the unsung poet . . . Sculpture at its greatest and most monumental is about simple, abstract, emotional states, like fear, pride, love and envy. "

Periodicals

All Things Considered (transcript), April 25, 1997.
Dallas Morning News, October 21, 1984.
Independent, June 8, 2000.
Jewish Bulletin, May 2, 1997.
Newsday, May 6, 1992.
Omaha World-Herald, June 13, 2000.
Portland Press Herald, August 22, 1999; August, 12, 2001.
San Francisco Chronicle, July 23, 2000.
Scotsman, August 1, 2000.
Seattle Post-Intelligencer, March 19, 1999.
Times of London, June 7, 2000.
Washington Post, June 6, 2000.

Online

"Leonard Baskin," *artnet.com,* http://www.artnet.com/ag/artistdetails.asp?aid+2067 (February 4, 2002).
"Leonard Baskin," *Davidson Galleries,* http://www.davidsongalleries.com/artists/baskin/baskin.html, (February 4, 2002).
"Leonard Baskin (1922-2000)," *Ro Gallery,* http://www.rogallery.com/baskin-biography.htm, (February 4, 2002).
"Leonard Baskin: The Ultimate Need," *Sheldon,* http://sheldon.unl.edu/HTML/PR/2000?Baskin.html, (February 4, 2002).
"R. Michelson Galleries, Leonard Baskin," *Michelson Galleries,* http://www.rmichelson.com/Leonard_Baskin_galleries.html (February 4, 2002). □

Barbara Baynton

Barbara Baynton (1857-1929) was an Australian novelist and short-story writer. Her work is notable for its rejection of Australian nationalism and the Australian bush, especially tales of women struggling to cope with the harsh realities of bush life.

Conflicting Stories

Baynton was born in Scone, in the Hunter Valley area of New South Wales, Australia, on June 4, 1857. For many years, the date of her birth and the identities of her parents were uncertain, because Baynton altered her birth date and disguised her parents' identities. She claimed to have been born in 1862, to Penelope Ewart and Captain Robert Kilpatrick, who were supposedly Irish immigrants to Australia and fell in love on the ship en route to Australia.

Although Penelope Ewart was supposedly married at the time, she began a relationship with Kilpatrick and later married him when her husband died. This story, which was believed even by Baynton's own grandchildren, was later proven false. Her parents' names were John Lawrence and Elizabeth Ewart. Baynton was born Barbara Lawrence, not Barbara Kilpatrick, and her father was a carpenter, not the rich landowner she claimed him to be.

As Sally Krimmer and Alan Lawson commented in *Barbara Baynton,* it is not clear why Baynton invented these things. In particular, her motives for saying that her parents were not married when they began their relationship are especially difficult to understand, especially since she lived in an era when unmarried relationships were considered scandalous. The authors speculated that Baynton and her social circle may have found the story romantic, or that she preferred people to think that her father was wealthy. *Contemporary Authors Online* quotes Baynton's grandson, H.B. Gullett: "She was a highly imaginative woman with no strict regard for truth. She told her children many conflicting stories of her early years . . . and it rather seems as if the truth to her was what she chose to believe it ought to be at any given moment. . . ."

However, Baynton's family life as a young girl may have helped with her fantasy about her parents. She was the seventh child of John and Elizabeth Lawrence, but when she was three years old, her mother had another child. This child was not John Lawrence's, although he raised the boy as part of his family.

Despite these stories, Baynton grew up in the Scone district, where her father did carpentry work. In the early 1860s, her family moved twenty-five miles north to Murrurundi, where one of Baynton's brothers established a blacksmith shop. Two other brothers set up a sawmill in Spring Ridge. Meanwhile, Baynton became a governess at Merrylong Park, in the Quirindi district, where she met Alexander Hay Frator, a selector. The couple married in 1880; Baynton was 23. They had three children, Alexander Hay, Robert Guy, and Penelope. However, Frater left Baynton for one of her cousins while the children were still young.

Began to Write

Baynton moved to Sydney and took various jobs, including selling Bibles door-to-door, in order to survive and provide for her family. On March 4, 1890, she and Frater officially divorced; she married 70-year-old Dr. Thomas Baynton the next day. On the marriage certificate, she wrote that she was widowed not divorced. Their marriage lasted fifteen years, and they had one son, who died in infancy. Thomas Baynton supported his wife and her children and introduced her to a wide variety of people. By 1903 she was friends with one-time Australian prime minister Billy Hughes; High Commissioner for Australia in London George Reid; and Federal Chief Justice Sir Samuel Griffith, among others.

Baynton's husband was an antique collector, a hobby she picked up as well. Her collection was famed throughout Australia, as was her collection of black opals. The couple bought "Fairmont," an impressive house in Sydney. Baynton, with her new financial security and high social standing, began to write. Despite the fact that she was now far removed from her rough childhood in the Australian bush, she drew most of her ideas from that time. Her first story, "The Tramp" (later retitled "The Chosen Vessel"), was published in the *Bulletin* in 1896. The *Bulletin*'s editor, A.G. Stephens, became Baynton's friend and encouraged her to keep writing.

Baynton wrote a short story collection titled *Bush Studies* but had trouble finding a publisher in Sydney or in London. Edward Garnett, a critic and publisher's reader, persuaded Duckworth & Company of London to publish *Bush Studies* in 1902. Her later works, *Human Toll* (1907) and *Cobbers* (1917), were published by the same company.

Thomas Baynton died in 1904, after which Baynton moved to London and frequently visited Australia. She divided her time between writing and collecting antiques. By 1917 Baynton had written two more stories, "Trooper Jim Tasman" and "Toohey's Party," which she added to *Bush Stories* to make *Cobbers*. These stories arose from Baynton's experience of hosting "open houses" for soldiers at her homes in London and in Essex during World War I.

In 1921, Baynton married Lord Headley in London. Headley was the fifth Baronet of Little Watley, Essex. He had converted to Islam, was the president of the Muslim Society, and had made a pilgrimage to Mecca in 1923. When they married, Baynton received Ardoe House, a gracious mansion in Ireland, but the marriage did not last long; they were separated in 1924 after a year and a half of legal wrangling. Baynton continued to live in London and Melbourne and kept up her passion for antiques. Her health, never robust, began to deteriorate, and she spent several periods in health resorts and nursing homes between 1905 and her death in 1929.

Krimmer and Lawson wrote that Baynton was "a grand lady with a strong character," and commented that her friends said she was "lovable, rash, clever, impulsive, generous," as well as "quick to anger, liable to be unjust, but always ready to forgive and make friends." She was also notably tasteful in her dress and memorable for her "dramatic nature."

Critical Response to Stories

The tales in *Bush Studies* reflect some of Baynton's intensity. The stories emphasize the brutality and violence of the bush, as well as the starkly unequal relationship between men and women there. In Baynton's tales, men are associated with the bush and its malevolent nature, and women, as representatives of civilization and gentleness, are forced to succumb to their exploitation. Unlike other Australian literature of the time, which celebrated the bush community as a place of hospitality, camaraderie, and compassion, Baynton mocks bush people and their ways. However, she balances this negativity by emphasizing motherhood as a source of hope, redemption, and creativity. *Contemporary Authors Online* explains: "Considering Baynton's own experience of motherhood . . . it is scarcely

surprising that ambivalence toward the maternal haunts Baynton's fiction."

Krimmer and Lawrence wrote of Baynton's work that her "stories are powerfully expressed and closely unified. Her vision is communicated through a straightforward yet intense style. Each story has a clear, almost single-minded impulse and each contributes to a cumulative effect which is memorable and convincing." They also commented that each story "sets out to investigate a particular situation, to explore a particular emotion, and to develop a particular motif. . . . Each story has an inexorable progress towards a dire conclusion—death, rape, rejection or some combination of these—and the progress itself is in the form of an ordeal which serves to heighten the victim's . . . perception of the horror of his or her vulnerability."

One of Baynton's most famous stories is "Squeaker's Mate." The title character of the story is married to Squeaker, a farmer. She is described as "the best long-haired mate that ever stepped in petticoats." A branch falls and breaks her back, and she is incapacitated, although her husband is too self-absorbed to notice. Forced to lie in bed, she must now rely on her husband for subsidence. As Squeaker brings his mistress into the home, his wife is forced to stay into a lean-to. However, she can still use her upper body, and when her husband's mistress comes to the lean-to to take away her food and water, she relies on it to strangle the other woman. Her loyal dog, in turn, attacks Squeaker. In *A History of Australian Literature,* Ken Goodwin commented, "Here is rage externally suppressed and then breaking out in a more positive and frightening way. . . ." and that this violence is "approved of by the author, not the fierce predatoriness of a peripheral marauder." The two stories that Baynton added to *Cobbers* are, according to Krimmer and Lawson, "of little interest in themselves," but they do show Baynton's interest in using local dialect as well as dark humor.

Human Toll

Baynton wrote only one novel, *Human Toll,* which was published in 1907. It has never been reprinted and is consequently rare and little known. Like her stories, it is drawn from her life in the bush, but it is difficult to determine how much of it is autobiographical. It does not have a strong structure but presents many short scenes of bush life. Ursula, the main character, wants to write but feels that she cannot do so until she moves away from the bush. The novel examines the effect of the bush on the men and women who live there, especially the toll the environment takes on them. Like her short stories, the novel also emphasizes women's vulnerability and men's exploitation and greed. It also emphasizes the positive value of maternity. Krimmer and Lawton commented that although the book is sometimes slow or discursive, some of the scenes "have a self-contained unity and intensity which echo the achievements of *Bush Studies.*" They also wrote that the most vibrant scene in the book is the last one, with Ursula lost, carrying the dead baby through the trackless bush. A.A. Phillips of *The Australian Nationalists,* praised Baynton's grounding of her fiction in very real life; the "bread-and-butter directness" of her style, her clear visualization, and her skill in exposition. Baynton begins her stories at points of crisis, and shows events though characters' actions and dialogue, rather than through authorial explanation.

Baynton died on May 28, 1929, at her home in Melbourne, after breaking her leg and contracting pneumonia. Phillips wrote that Baynton represented "with rare directness, [a] revolt against self-confident Australianism, despite the fact that she is not a social writer." Krimmer and Lawson summed up Baynton's literary impact by writing that although she has long been unknown and unread, "in the past decade she has been enthusiastically 'discovered' by a large number of readers. . . . Now that her name is relatively well known the time is ripe to make available for assessment the whole range of her literary work."

Books

Goodwin, Ken, *A History of Australian Literature,* St. Martin's Press, 1986, pp. 43-44.

Krimmer, Sally, and Alan Lawson, editors, *Barbara Baynton,* University of Queensland Press, 1980.

Pierre, Peter, editor, *Oxford Literary Guide to Australia,* Oxford University Press, 1993.

Phillips, A. A., "Barbara Baynton and the Dissidence of the Nineties," in *The Australian Nationalists,* edited by Chris Wallace-Crabbe, Oxford University Press, 1971. □

Alan Bean

American astronaut Alan Bean (born in 1932) was the fourth person to ever walk on the moon. In November 1969, he and Pete Conrad made the second moon landing in history in their Apollo 12 Lunar Module *Intrepid,* while their crewmate Dick Gordon orbited the moon in Apollo 12's Command Module *Yankee Clipper.*

Alan Bean was born in Wheeler, Texas on March 15, 1932. He grew up in Fort Worth, Texas, where he became enamored of flight at an early age. "When I was a boy, growing up during WW II," he said on the National Space Society's Web site, "I saw pictures of people flying aircraft, and I grew up near an airbase, so I wanted to be an aviator."

Bean began flight training when he was just 17 years old and still in high school, when he joined the Naval Air Rescue. He graduated from Paschal High School in Fort Worth, and went on to the University of Texas, where he received a Bachelor of Science degree in aeronautical engineering in 1955. A Reserve Officer Training Corps (ROTC) student, he was commissioned as an ensign in the United States Navy on graduation.

After completing flight training in 1956, Bean was assigned to the Jacksonville Naval Air Station in Jacksonville, Florida. At the age of 24, he became the youngest member of attack squadron VA-44. But painting, a career he was to

follow after he retired from the Navy, was in his blood too. Even as other pilots tinkered with their hot rods on weekends, Bean took classes in oil painting. Known as "Sarsaparilla" by his fellow fliers because he didn't drink alcohol, he also became known as "Beano," a nickname that would stick with him through his astronaut days.

After completing a four-year tour of duty, Bean attended the Navy Test Pilot School at Patuxent River, Maryland. He trained under the direction of Pete Conrad, who would later become commander of the Apollo 12 moon flight, and who would be instrumental in getting Bean assigned to that mission. After Pax River, Bean went on to another attack squadron in Cecil Field, Florida.

"Even More Fun"

By 1962, Bean knew he wanted to join the elite cadre of America's newest test pilots known as astronauts because, as he later said on the National Space Society's Web site, "I thought it might be even more fun than flying airplanes." In that year he applied and made the final cut of 35 candidates, along with his old instructor, Pete Conrad. Bean was rejected, even as Conrad made it in. Undaunted, Bean applied again the following year and was accepted.

However, Bean was not good at playing the office politics that dominated the astronaut group at the National Aeronautics and Space Administration (NASA). He got sidelined away from the Gemini flights that were in progress and away from the later Apollo missions to the moon. Instead, Bean was assigned to the Apollo Applications program, which was concerned with low earth orbit flights planned for after the moon landings. There he would have languished if it weren't for the intervention of Conrad, who successfully lobbied NASA officials to have Bean assigned to his Apollo 12 crew. And so it was that Pete Conrad, mission commander, Dick Gordon, Command Module pilot, and Alan Bean, Lunar Module pilot, got in line for the second mission ever to land people on the surface of the moon.

Since the actual landing site of Apollo 11, the first moon mission, turned out to be as much as four miles off target, one of Apollo 12's prime objectives became to perfect a pinpoint landing. Planners chose as the target the landing site of Surveyor 3, an unmanned probe that had touched down in the Ocean of Storms, a large plain, in April 1967. If the Apollo 12 crew could walk to Surveyor 3 after they landed, they would know their mission was a success.

No Longer a Rookie

Apollo 12 was launched on November 14, 1969. A perfect liftoff was marred just 36 seconds into the flight, when the moon rocket was hit by lightning, overloading the ship's electrical system and scrambling its navigation platform. As Bean later said on National Public Radio, "when all these warning-lights came on. . . , it was unlike anything we'd been trained for years, maybe five years beforehand . . . we had no idea whatsoever what had happened." With the help of Mission Control, however, the crew recovered the mission, reached Earth orbit, and continued on to the moon. After a three-day journey, Apollo 12 did indeed achieve its main objective, setting down within sight of Surveyor 12.

Bean became the fourth person in history to set foot on the moon after he followed Pete Conrad from their lander. One of Bean's first acts upon stepping onto the moon was to toss his astronaut pin, worn by rookie astronauts, into a crater. "When you become an astronaut, after about a year of training, you get a silver one," Bean later said on an ABC Good Morning America television broadcast, referring to the astronaut pins he and his fellow astronauts wore. "When I went to the moon, I took my silver one with me and I threw it in the crater near Surveyor. I often think of it at night when I look up at the moon."

Bean and Conrad spent a total of 31.5 hours on the surface of the moon, including two moonwalks. This was a full ten hours longer than the crew of Apollo 11. They would spend more than seven hours outside of their spacecraft, far longer than two hours that Armstrong and Aldrin spent on the first moon mission. On their second moonwalk, Conrad and Bean took pictures of Surveyor and cut off pieces of the probe for analysis on earth.

The two astronauts had a little illicit mission of their own. Unbeknownst to NASA officials, they had brought along a store-bought timer for one of their cameras. Their plan was to secretly attach the timer to the camera, and get some pictures of the two of them together in front of Surveyor 3. Since only two crew members from their mission had landed on the moon, the big question when they returned to earth would have been "Who took that picture?"

The two were certain their startling photos would land them on the cover of Life magazine. Unfortunately, they lost the timer among the rocks in their sample bags and they could not find it again until after the mission was completed.

After the Apollo mission was over, Bean became the second commander of Skylab, the first American space station. This station was built of Apollo hardware left over from moon missions that had been cancelled. Bean lived nearly two months (59 days) in 1973 in low Earth orbit with crewmates Owen Garriott and Jack Lousma.

A New Career

After serving as backup commander for the Apollo-Soyuz Test Project, which saw the first docking of American and Russian spacecraft in 1975, Bean retired from the Navy in 1975. He remained with NASA as the head of Astronaut Candidate Operations and Training until the first flight of the space shuttle in 1981. He wanted to devote full time to painting and public speaking. "I loved being an astronaut," Bean told The Washington Times. "I would have loved flying the space shuttle, but there were people there who could do it as well as I could or better. Yet no one was interested in doing this other job, which was recording it artistically."

In his home in Houston, Texas, Bean paints about four pieces a year. His paintings almost exclusively feature the Apollo flights, with such titles as "Armstrong, Aldrin, and an American Eagle," "A Giant Leap," "Houston, We Have a Problem," "Sunrise Over Antares," and "Tiptoeing on the Ocean of Storms." Each sells for $18,000-70,000. Bean also commands $10,000-15,000 per appearance as a public speaker.

To lend his paintings an authentic ruggedness, Bean paints on plywood normally used to make aircraft frames, "and then I make it rugged with a hammer I used on the moon," as he told an interviewer on ABC's Good Morning America.

In 1998, Bean published a book of his paintings called Apollo: An Eyewitness Account By Artist/Astronaut/Moonwalker. As he told The Washington Times, "For the last ten years, I've painted on commission so when a painting is finished it goes into somebody's house never to be seen again, really, by groups. So I knew I needed to have a book."

John Glenn, the first American astronaut to orbit the Earth, wrote the introduction to Bean's book, saying, as quoted by The Washington Times, "He saw the same monochromatic world as the other astronauts, yet with an artist's eye he also saw intrinsic beauty in the rocks and boulders and their textures and shapes."

Bean lives with his wife Leslie and seven Lhasa Apso dogs in his native Texas. Of the moon flights and his paintings, he told Reuters, "It seems farther away now because there are no rockets going there. Nobody is going. Maybe all this will inspire some kid to go try to be a pilot or an astronaut." Asked if he felt disappointed by the current lack of human activity on the moon, Bean told the Web publication Astrodigital, "Look how long it was between when

Columbus discovered here and the Pilgrims came. 1492 to 1640's—a couple hundred years. . . . I don't feel the least discouraged. . . . Eventually, as the centuries unfold . . . there will be more human beings living off the Earth than live on it. It's just going to happen and we don't need to be anxious about it.''

Books

Chaikin, Andrew, *A Man on the Moon: The Voyages of the Apollo Astronauts*, Penguin Books, 1994.

Periodicals

Reuters, October 1, 1998.
Washington Times, October 18, 1998.

Online

''Alan Bean,'' Web site of the Astronaut Hall of Fame, http://www.astronauts.org/astronauts/bean.htm (October 31, 2001).
''Alan Bean,'' Web site of Strategic Events International, http://www.lordly.com/talent/sei/BeanAlan.html (October 31, 2001).
''Ask an Astronaut: Alan Bean,'' Web site of the National Space Society, http://www.ari.net/nss/askastro/Bean/answers2.html (October 31, 2001). (October 31, 2001).
''Astronaut Bio: Alan Bean,'' Web site of the Lyndon B. Johnson Space Center, http://www.jsc.nasa.gov/Bios/htmlbios/bean-al.html, August 1993.
Chaikin, Andrew, ''Thirty Years Ago: Lunar Explorers Take a Walk,'' *Space.com,* http://www.space.com/news/apollo_12_surveyor_112099, November 20, 1999.
Plaxco, Jim, ''An Interview with Alan Bean,'' *Astrodigital,* http://www.astrodigital.org/space/intbean.html (October 31, 2001). □

Sidney Bechet

Musically educated on the streets and cabarets of New Orleans, clarinetist and alto-saxophonist Sidney Bechet (1897-1959) emerged as a major exponent of early jazz. He was to the alto-saxophone what Louis Armstrong had been to the trumpet. Bechet helped set the standard for his instrument, inspiring jazzmen like John Coltrane to study the New Orleans master's tone and immaculate phrasing.

One of seven children, Sidney Bechet was born on May 14, 1897, in New Orleans, Louisiana. His father, the son of a slave who performed in the city's Congo Square dances, shared a passion for music. A shoemaker and able dancer, Bechet's father encouraged his children to take up the study of music. As a Creole of color, Bechet grew up within the musical world of New Orleans. Running along parades in ''the second line,'' he watched brass bands play marches and ragtime numbers. Accompanied by his mother Josephine, he attended operas and

listened to circus bands. Around age six, Bechet took his older brother Leonard's clarinet and began practicing behind the family home. After she discovered him playing, his mother, instead of punishing him for taking the clarinet, had Bechet play for his older brother. Impressed by his brother's precocious playing, Leonard eventually invited him to join his family-based brass band that featured four of his brothers. Soon after, he sat in with trumpeter Freddie Keppard, marched in Manuel Perez's band, and took lessons from clarinetists George Baquet, Louis de Lisle ''Big Eye'' Nelson, and Lorenzo Tio.

Introduction to Louis Armstrong

By age twelve Bechet performed with a number of bands including John Robichaux's Orchestra. Around 1908 he performed with trumpeter Bunk Johnson who introduced him to Louis Armstrong. Bechet and Armstrong, along with a drummer, played on the back of a furniture truck, advertising Saturday night boxing. Composer and bandleader, Clarence Williams, in search of a band to promote the sale of his sheet music, hired Bechet to accompany him on a tour. Presuming that the tour was heading north, Bechet and his fellow band members were disappointed when they found themselves in Texas, plugging Williams' numbers in local dime stores. In Galveston, Bechet and the band's pianist Louis Wade quit and made their way back to New Orleans.

Bechet continued to build a reputation as one of the premiere clarinetists in New Orleans. As Martin Williams pointed out in *Jazz Masters of New Orleans,* ''It is important to remember . . . that Bechet was then not just a kid in the opinion of New Orleans players. While still in his teens, he was acknowledged as one of the best clarinetists in the city—to many the best.''

In the summer of 1917 Bechet embarked on a Southern and Midwestern tour with the Bruce and Bruce Touring Company. The group's last stop was Chicago. Bechet remained in the city and joined Lawrence Duhe's band at the De Luxe Cafe. He then performed with Freddie Keppard's band at the Dreamland and occasionally worked with King Oliver at the De Luxe. In 1919 he briefly rejoined Keppard at the Royal Gardens and took a late-hour job at the Pekin Theatre with the band of ragtime pianist, Tony Jackson.

Joined Southern Syncopated Orchestra

While performing in Chicago Bechet attracted the attention of Will Marion Cook, a classically trained composer. Cook invited him to join his Southern Syncopated Orchestra. As Bechet recounted in his autobiography, *Treat It Gentle,* ''Will knew I couldn't read notes . . . and told me, 'Son, I want you to listen to the band and I'll let you know when to rehearse.'' After informing Cook that he did not need to sit out, Bechet took part in the rehearsal, playing along with the orchestra by ear.

With Cook's orchestra, Bechet toured New York and Europe. In London he bought a straight-model soprano saxophone and began to adapt it into his repertoire. At Buckingham Palace, he entertained the Prince of Wales with his original composition ''Characteristic Blues.'' Taken with Bechet's fine musicianship, Swiss conductor Ernest Amsermet attended a number of his performances. As quoted in *Jelly Roll, Jabbo, and Fats,* Amsermet stated: ''There is in the Southern Syncopated Orchestra an extraordinary clarinetist who is, so it seems, the first of his race to have composed perfectly formed blues on the clarinet . . . I wish to set down the name of the artist of genius; as for myself I will never forget it—it is Sidney Bechet.''

With the disbanding of Cook's Orchestra, Bechet remained in London with a remnant group led by drummer Benny Peyton. This small ensemble appeared at The Embassy Club and the Hammersmith Palais in London and, for a short time in 1920, played in Paris before returning to the Embassy and Palais. Despite Bechet's musical achievements in England, an arrest for allegedly assaulting a prostitute resulted in his deportation to America.

Returning to New York in the fall of 1921, Bechet performed with society orchestra leader Ford Dabney and played in Donald Heywood's production ''How Come?'' In Washington D.C. he met singer Bessie Smith. During his brief relationship and musical association with the talented and hard-drinking blues woman, Bechet took Smith to Okeh Records and recorded ''Sister Kate,'' a side that was never released.

Recorded with Clarence Williams' Blue Five

Bechet's earliest and most legendary recordings were with Clarence Williams' Blue Five—sessions that spanned a three year period between 1923 and 1925. Among these ground breaking sides, were ''Wild Cat Blues,'' ''Kansas City Man,'' ''Texas Moaner Blues,'' ''Mandy, Make Up Your Mind.'' Joined by his old-time New Orleans musical associate Louis Armstrong, Bechet performed on Williams' legendary composition ''Cake Walkin' Babies From Home.'' Proclaimed by many critics as the best of the Williams' series, the song exhibited the brilliant interaction between Bechet and Armstrong. In *Jazz Masters of the Twenties*, Richard Hadlock wrote that Bechet ''was probably the only jazzman in New York at the time who could match Armstrong's brilliance in every way. When the two improvised together, each prodding the other to more daring flights. As Hadlock added, ''Despite Armstrong's authority on most of the Clarence Williams dates, it was the more experienced Bechet who initially set the pace and tone of each performance.''

Bechet's next most important association occurred around 1924 when he took a brief job at a white, midtown-cabaret, the Kentucky Club, with the Duke Ellington Orchestra. Though Ellington held Bechet's talent in high regard, he could not tolerate his eccentric habit of bringing a large dog on-stage. As quoted in *American Musicians,* Ellington later related, ''When Bechet was blowing, he would say 'I'm going to call Goola this time!' Goola was his dog, a big German shepherd. Goola wasn't always there, but he was calling him anyway with a kind of throaty growl.''

Bechet soon left Ellington and opened a restaurant on Lenox Avenue, the Club Basha—a name derived from his nickname Bash. The restaurant proved a short-lived venture. Before long he took to the road once more with Claude Hopkins and Josephine Baker, in the 1925 production ''Revue Negre.'' When the tour broke up in Berlin the next year, Bechet traveled to Russia where he made appearances in Kiev, Kharkov, and Odessa. He was billed as the exemplar of the ''Talking Saxophone.'' Afterward, Bechet returned to Berlin and organized a new production of ''Revue Negre'' which toured Europe in 1927. Moving to Paris in the summer of 1928, he joined bandleader Noble Sissle at the Les Ambassadors Club. Being a product of a tough upbringing, Bechet carried a pistol for protection. Outside a nightclub he got into a dispute with a man which resulted in the accidental wounding of a French woman. Arrested and convicted, he served eleven months in jail and was finally deported.

Rejoining Noble Sissle in New York, Bechet embarked on a tour of Europe, along with trumpeter Tommy Ladnier. Since his earlier meeting with Ladnier in Europe, Bechet became drawn to his musicianship. In 1931 Bechet and Ladnier formed a six-piece band, the New Orleans Feetwarmers. Eventually establishing themselves at New York's Savoy, they initiated a long and musically creative collaboration. ''That was the best band,'' recalled Bechet in *Profiles in Jazz,* ''people liked it and we were all musicians who understood what jazz really meant.'' As jazz writer Graham Colombe' observed, in the liner notes for *An Introduction to Sidney Bechet,* ''Tommy Ladnier was Bechet's most important sideman of the thirties and they recorded together in 1932 some of the most boisterous and jubilant music of the decade." Among their excellent up-tempo numbers were "Shag," "Sweetie Dear," and "Blackstick." With few musical jobs, Bechet and Ladnier soon open the Southern Tailor Shop, a combination repair and cleaners operation which doubled as a musicians hangout.

During the 1940s a renewed interest in traditional jazz helped bolster Bechet's career. He worked with a trio at Nick's in Greenwich Village and, through the connections of banjo/guitarist Eddie Condon, appeared at New York Town Hall concerts. Organized by Nesuhi Ertegun, he played at an all-star concert in Washington D.C., with such talents as trombonist Vic Dickerson and pianist Art Hodes. In 1945 he was briefly reunited with Louis Armstrong at the Jazz Foundation Concert in New Orleans, and soon after he made several sides for the Blue Note label with another famous New Orleans trumpeter, Bunk Johnson.

Moved to France

By 1949 Bechet responded to offers by European promoters, and left for France to appear at the Paris Jazz Festival. After the festival he returned to America and played a short stint at Jimmy Ryan's in New York. In 1951 Bechet took up permanent residence in France and became an international celebrity, earning enough income to buy a small estate outside Paris. The relaxed racial atmosphere and artistic recognition he received in France was a welcome break from long years of traveling and economic hardship in America. His musical association with French musician Claude Luter's band provided Bechet with steady work until 1955. Around this time he appeared in a ballet and two films: Se'rie Noire with Eric Stroheim and Blues featuring Vivane Romance.

Bechet remained busy in the recording studio as well. In 1953 he signed his last contract with the French Vogue label. Despite the varying criticism of the Vogue sides, Bechet's musicianship remained in fine form. Unlike many of the musicians of his era, he was not opposed to perform with Be bop-inspired jazzmen. His Vogue sides with modernist drummer Kenny Clarke yielded several notable recordings such as "Klook's Blues."

In 1958 Bechet experienced stomach pains while playing a job in Boston, and was taken to Boston General Hospital. More trustful of the French, he waited to return to his home outside Paris before undergoing surgery. Despite his weakened condition brought on by cancer, Bechet expressed intentions to return to America. Before he was able to complete these arrangements, Bechet died on his birthday, May 14, 1959. Years later, Duke Ellington, in The Duke Ellington Reader, paid tribute to his former band member: "Of all the musicians, Bechet was to me the very epitome of jazz. He represented and executed everything that had to do with the beauty of it all, and everything he played in his whole life was original . . . I honestly think he was the most unique man ever to be in this music—but don't ever try and compare because when you talk about Bechet you just don't talk about anyone else."

Books

Baillet, Whitney, *American Musicians: Fifty-Six Portraits of Jazz,* Oxford University Press, 1986.
Baillet, Whitney, *Jelly Roll, Jabbo, and Fats: 19 Portraits in Jazz,* Oxford University Press, 1983.
Bechet, Sidney, *Treat it Gentle,* 1960.
The Duke Ellington Reader, edited by Mark Tucker, Oxford University Press, 1993.
Hadlock, Richard, *Jazz Masters of the 20s,* Da Capo Press, 1972.
Horricks, Raymond, *Profiles in Jazz: From Sidney Bechet to John Coltrane,* Transition Pub., 1991.
Williams, Martin, *Jazz Masters of New Orleans.*

Periodicals

Periodicals Jazz Journal International, February, 1984. □

William Beebe

William Beebe (1877-1962) was a naturalist, oceanographer, ornithologist, and an executive of the New York Zoological Society. With Otis Barton, he was the first to use the bathysphere, a deep-sea diving device, and set a dive record in 1934 that was not broken until 1949. Beebe wrote over 800 articles and 24 books on natural history.

Beebe was the son of Charles Beebe, a paper company executive, and Henrietta Marie Younglove. He was born in Brooklyn, New York on July 29, 1877. When Beebe was a small child, his family moved to East Orange, New Jersey, where he experienced a happy childhood and was able to expand his innate interest in the outdoors. He was deeply interested in birds, and his first publication was a letter to the editor of *Harper's Young People* in 1895. His parents, particularly his mother, encouraged his interest in natural history.

New York Zoological Society

Beebe took extra science classes at East Orange High School and entered Columbia University as a special student in zoology in 1896. He was not a degree candidate, although later in life he would claim that he earned a B.S. Beebe was deeply influenced by Henry Fairfield Osborn, a professor at Columbia. In 1899, when the New York Zoological Society began looking for an assistant curator of birds, Osborn suggested that they appoint Beebe. Osborn was vice-president of the Society, and three years later, Beebe was given the post. According to David Goddard in *Saving Wildlife: A Century of Conservation,* this began "an epochal association for the New York Zoological Society, which was to find in William Beebe a defining genius, and an epochal tie for William Beebe, who was to find in the Society a lifelong champion and home." On August 2, 1902, Beebe married Mary Blair Rice. They did not have children, and were divorced in 1913.

Although Beebe seemed perfectly suited to his new job, he was not happy with it. He was interested in field research, and the job was a largely indoor one, dealing with caged birds. In 1900 he began taking field trips throughout the eastern United States and Canada. Osborn supported these trips, but William Temple Hornaday, the zoo director, objected to them because Beebe was absent so much. They found a replacement, Lee Crandall, who could do Beebe's work while he was gone, and he was allowed to continue his travels. His first book, which he wrote with his wife, was titled *Two Bird Lovers in Mexico* and was published in 1905. His first scientific work was *The Bird, Its Form and Function,* published in 1906. By 1955, Beebe had written 22 more books, some for the general public, others aimed at scientists. Many were so popular that they were translated into several languages. Goddard noted, "His elegant prose is everywhere infused with an empathy for animals and a cosmic sense of the interconnectedness of life. . . . With a naked curiosity and never-failing reverence he probed the bodies and pondered the minds and souls of birds, mammals, reptiles, amphibians, fish, and invertebrates, looking for connections."

In 1909, Anthony R. Kuser, a wealthy New Jersey businessman, commissioned Beebe to write a monograph on the pheasants of the world. Beebe spent several years doing research on pheasants, mainly in Southeast Asia. World War I caused publication of the work to be delayed. It was finally published in four volumes between 1918 and 1922, According to Keir B. Sterling in the *Dictionary of American Biography,* one authority of the time described *A Mono-*

graph of the Pheasants as "perhaps the greatest ornithological monograph of the present century."

Began Tropical Research

Beebe traveled to Trinidad, Venezuela, Brazil and British Guiana. In 1916, he established the New York Zoological Society's Department of Tropical Research in Bartica, British Guiana. He was director of the department, as well as honorary curator of birds at the New York Zoo. The tropical research program, which was later moved to Kartabo, operated until 1922.

In 1917 and 1918, while World War I raged, Beebe enlisted in the French Aviation Service. His service was ended by a wrist injury sustained in a fall, so he went back to British Guiana to collect small mammals for the New York Zoo. Later, he visited the Galapagos Islands. On this trip, he went helmet diving to study marine species in their own habitat. In 1927 he studied fish and coral near Haiti. In September of that year, he married Elswyth Thane Ricker, a writer. They did not have children.

In 1928, Beebe founded a tropical research station in Nonsuch, Bermuda, in buildings that had previously been used as quarantine huts for yellow fever patients. At Nonsuch, he set out on his tugboat, collecting sea creatures with nets, or descending below the surface with a copper diving helmet, breathing air through an ordinary hose. However, these expeditions were unsatisfying, because deep-sea creatures are often mutilated by changes in pressure when they are brought up from the depths, and he wanted to watch them living their lives in their own habitat. The problem with doing this is that as one descends deeper into the ocean, the pressure of the water becomes too great for a human being to withstand. For example, at only a half a mile down, the ocean pressure is over half a ton for every square inch of a person's body. Because of this, the deepest anyone had ever gone in the ocean at that time was 525 feet.

Beebe had previously discussed this problem with Theodore Roosevelt, who suggested diving while inside the protection of a rigid metal sphere. In 1929, American inventor Otis Barton had designed and created a diving device that was a round metal sphere with two inset portholes. This device, which Beebe eventually called a "bathysphere," weighed 5,000 pounds, was four feet nine inches in diameter, and had walls that were an inch and a half thick. Inside, there was just enough room for two men to crouch tightly together. The two portholes were made of three-inch-thick fused quartz, a clear mineral that is stronger than glass. The bathysphere had an air supply, electric lights, and a telephone line for communications with the surface.

Descended into Ocean Depths

Beebe teamed up with Barton to make over 30 descents into the ocean. Their first dive was to 800 feet, a record. On June 11, 1930, they dropped to 1,426 feet. During the dive, they were connected to the surface by a cable and a telephone hookup, and millions of listeners eagerly awaited the news from a place so deep that no human being had ever been there before. As they dropped, Beebe took a position at the window, and Barton watched over the instruments and put on the earphones that allowed them to communicate with people on the surface. Beebe commented on each depth; for example, he noted at 383 feet, "We are passing the deepest submarine record," and at 600 feet, "Only dead men have sunk below this." Beebe was thrilled to write at a depth of a quarter of a mile, in the pitch-black ocean, "A luminous fish is outside the window." He later wrote, "I knew that I should never again look upon the stars without remembering their active, living counterparts swimming about in that terrific pressure." He frequently compared the exploration of the ocean deeps to that of space, and never lost his sense of wonder about being involved in such exploration.

In 1934 Beebe and Barton descended to a record depth of 3,028 feet in 1934; this record was not beaten until 1949. This dive generated a great deal of interest and publicity, but Beebe was more interested in its scientific value. Using the bathysphere, he discovered and described species of sea life that were previously unknown. Beebe also studied changes in water color resulting from the loss of surface light at greater depths. He was fascinated with the use of such technology to allow humans to penetrate places that were unreachable without it. According to Jean Ann Pollard, Beebe wrote in 1934 that one day, "a human face will peer out through a tiny window and signals will be passed back to companions, or to breathlessly waiting hosts on earth, with such sentences as: 'We are above the level of Everest,' 'Can now see the whole Atlantic coastline,' 'Clouds blot out the earth.'"

However, Beebe ultimately discovered that he could learn more by wearing a diving helmet and exploring shallower water, where he would observe sea creatures in great detail. He continued his oceanographic research in Baja California and along the Pacific Coast of Central America. He was the first well-known and well-trained scientist to use helmet-diving as a part of his field research.

In 1942 the New York Zoological Society reestablished its tropical research unit in Venezuela. In 1948, Beebe bought 228 acres of land in Simla, in the Arima Valley of Trinidad, and founded a research station there. Although he officially retired from his post as director of tropical research in 1952, he worked at Simla for part of each year until his death on June 4, 1962. The property was deeded to the New York Zoological Society.

Beebe's Legacy

Beebe was given honorary Sc.D. degrees from Colgate and Tufts. He discovered hundreds of animals, many of which were named for him, and one bird, but much of his scientific work has since become obsolete. However, Goddard noted, he was the world's first "neotropical ecologist." According to Sterling, Beebe was a demanding boss to subordinates, but balanced his high standards with a good sense of humor. His major contributions were "the breadth and detail of his field observations, his emphasis upon the interrelationships of living forms, his abiding concern with conservation, and the felicity with which he expressed himself in his writings." Another great gift was his ability to

make natural history accessible and interesting to the general public. Perhaps because of this, Sterling noted, he was not recognized as a major figure in science despite his wide-ranging knowledge and publications. Sterling wrote, "Doubtless many [other scientists] were reluctant to accord serious standing to a successful populizer." Sterling also noted that Theodore Roosevelt wrote of Beebe's book *Jungle Peace,* "It will stand on the shelves of cultivated people, of people whose taste in reading is both wide and good, as long as both men and women appreciate charm of form in the writing of men."

Beebe summed up the value of nature and the necessity for conservation in *The Bird* (1906), when he wrote, "The beauty and genius of a work of art may be reconceived, though its first material expression be destroyed; a vanished harmony may yet again inspire the composer; but when the last individual of a race of living beings breathes no more, another heaven and another earth must pass before such a one can be again."

Books

Biographical Dictionary of American and Canadian Naturalists and Environmentalists, edited by Keir Sterling, Richard P. Hurmond, George A. Cevasco, and Lorne P. Hammond, Greenwood Press, 1997.

Dictionary of American Biography, Supplement 7, 1961-1965, edited by John A. Garrity, Charles Scribners Sons, 1981.

National Cyclopedia of American Biography, James T. White and Co., 1927.

Saving Wildlife: A Century of Conservation, edited by Donald Goddard, Wildlife Conservation Society and Harry N. Abrams, 1995.

Periodicals

Sea Frontiers, August, 1994. □

Gertrude Bell

Gertrude Bell (1868-1926) was the best known traveler in the Middle East and Arabia in the years before World War I. The British intelligence bureau in Cairo hired her as an advisor on Arabia. After the war, she was very involved in the political negotiations that divided the Arab world into new countries and established British political influence in the region.

Gertrude Bell was born into a wealthy family in the English county of Durham on July 14, 1868. Her father owned an iron works. Her mother died in childbirth two year after Bell's birth, and a stepmother raised the young child. At sixteen she attended Queens College and then went to Lady Margaret Hall, a womens college at Oxford University. She graduated with high honors in history.

First Trip to the Middle East

Bell traveled to the Middle East for the first time in 1892 to visit her uncle, who was the British ambassador to Tehran in Persia (now Iran). There she met a young diplomat and wrote to her parents asking for permission to marry him. They ordered her home instead (the young man died nine months later). She wrote a book about her experiences called *Persian Pictures, A Book of Travels* that was published in 1894.

In 1899 Bell studied Arabic in Jerusalem. During the spring of 1900 she went to visit the Druse in the mountains of southern Lebanon. Bell also visited Palmyra, the ruins of a Roman city in Jordan. She described it as "a white skeleton of a town, standing knee-deep in the blown sand." She then went mountain climbing in the Alps and took two trips around the world with her brother.

In January 1905 Bell made her first extended trip to the Middle East. She traveled through Syria to Cilicia and Konya in Asia Minor (Turkey). Bell was alone except for Arab servants and stayed in tents as well as in the houses of the wealthy, where her family could provide her with introductions. At the city of Alexandretta in southern Turkey she hired a servant, Fattuh, who was to stay with her for the rest of her life. She visited many ruins along the way and became interested in archeology. Bell wrote about her experiences in *Syria: The Desert and the Sown*, published in 1907.

Excavated Christian Churches

In 1907 Bell returned to Asia Minor with the British archeologist Sir William Ramsay to help excavate early Christian churches. The two of them collaborated on a picture book of their discoveries. In 1909 she left from Aleppo in Syria and traveled through the valley of the Euphrates River to Baghdad, visiting Babylonian sites along the way. She also went to the Shi'ite holy city of Karbala. Along the way Bell was robbed of her money and, most importantly, her notebooks. The whole countryside turned out to try to find the thieves, but the objects reappeared on a rock above her camp. When the Turkish soldiers of the Ottoman government arrived, they found a nearby village deserted, the inhabitants having fled for fear of retribution. Bell blamed herself for having been careless and causing all the difficulty.

Bell returned in 1911 to revisit the great castle at Kheidir and crossed the desert between Damascus and Baghdad. She then returned to England where she joined a movement that opposed women's suffrage. She also had an unhappy love affair with a married man.

Bell decided to return to Arabia to forget her unhappiness. This time she traveled to the city of Ha'il in the center of Arabia that had rarely been visited by Westerners. There, in 1913, Bell was held captive and robbed. When she was finally released, Arab hostility forced her to cut her journey short rather than continue to Riyadh as she had originally intended. Bell returned to Damascus in May 1914, having gained an unprecedented knowledge about the deserts of northern Arabia and the ruined cities that are found there.

Advisor to British Intelligence

This knowledge was to be of great value. When war broke out in Europe in August 1914, Turkey, which then controlled all of the Middle East, joined Germany in the fight against Great Britain. The British intelligence bureau in Cairo hired Bell as an advisor on Arabia. She became friends with T.E. Lawrence (the famous "Lawrence of Arabia") and helped formulate the British strategy of encouraging the Arabs to revolt against the Turks.

In 1916 Bell was sent to Basra in Iraq as an assistant political officer. She was transferred to Baghdad the following year, where she made her home for the rest of her life. Bell was very involved in the political negotiations that divided the Arab world into new countries and established British political influence in the Middle East. She also started and directed the Iraq Museum. Bell died of an overdose of drugs on the night of July 11-12, 1926 at her home in Baghdad.

Books

Burgoyne, Elizabeth. *Gertrude Bell, from Her Personal Papers,* 2 vols. E. Benn, 1958 and 1961.
Goodman, Susan. *Gertrude Bell,* Berg, 1985.
Kann, Josephine. *Daughter of the Desert: The Story of Gertrude Bell,* Bodley Head, 1956.
Tibble, Anne. *Gertrude Bell,* A. and C. Black, 1958.
Winstone, H.V.F. *Gertrude Bell,* Jonathan Cape, 1978. □

August Belmont

August Belmont (1816-1890), for whom the prestigious Belmont Stakes thoroughbred racing cup is named, was one of the influential bankers who helped define America's Gilded Age. In addition to heading a Wall Street firm that bore his name, Belmont served various Democratic administrations as a diplomat, amassed an impressive art collection, and was a key figure in establishing thoroughbred racing as a sport in the United States. Known for his penchant toward lavish entertaining, Belmont was said to have been the inspiration for a character in Edith Wharton's 1920 novel, *The Age of Innocence.*

Belmont's Jewish family had roots in Alzei, a town in Germany's Rhenish Palatinate. He was born there on December 8, 1816, to Simon and Frederika (Elsaas) Belmont. His father owned land in the area. Because of the family's relative affluence, young Belmont was able to choose his career freely. After attending a commercial school, at the age of 14 Belmont became an assistant at the offices of the House of Rothschild. The Rothschilds ran Europe's most important bank, and had made their fortune by financing various royal follies over the years; they were perhaps most appreciated for loaning the necessary funds to help turn back Napoleon's armies just before the year of Belmont's birth. To work for their House was considered to be a great honor for a young man, and Belmont's mother had secured this appointment for him through an acquaintance of hers, who had married into the family.

One of Belmont's duties as a lowly assistant was to sweep the floors at the Rothschilds' Frankfurt-am-Main headquarters. However, he proved himself a quick study, and was promoted after three years. He was sent to Naples, Italy in order to negotiate financial contracts with emissaries of the Papal Court. His time there was spent wandering through the city's art museums and galleries. This instilled in him an appreciation for art that would fuel a collecting mania later in life.

Became Rothschilds' Wall Street Representative

In 1837, the House of Rothschild posted Belmont to Havana, Cuba, to look after the firm's interests there. At the time, the island was a possession of the Spanish empire, and an ongoing civil war in Spain gave reason to believe that its monarch, Queen Christina, was extracting large sums from the island in order to finance her side against the Carlist claimants to her throne. On his sea journey there, however, a financial panic erupted in the United States. Belmont transacted his business in Havana hurriedly and then went on to New York. Having learned that the American banking firm which had handled all the Rothschilds' business in the U.S. had failed, Belmont offered to set up his own firm to fill the void; it was said that August Belmont and Company was

founded with almost no capital, save for its principal's ties to the famed Rothschild name.

Belmont and Company had an office on Wall Street, and primarily handled foreign exchange transactions. In a few years the firm was thriving. However, the currency business did not offer the chance for large profit margins. "Had he been as bold in business as he was outside it . . . he might have been the richest banker in America," Belmont's obituary in the New York *Herald* later noted. From his earliest days in New York, however, Belmont also enjoyed a reputation as somewhat of a bon vivant. He frequented a popular nightspot called Niblo's Garden Theater, where in the summer of 1841 he became involved in a quarrel with one William Hayward of South Carolina, reportedly over a woman. A duel between the two to resolve the matter resulted in a groin injury that left Belmont with a permanent limp. He was also fond of gambling, and allegedly lost $60,000 one night in a game of baccarat. In conservative New York, he seemed to enjoy defying social conventions. However, his established business reputation gave him a certain gravitas, and the raconteur stories that circulated about him only added to his allure.

Marriage to Prominent Socialite

Belmont became an American citizen and joined the Democratic Party to further establish himself. In 1844 he was named the U.S. consul general for Austria in New York City. Five years later, he married Caroline Slidell Perry, the niece of Oliver Hazard Perry, the War of 1812 naval hero whose fleet defeated the British on Lake Erie. She was also the daughter of Commodore Matthew Calbraith Perry, another famed naval officer. Four years after the marriage, in 1853, Belmont's father-in-law would sail to Japan and persuade its feudal rulers to allow Western ships in their harbor after a 250-year ban.

Such a union added immeasurably to Belmont's status. The newlyweds lived in one of the first residences built on Fifth Avenue, below 14th Street. They later acquired a mansion at 109 Fifth Avenue, where he lived the remainder of his life. He served as the consul general for Austria until 1850, resigning in protest after a newly-formed Hungarian republic was overthrown by Austrian and Russian troops. In 1853, President Franklin Pierce appointed Belmont minister to the Netherlands, and Belmont spent four years in The Hague. His time overseas allowed him to add to his growing private collection of European paintings; when he returned to New York in 1857 he was said to be the owner of over a hundred works of art. The collection even necessitated the renovation of his home to create a gallery space for them.

Democratic Party Executive

In addition to his duties in running the Wall Street firm that bore his name, Belmont also spent a dozen years as the Democratic Party's national chairperson. He rose to the post after the contentious split with the Southern Democrats just before the American Civil War in 1860. At the Charleston convention that year, the delegates were bitterly divided over the issue of slavery, though Belmont had made a rousing speech urging party unity. Belmont was opposed to slavery on principal, but did not believe in abolishing the institution altogether. He was not a supporter of Republican president Abraham Lincoln, but feared the breakup of the Union more. According to a *Dictionary of American Biography* profile, Belmont harbored deeply patriotic feelings for his adopted country. "I prefer," Belmont wrote to John Forsyth of Mobile, Alabama, in 1860, "to leave to my children, instead of the gilded prospects of New York merchant princes, the more enviable title of American citizens, and as long as God spares my life I shall not falter in my efforts to procure them that heritage."

During the Civil War, Belmont was integral in raising and equipping the first German regiment of the Union Army from New York City. He also worked behind the scenes to assure the Rothschilds and other influential names in Europe that the North would prevail, and cautioned them against providing financial support to the secessionist Confederacy. After the war, Belmont continued his activism inside Democratic Party circles, but fell out with some over the nomination of controversial war General George McClellan to oppose Lincoln in the 1864 presidential race.

Wharton Character Modeled After Him

During what became known as the Gilded Age, Belmont and his wife were counted among New York City's social elite, along with such prominent names as the Astors and the Rhinelanders. When the New York Stock Exchange closed at 4 p.m., he and several other scions of American finance enjoyed riding their carriages through Central Park in a daily promenade. The New York *Sun* reported in 1877 on the Belmonts' stature: "It is no exaggeration to say that on the whole of this continent there is not another house of which the appointments are as perfect as those of Mr. Belmont's. He is not a mere gastronome, a collector of works of art, or a blind follower of fashion. He is an artist in his household." The paper also commented favorably on Belmont's wine cellar, which it called perhaps the finest in America at the time. There were rumors that Belmont's wine bills sometimes exceeded $20,000 in a single month, and he was occasionally criticized for asking his esteemed, but then elderly father-in-law, Commodore Perry, to fetch a vintage from the cellar.

Belmont's connoisseurship was not without its detractors. His love of French painting was slyly mocked in *The Age of Innocence,* a novel of Old New York which won Edith Wharton the 1921 Pulitzer Prize for fiction. The wealthy Beaufort character was allegedly based on Belmont; Newland Archer, another character, dislikes the nattily-dressed banker and raconteur. In one exchange that takes place at the home of the Countess Olenska, the two men vie for her attention. "'Painters? Are there painters in New York?' asked Beaufort, in a tone implying that there could be none since he did not buy their pictures," Wharton's novel reads. Archer is secretly elated when Olenska dismisses Beaufort a moment later.

Leading Name in Horse Racing

Belmont had a summer home in the elite enclave of Newport, Rhode Island, and acquired a Long Island prop-

erty when he became more deeply involved in thoroughbred racing after the Civil War. A friend of his, publisher and financier Leonard W. Jerome, organized the American Jockey Club and established Jerome Park, the first genuinely modern track in the United States. Belmont served as the Club's president for many years. In 1867 the first running of the Belmont Stakes occurred at Jerome Park. The Stakes became the first of the Triple Crown contests in American thoroughbred racing, with the Kentucky Derby and the Preakness following. Belmont's thousand acres near Babylon, in Long Island's Suffolk County, was home to a number of prize horses, some of them considered the best in the country at various times in their career. Belmont, true to form, also constructed an opulent home there. The *Spirit of the Times* reported in 1870 that "All the sports and recreations which render a sojourn at a fine country house so agreeable have been provided for at the Nursery. Riding, shooting, fishing, rowing, billiards, and croquet, to say nothing of the more business-like walks, talks and inspections of the thoroughbred horses, the Alderney cattle, the Chester hogs, the deer, etc." But Belmont eventually moved his thoroughbred stable to a farm near Lexington, Kentucky in the 1880s, believing that the climate there was better for breeding and training winning horses. In 1889, his thoroughbreds took $125,000 in prize purses.

Belmont's life was marked by some personal tragedies. One of his two daughters died at a young age, and a son committed suicide. In his later years the banker suffered from dyspepsia, and was known to become cantankerous at times. In November of 1890, he presided over a horse show at Madison Square Garden. The chill in the drafty hall sent him home with a cold. It turned to pneumonia, and he died on November 24. He is buried in the Belmont Circle at Island Cemetery in Newport. At the time of his death, Belmont was worth an estimated five to ten million dollars. When St. Blaise, one of his stallions, was sold at auction the following year, it became the first thoroughbred in America to fetch $100,000. His son August Jr., a Harvard graduate, took over Belmont and Co., and eventually became one of the main investors in the construction of New York City's subway system.

Books

Bowmar, Dan M. III, *Giants of the Turf: The Alexanders, the Belmonts, James R. Keene, and the Whitneys,* Blood-Horse, 1960.

Dictionary of American Biography Base Set, American Council of Learned Societies, 1928-1936.

Wheeler, George, *Pierpont Morgan and Friends: Anatomy of a Myth,* Prentice-Hall, 1973. □

John Shaw Billings

As the first director of the New York Public Library, John Shaw Billings (1838-1913) was the early guiding force behind that institution's reputation as one of the premier information providers in the world. A physician by training, Billings was instrumental in

the establishment of the first comprehensive national medical library and provided much of the ideas and innovations that made the medical school of Johns Hopkins University the foremost learning center of its kind. Billings, noted Frank B. Rogers in a memorial essay that appeared in *John Shaw Billings Centennial,* did "more to advance American medical education than any other individual of his generation."

Trained as Doctor in Cincinnati

Billings was born on December 12, 1838, in southeastern Indiana in Cotton Township. His father's family had emigrated from England in the century before, and settled in Syracuse, New York. His mother, Abby Shaw Billings, was descended from Mayflower settlers. As a child, Billings spent time back East and even attended school in Providence, Rhode Island, for a time. The family eventually returned permanently to Indiana, where his father ran a general store in Switzerland County. Abby Billings was an avid reader, and her son inherited the habit. Billings even taught himself Latin and Greek and as a teen made a pact with his father that he would forego any inheritance if his father agreed to send him to college.

The nearest institution of merit was Miami University in Oxford, Ohio, about 50 miles from Switzerland County. Billings entered it in 1852. He was disappointed to learn that its library was only open to students a mere three hours a week, and he could only check out two books at a time. He borrowed his friends' cards and even revealed later in life that he found a way to enter the building during the summer break and enjoy its resources in solitude. Billings graduated second in his class in 1857. He worked for a traveling sideshow for a time and entered Cincinnati's Medical College of Ohio in 1858.

Career Interrupted by War

Billing's felt that the college's two-year curriculum was inadequate. Instead he read medical texts on his own, spent time in the sole dissection room, and for a time even lived at a Cincinnati hospital cleaning its dissecting room for pay. Funds were still tight, and Billings claimed to have budgeted just 75 cents a week for food one winter. An attempt to write his dissertation, "The Surgical Treatment of Epilepsy," aroused his interest in medical librarianship. He spent six months poring over a thousand journals and books in libraries in Cincinnati, Philadelphia, and New York. He imagined that students and physicians alike might make great progress in their research if there was one single source available with a reliable index to its titles for all medical books.

For a year after he finished medical school, Billings served as a demonstrator of anatomy at the Medical College. With the outbreak of the American Civil War, he took and passed the three-day exam of the Army medical board. He had the highest scores. He was commissioned first lieutenant and given charge of a makeshift military hospital in the Georgetown area of the District of Columbia. The facilities, which were merely filthy barracks, were entirely unsuited to caring for the wounded. They lacked sinks and drainage and no water was available for half a mile. Billings saw that plumbing was installed and ventilation improved. During this period he married Katharine Stevens, the daughter of a Michigan congressman.

Became Assistant to Surgeon General

Billings went on to supervise a Philadelphia military hospital and in April of 1864 was made medical inspector for the Army of the Potomac. From the field, he wrote to his wife that he was sometimes operating for 24 hours at a stretch. Later that year he was called to Washington, marking the end of his field service. He was eventually posted to the office of the U.S. Surgeon General. After the war ended, he oversaw the closing of army hospitals and the discharge of civilian doctors. In 1869 he was given a project involving the United States Marine Hospital Service. He formulated a reorganization plan for the network of facilities that turned it into the United States Public Health Service.

During this time Billings was moving toward the realization of a national medical library. His first order of business was to expand the holdings in the Surgeon General's office. With donations Billings solicited from around the country and even overseas, the number of titles in the library began to grow. A new home for the collection was found in the old Ford Theater building on Tenth Street, the site where President Lincoln was assassinated. The collection expanded from 1,800 to 50,000 volumes by 1873, but Congressional funding to expand, store, and utilize it was not forthcoming. Fortunately, Billings was allowed to use an $80,000 windfall that came from the budgets of closed army hospitals. He also began working on related bibliographic materials. In 1876 he published *Specimen Fasciculus of a Catalogue of the National Medical Library,* which became the *Index Catalogue of the Library of the Surgeon General's Office* four years later. Physicians deemed it an invaluable resource, and Billings and his assistant, Dr. Robert Fletcher, issued one volume per year for the next 15 years. Fletcher also helped Billings compile the *Index Medicus,* which first appeared in 1879 as a monthly guide to current medical literature.

Planned Johns Hopkins Hospital

In 1873, Baltimore banker Johns Hopkins died and left a large endowment for the foundation of a hospital and medical school. Billings was asked by the trustees to submit plans for a state-of-the-art hospital facility, and his were approved and then adapted by architects. Construction began in 1877. Billings was also granted permission by the Surgeon General's office to serve as medical adviser to the institution and as such was the author of several reports on hospital construction and organization, nursing education, and a proper medical-school curriculum. "A sick man enters the Hospital to have his pain relieved—his disease cured," Billings wrote in one paper. "To this end the mental influences brought to bear upon him are always important, sometimes more so than the physical. He needs sympathy and encouragement as much as medicine. He is not to have his feelings hurt by being, against his will, brought before a large class of unsympathetic, noisy students, to be lectured over as if he were a curious sort of beetle. . . . In this Hospital I propose that he shall have nothing of the sort to fear."

At the time, medical students usually attended classes in an amphitheater, where the patient served as passive demonstrator. Billings urged bedside instruction in smaller groups and better diagnostic training. His ideas were implemented into the curriculum, and Billings recruited top names in the field to lead the hospital and medical school. He was a strong advocate of the necessity of medical students earning a bachelor's degree first, a maverick idea at the time that was not enforced until much later, and provided guidelines that made the Johns Hopkins Medical School the first to have a resident system for specialist training. He taught some of the school's first courses in medical history himself.

Idea Led to Punched-Hole Card

Billings's innovations helped change the public perception of hospitals as unsanitary, even gruesome places. His ideas helped shape the American Public Health Association, which he served as founding member in the 1870s, and the National Board of Health. Billings' talents brought him to the attention of the U.S. Census Bureau, and he was named head of its division of Vital Statistics for the 1880 and 1890 federal censuses. Between those two counts alone, there was a massive increase in the U.S. population, a change of 12 million, and the Census Bureau struggled to keep pace with its task. Billings' daughter was romantically linked with a statistical engineer named Herman Hollerith at the time, and over dinner one evening Billings suggested that Hollerith consider some sort of system of tabulation involving punched cards, similar to those used for the Jacquard loom. The result was Hollerith's invention of the punched card, which remained in existence as a method of tabulating data by computer well into the 1970s.

A New and Vast Project

Billings oversaw the opening of the new Surgeon General's Library in 1887; in 1890 he accepted a post as director of the University of Pennsylvania Hospital and professor of hygiene. He officially retired from the Army and the Surgeon General's office in 1894, and many prominent names in medicine journeyed to the Philadelphia banquet held in his honor. Not long after that, however, Billings was invited to take a post of great prestige, but also herculean effort: he was selected as the first director of the newly established New York Public Library. The Library, however, existed in name only, for the city boasted three separate facilities at the time, each created by private endowment. There was the research library named in honor of its benefactor, John Jacob Astor, the wealthiest man in the United States at time of his death in 1848. There was also the James Lenox rare book collection at another site. The former governor of New York, Samuel J. Tilden, also left a bequest in his will for the establishment of a library. The trustees of each of the three libraries agreed to consolidate their holdings into a central library for New York City and recruited Billings to organize it.

Billings's initial task was to thoroughly catalogue all three collections and their holdings. Negotiations with city and state authorities to choose a site large enough for a building and obtain the necessary funding to erect one took years to complete. Once the land was donated, however, Billings sketched the proposed library and interior. His plans called for a large reading room and seven floors of stacks, as well as a rapid delivery system for patrons that was one of the most modern of the time. The architects chosen for the job incorporated each of the ideas into a large Beaux-Arts building at Fifth Avenue and 42nd Street. At the time, it was the largest marble structure ever attempted in the country. Billings also worked to finesse an agreement with another organization, the New York Free Circulating Library, to consolidate its holdings into the Central Library and convinced steel magnate Andrew Carnegie to donate $5 million to build a system of branch libraries. The New York Public Library, which quickly became a landmark of the city and one of its grandest cultural achievements, opened its doors in May of 1911.

Legacy Continued Well After Death

Billings was still keenly interested in medicine. He served as a consultant to Boston's planned Peter Bent

Brigham Hospital between 1905 and 1908 and chaired the board of trustees of the Carnegie Institution of Washington, which furthered research in science. Throughout his life he was known as a tireless executive and an imposing, formidable personality. In his final years he suffered from a form of cancer of the face as well as kidney problems. He was said to be grief-stricken after the death of his wife in 1912 and underwent his eighth operation seven months later. He died after contracting pneumonia on March 11, 1913, in New York City. He was buried with military honors at Arlington National Cemetery.

Billings' achievements were enduring ones: the *Index Medicus* became a computer index of medical abstracts, Medline, and the Johns Hopkins University is considered one of the foremost research and training centers for the science of medicine in the world. He was a man to whom no task seemed too large. As the *John Shaw Billings Centennial* volume noted, he had once told a colleague: "I'll let you into a secret—there's noting really difficult if you only begin—some people contemplate a task until it looms so big, it seems impossible, but I just begin and it gets done somehow. There would be no coral islands if the first bug sat down and began to wonder how the job was to be done."

Books

John Shaw Billings Centennial: Addresses Presented June 17, 1965, National Library of Medicine, 1965.
Lydenberg, Harry Miller, *John Shaw Billings,* American Library Association, 1924.

Online

Dictionary of American Biography Base Set, American Council of Learned Societies, 1928-1936. Reproduced in *Biography Resource Center,* http://galenet.galegroup.com/servlet/BioRC (January 21, 2002). □

Osama bin Laden

The Islamic fundamentalist leader Osama bin Laden (born 1957), a harsh critic of the United States and its policies, is widely believed to have orchestrated the 1998 bombings of two U.S. embassies in East Africa, as well as the October 2000 attack on the *USS Cole* in the Yemeni port of Aden. But it is his role as the apparent mastermind of the September 11, 2001, attacks on the World Trade Center and the Pentagon that have made bin Laden one of the most infamous and sought-after figures in recent history.

The 6-foot-5, lanky, bearded leader—soft-spoken and effeminate, even when he rails against America—is a man of tremendous wealth, and makes an unlikely spokesman for the poor and oppressed people of Islam whom he claims to represent. Nevertheless, his call for a *jihad,* or holy war, against the United States and Israel, has been heeded by like-minded fundamentalist Muslims.

Raised in Great Wealth

Born in Riyadh, the capital city of Saudi Arabia, Osama bin Laden was the son of Mohammad bin Laden, one of the country's wealthiest business leaders. Some sources state that he is the seventh son, while others claim that he is the seventeenth of some 50 children born to the construction magnate and his various wives. Young bin Laden led a privileged life, surrounded by pampering servants and residing in air-conditioned houses well insulated from the oppressive desert heat. He may have heard tales of poverty from his father, who started his career as a destitute Yemeni porter. He moved to Saudi Arabia and eventually become the owner of the kingdom's largest construction company.

Mohammed bin Laden's success was in part due to the strong personal ties he cultivated with King Saud after he rebuilt the monarch's palaces for a price much lower than any other bidder. Favored by the royal family, Mohammed served for a time as minister of public works. King Faisal, who succeeded Saud, issued a decree that all construction projects go to Mohammed's company, the Binladin Group. Among these construction projects were lucrative contracts to rebuild mosques in Mecca and Medina. When Mohammed died in a helicopter crash in 1968, his children inherited the billionaire's construction empire. Osama bin Laden, then 13 years old, purportedly came into a fortune of some $300 million.

A Passion for Religious Politics

Young bin Laden attended schools in Jedda, and was encouraged to marry early, at the age of 17, to a Syrian girl and family relation. She was to be the first of several wives. In 1979 he earned a degree in civil engineering from King Abdul-Aziz University. He seemed to be preparing to join the family business, but he did not continue on that course for long.

Former classmates of bin Laden recall him as a frequent patron of Beirut nightclubs, who drank and caroused with his Saudi royalty cohorts. Yet it was also at the university that bin Laden met the Muslim fundamentalist Sheik Abdullah Azzam, perhaps his first teacher of religious politics and his earliest influence. Azzam spoke fervently of the need to liberate Islamic nations from foreign interests and interventions, and he indoctrinated his disciples in the strictest tenets of the Muslim faith. Bin Laden, however, would eventually cultivate a brand of militant religious extremism that exceeded his teacher's.

Joined the Afghan War

As a student in the late 1970s, bin Laden was galvanized by events that seemed to pit both the Western world and communist Russia against Muslim nations. One of these was the Camp David peace accords between Egypt and Israel; another was the Soviet invasion in Afghanistan. In December 1979, when the Soviet Union invaded Afghanistan, bin Laden, like many other Muslims, rose to join the jihad declared against the attackers. He did not initially enter the fray as a soldier, but instead channeled his efforts into the organization and financing of the *mujahedeen,* or Afghan resistance. Over the next ten years, he used his tremendous wealth to buy arms, build training camps, and provide food and medical care. He was said to have occasionally joined the fighting, and to have participated in the bloody siege of Jalalabad in 1989, in which Afghanistan wrested control from the Soviet Union.

The United States, then embroiled in the Cold War with the Soviet Union, provided help to bin Laden and his associates. Although in many respects he worked side by side with the Americans to defeat the Soviets, bin Laden remained wary of the Western superpower. "To counter these atheist Russians, the Saudis chose me as their representative in Afghanistan," bin Laden later told a French journalist in an interview quoted by the Public Broadcasting System's (PBS) *Frontline.* "I did not fight against the communist threat while forgetting the peril from the West. . . . [W]e had to fight on all fronts against communist or Western oppression."

Formed "Al Qaeda"

During the war, bin Laden forged connections with the Egyptian Islamic Jihad, the militant group linked with the 1981 assassination of President Anwar el-Sadat. Under the influence of this group, bin Laden was persuaded to help expand the jihad and enlist as many Muslims as possible to rebel against so-called infidel regimes. In 1988 he and the Egyptians founded Al Qaeda, ("The Base"), a network initially designed to build fighting power for the Afghan resistance. Al Qaeda would later become known as a radical Islamic group with bin Laden at the helm, and with the United States as the key target for its terrorist acts.

After the war, bin Laden was touted as a hero in Afghanistan as well as in his homeland. He returned to Saudi Arabia to work for the Binladin Group, but he remained preoccupied with extremist religious politics. Now it was his homeland that concerned him. In 1990 Saudi Arabia's King Fahd, worried about a possible invasion by Iraq, asked the United States and its allies to station troops that would defend Saudi soil. Eager to protect its interests in the oil-producing kingdom, the United States complied. Bin Laden, euphoric after the Afghan victory and proud of the power of Muslim nations, was outraged that Fahd had asked a non-Muslim country for protection. He now channeled his energy and money into opposition movements against the Saudi monarchy.

As an outspoken critic of the royal family, bin Laden gained a reputation as a troublemaker. For a time, he was placed under house arrest in Jedda. His siblings, who had strong ties to the monarchy, vehemently opposed his antics and severed all ties—familial and economic—with their upstart brother. "He was totally ostracized by the family and by the kingdom," Daniel Uman, who worked with the Binladin Group, told an interviewer for the *New York Times.* The Saudi government, ever watchful of bin Laden, caught him smuggling weapons from Yemen and revoked his passport. No longer a Saudi citizen, he was asked to leave the country.

With several wives and many children, bin Laden relocated with his family to Sudan, where a militant Islamic government ruled. In Sudan, he was welcomed for his great wealth, which he used to establish a major construction company as well as other businesses. He also focused on expanding Al Qaeda, building terrorist training camps and forging ties with other militant Islamic groups. His primary aim had become to thwart the presence of American troops in Muslim countries.

Orchestrated First Terrorist Attacks

Bin Laden regarded even American humanitarian efforts as disgraces to Muslim countries. The first terrorist attack believed to trace back to bin Laden involved the December 1992 explosion of a bomb at a hotel in Aden, Yemen. American troops, en route to Somalia for a humanitarian mission, had been staying at the hotel, but they had already left. Two Austrian tourists were killed. Almost a year later, 18 American servicemen were shot down over Mogadishu in Somalia. Bin Laden initially claimed not to be involved in the attack, yet he later admitted to an Arabic newspaper that he had played a role in training the guerrilla troops responsible for the attack.

Several months later, on February 26, 1993, a bomb exploded in the parking garage of the World Trade Center in New York City, killing six and injuring more than 1,000. Though it has not been proven, bin Laden is widely suspected of being the mission's ringleader. Many believe it was the terrorist leader's first attempt to destroy the towers, which suicide hijackers succeeded in toppling in 2001.

United States and Saudi leaders pressured the Sudanese government to expel bin Laden. In 1996 he left the country voluntarily, according to Sudanese officials.

Declared Holy War Against United States

That same year, bin Laden openly declared war on America, calling upon his followers to expel Americans and Jews from all Muslim lands. In a statement quoted by PBS's *Frontline*, he called for "fast-moving, light forces that work under complete secrecy." Interviewed by Cable News Network (CNN) in 1997, bin Laden said, "[The United States] has committed acts that are extremely unjust, hideous, and criminal, whether directly or through its support of the Israeli occupation." The following year he issued an edict evoking even stronger language: "We—with God's help—call on every Muslim who believes in God and wishes to be rewarded to comply with God's order to kill the Americans and plunder their money wherever and whenever they find it."

After the Sudanese government asked him to leave, bin Laden operated out of Afghanistan. He is believed to have orchestrated at least a dozen attacks, some successful, some not. Among the worst of these were two truck bombings, both on August 7, 1998, of U.S. embassies in Nairobi, Kenya, and Dar es Salaam, Tanzania. The Nairobi bombing killed 213 people (only 12 were Americans) and wounded 4,500. The Dar es Salaam attack left 11 dead and 85 wounded. This news, compounded by intelligence reports suspecting that bin Laden had been attempting to acquire chemical and biological weapons, prompted U.S. action. President Bill Clinton responded with cruise missile attacks on suspected Al Qaeda training camps in Afghanistan and a pharmaceutical plant in Sudan. In November 1998 the U.S. State Department promised $5 million to anyone with information leading to bin Laden's arrest.

Despite attempts to apprehend him, bin Laden eluded the American government and continued plotting against it. Not all of his efforts were successful. A failed plan to bomb Los Angeles International Airport on New Year's Eve, 1999—suspected to be one of several failed attacks designed to correspond with the millennium—was linked to Al Qaeda. Bin Laden is also suspected of orchestrating a botched attack on the *USS The Sullivans,* a U.S. warship stationed off the coast of Yemen. "[I]n what seemed to us a kind of comic presentation of what happened," recalled *New York Times* reporter Judith Miller, "the would-be martyrs loaded up their boat with explosives and set the little dingy out to meet *The Sullivans* and the [dingy] was overloaded and sank."

The same group, with bin Laden at the helm, is widely believed to be responsible for the October 2000 suicide bombing of the *USS Cole,* carried out in the same waters only a few months after the *Sullivans* failure. The terrorists had apparently learned from their mistakes. The attack killed 17 U.S. navy personnel and left many wounded. Yemeni officials later reported that five suspects in the incident had admitted to training in bin Laden's Al Qaeda camps.

Prime Suspect in Attacks on America

Bin Laden's hatred for America had become well known, but nothing had prepared Americans for the most extravagant and heinous plot allegedly hatched by the terrorist leader: the September 11, 2001, attacks on the World Trade Center and the Pentagon. On the clear, late-summer morning, two hijacked commercial jets flew into the twin towers of the World Trade Center. About an hour later, another hijacked airliner slammed into the Pentagon in the nation's capital. A fourth hijacked jet did not reach its target, crashing in Western Pennsylvania instead. When the massive towers collapsed in flames, thousands perished. Among those lost in New York, Washington, D.C., and Pennsylvania were the 19 hijackers, most of whom have been linked to Al Qaeda operations. Bin Laden denied involvement in the attacks, but he praised the hijackers for their acts.

The U.S. government nevertheless regarded the terrorist leader as their prime suspect. President George W. Bush demanded that Afghanistan's Taliban government turn him over or face war, but to no avail. In early October, U.S. forces began striking Afghan targets, declaring a war on terrorism and on the countries that harbor terrorists.

Bin Laden's followers, who support a radical fundamentalist brand of Islam, remain devoted to their leader and continue to heed his call for a holy war. Ever wary of the price America has put on his head, he has reportedly chosen a successor: Muhammad Atef, an Egyptian Muslim who married bin Laden's daughter in January 2001.

Periodicals

Anonymous, October 12, 2001.
Los Angeles Times, September 15, 2001.
New York Times, September 14, 2001; October 28, 2001.
Reuters, October 3, 2001.

Online

"Hunting bin Laden," *Frontline,* http://www.pbs.org/wgbh/pages/frontline/shows/binladen (October 24, 2001).
"Laden, Osama bin," *Biography.com,* http://www.biography.com (October 24, 2001). □

Harrison Birtwistle

Sir Harrison Birtwistle (born 1934) is one of the most challenging, original, and controversial musicians of his generation. Though angular and modern, his work nevertheless is indebted to tradition. Birtwistle composes music for a variety of ensembles, but remains best known for his stage operas. His most famous opera is perhaps his massive medieval work *Gawain* (1991).

Harrison Birtwistle, the son of Frederick and Margaret Harrison Birtwistle, was born on July 15, 1934, in the Lancashire industrial town of Accrington in

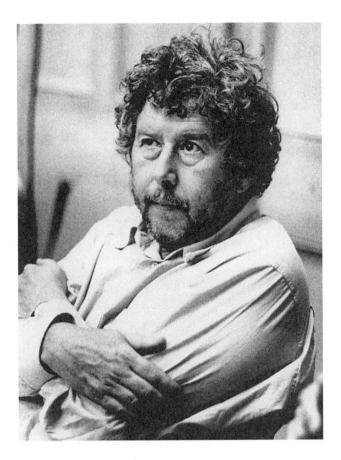

northern England. Interested in music early on, Birtwistle began taking clarinet lessons at the age of seven with a local bandmaster. Soon thereafter, he joined the Accrington military band and later played for local drama society performances. Although he had few encounters with contemporary music and little access to classical scores as a child, Birtwistle started composing his own music at around age eleven. "I think what I'd always wanted to do, right from the beginning, was to write music," he once claimed, as quoted by biographer Michael Hall.

The New Music Manchester Group

It was as a clarinetist that Birtwistle won a scholarship in 1952 to attend the Royal Manchester College of Music (now known as the Royal Northern College of Music), where he studied the clarinet with Frederick Thurston and composition with Richard Hall. He also delved further into contemporary music, making contact with a highly talented group of fellow students that included composers Peter Maxwell Davies and Alexander Goehr, pianist John Ogden, and trumpeter and conductor Elgar Howarth. Together, they formed in 1953 the "New Music Manchester Group," dedicating themselves to performances of the works of Schoenburg, Webern, and others. The Manchester group proved groundbreaking in many ways. Uninhibited by the constraints of convention, they enthusiastically embraced the European avant-garde, forever altering the face of British music.

However, the Manchester group did not intend to abandon tradition altogether. Like his colleagues, Birtwistle was opposed to the goal orientation found in classical or romantic music, but still believed in the preservation of continuity and a sense of line. In contrast to the Darmstadt school, which produced mostly static music, Birtwistle wanted his pieces to feel active and move freely without heed of destination. "I make up a set of rules, then rub them out," he once said of his approach, as quoted in the *National Review*, "and don't tell you what they are." Birtwistle published his first work, *Refrains and Choruses,* for flute, oboe, clarinet, horn, and bassoon, in 1957. It was first performed on July 11, 1959, in Cheltenham, England, by the Portia Wind Ensemble.

In the late-1950s and early-1960s, Birtwistle both composed and taught music. From 1962 until 1965, he served as director of music at the Cranborne Chase School. His compositions during this period included *Monody for Corpus Christi* (1959), for soprano, flute, horn, and violin; *Precis* (1960), a piano solo; *Entr'actes* (1962), for flute, viola, and harp; *Chorales for Orchestra* (1963); and *Three Movements for Fanfares* (1964), for chamber orchestra. In 1965, Birtwistle completed his first critical success, *Tragogoedia,* for wind quintet, string quartet, and harp. The Melos Ensemble, under conductor Lawrence Foster, premiered the work that same year at Wardour Castle.

Devoted to Composing

1965 marked a turning point in Birtwistle's career, as he sold all his clarinets to devote himself entirely to composing. In 1966, as a Harkness fellow, he traveled to Princeton University in the United States, where he completed his 1967 opera *Punch and Judy,* a one-act tragic comedy. This major accomplishment, along with *Verses for Ensembles,* for woodwind, brass, and percussion (1969), and *The Triumph of Time,* an orchestral piece (1972), firmly established Birtwistle as a leading voice in modern British music.

From 1973 to 1974, Birtwistle took a position as visiting professor of music at Pennsylvania's Swarthmore College and in 1975, served as a visiting professor at New York State University, Buffalo. Afterwards, he returned to Great Britain as associate director of the National Theatre, South Bank, London, a position lasting until 1983. While with the National Theatre, Birtwistle composed several instrumental pieces for production, including *Bow Down* (1977), a work for five actors and four musicians with text by Tony Harrison. As for Birtwistle's other composing endeavors, the early-1970s through the mid-1980s were largely dominated by his monumental lyric tragedy *The Mask of Orpheus,* based on the myth of Orpheus. He finished the first two acts in 1975 and wrote the third between 1981 and 1984. On May 21, 1986, the work premiered at the English National Opera in London.

In the 1980s, Birtwistle also dabbled with electronic and computer-generated materials and other medium in an attempt to create his vision of a total theater. Sometimes, the extreme measure almost seemed unworkable. For instance, in *The Mask of Orpheus* Birtwistle included several electronic inserts wherein dancers acted out the stories of

Orpheus told to animals, rocks, and trees from his mountaintop. Further, the action plays out at an accelerated pace, similar to that found in the films of Mack Sennett, Max Linder, Buster Keaton, or Charlie Chaplin. Although not impossible to stage, the work has often presented problems for directors unable to cope with Birtwistle's stylized procedures.

Birtwistle followed *The Mask of Orpheus* with a series of ensemble scores and operas performed by the world's most renowned new music groups. The mechanical pastoral piece *Yan Tan Tera* and *The Secret Theatre,* for 14 players, both from 1984, proved highly successful, as did the 1986 orchestral score *Earth Dances*. In 1991, Birtwistle completed his most famous work, *Gawain,* an opera in two acts based on the allegorical medieval poem "Sir Gawain and the Green Knight." Conducted by Elgar Howarth, it premiered on May 30 of that year at the Royal Opera House, Covent Garden. "His score is grainy, provocative and, often, mesmerizing," concluded a 1991 review in the *Economist.* "He has a remarkable ear for gripping sonorities, quirky rhythms and strange, keening melodies. The combination makes *Gawain* a powerful, indeed unforgettable experience."

Birtwistle's next opera, *The Second Mrs. Kong,* set to a libretto by American writer Russell Hoban, was completed in 1994 and opened that year under Howarth at the Glyndebourne Touring Opera on October 24. Covering a range of multi-layered territory, *The Second Mrs. Kong* stretches through the mythic underworld of the past to present-day London. The setting—complete with skinheads, computers, and a high-tech penthouse—serves as the backdrop to a romance between King Kong, from the classic 1933 film, and Pearl, the subject of a Vermeer painting entitled "Girl with Pearl Earring."

The remainder of the 1990s and beyond garnered Birtwistle continued recognition. *Panic* (1995), a score for saxophone, drums, and orchestra, received a high profile when it played for an audience of some 100 million people worldwide during the BBC Proms in 1995. His orchestral work, *Exody* (1998), was premiered by Daniel Barenboim and the Chicago Symphony Orchestra on February 5 of that year to critical favor. *Harrison's Clocks* (1998), a piano solo written for Joanna MacGregor, performed in its entirety for the first time on July 13, 1998, in Cheltenham. It also earned acclaim. Written in 1998 and 1999, Birtwistle's recent stage work *The Last Supper* premiered at the Deutsche Staatsoper in Berlin on April 18, 2000. Forthcoming projects include a work for the Cleveland Symphony Orchestra, as well as stage works for the Royal Opera House, Covent Garden.

Over the course of his career, Birtwistle won numerous awards and honors, including the Grawemeyer Award and the Chevalier des Arts et des Lettres, both in 1986; a British knighthood, 1988; the Siemens Prize, 1995; and a British Companion of Honor, 2001. From 1993 through 1998, Birtwistle served as composer-in-residence for the London Philharmonic and continued teaching. He was a Henry Purcell professor of music at King's College of Music in London, from 1995 until 2001, then became director of composition at the Royal College of Music in London. The music of Birtwistle attracted esteemed conductors from all over the world, among them Howarth, Barenboim, Pierre Boulez, Peter Eotvos, Oliver Knussen, Sir Simon Rattle, and Christoph von Dohnanyi.

In spite of such attention, Birtwistle never courted popularity or worried about critical reaction to his work. "If they don't like it, that's their problem," he told the *Economist* in 1994. "I'm not trying to be difficult. I write the stuff as clearly as I can." Birtwistle married Sheila Margaret Wilhelmina in 1958. The couple had three sons: Adam, born in 1959; Silas, born in 1963; and Thomas, born in 1965.

Books

Complete Marquis Who's Who, Marquis Who's Who, 2001.
Cross, Jonathan, *Harrison Birtwistle: Man, Mind, Music,* Cornell University Press, 2000.
Debrett's People of Today, Debrett's Peerage, 2001.
Hall, Michael, *Harrison Birtwistle,* Robson, 1984.
International Dictionary of Opera, St. James Press, 1993.

Periodicals

Economist, June 8, 1991; November 12, 1994.
National Review, March 30, 1992.
Notes, June 1996.
Opera News, July 1994; October 1997. □

Isabel Bishop

Isabel Bishop (1902-1988) was a painter and printmaker who depicted life in Union Square, New York, from the 1930s through the 1970s. She was best known for painting common American women performing their daily activities.

Artist Isabel Bishop came from an intellectual household. Her parents were both scholars and educators. Her father, Dr. J. Remsen Bishop, was a Latin and Greek scholar. Her mother, a Suffragist and feminist, wanted to be a writer, but was never published. She learned Italian in order to translate Dante's *Inferno* into English. The couple had founded a prep school in Princeton, New Jersey, but abandoned their project when family life and work combined became overwhelming. The family moved to Cincinnati where Dr. Bishop taught and eventually became principal at the Walnut Hills School.

Thirteen years after they had two sets of twins, they had Isabel on March 3, 1902, in Cincinnati. The family was often struggling financially, and her father's cousin, James Bishop Ford, was their wealthy benefactor. The family moved from Cincinnati to Detroit, where her father was principal of Eastern High School and taught Greek and Latin. He also wrote textbooks in these fields. They lived on the edge of a working class area, and Isabel was not allowed to play with the neighborhood's children. It was in Detroit in 1917, where Bishop studied at the Wicker School, that

Bishop developed her interest in art, however. During Saturday morning art classes, she learned to draw from life.

New York and the Art Students League

In 1918, a 16-year-old Bishop moved to New York City, with the financial help of Ford, to study illustration and design at the New York School of Applied Design for Women. She lived at the Misses Wilde's boarding house for young women on the Upper East Side. She was impressed by modernism, a trend following from the 1913 Armory Show.

"I remember us art students in our smocks, walking in the Armistice Day parade. Then I learned about modern art and put commercial art behind me. I enrolled at the Art Students League and moved to the Village with two other girls," Bishop told biographer Helen Yglesias.

It was then that she decided to abandon illustration and enter the world of fine art. From 1922 to 1924, she attended classes at the Art Students League of New York. First, she studied with modernist Max Weber, then with realist painter Kenneth Hayes Miller. She studied the techniques of the European Masters, but was also influenced by a group of New York social realists led by painter Robert Henri and known as the Ash Can School for their depictions of back yards, alleys, and trash cans.

The Fourteenth Street School

She became friends with Reginald Marsh who also admired Miller. Marsh, also a student at the League, was a Yale grad, whose first job in New York was reviewing burlesque shows for the *Daily News*. She was influenced by Marsh's drawings and prints of working-class subjects. She also developed a friendship with Guy Pene du Bois, another teacher at the League who painted satiric pictures of the New York café scene.

When Bishop left the League, she set up her first studio on Union Square. In 1926, she lived and worked at 9 West Fourteenth Street in a loft. It was here that she became part of the group known as "The Fourteenth Street School," along with Reginald Marsh and the Soyer brothers. She later returned to the Art Students League to study mural painting with Miller. That same year, at age 24, she tried to commit suicide on three different occasions because of a love affair that ended badly. She jumped into the Hudson River in the middle of the night. She commented later that her body wouldn't die, that it started swimming.

In 1931, Ford funded a trip to Europe for Bishop. She traveled with Kenneth Hayes Miller, Reginald Marsh, and Edward Laning. She toured museums and studied the techniques of the Great Masters. When she returned to Union Square, she started her first drawings of the Square and its people. In 1932, she painted "Virgil and Dante in Union Square," now housed at the Delaware Art Museum in Wilmington. A favorite of Bishop's, for many years it hung in her house at Riverdale.

Around 1930, Alan Gruskin started the Midtown Galleries, a cooperative gallery where new artists could show their work for five dollars a month. She developed an association with Midtown Galleries from the start. On May 21, 1932, Bishop signed a contract with the Galleries. The following year in October, she held her first solo exhibition at the Galleries.

Marriage and a New Studio

Donning a white smock and tennis shoes at her studio, Bishop was a very private person who worked slowly. She never needed to depend on her work to earn a living, however. On August 9, 1934, at the age of 32, she married Harold G. Wolff, a leading neurologist. The couple had a son, Remsen, born on April 6, 1940. Their happy 28-year marriage ended with the death of Dr. Wolff on February 21, 1962.

The doctor had a keen interest in art and wholeheartedly supported her work. As Bishop once said, "He found no contradiction between science and art. As far as truth and reality were concerned, there was no either/or about it."

Also in 1934, Bishop took a studio on the top floor of an office building at 857 Broadway on Union Square. She kept that same studio, taking the subway from 242nd St. near her home in Riverdale, the Bronx, to Union Square until she had to give it up in 1984 after the onset of illness.

Painted the Working Girls

The first painting to bring Bishop national recognition was her "Two Girls," which was purchased in 1936 by the Metropolitan Museum of Art in New York. The two girls were a waitress, Rose Riggens Hirschberg, and her friend Anna Abbott Sweeters. Rose was quoted in the New York World-Telegram, "I can't get over it—this picture causing all the commotion. I never thought much about it. I thought about how Miss Bishop used to come into Childs in the morning and have three cups of black coffee and toast for breakfast."

Bishop became most famous for her portraits of the working girls of New York. Suspended in time, female friends were pictured in parks, soda fountains, and snack bars from the 1930s through the 1960s. She described these pictures as an effort "to catch the fleeting moment without freezing its flight." Bishop is also known for her introspective nudes. Her figures are almost always depicted in motion, doing some activity, undressing, clipping toenails, bending, or reaching.

In March 1936, Bishop held her second solo exhibition at Midtown Galleries. She also showed her work at the Art Students League where she was employed as an instructor that year. In 1938 she painted a mural for the New Lexington, Ohio, Post Office. The work, an 11-foot long oil on canvas, called Great Men Come From The Hills, was commissioned by the Section of Fine Arts of the U.S. Treasury Department.

In January 1939, an art critic at *Time* wrote, in an article titled, "Bishop's Progress": "In the last few years Isabel Bishop's paintings have mildly haunted many a visitor to bit exhibitions. Her style, formed by thorough study at Manhattan's Art Students League and exceptional resistance to its influence, is noted for: (1) sensitive modeling of form, and (2) a submarine pearliness and density of atmosphere. The thing she feels about (the working girls) and tries to communicate in her painting, she says is their 'mobility in life,' the very fact that they do not belong irrevocably to a certain class, that anything may happen to them."

Years of Recognition and *Reality*

During the 1940s, she continued to develop a name for herself in the art world. In 1940, she exhibited her work at the New York World's Fair, won first prize at the American Society of Graphic Artists show, and was elected an Associate of the National Academy of Design in New York. She also held a solo exhibition at the Herbert Institute, Atlanta. The following year, she was elected an Academician of the National Academy of Design in New York.

In 1942, she held a third solo exhibition at Midtown Galleries, and she was awarded the Adolph and Clara Obrig Prize of the National Academy of Design, New York, for oil, "Nude by Stream." She also developed a relationship with the National Institute of Arts and Letters in New York: In 1943, she was presented the Arts and Letters Award, the following year, she was elected a member of the Institute, and in 1946, she became the first woman to be elected an officer of the Institute when she was elected vice president. She continued to hone new skills as well, studying engraving at the New School for Social Research in New York in 1945.

In the 1950s, she became one of the founding members of a new journal called *Reality*. Raphael Soyer started the

journal for realist artists. She told interviewer Barbaralee Diamonstein in *Inside New York's Art World* in 1979, "In four years we issued four copies—four copies in four years—and these weren't sold, we sent them to universities and libraries and so on. Art magazines became absolutely furious. They wrote long diatribes . . . after four issues there was no use going on—we had all said what we had to say. But it is remembered now as a sort of collector's item."

During the mid-1950s, she continued to collect honors for her work. In 1954, she was awarded an honorary Doctor of Fine Arts Degree from Moore Institute of Art, Science and Industry in Philadelphia. She was awarded the first Benjamin Altman Prize of the National Academy of Design in New York for "Girls in the Subway Station" in 1955. During the summers of 1956, 1957, and 1958, Bishop taught at Skowhegan School of Painting and Sculpture in Skowhegan, Maine. She resumed teaching there in 1963.

Pride and Prejudice and Honors from a President

The Whitney Museum held a retrospective of her work in 1975. In 1976, E.P. Dutton & Co. published a new version of Jane Austen's *Pride and Prejudice* with Bishop's illustrations, as well as an afterword written by the artist. Bishop's work for the book had been commissioned in the mid-1940s, but for various reasons, the publication had been delayed some thirty years.

The late seventies and the eighties saw Bishop receiving more recognition. In 1979, President Jimmy Carter presented her with an Outstanding Achievement in the Arts Award. In 1982, she received the Skowhegan Governors Award, and in 1987, she was awarded the Gold Medal for Printing of the American Academy and Institute of Arts and Letters.

Bishop died of Parkinson's disease at her home in Riverdale, the Bronx, in February 1988 at 85. Funeral services were held at Christ Church in Riverdale. Yglesias met with her only weeks before she died. She commented, "Always meticulously groomed, even during the last days of her life, her hair smoothly done, her skin surprisingly luminous and unlined, Isabel Bishop was the epitome of the perfect lady, the perfect hostess."

In 1975, biographer Karl Lunde appraised Bishop's work: "She speaks to a sophisticated audience, to viewers aware that the woman reading a letter in a Vermeer or the peaches in a Chardin are only superficially the subjects of those paintings. The real subjects are problems of art taking one beyond mere appearance. The artist, with each stroke of the brush, transforms, reforms, rearranges, selects, magnifies, rejects, organizes and reorganizes. Relationships are Isabel Bishop's theme; the human figure, the means."

Books

Contemporary Women Artists, edited by Laurie Collier Hillstrom and Kevin Hillstrom, St. James Press, 1999.
Lunde, Karl, *Isabel Bishop,* Harry N. Abrams, Inc., 1975.
Yglesias, Helen, *Isabel Bishop,* Rizzoli International Publications, Inc., 1989.

Periodicals

Associated Press, February 22, 1988.
Chicago Tribune, April 21,1989.
Los Angeles Times, March 21, 1985; February 25, 1988.
Magazine Antiques, December 1, 2000.
Newsday, June 5, 1987; February 23, 1988.
Richmond Times-Dispatch, July 29, 1990.
Washington Post, July 25, 1990.
Washington Times, July 25, 1990.

Online

''Isabel Bishop,'' *artnet.com,* http://www.artnet.com/ag/
artistdetails.asp?aid = 2532 (February 4, 2001). □

Helena Petrovna Blavatsky

One of the most influential occult thinkers of the nineteenth century, Helena Petrovna Blavatsky (1831-1891) left behind conflicting images of adventuress, author, mystic, guru, occultist, and charlatan. With the aid of Col. Henry Olcott and William Q. Judge, she founded the Theosophical Society in New York in 1875.

Born at Ekaterinoslav, Russia, on July 31, 1831, Blavatsky was the daughter of Col. Peter Hahn, a member of a Mecklenburg family settled in Russia. In order to gain converts to Theosophy, she felt obliged to appear to perform miracles. This she did with a large measure of success, but her methods were on several occasions detected as fraudulent. Nevertheless, her commanding personality secured for her a large following.

Surrounded with Mystery

An enigmatic personality, Blavatsky was raised in an atmosphere saturated with superstition and fantasy. She loved to surround herself with mystery as a child and claimed to her playmates that in the subterranean corridors of their old house at Saratow, where she used to wander about, she was never alone, but had companions and playmates whom she called her ''hunchbacks.'' Blavatsky was often discovered in a dark tower underneath the roof, where she put pigeons into a mesmeric sleep by stroking them. She was unruly, and as she grew older she often shocked her relatives by her masculine behavior. Once, riding astride a Cossack horse, she fell from the saddle and her foot became entangled in the stirrup. She claimed that she ought to have been killed outright were it not for the strange sustaining power she distinctly felt around her, which seemed to hold her up in defiance of gravitation.

According to the records of her sister, Blavatsky showed frequent evidence of somnambulism as a child, speaking aloud and often walking in her sleep. She saw eyes glaring at her from inanimate objects or from phantasmal forms, from which she would run away screaming and frighten the entire household. In later years she claimed to have seen a phantom protector whose imposing appearance had dominated her imagination. Blavatsky's powers of make-believe were remarkable. She possessed great natural musical talents, had a fearful temper, a passionate curiosity for the unknown and weird, and an intense craving for independence and action.

Led a Wild Life

At the age of 17, she was married to General Blavatsky, an old man from whom she escaped three months later. She then fled abroad and led a wild, wandering life for ten years all over the world, in search of mysteries. When she returned to Russia she possessed well-developed mediumistic gifts. Raps, whisperings, and other mysterious sounds were heard all over the house, objects moved about in obedience to her will, their weight decreased and increased as she wished, and winds swept through the apartment, extinguishing lamps and candles. She gave exhibitions of clairvoyance, discovered a murderer for the police, and narrowly escaped being charged as an accomplice.

In 1860 Blavatsky became severely ill. A wound below the heart, which she received from a sword cut in magical practice in the East, opened again, causing her intense agony, convulsions, and trance. After Blavatsky recovered, her spontaneous physical phenomena disappeared, and she claimed that they only occurred after that time in obedience to her will.

Blavatsky again went abroad and, disguised as a man, she fought under Garibaldi and was left for dead in the battle of Mentana. She fought back to life, had a miraculous escape at sea on a Greek vessel that was blown up and, in 1871 in Cairo, she founded the Societe Spirite. It was a dubious venture that soon expired amid cries of fraud and embezzlement, reflecting considerably on the reputation of the founder.

Arrived in New York

Her closer ties with Spiritualism dated from her arrival in New York in July 1873. Blavatsky first worked as a dressmaker to obtain a living and, after her acquaintance with Col. Henry Steel Olcott at Chittenden, Vermont, in the house of the Eddy Brothers, she took up journalism, writing mostly on Spiritualism for magazines and translating Olcott's articles into Russian. "For over 15 years have I fought my battle for the blessed truth," she wrote in *The Spiritual Scientist,* published in Boston (December 3, 1874); "For the sake of Spiritualism I have left my house; an easy life amongst a civilized society, and have become a wanderer upon the face of this earth.'

Her second marital venture, which occurred during this period, ended in failure and escape. The starting point of her real career was the founding of the Theosophical Society in 1875. It professed to expound the esoteric tradition of Buddhism and aimed at forming a universal brotherhood of man; studying and making known the ancient religions, philosophies, and sciences; investigating the laws of nature; and developing the divine powers latent in man. It was claimed to be directed by secret Mahatmas, or Masters of Wisdom.

Olcott, who was elected president, was a tireless organizer and propagandist. His relationship to Blavatsky was that of pupil to teacher. He did the practical work and Blavatsky the literary work. Their joint efforts soon put the society on a prosperous footing and, at the end of 1878, a little party of four left, under their leadership, for Bombay. Soon after the theosophical movement gained added impetus from the publicity launched by A. P. Sinnett, editor of the *Pioneer,* who had embraced Buddhism in Ceylon.

Practices Under Investigation

The publicity had its disadvantages as well. The attention of the Society for Psychical Research (SPR) was aroused by reports of the theosophic marvels, and Richard Hodgson was sent to Adyar, India, where the central headquarters of the theosophical movement was established, to investigate. The investigation had a disastrous effect for Blavatsky and dealt a nearly fatal blow to Theosophy. Hodgson reported that he found nothing but palpable fraud and extreme credulity on the part of the believers. The Coulombs, a couple who had joined Blavatsky in Bombay in 1880 and were her acquaintances from the time of the Cairo adventure, confessed to having manufactured, in conspiracy with Blavatsky, a large number of the theosophical miracles: they revealed the secret of the sliding panels of the shrine in the Occult Room through which, from Blavatsky's bedroom, the "astral" Mahatma letters were deposited; disclosed impersonation of the Mahatmas by a dummy head and shoulders; declared that the Mahatma letters were written by

Blavatsky in a disguised hand and that they were projected through cracks in the ceiling by means of spring contrivances; and they produced the correspondence between them and Blavatsky in proof of their self-confessed complicity. Hodgson's investigations, which lasted for three months, entirely demolished the first private and confidential report of the SPR issued in December 1884, which was theoretically favorable to Blavatsky's claims. Hodgson's conclusions were published in the *Proceedings* of the SPR.

The publication of the report, which followed the printing of the Coulomb letters in the *Madras Christian Magazine,* created an immense sensation. In response, Olcott, whose honesty was not impugned by the report, banished Blavatsky from Adyar. The proofs of her guilt were overwhelming, for the defense was built up with great difficulties. With the Theosophical Society thus discredited, recovery looked hopeless.

Nevertheless, Annie Besant, who would become Blavatsky's successor, and Sinnett valiantly took on the task. Hodgson answered and insisted on his conclusions. In the literature that subsequently grew up on the subject, V. S. Solovyoff claimed in *A Modern Priestess of Isis* (1895) that Blavatsky acknowledged her fraudulent practices to the author. *Blavatsky's Posthumous Memoirs* (1896) was a most curious artifact of the time that was said to have been dictated by Blavatsky's spirit. The text (which furnished strong, internal proofs of its apocryphal character) was obtained in independent typewriting on a Yost machine under the supervision of the spirit of its inventor, Mr. G. W. N. Yost.

The Secret Doctrine was Published

Blavatsky nevertheless succeeded in living down every attack during her lifetime, continued her work, gained many new adherents to Theosophy, and published a work, *The Secret Doctrine,* which was claimed to have been written in a supernormal condition. Whatever conclusions are reached about her complex character, it must be admitted that she was an extraordinarily gifted individual and it does seem probable that she indeed possessed psychic powers which, however, fell far short of the miraculous feats she constantly aimed at. Even Solovyoff admits some remarkable experiences, and though he furnished natural explanations for many of them, the assumption that withstands challenge is that she had, as plainly pointed out by Olcott himself, unusual hypnotic powers.

Her famous feats of duplicating letters and other small objects are plainly ascribable to this source when common fraud does not cover the ground. She never troubled about test conditions. Most of her phenomena were produced under circumstances wide open to suspicion and strongly savoring of a conjuring performance. These included the finding of an extra cup and saucer at a picnic at Simla in 1880 in the Sinnett garden under the ground at a designated spot, the clairvoyant discovery of the lost brooch of Mrs. Hume in a flower bed, the astral dispatch of marked cigarettes to places she indicated, and the Mahatma scripts imposed over the text of private letters which the post had just delivered.

Special Powers

There is no end of these and similar miracles, and the testimony of the truth is sometimes so surprising that one can conclude that imposture occasionally blended with genuine psychic performance. The general character of Blavatsky's phenomena is of a different order from those of the Spiritualist medium. Her early physical phenomena subsided at a later age, although the power to cause raps remained. Once, in New York, Olcott claimed that he witnessed the materialization of a Mahatma from a mist rising from her shoulders. As a rule the Mahatmas were not supposed to depend upon Blavatsky's organism for appearance, and controlled her body but seldom. *Isis Unveiled* and the *Secret Doctrine* were claimed to have been produced under such control.

Whereas there is a limit to the phenomena of every Spiritualistic medium, Blavatsky apparently knew none. From the materialization of grapes for the thirsty Col. Olcott in New York to the duplication of precious stones in India, or the creation of toys for children out of nothingness, she undertook almost any magical task and successfully performed it, to everyone's amazement.

The Hodgson Report left a deep shadow over Blavatsky's final years. Besant's conversion to Theosophy resulted after she had been requested by W. T. Stead to review *The Secret Doctrine* in 1889. Blavatsky suggested that she read the Hodgson Report before forming any firm conclusions, but Besant was not adversely affected and requested to be Blavatsky's pupil. Thereafter Besant provided a secure refuge for the aging Theosophist at her own home in London. In her last years, Blavatsky became the center of a memorable group of talented individuals. She died peacefully May 5, 1891.

Books

Besant, Annie. *H. P. Blavatsky and the Masters of Wisdom,* 1907.
Butt, G. Baseden. *Life of Madame Blavatsky.* Rider, 1926.
Cleather, Alice L. *H. P. Blavatsky: A Great Betrayal.* Thacker, Spink, 1922.
Endersby, Victor. *Hall of Magic Mirrors.* Carlton Press, 1969.
Fuller, Jean Overton. *Blavatsky and Her Teachers: An Investigative Biography.* East-West Publications/Theosophical Publishing House, 1988.
Kingsland, William. *The Real H. P. Blavatsky.* Theosophical Publishing House, 1928.
Lillie, Arthur. *Mme. Blavatsky and Her Theosophy.* Swan Sonnonschein, 1895.
Meade, Marion. *Madame Blavatsky: The Woman Behind the Myth.* G. P. Putnam's Sons, 1980.
Olcott, Henry Steel. *Old Diary Leaves.* 4 vols. Reprinted as *Inside the Occult: The True Story of Madame H. P. Blavatsky.* Running Press, 1995.
Sinnett, A. P. *Incidents in the Life of Madame Blavatsky.* George Redway, 1886.
Solovyoff, V. S. *A Modern Priestess of Isis.* Longmans, Green, 1895.
Wachmeister, Countess Constance. *Reminiscences of H. P. Blavatsky and the Secret Doctrine.* Theosophical Publishing Society, 1893.
Waterman, Adlai E. [Walter A. Carrithers] *Obituary: The Hodgson Report on Madame Blavatsky, 1885–1960.* Theosophical Publishing House, 1963.
Williams, Gertrude M. *Priestess of the Occult: Madame Blavatsky.* Alfred A. Knopf, 1946.
Yost, G. W. N. *Blavatsky's Posthumous Memoirs.* Joseph M. Wade, 1896. ☐

Leonardo Genezio Darci Boff

Leonardo Boff (born 1938) is recognized as one of the most outspoken, controversial, and articulate proponents of Roman Catholic liberation theology. A staunch supporter of the ordination of women priests, Boff's controversial writings put him at odds with the Vatican and eventually led to his resignation from the priesthood.

Leonardo Boff is an ordained Franciscan priest who resigned his vocation in 1992 to become a member of the Franciscan lay clergy. Protesting the hierarchical structure of the Roman Catholic Church as it existed in his native Brazil, Boff has advocated the ordination of women as priests and promoted social justice for the poor. The Vatican officially silenced Boff for eleven months in the mid-eighties as the result of his publishing several controversial works in the 1970s and 1980s because his books had an ideological alignment with liberation theology. Liberation theology evolved in South and Central America following the 1968 Second Latin American Bishops Conference and gained popularity in the 1970s. The theology calls for the Church to engage itself in the political and economic struggles of poor people. The Vatican, however, views liberation theology as a justification for violent revolution and Marxist economic policies. Roman Catholic theologians dismiss the socio-economic concentration of liberation theology because they believe it places too much emphasis on earthly, temporal matters rather than on spiritual matters. The church believes that the Word of Jesus is not concerned as much with political freedom as it is with freedom, or liberation, from sin.

While accepting Marx's views opposing capitalism, Boff told interviewers that he considered himself more anti-capitalist than pro-Marxist, and more a Franciscan Catholic than a Roman Catholic. He told *Time* reporter Richard N. Ostling: "The Vatican wants to centralize the church around the Pope and Rome. Liberation theology challenges that view, opting for a more decentralized church." He has also commented on his dissatisfaction with Catholic bishops living in relative luxury and controlling how parish monies are spent while Catholics with no say in church matters live in poverty. Addressing the politicized nature of Boff's beliefs, Richard Ouebedeaux in the *Catholic Century* wrote: "In giving such priority to the political dimension, one is led to deny the radical newness of the New Testament and above all to misunderstand the person of Our Lord Jesus Christ, true God and true man, and thus the specific character of the salvation he gave us, that is above all liberation

from sin, which is the source of all evils." Ouebedeaux balances the statement by adding: "Boff does not link his activist Jesus unequivocally with Marxist programs for social reconstruction in the manner of some liberation theologians. Also, despite the fact that the humanity of Jesus is stressed, his divinity—deity, really—is affirmed too." When the Vatican attempted to silence him again in the early 1990s, Boff resigned as priest. He told Mac Margolis of *Newsweek:* "The first time [of official discipline] was an act of humility and I accepted. The second time was humiliation, and I couldn't accept it." In works published since his resignation as priest, Boff expanded his liberation theology views to include ecological and feminist issues.

Born in Brazil

Boff was born December 14, 1938, in Concordia, Santa Catarina, Brazil. His father was a teacher, and his mother was raised in a farming family. He was ordained a priest in 1964 and continued his education at the University of Munich, where he earned a doctorate in 1972. Bonaventura Kloppenburg, who was to become an opponent of liberation theology, oversaw his doctoral dissertation. Another of Boff's doctoral instructors, Joseph Ratzinger, eventually became a Cardinal who served as the Vatican's chief spokesperson against liberation theology. Boff was notably a member of the Franciscan order of Roman Catholics. Boff has likened himself to the order's founder, St. Francis of Assisi, because rather than subjugating himself to the Catholic church's hierarchal structure, St. Francis established his own order. Boff told Margolis: "I define myself more as a

Franciscan Catholic than Roman Catholic. Never forget, St. Francis was a layman, he wasn't a priest or part of the hierarchy." After returning to Brazil, Boff taught theology at the Institute Teologico Franciscano in Petropolis and assumed editorial responsibilities for the Brazilian theological review *Revista Eclesiastica Brasilieira.* He attracted widespread attention in 1978 with the translation of his 1972 work *Jesus Christ Liberator: A Critical Christology for Our Times.* In this work, Boff applied liberation theology to the study of the life and works of Jesus Christ, characterizing Jesus as a revolutionary working on behalf of the economically oppressed against the corrupt Roman occupation of the Holy Lands as well as the hierarchal structure of the Jewish faith.

In his most controversial work, *Church: Charism and Power,* Boff employed Marxist theory to attack not only the economic oppression of the poor, but also the entire structure of the Roman Catholic Church. Equating the Church with industrialists who controlled the means of production, Boff asserted that the Church believed that it held a monopoly on God's grace. Writing in the *Los Angeles Times Book Review,* Marianne Sawicki refuted Boff's assessment: "A thoughtful reader would object that this comparison limps because grace is not a material thing. Grace is more like love, which increases as it is shared, than like the proverbial cake that you cannot both have and eat." However, Sawicki, stated: "One can fault Boff for this poor analogy, and his publisher for neglecting to inform the uninformed reader of the culture-specific character of the work. But such faults make the a book 'dangerous' only to an authority that has lost faith in the good sense and good will of its people." Boff's assertions caused Joseph Cardinal Ratzinger, by now head of the Vatican's Sacred Congregation, to demand an audience with Boff in 1984. One of the Vatican's primary concerns was Boff's interpretation of the Second Vatican Council's assertion that the "sole church of Christ . . . subsists in the Catholic Church." Ratzinger stated that Boff supported a thesis that refuted the Roman Catholic church as the one church of Christ by allowing that Christ "also may subsist in other Christian churches," which the cardinal stated, "could be characterized as ecclesiological relativism" and that, following such a belief, "no institutional church could affirm being that one church of Jesus Christ willed by God himself." Ratzinger officially silenced Boff for one year, prohibiting him from publishing, public speaking, or otherwise promulgating his liberation theology beliefs. Eleven months later, the silence was lifted, and the Sacred Congregation issued an extensive refutation of liberation theology.

Continued Controversy

In 1987, Boff published the English-language version of *The Maternal Face of God: The Feminine and Its Religious Expressions,* in which he advocated the ordination of women as priests. Because the Roman Catholic Church believes that "the ordination of women is not possible" due to being bound by Christ's choice of men as apostles, Boff was again at the center of controversy. He furthered the Vatican's displeasure by publishing a series of articles in 1991 that favored married priests. When the Vatican denied publication approval for his next work, Boff resigned from the priesthood. He told Margolis in 1999: "Strangely, to this day the Vatican has not recognized my renunciation. Officially, legally, I am still a priest and a friar. This is very rare. Usually Rome accepts your resignation or expels you."

Despite the collapse of the communist bloc countries in the late 1980s, Boff believed that the political ideas of Karl Marx concerning what he perceived to be inherent flaws in capitalism were still valid. Following his resignation from the priesthood, he continued to administer to the poor and publish works that are more ecumenical and reveal his readings from other faiths and religious practices, including Buddhism and Yoga, as well as his continued support of liberation theology. For example, in *The Lord's Prayer: The Prayer of Integral Liberation,* Boff explains that humankind cannot separate prayer from worldly concerns. In *Saint Francis: A Model for Human Liberation,* Boff writes that the life of St. Francis serves as an example of how the economically disadvantaged should receive preferential treatment. *Ecology and Liberation: A New Paradigm* prompted Catherine Keller to note in *The Journal of Religion:* "The great contribution of this book is the integration of ecology into the liberation model. . . . [Boff] is not content to embed class analysis within the ecological crisis and vice versa but also to infuse his now cosmologically widened liberation model with 'religious feeling'." Writing in the *National Catholic Reporter,* Stephen B. Scharper added: "He masterfully refutes triumphalistic paeans to global capitalism, noting how under its sweeping mantle the rich get richer, the poor get poorer, more and more species are driven to extinction, more toxins are released into our water and air and our overall quality of life is eroded."

Books

Catechism of the Catholic Church, Doubleday, 1995.
"Liberation Theology," *The Columbian Encyclopedia, Edition 6* Columbian University Press, 2000.

Periodicals

America, November 23, 1996, p. 26; March 18, 2000, p. 4.
Christian Century, November 1, 1978, pp. 1051-52; July 2-9, 1986, pp. 615-17.
Commonweal, June 15, 1990, pp. 395-97.
The Journal of Religion, January 1998, p. 134.
Los Angeles Times Book Review, May 5, 1985, p. 6.
The Nation, December 25, 1989, p. 778.
National Catholic Reporter, September 8, 1995, p. 24; March 17, 2000, p. 11.
Newsweek, June 28, 1999, p. 66.
Time, September 3, 1984, p. 86; September 17, 1984, p. 76; May 20, 1985, p. 44; April 14, 1986, p. 84.
Whole Earth Review, Winter 1995, p. 26.

Online

"Boff, Leonardo," *Contemporary Authors Online,* The Gale Group, 2000. □

Edward William Bok

A longtime editor of the influential magazine *The Ladies' Home Journal,* Edward W. Bok (1863-1930) embodied the ideals of Progressive Era America. Espousing free enterprise, civic responsibility, and the ideals of American womanhood, Bok was one of the best-known magazine editors of his day. He also wrote a series of books which included his Pulitzer Prize-winning autobiography, *The Americanization of Edward Bok.*

A household name in America during his editorship of *The Ladies' Home Journal* from 1889 until 1919, Edward W. Bok built the magazine into one of the most successful publications of its era. Moreover, Bok used his position to encourage a number of reforms ranging from civic beautification to sex education. He also used his pulpit to speak out on issues that included Americanization programs for immigrants, a limited role for women in the nation's political life, and the continued promise of free enterprise to alleviate the problems of poverty. In his retirement, Bok maintained his high profile by writing a series of books, one of which, *The Americanization of Edward Bok,* won the Joseph Pulitzer Prize in 1921. Bok was also actively engaged in philanthropic work throughout his life. In addition to endowing professorships in literature and government, he also sponsored the American Peace Prize to encourage the participation of the United States in international affairs. Bok died in 1930, but his legacy lived on through his sons, one of whom served on Pennsylvania's Supreme Court, and his grandson, Derek Bok, who was named president of Harvard University in 1971.

Emigrated from The Netherlands

Edward William Bok was born on October 9, 1863 in the Dutch city of Helder. The Boks were one of the leading families of the Netherlands: Edward's grandfather served as the chief justice of the Supreme Court and his father, William J.H. Bok, was a well connected diplomatic figure in the Dutch government. Unfortunately, Bok's father lost much of the family's fortune with a series of bad investment decisions. Seeking a fresh start, the family moved to the United States when Bok was six years old. Making their new home in Brooklyn, New York, Bok and his younger brother were enrolled in the city's public schools, even though they did not speak English. Later writing of the difficulty in adjusting to his new life as an American schoolboy, Bok referred bitterly to this experience as the beginning of his Americanization.

With the constant financial difficulties of his family, Bok contributed to the family coffers by performing whatever odd tasks would bring in some money. The strain on the family became so great that at the age of thirteen Bok left school for good to work as a messenger for Western Union. As he recalled in his book *Twice Thirty*, "There was no choice. My father, a stranger to American ways, could not readjust himself at his age to the new conditions of a strange country. My mother had not the health to endure housework; she had not been brought up to it. There was nothing for us boys to do but to get out and help to make the domestic machinery run a bit easier." Indeed, his father, who never achieved the success he had hoped for in America, died when Bok was eighteen, leaving the two sons to support their mother. By that time, Bok had decided to enter into a career in publishing. The ambitious young man began reporting for the *Brooklyn Eagle* in addition to taking classes to sharpen his office skills. After working as a stenographer for the New York publishing house of Henry Hold and Company in 1882, Bok started to edit the *Brooklyn Review*, a magazine affiliated with the Plymouth Church of renown minister Henry Ward Beecher. Taking advantage of his connection to the famous preacher, he founded the Bok Syndicate Press in 1886 to sell feature articles that included essays by Beecher. Adding to his responsibilities, Bok also worked for another New York publishing house, one founded by Charles Scribner. Bok rose to the position of head of advertising at Scribner's; still in his early twenties, it seemed that the once poor immigrant was a true American success story.

Success with *The Ladies' Home Journal*

In 1889 the young advertising director was offered a position as head of the editorial and art departments at a new magazine, *The Ladies' Home Journal.* The magazine

had first appeared as a supplement to the weekly *Tribune and Farmer,* a journal aimed squarely at the rural market. Its founders, Cyrus and Louisa (Knapp) Curtis, expanded the supplemental women's section into the *Ladies' Home Journal and Practical Housekeeper* in December 1883 and by 1889 the magazine had about 440,000 subscribers. Eventually, the magazine dropped the "Practical Housekeeper" from its name. The Curtises decided to refocus their publication away from its rural audience and appeal to the growing middle-class, urban market.

Bok's first challenge at *The Ladies' Home Journal* was to reshape the magazine into a far more prestigious publication than it was perceived to be. He actively solicited advertisements for luxury products while gradually purging the pages of solicitations for products such as patent medicines of dubious medical value. Bok and the Curtises also attempted to link the magazine with the wealthiest families in urban centers across the United States in their presentations to advertisers. The efforts paid off, and *The Ladies' Home Journal* quickly cast off its image as a rural publication aimed at farmers' wives. Once the image makeover had been substantially completed, the publishing team worked at increasing its circulation to reach a broader urban and suburban audience. In 1891 *The Ladies' Home Journal* reached the 600,000 mark in paid subscriptions; the figure passed one million subscribers in 1903. By fashioning itself into an upper-class publication accessible to the mass market, the magazine became one of the first to capture a middle-class readership aspiring for upward mobility and respectability.

With the groundbreaking success of *The Ladies' Home Journal,* Bok became something of legend in the magazine field by the time he was thirty years old. He married Louise Curtis, the daughter of Cyrus and Louisa Curtis, on October 22, 1896. Making their home in the Philadelphia area, the center of Curtis Publications, the young couple raised two sons: William Curtis Bok was born in 1897 and Cary William Bok arrived in 1905. The elder son, who went by his middle name, eventually served on the Pennsylvania Supreme Court and was the father of Derek Bok, who became the president of Harvard University in 1971.

Typified Progressive Era America

As an influential magazine editor and frequent contributor to *The Ladies' Home Journal,* Bok typified many of the sentiments of the Progressive Era of American history, a period that spanned the years from 1890 to World War I. At a time of explosive growth, as immigrants arrived by the hundreds of thousands, many Americans were concerned at the possible effects on the social, economic, and political life of the country. The far-reaching effects of industrialization and mass marketing also seemed to threaten the established social order. In response, Progressive Era leaders called for a variety of reforms; although few argued for a fundamental overhaul of American institutions, the period was nevertheless marked by a nationwide preoccupation with reform measures.

Considering the target audience of his magazine, Bok was especially concerned with the role of women in American life and their participation in keeping the country safe and sound in a turbulent era. Like many of his contemporaries, Bok esteemed the American woman as a source of morality and virtue in the nation's life through her role as mother and wife, a point of view that later historians described as the cult of true womanhood. Notwithstanding the moral authority of American women, however, Bok did not believe that women should play an active role in public life. He opposed extending the vote to women; as he wrote (in the third person) in *The Americanization of Edward Bok,* "He felt that American women were not ready to exercise the privilege intelligently and that their mental attitude was against it." Indeed, Bok favored the idea of *noblesse oblige,* or leadership by the privileged for the benefit of the masses, when it came to governance. Writing in *Twice Thirty,* Bok stated, "Those who were born under favorable conditions should be leaders of men and the doers of things, provided they take their America right and see its people truly."

Although he had become a citizen as a child at the time of his father's naturalization, Bok's attitude toward other immigrants was a contradictory one. He always took pride in his Dutch heritage, writing about it at length in his personal reminiscences. However, Bok was convinced that other immigrant groups posed a threat to American life, especially to native-born women and children. He expressed concern, for example, that foreign-born men such as Greek vendors could take sexual advantage of American women, and that Irish-born nannies did not have the innate control over their temperaments to raise American children properly. Despite these misgivings, however, Bok avoided most of the worst ethnic stereotyping of the day. Indeed, as a magazine that steered clear of the most controversial topics, *The Ladies' Home Journal* rarely covered inflammatory subjects such as race relations, prison reform, or poverty. One typical call for reform included demands for better labeling laws in food and drugs to assure consumers of their purity. Other appeals attempted to convince communities to undertake civic beautification drives and to reform the public schools. An exceptional reform crusade in Bok's final decade as editor was his encouraging of educators to take up sex education as a civic responsibility and to safeguard the health of women and children.

Won the Pulitzer Prize

In the wake of World War I, Bok's persistent calls for reform fell out of step with the times. With Americans retreating from international involvement after the war, many sensed that the era of domestic reform had also ended. Stepping down from the editorship of *The Ladies' Home Journal* in 1919, Bok's passage also seemed to mark the end of an era. However, he did not disappear from public sight once his days as an editor were over; if anything, his role as a reformer picked up pace in the last decade of his life.

In 1921 Bok published *The Americanization of Edward Bok,* an autobiography that topped the bestseller lists. Bok also received the Joseph Pulitzer Prize for his book, which recounted the author's many triumphs over adversity through hard work, persistence, and optimism. Indeed, the

entire tome read as an homage to the free enterprise system and the ability of individuals to become successful by taking advantage of their own talents in the land of opportunity. Bok followed the prize-winning volume with another book of autobiographical sketches, *Twice Thirty,* which was regarded as somewhat more revealing of the author's life.

In 1923 Bok donated $100,000 to the American Peace Prize, a contest to develop a plan that would engage America in international affairs and prevent another world war. Bok also donated money to endow professorships at Princeton University and Williams College, and undertook philanthropic efforts to beautify the city of Philadelphia. He spent much of his retirement time in Florida, where he created a nature preserve in Lake Wales that opened in 1929. One year after the dedication of the preserve, Bok died in Lake Wales on January 9, 1930.

Books

Bok, Edward W., *The Americanization of Edward Bok: The Autobiography of a Dutch Boy Fifty Years After,* Charles Scribner's Sons, 1921.
Bok, Edward W., *Twice Thirty: Some Short and Simple Annals of the Road,* Charles Scribner's Sons, 1925.
Steinberg, Salme Harju, *Reformer in the Marketplace: Edward W. Bok and The Ladies' Home Journal,* Louisiana State University Press, 1979.

Periodicals

Saturday Evening Post, September-October 2001.

Online

"Edward William Bok: Founder of Bok Tower Gardens," *Bok Tower Gardens Web Site,* http://www.boktower.org/bok.html (October 23, 2001). □

Louise Arner Boyd

Louise Arner Boyd (1887-1972) financed and led several expeditions to the Arctic. She became an expert on the fiords and glaciers on the east coast of Greenland.

Louise Arner Boyd was born in San Rafael, California, north of San Francisco, on September 16, 1887. She came from a wealthy family, her grandfather having made a fortune in the California Gold Rush. Both of Boyd's brothers were sickly and died in childhood; her parents were also not well and traveled frequently for their health. Her mother died in 1919 and her father in 1920. They left the family fortune to their daughter, who succeeded her father as president of the Boyd Investment Company in San Francisco.

Interest in the Arctic

Boyd had traveled to Europe and Egypt and had worked as a nurse during the influenza epidemic of 1918. After her

tion with the American Geographical Society, which sponsored her expedition in the summer of 1933 to Jan Mayen Island in the North Atlantic and to the fiord region of the east coast of Greenland. The expedition included several scientists, but the botanists became ill and Boyd took on the job of collecting plant specimens. She undertook expeditions to the same area in 1937 and 1938.

Investigated Magnetic and Radio Phenomena

As a result of her increasing knowledge of these areas, Boyd was asked to represent several American learned societies at international conferences in Europe in 1934. The knowledge she had gained about the east coast of Greenland became very valuable after World War II broke out. The United States government requested that she not publish a book she was writing. Instead she was sent at the head of an expedition to investigate magnetic and radio phenomena in the Arctic in 1940. Her book, *The Coast of Northeast Greenland*, was published in 1948, after the war had ended. During the remainder of the war Boyd worked on secret assignments for the U.S. Department of the Army.

By the time the war was over, Boyd was almost 60 and did not take part in any further Arctic expeditions. She did, however, charter a private plane and fly across the North Pole in 1955, the first woman to do so. Boyd died in San Francisco on September 14, 1972, having spent most of her fortune to finance her Arctic explorations.

Books

Olds, Elizabeth Fagg, *Women of the Four Winds,* Houghton Mifflin, 1985.

Rittenhouse, Mignon, *Seven Women Explorers,* J.B. Lippincott Company, 1964.

Robinson, Jane, *Wayward Women: A Guide to Women Travellers,* Oxford University Press, 1990.

Tinling, Marion, *Women into the Unknown,* Greenwood Press, 1989. □

parents' death she returned to Europe with a friend and then went there a third time in 1924. She traveled on a Norwegian ship past North Cape, the northernmost point in Europe. As a result of that trip she developed an interest in exploring the Arctic.

Boyd made her first trip to the Arctic in the summer of 1926. She traveled to Franz Josef Land, a group of islands north of Siberia, to hunt for polar bears with friends. Boyd chartered the supply ship that had been used by the explorers Roald Amundsen and Lincoln Ellsworth. She returned with thousands of feet of film, 700 photographs, and a great desire to return.

Search for Umberto Nobile

Boyd returned to the Arctic in 1928 and chartered the same ship. She arrived just as a search was underway for Umberto Nobile, the Italian aviator whose airship had crashed on the polar ice. Nobile was rescued, but in the search operations Amundsen was lost and never found. Boyd offered her ship to those who were searching for Amundsen and spent four months with her crew looking for him. They were unsuccessful. However, as a result of her efforts, she was presented with a medal by the King of Norway.

Boyd set out again in 1931. This time she hired several scientists to make the trip a scientific venture. It also satisfied her longing for adventure. The expedition sailed up the east coast of Greenland, and later part of that coast was named Louise Boyd Land. This expedition began Boyd's associa-

Joseph P. Bradley

American attorney Joseph P. Bradley (1813-1892) rose from his rural roots to become one of the most respected Supreme Court justices of the post-Civil War era. Appointed by President Grant following the end of the civil war, Bradley favored a conservative interpretation of the Constitution, particularly with respect to the Thirteenth and Fourteenth Amendments passed by Congress to end slavery and extend citizenship to African Americans.

As an associate justice of the U.S. Supreme Court during the late nineteenth century, Joseph P. Bradley was a loyal member of the Republican party who supported the federal government's role in interstate

commerce but opposed federal intervention in civil matters. His decision-making role on the Supreme Court was somewhat eclipsed in the historical record by his position—as a member of a special electoral commission—as the man casting the deciding vote that certified the disputed election of Rutherford B. Hayes as president of the United States in 1877. Separate from this political controversy, however, Bradley remains one of the most noted jurists of his era, standing second only to his respected colleague Justice John Marshall Harland. Harlan wrote the famous dissenting opinion condemning the "separate but equal" clause in *Plessy vs. Ferguson* in 1896.

Intellectual Promise at an Early Age

Born in Berne, New York, on March 14, 1813, Bradley was the oldest of eleven children born to Philo and Mercy (Gardner) Bradley. He was given no middle name at birth, but his middle initial "P" was likely Bradley's expansion of his own name in honor of his father. Growing up on the family's small farm in upstate New York, Bradley spent his summer months engaged in hard labor, although he soon displayed the intelligence and strength of character that his parents knew would benefit from education. Bradley attended school in the winter months as was the standard for farm children. He became a school teacher at the age of 16. The family's Lutheran minister instructed the young Bradley in Latin and Greek, which enabled the 20 year old Bradley to gain admission at Rutgers College in New Jersey in 1833.

Bradley arrived on campus wearing wool garments spun from his family's sheep and woven by his mother. He also wore homemade leather shoes. Despite his unusual appearance, he quickly showed himself to be an outstanding scholar and he graduated with honors three years later at the top of his class. After Rutgers, Bradley undertook the study of law by working alongside attorney Archer Gifford, collector of the port of Newark. He was admitted to the New Jersey Bar in late 1839. Five years later Bradley married Mary Hornblower, the daughter of the chief justice of the New Jersey Supreme Court. The couple had seven children.

Beginning in 1840 when he entered into private practice in Newark, Bradley worked to establish himself within the legal field and gained a reputation for his handling of patent and commercial law due to his knack for math. Among his major clients was the Mutual Benefit Life Insurance Company—later to be the Prudential Insurance Company—for whom he worked as an actuary. He also counselled several railroads as well. It was on behalf of one of his railroad clients that Bradley made his first appearance before the U.S. Supreme Court in December of 1860 in the case of *Milnor vs. the New Jersey Railroad and Transportation Co.*

Appointed to High Court

Bradley was a member of the Whig party, which had formed during the 1830s in opposition to Andrew Jackson's policies and which favored protective tariffs and a strong federal government. When the issue of slavery fragmented the party during the 1850s, like many northern Whigs, Bradley joined the Republican Party. As a Republican, he supported Abraham Lincoln's run for the presidency in 1860 and opposed the expansion of slavery to the western states. In the winter of 1860-61, after the eleven states representing the Confederacy seceded from the Union, Bradley traveled to Washington, D.C., to urge a compromise between the factions. However, in April of 1861, the attack on the Union-held Fort Sumter by South Carolina troops erased all hopes of avoiding a war, and Bradley became a staunch Unionist. Supporting both President Lincoln and the passage of the Thirteenth Amendment abolishing slavery, Bradley became caught up in politics to the point that he attempted a political career of his own. His 1862 bid for a seat in Congress was unsuccessful.

Bradley's backing of war hero Ulysses S. Grant in the 1868 presidential election gained him a nomination—as one of two Republicans—to the U.S. Supreme Court in February of 1870. He was confirmed by the Senate on March 21 of that year. Bradley's appointment brought the court's membership to nine justices out of a possible ten members, following the recent death of justices John Catron and James Moore Wayne and the retirement of Justice Robert Cooper Greer. Bradley's position as a stalwart Republican was viewed cynically by some as a move by Grant to "pack" the court and allow passage of several controversial cases.

During his tenure on the high court, Bradley continued to focus on business and commercial matters. His opinions on cases involving interstate commerce reflect his belief that the U.S. government has the power to regulate commerce among and between individual states. Significant among such cases were what became known as the "Slaughterhouse Cases," which reached the bench in 1873. The cases involved a group of New Orleans butchers who claimed that the Fourteenth Amendment, by protecting the right to work, did not just refer to African Americans but to all Americans through its first clause: "No state shall make or enforce any law which shall abridge the privileges or immunities of citizens of the United States . . . ; nor shall any state deprive a person of the right to life, liberty, or property without due process of law." The butchers felt that the Fourteenth Amendment prohibited the state of Louisiana from restricting butchers' rights to slaughter their own animals or mandating butchers to utilize specific privately owned slaughterhouses within the city on the basis of health concerns. Siding with the plaintiffs in one of three separate dissenting opinions in a divided Court, Bradley said the restrictions imposed by the state of Louisiana were "unreasonable, arbitrary, and unjust." Together with Justice Noah Swayne, Bradley interpreted the Fourteenth Amendment as applying not only to former slaves but to "all citizens," and argued that the Louisiana regulation deprived the plaintiffs of property without due process of law. In later years, Bradley's dissenting opinion became significant for its promotion of the concept of "due process of law" as a part of constitutional interpretation.

Conservative in Interpretation of Constitution

Determining limits on the power of the federal government to regulate interstate commerce as well as on the states to levy taxes also figured prominently in Bradley's Supreme Court rulings. Also incorporated within his opinions was the Court's interpretation of the fourth and fifth amendment protections against self-incrimination by the forced production of documentary evidence (*Boyd vs. United States*).

From a twenty-first century perspective, Bradley's opinions in the area of civil rights law seem almost radical in their conservatism. In 1872, Bradley sided with the majority in *Bradwell vs. Illinois*. *Bradwell vs. Illinois* was the case of Myra Bradwell, who argued that she had been denied admittance to the Illinois State Bar on the basis of her gender. Bradwell argued that, under the Fourteenth Amendment, the defendant state had no right to prevent her from pursuing a career in law. Bradley countered that civil laws should be subordinate to those traditions, or "laws of nature," giving women the responsibility of caring for family, citing that these traditions promote the overall good of society.

In the so-called civil rights cases that came before the Court over a decade later, Bradley adopted a conservative interpretation of the thirteenth and fourteenth Amendments protecting the rights of free citizens. Bradley declared the first two sections of the Civil Rights Act of 1875 unconstitutional, explaining that they were designed to prevent discrimination against African Americans in private establishments such as restaurants and inns, as well as in public transportation, etc. He argued that the protections

afforded by these amendments apply to actions of state governments, not to those of private enterprises. In his majority opinion he wrote that to "deprive white people the right to choose their own company would be to introduce another kind of slavery." Until the mid-twentieth century and the passage of the Civil Rights Act of 1964, the federal government remained silent on matters of civil rights enforcement, leaving such matters up to the individual states.

Electoral Dilemma Proved Unpopular

The year 1877 proved significant to Bradley, who had become a respected Supreme Court justice. The popular vote in the 1876 presidential election had found Democrat Samuel J. Tilden ahead by over 250,000 ballots over his Republican challenger, Rutherford B. Hayes. The electoral vote also favored Tilden. However, a dispute soon arose regarding the electoral votes in four states, which included Florida, Louisiana, South Carolina, and Oregon. Congress decided to call a fifteen-member bipartisan commission to sort the mess out. All members of the commission voted along party lines, with the result that the last man appointed—in this case Bradley—found his vote to be the decisive one. Although many considered Bradley's action to be counter to the intent of the commission, few could argue that he acted outside his honestly held Republican beliefs and talk of scandal soon ceased. Hayes, the former governor of Ohio, took the oath of office shortly after the commission vote and led the nation into a period of economic prosperity, in which the interests of the southern states were integrated with those of the north.

During the twenty-two years he served on the Supreme Court, Bradley's judicial record was widely respected due to his grasp of the law, his business acumen, and his analytical skills. Bradley also had many other intellectual interests including genealogy, philosophy, and the natural sciences. In addition to completing a history of his family that was published posthumously, Bradley devised a perpetual calendar for determining the day of the week in any year.

Bradley died on January 22, 1892, at the age of 78 in Washington, D.C. His extensive library, which contained over six thousand books of general interest as well as ten thousand legal tomes, was divided between his heirs and the Prudential Life Insurance Company of Newark, New Jersey. After his death, Republican President Benjamin Harrison nominated George Shiras Jr. to the Court. Shiras was confirmed by the U.S. Senate in July of 1892, ensuring that the Court retained a conservative bent after the arrival of the Democratic administration of Grover Cleveland later that same year. Bradley's son, Charles Bradley, organized his father's court opinions, lectures, and other writings after the justice's death and published selected works in 1901.

Books

Bradley, Charles, compiler, *Miscellaneous Writings of the Late Hon. Jos. P. Bradley . . . and a Review of His "Judicial Record,"* [Newark, NJ], 1901.

Lanman, Charles, *Biographical Annals of the Civil Government of the United States,* D. Appleton & Co., 1888-1889.

Stern, Horace, "Biography of Joseph P. Bradley," *Great American Lawyers,* Volume 7, John C. Winston Co., 1909.

Urofsky, Melvin I., editor, *The Supreme Court Justices: A Biographical Dictionary,* Garland Reference Library, 1994.

Online

"Hall of Distinguished Alumni," *Rutgers University Alumni Web site,* http://info.rutgers.edu/University/alumni (1991).
Joseph P. Bradley," *Biography Resource Center Online,* http://galenet.galegroup/servlet/BioRC. (February 4, 2002).
"Joseph P. Bradley," *Dictionary of American Biography* Base Set. American Council of Learned Societies, 1928-1936, http://galenet.galegroup.com/servlet/BioRC (February 4, 2002).
"Memorials and Inscriptions: Joseph P. Bradley," *University of Pennsylvania Law Library Web site,* http://www.law.upenn .edu (February 2, 2002). □

John Cabell Breckinridge

At the time of his election as vice president of the United States, John Cabell Breckinridge (1821-1875) was considered to be one of America's most promising young leaders. Caught up in the battle over the extension of slavery, this once moderate Democrat became the presidential candidate of the extreme Southern wing of his party in 1860. Joining the Confederacy, he served with distinction in the Civil War and later became an advocate of national reconciliation during Reconstruction.

Few American leaders of the mid-19th century underwent as tragic a political evolution as did John Cabell Breckinridge. A rising star in his native Kentucky by age 30, he advocated compromise and understanding between North and South at the start of his career. A strikingly handsome man with impressive oratorical skills, he advanced from a seat in the U.S. House of Representatives to serve as vice president under James Buchanan from 1857 until 1861. Many saw him as a potential president until events caused him to align himself with the Democratic Party's most vehement states' rights faction. After running on a pro-slavery ticket and losing to Republican Abraham Lincoln in 1860, Breckinridge reluctantly joined the newly formed Confederacy and took up arms against the nation he loved. He fought valiantly in some of the bloodiest conflicts of the Civil War as a Confederate general and went into exile at the war's end. He eventually returned home and, at the time of his death, was hailed by old friends and opponents alike as a statesman of courage and integrity.

A Political Family

Breckinridge seemed destined to enter politics. His grandfather had served as a U.S. senator and attorney general under Thomas Jefferson; his father had been a Speaker of the Kentucky House of Representatives. After graduating from Centre College in Danville, Kentucky in 1839, Breckinridge read law under Judge William Owsley, a future Kentucky governor. He attended the College of New Jersey (now Princeton University) and completing his legal studies at the Transylvania Institute in Lexington, Kentucky. Admitted to the bar in 1840, he moved to Iowa Territory a year later and practiced law there. His ties to Kentucky remained strong, however, and he returned to his native state in 1843. That same year he married Mary Cyrene Burch, a cousin of his law partner, Thomas Bullock.

Unlike most of his family, Breckinridge chose the Democrats over the Whigs for his party allegiance. He began to attract notice as an orator and potential candidate for office while still in his early twenties. Service as a major of Kentucky volunteers in the Mexican War delayed his entry into public life. Returning home, he was elected to the Kentucky House in 1849. Two years later, he ran for a seat in the U.S. House of Representatives once held by Henry Clay, the famed Whig leader. His victory was considered a significant one for the Democrats and marked Breckinridge as an emerging party leader.

Southern Sympathies

Arriving in Washington D.C. as the crisis over slavery was escalating, Breckinridge initially positioned himself as a staunch Unionist. As the controversy over territory won during the Mexican War grew more heated, he began to adopt more overtly pro-Southern positions. He favored repeal of the Missouri Compromise and supported the pro-slavery tilt of President Franklin Pierce. His personal views about slavery were more complex—on several occasions,

Breckinridge expressed support for voluntary emancipation and favored colonization of freed slaves in Liberia.

Breckinridge's support for the divisive Kansas-Nebraska Bill further aligned him with militant States Rights supporters. After winning a second term in the U.S. House, he was chosen by the Democrats as James Buchanan's running mate in the 1856 presidential contest. Breaking with tradition, Breckinridge campaigned actively for his ticket, which went on to defeat Republican John C. Fremont and American Party (or "Know-Nothing") nominee Millard Fillmore. At 35, he became the youngest vice president in American history.

Favored Protection for Slavery

In the midst of increasing bitterness in Washington, Breckinridge earned a reputation for fairness as the Senate's presiding officer. Personal friendships with political opponents didn't keep him from expressing increasingly extreme views, however. In a 1859 speech in Frankfort, Kentucky, he insisted that the federal government act to protect slavery in U.S. territories. Such guarantees of slaveholders' rights were unacceptable to Illinois senator Stephen Douglas, who went on to secure the 1860 Democratic presidential nomination. Southerners opposed to Douglas convened their own convention and nominated Breckinridge as a competing Democratic candidate for president, with Oregon senator Joseph Lane as his running mate. Breckinridge had no desire to head this doomed ticket—he had already been elected to the U.S. Senate and expected to take office following his vice-presidential term. He consented to run out of a sense of duty, and hoped that Douglas could be persuaded to withdraw in favor of a new Democratic nominee. In the end, both he and Douglas remained in the race against Republican candidate Abraham Lincoln. A fourth candidate, Constitutional Union nominee John Bell, also competed for the anti-Lincoln vote.

Widely seen as the candidate of Southern disunionists, Breckinridge insisted that he was the true Unionist in the race. However, it became clear that his ticket would only attract support in the South and, barring a combination with Douglas and Bell, Lincoln would be elected. Attempts at combining forces were only partially successful, and the 1860 presidential election resulted in Lincoln sweeping the North while winning only 39 per cent of the national popular vote. Breckinridge came in third in the popular vote, carrying 12 of the 15 slave states for a total of 72 electoral votes. He failed to carry a single free state and, to his particular disappointment, was defeated in Kentucky.

The results of the 1860 election revealed how polarized the nation had become. Taking his seat in the U.S. Senate, Breckinridge worked hard to promote compromise proposals that would allay Southern fears of Republican anti-slavery policies. As the Union began to unravel, he felt compelled to first defend the rights of secessionists, then to join them. When the Kentucky legislature voted to support the Union on September 18, 1861, his position became untenable. Breckinridge's loyalty was questioned and he barely managed to avoid arrest by fleeing Lexington. Reacting to his expulsion from the Senate, he declared, "I ex-

change with proud satisfaction a term of six years in the Senate of the United States for the musket of a soldier."

Though he lacked military training, Breckinridge was appointed brigadier general by Confederate president Jefferson Davis and placed in command of the First Kentucky Brigade. His initial hope was to return to his native state and spark a pro-Confederate uprising. When this failed to happen, he retreated to Tennessee in the spring of 1862 and served under General Albert Sidney Johnston's forces during the Battle of Shiloh. His heroic performance there raised his rank to that of major general. From there, he led an infantry assault at the Battle of Stones River near Murphreesboro, Tennessee that proved valiant but unsuccessful. After fighting Union forces in Mississippi, he helped achieve victory for the Confederate army at the Battle of Chickamauga. As a commander, Breckinridge proved to be resourceful and courageous, inspiring great loyalty in his troops.

1863 found Breckinridge in command of the Confederacy's Department of Western Virginia. In this strategic region, he defeated Union general Franz Sigel at New Market and held the line against General Ulysses S. Grant's assault at Cold Harbor. In July, he took part in a bold attack on Washington D.C. that came within five miles of reaching the city. In his final major engagement, Breckinridge was bested by General Phillip Sheridan at the Battle of Winchester.

Joined Confederate Government

On January 28, 1865, Breckinridge accepted the post of secretary of war in the Confederate government. He became increasingly convinced that the South's cause was lost and, as the end of the war drew near, he met with Union general William T. Sherman to discuss surrender terms. When these discussions fell through, Breckinridge helped Jefferson Davis make his way through the Deep South to avoid capture. Indicted by the Federal government for high treason, Breckinridge led a small party of Confederates into the wilds of Florida. Commandeering a small sloop, he survived a rough voyage across the Caribbean and found asylum in Cuba.

For over three years, Breckinridge lived as an exile, rejoining his family in Canada and moving to a house within sight of the United States border. He traveled to England, France and the Middle East during this period. With Jefferson Davis a prisoner back in the States, Breckinridge was the highest ranking official of the Confederacy still at large. He longed to return to his country, but refused to actively seek a pardon from the Federal government.

Returned from Exile

Finally, President Andrew Johnson proclaimed a universal amnesty for all former Confederates on December 25, 1868. Breckinridge returned with his wife to Lexington the following February. Refusing all requests (including one from President Grant) to seek public office, he nonetheless remained involved in civic affairs as a private citizen. He spoke out in favor of the legal rights of freedmen and denounced the Ku Klux Klan as "idiots or villains." Most of all, he urged forgiveness and harmony between the North and South. Though he never said so publicly, he intimated to friends that the South had been wrong to leave the Union.

Various business ventures occupied much of Breckinridge's time in his final years. He practiced law and served as president of the Elizabethtown, Lexington and Big Sandy railroad. His health began to decline in 1873, in part due to a Civil War battlefield injury to his liver. He died at his home on May 17, 1875 and was buried in Lexington Cemetery. His passing was mourned throughout the Union. An unfortunate symbol of sectional hatreds, John C. Breckinridge suffered for his political convictions and went on to become a champion of national healing.

Books

Davis, William C., *Breckinridge: Statesman, Soldier, Symbol,* Louisiana State University Press, 1974.
Heck, Frank, *Proud Kentuckian, John C. Breckinridge, 1821-1875,* University Press of Kentucky, 1976.
McPherson, James M., *Battle Cry of Freedom: The Civil War Era,* Oxford University Press, 1988.
Nevins, Allan, *The Emergence of Lincoln: Prologue to Civil War 1859-1860,* Charles Scribner's Sons, 1950.

Online

"Breckinridge, John Cabell (1821-1875)," *Biographical Directory of the United States Congress,* http://bioguide.congress.gov (October 26, 2001).
"New Market Personality: John C. Breckinridge," *The Insiders' Guide to Civil War Sites,* http:www.insiders.com (October 26, 2001). □

St. Brendan

St. Brendan the Navigator (c. 486-c. 578), also known as St. Brendan of Clonfert, is perhaps best known as the subject of the fictionalized romance *Navigato Sancti Brendani* (Brendan's Voyage), which according to the Clonfert-Monastic Settlement in Galway website, was "written by an Irish monk in the ninth or tenth century and describes the seven year voyage of Saint Brendan."

Navigato Sancti Brendani depicts St. Brendan as an explorer who discovers a land widely believed to be a representation of North America before the Norse Vikings, Amerigo Vespuci, or Christopher Columbus ever set foot on the continent. The seven-year voyage to locate the legendary island—alternately referred to as the Island of the Saints, Land of Delight, or Land of Promise—occurred while Brendan was older than 80 and features meetings with St. Patrick (who died in the century preceding Brendan's birth) and Judas Iscariot, betrayer of Jesus Christ. The tale also tells of encounters with sea monsters, talking birds, and a whale that allows Brendan and his crew to conduct Easter Mass on its back. While the tale contains these fantastic elements, some historians grant credence to

the theory that Brendan actually carried out a lengthy sea exploration that might have resulted in his visiting North American shores. Despite the conjectures surrounding his travels, it is known conclusively that Brendan was a tireless missionary on behalf of the Catholic Church, and that he established a number of abbeys and monasteries throughout Ireland, Scotland, Wales, and France.

Educated by Saints

The patron saint of Kerry, Ireland, Brendan was born around 486 in Ciarraighe Luachra near Tralee Bay in County Kerry, Ireland, now called Church Hill. Irish legends state that angels presented themselves in a bright light over the house when he was born. Some historians believe that he was the son of Findlugh and a descendant of a noblemen. The Bishop of Kerry, named Erc (later canonized St. Erc), baptized the infant. According to the custom of the time, the boy was then taken from his parents when he was one-year old and placed under the foster care of Ita (also spelled Aida; later canonized St. Ita) of Killeedy. Ita was a female mystic who became a lifelong confidante of Brendan's. She provided Brendan with his early education until he was six when his education was turned over to St. Erc. Erc instructed Brendan, and he also indulged his pupil's studies with St. Jarlath in Tuam, St. Enda in the Aran Islands, and St. Ninian in Whithorn, Galloway. It is believed that Brendan also studied with St. Finian and St. Gildas in Llancarfan, Wales. Erc ordained Brendan to the priesthood in 512.

Brendan is considered a member of what became known as the Second Order of Irish saints, also called the Twelve Apostles of Ireland. This group is credited with defining early Christian civilization as an amalgamation of religious, intellectual, and artistic pursuits. Their missionary zeal resulted in converting Ireland into a Christian haven from where they launched further missionary work to Scotland, Wales, and Brittany. The Irish monks, priests, and abbots are also credited with preserving much of the great works of civilization during the Dark Ages, when, due to the collapse of the Roman Empire and the subsequent barbarian raids on Europe's cultural centers, many books and cultural artifacts were destroyed.

Following his ordination, Brendan set about establishing monasteries in Ardfert and Shanakeel. He recruited many disciples and, during the next thirty years, Brendan founded monasteries in Kilbrandon and Kilbrennan Sound in Scotland and Inis-da-druim, which is north of Limerick in Ireland. Around 558, Brendan established a monastery at Clonfert in Galway, which remained one of Ireland's most prestigious schools until the sixteenth century. He founded a convent at Annagdhdown, County Galway, and named his sister, Brig, to head the institution.

St. Brendan the Navigator

While many details of Brendan's missionary work is documented, much of what is written about Brendan's other explorations is widely speculative. Historians conjecture that Brendan's passion for sea travel was nurtured by a childhood spent by the sea and led him to travel as far west as Iceland, Greenland, and perhaps the shores of North

America. These missionary travels led him to construct boats called curraghs (or currach), which were built by stretching animal skins over wooden frames. Traveling throughout the British Isles and Northern France, he would be accompanied by as many as sixty monks. During these travels, he is reported to have met St. Columba on Hynba Island in Scotland, traveled to Brittany with the Welsh monk St. Malo, and to have visited the Welsh monastery of Llancarfan founded by St. Cadoc.

His missionary travels, however, often are relegated beneath the supposed seven-year journey to the Land of Promise. While meditating in a chapel at the peak of what is now Mount Brandon, Brendan is said to have experienced a vision of Hy-Brasil, the legendary Land of Promise. He constructed a thirty-six-foot curragh, and, after fasting for forty days, set out with a crew of more than twelve men from Dingle Bay.

According to the *Navigatio Sancti Brendani,* Brendan's vision of the Land of Promise was inspired by the boasts of another abbot, who lived in the north of Ireland. The abbot had said that he had visited the Land of Promise many times by traveling only a short distance in the North Atlantic Ocean. Without any navigational coordinates, Brendan and his crew set out, trusting that God would guide their craft to their desired destination. On their travels, they encounter Judas Iscariot, who—allowed a temporary reprieve from Hell—clings to a rock above the sea. They also enjoy a conversation with the spirit of St. Patrick.

During their journey, the travelers encountered floating crystal palaces, "mountains in the sea spouting fire," and sea monsters with catlike heads and horns emanating from their mouths—which some scholars read as, respectively, icebergs, volcanoes, and walruses—leading them to believe that Brendan made it at least as far as Iceland. This postulation is supported elsewhere in the *Navigatio* when Brendan visits an island inhabited by former seekers of the Land of Promise. The island—inhabited by the Irish monks of the Community of Ailbe—is described as containing warm muddy pools and crystal, which some scholars believe are the natural hot springs and ice spar of Iceland.

In another part of the *Navigatio,* the narrators relate the story of Jasconius, a whale mistaken for an island by Brendan and his crew. The explorers realize their mistake when they light a fire on the surprised whale's back. Jasconius eventually befriends the monks, however, and allows them to conduct Easter Mass on his back for seven consecutive years. In other portions of the tale, the monks arrive in a tropical climate, visiting islands that may be fictional or, as some scholars suggest, may also be the Canary Islands, Jamaica, or the Bahamas. These islands featured "grapes as big as apples," which could either be oranges or grapefruit. The journey concludes when the crew returns to Donegal Bay, after traveling through lands and bodies of water that resemble Newfoundland, Greenland, and Iceland in their respective descriptions.

Navigatio Sancti Brendani was widely translated and distributed throughout Europe during the Middle Ages, leading some cartographers and explorers to believe its veracity and include St. Brendan's Island on maps of the era.

Whether he actually traveled to North America remains a mystery, but, in 1976, explorer Tim Severin built a curragh that he christened BRENDAN in the same manner as Brendan and traveled through the North Atlantic to the Faroe Islands—believed to be the Island of Sheep that Brendan described—and wintered in Iceland. Severin eventually landed in Newfoundland in June 1977, proving at least the possibility of Brendan's visit to North America.

After St. Patrick, Brendan remains the second-most popular Irish saint, and his name is given to several Irish landmarks, including Brandon Bay. St. Brendan's Feast Day is celebrated by Roman Catholics on May 16, and he is honored as the patron saint of boatmen, mariners, sailors, travelers, and whales. He is believed to have died when he was more than 90 years old while visiting his sister, Briga, who was serving as abbess at the Enach Duin convent in Annaghdown. He is buried facing the front door of the Cathedral of Clonfert. St. Brendan was a man of staunch faith. Nevertheless, his dying words, according to the Saints Preserved website, were to his sister: "I fear that I shall journey alone, that the way will be dark; I fear the unknown land, the presence of my King and the sentence of my judge."

Books

Ashe, Geoffrey, *Land to the West: A Search for Irish and Other Pre-Viking Discoverers of America,* New York: The Viking Press, 1962.
Cross, F. L., and Livingstone, E. A., *The Oxford Dictionary of the Christian Church,* New York: Oxford University Press, 1997.
Farmer, David, *Oxford Dictionary of Saints,* New York: Oxford University Press, 1997.
New Catholic Encyclopedia, Vol. II: Baa to Cam, The Washington, D.C.: Catholic University of America, 1967.

Online

Catholic Encyclopedia, http://www.newadvent.org/cathen/02758c.htm, (January 22, 2002).
Catholic Forum, http://www.catholic-forum.com/saints/saintb21.htm, (January 22, 2002).
Garland, Patrick V., "Who Really Discovered America," http://www.louthonline.com/html/who_really_discovered_america.html, (January 22, 2002).
Haggerty, Bridget, "St. Brendan, the Navigator," Irish Culture and Customs, http://www.irishcultureandcustoms.com/article1034.html, (January 22, 2002).
Ireland's Eye, http://www.irelandseye.com/aarticles/history/people/saints/brendan.shtm, (January 22, 2002).
"My Place amongst the Stones," Clonfert-Monastic Settlement in Galway, http://www.moytura.com/clonfert2.htm, (January 22, 2002).
St. Brendan's Isle, http://www.boatmail.net/page19.html, (January 22, 2002).
Saints Preserved, http://www.saintspreserved.com/brendan.htm, (January 22, 2002). □

Andre Philippus Brink

A voice of conscience within South Africa's Afrikaner community, novelist Andre Brink (born

literature in 1955. He later earned a master's degree in English literature from Potchefstroom in 1958 and a master's in Afrikaans and Dutch literature in 1959. That same year he married Estelle Naude. The couple had a son and were later divorced.

Off to Paris

Brink left South Africa in 1959 and headed for Paris, where he studied at the Sorbonne for the next two years. It was during his stay in Paris that his eyes were opened to the gross injustice of apartheid. In 1993 he told *UNESCO Courier:* ''I needed to see my country in perspective, and that only happened when I was living in Paris, between 1959 and 1961, at the time of the Sharpeville massacre. Sharpeville was the shock that forced me to see what was happening in my country, with the clarity that distance can provide.''

For the first time in his life, Brink had an opportunity in Paris to meet and socialize with blacks on equal terms. The only blacks he'd known back home in South Africa had been domestic servants and field workers. Now he was surrounded by black students, many of whom knew more about literature than he did, even after seven years of study. ''It was a cultural shock, a very pleasant shock, what's more, a discovery that opened up entirely new horizons for me,'' he told *UNESCO Courier.* ''It was a voyage of discovery into unknown territory.'' Brink's earliest novels, including *Eindelose wee,* published in 1960, *Lobola vir die lewe,* 1962, and *Die Ambassadeur,* 1963, were all written in his native Afrikaans and skirted the touchy issue of apartheid.

After his return to South Africa from Paris in 1961, Brink was hired as a lecturer at an English-language university. The school had a far more liberal tradition than the Afrikaner college at which he had studied earlier, and he began to meet South African blacks from the academic and professional worlds. Through his conversations with them and his observations of what was happening in his country, he gradually deepened his understanding of the plight of blacks in South Africa. However, he continued to avoid confronting these issues in his writing, focusing instead on some of the literary and philosophical ideas he had picked up in Paris. Major influences on his early writings, which were existentialist in style and mood, were Jean Paul Sartre and Albert Camus, particularly the latter. He had begun reading Camus before going to Paris in 1959. The French author died shortly after Brink arrived in Paris. ''For me his death was a shock that gave an extraordinary significance to his work,'' Brink told *UNESCO Courier.*

Not surprisingly, Brink gravitated toward others of his countrymen who had been exposed to the world outside South Africa. He'd met none of them in Paris but got in touch with them after his return to talk of their experiences overseas. There were five or six other Afrikaner writers who, like Brink, were interested in novels and the theater and all of whom had lived in Europe for a time. This handful of writers represented something new in Afrikaner literature, which theretofore had focused on a relatively narrow range of topics, including the lives of poor whites living off the land, drought, and farming problems. The changes that

1935) earned both governmental censure and the enmity of many of his countrymen for his longstanding opposition to apartheid. In the years since his country's exclusionary racial policies have been abandoned, Brink's stature as an author has increased significantly. An educator and playwright as well, Brink in recent years has championed Afrikaans, his native tongue, a language derived from Dutch. "There's a certain virility, a certain earthy, youthful quality about Afrikaans because it is such a young language, and because, although derived from an old European language like Dutch, it has found completely new roots in Africa and become totally Africanized in the process. . . . ," Brink told *Contemporary Authors Online.*

Son of Daniel (a magistrate) and Aletta (Wolmarans) Brink (a school teacher), he was born Andre Phillipus Brink on May 29, 1935, in Vrede, Orange Free State, South Africa. He grew up in a conservative Afrikaner family in a country where apartheid was the official policy. Of his youth, he told *UNESCO Courier:* "The opportunity never arose for me to question apartheid because I didn't have anything to compare it with." After graduating from Lydenburg High School, Brink attended Potchefstroom University in the Transvaal, earning his bachelor's degree in

Brink and his small circle of Afrikaner colleagues brought to Afrikaans literature was not welcomed at all. These forward-looking writers were condemned for writing in the European style, and their novels were condemned from the pulpits of hundreds of Afrikaner churches throughout South Africa. Even more ominously, South Africa's Directorate of Publications accused the writers of moral, religious, and sexual subversion. In some extreme instances, the writers' books were even burned.

Novel Is Critical of Religion

Brink took an even bolder step in writing *Die Ambassadeur,* later translated into English and published as *The Ambassador:* He criticized religion. This managed to alienate him to a degree from most Afrikaners, for whom religion is the cornerstone of morality. His personal rejection of religion further strained his relationship with his family, who had difficulty accepting his new political ideology. He later recalled for *UNESCO Courier* a number of fierce arguments with his father "before we realized that we had not common ground, politically speaking. So we took a calm rational decision not to talk about politics any more." In the fall of 1965, Brink married for the second time, wedding Salomi Louw, with whom he had a son, Gustav.

A major turning point in Brink's life and career came in 1968. Newly divorced and increasingly uncomfortable with the political climate in South Africa, he returned to Paris, considering seriously settling there for the rest of his life. However, the student riots in the French capital that year prompted Brink to reassess his obligations as a writer. Eventually he decided that he needed to return to South Africa "in order to accept full responsibility for whatever I wrote, believing that, in a closed society, the writer has a specific social and moral role to fill," he told *Contemporary Authors Online.* "This resulted in a more committed form of writing exploring the South African political situation and notably my revulsion of apartheid." Not long after his return to South Africa, Brink married potter Alta Miller. The couple later divorced.

Brink's 1973 novel *Kennis van die aand,* later translated into English and released as *Looking on Darkness,* was the author's first overtly political work. The government's reaction was not long in coming. Brink's novel was the first Afrikaans novel to be banned under South Africa's 1963 censorship legislation. The publicity surrounding the South African censorship created a strong international demand for Brink's work. The novel tells the story of the ill-fated love affair between Joseph Malan, a colored South African actor, and a white woman of British descent. In the end, Malan kills his white lover, after which he is beaten nearly to death by security police but later sentenced to death. The tale is recounted by Malan from his cell on death row. Although the novel brought down the wrath of official South Africa, literary critics were considerably more positive in their appraisal of Brink's work. Writing in the *Saturday Review,* Jane Larkin Crain said of the novel that "a passionately human vision rules here, informed by an imagination that is attuned at once to complex and important abstractions and to the rhythms and the texture of everyday experience." In the

Times Literary Supplement, C.J. Driver wrote that "within its context, this is a brave and important novel and in any terms a fine one." Fellow South African Nadine Gordimer, however, suggested that the novel suffered from the "defiant exultation and relief" of Brink's first attack on the political system within the country.

Novels Written in Two Languages

Although he remains a passionate champion of Afrikaans, Brink has completed the first "final" draft of all his novels since the mid-1970s in English. He admits, however, that he feels far more comfortable and idiomatic in Afrikaans. He followed the success of *Looking on Darkness* with *An Instant in the Wind* in 1976. The novel, another tale of interracial romance, touches on many of the same South African themes as its predecessor, but some critics found Brink's handling of the love story more appropriate to the pages of popular romance fiction. Far more successful was *Rumors of Rain,* published in 1978. To many, this was—and remains—Brink's finest novel. In an interview with *Contemporary Authors Online,* Brink offered this synopsis: "The apartheid mind is demonstrated in the account given by a wealthy businessman of the one weekend in which his whole familiar world collapsed through the conviction of his best friend for terrorism, the revolt of his son, the loss of his mistress, and the sale of his family's farm. In spite of his efforts to rigorously separate all the elements of his life, he becomes the victim of his own paradoxes and faces an apocalypse."

Published in 1979, *A Dry White Season* was eventually made into a motion picture starring Kevin Kline and Marlon Brando. Like *Rumors of Rain,* its story line is deceptively simple. While being detained by the security police, a black man dies, prompting his white Afrikaner friend to launch a probe into what really happened. In launching this private investigation, Afrikaner Ben Du Toit, the novel's protagonist, finds himself pitted against the awesome power of the state. Writing in the *New York Times Book Review,* Mel Watkins found the novel "demonstrates Andre Brink's continuing refinement of his fictional technique, without sacrificing any of the poignancy that his previous books have led us to expect."

A Chain of Voices, published in 1982, provides Brink's fictionalized account of a Cape Colony slave uprising in the early 19th century. This is among the novelist's most critically acclaimed works, but it was followed in 1984 with one of his more mediocre offerings, *The Wall of the Plague.* Brink was in excellent form once again in 1988's *States of Emergency,* a love story set against the backdrop of South Africa's State of Emergency of the 1980s. This was followed in 1991 by *An Act of Terror* and in 1993 by *On the Contrary.* Brink's more recent novels have included *Imaginings of Sand* in 1996, *Devil's Valley* in 1999, and *The Rights of Desire* in 2001.

Married since 1990 to Maresa de Beer, Brink occupies a chair in English literature at the University of Cape Town. He previously taught a course in Afrikaans literature at Rhodes University. Though he was nominated three times for the Nobel Prize for Literature, he has yet to win that coveted award. He has been twice honored by France, being made a chevalier of the Legion of Honor in 1982 and a commander of the Order of Arts and Letters in 1992.

Books

Contemporary Authors Online, Gale Group, 2001.
Contemporary Novelists, 7th ed. St. James Press, 2001.

Periodicals

Economist, June 18, 1988, p. 96.
Publishers Weekly, November 25, 1996, p. 50.
UNESCO Courier, September 1993, p. 4. □

Henry Peter Brougham

Henry Brougham (1778-1868) was one of Britain's leading reform politicians of the nineteenth century. Through the force of his oratory before Parliament, Brougham helped win passage of some of the country's most important legislative efforts in his generation. As the first Baron Brougham and Vaux, he was sometimes referred to as "the Terror of the Senate" and enjoyed great fame throughout the land.

Precocious Youth

B rougham was a native of Edinburgh, Scotland, and was born on September 19, 1778, into a family of minor nobility. His father held literary ambitions, but never pursued them with much vigor. The eldest Brougham son, however, proved much more ambitious, even at an early age. At school, he gained a measure of fame for successfully challenging his Latin master, who was forced to admit an error before the class. After finishing at the age of 13, Brougham was tutored for a year and entered Edinburgh University in 1792. There, he studied science and mathematics and even wrote a paper on optics that was published by the Royal Society in 1796. By that point, Brougham had begun studies toward the bar exam and was admitted to the Scottish bar in 1800.

In the early years of Brougham's career, the British criminal justice system still followed some harsh, medieval practices. Petty thieves were regularly hanged, prisons were filthy, and a fair trial was unlikely. This unenlightened attitude extended to other legal realms as well. Dissent and freedom of the press were greatly restricted, and even public meetings were outlawed. There was a growing movement toward reform, especially from the younger generation. Brougham and some of his college friends, many of whom would also achieve prominence later in life, founded the *Edinburgh Review* in 1802. The journal was a lively and opinionated magazine, and Brougham penned many of the anonymous articles himself. From there followed his first book, *An Inquiry into the Colonial Policy of the European Powers.* It discussed the slave trade in part, and his vocal

opposition to the practice drew him into the abolitionist cause.

Foe of Slavery

At the age of 25, Brougham moved to London in 1803 and immersed himself in political circles sympathetic to the Whig Party. At the time, the Whigs were Britain's liberal party, and the party was defiant in its belief that the power of Parliament was superior to that of the Crown. In contrast, the Tory Party was a conservative, tradition-minded institution and largely the province of the aristocracy and Church of England leaders.

The Whigs were committed to eradicating slavery, or at least England's role in the trade. Commercial interests— namely the shipping and trade magnates who profited from it—were adamantly opposed to any form of parliamentary restraint. It was argued that ending British involvement in the procurement and shipment of Africans to the New World would have a ruinous effect on the British economy. In 1807, Brougham was tapped to organize the press campaign for the Whig Party, and later that year British statesman William Wilberforce secured passage of a law that ostensibly ended the slave trade.

Brougham enjoyed great social success in London as an erudite and witty guest. His increasing prominence helped him gain a seat in House of Commons when a vacancy in the Camelford area occurred. This was known as a "pocket" borough and contained just twenty eligible voters, all of whom were in the service of the major landholder in the area, the Duke of Bedford. Elected in 1810, Brougham served two years and rose quickly within the Whig Party to a leadership role. He was a masterful, entertaining speaker, and early on made his mark with a fiery anti-slave trade bill before Parliament in June of 1810. Wilberforce's earlier bill had resulted in a law that made slave trading illegal, but it was punishable by a small fine. Brougham asserted that ships built in Liverpool yards dodged the law by sending carpenters out to sea with its first sailing, who then outfitted the vessel with the bunks necessary for human cargo. He argued for a law that would make slave trading a felony: "While you levy your pence, the wholesale dealers in blood and torture pocket their pounds and laugh at your twopenny penalty," Brougham thundered, according to Frances Hawes's biography, *Henry Brougham.*

Professional Accolades, Personal Woes

Brougham went on to argue many precedent-setting cases of the era. At the time, British sailors and soldiers were still flogged for infractions, and when one newspaper ran an article criticizing the barbaric practice, its publishers were sued by the Crown for libel. Brougham successfully defended them. He also gained an acquittal for 38 weavers from Manchester, a major textile center, accused of attempting to unionize. He lost his Camelford seat in 1812 but was elected again in 1816 from another pocket borough, Winchelsea. Political cartoonists of the era took great pleasure in caricaturing the outspoken M.P. and barrister, with his long nose and trademark plaid trousers. He gained further admiration from this quarter by proposing to guarantee freedom of the press.

Brougham had less success in his personal life. In the summer of 1819, he secretly wed Mary Anne Spalding, a widow with two children, and the couple had a daughter, who was born that November. It was said to be an unhappy union, an intellectual mismatch. Furthermore, their child died in 1821; another daughter, named after Brougham's mother Eleanor, who lived with him for many years, did survive until adulthood.

Still, Brougham's marital woes were trifling compared to those of his most famous client, the Princess of Wales. The corrupt prince, who had roused the ire of his family and parliament by marrying a Roman Catholic woman, finally agreed to marry a suitable bride in exchange for an increase in his royal allowance. A niece of the Queen, Caroline, a German princess of Braunschweig, was chosen. Caroline was immediately reviled by members of the royal family, who treated her shamefully. Elsewhere, political powers hostile to the prince used Caroline to attack him. The new Princess of Wales was said to be unattractive, with bad teeth and poor personal hygiene. Moreover, she was prone to incessant talk punctuated by vulgar jokes. After the birth of a daughter, the Prince refused to co-habit with his wife again, and Caroline was left to amuse herself. There was an inquiry into an allegedly indigent child she adopted, after rumors arose that it was her own, but she was acquitted. Brougham became her advisor in 1809, three years after these proceedings. She eventually left England for Europe and en-

gaged in further scandalous behavior there. When King George III died in 1820, she planned to return for her husband's coronation, but he refused to receive her. She was accused of adultery with her couturier in Italy and a bill to annul the marriage was introduced in Parliament.

Famed for Defense of Beleaguered Princess

At this point, Brougham became Caroline's attorney general. He delivered an impassioned speech before the House of Lords in her defense and skillfully discredited the witnesses brought in against her. According to Hawes, he enjoined the assembled lords to "save the country, that you may continue to adorn it—save the Crown, which is in jeopardy—the Aristocracy which is shaken—save the Altar, which must stagger with the blow that rends its kindred throne." The speech reduced some to tears, and though the Lords voted to annul the marriage, it was only by narrow majority, and there was no hope of its passage in the House of Commons. The bill was withdrawn, and public sentiment turned against the King. Brougham became a major celebrity of the era for his defense of Caroline, and large crowds often turned out when he visited towns outside the capital.

Ignited Generation of Political Change

Brougham's other achievements made a lasting mark on English society during his century. He introduced a Public Education Bill in 1820, which failed to pass, and subsequent proposals that would have created a vastly improved system of publicly funded schools in what was, at the time, virtually an educational vacuum. There were few schools, teachers were unqualified, corporal punishment common, and high rates of illiteracy persisted in the countryside. Many of the ideas Brougham proposed were adopted later in the century.

Brougham had better success as one of the primary founders of London University in 1828. At the time, the country's two major institutions of higher learning, Oxford and Cambridge, admitted only students who belonged to the Church of England. Brougham imagined a nonresidential university open to all religious denominations, with a focus on the sciences. He secured money from the government to help establish it, though it was initially derided as "Brougham's Cockney College." Still, the Anglicans formed a competing city college, and the two were formally joined as London University in 1836.

In 1830 Brougham accepted an offer from the Whig government to become Lord Chancellor under the Prime Minister, Earl Grey. With it he received a baronetcy. It was a brief tenure, but one stamped with a tremendous achievement. Brougham was instrumental in securing passage of the famous Reform Bill of 1831, which vastly modernized the nation's parliamentary election system. It had been largely unchanged since the 1600s. There were many of the aforementioned pocket boroughs, and so-called "rotten" boroughs as well. These were districts that had suffered a major loss of population, but still held a seat in House of Commons. Old Sarum, near Salisbury, was the most famous rotten borough; it had once been the site of a Roman garrison, but fell into decline by the 1300s. Moreover, major population shifts resulting from the Industrial Revolution had not remedied the situation; large cities like Manchester and Birmingham had little or no representation in the House of Commons. Voting was still restricted, and out of a nation of 24 million, only 435,000 men were eligible.

Passed Reform Bills

The Reform Bill vastly expanded the voting franchise and resulted in an entirely new group of voters from Britain's growing middle class. Passage of the bill, however, was hard-won. A new king in 1830, William IV, had Whig sympathies, and in 1831 he agreed to dissolve Parliament so that the necessary reforms could pass. He walked back to Buckingham Palace and was cheered by massive crowds. The bill failed to pass in the House of Lords, however, and reform riots took place in several British towns, most notably in Bristol. Grey and Brougham met with the King and asked him to create a number of Whig barons that would secure passage of the bill in the House of Lords, but he had a change of heart about the matter and refused. Grey's government then resigned, other parties failed to form a government, and Grey was invited back. When the King agreed to create new peers, the House of Lords decided to back the Reform Bill.

Brougham also helped secure passage of several other reform bills. One concerning criminal law brought speedier procedure for suspects regarding detention and trial and the creation of a central criminal court. The Privy Council judicial committee was remodeled on his plan in 1833. He lost office in 1834 with the defeat of the Whig Party, but when it returned to power the next year he was not given a post. He was, however, instrumental in the passage of the Municipal Reform Bill of 1835, which allowed taxpayers in England's 178 boroughs to form their own local councils and elect their own mayor. One of his last great political achievements was the Matrimonial Causes Act of 1857, which permitted divorce cases to be heard in the court system; prior to this it required petitioners to ask for a Private Act of Parliament, which was slow and costly.

Brougham had nicknamed his second daughter, born in 1821, "Tullia." She was in poor health throughout her life and died in 1839. The loss was said to devastate him. She was the first woman to be buried at Lincoln's Inn. In 1844, Brougham wrote a novel, *Albert Lunel, or the Chateau of Languedoc,* set in the south of France where he preferred to vacation. His presence helped make Cannes a popular spot for Britons of a certain class. He died there in May of 1868, at a house he had named after his daughter.

Books

Aspinall, Arthur, *Lord Brougham and the Whig Party,* Manchester University Press, 1917.
Hawes, Frances, *Henry Brougham,* St. Martin's, 1958. □

Thomas Alexander Browne

Thomas Alexander Browne (1826-1915), who wrote under the pen name of Rolf Boldrewood, was born in England but moved to Australia with his family at the age of five. He was known for his adventure novels set in the Australian bush.

Browne's father, Sylvester Brown (the family did not use the final "e" until about 1864) led a life of adventure worthy of one of the heroes in Browne's novels. After running away to sea from his home in Galway, Ireland, at the age of ten, he eventually rose to be a successful officer in the East India Company and later became the captain of his own ships. He met his wife when she was a passenger on one of his ships; they married in Mauritius and then settled briefly in London, where Browne was born on August 6, 1826. Five years later, Captain Browne took a shipload of convicts to Australia and moved to Sydney with his family. In Sydney, he became a whaler and built a large villa, named Enmore, for which the suburb of Enmore was later named. He was a large landowner in and around Melbourne and also founded the first ferry between Melbourne and Williamstown. Eventually the couple settled in Heidelberg, Australia, where they had nine more children. Browne was educated at Sydney College, largely in the classics. He completed his education at Melbourne in 1843.

Several Disastrous Ventures

In 1841, Browne's father was financially ruined by an economic depression. Browne did his part to support the family; he traveled to the Western District of Victoria, where he took over 32,000 acres of land, farming potatoes and keeping cattle and horses. He later described his experiences in this hard-working but pastoral setting in *Old Melbourne Memories* (1884). Later, during the Australian gold rush, he traveled to Ballarat to sell meat to the miners. After about fifteen years of raising cattle and horses, he decided to raise sheep instead and moved near Swan Hill to do so. Shortly before moving he visited England, Ireland, and Scotland, later writing about his travels in *Incidents and Adventures of My Run Home* (1874). He married Margaret Maria Riley in 1861, six months after the trip.

The sheep farming venture ended disastrously as a result of drought, and he sold the property at a tremendous loss in 1863. The following year he leased Bundidgaree station in Narrandera, but because of his financial difficulties, he needed the help of his two brothers-in-law to do so. Although he claimed to own the property, it is likely that the official owners were his brothers-in-law, and that he managed the property in return for the loan. Like his sheep farming business, this venture would end in disaster when four years of drought forced him to leave. He decided to move to Sydney with his wife and four children. In Sydney his wife gave birth to twins. Desperate to make some money, Browne herded cattle for a while until he discovered that he could sell his stories. His pen name, Rolf Boldrewood, is from a character in the novel *Marmion* by Sir Walter Scott. Scott's work also provided inspiration for much of Browne's fiction.

Browne's first published work was a story about a kangaroo hunt, which he sold to the English *Cornhill Magazine* in 1866. In 1871, the periodical published another of his stories. He also sold several articles on bush life to the *Australian Town and Country Journal*.

In 1871, he was appointed police magistrate and clerk of petty sessions for the gold rush town of Gulgong, despite his lack of experience in such a field, and in 1872, he was appointed goldrush commissioner at Gulgong. However, Browne was still in debt because he now owed money to a third brother-in-law who had paid off some of his other debts. The debt to his brother-in-law gave Browne a great incentive to write. According to Alan Brissenden in *The Portable Rolf Boldrewood,* he once said: " . . . my best work was done when I was half-drowned in debt."

By 1881, when he was appointed police magistrate in Dubbo, Browne had written seven serial novels for the *Town and Country Journal.* Four were romances about life in the bush, one was based on his trip to the British Isles, one was a novel set in England, and one was set in the goldfields.

Robbery Under Arms

In 1882, Browne began to write his most well-known work, *Robbery Under Arms.* The first two chapters of the series were rejected by both *The Australasian* and *Town and Country Journal.* Their editors claimed that the tale was more gloomy than anything else he had written, and they did not believe the story would get any better. However, Browne finally sold *Robbery Under Arms* to *The Sydney Mail,* which published the first chapter on July 1, 1882, and continued publishing the rest of the chapters over a period of a year. During this time, Browne's fame grew, as his *Old Melbourne Memories* were also appearing in serial form in *The Australasian.* Browne's stories, told in what Brissenden called a "freely running vernacular style," emphasized adventure and starred outlaws, goldrush miners, and other daring men.

Robbery Under Arms was first published in book form by Remington of London in 1888. Macmillan, a larger publisher, bought the rights to the book and published a shorter version of it in 1889. This version quickly became successful and was reissued two more times in 1889, four more times in 1890, and has never been out of print since. It has been adapted for the stage and radio and has been made into at least three films.

The novel stars Dick Marston, who narrates a tale of cattle-herding, bushranging, horse thievery, convicts, and aborigines. As the story opens, Marston is in jail, waiting to be executed for bushranging or banditry. He tells the story of his life, including twelve years in prison, his release from prison, and his love for and marriage to the faithful Gracey Storefield, his childhood sweetheart. Many of the book's events star the criminal Captain Starlight, who encounters Marston after he has been shot in the shoulder by another character, Sergeant Goring. Starlight is described in romantic style: "Starlight, with the blood dripping on to his horse's shoulder, and the half-caste [Warrigal], with his hawk's eye and glittering teeth, supporting him."

When Starlight takes his final stand, he kills Goring, and with his last breath engages in polite chat with his old clubmate and enemy, Sir Ferdinand Morringer, Inspector of Police. He also names his beloved, Aileen Marston. Warrigal, his sidekick, rides up and laments for him at his death. In *A History of Australian Literature,* Ken Goodrich wrote that the energy of the narrative is somewhat slowed by Marston's rambling, although his common Australian way of speaking "has its own interest. Nothing is to be taken too seriously in this romantic entertainment, just as the local and Sydney papers do not take too seriously the exploits of Starlight and the efforts of the police to track him down. There is an air of the school practical joke about it all."

In the novel, Browne's attitude toward Australia is ambiguous; he refers to England as "home" and "the mother country" and views Australia as "that other England growing up in the South." Although this was quite different from the nationalism and pride in Australia that was then developing among many Australians, it did not seem to hurt the novel's success. Some critics, according to Brissenden, claimed that Browne wrote for English readers and presented a version of Australia that fit with English prejudices and expectations. Brissenden, however, wrote that certain scenes in the novel indicate that Browne was not entirely sure about his own attitude toward Australia. For instance, although Browne believed in the worth of the English class system, which many other Australians viewed as repressive, characters in the novel speak up against it.

War to the Knife

Between 1884 and 1890, Browne wrote three more serials, notably *The Sealskin Mantle*, which was a romance written in a florid style. It appeared in the *Mail* beginning in February of 1884. In 1889, he wrote *War to the Knife*, set in the North Island of New Zealand, among the Maori people. *War to the Knife* describes the hero's fascination with the Maoris coupled with his revulsion for their communal system of land tenure. Roland Massinger, at age 28, is looking for a wife and an heir for his family's grandest possession, his ancestral home, Massinger Court. However, he is jilted by the aristocratic but feminist Hypatia Tolemache, who is more interested in her career than in marriage. Spurned, Massinger emigrates to New Zealand, where he becomes fascinated with a Maori woman, Erena Mannering. She is beautiful and innately aristocratic, but Mannering worries about the fact that he and she are of different races. Browne, like most Europeans of his age, found the idea of mixed-race unions titillating but shocking. Meanwhile, other tensions are building as Maoris clash with settlers, and eventually Erena is killed while trying to save Mannering's life. As Robert F. Dixon wrote in*Authority and Influence: Australian Literary Criticism 1950-2000*, "These details have a fictional source in James Fenimore Cooper's *The Last of the Mohicans* (1826), to which Boldrewood refers many times in *War to the Knife*."

Dixon also commented that the novel was "a formulaic tale of frontier adventure," and that "its sources are palpable, its characters and events predictable." However, readers loved it, as they loved Browne's other tales. By 1890, Browne was famous as an author. He moved with his family to Albury, where he lived until he retired from public service in 1895 and then moved back to Melbourne.

After retiring, Browne still enjoyed an active social life, engaging in Shakespearean readings, political discussions, and visits with aristocratic friends. In 1901, he published *Bad Company*, a short story collection set in the sheep-shearers' strike of the early 1890s. Browne's sympathies were against the strikers. This showed a change in his attitudes over time because more than two decades before, he had written "Shearing in Riverina, New South Wales," a story that was much more sympathetic to the workers' grievances. Browne's last published work was "The Truth About Aboriginal Outrages" (1906), in which he claimed aboriginal people were inherently violent and untrustworthy. Browne died on August 1, 1915, in Melbourne.

Over the course of Browne's prolific career, he wrote sixteen novels, three story and essay collections, and two handbooks for immigrants to Australia. Brissenden wrote that Browne's "prolific pen, supported by an unusually wide range of experience, excellent health and optimistic confidence, produced a great deal that is deservedly forgotten. Yet, little known parts of his writing can still give enjoyment by their readability and by the insight they provide into aspects of Australian life as the country was about

to emerge from the colonial stage." Dixon commented that Browne was "a popular writer of limited understanding whose novels are nevertheless deeply significant portraits of Australian society in the years before Federation."

Books

Brissenden, Alan, "Introduction," in *The Portable Rolf Boldrewood*, University of Queensland Press, 1979.

Dixon, Robert, "Narrative Form and Ideology," in *Authority and Influence: Australian Literary Criticism 1950-2000*, University of Queensland Press, 2001.

Goodwin, Ken, *A History of Australian Literature*, St. Martin's Press, 1986.

Pierre, Peter, *Oxford Literary Guide to Australia*, Oxford University Press, 1993. ☐

Edward Bulwer-Lytton

British author Edward Bulwer-Lytton (1803-1873) wrote *Falkland*, *Pelham*, and *Eugene Aram*. These novels won instant success and made him a wealthy man. As a result, he entered Parliament as a liberal member representing St. Ives, Huntingdonshire. Bulwer-Lytton remained an active politician yet still found time to produce many novels, plays, and poems.

According to his baptismal certificate, the full name of this once famous author was Edward George Earle Lytton Bulwer-Lytton. He was born in London May 23, 1803. His father was a Norfolk squire, William Bulwer of Heydon Hall, colonel of the 106th regiment (Norfolk Rangers); his mother was Elizabeth Barbara Lytton, a lady who claimed kinship with Cadwaladr Vendigaid, the semi-mythical hero who led the Strathclyde Welsh against the Angles in the seventh century.

As a child the future novelist was delicate, but he learned to read at a surprisingly early age and began to write verses before he was ten years old. Going first to a small private school at Fulham, he later attended school at Rottingdean, where he continued to manifest literary tastes, Lord Byron and Sir Walter Scott being his chief idols at this time.

Bulwer-Lytton was so talented that his relations decided it would be a mistake to send him to a public school. Accordingly he was placed with a tutor at Ealing, under whose care he progressed rapidly with his studies. Thereafter he proceeded to Cambridge, where he earned his degree easily and won many academic awards. After graduation he traveled for a while in Scotland and France, then bought a commission in the army. He sold it soon afterward, however, and began to devote himself seriously to writing.

Although busy and winning great fame, Bulwer-Lytton's life was not really a happy one. Long before meeting his wife, he fell in love with a young girl who died prematurely. This loss seems to have left an indelible sorrow. His

marriage was anything but a successful one, the pair being divorced comparatively soon after their union.

Early Works

His first publications of note were the novels *Falkland, Pelham,* and *Eugene Aram.* These won instant success and made the author a wealthy man. As a result, he entered Parliament as a liberal member representing St. Ives, Huntingdonshire in 1831. During the next ten years he was an active politician yet still found time to produce many stories, such as *The Last Days of Pompei, Ernest Maltravers, Zanoni,* and *The Last of the Barons.* These were followed by *The Caxtons.* Simultaneously he achieved some fame as a dramatist, perhaps his best play being *The Lady of Lyons.*

Besides further novels, Bulwer-Lytton issued several volumes of verses, notably *Ismael* and *The New Union,* while translating works from German, Spanish, and Italian. He produced a history of Athens, contributed to endless periodicals, and was at one time editor of the *New Monthly Magazine.*

Active Political Career

In 1851 Bulwer-Lytton was instrumental in founding a scheme for pensioning authors and also began to pursue an active political career. In 1852 he was elected conservative Member of Parliament for Hertfordshire and held the post until his elevation to the peerage in 1866. He became Secre-

tary for the Colonies in Lord Derby's ministry (1858–59) and played a large part in the organization of the new colony of British Columbia. He became Baron Lytton of Knebworth in July 1866 and thereafter took his place in the House of Lords.

In 1862 Bulwer-Lytton increased his stature by his occult novel entitled *A Strange Story.* Toward the end of the decade he began to work on another story, *Kenelm Chillingly,* but his health was beginning to fail, and he died on May 23, 1873, at Torquay.

Even as a child, Bulwer-Lytton had demonstrated a predilection for mysticism. He had surprised his mother once by asking whether she was "not sometimes overcome by the sense of her own identity." Bulwer-Lytton's interest in the occult increased, and it is frequently reflected in his literary output, including his poem "The Tale of a Dreamer," and in *Kenelm Chillingly.* In *A Strange Story* he tried to give a scientific coloring to old-fashioned magic.

Interest in Psychic Phenomena

Bulwer-Lytton was a keen student of psychic phenomena. The great medium D. D. Home was his guest at Knebworth in 1855. Home's phenomena greatly aroused his curiosity. He never spoke about his experiences in public, but his identity was at once detected in an account in Home's autobiography (*Incidents in My Life*), "Immediately after this another message was spelt out: 'We wish you to believe in the . . . ' On inquiring after the finishing word a small cardboard cross which was lying on a table at the end of the room was given into his hand."

When the press asked Bulwer-Lytton for a statement, he refused to give any. His wariness to commit himself before the public was well demonstrated by his letter to the secretary of the London Dialectical Society, February 1869: "So far as my experience goes, the phenomena, when freed from impostures with which their exhibition abounds, and examined rationally, are traceable to material influences of the nature of which we are ignorant. They require certain physical organizations or temperaments to produce them, and vary according to these organizations and temperaments."

Bulwer-Lytton sought out many mediums after his experiences with Home and often detected imposture. His friendship with Home continued for ten years. When he began the wildest of his romances, *A Strange Story,* he intended initially to portray Home, but abandoned this plan for the fantastic conception of Margrave. The joyousness of Home's character, however, is still reflected in the mental make-up of Margrave.

Bulwer-Lytton also became acquainted with the French occultist Eliphas Levi, whom he assisted in magical evocations, and Levi was clearly a model for the character of the magus in *The Haunted and The Haunters.*

Books

Howe, Ellic. *The Magicians of the Golden Dawn.* Routledge and Kegan Paul, 1972. □

C

Emma Carr

Emma Carr (1880-1972) was one of the most renowned chemical educators of the first half of the twentieth century. She was known not only for the chemistry program she established at Mount Holyoke College, which became a model for group research, but also for her groundbreaking work on the structure of unsaturated hydrocarbons. Employing absorption spectroscopy and later, far ultraviolet vacuum spectroscopy, Carr and her faculty and student collaborators made significant contributions to the understanding of the make-up of certain organic compounds.

Carr was the first recipient of the Francis Garvan Medal to honor an outstanding woman in American chemistry. In addition to her research and teaching skills, she also proved to be a formidable administrator, making Mount Holyoke College one of the premier chemistry schools in the nation at the time. At her instigation, Mount Holyoke became one of the first institutions in the United States to use ultraviolet spectrophotometry to illuminate the structure of complex organic molecules. Her 33 years as head of the chemistry department, from 1913 to 1946, were marked by her personal approach to teaching and her rigorous techniques in research. Active in both community and college, Carr became a much sought-after speaker following her retirement from teaching. She lived until the age of 92, mostly on or near the campus of Mount Holyoke, the center of both her public and private life.

Emma Perry Carr was born on July 23, 1880, in Holmesville, Ohio, the third of five children to Anna Mary (Jack) and Edmund Cone Carr. Her father and grandfather were both highly respected doctors, as was her brother. Carr was to follow in this scientific tradition. Her mother was a devout Methodist, active in church and community affairs. This also heavily influenced the young Carr. Raised in Coshocton, Ohio, and dubbed "Emmy the smart one" in high school, Carr went on to Ohio State University for her freshman year in college, one of very few women attending that institution in 1898. There she studied chemistry with William McPherson, but decided at the end of her freshman year to transfer to Mount Holyoke College in South Hadley, Massachusetts.

After successfully completing two years of college, she worked as an assistant in the Mount Holyoke chemistry department for three years. Carr then completed her B.S. degree at the University of Chicago in 1905. Thereafter, she returned to Mount Holyoke to teach for another three years until taking up graduate studies in 1908. During her graduate studies in physical chemistry at the University of Chicago, she received the Mary E. Woolley and the Lowenthal fellowships. She worked and studied with Alexander Smith and Julius Stieglitz, the latter being her primary advisor in her Ph.D. work on aliphatic imido esters. Carr was only the seventh woman to be awarded a doctorate from the University of Chicago.

Carr of Mount Holyoke

The name of Emma Carr and Mount Holyoke College are indelibly connected. It was at that institution where she did her major work and it was that institution which benefited so greatly from her teaching and administrative skills. Returning there to teach in 1910, she was made full profes-

89

pounds were subsequently analyzed, using a Fery spectrograph that Carr had persuaded the college to purchase. Initial research results, published in 1918 under the title of "The Absorption Spectra of Some Derivatives of Cyclopropane," established the college as a research institution of note and solidified research in the educational curriculum.

To gain further knowledge of spectroscopic techniques, Carr studied at Queen's University, Belfast, Northern Ireland, in 1919. These studies, and her expertise in spectroscopy, led to an invitation in 1925 to participate in the preparation of the International Critical Tables (ITC), an authoritative compilation of chemical data, including spectroscopic information. Carr traveled to Europe in 1925, taking a 12-month leave to complete her work on this project in the laboratories of two co-compilers, Jean Becquerel of the College de France in Paris and Victor Henri of the University of Zurich. Carr returned to Zurich after receiving the Alice Freeman Palmer Fellowship to study vacuum spectroscopy with Henri in 1929.

Won Fame for Ultraviolet Spectrographic Measurements

Carr and her research colleagues began to understand limitations to their work by the late 1920s. Specifically, they could not answer why certain molecular atomic groups absorbed some wavelengths of light, nor could they explain what mechanics were at play within the molecule when such light was absorbed. To answer these questions, Carr determined that simpler molecules with fewer variables needed to be studied. Again, undergraduates, graduate students, and professors teamed up in 1930 to prepare highly purified hydrocarbons with known positions of the carbon-carbon double bond in the molecule. These then were employed in the measurement of the absorption spectra in the far ultraviolet spectrum, employing vacuum spectroscopic techniques Carr had learned in Europe. Funds from the National Research Council aided in this research which shed new light on the spectra of aliphatic hydrocarbons, or those organic compounds in which the carbon atoms form open chains, especially the olefins. Carr and her students used these techniques to attempt to understand the causes of selective absorption of radiant energy in these simple structures.

While Carr's theories on the spectral absorption and heats of combustion of hydrocarbons did not gain widespread acceptance, her work with vacuum spectrographic analysis of purified hydrocarbons altered the understanding of the carbon-carbon double bond and also resulted in a better theoretical understanding of energy relationships in ehtylenic unsaturation. Carr's further work on this project, partly funded by the National Science Foundation and the Rockefeller Foundation, continued throughout the 1930s and into the 1940s and had lasting import, especially for the petroleum industry. Her research was later expanded upon by the Nobel laureate, Robert S. Mulliken, in developing theories about energy relationships in organic compounds.

sor and head of the Department of Chemistry in 1913. She retained that position until her retirement in 1946. Under her guidance, the chemistry department became one of the strongest at Mount Holyoke and one of the most important in the country. Though a liberal arts institution, Mount Holyoke had a strong science tradition from the time of its founding by Mary Lyons in 1837. Lyons herself taught chemistry, and subsequent directors of the college continued this emphasis. Carr, however, attracted top-notch instructors to the program such as Dorothy Hahn and Louisa Stephenson, establishing a curriculum every bit as challenging as those found at Ivy League schools. Known as a charismatic teacher, Carr was intimately involved with her students, and was a staunch believer in having the best instructors teach introductory courses so as to interest young students in the sciences. Moreover, she involved her students in active research, developing important research projects for the college to pursue.

From her survey of the literature, Carr came to see that British and European researchers were increasingly intrigued with the relationship between ultraviolet absorption spectra and the electronic configurations of organic molecules. Carr had been searching for some manner in which she could apply physical chemistry to organic problems, and this seemed the perfect project, for very little research on the subject was being conducted in North America at the time. In 1913 she initiated work on the project, working with Hahn to synthesize hydrocarbons. Students also participated in the research project as part of their hands-on training, an innovative approach then. These organic com-

A Life for Science

Carr continued to live in college dorms until 1935, when she and another researcher at Mount Holyoke, Mary L. Sherrill, began sharing a house on campus. Internationally recognized as a first class researcher, Carr continued to maintain close contact with her students, putting as much emphasis on the classroom as the lab. In 1937, she was awarded the first Francis Garvan Medal by the American Chemical Society to honor an outstanding woman in American chemistry. As part of the selection committee, she was embarrassed to find herself nominated while absent from one of the meetings.

During the Second World War, Carr and her students worked on a project to synthesize quinine. Though there were many near misses, her team was unable to come up with a successful synthetic form of the anti-malaria drug. In 1944, she gave a series of seminars at the fledgling Institute of Chemistry in Mexico City. Honorary degrees were conferred on Carr from Allegheny College in 1939, from Russell Sage College in 1941, and from Mount Holyoke in 1952.

Though she retired in 1946, Carr's professional life was far from over. She continued to speak at colleges and clubs well into her seventies, promoting the scientific ethos as well as her beloved baseball. In 1957, she shared the James Flack Norris Award for outstanding achievement in the teaching of chemistry with her friend and collaborator, Sherrill. When Sherrill retired in 1954, the two traveled extensively. A lover of music, Carr played the organ in the Methodist Church and also played the cello until arthritis forced her to become a listener rather than player. With failing health, Carr had to leave Mount Holyoke, moving to the Presbyterian Home in Evanston, Illinois, where she died on January 7, 1972 of heart failure. It is a lasting tribute to this renowned woman of science that the chemistry building at Mount Holyoke College bears her name.

Books

American Chemists and Chemical Engineers. Edited by Wyndham D. Miles. American Chemical Society, 1976.
Bailey, Martha J. American Women in Science: A Biographical Dictionary. ABC-CLIO, 1994.
Banville, Debra L. Women in Chemistry and Physics. Greenwood Press, 1993.
Notable American Women: The Modern Period. Edited by B. Sicherman and C.H. Green. Belknap Press, 1980.
Rayner-Canham, Marelene and Geoffrey Rayner-Canham. Women in Chemistry: Their Changing Roles from Alchemical Times to the Mid-Twentieth Century. American Chemical Society, 1998.

Periodicals

Mount Holyoke Quarterly, August 1946.
New York Times January 8, 1972.
Nucleus, June 1957. □

Jose Maria Carreras

Considered to be one of the world's three great operatic tenors living at the end of the 20th century, Jose Carreras (born 1946) waged a successful battle against a deadly form of leukemia to return to his beloved singing career. He won international acclaim touring with fellow tenors Luciano Pavarotti and Placido Domingo.

Born in Barcelona, Spain, on December 5, 1946, Carreras was the youngest child of traffic cop, Jose Carreras-Soler, and hairdresser, Antonia Coll-Saigi. His was not a particularly musical family, but Carreras became interested in opera at only six years old. His father, a teacher who'd been forced into police work by the repressive Franco regime, took young Jose to see The Great Caruso, a film biography of operatic singer Enrico Caruso starring Mario Lanza. From that moment on, there was no doubt in Carreras' mind about what he wanted to do with his life. The very next day, Jose's voice filled the Carreras household with arias he remembered from the film. In his autobiography, Carreras recalled that his performance of these arias amazed his family, for he "repeated them to perfection," despite the fact that he had never heard them before. His family, impressed at how profoundly Jose had been affected by the film, arranged for him to take music lessons.

Enrolled at Conservatory

At the age of eight, Carreras enrolled at the Barcelona Conservatory, where he studied music for the next three years. During this same period he saw his first live opera, attending a performance of Verdi's *Aida* at Barcelona's Gran Teatro del Liceo. In his autobiography, Carreras said of that experience: ''In every person's life, there are certain moments that can never fade or die. For me that night was one of those occasions. I will never forget the first time I saw singers on a stage and an orchestra. It was the first time in my life that I'd stepped into a theater, but the place was as familiar to me as if I had always known it. At the time, I couldn't understand my feeling. Today I can describe it this way: from the moment I crossed the threshold, I knew it was my world., I knew it was where I belonged.''

Shortly after seeing his first opera, Carreras made his singing debut in public, performing in a benefit concert broadcast over National Radio. When he was 11, he was invited to sing the role of Trujaman in *El Retablo de Maese Pedro,* an opera written by Spanish composer Manuel de Falla. Only three years after seeing his first opera at the Gran Teatro del Liceo, he had returned to its stage to make his operatic debut. He performed twice more in small parts at the Liceo before his changing voice forced him to temporarily decline all offers.

Took Formal Voice Lessons

Carreras began taking formal voice lessons in 1964. The following year he enrolled at the University of Barcelona, studying chemistry for the next two years. However, he remained interested mainly in pursuing a career in opera. After a year of voice lessons from Juan Ruax, Carreras dropped his chemistry studies in 1967. His adult debut in opera came in 1970, when he performed the role of Flavio in Bellini's *Norma*. The famous Spanish soprano Monserrat Caballe was so favorably impressed with Carreras' performance in *Norma* that she invited him to appear opposite her in Donizetti's *Lucrezia Borgia,* performing the role of Gennaro. Under the wing of Caballe, who Carreras later described as ''like family,'' the young tenor's operatic career was formally launched. In addition to the role of Gennaro, Carreras sang the role of Ismael in *Nabucco*. In 1971, he won the Verdi Singing Competition in Parma, Italy, which opened the door to the opera houses of the world for Carreras. That year he also married the former Mercedes Perez. The couple, who separated in 1992, had two children, Albert and Julia.

Carreras' repertoire eventually grew to include more than 40 operas. Among his more notable roles are Rodolfo in *La Boheme,* Don Jose in *Carmen*, Cavaradossi in *Tosca,* and Riccardo in *Un ballo in maschera*. Notable among the many conductors with whom he's worked was the late Herbert von Karajan, who called Carreras ''my favorite tenor.'' The two worked closely together from 1976 until 1989, the year of von Karajan's death. It was the conductor who

encouraged him to take on heavier roles, some of which were not really suited to his voice. One such role—Radames in *Aida*—was debuted in Salzburg in 1979 and was later dropped from his repertoire by Carreras.

In addition to appearing in most of the major opera venues worldwide, including La Scala in Milan, the Staatsoper in Vienna, and the Metropolitan and City Center in New York, Carreras has recorded extensively. His recordings are not limited to operatic performances but include popular music, folk songs, and excerpts from *zarzuelas,* the distinctive light operas of Spain.

Diagnosed with Leukemia

Carreras' greatest challenge came in 1987. The singer had felt profoundly fatigued for months, but when he arrived in Paris to begin shooting the film version of *La Boheme,* he felt so nauseated that a friend drove him to a hospital in the French capital. Within 48 hours, French doctors handed him their devastating diagnosis: acute lymphoblastic leukemia. Doctors gave him only a ten percent chance of survival. From Paris, he was transferred home to Barcelona, where he entered El Clinco Hospital. So popular was the tenor in his native country that Spanish television broadcast bulletins on his condition three times each day. When it was determined that the best treatment options for his particular form of leukemia were available in the United States, Carreras was transferred to the Fred Hutchinson Cancer Research Center in Seattle.

In Seattle Carreras underwent painful surgery in which bone marrow was extracted from his hip, cleaned of cancer cells, and then reinjected into his body. Fearful that breathing tubes might damage his voice, he insisted that he be given only partial anesthesia for the operation. The surgery was followed by weeks of radiation and chemotherapy. To sustain himself through this ordeal, he focused on his first love—the opera. To get through the radiation treatments, he would measure time by running through some of his favorite arias in his head. He later told *Time* reporter Margaret Hornblower: ''I'd say to myself, 'Only three more minutes of torture. That's the length of Celeste Aida.' So I'd sing it in my head better than I'd ever sung it onstage.'' The ravages of radiation treatments and chemotherapy took their toll on Carreras. He lost all his hair, his fingernails dropped off, and his weight fell sharply.

Never Feared Dying

Looking back on his fight with cancer, Carreras told *Time*: ''For nine months in the hospital, I knew I was facing death. But I always saw a light at the end of the tunnel. Sometimes it was bright; sometimes it was almost extinguished. But I tell you something: I was not afraid to die. I was worried for my children. But afraid of dying? Never.''

Against all odds, Carreras won his fight against leukemia, but he worried that the massive amount of radiation he'd received along with hours of nauseating chemotherapy might have damaged his voice beyond repair. Throughout his months in the hospital, he received support not only from his fans but also from fellow tenors Placido Domingo and Luciano Pavarotti. Domingo flew to Seattle to talk for two hours to his beleaguered countryman through a wall of plastic. Pavarotti sent a telegram that read in part: "Get well soon. Without you I have no competition!" Interviewed in 1992 by *Stereo Review,* Carreras recalled the importance of his fans' support. "The thousands of letters I received from people I didn't know touched me deeply and were fundamental to my recovery."

In July 1988, Carreras made his comeback in an open-air concert performed in the shadow of Barcelona's Arch of Triumph. More than 150,000 people attended the performance. Normally a modest man, Carreras couldn't resist telling one interviewer that "Michael Jackson, in the same city, got only 90,000." He followed his comeback in Barcelona with concert appearances in more than a dozen cities, including Vienna where the Staatsoper set up a video screen so that hundreds of fans in the streets who'd been unable to get tickets could see Carreras perform. Inside the prestigious opera house, Carreras was given a standing ovation of more than an hour. The tenor received equally warm receptions in New York City and London, where fans showered Carreras with flowers during five ovations. Late in 1988, Carreras established the International Foundation Against Leukemia, the main aim of which is "to help scientific research with funding and grants," he told the *Unesco Gazette.* "Scientists believe that the best way to fight the disease is to step up research efforts."

In September of 1988, Carreras traveled to Merida in the south of Spain to make his first operatic appearance since his diagnosis with cancer. Interviewed by a television crew before his performance, the tenor said, "This is a special moment in my life. It is a triumph over myself." And Carreras did not disappoint the thousands of fans who had flocked to Merida to see him sing the role of Jason in Cherubini's *Medea.* Although still weak from his months of treatment, he "proved that he was back, ready to compete again on the operatic stage," according to *Time* magazine's assessment of his appearance. Shortly after his appearance in Merida, Carreras returned to his hometown to premiere a new opera called *Christopher Columbus.*

Sang to Benefit Cancer Center

One of Carreras' first American concerts after his recovery was a 1989 benefit for Seattle's Hutchinson Cancer Research Center, where he had been successfully treated for leukemia. Perhaps the crowning jewel in Carreras' return to singing after his illness was his appearance with Domingo and Pavarotti in the "Three Tenors" concert of 1990. Staged in an outdoor arena in Rome, the concert preceded a game in the World Cup soccer championship and was seen by more than 800 million fans on television worldwide. A stunning success, the concert was repeated at the 1994 World Cup Finals in Los Angeles before a live audience of more than 50,000. An estimated 1.3 billion saw the concert on television. Records and videos from the two concerts have sold in the millions. In subsequent concerts the "Three Tenors" performed at New Jersey's Giants Stadium, outside New York City, in the summer of 1996, at Detroit's Tiger Stadium in July 1999, and again in Beijing's Forbidden City in June 2001.

Carreras' autobiography, *Singing from the Soul,* which focused on the singer's battle with cancer, was published in the United States in 1991. Although the reviews were mixed, the book sold well, racking up sales of about 650,000 copies.

Concerts, such as the "Three Tenors" performances with Domingo and Pavarotti, are seen by Carreras as a way to bring opera to the masses. Of his quest to win a wider audience for opera, he told the *Unesco Courier:* "Like any other form of artistic expression, music needs an audience. It can only be decoded and become accessible if it reaches the public—you can't love anything until you know it." In June of 1994, he joined an Italian opera company in a musical tribute to those who lost their lives in the ethnic fighting over the future of Bosnia. The concert, which was televised, was staged amidst the ruins of the National Library in war-torn Sarajevo. Conductor Zubin Mehta led Carreras, singers from the Italian opera company, and the Sarajevo symphony orchestra and chorus in Mozart's *Requiem Mass.*

Books

Dictionary of Hispanic Biography, Gale Research, 1996.

Periodicals

Commentary, October 1, 1996.
Time, September 25, 1989.
Washington Post, September 30, 2001. □

W. J. Cash

Although W.J. Cash (1900-1941) wrote only one book, *The Mind of the South,* before his untimely death in 1941, his work is recognized as one of the best single-volume histories of the American South ever published.

A native son of the Carolinas, W.J. Cash grew up with an intimate knowledge of the region's culture, society, and history. An aspiring writer, Cash first taught English after graduating from North Carolina's Wake Forest College, a career that fell short of his long-term literary ambitions. Cash then pursued an intermittent career as a journalist, honing his insights on the American South by working for a number of newspapers. Yet his failing health and high-strung temperament allowed him to work for only short periods before retreating to his parents' home to regain his mental and physical strength. In 1936, based on a series of articles that he had written for the nationally renowned *American Mercury* magazine, Cash received a contract from publisher Alfred A. Knopf to produce a single-volume history of the South. Cash began work on what would turn out to be his only book, *The Mind of the South,* that same year. Hailed by critics from across the nation upon its publication in 1941, Cash's book was recognized as a classic work and the author was transformed from a struggling journalist into a leading intellectual authority. Tragically, Cash's poor health, which contributed to an increasingly unstable personality, prevented him from enjoying his success. Less than a year after the publication of *The Mind of the South,* Cash committed suicide while staying in Mexico City on a Guggenheim grant.

Milltown Childhood

Cash's authority as an expert on the South derived in part from his family's deep roots in the region. For several generations, various branches of the Cash family spread out around North and South Carolina, mostly as small farmers. A few Cash ancestors may have owned slaves, but none of them ever ascended into the South's dominant planter class. Cash's father, John William Cash, was born on one such small farm in Clifton, South Carolina, in 1872. His father also ran a sawmill in Clifton, but the size of the family, which grew to include ten children, meant that John William Cash had to look for career opportunities elsewhere. Moving to Gaffney, South Carolina at the age of seventeen, Cash followed his brother, who had secured a job as the manager of a new cotton mill there. The town numbered less than 5,000 people, but the arrival of the mill promised a bright economic future for Gaffney, located just south of the border with North Carolina. Cash became a clerk at the Gaffney Manufacturing Company Mill's store, and impressed his bosses with his steady work habits, polite bearing, and God-fearing ways. The fact that he had little formal education beyond a few years at the Gaffney Male and Female Seminary was not a barrier to the honest and hardworking young man.

A regular worshiper at the Cherokee Avenue Baptist Church in Gaffney, John William Cash began courting music teacher Nannie Mae Lutitia Hamrick, who also served as the church's organist. Married on December 30, 1896, the Cashes began married life in a modest wood frame house in Gaffney. Their first child, a daughter, died at the age of two from Bright's Disease; thus, when Joseph Wilbur Cash arrived on May 2, 1900, he was the eldest child in the family. Wilbur Cash, as his family always called him, was later joined by two brothers and a sister; two other children died in infancy. Later, Cash used the reverse of his initials, W.J. Cash, as his professional byline, although his colleagues called him Jack. In his childhood, however, Cash earned another nickname, ''Sleepy,'' in reference to both his droopy eyelids and his sometimes distracted nature. One often repeated anecdote even had Cash falling asleep while reading a book, causing him to fall off of his front porch.

Indeed, although he loved reading, Wilbur Cash was an indifferent student in his early years. After his family moved to his mother's hometown, Boiling Springs, North Carolina in 1913, however, his work habits improved. At the time of his Boiling Springs High School graduation in 1917, Cash was named class historian, a mark of his scholastic achievement. By that time, Cash's father was running a general store founded by his father-in-law and added to the family's income by starting a taxi service for soldiers stationed in nearby Spartanburg, South Carolina. Given the

Cash family's economic status and Wilbur Cash's own intellectual promise, he surprised everyone by foregoing college to enlist in the Students' Army Training Corps, part of the American military effort on the home front during World War I. In 1917 and 1918 he served at a number of military encampments in the United States, performing everything from carpentry work to clerical duties. Unfortunately, a bout with frostbite left Cash's eyelids with a greater permanent droop. Combined with his rather squat stature, Cash's dowdy appearance contributed to his already introverted nature.

Upon his discharge at the conclusion of the war, Cash entered Wofford College in Spartanburg. Wanting more independence, Cash transferred to Valparaiso University in northern Indiana for the 1919-1920 academic year; however, the cold weather did not agree with him and he returned to the Carolinas to enter Wake Forest College in Wake Forest, North Carolina in 1920. Settling in at Wake Forest, Cash gained an outstanding scholastic reputation, particularly for his work on the school's newspaper, the *Old Gold and Black.* After his graduation in 1922, Cash remained at Wake Forest to begin law school; after finishing a year towards his law degree, however, he abandoned his legal studies. Instead, he began a career as an English teacher at Georgetown College in Kentucky. Cash's year at Georgetown College ended badly, however. After falling in love with a student, Cash found that he was impotent during their first tryst. Badly shaken by the episode, Cash did not return to Georgetown for a second year; he was also tormented by his sexual failing and questioned whether he would ever recover his sense of masculinity.

Intermittent Career as a Journalist

Cash taught at the Hendersonville School for Boys in North Carolina in 1924, but put aside his career as an educator to take up journalism as a reporter for the Chicago *Post* in 1925. Cash already had some experience in the field, as he had worked for the Charlotte *Observer* the summer after he abandoned law school in 1923. Although he was a well regarded staff member at the *Post,* his tenure there was brief. Stricken by failing health related to hypothyroidism—a glandular deficiency of the thyroid, which gave him bouts of goiter as an adult—Cash returned to his parents' home to recover. He attempted to work for the Charlotte *News* in 1926, but his return to work was once again ended by health problems, which doctors also attributed to an underlying nervous condition. Following his doctors' advice to exercise and relax his mind, Cash spent much of 1927 touring Europe. He worked for the *News* briefly upon his return, and in 1928 accepted a short-lived assignment as editor of the *Cleveland Press* in Shelby, North Carolina.

Although the *Cleveland Press* folded soon after Cash's arrival, his career as a writer took off after 1929 with a series of articles published in the nationally respected *American Mercury* magazine, edited by the legendary H.L. Mencken. One article, ''The Mind of the South,'' which appeared in *American Mercury* in October 1929, later served as the title of his book. Combined with the other essays, Cash's profile as an observer of all things southern gained him a book contract with New York publisher Alfred A. Knopf in March 1936. Cash's career as a journalist also picked up steam; he rejoined the Charlotte News in November 1935 and was promoted to associate editor at the paper in late 1937. Although his unsteady temperament and health—and a growing dependence on alcohol—caused Cash to miss work on a fairly routine basis, he remained at the News until 1940. Cash also conquered his innate shyness towards women when he met Mary Northrop in Charlotte in 1938. Like-minded in their love of literature, the couple married on Christmas Day in 1940.

Wrote *The Mind of the South*

Cash delivered the final pages of his manuscript for *The Mind of the South* to his publisher in late July 1940, over a decade after he first published the article that gave the volume its title. An ambitious work, the book affirmed that the South's history, as envisioned in the image of "the Old South," remained a strong influence on twentieth-century southern society. Unlike other regions of the United States, the past bound the South to specific patterns of race relations, gender roles, and community identities that prevailed despite the upheavals of technology, mass marketing, and urbanization. "So far from being modernized," Cash wrote in his introduction about the region, "In many ways it has actually always marched away, as to this day it continues to do, from the present toward the past."

While emphasizing the importance of a frontier mentality on the southern mentality, Cash looked to the cotton boom years from 1820 to 1860 as the crucial years of southern history. It was the latter period that southern elites used after the Civil War to create a mythological past for the South, one based on the dominance of the planter class in unity with other whites, regardless of economic status. This racist bond worked not only to the detriment of African-Americans, but against poor whites as well. As Cash observed, the myths that the southern elites invoked to retain their dominance over the rest of society were so powerful that "The grand outcome was the almost complete disappearance of economic and social focus on the part of the masses." Translated into a "democracy of feeling" that demanded political and economic deference from poor whites in exchange for recognition of "the common brotherhood of white men," this bond reinforced the racial hierarchy of slavery well into the twentieth century. As Cash wrote, modern southern society fixed upon a seemingly "ever-growing concern with white superiority and an ever-growing will to mastery of the Negro" in order to reassure poor whites that "a white man, any white man, was in some sense a master." As in the Old South, "Economic and social considerations remained, as ever, subordinate to those of race—and country."

In addition to detailing the racist bond among southern whites, Cash also observed the ways in which the region's frontier mentality reasserted itself in the modern era through its emphasis on individualism. Not only did white southerners refuse to admit to having any "primary dependence" on others; in Cash's analysis, they also developed "an intense distrust of, and, indeed, downright aversion to, any actual exercise of authority beyond the barest minimum essential to the existence of the social organism." This anti-authority trait led to a tendency toward outright violence, as Cash noted, particularly when one's honor or racial status was offended. It was not a coincidence, then, that the South became "peculiarly the home of lynching," and that southern cities had violent crime rates that far surpassed every other region of the country.

Success and Untimely Death

In explaining how the mindset of the Old South had persisted despite the upheavals of the Civil War, Reconstruction, Populism, the Great Depression, and the New Deal, Cash's work was almost universally hailed as a masterpiece upon its publication in 1941. Critics were especially impressed with the author's ability to explain the importance of racism in working to the benefit of southern elites, a topic that had rarely been explained in such convincing detail. Not only did *The Mind of the South* receive excellent reviews in national publications such as *Time, Atlantic,* the *New York Times,* and the *Saturday Review of Literature,* but in the leading regional newspapers such as the Dallas *Morning News* and Baltimore *Evening Sun* as well. Although a few southern critics were taken aback by Cash's unflinching analysis, the critical raves far outnumbered the negative reviews.

After he got word that he had won a prestigious Guggenheim fellowship, Cash looked forward to writing his first novel. With his wife, he traveled to Mexico City in June 1941 to begin work. Tragically, however, Cash suffered a series of psychotic episodes that increased his anxiety, paranoia, and depression; convinced that Nazi agents were following him, he ran away from his wife and checked into another hotel, where he was later found hanging from his own necktie. At the time of his death on July 1, 1941, Cash was only 41 years old.

Although he produced only one book, Cash's contribution to the understanding of the American South was a masterpiece. Never out of print since its initial publication, *The Mind of the South* remains essential reading to any student of southern history, society, and culture. As Louis D. Rubin, Jr. wrote in the *Virginia Quarterly Review* upon the 15th anniversary of the book's publication in 1991, "If I wish to get a sense of the workings of that elusive but very real entity known as the 'mind' of the Southern community, and how it operated at those and other points in history, Cash's book will offer certain kinds of insights that no other study can provide."

Books

Clayton, Bruce, *W.J. Cash: A Life,* Louisiana State University Press, 1991.
Morrison, Joseph L., *W.J. Cash: Southern Prophet,* Alfred A. Knopf, 1967.

Periodicals

Backlist, July-August 2000.
Sewanee Review, Summer 1998.
Virginia Quarterly Review, Spring 1991. □

John Cassavetes

John Cassavetes (1929-1989) was one of the most highly acclaimed independent filmmakers in America. He was widely honored for motion pictures that successfully brought to the screen believable portrayals of real human emotion.

The younger of two sons of Greek immigrants, Nicholas and Katherine Cassavetes, he was born in New York City on December 9, 1929. Shortly after his birth, his family moved to nearby Long Island, where John grew up and attended public schools in Sands Point and Port Washington. He attended Mohawk College and Colgate University, both in upstate New York, before enrolling at the New York Academy of Dramatic Arts, from which he graduated in 1950.

Failed to Win Broadway Parts

Cassavetes' hopes of launching his acting career on the New York stage were frustrated, sending him to Rhode Island where he appeared with a theatrical repertory company in Providence from 1950 until 1952. His film career began in 1952 when he was given a small role in *Taxi,* a motion picture directed by Gregory Ratoff. In 1954, Cassavetes began acting in live television productions, including those produced for *Omnibus, Studio One, Playhouse 90,* and *Kraft Theater.* In most of these early dramatic roles, Cassavetes was cast as a "troubled youth." He later appeared in a handful of motion pictures that had been adapted from these early teleplays.

While teaching method acting at a theater workshop in New York, Cassavetes came up with an idea for his first independent film project. He became convinced that one of the improvisations done in the drama workshop could be developed into a film. Appearing on Jean Shepherd's late-night radio talk show, he invited listeners who wanted to see an alternative to what was being turned out by the big Hollywood studios to send him some money to fund the project. He received donations totaling about $20,000. An additional $20,000 was raised from among his friends in show business and from his own savings. With this meager financing, Cassavetes began work on his first feature film, a daring statement on race relations called *Shadows.* The film related the story of a light-skinned black girl and her two brothers in New York City. But it was the manner in which it was made that clearly set *Shadows* apart. Cassavetes laid out roughly defined parameters and set his actors free to improvise within those scenarios. In this manner, the film's story line gradually evolved as the film was shot intermittently over a period of two years. He filmed the action with a hand-held 16mm camera and arranged to have the film's musical score composed by jazz bassist Charlie Mingus. The finished sound track featured horn solos by Shafi Hadi. Village Voice film critic Jonas Mekas said of *Shadows*: "The tones and rhythms of a new America are caught in *Shadows* for the very first time."

American Distributors Showed No Interest

Cassavetes was unable to interest any American distributors in *Shadows* and took the film to Europe where it was received enthusiastically, most notably at the Venice Film Festival where it won the Critics Award. A British distributor finally agreed to release the film in the United States. Impressed by the filmmaker's first outing, Paramount hired Cassavetes to make a series of films. However, the studio sacked him after his first attempt in the series, *Too Late Blues,* was poorly received both critically and popularly. He next directed *A Child is Waiting* for United Artists and Stanley Kramer. This creative collaboration, fractious from the start, ended badly when Kramer gave Cassavetes only two weeks to edit the film. Kramer than re-cut Cassavetes' finished product, producing a final version that Cassavetes complained was overly sentimental. These experiences soured Cassavetes on the idea of working for the big Hollywood studios. He longed for an opportunity to retain total artistic control over his projects.

Once again Cassavetes fell back on acting to raise the money he needed to finance his filmmaking projects. He appeared in a number of high-profile films, including Roman Polanski's *Rosemary's Baby* and *The Dirty Dozen.* For the latter he was nominated for an Oscar as best supporting actor. Although he was only interested in making films that he liked and believed in, his standards were relaxed a good deal when it came to choosing acting assignments. "I'd rather work in a sewer than make a film I don't like,"

Cassavetes was quoted in *People* magazine. "Sometimes I will act in them however."

His next project, after he accumulated enough money from acting, was the critically acclaimed *Faces,* which was again filmed in 16mm and shot over a period of three years. Like *Shadows,* the film was shot in cinema verite style. However, unlike its predecessor, it was both a critical and financial success, earning more than ten million dollars at the box office. Moreover, the motion picture won five awards from the Venice Film Festival and was nominated for three Academy Awards.

Worked with Studios

On the heels of *Faces,* Cassavetes returned to the studios, but this time with the promise that he would be guaranteed complete artistic control. Among his films made with studio backing were 1970's *Husbands* for Columbia and *Minnie and Moskowitz,* a comedy for Universal in 1971. *Husbands* focused on the relationship between three men forced to confront their own mortality when they attend the funeral of a mutual friend. Cassavetes not only directed the film but also acted in it with close friends Peter Falk and Ben Gazzara. Vincent Canby of the *New York Times* hailed *Minnie and Moskowitz* as Cassavetes' most ambitious work up to that point, but suggested that it failed as a comedy. "Mr. Cassavetes' use of exaggerated slapstick gestures to underscore the loneliness and fears of his characters is more interesting in theory than funny or moving in actual fact." Canby, however, was impressed by Cassavetes' selection of actors for the project. "As an actor," Canby wrote, "he appreciates actors and their mysterious art, as well as their awful dependence on the work of others. This explains why he casts his films so abundantly."

Returning to projects he financed on his own, Cassavetes in 1974 released *A Woman under the Influence,* which starred his wife of 20 years, Gena Rowlands. Considered by many to be his most commercial film, *Woman* also featured close friend Falk and earned Cassavetes an Academy Award nomination as best director. The motion picture related the story of middle-aged Mabel Longhetti (played by Rowlands) who is committed to a mental institution by her mother and husband, acting in concert. Of Cassavetes' directorial skill, film critic Pauline Kael wrote: "His special talent is for showing intense suffering from nameless causes; Cassavetes and Pinter both give us an actor's view of human misery. It comes out as metaphysical realism: we see the tensions and the power plays but never know the why of anything." Kael's review was not without criticism of Cassavetes, suggesting that his direction had "a muffled quality: his scenes are often unshaped and so rudderless that the meanings don't emerge."

Cassavetes himself acknowledged that he'd taken chances with *Woman,* saying, "It's naive in that sense, because we weren't sure that people would want to see family life, family life with problems, not hyped up. . . ." Also favorably impressed with the film was critic Paul Zimmerman, who wrote: "Every film is a risk, but Cassavetes is the biggest gambler around, betting that he can make enough magic out of inspiration and improvisation to keep his characters from boring us to death. For two and a half hours, he wins and loses from scene to scene until, battered, exasperated but close to tears, we surrender."

Far less successful than *Woman* was Cassavetes' next film, *The Killing of a Chinese Bookie,* the tale of a strip-joint owner who resorts to murder to handle a gambling debt. It was panned by most film critics. Typical of the reviews was this observation from Frank Rich: " . . . the style intentionally obscures what paltry drama there is." Even less kind was Judith Crist, who called *Killing* "a mess, as sloppy in concept as it is in execution, as pointless in thesis as it is in concept."

Final Three Projects

During the final decade of his life, Cassavetes worked on three major projects, all of which were backed by Hollywood studios. *Gloria* was taken on largely as a favor to his wife, who played the title role. Although he considered the story to be a potboiler, he undertook the project to provide Rowlands with a chance to play the role of a "sexy but tough woman who doesn't really need a man," a way in which she sometimes thought of herself. Of the story line, Cassavetes later observed: "*Gloria* celebrates the coming together of a woman who neither likes nor understands children and a boy who believes he's man enough to stand on his own." Shortly before shooting began on *Gloria,* Cassavetes' father died, contributing perhaps to the film's seeming preoccupation with the theme of death.

Although critics hailed *Gloria* as his "finest work," the film enjoyed only modest success at the box office. Cassavetes felt in retrospect about the film much as he had before taking it on. He later recalled: "It was television fare as a screenplay but handled by the actors to make it better. It's an adult fairy tale. And I never pretended it was anything else but fiction. I always thought I understood [it]. And I was bored because I knew the answer to that picture the minute we began. And that's why I could never be wildly enthusiastic about the picture—because it's so simple."

Other films made by Cassavetes during the 1980s included *Love Streams,* released by Cannon in 1984, and the disastrous *Big Trouble,* released in 1985. It was to be Cassavetes' final project, which was unfortunate because the film was so bad he was embarrassed to have his name attached to it. When the film's screenwriter and original director, Andrew Bergman, quit the project, Cassavetes stepped in to replace him as director.

Cassavetes died before independent films began to break into the commercial mainstream. As Jacob Levich wrote in a 1994 tribute in *Cineaste,* it is doubtful that Cassavetes' work ever would have found wide favor with backers, distributors, or audiences. "It is hard to believe that the irascible, fiercely individualistic Cassavetes—who never gave a damn what people thought of his films, or whether they made money—would be any more welcome among today's newly chic independent crowd than he was in the 'new Hollywood' of the Seventies." Levich wrote that in Cassavetes' view, "the filmmaker's highest calling was not to amuse, but to challenge, provoke, even exasperate. He was prepared, like a Brecht without politics, to do whatever might be necessary to interfere with the expectations of an increasingly complacent public."

Cassavetes died in Los Angeles on February 3, 1989, of complications arising from cirrhosis of the liver. Ben Gazzara, a close friend and one of the handful of actors that Cassavetes used regularly in his films, remembered the director fondly. "John was more interested in the surprise the actors gave him if let free with their imaginations," Gazzara told *People* magazine. "He hated the word auteur. He felt he made actors' films."

Books

Contemporary Theatre, Film, and Television, Volume 7, Gale Research, 1989.
Newsmakers 1989, Gale Research, 1989.

Periodicals

Cineaste, January 1, 1994.
People, February 20, 1989.

Online

"Cassavetes' Biography," http://people.bu.edu/rcarney/newpages/html/bio.htm (November 3, 2001).
"Chapter on the Making of *Gloria* (1979-1980)," http://people.bu/edu/rcarney/cassoncass/Gloria.htm (November 4, 2001).
"John Cassavetes," *Contemporary Authors Online,* http:www.galenet.com/servlet/BioRC (November 2, 2001). □

Bennett Cerf

Bennett Cerf (1898-1971) helped to shape the American publishing business into what it is today. A writer and television personality, Cerf was also an active editor and enthusiastic promoter of the writers published by his company, Random House. In the 1930s he led a successful challenge against censorship in the United States.

Bennett Alfred Cerf, the only child of Gustave Cerf, an elocution teacher and lithographer, and Frederika Wise Cerf, was born on May 25, 1898, in New York City. His mother died when he was only 15, leaving Cerf $125,000 that his maternal grandfather had placed in trust for him. Shortly after his mother's death, her brother, Herbert Wise, moved into the New York City home of the Cerfs, bringing the teenager "the greatest influence on my young life."

Educated in New York Public Schools

Cerf was educated in the public schools of New York City. He first attended Public School 10, where a fellow classmate was Howard Dietz, who grew up to become a lyricist and head of publicity for MGM Studios in Hollywood. After P.S. 10, Cerf went to Townsend Harris High School and Packard Commercial School. While attending Packard, he worked part-time for an accountant. In 1915, at

the age of 17, he began classes at Columbia University's School of Journalism, where he quickly joined the staff of the student newspaper, the *Daily Spectator,* and the student humor magazine, *The Jester.* In his freshman year, he wrote a column entitled "The Stroller" for the former. In his second year at Columbia, he served as editor of *The Jester* and was instrumental in adding a book review column to the magazine.

Cerf's college education was interrupted by World War I. After the United States became involved in the conflict, Cerf enlisted in the Army and was stationed at Camp Lee in Virginia. After the war, he returned to Columbia and resumed his studies. In 1919, Cerf graduated from Columbia College, receiving his bachelor of letters degree from Columbia's School of Journalism the following year.

Cerf had a short-lived career writing a financial advice column for the *New York Tribune.* He advised against investing in a bankrupt company. Unfortunately, the company in question took exception to Cerf's remarks and threatened to sue the newspaper, quickly ending his career as a financial columnist. At the time he was writing a column for the *Tribune,* Cerf was working for the New York brokerage firm of Sartorius, Smith and Lowei. Although he found the world of Wall Street somewhat dull, he continued to work for the company until 1923, when he finally found his niche in the publishing world.

Found Niche in Publishing

Columbia classmate Richard L. Simon, a vice president at the publishing house of Boni and Liveright, recommended that Cerf replace him when he left the firm to launch his own publishing company with Max Schuster. Cerf got the job. Two years later he and Donald S. Klopfer, a close friend, bought from Boni and Liveright the Modern Library imprint, which specialized in publishing low-cost editions of classic works of literature. Cerf and Klopfer immediately set about to make Modern Library distinctly their own. While Klopfer concentrated on finances and production, Cerf dealt almost exclusively with editorial matters. The two hired some of the best designers and artists of the period to give Modern Library books a new look. Elmer Adler encouraged them to drop the imitation leather bindings; Rockwell Kent designed new endpapers; and Lucien Bernhardt drew a new colophon.

The Cerf-Klopfer publishing combine soon was expanding beyond Modern Library. In 1927, Cerf became the American agent for England's Nonesuch Press. However, Cerf and Klopfer also wanted to publish their own books. Cerf came up with a name for their new enterprise. Discussing the prospective venture with his partner and artist Kent, he said: "I've got the name for our publishing house. We just said we were going to publish a few books on the side at random. Let's call it Random House." The Random House imprint made an impressive debut in 1928 with a beautifully bound edition of *Candide* by Voltaire. In the wake of the collapse of the stock market only a year later, Random House began focusing on trade publishing, the market for fine editions having all but vanished. Random's Modern Library imprint, with books selling at less than one dollar each, helped the company to survive the Depression.

An important addition to the editorial staff of Random House came in 1933 when Cerf acceded to the demands of Eugene O'Neill—a recent addition to the publisher's stable of writers—and hired Saxe Commins as an editor. Commins proved to be one of Random House's most discerning editors, an excellent judge of what readers wanted and a fiercely dedicated advocate for the authors he edited.

Took on Censorship Case

After signing O'Neill and Robinson Jeffers for Random House, Cerf set sail for Europe in the early 1930s to discuss with James Joyce the publication of *Ulysses* in the United States. Upon his return to New York, U.S. Customs seized Cerf's copy of Joyce's book on the grounds that it was obscene. Cerf decided to challenge the obscenity ruling and hired attorney Morris Ernst to take the case to court. On December 6, 1933, Federal Judge John M. Woolsey ruled, in a landmark decision, that Joyce's book was not obscene. He added that the book was "an amazing tour de force when one considers the success that has been in the main achieved with such a difficult objective as Joyce set for himself." Not only did the decision clear the way for the American publication of *Ulysses*, but it gave Random House an incredible amount of publicity. On October 2, 1935, Cerf married actress Sylvia Sidney, but the marriage soon ended in divorce.

In 1936 Random House merged with Haas and Smith, publisher of such notable authors as Isak Dinesen, William Faulkner, Robert Graves, and Andre Malraux. Shortly thereafter Harrison Smith's interest in the merged company was bought out, leaving Cerf, Klopfer, and Robert Haas each with a one-third share in the company. In September of 1940, Cerf married again, this time wedding Phyllis Fraser. The couple had two sons.

In 1942 Klopfer joined the Air Force, increasing Cerf's workload significantly. During the war years, Random House published war-related works by Quentin Reynolds, Robert Considine, John Gunther, and William L. Shirer. A big fan of humor and something of a wit in his own right, Cerf edited *The Pocketbook of War Humor,* published in 1943, and *Try and Stop Me: A Collection of Anecdotes and Stories, Mostly Humorous* in 1944.

In the early 1940s, Cerf began writing a column entitled "Trade Winds" for the *Saturday Review of Literature.* For the King Features syndicate, he also began turning out a daily humor column entitled "Try and Stop Me." However, it was television that truly made Cerf a household name. In 1951, he began appearing as a panelist on the popular CBS game show *What's My Line?* He continued to appear on the show, along with Arlene Francis, Dorothy Kilgallen, and others, until 1967.

Kept His Authors Happy

A good deal of Cerf's time was spent playing nursemaid to some of his more temperamental authors. Among the writers in that category was Sinclair Lewis. Cerf later recalled an occasion when Lewis was spending the night at his apartment and William Faulkner called to announce that he was in town. "I told Lewis and asked him, could Bill come over? Lewis said, 'Certainly not. This is my night!' " Later that night, according to Cerf, about an hour after Lewis had retired, the author called down for Cerf from upstairs. "I answered him, and he said, 'I just wanted to see if you sneaked out to see Faulkner.'"

Random House's acquisition of Haas and Smith in 1936 gave the publishing house added clout in the field of juvenile books. Haas and Smith had published *Babar the Elephant* by Jean de Brunhoff, and Haas's secretary, Louise Bonino, later became Random House's editor of juvenile books. Cerf's wife, Phyllis, also felt strongly that Random House needed to turn out better children's books, convincing Cerf to launch the Landmark Books imprint. Books in the Landmark series focused on important events in American history. They were written by top-notch authors, such as Dorothy Canfield Fisher, who wrote *Paul Revere and the Minute Men,* which was published as part of the series in 1950. Phyllis Cerf drafted Theodor Geisel (Dr. Seuss) to join her in launching a publishing company specializing in books for children who were just beginning to read. That company, Beginner Books, was so successful that Random House eventually bought it.

As its fortunes increased, Random House sought out a headquarters building befitting its stature. Eventually Cerf and his partners settled on a mansion at 457 Madison Avenue that had been designed by Stanford White and built by

Henry Villard. The company was headquartered there from 1946 until 1969.

Some of the most popular writers of the 1950s were published by Random House. This stellar group included Truman Capote, Ralph Ellison, James Michener, John O'Hara, Ayn Rand, Irwin Shaw, Karl Shapiro, and Robert Penn Warren. At the end of the 1950s, 30 percent of Random House stock was offered to the public. The following year, Random House acquired the imprint of Alfred A. Knopf, and Alfred and Blanche Knopf joined its board of directors. The next step in Random House's expansion came in 1961 when it acquired Pantheon Books, publisher of such authors as Gunter Grass, Anne Morrow Lindbergh, Jan Myrdal, and Boris Pasternak.

Never Forgot His Business Roots

Although Cerf concentrated on the editorial side of Random House's operations, he was still a keen and insightful businessman, perhaps a reflection of his days on Wall Street early in his career. This became very clear in Cerf's negotiations to sell Random House to RCA in 1965. According to Cerf's own recollections of the discussions with RCA, David Sarnoff and other RCA negotiators seemed to have sized up Cerf as a lightweight when it came to business dealings. Cerf carefully avoided doing anything to disabuse them of this notion. Sarnoff offered Cerf three-fifths of an RCA share for every share of Random House, but Cerf was holding out for a pledge of total editorial independence and sixty-two-hundredths of a share, a difference that in total would amount to about $1 million. When Sarnoff suggested they break off talks and resume the following day, Cerf calmly announced that he and his wife had vacation plans the next day, plans they intended to keep. RCA met Cerf's demands, and the deal was closed. First impressions, Cerf made clear, can be deceiving.

After selling Random House, Cerf and his wife spent much of their time at their country home in Mount Kisco, New York, less than an hour from the city. It was there that he died at the age of 73 on August 27, 1971. Throughout his career, some in the publishing business had dismissed Cerf as superficial and somewhat frivolous, pointing to his obvious delight at basking in the public spotlight. This more measured assessment of Cerf came from the *Saturday Review* shortly after his death: "He gave full measure to his profession. Everyone connected with the world of books is in his debt."

Books

At Random: The Reminiscences of Bennett Cerf, Random House, 1977.

Dictionary of American Biography, Supplement 9: 1971-1975, Charles Scribner's Sons, 1994.

Online

"Bennett (Alfred) Cerf," *Contemporary Authors Online,* The Gale Group, 2000. Reproduced in *Biography Resource Center.* The Gale Group, 2001, http:www.galenet.com/servlet/BioRC (November 2, 2001).

"A Brief History of Random House," Random House, http://www.randomhouse.com/backyard/corphist.html (November 13, 2001).

"Modern Library: History," Modern Library, http://www.randomhouse.com/modernlibrary/history/ (November 13, 2001). □

Gene Cernan

Gene Cernan (born 1934) was the commander of a manned mission that touched down on the moon's surface in December 1972. Harrison ("Jack") Schmitt accompanied him, becoming the first professional scientist to walk on the moon. Cernan and Schmitt lived for three days on the moon, using their small Lunar Module as a kind of tent on the ultimate geologist's field trip, while their crewmate Ron Evans waited for their return in the orbiting Command Module.

Cernan was born on March 14, 1934 in Chicago, Illinois. At an early age he wanted to be an aviator, and joined the Navy to follow his dream. Cernan received his navy commission from the Reserve Officers Training Corps (ROTC) program at Purdue University in West Lafayette, Indiana, and immediately began flight training. He flew on Attack Squadrons 26 and 112 based at the Miramar, California, Naval Air Station, and then went to Naval Postgraduate School.

To Boldly Go

In 1959 the United States selected the first seven of the pilots it called "astronauts"—who would fly higher and faster than anyone before them. This was in response to the unspoken challenge presented by the Soviet Union when it launched the world's first artificial satellite, Sputnik, in 1957, and the space race was on. Cernan, already a Navy pilot, was "fascinated," as he put it in his 1999 book, *The Last Man on the Moon.* "I had joined the Navy to fly, and the idea of riding a rocket ship into space had instant appeal. A new dream formed inside my crew-cut head."

The opportunity Cernan had been waiting for dropped into his lap in 1963 in the form of a telephone call from a high ranking Navy officer asking if he would like to be considered as an astronaut for Apollo—the U.S. space program whose goal was to land a man on the moon. "There was a moment of silence on my end," Cernan recalled in his book, "while my heart jumped into my throat. I hadn't even applied. Last time I looked, I wasn't even qualified. But this guy was saying the Navy was recommending me to NASA for astronaut training. Was he talking to the right Lieutenant Cernan? It took a moment for the meaning of his question to sink in, then I came out of my fog and shot back with snappy military enthusiasm, 'Well, yes sir! Not only that, sir, but hell, yes! Sir!'" Cernan passed the National Aeronautics and

Space Administration's (NASA's) strenuous tests and was officially selected as an astronaut in October 1963.

Into the Final Frontier

Cernan's first space flight came in 1966, aboard Gemini 9. The Gemini program had been developed to test and prepare the hardware and skills in earth orbit needed to land people on the moon and return them safely. The Gemini space craft were two-man ships, and tiny. Cernan and his crewmate, Tom Stafford, spent three days in their capsule, orbiting 161 miles above the earth. While there, the astronauts perfected spacecraft rendezvous techniques that were later used on the moon flights. On this flight, Cernan became the second American, after Ed White, to leave a spacecraft while in flight on a space walk. Cernan's space walk, or extravehicular activity (EVA), lasted two hours and ten minutes.

Cernan's next mission came in May 1969, when he flew as lunar module pilot on Apollo 10. This was the mission that preceded the flight that landed the first people on the moon, and it was only the second mission, after Apollo 8, to send people into lunar orbit. Apollo 10's purpose was to perform a full dress rehearsal for the first manned landing without actually touching down. In their lunar module Cernan, and his old crewmate Tom Stafford, descended to within eight miles of the lunar surface. The mission went smoothly except for a brief moment when the astronauts lost control of their ship, named *Snoopy* after the famous comic strip character by Charles M. Schulz. The

command module was called *Charlie Brown*, also from Schulz's comic, and was piloted by John Young, who later commanded the first Space Shuttle mission.

Disaster Narrowly Averted

On the way down to the moon, at just 47,000 feet from the lunar surface, and hurling through space at some 3,000 miles per hour, the Apollo 10 lunar module went out of control for several very tense seconds when Cernan and Stafford mistakenly switched on the wrong guidance system. The spacecraft's computers became confused, and, as Cernan noted in *The Last Man on the Moon*, "all hell broke loose. *Snoopy* went nuts. We were suddenly bouncing, diving and spinning all over the place . . . The spacecraft radar that was supposed to be locking onto *Charlie Brown* had found a much larger target, the Moon, and was trying to fly in that direction instead of toward the orbiting command module."

Finally, Stafford regained control by switching off the computers and flying the ship manually. "After analyzing the data," Cernan reported in his book, "experts later surmised that had we continued spinning for only two more seconds, Tom and I would have crashed. Things had been more than a little tense. Hell, I was scared to death. But we got back on track immediately." In spite of this potentially disastrous episode, the mission was a success, paving the way for Apollo 11, which landed the first men on the moon in July, 1969. "Apollo 10," said Cernan in his book, "had painted a big stripe right down the middle of the space highway that led from Cape Kennedy to the Sea of Tranquility."

No Regrets

In his book, Cernan responded to the question of whether he was disappointed that Apollo 10 did not make the first landing, thus rocketing him into the pages of history instead occupied by Neil Armstrong and Buzz Aldrin of Apollo 11: "Would I liked to have had a shot at it? You bet I would. However, we all believed in the importance of our mission because we knew Apollo 11 was going to need every scrap of information we could gather if it was to have a successful flight of its own. Our crew had the know-how, but not the right equipment because *Snoopy* was too heavy, and there were too many things still unknown about landing on the Moon before we made our flight. . . . Anyway, I had an idea—I planned to go back."

Go back he did, on the last manned flight to the moon, Apollo 17. But not before another close call that almost cost him the mission—and his life. With just months to go before the final Apollo mission to the moon, Cernan took a small helicopter out over the Indian River near the Kennedy Space Center to practice moon landings. "After so many months of hard work and concentration," he said in his book, "I couldn't resist the temptation for a bit of mischief known among pilots as 'flat-hatting.'" He flew too low to the water, and the machine crashed and exploded. Miraculously, he escaped serious injury, and remained on active flight status.

Back to the Moon

Apollo 17 was launched on December 6, 1972. This was the first manned spacecraft to launch at night, and it returned to the earth on December 19, 1972. Cernan, the commander of the mission, flew to the lunar surface in the lunar module *Challenger* with geologist and lunar module pilot Harrison H. ("Jack") Schmitt. Ronald Evans awaited their return in lunar orbit aboard command module *America*. *Challenger* touched down at Taurus-Littrow, on the southeast edge of Mar Serenitatis. The moon was Cernan and Schmitt's home for more than three days. This mission marked the longest stay for people on the moon (301 hours and 51 minutes), and the largest amount of lunar material returned to Earth for study (249 pounds).

Cernan described his first moments on the lunar surface in his book: "I slowly pivoted, trying to see everything, and was overwhelmed by the silent, majestic solitude. Not so much as a squirrel track to indicate any sort of life, not a green blade of grass to color the bland, stark beauty, not a cloud overhead, or the slightest hint of a brook or stream. But I felt comfortable, as if I belonged there. From where I stood on the floor of this beautiful mountain-ringed valley that seemed frozen in time, the looming massifs on either side were not menacing at all. It was as if they, too, had been awaiting the day when someone would come and take a walk in their valley." And, "As I stood in Sunshine on this barren world somewhere in the universe, looking up at the cobalt Earth immersed in infinite blackness, I knew science had met its match."

End of the Road

Cernan stayed on with NASA after Apollo 17, although the mission was his last space flight. He worked as special assistant to the program manager of the Apollo spacecraft program at the Johnson Space Center, where he helped in the development of the Apollo-Soyuz project, which saw the first dockings of American and Russian spacecraft. He left NASA in 1976, and at the same time retired from the Navy with the rank of captain.

His next venture was with Coral Petroleum, Inc., based in Houston, Texas. He served the company as executive vice president-international, helping to promote company business around the world. He started his own aerospace and energy consulting business in 1981, The Cernan Corporation. Also in the 1980s, he provided onscreen commentary for ABC-TV's coverage of the space shuttle launches. He subsequently became chairman of the board of Johnson Engineering Corporation, consulting with NASA on the development of space habitats.

Cernan met his first wife, Barbara, in 1959. The two were married in 1961 and lived together until their 1980 separation. "She got tired of being Mrs. Astronaut," Cernan told CNN.com. In 1984 he met Jan Nanna, who became his second wife in 1987.

Online

"Astronaut Bio: Eugene A. Cernan," Web site of the Lyndon B. Johnson Space Center, http://www.jsc.nasa.gov/Bios/htmlbios/cernan-ea.html, December 1994.

"Cernan Center: Captain Eugene Cernan," *Cernan Earth and Space Center Online,* http://www.triton.cc.il.us/cernan/genecernan.html, May 23, 2001.

"Discover the Heroes: Eugene Cernan," Web site of the U.S. Astronaut Hall of Fame, http://www.astronauts.org/discover_heroes/cernan.htm (October 23, 2001).

O'Brien, Miles, "Moon's Last Visitor Spins Tale of Guts, Glory, and Loss," *CNN.com,* http://www3.cnn.com/TECH/space/9907/14/downlinks, July 14, 1999. □

Gabrielle-Emilie Marquise du Chatelet

Gabrielle-Emilie Chatelet (1706-1749) played a major role in the scientific revolution of the eighteenth century. By popularizing the theories of Isaac Newton she brought them more widespread acceptance in Europe, where most people still followed the ideas of Rene Descartes. Chatelet's scientific contribution has been largely overshadowed by her relationship with the philosopher Voltaire.

B orn Gabrielle-Emilie Le Tonnelier de Breteuil in Paris on December 17, 1706 into an aristocratic family, she received an exceptional education at home, which included scientific, musical, and literary studies. In 1725, she married the marquis du Chatelet, who was also the count of Lomont. It was a marriage of convenience, but she nevertheless had three children with him. After spending some years with her husband, whose political and military career kept him away from Paris, the marquise du Chatelet returned to the capital in 1730.

Initially leading a busy social life, Chatelet became the lover of the philosopher Francois-Marie Arouet de Voltaire in 1733. One of the greatest intellectual figures of 18th-century France, Voltaire recognized her exceptional talent for science, and encouraged her intellectual development. Chatelet consequently embarked on a study of mathematics, taking private lessons from the prominent French philosopher and scientist Pierre-Louis Moreau de Maupertuis. Both Voltaire and Maupertuis were enthusiastic supporters of Isaac Newton's scientific theories and world view, and it seems that the marquise was, as a result, immersed in Newtonian philosophy.

Created Intellectual Center at Cirey

In 1734 Voltaire faced arrest because of his criticism of the monarchy. He was offered sanctuary at Chatelet's chateau at Cirey, in Lorraine, where they spent many productive years. The two welcomed Europe's intellectual elite, thus creating a remarkable cultural center away from Paris. Chatelet was involved in a variety of literary and philosophical projects, eventually concentrating on the study of Newton's philosophy. She assisted Voltaire in the preparation of his 1738 book, *Elements of Newton's Philosophy.*

In 1737, Chatelet, like many other 18th-century scientists, attempted to explain the nature of combustion, submitting an essay entitled "Dissertation sur la nature et la propagation du feu," as an entry for a contest organized by the Academie Royale des Sciences. Voltaire also participated in the contest, but was unaware of her work. When Leonhard Euler and two other scientists were declared the winners, Voltaire arranged that Chatelet's essay be published with the winning entries. In her study, she correctly argued that heat was not a substance, a view defended by the proponents of the phlogiston theory, which the great French chemist Antoine-Laurent Lavoisier empirically disproved in 1788. Furthermore, Chatelet put forth the original idea that light and heat were essentially the same substance.

Incorporated Ideas of Leibniz

While writing her *Institutions de physique*, a work on Newtonian physics and mechanics, Chatelet became acquainted with the ideas of Gottfried Leibniz, particularly his conception of *forces vives*, which she accepted as true. While Rene Descartes described the physical world geometrically as extended matter, to which force can be applied as an external agent, Leibniz defined force as a distinctive quality of matter. In view of Chatelet's general Newtonian orientation as a scientist, her passionate interest in Leibnizian metaphysics, which essentially contradicts the Newtonian world view, may seem odd. However, as Margaret Alic argues, the marquise sought a synthesis of the two world views. "*Institutions*," Alic has written, "remained faithful to Newtonian physics, but Newton's purely scien-

tific, materialistic philosophy did not completely satisfy the marquise. She believed that scientific theory demanded a foundation in metaphysics and this she found in Leibniz. She never doubted that Leibnizian metaphysics was reconcilable with Newtonian physics, as long as the implications of the Newtonian system were limited to empirical physical phenomena." Chatelet's acceptance of the metaphysical foundations of science was an implicit rejection of any mechanistic world view, Cartesian or Newtonian. French scientists, most of whom tacitly accepted the Cartesian scientific paradigm, found the marquise's ideas offensive. For example, the eminent Cartesian physicist and mathematician Jean-Baptist Dortous de Mairan, whom she had singled out for criticism, responded sharply in 1741, representing a majority view which Chatelet was unable to refute alone.

Translated Newton's Masterpiece

Retreating from the philosophical war between the Cartesians and the Leibnizians, Chatelet focused on her Newtonian studies, particularly the huge task of translating Newton's *Principia mathematica* into French, an undertaking which she devoted the rest of her life. An excellent Latinist with a deep understanding of Newtonian physics, she was ideally suited for the project. Despite many obstacles, which included a busy social life and an unwanted pregnancy at the age of 42, Chatelet finished her translation. On September 4, 1749, she gave birth to a daughter, and died of puerperal fever shortly thereafter. Her translation of Newton's work remains one of the monuments of French scientific scholarship.

Books

Alic, Margaret. *Hypatia's Heritage: A History of Women in Science from Antiquity through the Nineteenth Century*. Beacon Press, 1986.

Copleston, Frederick. *Modern Philosophy: From Descartes to Leibniz*. Vol. 4: *A History of Philosophy*. Image Books, 1960.

Klens, Ulrike. *Mathematikerinnen im 18. Jahrhundert: Maria Gaetana Agnesi, Gabrielle-Emilie du Chatelet, Sophie Germain*. Centaurus-Verlagsgesellschaft, 1994.

Mitford, Nancy. *Voltaire in Love*. Greenwood Press, 1957.

Olsen, Lynn M. *Women in Mathematics*. MIT Press, 1974.

Smelding, Anda von. *Die gottliche Emilie*. Schlieffen Verlag, 1933.

Vaillot, Rene. *Madame du Chatelet*. Albin Michel, 1978.

Wolf, A. *A History of Science, Technology, and Philosophy in the Eighteenth Century*. 2d ed. George Allen and Unwin, 1952. □

Joseph Hodges Choate

Joseph H. Choate (1832-1917), a diplomat and lawyer, was considered the quintessential New Englander, though much of his life was spent in New York City at the apogee of America's Gilded Age. As a partner in a successful law practice there, Choate was involved in some of the country's most publicized legal cases during the latter decades of the

nineteenth century. President William McKinley named him U.S. ambassador to Great Britain in 1899, where he proved himself a skilled diplomat.

Old New England Name

Choate was the scion of one of Massachusetts's Puritan-era families. An ancestor, John Choate, sailed there from England in 1643, and a number of his descendants had distinguished themselves by the time of Joseph Hodges Choate's birth in 1832. There were farmers of Hog Island, sometimes called Choate Island, in Ipswich Bay of Massachusetts; another served in the state legislator in the 1700s; and a cousin of his father's was a highly regarded U.S. congressman. Choate was born in Salem, where his father was a physician, into a family of five. His education began as a toddler when his brother took him along to a local "dame school," one of New England's informal schoolhouses run by older women. He attended public school later and followed his three older brothers into Harvard College. During the academic year of 1848-49, all four Choate brothers were enrolled at Harvard. Choate joined the Hasty Pudding Club and graduated in 1852 at a ceremony in which his brother William, later a renowned judge, gave the valedictory address; he himself held the rank of class salutatorian.

Choate went on to Harvard Law School, finishing in 1854, and began as an associate with the Boston firm of Hodges and Saltonstall. He was admitted to the Massachusetts bar in October 1855. Moving to New York City later in the year, he was hired at the firm of Butler, Evarts and Southmayd with a letter of introduction from Rufus Choate, the U.S. senator, and was made partner within five years. As such he earned around $3,000 a year. He became active in city politics and Republican circles and was a staunch opponent of the Tweed Ring that ran City Hall. Choate helped rouse sentiment against the Tweed Ring's flagrant corruption at a public meeting in Cooper Union that took place in September 1871.

Energetic Fundraiser and Board Member

Choate married Caroline Dutcher Sterling of Cleveland, Ohio, in 1861. In his after-work hours, he played a key role in the foundation of some of New York City's finest institutions. He was a member of the founding board of the American Museum of Natural History and a trustee of it until his death. For the Metropolitan Museum of Art, he served as an incorporator and trustee and headed its legal committee and served as board vice president. He was governor of the New York Hospital for forty years and twice president of the board of the New York State Charities Aid Association. Choate's energies were also devoted to the New York Association for the Blind, the American Society for the Judicial Settlement of International Disputes, and the Carnegie Endowment for International Peace, for each of which he served in executive posts.

Yet Choate was by profession an attorney and practiced for 55 years. He was involved in a number of prominent or historic cases and earned a reputation as a formidable jury lawyer. He argued in the estate battles of railroad magnate Cornelius Vanderbilt and former New York governor Samuel J. Tilden and was involved in anti-trust cases involving both the Standard Oil Company and a consortium of tobacco growers and manufacturers. A court-martial case involving General Fitz-John Porter he once claimed was the toughest challenge of his career and his most satisfying victory. Rumor held that he earned $250,000 for an 1895 case argued successfully before the U.S. Supreme Court that challenged a new income tax law. Choate pointed out that the law was iniquitous, since four-fifths of the revenues collected came from some of the country's wealthiest landowners in the Northeastern states. He declared it opposed the spirit of the preservation of private property on which America had been founded 115 years earlier. "If this law is upheld, the first parapet would be carried, and then it would be easy to overcome the whole fortress on which the rights of the people depend," Choate urged, according to his biography by Strong.

As he rose in prominence, Choate became a gifted and popular after-dinner speaker. He added more board and committee memberships to his schedule of commitments. He served on a commission that made revisions to New York state's judicial system, was elected president of the Association of the Bar of the City of New York and the American Bar Association as well, and was president of the

Harvard Alumni Association. He also served as president, at various times, of the prestigious Union League Club, the New England Society of New York, and the Pilgrim Society. As president of the New York Exchange for Women's Work, he was integral to fundraising efforts for a new building, enjoining his audience, "There are said to be twelve hundred millionaires in this city. Their money is corrupting them and their families. Now each of you select your millionaire or millionaires and get this money from them," according to Strong's biography.

Made Irish Enemies

Not surprisingly, Choate was known for a biting wit that sometimes bordered on sarcasm. He earned a fair amount of enmity among Americans of Irish descent for a speech he delivered in 1893 before the St. Patrick's Society of New York. There were many Irish-American politicians in the audience, and the question of Home Rule for Ireland, free of English domination, was a hotly debated topic at the time. In his speech, Choate wondered why so many Irish had succeeded in America, while their counterparts at home had trouble having their demands met. "For what offices, great or small, have the Irishmen not taken? What spoils have they not carried away? But, now that you have done so much for America, now that you have made it all your own, what do you propose to do for Ireland? How long do you propose to let her be the political football of England?" Choate, according to a biography from Theron G. Strong, then told the assembled that they should, with families and fortunes earned, "set your faces homeward" and take Ireland themselves. "It would be a terrible blow to us. It would take us a great while to recover. Feebly, imperfectly, we should look about us and learn, for the first time in seventy-five years, how to govern New York without you."

Later that decade, Choate defended a U.S. Marshal who was serving as a bodyguard to a U.S. Supreme Court justice. The marshal was accused of shooting David Terry, a former judge on California's state supreme court, who had made threats to assassinate Justice Stephen J. Field. Terry had been legal advisor to a woman who tried to make a claim on the estate of a senator and then married her. When Field, then judge of the U.S. Circuit Court in California, delivered his verdict, Terry pulled a knife and was jailed. After his release, he made threats on Field's life and surprised both the judge and his bodyguard on a train one day. The case went before the U.S. Supreme Court, and Choate's arguments resulted in the marshal's acquittal.

Served Six Years as Ambassador

In 1899 Choate was appointed Ambassador to the Court of St. James, one of the most coveted of all diplomatic postings, by President McKinley. The appointment aroused an outcry from some Irish-Americans, and one journal termed it "a cruel insult" on the part of McKinley. Choate met both Queen Victoria and her successor, Edward VII. His six years in London were marked by several notable diplomatic achievements, including the settling of a boundary dispute between the United States and Canada over the Alaska Territory. The contested area was near to the gold discoveries of the Klondike in the mid-1890s, and a Joint High Commission in 1898 had failed to reach agreement. A new tribunal was called, consisting of three English jurists and three American counterparts, and Canada was initially confident that Britain would support its claims. Thanks to Choate's work, however, Britain decided that maintaining good relations with the United States was paramount, and the 1903 ruling decided in favor of the American claims.

Choate was also a vital part of settling preliminary negotiations over a planned Panama Canal. The United States desired full control, but the Clayton-Bulwer Treaty of 1850, between United States and Great Britain, specified that any canal built through the Central American isthmus would be jointly controlled by both nations. U.S. Secretary of State John Hay directed Choate to nullify the terms of that treaty by securing Britain's acquiescence to the American promise that the canal would give ships of all nations free and open passage. Choate also helped with Hay's "Open Door" policy regarding freedom of trade in China. Some European powers were against it, since they had made their own agreements with the Chinese government, but the American ambassador secured Great Britain's acceptance of the free trade agreement.

Active in International Peace Efforts

Choate's time in London was a pleasant and prestigious one, but he was sometimes known to ruffle the more formal English aristocracy. Once, as guest at a manor home, he was reportedly mistaken for a butler by an English aristocrat, who gave the ambassador the command, "Call me a cab," according to Strong's 1917 biography. Choate allegedly replied, "You are a cab." He returned to the United States in 1905, at the age of 73, and devoted his final years to the aims of international peace organizations. In 1907 he headed the American delegation to the Second Hague Conference for the reduction on world armaments. The nations failed to reach an agreement, but many resolutions were adopted regarding laws of war and the rights of neutral shipping during wartime. The conference was a predecessor to the League of Nations and United Nations, formed respectively after each world war.

Choate and his wife celebrated their fiftieth wedding anniversary at their Naumkeag estate in Stockbridge, Massachusetts, in 1911, with a party attended by a thousand guests. Naumkeag, which boasted 26 rooms, was designed by renowned Stanford White as a summer home for the Choates. The home is now a national historic landmark and is open to the public. At the outbreak of World War I in 1914, Choate was a firm supporter of U.S. intervention. When that occurred in 1917, his distinguished diplomatic career gained him appointment as chair of the New York committee for the reception of the Commissions from England and France. At closing ceremonies on May 13, he told the Earl of Balfour, Britain's Foreign Secretary at the time, "Remember, we meet again to celebrate the victory," but Choate died the next day.

Books

Dictionary of American Biography Base Set, American Council of Learned Societies, 1928-1936.

Strong, Theron G., *Joseph H. Choate: New Englander, New Yorker, Lawyer, Ambassador,* Dodd, Mead and Company, 1917. □

Rufus Choate

Ranked among the greatest trial lawyers of his era, Rufus Choate (1799-1859) was also an active participant in American politics. His brilliant legal mind and flamboyant oratorical skills helped him win numerous high-profile courtroom battles. As a U.S. representative and senator, Choate opposed sectional extremists and fought for preservation of the Union.

A colorful, somewhat eccentric figure, Rufus Choate earned his greatest renown in the courtrooms of his native Massachusetts. For over 30 years, he dazzled juries with his emotional, yet carefully-reasoned rhetoric, winning victories in some of the most celebrated criminal cases of his day. He combined a scholar's diligence with an actor's feel for drama and audience psychology. An early supporter of the Whig Party, Choate entered public life in the 1820s and went on to serve in both the U.S. House and Senate. Towards the end of his life, he became a forceful advocate of compromise between Northern abolitionists and Southern States Rights partisans. Politics, though, remained secondary to his abiding love for the law. While not identified with any landmark constitutional decisions, Choate was highly regarded for his exceptional intellect, oratorical powers, and personal graciousness.

Early Life

The fourth of six children, Choate born on Hog Island, off of the Atlantic coast near Essex, Massachusetts. His father David Choate (a Revolutionary War veteran and former teacher) and mother Miriam Foster encouraged his studious nature at an early age. After studying at local schools and at an academy in Hampton, New Hampshire, he went on to enroll at Dartmouth College, graduating in 1819. It was during his Dartmouth years that Choate first gained notice as a public speaker. He delivered an outstanding valedictory address at his class's commencement exercises after suffering a nervous breakdown; among those present was statesman Daniel Webster, who would become a political mentor for Choate in later years.

After going on to study at Dane Law School in Cambridge, Choate worked in the law office of former U.S. Attorney General William Wirt. In 1822, he was admitted to the Massachusetts bar and began his practice in Danvers, near Salem. He soon gained recognition as the most impressive criminal lawyer in his area, renowned for his meticulous preparation in even the most low-paying cases. He

matched his thoroughness with a persuasive courtroom speaking style that rarely failed to sway jurors. His ability to touch emotions with humor, sarcasm, and pathos led some to consider him more of a stage performer than a keen legal mind. Among those who disagreed was Webster, who commented to a colleague, "It is a great mistake to suppose that Mr. Choate, in that flowery elocution, does not keep his logic all right. Amid all that pile of flowers there is a strong, firm chain of logic," according to Fuess's biography.

Political Career

In 1825, Choate married Helen Olcott, the daughter of a Dartmouth board of trustees member. That same year, he was elected to the lower house of the Massachusetts General Court. Two years later, he was elected to the State Senate and, in 1830, he won a seat in the U.S. House of Representatives. An opponent of President Andrew Jackson's policies, he aligned himself with Webster, Henry Clay, and other leaders of the National Republican Party. After his re-election in 1832, he resigned his seat and relocated with his family to Boston. In the midst of a thriving law practice, he worked to organize the Whig Party in his state in opposition to the Democrats. He was sent to the U.S. Senate in 1841, completing the term of Webster, who had become Secretary of State in President William Henry Harrison's cabinet. In the Senate, Choate supported the protective tariff and opposed annexation of Texas. He unsuccessfully worked to heal the rift between President John Tyler and his fellow Whigs over the chartering of a national bank. Eager to return to the law, he left the Senate in 1845. Fuess's biography includes Choate's comment: "If I could be permanently and happily in the Senate," he told a friend, "I should like that better than anything in the world; but to be just enough in the Senate to be out of the law, and not enough in the Senate to be a leader in politics, is a sort of half-and-half business very contemptible."

Legal Advocate

In partnership with B.F. Crowninshield and, later, his son-in-law Joseph M. Bell, Choate rose to the front ranks of the Boston bar during the 1840s. His most celebrated cases included his successful defense of Albert Terrill, accused of murder and arson. During the trial, Choate advanced the theory that his client committed his acts of violence while sleepwalking, the first use of such a defense in U.S. history. He also gained an acquittal for a Roman Catholic priest charged with assault from a Protestant jury during a time of widespread prejudice against Catholics in Massachusetts. A tireless worker, he took on cases from rich and poor alike, with the ability to pay largely irrelevant. Some criticized him for defending the obviously guilty. Political foe Wendell Philips, as quoted in Fuess's biography, referred to him as someone "who made it safe to murder, and of whose health thieves asked before they began to steal." Whatever the moral implications, there was no disputing his abilities as a legal advocate. His contemporary Edwin P. Whipple remarked on Choate's "imaginative power of transforming himself into the personalities of his clients, of surveying acts and incidents from their point of view . . . He not only could go in, but could get out of, every individuality he assumed for the time."

Beyond the courtroom, Choate was considered one of the great public speakers of the pre-Civil War era. His rich, intricate speeches were delivered in a dynamic, well-modulated voice embellished with dramatic gestures. His role models were such Greek and Latin orators as Demosthenes and Cicero. Even by the standards of his time, his sentences were lengthy—his 1853 eulogy of Webster included one that ran to four pages and took ten minutes to deliver. Remarkably, he could maintain his clarity of expression even during such unwieldy passages. His most famous addresses included "The Age of the Pilgrims," "The Romance of the Sea," and "The Eloquence of Revolutionary Periods." Choate's appearance added to the striking effect of his words. His unkempt hair, deep-set eyes, and grim expression were accentuated by his nervous manner and carelessly-chosen clothing. Chronically overworking, he was subject to excruciating headaches, particularly after delivering an important speech. Intense to the point of mania, his personal oddities did not interfere with his ability to move lecture audiences to tears.

Choate refused public honors after leaving the U.S. Senate. He turned down a seat on the bench of the supreme judicial court of Massachusetts and, in 1851, took himself out of consideration for nomination to the U.S. Supreme Court. He did re-enter the public eye as a defender of the Compromise of 1850 and an opponent of anti-slavery agitation. While morally opposed to slavery, he supported his friend Webster in promoting peace between North and South and saw abolitionism as dangerous. At the 1852 Whig convention in Baltimore, he delivered a memorable (though futile) nominating speech for Webster. Choate remained a supporter of the Whig Party until its demise in 1855. He was unwilling to join the newly-launched Republican Party, viewing it as sectional and disunionist. In the 1856 presidential campaign, he announced his support of Democrat James Buchanan over Republican John C. Fremont, a move that angered many of his former Whig allies in Massachusetts.

In 1855, Choate injured his knee while trying a court case. The resulting surgery led to a decline in his health and vitality, with Bright's Disease a contributing factor. On the advice of his physician, he sailed to Europe with his son in 1859. His condition worsened during the voyage and, after landing in Halifax, Nova Scotia, he died on July 13. He was buried at Mount Auburn Cemetery in Boston. Choate was widely mourned as a man of integrity and generosity, a dedicated legal professional with a poet's gift for language. His unwillingness to seek a leadership role in American politics kept him from achieving the stature of a Webster or Clay. He is best remembered by historians as an attorney of great distinction and an orator of brilliance.

Books

Fuess, Claude M., *Rufus Choate*, Milton, Balch & Co., 1928. Reprint. Archon, 1970.

Holt, Michael F., *The Rise and Fall of the Whig Party*, Oxford University Press, 1999.

Matthews, Jean V., *Rufus Choate*, Temple University Press, 1980.

Whipple, Edwin P., *Recollections of Eminent Men*, Houghton, Mifflin & Co., 1892.

Online

"Choate, Rufus, 1799-1859,"*Biographical Directory of the United States Congress*, http://bioguide.congress.gov (February 1, 2002). □

Camille Claudel

The French sculptor Camille Claudel (1864-1943) was the muse, pupil, and lover of Auguste Rodin, as well as a major artist in her own right. She is perhaps better known for her tempestuous relationship with Rodin than for her moving works of art, many of which can be found at the Musee Rodin in Paris.

After her breakup with Rodin in 1898, Claudel composed some of her best sculptures, yet she grew increasingly reclusive and paranoid. In 1913 her family committed her to an insane asylum, where she remained for the last 30 years of her life.

Camille Claudel was the eldest of three children born to Louis-Prosper Claudel, a civil servant, and Louise-Athenaise Cervaux Claudel, a middle class country housewife on December 8, 1864 in Fere-en-Tardenois, France.

The family moved occasionally as Louis-Prosper's work demanded, living for a time in the small town of Bar-le-Duc, where Claudel first attended school at the age of six. However, the family returned often to its ancestral home in the small village of Villeneuve in the Champagne region of France. Though not wealthy, the Claudels were well established in the community and lived comfortably.

At an early age Claudel took an interest in modeling with clay, finding in the art of sculpture an outlet for her active imagination. A willful and precocious child, she quickly adopted the identity of an artist and never doubted her talents. Before she had even taken lessons in sculpture, Claudel coaxed every family member—her father, mother, brother, and sister—into posing for clay-modeled portraits.

While Claudel's father encouraged his daughter in her pursuit of art, the young sculptor's mother never accepted what she regarded as her daughter's unconventional, proud, and wayward disposition. Of her three children, Louise-Athenaise favored Claudel the least, preferring her obedient and traditional younger sister, Louise. In a household filled with discord, Claudel turned for affection to her father, and especially to her brother, Paul, to whom she grew very close.

Like his sister, Paul had an artist's temperament. He crafted a talent for writing that would make him one of France's leading poets and playwrights. The two artists shared a deep love and understanding, and from an early age they motivated and inspired each other in their creative endeavors. The unusually intense bond between the sculptor-sister and poet-brother would later become a subject of fascination and curiosity among cultural historians.

By the age of 15 Claudel had completed her first significant sculptures, which included busts of Napoleon and Bismarck (who defeated Napoleon III) as well as a group of figures depicting the tale of David and Goliath. (None of these works survives.) At this time she and her family were living in Nogent-sur-Seine, a Champagne town about 60 miles from Paris. The location was an auspicious one for Claudel, as the town was home to two respected nineteenth-century sculptors, Alfred Boucher and Paul Dubois. Boucher, asked by Claudel's father to give his opinion on the young girl's work, expressed astonishment at her talent and encouraged Louis-Prosper to send his daughter to study at an art academy.

At that time only men could attend the Ecole des Beaux-Arts, the prestigious academy in Paris, but some private art schools admitted female students. In 1881, before she turned 17, Claudel entered the Colarossi Academy in Paris, sharing a studio with three female British art students. One of these, Jessie Lipscomb, would remain a lifelong friend.

The first sculptures Claudel completed at the school are among the earliest surviving examples of her formative works. These include a bronze bust of her brother at age 13 (made in 1881) and *La Vieille Helene* (1882), modeled after the family housekeeper. The latter piece would become her first exhibited work in 1885.

Became Rodin's Assistant

Boucher took an interest in his young protege's progress, and every Friday he would visit the studio to give advice to Claudel and Lipscomb. When Boucher relocated to Italy in 1883, he arranged for another sculptor to continue these weekly tutorials. His replacement was Auguste Rodin, then 43 years old and considered perhaps the foremost sculptor of his day, though not yet celebrated as a master.

The first meeting between Claudel and Rodin is a subject of much speculation, although little is known of the fateful day. At 19, when she met Rodin, Claudel was strikingly beautiful, with large blue eyes and chestnut hair. The young sculptor displayed a passion for her art that Rodin doubtless found disarming as well. In 1884 he completed his first bust of the woman who would become his collaborator and muse.

The following year, Claudel and Lipscomb had become habitues in Rodin's studio, hired as assistants to help complete his masterpiece, *The Gates of Hell.* Rodin had begun this large-scale work in 1880, and it would continue to consume him until 1917. Claudel became Rodin's most active assistant, posing as figures and helping to compose various elements of the sculpture. Many art historians believe that Claudel also sculpted the hands and feet of the *Burghers of Calais,* Rodin's monument to six citizens who gave their lives to save the French town of Calais in the fourteenth century.

Thus began a long period of intense relations between Claudel and Rodin, who had become lovers as well as partners in artistic creation. Art historians continue to disagree about which of the two sculptors most influenced the other. Many contend that their influence was mutual. What is clear is that Rodin produced much more artwork than Claudel during this time, and that she helped him do so. All of Rodin's assistants (and there were many) helped build the legendary sculptor's reputation as a prolific artist of almost superhuman productivity—especially during the late 1880s and early 1890s, when Claudel was at his side.

The love affair and creative collaboration between Claudel and Rodin would last nearly 15 years. Letters from Rodin in the mid-1880s reveal just how smitten he was with the female sculptor who was 24 years his junior. In 1886 he followed Claudel to England, where she was visiting Lipscomb. Accounts of this early stage in their relationship depict Claudel as elusive and perhaps teasingly coy with the famous sculptor. Rodin, meanwhile, held a longstanding reputation as a womanizer, a sculptor specializing in the female nude who required fresh models regularly. He also remained involved with one woman whose presence preceded—and long outlasted—that of Claudel. This was Rose Beuret, a seamstress whom Rodin had met in the mid-1860s as well as the mother of his son, Auguste.

A Love Triangle

As relations intensified between Rodin and Claudel, Beuret naturally became a subject of contention between the lovers. Claudel repeatedly asked Rodin to choose between them, but he refused, desiring to keep both women in his life. Beuret, who lived with the sculptor, kept his house, and raised his child, seemed willing to accept her lover's infidelities and his lack of interest in marriage. In most circles, Beuret was known as Madame Rodin, despite their unmarried status. Rodin's unwillingness to leave Beuret would ultimately drive Claudel away. Some believe it also drove her mad.

In 1888 Claudel moved out of her parents' house and rented a small apartment in Paris. Shortly after, Rodin purchased a house nearby known as La Folie-Neufbourg. Here the lovers were said to have occasionally lived together, while Beuret remained at Rodin's primary residence. During this time, Rodin sculpted several portraits of Claudel, and Claudel sculpted her *Bust of Rodin* (1892), the artist's favorite portrait of himself. Claudel also began working on her minor masterpiece *The Waltz* (begun 1891), which depicts a couple entwined in a dance.

While Rodin's infidelities are well-documented, less is known of affairs Claudel may have had with other men. Some historians believe she had a brief romance with the composer Claude Debussy in or around 1890. Whatever passion may have existed between them was over by early 1891, however, when they ceased seeing each other. Debussy was said to have kept a small cast of *The Waltz* on his piano until his death.

Matured as an Artist

In 1893 Claudel exhibited two sculptures at the Paris Salon: *The Waltz* and *Clotho,* a moving depiction of one of the Fates from Greek mythology. Claudel depicts Clotho as an elderly woman with a hauntingly wasted body, tangled in the threads of destiny she must weave. Both pieces were received well by critics, and it seemed that Claudel, about to turn 30, was entering her peak as an artist.

While Claudel's work flourished in the 1890s, her relationship with Rodin progressively deteriorated. She did not want to share Rodin with Beuret, but she was not content, either, merely to be the muse of her famous lover; she wanted a successful career of her own. The break between the lovers took years, but by 1889 the relationship was over. Claudel would not let Rodin enter her studio, though she is said to have often hidden in the bushes near the artist's house to watch him return home at night.

Immediately following the breakup, Claudel was perhaps her most productive, completing some of her most original and mature works, including *L'Age Mur* (1898), an autobiographical sculpture depicting a love triangle, and *La Vague* (1900), with three female figures bathing under an enormous wave. The latter work was indicative of a new style for Claudel, who now used onyx, a rare material, and based her compositions on an eloquent play of curves. She composed large works as well as sculptures of a more intimate scale, making quick sketches of people in the streets of Paris and returning home to sculpt them. Unfortunately, these small figures do not survive; she destroyed them all.

Descended into Madness

In the early years of the twentieth century, Claudel had begun a pattern of working obsessively for months, and then destroying her creations. She had become reclusive, losing touch with the world, taking in stray cats, and letting her apartment fall into a state of filthy disrepair. She struggled with poverty, and turned down social invitations with the excuse that she had nothing to wear. Increasingly, she grew paranoid of Rodin, imagining that he was plotting against her.

Claudel's family became aware of her circumstances and her apparent descent into madness. Upon his return to France in 1909 after four years of diplomatic service, Paul Claudel found his sister appallingly changed. In his journal (quoted in the *Smithsonian*) he described her as "insane, enormous, with a soiled face, speaking incessantly in a monotonous metallic voice."

For a few more years Claudel lived in her disheveled studio, with her shutters closed to the light and neighbors warning their children not to speak to her. Then, on March 5, 1913, three days after the death of their father, Louis-Prosper, Paul arranged for his sister's internment at a mental asylum in Ville-Evrard, near Paris. Five days later two orderlies broke into Claudel's apartment and took her to the asylum in an ambulance. She was 39 years old.

For the remaining 30 years of her life, Claudel languished in an insane asylum, transferring once to a facility in Montdevergues, near Avignon. Her life as a sculptor was over, although she wrote letters begging her brother and mother to release her and let her return to the artist's life. When Claudel's doctors tried to interest her in sculpting and presented her with clay, she angrily rejected it. Diagnosed as suffering from a persecution complex, she remained deeply paranoid of Rodin, and blamed him for her troubles.

Whether or not Claudel was truly insane and needed to stay in an asylum remains unclear. She wrote lucid letters to her family and friends, and even her doctors recommended that she be released on at least two occasions. But her brother was often abroad, and her mother would not allow her release, claiming that she was too old to care for her daughter.

"I live in a world that is so curious, so strange," Claudel wrote in a letter to a friend in 1935. "Of the dream which was my life, this is the nightmare." She died eight years later, on October 19, 1943 in Montdevergues, France.

Books

Paris, Reine-Marie, *Camille: The Life of Camille Claudel, Rodin's Muse and Mistress,* Seaver Books, 1988.
Schmoll Eisenwerth, J. A., *Auguste Rodin and Camille Claudel,* Prestel-Verlag, 1994.

Periodicals

Smithsonian, September 1985.

Online

"Artist Profile: Camille Claudel," http://www.nmwa.org/legacy/bios/bclaudel/htm (October 24, 2001).

"Camille Claudel," http://www.musee-rodin.fr/claud-e.htm (November 1, 2001). □

Beverly Cleary

The writings of Beverly Cleary (born 1916) include realistic and humorous portraits of American children. They have gained critical acclaim as "classics" of children's literature.

Born Beverly Bunn on April 12, 1916 in McMinnville, Oregon, Cleary was the only daughter of Chester Lloyd and Mable Atlee Bunn and a descendant of Oregon pioneers. She grew up on an 80-acre farm in Yamhill, Oregon, where her uncle was mayor and her father was on the town council. In her autobiography *A Girl from Yamhill,* she wrote that living there taught her "that the world was a safe and beautiful place, where children were treated with kindness, patience, and tolerance." All of these qualities would later be apparent in her books.

Yamhill had no library; her mother arranged for the State Library to send books to Yamhill, and created a small lending area in a lodge room over the Yamhill Bank. Cleary later recalled in an article in *Top of the News* that this was "a dingy room filled with shabby leather-covered chairs and smelling of stale cigar smoke," but that she was amazed at the variety of books available for children.

Became Interested in Reading

When she was six, low income forced her father out of farming, and the family moved to Portland, Oregon. Beverly was excited about the move, and looked forward to playing with other children. Although she was excited by the big city and by the immense children's room in the Portland Library, Cleary felt out of place in school, particularly after a bout of chicken pox left her behind the other students. By the time she got back to school after her illness, the class had been divided into good readers, next-best readers, and worst readers, and Cleary was in the bottom group. Bored and discouraged, she decided reading and school were miserable experiences. At the same time, she became consumed with fears that an earthquake would hit, that her father would be hurt, or that she would die. These fears receded somewhat between first and second grade, but she still refused to read except while in school. When she was eight years old, she finally found a book that aroused her interest, Lucy Fitch Perkins's *The Dutch Twins.* In this story about two ordinary children and their adventures, Cleary found release and happiness. She told a writer for *Publishers Weekly,* "With rising elation, I read on, I read all afternoon and evening, and by bedtime I had read not only *The Dutch Twins* but *The Swiss Twins* as well. It was one of the most exciting days of my life." The book opened the door for her to read more books for pleasure. Soon she was reading all the books for children in the library.

When Cleary was in seventh grade, a teacher suggested that she write books for children. This suggestion struck home. She vowed to write "the kind of books I wanted to read," she wrote in *Top of the News.* When her mother reminded her that she needed a steady job too, Cleary decided that she would become a librarian.

Cleary earned a BA in English at the University of California-Berkeley in 1938. The following year she earned a BA in librarianship from the University of Washington-Seattle. She then got a job as children's librarian in Yakima, Washington, where she learned to tell stories to children and found out what stories children liked to read and hear.

Wrote Her First Book

In 1940 she married Clarence T. Cleary, whom she had met in college. They moved to Oakland, California, where they had twins, Marianne Elisabeth and Malcolm James. During World War II she worked as post librarian at the Oakland Army Hospital. After the war, she worked in the children's department of a Berkeley bookstore. David Reuther noted in *Horn Book,* "Surrounded by books, she was sure she could write a better book than some she saw there, and after the Christmas rush was over, she said, 'I decided if I was ever going to write, I'd better get started'" According to Pat Pflieger in *Beverly Cleary,* she said to her husband, "I'll have to write a book!" He replied, "Why don't you?" She said, "Because we never have any sharp pencils," so the next day he brought home a pencil sharpener. "I realized that if I was ever going to write a book, this was the time to do it," she later wrote. She began writing on January 2. Since then she has begun all her books on that same date. Although she had planned to write a book about a little girl who wanted to write, the story turned out to be that of a boy who would be allowed to keep a stray dog if he could find a way to get it home on the bus. She wrote in *Top of the News*, "When I finished the chapter I found I had ideas for another chapter and at the end of two months I had a whole book about Henry Huggins and his dog Ribsy."

The book was accepted six weeks later and was published in 1950 by William Morrow and Company, which has published almost all of her books since then. *Henry Huggins* was different from many other books of the time, which either presented an idealized version of "goody-goody" children, or told unrealistic tales of children who solved crimes or found long-lost wealthy relatives. As a *People Weekly* writer commented, "Cleary had written a story that was simply a delightful slice of life."

Timeless Characters

Cleary went on to write many more books about Henry and other children in his neighborhood, including Ellen Tebbits, Otis Spofford, and Ramona and her older sister Beezus. She also wrote books for older, teenaged readers about teen romance, but these were not as well loved as her books for younger readers. In *Twentieth-Century Authors*, Cathryn M. Mercier commented about her young adult novels, "[They] do not possess the timeless qualities of the Ramona and Henry books . . . [and] do not speak to contemporary young adults." However, in *Bookpage.com*, Cleary defended these books, saying to Miriam Drennan, "Some people have said that those books are dated, but they're not. They're true to the period [the 1950s]."

Henry Huggins and Cleary's other most-loved characters all live on or near Klickitat Street in Portland, Oregon; one of the best-loved is Ramona, who first appeared as a minor character ("a nuisance," Cleary told Miriam Drennan in *Bookpage.com*) in *Henry Huggins*. Cleary told Drennan, [Ramona] was an accidental character. It occurred to me that as I wrote, all of these children appeared to be only children, so I tossed in a little sister, and at that time, we had a neighbor named Ramona. I heard somebody call out, 'Ramona!' so I just named her Ramona." Ramona came into her own in the 1968 *Ramona the Pest*, where she was the star character. Of all of Cleary's characters, Ramona would become a favorite of readers.

Cleary drew on some of her own experiences to create Ramona, but said she often used people she knew to create other characters. Otis Spofford was based on a "lively" boy who sat across the aisle from her in sixth grade, she told Drennan, and her best friend "appears in assorted books in various disguises." She said of her friend, "She's a very warm and friendly person; the sort of person everybody likes. I've known her since we were in the first grade. I don't think we've ever exchanged a cross word."

Pflieger wrote, "Material for Cleary's books has come from her own life, from the nostalgic glow of Yamhill . . . and the dark fears of her early years in Portland . . . to her

[adolescent romances], which inform the difficult relationships in some of her works for adolescents." She also noted that Cleary wrote the books that she would have wanted to read as a child, and that she had very clear ideas about what she did *not* want to read: "Any book in which a child accepted the wisdom of an adult and reformed, any book in which a child reformed at all. . . . [and] any book in which education was disguised like a pill in a spoonful of jelly." In her Regina Medal acceptance speech, she spoke bitterly about a book that she thought was a "real" story, but which turned out to be a phonics lesson in the end. She said the author had "cheated" her. "He had used a story to try to teach me. I bitterly resented this intrusion into my life."

Cleary has occasionally been criticized because her books don't address contemporary problems or social ills. She told Drennan, "I feel sometimes that [in children's books] there are more and more grim problems, but I don't know that I want to burden third- and fourth-graders with them. I feel it's important to get [children] to enjoy writing." She also said, in her Regina Medal acceptance speech, "I feel that children who must endure such problems want to read about children who do *not* have such problems." In *Horn Book*, Barbara Chatton noted that "A third-grader whose family was going through a painful divorce read and reread the Ramona books because they were stories about the way her family used to be, and she could laugh and remember; and, she said wisely, 'They comfort me.'"

Cleary writes in longhand on yellow legal pads, and often begins books by writing scenes at the middle or the end of the story. She does not outline them before writing; she simply dives in and plays with the characters.

"Reading is a Pleasure"

In 1999, Cleary presented a new Ramona story in *Ramona's World*. She didn't warn her editor that she was working on a new Ramona book, but simply handed the manuscript to her when the editor visited her at home. The editor, Barbara Lalicki, told Heather Vogel Frederick in *Publishers Weekly*, "I had no idea what it was, and the curiosity was killing me. "I was driving back to my hotel and got caught in a traffic jam, so I opened it up and read the first few lines and thought, 'Wow!' Ramona was back with all the immediacy—it was just as if 15 years hadn't gone by."

Cleary told Drennan, "Children should learn that reading is pleasure, not just something that teachers make you do in school. If her readers' response is any indication, she has succeeded admirably in showing them just that. She still receives hundreds of letters each week from fans, mostly schoolchildren. An article in *People Weekly* quoted one, which sums up the impact of Cleary's work on children: "I read everything you ever wrote. When I feel sad, I pick up one of your books and it makes me feel better." And another one, which commented, "You're my number one author in the universe."

Books

Pflieger, Pat, *Beverly Cleary: Twayne's United States Authors Series*, G.K. Hall and Co., 1999.

Twentieth-Century Children's Writers, edited by Laura Standley Berger, 1995.

Periodicals

Catholic Library World, July-August, 1981.
Horn Book, Vol. 60, 1984; May-June, 1995; November-December, 1995.
People Weekly, October 3, 1988.
Publishers Weekly, October 11, 1993; February 20, 1995; July 17, 1995; September 16, 1996; November 22, 1999.
Top of the News, December, 1957.

Online

Drennan, Miriam, "I Can See Cleary Now," *Bookpage,* http://www.bookpage.com/ (November 14, 2001).
"The World of Beverly Cleary," *Beverlycleary.com,* http://www.beverlycleary.com/ (November 14, 2001). □

Jewel Plummer Cobb

Largely known for her work with skin pigment, or melanin, cell biologist and cell physiologist Jewel Plummer Cobb (born 1924) has encouraged women and ethnic minorities to enter the sciences. An educator and researcher, she contributed to the field of chemotherapy with her research on how drugs affected cancer cells.

Followed the Path of Science

Cobb was born in Chicago, Illinois, on January 17, 1924, and spent her childhood as an only child. She is from the third generation of the Plummer family who sought a career in medical science. Her grandfather, a freed slave, graduated from Howard University in 1898 and became a pharmacist. Her father, Frank V. Plummer, became a physician after he graduated from Cornell University, where he helped found the Alpha Phi Alpha Fraternity. Her mother, Carriebel (Cole) Plummer, taught dance and was a physical education teacher.

Becoming a noted cell biologist was a difficult road for Cobb. Because she was African American, she faced segregation during the course of her education. Although she came from an upper-middle-class background, Cobb found that she had to go to black Chicago public schools. Cobb was in constant contact with African American professionals and was well aware of their accomplishments. She decided not to let anything stand in the way of her own success.

Supplementing her education with books from her father's library, Cobb had access to scientific journals and magazines, current event periodicals, and materials on successful African Americans. Although Cobb was at first interested in becoming a physical education teacher like her mother and aunt, she found that she was interested in biology when, in her sophomore year in high school, she studied cells through a microscope. An honors student, Cobb showed academic promise. She had a solid education and a drive to learn.

Although her interest in biology could have led her to become a medical doctor, Cobb was not interested in working directly with the sick. She was, nonetheless, interested in the theory of disease, an interest that later led her to become one of the leading cancer researchers in the United States.

Academic Career

When it came time to enroll in college, Cobb selected the University of Michigan. Due to the segregation of the dormitories at the university, all African Americans, regardless of their year of study, were forced to live in one house. In disgust at the racism still found there, Cobb left the University of Michigan after three semesters and earned her B.A. in biology from traditionally black Talladega College in Alabama.

Cobb applied for a teaching fellowship at New York University. Because of her race, she was at first turned down for the position. Cobb refused to accept the rejection and personally visited the college, which then accepted her because her credentials were so impressive. In 1945, Cobb started her career in teaching as a fellow there. In 1947, she earned an M.S. in cell physiology and in 1950 she earned a Ph.D. in cell physiology from New York University. Her dissertation was titled "Mechanisms of Pigment Formation."

Cobb was named an independent investigator for the Marine Biological Laboratory in 1949. She completed a postdoctoral fellowship at the Cancer Research Foundation of Harlem Hospital and at Columbia University College of Physicians and Surgeons.

Attracted by theoretical approaches to biology, Cobb entered the field of research. Understanding the processes of living cells was at the heart of her studies. In particular, she found that tissue cultures were an interesting area of research. Determining which cells grew outside the body led to her study with Dorothy Walker Jones that looked at how human cancer cells were affected by drugs.

Entered Research and Administration

After she earned her doctorate, Cobb became a fellow at the National Cancer Institute. From 1952 to 1954, she directed the Tissue Culture Laboratory at the University of Illinois. Cobb took to the university life and went on to work for New York University and Hunter College in New York. She stayed at New York University from 1956 to 1960 as an assistant professor in research surgery. In 1960 Cobb became a professor at Sarah Lawrence College, where she continued her research until 1969.

Focusing on skin pigment and how melanin can protect skin from ultraviolet damage, Cobb looked at skin cancers, or melanomas. She also studied the differences between normal and cancerous pigment cells. Her research looked at neoplastic pigment cells and their development as well as exploring how hormones, chemotherapeutic drugs, and other agents could cause changes in cell division. She experimented with comparisons between how chemotherapy drugs performed in cancer patients and how they performed in vitro, or in other words, in laboratory test tubes, flasks, and dishes.

From 1969 to 1976, Cobb became dean of Connecticut College in New London, where she taught zoology. From 1976 to 1981, Cobb was a professor of biological sciences at Douglass College, a women's college at Rutgers University. She also served as dean. As she moved into administrative positions, Cobb used her influence to further the educational facilities and opportunities for those interested in studying the sciences.

In 1981, Cobb became president of California State University, Fullerton. There she was able to get state funding for a new science building and a new engineering and computer science building. She also raised private funds to found a gerontology center in the Orange County community. On campus, she was responsible for having an apartment complex built that ended Fullerton's status as a commuter college. In 1990, Cobb became a trustee professor at California State University, Los Angeles.

As administrative duties consumed much of her time, Cobb found less time for research. But she worked to ensure that others would have opportunities to pursue studies in the sciences.

Encouraged Others

Cobb never forgot the years of frustration she faced discrimination when pursuing her education. To help pave the way for other minorities who wanted to enter the sciences, Cobb established a privately funded program for minority students in premedical and predental studies at Connecticut College. She was tireless in her efforts to extend opportunities to women as well.

In her quest for equal access to opportunity, both educational and professional, Cobb sought to increase diversity among faculty and students during her time at Fullerton. Also at Fullerton, Cobb started a president's opportunity program for minority students. She recognized a great difference between the number of blacks who pursued sports careers and the number of blacks who pursued research careers, so she set up teams of faculty members to tutor students on math skills. A solid foundation in math, Cobb believed, would help minorities prepare for a career in the sciences.

Cobb spent much of her time trying to start minorities on the path of science that she had followed. As a university trustee professor, Cobb worked with six colleges to find funding for minority grants and fellowships. When government funding for such programs was reduced, Cobb worked to find private funds to fill the void.

Education, according to Cobb, is a key factor in determining whether someone will be successful and independent or encounter failure and have to depend on welfare. She maintains that one of the best pathways to success is education, and it is the route she took to achieve her own personal accomplishments. She believes more minorities should have the chance to find their niche in society through education.

"There's been a deprivation of certain educational experiences that would give young people a proper boost and encouragement to study science [and technology]," Cobb told *Black Enterprise.* "I don't think there's anything wrong with [black children's abilities to learn.] It is a matter of being stimulated, having a curiosity about science early on, and developing the commitment and discipline to study."

In 1991, Cobb became principal investigator at Southern California Science and Engineering ACCESS Center and Network, which helps middle school and high school students from economically disadvantaged backgrounds pursue careers in engineering, mathematics, and the sciences. She continued to help in efforts to bring opportunities to minorities. In 2001, she was principal investigator for Science Technology Engineering Program (STEP) Up for Youth—ASCEND project at California State University, Los Angeles.

For her work helping minorities discover the rewards of a career in science, Cobb received the 1993 Lifetime Achievement Award. This was given by the National Academy of Science for her contributions to the advancement of women and underrepresented minorities. Her photograph hangs in the academy's hall reserved for distinguished scientists.

Led a Distinguished Career

Cobb's many accomplishments include an honorary doctorate of science from Pennsylvania Medical College. She also holds honorary doctorates from the Medical College of Pennsylvania, Northern University, Rensselaer Polytechnic Institute, Rutgers University, and Tuskegee University. A trustee at a number of colleges, Cobb holds twenty-one honorary degrees.

Memberships include Human Resource Commission, Sigma Xi, National Academy of Sciences (Institute of Medicine), and National Science Foundation. She was a fellow of National Cancer Institute and New York Academy of Science. She also served on Allied Corporation's board of directors. From 1972 to 1974, she was a member of the Tissue Culture Association of the Education Committee. She received research grants from the American Cancer Society from 1971 to 1973 and from 1969 to 1974. She also developed and directed a fifth-year postbaccalaureate pre-medical program.

Since 1972, Cobb has been a member of the Marine Biological Laboratory. Since 1973, she has been on the Board of Trustees for the Institute of Education Management. After Cobb retired, Fullerton named her named president and professor of biological science, emerita.

Cobb is the author of many publications, including articles, books, and scholarly reports. She is a recipient of the Achievement in Excellence Award from the Center for Excellence in Education and the Reginald Wilson Award from the American Council on Education, Office of Minorities in Higher Education.

Cobb's struggles as an African American female left her with the conviction that racism and sexism were challenges that made it tougher for those like her to succeed. But, once she succeeded, she was determined to share her success with others.

Cobb married Roy Cobb, an insurance salesman, in 1954 and had a son, Jonathon Cobb, in 1957. They divorced in 1967.

Periodicals

Black Enterprise, February 1985, pp. 49-54.
Ebony, August 1982, pp. 97-100.

Online

"CSU Trustee Professor at Cal State L.A. Receives the Inaugural Reginald Wilson Award," *Cal State L.A.,* http://www.calstatela.edu/univ/ppa/newsrel/jpcobb2.htm (January 6, 2002).
"Jewel Plummer Cobb," *Learning Network,* http://www.globalalliancesmet.org/prom_cobb.html (January 6, 2002).
"Jewel Plummer Cobb," *Princeton University—Faces of Science: African Americans in the Sciences,* http://www.princeton.edu/~mcbrown/display/cobb.html (January 6, 2002).
"Jewel Plummer Cobb," *Think Quest,* http://library.thinkquest.org/20117/cobb.html (January 6, 2002).
"Jewel Plummer Cobb, 1924-," *African American Publications,* http://www.africanpubs.com/Apps/bios/1109CobbJewel.asp?pic=none (January 6, 2002).

"Jewel Plummer Cobb, (b. 1924)," *Marine Biological Library,* http://hermes.mbl.edu/women_of_science/cobb.html (January 6, 2002).
"Jewel Plummer Cobb, (b. 1924): Biologist," *Hill AFB—Women in Science,* http://www.hill.af.mil/fwp/cobbbio.html (January 6, 2002).
"Jewel Plummer Cobb: Biologist, Physiologist," *InfoPlease.com,* http://www.infoplease.com/ipa/A0775685.html (January 6, 2002).
"Jewel Plummer Cobb: Cell Biologist/Cell Physiologist," *The Just/Garcia/Hill Science Web Site,* http://hyper1.hunter.cuny.edu/JGH/biographies/jpcobb.html (January 6, 2002).
"Jewel Plummer Cobb Honored," *Emeritopics on the Web, CSU, Fullerton,* http://www.fullerton.edu/emeriti/fall00topics.html (January 6, 2002). □

Pete Conrad

Charles "Pete" Conrad (1930-1999) was the third person, after Neil Armstrong and Buzz Aldrin, to walk on the moon's surface. In November, 1969, he and Alan Bean made the second moon landing in history in their Apollo 12 lunar module *Intrepid*.

Conrad was born in Philadelphia, Pennsylvania on June 2, 1930, to a wealthy stockbroker. He attended Princeton University, graduating in 1953 with a degree in aeronautical engineering. After college, Conrad joined the U.S. Navy and became a pilot. He later transferred to the test pilot school at Patuxent River Naval Air Station in Maryland, a proving ground for many future astronauts, including Wally Schirra and James Lovell.

A Space Pioneer

When the National Aeronautics and Space Administration (NASA) made its selection of the "Mercury Seven" astronauts in 1959, Conrad jumped at the chance to become one of the first Americans in space. He made it to the final rounds of selection, but his open disgust with many of the physical and mental tests required of astronaut candidates earned the disapproval of NASA administrators, and he was edged out of the competition. Undaunted, he applied again with NASA's second group of astronauts in 1962, this time successfully.

Three years later, Conrad rocketed into space for the first time aboard the tiny two-man capsule, Gemini 5, with crewmate Gordon Cooper, one of the Mercury Seven astronauts. The two remained in space for a record-breaking five days in the phone-booth-sized ship before returning to Earth. Conrad flew another Gemini flight before that program ended, this time as commander of Gemini 11. He and crewmate Richard Gordon spent three days in Earth orbit, achieving a new altitude record, 850 miles, high enough to clearly see the curvature of the planet.

"We burned the Agena to make our climb to altitude," he later recalled on the Smithsonian Institution's *Air and Space Magazine* Web site. "That was really spectacular. I made the remark when we went over the top, 'Eureka,

Houston, the Earth is really round,' and when I got back to Houston, I got all this mail from members of the Flat Earth Society telling me I didn't know what I was talking about."

This flight also tested the concept of artificial gravity in space for the first time, tethering the Gemini ship to the unmanned Agena booster, which had been launched separately, and spinning the two craft around each other to create centrifugal force. As Conrad said on the *Air and Space Magazine* Web site, "You have the Agena out on the end, and it's roughly the same weight as we were. I kept trying to back out to get the line taut before I tried to spin up, and no matter how gently I did it, it would always just get to the end and act like a rubber band and make the Agena start to wobble around or move towards us . . . and then we'd whip off into night and I wasn't exactly sure where the Agena *was*. Made it real interesting. Finally I just decided what I got to do is just keep thrusting back, away, and also radially to get the thing going, and once I finally decided to do it that way, why, it spun up right away."

Third on the Moon

But it was with the Apollo program that Conrad achieved the astronaut's ultimate dream, a walk on the moon. In November, 1969, just four months after Neil Armstrong and Buzz Aldrin made their historic first moon landing, Conrad and crewmate Alan Bean touched down on the Ocean of Storms in the second moon landing. Betting that no one would remember the first words of the third man to walk on the moon, Conrad said, "Whoopee! Man, that

may have been a small one for Neil, but that's a long one for me." As he later told *Apollo Lunar Surface Journal* editor Eric M. Jones, "I . . . had $500 riding on it, but I never got paid."

One of Apollo 12's primary missions was to perfect a pin-point landing on the moon's surface (Apollo 11's flight had been off by some four miles). Mission planners chose as a target the landing site of Surveyor 3, an unmanned probe that had been launched some two years before. If Conrad could land *Intrepid* within walking distance of the probe, he would know the mission was a success. Conrad did succeed in setting his and Bean's ship down within sight of Surveyor. It was an easy walk from *Intrepid* to Surveyor, and on their second moon walk (the early Apollo missions lacked the lunar rover of later missions), Conrad and Bean strolled over to take pictures and to remove the probe's television camera to return it to Earth for analysis. Conrad later noted that Surveyor's TV camera yielded what he called the most significant discovery of the Apollo missions to the moon. Bacteria from Earth accidentally deposited on Surveyor before its launch not only survived launch, but also two years in the vacuum and extreme temperatures of the lunar surface.

Conrad and Bean had also planned an illicit little task of their own at the Surveyor landing site. The task was written as "Perform D.P." on the checklists they wore on their spacesuit cuffs. "D.P." was known only to the two astronauts as "dual photo." Unbeknownst to NASA, the two had taken along a little store-bought timer for one of their cameras, and, as Conrad later told Jones, "We were going to put the camera on the stake and both of us were going to walk over to the Surveyor and have our picture taken. . . . We knew that PAO (Public Affairs Office) would put that photograph out before they'd put anything else out. Then somebody was going to ask the question 'Who took the picture?'" Unfortunately, the timer got buried under moon rocks in one of their sample collection bags, and they couldn't find it when the time came to take the picture, so the picture was never taken.

Conrad and Bean spent 7 hours and 45 minutes walking on the surface of the moon, in two separate excursions outside of their spacecraft. This was much longer than the little more than two hours that Armstrong and Aldrin had spent on their historic single moon walk.

Space Station Commander

Conrad's next trip into space was in 1973 aboard another Apollo ship, this time to the Skylab space station in low Earth orbit. This was America's first space station. Built from hardware left over from cancelled moon missions, it was launched without people aboard. Conrad was commander of the mission, the first to Skylab. His crewmates were Joseph Kerwin and Paul Weitz. Their first task was to repair the station since it had been damaged on launch. On a risky space walk, Conrad and Kerwin rescued the damaged station by manually pulling open a solar panel that had failed to deploy. The crew spent a record-breaking 28 days in space aboard the station.

Back to Civilian Life

Conrad retired from NASA and the Navy in 1973 after completion of his Skylab mission. He joined the McDonnell Douglas Corporation as an executive, where he served for 20 years. Early in the 1990s, Conrad led a McDonnell Douglas team that tested a scale model of the innovative single stage to orbit (SSTO) spacecraft called the Delta Clipper. Designed to take off and land on its tail like the science fiction rockets of old, the Delta Clipper sought to reduce launch costs with a fully reusable spacecraft built of very lightweight materials. That project was cancelled after a successful test flight of a 1/3 scale model, but before a working full-scale prototype was built.

In 1995, Conrad helped to found Universal Space Lines, a company committed to establishing profitable commercial space travel. As he testified at a U.S. House of Representatives hearing in 1998, "Our long-term company goal is to position ourselves as the world's premier provider of affordable commercial space transportation services, including purchase and operation of both expendable and reusable launch vehicles."

Conrad died on July 8, 1999 in Ojai, California, after losing control of the motorcycle he was riding on a winding highway. His wife, four sons, and seven grandchildren survived him. At the time of his death Conrad was 69 years old.

Books

Chaikin, Andrew, *A Man on the Moon: The Voyages of the Apollo Astronauts,* Penguin Books, 1994

Stine, G. Harry, *Halfway to Anywhere: Achieving America's Destiny in Space,* M. Evans and Company, Inc, 1996

Online

"Apollo 12 Astronaut Pete Conrad Killed in Motorcycle Accident," *CNN.com,* http://www.cnn.com/TECH/space/9907/09/conrad.obit.02/, posted July 9, 1999.

"Astronaut Bio: Charles Conrad, Jr.," Web site of the Lyndon B. Johnson Space Center, http://www.jsc.nasa.gov/Bios/htmlbios/conrad-c.html, July 1999.

Bond, Peter, "Charles 'Pete' Conrad, Third Man on the Moon, Dies in Motorcycle Accident," *Astronomy Now Online,* http://www.astronomynow.com/breaking/9907/09conrad/, posted July 9, 1999.

"Charles 'Pete' Conrad," Web site of the Astronaut Hall of Fame, http://www.astronauts.org/astronauts/conrad.htm (November 9, 2001).

Conrad, Jr., Charles "Pete," NASA 1998, Life Begins at Forty: Testimony Before the Subcommittee on Space and Aviation of the House Committee on Science," http://www.house.gov/science/conrad_10-01.htm, October 1, 1998.

"Former Astronaut Pete Conrad Dies," *SpaceViews: The Online Publication of Space Exploration,* http://www.spaceviews.com/1999/07/09a.html, posted July 9, 1999.

Jones, Eric M., editor, *Apollo Lunar Surface Journal,* http://www.hq.nasa.gov/office/pao/History/alsj/frame.html, November 9, 2001.

"Pete Conrad Remembers: Doin' the Agena Swing," Web site of *Air & Space Magazine,* http://www.airspacemag.com/ASM/Web/Site/QT/AgenaSwing.html (November 9, 2001).

"Pete Conrad Remembers: The Flat Earth Society," Web site of *Air & Space Magazine,* http://www.airspacemag.com/asm/web/site/QT/FlatEarth.html (November 9, 2001). □

Thomas McIntyre Cooley

American judge and legal scholar Thomas McIntyre Cooley (1824-1898) served as a State Supreme Court Justice in Michigan and led the court to a national reputation with a distinguished record. In addition, his book, *A Treatise on the Constitutional Limitations Which Rest Upon the Legislative Power of the States of the American Union,* written in 1868, became the most widely-read and important work of its day on constitutional law.

Early Life

Thomas McIntyre Cooley was born on January 6, 1824, on a small farm in Attica, New York, in a rural part of western New York state. The son of Thomas and Rachel Cooley, he was part of a large, Protestant family. His father had come from Massachusetts to western New York 20 years earlier, and the Cooleys were a farming family.

Although the family was poor, learning was important to young Cooley. As a child he loved history and literature. He balanced his time between working on his father's farm and going to school. When he could not go to school, Cooley taught himself at home, but he did complete three years of high school. Later, he taught school in order to earn money for his education. As noted in *American Biographical History of Self-Made Men,* Cooley left the family farm in 1842 and became a lawyer's apprentice to Theron R. Stong in Palmyra, New York.

Settled in Michigan, Became a Lawyer

At the age of nineteen, Cooley moved west. As noted on the *Michigan Supreme Court Historical Society website,* Cooley had planned to continue his studies in Chicago, but during his travels, he ran out of money. He settled in Adrian, Michigan, in 1843, and finished his law studies in the firm of Tiffany and Beaman. His biography in *American Biographical History of Self-Made Men* commented that Cooley was a "careful student . . . quick, through, and methodical."

Soon, there were many changes in Cooley's personal and professional life. In December 1846, he married Mary Horton, and the couple would have six children. Also in that year, he was admitted to the Michigan Bar. As noted in his biography on the *Michigan Supreme Court Historical Society website,* Cooley began a fast-paced professional life upon his admission to the bar. He worked as a deputy county clerk and later, his biography noted, "worked in two law firms while editing the *Adrian Watchtower,* serving as court commissioner and recorder for Adrian, and cultivating his 100-acre farm."

As an attorney, the *American Biographical History of Self-Made Men,* noted, Cooley was known for his "great care and faithfulness, clearness, and logical force." His

reputation likely led to his selection by the state legislature to compile the statutes of the state, which he completed in one year. As noted on the *Cooley Law School website,* after Cooley completed this task in early 1857, he was appointed reporter of the State Supreme Court, a position he would hold until 1864.

Accepted Position as Law Professor

In his biography on the *Michigan Supreme Court Historical Society website,* it was noted that early in his career, Cooley was offered a number of teaching positions at various law schools around the country, but he declined. In 1859, when a department of law was being organized at the University of Michigan in nearby Ann Arbor, he accepted a position. He would remain at the school as a professor until 1884 and also served as dean of the law department and chair of the history department.

The *Cooley Law School website* noted that Cooley "taught constitutional law, real property, trust, estates, and domestic property." In addition, he "authored countless articles on legal subjects and wrote several full-length works." Once he began his professional relationship with the University of Michigan, Cooley moved to Ann Arbor permanently. Wilfred Shaw, who once served as general secretary of the Alumni Association and was editor of the *Michigan Alumnus,* reflected that Cooley's home "was long a center of the intellectual and social life of Ann Arbor."

The State Supreme Court Justice

In 1850, according to the *Michigan Supreme Court Historical Society website,* Michigan's State Constitution read that circuit court judges would also serve as justices of the State's Supreme Court, serving six-year terms. This plan failed. In 1857, the Michigan State Legislature created a permanent State Supreme Court.

As added by *American Biographical History of Self-Made Men,* Cooley was appointed to the State Supreme Court in 1864, while serving as the dean of the University of Michigan Law School (as it was now known). He joined colleagues James V. Campbell and Isaac P. Christiancy on the bench. In 1868, Cooley became Chief Justice of the Court, and Benjamin F. Graves joined the Court, filling the Justice position vacated by Cooley. Together, these four men became known as "the Big Four."

As both a justice and chief justice, Cooley faced many challenges as the state of Michigan grew and changed. Yet, as it was noted in his profile in *American Biographical History of Self-Made Men,* Cooley had an "enviable reputation" and possessed "genial qualities . . . a delicate sense of honor . . . and strict integrity." His profile added, "his eminent public services entitle him to rank among the foremost men of Michigan."

One of the best known cases Cooley and the State Supreme Court heard involved the establishment of public high schools. In his book *Michigan: A History of the Wolverine State,* Willis F. Dunbar explained that the Michigan State Legislature passed an act in 1859 that authorized any school district with more than 200 children to establish a high school. The school board would then put forth a proposal to its residents, who would vote on a tax to support the high school. Some school districts ran into resistance, as their residents believed a primary school education was sufficient.

As told by Bruce A. Rubenstein and Lawrence E. Ziewacz in their book *Michigan—A History of the Great Lakes State,* a group of Kalamazoo, Michigan, citizens filed suit in 1873. They were opposed to taxes supporting a local high school. The citizens lost, but the decision was ultimately appealed to the State Supreme Court.

On July 21, 1874, the Court voted to uphold the lower court's decision, and Cooley spoke for the majority opinion. Rubenstein and Ziewacz noted that "Cooley's opinion helped convince state residents of the propriety of state-funded education." *American Biographical History of Self-Made Men* added that "the 'Kalamazoo Case' laid the legal foundation for the growth of high schools not only in Michigan, but in other states. . . . [T]he case is cited in the major histories of American education."

Cooley wrote many of the opinions for the State Supreme Court, including, as the *Cooley Law School website* noted, the "*People ex rel. Sutherland v. Governor,* 29 Mich. 320 (1874), which remains a benchmark in the separation of powers among the three branches of government."

The *Michigan Supreme Court Historical Society website* noted that during these years, Michigan's State Supreme Court, led by Cooley and the rest of the "Big Four," was soon "recognized throughout the United States as a strong judiciary, ranking with the best in the land. The Court worked with a new Constitution in the formative years of Michigan's statehood. It was instrumental in sharpening judicial procedures and resolving constitutional issues." The professional relationship of the "Big Four" would end in 1875, when Justice Christiancy was elected to the United States Senate.

Cooley the Writer

As noted on the *Michigan Supreme Court Historical Society website,* Cooley was also known for his literary works. He wrote a number of law articles, manuals, and books, the most famous being *A Treatise on the Constitutional Limitations Which Rest Upon the Legislative Power of the States of the American Union.* In this book, written in 1868, Cooley was the first to interpret 'due process of law,' mentioned in the Fifth and Fourteenth Amendments to the Constitution, as a means of broadly protecting property and liberty of contract.

Cooley also wrote *The Law of Taxation* (1876, 4th edition in 1924), *Michigan, a History of Governments* (1885, rev. ed. 1905), *The Element of Torts,* and *General Principles of Constitutional Law,* (2nd edition in 1891) and served as assistant editor of the *American Law Register.* In one of his writings, he also coined the phrase "A public office is a public trust."

Later Years

Cooley was committed to the ideals of private property, equal rights, and political liberty for all citizens. These influences also led to his intense dislike of special privileges for corporations. As a justice on the Michigan State Supreme Court, Cooley used common law in his opinions to place clear limitations on government power. He did this to keep corporations from influencing the government or violating public trust. He felt a distinct division between public and private activity was necessary.

Cooley retired from the State Supreme Court in 1885, and then, the *Michigan Supreme Court Historical Society website* noted, "The later part of Cooley's career was played out on a national level. He was placed on a commission to investigate issues involving railroads." During Cooley's time, the railroad companies committed many unfair practices. He believed the separation of public and private spheres of activity would keep the railroads from financing their own development with public credit and tax revenues.

Because of the abuses perpetrated by the railroads, the Interstate Commerce Act became law in 1887. The Interstate Commerce Commission (ICC) was established to enforce the Act. In 1887, U.S. President Grover Cleveland appointed him to the newly-established ICC. He was elected chairman and established the guidelines for the administration of this first important federal regulatory agency. He retired from the commission in 1891.

In his later years, Cooley received honorary degrees (LL.D.) from the University of Michigan, Harvard University, and Princeton. He continued to be highly regarded at the University of Michigan Law School. In 1895, a bronze bust statue of Cooley was placed in the University of Michigan Law Library. Shaw added, "Cooley's great work, with its high scholarship and profound learning, added greatly to the reputation of the University."

After he resigned from the Interstate Commerce Commission, Cooley continued to write legal articles until his death. He died on September 12, 1898, in Ann Arbor, at the age of 74.

The Cooley Legacy

In 1972, Cooley's contributions to law were permanently recognized when "The Thomas M. Cooley Law School" was founded in Lansing, Michigan, the state's capital. Thomas E. Brennan Sr., one of the founders of the law school, as well as its president, commented on Cooley's accomplishments, noting that "Justice Cooley, a law teacher, constitutional scholar, and small town practitioner, combined true scholarship with professional accomplishment, business acumen, and public service."

In addition to the law school, Cooley's legacy lives on in the 21st century. The law school's website noted that Cooley's writings are still cited in court opinions, and legal scholars continue to discuss his interpretations. Papers that Cooley wrote between 1850 and 1898 can also still be found at the University of Michigan Bentley Historical Library. Dunbar perhaps summed it up best when he wrote, "Cooley was the most notable jurist Michigan has ever produced."

Books

American Biographical History of Self-Made Men—Michigan Volume, Western Biographical Publishing Company, 1878.

Cooley, Thomas M., *General Principles of Constitutional Law,* Weisman Publications, 2 Ed edition, 1998.

Dunbar, Willis F., *Michigan: A History of the Wolverine State,* William B. Eerdmans Publishing Company, 1995.

Dunbar, Willis Frederick, PhD, *Michigan Through the Centuries,* Lewis Historical Publishing Company, Inc., New York, 1955.

Jones, Alan, *The Constitutional Conservatism of Thomas McIntyre Cooley: A Study in the History of Ideas,* Garland Publishing, 1987.

May, George S., *Michigan: An Illustrated History of the Great Lakes State,* Windsor Publications, Inc., 1987.

Paludan, Phillip, *A Covenant with Death: The Constitution, Law, and Equality in the Civil War Era,* University of Illinois Press, 1975.

Rubenstein, Bruce A., and Lawrence E. Ziewacz, *Michigan—A History of the Great Lakes State,* Forum Press, 1981.

Shaw, Wilfred, (General Secretary of the Alumni Association and editor of the Michigan Alumnus), *The University of Michigan,* Harcourt, Brace, and Howe, 1920.

Online

"The Big Four," *The Michigan Supreme Court Historical Society website,* http://www.micourthistory.org (January 13, 2002).

"History & Mission," *Thomas M. Cooley Law School website,* http://www.cooley.edu (January 13, 2002).

"Thomas M. Cooley," *Amazon.com,* http://www.amazon.com (January 17, 2002).

"Thomas M. Cooley," Biography Resource Center Online, Gale Group, 1999.

"Thomas M. Cooley, 25th Justice," *The Michigan Supreme Court Historical Society website,* http://www.micourthistory.org (January 13, 2002).

"Thomas M. Cooley—The Man," *Thomas M. Cooley Law School website,* http://www.cooley.edu (January 13, 2002).

"Welcome from the President," *Thomas M. Cooley Law School website,* http://www.cooley.edu (January 13, 2002). □

Annie Cooper

Annie Cooper (1858-1964) expressed strong concerns for justice, right conduct, gender equality, racial pride, and fairness in social matters. As an educator, writer, and scholar, she did not make headlines. However, as a teacher and thinker who had known and learned from some of the greatest minds of her time, Cooper affected the lives of untold numbers of young people in ways that headlines never could.

Anna Julia Haywood Cooper was born on August 10, 1858 or 1859, in Raleigh, North Carolina. Her mother was Hannah Stanley (Haywood), a slave, and her father was most likely George Washington Haywood, the owner. A precocious child, Cooper was admitted to Saint Augustine's Normal School and Collegiate Institute (now Saint Augustine's College), an Episcopalian establishment that opened in Raleigh in 1868. There she soon distinguished herself and even became a tutor in those important years that followed Emancipation. When she finished her studies, she became a teacher at that same institution, where she met and, in 1877, married a fellow teacher. Her husband, George A. C. Cooper, was a 33-year-old former tailor from Nassau who had entered Saint Augustine's in 1873 to study theology; he died prematurely in 1879 just three months after his ordination. Anna Cooper never remarried.

In 1881 the young widow entered Oberlin College, one of the few institutions that accepted blacks and women at the time. She earned her A.B. degree in 1884 and taught modern languages at Wilberforce University (1884-1885). She returned to Raleigh the following year to teach mathematics, Latin, and German at Saint Augustine's. Oberlin awarded Anna Cooper an M.A. degree in mathematics in 1887. That same year she accepted a position in Washington, D.C., at the Preparatory High School for Colored Youth, which in 1891 became the M Street High School and in 1916 was renamed the Paul Laurence Dunbar High School. Most of her career as an educator would be at this distinguished institution.

Cooper's first important work, *A Voice from the South: By a Black Woman from the South* (1892) consists mainly of essays and papers that she had delivered at various meetings and conferences. It demonstrates clearly the concerns that were to preoccupy her throughout life: women's rights and the uplifting of African-Americans—who at that time were just one generation removed from bondage.

The 1890s were peak years of experience and achievement for Cooper; while racist terrorism escalated, she and other black intellectuals organized and mobilized both to arouse public opinion and provide direction. During this decade Cooper attended numerous conferences, making addresses and presenting papers to such diverse groups as the American Conference of Educators (1890), the Congress of Representative Women (1893), the Second Hampton Negro Conference (1894), the National Conference of Colored Women (1895), and the National Federation of Afro-American Women (1896). In addition to her teaching duties at the M Street School, Cooper also found time to do her first foreign travel: Early in the decade she went to Toronto on a summer exchange program for teachers, and in 1896 she visited Nassau. Cooper traveled to London in July 1900 to attend the first Pan-African Conference, where she presented a paper on "The Negro Problem in America"—the text of which has apparently not survived. Her London stay was followed by a tour of Europe, including a visit to the Paris Exposition, a stop at Oberammergau for the Passion Play, and a journey through the Italian cities of Milan, Florence, Naples, Rome, Pisa, and Pompeii.

Cooper was principal of the M Street School from 1902 until 1906. When she disputed the board of education's design to dilute the curriculum of "colored" schools, she was dropped from her position. She served as chair of languages at Lincoln University in Jefferson City, Missouri, from 1906 to 1910, then returned to the M Street School as a teacher of Latin.

In 1904, during her stint as principal, Cooper had impressed a visiting French educator, the abbe Felix Klein, who would later serve as an important contact when she decided to pursue the doctorate in France. Study at the Guilde Internationale in Paris during the summers of 1911, 1912, and 1913, then at Columbia University in the summers of 1914 through 1917, allowed Cooper to finish her course requirements for the Ph.D. With credits transferred, and two theses completed—an edited version of the medieval tale, *Le Pelerinage de Charlemagne*, and an important historical study of French racial attitudes, *L'Attitude de la France a regard de l'esclavage pendant la Revolution*, Cooper successfully defended her dissertation at the Sorbonne on March 23, 1925. At the age of 66 she was only the fourth known African-American woman to earn the doctorate degree and among the first women to do so in France. This feat is all the more admirable when one considers the obstacles that Cooper had to overcome: Born in slavery, reared in a sexist and racist country, she had worked her way through school, and raised two foster children while in her forties. She then adopted her half brother's five orphaned grandchildren (ages six months to twelve years) when she was in her late fifties

In the latter years of her life, Anna Cooper retained a lively interest in education. Even before her retirement she became involved with Frelinghuysen University in Washington, of which she served for a short while as president. Named for a senator who had been sympathetic to the struggle for equal rights, Frelinghuysen was a unique institution that only briefly became a university before socioeconomic conditions and accrediting requirements combined to close it. Frelinghuysen was intended primarily for adult education and offered evening classes at several centers, providing academic, religious, and trade programs. These were particularly important for the many adult working people in the Washington area who had moved in from points south where educational opportunities for blacks were limited.

Anna Julia Cooper died in her 105th year, on February 27, 1964 in Washington DC. She was interred in the Hargett Street Cemetery in Raleigh next to her husband, whom she had outlived by 85 years.

Gender and Racial Issues in Writings

Cooper's earliest writings, collected in *A Voice from the South*, mark her both as a dedicated feminist and an advocate for her race, with a firm position clearly and logically thought out. Her concern for women's rights grew out of her own experiences. As a student she was not encouraged in her schoolwork in the way that male students were, and her announced intention of going to college "was received with incredulity and dismay". "A boy," she wrote in later years, "however meager his equipment and shallow his pretentions, had only to declare a floating intention to study theology and he could get all the support, encouragement and stimulus he needed". Not all colleges would admit women in those days. Of those that did, only a

handful had ever graduated any African-American women—Fisk leading the way with twelve.

Throughout the years, Cooper's commitment endured, but her vision expanded from the obvious signs of inequality and injustice to the overall situation that created and maintained those conditions in the first place. By the time she did what should be considered her major work—her doctoral thesis at the Sorbonne—Cooper had matured and broadened her perspective considerably. *L'Attitude de la France a l'egard de l'esclavage pendant la Revolution* (Paris: Imprimerie de la Cour d'Appel, 1925) incorporates both sides of the Atlantic and studies the social and racial complexities of the Americas in a global and historical framework. The immorality of the abuse of force is a recurring theme in Cooper, as is the view that slavery could have been very easily ended if only the will had been present.

Although her dissertation at the Sorbonne is labeled as a study of French racial attitudes, it is equally a study of the successful struggle of slaves to throw off an oppressive system and to attempt the creation of a new order. And although this work centers on Haiti and France, Cooper shows that it is not limited geographically or historically, because the whole phenomenon of colonial plantation slavery impacted both sides of the Atlantic over a period of several centuries. In a word, events that took place in antebellum North Carolina, in pre-1843 Bahamas, and in revolutionary Saint Domingue/Haiti were all chapters in the same book of history.

Cooper's *L'Attitude* may at first glance appear to be a very ordinary work, one among many of the studies of events in Saint Domingue that led to the establishment of a black state by slaves who revolted. Indeed, her sources are far from extraordinary; official documents in the Archives de la Guerre and the Archives Nationales, contemporary journals, memoirs, polemic works on slavery, travelogues, and histories. Yet Cooper's work, if it does not make major discoveries or revelations, does possess the unique characteristic of its point of view: it is the work of an African-American scholar who was born a slave, and as such benefits from an insight and sensitivity that elude most histories. For one thing, she holds up positive African images and she praises black achievements; she emphasizes the fact that Toussaint L'Ouverture—the brilliant military strategist and leader of the slaves—was of pure and unmixed African descent.

Intellectual Evolution Mirrored Social Development

Anna Cooper's intellectual evolution mirrored her social development. From the confined environment of a small, newly emancipated rural community, she grew to become a broadly educated and knowledgeable scholar and teacher. From a young woman concerned with sexism and racism, she expanded her horizons to international proportions where her concerns could be viewed and addressed in a much broader context.

This process must have begun with her education at Saint Augustine's, particularly in the classics, when she studied the history of ancient Greece and Rome. Later she would have read some of the more recent European writers and thinkers, particularly those in France and Germany, which she was able to read in the original—as she did also the classics. But her personal contacts appear to have been particularly fruitful, beginning with her husband, George Cooper, who was born a free man in Nassau in 1843 or 1844 (emancipation in the British colonies occurred beginning in 1834). His experiences must have provided new perspectives to the curious and intelligent young Anna Cooper, who later went to see Nassau for herself.

Another important contact was the Reverend Alexander Crummell, founder of the American Negro Academy, with whom Anna Cooper had a long acquaintance. A former missionary in Liberia for twenty years (1853-1873), Crummell was the American grandson of an African dignitary and a graduate of Queen's College, Cambridge His positive views on Africa and on the importance of education find echoes in Cooper's writings. Other significant contacts in Washington were made through Cooper's circle of friends, which, besides the Crummells, included the Grimkes—brothers Archibald and Francis, and the latter's wife, Charlotte Forten Grimke. The Reverend Francis James Grimke, a former slave and graduate of Princeton Theological Seminary, was active in civic affairs in the capital; his wife, Charlotte, the granddaughter of Philadelphia free black abolitionist James Forten (1766-1842) was an activist and a teacher; Archibald Grimke—also a former slave—was a graduate of the Harvard Law School, and served as United States consul to Santo Domingo from 1894 to 1898. These, and others—like W. E. B. Du Bois, Sylvester Williams, and Edward Wilmot Blyden—were individuals with international connections and interests.

It is not surprising, therefore, that Cooper would take the opportunity to travel when she had the chance. Her summer's stay in Canada had a positive impact on her; a glowing letter to her mother speaks of the beauty of Toronto and of the kindness of her hosts. Some years later, Cooper would be similarly impressed and pleasantly surprised by public civility in France, when she visited the Chambre des Deputes, where it was customary in the public gallery for gentlemen to rise when a lady entered, and to remain standing until she was seated.

The 1900 Pan-African Conference in London must have been another important event in Cooper's formation. Arranged by the Trinidadian barrister, Henry Sylvester Williams, and attended by W. E. B. Du Bois, the composer Samuel Coleridge-Taylor, bishop Alexander Walters of Jersey City, former attorney general of Liberia F. S. R. Johnson, and the bishop of London, among others, the conference was held at the Westminster Town Hall and attracted considerable interest. Participants from the Caribbean, Africa, Europe, and the United States—Cooper among them—spoke on a variety of topics relating to peoples everywhere of African descent. The conference ended-after electing to honorary membership Emperor Menelek of Ethiopia and the presidents of Haiti and Liberia—with an address to the governments of all nations to respect the rights of colonized peoples everywhere.

Such exposure on an international scale surely gave Cooper an impetus to undertake the research necessary for her important work that was to earn her the Ph.D. degree. Cooper's great achievement is that she came to understand the importance of these wider, international dimensions, and, as a teacher, to communicate them to her students.

Books

The Afro-American Woman: Struggles and Images. Edited by Sharon Harley and Rosalyn Terborg-Penn. Kennikat Press, 1978.

Black Women in Nineteenth-Century American Life: Their Words, Their Thoughts, Their Feelings. Edited by Ruth Bogin and Bert Loewenberg. Pennsylvania State University Press, 1985.

Gabel, Leona Christine. *From Slavery to the Sorbonne and Beyond: The Life and Writings of Anna J. Cooper.* Department of History of Smith College, 1982.

Giddings, Paula. *When and Where I Enter.* Morrow, 1984.

Hooks, Bell. *Ain't I A Woman?: Black Women and Feminism.* South End Press, 1981.

Hutchinson, Louise Daniel. *Anna J. Cooper, a Voice from the South.* Smithsonian Press, 1981.

Sewall, May Wright. *World's Congress of Representative Women.* 1893.

Shockley, Ann Allen. *Afro-American Women Writers, 1746-1933.* G. K. Hall, 1988.

Who's Who in Colored America. 6th ed. Thomas Yenser, 1942.
☐

James Couzens

From an early age, James Couzens (1872-1936) demonstrated determination and incisiveness. The former enabled him to set a course of action, and the latter to carry it out. These qualities drove the naturalized U.S. citizen to achieve successes in business, industry, and politics. He was an executive of the Ford Motor Company, mayor of the city of Detroit, and U.S. senator from Michigan.

According to folk legend, a child born with a caul (fetal membrane) covering the head will have good fortune in life. The legend proved true for James Joseph Couzens, Jr. Born in Chatham, Ontario, on August 26, 1872, his mother, Eunice Clift Couzens, an English immigrant, kept the caul in a silk sack, giving it to Couzens' wife when he married. His father, James Joseph Couzens, also an English immigrant, was a grocer's clerk before becoming a laborer and salesman for a soap factory.

The senior Couzens introduced his son to the business world by taking him on his sales rounds, where he learned about consumer behavior. By the age of nine, Couzens held multiple jobs. He pumped the organ at St. Andrew's Presbyterian Church, was a lamp-tender for the town, and sold soap for his father, who had started his own soap works. Throughout his life, Couzens would always be happiest when working the hardest. At the age of 12, he left the soap

factory and found work as a bookkeeper at a flour mill, without any experience. However, he lost this job when his employer decided Couzens was too young. In order to avoid the soap works, he returned to school. Couzens enrolled in a two-year bookkeeping course at Canada Business College in Chatham, after completing two years of high school. His first job after school was as a newsbutcher (vendor) on the Erie and Huron Railroad.

Serious Worker

Couzens moved to Detroit, Michigan, in 1890 and was hired as a car-checker by the Michigan Central Railroad, working twelve hours a day, seven days a week He didn't make many friends. Couzens was standoffish, blunt, and had the appearance of a well-groomed banker or divinity student, even when in the rail yards. By asking for the job, he passed up others to become the boss of the freight office in the yards when he was 21. A strict disciplinarian, he wasn't a popular boss, but he did admit his mistakes. Couzens also had no qualms about speaking honestly to his patrons. Alex Malcomson liked Couzens' no-nonsense approach and hired him as an assistant bookkeeper and private car-checker in 1895.

Before leaving Michigan Central, Couzens met his future wife, Margaret Manning. Her uncle was a banker and shipping company executive. Her nephew was a journalist. He rented a room in the Manning house, and the couple lived with her widowed mother after their marriage on August 31, 1898. The same year Couzens became a natural-

ized citizen. The couple would eventually have three sons (one dying in infancy, another as a teenager) and three daughters.

Ford Motor Company

In 1902 Malcomson entered into a secret agreement with Henry Ford to supply the credit needed for building a car. Because of previous business failures, Ford had difficulty obtaining credit and his scheme was considered to be a risky investment. Couzens was brought in to monitor Ford's expenditures, and later for project negotiations. Without sales, however, Malcomson was unable to meet obligations and investors had to be sought. On June 16, 1903, the Ford Motor Company was incorporated with 12 shareholders. Couzens, the next lowest shareholder, managed to purchase $2,500 in shares; his sister Rosetta put up $100 of the sum. Banker John S. Gray was named president, Couzens became business manager and secretary, while Ford held the titles of vice president and general manager of mechanics and production.

Ford and Couzens did not regard each other highly, but were able to cultivate a relationship. Ford was a perfectionist. He didn't want to ship any cars until they ran well. At Couzens' insistence (and with his help in crating them for rail shipment), the first cars shipped on July 23, 1903. Complaints were heard that the cars couldn't climb hills. Ford wanted to halt production, but Couzens convinced him to send mechanics to customers to solve their problems, while continuing to build cars. Reorders came in. By the end of the year, the company had sold some 1,000 cars and all the shareholders had a 100 percent return on their investments. Couzens added the title of sales manager to his responsibilities. Under him, the company experienced phenomenal growth. Describing Couzens' immersion in the company, Harry Barnard in his book *Independent Man: The Life of Senator James Couzens* as quoted in the *Ford Times:* "J.C. was the entire office management—he hired and fired—he kept the books, collected, spent, and saved the cash, established agencies, and dictated policy."

Although a cautious financial manager and administrator, Couzens came up with innovative policies that most thought would lose the company money. Instead they boosted growth. He organized a network of salaried branch managers, then developed an incentive system that paid them bonuses when certain sales figures were topped. In cooperation with banks, he established a loan program for dealers to buy Ford cars through bank deposits. The company and the banks shared the interest. Retaining employees was a major problem—even after stripping foremen of their authority to fire workers, raising wages 15 percent, and reducing the workday to nine hours. Couzens did not believe that the company was sharing enough of its wealth with workers to enable them to save for pensions and periods of unemployment. In 1914, Couzens, who had been promoted to vice president, "issued a revolutionary order" raising the minimum wage at the Ford plant to five dollars a day and reducing the work day to eight hours. Refusing to be cowed, he persisted until the executive board approved the plan. News of the plan spiked sales, enabling Couzens to push for expansion in other cities.

The Ford Motor Company's legal wrangling with the Association of Licensed Automobile Manufacturers, which had begun in 1911, also turned out to be good for business. As Couzens later claimed, "The Selden suit was probably better advertising than anything we could put out." George Selden claimed to hold a patent covering all gasoline automobiles, which the association licensed. Lawsuits were threatened against manufacturers, dealers, and buyers of unlicensed cars, like the Ford. As noted by Barnard, Couzens "became the official voice of the opponents of the monopoly manufacturers." He organized and presided over the rival American Motor Car Association. He read law books, becoming so well versed on patent law that he could discuss and advise attorneys on the subject. Most importantly, he "assured prospective car buyers, 'we will protect you.'" The company had sold 34,000 cars and netted more than six million in profits by the time a court found, in 1911, that Ford Motor had not infringed on Selden's patent.

During his years at Ford, Couzens became a respected businessman, assuming directorates of several companies and serving as president of the Detroit Board of Commerce. He also had other business interests. He built the Couzens Building on Woodward Avenue in Detroit and was president of a shoe company. In 1909, he organized and presided over the Highland Park State Bank (and later, other banks), that became a banking subsidiary of Ford Motor Company. Couzens negotiated a deal with William C. Durant for General Motors to buy Ford Motor. However, a bank committee would not approve the loan, so the deal fell through.

However, as Couzens' prestige and expertise as a business manager increased, his partnership with Henry Ford faltered. Ford had purchased enough shares to become majority shareholder in Ford Motor Company, and he was gradually taking a more active role in the company's activities. Ford overruled Couzens on a supplier contract, vetoed him on sales/promotion campaigns, and, during a tiff in 1914, withdrew his personal money from Couzens' Highland Park bank. Meanwhile, Couzens "found himself shocked by certain points of view taken by Ford," wrote Barnard. Among these were Ford's anti-Semitism and his idea to store the payroll in cash in a company vault. The final flare-up between the two occurred on October 12, 1915. Saying that it did not reflect the company view, Couzens had removed a pacifist article on the war (World War I) that Ford had approved for publication in the *Ford Times*. Ford had an outburst when he learned of Couzens' action. This gave Couzens the excuse he needed to resign, a move he had been contemplating for some time. Before Ford could release a statement, Couzens contacted his friend Jay G. Hayden, a journalist, who spread the story of the resignation to other papers. That day the resignation of the chief executive of the business known as "The Seventh Wonder of the World" subordinated European war dispatches.

Public Servant

Couzens was 43 years old and worth $40-$60 million when he resigned. He could have become a man of leisure. However, he was a workaholic, and one who had developed a social conscience. Couzens remained a Ford Motor Company director and president of the Highland Park State Bank. He also retained his position with the Detroit Street Railway Commission. In 1913 Mayor Oscar B. Marx had appointed him to the commission, whose aim was to convert the streetcar lines to municipal ownership. As an employee of Michigan Central, Couzens complained about the lack of lines. He even threw a few bricks during the 1891 railway strike. Now he forced a referendum on the issue, using his own money to print literature and fight injunctions; but the proposition failed, as it did a second time in 1918.

In 1916 Couzens became more involved in politics. He served as treasurer of Senator Charles E. Townsend's campaign and was a delegate to the state and national Republican conventions. Mayor Marx appointed Couzens to head the police department. This appointment helped to win his reelection, which had been in doubt because of lax oversight of the police. Couzens accepted the appointment on the condition he be given a "free hand without political interference of any kind." His personal survey of police conditions revealed things to be worse than thought. With the goal of "a disciplined city," he ordered officers to enforce laws, took down the license numbers of cars parked near brothels, and eliminated parking in the busiest downtown sections. The city council rescinded the parking order, but later passed similar traffic control legislation. Noted Barnard, "Thus [Couzens] became the father of the city's modern traffic code." In 1917 Couzens became an inmate in his own jail. After issuing a statement about a municipal judge who gave blanket releases (let others fill in the names of those arrested), Couzens ordered the police officers to ignore the releases. When two officers did just that, he was called before the judge for contempt of court. He refused to pay a fine and was taken to jail. Couzens' fight with the judge went to the State Supreme Court and resulted in the outlawing of the giving of blanket releases.

Mayor Couzens

Detroit had just adopted a "strong mayor charter" when Couzens announced he would run for mayor. He reached this decision, not because anyone had encouraged him to, but because he thought he would make "a good mayor." Oddly, it was the streetcar system that probably led to his election. In protest against a fare increase, Couzens got on a car and paid the old fare. The newspapers and photographers were there to record his being pushed off the car. The stunt was repeated by others and led to riots, and abandonment of the rate increase.

Couzens took the helm of the nation's fourth largest city in 1919 and embarked on an aggressive program of construction projects. During the first three years of his administration, he directed the expenditure of $243 million on schools, sewers, hospitals, and streets. Another project was the building of street railways. The city had finally passed the referendum in 1919. However, the Detroit Urban Railway refused to surrender its lines to the city until 1922, thereby establishing the nation's largest municipal-owned railway. Couzens assumed management of the street railway lines in addition to his mayoral duties.

During his tenure as mayor, Couzens tackled the problem of postwar unemployment by creating city jobs and providing doles to needy families. Herbert Hoover, who was then secretary of commerce, would model unemployment relief on Couzens' program. In addition, the city expanded to its present 138-square-mile boundaries. No scandals marred his two terms in office, and he made appointments based on merit alone.

The Philanthropist

Speaking of his wealth, Couzens once said to his daughter, "It's a trust. It's a responsibility, and a tough one." As early as 1915, he began distributing money. He gave Blanche Leuven Brown $10,000 for her home for crippled children. In 1918 he paid the salary for an executive to set up the Detroit Patriotic Fund, the forerunner of the Detroit Community Fund and Community Chest, then served as its president and gave it yearly gifts averaging $150,000 for several years. A million-dollar gift in 1919 helped crippled children by converting the Brown home into a scientific institution. This institution later merged with the Michigan Hospital School, then Children's Free Hospital of Detroit (the "Free" has since been dropped). Another million dollar gift in 1922 paid for a branch of the hospital in Farmington, Michigan.

Other Couzens' gifts built residences for nurses and established a fund for providing loans for business startups to physically handicapped veterans. However, Couzens' most impressive philanthropic project was the launch, in 1929, of the Children's Fund of Michigan. The fund, begun with an irrevocable gift of ten million dollars, to which Couzens added nearly two million more in 1934, supported existing agencies helping children and initiated activities in neglected fields. Principal areas of interest were public health, mental hygiene, research, and orthopedic treatment. The fund established clinics and laboratories in Detroit and out of state. Couzens oversaw the fund as its chairman until his death. Per his wishes, the fund was liquidated 25 years after its establishment. Couzens' charitable contributions totaled $30 million—the sum he received when he sold his Ford Motor Company stock in 1919.

Senator Couzens

Governor Alex J. Grosbeck's appointment of Couzens to replace Commodore Newberry in the U.S. Senate caused quite a stir. "His career in industry as well as in municipal government, plus his wealth and his reputation as a fighter formed a combination that caught the public fancy. . . . Indeed, he rivaled in public attention, quite successfully, that distinctive feature of the year 1922—the flapper," exclaimed Barnard. As a senator he remained true to his convictions. Unlike most politicians, he didn't kowtow to party lines, though often acting with Progressives. Consequently he never built a political bloc for himself. He was

chairman of the Committee on Civil Service for one term, and sat on the Committee on Education and Labor and the Committee on Interstate Commerce during other terms.

"Though wealthy himself, Couzens often employed class-warfare rhetoric as an advocate of 'soak-the-rich' tax policies, and his principal nemesis was Treasury Secretary Andrew Mellon," declared Lawrence W. Reed and David Bardallis in "Jeffords's False Parallel." After Mellon proposed reducing income taxes, Couzens introduced a resolution in February 1924 calling for an investigation of the Bureau of Internal Revenue, which had never been examined before. President Calvin Coolidge, in an attempt to cut Couzens out of the investigation, offered him an ambassadorship to the Court of St. James. His answer: "I won't be kicked upstairs." The inquiry ultimately found nothing illegal, just loose interpretations of the law resulting in large tax refunds and special deference. After the investigation, President Herbert Hoover signed an executive order stating that tax refunds greater than $20,000 be made public, and Congress created the Joint Committee on Taxation of the Senate and House, the first continuously staffed committee on a legislative subject. In 1925 Mellon brought suit for underpayment of taxes against Couzens and others who had sold their Ford stock to the Fords. Couzens was vindicated three years later when it was determined that he had overpaid his taxes by $900,000.

Couzens was undecided whether to run for election in 1924. The Anti-Saloon League, chambers of commerce, manufacturers' associations, and the Ku Klux Klan (because Mrs. Couzens was a Catholic) all opposed him, and he had refused to sign a pledge of support for Republican candidates. When he did declare his candidacy on the 4th of July, he made it clear that party bosses could not dictate to him. He won the election by an enormous majority. During this term he was concerned about the speculation in banking securities. On the Senate floor, wrote Barnard, Couzens "criticized the Federal Reserve Board for encouraging 'a great orgy of speculation.' This, he said, was a 'dumb' policy that could only end in disaster." The stock market crash and bank closings would prove him prophetic. The issues of guaranteed wages for industrial workers, which he promoted after the crash, as well as the need for unemployment insurance and old-age pensions, were also of concern to Couzens.

In 1930 Couzens almost ran unopposed when he stood for reelection. Back in the Senate, he led a revolt that blocked a national sales tax and pushed for relief for the unemployed. Although he tried to keep Detroit banks open, he was blamed for Governor William A. Comstock decision to close them on February 14, 1933. The "Couzens Resolution" presented a plan for reopening the banks, but the plan fell through. On Inauguration Day, March 4, nearly all banks nationwide were closed. One of Franklin Roosevelt's first acts as president was to declare a nationwide bank holiday and devise a plan for their reopening. After serving as a delegate to the World Economic and Monetary Conference in London, Couzens returned home to find a Detroit grand jury blaming him again for the bank failures. The smear campaign ended with his exoneration by a Senate committee.

Declining to participate in partisan politics, Couzens supported the New Deal. He initiated an amendment for a ten percent surtax on large incomes to pay for unemployment relief, which garnered attacks, especially by publisher William Randolph Hearst. Because he wouldn't oppose Roosevelt and had voted against Republican legislation, Couzens knew his party probably would not support him for reelection. In 1935 Democrats began approaching Couzens about switching parties. In 1936 Michigan's state Democratic Party passed a resolution endorsing Couzens for reelection on their ticket. He turned down the overture, saying he wanted to maintain his independence by not being a "turncoat." Couzens also considered running as both a Republican and Democrat in the primary, but decided against this after Michigan's attorney general said he would have to declare a party for the general election, which might be Democratic. He also considered running as an independent, or not running at all.

Further complicating Couzens' decision was his ill health. For years, he had suffered from various ailments. He had undergone numerous operations and hospitalizations. The year 1935 was no exception. However, he could not stand inactivity. Therefore, against his doctor's advice and wracked with pain, he was back in the Senate on January 3, 1936. It was impossible for him to imagine not being busy.

On June 15, Couzens announced that he would be a Republican candidate for the Senate. In the only speech he made after his declaration, he told the Detroit Optimist Club: "I will be entirely content if the people of Michigan say I am through, if they are dissatisfied with my work." He then chartered a yacht and cruised through the Great Lakes with his son and friends instead of campaigning. In August he cancelled the campaign ads that had been developed, then cemented the end of his political career by issuing a statement in support of Roosevelt, saying "the outcome of my own candidacy is neither important to the nation nor to me, . . ." Roosevelt had confided to Couzens that he thought war might be coming; Couzens believed Roosevelt was the leader that the country would need.

For his honesty and convictions, Couzens was defeated at the polls. Within days, Roosevelt declared that "the country needs you in public service," and offered him the chairmanship of the Maritime Commission. Although in and out of the hospital with serious illnesses after the September 12 primary, Couzens mustered the strength to be the honorary chairman of the committee for the Detroit reception of the president. On October 15, he left his hospital bed to meet with Roosevelt in his campaign rail car and join him in a parade and rallies. Couzens was pleased to hear the president giving voice to many of the government policies he had championed. Afterward he was taken back to the hospital. He never survived his final surgery and died in Detroit on October 22, 1936.

Admiration for Couzens was demonstrated after his death. "Suddenly, it was remembered that he had been one of the great builders of American industry, starting from scratch; that he had struck mighty blows for the work-ingmen while still an industrialist; that, after making millions, he had retired not to leisure, but to public service; that he had been a great and constructive mayor before he had become an outstanding senator; that he had been a benefactor of children through philanthropy equaled by few; that he was that rare thing, an honest man in politics," summarized Barnard. The Detroit City Council honored him by passing a resolution to have his body lie in state at City Hall and the flags in the city flown at half-mast for 30 days.

Books

Barnard, Harry, *Independent Man: The Life of Senator James Couzens,* Charles Scribner's Sons, 1958.

Online

"James Couzens," *infoplease.com,* http://www.infoplease.com/cele/people/A0813832.html (October 17, 2001).
"James Couzens," *Political Graveyard,* http://www.politicalgraveyard.com/bio/courts-covode.html (October 17, 2001).
Reed, Lawrence W. and David Bardallis, "Jeffords's False Parallel," *Guest Comment on NRO,* http://www.nationalreview.com/comment/comment-reedprint052501.html (October 17, 2001). □

Ellen Craft

American activist Ellen Craft (c. 1826-1897) is known for her remarkable escape from slavery, narrated in *Running a Thousand Miles for Freedom* (1860). In a daring journey, she posed as a young male slave owner. Craft stands out as a determined and resourceful woman.

Ellen Craft was born about 1826 in Clinton, Georgia, the daughter of a slave named Maria. Her father was Major James Smith, the mother's owner. Often mistaken for a member of her father/master's family, Craft especially incurred the displeasure of her mistress. When she was eleven, Craft was removed from the household and taken to Macon, Georgia, having been made a wedding gift for a Smith daughter. In Macon, she met her future husband, William Craft, also a slave.

William and Ellen Craft are most famous for their remarkable escape from slavery, narrated in *Running a Thousand Miles for Freedom* (1860). In a daring journey, Ellen posed as a young male slaveowner and William as his slave. The determination to flee came from Ellen. She was particularly adamant about not wanting to bear children into slavery. William noted that being separated from her own mother at an early age had strengthened Ellen's resolve: She had seen so many other children separated from their parents in this cruel manner, that the mere thought of her ever becoming the mother of a child, to linger out a miserable existence under the wretched system of American slavery, appeared to fill her very soul with horror.

With her hair cut short, and wearing men's clothing, she became a most respectable looking gentleman.

The plan succeeded. Traveling primarily by train but with steamer and ferry connections, they went through parts of Georgia, South Carolina, North Carolina, and Virginia. Baltimore, Maryland, was their last stop in slave territory. They reached Philadelphia on Christmas Day 1848. From plan to completion, the trip took eight days.

Despite understandable fears, Ellen carried out her part with fortitude and quick thinking. William states that several times alone with him she burst into tears at the thought of the difficulty of the endeavor. Yet she did not falter when faced with the challenges of maintaining her disguise. For example, when she boarded the train in Georgia, she was terror stricken to see sitting beside her an old white man who knew her well and who had in fact dined at Ellen's owners' home the previous day. Rather than have him recognize her or her voice, she gazed out the window, pretending to be deaf. Forced to say something when the old man talked louder and louder, she answered in a single word, lessening the chances of her voice being recognized.

In Baltimore, threatened with detainment for being without documentation of William's ownership, Ellen questioned the official with more firmness than could be expected. Once they reached the safety of Philadelphia, William remembered Ellen's weeping like a child; he also remembered that "she had from the commencement of the journey borne up in a manner that much surprised us both".

Befriended by Quakers

In Philadelphia, the Crafts were befriended by Quakers and free blacks. At first, Ellen Craft was distrustful of all whites. She did not believe that the Barkley Ivens family, white Quakers, could mean them any good. But the Ivens's generosity and gentle ways convinced her otherwise during the three weeks she and William spent with them recuperating from the strain of the journey. While regaining their strength, the Crafts received tutoring in reading and writing. William noted that both he and Ellen had learned the alphabet by stratagem while enslaved. In their time at the Ivens's home, they began to learn to read and they learned to write their names.

The Crafts then moved on to Boston. They were assisted by abolitionists, including William Lloyd Garrison, Theodore Parker, and William Welles Brown. Brown arranged appearances for them, sometimes charging an admission fee, an almost unprecedented practice in abolitionist circles. Continuing to develop her skills as a seamstress, Ellen Craft studied with an upholsterer. (She had already made good use of her ability to sew by making the trousers she wore in the escape from Georgia.)

Fled to England

The Crafts remained in Boston two years. They became the center of highly publicized events once again in 1850. They were forced to flee to England because of attempts to return them to slavery by means of the Fugitive Slave Law. Their former owners sent two slavecatchers with warrants for their arrest. William was ready to resist with force if

At first, the Crafts hoped to avoid the potentiality of such a horror by not marrying until they could escape, but they could devise no plan to flee. They then received their owners' permission to marry and toiled on until December 1848. William stated that it was he who thought of a plan and together they worked out the details. According to another contemporary account, however, Ellen herself proposed the plan of her traveling as white, along with the details of the disguise. In the latter account, it was William who hesitated, with Ellen admonishing him not to be a coward. Whatever the origin of the ideas, Ellen's role was clearly the more difficult one, for she had both to impersonate someone of a different gender and to appear educated. William, on the other hand, was not stepping out of his familiar role, that of a slave.

Plan for Daring Escape

The plan was as follows: Given the great distance they would have to cover, they could not hope to make a successful journey on foot. Since Ellen looked white, however, they might be able to travel by train and other public transportation with William posing as Ellen's slave. She needed to play the role of a male because a white woman would not be traveling alone with a male slave. Suspicion would be aroused in that Ellen would be beardless. She would also be expected to sign in at hotels, something she could not do since she could not write. Her disguise was thus that of a sickly young man whose face was almost completely covered in a poultice of handkerchiefs and whose writing arm was in a cast. She also wore eyeglasses with green shades.

necessary. Abolitionists in the Vigilance Committee of Boston played a strong role in sheltering the Crafts and in helping them get out of the city.

Once again, Ellen Craft showed firm resolve even as she recognized the depth of the danger. Mrs. George Hilliard, who informed Craft of the new threat, wrote: "My manner, which I suppose to be indifferent and calm, *betrayed* me, and she threw herself into my arms, sobbing and weeping. She, however, recovered her composure as soon as we reached the street, and was *very firm* ever after".

Before fleeing Boston, the Crafts were married for a second time. Theodore Parker performed this ceremony on November 7, 1850. Because the ports in the Boston area were being watched, the couple went by land to Portland, Maine, and then on to Nova Scotia before they were able to book passage on a steamer from Halifax to Liverpool. They encountered racial prejudice and delays on the journey from Boston to Halifax, but they were finally able to leave American shores.

In England by December 1850, the Crafts continued to evoke interest. An interviewer for *Chambers' Edinburgh Journal* retold the story of their escape. Although the Crafts were clearly on really free soil for the first time, as the interviewer stated, attitudes toward skin color showed consistency with American views. The interviewer described Ellen Craft as "a gentle, refined-looking young creature of 24 years, as fair as most of her British sisters, and in mental qualifications their equal too." William, on the other hand, was described as "very dark, but of a reflective, intelligent countenance, and of manly and dignified deportment."

For six months after their arrival in England, the Crafts and William Welles Brown (who had gone to England in 1849), gave immediacy to the antislavery cause in travels within England as well as in Scotland. When they attended the Crystal Palace Exhibit in London with Brown several times during the summer of 1851, the ex-slaves were something of an exhibit themselves. White abolitionists made a point of promenading with them "in order that the world might form its opinion of the alleged mental inferiority of the African race, and their fitness or unfitness for freedom".

In the fall of 1851, the Crafts continued their education at the Ockham School near Ripley, Surrey. This was a trade school for rural youth founded by Lady Noel Byron, widow of the poet. The Crafts were able to teach others manual skills as they themselves improved their literacy.

In October 1852, Ellen Craft gave birth to Charles Estlin Phillips. The Crafts had four other children, all born in England: Brougham, William, Ellen, and Alfred. True to her resolve, Ellen Craft bore no children into slavery. And if there were any question about her continued determination to be free, she spoke clearly in a letter published shortly after Charles's birth. In response to rumors that she was homesick for family still enslaved and would like to return to that life, Ellen Craft wrote that she would much rather starve in England, a free woman, than be a slave for the best man that ever breathed upon the American continent.

Running a Thousand Miles for Freedom was published in London, where the Crafts made their home beginning about 1852. William Craft remained a primary spokesman and the more public figure of the two. During the American Civil War, he was active in working against support for the Confederacy, and between 1862 and 1867, he made two trips to Dahomey. Ellen was active in the British and Foreign Freed-men's Aid Society. In November 1865, the Lushingtons, English abolitionists who had helped the Crafts attend the Ockham School, brought Ellen Craft's mother to London.

Returned to U.S.

In 1868 the Crafts returned with two of their children to the United States. After working for a while in Boston, they returned to Georgia, where they purchased land in Bryan County, near Savannah. They opened an industrial school for colored youth. Ellen Craft must have had a major role to play, for she forbade whippings in her school and made the plan that when the parents wanted to whip their children, they should take them into the grave yard, and when they got there to kneel down and pray.

In the 1890s Ellen Craft made her home with her daughter, who had married William Demos Crum, a physician and later United States minister to Liberia. She died in Charleston, South Carolina in 1897. By her request, [Ellen Craft] was buried under a favorite tree on her Georgia plantation. William Craft survived her by several years, dying in Charleston in 1900.

The Crafts' achievements as a couple stand out against the backdrop of more typical examples of the fragmented families in slavery. At the same time, Ellen Craft stands out on her own as a talented, determined, intelligent, resourceful woman.

Books

Dannett, Sylvia G. L. *Profiles of Negro Womanhood, 1916-1900.* Educational Heritage, 1964.

The Mind of the Negro as Reflected in Letters Written During the Crisis, 1800-1860. Edited by Carter G. Woodson. Association for the Study of Negro Life and History, 1926.

Nichols, Charles H. *Many Thousand Gone: The Ex-Slaves' Account of Their Bondage and Freedom.* Indiana University Press, 1963.

Notable American Women. Harvard University Press, 1971.

Quarles, Benjamin. *Black Abolitionists.* Oxford University Press, 1969.

Slave Testimony: Two Centuries of Letters, Speeches, Interviews, and Autobiographies. Edited by John Blassingame. Louisiana State University Press, 1977.

Starling, Marion Wilson. *The Slave Narrative: Its Place in American History.* 2nd ed. Howard University Press, 1988.

Still, William. *Underground Railroad Records.* Rev. ed. William Still, 1886.

We Are Your Sisters: Black Women in the Nineteenth Century. Edited by Dorothy Sterling. Norton, 1984. 62-64. □

George Croghan

George Croghan (1720-1782) was instrumental in negotiating Native American treaties that resulted in

several tribes switching allegiances from the French to the British during the French and Indian War and the 1763 Anglo-Indian War fought on the North American continent.

In his extensive travels in the wilderness areas of pre-Revolutionary War America, Croghan became adept in Native American customs and, in more than one case, languages. These skills prompted the British occupational forces to enlist him to negotiate with several tribes to be more friendly toward the French. On one occasion, Croghan was held hostage by Native Americans, but otherwise he moved freely throughout the areas of Kentucky, Ohio, Pennsylvania, and Michigan. In addition to serving as an appointed British official in the areas west of the Appalachian Mountains, Croghan was also a fur trapper and land speculator intent on capitalizing on Western expansionism by white settlers. His official capacity with the British government, however, led American colonialists to suspect him of working covertly against their efforts in the American Revolution, and he was twice accused of treason. He was a staunch defender of Native American culture, customs, and religion and also a land speculator who attempted to amass a fortune by purchasing land from Native Americans and selling it at a tremendous profit to white settlers.

Fur Trader and Government Agent

Little is known about Croghan's early life. His parents are unknown, as is the name of his first wife. He had a half-brother named Edward Ward Sr. and a brother-in-law named William Trent with whom he partnered in the fur trade. He fathered one European daughter and another by a Native American woman. He traveled to America in 1741 and became a fur trader in Lancaster, Pennsylvania. His success was attributed to his practice of traveling to Native American villages to purchase pelts rather than waiting for the furs to be delivered to him. During this period he learned much about Native American customs and traditions. He had great admiration for these traditions, which his letters of the time state. He learned the Delaware and Iroquios languages. It is surmised that he learned the Mohawk language as well. Croghan was among the first English colonists to visit Kentucky, and he expanded his fur-trading operations throughout the Ohio and Illinois valleys. By the early 1750s, Crogan had established several trading posts throughout Pennsylvania. His rapid expansion and inability to protect his storehouses from thieving competitors, however, forced him into bankruptcy in 1853.

Croghan's work as a government agent working to secure peace with the Native American tribes began in February 1750, when he and Andrew Montour represented the colonial government of Pennsylvania at Big Mineamis Creek. In 1751, he accepted a mission in Logstown, where several Native American tribes held a large council. In June 1753, his Native American trading partners were captured by Native Americans in collusion with the French and sent to Montreal. Croghan opened another post near Cumberland, Maryland, the following year. He served as a captain with General Edward Braddock during the French and Indian War in 1754 and 1755 and was with George Washington at Fort Necessity. In 1756, Superintendent Sir William Johnston appointed Croghan deputy superintendent of Indian affairs for the northern colonies. Headquartered at Fort Pitt from 1758 to 1772, he helped negotiate treaties with the tribes west of the Six Nations and north of the Ohio River, including the Shawnees, Delawares, Miamis, Wyandots, and Ottawas, many of the same groups he had become familiar with as a fur trader. Following the conclusion of the French and Indian War in 1760, the responsibility fell upon Croghan to inform the tribes allied with the French that the British would be taking over the French forts.

In 1761, Croghan and Johnson represented British interests at another council of Native American tribes held in the Michigan-territory outpost of Detroit. Croghan was instrumental in ending the Anglo-Indian War of 1863, which began when Sir Jeffery Amherst ordered an end to gift giving by the British to Native Americans. Failing to make Amherst understand the value Native Americans placed upon this custom, Croghan purchased gifts from his own monies to forestall armed conflict. He attempted to resign from his deputy supervisor position in 1762 and 1763, but both resignations were rejected. The Seneca and Shawnee tribes attempted to drive the British out of the territory previously occupied by the French, and the British monarchy attempted to settle the dispute by forbidding new settlements west of the Appalachian Mountains in the Proclamation of 1763. In 1765, Croghan was commissioned to accept a French surrender at Fort de Chartres. En route, his contingent was attacked by Kickapoo and Mascouten tribe members, who killed three Shawnee chiefs escorting him and captured Croghan. He wrote to his friend Captain Murray about the incident: "I got the stroke of a Hatchet on the Head, but my skull being pretty thick, the hatchet would not enter, so you may see a thick skull is of service on some occasions." The angered Shawnee threatened retaliation against the Kickapoo, who in turn released Croghan to the Miami tribe and instructed the Miami to tell the British to massacre the Shawnee. While in custody of the Miami tribe, Croghan corresponded with Chief Pontiac, and the two men met in Detroit to sign a peace treaty. Croghan was able to later negotiate Kickapoo and Mascouten consent for the British to occupy the French forts.

Land Speculator

While arguing for fair treatment of Native Americans, Croghan clearly intended to remove them from their lands and replace them with white settlers and amass a huge profit for himself. Croghan visited England in 1764 to discuss the status of Native American relations. He particularly wanted all treaties to be negotiated between the tribes and the British Crown rather than the American colonies. Croghan also attempted to secure for himself a deed for 200,000 acres in New York. His request was denied, but the Crown issued him 10,000 acres in 1768. Throughout the 1750s and 1760s, Croghan amassed enormous parcels of land along the Susquehanna and Ohio rivers on behalf of business partners and other speculators. In 1868, he negotiated a 2.5-million-acre grant from a consortium of Native American tribes as restitution for his own losses during the Anglo-Indian War. This land extended from the borders of Pennsylvania and Ohio to the Little Kanawha and Monongahela rivers. Called the Indiana Grant, Crogan arranged to include it as part of the 1768 Treaty of Fort Stanwix, which angered many colonialists. Hedging his bets, Croghan attempted to supersede the Indiana Grant with his idea for the Vandalia colony. The 20-million-acre Vandalia included the Indiana Grant acreage and was supported by Virginia politicians. However, the Crown, concerned about the rebellious attitude in the colonies, decided to cancel the Vandalia project to appease potential unrest with Native Americans. According to *Dictionary of American Biography,* ''the outbreak of the Revolution, however, wrecked all of Croghan's extensive land operations.'' He would not recover his losses.

In 1775, Croghan declared his allegiance to the American colonies in their attempt to seek independence from Britain. His service for the British department of Native American affairs, however, prompted suspicions concerning his loyalty. Furthering these suspicions were the facts that many of his former workers in the department had sworn fealty to the Crown, and that Croghan's own son-in-law, Augustine Prevost, was a commissioned officer in the British military. Croghan's resignation was forced in 1777, and, one year later, his name appeared on a list of traitors. He was brought to trial but acquitted. General George Washington tried him later for treason in 1782, but some historians believe that Washington was seeking revenge for a land dispute with Croghan. The two men reportedly had laid opposing claims for the same parcel of land at separate times, and Croghan's claim preceded Washington's. Called Croghan Plantation, the property extended from the forks of the Ohio River to Turtle Creek in Pennsylvania. The Plantation was burned to the ground in 1763 during Chief Pontiac's uprising. Rather than rebuild it, Croghan offered to sell it to Washington in 1770. This angered Washington and, in 1782, he charged Croghan with treason. Croghan died two weeks later on August 31, in Passyunk near Philadelphia, before he could be brought to trial.

Books

Dictionary of American Biography Base set. American Council of Learned Societies, 1928-1936, http://www.galenet.com/servlet/BioRC (March 7, 2002).

Garrity, James A., and Mark C. Carnes, editors, *American National Biography, Volume V,* Oxford University Press, New York, 1999, pp. 753-54.

Johnson, Alan, and Dumas Malone, editors., *Dictionary of American Biography, Volume IV,* Charles Scribners Sons, New York, 1930, p, 557.

Stephens, Sir Leslie, and Sir Sidney Lee, editors, *Dictionary of National Biography, Volume V,* Oxford University Press, New York, 1963-64.

Online

''Captain Croghan to General John Stanwix,'' *The Ohio Valley-Great Lakes Ethnohistory Archives: The Miami Collection,* www.gbl.indiana.edu/archives/miamis12/miamitoc14.html, January 29, 2002.

''Croghan's Plantation,'' *Etna, Pennsylvania History,* http://freepages.genealogy.rootsweb.com/~njm1/etna1.htm, (January 29, 2002).

'' George Croghan,''*Central Michigan University Clarke Historical Library,* www.lib.cmich.edu/clarke/detroit/croghan1760.htm, (January 29, 2002).

''George Croghan,'' *Trade Goods: Midwestern Genealogy/History prior to 1840,* http://www.usinternet.com/users/dfnels/croghan.htm, (January 29, 2002). □

D

Datsolalee

One of the most famous weavers in the world, Datsolalee (1835-1925) was a major influence on the evolution of Washo fancy basketry and is recognized as the greatest basket weaver and designer among the Washo people.

Born in Nevada's Carson Valley of unknown parentage in 1835, Datsolalee learned the skills of traditional Washo basketry, perfecting the intricate design that used up to 36 stitches to the inch. Datsolalee was married twice, first to a Washo man named Assu, by whom she had two children, and second to Charley Keyser in 1888. With her marriage to Keyser, Datsolalee took the name Louisa. However, it was her friendship with and patronage from a man named Dr. S. L. Lee of Carson City in the 1860s that earned her the nickname Datsolalee—a name she was known by for the remainder of her life.

In 1851, disaster struck the Washo tribe when it was attacked by the Northern Paiute, a tribe that had come to Carson Valley when white settlers forced it from its own homeland during the California Gold Rush. In a dispute over the use of certain lands, the Paiute defeated the Washo, imposing two penalties: the Washo could own no horses, and, more importantly for Datsolalee and her tribe, they could weave no baskets. The Paiute wanted to eliminate the competition in order to sell their own basketry. This restriction was disastrous for the Washo people, who had very little to offer for trade or sale without their basketry.

Defied Basket Prohibition

By 1895, the Washo people were living in utter poverty and their financial condition was desperate. In a defiant move, Datsolalee took some glass bottles she had covered with weaving to a clothing store in Carson City, which eventually became the major outlet for her weavings and those of the Washo people. The Emporium Company was owned by Abram Cohn and his wife Amy (and later his second wife, Margaret), who regretted the loss of Washo basketry through the years of Paiute rule and were surprised to find that the Washo women had continued to weave despite the nearly half-century ban. Both recognized the high quality of Datsolalee's work and bought all of her baskets, requesting that she produce more and promising to purchase all of them.

After that, the Cohns handled all of Datsolalee's work, as well as baskets from other Washo weavers. Although Abram took credit for discovering Datsolalee, apparently Amy was the first to become interested in Washo basketry and in Datsolalee herself. Amy kept very detailed records of Datsolalee's work, compiling a written catalog of her basketry. Particularly with Datsolalee's major pieces, Amy's records show the dates each weaving was started and finished; Datsolalee's minor works were usually given only a finishing date or a date when she brought a group of works to the Emporium. With each sale, Amy issued certificates of authentication. In addition, she published pamphlets about Datsolalee's work and took promotional photographs, all in an effort to raise the value of her baskets.

Datsolalee's baskets combined creative and unusual design work with a rare technical skill. She wove her baskets with tiny, detailed stitches, pulled tightly into a coil. In addition, the geometrical designs in Datsolalee's baskets delineated her perception of Washo life and history. It is believed that Datsolalee interwove designs that were part of her dreams and visions. All of her baskets are distinguished by small, repetitive designs—often lines or triangles—woven with exact spacing. Her designs can be found on three major types of baskets: the singam, shaped like a truncated cone; the mokeewit, a conical burden basket; and the degikup, a spherical ceremonial basket and Datsolalee's preferred style. For tools, she used her teeth, her fingers, a piece of sharp stone or glass, and a bone or iron awl.

Found a Second Patron

Most of the Washo weavers first sold their work through the Emporium, but eventually found their own patrons or sold directly to tourists at Lake Tahoe. So, too, Datsolalee found another patron for her work. Every summer, the Cohns took their inventory of baskets to their branch shop in Tahoe City, and Datsolalee attracted attention by weaving her baskets outside this store. Here Datsolalee met William F. Breitholle, who worked as a wine steward at a resort hotel at Lake Tahoe from 1907 to 1916. Because the Cohns gave her Sundays off from weaving, Datsolalee would visit the Breitholle's for breakfast and, ultimately, developed a close relationship with them. William's son, Buddy, who currently owns 17 pieces of a private collection of Datsolalee's work, has said that the baskets were given to his parents without the Cohns' knowledge and are not recorded in the Cohn ledger. Art historians have speculated that either Amy was unaware that Datsolalee was weaving on Sundays for Breitholle, or she felt she had no right to the baskets Datsolalee was making in her spare time.

The Cohn ledger lists approximately 120 of Datsolalee's pieces; however, it is estimated that she wove nearly 300 in her lifetime, including approximately 40 exceptionally large pieces. During 1904 and 1919, Datsolalee worked primarily on these large pieces, some of which took an entire year to complete. One of her most famous, called "Myriads of Stars Shine Over the Graves of Our Ancestors," contains 56,590 stitches.

Though nearly blind in the latter years of her life, Datsolalee worked until her death in 1925 in Carson City at the age of 90. She experimented considerably with design, technique, and color, and, as Marvin Cohadas pointed out in "The Breitholle Collection of Washoe Basketry" in *American Indian Art* magazine, was a pioneer in "introducing most of the innovations that characterize the Washo fancy or curio style, including the incurving spheroid degikup basket form, fine stitching, two-color design and expanded pattern area." Five years after her death, one of Datsolalee's baskets sold for $10,000. In the 1990s, her baskets were considered collectors' items and sold for close to $250,000.

Books

Dockstader, Frederick J., *Great North American Indians,* Van Nostrand Reinhold, 1977.
Leitch, Barbara A., *A Concise Dictionary of Indian Tribes of North America,* Reference Publications, 1979.
Terrell, John Upton, *American Indian Almanac,* World Publishing, 1971.
Waldman, Carl, *Who Was Who in Native American History,* Facts on File, 1990.

Periodicals

American Indian Art, 1, autumn 1976; 4, autumn 1979; 9, autumn 1984.
Newsweek, December 13, 1993. □

Sir Colin Rex Davis

Sir Colin Davis (born 1927) is considered by critics as one of Britain's greatest conductors. His illustrious career has been marked by extended relationships with the Symphony Orchestra of the British Broadcasting Corporation and the Royal Philharmonic Orchestra. He is well known for his interpretations of Mozart, Berlioz, and Stravinsky.

Obsession with Music

Sir Colin Davis was born on September 25, 1927, in Weybridge, Surrey, England. He was the fifth of seven children born to Reginald George, a bank clerk, and Lillian Constance (Colbran) Davis. The large family lived in a flat above a shop. Although his mother played the piano occasionally and his father was known to have a soothing tenor voice, neither of his parents were musicians, but rather simply music lovers. From a very early age, Davis showed a tremendous interest in music. His father had a large collection of classical music, and Davis spent hours listening to composers such as Elgar, Delius, Debussy, Sibelius, and Wagner. By the age of nine, Davis had become something of a loner, spending a great deal of time reading and listening to music. Davis applied for a scholarship to attend King's School in Wimbledon, where the family had since moved. After he failed the scholarship exam, his mother convinced the authorities at the boarding school to allow Davis to take it again. He did and, much to his mother's delight, passed. However, by that time, one of his brothers had graduated from Christ's Hospital Boys School, thereby leaving a space for Davis to enroll, which he did in 1938.

Upon entering the boarding school, Davis began studying the clarinet. He had already set his sights on becoming a musician, a career path generally discouraged by his instructors who wanted rather to push him toward the fields of biology or chemistry, subjects at which Davis also excelled. At the age of 13, music turned from a deep love to a strong obsession after listening to Beethoven's Eighth Symphony on a record his brothers had given him. His family did not exactly understand Davis's musical obsession, but nonetheless remained supportive. One of his two older sisters, Yvonne, told Davis's biographer Alan Blyth about Davis's visits to the family over school holidays. "He thought we were half-baked, probably because we didn't appreciate his

In 1946 Davis was called into military service. He joined the Household Calvary and played clarinet in His Majesty's Life Guards Band. A rather easy assignment, the band played at parades and events for George VI. Stationed in Windsor, Davis was conveniently close to London and often found time to attend concerts. During his two years of military duty, he was able to experience the talents of important conductors such as Beecham, Bruno Walter, and Eduard van Beinum. After his discharge in 1948 Davis began his apprenticeship as a conductor.

In 1949 when a group of musicians from the Royal College who regularly played together to hone their skills and learn new music decided to delve into orchestral arrangements, they needed a conductor, and Davis was asked to fill the job. Forming themselves as the Kalmar Orchestra, the group practiced every Wednesday in the basement of the Ethical Church in Bayswater. The following year he was tapped to conduct the semi-professional Chelsea Opera Group, a small orchestra that attracted attention for its performances of Mozart operas in London, Oxford, and Cambridge. He made his professional debut in 1952 at the Royal Festival Hall in London, where he conducted ballet performances. He also gained experience working with the Ballet Russe and the Ipswich Orchestral Society.

Although Davis was gaining recognition for his conducting, he still had to supplement his income as a concert clarinetist. During this time of transition, steady work was difficult to come by for Davis. Those looking for a conductor still considered him primarily a clarinetist; those looking for a clarinetist had already relabeled him a conductor. The result was several financially lean years during which Davis conducted as often as he could, but also took odd jobs, such as conducting at music camps and summer schools and giving lessons at Cambridge. Davis felt the added pressure of supporting his growing family. He had married soprano April Rosemary Cantelo in 1949; the couple had two children, a daughter and a son, before divorcing in 1964.

Davis's first significant break came in 1957. After applying twice previously for a post as an assistant conductor for the British Broadcasting Corporation (BBC) Scottish Orchestra in Glasgow, Davis's third application was accepted. Over the next two years with the BBC, Davis honed his skills, expanded his repertoire, and gained much needed experience. He also continued his relationship with the Chelsea Opera Group and served as a guest conductor for the Scottish National Orchestra. During this time, Davis's varied works included *Falstaff, Fidelio, The Merry Wives of Windsor, The Seraglio,* and a highly touted *Don Giovanni* at the 1959 Edinburgh Festival.

Don Giovanni

In 1959 Davis was invited to become the music director of Sadler's Wells, an opera company based in London. Just a few months after accepting the job, Davis received his second, and most important, break of his career. On October 18, 1959, famed conductor Otto Klemperer fell ill before a performance of the London Philharmonic that he was scheduled to conduct at the Royal Festival Hall. Davis was asked to step in. The performance was Mozart's *Don*

music enough. We tried to tell him that there *were* other things besides music. Not that we were against his interest in it; in fact we always gave him miniature scores for his birthday.'' By the age of fourteen, Davis had still not been dissuaded from pursuing music. He also had a new, as yet undisclosed, desire: He wanted to become a conductor.

The Road to Conducting

Despite the lack of enthusiasm expressed by his instructors at Christ's Hospital, Davis won a clarinet scholarship to the Royal College of Music. There he expressed his wish to be a conductor. The school, however, found him lacking in piano, an instrument not to his liking, and music theory, prerequisites for conducting classes. Davis told *The Economist* in 1991: ''I was given a clarinet at the age of 11. You can never make up for the earliest years that a child spends practicing the piano. I don't like the sound of a piano. Conducting has more to do with singing and breathing than with piano-playing. I studied singing, and breathing has lots to do with the length of a musical phrase. The difference between something alive and something dead is that the living thing breathes.'' Forbidden to study conducting, Davis began to doubt his ability to fulfill his dream, yet he also believed that musicians were confronted by challenges that tested their resolve. With no formal training, Davis learned his conducting skills by independent study, memorizing musical scores and developing his baton technique by ''conducting'' classical records.

Giovanni, an opera with which Davis was extremely familiar. With a highly talented cast on stage and in the orchestra, Davis's performance over the next two nights was received with spectacular reviews. He had, at the age of thirty two, been "discovered" as the next great British conductor.

Davis's career had struggled to get off the ground, but after October 18, 1959, he became an instant celebrity. "I wasn't ready," he told Blyth, "to be the kind of success that I was supposed to be." Despite his misgivings about his sudden fame, Davis set off on several extended tours, including a series of guest appearances with the Canadian Broadcasting Corporation Symphony Orchestra. The following year, in 1960, he once again stepped into the limelight when he filled in for another famed conductor. This time, Sir Thomas Beecham had fallen ill, and Davis was called on to lead a performance of *The Magic Flute* at the Glyndebourne Festival. Again, Davis's conducting was lauded by the public and critics alike.

Life in the Spotlight

In 1960 Davis was named principal conductor at Sadler's Wells, a position he maintained until 1965. In 1964, he married Ashraf Nani, a student of Persian descent. Also during this time he made his debut in the United States. In 1961 he appeared with the Minneapolis Symphony, and in 1964, he performed at Carnegie Hall in New York as part of a worldwide tour of the London Symphony Orchestra. These appearances greatly increased Davis's international fame. In 1965 he was named Commander of the Order of the British Empire; he was knighted in 1980. At the end of 1965 Davis was rumored to be in line to become the next chief conductor of the London Symphony Orchestra; however, the position was given to Istvan Kertesz. Instead, Davis accepted an offer to become the chief conductor of the BBC Symphony Orchestra, a position that became effective in 1967. During the interim, Davis most often affiliated himself with the London Symphony Orchestra and traveled to the United States for several extended engagements. He also produced recordings under the Philips label, including the London Symphony Orchestra Chorus's performance of Handel's *Messiah,* which won France's Grand Prix du Disque Mondiale. A 1966 performance of Berlioz's' opera *Les Troyens* in London established Davis as the preeminent interpreter of Berlioz's' works.

During the late 1960s rumors spread again, this time that Davis would be asked to take the place of the revered Leonard Bernstein at the podium of the New York Philharmonic. As it happened, Davis was invited to become chief conductor of the Boston Symphony; however, he chose rather to accept an offer in 1971 to become the musical director of the Royal Opera at Covent Garden, a prestigious post he held with distinction for fifteen years. During his tenure at Covent Garden, Davis produced over 30 operas. Most notable were his performances of Mozart, Berlioz, Verdi, and contemporary composer Sir Michael Tippett. Davis served as the principal guest conductor of the Boston Symphony Orchestra from 1972 to 1983. In that year he was named the principal conductor and music director of the renowned Bavarian Radio Symphony Orchestra in Munich,

Germany. In 1985 he resigned from his duties with the Royal Opera to devote himself to his work in Munich and a heavily booked schedule of performances worldwide. In 1988 he was named to an international chair at the Royal Academy of Music. Davis returned to England in 1992 to become the principal conductor of the Royal Philharmonic Orchestra. Having retained his ties to the London Symphony Orchestra, he became the company's chief conductor in 1995. In the same year he was awarded a Gold Medal from the Royal Philharmonic Society. He also served as the principal guest conductor for the Dresden Staatskapelle from 1990 and for the New York Philharmonic from 1998.

Continuing Success

Along with his nearly unmatched career as one of the world's most important maestros to step behind the podium, Davis has also had a productive career in recorded music. His discography is long and impressive. Of particular note are his recordings of the music of Sibelius and Berlioz, which have spanned the entirety of the composers' works. In a review Berlioz's' *Les Troyens,* released in 2001 on the album *LSO Live, Opera News* reviewer Joshua Rosenblum commented on Davis's skill on both this album and his original release of *Les Troyens* in 1969: "The real hero of both recordings is Davis, whose lifelong devotion and impressive discography have probably done more for Berlioz appreciation than anyone or anything else." Rosenblum called Davis's 2001 version "splendid by any standard, with superb sonics and an exceptional supporting cast."

Davis continues his work with the London Symphony Orchestra. He maintains his position void of any administrative duties, but actively leads from the podium and retains his passion for music. In an interview in 2001 with *Opera News* Davis explained, "[Music] isn't in the notes. It's in the human heart. And you can theorize too much. We use our brains too much. These pieces are so emotional. Mozart is expressing something that is more than human."

Books

Blyth, Alan, *Colin Davis,* Drake Publishers, 1973.
Kuhn, Laura, *Baker's Dictionary of Opera,* Schirmer Books, 2000.
Larue, C. Steven, ed., *International Dictionary of Opera,* St. James Press, 1993.
Sadie, Stanley, ed., *The New Grove Dictionary of Music and Musicians,* Macmillan Publishers, 2001.
Slonimsky, Nicolas, ed., *Baker's Biographical Dictionary of Musicians,* Schirmer Books, 2001.

Periodicals

Economist, September 28, 1991.
Opera News, October 21, 2001; November 2001. □

Elmer Holmes Davis

Elmer Holmes Davis (1890-1958) was a respected newspaper journalist, novelist, essayist, and radio announcer. His insightful and candid commentary

**on Columbia Broadcasting System (CBS) Radio pro-
vided the people of the United States with a trusted
voice of reason and authority during the tumultuous
years of World War II. Later, during the 1950s, Davis
helped rally popular opinion against the Communist
conspiracy theories of Senator Joseph McCarthy.**

Davis was born on January 13, 1890, in Aurora,
Illinois. His father, Elam Holmes Davis, was a
cashier at the First National Bank of Aurora and
his mother, Louise (Severin) Davis, was the principal of a
local high school. Davis began his lifelong career in the
news industry after his freshman year in high school, landing a summer job with the *Aurora Bulletin* as a printer's
devil. In 1906, at the age of 16, Davis entered Franklin
College, where he served as editor of the school newspaper.
That same year, he sold his first story to the *Indianapolis Star*
for $25 and subsequently began work as the paper's Frank-
lin correspondent. Davis earned a bachelor of arts degree
from Franklin College in 1910, graduating magna cum
laude.

Upon graduation, Davis was awarded a Rhodes Scholarship to study at Queen's College at Oxford University.
While at Oxford, Davis studied Greek language, literature,
and history. In 1911 he was awarded a master's degree from
Franklin College for courses completed while in residence.
Despite cutting his Oxford experience short by a year because of his father's deteriorating health and subsequent

death, Davis managed to graduate from Oxford with a
bachelor of arts degree in 1912. He was also able to spend a
significant amount of time traveling around Europe.

Began Newspaper Career

Returning to the United States in 1913, Davis took a job
as an editor for *Adventure* magazine. However, in early
1914, after only a few months on the job, he was offered a
position as a junior reporter for the *New York Times*. Over
the course of ten years, Davis moved from sports writing to
become a foreign correspondent and editorial writer. He
covered Henry Ford's 1915 Peace Ship voyage, which was
aimed at putting an end to World War I. In 1920 he created
the cartoon Godfrey G. Gloom, who was a columnist and
political commentator. Gloom became a popular character
whose quick-witted remarks were highly popular among
readers until Davis retired the cartoon in 1936. On February
5, 1917, Davis married Florence MacMillan from Mount
Vernon, New York, whom he had previously met during his
travels across Europe. The couple had two children, a son
and a daughter.

Along with working for the *New York Times,* Davis also
began writing stories, novels, and political and historical
essays. He published *The Princess Cecilia* (1913), *History of
the New York Times* (1921), and the popular novel *Times
Have Changed* (1923). On December 31, 1923, Davis quit
his job with the *Times* to become a freelance writer. As a
freelancer, Davis contributed stories and essays to such
publications as *Saturday Review of Literature, New Republic, Harper's, Liberty Magazine,* and *Collier's.* He also continued to write novels, publishing nine fictional titles by
1936, several of which proved to be popular if not critically
acclaimed, including the novel *Love Among the Ruins
(1935).* During the early 1930s his political commentary
focused on the domestic issues surrounding the Great Depression and President Franklin D. Roosevelt's New Deal. In
1940 he published his first collection of essays entitled *Not
to Mention the War.*

Joined CBS Radio

In 1936, with the world's eyes focused on Hitler's
military aggression in Europe, Davis's attention turned to
foreign affairs. In 1937 and 1938 he published a series of
articles in *Harper's* that examined the deteriorating political
situation in Europe. In August of 1939, while working on a
mystery series for the *Saturday Evening Post,* Davis was
invited by the Columbia Broadcasting System (CBS) to fill in
for popular radio broadcaster H. V. Kaltenborn, who had
gone to Europe to cover the news. Leaving his mystery serial
unfinished, Davis, who had filled in for Kaltenborn briefly
during the summer of 1937, stepped in front of the micro-
phone to become a radio news analyst. What had been
intended as a temporary assignment soon became Davis's
new career.

With the onset of World War II, radio news became
increasingly important. For the first time radio networks
were deploying reporters overseas to keep the public informed with accurate, up-to-date news. Thus, when Nazi
Germany invaded Poland just ten days after Davis joined

CBS, he was in the right place at the right time to be heard by millions of American listeners who relied on radio broadcasts to stay in touch with the dramatic happenings in Europe. Davis quickly became popular among listeners who found his commentary insightful. His monotone voice tinted with a Midwestern accent also helped endear him to the nation. Before long he had an audience of more than 12 million listeners, and CBS responded by offering him a permanent position. According to Alfred Haworth Jones in his essay "The Making of an Interventionist on the Air: Elmer Davis and CBS News, 1931-1941," published in the *Pacific Historical Review*, "Davis's nightly five-minute news summary became the standard of the profession. [Radio commentator Edward R.] Murrow claimed that no one else could explain the *why* of the news in such brief compass; and even Davis's rivals conceded his ability to condense effectively more information into less time than any other newscaster."

Before long Davis's voice could be heard in mid-morning and during the peak listening hours of early evening. He also frequently anchored CBS's international report, "World News Roundup," and provided occasional 15-minute commentaries on foreign affairs. He continued to contribute written commentary to such publications as *Harper's* and the *Saturday Review*. Although he prided himself on maintaining an objective stance during his broadcasts, he advocated a policy of nonintervention in his essays. Having covered World War I, he believed that no good would come from sending American troops to Europe once again. He published articles explaining his position, including "The War and America" and "We Lose the Next War." Underlying Davis's noninterventionist opinion was the belief that the Allies could win the war without the direct involvement of the United States. However, as the Germans marched across Europe, advancing on Norway and Denmark, taking over France, and attacking England, Davis was challenged to retain his isolationism.

In March of 1941 CBS sent Davis to England for five weeks. During this time, Davis, often accompanied by Murrow, toured the war-torn city of London and outlying areas, reporting back to the United States what he had seen in nightly broadcasts. The experience was a turning point for Davis, who came to believe that the United States was under a direct threat from Nazi German. He returned to the United States now believing that for the Allies to defeat Hitler, the direct involvement of the United States would be necessary. Davis's broadcasts helped rally support for the war even though the majority of Americans, like Davis himself, had previously wished to remain militarily uninvolved. For his opinions, Davis incurred the wrath of isolationists, including Senator Gerald P. Nye, a Republican from North Dakota and a member of the America First Committee, which later called for an investigation into interventionist propaganda in radio.

Director of the U.S. Office of War Information

During a March 1942 broadcast, Davis, who had consistently complained on air about the chaos of governmen-

tal news dissemination, advocated the creation of a government organization that could coordinate the war news. As a result, in June 1942 President Roosevelt established the U.S. Office of War Information (OWI) and named Davis as its director. Although Davis had not considered himself the best choice, he rather reluctantly accepted the position out of a deep sense of national duty. According to Allan M. Winkler in *The Politics of Propaganda: The Office of War Information, 1942-1945*, "Davis['s appointment] was welcome in all quarters. The fifty-one-year-old Hoosier with the white hair, black brows, and dark eyes behind horn-rimmed glasses inspired confidence and seemed to be the perfect man to bring order out of the information mess." With a budget reaching nearly $25 million and some 30,000 people on staff, Davis developed a federal news agency that employed the services of writers, editors, advertisers, lawyers, and publicists. The staff also included sociologists, psychologists, playwrights, and poets.

With the slogan "This is a people's war, and the people are entitled to know as much as possible about it," Davis began his job at the OWI. However, obtaining reports from military officials who wished to guard information pertaining to the war proved to be a serious obstacle for Davis. Charged with the task of keeping the public well informed, Davis was only moderately successful in prying loose information from the Army, Navy, and Air Force. With minimal support from Roosevelt, who had created the agency only because of public pressure to do so, Davis was without authority to demand the information he wanted. The military consistently invoked silence on the grounds that releasing information would threaten forces in the field by giving away military tactics and strategies to the enemy.

Davis seemingly proved himself correct about not being the best person for the OWI directorship. He had no managerial experience, and his tendency to look for compromises allowed those within the organization with stronger personalities to take advantage. Along with squabbles among the personnel, there was the larger issue of ideology. Davis believed his job was to do as he had done as a news commentator: provide the public with objective, accurate accounts of events related to the war. Others, however, saw the OWI as a vehicle for propaganda that could serve the war by enlisting and retaining the support of the American public. Thus, during the three and a half years of the OWI's existence, Davis spent much of his time being stonewalled by the military and doing damage control within his organization. He also came under attack from congressional members who declared that he was a pawn of the Roosevelt administration; some even wildly suggested Davis was a Communist. The OWI's image improved toward the end of the war as an Allied victory appeared imminent. With only successes to report, the military opened its communication lines, and Davis was able to put the OWI into more effective service.

Battled McCarthyism

In September of 1945, with the war at an end, the OWI was dissolved and Davis returned to radio as a commentator for the American Broadcasting System (ABC), later becoming a television broadcaster with the ABC network. During the 1940s Davis tried to strike a balance in his understanding of Communist aggression that was feared by much of the American public. Although he condemned Communism and abhorred the Soviet invasion of Czechoslovakia, he understood there to be a difference between external aggression and internal, popular revolution, such as the Chinese communist revolution. He strongly condemned the House Un-American Activities Committee for attempting to rout out supposedly subversive individuals. Senator Joseph McCarthy of Wisconsin set off a massive, nationwide campaign against Communism with the announcement on February 9, 1950, that he could name 205 Communists within the State Department. Davis felt it his duty to speak out against what became known as McCarthyism. During 1953 he traveled across the United States to advocate for rational thinking, defend freedom of thought, and promote the need for civil liberties. Davis won the George Foster Peabody Radio Award in 1951.

In 1954 Davis published the bestseller *But We Were Born Free,* a collection of his speeches and essays. Throughout the book he expounds on the need for optimism, clearheaded thinking, and the courage to stand against those who wished to tear the country apart through intolerance and willful ignorance. As Gerald Weales noted in his essay "The Voice of Elmer Davis," published in the *Virginia Quarterly Review,* "There is never any doubt about the urgency of his message, but he gives it in a deliberate, intelligent, unhurried, and unharried voice, one—his work always is—with wit and irony." *But We Were Born Free* sold almost 100,000 copies. By the end of 1954 McCarthyism had come to an end after the Army-McCarthy hearings resulted in the denouncement and congressional censorship of McCarthy. In 1955 Davis published his last book, an examination of the threat of nuclear war entitled *Two Minutes Till Midnight.* In March 1958, Davis suffered a stroke. He died two months later on May 18, 1958, in Washington, D.C.

Books

American National Biography, edited by John A. Garraty and Mark C. Carnes, Oxford University Press, 1999.
Dictionary of American Biography, supplement six, edited by John A. Garraty, Charles Scribner's Sons, 1980.
Encyclopedia of American Biography, 2nd ed., edited by John A. Garraty and Jerome L. Sternstein, HarperCollins, 1996.
Winkler, Allan M. *The Politics of Propaganda: The Office of War Information, 1942-1945,* Yale University Press, 1978.

Periodicals

Pacific Historical Review, February 1973.
The Virginia Quarterly Review, summer 1995. □

Ella Clara Deloria

Ella Clara Deloria (1889-1971) was a well-known linguist, ethnologist, and novelist whose work is only recently being appreciated for its depth and volume

of detail, as well as for its artistry. Her contributions to the field of Native American ethnography is vast, encompassing translations of primary sources, linguistic texts on Sioux grammar, and even a Sioux-English dictionary. These accomplishments earned her a reputation as the leading authority on Sioux culture by the 1940s.

Ella Clara Deloria was born into the prominent Deloria family on January 31, 1889, at White Swan, South Dakota, on the Yankton Sioux Reservation. Her brother Vine Deloria, Sr., like her own father, was a prominent minister and leader in the community. Her nephew Vine Deloria, Jr., is a well-known writer and lawyer. The Deloria family's involvement in the leadership of their community goes back a long way. In 1869, Ella's grandfather, Chief Francois Des Laurias (medicine man and leader of the White Swan band), called for the establishment of an Episcopal mission among his people. Her father, Phillip Deloria, was ordained an Episcopal priest in 1891. His first two wives died. In 1888, he married Mary Sully Bordeaux, a widow who also had children from a previous marriage. Mary, Ella's mother, was a devout Christian and, though only one-quarter Indian, had been raised as a traditional Dakota. Thus Ella was raised in a home that valued Christian principles balanced with adherence to traditional Sioux ways; Dakota was more often than not the language spoken at home.

Deloria's first schooling took place at St. Elizabeth's school, attached to her father's church, St. Elizabeth's, on the Standing Rock Reservation. In 1902 she attended All Saints, a boarding school in Sioux Falls, South Dakota. In 1910 she matriculated at Oberlin College. She received her Bachelor of Science degree from New York's Columbia Teacher's College in 1915. In the same year she returned to All Saints as a teacher and stayed until 1919, when she took a job that afforded her the opportunity to travel extensively throughout the western United States. Her position as a YWCA health education secretary for Indian schools and reservations also brought her into contact with many Indian groups. In 1923 she became a physical education and dance instructor at the Haskell Institute, an Indian School in Lawrence, Kansas.

Affiliation with Franz Boas and Ethnography

Deloria is held in high esteem as an ethnologist, but in fact she never studied anthropology in an institutional setting. In a 1935 letter to anthropologist Franz Boas, published in Raymond DeMallie's afterword to *Waterlily,* she addressed the question of whether she should have gotten a degree and become an academic anthropologist: "I certainly do not consider myself as such." It was her knowledge of the Lakota language, as well as her general scholarly abilities that attracted the attention of Boas, who taught at Columbia University from 1899 to 1942. Deloria was a student at Columbia Teachers College in 1915, when Boas hired her to work on a collection of Lakota texts that had been assembled in 1887 by George Bushotter, a Sioux, under the supervision of Smithsonian ethnologist James Owen Dorsey. She found the job of translation and linguistic analysis rewarding. Twelve years later, when Deloria was at Haskell Institute, Boas contacted her again, and work on the texts resumed. She translated some additional texts as well, and in 1929 published her first work, an article on the Sun Dance in the *Journal of American Folk-Lore*.

In 1928, Deloria moved to New York to work for Boas. It was in this year that the anthropological study of her people became her primary occupation. While in New York, she met Ruth Benedict, who encouraged her to focus on kinship, tribal structure, and the roles of women—issues that are deftly and comprehensively treated in her novel. Over the next 20 years, she worked closely with Boas and Benedict (until Boas' death in 1942 and Benedict's in 1948) and completed a body of work that added greatly to the field of Native American ethnography. She finished translation of the Bushotter collection and translated manuscripts of Oglala Sioux George Sword written around 1908, plus an 1840 text by Santee Sioux Jack Frazier. During this time, she published several books, including *Dakota Texts, Dakota Grammar*, and *Speaking of Indians*, which she wrote during the 1940s. She also assembled a Sioux-English dictionary and amassed such a wide array of Lakota and Dakota texts (conversations, autobiographies, stump speeches, jokes) that no comparable body of written work exists for any other Plains tribe. In 1943 she was awarded the Indian Achievement Medal and was esteemed the foremost authority on Sioux culture.

After Boas' death, Deloria began approaching her compiled data from an analytical standpoint. A manuscript, which she sometimes called "Camp Circle Society" and sometimes "Dakota Family Life," would later serve as the germ for her novel, *Waterlily*. The manuscript, which was never published, attempts to describe ancestral Sioux culture in all its aspects. In this sense it is impressionistic and idealistic, making the novel format a well-suited way to present the diverse and voluminous ethnographic material. In a 1952 letter to H. E. Beebe, she described her motivation for preparing such a work: "I feel that one of the reasons for the lagging advancement of the Dakotas has been that those who came out among them to teach and preach, went on the assumption that the Dakotas had *nothing*, no rules of life, no social organization, no ideals. And so they tried to pour white culture into, as it were, a vacuum. And when that did not work out, because it was not a vacuum after all, they concluded that the Indians were impossible to change and train. What they should have done first, before daring to start their program, was to study everything possible of Dakota life, to see what made it go, in the old days, and what was still so deeply rooted that it could not be rudely displaced without some hurt. I feel that I have this work cut out for me." Deloria's sense of mission and her personal stake in the material she collected undoubtedly made it difficult for her to be the detached and objective observer that was expected of serious academic anthropology in the 1940s. She always favored a more subjective approach.

From the time when she was a student at Columbia Teacher's College onward, Deloria gave informal lectures and presentations of Sioux songs and dances at churches, schools, and civic organizations. She wished to bridge the gap of misunderstanding and ignorance between Indian and white on a directly personal level that could not be obtained through scientific monographs. In the letter quoted above, she also wrote, "This may sound a little naive, Mr. Beebe, but I actually feel that I have a mission: To make the Dakota people understandable, as human beings, to the white people who have to deal with them." Her non-technical description of American Indian culture of the past and present, *Speaking of Indians*, was assembled with this goal in mind, and was published by one of the organizations that invited her to speak, the YMCA.

Published Novel

Boas' circle of colleagues tended to search for non-technical media, perhaps even fiction, to get an anthropological point across to a wider audience. Zora Neale Hurston was a Boasian anthropologist who did just this to paint a picture of the life of African American women in the South. Similarly, Elsie Clews Parsons was a student and colleague of Boas who edited a book of fictional sketches of the Native Americans of the past entitled *American Indian Life* in 1922. Boas and Benedict believed that Deloria was eminently qualified for this kind of work and suggested that she write a novel about the life of a nineteenth-century traditional Sioux woman. That idea would become Deloria's best known work today, *Waterlily*.

In *Waterlily* Deloria synthesized diverse aspects of her collected data and life experience. This included the texts of George Bushotter and George Sword, interviews with living elders, and the stories and values of her own family. It is in many ways a book that defies categorization. It is a work of ethnographic description, dense with cultural details. It is an historical novel firmly grounded in its geographical and chronological setting. It is a monograph on the social organization of a highly complex society. Finally, it is a work of narrative fiction with an intricate plot and finely tuned characterizations. Like Hurston's 1937 *Their Eyes Were Watching God, Waterlily* does not focus on the tragedy of an embattled and degraded people, but chooses instead to celebrate a rich, vibrant, and healthy culture. References to the impending doom faced by *Waterlily*'s people are oblique and subtle, such as the happy chanting of the children: "While the buffalo live we shall not die!" The book did not achieve publication during the author's lifetime: Macmillan turned it down, as did the University of Oklahoma Press; both houses admired the book's depth of detail, but feared the reading public would not buy it. It was not until 1988 that the book was published by the University of Nebraska Press.

In 1955 Deloria returned to her grade school alma mater, St. Elizabeth's, to serve as director. She held that post until 1958. From 1962 to 1966 she continued her work at the University of South Dakota. Deloria died in Vermillion, South Dakota in 1971. Her work remains invaluable, both to academic linguists and anthropologists for her translations and researches, and to the general reading public for her rich and polished novel, *Waterlily*.

Books

Native American Women, edited by Gretchen M. Bataille, Garland Publishing, 1993. □

Alfred Thompson Denning

Lord Alfred Thompson Denning (1899-1999) was a Populist English judge whose career spanned 37 years. He was known as a fighter for the underdog and a protector of the little man's rights against big business. He served for 20 years as the head of the Court of Appeals, one of the most influential positions in the English legal system. Denning was a controversial judge who was often the dissenting voice on the bench. His decisions were based more on his religious and moral beliefs than the letter of the law and he was often criticized for his subjectivity. Denning retired from the bench in 1982 under a cloud of controversy regarding some racially insensitive views that he published. Denning continued to publish books during his retirement and died at the age of 100.

Early Education

Alfred Thompson (Tom) Denning was born on January 23, 1899, at Whitchurch in Hampshire, England. He was the youngest child of five born to Charles Denning and Clara Thompson. His father owned a draper's shop and his mother did the bookkeeping for the business. Denning attended elementary school at Whitchurch and then joined two of his brothers at Andover Grammar School. Denning excelled in both English and mathematics and won a scholarship to Magdalene College, Oxford.

After one year at Oxford, Denning was called to military service in the summer of 1917. He served a year and a half on the Western Front in the 151st Field Company of the Royal Engineers and then returned to his education. In 1920 Denning graduated First Class in mathematics. He then taught for a year at a prominent public school. However, as Jowell and McAuslan described in *Lord Denning: The Judge and the Law,* "he was ambitious and desired to be a man amongst men." Denning returned to Oxford on another scholarship and graduated First Class in the law school in 1922.

From the Bar to the Bench

In 1923 Denning was called to the Bar and began working in private practice. His early career consisted

mainly of small civil work, such as landlord disputes and traffic accidents. Denning also began writing at this time. He published two articles in the *Law Quarterly Review* and co-edited a book on prominent common law cases. Denning married Mary Harvey, the daughter of the Vicar of Whitchurch, in 1932 and the couple had one son, Robert, who eventually became a professor of chemistry at Oxford University. In 1941 his wife died and Denning remarried four years later. His second wife, Joan Elliot Stuart, was a widow with three children who remained married to Denning until her death in 1992.

After fifteen years of private practice, Denning became king's counsel in 1938. When World War II broke out, he volunteered as a legal adviser to the Regional Commissioner of the North-East Region. After the war, he was appointed judge to the Probate, Divorce, and Admiralty Division. He was not very enthusiastic about the appointment because he considered divorce work inferior to other kinds of legal practice. However, he accepted the position with the hope that it would further his career. He was 45 years old when he started working as a judge. In October 1945 Denning was transferred to the King's Bench Division and became the Chairman of the Committee on Procedure in Matrimonial Causes. Three years later Denning was promoted to the Court of Appeals. Initially the court only handled civil appeals until criminal cases were allowed in 1967. Denning's career, however, focused mainly on civil matters.

Controversial Judgements

During the 1950s Denning began to earn a reputation for his controversial judgements, which were often at odds with the opinions of the other judges on the Court of Appeals. Despite the tension in the courtroom, Denning found the work to be very satisfying. On April 24, 1957, he was appointed to fill a vacancy among the Law Lords. The pace of the work was much slower in his new position and he did not enjoy the work as much as the appeals court. Five years later an opportunity arose for Denning to return to the Court of Appeals. The Master of the Rolls, the head of the Court of Appeals, wanted to step down because of the administrative burden of the position and Denning was appointed to take his place. Denning retained this role for 20 years until his retirement.

A year after being appointed Master of the Rolls, Denning heard a high profile case that bolstered his popularity among the general public. In 1963 he was assigned to investigate a sex scandal involving Secretary of State John D. Profumo. Profumo had had an affair with a young woman who was also involved with a Russian intelligence officer. Even though Denning did not find evidence that government secrets were compromised, his report on the Profumo Affair became a best-seller. Denning supplied the public with the racy details of the scandal and 10,000 copies of the report sold in two days. He also publicly criticized the Prime Minister for not properly handling the situation. A month after the publication was released, the conservative British Prime Minister Harold Macmillan resigned. While the public enjoyed reading about the scandal, many of Denning's colleagues believed that the level of detail in the report and the "gossipy" style were unprofessional.

Professional Legacy

Denning was a deeply religious man who allowed his personal ethics to influence his judgements. He was president of the Lawyers' Christian Fellowship and he noted that the book he read most often was the Bible. He had a strong view of what justice meant and achieving justice was more important to him than statutes or previous rulings. According to *The Lawyer,* Denning once said, "Unlike my brother judge here, who is concerned with the law, I am concerned with justice." This was more than just a philosophy for Denning, but rather was a way of life. In a 1974 speech entitled *Let Justice Be Done,* Denning concluded, "In our society, if we are to maintain civilization as we know it, it is essential that each one of us does all he can to 'Let Justice Be Done.'" Despite such noble intentions, the subjectivity of Denning's decisions made him the target of much professional criticism. To respond to the controversy surrounding many of his decisions, Denning published *The Discipline of Law* in 1979 when he was 80 years old. In this book he explained that the law was outdated and it was up to judges to shape it to fit contemporary needs.

Though Denning was often the dissenting opinion on rulings, he nonetheless introduced important changes to the legal system. Denning impacted the language of the law through his emphasis on using simple sentences to commu-

nicate legal issues so that lay people could understand the law. He tried to communicate his points in a clear, direct manner and often liked to present facts in the form of a story. Many of his decisions were also of historic importance. According to his obituary in *The New York Times,* "He went on to build a reputation as the champion of the underdog, with decisions protecting individuals from exploitation by bureaucrats, large companies, and trade unions." In particular, he upheld the idea that oral contracts could be binding and he introduced the Mareva injunction, which freezes assets during litigation. Another notable decision was allowing Sir Freddie Laker the right to operate a transatlantic airline to New York, introducing competition to British Airways and sharply reducing the price of air travel across the Atlantic.

Denning also fought for the property rights of deserted wives and unmarried women. His judgements in these cases were not always upheld and many men wrote to him objecting to his interference in what was considered a personal matter. In a speech presented in 1959 for the Eleanor Rathbone Memorial Lecture entitled *The Equality of Women,* Denning elaborated his views on women in society. "There is no question of retracing our steps about the equality of women, nor would anyone wish to do so. If women are able to live up to the responsibilities which freedom entails, their equality is not only a matter of absolute justice, but is also capable of great benefits to the human race; and of all their responsibilities, the chief is to maintain a sound and healthy family life in the land."

Retirement

Denning fell out of professional and public favor during his last two years on the bench. He was sharply criticized by members on the House of Commons. To make matters worse, he offended black lawyers and judges with a ruling on a case involving a riot in Bristol when he asserted that the accused were acquitted because of black members on the jury. In *Lord Denning: The Man and His Times,* Jowell and McAuslan quote a 1980 article from the *Cambrian Law Journal* in which the author pointedly stated, "We are witnessing the tragic drama of a great judge whose acute sense of rightness has become a conviction of righteousness, whose consciousness of the need for justice has led him to become a self-appointed arbiter in the politics of society and whose desire to draw attention to defects in our law has noticeably drawn attention to himself." Jowell and McAuslan went on to clarify that, "But whatever criticisms were made of the substance or style of the judgement of the Master of the Rolls, nobody doubted that his physical capacities to preside over his court were unaffected by his years."

In 1982 Denning published another book called *What Next in the Law.* The book outraged the Society of Black Lawyers because some passages questioned the capacity of Blacks to serve as jurors. There was such controversy over the book that the publishing company had to recall it, change the offensive passages, and then republish it. In addition, some black jurors from the 1981 Bristol riots trial threatened to sue Denning for libel. Amidst the controversy,

Denning resigned from his position as Master of the Rolls on September 30, 1982, citing "advanced age" as the reason for his decision. According to *The New York Times,* Denning explained "I want to go while I'm still at my peak."

Denning continued to work after retirement writing three more books including *The Closing Chapter,* which gives his account of the events leading to his retirement. At the age of 88 Denning was still active and even tried a small pro bono case regarding private property in Andover. In 1997 Denning was appointed by the Queen of England to the elite Order of Merit. Denning died on March 5, 1999, at the age of 100 in Winchester, England. He was a prolific writer and an influential judge who significantly impacted the legal system during his tenure. Despite the controversy he generated with his legal rulings, personal style, and sometimes inappropriate remarks, Denning was a well respected lawyer and one of the best known judges of his time.

Books

Denning, Alfred, *The Discipline of Law,* Butterworth, 1979.
Denning, Alfred, *The Equality of Women,* Liverpool University Press, 1960.
Denning, Alfred, *The Family Story,* Butterworth, 1981.
Denning, Alfred, *Leaves from My Library: An English Anthology,* Butterworth, 1986.
Denning, Alfred, *Let Justice Be Done,* Birbeck College, 1974.
Jowell, L.L., and J.P.W.B. McAuslan, *Lord Denning: The Judge and the Law,* Sweet and Maxwell Limited, 1984.
Justice Lord Denning and the Constitution, edited by P. Robson and P. Watchman, Gower Publishing Company Limited, 1981.

Periodicals

Daily Telegraph, March 6, 1999.
Financial Times, March 6, 1999.
Independent, March 6, 1999.
Lawyer, December 20, 1999.
New York Times, March 6, 1999.
Times, August 2, 1987; November 26, 1997.
Washington Post, March 7, 1999.

Online

"Lord Denning," http://www.ciltpp.com/bio_denn.html (January 31, 2002).
"Lord Denning: Judged by Words," http://www.news.bbc.co.uk/hi/english/uk/newsid_291000/291053/stm (January 31, 2002).
"Magdalen History: Some Famous Alumni," http://www.magd.ox.ac.uk/history/alumni.shtml (January 31, 2002).
"Profile of Lord Denning," http://www.muklaw.ac.ug/profiles/denning.html (January 31, 2002). □

Juliette Derricotte

American educator Juliette Aline Derricotte (1897-1931) was the first female trustee at Talladega College and a member of the general committee of the World Student Christian Federation. Feeling a spe-

cial call to participate in black education in the South, Derricotte accepted a position at Fisk University as its dean of women in 1929. Her promising career was cut short by a fatal automobile accident at the age of 34.

Juliette Aline Derricotte was born on April 1, 1897, in Athens, Georgia. She was the fifth of nine children of Isaac Derricotte, a cobbler, and Laura (Hardwick) Derricotte, a seamstress. Her parents managed to provide a home that was warm, affectionate, and secure. The lively and sensitive Derricotte, growing up in Athens, soon became aware of the racial mores of a small southern town in the early 1900s. For example, she learned that her family would always be the last to be waited on in a store. Her desire to attend the Lucy Cobb Institute, located in a section of Athens with spacious homes and tree-lined streets, was dashed when her mother told her that it would be impossible because of her color. The recognition of that limitation was traumatic for Derricotte but critical in forging her determination to do whatever she could to fight discrimination.

Admitted to Talladega College

After completing the public schools of Atlanta, Derricotte hoped against all odds that she would be able to go to college. A recruiter was able to convince her parents to send her to Talladega College. They could just manage the fifteen dollars a month for tuition and room and board.

That fall, Derricotte made the long, rumbling train ride across the red hills of Georgia and Alabama to the town of Talladega. It was love at first sight when she saw the campus, with its large trees and graceful buildings. However, she was shocked almost to the point of returning home when she discovered that all of the professors were white.

At Talladega Derricotte was a popular student and her warm personality made her many friends. One of her professors, recognizing her potential, suggested that she try for a public-speaking prize that included tuition. "Of course, I can't do it," she almost managed to convince herself. But with some coaching, she won the contest and self-confidence as well. Derricotte became the most important young woman on campus, always in charge of something. She joined the intercollegiate debating team, made speeches, became president of the YWCA, and helped to plan student activities. When disputes arose between students and faculty, as they often did, Derricotte would be the spokesperson for whichever side she felt to be correct, yet she maintained the goodwill of both. It was during her years at Talladega that she came to the realization that one should work for something bigger than oneself.

After graduation from Talladega in 1918, Derricotte enrolled in a summer course at the National YWCA Training School in New York. In the fall she was made a secretary of the National Student Council of the YWCA. In this position she visited colleges, planned conferences, and worked with student groups, bringing ideas and building leadership. She is credited with pioneering the methods of work and organizational structure that made the council an interracial fellowship. Through the warmth and forcefulness of her personality, Derricotte succeeded in making people understand each other in the most practical manner. She remained in this post for eleven years.

World Student Christian Federation

Derricotte had become a member of the general committee of the World Student Christian Federation and, in 1924, was sent to England—one of two black delegates—to represent American college students. Four years later she was sent to Mysore, India. In these international settings, among representatives from around the world, Derricotte was always a curiosity and the center of attention, which gave way to respect. In India she learned first-hand from her fellow delegates of the worldwide extent of repression and discrimination in all forms. She learned from a young Indian woman who had been told upon entering church that all the whites must be seated before she could be seated. From a young Korean tentmate who kept her awake until two A.M. she learned that to know the meaning of prejudice, segregation, and discrimination, she would have to be a Korean under Japanese government occupation. She remained in India for seven weeks, living in YWCAs, student hostels, mission schools, the furnished camp of a maharajah, a deserted military camp with five hundred students from India, Burma, and Ceylon, and in Indian homes. She gained valuable insights, for she came to realize that the general committee, with its 90 or so delegates from around the world, was prophetic in the sense that: "This is what can happen to all the world. With all the differences and difficulties, with all the .7]entanglements of international attitudes and policies, with all the bitterness and prejudice and hatred that are true between any two or more of these countries, you are here friends working, thinking, playing, living together in the finest sort of fellowship, fulfilling the dream of the World Student Christian Federation."

Employment at Fisk University

In 1927 .7]Derricotte received a master's degree in religious education from Columbia University. From 1929 to 1931 she was the only female trustee of Talladega College. Feeling a special call to participate in black education in the South, Derricotte resigned from the YWCA in 1929 and went to Fisk University as its dean of women. She entered a campus roiling with the problems of change and in revolt against long-outdated rules, particularly for young women. She eventually gained the confidence of the female students and gradually began to introduce the idea of freedom of action and responsibility for oneself. The students were beginning to feel comfortable. In November 1931, almost fully recovered from illness that had troubled her all summer, Derricotte decided to go to Athens to visit her mother. Making the trip with her were three Fisk students from Georgia. One of them, a young man, was to do the driving. They stopped for lunch with friends in Chattanooga and headed south towards Atlanta with Derricotte driving. About a mile outside Dalton, Georgia, their car collided with that of a white couple. The details of the accident have never been known. Derricotte and a student were seriously injured. They were given emergency treatment in the offices of several white doctors in Dalton, and two students were released. As the local tax-supported hospital did not admit blacks, Derricotte and the seriously injured student were then removed to the home of a black woman who had beds available for the care of black patients. The student died during the night, and Derricotte was driven by ambulance to Chattanooga's Walden Hospital, where she died the next day, November 7, 1931.

Perhaps .7]Derricotte is best remembered today for her death and the national outrage it caused. There was a series of investigations; the NAACP became involved; the Commission of Interracial Co-operation of Atlanta made an investigation at the request of Fisk University and other organizations. Memorial services were held all over the country, and her friend, noted theologian Howard Thurman, delivered the eulogy at the service held in her hometown.

Books

Cuthbert, Marion V. *Juliette Derricotte*. Woman's Press, 1933.
Dictionary of American Negro Biography. Edited by Rayford Logan and Michael Winston. Norton, 1982.
Jeanness, Mary. *Twelve Negro Americans*. Friendship Press, 1925.
Richardson, Joe M. *A History of Fisk University, 1865-1946*. University of Alabama Press, 1980.

Periodicals

Crisis, March 1932.
New York Herald Tribune, December 31, 1931. □

Grenville Mellen Dodge

Civil engineer Grenville Mellen Dodge (1831-1916) distinguished himself as a Civil War general and railroad builder. He served as the chief engineer of the Union Pacific leg of the first transcontinental railroad in the United States. An opportunist as well, Dodge amassed a fortune through land speculation and other ventures. Theodore Roosevelt once confessed publicly to Dodge: "I would rather have had your experience in the Civil War and have seen what you have seen and done than to be President of the United States."

Dodge was born in Danvers, Massachusetts on April 12, 1831 to Sylvanus and Julia Theresa Phillips Dodge. From the time of his birth until he was 13 years old, Dodge moved frequently while his father tried various occupations. In 1844 the fortunes of Sylvanus Dodge improved. An ardent Democrat, he became postmaster of the South Danvers office and opened a bookstore. Good fortune also was in store for the young Dodge. While working at a neighboring farm, the 14-year-old met the owner's son, Frederick W. Lander, and helped him survey a railroad. Lander, who was to become "one the ablest surveyors of the exploration of the West," according to Charles Edgar Ames in *Pioneering the Union Pacific*. Lander was impressed with Dodge and encouraged him to go to his alma mater, Norwich University, and become a civil engineer. Dodge prepared for college by attending Durham Academy in New Hampshire.

Dodge entered the military and scientific Norwich University in Vermont at the age of 18. Despite its military discipline, the university failed to tame the young man's spirit. Somewhat cocky, he often was in scrapes. That same trait would serve him well later in life as he dealt with railroad officials and politicians. A story describing Dodge's treatment of a Negro servant while in college exemplifies his cockiness, though not his subsequent treatment of blacks. The student Dodge, dressed in his military uniform, publicly humiliated his servant for looking at the wrong part of his uniform. Later, as a Civil War general, Dodge would delegate important responsibilities to black men. He also urged President Theodore Roosevelt to expand the civil rights of Southern blacks.

Like his mentor Lander and other scholars at Norwich, Dodge dreamed of a transcontinental railroad. At Norwich, he took studies that gave him the knowledge to help implement the dream. Following his graduation as a civil engineer in 1850, he made a brief visit home then headed to Peru, Illinois, to join classmates. He never would live in New England again.

Pioneer and Surveyor

Dodge's first job in Illinois was surveying for the Illinois Central Railroad. In 1852 he became the principal assistant of well-known surveyor Peter M. Dey. Together they made the first railroad survey across Iowa, from Davenport to Iowa City, for the Mississippi and Missouri Railroad. This survey reached a point near Council Bluffs, Iowa, in 1853— the area that Dodge would promote as the eastern terminus of the Pacific Railway. On May 28, 1854, Dodge married Ruth Anne Brown of Peru. He took his bride to Nebraska Territory, where the couple tried homesteading on his Elkhorn River claim. Relentless Indian attacks on settlers caused them to move to Omaha by the fall. Their daughter, Lettie, was born there in 1855. The next year the family moved to Council Bluffs, where Dodge opened a banking and real estate business. The Baldwin and Dodge Bank merged into the Pacific National Bank, with Dodge as president. Later it became the Council Bluffs Savings Bank. The main activity of Dodge's firm was selling lots and locating land warrants, to which land speculation and bribery of public officials were later added. One of his speculative deals involved buying land along the route he and Dey proposed for the Mississippi and Missouri Railroad and persuading the towns of Omaha and Council Bluffs to sell bonds for it. A financial panic canceled the project, but Dodge would go on to make a fortune speculating on real estate along other railroad routes he surveyed. Another Dodge venture in Council Bluffs was a general store. His second daughter, Ella, was born in 1858.

Over his lifetime Dodge is said to have been associated with the building of more than 10,000 miles of railroad on the estimated 60,000 miles he had surveyed. Along those routes he also platted and established communities, including Cheyenne, Dodge City, and Laramie. Dodge had already made surveys of the Platte River Valley in Nebraska Territory for the Chicago and Rock Island Railway when he met an attorney for the railroad, Abraham Lincoln. Not yet a candidate for president in 1859, Lincoln nevertheless was making political speeches. Americans were interested in a transcontinental railroad even as war was becoming imminent. After Lincoln finished a speech one August night in Council Bluffs, his host "pointed out Dodge to [him] and said the young engineer knew more about railroads than any 'two men in the country'," related Stephen E. Ambrose in *Nothing Like It in the World.* For two hours, Lincoln questioned him about possible routes and the best site for the eastern terminus. Dodge told Lincoln that the best railroad route would be from Council Bluffs out the Platte Valley, a route he had surveyed. Building of the eastward railroad had already been begun using private and state funding. Starting in Sacramento, the Sacramento Valley Railroad, was just 22 miles long. Funding for the westward leg hit hurdles causing its delay. In 1860, Dodge, then a Council Bluffs city council member, appeared before the Congressional railroad committee which was debating the issue of funding. The country faced more pressing matters. Before Dodge attended Lincoln's inauguration in 1861, six states had left the Union. The Pacific Railroad Act of 1862 enabled westward construction to begin; the Act of 1864 solved the financial problems that had blocked the progress of both routes.

Iowa's Greatest Civil War General

Soon after settling in Council Bluffs, Dodge became captain of the Council Bluffs Guards, which he had organized and equipped. The group, later known as the Dodge Light Guard, "played an important role in the opening days of the Civil War," claimed Ames. The *History of the Iowa National Guard: The Civil War,* related how Governor Samuel Kirkwood sent Dodge to Washington in 1861 "to secure arms for Iowa troops. [There] he obtained 6,000 muskets and was offered a commission in the Regular Army. He declined, preferring to serve in the Iowa Militia." Dodge was named colonel of the 4th Iowa Infantry on June 17, 1861, and drilled alongside his men. When other regiments confiscated weapons from his troops, Dodge gave his store the business of re-outfitting the regiment.

Dodge suffered two wounds during the Missouri campaigns of 1861 and 1862. A thigh wound resulted when the pistol in his flapping coat struck the saddle and discharged, explained Stanley P. Hirshson in *Grenville M. Dodge.* The second injury occurred at Pea Ridge. An enemy shell severed a tree branch, striking Dodge in the head. For his service in Missouri, Colonel Dodge was promoted to brigadier general and put in command of the Central Division of the Army of the Tennessee," as stated in the *History of the Iowa National Guard.*

For General Ulysses S. Grant, Dodge undertook special assignments. He and his troops aided Generals Grant and William T. Sherman by rapidly repairing and rebuilding the railroads, bridges, and telegraph lines destroyed by the Confederates. In the *History of the Iowa National Guard* a

source was quoted that described how the troops, using just axes, picks, and spades, reopened the Nashville and Decatur Railway: "General Dodge had the work assigned to him finished within forty days of receiving his orders. The number of bridges to rebuild was 182, many of them over wide and deep chasms; the length of the road repaired was 102 miles." Rebuilding the 150-mile Mobile and Ohio Railroad, the troops had to contend with the Confederates and guerillas ripping up track, wrecking bridges, and killing pickets. Dodge partially solved the problem by building two-story blockhouses near the bridges.

Dodge also organized and ran an effective espionage network. His "spies," declared Hirshson, "saved the Army of the Southwest from annihilation." Dodge identified some 100 secret agents by number and would not reveal their names to anyone, including his superiors. He devised a method to estimate the size of an enemy force based on the space it occupied on a road. The estimates, coupled with locations, of the Confederates, enabled Union officers to make shrewd strategic decisions. Women and blacks were among Dodge's spies. He organized the First Tennessee Cavalry, First Alabama Colored Infantry Regiment, and the First Alabama Cavalry Regiment as agents and messengers. He also armed a detachment to guard runaway slaves. Because Southern pickets seldom stopped and questioned blacks, they made good messengers. Communications also came through wives and parents of certain regiment members. Because of the intelligence his spies gave Grant at Vicksburg, Dodge was given command of the large left wing of the Sixteenth Corps of Army of Tennessee. In the spring of 1863, fearing a reprimand for arming blacks, Dodge answered a summons to Washington. Instead President Lincoln wanted advice once again on the eastern terminus of the transcontinental railroad and related matters.

During the Atlanta campaign of 1864, Dodge commanded the 16th Army Corps, which included the 2nd, 7th, and 39th Iowa regiments. His troops held the right flank for General Sherman's army, earning him the rank of major general. On August 19, Dodge received a third wound that was so serious the New York newspapers reported his death. Hirshson described the incident: "Dodge went to his front lines and looked through a peephole. Almost immediately a Minie ball glanced off his forehead, went through his black slouch hat, peeled a ribbon of skin off his scalp, and laid bare a portion of his skull. Dodge was knocked senseless, fell back into a ditch, and was carried to the rear in a blanket. He had suffered a fracture of the external table of the frontal bone and a severe brain concussion." The injury was not as serious as first thought; he was given a 30-day leave. In November he was made commander of the Department of Missouri. Two months later he was given command of the Departments of Kansas, Nebraska, Colorado, and Utah. As stated in the *History of the Iowa National Guard,* Dodge "oversaw the Indian campaigns on the plains, protecting overland routes to California."

Dodge practiced a tough policy towards the Native Americans through psychological warfare, brutal exterminations, and worthless treaties. In the 1850s the Indians had nicknamed him "Long Eye," "Sharp Eye," and "Hawk Eye" because he could see for miles through his surveyor's equipment, and presumably shoot as far. "Dodge's spies constantly warned the enemy how useless it was to fight Long Eye, who, besides his other powers, could send messages long distances at great speeds over the 'Big Medicine,' or telegraph." Dodge offered the Union Pacific Railroad captured Indians as laborers, who would work for food and clothes, and guards to watch them. When Dodge called for volunteer troops to fight the Indians, most men said the war was over and declined the service. Five regiments of "Reconstructed Rebs" provided the necessary forces. They were made up of Southern war prisoners willing to fight Indians for their freedom. Before the Indians were eradicated, President Johnson instituted leniency. Dodge resigned from the Army effective May 30, 1866.

Political and Railroad Career

The year 1866 was a banner one for Dodge. On March 7, his third daughter, Annie, was born. He also accepted the position of chief engineer of the Union Pacific Railroad and was elected to Congress. Dodge epitomized the politician of the time: a Republican general, lobbyist, and business speculator. His nomination came on the 78th ballot at the convention, after promising employment to a third candidate. Throughout the summer and fall he worked on the railroad. Dodge was in the Rockies on Election Day, unmindful that voters in Iowa were going to the polls. Ambrose related that Dodge "figured himself to be the only man 'elected to Congress who forgot the day of the election.' He never campaigned for the office and hardly ever went to Washington to serve." He declined re-nomination in 1868, but continued to be active in politics, serving as a delegate to the Republican National Convention in 1868, 1872, and 1876. Dodge also headed a commission that investigated the management of the war with Spain.

As chief engineer, Dodge was responsible for supervising the surveyors and choosing the route for the road. Though capable, he was not in charge of construction of the transcontinental railroad or its workers, as he liked people to think. "Still," Hirshson pointed out, "Dodge passed on to the Union Pacific's workers things no one else supplied. Dynamic, forceful, efficient, and fearless, he gave strength and direction to those in the field." As he had done during the Civil War, Dodge took action as he saw fit. He struck back when Indians attacked his surveyors and saw to it that the troublemakers were eliminated from one particularly lawless town at the head of the road construction. On May 10, 1869, Dodge and Samuel Montague, the Central Pacific's chief engineer, set the final spike of the transcontinental railroad at Promontory Point, Utah. Resigning from his engineering position with the Union Pacific, Dodge left his 14-room mansion that overlooked the railroad and Missouri River for New York. He would live in Manhattan for the next few decades.

Opportunist and Self-Promoter

Dodge loved to make money, "irrespective of whether it were ethical or permanent," concluded Hirshson. He speculated in land along the railroad routes that he pro-

posed and won government contracts to supply Indian agencies, even though he had the highest bid and substituted items in the contracts. Between 1860 and 1870 his wealth increased from $12,000 to $350,000. Enterprises run by Dodge and his brother supported hundreds of Council Bluffs families. However, despite his wealth and substantial government contracts, and the fact that he helped build the Union Pacific, the Texas and Pacific, and other railroads, the federal government granted him a pension in 1873 because his war wounds disabled him so he could not "obtain subsistence from manual labor." The pension was made retroactive to his discharge in 1879. From the mid-1870s until his return to Council Bluffs in 1907, Dodge built and consulted on railroads in the Southwest as well as in Europe—on German, Italian, and Russian railroads. Ames related that Dodge "became president of the American, the Pacific, and the International Railway Improvement Companies, and of the Missouri, Kansas and Texas Railroad, as well as of others, and built a line to Mexico City. He was Director of the UP during most of the years between 1869 and 1897." He completed his last project, the Cuba Company Railroad, in November 1902.

In the mid-1880s, Dodge began writing his memoirs. He hired an assistant to compile information and interview people who knew him. The research resulted in the Dodge Records, 23 laudatory volumes on Dodge's life. As noted by Hirshson, Dodge "conveniently passed over [in his lectures and writings] his connections with politics, lobbying, and various scandals. And shrewdly but discreetly he upgraded his role in significant events and downgraded his opponents." Among Dodge's writings are *Address to Army Associations,* a collection of essays, *How We Built the Union Pacific Railway, The Battle of Atlanta,* and *Personal Recollections of President Abraham Lincoln, General Ulysses S. Grant and General William T. Sherman.* Regardless of how he presented events, there is no denying that the railroads he built helped develop and populate the western United States.

Retiring to Council Bluffs in 1907, Dodge spent much of his time organizing his memoirs and being active in patriotic organizations. He donated his records to libraries, but never could arrange for someone to write his biography during his lifetime. In 1915 he fell ill with cancer. He returned briefly to New York for radium treatment and also had an operation without anesthesia. He died in Council Bluffs on January 3, 1916. A caisson carried his body to Walnut Hill Cemetery for entombment. Camp Dodge, the state headquarters of the Iowa National Guard, established in 1905 as a militia training camp, continues to honor Dodge's memory as does a statue of him at the Soldiers and Sailors Monument at the state Capitol in Des Moines.

Books

Ambrose, Stephen E., *Nothing Like It in the World: The Men Who Built the Transcontinental Railroad 1863-1869,* Simon and Schuster, 2000.

Ames, Charles Edgar, *Pioneering the Union Pacific: A Reappraisal of the Builders of the Railroad,* Appleton-Century-Crofts, 1969.

Hirshson, Stanley P., *Grenville M. Dodge: Soldier, Politician, Railroad Pioneer,* Indiana University Press, 1967.

Latham, Frank B., *The Transcontinental Railroad, 1862-69: A Great Engineering Feat Links America Coast to Coast,* Franklin Watts, 1973.

McCagne, James, *Moguls and Iron Men: The Story of the First Transcontiental Railroad,* Harper and Row, 1964.

Online

"Grenville M. Dodge," *History of the Iowa National Guard: The Civil War,* http://www.guard.state.ia.us/pages/Pub_Affair/history/Civil_War.htm#Generals (October 17, 2001).

Longdon, Tom, "Grenville Dodge: Railroad Engineer 1831-1916," *Famous Iowans,* http://desmoinesregister.com/extras/iowans/dodge.html (October 17, 2001). □

Fats Domino

Fats Domino (born 1928) brought a unique blend of sounds to the rhythm and blues scene in the 1950s and 60s that appealed to a wide audience. His rendition of "The Fat Man," recorded in December of 1949, is considered by many to be the first rock-and-roll song ever. Domino continues to perform in his own nightclub in New Orleans, the city of his birth.

Born Antoine Domino Jr. on February 26, 1928 in New Orleans, he grew up in a large, musical family of nine children. He began his love affair with the piano at a very young age. Domino taught himself to play with help from his brother-in-law, Harrison Verrett, a local musician and well-regarded guitarist. He loved all the popular styles of music: boogie, ragtime, and blues. Domino left school in order to focus all of his energies on music.

Shortly after leaving school, Domino found a job at a local bedspring factory. He worked at the factory during the day and played music by night in local nightclubs. A mishap on his day job came very close to costing him his future in music. One of his hands was severely injured by a heavy spring, an injury that required multiple stitches. For a while, it was uncertain whether Domino would ever recover use of the hand for the piano. However, with sufficient exercise he was able to regain most of his previous use of that hand.

Discovered at Hideaway Club

One of Domino's nighttime jobs was at a New Orleans club called the Hideaway, where he earned three dollars a week. By the age of 19 he had become a fixture there, along with prominent New Orleans pianists such as Professor Longhair and Amos Milburn. Like them, Domino was inspired by the rich musical styles of New Orleans. It was here that he got his first big break. Lew Chudd, head of Los Angeles-based Imperial Records, was touring the city in search of promising new artists when he happened to catch Domino's act. Duly impressed, he quickly signed the young musician to a recording contract and paired him up with Dave Bartholomew of Imperial to write the song that be-

came his signature number and established him forever as "Fats" in the mind of his fans. "The Fat Man," that drew heavily from a song entitled "Junkers Blues," was recorded in December 1949 in the J and M Studios of Cosimo Matassa, along with seven other tracks. The song became Domino's first big rhythm and blues hit and is considered by many music industry observers to be the first genuine rock and roll song ever recorded. Fred Ward, writing in *Rock of Ages: The Rolling Stone History of Rock and Roll,* said of Domino's first big hit: "What better song to introduce the young singer than the one he opened with. . . ." The record took off, Ward reported, "winning Imperial some prominence in the rhythm-and-blues world and, more important, on its charts.

Chudd's Imperial recording label, which focused on unknown rhythm and blues talent from the Deep South, had experienced rapid growth in the years following the end of World War II. Bartholomew, a prominent trumpet player and composer, became Domino's producer and bandleader for most of the 1950s and 60s and co-wrote virtually all of the performer's best-known hits. Bartholomew, who remained closely involved with Domino well into the 1980s, was a trained musician who perfectly complemented Domino's unschooled but brilliant musical instincts. Domino never learned to read music. He once described to Irwin Stambler, author of *The Encyclopedia of Pop, Rock, and Soul,* how he and Bartholomew collaborated on their now-famous songs: "When I get an idea for a song, I sit down at that piano [in his special music room in his home] and sing it into the tape. Then I've got it so I can talk with Dave about it. Dave works on all my recordings and on my band arrangements, and we're together a lot of the time."

Several hits followed "The Fat Man." These included "Rockin' Chair," "You Done me Wrong," "Please Don't Leave Me," and the 1952 hit, "Goin Home." The latter reached number one on the rhythm and blues charts in 1952. Domino dominated the R and B charts with these and other releases from 1952 to 1959. In 1954 Domino impressed audiences at the Moondog Jubilee of Stars Under the Stars, promoted by famed disk jockey Alan Freed, at Ebbets Field in Brooklyn, New York. Other entertainers performing at Moondog Jubilee included Muddy Waters, Little Walter, the Orioles, and the Clovers.

Took Rock and Roll by Storm

Domino took the rock and roll scene by storm in 1955 when he released "Ain't That a Shame," a song that had been previously popularized by cowboy movie star, Gene Autry. His success with the recording of this song was somewhat overshadowed by Pat Boone's "cover" version of the same song. Although Domino's version hit number one on the R and B charts, it made it only to number ten on the pop charts for this reason. White record producers in the 1950s were quick to pick up on the popularity of rhythm and blues for its white singers. However, Domino and collaborator Bartholomew shared in the royalties of Boone's recording. It was with this hit that Domino crossed over from R and B to the pops charts.

Other Domino songs that rose to the top of the R and B charts in 1955 included "All by Myself" and "Poor Me." That same year, Imperial Records cut his first long-playing (LP) album. Entitled "Rock and Rollin' With Fats Domino," the album was released on March 1, 1956. Among his big hits in 1956 were "I'm in Love Again," "My Blue Heaven," "Blue Monday," and "Blueberry Hill," Domino's version of a song first made popular by Louis Armstrong. In July of 1956, "I'm in Love Again" hit the top of the R and B charts and climbed to number three on the pop charts. At year's end, "Blueberry Hill" topped out at number two on the pop charts, having already occupied the top spot on the R and B charts for 11 straight weeks. Domino's success in the mid-1950s made him a fixture in most of the period's touring rock and roll shows. In early 1957, Domino got top billing in the three-month "Biggest Show of Stars for '57," a tour that also featured such popular rock and R and B performers as Chuck Berry, Laverne Baker, Clyde McPhatter, and the Moonglows. Gene Busnar, author of *It's Rock'n' Roll,* explained Domino's success on the pop charts this way: "Most of Fats' songs were less raw and sexually explicit than most other blues-based singers. He was, therefore, more acceptable to the pop audience."

Debut in Films

Hoping to expand his horizons, Domino looked to Hollywood. He first appeared with Big Joe Turner in *Shake, Rattle, and Roll,* singing three of his big hits. In 1957 he appeared in *The Girl Can't Help It,* a rock and roll movie that is still considered by many to be the best ever made. The film featured Domino singing his big hit, "Blue Mon-

day." Other motion pictures in which Domino appeared included *Jamboree* and *The Big Beat.*

Other Domino songs that fared well on the pop charts included "I'm Walkin'," which made it to number four in April of 1957; "I Want to Walk You Home," climbing to number eight the week of September 14, 1959; and "Walking to New Orleans," which made it into the top ten on the pop charts in mid-1960. "Walking to New Orleans," which climbed to number two on the R and B charts, was the last of Domino's songs to hit the top ten on the pop charts.

In April of 1963, Domino left the Imperial label after nearly 14 years to sign with ABC-Paramount. For ABC-Paramount, he had a modest hit with "Red Sails in the Sunset." He switched labels fairly often in the 1960s, recording also on the Mercury and Reprise labels. In 1968 Domino released his version of "Lady Madonna" on the Reprise label. Written by Paul McCartney for the Beatles in a style reminiscent of Domino's, the song was given the full New Orleans treatment in Domino's cover version. It was the last of Domino's songs to make it onto *Billboard's* Top 100 Pop Singles chart. When recording industry executives began pressuring Domino to update his style in order to appeal to changing musical tastes, he quit recording altogether. Interviewed by Hans J. Massaquoi of *Ebony,* Domino explained, "I refused to change. I had to stick to my own style that I've always used, or it just wouldn't be me."

Focused on Personal Appearances

With his recording career at least temporarily terminated, Domino began concentrating most of his energies on public appearances, focusing in particular on Las Vegas. He signed a long-term contract with the Flamingo Hotel and Casino but soon got himself into trouble gambling during his off-hours. He got started on the slots but soon graduated to playing craps. According to Massaquoi of *Ebony,* Domino gambled away about two million dollars over a ten-year period. It took the performer a while to admit that he had a serious problem with gambling. However, he eventually took steps to wean himself away from the craps tables, a goal Domino claimed to have reached by 1972.

On January 23, 1986, Domino was formally inducted into the Rock and Roll Hall of Fame at its first induction dinner, held in New York City. Presenting Domino with a plaque marking his selection for this honor was popular singer/pianist Billy Joel. It seemed altogether fitting that Domino was among the first to be enshrined in the Rock and Roll Hall of Fame, considering that he had sold more records—some 65 million—than any other Fifties-era rocker except Elvis Presley. The following year, Domino received the Grammy Lifetime Achievement Award.

In 1991, EMI-owner of the Imperial label's music catalog released a boxed set of Domino's greatest hits. Domino returned to the recording studio two years later—the first time he'd done so in a quarter-century. The recording session produced an album entitled *Christmas is a Special Day,* released on the EMI/Right Stuff label on November 1, 1993. Interviewed during the recording session, Domino looked back on his long and rewarding career, saying: "People don't know what they've done for me. They always tell me, 'Oh, Fats, thanks for so many years of good music.' And I'll be thankin' them before they're finished thankin' me!"

In March of 1995, the Rhythm and Blues Foundation of Washington, D.C., honored Domino. As one of the recipients of the foundation's annual Pioneer Awards, he was given the Ray Charles Lifetime Achievement Award. This foundation honors those who create "an art form that is a fountainhead for contemporary popular music and a life-blood of American culture." Other recipients of these awards included the Moonglows, the Marvelettes, Inez and Charlie Foxx, and Cissy Houston. That same year Domino toured Great Britain with fellow rock artists James Brown and Chuck Berry. However, the trip was cut short when the 67-year-old Domino was hospitalized for an infection and exhaustion.

Domino and his wife, Rosemary, continue to live in New Orleans, the city of the singer's birth. They have raised eight children—Antoinette, Antoine III, Andrea, Andre, Anatole, Anola, Adonica, and Antonio. Domino still performs occasionally at his club in the city's French Quarter.

Books

Busnar, Gene, *It's Rock'n' Roll,* Messner, 1979.
Contemporary Musicians, Gale Research, 1989.
Ward, Ed, Geoffrey Stokes, and Ken Tucker. *Rock of Ages: The Rolling Stone History of Rock and Roll,* Summit Books, 1986.

Periodicals

Billboard, January 28, 1995.
Time, May 29, 1995.

Online

"Fats Domino," Chuck Berry-Mr. Rock and Roll, http://www .chuckberry.de/fatsdomino.htm (November 4, 2001).
"Fats Domino-Biography," Yahoo! Music, http://musicfinder .yahoo.com (November 4, 2001).
"Fats Domino: Performer," Rock and Roll Hall of Fame and Museum, http://www.rockhall.com/hof/inductee.asp?id=91 (November 4, 2001). □

William Joseph Donovan

The first head of the Office of Strategic Services (OSS) during World War II, William J. Donovan (1883-1959) ran the agency that served as the direct precursor to the Central Intelligence Agency (CIA). Before his career in intelligence, however, Donovan was one of the best known lawyers in the country, reaching the post of assistant Attorney General during the administration of Herbert Hoover in the 1920s. After his term at OSS, Donovan remained both an influential lawyer and an expert in the world of espionage. Appointed ambassador to Thailand in 1953 for a brief period, Donovan continued to use the latter skills in building up America's resistance to

Communism in the Far East. At the time of his death in 1959, Donovan was remembered as a public servant and statesman in addition to his success as an attorney and businessman.

In contrast to his later elite connections and world travels, William Joseph Donovan was born into working-class surroundings in Buffalo, New York, on January 1, 1883. His father, the son of Irish immigrants, dropped out of school early in life and eventually worked as a railroad superintendent. However, Donovan's father insisted that his children be well read and managed to send them to parochial schools at significant expense. The oldest surviving child in the family, William Donovan realized his father's ambition; after completing his college degree at New York City's Columbia University, where he gained a reputation as "Wild Bill Donovan" for his exploits on the football field, he then entered the university's law school. Although his grades were bad enough to put him on the verge of flunking out, Donovan nevertheless obtained his law degree in 1908. According to one story, it was future Supreme Court Justice Harlan Stone, then the dean of the law school, who intervened to keep Donovan from being expelled. While Donovan's academic work was substandard, Stone was impressed by his forceful personality and ability to maintain a clear argument during debates.

Returning to Buffalo to enter private practice, Donovan soon joined the elite of the city as a successful lawyer with a promising future. His status was confirmed when he married the former Ruth Rumsey in July 1914; a product of a family said to be Buffalo's wealthiest, the marriage elevated Donovan into the city's upper crust. By the time he was thirty, then, Donovan had traveled far from his rather humble origins in Buffalo's First Ward, an Irish enclave for generations. His rise was not without criticism, however; when he formed a National Guard unit that took up arms against striking railcar workers in 1914, Donovan was assailed as an agent of class warfare. The charge would later be revived against Donovan during his political campaign for governor of New York in 1932 and helped to defeat him at the polls. Yet Donovan refused to see his actions as anything more than enforcing law and order in the streets, even if such a position made him unpopular with voters.

Lawyer and War Hero

Although he was a wealthy and influential lawyer at the time of World War I, Donovan answered a request to help out with relief efforts under Herbert Hoover in 1916, just before America entered the conflict. Traveling to Europe, Donovan aided efforts to get food to starving people in neutral nations; after America entered the war, he also served as the leader of the First Battalion of the 69th Infantry Regiment of the New York National Guard. In this capacity, he was wounded in October 1918, just a month before the war ended. For his effort, he received the Purple Heart.

Donovan returned to private practice in Buffalo after World War I; by that time, his family had grown to include a son, David, born in 1915 and a daughter, Patricia, born in 1917. Tragically, Patricia would die in a car accident in 1940; David Donovan's daughter, Sheilah, also died from a freak accident after ingesting silver polish in 1951, and his wife succumbed to a drug and alcohol overdose in 1955. Given the magnitude of the losses, William Donovan's marriage endured its own tensions over the years. Although he was devoted to his wife, his frequent travel, especially when she was suffering from one in a series of gynecological illnesses, tested their bonds. Unlike her husband, Ruth Rumsey Donovan was uncomfortable in the spotlight, particularly in the fishbowl atmosphere of Washington, D.C., where the family moved in 1925.

Failed Run for New York Governor

While Donovan's private practice had made him a wealthy corporate lawyer, his turn to public office as the U.S. District Attorney for the Western District of New York in 1922 was not without controversy. Personally opposed to Prohibition, Donovan nevertheless was expected to enforce the laws against the manufacture, sale, and consumption of liquor. When he refused to press charges against patrons of an exclusive, private Buffalo club that had been raided, however, Donovan was accused both of being soft on Prohibition as well as deferential to his social peers. The scandal later resurfaced and was cited as one of the reasons that his legal career in Washington, D.C., never reached the heights that he expected. Appointed as an assistant to the U.S. Attorney General in 1925, Donovan was never elevated to the higher post. While some pointed to his soft

stance on Prohibition as the reason, other observers noted that the potential appointment of a Roman Catholic as Attorney General would instigate enormous opposition, especially from the then-powerful Ku Klux Klan. It was not the first time that Donovan experienced prejudice because of his Irish-Catholic background; when he had married Ruth Rumsey, a Protestant, some had criticized his insistence that their children be raised as Catholics.

Donovan was rumored to be a potential vice-presidential candidate alongside Herbert Hoover in 1928. The two men had close ties from their days as relief workers in World War I, however, Hoover feared another controversy if he chose a Catholic to share the ballot. Instead, Donovan left public service to open his own law partnership with offices in Washington, D.C., and New York City. Given Donovan's ties to the political and business arenas, the venture was an immediate success. Indeed, Donovan suffered little, if any, from the onset of the Great Depression and continued to spend lavishly on his own comforts. Unfortunately, his air of privilege and success worked against him in his first major run for political office in 1932. Running to replace president-elect Franklin Delano Roosevelt (FDR) as the Governor of New York, Donovan ran a campaign that leveled an unmitigated attack against FDR's New Deal proposals. Although Donovan referred to his own life as an example of the self-made man and heralded his wartime heroism, voters were not swayed. In addition to criticism of his attacks on government relief efforts, old charges of his anti-labor tactics resurfaced, and Donovan lost the election by a huge margin.

Established Office of Strategic Services

During the rest of the 1930s, Donovan continued to build his private law practice with a number of important corporate clients. With tensions building in Europe, however, he was once again prevailed upon to take up public service. Ironically, it was FDR, whom Donovan had attempted to succeed as New York governor, who asked Donovan to serve as a special envoy for the U.S. in 1941. In this capacity, Donovan undertook a series of intelligence-gathering trips, most notably to Great Britain and then the Balkans in 1941. Not only did such trips cement Donovan's ties to the military intelligence personnel of America's future wartime allies, it also placed him in a strategically important position within the U.S. government itself. Soon after completing his trip to the Balkans, Donovan was appointed the chief of the Office of Coordination of Information (COI), one of the first comprehensive efforts of the U.S. government to gather military information in preparation for actual maneuvers. The following year, on June 13, 1942, the office was reorganized into the Office of Strategic Security (OSS), with Donovan once again as its head.

While America had been lackluster in its intelligence gathering during the interwar period, the establishment of the OSS carried with it several ambitious goals. First, its secret intelligence branch would carry out the actual field espionage to gather information in countries around the world. Second, a staff of highly trained analysts would interpret the data and add background information as needed. Third, a counterespionage section would keep track of other countries' efforts to spy on the United States. Fourth, a special operations team would undertake covert efforts to instigate or dampen civil unrest in other countries to further American objectives. Finally, the OSS would also direct morale operations to spread propaganda aimed at undermining public support of the war in enemy nations.

Given the initial lack of espionage experience among his team, Donovan delivered impressive results with the OSS that significantly aided the Allies' efforts in the duration of the war. The OSS was particularly helpful in gathering intelligence in preparation for the Allied invasion of southern Europe, an effort that was crucial in reducing the casualty rate among Allied troops. For his work, Donovan received awards including the Knight Commander of the Most Excellent Order of the British Empire in 1945 and the Oak Leaf Cluster added to his U.S. Distinguished Service Medal in 1946. Just weeks after the war's end in early September 1945, however, the OSS was disbanded. While most observers praised Donovan's ability to raise the professionalism of American intelligence-gathering efforts, others deemed him too controversial and partisan a figure to continue leading such a program. Instead, the CIA was created under the National Security Act of 1947 as an independent agency that would undertake both wartime and peacetime espionage efforts.

Cold Warrior

After his departure at the demise of the OSS, Donovan once again took up his private practice and business concerns; however, he remained keenly interested in public affairs. Although his efforts to secure the Republican Party nomination as a Senate candidate failed, he remained well respected as a government advisor. As a sign of his stature during the Cold War, Donovan secured an appointment as U.S. Ambassador to Thailand (or Siam, as the country in Southeast Asia was then known) in 1953. Although the post might have seemed an unusual one for the longtime government official, Donovan's intelligence-gathering capabilities were crucial in furthering America's efforts in the region. In particular, the Eisenhower administration had cast a suspicious eye on the designs of the People's Republic of China over the region, tensions that would eventually lead to the Vietnam War.

A series of strokes limited Donovan's effectiveness as ambassador, however, and he returned to the United States in 1954. Faced with the tragic deaths of his granddaughter in 1951 and daughter-in-law in 1955, Donovan's own health deteriorated in the last year of his life, when he was largely incapacitated. Donovan died on February 8, 1959, in Walter Reed Hospital in Washington, D.C. Remembered at the time of his death as an effective administrator and supreme loyalist to America's interests, Donovan was later viewed as a symbol of America's efforts against Communism and Third World movements during the early years of the Cold War.

Books

Brown, Anthony Cave, *Wild Bill Donovan: The Last Hero,* Times Books, 1982.

Dunlop, Richard, *Twice Thirty: Donovan: America's Master Spy,* Rand McNally and Company, 1982.

Hersh, Burton, *The Old Boys: The American Elite and the Origins of the CIA,* Charles Scribner's Sons, 1992.

McCormick, Thomas J., *America's Half-Century: United States Foreign Policy in the Cold War and After,* Johns Hopkins University Press, 1995.

Troy, Thomas F., *Donovan and the CIA: A History of the Establishment of the Central Intelligence Agency,* Aletheia Books, 1981. □

Thomas Andrew Dorsey

Thomas Andrew Dorsey (1900-1993), often called the Father of Gospel Music, migrated from Atlanta to Chicago as a young man, thus exemplifying the experience of many southern blacks of his day. This journey is also critical to an understanding of what Michael W. Harris called "the rise of gospel blues" in his book of that title, which chronicles the role Dorsey's music played in urban churches.

There was a great deal of early resistance to Dorsey's work, partly because it was rooted in the rural southern African American culture from which the old-line urban churches sought to distance themselves in favor of assimilation. These churches discouraged expressive congregational participation and attempted to incorporate white church traditions in both service and music. In addition, the blues factor of the gospel blues equation had associations with secular venues and activities often discouraged by the church. It is perhaps Dorsey's greatest achievement that he was able to overcome this opposition and thus preserve important aspects of black musical expression as it had existed in both the spiritual and secular realms.

Dorsey, one of five children, was born in Villa Rica, Georgia on July 1, 1900, but soon moved with his family to Atlanta. His father was a Baptist minister with a flamboyant pulpit style. His mother played a portable organ and piano wherever the elder Dorsey preached. Young Dorsey was influenced musically by his mother's brother, an itinerant blues musician. He also was influenced by her brother-in-law, a teacher who favored shaped note singing—also known as "fasola" (fa-so-la), a rambunctious, 19th-century congregational style propagated by songbooks and popular in the rural South in which four distinct shapes (the diamond, for one) correspond to specific notes on the musical scale. In *The Rise of Gospel Blues* Michael Harris noted, "Other than slave spirituals, the white Protestant hymns and shaped note music, Dorsey describes a type of 'moaning' as the only other style of religious song he recalls." He left school early and was soon hanging around theaters and dance halls. His association with musicians there encouraged him to practice at home on his mother's organ, and by age 12, he claimed that he could play the piano very well. Before long he was earning money playing at private parties and bordellos. In order to improve his skills and identify himself as a professional, he briefly took piano lessons from a teacher associated with Morehouse College, as well as a harmony course at the college itself.

Moved to Chicago

Dorsey's desire to become a professional musician motivated him to move to Philadelphia in 1916. However, his plans soon changed and he settled in Chicago, then abuzz with both migrant workers and migrant musicians. According to Harris, Dorsey's piano style was already somewhat out of vogue by then. Although he was still able to find work, he remained on the periphery of the music community. Harris observed the Dorsey was held back by his lack of technique and repertoire, which prevented him from joining the union. A further obstacle was the sheer size and wealth of the musical community. In order to increase his chances for employment, he enrolled in the Chicago School of Composition and Arranging. Thus, for the rest of his life, Dorsey able to find work as a composer and arranger. By 1920, he was prospering. However, the demanding schedule of playing at night, working at other jobs during the day, and studying in between led him to the first of two nervous breakdowns. He was so ill that his mother had to go to Chicago to bring him back to Atlanta.

Dorsey returned to Chicago in 1921. His uncle encouraged him to attend the National Baptist Convention, where he was impressed by the singing of W. M. Nix. As Dorsey related in The Rise of Gospel Blues: "My inner-being was thrilled. My soul was a deluge of divine rapture; my emotions were aroused; my heart was inspired to become a great singer and worker in the Kingdom of the Lord—and impress people just as this great singer did that Sunday morning." Dorsey soon began composing sacred songs and took a job as director of music at New Hope Baptist Church on Chicago's South Side, where he described the congregation's singing of spirituals "like down home," noting that the congregants also clapped to his music.

Dorsey's conversion was fleeting. He was soon playing with the Whispering Syncopators, making a salary commensurate with professional theater musicians. As the popularity of the blues increased in New York and Chicago, especially among non-black audiences, Dorsey was able to adapt his style to the tastes of the day. Singers like Bessie Smith, who embodied the southern tradition, were also popular, especially among black Americans.

Debut at Grand Theater

In 1924, Dorsey made his debut as "Georgia Tom" with Ma Rainey at the Grand Theater. He continued to tour with her, even after he wed in 1925, until he suffered the second of his breakdowns in 1926. The pressures of touring overwhelmed him and Dorsey considered suicide. His sister-in-law convinced him to attend church. While at a service, he had a vision, after which he pledged to work for the Lord. It was not long before he penned his first gospel blues,

"If You See My Savior, Tell Him That You Saw Me," which was inspired by the death of a friend.

But the Lord's work would not be easy for him. Dorsey was convinced that the same experiences that had engendered secular blues should also inform church music. As he was quoted as saying in The Rise of Gospel Blues: "If a woman has lost a man, a man has lost a woman, his feeling reacts to the blues; he feels like expressing it. The same thing acts for a gospel song. Now you're not singing blues; you're singing gospel, good news song, singing about the Creator; but it's the same feeling, a grasping of the heart." In a purely musical sense, the blues was merely a collection of improvisational techniques to Dorsey. Nevertheless, imparting a bluesy feel to a traditional arrangement was shocking to many, though Dorsey was able to vary the effect depending on his audience and their reaction. He was soon making printed copies of his gospel blues. However, since he relied on the performer to embellish the music, they did not sell well. Before long he was back to writing and performing secular blues. In 1928, "It's Tight Like That" became a hit, selling seven million copies.

Although Dorsey claimed to have been thrown out of some of the best churches, Harris observed that the time was right for Dorsey's eventual success. There were increasing numbers of store-front churches that appealed to southern migrants, and there was a booming trade in recorded sermons of the type Dorsey's father might have delivered. Harris even linked the blues soloist to the preacher, as each embodies the yearning of a people and manifests that yearning principally through improvisation. There were also a growing number of influential choirs in Chicago, challenging the musical norms of the established churches, though Dorsey was usually more associated with the rise of the solo tradition. In the late 1920s, he would begin work with one of the great gospel soloists of all time, Mahalia Jackson. According to Dorsey, she asked him to coach her, and for two months they worked together on technique and repertoire. They would tour together in the 1940s.

Personal Tragedy

In 1931, Dorsey again experienced great personal tragedy. The death in childbirth of both his wife and newborn son devastated him. As he related in the documentary Say Amen Somebody, "People tried to tell me things that were soothing to me . . . none of which have ever been soothing from that day to this." Out of that tragedy he wrote "Precious Lord," the song for which he is best known. This work has been translated into 50 languages and recorded with success by gospel and secular singers alike, including Elvis Presley. A second song, "Peace in the Valley," was a hit for Tennessee Ernie Ford and others. In 1932 Dorsey was appointed musical director of Pilgrim Baptist Church in Chicago, a post he held until his retirement in 1983. 1932 was also the year he formed the National Convention of Gospel Choirs and Choruses with blues singer Sallie Martin. Their collaboration would continue over the years as his fame spread, Martin often accompanying him on his tours around the country. She also helped him with his publishing business, which quickly became so successful that people nationwide called any piece of gospel sheet music a "Dorsey."

Dorsey remarried in 1941. His career continued to flourish. He would eventually compose over 3,000 songs. Well known within the African American community, Dorsey nonetheless remained relatively obscure outside of it—though people were singing his songs all over the world—until he became the subject of a BBC documentary in 1976. His appearance with another great gospel singer, Willie Mae Ford Smith, in the documentary *Say Amen Somebody* also afforded him considerable exposure. In that film, after being helped into a room, he addresses a group of people, moving comfortably in and out of song all the while. He was ordained a minister in his sixties, formalizing the union of song and worship. The Pilgrim Baptist Church created the T. A. Dorsey Choir to honor him in 1983. Dorsey died of Alzheimer's disease on January 23, 1993 in Chicago, Illinois. However, he lives on each Sunday as voices rise in praise, singing the gospel across the land.

Books

Harris, Michael W., *The Rise of Gospel Blues: The Music of Thomas Andrew Dorsey in the Urban Church,* Oxford University Press, 1992.
We'll Understand It Better By and By: Pioneering African American Gospel Composers, edited by Bernice Johnson Reagon, Smithsonian Institution Press, 1992.

Periodicals

Ann Arbor News, February 24, 1993.
Chicago Tribune, January 25, 1993.
Down Beat, April 1993.
Entertainment Weekly, February 5, 1993.
Jet, February 8, 1993.
Newsweek, February 8, 1993.
New York Times, January 25, 1993.
Time, February 8, 1993.
Village Voice, October 5, 1982.
Washington Post, January 25, 1993; January 31, 1993. □

Giulio Douhet

Giulio Douhet (1869-1930) is regarded as one of the first military strategists to recognize the predominant role aerial warfare would play in twentieth-century battle. Known as the father of airpower, Douhet's theories are still popular among modern military aviators.

Douhet's service in the Italian Army before and during World War I provided him with the experiences he would use to develop his theories of the function of aerial combat in subsequent warfare. Among the revolutionary ideas put forth by Douhet in his most famous work, *Il domino dell'aria (The Command of the Air),* was the necessity of a warring nation to possess first-strike capabilities via aircraft. Douhet argued that these capabilities

should be used before an official declaration of war to ensure a swift, decisive, and demoralizing victory that would shorten any potentially drawn-out naval or land campaign. Believing the airplane to be "the offensive weapon par excellence," he also established the air warfare strategy of the bombing of an opponent's industrial centers and metropolitan infrastructures, reasoning that, even if the attacked nation had advance warning of imminent air strikes, they could never be certain of the specific targets.

Douhet predicted that the future of war would abandon distinctions between civilian and military personnel and justify the bombing of civilian targets by declaring total war in the modern world as an uncivilized pursuit unbound by previous notions of civilized warfare conduct. To support his theory that wars are won by eliminating the will of an opposing country to fight back, which occurs most effectively by attacking the enemy's cities, Douhet wrote: "Victory smiles upon those who anticipate the changes in the character of war, not upon those who wait to adapt themselves after the changes occur." Ultimately, Douhet believed that such a strategy would shorten any war effort significantly, thus resulting in a minimum of casualties because the enemy would be forced to surrender more quickly. He further argued that governments should establish air forces separate from other military branches and appropriate the majority of defense budgets to the development of fighter planes. Douhet also believed that, because most land and naval combat were primarily defensive in nature, they were prone to stalemates. He predicted incorrectly that neither would possess significant value in future warfare.

Despite his forecasts for the inherent primacy of aerial warfare and the shortcomings of his forecasts for aerial technology, Douhet's theories and strategies were employed extensively by both Allied and Axis forces during World War II—most notably against Dresden, Germany, and Hiroshima and Nagasaki, Japan, by the Allies; and against London, England, by the Axis Luftwaffe. His theories continued to be employed in such campaigns as Vietnam and Cambodia in the 1960s and 1970s, the Balkans in the 1990s, and Afghanistan in 2001 and 2002.

Pioneered Aerial Combat

Born in Capreta, Italy, in 1869, Douhet belonged to a family with a long history of military service to the House of Savoy. While dabbling in writing poetry and dramatic pieces, Douhet was also found to be adept in military matters. He expressed his views on the increasing mechanization of warfare in several works prior to World War I, including a journal article in which he wrote: "It must seem that the sky, too, is to become another battlefield no less important than the battlefields on land and at sea. For if there are nations that exist untouched by the sea, there are none that exist without the breath of air." He concluded that, "[t]he army and the navy must recognize in the air force the birth of a third brother—younger, but nonetheless important—in the great military family."

Douhet, who had never flown an aircraft, became involved with the aerial unit of the Italian Army in 1909. By

1911, he was commanding a contingent of nine airplanes in Italy's campaign against the Turkish Empire on the Libyan front. The conflict marked many firsts in aerial combat reconnaissance. It marked the first aerial photo reconnaissance, the first aerial bombing mission, and the first aircraft shot down. Douhet's successes led his superiors to appoint him commander of the entire Italian Army aviation battalion. However, he became frustrated with military protocol and bureaucracy and proceeded to commission the building of a three-engine military aircraft with a combined horsepower of 300. He also sent very impatient and caustic memos to his military superiors. These memos became public and resulted in his being court-martialed and imprisoned for more than a year. Upon his release near the end of World War I, Douhet resumed his responsibilities and was promoted to brigadier general in 1921. That same year, he published the first edition of *Il domino dell'aria*, which he revised for its definitive version in 1927. In 1922, he was named Commissioner of Aviation, serving under Fascist ruler Benito Mussolini. He resigned later that year to dedicate his time to writing.

If the beliefs espoused by Douhet during World War I served to anger his superiors, they were to prove prophetic following the publication of *Il domino dell'aria*. Expressing the need for a more updated model of modern warfare, he argued for the creation of an independent air force. Air warfare, he predicted, would become the decisive factor in future wars. Douhet advocated the use of incendiary bombs, chemicals, gasoline, and high explosives on population centers, reasoning that the "time would soon come when, to put an end to horror and suffering, the people themselves, driven by the instinct of self-preservation, would rise up and demand an end to the war." He recommended that initial attacks employ explosives to frighten the population on the ground; incendiaries to set massive and wide-spread fires; and chemical weapons to deter fire fighters. At first, these theories shocked military strategists who remembered the long-term debilitating effects of the use of mustard gas in the World War I trenches, but Douhet argued that war is already amoral, and that any method used to shorten a war is therefore justifiable. He also defended the establishment of an air force that was completely separate from all other military divisions. He discounted notions that an army or navy might require their own fleet of aircraft that could, at the very least, defend the air force's bombers, believing that an aerial bomber would be able to defend itself from ground and air retaliation.

Following the nineteenth-century theories of military strategists Albert Thayer Mahan and Henri Jomini, Douhet also believed that military targets were of secondary importance, asserting that industrial centers and supply lines were the more decisive targets. He wrote that the country that possessed the strongest air power would achieve military primacy and that total command of the air would render land and sea forces comparatively insignificant because they could not achieve such swift, economical, or effective results as an aerial bombing. Douhet wrote that since the advent of aerial warfare capabilities, the entire history of warfare had been rendered irrelevant, including the concept of differentiating between civilian and military popula-

tions. Since World War I, Douhet reasoned, all wars in the future would be total wars between entire nations that involve every man, woman, and child. Knowing that all of a nation's population was subject to casualties would serve to abbreviate prolonged hostilities.

Books

MacIsaac, David, "Voices from the Central Blue: The Air Power Theorists," in *Makers of Modern Strategy from Machiavelli to the Nuclear Age,* Peter Paret, editor, Princeton University Press, Princeton, New Jersey, 1986.

Pisano, Dominic A., Gernstein, Joanne M. Schneide, Karl S., *Memory and the Great War in the Air,* University of Washington Press, Seattle, Washington, 1992.

Tucker, Spencer C., *Who's Who in Twentieth-Century Warfare,* Routledge, London and New York, 2001.

Online

Cassin, Eddy, "Giulo Douhet: Father of Air Power, 1869-1930," http://www.comandosupremo.com/Douhet.html (January 30, 2002).

Estes, Lieutenant Colonel Richard H., "Giulo Douhet: More on Target than He Knew," http://www.airpower.maxwell.af.mil/airchronicles/apj/6win90.html (January 30, 2002).

"General Giulio Douhet: The First and Most Famous Air War Theoretician," *Air Way College: Gateway to Military Theory & Theorists,* http://www.au.af.mil/au/awc/awcgate/awc-thry.htm.

Shiner, Colonel John F., "Reflections on Douhet: The Classic Approach," http://www.airpower.au.af.mil/airchronicles/aureview/1986/jan-feb/shiner.html (January 30, 2002). □

Carl Theodor Dreyer

Although the output of Danish film director Carl Dreyer (1889-1968) was slim by Hollywood standards, he was nonetheless a master of early cinema. His insistence on artistic independence and the personal, idiosyncratic style of his films have influenced generations of European filmmakers.

Born in Copenhagen on February 3, 1889, Dreyer's childhood is somewhat clouded in mystery. What facts are known are those he himself revealed to his friend and biographer, Ebbe Neergaard. According to some sources (and his own claim) he was the illegitimate son of a Swedish woman and that his father was unknown; other sources mention that his father was the Swede and his mother a Danish housekeeper. At any rate the boy was orphaned at an early age and was adopted by the Dreyer family. Dreyer's original family name remains unknown. His early life had something of a Dickensian tone about it. David Bordwell, in *The Films of Carl-Theodor Dreyer,* quotes one of Dreyer's recollections to Edde Neergaard, saying that his adopted family "consistently let me know that I had to be very grateful for the food I got and I really had no claim on anything because my mother had cheated her way out of paying for me by going off and dying. . . ."

One cannot, however, discount Dreyer feeding his own legend as the gloomy, independent-minded artistic genius.

A Dickensian Background

Dreyer claimed his family wanted him to earn his way by playing piano in a cafe, for which he had no aptitude. Instead, after completing school he left home at the age of 17 and embarked on a series of office jobs: the young Dreyer worked in the municipal administration, a power company, and a telegraph company. In 1909 he quit the telegraph company job in a moment of existential despair and went to work as a journalist. During the next three years Dreyer wrote for the Copenhagen newspapers, *Berlingske Tidende* and *Riget,* concentrating on aviation and nautical reporting. In 1912 Dreyer moved to the daily newspaper, *Ekstrabladet,* where in October of that year, writing under the pseudonym "Tommen," he introduced a series of feuilletons (literary sketches of people and events) titled *Vor Tids Helt* (Heroes of Our Time), which where profiles of Copenhagen's celebrities. This proved fortuitous for Dreyer because in the years just prior to the First World War many of Copenhagen's celebrities were associated with the film industry. In these years the Nordisk Films Kompagni dominated the Danish film industry and earned a good profit from its foreign market (which included the United States, France, Britain, and Germany). Dreyer profiled Ole Olsen, the head of Nordisk Films, and director Asta Nielsen among others. Eventually he tried his hand at film writing.

Held Various Jobs at Nordisk Films

Dreyer wrote or co-wrote three film scripts for a small studio, Skandinavisk-Russiske Handelshus, before joining Nordisk Films in 1913. His first two years at Nordisk were part-time positions. Dreyer began by writing intertitles (brief verbal plot explanations that were flashed on the screen and which served as narrative bridges in silent movies). He was also a reader of film script submissions and acquired the film rights to literary works for the company. Soon Dreyer started writing adaptations of these acquired works and also original screenplays. Including his three pre-Nordisk screenplays, there are 23 films, shot between the years 1912 and 1918, which had Dreyer's name in the credits as scriptwriter, though nearly all have been lost. These include originals as well as adaptations of works by Zola, Balzac, and others. Dreyer also wrote another 17 film scripts for Nordisk, but it is unclear whether or not they were filmed.

Nordisk Films was hit hard financially by the First World War, forcing the exodus of numerous personnel, including directors. The vacuum gave Dreyer his opportunity. The first of the 15 films on which Dreyer's reputation as director rests was *Pr3sidenten* (The President), based on a novel by Karl Emil Franzos. In his acquisitions capacity at Nordisk, Dreyer had purchased the film rights. Completed in 1918, *Praesidenten* was released in Sweden in 1919, but not screened in Denmark until 1920. Critics have recognized influences as varied as German avant-garde theater and the innovative American director, D.W. Griffith. His second film was *Blade af Satans Bog* (Leaves from Satan's Book), loosely based on a novel by Marie Corelli. It was filmed in 1919, but not released in Denmark until 1921. During the pre-production of the film Dreyer quarreled with his superiors at Nordisk over the budget. For Dreyer, however, the quarrel was more than that: he saw it as a battle between art and commercialism. In the end he was forced to accede to Nordisk's demands for a smaller budget. Despite the budget constraint, edits that Dreyer had not authorized and criticism leveled against the film by political and religious groups, *Blade af Satans Bog* established Dreyer as a director. It was also his final film for Nordisk.

Dreyer next went to work for Svensk Filmindustri, but he would leave after making only one film, *Prastankan* (The Parson's Widow), in 1920. The film was shot in Sweden. Because Svensk Filmindustri, like Nordisk, was experiencing postwar financial troubles Dreyer went to Berlin the next year. Thus began his period as a nomad, working wherever in Europe he could find financing—a recurrent problem for Dreyer since he refused to compromise his artistic vision. In Berlin, he made *Die Gezeichneten* (The Stigmatized One) for Primusfilm in 1921. Considered by critics to be one of the great films about the plight of Jews in pre-Revolutionary Russia (certainly the best by a non-Russian filmmaker), it was an adaptation of a Danish novel, *Love One Another,* by Aage Madelung and featured Richard Boleslawski, who had been a member of Stanislavsky's acting troup before the Revolution. Actors from Max Reinhardt's troupe as well as Scandinavians such as Johannes Meyer (a Dreyer favorite) were also in the film. It was *Die Gezeichneten* which caught the eye of film critics in France.

For his next film Dreyer returned to Denmark. In 1922 a theater owner, Sophus Madsen, agreed to finance *Der Var Engang* (Once Upon a Time), a sentimental operetta. (During the early years of the film industry it was not uncommon for production companies to own theaters, or vice versa.) The most interesting aspect of this film (slightly more than half of *Der Var Engang* remains) was Dreyer's plan to build sets within sets to economize during filming. However conflicting schedules forced him to abandon this plan. Dreyer returned to Berlin in 1923. The following year he directed *Michael* for UFA—actually Decla-Bioskop, which David Bordwell describes as "the artistic wing of UFA." *Michael* was a remake and again Dreyer quarreled with his producer, Erich Pommer, who made changes to the ending without consulting him. The assistant cameraman for this production was Rudolf Mate, who would work with Dreyer on some of his most famous films, and later went to Hollywood.

By 1925 Palladium Films had taken control of the Danish film industry from Nordisk and Dreyer signed on to direct the tragicomedy, *Du Skal AEre Din Hustru* (translated as both Thou Shalt Honor Thy Wife and The Master of the House). The film starred Johannes Meyer and proved to be a huge success in Europe, especially France, where it was named one of the year's best by a film magazine. In 1942 it was remade as *Tyrannens Fald*—the title of the play on which it was based. Dreyer also shot *Glomdalsbruden* in Norway in 1925. It was primarily an improvised affair that was far overshadowed by his next film. Indeed, everything Dreyer had done to date would be overshadowed by *La Passion de Jeanne d'Arc*.

Directed a Silent Classic

Produced by Societe Generale de Films, in Paris, the film follows the last day in the life of Joan of Arc, who had been canonized as a saint only in 1920. The Societe Generale de Films allowed Dreyer a free hand; Rudolph Mate was his cinematographer and he used primarily stage actors including Renee Falconetti (Jeanne), who never again acted in film, and Antonin Artaud. The film was shot in chronological order and the actors appeared without make-up, which intensified the film's "realism" all the more since it relies upon an extraordinary number of close-ups. *La Passion de Jeanne d'Arc* premiered in Copenhagen in April 1928 and was first shown in Paris in October 1928, though it wasn't until June 1929 that French audiences finally saw an uncensored version. Unfortunately the film was a financial failure (as was Abel Gance's *Napoleon*, another picture produced by the Societe Generale de Films) and Dreyer never worked for them again.

The subsequent history of the film is somewhat murky. There are conflicting accounts by Dreyer himself as to whether or not he edited it, though evidence seems to point that he did. Also the original negative was destroyed in a fire and various versions of the film have been floating around since. A print discovered in 1952 was for years the standard version, but in the early 1980s a copy of the original print that was submitted to the censor was discovered in a Norwegian mental hospital and was proclaimed the authentic

version. In 1990 *La Passion de Jeanne d'Arc* was voted by film critics as sixth among the world's ten best films; directors gave it ninth place. In 1992 noted film critic David Robinson declared in the (London) *Times,* "The film has no parallel, either in stylistic austerity or emotional force." David Cook in his study, *A History of Narrative Film,* regarded *La Passion de Jeanne d'Arc* as "the last great classic of the international silent screen." It was the first of the five films (each filmed in a different decade) on which Dreyer's reputation rests.

Film legend has it that Dreyer's next film, *Vampyr,* (1932) was a response to Todd Browning's *Dracula.* Dreyer's first sound film was financially backed by the young Baron Nicolas de Grunzburg, who was credited as co-producer along with Dreyer. De Grunzburg, under the pseudonym Julian West, played the role of David Gray, the film's protagonist. The film premiered in Berlin to only mixed success. In subsequent years it has become a classic. However a decade passed before Dreyer made his next film, *Modrehjaepen* (Good Mothers). It was financed by a consortium, which included Nordisk. It is a wartime documentary (at the time Denmark was occupied by Nazi Germany) showing how the state assists an unmarried mother.

Wartime and Post-War Features

In 1944 Dreyer made *Vredens Dag* (Day of Wrath) for Palladium Films. The film is about witchcraft, persecution and murder in the 17th century. However, as Derek Malcolm pointed out in the *Guardian,* it is "sometimes seen as an allegory of the German occupation of Denmark." It is the third of Dreyer's five great films and Bordwell (in *The Films of Carl-Theodor Dreyer*) observes that "it is a moment of equilibrium in Dreyer's career . . . but not in any simple way." As with *La Passion de Jeanne d'Arc* Dreyer used established stage actors (this time from the Danish Royal Theatre) and wanted to film in chronological order, but could not because of previous commitments of one of the actors. The Danish critics hated the film, but as Bordwell points out Andre Bazin (in *Jours de colere*) wrote, "like its contemporary *Ivan the Terrible,* this is a film which is not of the moment, a masterpiece at once anachronistic and ageless." In 1944 Dreyer also made *Tva Manniskor* (Two People) for Svensk Filmindustri. It was an artistic and commercial failure, all but disowned by both Dreyer and his producer.

During the ten years following the Second World War Dreyer worked on a dozen short documentary films. In not all of these was he the director, sometimes working only on the script, sometimes only the editing. It was an extremely fallow period for him as he struggled to find financing and uphold his personal artistic vision. This came about in 1954 when Palladium financed *Ordet* (The Word). *Ordet* has a Romeo and Juliet plot interwoven with the symbols of religious mystery and theological differences as two families seek to reconcile their different beliefs. Dreyer employed long takes that effectively highlighted his slow, deliberate style. The film was a commercial and critical success, and was awarded the Golden Lion at the 1955 Venice Film Festival.

It was another ten years before Dreyer made *Gertrud* (1964), his final film. The distinguishing aspect of the film is that sound, particularly speech, supercedes image: Dreyer had the characters realistically speak past one another's lines. For this reason the film was initially poorly received in France (where Dreyer was revered) and elsewhere. Dreyer remained undaunted. For years he had been researching and writing a film, *Jesus,* but had unsuccessfully sought backing. In late 1967 and early 1968 the Danish government and RAI, the Italian film and television company, decided to finance the film. However Dreyer died on March 20, 1968 before work could proceed.

Books

Bordwell, David, *The Films of Carl-Theodor Dreyer,* University of California Press, 1981.
Cook, David A., *A History of Narrative Film,* W.W. Norton and Co., 1981.

Periodicals

Guardian (London), April 6, 2000.
Los Angeles Times, August 1, 1989.
Newsday, April 9, 1947.
Times (London), December 10, 1992.

Online

"Biography of Carl Theodor Dreyer," http://clickit.go2net.com (October 21, 2001). □

E

Dale Earnhardt

Dale Earnhardt (1951-2001) was a race car driver who drove on the NASCAR circuit for 22 seasons, won 7 Winston Cups, had 76 career wins, and made more money driving than any other driver in NASCAR history. His life was ended with an automobile crash that occurred during the 2001 Daytona 500.

Racing in the Family

Earnhardt was born in the Kannapolis, North Carolina, a textile mill town. His father, Ralph Earnhardt, was known as "Ironheart" on the short-track racing circuit, and he taught his son how to drive stock cars and work with engines. He had converted a barn behind the family home into a garage, and was well-known for his skill with engines. Earnhardt's earliest memory is of watching his father race.

Earnhardt dropped out of high school after eighth grade; according to Bill Hewitt in *People Weekly* he later said, "I tried the ninth grade twice and quit. Couldn't hang, man. Couldn't hang." He worked odd jobs, argued with his father, who wanted him to complete high school, and drove on dirt tracks.

Although Earnhardt became famous for driving a black car emblazoned with the number 3, his first dirt-track car was a 1956 hot-pink Ford Sedan, which he got from his neighbors, David and Ray Oliver. His father had built the engine, and some other friends, Frank and Wayne Dayvault

and their cousin Gregg, tuned it. They intended to paint the car avocado green, but a paint mishap resulted in the car being pink. They could not afford to repaint it, and he raced the pink car on dirt tracks around Charlotte, North Carolina.

Earnhardt married for the first time at 17, and at age 18 had a son, Kerry. Earnhardt divorced his first wife at 19 and married a second time. This marriage would last five years before he divorced again. Earnhardt had two children with his second wife, a daughter, Kelley, and a son, Dale Jr., who would both follow him into racing.

When he was 22, his father died of a heart attack. According to Hewitt, Earnhardt said, "He was against me dropping out of school to go racing. But he was the biggest influence on my life."

Earnhardt's mother gave his father's race cars to Earnhardt. Along with the cars, he inherited the business side of racing that came with them. Mark Bechtel wrote in *Sports Illustrated* that Earnhardt once said, "Daddy had begun to help me with engine work and give me used tires, and he'd talked to Mama about putting me in his car. Then he died. It left me in a situation where I had to make it on my own. I'd give up everything I got if he were still alive, but I don't think I'd be where I am if he hadn't died."

Earnhardt's Big Break into Racing

Racing was not an easy way to make a living, and Earnhardt considered getting some other job. However, in 1975 he drove in his first Winston Cup race, coming in at 22nd. For him, unlike some other drivers, driving was not a hobby—it was almost his only means of support. If he was short of money, he borrowed from other drivers, hoping that he would win the next Sunday's race so he could pay them back on Monday.

Earnhardt was fearless, but he was also astonishingly precise. According to Bechtel, NASCAR historian Greg Fielden once watched Earnhardt taking practice laps around the Myrtle Beach Speedway, where ivy covered the wall along the frontstretch. On each pass, Earnhardt went close enough to the wall to clip off some of the ivy without actually touching the wall with the car. Fielden later commented, "I said to myself, This kid's good, and it didn't take long for the rest of the world to find that out."

Earnhardt's big break into racing came in 1978, when he replaced another driver for the World 600 Cup in Charlotte, North Carolina. He finished seventh in one race, the Firecracker 400, and caught the eye of Rod Osterlund, who owned a Winston Cup car and was not satisfied with his current driver. He replaced him with Earnhardt for the next-to-last race of that season, and Earnhardt drove with his characteristic fearlessness, refusing to be intimidated by the experienced drivers he was competing against. This won him a full-time position driving for Osterlund, and in only his 16th start, he had his first win.

By 1979, Earnhardt was named NASCAR Rookie of the Year, and in 1980 he won the first of seven Winston Cup titles. He became known for his aggressive driving style, earning the nicknames "The Intimidator" and "Ironhead."

The Most Famous Driver in NASCAR

He invested his winnings in a business, Dale Earnhardt Inc., He later acknowledged that his second marriage broke up because of his racing; all his money and attention went to his racing cars. According to Bechtel, he said that his family "probably should have been on welfare" because he was not providing properly for them. The family cars were "old junk Chevelles—anything we could get for $200." In 1982, after the breakup of his second marriage, he married a third time and had a daughter, Taylor Nicole.

Earnhardt won six more Winston Cup titles and eventually became the most famous driver in the sport. As Ken Willis observed in *Auto Racing Digest,* "For two decades ... Earnhardt was part of the national Sunday fabric in a way known only by the likes of Ed Sullivan and Billy Graham. The entire industry benefited." NASCAR gained increasing attention and legions of fans, many of whom were drawn by Earnhardt's charisma and legend. By 2000, 25 percent of NASCAR's $1.1 billion merchandising sales went to Earnhardt-related items, according to Willis.

Earnhardt's auto-racing business, Dale Earnhardt, Inc., expanded exponentially, eventually making $41.6 million, with 200 employees and three cars on the NASCAR circuit. The company had a corporate jet, a helicopter, and a 76-foot yacht, and as Hewitt noted, the work area there was so big that his mechanics called it the "garage-mahal."

Aggressive and bold on the track, Earnhardt could be generous off it. According to Hewitt, when North Carolina farmers were facing financial ruin in the wake of a flood that had destroyed crops, Earnhardt told them to get their tractors ready to roll. At his own expense, he bought and sent them tons of seed to replant their devastated acreage. Earnhardt was also generous with fans, signing autographs and posing for pictures.

Daytona 500

Before the 2001 Daytona 500 race, NASCAR officials instituted some changes in the cars in order to make the races more exciting for viewers. More excitement meant more viewers, and more viewers meant more revenue for the officials and sponsors. In previous races, drivers often took the lead early and stayed there, and there were few changes in the lead, and less exciting jockeying for position on the track. In order to make races more exciting to watch, the officials decided to install restrictor plates on the carburetors, in order to reduce horsepower, and to add aerodynamic spoilers to the cars' surfaces, in order to increase drag. These changes made the cars slower, allowing drivers to catch up to each other, pass, and change position.

Earnhardt was not in favor of these measures, saying that people who were afraid of cars going too fast should stay home, that they were "chicken," according to an article in *Time.* He also refused to wear a new head and neck support system, which helped protect a driver from getting whiplash in a crash.

In the Daytona 500, the changes NASCAR had instituted had a notable effect: over the course of the race, there were 40 more lead changes than in the previous year. With 27 laps to go, 19 cars piled up in a crash. The crash looked horrendous, with one car flipping, flying through the air, and tearing the hood off another, and many others badly damaged, but no one was seriously hurt. Earnhardt's car received some minor damage that he knew would put him out of the running for first place, but on the whole, the race was going well, and it was likely that either Dale Jr. or Michael Waltrip, who drove an Earnhardt car, would win. Over the last ten laps, Earnhardt talked with his pit crew and teammates on his car radio. According to *Time,* his friend and crew chief Larry McReynolds said, "Those last ten laps, I saw such a different Dale Earnhardt. I can't imagine how proud he was to look out his windshield to see his son and good friend up there."

Fatal Crash

Waltrip did win, with Dale Jr. in second place. Earnhardt was not far behind, and was jockeying for position with Sterlin Marlin, battling for third place. On the final turn of the last lap, Earnhardt's car collided with Marlin's car. The contact was minimal, but Earnhardt's black Chevy Monte Carlo veered right, smashed into the wall, and bounced back right into the path of Ken Schrader's car, which broadsided it, slamming Earnhardt's car head-on into the concrete wall. A writer in *Time* commented, "The crash was undramatic. Ironhead had survived much worse." However, when members of his pit crew called him, saying, "Talk to us, Dale!" there was no answer. Even though firemen and medical personnel were on the scene in seconds, it was too late. Earnhardt was dead. According to Bechtel, the emergency medical director at the scene said that he had died instantly from a severe injury at the based of his skull.

Later investigations revealed that Earnhardt's left lap seat belt had failed, tearing apart and allowing him to be thrown into the steering column of the car. However, because this had never happened before, officials did not immediately institute new safety rules, and the next week's race would be held as scheduled, in Rockingham, North Carolina. Dale Earnhardt Jr. announced that he would drive his own car, in honor of his father. Alex Tresniowski wrote in *People Weekly* that Dale Jr. said, "I miss my father, and I've cried for him. I just try to . . . remember that he's in a better place." Earnhardt's legions of fans mourned his loss deeply, creating shrines and memorials all over the country, particularly in his hometown of Mooresville.

According to Hewitt, Earnhardt once summed up his driving style by saying, "I want to give more than 100 percent every race, and if that's aggressive, then I reckon I am." He also said of driving, "It's not a sport for the faint of heart." Fellow driver Bobby Hamilton, who sometimes came head-to-head with Earnhardt over Earnhardt's aggressive style, said, "There is never, ever gonna be anybody as good as Earnhardt."

Bechtel quoted long-time friend H.A. Wheeler, who said, "Here's a kid who came from the bottom, worked hard for everything he got and didn't have any airs about him. . . . Truck drivers, dockworkers, welders and shrimp-boat captains loved that. He was everything they dreamed about being."

Periodicals

Auto Racing Digest, July 2001.
Hot Rod, June 2001.
People Weekly, March 5, 2001; March 12, 2001.
Sporting News, February 12, 2001.
Sports Illustrated, February 28, 2001.
Time, March 5, 2001. □

Alice Eastwood

Botanist Alice Eastwood (1859-1953) amassed a startlingly detailed amount of research on the flowering plants and herbs native to the California coast and the Colorado Rocky Mountains. It was her ardent collecting of plant specimens that helped establish a definitive classification table for the flora of North America.

Born on January 19, 1859, in Toronto, Canada, Eastwood was the daughter of Eliza Jane Gowdey and Colin Skinner Eastwood. Her father was the steward at the Toronto Asylum for the Insane in Ontario, and she lived on the grounds of the institution as a young child. Her paternal ancestry reached back several generations in Canada, and her grandfather had built the first paper mill in Ontario. When she was six, her mother died, and Eastwood took on many household duties involving her younger brother and sister. When their father began to suffer financial troubles, the children were taken in by relatives, and Eastwood lived for a time with a physician uncle. He was an avid gardener and amateur botanist, and from him she began to learn the scientific names of plants.

At the age of eight, Eastwood was sent to a Roman Catholic convent school outside of Toronto where she and her sister were the only boarders. There she came to know another amateur botanist, a priest, who also encouraged her interest in plants and nature. After some six years at the convent, Eastwood moved to Denver, Colorado, to join her father and attend East Denver High School. Again she shouldered much of the cooking and cleaning for her household, and the family's circumstances forced her to take after-school work as a seamstress as well. As a result, she endured long days and nights; once, when her father was working as a janitor at her high school, he and Eastwood's younger brother took on a paper route. This meant that Eastwood had to rise at 4 a.m. in order to start the fires in the basement of the school, but she used the time to do her homework.

Taught High School

Despite these obstacles, Eastwood graduated first in her class in 1879. Unable to afford college, she became a high school teacher in the city for the next decade, a job that left her summers free to hunt for plant specimens. By this time she was an avid collector, but she needed to live frugally in order to afford the expensive scientific books on her pet subject. Though it was considered somewhat improper for a woman to roam about the countryside by herself collecting plants, Eastwood cared little about convention and borrowed a horse, shortened her skirts at the ankles so she

the curator of botany at the California Academy of Sciences. Brandegree gave her Eastwood a job as a writer for the Academy's botanical magazine, *Zoe,* and a job in its herbarium as well. At the time, the Academy's collection of flora was the largest in the western United States. She accepted the job, but returned to Denver to her finish book, *A Popular Flora of Denver, Colorado,* which she and her father published in 1893. She also made another journey with the Wetherills to Montezuma Canyon; she was the first botanist of record to investigate Utah's Great Basin, a vast desert area.

In between stints at the Academy, Eastwood continued to explore on her own and gather specimens; many of these were "type" specimens-in botany parlance, the first sample of a species to be described and named. She usually did so under the roughest of conditions; once, in a California's San Joaquin Valley, she slept in an abandoned shed for two nights, but discovered a new member of the sunflower family. Eastwood knew by heart all the stagecoach routes to the counties surrounding the Bay Area and on foot was known to clock a rate of four miles per hour. Eastwood, perhaps because of the hardships of her early life, was never interested in marriage and had stated on occasion that she feared a romantic attachment might stand in the way of her first love, botany.

Offered Prestigious Post

Back in San Francisco, Eastwood became curator of botany when Brandegree and her husband left the Academy. Her first task was to organize the Academy's vast collections of specimens, and then to bring in more to fill in the gaps. Some of her work and much from the Academy was lost as a result of the great San Francisco earthquake in April of 1906. At the time, the rumblings woke Eastwood from her lodgings in a garret room on Nob Hill. She dressed and ran to the Academy building on Market Street and began working with her assistant to retrieve as many specimens as possible. The herbarium was located on the sixth floor of the building, a considerable danger due to an adjacent paint plant that had erupted in flames. Eastwood arranged to have the specimens safely stored, then took shelter with friends in Berkeley. In all, 1,497 plant specimens were rescued from the Academy that day. Her own personal collection, which Eastwood began assembling in her teens, was lost.

As cited in Carol Green Wilson's *Alice Eastwood's Wonderland: The Adventures of a Botanist,* Eastwood penned a letter to the journal *Science* a few weeks later about the city's tragedy and the tremendous civic spirit she witnessed in the hours following: "[N]obody seemed to be complaining or sorrowful. The sound of trunks being dragged along I can never forget. This seemed the only groan the city made. . . ." As for the Academy itself, "I did not feel the loss to be mine," she wrote, "but it is a great loss to the scientific world and an irreparable loss to California. My own destroyed work I do not lament, for it was a joy to me while I did it, and I can still have the same joy in starting it again. . . ."

might hike hills more easily, and carried a plant press on her back. Yet she also lived in an age when the American West was still uncharted territory in some places. She was robbed on one occasion, and on another became lost near Colorado's border with Utah and spent the night on a canyon ledge.

Over the next few years Eastwood became well known in Denver for her knowledge in all matters botanical. When a highly regarded British naturalist, Alfred Russel Wallace, planned a visit to the city, her name was recommended to serve as his guide for a collecting hike on Gray's Peak. Eastwood also became friends with the Wetherill brothers, who owned a large ranch near the Utah border. They had discovered Mesa Verde, a vast complex of pre-Columbian cliff dwellings that quickly became a renowned archeological site. When a more modern real-estate boom occurred in Denver in 1890, Eastwood was surprised to find that she and her father each pocketed $10,000 from the sale of a building they had acquired. The windfall allowed her to quit teaching for good, and she reinvested the funds in other real estate holdings that would give her a steady income for the rest of her life.

Roamed the Wild West

Eastwood had always been eager to visit California and add specimens from its flora to her growing collection. She journeyed to San Diego, and then explored the Santa Cruz and Monterey Peninsula areas as well. When she arrived in San Francisco, she was introduced to Katharine Brandegree,

Traveled Extensively

True to her nature, Eastwood returned to San Francisco after the fires had died down and explored the broken walls and open basement sites of the rubble to see which kinds of plants remained. Her job at the Academy was on temporary hiatus, so she took advantage of assistantships and posts offered to her by the renowned scholars she had come to know. She worked at the University of California at Berkeley and made a trip across the United States. She was a guest at Theodore Roosevelt's White House and worked at the celebrated Asa Gray Herbarium in Cambridge, Massachusetts. She also visited Europe in 1911, spending time at the famed hothouses of Kew Gardens in London and enjoying a stint as an unregistered student at Cambridge University.

The following year the Academy reopened, and she became curator of botany once again. The specimens she had saved, along with a shipload of plant and animal specimens that arrived after the earthquake from the Academy's famed Galapagos Islands expedition, would become the institution's cornerstones. Over the next 40 years, Eastwood oversaw the acquisition of 340,000 specimens for its botany collection and helped make the Academy's library of botanical literature an impressive one. She became a celebrated Bay Area fixture as an active member of the San Francisco Floral Society who curated its lavish annual shows. She was also a key player in the city's efforts to make its Golden Gate Park a renowned arboretum and horticultural spot. For several years she held weekly classes for its gardeners. The sunflower-type bush she had discovered in the San Joaquin Valley had been named *Eastwoodia elegans* in her honor, and she was pleased to learn that whenever oil was discovered somewhere in California, the shrub was likely to be near.

Studied Aftermath of Brush Fires

Eastwood lived in the Russian Hill district of the city but also kept a mountain cabin in the Tamalpais section of Marin County. This served as her hiking headquarters for many years, but it was a leveled by a brush fire. She revisited the area some seven years later and was surprised to see some things that she had planted still growing. She wrote an article for a journal, as cited by Wilson, called "The Aftergrowth of a Mountain Fire," noting that the roots of the manzanita and California lilac seemed to endure conflagration. "Stranger than the behaviour of these woody plants," she wrote, "is that of some of the humble herbs. These appear for a year or two, then are not seen again until another fire when once again they spring forth." It was one of 300 published articles she wrote in her lifetime.

Eastwood's plant-collecting forays into the California countryside continued unabated until 1932 when she was struck by a car at the entrance to Golden Gate Park. Her knee was permanently damaged. That same year, she also launched *Leaflets of Western Botany* with her assistant (and later successor), John Thomas Howell, a highly regarded forum for botanical research. Eastwood enjoyed an international reputation. Her eightieth birthday was the occasion of a series of honors at the Academy; proceeds from a banquet became the first contributions to the Alice Eastwood Herbarium there.

Eastwood retired from the Academy in 1950 at the age of ninety and was given the title Curator-Emeritus. That same year, she journeyed to Stockholm, Sweden, to accept an award from the Seventh International Botanical Congress. Eastwood died of cancer on October 30, 1953, in San Francisco. The plant specimens she collected remain a vital part of the plant archives at the California Academy of Sciences.

Books

Notable Women Scientists, Gale Group, 2000.

Wilson, Carol Green, *Alice Eastwood's Wonderland: The Adventures of a Botanist,* California Academy of Sciences, 1955. □

Marriner Stoddard Eccles

Marriner Eccles (1890-1977), a Republican Mormon, rose to great power in Franklin Delano Roosevelt's administration as the head of the Federal Reserve. The banker from Utah helped ease the Great Depression by urging a change in how the government used money to control the economy.

Although he never attended college, Eccles ideas about the economy anticipated those of the famed economist John Maynard Keynes. Eccles argued for deficit spending during the Depression and pushed for a balanced budget during World War II.

Unlikely Beginnings

Marriner Eccles's father, David, as an illiterate teenager, emigrated from Scotland to America in the 1860s. Settling in Utah, he made a fortune, starting with the ownership of a sawmill and continuing on the road to riches by owning or investing in railroads, coal mines, sugar production, construction, and banks.

David Marriner was a Mormon. He had two wives, who produced 21 children. Marriner was the eldest son of the second wife, Ellen. Marriner Eccles attended schools in his birthplace, Logan, Utah, and spent four years at Brigham Young College. In 1909, he traveled to Scotland, where he spent two years as a missionary. He returned to America with May Campbell Young, whom he married in 1913. The couple had three children.

David Eccles died unexpectedly in 1912. Marriner, at the age of 22, became responsible for his mother, Ellen, and his eight siblings. He was a remarkable business person, as was his father. In 1928, he founded one of the first bank holding companies in the United States, First Security Corporation, which ran 28 banks in the western United States. Eccles's Utah Construction helped build Boulder Dam.

The Great Depression began in 1929 when the stock market experienced its worst plunge ever and lost more than

$10 billion in value. Over the next three years unemployment rose by the millions, until in 1933, when Franklin D. Roosevelt took office as president, it had reached 13 million. Many banks, farms, and industries failed, and homelessness skyrocketed. When the Great Depression struck, Eccles spent three years trying to prevent "runs" on his bank. (A bank run is when so many depositors withdraw their money that the bank runs out of money and fails.) Eccles succeeded in preventing runs on his banks, but he realized that something needed to be done to solve the economic problems of the country.

Eccles Pushed Deficit Spending

Although he had no formal training in economics, Eccles's reading and thinking led him to certain conclusions about the causes of the Depression. Eccles wrote, "Had there been a better distribution of the current income from the national product—in other words, had there been less savings by business and the higher-income groups and more income in the lower groups—we would have had far greater stability in the economy. Had the $6 billion, for instance, that was loaned by corporations and wealthy individuals for stock-market speculation been distributed to the public as lower prices or higher wages, with less profits to the corporations and the well-to-do, it would have prevented or greatly moderated the economic collapse that came at the end of 1929."

Eccles concluded that the most important thing in preserving a sound economy is to keep money moving. To transfer it from those who had an excess to those who did not have an adequate amount, the federal government would have to step in. Eccles realized that the government could borrow money from the people who had it and spend it on those who needed it, a principle called deficit spending. In his memoir, *Beckoning Frontiers: Public and Personal Recollections,* edited by Sidney Hyman, Eccles explained, "A policy of adequate governmental outlays at a time when private enterprise is curtailing its expenditures does not reflect a preference for an unbalanced budget. It merely reflects a desire and the need to put idle men, money and material to work. As they are put to work, and as private enterprise is stimulated to absorb the unemployed, the budget can and should be brought into balance, to offset the danger of a boom on the upswing, just as an unbalanced budget could help counteract a depression on a downswing." The concepts described by Eccles were written about three years later by the famous British economist John Maynard Keynes and came to be known as "Keynesian economics."

Eccles Became a New Dealer

When the democrat Franklin D. Roosevelt became president, he began what was called the "New Deal," a series of strong governmental interventions in the economy intended to ease the hardships of the Great Depression, to lift the nation out of depression, and to prevent another one through reforms.

The United States began to rebound from the stock market crash of October 1929 in the spring of 1933, when a shaky recovery began. Although economic output increased, prices rose, and the stock market went up, the recovery was weak. In 1933, 15 million people were still without jobs.

In 1933, Eccles testified at a Senate hearing about his ideas and about how to ease the effects of the Depression. He suggested that the federal government spend money on unemployment relief, public works, and aid to farmers. Eccles also advised some long-term solutions such as federal insurance for banks, a centralized Federal Reserve System, tax reforms, a minimum wage, unemployment insurance, pensions for the elderly, and governmental regulation of the stock market.

Roosevelt's advisers were impressed with Eccles and asked him to help them create new legislation. As William Greider described it in his book, *Secrets of the Temple: How the Federal Reserve Runs the Country,* "One summer, Marriner Eccles was struggling to save his small-town banks from failure. The next summer, he was at the center of American political power, an intimate of the President's and a principal architect of the New Deal's reforms."

In September 1934, the president asked Eccles, then a special assistant to Treasury Secretary Henry Morgenthau Jr., to become the next governor of the Federal Reserve Board. The Federal Reserve System, known as "the Fed," had been established in 1913 to create a flexible and sound currency and to make money available to all areas of the country. Eccles told the president that he would only be interested in the position if fundamental changes were made in the Federal Reserve System. Roosevelt asked Eccles to prepare a memorandum on the fundamental changes that he had in mind. Eccles presented his ideas to Roosevelt in November 1934.

The focus of Eccles's suggestions was control of open market operations. This refers to the buying and selling of securities to expand or contract bank reserves, money, and credit. (Open market operations were eventually considered the Fed's most powerful tool.) Eccles recommended that "the power over open market operations . . . should be taken away from the privately run Federal Reserve banks . . . [and] vested in an Open Market Committee of the Federal Reserve Board in Washington."

On November 10, 1934, Roosevelt nominated Eccles as head of the Fed. Eccles immediately began writing his Fed reform bill, which reduced the size of the board from eight to five members. Authority over open market operations was given to a new Federal Open Market Committee, formed only of board members, with Federal Reserve banks represented as advisers. The bill lessened the power of the Federal Reserve banks' boards of directors and formed new offices of bank presidents, whose nominations were subject to a Fed board veto. The board also was given more power over discount rates and reserve requirements. Eccles knew that his ideas would cause controversy. Roosevelt told him, "Marriner, that's quite an action program you want. It will be a knockdown and drag-out fight to get it through."

The Eccles bill was introduced in the House of Representatives on February 5, 1935, and in the Senate on February 6. On May 9, the House passed the Banking Act of 1935 on a vote of 271 to 110, with only minor changes. In August, the Senate passed the bill, the basic outlines of which were the same as Eccles had originally proposed: the board's power was increased; the public character of the Fed was enhanced; the independence of the Federal Reserve banks was lessened; and bankers' influence over the system was reduced. The board now had control over open market operations and monetary policy. Roosevelt signed the act into law on August 23. Soon after, he named Eccles chairman of the new Board of Governors of the Federal Reserve System, a position Eccles held until 1948. He served on the Board as a member until 1951.

Recovery Unraveled

In August 1937, a serious recession began. One of the causes of this recession was the government's decision to balance the budget, instead of allowing deficit spending to continue. In 1936, the federal deficit was cut in half, with this same halving occurring again in 1937. While the government was slashing the deficit, the Fed was increasing the reserves required of banks, known as tightening, and boosting interest rates. These policies combined to kill the recovery and raise unemployment, although Eccles would not acknowledge any blame for the recession.

After the recession of 1937, Eccles finally convinced Roosevelt that deficit spending was essential, but the amount of spending was still too small to bring about full recovery. By 1939, the United States had achieved a partial economic recovery, but more than 8 million people were still unemployed. The Great Depression did not end until the economy was improved by the national defense program and American involvement in World War II.

War Time Disagreements

During World War II, Eccles argued against the government's cheap-money policies, and he fought the Treasury on how to finance the country's war efforts. Eccles argued for limiting bank activity on the buying and selling of government bonds, but he could not convince the government to do so. He also pushed for higher taxes during the war, which did occur. Although he had earlier promoted deficit spending, Eccles now encouraged Roosevelt to borrow less money and raise more through taxation. David Hage, in a 1995 article in *U.S. News & World Report,* notes, "The last episode of formal cooperation [between the Fed and the president] occurred in the mid-1940s, when the cost of World War II had driven the federal debt to a staggering 128 percent of gross domestic product, versus about 71 percent today. The Fed agreed to buy any Treasury securities that the public would not, while pegging long-term interest rates at a low 2.5 percent to help America's postwar recovery. The strategy worked: Washington reduced spending by some two thirds after the war, triggering a brief downturn, but low interest rates soon had the economy humming." This cooperation marked some loss of independence for the Fed.

After the war, Eccles pushed for a balanced budget and tighter credit policies. In 1948, President Harry Truman did not reappoint Eccles to the position of chairman of the Fed, however, he remained on the board until 1951.

By 1950, the Fed was concerned about inflation, which had reached almost 7 percent, and wanted its independence back. Eccles embarrassed Truman by leaking the transcript of a meeting at which Truman asked for easy money. After a month of fighting between the Fed and the president, Treasury/Federal Reserve Accord resulted, re-establishing the Fed's independence.

Eccles died in 1977. Although history has largely forgotten his name, he was memorialized on the seventieth anniversary of the Federal Reserve by having its building renamed in his honor. He is considered the first great chairman of the Federal Reserve and one of the three greatest. The bank holding company he founded, First Security, still exists and consists of 270 branches. It is run by Eccles's nephew, Spencer Eccles.

Books

Eccles, Marriner S., *Beckoning Frontiers: Public and Personal Recollections,* edited by Sidney Hyman, Alfred A. Knopf, 1951.

Greider, William, *Secrets of the Temple: How the Federal Reserve Runs the Country,* Simon and Schuster, 1987.

Periodicals

American Banker, August 22, 1985, p. 4.
New Leader, March 23, 1992, p. 8.
U.S. News & World Report, June, 26, 1995, p.46. □

Tilly Edinger

**Tilly Edinger (1897-1967) was born Johanna Ga-
brielle Ottelie Edinger and is recognized as a pioneer
in the field of paleoneurology, which is the study of
the brain through fossil remains. Her major work is
titled *Evolution of the Horse Brain.***

Edinger applied her knowledge of neurology to the
study of paleontology to determine how the brains of
a species evolved. Because brains decompose, she
focused on the study of the fossilized remains of the skulls
and cranial cavities of many species to hypothesize that
brains of any given species evolve differently based upon
immediate external stimuli. Rejecting previous scientific notions from the eighteenth- and nineteenth-centuries, which
asserted that evolution was a linear progression resulting in
such lower animals as rodents eventually evolving into
higher beings such as humans, Edinger postulated that evolution follows a complex branching process. This is a process by which different environmental factors that include
climate and weather cause a species to evolve in radically
different ways. In *Evolution of the Horse Brain,* Edinger
proposed that the rate of evolution varies according to the
individual lineage of any member of a particular species,
and it is based upon that individual's ability to adapt, as well
as the capacity of the brain's components to evolve new
methods of interaction.

Edinger was born on November 13, 1897, in Frankfurt,
Germany. Her Jewish parents were members of Germany's
upper class, and they provided her with a financially secure
childhood in her hometown of Frankfurt am Main. The
ready availability of money provided Edinger and her two
older siblings with ample educational, travel, and leisure
opportunities. Her father, Ludwig E. Edinger, was a professor of neurology at the University of Frankfurt, a respected
researcher, and one of the founders of comparative neurology. He was held in such high esteem that the city of
Frankfurt am Main named a street after him following his
death in 1918. Edinger's mother, Anna Goldschmidt
Edinger, was a descendent of the Warburg family of
bankers. Her active engagements in charity and social work
resulted in the city honoring her with a bronze bust in the
municipal park.

Edinger attended several universities, including schools
in Heidelberg and Munich, before graduating from the
Schillerschule in Frankfurt am Main. She had originally
intended to study geology because she was convinced it
would be easier for a woman to obtain a position in the field
of zoology. Her focus was vertebrate paleontology. Edinger
received her doctorate in natural philosophy from the University of Frankfurt in 1921, after her dissertation on the
cranial capacity of the extinct Triassic era marine reptile
Nothosaurus was accepted. Following her doctorate,
Edinger pursued her interest in neurology and paleontology
as a research assistant at the University of Frankfurt until
1927. Financially independent because of her family's
wealth, she accepted an unpaid position in 1927 as curator
of the vertebrate collection at Frankfurt's Senckenberg Museum. After publication of her first major work, *Die fossilen
gehirne (Fossil Brains)* in 1929, the museum offered her a
paid position.

When the Nazi party took political control of Germany
in 1933, Edinger chose to remain in Frankfurt am Main.
While her supervisor at the Senckenberg Museum was a
member of the Nazi party, he allowed Edinger to continue
her work as museum curator. In return, the supervisor requested that Edinger remove her name from her office door
and vacate the building whenever there was a Nazi visitor.
She worked under these circumstances until 1938, when
the Nazi party increased its pressure on the German Jewish
community. She applied for an exit visa in order to immigrate to the United States in 1938 but was placed on a
waiting list. In May 1939, she was granted temporary permission to leave Germany. Her brother Friedrich (Fritz),
however, was less fortunate and perished in the Holocaust.
In addition, the Nazis removed the statue of Edinger's
mother from the municipal park and changed the name of
the street bearing her father's name. Edinger settled in London and worked as a wartime translator of medical texts. In
1941, she immigrated to the United States and accepted a
tenured faculty appointment at Harvard University. Alfred
Sherwood Romer, director of Harvard's Museum of Comparative Zoology, appointed Edinger to the position of research assistant at the museum. With the exception of one
year of teaching at Wellesley College, she retained her
position at the museum until 1966.

Published in 1929, Edinger's *Die fossilen gehirne* is considered her first major study. In this book, she argued persuasively that scientists should study fossils in order to determine the evolution of a specie's brain. This method was in opposition to the prevailing scientific method of the previous 150 years, in which scientists used the skulls and brains of contemporaneous animals to explain the evolution of its species. Edinger argued that such a method resulted in erroneous conclusions, because each generation of species possessed its own identifying creatures incumbent upon the climate, environment, and other determining factors specific to that generation. She argued that these factors directly led to brain development changes that were unique to that generation. To prove her theory, Edinger pioneered the method of using plaster casts of the fossilized remains of animal skulls and cranial cavities. Once the cast is made, scientists can make educated guesses on the size and shape of the different components of the animal's brain and how those components interact. Once these determinations were made, they could be compared to previous or subsequent generations of fossil remains.

Her second major work, *The Evolution of the Horse Brain* continued her explorations into the evolution of mammalian brains. In this work, she presented a convincing argument for the independent development of an enlarged forebrain in several species of mammal, focusing on the horse as an example. She argued that previous assumptions of linear evolution could not account for such a widespread occurrence among so many different species. She thus was able to explain how animals, including humans, developed at different rates in varying geographical locations and in different time periods based upon the lineage of the species member and the physical demands placed upon it by that location's climate and environment.

In 1950, Edinger received a fellowship from the American Association of University Women to study fossils. Her research took her to five countries in western Europe and produced several papers on her findings. She continued her studies with the help of a Guggenheim Fellowship. In 1963, her membership in the American Academy of Arts and Sciences led to her election as the president of the Society of Vertebrate Paleontology. She later earned honorary doctorates from Wellesley College and the German universities in Giessen and Frankfurt am Main. On May 26, 1967, prior to an anticipated return visit to Frankfurt, Edinger received serious injuries while walking near her home in Cambridge. Suffering a serious hearing impairment since birth that also increasingly prevented her from teaching, she did not hear the approaching automobile that eventually struck her. She died the following day.

Books

Kass-Simon, G., and P. Farnes, *Women of Science: Righting the Record,* Indiana University Press, 1990.
Notable Twentieth-Century Scientists, Gale Group, 1995.
Notable Women Scientists, Gale Group, 2000.
Sicherman, B., and C. H. Green, editors, *Notable American Women: The Modern Period,* Harvard University Press, 1980.
Women in World History: A Biographical Encyclopedia, Yorkin Publications/Gale Group, 2000.

Periodicals

Society of Vertebrate Paleontology News Bulletin, no. 81, 1967.
□

David R. Einhorn

Anti-slavery proponent and Jewish theological writer David R. Einhorn (1809-1879) was one of the leaders of the Reform movement of Judaism in the United States. Influenced by the ideas of Friedrich Schelling, he had a turbulent career as rabbi in central Europe before he moved to the United States. Like Abraham Geiger, Einhorn took a more liberal view on the practice of Judaism than did orthodox Jews.

Turned to Radical Jewism

Einhorn was born on November 10, 1809, in Dispeck, Bavaria. Son of Maier and Karoline Einhorn, the reform rabbi David Einhorn had a traditional Jewish education at the Furth yeshiva. He did exceptionally well in his studies and earned his rabbinical diploma at age 17. When Einhorn's father died, his mother helped him attend the universities of Erlangen, Wurzburg, and Munich.

Einhorn was a religious radical. He was raised in the strict traditions of his Judaism, but the more liberal environment of the university helped to change his views. His views included abandoning ceremonial laws that seemed cumbersome in the modern age. He preferred using German rather than Hebrew; he also wanted to eliminate prayers for the restoration of the temple in Jerusalem and for the furtherance of Zion. Because of these views, Einhorn was barred from becoming a rabbi in Germany. It was ten years later, in 1842, that he finally was given an appointment of Landesrabbiner of Birkenfeld, Oldenburg. He married Julia Ochs in 1844, and the couple had nine children.

At the Frankfurt Reform Rabbinical Assembly in 1844, Einhorn staunchly argued for reforms, such as preaching in the German vernacular rather than in Hebrew and leaving out prayers for a Jewish nation. In 1847, Einhorn replaced Samuel Holdheim as chief rabbi of Mecklenburg-Schwerin and found himself influenced by Holdheim and by the philosopher F.W. Schelling. More and more opposed to serving in a reactionary state, Einhorn was soon in the midst of controversy. Most people in his congregation were orthodox and were opposed to his views. When Einhorn gave an uncircumcised boy a blessing in the synagogue, the congregation did not approve. Due to the clash of views between Einhorn and his congregation, Einhorn left his position as chief rabbi, and he left Germany altogether.

In 1851, Einhorn went to Hungary, where he served at Budapest's Reform synagogue. The government felt threatened by the religious liberalism preached there. Confusing

the religious liberalism with political liberalism, the Hungarian government closed the temple only two months after Einhorn took the pulpit. After the temple was closed, Einhorn began to think about relocating to a place where he could preach his radical religious ideas. He considered the United States as a possibility for his new home but did not leave until 1855.

While he waited for the right conditions to sail for America, Einhorn wrote his *Das Prinzip des Mosaismus* (*The Principles of Mosaic Faith*). Published in 1854, this volume reflected his thinking on Jewish philosophy. One of his beliefs echoed that of Abraham Geiger and other reform leaders. These leaders did not accept that revelation from God occurred only in the past; Einhorn believed that God revealed truths to his people over time, so that religious ideas could be perfected.

Campaigned against Slavery

In 1855, Einhorn left Germany for the United States. Once in America, he became the religious leader at Har Sinai Synagogue in Baltimore. Again he found himself in the midst of controversy. Einhorn opposed slavery. Opposition to slavery in a pro-slavery state put Einhorn in danger. Some of Einhorn's contemporaries felt that slavery was a traditional way of life, although they might not themselves practice it. Einhorn, in direct opposition to these contemporaries, did not share those views. Neither did he support the idea that slavery was ordained of God.

Einhorn felt that using the Bible to support slavery was akin to wielding the whip of slavery. It was following the letter of the law in direct opposition to the spirit of the law. In his sermon "War with Amalek!" based on Exodus 17, Einhorn said, "We are told that this crime [slavery] rests upon a historical right! . . . Slavery is an institution sanctioned by the Bible, hence war against it is war against, and not for, God! It has ever been a strategy of the advocate of a bad cause to take refuge from the spirit of the Bible to its letter. . . ."

Outspoken in his views that slavery was a moral sin, Einhorn took a firm stance against it. Although Einhorn preached in German—indeed, he continued to be a proponent of German as the language of biblical scholarship and criticism—his words nevertheless incited a riot on April 19, 1861. According to David E. Lipman of the *Gates to Jewish Heritage,* "a mob threatened to tar and feather him, and he was forced to flee north." He first fled to Philadelphia and became rabbi of Keneseth Israel Congregation. In 1866, he went to New York and became rabbi of the Congregation Adath Israel. The congregation eventually merged with an orthodox congregation and was renamed Beth El.

Einhorn was staunch in his refusal to give way to the view that slavery had a right to exist. Even though he acknowledged that honorable men could be slave holders, as was Abraham, he nevertheless condemned slavery as a moral evil. Pointing to the bondage of the Jews in Egypt, he noted that they rejoiced when God delivered them; there was no justification for viewing slavery as a state of man established by God. Jews, of all people, should abhor slavery, Einhorn pointed out. He noted that the Jewish race was under the bondage of slavery in places throughout the world; therefore the Jewish race should certainly be against slavery, in all its forms.

In 1856, Einhorn began publishing a monthly magazine on Judaism reform, *Sinai.* Written in German, the magazine was published for seven years before it folded, due to its anti-slavery message. *Sinai* was a vehicle used by Einhorn to voice his opposition to the views of his colleagues who accepted slavery as a necessity. When one of his peers, Rabbi Morris Raphall, delivered pro-slavery words from the pulpit, Einhorn fiercely opposed him in *Sinai.* Calling Raphall's sermon a "deplorable farce," Einhorn refuted the notion that slavery was acceptable because it was mentioned in the Bible, any more than murder was acceptable because Cain committed it. Einhorn further explained in volume. VI of *Sinai* that "to proclaim slavery in the name of Judaism to be a God-sanctioned institution—the Jewish-religious press must raise objections to this, if it does not want itself and Judaism branded forever. Had a Christian clergyman in Europe delivered the Raphall address, the Jewish-orthodox as well as Jewish-reform press would have been set going to call the wrath of heaven and earth upon such falsehoods, to denounce such a disgrace."

Einhorn accused Jews who supported slavery of putting money before their values, because the economic advantages some enjoyed because of slavery did not mean that it should be tolerated. The Jews, once in slavery themselves and now free, should not feel that they practiced a humane religion if they were willing to believe that religion allowed for the justification of slavery. Because of his outspoken views against slavery, Einhorn was elected as an honorary member of the Union League Club of Philadelphia.

Influenced American Reform

In 1855, Einhorn opposed the decision of the Cleveland Rabbinical Conference that the Talmud was the only acceptable interpretation of the Bible. Led by Isaac Mayer Wise, the conference adopted a unified approach that allowed for incorporating broad practices present in American Judaism. Einhorn considered this to be false to the Reform's cause; his disagreement sparked a lasting feud between him and the more moderate Wise.

At the same time that Einhorn opposed recognizing the Talmud as divine, he never deviated from his belief that the Law of Moses held true and lasting principles that guided his people. He compared Mosaic law to a weapon against the enemies of the Jewish people. His people could not afford to lose this weapon, he said. Einhorn maintained that for Jews to curry favor with those in power by departing from the time-tested principles given by Moses was to agree to their own destruction.

Although a radical, Einhorn still believed the scripture in Exodus 19:6 that spoke of the Jews as a priestly people: "And ye shall be unto me a kingdom of priests, and an holy nation. These are the words which thou shalt speak unto the children of Israel." Einhorn believed that in order to be holy, Jews needed to keep the covenants their ancestors made with God. He did not subscribe to a defeatist mentality found in the *Wissenschaft des Judentums.*

But to maintain their status of a holy people, Einhorn maintained that Jews should not intermarry. In *Sinai* he wrote that marrying into other races was "a nail in the coffin of the small Jewish race." Although he once blessed an uncircumcised boy, Einhorn insisted that male converts be circumcised. He believed that the Jews had to preserve their heritage in order to maintain their identity as the people of God. At the same time that he wished to continue the practice of circumcision, Einhorn wished to cast off other practices of the "Ceremonial Law" that he considered to be outdated. He was against practices such as wearing phylacteries twice a day; refraining from 39 different kinds of work on the Sabbath; and following dietary restrictions. Einhorn was interested not in the outward forms of the Mosaic law, but in the moral aspects of it.

In 1856, Einhorn published his prayer book and called it *Olat Tamid,* which means "Eternal Sacrifice." The title of his prayer book might seem ironic, given the fact that Einhorn had agreed with Geiger that the Talmud had no divine authority. But unlike Wise's prayer book *Minchag America,* Einhorn's work was more than just a shortened version of the existing service. *Olat Tamid* was a creative expression on universal human values that served as a model for the original *Union Prayer Book. Olat Tamid* was a more modern approach to religious practice than the traditional worship for it did not emphasize the chosen status of Israel. It also removed mention of a Messiah and eliminated references to a return to sacrificial practices and a return to Israel.

As Wise's moderate approach to Judaism eventually became the standard for Jewish reform in America, Einhorn's influence lived on. His son-in-law, Rabbi Kaufmann Kohler, collected a volume of Einhorn's sermons and published it in 1880. Kohler was responsible for forming the Pittsburgh Platform of 1885, which became a foundation for American Reform. Kohler also helped incorporate material from Einhorn's *Olat Tamid* into the *Union Prayer Book.*

Einhorn retired in 1879 and died just four months later on November 2, 1879. He will be remembered as an eloquent man who refused to change his opinions. His theological writings have a rational strain that apply universally to the human race. A leading reform theologian in his day, Einhorn was instrumental in bringing Jewish reform to a modern school of thought.

Periodicals

American National Biography, Volume 7, p. 364-365.
The New York Times, January 15, 2000, p. B11.

Online

"Anti-Slavery Answer to Dr. Raphall by Dr. David Einhorn," *Jewish-American History on the Web,* http://www.jewish-history.com/einhorn.html (January 6, 2002).
"David Einhorn," *Dictionary of American Biography,* Base Set. American Council of Learned Societies, 1928-1936, http://galenet.com/servlet/BioRC (January 15, 2002).
"David Einhorn," *Encyclopedia.com,* http://www.encyclopedia.com/articlesnew/14885.html (January 6, 2002).
"David Einhorn," *Infoplease.com,* http://www.infoplease.com/ce6/people/A0816890.html (January 6, 2002).
"David Einhorn: Radical American Reformer," *Gates to Jewish Heritage,* http://www.jewishgates.org/personalities/einhorn.stm (January 6, 2002). □

Paul Erdos

For Paul Erdos (1913-1996), mathematics was life. Number theory, combinatorics (a branch of mathematics concerning the arrangement of finite sets), and discrete mathematics were his consuming passions. Everything else was of no interest: property, money, clothes, intimate relationships, social pleasantries—all were looked on as encumbrances to his mathematical pursuits.

A genius in the true sense of the word, Erdos traveled the world, living out of a suitcase, to problem solve—and problem pose—with his mathematical peers. A small, hyperactive man, he would arrive at a university or research center confident of his welcome. While he was their guest, it was a host's task to lodge him, feed him, do his laundry, make sure he caught his plane to the next meeting, and sometimes even do his income taxes. Cosseted by his mother and by household servants, he was not brought up to fend for himself. Gina Bari Kolata, writing in *Science* magazine, reports that Erdos said he "never even buttered his own bread until he was 21 years old."

Yet this man, whom Paul Hoffman called "probably the most eccentric mathematician in the world" in the *Atlantic Monthly*, more than repaid his colleagues' care of him by giving them a wealth of new and challenging problems—and brilliant methods for solving them. Erdos laid the foundation of computer science by establishing the field of discrete mathematics. A number theorist from the beginning, he was just 20 years old when he discovered a proof for Chebyshev's theorem, which says that for each integer greater than one, there is always at least one prime number between it and its double.

Erdos was born in Budapest, Hungary, on March 26, 1913. His parents, Lajos and Anna Erdos, were high school mathematics teachers. His two older sisters died of scarlet fever when he was an infant, leaving him an only child with a very protective mother. Erdos was educated at home by his parents and a governess, and his gift for mathematics was recognized at an early age. It is said that Erdos could multiply three-digit numbers in his head at the age three, and discovered the concept of negative numbers when he was four. He received his higher education from the University of Budapest, entering at the age of 17 and graduating four years later with a Ph.D. in mathematics. He completed a postdoctoral fellowship in Manchester, England, leaving Hungary in the midst of political unrest in 1934. As a Jew, Hungary was then a dangerous place for him to be. During the ensuing Nazi era, four of Erdos's relatives were murdered, and his father died of a heart attack in 1942.

In 1938, Erdos came to the United States. However, because of the political situation in Hungary, he had difficulty receiving permission from the U. S. government to come and go freely between America and Europe. He settled in Israel and did not return to the United States until the 1960s. While in the U.S., he attended mathematical conferences, met with top mathematicians such as Ronald Graham, Ernst Straus and Stanislaw Ulam, and lectured at prestigious universities. His appearances were irregular, owing to the fact that he had no formal arrangements with any of the schools he visited. He would come for a few months, receive payment for his work, and move on. He was known to fly to as many as fifteen places in one month—remarking that he was unaffected by jet lag. Because he never renounced his Hungarian citizenship, he was able to receive a small salary from the Hungarian Academy of Sciences.

An Erdos Number Conveyed Prestige

So esteemed was Erdos by his colleagues that they invented the term "Erdos number" to describe their close connections with him. For example, if someone had co-authored a paper with Erdos, they were said to have an Erdos number of one. If someone had worked with another who had worked with Erdos, their Erdos number was two, and so on. According to his obituary in the *New York Times*,

458 persons had an Erdos number of one; an additional 4,500 could claim an Erdos number of two. It is said that Albert Einstein had an Erdos number of two. Ronald Graham, director of information sciences at AT and T Laboratories, once said that research was done to determine the highest Erdos number, which was thought to be 12. As Graham recalled, "It's hard to get a large Erdos number, because you keep coming back to Erdos." This "claim to fame" exercise underscores Erdos's monumental publishing output of more than 1,500 papers, and is not only a tribute to his genius but also to his widespread mathematical network.

Throughout his career, Erdos sought out younger mathematicians, encouraging them to work on problems he had not solved. He created an awards system as an incentive, paying amounts from $10 to $3,000 for solutions. He also established prizes in Hungary and Israel to recognize outstanding young mathematicians. In 1983, Erdos was awarded the renowned Wolf Prize in Mathematics. Much of the $50,000 prize money he received endowed scholarships made in the name of his parents. He also helped to establish an endowed lectureship, called the Turan Memorial Lectureship, in Hungary.

Perfect Proofs from God's "Great Book"

Erdos's mathematical interests were vast and varied, although his great love remained number theory. He was fascinated with solving problems that looked—but were not—deceptively simple. Difficult problems involving number relationships were Erdos's special forte. He was convinced that discovery, not invention, was the way to mathematical truth. He often spoke in jest of "God's Great Mathematics Book in the Sky," which contained the proofs to all mathematical problems. Hoffman in the *Atlantic Monthly* says "The strongest compliment Erdos can give to a colleague's work is to say, 'It's straight from the Book.'"

Mother's Death Brought on Depression

Erdos's mother was an important figure in his life. When she was 84 years old, she began traveling with him, even though she disliked traveling and did not speak English. When she died of complications from a bleeding ulcer in 1971, Erdos became extremely depressed and began taking amphetamines. This habit would continue for many years, and some of his extreme actions and his hyperactivity were attributed to his addiction. Graham and others worried about his habit and prevailed upon him to quit, apparently with little result. Even though Erdos would say, "there is plenty of time to rest in the grave," he often talked about death. In the eccentric and personal language he liked to use, God was known as S.F. (Supreme Fascist). His idea of the perfect death was to "fall over dead" during a lecture on mathematics.

Erdos's "perfect death" almost happened. He died of a heart attack in Warsaw, Poland, on September 20, 1996, while attending a mathematics meeting. As news of his death began to reach the world's mathematicians, the accolades began. Ronald Graham, who had assumed a primary role in looking after Erdos after his mother's death, said he received many electronic-mail messages from all over the world saying, ''Tell me it isn't so.'' Erdos's colleagues considered him one of the 20th century's greatest mathematicians. Ulam remarked that it was said ''You are not a real mathematician if you don't know Paul Erdos.'' Straus, who had worked with Einstein as well as Erdos, called him ''the prince of problem solvers and the absolute monarch of problem posers,'' and compared him with the great 18th-century mathematician Leonhard Euler. Graham remarked, ''He died with his boots on, in hand-to-hand combat with one more problem. It was the way he wanted to go.''

Books

Mathematical People, Profiles and Interviews. Edited by Donald J. Albers and G.L. Alexanderson. Contemporary Books, Inc., 1985.

Ulam, S. M. *Adventures of a Mathematician.* Charles Scribner's Sons, 1976.

Periodicals

The Atlantic Monthly, November 1987.
The New York Times. September 24, 1996.
Science, April 8, 1977.
Two-Year College Mathematics Journal, 10, 1979.

Online

''In Memoriam: Paul Erdos.'' February 11, 1997. http://www.cs .uchicago.edu/groups/theory/erdos.html (July 20, 1997). □

Thomas Erskine

Eighteenth-century Scottish jurist and historian Thomas Erskine (1750-1823) was noted for his contributions to British law, his spirited defense of American patriot Thomas Paine, and his support for the French Revolution.

The youngest son in a noble Scottish family, Thomas Erskine excelled at law and gained renown as one of the most eloquent orators of his day. He had a brief tenure in the British Parliament, but his most significant contributions lay in the area of commercial law, where he maintained a substantial practice. His historical significance was the result of his defense of the revolutionary ideals of the age and his support of freethinkers against King George III.

Naval and Military Training

Born in Edinburgh, Scotland, in 1750, Erskine was the third son of the tenth earl of Buchan. Despite their grand title, the Erskines lived on limited means; rather than an ancestral home, they lived in a flat in a middle-class area of Edinburgh. Thomas Erskine was not in line to inherit his father's title; his oldest brother, David, would become the 11th earl of Buchan. Seeking to regain some of the dignity of his ancestors, Thomas Erskine vowed to follow his other brother, Henry, into the practice of law. After getting a basic education in Latin and the English classics, Erskine decided to see the world, and at age 14 he went to sea as a midshipman aboard a Navy ship, the *Tarter,* sailing for the West Indies. He would not return to Scotland for 56 years.

Four years after joining the navy, in 1768, Erskine purchased a commission in the British army, using inheritance money given him after the death of his father. He also married, and his wife accompanied him on his assignments. While posted to the Spanish island of Minorca from 1770 to 1772, he passed his free time studying English literature. Like many educated young men of his generation, he also became interested in the philosophical writings of thinkers such as Voltaire, Jean-Jacques Rousseau, and others associated with the French Enlightenment. On leave to London in 1772, he ingratiated himself with many influential men, such as Samuel Johnson, Edmund Burke, and historian Edward Gibbon, using his noble birth, his good looks, and his conversational abilities to make his way into polite society.

Became a Successful Jurist

In 1775 Erskine resigned his commission in the British army and entered Lincoln's Inn and Trinity College, Cambridge, earning an honorary M.A. in 1778. Admitted to the bar the following year, he gained immediate success in court. A capable speaker with a solid grounding in commercial law, Erskine was an excellent debater, quick on his feet and with a ready wit. He also was a great lover of animals and became known for sometimes bringing his pet Newfoundland dog, Toss, into chambers, where the dog sat on a chair with its paws on the table.

Many of Erskine's early cases involved high-profile clients. After his successful defense of Captain Thomas Baillie, lieutenant governor of Greenwich Hospital, against Lord Sandwich's criminal charge of libel, Erskine became highly sought among the better class of accused. His successful defense of Admiral Lord Keppel in 1779 against charges of neglect of duty while in command of the British fleet off Ushant was followed by an equally well-publicized acquittal in the case of Lord George Gordon in 1781. Gordon, tried for high treason after leading a mob of 50,000 Protestant rioters to disrupt Catholic buildings and the home of the chief justice, escaped both the charge and the bill for over 180,000 pounds in damages, even though 21 of the 139 rioters arrested with Gordon were executed on similar charges.

Word of Erskine's legal triumphs quickly spread and he soon found himself propelled into the civil service. In 1783 he was appointed a king's counsel and member of Parliament for Portsmouth. Although his first appearance in Parliament was uninspired, he returned for several terms, serving intermittently from 1783 to 1806. He was appointed attorney general to the Prince of Wales in 1789.

Defended Revolutionaries

Inspired by a visit to France in 1790 and his long-held Whig beliefs, Erskine joined the Friends of the People, a group formed by Charles Grey and several members of Parliament in April 1792. The goal of the group was to gain greater representation for English citizens in Parliament through peaceful means. In line with this goal, Erskine defended many people arrested on political grounds between 1793 and 1794.

Erskine's agreement to defend British-born American revolutionary Thomas Paine in 1793 cost the attorney his position with the Prince of Wales. Paine, who had fomented the uprising in England's North American colonies with his pamphlet *Common Sense,* returned to England in 1787. Four years later, when he published his pamphlet *The Rights of Man* in defense of the French Revolution, King George III moved to curb his influence. Paine's book was banned and its author arrested on the charge of sedition. Erskine successfully defended Paine in the case and another stemming from his subsequent publication, *The Age of Reason,* written while its author was in jail in France in 1794. In his first defense of Paine, Erskine quoted Burke and John Milton, recounted the history of the Glorious Revolution, and noted, as his core argument, the following: "That every man, not intending to mislead, but seeking to enlighten others with what his own reason and conscience . . . have dictated to him as truth, may address himself to the universal reason of a whole nation, either upon the subject of governments in general, or upon that of our own particular country;—that he may analyze the principles of its constitution,—point out its errors and defects,—examine and publish its corruptions,—warn his fellow citizens against their ruinous consequences, and exert his whole faculties in pointing out the most advantageous changes in establishments which he

considers to be radically defective, or sliding from their object by abuse.—All this every subject of this country has a right to do, if he contemplates only what he thinks would be for its advantage, and but seeks to change the public mind by the conviction which flows from reasoning dictated by conscience."

English politician John Horne Tooke also needed Erskine's legal abilities after he was accused of treason. Tooke was a founding member of the London Corresponding Society, a group with the same aim as that of Friends of the People, and Erskine helped him win acquittal. Other political rebels Erskine aided included Scottish radical Thomas Hardy, a middle-aged shoemaker and associate of Tooke who was accused of conspiring to kill the king of England, and John Thelwall, a journalist and former tailor's apprentice who was acquitted of the charge of high treason in 1794 with Erskine's help.

Advanced Legal Theory

In addition to gaining a reputation as both a liberal and a defender of the constitution, Erskine also established a number of important legal precedents. In his 1798 defense of Hadfield, a man indicted for attempting to shoot George III, Erskine made a "destructive analysis of the current theory of criminal responsibility in mental disease," and his defense of the dean of St. Asaph resulted in a 1792 revision of the laws regarding libel.

In 1806 an ancient office was revived in his honor and Erskine was appointed chancellor to the Prince of Wales. He was also elevated to the peerage as 1st Baron Erskine. Despite such honors, he tired of public life and resigned from his position the following year. His decisions as chancellor were later published under the title *Apocrypha.* His other written works included a 1772 pamphlet on army abuses; a 1797 discussion of the war with France; *Aramata,* a political romance; a pamphlet in support of the Greeks; and several works of poetry.

Erskine's forensic abilities were unrivaled in the history of the English Bar. While he had a long and active legal career, it did not bring him great fortune, because he took many cases pro bono to defend political rights. After years of ill-advised investments and extravagant spending, Erskine was reduced to poverty by 1818. He returned to his family in Edinburgh in February 1820 at the age of 70 and was widely praised for his wit and character at a large public gathering. A strong supporter of the constitution despite his return to Scotland, Erskine remained loyal to Queen Caroline, consort of King George IV, despite the king's decision to divorce her on charges of adultery in 1821. He died in 1823 at the home of his brother, David Erskine, and was buried in the family's tomb in Linlithgow. As a fitting epitaph, Erskine was immortalized in the lines of the poem "The Author's Earnest Cry and Prayer," written by his friend and fellow Scot, Robert Burns: "Erskine a spunkie Norland billie." In legal circles, he remained known for many years as "England's foremost advocate."

Books

Hostettler, John, *Thomas Erskine and Trial by Jury,* Barry Rose Law Publishers, 1996.

Online

Gabb, Sean, "Thomas Erskine: Saviour of English Liberty," *Libertine Alliance,* http://freespace.virgin.net (May 11, 1997).

"Mr. Erskine's Speech in Defense of the Liberty of the Press," *Cambridge and Oxford Free Speech Seminar/University of Arkansas Web site,* http://wwwuark.edu/depts/cmminfo/cambridge/paine.defense.html (February 2, 2002). □

F

John Arbuthnot Fisher

An ordnance and torpedo specialist and brilliant military tactician, John Arbuthnot Fisher (1841-1920) boosted Britain's Royal Navy to new heights prior to World War I. In combat and on sea patrol, he served admirably in China, the Crimea, Egypt, the West Indies, and the Mediterranean. An able administrator, at a time when Germany vied for supremacy at sea, he oversaw officer training, manpower, ship construction, fuel efficiency, fleet formation, and ordnance.

Rose through the Ranks

Born in Ceylon on January 25, 1841, John "Jackie" Fisher joined the navy in 1854 as a penniless boy and, during service in the Crimean War in his mid-teens, rose to midshipman. At age 18 in China during the Second Opium War, he aided in the seizure of Canton and the Pei forts. After twenty years of experience, he helped to revise *The Gunnery Manual,* a handbook on marksmanship and gun maintenance.

By age 33, Fisher attained the rank of captain and commanded the superior battleship H.M.S. *Inflexible* at the 1882 bombardment of Alexandria's forts during the Egyptian War. He and his naval brigade mounted an overland attack on Ahmed Arabi Pasha, who led the nationalist revolt. As a result of the offensive, Britain established a 40-year occupation in North Africa.

Fisher progressed to captain of the H.M.S. *Excellent,* the navy's name for its gunnery school. After five years instituting innovations to torpedo design, Fisher directed naval ordnance and torpedoes and served on the admiralty board. He rose to Third Sea Lord and controller of the navy in 1892. Within four years, he achieved the rank of rear admiral and then vice admiral and received a knighthood.

A Leader during Peacetime

From 1897 to 1899, an era of relative calm in the Western Hemisphere, Fisher commanded military readiness in North America and the West Indies. At the end of his tour, after taking charge of the British military in the Mediterranean, he helped negotiate terms at the First Hague Peace Conference, which initiated a permanent court of arbitration for settlement of international disputes. A blunt champion of a strong military, he startled fellow delegates with the statement that "war is the essence of violence" and proposed that nations make war so terrible that challengers would go to great lengths to avoid combat. His concept of preparedness was priming the British fleet to strike first and hardest and to keep up the pace. In 1902, a year after he was made full admiral, he received a chance to apply his philosophy as Second Sea Lord of training and recruitment for the Home Fleet.

Fisher's responsibilities in the navy required that he upgrade fleet efficiency, improve sailors' welfare with better food and firm discipline, and overhaul the training for officers. He accomplished all of these objectives with the aid of a group of experienced naval captains. In 1904, he headquartered at Portsmouth, England, as First Sea Lord and began honing the British Navy for war with Germany. At the Royal Naval College at Osborne, he controlled the training of cadets. In this same period, through a review commis-

171

December 1906, the prototype ship stood ready for use. Fisher approved of its speed and deadliness and acquired eight more new fighting ships for the British navy. True to his prediction, the dreadnought concept revolutionized warfare at sea.

Fisher supported his heavy gun ships with light, maneuverable armored battle cruisers, beginning with the H.M.S. *Invincible,* which was capable of traveling at 25 knots. His intent was to surround heavy gun ships with lightweight cruisers that would act as scouts. For instant manpower, he designed a system that removed battle-ready crew and officers from the Mediterranean Sea, familiarized them thoroughly with ships and strategy, and placed them on England's coast for immediate call-up.

Replaced Traditions

Fisher fearlessly retired the preferential treatment system for which the old-style military was known. He ended a promotions system based on social class and replaced it with promotion based on talent and experience. To open military careers to all young men, he abolished tuition to Dartmouth and Osborne, the training centers for the Royal Navy. Fisher advocated four or more years of sea duty in addition to classroom training at the newly established Royal Naval College at Osborne. To better defend Great Britain, he ordered that the cream of the navy form a home fleet to remain in England at shore barracks ready for deployment. With men kept in tip-top form by constantly familiarizing themselves with the latest in equipment, ships and crew functioned at peak efficiency.

The concept of a home fleet earned sharp criticism from Admiral Lord Charles Beresford, who commanded the Channel Fleet. Beresford chafed at Fisher's taking a lead in developing Britain's battle plans. The tug of war between naval heads polarized the high command, endangering military readiness. True to Beresford's warning, Fisher's reshaping of the British fighting fleet and its crews failed in competition with Germany's big gun ships. Beresford called for an investigating committee to determine whether Fisher's dispersal of warships was at fault. The internal inquiry into Beresford's charges neither confirmed them nor advanced Fisher's theories.

In 1909, a year before his retirement on January 25, 1910, Fisher became one of the few naval officers raised to the British peerage when he was named Baron Fisher of Kilverstone. Severely weakened by his detractors' campaign, he continued to advise another of his critics, First Lord of the Admiralty Winston Churchill, on equipping the navy and on building the Queen Elizabeth class of fast, oil-powered battleships. Churchill reciprocated by appointing him to chair a commission on fuel oil purchase, which completed its report in 1913.

Prepared for War

Recalled into service in October 1914 to replace Prince Louis of Battenberg, Fisher once more assumed the role of First Sea Lord under Churchill. Fisher's attitude toward war had not softened with age. He wrote that supremacy was Britain's best security and the source of world peace: "If you

sion, he advised the British cabinet to reorganize the War Office to resemble the admiralty board. This tactless proposal prompted a vocal campaign against him that continued until his retirement.

A Bold Reformer

To bolster home defense against the mounting threat from Germany, Fisher weeded out weak or useless vessels and reassigned men to reserve crews. He reorganized and modernized the fleet and oversaw the Portsmouth dockyards and the construction of lighter, faster ships. To increase Britain's chances of surviving all-out war, he developed firepower and submarines, which he saw as the offensive wave of the future.

Fisher surprised and dismayed his critics by converting ships from coal to oil. His support of petroleum as the fuel of the future earned him the nickname "godfather of oil." The switch in fuel for steam boilers forced England away from dependence on native coal and into ongoing political involvement in the Middle East, the source of British crude oil. In 1905, his wisdom and fighting spirit earned Fisher the Order of Merit and command of the entire fleet.

Fisher created the British military model based on rapid and all-out response to war to shorten conflict and lessen damage. For this goal of brief but lethal engagement, he developed torpedoes and oversaw design and construction of the battleship *Dreadnought,* modeled on the German warship and armed with ten 12-inch guns. He described it as "the hard-boiled egg—because she cannot be beat." By

rub it in, both at home and abroad, that you are ready for instant war, with every unit of your strength in the first line and waiting to be first in, and hit your enemy in the belly and kick him when he is down . . . then people will keep clear of you." In a letter to German Grand Admiral Alfred von Tirpitz in March 1916, Fisher barked, "You're the sailor who understands war. Kill your enemy or be killed yourself."

Already steeled for World War I, Fisher faced a test of readiness in November 1914, after Sir Christopher Cradock lost two major cruisers in the Pacific at the battle of Coronel. Fisher amassed an armada of 600 ships to ward off German submarines and commissioned military blimps to scout for German U-boats. The added muscle and surveillance enabled the British to trounce the fleet of German Admiral Graf von Spee on December 8 at the battle of the Falkland Islands.

War and Retreat

Fisher's impressive military history ended in a disagreement over Churchill's chancy assault on the Dardanelles. Vigorous, combative, and original in his thinking, Fisher did not work well as Churchill's underling. As World War I worsened, Churchill rejected Fisher's proposal for an amphibious assault on Germany's Baltic coast. Instead, Churchill called for an expedition against the Dardanelles in the eastern Mediterranean to assure that the fleet could pass through unharmed. Because Fisher feared that heavy concentrations of firepower off Turkish shores would weaken protection of the Baltic Sea, he proposed instead an Anglo-Russian assault on Germany's northern shores. On May 15, 1915, the day after Churchill announced his intent to attack the Dardanelles, Fisher resigned. The British failed in the assault, and Fisher's analysis proved correct.

A patriot and friend to the British military, Fisher spent his last years serving in various ways. In July 1915, he chaired a board of invention and research to help the Royal Navy absorb the latest scientific breakthroughs. In vain, he hoped for reappointment to naval command. During his second retirement, he compiled the two-volume *Memories and Records* (1919), containing autobiography, combat philosophy, and speculation on air-based wars of the future. Witty and fun-loving, he developed his interests in dancing, the Bible, and military history. Evaluating Fisher's contributions to British military preparedness, Churchill later commended him for his reforms during a critical era in world history.

Books

Almanac of Famous People, 6th edition, Gale Research, 1998.
Columbia Encyclopedia, Edition 6, Columbia University Press, 2000.
Davis, H.W.C, and Weaver, J.R.H., editors, *Dictionary of National Biography, 1912-1921,* Oxford University Press, 1927.
Drexel, John, editor, *Facts on File Encyclopedia of the Twentieth Century,* Facts on File, 1991.
Harris, William H., and Levey, Judith S., editors, *New Columbia Encyclopedia,* Columbia University Press, 1975.
Keegan, John, and Andrea Wheatcroft, *Who's Who in Military History,* William Morrow & Co., 1976.
Kemp, Peter, editor, *Oxford Companion to Ships and the Sea,* Oxford University Press, 1976.
Seldes, George, *The Great Quotations,* Pocket Books, 1967

Periodicals

Washington Report on Middle East Affairs, October/November 1997.

Online

Biography Resource Center, http://galenet.galegroup.com/servlet/BioRC.
Churchill Archives Centre, http://www.chu.cam.ac.uk/archives/collections/full.shtml#FISHER
"History of the Oil Industry,"*University of Pennsylvania Political Science,* http://www.ssc.upenn.edu/polisci/psci260/OPECweb/OILHIST.HTM.
The Royal Navy, http://www.royal-navy.mod.uk/ □

Max Fleischer

A pioneer of film animation, cartoonist Max Fleischer (1883-1972) created cartoon characters Betty Boop and Popeye. He is also remembered for his more than 20 motion picture production inventions, particularly the rotoscope.

Max Fleischer was born into a family of inventors on July 17, 1883, in Vienna, Austria. His mother immigrated with him to the United States when he was four years old, and he was raised on the Lower East Side of New York City. Fleischer was one of five sons. Animator Dave Fleischer was his younger brother.

Fleischer didn't finish high school, but attended numerous trade schools and art programs in his youth. He worked for the *Brooklyn Daily Eagle* as a cartoonist, photographer, and photo-engraver before becoming art director for the magazine *Popular Science.* Fleischer's animation career began at Joseph Randolph Bray's studio, where he made instructional films during a short World War I commission.

Invented the Rotoscope

Fleischer were granted a patent in 1917 for the rotoscope, a mechanism used for transferring live action film into animated cartoon through tracing. Still used in modern animation and video game production, this process involves the projection of single frames of film onto a drawing surface for tracing. Re-photographing the sequence of drawings results in very lifelike animation. This invention was prompted by Fleischer's frustration with cel animation, which didn't allow a realistic enough product. Creating their first rotoscoped cartoon character, the Fleischer brothers shot a normal filmstrip of a body in motion. Dressed as a clown, Dave was the body. Using the rotoscope, the Fleischers then magnified each frame of the filmstrip onto a piece of glass. The next step involved tracing Dave's changing positions onto celluloid frame by frame, changing his features into those of their new character, Koko the Clown.

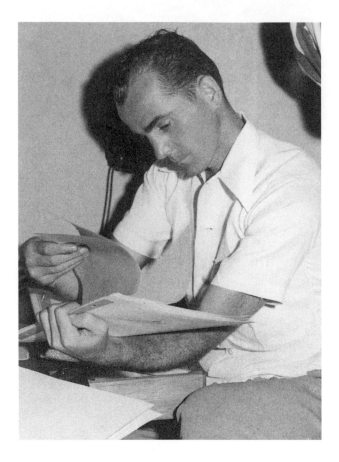

The final stage was photographing each piece of celluloid onto a single frame of motion picture film. The finished product was the first Koko the Clown filmstrip, in which the star's body reflected all of the subtle changes made by a moving human form. Fleischer was quoted in Film100.com's Fleischer biography as calling rotoscoping "the greatest achievement in pen-and-ink production." The brothers' invention caught the attention of animator John R. Bray, who hired them to work in Paramount's New York studios.

Fleischer and his brother, Dave, founded Out of the Inkwell Films, Inc. in 1921. They renamed the business Fleischer Studios in 1928. Their "Out of the Inkwell" cartoon series, featuring Koko the Clown, was their first series of films and was produced through 1929. Fleischer continued to experiment with cartoon mechanics and soon developed the rotograph. Using this method the animators could draw characters in real-world settings. A live action film was projected to the underside of the artist's table, and Koko the Clown was drawn into each frame. This system was a trailblazer for films like Mary Poppins (1964) and Who Framed Roger Rabbit (1988).

Fleischer never grew tired of experimenting, and he was always trying out new color, sound, and optical tricks in his films. His constant tinkering didn't allow him to refine these new processes, so Fleischer's films lacked consistency. His audiences were always entertained, and his rivals were always worried about his next invention. Fleischer's major rival was Walt Disney. While Fleischer clearly had

the most ingenuity, Disney shone in showmanship, discipline, and vision. While Disney slowly built on each success, Fleischer was always moving forward and rarely looking back. Howard Beckerman discussed their relationship in *Back Stage,* "Both Fleischer and Disney had a great deal of respect for each other. The older man had pioneered many of the early innovations in the medium. The younger man, Disney, had wanted to be another Fleischer (Max had a mustache first)." Disney recognized the importance of Fleischer's discoveries and was quoted in Film100.com's Fleischer biography as saying, "Without his pioneering spirit and additions to the technology of animation, few, if any of us, would be where we are today."

Betty Boop Made Her Debut

Fleischer created a number of firsts with his brother, including the "bouncing-ball" sing along cartoons, which were silent but synchronized to the cinema orchestras. His cartoon "Song Car-Tune" was the first cartoon with a soundtrack, and was produced in 1924. Betty Boop was the first female cartoon star, making her debut in 1930. She was the girlfiend of an unpopular character named Bimbo, who starred in *Dizzy Dishes,* and she soon had her own series. The Fleischer brothers' creation was a sexy woman in the form of a cartoon character. Gary Morris recalled her appearance in *Bright Lights Film Journal,* "Betty is best remembered for her red-hot jazz baby persona. With a head like a giant peanut, vast mascara'd eyes, too-kissable lips, baby-doll voice (courtesty of singer Mae Questel), flattened marcelled hair, and mere threads of a dress exposing miles of hot flesh, she was the perfect celluloid sex toy."

A far cry from the wholesome characters being created at the Disney Studios, Betty Boop not only appeared sexy but acted the part. She was often shown undressing and kissing clowns, cats, and other creatures. While other cartoons of the time were focusing on the charming lives of adorable animals, the Fleischers had Betty running around in her slinky costumes, living the life of a provocative young woman. The general trend in movies and cartoons was more respectable, and Betty Boop was bucking this trend. Amelia S. Holberg discussed the differences between Disney and the Fleischers in *American Jewish History,* "By the time Pinocchio was released, Disney had redefined animation as a children's genre. The very adult Betty Boop, on the other hand, was a flapper, a flashy city party girl, not a respectable lady and definitely not an appropriate character for children's films." The Hays office Production Code was instituted in 1934, and censors transformed Betty Boop into an all-American girl, clothing her more fully and temporarily banning her garter. The series ended in 1939, but there was a Betty Boop revival in the 1970s. She starred in a touring film festival, "Betty Boop's Scandals," and was featured in Macy's Thanksgiving Day Parade in 1984. 1985 saw Betty Boop's network television debut, and her sixtieth birthday was celebrated in the animated special, "Betty Boop's Hollywood Mystery."

Popeye the Sailor Man

Max and Dave Fleischer followed up their Betty Boop success with another popular character's introduction in 1933. Popeye was a result of stiff competition among animation studios. A key part of the studios' business strategies was the development of cartoon characters whose popularity would guarantee bookings by major theater chains. Disney's Donald Duck and Goofy were developed from smaller roles in Mickey Mouse cartoons, and Warner Bros. created Bugs Bunny and Daffy Duck after their initial success in films featuring other animated animals. E.C. Segar created a comic strip called "Thimble Theater" in 1919. He introduced Popeye into the strip as a temporary character, but when Segar attempted to write Popeye out, fans complained and he returned as Olive Oyl's love interest. Max Fleischer requested the right to use Popeye from Hearst's King Features Syndicate and was granted permission two years after Betty Boop's debut.

Due to the very satisfying quality of the first Popeye production, the agreement between Fleischer and King Features was extended to a five-year term even before the film's release. The movie, entitled *Betty Boop Presents Popeye the Sailor,* marked the beginning of Popeye's highly successful series. Within five years, Popeye was the most popular American cartoon character. Fleischer was so confident, he attempted to convince film distributor Paramount to back a feature-length Popeye movie, but the shorts they created were the most profitable Popeye productions.

Disney moved into feature films in 1937 with the success of *Snow White and the Seven Dwarfs,* forcing the Fleischers into entering this new arena. They produced the feature-length cartoons *Gulliver's Travels* and *Mr. Bug Goes To Town* in 1938 and 1941, both of which bombed. Their expansion, which involved enlarging their staff to produce the features, proved unsuccessful. In 1942 Paramount forced the brothers out of their own studio. Amidst this disappointment, the Fleischers premiered the first Superman short in 1941.

Max Fleischer went on to direct films, which include *20,000 Leagues Under the Sea, Dr. Doolittle, Compulsion, Tora Tora Tora,* and *The Jazz Singer.* After Paramount bought his studio, Fleischer worked for that company as production chief of cartooning until he retired in the 1960s. Fleischer died of heart failure on September 11, 1972, in Woodland Hills, California. He was survived by his wife, Essie, and two children.

Books

Almanac of Famous People, 7th ed., Gale Group, 2001.
Contemporary Theatre, Film, and Television, Gale Research, 1998.

Periodicals

American Jewish History, v. 87 no. 4, December 1999.
Animation World Magazine, July 1997.
Back Stage, April 12, 1985.
HFD-The Weekly Home Furnishings Newspaper, February 12, 1990.
Newsweek, Summer 1998.

Online

Furniss, Maureen, "The Fleischer Studio and Modeling," *AFI Online Cinema,* http://www.afionline.org/cinema/archive/alice/koko.html (January 31, 2001).
"Max Fleischer," *Contemporary Authors Online,* http://www.galegroup.com (January 22, 2001).
Morris, Gary, "Betty Boop," *Bright Lights Film Journal,* http://www.brightlightsfilm.com/16/betty.html (January 31, 2001).
"The One Hundred Most Influential People in the History of the Movies," *The Film 100,* http://www.film100.com/cgi/direct.cgi?v.flei (January 31, 2001). □

Williamina Fleming

The first of the famous women astronomers at the Harvard College Observatory, Williamina Fleming (1857-1911) helped to revolutionize astronomy in the late nineteenth and early twentieth centuries. She discovered ten novae, or exploding stars, and more than 200 variable stars. She also developed a new star classification system. Fleming was considered to be the leading female astronomer of her day and her achievements opened up the field of astronomy for women.

Born in Dundee Scotland on May 15,1857, Williamina (known as Mina) Fleming was the daughter of Robert and Mary (Walker) Stevens. Her father had a profitable carving and gilding business and was well known for his picture frames. He was also one of the first in Dundee to experiment with photography. He died when his daughter was seven. Fleming attended public schools in Dundee until she was 14. She then worked as a student teacher until she married James Orr Fleming at the age of 20. In 1878, the couple emigrated to the United States, settling in Boston, Massachusetts. Soon after their arrival, her husband deserted her. To make matters worse, she was pregnant. Fleming was forced to work as a maid to support herself. Her choice of employers would change her life

From Housekeeper to Astronomer

In 1879 Fleming went to work for Edward C. Pickering, an astrophysicist and the new director of the Harvard College Observatory. She returned briefly to Scotland that fall to give birth to her son. Presumably, she wanted to be with her family for the birth. Pickering must have made a great impression on her in the brief time they knew one another, because she named her son Edward Pickering Fleming. Pickering was an advocate of higher education for women and an exacting employer. Frustrated with the inefficiencies of his male assistant, the story goes that he proclaimed that even his Scottish maid could do a better job and he set out to prove it. Soon, the 24-year-old Fleming had progressed from housework to astronomical observations.

The major work of the Harvard Observatory, made possible by the Draper Memorial established by Mary Anna Palmer Draper in 1886, was to use photographs to analyze the spectra, brightness, positions, and motions of stars. Photographs revealed wavelengths of light that were invisible to the human eye and therefore had never been seen with telescopes. The photographs of star spectra, the pattern of bands and lines that form when a star's light is dispersed through a prism, provided an entirely new way of classifying and analyzing stars. Nettie A. Farrar, an assistant at the Observatory who was leaving to marry, trained Fleming to analyze the spectra. Fleming's most important contribution to astronomy was her classification of 10,351 stars into 17 categories for the *Draper Catalogue of Stellar Spectra*, published in 1890. Her system of classification, known as the Pickering-Fleming System, supplanted the original classification system devised by Pickering.

In the course of her career, Fleming examined nearly 200,000 photographic plates, made at Cambridge and at Harvard's southern observatory in Arequipa, Peru, and supervised their classification. Fleming's studies of these photographic plates of star spectra led to her discoveries of ten of the 24 novae that were known at the time of her death in 1911. Novae are stars whose light suddenly increases dramatically and then fades. She also discovered 59 gaseous nebulae. Gaseous nebulae are high density interstellar dust or clouds, belonging to two groups of nebulae—planetary and diffuse. One of her most important discoveries concerned long-period variable stars, which were thought to be very rare, since their brightness changed so slowly that the magnitude of brightness was not observed to vary. Fleming discovered that variable stars could be identified by certain spectral characteristics. This enabled her to identify and analyze 222 of these of stars. Furthermore, she selected comparison stars that enabled the brightness of the variable stars to be determined with accuracy. This was the first photographic standard for determining the magnitude of star brightness. Of the 107 unusual Wolf-Rayet stars known at the time, Fleming discovered 94. In 1891, Fleming discovered spectral variations corresponding to changes in the light from the star Beta Lyrae, indicating that it was a double star. The latter discovery is usually credited to Pickering. Fleming's early work was published under Pickering's name, although by 1890, "M. Fleming" was appearing on the reports as Pickering's coauthor.

Directed the Women of the Harvard College Observatory

Fleming's work at the observatory was so outstanding that Pickering put her in charge of hiring and supervising a team of women to sort and study the immense collection of photographs of star spectra. Over the next 15 years, Fleming hired some 20 women. Some of them were college graduates who had majored in astronomy and went on to become famous astronomers in their own right. Among these women were Antonia Maury, Henrietta Leavitt, and Annie Jump Cannon. In 1893, Fleming gave a speech on women's work in astronomy at the Chicago World's Fair, and following this, astronomy as a scientific profession for women

became a subject for the popular press. As a result, other observatories around the United States began hiring women.

In 1898, Fleming was made curator of astronomical photographs at the Observatory, the first woman appointed by the Harvard Corporation. She directed the work of the other women, assisted Pickering at the Observatory, and prepared the work of other astronomers for publication. Much of her time was occupied with editing the *Annals of the Harvard College Observatory*, which she resented because this distracted her from her own astronomical research. Fleming worked 60-hour weeks for a salary of $1,500 per year, which was far below what the newest male assistant at the Observatory received. Her recently discovered journals from 1900 reveal her frustration with this situation, particularly because she was putting her son through the Massachusetts Institute of Technology at the time. She had to struggle to make ends meet, but she was even more indignant at having her work and expertise undervalued.

Fleming was awarded honorary memberships in the Royal Astronomical Society and the French and Mexican astronomical societies. The latter presented her with a gold medal for her discovery of new stars. She was one of 11 women charter members of the American Astronomical Society and an honorary fellow of Wellesley College. After her death from pneumonia at the age of 54, Fleming was succeeded as curator by her protege, Annie Jump Cannon.

Books

Jones, Bessie Z. and Lyle Boyd. *The Harvard College Observatory: The First Four Directorships, 1839-1919*. Harvard University Press, 1971.
Notable American Women 1607-1950: A Biographical Dictionary. Edited by Edward T. James, Janet Wilson James, and Paul W. Boyer. Harvard University Press, 1971.
Rossiter, Margaret W. *Women Scientists in America: Struggles and Strategies to 1940*. Johns Hopkins University Press, 1982.

Periodicals

Science, June 30, 1911. □

Judah Folkman

In the battle against cancer, Dr. Judah Folkman (born 1933) has found a new approach: to attack the blood vessels that nourish cancer cells. The results of initial tests in cancer-bearing mice performed in 1998 were promising enough to raise the hopes of both cancer patients and physicians worldwide.

A noted professor, physician, and former surgeon-in-chief at the Boston Pediatric Hospital, Dr. Judah M. Folkman has demonstrated that by cutting off the blood supply nourishing cancer cells, cancer tumors can be

killed with only negligible side effects. Theorizing on a method to prevent the growth of existing tumors, Folkman decided to try blocking the signals sent out by these tumors to perform angiogenesis—the formation of new blood vessels. To test his theory, he used two agents—angiostatin and endostatin—to treat cancer in laboratory mice. Although the results were positive, they were not conclusive, for other cancer-fighting drugs had a history of working well on mice but not as well on humans. By 2000 there remained the task of completing extensive tests on humans before EntreMed Inc., a Rockville, Maryland-based biotech company, could begin to put the new compounds on the market.

Discovered How Cancer Cells Grow

The son of Rabbi Jerome Folkman and his wife, Bessie, Folkman came to a love of medicine early in life. At his bar mitzvah his father told him to be a credit to his people; as an adult Folkman determined to dedicate himself to cancer research as a way of following his father's advice. In 1961 he made an astounding discovery. While doing medical research in a U.S. Navy laboratory, he found that cancer cells grow because they have an abundant blood supply. From this discovery Folkman developed the theory of angiogenesis and hypothesized further that cancers could not thrive without this abundant blood supply. A tumor formed, he theorized, because it could somehow stimulate new blood cells to deliver to it the nutrients it required in order to grow. Without sufficient blood, a cancer would not be able to grow any larger than a pin head.

Folkman's theory led him to look for ways to block blood vessel growth. He worked for years before he was able to develop compounds that sufficiently inhibited angiogenesis. These compounds, the human proteins endostatin and angiostatin, seemed like the answer to a prayer for people affected by cancer. Endostatin in particular showed promise; its marked lack of toxicity seemed to make it safe for human testing and two small-scale clinical trials at the U.S. National Cancer Institute (NCI) were authorized to further examine its effects on humans.

In February 1999, the NCI verified that Folkman's results with endostatin could be replicated. The human protein endostatin not only inhibited tumor growth in mice, but also showed no side effects when tested on in monkeys, even when administered in high doses. In an exciting announcement, the NCI confirmed that endostatin's anti-angiogenesis properties dramatically shrank cancerous tumors in laboratory mice.

The NCI's announcement came at the end of 30 years of arduous work on the part of Folkman. Years of work resulted in his discovery that blood vessels provided the key to cancer's survival, and much more research was subsequently undertaken in order for him to determine the basic process by which cancerous tumors spark the formation of the new blood vessels required to feed their growth. "Most research is failure," Folkman told *NOVA* producer Nancy Linde. "You go years and years and years, and then every once in a while there is a tremendous finding, and you realize for the first time in your life that you know something that hour or that day that nobody else in history has ever known, and you can understand something of how nature works."

Perhaps most frustrating for Folkman during his decades of research was the time it took him to convince the medical community that his theory had merit. Although he encountered skepticism from researchers, Folkman persisted because he knew that as a surgeon he had the hands-on experience with live human cancer tissues that researchers lacked. During surgery, Folkman had seen small tumors in the thyroid gland and the lining of the abdomen that never grew very large because they could not stimulate blood vessel growth. That led him to think that some kind of angiogenesis factor, possibly a diffusible protein, could stimulate the growth of blood vessels in certain tissues. But where the factor could not stimulate the formation of new blood vessels, the cancer did not grow. That meant cancer could be kept from growing if it could not attract the formation of a nutrient source. Folkman focused on determining what the factor was and if it could be blocked.

Discovered the Angiogenic Factor

Folkman maintains that being a researcher is one of the hardest jobs around, because, unlike a surgeon, a researcher doesn't get feedback from patients. That means that years of criticism, along with funding problems, must be faced before any positive reinforcement results from one's work. His own research experience was no exception to that rule. Fortunately, he was persistent; his knowledge as a practicing surgeon gave him the courage to continue presenting his ideas.

Although Folkman's ideas were at first largely discounted, by the 1970s that began to change. Researchers agreed that tumors did seem to cause the presence of new blood vessels, but most thought it was a side effect of dying cancer cells. They did not believe that the live cells actually stimulated the formation of new blood vessels.

When Robert Auerbach came to Folkman's lab, the two researchers conducted an experiment that proved the cancer cells were in fact causing the formation of blood vessels as a means of feeding their growth. Auerbach put live tumor cells in one eye of a rabbit and dying tumor cells in the other eye. The results showed that blood vessels formed around the live cells, not the dying ones. This proved that live cancer cells were actually causing the growth of the blood vessels.

In 1971 the *New England Journal of Medicine* published Folkman's paper that discussed the angiogenesis factor. Folkman began by noting that new blood vessels were recruited by tumors. Second, he maintained, the tumors sent out a factor that caused angiogenesis, or the formation of new blood vessels. Third, he said, this factor would stimulate the growth of new blood vessels. If this factor could be blocked, he hypothesized, tumors would stay small.

In 1984 Folkman and his team of researchers published a paper about the first angiogenic factor, a molecule that stimulated angiogenesis. He was later to discover 17 molecules, but the discovery of the first convinced him that he was on the right track. When he was unable to find the biological factor that stimulated blood vessel growth, Folkman began to wonder if he was being headstrong about his ideas rather than persistent. Realizing that he was right took time, but it was worth it in the end, when the medical community realized that through his work there was new hope for cancer patients: their disease could be stopped without debilitating side effects.

Experimented with Inhibitors

Killing cancer is a daunting task that often requires extensive drug treatments, chemotherapy, and radiation, which takes a heavy toll on healthy cells in the body. Cancer cells are more resistant to drugs than are normal cells, which is part of the reason why they are so hard to kill. The genius of Folkman's solution is that blood vessels are normal cells that respond readily to drugs. When subjected to angiostatin and endostatin treatments, blood vessels disappear, and with them, the tumors that feed on them. The anti-angiogenesis process might be compared to starving an enemy out by laying siege to his castle. No food supplies can get in, so the enemy eventually weakens. "We have been leveling out in our ability to stop cancer using available tools," Robert Siegel, director of hematology and oncology at George Washington University Medical Center, told *Insight on the News:* "The idea of having a completely new approach that is effective with some cancers is exciting."

Following testing on endostatin and its approval for use on human subjects, Duane Gay was one of the first to be treated with the substance. Although a tumor in his rib grew, those in his liver, lungs, and kidney stabilized. With the anti-angiogenic benefits of the drug interferon-alpha, Folkman also had successes treating children with hemangiomas, or life-threatening masses of blood capillaries. By the year 2000, 30 drugs were considered angiogenic inhibitors.

The Value of Observation

That Folkman perceived something no one else had noticed while working with cancer patients was not surprising to the people who know him best. Dr. C. Everett Koop, one of Folkman's colleagues at Boston Children's Hospital, found his colleague's power of observation startling. For example, when Folkman started in pediatric surgery, he had no experience working on young children. Koop painstakingly showed him the difference between pediatric tissues and adult tissues. While watching Koop, Folkman discovered that Koop's technique largely depended on steadying things with his left thumbnail against his left forefinger. Fingernails, Folkman decided, made all the difference. Koop had never realized how important his fingernails were before, but he knew Folkman was right.

Folkman's skill as a pediatric surgeon grew, as did his skill as a physician and researcher. He also became s a noteworthy professor whose students at Harvard Medical School counted him among their best teachers. Throughout the years Folkman conveyed to his students the importance of staying connected to patients. As a doctor, he gave his home telephone number and beeper number so that his patients could contact him. As a surgeon, he believed there was no such thing as "false hope." He advised his students never to tell a patient that there was nothing they could do to help him or her, because there was always something, even if it was only making the patient feel better.

In all his years of research, Folkman never lost sight of the people he was helping. Despite repeated criticism, he persevered with his assertions regarding cancer treatments until the medical community finally acknowledged that his research had in fact expanded their understanding of the disease. In fact, Folkman's research has applications for 26 diseases, including arthritis, cancer, Crohn's disease, endometriosis, and leukemia.

Robert Cooke, author of *Dr. Folkman's War: Angiogenesis and the Struggle to Defeat Cancer,* wrote that by 2000 Folkman's work was clearly recognized as having contributed to the sum of medical knowledge. "Finally it seemed that his peers were judging him to be persistent, not obstinate," Cooke wrote. "This was a distinction he had long sought. Now it seemed clear that great strides had been made largely because one man worked, pushed, and badgered one idea for so many years. Step by painful step, at first alone and then with colleagues he had engaged the struggle, Folkman had faced the objections and surmounted all the barriers that inflexible critics and doubters threw in his path. This experience had bred an enduring confidence and had even given him a sense of peace."

Books

Cooke, Robert, *Dr. Folkman's War: Angiogenesis and the Struggle to Defeat Cancer,* Random House, 2001.

Periodicals

Cancer Weekly Plus, September 27, 1999.
Insight on the News, June 8, 1998.
Maclean's, May 18, 1998.
Newsweek, February 19, 2001.
People Weekly, May 25, 1998.
Scientist, May 14, 2001.
U.S. News and World Report, December 9, 1996.

Online

"Dr. Folkman Speaks," *NOVA,* http://www.pbs.org/wgbh/nova/cancer/folkman.html (January 6, 2002).
"Judah Folkman: Inventing the Future," *Biospace,* http://www.biospace.com/articles/010600_Judah.cfm (January 6, 2002).

□

Lavinia Fontana

A producer of over 135 sophisticated oil paintings, Lavinia Fontana (1552-1614) was one of the first female portraitists to seek commissions. Her prolific body of work encompasses numerous categories of art, including single and group portraits, church altar art, and narrative and historic scenes. She was the first Bolognese female to earn renown throughout Italy.

Born in Bologna in 1552, Lavinia Fontana was the daughter of cosmopolitan fresco artist and teacher Prospero Fontana, who established his reputation in Rome and joined Giorgio Vasari in adorning Florence's Palazzo Vecchio. Unlike most female artists of the period, Lavinia received encouragement at home, where her father taught her to paint. She came under the influence of one of her father's pupils, Ludovico Carracci, founder of Bologna's academy. Beyond other women seeking careers in art, she flourished in an open-minded city that claimed painter Caterina dei Vigri as patron saint and which had welcomed women to its university since its opening in 1158.

A Life Dedicated to Art

At her father's studio Fontana met painter Giano Paolo Zappi and married him when she was twenty-five. They formed a working partnership that supported her career, allowing her to accept a growing number of commissions for baroque portraits, small paintings, and religious art. To assist her work, Zappi abandoned his career, kept Fontana's accounts, and tended the couple's 11 children, of whom only three outlived their mother. Art critics surmise that Zappi also painted some of the drapery and background in Fontana's paintings.

Both financially and critically successful, Fontana was a representative painter of the Italian mannerist school, earning a reputation for pose, detail, and the use of a delicate palette. Such qualities are reflected in Fontana's self-portrait that now hangs in the Uffizi Gallery at Florence. Therein she is elegantly dressed in lace and jewels and studying archeological finds on shelves and a table, likely as preparation for sketching them. Venturing beyond traditional still lifes and set poses into high drama, she painted mythic and biblical figures on a grand scale and used as models female and male nudes. At age 27 she received a commission from Dominican scholar and church historian Pietro Ciaconio for the first of her two self-portraits, "Self-Portrait Seated at Her Desk," which features her in a composed, contemplative posture. Painted the following year, "Portrait of a Noblewoman" depicts a standing female figure holding a decoratively jeweled marten skin and absently petting a lap dog. Characteristic of Fontana's images is the incorporation of textured and embroidered fabrics and rich gold jewelry set with pearls and rubies.

Fontana excelled at the depiction of the female form, either alone or in groups, as exemplified in "Portrait of the Gozzadini Family" (1584), a psychologically complex grouping. In the undated "Allegory of Music" she painted a female keyboardist at the virginal accompanied by three males, two lute players and a vocalist. She surrounded this musical group with a variety of instruments: cittern, cornetto, harp, hurdy-gurdy, recorder, viol, and viola da braccio. For "Visit of the Queen of Sheba," which now hangs in Dublin's National Gallery, Fontana improvised a demanding narrative scene that depicts the unnamed queen's royal presentation to Solomon albeit in Renaissance costume and court.

Expanding Challenges

By the time she reached her thirties, Fontana was respected as a painter of devotional art. In 1581 she completed "Jesus Appears to Mary Magdalen" in the balanced dark-against-light style of Antonio Correggio. The painting, now housed in Florence's Uffizi Gallery, captures the rapt attention of a familiar bible figure moved by a glimpse of Christ. In this same period, Fontana completed "The Dead Christ with Symbols of the Passion" and "The Holy Family," the latter an undated piece that creates an adult triad of the Virgin Mary and Elizabeth comparing the virtues of their toddler sons Jesus and John the Baptist, while the third figure, a colorless Joseph, looks on in the background. At the request of the Vizzani Chapel at the church of Santa Maria della Morte in Bologne, in 1590 Fontana painted "St. Francis of Paola Blessing a Child," now displayed in the city's Pinacoteca Nazionale. The work contrasts a bevy of overdressed aristocratic ladies with the simple demeanor of a saint performing a sacred task.

Fontana used imagination to recreate images from the past. In a 1585 painting she depicted Egyptian monarch Cleopatra cloaked in red and adorned with a jeweled hat and veil. Standing before an urn, the regal figure suggests the Renaissance era's immersion in Eastern subjects. That same year, Fontana created a likeness of Venus and Cupid, the mother and son from classic mythology who superintend passion and infatuation. Desiring a work to grace the grand Escorial Palace in Madrid, Philip II of Spain commissioned Fontana to paint an altarpiece, "The Holy Family with the Sleeping Christ Child."

From Bologna to Rome

In 1603, after her father's death, Fontana was a recipient of a rare honor, particularly for a female artist, when Pope Clement VIIII summoned her to an audience in the papal palace. At Clement's request, she executed her most famous public work, a 20-foot altarpiece titled "The Stoning of St. Stephen Martyr," which pictures the pathos of the first Christian to die for the faith. The altarpiece adorned one of Rome's seven pilgrimage centers, the church of San Paolo Fuori le Mura, until the building was consumed by fire in 1823 and the painting was lost.

In 1611, during Fontana's residence in Rome, sculptor Felice Antonio Cassoni cast a medal to honor her contribution to the arts. The obverse pictures her in profile; the reverse depicts her as the symbolic female artist, too immersed in her work to tame her flowing hair. As the first woman to be commissioned for public paintings, Fontana earned membership in the prestigious Roman Academy.

Fontana's work was lucrative enough to support her family. Popes Gregory XIII and Clement VIII each posed for her in ceremonial regalia and the Vatican offered her commissions normally contracted to male artists. Of her 135 works—the largest corpus of artwork by any woman from the Renaissance or before—only 32 are signed and dated. In 1998, Professor Vera Fortunati of the University of Bologna arranged for the first U.S. exhibition of Fontana's canvases at the National Museum of the Arts in Washington, D.C.

Books

A Dictionary of Art & Artists, Penguin, 1976.
The Women's Chronology, edited by James Trager, Holt, 1995.
Women's World, edited by Irene Franck and David Brownstone, HarperPerennial, 1995.

Periodicals

Art in America, August 1, 2001.
Instructor, March 1992.
San Francisco Chronicle, March 30, 1998.
Washington Post, February 13, 1998.
Washington Times, April 29, 1998.

Online

"Lavinia Fontana," http://www.nmwa.org/legacy/bios/bfontana .htm (January 15, 2002).
The Lives of Renaissance Women, http://www.bctf.bc.ca/ lessonaids/online/LA9245.html (January 15, 2002). □

Dion Fortune

Occultist, medium, and author Dion Fortune (1890-1946) presented her beliefs in Christian mysticism, pantheism, magic, and psychology through her published works and her association with the Hermetic Order of the Golden Dawn and the establishment of the Fraternity of the Inner Light.

As a medium, Fortune went to lengths to explain that she did not disturb the spirits of the dead, but rather channeled an intelligence from a higher plane of existence. Her first essays to contain such explanations appeared in the British magazine The Occult Review in the mid-1920s and, later, in her own magazine, The Inner Light, which she edited from 1927 to 1940. Much of this work reflects her interest in the legends of King Arthur and the Knights of the Round Table as well as the legends of the Welsh poem The Mabinogian. Believing that the historical basis of the Arthurian legends existed in the English countryside at Glastonbury in Somerset, she established a retreat for the Fraternity of the Inner Light there. According to Fortune biographer and essayist Gareth Knight in his introduction to Aspects of Occultism, "She maintained a deep sympathy for the renaissance of native tradition, where she felt this tradition had its heart, combined with an early form of Christianity via the legends of Joseph of Arimathea and of the Holy Grail."

Fortune also examined these concerns in several works of fiction, including her novels The Winged Bull and The Goat-Foot God, which displayed the pantheistic thematic concerns of D. H. Lawrence. Some later works attributed to Fortune's authorship were reputedly dictated from the afterlife to the medium Margaret Lumley Brown. In other essays and fiction, she examined feminine mythological archetypes, human sexuality as a generator of psychic energies, and the visionary and magical concept of pathworkings, an expanded method of the Golden Dawn's explorations of the Tree of Life.

Studied Psychology and Mysticism

Fortune was born Violet Mary Firth in the village of Bryn-y-Bia, in Llandudno, Wales, on December 6, 1890, to parents who followed the Christian Science religion. Her father, Arthur Firth, was a solicitor, and her mother was a registered Christian Science healer. Reportedly cognizant of her mystical abilities from an early age, Fortune claimed to have received visions of Atlantis when she was four years old and believed that she had been a temple priestess there in a former life. Fortune claimed that she first recognized her mediumistic abilities during her adolescence. She is said to have joined the Theosophical Society of Madame Helena Blavatsky briefly in 1906 when her family moved to London, but rejected the theosophists' reliance on Eastern thought, largely due to Indian revolts against British rule. In April 1908, Fortune published a poem, "Angels," in the Christian Science Monitor.

Prior to World War I, Fortune said she had a nervous breakdown, brought on by the "psychic attacks" of a woman with whom she had worked. During this period, she also studied the works of Sigmund Freud and Carl Jung as a student of Professor Flugel at the University of London, who was a member of the Society of Psychical Research. She preferred Jung's work to Freud's, particularly Jung's examination of the archetypes of the collective unconscious, but she ultimately rejected both men as unable to comprehend the full range of the human mind's capabilities. During World War I, Fortune worked with a government agency on the development of protein supplements from soybeans; she subsequently advised her father in a business venture to manufacture and sell dairy substitutes derived from soybeans.

Fortune worked as a lay psychoanalyst in a medico-psychological clinic in London and became a therapist in 1918. While working at the clinic, Fortune is believed to have met Dr. Theodore Moriarty, an Irish Freemason who expressed his metaphysical and theosophical beliefs in a series of lectures on the esoteric subject of astro-etheric psychological conditions. Moriarty's lecture topics included the lost continent of Atlantis, Gnostic Christianity, reincarnation, and psychic disturbances that result in illness. Perhaps more influential on her occult interests, however, was Fortune's childhood friend, Maiya Curtis-Webb, who introduced her to the Hermetic Order of the Golden Dawn. Beginning in 1919, Curtis-Webb instructed Fortune in trance mediumship at the Golden Dawn Temple of the Alpha and Omega Lodge of the Stella Matutina, which was led by J. W. Brodie-Innes. She became disillusioned with the group, however, when she saw that its ranks had been reduced to widows and elderly men because of World War I, and she joined the London-based Golden Dawn group led by Moina Mathers, widow of the group's original founder, MacGregor Mathers. It was during this period that the former Violet Firth adopted the phrase *Deo Non Fortuna,* which translates as "by God and not by luck," as her name. Intended to be her Golden Dawn magical name, it is also the Latin motto that appeared on the Firth family crest. She subsequently shortened her new appellation to Dion Fortune.

Formed the Fraternity of the Inner Light

In 1921, Fortune worked with Frederick Bligh Bond in a group of Arthurian enthusiasts called the Watchers of Avalon. In 1922, Fortune established her own outer-court Golden Dawn lodge called the Christian Mystic Lodge of the Theosophical Society. Agreeing with Moriarty's conjecture that the Christian Gospels are essentially allegories, Fortune also agreed with her mentor that Jesus Christ was a prophet of the same rank as Orpheus, Mithra, and Melchizedek, while remaining steadfastly resolute in her conviction that the "Master Jesus" was her spiritual guide. Her affinity to Blavatsky's teachings is reflected in her appropriating the term "theosophical" for her new group. Fortune published her first book, *Machinery of the Mind* in 1922, under her birth name, Violet Firth. It was her subsequent works, however, that brought Fortune fame and notoriety.

In 1922, she and Charles Thomas Loveday, who served as both Fortune's patron and secretary, worked together to produce *The Esoteric Philosophy of Love and Marriage,* which Fortune narrated from a psychic trance to Loveday, who then transcribed Fortune's narration. The book had repercussions, however, when Moina Mathers became annoyed at what she perceived as Fortune's disclosure of Golden Dawn secrets. In the book, Fortune discussed that human sexuality could be a mystical as well as a physical union, and that the sexual act could be used to generate otherworldly energies. Mathers was infuriated further by articles that were eventually published in Fortune's books *The Cosmic Doctrine* and *Sane Occultism,* the latter republished as *What Is Occultism?* In this work, Fortune questioned why the occult sciences attracted charlatans rather than the world's leading intellectual thinkers. She also disparaged the sentimentality and unscientific nature of most published works on the occult and declared that most occult practitioners were inept. She also offered recommendations on how to identify past lives, as well as discussions on numerology and astrology, yoga, and vegetarianism. She also staunchly opposed drug use, homosexuality, promiscuity in general, and premarital and extramarital sex.

Mathers suspended Fortune temporarily from the Golden Dawn and eventually terminated Fortune's membership permanently. Fortune responded by aligning herself with the Golden Dawn splinter sect of the Stella Matutina. She believed that Mathers engaged in psychic attacks on her during this period, employing magic to block Fortune's astral projections and inundating her home with black cats and simulacrums, which are apparitions conjured by an individual possessing magical powers. Fortune detailed these claims, as well as her previous nervous breakdown, in an article for the *Occult Review* entitled "Ceremonial Magic Unveiled," and in her 1929 book *Psychic Self-Defense: A Study in Occult Pathology and Criminality,* in which she also offered remedies for supernatural aggressions.

After severing her ties with the Golden Dawn, Fortune embarked upon a busy and productive period that included establishing the Community of the Inner Light, which later became the Fraternity of the Inner Light in 1927, and existed into the twenty-first century as the Society of the Inner Light. Her fascination with Celtic mythology also blossomed during this period following an extended stay in Glastonbury in 1923 and 1924. She believed during this time that she had been contacted by the spirits of Greek philosopher Socrates and Arthurian magician Merlin, which she chronicles in her book *Glastonbury: Avalon of the Heart.* The Fraternity of the Inner Light purchased an unused Army barrack, which they rebuilt as a lodge in Glastonbury and which Fortune named the Chalice Orchard Club to complement the group's London headquarters.

In 1922, Fortune launched her career as a writer of fiction with the first of a series of short stories featuring the character of Dr. Traverner, whom many critics believe was inspired by her friendship with Moriarty. Originally published in *Royal Magazine,* Fortune's 1926 short story *The Secrets of Dr. Traverner* details the adventures of an occult investigator who explores the negative psychic aftereffects of World War I, including a soldier possessed by a vampire in the book's opening story, "Blood-Lust." In other stories, Fortune presents Dr. Traverner as an explorer of themes of reincarnation and psychic revenge. While critics usually judge her fiction writing abilities negatively, most agree that Fortune's work often presents lucid explanations for her own theories and concerns. Reception of Fortune's first novel, *The Demon Lover* in 1927, was more positive. In this novel, Fortune presents the corrupt Lucas, who intends to manipulate the innocent medium, Veronica Mainwaring, in order to apply his black arts in the spiritual realm. He is killed, but condemned to vampirism until Veronica, Lucas's unrequited lover from a previous life, returns him to life. Fortune married Thomas Penry Evans in 1927.

Published *The Mystical Qabalah*

Fortune continued writing and publishing prodigiously into the early 1930s, then her output slowed considerably. Fortune moved away from Christianity during this period, an action that many critics attributed to her affinity to the paganistic novels of D. H. Lawrence; the influence of her husband, who focused on the Greek pagan spirit, Pan; and her magic partner from 1934 to 1937, Charles Seymour, who was convinced that twentieth-century Christianity was spiritually bankrupt. *The Winged Bull* and *The Goat-Foot God* reflect these influences but are considered among her weakest fictional efforts due to what critics perceived as weak characterizations. In 1936, Fortune attended a series of university lectures on tantra given by Bernard Bromage, which led to the pair conducting a series of evening discussions on literature and the occult. She published what many of her followers consider to be her most important work that same year, *The Mystical Qabalah.* In this work, Fortune discussed perhaps most fully her design for a Western-based esoteric belief system based on the Kabbalah. Employing Carl Jung's concept of the archetypal symbols of humankind's mass unconscious, Fortune postulated that the human mind helped shape the true nature of its gods through human contacts in the astral plane.

In her final two novels, *The Sea Priestess* and *Moon Magic,* Fortune introduces the character Lilith Le Fay Morgan. Morgan revives the cult of the ancient goddess Isis and conducts elaborate rituals in her honor. The former novel was completed in 1936, but Fortune was unable to find a publisher for two years. She eventually published the novel herself two years later. Both works serve to introduce the rituals that Fortune herself was conducting in a converted London church. Nicknamed the Belfry, the building was dedicated to the worship of the mysteries of Isis, whom Fortune depicted as a feminine expression of God which the Virgin Mary was also a component. The final chapter of *Moon Magic* is believed by Inner Light members to have been written after Fortune's death through her close friend and Inner Light medium, Margaret Lumley Brown.

Fortune ceased writing in 1939, which some biographers speculate resulted from three personal upheavals that occurred that year, including divorce, the outbreak of World War II, and the dissolution of her partnership with Seymour. She did continue contributing articles to the *Inner Light* which illustrated her return to Christian thinking. Other historians speculate that she turned in a new direction and had sought the help of Aleister Crowley in her efforts. During World War II, Fortune continued the work of the Fraternity of the Inner Light during Nazi bombing of London. She attempted to apply magic against Great Britain's enemies in a project she eventually published as *The Magical Battle of Britain*. She died in 1946, one week after being diagnosed with leukemia. The Society of the Inner Light continued, however, and Fortune's works and the Society continued to inspire occultists, pagans, and students of magic.

Books

Buckland, Raymond, *The Witch Book: The Encyclopedia of Witchcraft, Wicca, and Neo-Paganism,* Visible Ink Press, 2002.

Chapman, Janine, *Quest for Dion Fortune,* Samuel Weiser, 1993.

Drury, Neville, *The History of Magic in the Modern Age: A Quest for Personal Transformation,* Carroll & Graf Publishers, Inc., 2000.

Fielding, Charles, and Clark Collins, *The Story of Dion Fortune,* Samuel Weiser, 1985.

Fortune, Dion, *Aspects of Occultism,* Samuel Weiser, Inc., 2000.

Fortune, Dion, *What Is Occultism?* Samuel Weiser, Inc., 2000.

Hutton, Ronald, *The Triumph of the Moon: A History of Modern Pagan Witchcraft,* Oxford University Press, Inc., 1999.

Richardson, Alan, *Priestess: The Life and Magic of Dion Fortune,* Aquarian Press, 1987.

St. James Guide to Horror, Ghost & Gothic Writers, St. James Press, 1998.

Online

"About Dion Fortune," http://www.angelfire.com/az/garethknight/aboutdf.html (March 8, 2002).

"Fortune, Dion," http://themystica.com/mystica/articles/f/fortune_dion.html (March 8, 2002)

"Mystical-WWW: Dion Fortune" http://www.mystical-www.co.uk/glastonbury/dionf.htm (March 8, 2002). □

John Frankenheimer

Though American director John Frankenheimer (born 1930) is best known for his challenging films of the early 1960s, he got his start directing live television dramas in the 1950s and revived his career in that medium in the 1990s.

Frankenheimer was born on February 19, 1930, in Melba, New York. His father was a German Jewish stockbroker, while his mother was Irish Catholic. Frankenheimer was raised in the Catholic faith and received his education at LaSalle Military Academy, a Catholic military school. After graduating from LaSalle in 1947, Frankenheimer entered Williams College. By this time, he had developed an interest in acting and studied drama. Frankenheimer earned his B.A. degree from Williams in 1951.

Became Involved in Production

When Frankenheimer completed his education at Williams, the Korean War was underway. He served in the U.S. Air Force between 1951 and 1953. It was during this time that Frankenheimer became interested in the production of film and television and lost his interest in acting. He became attached to the film squadron that was based in California where he learned about production. Frankenheimer loved working with cameras, often taking some home on the weekend to learn more about them. Deciding to become a filmmaker, Frankenheimer produced some documentary shorts.

While still in the Air Force, Frankenheimer had his first experiences as a director. He had been writing for a local series in Los Angeles called either *Harvey Howard's Ranch Roundup* or *The Harry Howard Ranch Hour* (sources vary) that aired on KCOP. When the show's director was unable, he was forced to make his debut as director. The show featured cows and the rancher Howard. Despite his inexperience, Frankenheimer was kept on as director for three more months, until the show was taken off the air by the Federal Communications Commission.

Early Work in Television

When Frankenheimer's tour of duty in the military was completed, he decided to pursue his goal of directing. Returning to the East Coast, Frankenheimer was hired as an assistant director for CBS-TV in New York City. This was the era of live television and television plays. Between 1953 and 1954, Frankenheimer was the assistant director on shows such as *Person to Person*, *The Garry Moore Show*, and *You Are There*. Frankenheimer did the work of a cinematographer as well, by setting up shots in the control room for the director.

When Sidney Lumet, the director of *You Are There*, left the show to begin a film directing career in 1954, Frankenheimer was promoted to director. While Lumet went on to have a solid film career, Frankenheimer also made the most of his opportunity. He built a significant career directing live television plays that received much praise from critics and audiences alike.

While directing over 150 television plays for series like *Climax*, *Ford Startime*, *Buick Electra Playhouse*, *Playhouse 90*, and other anthology series, Frankenheimer worked with a number of accomplished actors, as well as future stars. They included Claudette Colbert, Ingrid Bergman, John Gielgud, and Paul Newman. Some of the more famous episodes that Frankenheimer directed were "The Snows of Kilimanjaro" and "Journey to the Day."

For Frankenheimer, live television was challenging. It allowed him the freedom to try out new things, including deep focus photography, distinctive angles, and other interesting camera work. Frankenheimer told Jay Carr of the *Boston Globe* that "I did an awful lot of television, and out of that I developed a very fluid camera style. I learned through doing it how to stage very complicated scenes and how to photograph them. So it gave me a great freedom when I got into movies—that I wasn't scared of it, that I didn't worry what I'd do with the camera, that I'd find a way to photograph the scene."

Directed First Film

Frankenheimer made his first foray into film directing in 1956. He turned an episode of the *Climax* series into a movie entitled *The Young Stranger*. As a film director, he tried to bring the same creativity that he employed in live television, but found his crew to be unresponsive and the medium too restrictive. Though critics generally were impressed, Frankenheimer returned to television and did not make another film for five years.

In the early 1960s, Frankenheimer left television and worked primarily in film for the next 30 years. This period proved to be his most fruitful as a filmmaker. He earned a reputation as an innovative, technically skilled filmmaker. Frankenheimer was not afraid to use fast film stocks and new light cameras. Many of these early successes featured themes of social and political intrigue.

After 1961's *The Young Savages*, a courtroom drama that dealt with social problems of the day, Frankenheimer made arguably the three most significant films of his career in 1962. The first *All Fall Down* was often overshadowed by the other two. This striking film about brothers was well-received by critics. A more popular film with audiences was *Birdman of Alcatraz*, a biopic of Robert Stroud that starred Burt Lancaster. Frankenheimer took over the production from Charles Crichton; he would perform such a task a number of times over his career.

The most important film by Frankenheimer in 1962 was *The Manchurian Candidate*. This political suspense thriller starred Frank Sinatra and Angela Landsbury. Both a commercial and critical success, it has retained an enduring following. Riding the success of these films, he formed his own production company, John Frankenheimer Productions, in 1963.

Frankenheimer made several more important films in the mid-1960s. *Seven Days in May* (1964) was, like *The Manchurian Candidate*, another Cold War suspense thriller. This film portrays a military coup attempt against the U.S. government. Frankenheimer took over the production of *The Train* (1964) after its first director, Arthur Penn, was fired. Set in Europe during World War II, the story focused on a train bound for Nazi Germany loaded with French art and the intrigue that surrounded it.

Decline in Reputation

By the late 1960s, the quality of Frankenheimer's work was seen as being in decline. His films were not as technically fresh and lacked the strong stories of his previous works. Critics believed that he made a misstep with his two 1966 releases, *Grand Prix* and *Seconds*. The former was about auto racing. Business demands forced Frankenheimer to cut the film in a way he believed was detrimental. The latter was about a man who changes his appearance.

On a more personal level, Frankenheimer suffered a great loss in the late 1960s. A close of friend of Senator Robert F. Kennedy, Frankenheimer had been hosting the presidential candidate at his home in Malibu in 1968 when Kennedy was assassinated. Frankenheimer was devastated by the loss. Soon after Kennedy's death, he moved to Europe with his second wife, actress Evans Evans. Though he continued to make films there, few were commercial successes. During his time in Europe, Frankenheimer also went took cooking lessons at the Cordon Bleu, emerging as a trained chef.

Returned to the United States

When Frankenheimer came back to the United States in the early 1970s, he enjoyed some successes as a filmmaker, though the quality of his work did not match his early films. After the relative failure of *The Iceman Cometh* (1973), Frankenheimer revived his career with *The French Connection II* (1975). He saw big box office success with *Black Sunday* (1977). The plot concerned a terrorist who planned to crash a blimp into the Superbowl.

After these high points, Frankenheimer had only a few releases scattered over the next decade. To many critics, his choice of projects was somewhat questionable. Many were made for the money. Among the undistinguished releases were *Prophecy* in 1979 and *The Challenge* in 1982. By the early 1980s, Frankenheimer had reached a low point in his career, stemming in part from a long-term problem with alcohol. After receiving treatment and dealing with many related issues, he stopped drinking in 1981 and was able to get his life back on track.

While Frankenheimer put his demons to rest, his professional life remained undistinguished. He was able to find work, but most of his projects were mediocre. In 1986, Frankenheimer directed *52 Pick-Up*, which was reasonably successful. Three years later, he took on *Dead Bang* (1989), which proved to be a commercial failure. *The Fourth War* (1990) was a political thriller in the same vein as *The Manchurian Candidate*, but without enjoying the same prestige.

Won Four Emmys

After the relative failure of *Year of the Gun* (1991), about a conspiracy that forms around an innocent American journalist in Rome, Frankenheimer did not make a film for five years. Instead, he focused on projects for television. These works were successful both with audiences and critics. His first movie was *Against the Wall* (1994) for the cable network, HBO. This was a personal story about the Attica prison riots that Frankenheimer shot in newsreel style. That same year, he took on another movie for HBO, *The Burning Season*, about Chico Mendes, the Brazilian activist who fought against the exploitation of workers in the Amazon rain forest. Both projects won Emmy Awards.

Frankenheimer then shot two movies for the TNT cable television network. *Andersonville* (1996) focused on the horrific Confederate prisoner-of-war camp in which thousands of Union soldiers died. The following year, TNT aired Frankenheimer's biopic *George Wallace*, about the former governor of Alabama who went from strict segregationist to support of the anti-segregation movement. Frankenheimer again won Emmys for both works. Though Frankenheimer had enjoyed much success as a film director, he told Nina J. Easton of the *Los Angeles Times*, "If they had live television today, I'd still be doing it. You had total control as a director. It was live, so we had final cut. And you had no such thing as a difficult actor."

Returned to Film

Frankenheimer's successes on television led to more film offers, though some of the projects were problematic. He took over the faltering production of *The Island of Dr. Moreau* (1996), after the film company, New Line Cinema, was forced to fire its first director. Frankenheimer agreed to take on the nightmarish production because he needed the money. Though the film was panned by critics, Frankenheimer delivered what New Line wanted: a completed film with a coherent, ordered story, that was reasonably successful at the box office.

His accomplishments with *Dr. Moreau* led to better film projects. In 1998, he directed *Ronin*, an action thriller that starred Robert De Niro and performed reasonably well at the box office. Frankenheimer's 30th film was another suspense thriller, this time focused on crime, called *Reindeer Games* (2000). While it received mixed reviews from critics, the film had some success connecting with audiences.

Still directing after the age of 70, Frankenheimer hoped to match, if not exceed, his early successes. He told Robert Wilonsky of the *Dallas Observer*, "You can't be burdened by your legacy. . . . People say, 'You'll never do a movie as good as *Manchurian Candidate*.' I say, 'I probably won't, but you know what? I'm just gonna keep on trudging along.' But the answer in my own heart is, I think I will."

Books

Barson, Michael, *The Illustrated Who's Who of Hollywood Directors Volume 1: The Sound Era*, Farrar, Straus and Giroux, 1995.

Katz, Ephraim. *The Film Encyclopedia*, HarperResource, 2001.

Pendergast, Tom, and Sara Pendergast, *International Dictionary of Films and Filmmakers-2: Directors*, St. James Press, 2000.

Periodicals

Adweek, June 5, 1989.
Boston Globe, October 27, 1991.
Dallas Observer, February 24, 2000.
Los Angeles Times, November 5, 1989; March 20, 1994; February 25, 2000.
Newsweek, March 4, 1996.
New York Times, March 24, 1994; January 18, 1996; September 13, 1998.
Washington Post, February 20, 2000.
Washington Times, February 18, 2000. □

John Frederick Charles Fuller

John Frederick Charles Fuller (1878-1966) was a prodigious writer of world and military history, and one of the progenitors of tank warfare strategy during and after World War I.

John Frederick Charles Fuller's career in the British military included service in the Second Boer War, service to the British Raj in India, World War I battlefield experience, and establishment of the Royal Tank Corps, where he earned respect as the man responsible for leading the first offensive in military history that employed tanks as the primary offensive weapon. After his retirement from the military in 1933, he dedicated himself as a military correspondent for the London *Daily Mail,* which provided him the opportunity to cover the Abyssinian War from 1935 to 1936 and the Spanish Civil War from 1936 to 1939. During this period, he met Adolph Hitler, Benito Mussolini, Francisco Franco, and various generals of Hitler's Third Reich. A controversial figure, Fuller was a member of Sir Oswald Mosely's fascist group, the British Union, during the 1930s and was a supporter of Europe's fascist governments, in addition to possessing ardent anti-Semitic views. Following World War II, he devoted himself to composing military histories, many of which are admired and remain in print. Fuller further incurred notoriety through his affiliation with occultist Aleister Crowley during the first decade of the twentieth-century, as well as his lifelong fascination with the occult.

Steeped in the Military and the Occult

John Frederick Charles Fuller (also known as J.F.C. Fuller) was born in Chichester, England, the son of Alfred, a minister, and Selma Fuller on September 1, 1878. Nicknamed "Boney," Fuller was educated at Malvern College and the Royal Military College in Sandhurst, England. His first commission was as a light infantry soldier in Oxfordshire and Buckinghamshire in 1898, before service in the Second Boer War. In 1903, he was commissioned to India, where he immersed himself in the country's mysticism. He was promoted to the rank of captain in 1905 and married Margaretha "Sonia" Karnatz the following year. In 1906, he also befriended Aleister Crowley. The friendship was initiated after Fuller read the poetry and occult writings of Crowley, which also caused Fuller to praise Crowley in his 1907 book, *The Star of the West.* In this work, Fuller declared Crowley "more than a new-born Dionysis, he is more than a [William] Blake, a Rabelais or a [Heinrich] Heine; for he stands before us as some priest of Apollo." Crowley's stated purpose was to replace Christianity with a new religion he dubbed Crowleyanity. To fulfill this end, he established a magical order, the Argenteum Astrum, or Silver Star. Besides Fuller, the Argentum Astrum included George Cecil Jones, Pamela Hansford Johnson, artist Austin Osman Spare, violinist Leila Waddell, and mathematics professor Norman Mudd from Bloemfontein. Essentially based on MacGregor Mather's secret rituals written for the Hermetic Order of the Golden Dawn, the Argenteum Astrum gradually incorporated Crowley's views on yoga and sex magic. Fuller co-edited with Crowley the Argentum Astrum magazine, *The Equinox,* and is credited also with introducing Crowley and Victor Neuburg, who became Crowley's most dedicated disciple and homosexual lover. It is important to note that Jean Overton Fuller, who wrote Neuburg's biography, was not related to J. F. C. Fuller. Legal enmity separated Fuller and Crowley in 1911, and Fuller disparaged his *The Star of the West* as "a jumble of undigested reading with a boyish striving after effect." He maintained until his death, however, that Crowley was "one of the greatest of English lyric poets." Fuller continued his interest in esoteric subject matter, publishing *Yoga: A Study of the Mystical Philosophy of the Brahmins and Buddhists* and *Atlantis: America and the Future* in 1925 and *The Secret Wisdom of the Quabalah* in 1937.

While indulging his passion for the occult, Fuller contemporaneously progressed in his military career. In 1907, he was assigned to the Second Middlesex Volunteers, which became known as the Tenth Middlesex Volunteers after 1908. Serving as an instructor allowed Fuller to refine his writing skills, which he employed to compose training manuals. By 1914, he had written two books upon entering the military staff college at Camberley. He proceeded to alienate his instructors and senior officers with an uncooperative and surly disposition that ultimately stifled his military career. The student papers he composed were refused by his commanding officer. He was placed in several staff positions in England before his transfer to the western front of World War I in July of 1915. The delay in sending him to the battlefield caused him to miss the First Battle of Ypres, which resulted in the slaughter of the regular British Expeditionary Force. In December of 1916, Fuller transferred to the Heavy Branch Machine Gun Corps, where he acquitted himself admirably by writing a series of papers on the ability of the tank to eliminate the devastating fatalities and time-consuming aspects of trench warfare. The methods outlined in his paper "Plan 1919" were based upon the successful British tank attack on Cambrai, inspired by Fuller and representing the first time a tank was used successfully as a primary offense weapon. Invigorated by the success at Cambrai, Fuller pressed the importance of mechanized warfare. He insisted that tanks should be used as a flanking device that, coordinated with aircraft support, could effectively frighten opponents into surrender.

Fuller's military career continued after World War I, but his insubordinate behavior and insistence on his principles for warfare prevented him from making an effective contribution as a military strategist. He was assigned to the Staff Duties branch at the War Office, and was assigned to the Tank Corps in 1922, which eventually became known as the Royal Tank Corps. In 1923, he was reassigned as a chief instructor at the Staff College, and his lectures were published later as *The Reformation of War* and *The Foundations of the Science of War.* In 1925, he began a long and fruitful editorial partnership with Captain Sir Basil Henry Liddell Hart, a prodigious writer of military history. Two years later, Fuller was given the opportunity to command the inaugural Experimental Brigade, but by all accounts ruined his chances by behaving in a belligerent fashion. Upset that his ideas were not put into practice, Fuller re-

signed but was reinstated shortly thereafter. The result, however, was that his hopes for military advancement were nullified. Instead of another prestigious appointment, he was transferred to serve as General Staff Officer at Aldershot and subsequently served as commander of the Second Rhine Brigade at Wiesbaden, Germany. He was promoted to Major General in 1930 but placed on half pay by the British Army after refusing the command of the Second Class District of Bombay, India. He wrote several military books in 1932, including *Lectures on Field Service Regulations, II, Lectures on Field Service Regulations, III,* and *The Dragon's Teeth: A Study of War and Peace.* By the end of 1933, Fuller was placed on the Army's retirement list.

Fascism and Military History

In 1934, Fuller joined Sir Oswald Mosely's British Union of Fascists and engaged in fascist propaganda leading up to World War II. His military background, however, rescued him from British arrest in 1940, while all other British Union leaders were incarcerated. Because of his membership in the British Union, he was refused military service during World War II. Much of the writing he produced during this period is vehemently anti-Semitic, which endeared him to such high-ranking officials of Hitler's Third Reich as Heinz Guderian, one of the German military's chief proponents of Panzer warfare. Such was his affinity to Fuller, that Guderian referred to him as his mentor. As a military correspondent for the London *Daily Mail* during the 1930s and 1940s, Fuller traveled to the fascist capitals of Europe and knew the era's chief fascist proponents. Following the war, Fuller dedicated himself to writing military histories on the campaigns of such generals as Ulysses S. Grant, Julius Caesar, Robert E. Lee, and Alexander the Great. He also contributed more than 400 articles to British and American periodicals.

Books

Chambers Biographical Dictionary, 6th edition, edited by Melanie Parry, Larousse Kingfisher Chambers, 1997.
Contemporary Authors, Permanent Series, Gale Research, 1975.
Dictionary of National Biography, 1961-1970, edited by E.T. Williams and C.S. Nicholls, Oxford University Press, 1981.
Drury, Neville, *The History of Magic in the Modern Age: A Quest for Personal Transformation,* Carroll & Graf Publishers, Inc., 2000.
The Encyclopedia of Occultism & Parapsychology, 5th Edition, edited by J. Gordon Melton, Gale Group, 2001.
Fuller, John Frederick Charles, *A Military History of the Western World, Volume 1: From the Earliest Times to the Battle of Lepanto,* Da Capo Press, Inc., 1954.
Historical Encyclopedia of World War II, edited by Marcel Baudot, Facts on File, 1980.
The Oxford Companion to Military History, edited by Richard Holmes, Oxford University Press, 2001.
The Reader's Companion to Military History, edited by Robert Cowley and Geoffrey Parker, Houghton Mifflin Company, New York, New York, 1996.
Who's Who in Twentieth-Century Warfare, edited by Spencer C. Tucker, Routledge, 2001. □

Casimir Funk

The discoverer of vitamins, Polish American bio-chemist Casimir Funk (1884-1967) found that vitamins B1, B2, C, and D were necessary to human health and that vitamins contributed to the normal functioning of the hormonal system. His work led to the prevention of beriberi, rickets, scurvy, and other diseases caused by vitamin deficiency.

Studied in Switzerland and Germany

Funk was born February 23, 1884, in Warsaw, Poland, then part of Russia. His mother was Gustawa Zysan and his father was Jacques Funk, a dermatologist. At the time, education for Poles was difficult. All public schools were under Russia's control. Getting into a school required the help of someone with influence.

Funk was tutored at home until he was admitted to public school, where he did well at his studies. Dissatisfied with the education Funk was receiving, his parents enrolled him in the Warsaw Gymnasium in 1894. Funk graduated in 1900 and continued his education. He studied biology under Robert Chodat at the University of Geneva in Switzerland, then transferred to the University of Bern in Germany, where he studied chemistry under Carl Friedheim and Stanislaw Kostanecki. (Funk and Kostanecki later published an article on the synthesis of stilbestrols.)

In 1904, Funk earned his Ph.D. after completing his dissertation on how to prepare two stilbene dyes, Brasilin and H„matoxylin. He then went to the Pasteur Institute in Paris, where he studied organic bases and amino acids under Gabriel Bertrand. During his time in Paris, Funk experimented with laccol, a phenol that caused him to suffer painful swelling. After he stopped those experiments, Funk began to study the building blocks of sugars and proteins.

In 1906, Funk held an unpaid position at the University of Berlin. There he worked in the laboratory of Emil Fischer. Under Fischer's assistant, Emil Abderhalden, Funk experimented with protein metabolism. A year later, Funk began a paid position as a biochemist at the Municipal Hospital in Wiesbaden, Germany. There, he found that when dogs were fed purified proteins they lost weight, but when they were fed horse meat and powdered milk, they gained weight. The results were not what Abderhalden expected; he decided that Funk's methods were at fault and discounted the data. When relations with Abderhalden did not improve, Funk transferred to the pediatric clinic at the University of Berlin.

Discovered "Vitamines"

In 1910, Funk left Germany and became a scholar at the Lister Institute of Preventative Medicine in London, England. In 1911 he published his first paper in English, on dihydroxyphenylalanine. Charles Martin, head of the institute, gave Funk another problem to study: beriberi. Beriberi

is a disease of the peripheral nerves that causes pain and paralysis. At the time of Funk's study, it was not known that beriberi is caused by a lack of B1, but only that the disease occurred in areas of the Orient where the population consumed polished rice.

Earlier work in how deficiencies in diet could cause health problems were the basis for Funk's work. In 1873, research had shown that dogs did not thrive on a diet of washed meat and that pigeons that ate synthetic food developed symptoms of disease. At the turn of the 20th century, Christiaan Eikjman found that chickens made sick by a diet of polished rice would recover if fed rice hulls. He determined that rice hulls could cure some diseases, but he assumed wrongly that the problem arose from a toxic factor in rice. In the early 1900s, Sir Frederick Hopkins found that mice fed a diet of carbohydrates, proteins, fats, and mineral salts stopped growing if their diet did not contain milk. He determined that milk contained a substance that maintained health.

Building on the work of such researchers, Funk looked at how food factors affected health. It was already known that including citrus fruit in the diet could prevent scurvy and that rice hulls could prevent beriberi. But it was not clear why. To find the answer, Funk experimented with extracts made from the dark outer coating of rice that was removed during polishing. He found that there was a substance within that coating that cured beriberi. Funk also fed pigeons a diet of polished rice and found that within a short time the birds lost weight and became unhealthy. Since the birds were consuming enough proteins, he knew that the problem was not a protein or amino acid deficiency.

Birds fed the extract made from rice polish soon began to recover. Also, birds that ate small amounts of yeast regained their health. Funk decided that there was a substance in the rice polish and the yeast that was required in small amounts to maintain health. He published an article on the subject titled "On the Chemical Nature of the Substance which Cures Polyneuritis in Birds Induced by a Diet of Polished Rice."

The study led Funk to realize that there were substances in food essential to good health. He found that diseases such as beriberi, rickets, and scurvy could be cured by introducing into the diet organic compounds that contained certain chemical substances. Funk also maintained that certain diseases could be prevented by making sure the chemical substances were present in the diet. He called the substances "vitamines," with "vita" meaning vitality and "amines" meaning a chemical compound containing nitrogen. (The "e" was dropped in the 1920s when it was found that amines, or organic compounds derived from ammonia, were not always present.)

In 1912, Funk published his paper, "Vitamines." His publication earned him public recognition and a Beit Fellowship from the University of London. In 1913, Funk began working at the London Cancer Hospital Research Institute. He published his first book, *Die Vitamine,* translated in 1922 by Dr. H.E. Dubin into English. (Dubin collaborated with Funk to produce the first cod liver oil vitamin concentrate, called Oscodal.)

Later Career

In 1915 during World War I, Funk decided to leave England and accept a position at the Harriman Research Laboratory in New York City. Upon his arrival, he found to his dismay that the laboratory did not have research funding or equipment. Anxiety over how he would support his family caused Funk to suffer serious health problems. But he recovered and in 1916 accepted a position with Calco Company in Bound Brook, New Jersey. A year later, in 1917, he started working for the pharmaceutical firm Metz and Company in New York City. From 1918 to 1923, he also held an academic position at Columbia University's College of Physicians and Surgeons, where he worked on the synthesis of adrenaline.

Funk became a United States citizen in 1920. In 1923, sponsored by the Rockefeller Foundation, he returned to Poland and worked as chief of the Department of Biochemistry at the State Institute of Hygiene. While there, he increased the quality of insulin produced in the laboratory. In 1928, because of political unrest in Poland, he accepted a part-time position with Gr,my, a pharmaceutical house in Paris. There he founded Casa Biochemica, a private laboratory that produced biochemical products. From 1927 to 1936, Funk also worked as a biochemist for the Rousell Company.

In 1936, Funk published *Vitamin and Mineral Therapy,* also translated by H.E. Dubin. In this publication he called vitamin deficiencies insidious because they occur without

warning and can cause irreparable damage. "Lack of a particular vitamin leads eventually to a particular nutritional disease," Funk wrote. "However, long before this deficiency disease becomes apparent, a shortage of one or more vitamins may—and usually does—give rise to some tissue changes which lower the general resistance of the body making it susceptible to the attack of certain infections."

After Germany invaded Poland in 1939, Funk returned to New York and began working for the U.S. Vitamin Corporation, a company for which he had previously worked and which owned the copyright to *Vitamin and Mineral Therapy.* In 1947, with the support of the U.S. Vitamin Corporation, Funk became head of the Funk Foundation for Medical Research. In 1963, Funk gave up an active role in research when he retired. He died in New York City on November 20, 1976.

Married in 1914 to Alix Denise Schneidesch, Funk had two children. During his lifetime, he published more than 140 articles, including material on gonadotropic hormones, ulcers, and diabetes.

Legacy of Improved Health

Funk advanced humankind's understanding of nutrition and revolutionized the way people looked at their health. He never isolated a pure vitamin, but he did prepare concentrations that contained several vitamins. His conclusion that lack of vitamins in the diet was responsible for disease helped develop effective preventive and curative measures for anemia, beriberi, osteomalacia, pellagra, rickets, scurvy, and sprue.

During the vitamin craze that followed Funk's discoveries, many people overlooked Funk's observation that only small amounts of the substances were necessary to maintain health. Nutritional supplements were said to cure diseases, and vitamin makers claimed that synthetic vitamins improved energy and health. Consumers began to ingest large amounts of vitamins, despite the fact that small amounts were sufficient and that too much of some vitamins, such as A and D, are toxic to the body.

Although he is remembered primarily for his work with vitamins, Funk was also instrumental in advancing studies on hormones, cancer, and diabetes. His contributions to science include developing accurate views of the relationship between diet and health that led to advances in child and adult nutrition. He also contributed to getting proper nutrients into manufactured foods.

Other contributions made by Funk include finding the connection between Vitamin B complex and carbohydrate metabolism, discovering that vitamins influence the speed at which cancer grows, separating Vitamin D from cholesterol, and realizing that bacteria are a necessary part of the diet.

Generations of children made to consume cod liver oil by their parents may not appreciate Funk's work, but it is certain that his contributions have improved the health of countless. Indeed, his work clearly contributed to the increased life span many people enjoy in modern society.

Books

American National Biography, Oxford University Press, 1999.
Dictionary of American Biography, Supplement 8: 1966-1970, American Council of Learned Societies, 1988.
Funk, Casimir and H.E. Dubin, *Vitamin and Mineral Therapy*, U.S. Vitamin Corporation, 1936.

Periodicals

Washington Post, October 16, 1985.

Online

"Funk, Casimir," *Encyclopedia.com*, http://www.encyclopedia.com/articles/04822.html (January 6, 2002).
"Polish Born Biochemist Casimir Funk Introduces the Name Vitamin," *Intellihealth*, http://www.intelihealth.com/IH/ihtIH/WSIHW000/23722/21250/245416.html?d=dmtContent (January 6, 2002).
"Year 1912—Casimir Funk Coins The Name 'Vitamin,'" *India Infoline*, http://www.indiainfoline.com/phar/mile/1912.html (January 6, 2002). □

Fürüzan

Fürüzan (born 1935), who uses only her first name as a pen name, is one of Turkey's best contemporary short story writers and one of its most famous female authors. She established her career by writing about the disadvantaged in society, particularly refugees and women and children. She has published two novels and five volumes of short stories, in addition to travel writing and producing a movie script. She has gained critical acclaim in Turkey and the international literary community. Her works have been translated into English, German, Russian, Dutch, Swedish, Arabic, and Persian.

Became Self-Taught Author

Fürüzan Yerdelen was born in Istanbul, Turkey, on October 29, 1935. When she was a child her father passed away and she had to quit school after the eighth grade. She went to work as an actress with the Little Theater acting company. In 1958, when she was 23 years old, Fürüzan married cartoonist Turhan Selçuk. The couple had one child together, but the marriage ended in divorce. Despite her brief formal education, Fürüzan enjoyed reading as a child. When she was a teenager she began writing poems and short stories. She became a serious writer in 1968 and after her divorce she began using only her first name as her pen name.

Fürüzan was a self-taught author who wrote two novels and five collections of short stories. She published her first collection of short stories in 1971 and soon gained public and critical acclaim. In 1971 she won the Sait Faik Short Story Award for her work *Parasiz Yatili* ("Free Room and Board"). In 1975 she also won the Turkish Language Association Novel Award for her first novel *47'liler* (*Those Born in '47*), about the 1947 generation's perspective on the 1971 coup in Turkey. Fürüzan is best known for her short stories, including *Tasrali* ("The Girl from the Provinces," 1968), *Iskele Parklarinda* ("In the Park by the Pier," 1971), *Kusatma* ("The Siege," 1972), *Benim Sinemalarim* ("My Cinemas," 1973), and *Nehir* ("The River," 1973).

Wrote as Voice of the Oppressed

Fürüzan established her reputation as a voice for the oppressed and downtrodden, particularly refugees and women and children. Her characters included elderly servants, migrant families, sexually exploited women, and unloved wives. She made the reader aware of the social problems facing her characters, and hence facing her country, but she did not offer her own solutions to these problems. Instead, Fürüzan tried to generate empathy in the readers and encouraged them to have the strength to address these social problems. Literary critics have described her work as psychologically insightful. Fürüzan was quoted in *Contemporary Turkish Writers* as saying, "Of the methods that I would like to apply in my writing, the first, I would say, is to be comprehensible. The second is to inspect, from a correct point of view, the problems of the country."

One of the social problems that Fürüzan has addressed in her writing is the difficult material conditions of refugees living in Turkey and the prejudices against them. These refugees are from many countries around Turkey, including Serbia, Croatia, Albania, Bosnia, Bulgaria, and Greece. They have not assimilated to Turkish culture because of their customs, dress, or accents, and therefore they have been discriminated against. Fürüzan has given a voice to this otherwise ignored population and has written about their virtues, such as cleanliness and strong family ties.

Represented Turkish Women

Another group that Fürüzan has given a voice is women. In a *World Literature Today* article entitled "The Woman in the Darkroom: Contemporary Writers in Turkey," Güneli Gün compared Fürüzan's work and her impact to that of Erica Jong. In particular, she explained, "These were women's voices that broke through womanly hopes and fears, and they stood in front of the reader, momentarily, utterly open: open eyes, open minds, open sexuality."

For example, in one of her first short stories, *Tasrali* ("The Girl from the Provinces," 1968), Fürüzan wrote about an elderly widow whose niece, a girl from the provinces, came to live with her in search of a higher education. The widow did not approve of the niece's ambitions despite the fact that she herself was educated. Fürüzan used the relationship of these two characters to explore gender stereotypes. In another example, Fürüzan wrote about the complications of duty, marriage, and love in *Nehir* ("The River," 1971). When a woman left her farmer husband and his country home for the beauties of city life in Istanbul, one of the characters explained, "There couldn't be a place more beautiful than here, but when you can't get on with your man every place is hell. A man is everything. What's a woman? The most wretched of creatures.''

One of her most popular works was *Benim Sinemalarim* (''My Cinemas''), a short story published in 1973. Fürüzan wrote about a teenage girl whose family was very poor. The girl worked in a sweatshop to help her parents financially, but she did not earn enough money to buy clothes and other things that she wanted. As a result, the young girl turned to prostitution, dating older men to finance her material desires. The story explored how the girl rationalized her decision as well as her parents' reaction to the news. In 1990 Fürüzan turned this short story into a film script and also directed the movie under the same title as the short story. The film was well received and won awards at the Cannes, Tehran, and Tokyo film festivals.

Fürüzan has been credited for her artful command of the Turkish language, in particular for her simplicity and clarity. She wrote from a deeply personal point of view and with a passion that was honest and often angry. An example of this pained honesty can be found in the English translation of her short story *Iskele Parklarinda* (''In the Park by the Pier,'' 1971). Fürüzan told the story of a poor thirty year old widow and her young daughter who spent the summer days by the pier. As they were sitting in the park, the woman lamented,'' Who would want to marry a woman with a seven-year-old child? I'm so thin. I'm flat chested. Maybe if I ate a little better. Oh, where are the husbands anyway? I don't really want to get married. But I haven't a penny.''

Later Career Included Travel Writing

In 1975 Fürüzan was invited by the West German government to come to Germany and write a series of newspaper articles about the plight of Turkish workers in that country. In 1975 she published her interviews with some of these workers in a book called *Yeni Konuklar* (*New Guests*). In 1981 she wrote another book, *ev Sahipleri* (*The Landlords*), about her travels in Germany. In the 1980s Fürüzan continued to write short stories, including *Gecenin Oteki Yuzu* (''The Other Face of the Night,'' 1982) and *Gul Mevsimidir* (''It's the Season for Roses,'' 1985). She also published her second novel, *Berlin'in Nar Cicegi* (*The Pomegranate Blossom of Berlin*) in 1988. Her most recent work, *Bizim Rumeli* (*Our Rumelia*) was published in 1994 and tells of her travels to Bosnia, Greece, and Bulgaria.

Fürüzan's work after her trip to Germany was not as well received as her earlier short stories. She has been criticized for adopting a journalistic approach to her subject matter and for using a journalistic writing style that is not as authentic as her earlier style. In addition, her political agenda, which was once subtly woven into her stories, has become more apparent. As Gun wrote in ''The Woman in the Darkroom: Contemporary Writers in Turkey,'' ''Her characters are more politically determined devices than they are people that have any basis in the author's experience. It seems as if she has broken into a dark room, where her urgent hunger for truth, beauty, and freedom has been replaced with a diet consisting of crusts of stale ideology, language, and consciousness that have been fed her from someplace else.''

Despite these criticisms of her more recent work, Fürüzan has established herself as one of Turkey's best modern writers and certainly one of its best known women writers. She has built her reputation as a voice for the voiceless, the poor, weak, and powerless segments of society. Her insightfulness and poignant writing have gained her popularity in both the general public and the literary community. English translations of some of her short stories can be found in anthologies of Turkish literature.

Books

Arat, Zehra F., editor, *Deconstructing Images of ''The Turkish Woman,''* St. Martin's Press, 1998.

Buck, Claire, editor, *The Bloomsbury Guide to Women's Literature,* Prentice Hall General Reference, 1992.

Mitler, Louis, *Contemporary Turkish Writers: A Critical Bio-Bibliography of Leading Writers in the Turkish Republican Period up to 1980,* Indiana University, 1988.

Reader's Adviser, edited by Marion Sader, R.R. Bowler, 1994.

Periodicals

Variety, May 9, 1990.

World Literature Today, Spring 1986.

Online

''Authors,'' http://courses.washington.edu/mtle/authors.html (January 31, 2002).

''Contemporary Turkish Literature,'' http://www.turkish-lit.boun .edu.tr (January 23, 2002). □

G

Robert Gallo

Robert Gallo (born 1937) is one of the most influential, yet controversial, researchers of the twentieth century. Working at the National Institutes of Health, Gallo was one of the first scientists to discover a human retrovirus, which proved to be an important breakthrough in the fight against cancer. He was also a co-discoverer of the AIDS virus and developed the test used to screen blood for AIDS.

Robert Charles Gallo was born in Waterbury, Connecticut on March 23, 1937. His grandparents immigrated to the United States from Italy. His parents, Francis Anton and Louise Mary (Ciancuilli) Gallo, were both born and raised in Waterbury, where his father worked as a metallurgist.

Gallo's early scientific influences were his father and his uncle, Joe Anthony, his mother's brother-in-law. His father had an extensive technical library. His uncle was a zoologist who had a passion for his work. However, it was a life-altering event in 1948 that had the biggest impact on Gallo's future career. When Gallo was only 11 years old his younger sister and only sibling, Judy, was diagnosed with leukemia at the age of five. She was one of the first patients to be treated with antimetabolite chemotherapy and one of the first to experience remission from drug therapy. Despite these efforts, Judy died in March 1949. Gallo was deeply affected by the images of his little sister in the hospital and by the toll the child's death took on his parents, particularly his father.

The only positive outcome of this family tragedy was that young Gallo was introduced to Dr. Marcus Cox, the pathologist at St. Mary's Hospital in Waterbury who first diagnosed his sister's illness. In his autobiography, *Virus Hunting,* Gallo described Cox as "a clinical pathologist by medical specialty, he had the attributes of a born scientist, ever curious, always seeking to find out why something happened the way it did, harshly critical of glib explanations." Dr. Cox became a close friend of Francis Gallo and a mentor to his young son, Robert.

Medical Training

As a teenager at Sacred Heart High School, Gallo had not given much thought to his career. Instead, he was preoccupied with the usual teenage activities, sports and socializing. Gallo was an avid basketball player, but an injury during his senior year kept him from playing. Instead he began to spend his free time with Dr. Cox at the hospital. By the time he entered Providence College the following year, he knew he wanted a career in medicine. Gallo majored in biology and then went on to Thomas Jefferson University School of Medicine in Philadelphia. At that time Jefferson was known for its strong clinical departments, but not necessarily for its research. Gallo, however, was fortunate to work with one of the great researchers, Alan Erslev, who had discovered the first growth factor for any type of blood cell. Erslev taught Gallo how to approach research problems, as well as valuable laboratory skills. He also introduced Gallo to the National Institutes of Health.

Gallo married Mary Jane Hayes after his second year of medical school. She was also a Waterbury native and her brother had been a friend of Gallo in high school. Gallo and Mary Jane began dating when he was a freshman in college.

The couple was married on July 1, 1961 and went on to raise two sons, Robert Charles and Marcus.

After finishing medical school Gallo wanted to pursue a career in research, particularly at the National Institutes of Health. Erslev, however, thought it would be better for his career if he first did a medical internship. Gallo followed his advice and went to the University of Chicago, which was an important center for blood cell biology. There he worked with Leon Jacobsen and Rudi Schmid.

Began Career at National Institutes of Health

In 1965 Gallo joined the National Institutes of Health in Bethesda, Maryland, where he would work for the next 30 years. He began his career in the National Cancer Institute where he conducted research on leukocytes, types of white blood cells. In 1971 he became head of the new Laboratory of Tumor Cell Biology. Gallo began to explore whether viruses could cause cancer. In particular, he began to research retroviruses. Once called RNA tumor viruses, retroviruses can convert RNA to DNA with the help of an enzyme called reverse transcriptase. As Gallo explained in his autobiography, this enzyme "in effect gave these viruses permanent access to a variety of cell mechanisms, which they put to use for their own replication and often to a cell's detriment." At that time, retroviruses had been found in animals, but it was not know if they also existed in humans.

In 1975 Gallo and a colleague, Robert E. Gallagher, announced the discovery of a human leukemia virus. This

would have been a major accomplishment in Gallo's young career. However, other scientists were unable to replicate his results. In fact, Gallo's samples were contaminated and the retroviruses he found were actually from animals and not humans. Gallo's premature announcement of his discovery was damaging to his reputation, but he continued to pursue this line of research.

Discovered First Human Retrovirus

Gallo next discovered a T-cell growth factor which would keep these white blood cells alive longer while outside of the body and thereby give researchers more time to look for retroviruses. This technique led to the first true discovery of a human retrovirus in 1981, which was called the human T-cell leukemia virus, or HTLV-I. This retrovirus was later linked to some forms of leukemia and neurological diseases. A year later Gallo discovered another retrovirus called HTLV-II.

Around this same time a new disease was gaining worldwide public attention, acquired immuno-deficiency syndrome (AIDS). Gallo noticed similarities between his HTLV retroviruses and AIDS, particularly with respect to how they were transmitted. He became one of the first scientists to suspect that AIDS was caused by a virus, possibly a retrovirus. In 1982 Gallo was asked to head a new AIDS task force at the National Cancer Institute.

Controversy Surrounding AIDS Virus

The following year Gallo succeeded in identifying the AIDS virus, which he named HTLV-III. He published his findings in the May 4, 1984 issue of *Science*. He then quickly developed a test to screen blood for antibodies to the virus and applied for a patent. However, Luc Montagnier, a French scientist from the Pasteur Institute in Paris, had published a paper in *Science* in May 1983 announcing the discovery of a virus called lymphadenopathy, or LAV. Unlike Gallo, Montagnier had not been able to prove that his virus caused AIDS. However, he did apply for a patent for an AIDS blood test seven months before Gallo.

The United States Patent Office awarded the patent for the AIDS blood test to Gallo. France responded by suing the U.S. government. This controversy led to several heated exchanges between Gallo and Montagnier in which accusations of impropriety were exchanged. The scientific community disapproved of the battle because it was taking time and energy away from treatment and further research on AIDS. In 1987 several scientists, including Jonas Salk who had weathered his own controversy with the polio vaccine, had encouraged Gallo and Montagnier to share credit for the discovery. In an unprecedented event in the scientific community, the two scientists agreed on a timeline of events and published their joint contributions in a 1987 article in *Nature*. The U.S. and French governments also decided to settle the patent dispute out of court and share the royalties from the AIDS blood test.

Charged with Scientific Misconduct

The controversy was renewed in 1989 when journalist John Crewdson published a lengthy expose of the discovery of the AIDS virus in the *Chicago Tribune*. Crewdson attacked Gallo's credibility and charged that HTLV-III and LAV were exactly the same virus. Since Montagnier discovered the virus a year before Gallo, it appeared that Gallo was taking credit for Montagnier's work. To make matters worse, Gallo's 1984 *Science* article announcing HTLV-III accidentally included a picture of Montagnier's LAV virus. The *Tribune* article led to a 1990 investigation by Congress. In December 1991 the Office of Research Integrity at the U.S. Department of Health and Human Services found Gallo and his colleague Mikulas Popovic guilty of scientific misconduct.

In 1991 Gallo published his autobiography, *Virus Hunting*, which was a detailed rebuttal of Crewdson's allegations. Gallo publicly acknowledged that his virus sample had been contaminated because the two researchers had been sending samples to one another. Gallo, however, still maintained that he was the one who had made the important link between HTLV-III or LAV and AIDS. He and Popovic both appealed the misconduct decision and they were cleared of all charges by December 1993. In 1994 the United States and France renegotiated their agreement regarding the AIDS blood test patent to make the distribution of royalties more equitable. In the same year Montagnier published his own autobiography called *Virus* documenting his view of the events leading to the discovery of the AIDS virus. He began by stating that "scientific discoveries are often a matter of circumstance and chance. This was true in Pasteur's time, and is equally so in ours, as we have seen with the discovery of the AIDS virus."

Continued AIDS Research

With the HTLV controversy behind him, Gallo continued his AIDS research. In 1995, after a 30-year career with the National Institutes of Health, he left to become the director of the new Institute of Human Virology at the University of Maryland. Gallo has since been working on a vaccine for AIDS. In September 2001 Gallo announced that he had developed such a vaccine that worked on monkeys. The next step would be to create a vaccine that could be used for human trials. Gallo has also been involved in the development of a blood test for mad cow disease.

Gallo's groundbreaking research on retroviruses has led to numerous scientific awards. In 1982 he won the prestigious Albert Lasker Award for his work on viral links to cancer and in 1986 he won it a second time for his work on AIDS. He also won the American Cancer Society Medal of Honor in 1983, the Armand Hammer Cancer Research Award in 1985, the Japan Prize for Science and Technology in 1988, and the Paul Erhlich and Ludwig Darmstaedter Prize for biomedical research in 1999. Gallo has also received 11 honorary degrees. The one award that has eluded him so far is the Nobel Prize. Some scientists speculate that, despite his groundbreaking discoveries, he has not yet won the most coveted scientific award because of the controversy surrounding the discovery of the AIDS virus. However, Gallo's continuing work on an AIDS vaccine keeps the possibility of a Nobel Prize alive.

Books

Hellman, Hal, *Great Feuds in Medicine: Ten of the Liveliest Disputes Ever*, John Wiley and Sons, Inc., 2001.
Montagnier, Luc. *Virus: The Co-Discoverer of HIV Tracks Its Rampage and Charts the Future*, W.W. Norton and Company, 2000.

Periodicals

Baltimore Sun, August 15, 1998.
Business Week, December 14, 1987.
Chicago Tribune, November 19, 1989.
Discover, October 1989; June 1997.
Economist, April 28, 1984; April 28, 1986; June 8, 1991.
Forbes, September 17, 2001.
Maclean's, June 15, 1987.
Nature, April 1987
New Scientist, July 23, 1994.
Newsweek, June 15, 1987; April 2, 1990; March 18, 1991; June 10, 1991; January 11, 1993.
San Diego Union-Tribune, December 24, 2000.
Science, June 22, 1990; November 15, 1991.
Sunday Times, September 2, 2001.
Time, May 20, 1991; November 22, 1993.
U.S. News and World Report, May 7, 1984; June 3, 1991.
USA Today, December 4, 2000.
Washington Post, August 9, 1987.

Online

"About the Institute of Human Virology," http://www.ihv.org/pages/about/about.html (October 29, 2001).
"By AIDS Obsessed," http://www.virusmyth.net/aids/data/bwobsessed.html (October 29, 2001).
In Their Own Words . . . Robert Gallo, M.D.," http://aidshistory.nih.gov/transcripts/bios/Robert_Gallo.html (November 4, 2001).
"Robert C. Gallo, M.D.," http://www.biblio.org/bronson/robert1.html (October 29, 2001). □

Erle Stanley Gardner

Erle Stanley Gardner (1889-1970) became one of the most successful mystery writers of all time. Most of his reputation stems from Perry Mason and other memorable characters that he created. Gardner's best novels offer abundant evidence of his natural storytelling talent.

Gardner was born in Malden, Massachusetts on July 17, 1889. He spent much of his childhood traveling with his mining-engineer father through the remote regions of California, Oregon, and the Klondike. In his teens he not only boxed for money, but also promoted a number of unlicensed matches. Gardner attended high school in California and graduated from Palo Alto High School 1909. He enrolled at Valparaiso University in Indiana that same year but was soon expelled for striking a professor.

In the practice of law Gardner found the form of combat he seemed born to master. He was admitted to the California bar in 1911 and opened an office in Oxnard, where he practiced law until 1918. As a lawyer he represented the Chinese community and gained a reputation for flamboyant trial tactics. In one case, for instance, he had dozens of Chinese merchants exchange identities so that he could discredit a policeman's identification of a client. Gardner worked as a salesman for the Consolidated Sales Company from 1918 until 1921. He then resumed his legal career in Ventura, California from 1921 until 1933.

Early Writings

In the early 1920s Gardner began to write western and mystery stories for magazines, often under the pseudonyms of A.A. Fair, Carleton Kendrake, and Charles J. Kenny. Eventually he was turning out and selling the equivalent of a short novel every three nights while still practicing law during the business day. With the sale of his first novel in 1933 he gave up the practice of law and devoted himself to full-time writing, or more precisely to dictating. Thanks to the popularity of his series characters—lawyer-detective Perry Mason, his loyal secretary Della Street, his private detective Paul Drake, and the foxy trio of Sergeant Holcomb, Lieutenant Tragg, and District Attorney Hamilton Burger—Gardner became one of the wealthiest mystery writers of all time.

The 82 Mason adventures from *The Case of the Velvet Claws* (1933) to the posthumously published *The Case of*

the *Postponed Murder* (1973) contain few of the literary graces. Characterization and description are perfunctory and often reduced to a few lines that are repeated in similar situations book after book. Indeed virtually every word not within quotation marks could be deleted and little would be lost. For what vivifies these novels is the sheer readability, the breakneck pacing, the convoluted plots, the fireworks displays of courtroom tactics (many based on gimmicks Gardner used in his own law practice), and the dialogue, where each line is a jab in a complex form of oral combat.

Perry Mason Novels

The first nine Masons are steeped in the hard-boiled tradition of *Black Mask* magazine, their taut understated realism leavened with raw wit, sentimentality, and a positive zest for the dog-eat-dog milieu of the free enterprise system during its worst depression. The Mason of these novels is a tiger in the social-Darwinian jungle, totally self-reliant, asking no favors, despising the weaklings who want society to care for them, willing to take any risk for a client no matter how unfairly the client plays the game with him. Asked what he does for a living, he replies: "I fight!" or "I am a paid gladiator." He will bribe policemen for information, loosen a hostile witness's tongue by pretending to frame him for murder, twist the evidence to get a guilty client acquitted and manipulate estate funds to prevent a guilty non-client from obtaining money for his defense. Besides *Velvet Claws,* perhaps the best early Mason novels are *The Case of the Howling Dog* and *The Case of the Curious Bride* (both 1934).

From the late 1930s to the late 1950s the main influence on Gardner was not *Black Mask* but the *Saturday Evening Post,* which serialized most of the Masons before book publication. In these novels the tough-guy notes are muted, "love interest" plays a stronger role, and Mason is less willing to play fast and loose with the law. Still the oral combat remains breathlessly exciting, the pace never slackens and the plots are as labyrinthine as before, most of them centering on various sharp-witted and greedy people battling over control of capital. Mason, of course, is Gardner's alter ego throughout the series. In several novels of the second period, however, another author-surrogate arrives on the scene in the person of a philosophical old desert rat or prospector who delights in living alone in the wilderness, discrediting by his example the greed of the urban wealth-and power-hunters. Among the best cases of this period are *Lazy Lover; Hesitant Hostess* which deals with Mason's breaking down a single prosecution witness; and *Lucky Loser* and *Foot-Loose Doll* with their spectacularly complex plots.

Television Work

Gardner worked without credit as script supervisor for the long-running *Perry Mason* television series (1957-66), starring Raymond Burr. Within a few years television's restrictive influence had infiltrated the new Mason novels. The lawyer evolved into a ponderous bureaucrat mindful of the law's niceties, just as Burr played him, and the plots became chaotic and the courtroom sequences mediocre, as happened all too often in the television scripts. But by the mid 1960s the libertarian decisions of the Supreme Court under Chief Justice Earl Warran had already undermined a basic premise of the Mason novels, namely that defendants menaced by the sneaky tactics of police and prosecutors needed a pyrotechnician like Mason in their corner. Once the Court ruled that such tactics required reversal of convictions gained thereby, Mason had lost his raison d'etre.

Several other detective series sprang from Gardner's dictating machine during his peak years. The 29 novels he wrote under the byline of A. A. Fair about diminutive private eye Donald Lam and his huge irascible partner Bertha Cool are often preferred over the Masons because of their fusion of corkscrew plots with fresh writing, characterizations, and humor, the high spots of the series being *The Bigger They Come* and *Beware the Curves.* And in his nine books about small-town district attorney Doug Selby, Gardner reversed the polarities of the Mason series, making the prosecutor his hero and the defense lawyer the oft-confounded trickster. But most of Gardner's reputation stems from Perry Mason, and his best novels in both this and other series offer abundant evidence of his natural storytelling talent, which is likely to retain its appeal as long as people read at all.

Gardner was married in 1912 to Natalie Talbert. The couple had one daughter and separated in 1935. Gardner married his second wife, Agnes Jean Bethell, in 1968. He died on March 11, 1970 in Temecula, California.

Books

Hughes, Dorothy B. *Erle Stanley Gardner: The Case of the Real Perry Mason,* Morrow, 1978.

Johnston, Alva. *The Case of Erle Stanley Gardner,* Morrow, 1947.

Van Dover, J. Kenneth. *Murder in the Millions: Erle Stanley Gardner, Mickey Spillane, Ian Fleming,* Ungar, 1984. □

Artemisia Gentileschi

The 16th and 17th centuries in Italy saw the emergence of an increasing number of accomplished female artists, who were often members of artistic families. The outstanding talent among them was Artemisia Gentileschi (1593-1652).

Gentileschi was born on July 8, 1593 in Rome. She was the daughter of the painter Orazio Gentileschi and was trained by him. Our perception of Gentileschi has been colored by the legend surrounding her. Her alleged rape by her father's colleague, the "quadratura" painter Agostino Tassi, when she was 17, was the subject of a protracted legal action brought by Orazio in 1611. Although she was subsequently "married off" to Pietro Antonio di Vicenzo Stiattesi in 1612 and gave birth to at least one daughter, she soon separated from her husband and led a strikingly independent life for a woman of her time—even if there is no firm evidence for the reputation

she enjoyed in the 18th century as a sexual libertine. After her marriage, Gentileschi lived in Florence until about 1620. She then worked in Genoa and settled in Naples in 1630. Gentileschi traveled to England in 1638-40, where she collaborated with her father on a series of canvasses for the Queen's House, Greenwich (now Marlborough House, London). Gentileschi died in Naples in 1652.

It is tempting to adduce the established biographical data in partial explanation of the context of her art: the sympathy and vigor with which she evokes her heroines and their predicaments, and her obsession with that tale of female triumph, Judith and Holofernes. But such possibilities should not distract attention from the high professional standards that Gentileschi brought to her art. In a letter, dated July 3, 1612, to the Grand Duchess of Tuscany, Orazio claimed that "Artemisia, having turned herself to the profession of painting, has in three years so reached the point that I can venture to say that today she has no peer." Despite the obvious exaggeration, one can agree that Gentileschi's art was of a consistently high quality virtually from the beginning.

Early Works

Her earliest surviving work may be a tender *Madonna and Child* of c. 1609 in the Spada Gallery, Rome. But two other pictures give a clearer idea of her consummate early style. They are *Judith and Her Maidservant with the Head of Holofernes* in the Pitti Palace, which could be a picture referred to in the transcript of the Tassi rape trial, and

Susanna and the Elders, dated 1610. Both pictures owe a good deal (in their crisp compositions, attractive physiognomies, and sparkling costumes) to Orazio, who might have contributed to both their design and execution. They are also, in their focussed realism, obviously works of the Caravaggist school—especially the former, with its bold *chiaroscuro.* But they introduce us to some distinctive traits of Gentileschi's own: in the *Judith* a greater freedom of brushwork than that of her father (at this stage not yet an altogether positive quality) and in both cases a certain authenticity of emotion (in the alert stare of Judith, for example; or the brilliantly evoked sense of violation conveyed by the defensive gesture and startled gaze of Susanna).

While Gentileschi's style during her Florentine and Roman years (1610s and 1620s) was a development of the idiom adumbrated by her father, her own vigorous sense of drama (more akin to that of Caravaggio than Orazio) lends most of the works a distinctive, cutting edge. The characterizations of her heroines (and nearly all of her pictures have female leads) are emotional without being sentimental. She is highly observant of both psychology and action and has a keen eye too for the natural disposition of flesh. Her sustained achievement can be seen in a series of masterpieces which includes the two versions of *Judith Slaying Holofernes; The Penitent Magdalen,* Florence, Pitti Palace, c. 1617-20; the powerful *Lucretia* of c. 1621 from the Palazzo Cattaneo-Adorno, Genoa; and *Judith and Her Maidservant with the head of Holofernes* (Detroit, c. 1625). These works are also distinguished by an opulent drapery style, with spirited highlights, that must have gone down well at the sartorially conscious Medicean court, where Gentileschi enjoyed the high patronage of Duke Cosimo II.

Explored Effects of Light

The Detroit *Judith and her Maidservant,* which is a candlelit night scene, also breaks new ground for Gentileschi in its thorough exploration of the effects of light radiating from an internal source. It was probably influenced by the fashionable candle-lit scenes of Honthorst executed in Rome in the late 1610s and well-known in Florence. But her employment of the flickering illumination is, as Spear has noted, predictably bolder than Honthorst's. Indeed this picture, like another of the very few of her works which have survived from the 1620s is redolent of the spirit of the emergent High Baroque. Painterly and sensuous handling, flow of action, theatrical deployment of light and gesture, and judicious selection of dramatic moment combine to effect a riveting illusion. In such pictures Gentileschi may be said to have played her part in the formulation of the new idiom, rather than merely imitating what others had initiated. The Burghley House *Susanna,* in particular, reveals her empathetic originality, since it parallels without, in any way being dependent upon, the early style of Guercino.

If the 1620s represent the high watermark of Gentileschi's achievement, her subsequent career, spent mostly in Naples, succumbed to a fragmentation of purpose. While retaining, on occasions, much of the vigor of her mature style (*Self Portrait as the Allegory of Painting,* London, Kensington Palace), she grew increasingly attracted to

the idealizations both of the Bolognese and, after her visit to England, of her father's late style. The former can be discerned in the poses and figure types of such works as the Capodimonte *Annunciation* of 1630; while the powerful impact of the latter is evident in the wholesale translation of the elongated, mannered figures of Orazio's Castle Howard *Finding of Moses* (c. 1633) into her own elegantly artificial *Bathsheba* (late 1640s, Potsdam, Neues Palast).

Gentileschi's influence on her contemporaries is still in need of detailed assessment. But it is clear that she greatly stimulated the imagination of Guerrieri in Florence (so much so that some of their works have been confused) and of Vouet in Rome, and her contribution to the development of the Neapolitan school, particularly through her impact on Stanzione and Cavallino, was arguably profound.

Books

Garrard, Mary D., *Gentileschi: The Image of the Female Hero in Italian Baroque Art,* 1989.
Moir, Alfred, *The Italian Followers of Caravaggio,* 2 vols., 1967.

Periodicals

Art Bulletin, 1968.
Scritti giovanili 1912-1922, vol. 1, 1961. □

Dan George

Chief Dan George (1899–1981), a member of the Coast Salish nation, gained fame as an actor relatively late in life. He is best remembered for his role as the Cheyenne elder, Old Lodge Skins, in the 1970 film *Little Big Man* alongside a young Dustin Hoffman. The success of *Little Big Man* gave George a platform from which to call attention to the plight of North America's indigenous peoples in the twentieth century.

A Vanishing Culture

George once delivered an open letter at a Canadian symposium on the matter of progress in the twentieth century and its effect on the indigenous cultures of North America. "I knew my people when they lived the old life," he said, according to a reprint of the speech in *UNESCO Courier,* "I knew them when there was still a dignity in their lives and a feeling of worth in their outlook; I knew them when there was unspoken confidence in the home and a certain knowledge of the path they walked upon. But they were living on the dying energy of a dying culture, a culture that was slowly losing its forward thrust." George was born during this transitional era, on June 24, 1899, near Vancouver, British Columbia, as the area was experiencing a timber boom and was rapidly being settled.

George's family was part of the Tell-lall-watt band of a Burrard Inlet group of Squamish, classified as a Coast Salish nation. He was named Geswanouth Slaholt, or "thunder coming up over the land from the water," but his name was Anglicized when he started school at the Roman Catholic Oblate Mission. His father believed it was best for his children's future to learn English, so he decided to send George's older brother to the Mission school. However, the boys were so close that Harry refused to go without his little brother, and so his father sent both boys. They knew no English when they arrived and were forbidden to speak their native language. George found the priests and nuns, in their strange garb, "terrifying for a little boy of my age," as he told biographer Hilda Mortimer in *You Call Me Chief: Impressions of the Life of Chief Dan George.* They saw their parents twice a month. "Every two weeks we'd catch the streetcar to the end of the line," he recalled, "then walk seven miles to get home on a Friday night."

Worked As Stevedore

George did well in school, but government funding for Native American education stopped when a student reached the age of 16. "I remember I cried when I left, for I felt that if I was to get anywhere in life I needed to study and learn more," he told Mortimer. "But I packed my clothes and walked the miles home." George worked as a logger, and, in 1917, he married Amy. Her father helped him get a coveted job as a stevedore in busy Vancouver Harbor. He worked loading timber beams onto ships for nearly 30 years, save for some lean times during labor strikes in the

1920s and the Great Depression in the 1930s, when he returned to logging to support his growing family. Sometimes they dug for clams or picked cascar bark, a typical Salish remedy for a stomach distress that was then sold to pharmaceutical companies for over-the-counter medicines.

The stevedore's life was typically a rough one, and George was an admitted gambler and drinker. His career was effectively ended when he was hit with a large load of lumber. "My bones were so tough nothin' was broken, but my leg and hip muscles were smashed to hamburger," he recalled in his biography. For the next ten years, George worked at odd jobs and even enjoyed a successful period as a country-and-western entertainer with his children as "Dan George and His Indian Entertainers." In 1951, he became tribal leader in lieu of his brother Harry, who had left the area.

A Star on "Cariboo Country"

By 1960 George had a grown son, Bob, who was enjoying minor success as a television actor. Bob George was cast in a new Canadian Broadcasting Corporation (CBC) series, *Caribou Country,* that was being filmed in British Columbia's Chilcotin Valley. When a white actor slated to play an Indian elder became ill, Bob George suggested his father as a replacement. George went on to appear in the series for the next few seasons and also won rave reviews for a stage performance as a heartbroken father whose daughter leaves the reservation for the city, only to be brutalized and eventually killed, in *The Ecstasy of Rita Joe.* The play premiered at the Vancouver Playhouse in 1967 and went on to performances at the National Arts Center in Ottawa in 1969.

By this point George was already using his prominence to call attention to the plight of Canada's First Peoples. In the summer of 1967, he was invited to read a declaration at Vancouver Stadium in honor of the country's Centennial Celebration. "How long have I known you, O Canada?, " George reflected. ". . . . I have known you when the forests were mine; when they gave me my meat and my clothing. . . . But in the long hundred years since the white man came, I have seen my freedom disappear, like the salmon going mysteriously out to sea. . . . O Canada, how can I celebrate with you this Centenary, this hundred years? Shall I thank you for my reserves that are left to me of my beautiful forests? For the canned fish of my rivers? For the loss of my pride and authority, even among my own people?"

In 1969, George appeared in the Walt Disney film, *Smith!* The movie was based on the Cariboo Country stories and starred Glenn Ford. That role led to the offer to appear in the 1970 film *Little Big Man* with Dustin Hoffman. The movie was directed by Arthur Penn, and it is based on a Thomas Berger novel, which chronicles a notorious event in American history, the slaughter of several hundred Cheyenne in Oklahoma by U.S. Cavalry troops under the leadership of General George A. Custer. The blatant display of hostility helped set the stage for "Custer's Last Stand," the 1876 battle in Montana in which U.S. government troops were decimated by a combined Cheyenne and Sioux force. Custer died in that battle and was usually portrayed thereafter in popular culture as a heroic figure. The Penn film, however, set out to show a far more flawed leader.

Civil Rights Spirit of 1960s

Prior to *Little Big Man,* Native Americans had usually been depicted as savages or double-crossers by Hollywood. George was cast as a Cheyenne elder, Old Lodge Skins, who befriends Hoffman's character, a cavalry soldier named Jack Crabb. In the film, Crabb is fascinated by Native American culture, and Old Lodge Skins serves as a mentor of sorts to the confused Crabb. Film critic Pauline Kael, in her *5001 Nights at the Movies,* described George's role as "part patriarch, part Jewish mother." In his death scene, George climbs a mountain to die alone. He later recalled that Penn, the director, allowed him a great degree of artistic license when it came time to shoot the scene. "That was my own song, my own dance, and my own way of talking to the great white spirit," he told Judy Klemesrud in a 1971 profile for the *New York Times.* "Those things were all my idea."

Little Big Man was a critical and commercial success and ushered in a new era in Hollywood's characterization of Native Americans. Other films followed that attempted to show U.S. history from a more balanced perspective. For his part George was honored with a New York Film Critics Award for best supporting actor. He was 71 years old at time. "I really don't feel I should be given credit for this part," he explained to Klemesrud. "I was an Indian chief for 12 years, so I really didn't have to do much acting."

Declined Larger Role

George was also nominated for an Academy Award for best supporting actor for his role as well. Tragically, his wife of more than 50 years died just before the ceremony. He returned to his two-room wood house on the Berard Reservation, where he lived with one of his daughters and her children. Despite his age, he joined a rock band in 1972 called Fireweed and toured with them. He also accepted other film roles, but was sometimes criticized by an increasingly political Native American and Canadian indigenous groups for taking roles deemed unsuitable for Native Americans. One of them was *Cancel My Reservation,* a 1972 farce that starred Bob Hope. When *The Ecstasy of Rita Joe* debuted in Washington in 1973, a group of militant Native Americans affiliated with the American Indian Movement (AIM) occupied the theater lobby in hopes of persuading George to serve as their spokesperson. George he refused the request. The group had recently taken over South Dakota's Wounded Knee Reservation by force for several weeks, demanding a review of the 300 treaties signed between Native American nations and the U.S. government. George refused to become involved, believing that using guerrilla tactics was counterproductive. According to Notable Native Americans, he was more "interested in changing predominant images of Native Americans in the media, as well as derogatory images that many Indians had of themselves."

Still, George did become an unofficial spokesperson for Native American causes and environmental issues. He was invited to a 1975 symposium on the future of northern Canada's indigenous peoples and used the open-letter format of his speech to call attention to the plight of all First Nations. "Do you know what it is like to feel you are of no value to society and those around you, to know that people came to help you but not to work with you, for you knew that they knew you had nothing to offer," he asked his audience. Such eloquent words were later published in two volumes of poetry, *My Heart Soars* and *My Spirit Soars.*

A Fitting Finale

George made guest appearances on popular television shows of the era, such as *High Chaparral, Bonanza,* and *Kung Fu.* He also appeared in many more films including *Harry and Tonto,* a 1974 box-office hit, and he appeared as Clint Eastwood's hapless traveling companion in *The Outlaw Josey Wales* the following year. His last role was another farce, *Americathon,* released in 1979. The film is set twenty years into the future—in 1998—and imagines the United States government is on the brink of bankruptcy. Foreclosure is imminent at the hands of a corporation run by a Native American group led by George's character. The film starred John Ritter as the beleaguered American president who decides to hold a telethon and featured guest appearances by Elvis Costello and Jay Leno.

George died in his sleep on September 23, 1981, on British Columbia's Berard Reservation where he had been born. He left behind six children and 36 grandchildren. In 1998 the American Indian Motion Picture Award Ceremony honored him posthumously on the occasion of a film documentary on his life, *Today Is a Good Day: Remembering Chief Dan George,* which included interviews with his family and Hoffman. The festival director, Mike Smith, spoke about George and the importance of his role in *Little Big Man* nearly three decades earlier. Smith called it "the first film that really showed the other side of Native people, the love and the respect of family and culture."

Books

Kael, Pauline, *5001 Nights at the Movies,* Holt , 1991.
Mortimer, Hilda, with Chief Dan George, *You Call Me Chief: Impressions of the Life of Chief Dan George,* Doubleday, 1981.

Periodicals

New York Times, February 21, 1971.
UNESCO Courier, December 2001, p. 16.
Windspeaker, December 1998, pp. 18-20.

Online

Contemporary Authors Online, Gale, 1999.
Contemporary Theatre, Film, and Television, Volume 17, Gale Research, 1997. Reproduced in *Biography Resource Center,* http://galenet.galegroup.com/servlet/BioRC (March 4, 2002).
Notable Native Americans, Gale Research, 1995. Reproduced in *Biography Resource Center,* http://galenet.galegroup.com/servlet/BioRC (March 4, 2002). □

Heinosuke Gosho

Heinosuke Gosho (1902–1981) was one of Japan's most important film directors for several decades of the twentieth century. He directed the first "talking" picture in Japan in 1931 and came to excel in what film historians classify as Japan's "shomingeki" genre, or movies that depict the lives of the lower and middle classes with both realism and humor. An essay in *International Dictionary of Films and Filmmakers* noted that "throughout his career, Gosho expressed his basic belief in humanistic values," and commended "the warm, subtle, and sentimental depiction of likable people" in his films.

Rags to Riches Tale

Gosho's own life seemed fodder for a Cinderella-style plot: he was born in Tokyo on February 1, 1902, to a mother who was a geisha and renowned beauty. His father was a well-to-do tobacco merchant who refused to marry her, and thus Gosho spent the first years of his life in Tokyo's old *shitamachi* district downtown, an area he later portrayed in films. When he was five years old, however, his father's legitimate son died, and Gosho became his heir and lived an affluent childhood thereafter. He was groomed to take over the family business by his father and grandfather—though he was never allowed to call his biological mother "mother" again. Meanwhile, she and the rest of his siblings lived in hardship. "What Gosho could not help but appreciate, in short," wrote Arthur Nolletti Jr., in an essay on the director for *Reframing Japanese Cinema: Authorship, Genre, History*, "were the contradictions in life—and the fact that nothing was black or white. . . . It is this knowledge, this unerring sense of life's injustices, contradictions, and complexities, that lies at the heart of Gosho's films, giving them an expansiveness and generosity of spirit."

Gosho's father and grandfather owned stock in theaters—urban Japanese had been enthusiastic cinema-goers since the onset of film-entertainment industry in late 1890s—and he enjoyed free passes to them, which ignited his artistic ambitions. He became a fan of German director Ernst Lubitsch and reportedly saw his *Marriage Circle* 20 times. He was also fascinated by the work of Charlie Chaplin. Gosho attended Keio Commerce School and graduated in 1921, but his decision to enter the film business instead of the family tobacco concern was greeted with much opposition.

Young Filmmaker in Breakthrough Era

Gosho's first mentor was Yasujiro Shimazu, a filmmaker at the prestigious Shochiku-Kamata Studio in Tokyo. He began working there in 1923, the same year the great Kanto earthquake destroyed much of Tokyo and Yokohama.

The studios and theaters were quickly back in business to provide respite for citizens rebuilding their lives. There was also a sense of revitalization and change in the national mood. Studios, eager to meet the demands of the growing numbers of cinema-goers, began making more and more of their own films instead of relying on imports from the United States and Europe, and Gosho was able to master the necessary skills quickly. He earned his director's certificate in 1925.

His first work was *Nanto no haru* ("Spring of Southern Island"), for which he also wrote the screenplay. This triumph, however, was marred by personal tragedy, for his beloved younger brother was diagnosed with polio and lost the use of a leg. Gosho grew despondent, as Joseph Anderson and Donald Richie's volume *The Japanese Film* quoted him as saying: "I lost my way for several years, and my personal life began to fall apart." He admitted to attempting suicide even, but "as in all my efforts during this period, I failed." Finding solace in work, Gosho began working at a fast pace, and in two years directed more than a dozen films. His fourteenth, *Sabishiki ranbomono* ("Lonely Hoodlum"), depicted a romance between a young city woman from a good family who falls in love with rough horse-cart driver from the countryside. *Sabishiki ranbomono* became Gosho's first box-office hit.

Created Sympathetic Characters

Perhaps because of his brother's difficulty, Gosho was interested in creating characters with physical or mental handicaps. This is explicit in *Musume* ("A Daughter"), from 1926, and 1928's *Mura no hanayome* ("The Village Bride"). The latter's story centers on a beautiful young woman from a rural village who is betrothed in an arranged marriage; before the wedding, she suffers an accident and is permanently disabled. Her parents decide to have her younger sister married in her stead. Critics and audiences did not rate the films favorably, and Gosho was stung by the negative reaction. "Gosho's intention, however, was to illustrate a kind of warm and sincere relationship born in pathos," according to an essay in *International Dictionary of Films and Filmmakers*. "Today, these films are highly esteemed for their critique of feudalistic village life."

In 1931, in part because of his lack of recent commercial success, Shochiku-Kamata bosses told Gosho that he would make Japan's first "talking" picture using the new sound technology. Other directors in Japan were leery of the form, fearing failure, but Gosho rose to the challenge and expanded a two-reel into a feature film that was a great success. The film was called *Madamu to Nyobo,* ("Next Door Madame and My Wife"). The comedy revolves around a playwright who suffers from writer's block and is increasingly plagued by noises that disturb his concentration, from the cry of a child to live jazz music emanating from the rakish couple next door. At one point the lead whistles a tune, the melody of which was Gosho's homage to a popular song featured in one of France's best known films from the era, Ren, Clair's first sound picture *Sous les toits de Paris* ("Under the Roofs of Paris"). The film had recently debuted in Japan.

Films Gently Satirized Japanese Society

Gosho went on to make several successful comedies in the 1930s. Among his best were *Hanayome no negoto* ("The Bride Talks in Her Sleep") from 1933 and *Hanamuko no negoto* ("The Bridegroom Talks in His Sleep"), released in 1935. Nolletti discussed these, along with *Madamu to Nyobo,* in his essay. "Regarded in their day simply as 'entertainment,' today they are considered classics. . . . Virtually plotless, these comedies take a wholly trivial matter and use it as a springboard for a succession of silly-some would even say 'stupid'-gags." The *Hanayome* and *Hanamuko* pictures each featured newlywed couples and their meddlesome family, friends, and neighbors. Both proved popular with the Japanese public, portraying the sense of community that it valued, while at the same time poking fun at the societal pressures individuals often faced because of that closeness.

Gosho also returned to the silent-film medium on occasion. These included *Lamuru* ("L'Amour"), about a country doctor worried about his son's decadent lifestyle, and *Izu no odoriko* ("Dancer of Izu"), a doomed romance between an itinerant dancer and a Tokyo college student. Both were released in 1933. The theme of the latter Gosho returned once more to one of his most acclaimed works, *Oboro yo no onna* ("Woman of Pale Night," also called "Woman of the Mist"), which premiered in 1936. He penned its screenplay himself. It is the story of a childless couple, Bunkichi and Okiyo, who run a dry-cleaning business in Tokyo. Bunkichi seems at first to be a henpecked husband, but reveals himself to be much slyer as the story progresses. Bunkichi's widowed sister Otuju works as a maid to help her son Seiichi become a lawyer and dreams only of success for him. Seiichi prefers novels and a geisha girl. On one hand, Gosho's film served as a standard social drama that upholds the conservative Japanese traditions of personal sacrifice toward a common goal and the exaltation of family values. However, it also depicts the younger generation defying its elders' wishes, and the ultimate futility of any sacrifice in the end.

Took Wartime Hiatus

By 1941, Japan had been drawn fully into World War II, and Gosho was offered a post at another prestigious studio, Daiei, the same year. The wartime era, however, was also one of a new government mandate for the film industry, decreeing "national policy" storylines which did not demean or diminish Japanese society or culture. Gosho found it nearly impossible to work within such constraints and made just four films between 1940 and 1945. He helped usher in a new era in Japanese cinema with the highly regarded *Ima hitotabi no* ("One More Time") in 1945, a love story set before, during, and after World War II.

In the 1950s, other Japanese directors such as Akira Kurosawa and Yasujiro Ozu gained international prominence for their groundbreaking films. Japan's film industry started to produce far more socially critical films, and Gosho's work became part of this new wave. In 1951, he founded his own production company, Studio 8 Productions, and he was happiest to make his own works, free from

studio dictates. One of these films was the 1953 *Entotsu no mieru basho* ("Four Chimneys"; also called "Where Chimneys Are Seen"). The film centered on the lives of two couples in a poor, industrialized section of Tokyo. *Entotsu no mieru basho* was awarded the International Peace Prize at the prestigious Berlin Film Festival that year. His 1955 project, *Takekurabe* ("Growing Up"), starred Hibari Misora, a teen pop star in Japan at the time. It was the singer's only serious film role, one in which she portrayed a young woman in nineteenth-century Japan whose origins predestine her career as a prostitute.

For a number of years Gosho served as president of the Japanese Association of Film Directors, retiring from the post in 1975. Eleven of his films won "Film of the Year" honors from *Kinema Jumpo,* Japan's leading film magazine. His final work was a filmed puppet play, *Meiji haruaki* ("Seasons of Meiji"), in 1968. He died on May 1, 1981, at the age of 79 in Shizuoka, Japan. Over the next few years his films enjoyed a revival among Japanese-cinema enthusiasts and were celebrated posthumously at retrospectives in Paris, London, and New York City. His earliest surviving work is *Madamu to nyobo,* the 1931 work that broke the sound barrier in Japanese film. Gosho's cinematic output-some 80 films over 40 years—ranged in theme from comedy to family melodrama to social commentary, and critics remember him as a director and screenwriter who adeptly captured the humanity in his stories, no matter what the genre.

Books

Anderson, Joseph, and Donald Richie, *The Japanese Film,* 1982.
Currents in Japanese Cinema: Essays by Tadao Sato, translated by Gregory Barrett, Kodansha, 1982.
International Dictionary of Films and Filmmakers, Volume 2: Directors, St. James Press, 1996.
MacDonald, Keiko I., *Cinema East: A Critical Study of Major Japanese Films,* Farleigh Dickinson University Press, 1983.
Reframing Japanese Cinema: Authorship, Genre, History, edited by Arthur Nolletti Jr. and David Desser, Indiana University Press, 1992. □

Catherine Littlefield Greene

Catherine Littlefield Greene (1755-1814) is credited with aiding Eli Whitney in his invention of the cotton gin—an invention that revolutionized the plantation economy of the American south. Her husband, Nathanael Greene, was a decorated army officer who served with distinction during the Revolutionary War.

A question that has appeared on history tests in public schools around the United States for over a century is "Who invented the Cotton Gin?" While most would answer "Eli Whitney," this answer may not be correct. In an 1883 pamphlet titled "Woman as Inventor," author and proto-feminist, Matilda Joslyn Gage, first put forth the contention that it was not, in fact, Whitney who invented the machine. The person who should receive credit for the cotton gin, explained Gage, was a woman: Catherine Littlefield Greene.

Wife of a Revolutionary Hero

Catherine Littlefield—known to family and friends as Kitty or Caty—was born on Block Island, Rhode Island, on February 17, 1755. She was the daughter of Phebe Ray and John Littlefield. After her mother's death, Catherine went to live with her maternal aunt, Catherine Ray Greene, who was the wife of the future governor of the state of Rhode Island. Aunt Catherine, an attractive, energetic woman who was known as a charming hostess, took over the role of mother to ten-year-old Caty, and supervised the young girl's education as befit a young woman of the upper classes.

Present during her aunt's many social gatherings, Catherine caught the interest of several of the Littlefield's bachelor acquaintances when she came of age. After a quick courtship, 19-year-old Catherine married Nathanael Greene on July 20, 1774, in Greenwich, Rhode Island. Fourteen years her senior, Nathanael was the son of Nathanael Greene Sr. and Mary Mott, born July 27, 1742 at Potowamut, Rhode Island. As a military man who keenly felt the looming threat of war in the American colonies, Nathanael realized that time spend with his young wife would be limited. His wedding invitation to Samuel Ward dated July 10, 1774 contained concerns shared by many in the colonies: "On the 20th this Instant I expect to be married to Miss Kitty Littlefield at your Uncle Greene's. . . . As she is not married at her fathers house she declined giving any an invitation but a few of her nearest relations and most intimate friends. . . . Your Daddy is appointed one to attend the Congress, for which I rejoice, as the mean motives of Interest . . . will have no influence upon his Virtuous Soul. . . . The [British] soldiers in Boston are insolent above measure. Soon, very soon, expect to hear the thirsty Earth drinking in the warm blood of American sons."

Following their wedding, the couple moved to Nathanael Greene's home in Coventry, Rhode Island, where they spent less than a year together before he was called into service. Greene—a pacifist Quaker with a limited education who suffered from recurring bouts of asthma and a limp—seemed an unlikely person to become known as the savior of the south. In 1775 his historic military career began when he was commissioned a brigadier general. Charged with raising the Rhode Island Army of Observation, he traveled to Massachusetts with his troops in May. In a letter dated June 2, 1775, he wrote to his young wife: "I have recommended you to the care of my brethren;. . . . It had been happy for me if I could have lived a private life in peace and plenty. . . . But the injury done my Country, and the Chains of Slavery foregoing for posterity, calls me fourth to defend our common rights, and repel the bold invaders of the Sons of freedom." On June 22 he was commissioned a brigadier general in the Continental Army. During the siege of Boston a month later Greene commanded troops on Boston's Prospect Hill.

With her husband now in Massachusetts, Catherine remained in Coventry, where she gave birth to their first child in February of 1776, naming him after General George Washington. Nathanael remained in Boston until the evacuation of British troops a few months later and then moved his army south to Long Island. In August 1776 he was commissioned a major general of the Continental Army. However, he was stricken almost immediately with a serious illness and prevented from joining the Battle of Long Island. He returned home to recover. Returning to his troops, General Greene commanded forces at the battles of Trenton (December 26, 1776) and Princeton (January 2-3, 1777).

Dedicated Wife Battles Childbirth

A daughter, which Catherine chose to name Martha Washington, was born to the Greenes in March of 1777. The pregnancy was not an easy one, and Catherine remained bedridden. She was instructed to partake of a common but potentially deadly cure by ingesting four grains of mercury a day. In a letter dated May 20th 1777, Nathanael chastised his young wife for not being a more attentive letter-writer. "I return'd last Night from Peeks Kill after a long, tedious and hard journey. To crown all I fell from my Horse upon the Top of an exceeding high Mountain, cut my lip through and otherwise bruised myself exceedingly. Never did I undergo more fatigue in less time. . . . My dear, it is now a month and upwards since I receiv'd a line from one of the family. I think it exceeding unkind; if you are unwell and incapable of writing surely some of the brothers might do me that friendly office. . . . Think how you would feel if I had been in an engagement and left your mind under the torture of Suspense for upwards of a month. O how cruel!" As an older man of some ambition, General Greene was careful that both he and his wife be approved of by polite society. "If you are in want of anything from Boston, write to Mrs. Knox. . . . ," he added. "But remember when you write to Mrs. Knox you write to a good scholar; therefore mind and spell well. You are defective in this matter, my love, a little attention will soon correct it. . . . It is said it is ungenteel for Gentlemen to make observations upon Ladies writeing [sic]. I hope you won't think it unkind in me. Nothing but the affection and regard I feel for you makes me wish to have you appear an accomplished Lady in every point of view."

Despite her lack of attention to writing like other military wives Catherine attempted to join her husband whenever practicable for the duration of the Revolutionary War. Until Nathanael was sent south to command the Army of the South in October of 1780, his wife remained near him a great deal of the time. While away from her home in Coventry, she left her young children with family members, despite the criticism of several friends and relatives. Catherine became pregnant with four of the couple's six children during her husband's tour of duty.

In early June of 1777, after several months of illness, Catherine felt well enough to travel south to her husband's side, and was welcomed at the Beverwyck, New Jersey country house of Abraham Lott, located ten miles northeast of Morristown and close to the site where Greene's army was billeted. Lott was a wealthy middle-aged merchant and patriot who, with his wife and daughters, had left New York City the year before. The Greenes and Lotts soon became close friends, and Catherine returned to Beverwyck on several occasions. Her second daughter would be named after Lott's daughter, Cornelia.

On September 11, 1777 Greene again engaged with British troops, this time under the command of General Howe, at the Battle of Brandywine. In November he returned to New Jersey in a vain attempt to protect the fort at Red Bank. A month later Washington and his troops set up winter headquarters at Valley Forge, Pennsylvania. Catherine joined her husband during this dismal encampment and shared his small, cramped quarters and the meager military fare. The following spring Greene was appointed quartermaster general. General Washington ordered him to Rhode Island, to aid General Lafayette in preparing for an attack on Newport. The attack came on August 29, 1778, forcing an American retreat.

In December of 1778 Catherine and her two-year-old son George returned to the Lotts' home in Beverwyck. On Christmas Eve, 1778, the Greenes sent an invitation: "General and Mrs. Greene beg that General and Lady Washington honor their poor quarters with their presence this evening at eight." The general responded: "Deliver to Mrs. Greene the compliments of Mrs. Washington and myself with the assurance that we will do ourselves the pleasure of being present at Van Veghten House this evening." Recalling that evening in her memoirs, Greene's friend Jane Stickle Crosier of Indianapolis provides a glimpse of Catherine Greene: "Not far from the two generals stands the fair hostess, surrounded by a bevy of bright young faces. How beautiful that face and form and how graceful her every movement! The 25 summers have left no mark of care upon that joyous mature. The expressive grey eyes respond to every mood, and the sweetest smile hovers ever upon the regular and animated features. Her quick perception and unusually retentive memory combine in making her conversation brilliant and her society a delight to all who come within the magic of her presence. The mass of reddish brown hair is coiled high upon the well-poised head, with dainty puffings to the front. The brilliancy of that beautiful, clear complexion is set off to wondrous advantage by the tiny bit of black court plaster placed near the dimpled chin. She wears a superb gown of heaviest old rose brocade. The square cut neck is filled in with rare old lace and the elbow sleeves have flounces of the same cob-web like texture.

Leaving New Jersey once again, Catherine traveled with her husband to Philadelphia, staying with patriot John Cox and his family in Trenton along the way. While Greene went on ahead due to the need to address Congress, his wife remained with the Cox family before continuing on to Philadelphia in mid-January of 1779. By February the family had returned to Camp Middlebrook, New Jersey. At the end of May Catherine was once again pregnant, and returned home to Rhode Island, where the Greene's third child, Cornelia Lott, was born in September. A month later Greene was ordered to rejoin Washington's army at Fredericksburg,

New York. Catherine joined her husband at his new encampment at West Point, New York, in mid-November 1779, but returned to Morristown to give birth to her second son, Nathanael Ray, in mid-January 1780.

Moved South at Close of War

On June 7, 1780 Greene commandeered the front line against a British advance at Connecticut Farms, New Jersey. Three days later, as the conflict again showed signs of escalating, Catharine returned with her children to her home in Rhode Island. For 11 days in September 1780, Washington placed Greene in temporary command of the Continental Army after he found himself delayed after returning from a meeting with French officers, due to Benedict Arnold's treachery at West Point. Greene presided over the military tribunal that convicted Major John Andre to death for aiding Arnold in his attempt to surrender West Point to British forces.

Although Nathanael missed his wife terribly during the fall of 1780, escalating military campaigns in the south prevented her from traveling to his side. In early December Greene arrived in Charlotte, North Carolina, and received command of the Southern Army, which had suffered several defeats under the recent leadership of General Gates. Greene rebuilt the army and fought the British at Guilford Courthouse, near Greensboro, North Carolina, on March 15, 1781. There he and fellow general, Daniel Morgan, distinguished themselves against General Charles Cornwallis, by inflicting heavy losses on the enemy and forcing a British retreat.

After the war for independence was won in 1783 Greene was offered the post of secretary of war in the new government. He twice declined it, preferring to return to his home in Rhode Island. That same year a third daughter, Louisa, was born to the Greenes. Catherine went on to have another child, also named Catherine, who died as an infant c. 1785.

In the fall of 1785 the Greenes left their family and friends in Rhode Island and moved south to Savannah, Georgia. They made their new home at Mulberry Grove, a plantation given in gratitude to General Greene by the states of Georgia and South Carolina. While the family's wealth had diminished during the course of the war and Mulberry Grove proved unprofitable because Greene's Quaker upbringing prevented him from utilizing slave labor, life at Mulberry Grove proved a happy one. After almost a year spent in the society of his beloved Catherine and their many friends, the 44-year-old general died at his home on June 19, 1786, a victim of severe sunstroke.

After her husband's death, 31-year-old Catherine continued to raise her five children, who now ranged in age from three to ten. She also showed herself to be a competent businesswoman in her management of the family plantation. President George Washington visited her during his trip through the south in 1791, calling at Mulberry Grove in mid-May to make sure the widow of one of his most trusted generals was well cared for.

Whitney and the Cotton Gin

In 1892 Catherine rented a room to a young Yale College graduate who had traveled south from Massachusetts in search of a teaching job. The young man's name was Eli Whitney, and his skills as a handyman were of use in maintaining the large plantation house. Although being a New England native and knowing little of cotton-farming, Whitney became intrigued when Greene explained how unprofitable it was to raise green-seed cotton, due to the time involved in cleaning it. Tradition holds that Greene suggested that Whitney build a machine that could clean seed cotton. Perhaps her prompting went only that far, or perhaps she provided a more detailed suggestion, maybe even a rudimentary design. In any case, Whitney's mechanical skills transformed Greene's suggestion into a reality.

By some reports, Greene financed the patent and fabrication of Whitney's cotton gin ("gin" being short for "engine"), perhaps because women were not then allowed to hold patents. Others claim that the young man went into partnership with Connecticut native Phineas Miller, a fellow Yale graduate a year older than Whitney, who owned a cotton plantation on Cumberland Island, Georgia. Either way, during the winter of 1792 Whitney worked on the machine and by April of 1793 his design was complete, although some sources suggest that Greene recommended improving his prototype by replacing its wooden teeth with wire ones. On March 14, 1794, Whitney received a patent for the cotton gin. However, he was unable to profit from his device because Congress did not renew the patent in 1807 and his design was adapted for use by other manufacturers. Due to the widespread use of the cotton gin, the United States quickly grew to become the largest producer of cotton fiber in the world.

Initially dubbed a "saw engine," Whitney's machine separated the cotton seeds from the cotton fibers mechanically, through the use of a rotating cylinder containing rows of saw-like teeth. When the cylinder revolved through the use of a hand-crank, these teeth passed through closely spaced ribs on a fixed comb. When a clump of cotton was inserted into the gin and the crank turned, fibers were caught by the teeth and pulled through the comb, while the seeds, too large to pass between the rib, were filtered out. Whitney's first gin was able to produce 50 pounds of cleaned cotton a day.

Whatever role she played in the development of Whitney's cotton gin, Greene ceased to be interested in the matter after the spring of 1793, when her oldest son, George Washington Greene, drowned during a canoe trip up the Savannah River with a friend. Eighteen years old when he died, George was buried on the plantation. In 1901 the remains of both George and his father, General Nathanael Greene, would be reinterred next to the Greene Monument in Johnson Square, Savannah.

On May 31, 1796 the widowed Catherine Littlefield Greene married Whitney's partner, Miller. He had grown in Greene's esteem while serving as both her plantation manager and a tutor to her younger children. Eventually Miller was elected to the state Senate. The marriage would last until his death in 1802. After her marriage Catherine left Mulberry Grove and moved to Miller's home on Cumberland Island, where she died on July 20, 1814, at the age of fifty-nine. As her surviving children were known to remark, there was irony in the fact that Catherine Greene, who disliked sea voyages, ended her life as it had begun: on a sea island.

Books

Greene, George Washington II, *Life of Nathanael Greene*, (3 vols., 1867-1871).

Ogilvie, Marilyn Bailey, *Women in Science: Antiquity through the Nineteenth Century*, MIT Press, 1986.

Stegman, John F., and Janet A. Stegman, *Caty: A Biography of Catharine Littlefield Greene*, University of Georgia Press, 1985.

Online

Greene's of the World: Nineteenth Century, http://www.uftree .com/UFT/WebPages/plgreene/ (November 10, 2001). □

Edward Marshall Hall

Sir Edward Marshall Hall (1858-1927) was the most celebrated legal figure of his era in England as the defense attorney for a large number of sensational murder trials that featured in British tabloids during the Edwardian era.

British barrister Edward Marshall Hall trained for a career in the law, but his successes in his chosen field came as a result of his abilities as an actor. The courtroom provided Hall with a rapt—and captive—audience, and he used his abilities as a persuasive speaker to convince countless juries that the "invisible weight" of the presumption of innocence should tilt the scales of justice in favor of the defendant. The details of Hall's courtroom antics, and the dedication with which he defended the lives of his clients, made Hall into a popular hero and one of the most widely known attorneys in England.

Used Courtroom as Theatre

Born in Brighton, England, in 1858, the son of an attorney, Hall grew up enjoying a privileged existence. While deciding early in his life that he would become a priest, he spent much of his youth perfecting his shooting skills. Educated at Rugby and then Cambridge, he became engaged to Ethel Moon shortly after graduation and decided to abandon his dreams of ordination in favor of a career either in acting or law. His inability to memorize material made an acting career impossible, and after a period of study Hall was admitted to the bar in 1888. He also married despite opposition from both his and Ethel's friends. Even on their honeymoon in Paris, Ethel was unfaithful, and she eventually abandoned her husband before dying at a young age.

Hall found consolation from his wretched marriage in his work. Setting himself up in private practice, he decided to dedicate his legal career to defending murder suspects—people he viewed as suffering the worst sort of torment as they hung in limbo between life and death. He quickly built his reputation through a series of high-profile murder cases. Among his early courtroom victories was the case of Robert Wood, a glass engraver and cartoonist tried in 1903 for the brutal murder of a prostitute. After a six-day defense and despite credible evidence against Wood, Hall cast enough doubt in the minds of the jury that Wood was set free.

Other wins for Hall included the 1909 trial of Edward Lawrence and the trial of Ronald Light the following year. Lawrence had left his wife of several years and was living with a barmaid who was discovered dead. Although Lawrence made an incriminatory statement during police questioning shortly after the crime was discovered, Hall did not let that deter him. His oratory captivated the jury and achieved a verdict of not guilty.

In 1920 Hall defended Welsh attorney Harold Greenwood, who was suspected of murdering his young wife for her sizeable fortune. When Greenwood and another woman announced their engagement a month after the death, Mrs. Greenwood's body was exhumed. Traces of arsenic were found and Greenwood was arrested, but Hall managed to convince the jury that Greenwood was not guilty. Hall's notoriety even attracted the attention of the infamous mass murderer Jack the Ripper, who wrote to Hall but never needed his services since he was never apprehended.

Created Doubt in Jurors

Hall was not noted for possessing a solid grounding in the law. His law clerks did most of the legal research and brief writing needed for his cases. But he had a talent for understanding and exploiting people's emotions, and he approached each new jury as if it were a new audience waiting to be won. One of Hall's techniques was to begin his defense argument with a list of the defendant's questionable attributes, and then, one by one, deny that they played any role in the charges leveled against him. "My client is not on trial for enjoying strong drink. He is not on trial for abandoning his ill wife and his three young children, though perhaps he should be," Hall would begin in such a defense. By exposing his client's shortcomings, Hall could then manipulate the jury into believing the defendant truthful, even contrite. Hall also had a habit of annoying the presiding judge to the point that the judge would snap at him. Then Hall would appear humbled, making all of the judge's subsequent objections seem to be motivated by a personal dislike of Hall rather than an appropriate point of law. By creating the impression that the court was prejudiced against his client, Hall often manipulated the outcome in his client's favor.

Not all of Hall's defenses were successful. When cases revolved more around circumstantial evidence than suspicion and emotions, Hall's shallow understanding of the law proved fatal. In the case of Lieutenant Frederick Rothwell Holt, for instance, the defendant suffered from both depression and shell shock, facts that should have prevented his execution for the 1919 murder of girlfriend Kitty Breaks. While Hall attempted to argue Holt's incompetence, he did not have the technical expertise to cite sufficient legal precedent to dissuade the jury from a guilty verdict.

In the case of Frederick Henry Seddon, Hall was hampered with a difficult client; far from eliciting sympathy during his trial for murdering his tenant, Seddon antagonized jurors with his arrogance. The case centered on the death of Miss Eliza Mary Barrow, a woman who rented the top floor of Seddon's Islington brownstone. After alienating most of her friends, Barrow began to look to Seddon for financial advice and gradually liquidated most of her assets in real estate and stocks, converting her wealth into gold coin. While it was believed that over four hundred pounds of gold coin was hidden in her room, no money was ever found after her sudden and mysterious death. Suspicion was aroused after family members called to visit and discovered Barrow dead and buried. When the body was exhumed, trace amounts of arsenic were found, and both Seddon and his wife were charged. On trial with his wife in 1912, Seddon was found guilty and hanged. But his wife—who the circumstantial evidence showed to have been the person who most likely administered the fatal doses of arsenic—was set free.

Hall suffered another loss in the trial of George Joseph Smith, charged with murdering three young brides in three successive years, 1912 through 1914, by drowning each young woman in a bath shortly after their wedding. Smith was executed in 1915.

Political Career at Midlife

Although most of his cases were criminal defenses, Hall also took on several civil cases, the most noteworthy of which was *Russell v. Russell* in 1923. While Hall was praised for his classical oratory, his ignorance of the nuances of the law and his tendency to get into heated arguments in court prevented him from advancing too far beyond sensational murder trials during his career. Knighted by the queen at the height of his popularity, Hall married again in the mid-1890s and had a daughter.

At the age of 42, Hall decided to enter politics. He was elected as a Conservative Member of Parliament for Southport in 1900 and remained in that house for six years; he then ran in East Toxteth and served his new constituents from 1910 until 1916. Hall's parliamentary career remained undistinguished, in part due to an embarrassing maiden speech on the floor of the House in 1901. The events of that day became legendary in the House of Commons. Hall, in deference to the daughter of one of his constituents, spoke on the issue of temperance reform, in particular the problems caused when young children were ordered by their fathers to enter public houses and buy ale to bring back home. The issue was brought up late in the day, at an hour when most MPs were looking forward to going out drinking themselves or returning home to their families. As Hall dramatically outlined his proposal to have beer and ale distributed throughout the city on carts and left on subscribers' doorsteps like milk, jeers rang out in the chamber. From that day on, Hall refrained from speaking in Parliament unless absolutely required to do so.

Hall died in 1927 at the age of 69. His career continued to fascinate the public and served as the basis for a number of British television programs, including a segment of the 1990 series *Crime Secrets* and an eight-part BBC-TV series, *Shadow of the Noose,* in 1988.

Books

Inge, W. R., *Post-Victorians,* Nicholson & Watson, 1933.
Marjoribanks, Edward, *For the Defense: The Life of Sir Edward Marshall Hall,* Macmillan, 1929.

Online

Murder—UK Web site, http://www.microwaredata.co.uk/murder-uk (February 2, 2002). □

Henry Wager Halleck

Henry Wager Halleck (1815-1872) was named General-in-Chief of the United States Union forces during the Civil War by President Abraham Lincoln to replace General George Brinton McClellan and was replaced, in turn, by General Ulysses S. Grant.

Halleck was elected to Phi Beta Kappa at Union College. In 1839, he graduated from West Point Military Academy, where he also taught as an undergraduate. He performed engineering consulting on the fortifications of New York Harbor and later traveled to France where he conducted similar tasks. After publishing *A Report on the Means of National Defence,* Halleck was invited to present a series of lectures at the Lowell Institute of Boston. The lectures were the basis of his popular *Elements of Military Art and Science.* While traveling by boat to California at the onset of the Mexican-American War, he translated Henri Jomini's *Vie Politique et Militaire de Napolean,* which he published in 1864.

Halleck's military tenure in California was marked by many successes, including serving as secretary of state of the military government of the territory, as well as serving as lieutenant governor of the Mexican city of Mazatlan. His engineering expertise led him to be named captain of engineers, and he served as a military inspector and engineer of California's fortifications and lighthouses. He resigned from the army in 1854 and established the law offices of Halleck, Peachy & Billings, which became the most prominent legal firm in California. He also contributed significantly to the constitution of the state. He turned down a seat on the state's supreme court as well as an opportunity to serve as a United States senator, choosing instead to reap a vast financial fortune as a lawyer, writer of books on legal issues, and mine owner. He married a granddaughter of Alexander Hamilton, which also made him the brother-in-law of Major General Schuyler Hamilton.

Called Back to Active Duty

When the United States Civil War began, the Union Army was lacking the quality of military leaders possessed by the Confederacy. Upon the recommendation of General Winfield Scott, President Lincoln appointed Halleck major general, the fourth-highest military officer in the Union Army. Following the teachings of his West Point instructor Dennis Hart Mahan, Halleck initiated strategies that emphasized tactical victories over battlefield victories. His concept required constant entrenchment of his troops in efforts to occupy Confederate territories in order to cut off their communications and supply lines rather than by direct attack. General McClellan, Halleck's commanding officer, named him head of the Department of the Missouri Union war effort in November 1861, whereupon he replaced General John Fremont. Known for his organizational skills, Halleck arrived in Missouri, where he wrote McClellan: "Affairs here in complete chaos. . . . Troops unpaid; without clothing or arms. Many never properly mustered into service and some utterly demoralized. Hospitals overflowing with sick." Halleck famously brought order to the chaos. Whereas the generals under his auspices commanded several decisive victories, notably General Grant at Forts Henry and Donelson, General Pope at Island No. 10, and General Samuel R. Curtis at Pea Ridge, Halleck notoriously moved his armies too slowly against Corinth, allowing the Confederate forces under General Beauregard to retreat unscathed. According to historians, Halleck's forces could have beaten Beauregard's troops decisively with the possible outcome a

Many Civil War historians regard Halleck's military successes as unwarranted credit for the strategies of such subordinates as Grant, General John Pope, and General Samuel R. Curtis. He first gained attention as a military strategist of note when he graduated third in his class at West Point Military Academy. He later published a volume of military strategy, *Elements of Military Strategy,* and served in the Army during the Mexican-American War. President Lincoln recalled him from civilian life to serve as a major general in 1861, and after initial successes, he was named to replace first General John C. Fremont as commander of the Missouri Department and, later, General McClellan as General-in-Chief of the Union Army. His battlefield methodology and unyielding and arbitrary adherence to the strategies of Frenchman Henri Jomini led to several costly delays and embarrassing battlefield defeats and he was demoted to chief of staff when President Lincoln replaced him as General-in-Chief with Grant. The breadth of his knowledge as a lawyer, engineer, and military historian earned him the nickname "Old Brains" early in his career, but his abrasive demeanor and ineffectuality led others to amend the nickname to the derisive appellation "Old Wooden Head." He has since become one of the Civil War's most vilified Union officers with few defenders.

From Farm Boy to West Point

Born on a farm in Westernville, New York, Halleck ran away from home due to his intense dislike of farmwork. His maternal grandfather subsequently adopted him and paid for his education. After studying at the Hudson Academy,

significantly abbreviated campaign on the Western front. Instead, he ordered Pope, Grant, and General Buell to amass the Union forces in a slow, deliberate advance to Corinth. Rather than march through the evening, he ordered the 110,000 troops to entrench each evening, a time-consuming effort that took more than one month to advance less than twenty miles, and allowed the 66,000 Confederate troops to abandon the city unbeknownst to the Union Army. Furthering the blunder, Halleck also castigated Grant for leading an unauthorized attack on Shiloh. Halleck was angered primarily by Grant's sacrificing thirteen thousand Union troops compared to the ten thousand Confederate casualties. Grant's victory, however, marked a significant triumph for the Union Army. Halleck's enduring reputation also was impacted negatively by a post he sent to President Lincoln that accused Grant of drunkenness, insubordinate behavior, and being unfit to command, which some historians say offers proof of Halleck's pettiness, competitiveness, and underhanded behavior. The Union victories, however, resulted in Halleck taking command of the newly named Department of the Mississippi, which included Missouri, Ohio, and Kansas.

Following the debacle of Corinth, assessments of Halleck's subsequent reputation diminished rapidly. Fearing that General McClellan's military leadership was resulting in a stalemate or, worse, defeat, President Lincoln replaced him as General-in-Chief with Halleck in July 1862. Generally considered to be a micromanager, Halleck proved more ineffectual than McClellan. Among the many complaints lodged against him was his insistence that troops in the field slow their advances against the enemy by repairing railroads, building roads, and fixing bridges. He is blamed also for hampering his generals—particularly Grant—with bureaucratic requests, paperwork, and unnecessary military advice. As General-in-Chief, Halleck is credited with withdrawing McClellan's forces from the Potomac Peninsula, but negatively criticized for his failure to adequately coordinate McClellan's and Pope's forces at the Second Battle of Bull Run. According to Russell F. Weigley in his *A Great Civil War: A Military an d Political History, 1861-1865:* "Through the rest of the campaign, however, Halleck never again did anything comparably correct. He hid from responsibility. The Union would have been better off without a General-in-Chief." By the time he was demoted in March 1864 to chief of staff and replaced by Grant, Halleck had earned the disrespect of both his superiors and subordinates. President Lincoln called him "little more than a first-rate clerk," and McClellan disparaged him as "the most hopelessly stupid of all men in high position." Numerous biographical resources also refer to his disagreeable demeanor, physical unattractiveness, and his consistent efforts to lay blame on his subordinates for his own mistakes. Following the Civil War, he was named commander of the Military Division of the James. In August 1865, he was given command of the Pacific. In 1869, he was reassigned to command the Division of the South, and he moved to Louisville, Kentucky, where he died in 1872.

Books

Boatner, Mark M. III, *The Civil War Dictionary,* David McKay Company, Inc., 1959.

Cozzens, Peter, *General John Pope: A Life for the Nation,* University of Illinois Press, 2000.

Hagerman, Edward, *The American Civil War and the Origins of Modern Warfare: Ideas, Organization, and Field Command,* Indiana University Press, 1992.

Hawkins, Vincent B., *The Harper Encyclopedia of Military Biography,* HarperCollins Publishers, 1992.

Pratt, Fletcher, *A Short History of the Civil War,* Dover Publications, 1976.

Warner, Ezra J., *Generals in Blue: Lives of the Union Commanders,* Louisiana State University Press, 1964.

Weigley, Russell F., *A Great Civil War: A Military and Political History, 1862-1865,* Indiana University Press, 2000. □

William Halsted

William Stewart Halsted (1852-1922) pioneered many methods of preventing surgical infection and introduced the use of general anesthesia.

In an era when more surgery patients died from bacterial infections than the illness prompting the initial surgery, William Stewart Halsted introduced new preventative methods that significantly reduced bodily infections introduced through invasive surgery techniques. His main concern was the prevention of infection through the methodical sterilization of all medical equipment, as well as pioneering efforts in the design and use of surgical gloves. More important, Halsted introduced new procedures for the handling of bodily tissues and organs that minimized trauma and infection, as well as methods to control and stop hemorrhaging. Well-versed in human physiology and anatomy, a knowledge not necessarily common nor applied in 19th-century medicine, he taught that bodily tissues that are damaged during surgery are more susceptible to infection, subsequently rendering the patient less likely to recover. He also pioneered the use of general anesthesia, which proved tremendously valuable in minimizing surgical pain for patients, which, in turn, enabled surgeons to devote more time to performing surgeries on patients prompted to move reflexively from pain.

Slow Rise to Medical History

Halsted was a descendent of Timothy Halsted, an English emigrant who came to America around 1660 and settled in Hempstead, Long Island, New York. Halsted was born in New York City to William Mills and Mary Louisa Haines Halsted on September 23, 1852. Halsted's father was the president of a textile-importing firm, Halsted, Haines and Co., and his mother came from the family of Richard Townley Haines, her husband's partner. When he was ten years old, Halsted's parents sent him to a private school. He subsequently attended Andover, graduating in 1869, and Yale University. At Yale, he distinguished himself more on the gridiron than in the classroom, serving as cap-

first transfusions in 1881 when his sister nearly died from a postpartum hemorrhage. He wrote: "After checking the hemorrhage, I transfused my sister with blood drawn into a syringe from one of my veins and injected immediately into hers." One year later, he successfully operated on his mother in order to remove gallstones.

In 1884, Halsted was impressed by an announcement of Carl Koller at the Opthalmological Congress in Heidelberg, Germany. Koller discovered that the entire conjunctiva and cornea area of a patient's eye could be anesthetized by injecting anesthetic directly into a nerve. Halsted subsequently began his own experiments in anesthesia. The most readily available anesthetics at the time, however, were cocaine and morphine, and Halsted succumbed to both drugs' highly addictive qualities through his experiments. For the remainder of his life, historians and biographers believe he remained addicted to morphine. He discovered, however, that an injection of cocaine into the trunk of a sensory nerve resulted in a numbing of pain in all that nerve's branches. Halsted concluded that a small amount of injected anesthetic could be used to anesthetize a wide portion of the patient's body, thereby introducing general anesthesia to modern medicine. The practice had its most widespread use in dental surgery and earned Halsted a gold medal from the American Dental Association in 1922.

A Changed Man at Johns Hopkins

By 1886, Halsted's morphine and cocaine addictions caused his surgical abilities to become dangerously unreliable, and his medical career was nearly destroyed by the time he was forced to leave New York City. He subsequently exhibited a withdrawn, reticent personality that sharply contrasted with his former outgoing self. He relocated to Baltimore, Maryland, where his former mentor, Dr. Welch, worked with him to overcome his addictions, and it is believed Welch was successful in curing Halsted of his cocaine addiction. Halsted reentered the medical profession by working in Welch's laboratory around which was built Johns Hopkins Hospital. In 1889, he was named acting surgeon and supervisor of the outpatient department at Johns Hopkins. His initial term was for one year, due to the hospital's concerns about Halsted's diminished capabilities from drug addiction. His exemplary performance resulted in a permanent appointment the following year. In 1890, he became surgeon-in-chief and married Caroline Hampton, the head operating room nurse at the hospital. Hampton had complained about the dermatitis she experienced due to Halsted's insistence that she use mercuric bichloride as a surgical antiseptic, resulting in her future husband drafting the Goodyear Rubber Company to produce surgical gloves to protect his staff. In 1892, he became the founding professor of surgery at Johns Hopkins Medical School.

Medical Breakthroughs

As professor of surgery at Johns Hopkins, Halsted instructed many students who would graduate to medical prominence, including Hugh Young, John M. T. Finney, and neurosurgery pioneers Harvey Cushing and Walter Dandy. Halsted was an ardent medical researcher, exploring new

tain of the school's football team during his academic tenure. He purchased copies of *Gray's Anatomy* and John C. Dalton's *Physiology* during his senior year and attributed much of his subsequent interest in medicine to those two works. Following his graduation from Yale in 1874, he enrolled in the College of Physicians and Surgeons in New York City. He served as assistant professor of physiology under Dalton until his graduation with honors in 1877. That same year, he interned at Bellevue Hospital under the auspices of William H. Welch, who later became a founding member of the Johns Hopkins Medical School. He was selected later that year to establish the medical service guidelines as house physician at the recently completed New York Hospital. In 1877, English surgeon Joseph Lister visited New York and impressed Halsted with his findings on the effectiveness of antiseptic surgical methods in preventing operation-induced infection.

In 1878, Halsted embarked for Europe, spending the majority of his time in Vienna, Austria, where he spent two years studying surgical procedures, as well as embryology and histology. He returned to the United States in 1880 and became a surgeon of renown. Over the course of the next five years, he became visiting surgeon to many New York City hospitals, including Bellevue, Roosevelt, the Charity, Emigrant, Chambers Street, and Presbyterian as needed during his afternoons and oversaw the outpatient program at Roosevelt Hospital each morning. During the evenings, he taught anatomy and conducted medical classes. Throughout the 1880s, Halsted revolutionized surgical medicine in the United States. He conducted one of modern medicine's

methods to operate on hernias, thyroid glands, and gall bladders and its ducts. He contributed to new procedures in intestinal sutures and treatment of tuberculosis, hernias of the groin, goiters, radical mastectomys for breast cancer, and circulatory problems, including aneurysms and surgery on blood vessels. He is admired also for establishing new procedures for training medical students, requiring that students study physiology and anatomy. His views were expressed in the article "The Training of the Surgeon," which was reprinted in the *Johns Hopkins Hospital Bulletin* in 1904. Halsted is credited also with changing the approach of modern medicine from its previously unrefined reputation to a more calculated manner that emphasized controlled blood loss and minimized tissue damage, which also marked his emphasis on physiological and anatomical knowledge. He was considered to be a slow and methodical surgeon, careful to not disrupt any area of the patient's body that was in close proximity to the operated area.

For the remainder of his life, Halsted traveled extensively throughout the medical capitals of Europe, visiting clinics in Germany, Austria, and Switzerland. He was an honorary member of the German Surgical Association and attended several of the group's congresses. His research and teaching made him an invaluable asset to Johns Hopkins, and he helped establish the institution as among the United States's most respected centers of medical research and knowledge. His breakthroughs in the medical use of anesthesia and antiseptics and his deliberate approach to surgery are credited as significant medical advancements. In 1919, he recovered from an operation to remove gallstones. He failed to recover from a second gallstone operation, however, and died in 1922. His medical writings, entitled *Surgical Papers in Two Volumes,* were published in 1924 and reprinted in 1961.

Books

American National Biography, Volume 9, edited by John A. Garraty and Mark C. Carnes, Oxford University Press, 1999.
Dictionary of American Biography, Volume IV, Part I, Charles Scribner's Sons, 1960. □

Edith Hamilton

Edith Hamilton (1867-1963) was an excellent teacher, scholar, and writer. She was a gifted storyteller and had a phenomenal memory. Starting at the age of 63, Hamilton published a number of acclaimed books on Greek and Roman culture, was made an honorary citizen of Athens, and was awarded several honorary doctorates.

Edith Hamilton was born in Dresden, Germany, on August 12, 1867, while her mother was visiting relatives. After two months her mother returned with her to the United States, but thereafter, many people thought that she was of German extraction. Her great grandfather,

the first of the family to come to North America, was the youngest son of a branch of the wealthy Hamilton family of Northern Ireland. Realizing that as the youngest son, he would not inherit much, he immigrated to Canada. His genteel status was not suited to manual labor, but he finally landed a job as a deck hand on one of the flat-bottomed boats used on frontier rivers and canals. On one such trip, he apparently jumped ship at Fort Wayne, Indiana, which was then part of Canada. He bought large tracts of land cheaply, and eventually became very wealthy. Hamilton sent for his son, Allen, from Northern Ireland.

Allen's son, Montgomery, married Gertrude Pond. Montgomery, Edith Hamilton's father, who never worked a day in his life, was a voracious reader and an educated man but was interested mainly in literature and religious heresies. According to his daughter, he was a horrible teacher. Her mother encouraged Hamilton to play outdoors and to learn foreign languages.

Hamilton, the eldest of five children from an exceptionally gifted intellectual family, was raised on a family estate with many servants, many relatives, and no need for outsiders. She was withdrawn, intense, moody, and somewhat depressive. However, she was also caring, a gifted storyteller, and had a phenomenal memory. She learned French at an early age from her mother and German from servants. Her father taught her Latin at the age of seven and Greek at eight. She was also a voracious reader, but was especially interested in ancient Greece. Her sister Alice says of her in *Edith Hamilton: An Intimate Portrait,* by Doris Fielding Reid,

''Edith had intense emotions. She had her times of joyous gaiety over the beauties of the outside world or a new book or some amusing family episode, but she had her sudden deep depressions that mystified me.''

Determined to be Educated

At the age of 16, Hamilton attended school for the first time at Miss Porter's School in Farmington, Connecticut, along with her three sisters, Alice, Margaret, and Norah. About this experience, Hamilton stated, ''We weren't taught anything.'' Since all courses were elective, a young woman did not have to take any she was weak in or did not like.

Hamilton decided to attend Bryn Mawr College in Bryn Mawr, Pennsylvania, near Philadelphia, even though Miss Porter did not believe in college for women, and her family objected strenuously. It was necessary for Hamilton to study subjects not taught at Miss Porter's School, such as trigonometry, which Hamilton taught herself from a book, in order to pass the college entrance examination.

While at Bryn Mawr, Hamilton successfully fought against a rule that smoking would automatically lead to expulsion. She majored in classics and finished in two years with a Master of Arts degree in 1894. She was awarded the European Fellowship given to the most outstanding woman in the graduating class to enable her to study for a year in any foreign country.

Travel and Study Abroad

In 1895, Hamilton traveled with her sister Alice, who had recently become a doctor, to Germany. She and Alice were the first women at the universities of Leipzig and Munich. They first studied at the University of Leipzig, where Hamilton was very disappointed in the sterility of the Greek and Roman courses. Although her professors were linguistically highly proficient, she felt they failed to see the bigger picture concerning what the ancient writers were saying. After several months of studying the grammar of the ancient Greek texts, Hamilton left Leipzig with her sister to attend the University of Munich. Her sister writes of the effect her admission to Munich had on the formerly all male bastion. ''Her admission to the University was a cause of such excitement among the students that a kind, elderly professor offered to see her through it on her first day.'' All sorts of suggestions were floated on how to avoid contamination with the sole woman on the campus. ''Finally, it came to a chair up on the lecturer's platform, where nobody could be contaminated by contact with her.'' Of course, this had the effect of making poor Hamilton even more conspicuous. She wrote that the head of the University used to look at her and shake his head sadly, while muttering about the ''woman question.''

Nevertheless, Hamilton liked being at Munich and enjoyed the notoriety. She felt that the professors there were much more interesting and kinder to her. She stated that one ''treated me as if he actually liked having me there!'' She might have stayed at Munich and earned her Ph.D. if two events had not happened. First, her father lost his money. At the same time, the dean of Bryn Mawr College, Miss M.

Carey Thomas, offered her a position as headmistress of the Bryn Mawr Preparatory School in Baltimore, Maryland.

Frightened but Frightening

When Hamilton arrived at the school in the autumn of 1896 at the age of 29, she was the first headmistress. Previously, a secreatry who reported to the dean at Bryn Mawr College had run the school. Not only had she no experience at running the only college preparatory school in the area, but she was a northerner and was faced with parents who did not necessarily believe that young women needed a real education. Hamilton remembered: ''I was very young and very ignorant when I first came to Baltimore and, I may say, very, very, frightened. I remember vividly saying to myself as I traveled down here, 'If I were put in charge of running this train, I could hardly know less how to do it than I know how to run the Bryn Mawr School.'''

If she were frightened, the impression she gave her children was terrifying. She was a remote eminence, but exacting and demanding. In spite of this, many remember her fondly. She instilled in them a love of learning and an ability to persevere, which she found in ancient Greek literature. Hamilton said, ''Nothing effortless was among the good things the early Greeks wanted. A wise and witty writer has said that the spirit of American education today is if at first you don't succeed, try something else. That spirit has never invaded our school.'' She also believed in the importance of the individual rather than of the aggregate.

Hamilton was headmistress of this school of approximately 400 students until 1922. She loved teaching, but too rarely had the opportunity. She apparently was an excellent teacher, able to inspire students with her love of learning. The fondest memories of her students revolve around her courses. One suggested Hamilton's classes were the highlight of her intellectual life. Another aspect of Hamilton's tenure was that she was highly religious and frequently quoted scriptural passages to her students. Finally, after 26 years, she was tired of her work and decided that it was time to retire. So it reads in her official biography by Doris Fielding Reid. However, a *New York Times* article of March 22, 1922, states that President Thon of Bryn Mawr College denied reports that she forced Hamilton to retire.

Bullied Into Writing

Hamilton's retirement led to a whole new career. She acquired a retreat at Sea Wall, Mt. Desert Island, Maine, where she would spend summers for 40 years with the future author of her official biography, her friend and former student, Doris Fielding Reid. Hamilton loved the outdoors and the wildness of Sea Wall's ocean and mountains. In the autumn of 1924, Hamilton moved into Reid's New York apartment for the winter and for all the subsequent 20 winters. Visitors were frequently entertained there. At one such meeting, a friend asked her to talk about the ancient Greek writers of tragedy Aeschylus, Hamilton's favorite, Sophocles and Euripides. Thereafter, the group met regularly, and Hamilton held court. After one such meeting, Rosamond Gilder, the editor of *Theatre Arts Monthly,* suggested she write about Greek tragedies for her magazine. At first, Hamilton refused, but finally prodded beyond endurance, she wrote an article and sent it off. After being published with high praise, she sent off several more articles. She was told, "You are that unusual combination, a gifted talker and a gifted writer. To be a gifted talker can be fatal to a writer."

The articles she wrote for *Theatre Arts Monthly* were remade into a book, *The Greek Way,* published in 1930, when she was 63 years old. Two years later, she published *The Roman Way.* Both books showed the relationship of ancient life to the present and are considered classics in their own right. When asked why she started writing books at an age when most people thought only of retirement, she said, "I was bullied into it."

Besides continuing to write articles, she also wrote further books, including *The Prophets of Israel* (W.W. Norton, 1936), *Three Greek Plays* (W.W. Norton, 1937), *The Great Age of Greek Literature* (W.W. Norton, 1942), *Mythology* (Little, Brown and Company, 1943), *Witness to the Truth: Christ and His Interpreters* (W.W. Norton, 1948), *Spokesmen for God: the Great Teachers of the Old Testament* (W.W. Norton, 1949), *The Echo of Greece* (W.W. Norton, 1957), *The Age of Heroes: An Introduction to Greek Mythology* (McClelland, 1957), *The Collected Dialogues of Plato* (Princeton University Press, 1961), and *The Ever-Present Past* (W.W. Norton), published posthumously in 1964.

Determined to Survive

While spending winters in Washington, D.C., from 1943 to 1963, Hamilton met many litterati, including novelist Isak Dinesen, historian Arnold Toynbee, and poets Robert Frost and Ezra Pound. In 1955, she was elected a member of the National Institute of Arts and Letters, and in 1957 became member of the American Academy of Arts and Letters. In 1957, at the age of 90, Hamilton was invited to Athens where she was given the Gold Cross of the Legion of Benefaction by King Paul of Greece, and made an honorary citizen of Athens. In 1958, she was awarded the Constance Lindsay Skinner Award for literature. Between 1949 and 1962, Hamilton was awarded honorary doctorates by the University of Rochester (1949), the University of Pennsylvania (1953), Yale University (1959), and Goucher College (1962).

Near the end of her life, she suffered a stroke from which her doctor said she would never recover. He told Reid, "You must face the fact that Miss Hamilton will never walk again and never talk again." At that instant, Hamilton opened her eyes and said "Pooh!" She recovered. She spent the following summer at Sea Wall in Maine, where she celebrated her 95th birthday. A week before she died, Hamilton decided to try to finish a book on the Greek philosopher, Plato. She passed away peacefully on May 31, 1963, in Washington, D.C.

Books

Reid, Doris Fielding, *Edith Hamilton: An Intimate Portrait,* W.W. Norton and Co., 1967.

Online

Browning, Benita, "Edith Hamilton," *Department of History at IPFW,* http://www.ipfw.edu (November 8, 2001).
"Edith Hamilton," *Distinguished Women of Past and Present,* http://www.distinguishedwomen.com (November 8, 2001).
☐

Lionel Hampton

One of the best-known orchestra leaders of the Big Band Era, Lionel Hampton (born 1908) formed his own jazz group after first playing vibraphone with bands led by Benny Goodman and Les Hite. Hampton's band played a major role in the shaping of American jazz and was the launching pad for such stellar performers as Dinah Washington, Quincy Jones, and Charlie Parker.

Although there seems to be some question about his actual birthdate, Hampton wrote in his autobiography, *Hamp,* that he was born on April 20, 1908. The son of Charles Edward and Gertrude Morgan Hampton, he was born in Louisville, Kentucky. Not long after his birth, his mother moved the family to Birmingham, Alabama, and later to Chicago. His father joined the U.S. Army shortly after the United States entered World War I and was declared missing only weeks after he was sent to France. He survived the war, however, and was reunited with his son two decades later in a Veterans Administration hospital in Dayton, Ohio.

Musical Talent Surfaced Early

While still quite young, Hampton showed a talent for music, with a particular leaning towards percussion instruments. When his mother could no longer tolerate his incessant drumming on whatever household object was handy, she invested in a set of drums for her son. In no time, he had worn it out and was ready for a new one. For awhile Hampton attended Holy Rosary Academy in Collins, Wisconsin, not far from Kenosha, where he was tutored on the drums by Sister Petra, one of the academy's Dominican nuns. Years later, in his autobiography, Hampton wrote of that experience: "She taught me the 26 rudiments on drums—drums have a scale just like the horn. She taught me the flammercue and 'Mama-Daddy,' and all that stuff on the drums." During his high school years in Chicago, Hampton worked as a news carrier for the *Chicago Defender,* mostly so that he could join the newsboys' jazz band as drummer. The jazz band's director was Major N. Clark Smith, who Hampton later praised in his autobiography as "about the greatest musician I guess I have ever known." Smith was a mentor for Hampton, schooling him in the basics of music theory, harmony, and sight-reading.

Hampton's maternal uncle, Richard Morgan, was an avid jazz fan and friendly with a number of the leading jazz musicians of the period, many of whom attended parties at

Morgan's home in Chicago. This gave young Hampton an opportunity to rub shoulders with the likes of Bix Biederbecke, Louis Armstrong, King Oliver, and Jelly Rose Morton. During his final years in high school, Hampton began playing drums in the band of Les Hite. Hite later relocated to Los Angeles and after he'd been on the West Coast for a year or so invited Hampton to come west and rejoin the band. Convincing his mother that he'd finish high school in California, Hampton headed west. For the next four years, he played drums with the Hite organization, earning a reputation as one of the best drummers on the West Coast.

Discovered Vibraphone

It was a recording session with Louis Armstrong in the fall of 1930 that first brought Hampton together with the instrument that would earn him his greatest fame. During a break in recording, Hampton noticed a vibraphone sitting in the corner. He had played the xylophone while he was a member of the newsboys' band in Chicago but had never tried his hand on the vibraphone. Writing about the incident in his autobiography, Hampton wrote: "So Louis asked me, did I know anything about the instrument, and I said, 'Sure.' I had never played the vibes before in my life, but I picked it up and played Louis' solo from his record 'Chinese Chop Suey' note for note." So impressed was Armstrong that he insisted Hampton play the vibes on a recording of Eubie Blake's "Memories of You," marking the first time the instrument had been used on a jazz recording.

Hampton's first encounter with the vibraphone marked a turning point in his career. Although he continued to play the drums, over the next couple of years he devoted progressively more of his time to the vibes until he was concentrating almost exclusively on the new instrument. In 1936, Hampton was invited by Benny Goodman to join a jazz quartet he was forming as a complement to his big band. Other members of the quartet included Teddy Wilson on piano and Gene Krupa on drums. Joining the Goodman quartet gave Hampton national exposure. It also marked the first time that a well-known band had been racially integrated. Recalling his years with Goodman, Hampton wrote in his autobiography: "With Benny, touring with two black musicians was a pioneering effort. Nobody had ever traveled with an integrated band before, and even though Teddy Wilson and I were only part of the Benny Goodman Quartet, not the whole orchestra, that was still too much for some white folks." Despite occasional racial hostility, the quartet was a smashing success. Among its more memorable hits were "Moonglow" and "Dinah," along with Hampton's own composition, "Flying Home." In addition to playing the vibes in the Goodman quartet, Hampton occasionally sat in on the drums or contributed a vocal. Shortly after joining Goodman's entourage, Hampton married his longtime business manager, Gladys Riddle.

Formed Own Band

After four years of touring with Goodman's quartet—exposure that helped make him one of the major figures of the swing era—Hampton struck out on his own in the summer of 1940. Wife Gladys served as manager for the new band, which was made up largely of young but talented musicians, most of who were unknown. Reflecting Hampton's boundless energy and innate sense of showmanship, the band soon became well known for its extended solos and bravura performances, with Hampton more often than not in the center of the spotlight. He displayed the full range of his musical talents, playing the piano, vibes, and drums.

Shortly after its formation, Hampton's band released a recording of Hampton's "Flying Home," which soon became an anthem of the swing era, helping to further establish Hampton as a star and also providing a platform for the rhythm and blues saxophone stylings of Illinois Jacquet. Music historians often credit the plaintive wail of Jacquet's sax and Hampton's jump-boogie records of the late 1940s with helping to lay the groundwork for contemporary rhythm and blues. Although music purists and critics have been disdainful of some of Hampton's antics, including playing the piano mallet-style with two fingers and dancing on the drums, his consummate skill as one of swing music's most innovative improvisers has never been in doubt.

Despite a fair amount of criticism from other jazz performers that Hampton and his band expended far too much energy grandstanding, audiences clearly loved the showmanship and flocked to Hampton concerts. Of the criticism from his fellow jazz musicians, Hampton later remarked in an interview for *Downbeat*: "They used to criticize my band and say, 'Here comes the circus.' And now all of them do it. As soon as they start singing, they're walking around the stage, they're sitting on the steps, they're singing out in the audience. And all that jive came from us."

Spawned Many Jazz Stars

The Hampton band spawned a number of the 20th century's most notable jazz stars, including Dinah Washington, Joe Williams, Dexter Gordon, Howard McGhee, Quincy Jones, Betty Carter, Clifford Brown, and Arnett Cobb. For the next 25 years Hampton and his band traveled the world, making a number of foreign goodwill tours to Africa, Australia, Europe, Japan, and the Middle East. The band also was seen frequently on TV, helping to build the group's—and Hampton's—reputation and popularity. In 1957, Hampton led his band in a performance at London's Royal Festival Hall. Two decades later he played for President Jimmy Carter at the White House.

By the mid-1960s changing musical tastes made it financially unfeasible for Hampton to keep the band operating on a regular basis. But Hampton himself was far from through. He continued to lead small groups that he put together and occasionally reassembled the big band for appearances at jazz festivals and concerts. Through the 1970s and 1980s he continued to perform and record with some of America's best jazz performers, including Chick Corea, Earl "Fatha" Hines, Charlie Mingus, Gerry Mulligan, and Woody Herman.

Hampton has been widely honored through the years, having received 17 honorary degrees from universities all over the world. In 1968 Pope Paul VI awarded Hampton the Papal Medal. He has been given the keys to the cities of New York, Los Angeles, Chicago, and Detroit, and in 1985 he received the Medal of the City of Paris. Among his other honors have been the *Ebony* Magazine Lifetime Achievement Award of 1989, the Kennedy Center Lifetime Achievement Award in 1992, and the 1996 National Medal of Arts, which was actually awarded in 1997.

Performed at White House

A lifelong Republican, Hampton campaigned actively for a number of GOP politicians through the years, including Nelson Rockefeller, Richard Nixon, Ronald Reagan, and George H.W. Bush. Perhaps as a reward for his political support, he's been invited frequently to perform at the White House. He did make one notable deviation from his straight-Republican allegiances in 1964, when he backed Democrat Lyndon B. Johnson. In his autobiography, Hampton explained his political shift in these words: "I may be a Republican, but I'm first of all an American, and I thought what President Johnson was doing was good for the country. So in 1964, when he ran for election as president, I jumped party lines to support him. I had nothing personally against Barry Goldwater—in fact, we were good friends—but Johnson had signed the 1964 Civil Rights Act, and said, 'We shall overcome,' and he was the man I wanted to support."

In 1995 Hampton suffered two mild strokes, only weeks apart. Although he recovered from the strokes, he was left dependent on a cane or wheelchair to get around. Perhaps even more devastating for Hampton was the January 7, 1997, fire at his New York City apartment, which

destroyed almost all of his belongings, including his vast collection of vintage recordings, several musical instruments, and other invaluable memorabilia from his years in music.

In February 2001, a couple of months before his 93rd birthday, Hampton donated the vibraphone he'd been playing for the previous 15 years to the Smithsonian Institution's National Museum of American History in Washington, D.C. At the ceremonies marking the formal handover of the instrument to the museum, Hampton was hailed as the "vibe president" of the United States by John Edward Hasse, the museum's curator of American music. Rep. John Conyers, a Democratic congressman from Michigan and a big jazz fan, recalled that when President Bill Clinton threw Hampton a birthday party in 1998, the vibraphonist managed to convince the chief executive to play a saxophone solo with Hampton's band. A few months later, at a 93rd birthday celebration in his New York apartment, Hampton told a reporter for *Jet* that the key to a long life is "the power of prayer and a strong belief in our Almighty God."

Books

Contemporary Black Biography, Gale Research, 1998.
Contemporary Musicians, Gale Research, 1991.
Notable Black American Men, Gale Research, 1998.

Periodicals

Jet, February 26, 2001; May 28, 2001.

Online

"Lionel Hampton: Biography," DownBeat, http://www.downbeat.com/sections/artists (November 6, 2001).
"Lionel Hampton: Biography & Early Life," Lionel Hampton's Home Page, http://www.duke.edu/~hlh2/ (November 6, 2001). □

James Harper

James Harper (1795-1869) established a printing firm in New York City that grew to become one of the largest and most influential American publishing houses of the nineteenth and twentieth centuries. As it expanded under the guidance of its founder and his three brothers, the firm published the works of such influential American authors as Washington Irving and Herman Melville. During his tenure, magazines were launched that have survived into the twenty-first century as *Harper's Bazaar* and *Harper's*.

Harper was born on April 13, 1795. He was the eldest of Joseph and Elizabeth Kolyer Harper's four sons. Harper had emigrated from England to the New York area before the American Revolution. By the time of the future publisher's birth, the family had settled in Newtown, Long Island, a distinctly rural area at the time.

The Harper boys were raised in a disciplined and pious Methodist household, and farm duties prevented the eldest son from attending school more than a few months out of every year. As a youth, however, he read the autobiography of Benjamin Franklin, one of the most admired Americans of the eighteenth century, and decided that he, too, would like to become a printer, as Franklin had been. Thus Harper was sent to the home of a family friend, Abraham Paul, who was the partner in a New York City printing shop, when he was 16. He learned the trade at Paul and Thomas as an apprentice, and lived with the Paul family, as was the custom.

Harper's next youngest brother, John, also entered the printing profession as an apprentice. In 1817, they established themselves in New York City as J. and J. Harper, in a shop at the corner of Dover and Front streets. Harper was 22 years old, his brother only 20. Their father loaned them the initial sum with which they purchased some printing presses and typesetting equipment. They also borrowed a horse from the family farm, since the presses literally ran on horsepower at the time: the yoked animal trod in a circle to power the machinery. The Harpers had researched the book market in New York City, and saw a business opportunity— a strategy that would be repeated throughout the nineteenth century inside their headquarters and make the firm an unparalleled success. There were 33 booksellers in New York City at the time, and some were publishers as well. The Harpers thought that they could contract directly with booksellers to publish various titles; in return the booksellers would receive title page credit.

Firm Grew Rapidly

The first order that Harper and his brother filled was from a seller named Evert Duycinck, who ordered 2,000 copies of *Seneca's Morals*. By this time the remaining Harper brothers were helping in the venture—Wesley was 16 and serving as a "printer's devil," while Fletcher, just 11 years old, assisted during his school holidays at the shop. In 1818, the brothers decided to publish something of their own and sell it. *Essay on the Human Understanding*, an influential work by English philosopher John Locke originally published in 1690, became the first title in the Harper catalog. Their business acumen and reputation for printing quality books and pamphlets soon made them the largest printer/publisher in the city. Rapid expansion forced them to move several times. By 1825 they were established in a series of buildings at 82 Cliff Street.

In the early 1820s, both Wesley and Fletcher had joined the business with partnership shares bought for $500 each. The name was officially changed to Harper and Brothers in 1833. When asked once who was the Harper and who were the brothers, James was said to have replied, "Any one is Mr. Harper, and the rest are brothers." Each fulfilled various duties in the operation: James served as the press operator, John was a skillful compositor of type and proofreader, and literary-minded Wesley often made the final decision on their list and wrote many prefaces to the early volumes.

Became Industry Leaders

The same year that the name change took place, the Harpers issued their first catalog, which listed 234 titles. Many of their first successes came from reprinting novels whose popularity had already been established in England. These they did so quickly that the firm was able to have a book finished less than 24 hours after its proofs had been delivered by ship. The novels of Sir Walter Scott were one example of the success that the firm enjoyed by giving eager American readers works of popular fiction. However, competition in the U.S. market for such titles was fierce, since there were no international copyright laws at the time. Over the years, the Harpers were instrumental in establishing some trade courtesies that served as a self-regularity effort in the industry. What became known as the "Harper Rule" specified that an American publisher could enjoy exclusivity for a planned title if the proofs were purchased from the English publisher or author first, and then an announcement placed in a local American newspaper heralding the forthcoming title from the firm.

A Fair-Minded Boss

As the business grew, Harper no longer ran the presses, but busied himself with the management of the physical plant. He was known to spend a good part of the workday on the floor, and was a well-liked boss. He cautioned his supervisors to treat all employees fairly. "Don't try to drive men too roughly. It is so much easier to draw than push," a company history, *The House of Harper*, quoted the founder as saying. The company became one of the first to use steam-run presses in the 1830s, and were finally able to retire the hardworking family horse; company legend asserts that when it returned to the Long Island family farm, it continued to walk in a circle for the remainder of its days around a tree, stopping and starting according to a twice-daily factory whistle from a nearby establishment.

Harper and his brothers expanded their business through several innovative practices. They launched the "Harper's Family Library" of travel, history, and biography titles, which concluded in 1845 with 187 volumes. Its titles included Washington Irving's *Life of Oliver Goldsmith* and Richard Henry Dana's *Two Years Before the Mast,* an 1840 account of Dana's years as a common sailor aboard one of the last wind-powered ocean-going vessels of the era. The Dana title was a huge success, and the Harper firm was said to have earned a small fortune from it. They held the copyright until 1868, for which they had originally paid just $250.

Lobbied in Albany

The Harper's Family Library series was famously popular—John Quincy Adams once recommended it as a worthy addition to American households—but it did have one well known detractor. Henry David Thoreau complained in his *Walden* that one family's taste should not have dictating power over the reading public. Other series followed that helped win the Harper firm more market share, such as the "Boy's and Girl's Library" for young readers. Harper himself traveled to Europe to collect fairy tales for one of its volumes, the best-selling *Fairy Book.* The founder's friendship with Thurlow Weed, who had apprenticed at the Paul firm with him years before and became the editor of the Albany *Evening Journal,* yielded introductions to state politicians. The result was an 1838 state law mandating that all New York school districts of a certain size must possess a library. Harper and Brothers filled the new demand with their "Harper's School District Library," which contained 50 volumes for just $20. Five years later, they offered many of the same titles in a pine cabinet called the New England School Library; each were tremendous sellers and earned the firm healthy profits.

Savvy business practices were the hallmark of the Harper firm. Early on, James and his brothers realized the potential of favorable mentions in newspapers for their titles, and urged editors to review their books. They also hired literary advisors who read manuscript and made recommendations, another first in the industry. They began to hire "readers" to help them sort through the numerous submissions they received. In the 1840s the Harper firm had a number of literary successes. They published an abridged edition of *Webster's Dictionary,* Charles Darwin's *Voyage of the Beagle* in 1845, and the classic Charlotte Bronte novels *Jane Eyre* and *Wuthering Heights.* Other authors in their roster included William Makepeace Thackeray, Charles Dickens, and George Eliot. By 1849 the Harper firm was printing two million volumes a year on 19 presses; they employed 350 in seven five-story buildings. In sheer numbers, the firm was the largest publishing company in the world.

Success with Magazine Publishing

James Harper provided the idea for a new venture, which was launched in 1850 as *Harper's New Monthly Magazine.* It came under the control of Fletcher, the youngest of the brothers. The following year it excerpted part of a new novel by Herman Melville that failed to arouse much attention. The finished work, *Moby Dick,* did not achieve fame until decades later. In 1857, the firm launched *Harper's Weekly,* also under the direction of Fletcher. In its day, the magazine enjoyed a healthy circulation and several historic firsts: political cartoonist Thomas Nast created the first image of Santa Claus for an 1863 cover, depicting the bearded figure distributing presents to Union Army soldiers. The magazine also featured the first images of two enduring American political symbols: the Republican Party elephant and the its Democratic Party counterpart, the donkey. In 1867, the Harpers launched *Harper's Bazar,* a weekly fashion magazine; it was acquired in 1913 by publishing magnate William Randolph Hearst, who added an "a" to the title.

At several points in its history, the Harpers weathered some difficult financial straits. A disastrous 1853 fire destroyed much of their plant and caused losses of one million dollars. By the end of the terrible day, however, the brothers had decided to rebuild and carry on—though each was by then quite well-off and could have retired. Each had sons and hoped to pass on their firm to a new generation.

First Reform Mayor of New York

Harper became active in New York political circles in mid-life. In 1844, he successfully ran for mayor on a platform that promised municipal reform after reports of widespread corruption had incensed citizens. Harper did manage to implement several internal reform measures during his tenure, but the political machine known as Tammany Hall regained control the following year. His name was even mentioned for the governorship of the state of New York, but the publisher was reportedly uninterested in running for higher office. He was married to Maria Arcularius, with whom he had one son. His wife died in 1847. Julia Thorne became his second wife. The family grew to include another son and two daughters. When his son Philip's wife died in 1856, Philip wed Julia's sister Augusta, which made the father and son brothers-in-law.

Harper's one passion, outside of his business, was driving his horses. He was enjoying his daily ride on the afternoon of Good Friday in 1869 when an accident caused the pole of the carriage to split. The horses became frightened and bolted. Both Harper and his daughter were ejected from the carriage, but his injuries were more serious than hers. He was taken to Knickerbocker Hospital, and died two days later, on March 27, 1869 in New York City. The City Hall flag flew at half-mast in his honor, and the New York papers ran lengthy obituaries.

Books

Dictionary of American Biography Base Set, American Council of Learned Societies, 1928-1936.

Exman, Eugene, *The House of Harper: One Hundred and Fifty Years of Publishing,* Harper and Row, 1967. □

Charles Harpur

Born in Australia, Charles Harpur (1813-1866) was the first important Australian poet and wrote the first sonnet sequence ever published in Australia. In addition, *The Bushrangers* was the first play by a native-born Australian both to be performed and published in book form in Australia.

Called "one of the best" of Australia's early poets by Judith Wright in *Authority and Influence: Australian Literary Criticism 1950-2000,* Charles Harpur's work has been largely neglected by both Australian literary critics and those outside Australia. As Wright pointed out, most of his work exists only in manuscript form, in many different versions, and no reliable or comprehensive collection of his work has yet been published. However, Wright wrote, "Harpur's claim to be regarded as the first poets of his country is better founded than has yet been allowed, and . . . he is also a better poet than many of those who followed him."

Harpur was one of the first Australian poets whose work embodied one of the great contradictions of Australian literature: Australian writers of his time were largely of European descent, and strove to carry on the literary traditions of Europe. At the same time, however, they were so far from Europe, and lived in such a different environment, that they could not help but regard themselves as a culture altogether separate from Europe.

Son of Convicts

Unlike many of his contemporaries, Harpur was born in Australia. His parents were both convicts, sent to Australia by the British government, which attempted to dispose of many criminals by shipping them off to the new country. His father, originally from Ireland, was transported for highway robbery in 1800, and his mother had been transported in her early teens.

Although people from many other walks of life also emigrated to Australia, many of those from non-criminal backgrounds tried to distance themselves from Australia's origins as a criminal colony. These people embraced English and European culture, were usually politically conservative, and thought of themselves as superior to those who were born in Australia.

Harpur's father eventually received a conditional pardon and became integrated into respectable life. During Harpur's youth he was a schoolmaster at Windsor, a prosperous settlement west of Sydney. He gave Harpur a basic education, and Harpur continued to read on his own, borrowing books from private libraries, most likely those of local clergymen, and studying whatever poetry he could find in them, particularly that of English poets such as Wil-

liam Wordsworth. According to Judith Wright in *The Literature of Australia,* from these poets Harpur gained an appreciation for the landscape of Australia, as well as pride in his own power to educate himself. In writing about the Australian landscape, he was the first poet to find beauty and mystery where others saw only a hostile, arid, and distasteful place. In his powerful convictions about his own value as a poet, he was able to lay a foundation for future Australian poetry by combining techniques of the great English poets with Australian material.

Wright commented, "Charles Harpur seems to have chosen his calling early. His life from his youth onward was to be remarkable for the tenacity and dedication with which he clung to the almost impossible task of laying the foundation for an Australian poetry, under conditions that would have discouraged most writers."

From the age of seventeen on, Harpur made a rather impoverished living as a clerk and journalist and began publishing poetry and sketches in Sydney newspapers. His earliest long poem was probably "The Kangaroo Hunt," which was never published. In it, he described contemporary Australian life, as well as the great forests of his time. According to Wright, the poem is of historical interest, and generally well-executed, but "relies too much on contemporary poetic tricks like the use of capital-letter abstractions which seem oddly out of place in the poem's setting." Harpur, showing the great amount of thought he gave to his poetry even as a young man, wrote in the manuscript preface to it that he deliberately used irregular versification, thinking that the poem could better be varied and modeled on a musical movement.

Harpur alternated his town jobs with bouts of hard physical work and frugal living in the countryside, where he continued to write. Wright noted, "His ambition [as a poet] and a certain uncompromising pride made him frequently a target for criticism and jealousy, and he was easily wounded into retaliation." Beginning in 1833, he published work in almost all the newspapers that would print poetry, particularly those that stressed radical politics. Before he was twenty, he also wrote a play in blank verse. Titled *The Tragedy of Donohoe,* it was based on the life of a bandit as described in a popular song," The Wild Colonial Boy." Harpur occasionally wrote political poetry in which he urged that the harshness of English law and the injustices of the English class system not be allowed to gain a hold in Australia, but as Wright noted, his political verses "tended to sound rather ponderously idealistic." Most of his work, however, was more serious.

In the early 1840s, he moved near Singleton, 100 miles north of Sydney in the Hunter River valley. There he published many poems in the *Maitland Mercury.* While living in this area, at the age of thirty, he met Mary Ann Doyle, whom he called "Rosa" in his sonnets. Although he had previously had a few relationships, this one would become lasting; they would eventually marry.

In 1845 Harpur published *Thoughts: A Series of Sonnets,* the first sonnet sequence published in Australia. The volume contained only sixteen sonnets, but they provide an almost chronological commentary on his courtship of

Doyle, its ups and downs, and their relationship. Doyle, unlike Harpur, came from a relatively wealthy family of settlers, and her family objected to her marrying the penniless son of convicts. Because of this, their courtship proceeded slowly, and Doyle did not accept his offer of marriage until they had known each other for seven years. According to Wright, the sonnets are "competent, pleasantly turned, and sometimes moving in their expression of his loneliness and frustration," but they are "not characteristic of Harpur at his best." She commented that longer poetic forms suited him better; in longer poems, his "occasional prolixity and awkwardness" are not as apparent.

Publication of *The Bushrangers*

In 1853, Harpur published *The Bushrangers: A Play in Five Acts, and Other Poems.* This was his only substantial publication. The play was a retitled version of *The Tragedy of Donohoe.* It was the first to be both performed and published in book form by an Australian-born writer. The volume also contained forty poems, some of which gained Harpur a great deal of attention, some of which was favorable, and some of which was unfavorable. His best-known poem from this collection is "The Creek of the Four Graves," which emphasizes descriptions of the Australian landscape and reveals his inspiration by the work of William Wordsworth. Another notable poem from the collection is "To an Echo on the Banks of the Hunter," which harks back to Harpur's own childhood, and expresses the frustration he felt about his lack of achievement of his youthful ambitions. Wright commented that the poem "has a somber strength and unity that mark Harpur's thought at its most effective."

In "The Dream by the Fountain," Harpur showed his love for poetry, and addressed the Australian Muse, the inspiring force of his own country. All of his poems show certain recurring themes: Harpur's love of the Australian mountains and valleys, and the inspiration he gained from Wordsworth's assertion that through nature, people can connect with purity and spirituality. In addition, his poems are fueled by an undercurrent of radical thought. Wright asserts that although some critics may think this theme was inspired by the work of Percy Bysshe Shelley, Harpur himself wrote that he did not read Shelley's work until 1842, by which time the theme was already evident in his writing. It came naturally from his own experience as the son of convicts; he had seen through his parents' experience, and his own, that some people are privileged and some are subject to poverty and oppression.

In 1862 Harpur published *The Poet's Home,* and in 1865 he published *The Tower of the Dream.* Harpur paid for these publications with his own money, or with gifts from friends. He tried to gather payments for a subscription volume of poems, but the plan fell through.

An Underestimated Poet

Because of his convict parentage, and because he was born in Australia at a time when the prevailing opinion was that nothing good could come of native Australians,

Harpur's work was largely neglected by the literary establishment during his lifetime. At that time, Australians were occupied with settling a vast and difficult country, unlike any place they had ever seen. They valued hard work, action, and success, and had little time for poetry, art, and ideas. In fact, many successful people had nothing but scorn for poets and artists, saying they had gotten where they were without wasting time on any education. In this environment, naturally, Harpur found few readers in Australia. In addition, because he was identified as an Australian and was not formally educated, his work was also scorned in England.

After Harpur's death, his widow gathered many of his poems and arranged to have them published. She hired a man named H. M. Martin to edit them, but Martin apparently had little or no qualifications for the job. Wright wrote, "His chief aim in editing [was] apparently to remove any passages which might excite controversy, regardless of meaning or unity." This chopped-up collection, published in 1883, remains the only collection of Harpur's work, but because it has never been corrected or revised, provides what Wright called "a very misleading guide to Harpur's work and thought."

Because Harpur's work was distorted in this way, it is difficult for critics to assess the real impact of his poetry. However, his manuscripts have been preserved and remain in Mitchell Library in Sydney, so it is theoretically possible that some scholar might someday revise the collection of his poems more accurately. In addition, newspapers preserved from his lifetime, according to Wright, "make clear the real complexity and breadth of his interests and of his ambitions."

Wright commented that Harpur's depiction of Australia "is a much more faithful and detailed one than his critics have believed." She noted that early settlers, used to the softer landscape of Britain, found it "difficult both to love and to absorb," and that "only after generations of living in it has it finally become part of our [Australian] vision; and this has come about precisely through the efforts of earlier artists and writers such as Harpur, to grasp and render its qualities."

In *The Oxford History of Australian Literature,* Leonie Kramer wrote that Harpur's life "is moving for its examples of endurance, loyalty and integrity to his art and his convictions, and his poetry deserves to be much more widely known and more highly esteemed."

Books

Goodwin, Ken, *A History of Australian Literature,* St. Martin's Press, 1986.

Jones, Joseph, *Radical Cousins: Nineteenth-Century American and Australian Writers,* University of Queensland Press, 1976.

Kramer, Leonie, editor, *The Oxford History of Australian Literature,* Oxford University Press, 1981.

Pierre, Peter, editor, *Oxford Literary Guide to Australia,* Oxford University Press, 1993.

Wright, Judith, "Australian Poetry to 1920," in *The Literature of Australia,* edited by Geoffrey Dutton, Penguin Books, 1964.

Wright, Judith, "Charles Harpur," in *Authority and Influence: Australian Literary Criticism 1950-2000,* edited by Delys Bird, Robert Dixon, and Christopher Lee, University of Queensland Press, 2001. □

Herbert Lionel Adolphus Hart

Herbert Lionel Adolphus Hart (1907-1992) became a leading scholar in the field of legal philosophy after publishing his most influential work, *The Concept of Law,* in 1961. Hart was a foremost proponent of legal positivism.

Law Career

H.L.A. Hart was born on July 18, 1907, in Harrogate, England, the son of Jewish parents, Simeon, a wool merchant, and Rose (Samson) Hart. He received his early education at Cheltenham College and Bradford Grammar School. He then enrolled in New College, Oxford, where he studied under H.W.B. Joseph. Hart was an exceptional student, especially in the classics, ancient history, and philosophy. He earned his bachelor's degree in 1929 and was admitted to the bar in 1932. For the next eight years Hart practiced as a barrister in the Chancery courts of London. He established a successful legal office handling complex cases involving trusts, family settlements, and taxes. Although he was asked to become a philosophy tutor at New College, he declined the offer and remained with his law practice.

During World War II, the British War Department called on Hart to serve in military intelligence. From 1939 to 1945, he was a civil servant with the MI5, the British intelligence division. While at this post, Hart worked with two Oxford philosophers, Gilbert Ryle and Stuart Hampshire. Their frequent philosophical conversations spurred Hart's interest in the subject. During this time he married Jenifer Fischer Williams; the couple had one daughter and three sons. He also managed to fulfill the requirements for an advanced degree and was awarded an M.A. from Oxford in 1942.

Oxford Professor

When the war ended, Hart was again invited to return to New College. He became a Fellow and Tutor in philosophy at Oxford from 1946 to 1952. He was also appointed as a university lecturer in philosophy in 1948. According to Neil McCormick in the book *H.L.A. Hart,* "After sixteen years of intensely practical work in the law and then in war service he returned to the academic life. His aims had nothing to do with applying philosophy to legal problems. But, as it turned out, his legal experience in the Chancery . . . was particularly relevant to the current concerns of his fellow philosophers, for whom the study of the uses of language in practical as well as theoretical ways had assumed a new urgency." Thus Hart came to the field of jurisprudence almost by accident.

After A.L. Goodhart's resignation in 1952, Hart was selected to replace him as the Chair of Jurisprudence at Oxford. From 1952 to 1968 Hart served as a professor of jurisprudence and an Oxford University Fellow. He was a visiting professor at Harvard University from 1956 to 1957 and at the University of California at Los Angeles from 1961 to 1962. From 1959 to 1960 he served as the president of the Aristotelian Society. In 1968 he resigned as the Chair of Jurisprudence and spent the next four years as a Nuffield Foundation Senior Research Fellow at University College, Oxford. In 1972 he was named Principal of Brasenose College, Oxford, where he remained until his retirement in 1978. He was a delegate of Oxford University Press beginning in 1960, a member of the Monopolies Commission from 1967 to 1973, and chairperson of the Oxford University Enquiry into Relations with Junior Members in 1969.

Advanced Legal Positivism

As a legal philosopher, Hart drew heavily on the tradition of legal positivism, especially the works of Jeremy Bentham (1748-1832) and John Austin (1790-1859), as well as their follower John Stuart Mills (1806-1873). Legal positivists based their theories on three basic tenets. First, they argued that what the law is and what the law should be are two separate questions; therefore, there is no connection between legality and morality. A law can be legitimized by a society but also be immoral, and an evil regime can still institute a system of laws. Second, they held that the analysis of legal concepts, such as a legal system, rules, and rights, is an important endeavor. Third, they argued that laws are commands issued by a sovereign whom the public obeys out of habit.

Hart concurred on the first two points. However, he disagreed that the foundation of a legal system rests in the power of a sovereign to command. Laws are not obeyed because of the coercive demands of the government, he argued; rather, obligation stems from the social rules of a given society.

The Concept of Law

In *The Philosophy of Law: An Introduction to Jurisprudence,* Jeffrie G. Murphy and Jules L. Coleman refer to Hart's *The Concept of Law* (1961), as being "universally regarded as the most significant contribution to legal philosophy of [the 20th] century. . . . Hart gives the theory of legal positivism the most systematic and powerful statement it has ever received and is ever likely to receive." In *The Concept of Law,* Hart argued that Austin laid a foundation for an excellent theory of law by delineating between laws and morals but erred in viewing law as a weapon of a large bully who demands compliance by force.

Hart argued that a legal system is not a compilation of individual laws, but rather a union of primary and secondary rules. Primary rules impose an obligation: what a citizen can or cannot do. Secondary laws define specifics of the primary rules. To exemplify his theory, Hart asked his readers to imagine a pre-legal society, that is, one that lacked laws, and then imagine the types of problems that might plague such a society. To make changes to eliminate these pathologies would be to make laws. The legal system is then, simply defined, those changes prescribed by a society to cure social problems.

Hart noted that even a pre-legal society would follow social norms. Even if there were no specific law against it, walking around naked in most societies would be considered outside the range of acceptable social behavior. Hart called these primary rules: rules directed to all individuals in a given society that impose obligations. Unlike Austin, who suggested that such rules are followed in order to avoid punishment, Hart argued that a primary rule imposes obligation because it sets a standard for criticism or justification within the society.

A society formed around primary rules alone, Hart acknowledged, would suffer from difficulties. First, uncertainty would arise concerning what the rules are, how rules are applied, and what to do if rules conflict. Second, primary rules are static and do not change as the social, economic, and political environment changes. Third, primary rules alone are inefficient because there is no systematically prescribed recourse for when there is conflict over the rules or the rules are broken. In response to these apparent difficulties, Hart suggested the addition of secondary rules, or rules about rules, as he noted in *The Concept of Law*: "They specify the ways in which the primary rules may be conclusively ascertained, introduced, eliminated, varied, and the fact of their violation conclusively determined." According to Hart, three basic secondary rules exist: rules of recognition, rules of change, and rules of adjudication. They are laws that establish the authoritative structure by which primary laws are defined and enacted.

Hart maintained that a legal system must be approached from an internal viewpoint. As a participant within the system, an observer brings an assumption that the law ought to be obeyed. In *The Legal Philosophy of H.L.A. Hart*, Michael Martin discusses Hart's theory of internalization: "Social actors can view their own behavior in different ways: they can accept the rules of a system and use them to guide their actions and to evaluate the actions of others or they can follow the rules without accepting them. Hart maintains that to have a legal system at least the officials of the system must take the internal point of view: they must accept the rules of the system and evaluate others' actions in terms of them."

The Concept of Law became the yardstick by which both Hart's supporters and detractors were measured. As McCormick noted, "It is a work of international eminence which even its strongest critics have acknowledged as a masterpiece worth at least the compliment of careful refutation."

Other Works

The Concept of Law was not Hart's only important book. In 1959 he published *Causation in the Law*, co-authored by A.M. Honore, which examined questions of causality in matters of civil and criminal liability. Hart and

Honore argued for a definition of cause that employed common, everyday language, which is fundamental to basic understanding of what is fair and just in punishment or compensation. In *Law, Liberty, and Morality*, published in 1963, Hart set forth an argument against legal moralism. He argued that laws and morals are not related by necessity. In 1965 he published *The Morality of Criminal Law*, in which he laid out a defense of the limits of law in regulating moral behavior. *Punishment and Responsibility: Essays in the Philosophy of Law* followed in 1968. In it, Hart offered a complex theory of punishment that combines elements of both retribution and utility.

Hart edited three books on Bentham: *Jeremy Bentham, Of Laws in General* (1970), *Bentham, An Introduction to the Principles of Morals and Legislation* (1970), and *Bentham, Comment on the Commentaries [and] A Fragment on Government* (1977). Hart published two more works after his retirement: *Essays on Bentham: Studies in Jurisprudence and Political Theory* (1982) and *Essays on Jurisprudence and Philosophy* (1983). Over the course of his distinguished career, Hart wrote numerous published essays. The most influential were "Definition and Theory in Jurisprudence" (inaugural lecture, Oxford, 1953), "Are There Any Natural Rights?" (1967), and "Positivism and the Separation of Law and Morals" (1958).

Books

Audi, Robert, *The Cambridge Dictionary of Philosophy, 2nd edition,* Cambridge University Press, 1999.
Blackburn, Simon, *The Oxford Dictionary of Philosophy,* Oxford University Press, 1994.
Bunnin, Nicholas and E.P. Tsui-James, editors, *The Blackwell Companion to Philosophy,* Blackwell Publishers, 1996.
Devine, Elizabeth; Michael Held, James Vinson, and George Walsh, editors, *Thinkers of the Twentieth Century: A Biographical, Bibliographical and Critical Dictionary,* Gale Research Company, 1983.
Edwards, Paul, editor, *The Encyclopedia of Philosophy,* Macmillian, 1967.
MacCormick, Neil, *H.L.A. Hart,* Stanford University Press, 1981.
Martin, Michael, *The Legal Philosophy of H.L.A. Hart: A Critical Appraisal,* Temple University Press, 1987.
Murphy, Jeffrie G., and Jules L. Coleman, *The Philosophy of Law: An Introduction to Jurisprudence,* Rowman & Allanheld, 1984.
Parry, Melanie, editor, *Chambers Biographical Dictionary, 6th edition,* Chambers Harrap Publishing, 1997. □

Patrick Gardiner Hastings

Sir Patrick Hastings (1880-1952) served as one of Britain's leading trial attorneys from the Edwardian era until well into the 1940s. Considered a brilliant legal mind and an impressive jury persuader, Hastings was involved in some of England's most highly publicized criminal cases of his day. As a young man studying for the Bar, he supported himself by working as a theater critic and noted later that this em-

ployment had served him well. Every trial lawyer should study the art of drama, his biographer H. Montgomery Hyde quoted Hastings as saying. "If he does, his speeches will be shorter, his judges will be grateful, and his own success may correspondingly increase."

As the result of his Irish lineage, noted British barrister Sir Patrick Hastings was named after the patron saint of Ireland when he was born on St. Patrick's Day (March 17), 1880. At the time, Hastings' family lived in the Regent's Park area of London, but they moved several times during Patrick's youth. His father, Alfred Hastings, was a solicitor, although he failed to establish much of a law practice and was perennially involved in spurious business schemes. "Bankruptcy in my family was not a misfortune, it was a habit," Hastings wrote later in life, according to Hyde. Hastings was often present at late-night parties during which his father and friends, fueled with strong drink, railed over financial matters and various legal woes. The youthful Hastings listened, and privately reasoned that the mens' flimsy arguments would likely never stand the scrutiny of a court of law.

Sent to boarding school at the age of ten, Hastings disliked school's harsh discipline and was physically beset by asthma. He attended the Charterhouse School next, a well-known private academy for boys in England. Such schools were considered training ground for a career in politics or the military, or as a preliminary to an elite education, and were infamous for their insularity and unspoken codes of behavior. Again, at Charterhouse he endured a miserable few years and left the school at age 16. Then, on the heels of another financial blunder by his father, with his older brother Archie and his mother, Hastings went to Europe. It was still a time when one could live cheaply in the countryside, and Hastings and his brother learned to hunt hedgehogs while living on the island of Corsica.

From Bleak Childhood to Study of Law

Hastings's fortunes changed after he served in the British Army in South Africa during England's Boer War. He returned to England in November of 1901 and resolved to become a barrister. The first step was admittance to the Honourable Society of the Middle Temple, one of the four Inns of Court, as a student. Next came a period of three years during which Hastings was expected to dine regularly at the Middle Temple, pass occasional exams, and then pay a rather large sum of 100 pounds for formal entrance. Hastings was penniless and paid for these costs by working as a journalist and writing a theater gossip column and theater reviews. He also worked for a time for a civil servant and regularly put in eighteen-hour workdays. Since he could not afford to buy his law books, much of his studying was done at the Middle Temple library. Hastings passed his exam in 1904 and paid the required entrance sum from his savings. For the ceremony, however, he was forced to buy his wig and robe on credit.

Hastings apprenticed for established attorneys and attended court sessions daily to learn how to argue a case. One of his mentors provided sound advice for a future trial lawyer, reminding Hastings to never ask a question of a witness on the stand unless he was already assured of its answer. In 1910 one of his superiors was made judge and offered Hastings the opportunity to take over his practice, generously deferring the rent until the young lawyer became more solvent. It was a stroke of good fortune, for Hastings by this time had a wife and growing family to support. His practice was confined to the County Court system until a 1912 police murder case helped make his name. "The Case of the Hooded Man," also known as the Eastbourne Murder, attracted national interest. It involved an attempted jewel thief, a dead police inspector, the betrayal of the suspect by a friend, and an unmarried, pregnant girlfriend. Hastings's client, the accused thief and murderer, was taken to and from court with his face covered by a veil and was billed in the press as "the Hooded Man." Although Hastings failed to gain his clients' acquittal, the case earned him a reputation as a brilliant strategist and skilled debater.

A Succession of Sensational Cases

Hastings moved to the High Courts just before World War I. At the height of the anti-German sentiment stemming from the European conflict, he won another highly publicized case involving a noted civil servant and a man named Gruban who, though born in Germany, had become a naturalized British citizen and a well-to-do machine-tool manufacturer. Gruban was befriended, then subsequently betrayed by a member of parliament, who attempted to extort money from Gruban, and then used his influence to have the business owner interned. Hastings won the case, and the M.P.'s career was duly ended. In 1919 Hastings became King's Counsel and added the honorary "K.C." after his name.

The same year Hastings became King's Counsel he also took on another sensational case, this one involving Britain's war effort. Violet Douglas-Pennant, the daughter of Welsh lord, was a highly regarded, though often personally disliked, public servant with a long list of charitable posts to her name. She was made commandant of the newly created Women's Royal Air Force in the spring of 1918, but was fired two months later. Douglas-Pennant claimed the women's service camps, which adjoined those of the men's air force, were dens of licentious behavior. As King's Counsel, Hastings represented Colonel Bersey, the commanding officer of one London-area camp named by Douglas-Pennant. Against charges that Bersey himself was party to some of the indiscretions, Hastings was able to prove Douglas-Pennant's accusations without merit. His closing arguments suggested that, in the end, the colonel would not be the one disgraced; rather it would be "the person who brought the whole of this dirty, filthy story into prominence solely for her own ends, and that is Miss Douglas-Pennant herself!"

Brief Interludes in Politics, Playwrighting

By age 40 Hastings enjoyed a very successful practice. He was elected a member of Parliament for the fledgling

Labour Party in the early 1920s, and since he was the only barrister of senior rank in the House of Commons at the time, he became party spokesperson on legal matters. This political dalliance led to a brief stint as attorney general in the government of Prime Minister Ramsay MacDonald, the first Labour government in British history. Hastings disliked the grind of the job intensely, finding himself involved in resolving a boundary dispute between the Irish Free State and Northern Ireland, as well as leftover war matters. He sometimes worked from seven in the morning until well past midnight, recalling: "Nothing that I began was I ever allowed to finish, and nothing was ever finished until something else was begun," according to Hyde. "Being an Attorney-General as it was in those days is my idea of hell."

In the early 1920s two cases came before the House of Lords for final decision that set legal precedent at the time. One was a divorce case so sensational that Parliament passed a statute banning the publication of details from divorce proceedings until the matter was decided. In the matter, a woman had become pregnant and her husband denied paternity; the first trial ended in a hung jury, and hinged upon the question of whether a husband's claim that there had been no relations—though they had shared the same bed—was admissible in court. In another well-publicized case, a Roman Catholic physician attacked noted birth control advocate Dr. Marie Stopes, who then sued him for libel. Though the doctor's book did not mention Stopes by name in its pages, he did claim in its pages that a female doctor's practice in a London slum involved harmful "experiments" on the poor. Hastings defended Stopes, and the jury returned a mixed verdict on the charges; the judge then decided in favor of the physician, but that decision was overturned on appeal, which appeal was subsequently overturned in the House of Lords.

"The Case of the Shrunken Heads"

In the 1920s, Hastings suffered increasingly from bouts of ill health, and he eventually retired from politics altogether. He enjoyed a second career as a playwright, and his first drama, *The River,* was produced in London in 1925. Set in Africa, the play earned bad reviews, but Hastings nonetheless sold the film rights to Hollywood. Another play, *Scotch Mist,* starred Tallullah Bankhead in its London production, and though critics panned it as well, it was a box-office success after being denounced as immoral by the bishop of London. In 1927 Hastings and his law practice were once again the subject of newspaper headlines when he was involved in a libel suit brought by a well-known explorer against London's *Daily Express* newspaper. The newspaper claimed that the explorer had participated in a highway robbery hoax in order to gain publicity for the Monomark, an identification device made by a company in which he had a vested interest. The explorer's missing briefcase, containing shrunken heads from his exotic travels, aroused much press attention.

Defended Libeled Royal's Honor

In 1934 Hastings took the case of Princess Irena Alexandrovna Youssopoff in her suit against Metro-Goldwyn-Mayer Pictures. Princess Youssopoff was the niece of Russia's last tsar, Nicholas II, and her husband, Prince Felix, was the man who masterminded the infamous 1916 death of Grigori Rasputin, the strange monk who came to hold great sway over Russia's doomed royal family. Prince Felix, descended from one Russia's wealthiest and venerable families, was sent to the country for his part in the crime, and when the Russian Revolution began several months later, he and his wife fled Russia. The death of the mystic was fictionalized in the M-G-M film *Rasputin the Mad Monk.* The names of the Youssopoffs were changed for the film, and they were portrayed as an engaged couple instead of married. Princess Irena was further dramatized as a supporter of the monk, and there was a hint of a romantic affair. The Youssopoffs were appalled when the film was released, and Hastings's compelling arguments in the princess's favor caused the jury to award her 25,000 pounds, one of the largest damage awards in British legal history at the time.

Hastings' prominent position brought offers of judgeships, but he declined them. During World War II he served briefly in the Royal Air Force's intelligence corps before poor health sent him home. He was elected Treasurer of the Middle Temple in 1940 and witnessed the Battle of Britain from his East Sussex farm. His playwrighting continued with a 1942 production of *The Admiralty Regrets,* a naval drama. In the immediate postwar era, Hastings argued one of the last of his greatly publicized cases. This one involved Harold Laski, an esteemed economist and top Labour Party executive. Laski was the architect of much of Britain's socialist-inspired programs under a new Labour government which nationalized many vital industries and established a generous social-service network. Laski campaigned for Labour candidates during the general election of 1946, and in a controversial speech, as a letter to the editor of a Nottingham newspaper claimed, commented that reform in Britain might have to take place by force. "If we cannot have [the reforms] by fair means, we shall use violence to obtain them," Laski was quoted by the newspaper as allegedly stating. The letter to the newspaper was written by a Conservative Party M.P., and the statement amounted to treason. In Laski's suit against the *Newark Advertiser,* the paper giving the account of the meeting, Hastings successfully defended the newspaper.

Hastings retired in 1948 after a mild stroke. One of his sons died in World War II, and the other moved to Kenya. Visiting Africa with his wife, Hastings suffered another stroke, then lost all his personal possessions in a fire at his son's home. He returned to England, his health declining further. Hastings died at his London home on February 26, 1952.

Books

Hyde, H. Montgomery, *Sir Patrick Hastings: His Life and Cases,* Heinemann, 1960. □

Henry Osborne Havemeyer

The dominant figure in the sugar-refining business of the late nineteenth century, Henry Osborne Havemeyer (1847-1907) controlled the so-called "Sugar Trust." He was also known for his extensive art collection, assembled with the help of his second wife.

Henry O. Havemeyer was born on October 18, 1847, in Commack on Long Island. He was the youngest of four sons born to Frederick Christian Havemeyer and his wife, Sarah Osborne (Townsend) Havemeyer. The Havemeyer family had been in the sugar-refining business for two generations in the United States. Havemeyer's grandfather, a German immigrant who came to America in the early 1800s, had established a modest sugar refining business with his brothers. This eventually made him a wealthy man. Upon his death, when Havemeyer was 14 years old, he left an estate worth $3 million. Partnering with his cousin William F. Havemeyer, who also was a three-term mayor of New York, Frederick Havemeyer further built on his father's success in the sugar-refining business in the firm Havemeyer & Elder.

Entered Family Business

Though Havemeyer was raised amid a life of privilege, his schooling left him less educated that a typical high school graduate of the period. What he lacked in formal education, however, he gained in practical experience by working in the family business. Beginning as an apprentice at Havemeyer & Elder. Havemeyer spent time working in the refinery and as an assistant sales agent, then headed the buying and selling department. Havemeyer also gained experience in the transforming technology of the industry, especially the refining process. The sugar-refining business was undergoing a massive change and expansion in the late nineteenth and early twentieth century.

At the time, the sugar-refining business was centered on imported sugar and companies like Havemeyer & Elder maintained large waterfront plants. When he had received enough training, Havemeyer partnered with his elder brother, Theodore, and began to run the family's sugar refineries in Brooklyn, New York. The brothers began working to expand and consolidate their controlling interest by 1887. Though Havemeyer was against such consolidation at first, this position soon changed and he eventually led the charge.

The Havemeyer brothers eventually merged all 15 of their major refineries in New York, including the Havemeyer & Elder plant located in Brooklyn, then the biggest, most cost-effective plant in the United States. They then formed the Sugar Refineries Company, which included all 15 sugar refining plants. Havemeyer, the company's president, became something of a financial expert. Over the next few years, he garnered made the contacts on Wall Street that would prove important in his business's future. Havemeyer became known for his strong, if not dominating personality, and his enthusiasm for taking risks.

Early Legal Problems

After the Havemeyers' aggressive consolidation, the Sugar Refineries Company found itself under investigation by legislative bodies and taken to court. Many considered the company a trust, some even dubbing it "the sugar trust." Corporate trusts such as Standard Oil were being attacked on such fronts because they controlled industries, fixed prices, and engaged in other monopolistic practices thought to inhibit free trade. In 1890, after many months of legal wrangling, Havemeyer's sugar trust was deemed illegal and dissolved as a result of the case of *State of New York vs. North River Sugar Refining Company.*

Despite this dissolution and the setbacks accompanying it, Havemeyer remained in the sugar-refining industry. The Sugar Refineries Company was reorganized as a holding company named American Sugar Refining Company and chartered in New Jersey. Havemeyer was appointed the holding company's financial head. Though the company faced no further legal hassles, Havemeyer continued to engage in business practices similar to those of a corporate trust. Essentially nothing changed about the way Havemeyer ran his company.

Using his economic contacts and clout, Havemeyer sought to eliminate competition and ensure his company's control over the sugar industry in the 1890s. He wanted to regulate both the price of refined sugar and the wages of those workers who labored in the factories. Among several questionable strategies, he created rebate arrangements with wholesalers, manipulated suppliers, and took advantage of railroad rebates. On the political/legal front, he argued for tariffs to be lowered on imported raw sugar and convinced Congress on this front. However, he also wanted his product, refined sugar, to be protected from competing imports.

Price cutting and price wars were also part of Havemeyer's tactics in the early 1890s. One such war was with Claus Spreckels, the dominant sugar refiner on the west coast. To gain ground in the east, Spreckels built a plant in Philadelphia. Havemeyer won this war, however, acquiring sugar-refining firms in Philadelphia, including the Spreckels Sugar Refining Company. Within several years the American Sugar Refining Company controlled about 90 percent of the industry.

Competition from Arbuckle and Others

Havemeyer's business strategies worked in the short term, but his company's market share continued to fall as the end of the 19th century neared. By 1894 the American Sugar Refining Company controlled only 75 percent of the sugar refining market. This drop was due in part to the emergence of at least two significant competitors just prior to 1900. One was a new concern founded by a former customer of the American Sugar Refining Company named John Arbuckle.

Arbuckle had made his start in business as a wholesale grocery salesman and coffee merchant; he bought refined sugar from Havemeyer to resell via his companies. Arbuckle questioned why the price of refined sugar sold by Havemeyer stayed high when the price of raw sugar fell. Havemeyer responded to Arbuckle's inquiry by raising the prices charged to Arbuckle's company. Because of the disagreement, Arbuckle founded his own sugar-refining company. Both companies suffered financial losses and caused each other long-term legal problems as the result of this competitive stance. They sued each other repeatedly, and both lost as much as $25 million. Arbuckle was almost destroyed, while the resilient Havemeyer survived and pressed forward.

Engaged in Risky Ventures

Though he suffered such financial losses, Havemeyer continued to look for ways to stay innovative in the sugar-refining business. He continued to chart a course of horizontal combination. In the late 1890s and early 1900s, sugar beets began to be used as a source of sugar. In response, Havemeyer acquired a controlling interest in the biggest sugar beet companies for the American Sugar Refining Company. By investing in the industry's development, he had the power to control it. One such company that he had control over was American Beet Sugar, founded in 1902.

Another significant investment by Havemeyer during this time was in the Cuban-American Sugar Company, which he bought into in 1906 with other partners. This expansion did not pay off in the manner that he wished: that is, industry dominance. The expansion into the sugar beet market and Havemeyer's investment in the Cuban-American Sugar Company were costly to Havemeyer's company to the tune of $20 million.

Despite such losses, Havemeyer continued to control the sugar-refining industry in other ways. Using his business savvy, he orchestrated the consolidation of American Sugar Refining Company's primary competition into one company, the National Sugar Refining Company, which was secretly controlled by Havemeyer's company. The buyouts cost American Sugar Refining $20 million between 1902 and 1907. Havemeyer also influenced the means through which refined sugar was marketed throughout the United States. In a 1903 article in *Cosmopolitan*, Robert N. Burnett wrote, "In business circles he is regarded as one of the most brilliant men of this generation."

Despite his stature as a businessman, Havemeyer made some costly missteps. The sugar beet investment never paid off, and while American Sugar Refining survived the war with Arbuckle, it was weaker for it. There was evidence of regular cheating on customs duties. In 1906 Havemeyer refused to raise the wages of striking workers to 18 cents per hour, though his company posted profits of $55 million. In 1907, the year of Havemeyer's death, the American Sugar Refining Company was found guilty of taking railroad rebates that were illegal. Most of these actions were taken by Havemeyer in an attempt to raise his company's profit margin, in part because the price of sugar for consumers had fallen significantly since the last quarter of the nineteenth century. The market for his product was also smaller.

By the time Havemeyer died on December 4, 1907, American Sugar Refining had only 49.3 percent of the United States' market despite its 25 plants. Havemeyer had been frustrated in his efforts to control the industry as fully as he wanted to. For example, he was unable to takeover sugar-refining enterprises in Baltimore, Maryland; New Orleans, Louisiana; California; and Hawaii. Upon his death it was revealed that he ruled American Sugar Refining by the brute force of his personality; the family really owned less than 1,000 of the company's 900,000 outstanding shares, though Havemeyer gave the illusion that they controlled much more. From its position as the sixth largest industrial corporation in the United States, the market share would continue to fall. After his Havemeyer's death, the American Sugar Refining Company changed strategies to vertical integration and soon sold off a number of holdings. Eventually the company developed its own brand of sugar for the consumer marketplace, Domino.

Significant Art Collection

A legacy of Havemeyer's life was his art collection. Throughout his life, he bought art, primarily with his second wife, Lousine W. Elder, whom he married in 1883 and with whom he had three children. Many of the couple's purchases were made under the guidance of Mary Cassatt, a significant painter in her own right. Their collection consisted of thousands of works, including at least 100 paintings by Monet, Degas, Rembrandt, Cassatt, and El Greco; ceramics from Asia; armor from Japan; and bronzes, Egyptian figurines, and textiles. During his and his widow's lifetime, the Havemeyer collection was housed at their mansion in Manhattan. The home itself was a work of art, featuring interior design by Louis Comfort Tiffany. After Lousine's death in 1929, the collection was donated to the Metropolitan Museum of Art.

As in his sugar refining business, Havemeyer was aggressive and sometimes made bad decisions. He once tried to buy Botticelli's "Birth of Venus," but was refused by Italian officials. Many of his purchases also turned out to be fakes, and therefore bad investments. Only three or four of the 16 paintings by Goya that he bought were real, while 12 of the 15 works by Renoir were fakes. Summing up the contradiction that was Havemeyer, Paul Richard of the *Washington Post* wrote, "Though a cultivated fellow—he played a Stradivarius and pored over rare books—he was easily cartooned as a capitalist class enemy. He had the black frock coat, the black silk hat, the bluffness and the paunch—and the requisite monopoly."

Books

Chandler, Alfred D., Jr., *The Visible Hand: The Managerial Revolution in American Business,* Belknap Press, 1977.
Eichner, Alfred S., *The Emergence of Oligopoly: Sugar Refining as a Case Study,* Johns Hopkins Press, 1969.
Garraty, John A., and Jerome L. Sternstein, editors, *Encyclopedia of American Biography,* HarperCollins, 1996.
Ingham, John N., *Biographical Dictionary of American Business Leaders,*, Greenwood Press, 1983.
Johnson, Allen, and Dumas Malone, editors, *Dictionary of American Biography,* Charles Scribner's Sons, 1960.

Periodicals

Century Magazine, January 1903.
Cosmopolitan, April 1903.
New York Times, March 25, 1993; March 26, 1993.
Washington Post, April 14, 1993.

Online

Bradley, James, "New York Food Museum: Sugar," http://www .nyfoodmuseum.org/sugar.htm (January 30, 2002). □

Harriet Hawes

Harriet Hawes (1871-1945) was the first female archaeologist to head an excavation. A classicist and scientist by training, she worked on the Greek island of Crete, discovering the ancient town of Gournia, one of Crete's "ninety cities" of Homer's *Odyssey*. Despite her international acclaim, Hawes devoted much of her free time to social activism, becoming involved with political issues of the day.

Harriet Ann Boyd Hawes was born in Boston on October 11, 1871, to Alexander and Harriet Fay (Wheeler) Boyd. The fifth child and the only girl, Hawes grew up in a family of men when her mother died suddenly during Hawes's infancy. She was close to her father, a leather-merchant, and to her brothers, especially Alexander, Jr., who shared her fascination with ancient history.

Hawes graduated from Prospect Hill School in 1888 before going on to Smith College. She graduated with a B.A. in 1892 and an M.A. in 1901. Between her years of schooling, Hawes taught classics—ancient and modern languages—in North Carolina and Delaware. From 1900 until 1906 she also taught modern Greek, epigraphy, and Greek archaeology at Smith.

Undaunted by Discrimination

In 1896, Hawes attended the American School of Classical Studies (ASCS) in Athens, Greece. As a woman, she was not permitted to take part in excavations sponsored by the ASCS. Hawes had been awarded the Agnes Hoppin fellowship in 1900, and she used the money to finance her own excavation. She wanted to follow up on recent archaeological work in Crete, and the fellowship allowed her to go.

Once in Crete, Hawes was advised by Arthur J. Evans, a British archaeologist excavating Knossos, to try the Kavousi region. In 1901, after securing funding from the American Exploration Society of Philadelphia, Hawes focused on the part of the region known as Gournia, in which she discovered an Early Bronze Age Minoan town site. The first woman to direct an excavation, she was also the first archaeologist to make such a discovery. Gournia was noted for its residents, artisans, and the part it played in the larger tapestry of Cretan society. The excavation, continued in 1903 and 1904, offered a significant amount of archaeological information to current studies. In fact, Hawes' discovery is still the only town from the Minoan age to be found in a well-preserved condition. In 1902, the Archaeological Institute of America sponsored her national lecture tour to describe her findings, which were later published in 1908.

Hawes met her husband, Charles Henry Hawes, a British anthropologist, in Crete, and they married on March 3, 1906. In December of that year, their son, Alexander, was born, followed by their daughter, Mary, in August of 1910. Hawes and her husband co-wrote a book on Crete during this time. After teaching appointments in Wisconsin and New Hampshire, Charles Hawes took a position as assistant director of the Boston Museum of Fine Arts in 1919. The following year, Hawes returned to teaching, this time at Wellesley College, where she lectured on pre-Christian art. She remained there until her retirement in 1936.

Political and Social Activism

A lifelong activist, Hawes devoted much of her life to political and social causes. She was a volunteer war nurse in Thessaly (1897), Florida (1898), and Corfu (1916). In 1917 she organized the Smith College Relief Unit to aid French civilians. Later, in 1933, she gave aid to union shoe workers who were on strike, and was subsequently sued for $100,000 by the company.

Hawes and her husband retired to a farm in Alexandria, Virginia. After Charles' death in 1943, Hawes moved to a Washington, D.C. rest home, where she died of peritonitis on March 31, 1945. Smith College loved its archaeologist, awarding Hawes the honorary L.H.D. degree in 1910, creating a scholarship in her name in 1922, and holding a memorial symposium in Crete in 1967.

Books

Bailey, Martha J. *American Women in Science*. ABC-CLIO, 1994.
Dictionary of American Biography. Supplement three. Edited by Edward T. James. Charles Scribner's Sons, 1973.
Liberty's Women. Edited by Robert McHenry. G and C Merriam Company, 1980.
Notable American Women 1607-1950. Edited by Edward T. James. Belknap Press, 1971.
Ogilvie, Marilyn Bailey. *Women in Science: Antiquity Through the Nineteeth Century*. MIT Press, 1986. □

Howard Winchester Hawks

Howard Hawks (1896-1977) was perhaps the greatest director of American genre films. He made films in almost every American genre, and his films could well serve as among the very best examples and artistic embodiments of the type: gangster, private eye, western, screwball comedy, newspaper reporter, prison picture, science fiction, musical, racecar drivers, and pilots. Into each of his narratives Hawks infused his particular themes, motifs, and techniques.

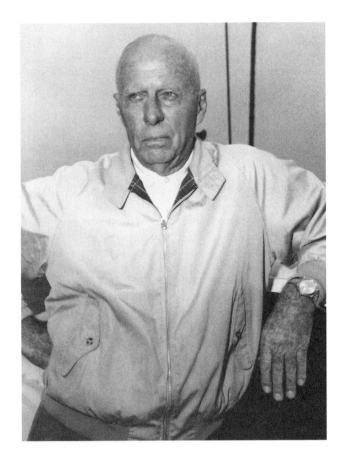

Born in Goshen, Indiana on May 30, 1896, Hawks migrated with his family to southern California when the movies did. He attended Pasadena High School from 1908 until 1913. Hawks went on to Exeter Academy in New Hampshire from 1914 until 1916. He spent his formative years working on films, learning to fly, and studying mechanical engineering at Cornell University. During vacations, he worked in the property department of Famous Players-Lasky in Hollywood. After graduating from college in 1917, Hawks served in the U.S. Army Air Corps until 1919. Following his discharge from the army, he worked as a designer in an airplane factory until 1922.

Hawks began his career in films as an editor, writer, and assistant director. He was put in charge of the story department at Paramount in 1924 and signed as director for Fox in 1925. Hawks directed his first feature film, *Road to Glory* in 1926. His initial work in silent films as a writer and producer would serve him well in his later years as a director, when he would produce and, if not write, then control the writing of his films as well. Although Hawks' work has been consistently discussed as exemplary of the Hollywood studio style, Hawks himself did not work for a single studio on a long-term contract. Instead, he was an independent producer who sold his projects to every Hollywood studio.

Whatever the genre of a Hawks film, it bore traits that made it unmistakably a Hawks film. The narrative was always elegantly and symmetrically structured and patterned. This quality was a sign of Hawks' sharp sense of storytelling as well as his sensible efforts to work closely with very talented writers: Ben Hecht, William Faulkner, and Jules Furthman being the most notable among them. Hawks' films were devoted to characters who were professionals with fervent vocational commitments. The men in Hawks' films were good at what they did, whether flying the mail, driving race cars, driving cattle, or reporting the news. These vocational commitments were usually fulfilled by the union of two apparently opposite physical types, who were spiritually one. In some cases, they represented the union of the harder, tougher, older male and a softer, younger, prettier male (John Wayne and Montgomery Clift in *Red River*, Wayne and Ricky Nelson in *Rio Bravo*). At other times, they united a sharp, tough male and an equally sharp, tough female (Cary Grant and Rosalind Russell in *His Girl Friday*, Bogart and Bacall in *To Have and Have Not* and *The Big Sleep*, John Barrymore and Carole Lombard in *Twentieth Century*). This spiritual alliance of physical opposites revealed Hawks' unwillingness to accept the cultural stereotype that those who are able to accomplish difficult tasks are those who appear able to accomplish them.

This tension between appearance and ability, surface and essence in Hawks' films led to several other themes and techniques. Characters talk very tersely in Hawks' films, refusing to put their thoughts and feelings into explicit speeches that would either sentimentalize or vulgarize those internal abstractions. Instead, Hawks' characters reveal their feelings through their actions, not by what they say. Hawks deflects his portrayal of the inner life from explicit speeches to symbolic physical objects—concrete visual images of things that convey the intentions of the person who handles, uses, or controls the piece of physical matter. One of those physical objects—the coin which George Raft nervously flips in *Scarface*—has become a mythic icon of American culture itself, symbolic of American gangsters and American gangster movies (and used as such in both *Singin' in the Rain* and *Some Like It Hot*). Another of Hawks' favorite actions, the lighting of cigarettes, became his subtextual way of showing who cares about whom without recourse to dialogue.

Consistent with his narratives, Hawks' visual style was one of dead-pan understatement, never proclaiming its trickiness or brilliance but effortlessly communicating the values of the stories and the characters. Hawks was a master of point-of-view, knowledgeable about which camera perspective would precisely convey the necessary psychological and moral information. That point of view could either confine us to the perceptions of a single character (Marlowe in *The Big Sleep*), ally us with the more vital of two competing life styles (with the vitality of Oscar Jaffe in *Twentieth Century*, Susan Vance in *Bringing Up Baby*, Walter Burns in *His Girl Friday*), or withdraw to a scientific detachment that allows the viewer to weigh the paradoxes and ironies of a love battle between two equals (between the two army partners in *I Was a Male War Bride*, the husband and wife in *Monkey Business*, or the older and younger cowboy in *Red River*). Hawks' films are also masterful in their atmospheric lighting; the hanging electric or kerosene lamp that dangles into the top of a Hawks frame became almost as much his signature as the lighting of cigarettes.

Hawks' view of character in film narrative was that actor and character were inseparable. As a result, his films used a lot of improvisation. He allowed actors to add, interpret, or alter lines as they wished, rather than force them to stick to the script. This trait not only led to the energetic spontaneity of many Hawks films, but also contributed to the creation or shaping of the human archetypes that several stars came to represent in our culture. John Barrymore, John Wayne, Humphrey Bogart, and Cary Grant all refined or established their essential personae under Hawks' direction, while many actors who would become stars were either discovered by Hawks or given their first chance to play a major role in one of his films. Among Hawks' most important discoveries were Paul Muni, George Raft, Carole Lombard, Angie Dickinson, Montgomery Clift, and his Galatea, Lauren Bacall.

Although Hawks continued to make films until he was almost seventy-five, there is disagreement about the artistic energy and cinematic value of the films made after 1950. For some, Hawks' artistic decline in the 1950s and 1960s was both a symptom and an effect of the overall decline of the movie industry and the studio system itself. For others, Hawks' later films—slower, longer, less energetically brilliant than his studio-era films—were more probing and personal explorations of the themes and genres he had charted for the three previous decades.

Hawks was married three times, each marriage ending in divorce. His second marriage to Nancy Raye Gross produced one daughter. His third marriage to Mary (Dee) Hartford produced two sons and two daughters. Hawks died in Palm Springs, California on December 26, 1977.

Books

Belton, John, *Cinema Stylists*, Metuchen, New Jersey, 1983.
Bogdanovich, Peter, *The Cinema of Howard Hawks*, New York, 1962.
Branson, Clark, *Howard Hawks: A Jungian Study*, Los Angeles, 1987.
Giannetti, Louis D., *Masters of the American Cinema*, Englewood Cliffs, New Jersey, 1981.
Gili, J.-A., *Howard Hawks*, Paris, 1971.
Mast, Gerald, *Howard Hawks, Storyteller*, New York, 1982.
McBride, Joseph, ed. *Hawks on Hawks*, Berkeley, 1982.
Missiaen, Jean-Claude, *Howard Hawks*, Paris, 1966.
Murphy, Kathleen A., *Howard Hawks: An American Auteur in the Hemingway Tradition*, Ann Arbor, Michigan, 1978.
Poague, Leland, *Howard Hawks*, Boston, 1982.
Simsolo, Noel, *Howard Hawks*, Paris, 1984.
Willis, D.C., *The Films of Howard Hawks*, Metuchen, New Jersey, 1975.
Wood, Robin, *Howard Hawks*, London, 1968, revised 1981.

Periodicals

Cahiers du Cinéma, (Paris), February 1956; January 1963; November 1964; July/August 1967.
Cine-Action! (Toronto), no. 13/14, 1988.
Cinema, (Beverly Hills), November/December 1963; March 1978.
Cinématographe (Paris), March 1978.
Film Comment (New York), May/June 1973; March/April 1974; May/June 1974; July/August 1977; February 1978; March/April 1978; September/October 1982.
Filmkritik (Munich), May/June 1973.
Films and Filming (London), July and August 1962; October 1968.
Films in Review (New York), November 1956.
Focus on Film (London), Summer/Autumn 1976.
Interviews with Film Directors, New York, 1967.
Journal of Popular Film (Washington, D.C.), Winter 1984.
Jump Cut (Berkeley), January/February 1975.
Movie, (London), November 5, 1962; December 5, 1962.
Movietone News (Seattle), June 1977.
Positif (Paris), July/August 1977.
Post Script (Jacksonville, Florida), Fall 1981.
Présence du Cinéma (Paris), July/September 1959.
Quarterly Review of Film Studies (New York), Spring 1984.
Sight and Sound (London), Summer 1962; Spring 1971.
Take One (Montreal), July/August 1971; November/December 1971; April 1972; March 1973; December 1975. □

Ferdinand Vandiveer Hayden

American geologist Ferdinand Vandiveer Hayden (1829-1887) explored the Great Plains and Rocky Mountain regions, his dedicated efforts providing the foundation for the U.S. Geological Survey and for the establishment of Yellowstone National Park.

Ferdinand Vandiveer Hayden studied to be a physician, until a chance encounter with a noted paleontologist drew him to the yet unmapped northwestern territories of the United States and a relentless career as a geologist and explorer. Through his work in mapping the states of Montana, Colorado, Wyoming, and Idaho, Hayden set the foundation for the activities of the U.S. Geological Survey, and his forward-thinking advocacy of preserving pristine wilderness areas resulted in the creation and preservation of Yellowstone National Park at a time when the nation's interests were in developing the wealth of natural resources west of the Mississippi.

Undeterred by Humble Beginnings

Hayden was born in Westfield, Massachusetts, in 1829, the son of Asa and Melinda (Hawley) Hayden. His father died when he was ten, and his mother remarried soon afterward. As was not uncommon in such circumstances, Hayden was sent to live with an uncle who owned a small farm outside of Rochester, New York. Helping on the farm during the summer months, Hayden spent the winter working as a teacher at a local school from the time he was sixteen. At age eighteen he determined to leave the farm and make it on his own. With little money, he hiked south to Ohio's Oberlin College, where he gained the help of the college president and enrolled in 1847. Shy, often distracted, and poorer than most of his fellow students, Hayden nonetheless proved to be an able student, and he graduated in 1850.

After graduating from Oberlin College, Hayden returned to upstate New York and enrolled at the Albany Medical College, having decided to pursue a career in medicine. During his years in Albany, he became the friend of James Hall, the New York state paleontologist, who introduced the young medical student to the increases in understanding of ancient history made as a result of evidence gleaned from the discovery of fossils. Despite receiving his M.D. from Albany in 1853, Hayden decided to postpone his career temporarily; instead he decided to explore the world of natural science shown to him by Hall.

Participated in First Trek Westward

In the spring of 1853, shortly after receiving his diploma, the twenty-four-year-old Hayden joined an expedition sponsored by Hall and led by paleontologist Fielding B. Meek that collected fossils in the Badlands located in southwest South Dakota, east of the Black Hills. The region gained its well-deserved name due to the difficulty of traversing its terrain due to the many deep gullies and steep hills that cut across its barren surface. The trip was a success—many fossils were uncovered and brought back to Albany—although as a novice Hayden participated little in the actual excavation. Instead, he spent his time mapping the vertical geological strata occurring in the area of the excavations, this work eventually incorporated into a larger study and published.

The following year, under the sponsorship of the American Fur Company, Hayden returned to the region and traveled the Missouri River basin; Within two years he mapped his way as far north as Fort Benton, Montana. The trip required physical strength, endurance, and perseverance, all qualities the then twenty-five year old Hayden possessed. Most of the trip was made on foot, passing through untraveled forests and over rocky terrain, and Hayden and his followers carried with them limited provisions so that they could cover maximum distances. Along the way temporary camps were established to facilitate scientific study of the area. At one such camp, made near the confluence of the Missouri and the Judith Rivers, Hayden and his party made a momentous discovery, although it did not perhaps seem so at the time. A collection of unusual teeth uncovered and collected at this location were later determined by paleontologist Joseph Leidy to be those of the dinosaurs *Trachodon, Troodon* and *Deinodon*, making Hayden's 1854 expedition the first in North America to uncover dinosaur remains.

In 1856 Hayden signed on with Lieutenant G. K. Warren of the Topographical Engineers to explore the Yellowstone and Missouri Rivers, as well as the Black Hills of the Dakota territory. Two years later he rejoined Meek in a trip through the Kansas wilderness, and in 1859 he traveled to Montana with Captain W. F. Raynolds to reconnoiter the headwaters of the Yellowstone, Gallatin, Snake, and Madison Rivers under the leadership of former trapper and topographer Jim Bridger. It was during this trip, as Hayden took in the natural beauty of this undisturbed region, that the idea of setting aside part of these western lands for posterity was first discussed. Although their expedition was cut short by bad weather, the Yellowstone region became the focus of several mapping expeditions over the next decade, Bridger often serving as guide.

Civil War Resulted in Interest in Western Resources

The outbreak of the U.S. Civil war in 1860 prompted Hayden to use his medical training in defense of his country. He enlisted in the Union army and worked as a surgeon near the battlefields of the Carolinas, retiring from active service at the war's end having attained the rank of lieutenant colonel. Three months later, Hayden accepted a position as professor of geology at the University of Pennsylvania.

The Civil War, by taxing the country's many resources, indirectly prompted the surveys that would uncover the beauty of the western United States, a region that was in 1867 still divided into territories. The General Land Office

(GLO) alerted Congress to the demands that the increasingly industrialized northeast was making on existing natural resources east of the Mississippi, and in response Congress, on March 2, 1867, authorized funding of a geological study to determine the location of natural resources along the fortieth parallel, the route of the Transcontinental Railroad then underway, to be undertaken by Clarence King and the Corps of Engineers, as well as a GLO-led survey of Nebraska, which had achieved statehood only the day before.

While his teaching duties occupied his time during the fall and winter months, Hayden meanwhile had continued to explore the northwestern regions of the United States. In the spring of 1866, with the sponsorship of the Philadelphia Academy of Natural Sciences, he returned to the Badlands. Now, in 1867, the thirty-eight-year-old professor was tapped as head of the newly formed U.S. Geological Survey for the Territories to undertake the needed survey of Nebraska for the GLO. Hayden's pioneering work for this organization—backed by only $5,000 in federal funds as opposed to King's $100,000—provided the basis for the U.S. Geological Survey.

Competing with fellow surveyors King, John Wesley Powell (the Colorado basin, 1870, 1872), and Lieutenant George Wheeler (Nevada and Colorado, 1870, 1871) for federal appropriations, Hayden continued to lead small, government-funded expeditions to Colorado, Idaho, Montana, Wyoming, and Utah between 1868 and 1869 and surveyed the geology and wildlife of much of this region. Cope often served as the official paleontologist on these travels, while invertebrate fossils were the domain of J. S. Newberry and fossil plants that of Lesquereux. William Henry Jackson often joined these excursions, serving as Hayden's photographer. In 1877 Hayden assisted the botanical survey of Hooker and Gray.

Hayden undertook his exploration of the Rocky Mountain region without reliable maps; these were developed during his travels. Roads and railways were rare west of the Mississippi; the only passages through the vast American west were made along the trails made by trappers and Native Americans, or on the trails used by pioneering families traveling westward. Despite such conditions, Hayden traveled quickly, determined to cover as much distance as possible before weather, waning provisions, or the start of fall classes at the University of Pennsylvania forced his return east.

By 1870 Hayden had created a system whereby uniformly scaled maps noting topography and geology throughout the territories could be created. He proposed this system to Congress and it was adopted by the Department of the Interior. Hayden married Emma C. Woodruff, daughter of a Philadelphia merchant, on November 9, 1871; in their forties at the time of their marriage, the couple would have no children. Hayden remained at the University of Pennsylvania until the following spring, resigning at that point to devote all his time to government work.

Staunch Advocate of Preserving Yellowstone Region

From 1871 to 1872 Hayden made what is considered his most noteworthy contribution to the nation when he requested funding to survey the Missouri and Yellowstone territories. His thirty-four-member team set out in seven wagons from Ogden, Utah, in the spring of 1871. Among Hayden's party were photographer Jackson and guest painter Thomas Moran, who captured the beauty of the region, while geologist George Allen, mineralogist Albert Peale, topographical artist Henry Elliot, botanists, and other scientists collected countless specimens and other data. Moran's paintings especially were useful in promoting Hayden's dream of preserving this area, and he made a concerted effort to bring images of Yellowstone before the American public by publishing articles in magazines, lecturing to groups, and otherwise advocating for preservation of the region. Following his presentation to Congress of a 500-page report containing pictures of the region, an area encompassing 2,219,791 acres in what would become southwestern Wyoming and spreading into the future states of Idaho and Montana, a bill was introduced setting aside Yellowstone as public land. Signed on March 1, 1872, by President Ulysses S. Grant, the bill's timing was crucial; eleven years had passed since the first rail line, the Northern Pacific, was laid to the north across Montana, and movement into the west by both settlers and business interests was on the rise. The nation's first national park, Yellowstone remained undisturbed except by tourists, a site of geothermal activity that takes the form of geysers such as "Old Faithful" and the Mammoth Hot Springs, as well as lakes, mud springs, waterfalls, and other areas of great natural beauty and geological interest.

The work of nineteenth-century surveyors such as Hayden and his colleagues gave definition to the vast western lands first traversed by Meriwether Lewis and William Clark's famous expeditions of 1804-1806. The results of Hayden's efforts—the topographical maps and reports of geological formations in the northwest territory, as well as the discovery of such interesting geological formations as the Mount of the Holy Cross in central Colorado—were combined with those of King, Powell, and Wheeler under the newly formed U.S. Geological Survey in 1879, with King as director. While leadership of this new organization was controversial due to the competition between its founding members and its work in collaboration with U.S. mining interests, Hayden accepted the position as chief geologist of the Montana territory.

Within a few years of his appointment in Montana, Hayden was forced to discontinue his travels, debilitated by years of arduous activity and the rapid progress of the disease locomotor ataxia. He resigned in 1886 and died the following year in Philadelphia at the age of fifty-eight. The Montana territory achieved division into various states shortly after Hayden's death: Montana in 1889, Wyoming in 1890.

Known for being impulsive and quick to action, Hayden was generous with his time and knowledge. His physical endurance and mental perseverance were qualities that allowed him to make outstanding contributions to the growth and appreciation of the western United States. During his career Hayden was an esteemed member of several societies, among them the National Academy of Sciences and geological societies in Great Britain, Austria, and Russia. In honor of his work, over forty organisms or geological features now bear his name, including towns and lakes in the states he traversed, a moth, a species of wildflower, and a fossil dinosaur.

Books

Bartlett, Richard, *North American Exploration,* Volume 3: *A Continent Comprehended,* University of Nebraska Press, 1997.

Cassidy, James G., *Ferdinand V. Hayden: Entrepreneur of Science,* University of Nebraska Press, 2000.

Foster, Mike, *Strange Genius,* 1994.

Merrill, Marlene D., editor, *Yellowstone and the Great West: Journals, Letters, and Images from the 1871 Hayden Expedition,* University of Nebraska Press, 1999.

White, C. A., "Frederick V. Hayden", *National Academy of Science Biographical Memoirs,* Vol. III, 1895.

Online

"The Four Great Surveys of the West," *U.S. Geological Survey Web site,* http://pubs.usgs.gov (April 10, 2000).

Yellowstone National Park.com, http://222 .yellowstonenationalpark.com (February 5, 2002). □

Robert Earl Hayden

Through his meticulously crafted and highly thoughtful poetry, Robert Hayden (1913-1980) often explored human dilemmas in the context of race. He was a college professor throughout his career, doing most of his work at Fisk University in Nashville, Tennessee, and at the University of Michigan in Ann Arbor. Hayden won the Grand Prix de la Poésie at the First World Festival of Negro Arts in Dakar, Senegal. In 1976 he was appointed consultant to the Library of Congress, becoming the first African American poet to receive this honor.

Robert Earl Hayden was born on August 4, 1913, in Detroit, Michigan, to Ruth Finn and Asa Sheffey. His parents had divorced by the time of their son's birth. Originally named Asa Bundy Sheffey, he was raised by foster parents, William and Sue Hayden. Robert Hayden (as he was now called) occasionally visited each of his biological parents while he was growing up. His mother lived nearby and, at times, with the Haydens. Although she was not well educated, Ruth Sheffey supported her son's ambitions. She was a vivacious woman, in contrast to her son's foster family. William Hayden, a laborer, was a strict Baptist fundamentalist. Sue Hayden was less austere in manner and outlook than her husband. Although they were not highly

educated, the Haydens did the best they could for young Robert. The family lived in an environment of poverty and danger in Paradise Valley, the ironic name for their inner-city Detroit community. Robert Hayden recalled in *Collected Prose* that in Paradise Valley, along with the "violence, ugliness, and cruelty, . . . there were people who retained . . . a sheltering spiritual beauty and dignity—my mother and my foster father among them—despite sordid and disheartening circumstances.

Very nearsighted as a boy, Hayden was introverted and spent much of his time reading. He enjoyed playing the violin until he had to give it up because of his vision problems. Because of his weak eyesight, he transferred from the inner city's predominantly black Miller High School to predominantly white Northern High School, which provided resources to assist visually-impaired students.

Hayden's graduated from high school in 1930, at the beginning of the Great Depression. His family lacked the financial resources to send him to college. Unable to find work, Hayden took some courses at Cass Technical High School. In 1932, he entered Detroit City College (now Wayne State University) where he majored in Spanish. Although he left college in 1936—just one semester hour short of graduation—he subsequently returned and received his B.A. in 1942.

From 1936 to 1938, Hayden worked as a researcher and writer with the Detroit unit of the Federal Writers' Project of the Works Progress Administration (WPA). Pontheolla Williams noted in *Robert Hayden: A Critical*

Analysis of His Poetry that he "completed. . .[essays] on the anti–slavery activities in Detroit and. . .in Illinois" and that he "supervise[d] research into local history and folklore." In addition to providing him a livelihood during the Depression, the research proved relevant to Hayden's poetry, for he often meditated on the implications of historical figures and events. The experience also enabled him to learn more about other black writers affiliated with the WPA, such as Richard Wright. However, unlike Wright, Hayden was not drawn to Marxist thought.

Hayden took some graduate courses at the University of Michigan in Ann Arbor during the summer of 1938. On June 10, 1940 he married Erma Inez Morris, a musician who had studied piano at Julliard. Their daughter, Maia, was born on October 5, 1942. The same year Hayden began full time graduate study at Michigan, receiving his Master's degree in 1944. He worked as a teaching assistant at Michigan from 1944 to 1946. From 1946 to 1969 he taught at Fisk University. After a brief period at the University of Louisville, he returned to the University of Michigan, his home base for the rest of his career. Hayden held visiting appointments at the University of Washington, the University of Connecticut, Connecticut College, Indiana State University, and Denison University in Ohio.

In 1943 Hayden became a member of the Baha'i faith. In a 1977 interview in *Collected Prose,* Hayden explained the meshing of Baha'i tenets and his own beliefs. He wrote: "I believe in the oneness of all people and I believe in the basic unity of all religions. I don't believe that races are important. I'm very suspicious of any form of ethnicity or nationalism; I think that these things are very crippling and are very divisive. These are all Baha'i points of view, and my work grows out of this vision."

Developed as a Writer

Hayden had become interested in writing while he was still in elementary school. Williams wrote that "he tried to rewrite the stories of plays and movies he had seen" and that while still in high school, he won an award for a short story entitled "Gold." He developed an interest in modern poetry as a teenager and was especially drawn to Countee Cullen's work. Hayden's poem "Africa," published by *Abbott's Monthly* in 1931, is reminiscent of Cullen's "Heritage." According to *Collected Prose,* Hayden met Cullen in 1941. The poet knew of Hayden's work and praised it during their conversation. Earlier, in the 1930s, Hayden had been thrilled to meet Langston Hughes, who read some of his poetry and encouraged him to find his own voice. Although the response dampened his spirits at the time, Hayden later recognized the accuracy and helpfulness of Hughes's critique.

As an apprentice volume, *Heart–Shape in the Dust* (1940) reflects Hughes's assessment. Even so, Hayden's merit as a poet was discernible, for the volume won the 1938 Jules and Avery Hopwood summer award at the University of Michigan. Hayden won another Hopwood for "The Black Spear," a poetry collection which to date has not been published. W.H Auden, who was a visiting professor at the University of Michigan, taught Hayden when he was in graduate school. Hayden characterized the experience in *Collected Prose* as a marvelous one. Auden's erudition and stimulation made him a memorable teacher. The two men subsequently maintained a warm, though not close, relationship.

Hayden received a Julius Rosenwald Fellowship in Creative Writing in 1947, during which time he worked on poems published in *The Lion and the Archer* (1948). The volume features six poems by Hayden and six by Myron O'Higgins. O'Higgins, a consultant and researcher at Fisk, had also received a Rosenwald Fellowship. *The Lion* contains "A Ballad of Remembrance," which became the title poem in a later volume. The cover art was provided by one of Hayden's students, William Demby, who was attending Fisk as a World War II veteran and who later became famous in his own right as a novelist. Hayden's next volume, *Figure of Time: Poems* (1955), consisted of 14 poems: 11 new ones and three reprints. The work was illustrated by Aaron Douglas, who had come to prominence for his murals during the Harlem Renaissance and was on the faculty at Fisk.

Both *The Lion and the Archer* and *Figure of Time* were published by Hemphill Press, a small black press in Nashville, Tennessee. The volumes were part of the Counterpoise Series at Fisk, a project for which Hayden edited four books. The introductory leaflet to the series reflects Hayden's view that it expresses opposition "to the chauvinistic, the cultish, to special pleading, to all that seeks to limit and restrict creative expression." In phrasing consistent with Baha'i beliefs, the statement supports "the oneness of mankind and the importance of the arts in the struggle for peace and unity," as noted in *Collected Prose.*

A Ballad of Remembrance (1962) contains some of Hayden's best known poems. "Middle Passage," revised from earlier versions, is a key example. The poem focuses on the Amistad rebellion, in which Africans being brought to the Caribbean took over the ship meant to deliver them to slavery and eventually won their freedom in a United States court. The poem is a collage of various of materials, including journals, depositions, and hymns. A refrain characterizes the middle passage as a "voyage through death / to life upon these shores." Other often anthologized poems from the volume are "O Daedalus Fly Away Home" and "Frederick Douglass," as well as "Home to the Empress of the Blues," a tribute to the blues singer, Bessie Smith.

A section of *Ballad* draws on Hayden's time in Mexico, where he was based in 1954 and 1955, having received a Ford Foundation Fellowship. The sojourn enabled Hayden to draw on his earlier study of Spanish. Another section of the volume draws on childhood memories in poems such as "The Whipping," "Those Winter Sundays," and "Summertime and the Living." *Ballad* was first published in London and then by the American firm, October House, as *Selected Poems* in 1966. "Runagate Runagate," Hayden's stirring tribute to Harriet Tubman and the Underground Railroad, had been published earlier, but was revised for *Selected Poems.*

Taken together, *A Ballad* and *Selected Poems* mark Hayden's maturity as a poet. The change in publishers and the international dimensions of publication also widened Hayden's audience. In 1966, *A Ballad of Remembrance* was awarded the Grand Prix de la Poésie at the First World Festival of Negro Arts in Dakar, Senegal. In the same year, Hayden was named poet laureate of Senegal.

Despite the accolades and greater fame in the sixties, Hayden was also subjected to negative criticism. At the Black Writer's Conference held at Fisk in 1966, Hayden was castigated by many of the conferees as the author of poems that were too erudite and too removed from political and social activism. The conference had been organized by John O. Killens, then writer–in–residence at Fisk. Hayden compared the experience at the Fisk conference to the criticism he received in college when he read his poems before the John Reed Club. There, according to *Collected Prose*, "he was scathingly criticized for his lack of political awareness. And he was often accused of being too much the individualist and not willing to submit to ideology." In any case, the Fisk experience was painful. In 1969 Hayden resigned from the university.

Williams characterized Hayden's next volume *Words in the Mourning Time* (1970) as "a cathartic work, his poetic response to the Fisk confrontation with the black militants, an affirmation of his humanism, and the rejection of what he sees as evil." The volume contains Hayden's tribute to Malcolm X, "El–Hajj Malik El–Shabazz." The opening lines show Hayden's "rejection of evil" as well as his attention to central issues of the African American experience. In accessible, economical use of language, Hayden declares: "The icy evil that struck his father down/ and ravished his mother into madness / trapped him in violence of a punished self / Struggling to break free." The title poem in the volume ponders the meaning of the deaths of Martin Luther King and Robert Kennedy, and it mourns "for America, self–destructive, self–betrayed."

Hayden's other volumes are *The Night Blooming Cereus* (1972), *Angle of Ascent: New and Selected Poems* (1975), and *American Journal* (1978 and 1982). These works continue to demonstrate his maturity of thought and concise crafting of language. The title, *American Journal*, for example, refers to the report of an extraterrestrial trying to discern American values. The alien observes that he will "disguise myself in order to study them unobserved / adapting their varied pigmentations white black / red brown yellow the imprecise and strangering / distinctions by which they live by which they / justify their cruelties to one another." *American Journal* also includes "The Snow Lamp," which focuses on Matthew Henson and his exploration of the North Pole, and "Letter from Phillis Wheatley," which draws on Wheatley's letters to her black friend Obour.

Hayden was also a critic and editor. He wrote the preface to the reissue of Alain Locke's *The New Negro*, reissued by Atheneum in 1968. He edited *Kaleidoscope: Poems by American Negro Poets* (1967), and for many years, he was the poetry editor for *World Order,* the Baha'i magazine. He collaborated with James E. Miller and Robert O'Neal in editing many Scott Foresman publications, including *American Models: A Collection of Modern Stories* (1973), *Person Place and Point of View: Factual Prose for Interpretation and Extension* (1974), *The Lyric Potential* (1974), and *The Human Condition: Literature Written in the English Language.* Another of Hayden's co–edited works, with David J. Burrows and Frederick Lapides, is *Afro–American Literature: An Introduction* (1971).

The city of Detroit recognized Hayden in 1969 for distinguished achievement by presenting him the Mayor's Bronze Medal. In 1970 he received an award from the National Institute of Letters for distinguished achievement in poetry. In 1975 he was elected a Fellow of the American Academy of Poets. Hayden served two terms as consultant in poetry to the Library of Congress, 1976—77 and 1977—78. He was the first African American poet to hold this post.

Hayden held honorary degrees from Grand Valley State College in Allendale, Michigan, Brown University, Benedict College in Columbia, South Carolina, Wayne State University, and Fisk University. On January 4, 1980, he was among a group of American poets honored by President Jimmy Carter at the White House. Hayden was too ill to attend a celebration held in his honor in Ann Arbor on February 24, 1980. He died the next day.

Although he saw the relevance of race to the human condition, Hayden refused to be limited in his subject matter. At the same time, he understood and demonstrated that poems on a racial theme inherently deal with the human condition. In an interview with John O'Brien for *Interviews With Black Writers,* Hayden summarized his philosophy. "I am convinced," he said, "that if poets have any calling. . .beyond the attempt to produce viable poems––and that in itself is more than enough––it is to affirm the humane, the universal, the potentially divine in the human creature." Hayden affirmed that calling unequivocally.

Books

Harris, Trudier, ed. *Afro–American Writers, 1940—1955.* Gale Research, 1988.

Hatcher, John. *From the Auroral Darkness: The Life and Poetry of Robert Hayden.* George Ronald, 1984.

Nicholas, Xavier, ed. "Robert Hayden and Michael S. Harper: A Literary Friendship." *Callaloo* 17 (Fall 1994): 975—1016.

O'Brien, John, ed. *Interviews with Black Writers.* Liveright, 1973.

Williams, Pontheolla T. *Robert Hayden: A Critical Analysis of His Poetry.* University of Illinois Press, 1987. □

Elwood Haynes

A pioneer in the American automobile industry, Elwood Haynes (1857-1925) built one of the first automobiles powered by a gasoline internal combustion engine in 1894. In 1898 Haynes co-founded the Haynes-Apperson Automobile Company, and Haynes continued to manufacture automobiles until 1924. He also held a number of metallurgical patents and built the Stellite Corporation into a multimillion dollar enterprise manufacturing an early form of stainless steel.

Although his name is not as well remembered as Henry Ford, Ransom Olds, or the Duryea Brothers, Elwood Haynes was one of the pioneers of the automobile age. While the debate has continued on who built the first automobile in America, Haynes was one of the first to make a successful trial run of a gasoline internal combustion-powered automobile in the United States. His mechanical innovations helped spur early automotive technology past its first challenges of durability and performance. After winning a number of awards in motor vehicle endurance contests in the 1890s, Haynes used his reputation to start one of the first car companies in the United States with his partners, the Apperson brothers. Haynes eventually split from the Appersons in order to concentrate on the luxury car market, and the Haynes Automobile Company reached its sales peak in 1916. Haynes also devoted his time to metallurgical experiments with tungsten and cobalt-chrominum alloys in order to develop a lightweight yet durable and strong metal. The result, patented in 1912, was manufactured and sold as "Stellite," and Haynes's new venture quickly grossed several million dollars in sales. Haynes's fortune later ebbed due to lawsuits over the patents for Stellite and the sudden failure of the Haynes Automobile Company in 1924.

High-Achieving Family

Born in the east central Indiana town of Portland on October 14, 1857, Elwood Haynes was the fifth of the eight surviving children of Jacob and Hilinda Sophia Haynes. The family was one of the wealthiest in the area. Jacob Haynes

had been born into a prosperous Massachusetts family that manufactured munitions and horse riding equipment, and he had studied at the exclusive Phillips Academy in Andover before moving west. After settling in Indiana around 1843, Jacob Haynes practiced law and eventually became a circuit judge. He also served as the county school commissioner. Most of the Haynes children excelled in their pursuits and completed their college degrees, a rare feat in an age when only a fraction of the population had access to higher education.

In comparison to his siblings, Haynes was a relative failure in his early years. Although he received good marks in grammar school and demonstrated an obvious interest in scientific pursuits—conducting his own early experiments with metals by melting down spoons—he also seemed easily distracted. After finishing his primary education, Haynes did not go into high school until one opened in the area. Haynes then entered the Worcester County Free Institute of Industrial Science in 1878. The school was later named the Worcester Polytechnical Institute and achieved a reputation as one of the finest engineering and math schools in the country. Haynes struggled to make it through his first year because he was not really prepared him for the rigors of university study. Under strong pressure from his family, Haynes completed his degree in 1881.

Early Careers

Returning to Indiana after three years in Massachusetts, Haynes got a job as a teacher in the Jay County public school system. After a year of teaching, he also served as Portland High School's principal. He enjoyed his experience as a novice teacher and made plans to continue his career at a new teachers' school established in Portland in 1883. There he taught chemistry, geometry, and other scientific subjects. In 1884 Haynes decided to pursue graduate work in chemistry at Johns Hopkins University in Baltimore, Maryland. Although his mother's death in 1885 cut short his stay in Baltimore, Haynes made good use of his time in the school's labs.

A series of events in the region changed his career path soon after his return home. Early in 1886, a promising natural gas deposit was discovered in Jay County. Seizing the opportunity, Haynes and a group of investors founded the Portland Natural Gas and Oil Company by the end of 1886. Exploiting Jay County's natural gas reserves proved a somewhat speculative venture, and, like most other deposits, the reserves were exhausted within a fairly short time. In the years immediately after the discovery of natural gas in north central Indiana, however, the industry grew by leaps and bounds. While the Portland Natural Gas and Oil Company was the first to bring gas into the town, two other competitors sprung up within a year.

With a promising future as a gas company executive and shareholder, Haynes felt financially secure enough to marry the woman he had courted for about ten years. Bertha Lanterman was raised in Portland, but her family relocated to Alabama when she was a teenager. She and Haynes kept in touch, and when the Lanterman family moved back to Indiana, the couple resumed their courtship. They were married on October 21, 1887, and had two children: a daughter, Bernice, born in 1892, and a son, March, in 1896.

Haynes continued his scientific experiments and developed a number of innovative devices during his time with the Portland Natural Gas and Oil Company. One device improved the accuracy of gas meters, and another, something like an early home thermostat, allowed consumers to regulate the amount of gas they used. At a time when much of the public feared bringing natural gas into their home, Haynes's devices helped to foster a safer and more dependable reputation for the new service. Joining the Columbus Construction Company in 1890—a division of the Indiana Natural Gas and Oil Company—Haynes helped to build an innovative high-pressure gas pipeline to bring gas across the state. With his new position, Haynes moved his family to Kokomo, a sizable city in north-central Indiana about forty miles from Indianapolis.

Pioneering Automotive Run

As early as 1891, Haynes had started to make some sketches of vehicles that would be powered by gasoline internal combustion engines. Since the mid-1880s, European inventors had tested such motor vehicles, including the Germans Gottlieb Daimler and Karl Benz, who conducted successful trial runs in 1885 and 1886. In 1891, the same year that Haynes started to take the pursuit seriously, Benz offered the first automobiles for sale in Europe. In 1893, the Duryea Brothers, Charles and Frank, claimed to have made the first automobile run in the United States in Springfield, Massachusetts; however, Haynes would later dispute their assertion. The Duryeas had essentially strapped an engine onto an existing carriage, but Haynes built a vehicle expressly designed as an automobile. While the distinction may not have mattered to some, Haynes and the Duryeas argued over the point in the years to come, particularly after they had entered the automobile manufacturing business and used the claim of being first in their advertisements.

Haynes's vehicle was one of the first on American soil that deserved to be called an "automobile." After numerous experiments with a gasoline engine, Haynes meticulously designed a vehicle that was lightweight yet strong enough not to rattle apart while being driven. Using Haynes's design, the car itself was built in the Riverside Machine Shop in Kokomo, a business owned by the Apperson brothers. They pledged to keep the automobile under wraps, for Haynes did not want to publicize his work until he could be assured that it would be a success. On July 4, 1894, the car was ready for its first test run. Taking a cautious approach—for the car had almost no steering capability—Haynes had the car pulled to a road outside of town so that pedestrians and horses would not get in the way. The test run on Pumpkinvine Pike outside of Kokomo was successful, with the car, named the Pioneer, reaching speeds of about seven miles per hour. Later, Haynes redesigned the Pioneer, improved its steering, and added pneumatic tires, taking its top speed up to about 12 to 14 miles per hour. Over the next year, the Pioneer became a familiar site on the streets of

Kokomo, as Haynes worked to improve its speed, reliability, and maneuverability.

Produced Luxury Cars

In February 1897, the Duryeas became the first automobile manufacturers in the United States when they offered a car for sale to the public. By 1900 over thirty other manufacturers had joined their ranks, including the Haynes-Apperson Corporation of Kokomo. Starting in 1895, Haynes and the Appersons produced a couple of cars for sale to individual clients. In 1898, they built their own automobile factory with the capacity to produce about 200 cars a year. With demand far outstripping the supply, most of their automobiles were sold before they were even built.

The year 1901 was pivotal for Haynes, who finally quit his job with the Columbus Construction Company and parted ways with the Appersons. While the brothers went on to produce smaller, less expensive cars, Haynes remained in the luxury market. Haynes also took a conservative approach in running his factory; producing 240 cars in 1901 and 350 in 1909. By that time, rival Henry Ford was producing and selling over 10,000 Model Ts annually, a figure that would expand greatly after he opened up his Highland Park, Michigan, plant in 1909.

In 1911 a fire at the Haynes factory finally spurred Haynes to modernize and enlarge its production capacity. After it reopened, the Haynes Corporation reached a production peak of 7,100 automobiles in 1916. At a time when Ford and General Motors aggressively sought a mass market for low- and medium-priced automobiles, Haynes continued to sell to the luxury market. In 1908, for example, Haynes sold two models, a five-passenger runabout for $2,500 and a seven-passenger touring car for $5,500. That same year, Ford sold the innovative Model T for $825.

Success with Stellite

Through his experiments with metal alloys, Haynes had long sought to create a lightweight yet stronger form of steel for use in the manufacturing process. In 1912 he received patents covering his invention of tungsten and cobalt-chromium alloys, which he marketed under the name "Stellite." As an early form of stainless steel, Stellite was immediately successful for use in machine parts and such consumer items as silverware, knives, and jewelry. His new company, the Stellite Corporation, reached over $1 million in sales in 1915-16 and grossed over $3.6 million in 1918.

Despite the success of Stellite, however, Haynes earned a reputation as an owner who was unconcerned with his workers' safety. According to some published accounts, injuries were a daily occurrence in Haynes's factories, but Haynes never improved his companies' safety records. Haynes was stingy with his wages, never giving bonuses and paying only 17.5 cents an hour in 1915 for an 11-hour day and six-day work week.

In 1920, Haynes transferred the Stellite Corporation to Union Carbide in exchange for an estimated $1.6 million in stock; the stock dividends provided Haynes with a $500,000 annual income. Unfortunately, Haynes's interest in his automobile company was not as lucrative. Refusing to budge from the luxury car market, the Haynes brand was hit hard by a slump in auto sales in 1921, and it never recovered from the loss. The company closed in September 1924, throwing at least 400 workers out of a job. The following year, on April 13, 1925, Haynes died in Kokomo, Indiana, after a brief illness probably brought on by heart failure.

Books

Flink, James J., *The Car Culture,* MIT Press, 1975.
Gray, Ralph D., *Alloys and Automobiles: The Life of Elwood Haynes,* Indiana Historical Society, 1979.
Lacey, Robert, *Ford: The Men and the Machine,* Ballantine Books, 1986.
Madison, James H., *The Indiana Way: A State History,* Indiana University Press, 1990.

Periodicals

Automotive News, June 26, 1996.
Indiana Business Magazine, August 1997.

Online

"Elwood Haynes," *Indiana Historical Society,* http://www.indianahistory.org/heritage/ehay.html (January 9, 2002). □

John Hemphill

John Hemphill (1803-1862) was the first significant Chief Justice of Texas. He served both as Chief Justice of the Supreme Court of the Republic of Texas and later, after Texas was incorporated into the Union, as the Chief Justice of the Texas State Supreme Court.

Years in South Carolina

John Hemphill, born on December 18, 1803, in Chester District, South Carolina, near the small town of Blackstock, was the fifth child of John and Jane (Lind) Hemphill. His father immigrated to the United States from Londonderry County, Northern Ireland, in 1783. He attended Dickinson College in Pennsylvania, and, upon graduating, relocated to South Carolina, where he became a licensed minister of the Associate Reformed Church. Hemphill's mother, also of Scotch-Irish descent, was a native of Pennsylvania and the daughter of an Associate Reformed Church minister. She was related to Robert Fulton, the inventor. After his mother's death when Hemphill was still a young child, he was reared by his father and, after 1811, his stepmother, Mary Nixon.

Hemphill attended the local one-room school and then enrolled in Monticello Academy. After teaching school for one year, he entered Jefferson College (now Washington and Jefferson College) in Pennsylvania in 1823, graduating second in his class in 1825. Returning to South Carolina, he taught in classical academies in the Abbeville and Richland

districts for the several years. Turning his attention to the legal profession, in 1829 he began his law studies under the tutelage of David J. McCord, a prominent attorney in Columbia, South Carolina. After being admitted to practice in the court of common pleas in November 1829, Hemphill opened a law office in Sumter district and began his practice. In 1831 he was admitted to practice in the equity courts.

In Sumter the young and zealous Hemphill became embroiled in the growing debate over slavery and nullification (i.e., the right of a state to nullify, or reject, federal laws). A staunch supporter of both slavery and nullification, Hemphill submitted regular essays to the local newspaper, the *Sumter Gazette,* expressing his views. In 1832 he engaged in a two-month debate with a reporter that was played out in the newspapers. Hostilities between the two men escalated into a brawl outside the Sumter courthouse. Hemphill eventually became editor of the *Gazette* and used his editorial power to spur the proslavery and nullification efforts. His opinions drew strong opposition, and in 1833 he actually entered into a duel with a local merchant over their differences. Played out with smooth-bore pistols, Hemphill was wounded in his hand, receiving a scar that stayed with him the remainder of his life.

Hemphill's law practice was interrupted in the beginning of 1836 when he volunteered to assist in putting down an insurrection of the Seminole Indians in Florida. He attempted to gather a company of volunteers from Sumter County, but failing to do so, he traveled to Columbia and enlisted as a second lieutenant. During his military expedition to Florida, Hemphill, like many of his comrades, contracted malaria, which necessitated his return to South Carolina after a just few months in ill health. Little else is known of Hemphill's seven years as a lawyer in Sumter County. His name appears in official court records in 1836 and 1838 as counsel in cases appealed to the court of last of resort.

Texas Jurist

In the summer of 1838 Hemphill moved to Texas, which at the time was the independent Republic of Texas. In September of the same year he was licensed to practice and subsequently established a law practice in the small, old town of Washington-on-the-Brazos in Washington County. Sometime before May 3, 1839, Hemphill relocated to the town of Bastrop, outside of Austin. Keenly aware of the importance of the Spanish language and Spanish civil law, which was still commonly practiced in Texas, Hemphill, according to legend, went into seclusion for a time while he mastered the language and the law books. His studies proved to be an important asset in his career and earned his significant respect for his learning and intellect.

Having declined a previous offer from President Mirabeau B. Lamar to become the Texas Secretary of the Treasury, on January 20, 1840, Hemphill was elected by the Texas Congress to serve as district judge of the Republic's fourth judicial district. According to the Texas constitution adopted in 1836, district judges filled the role as Associate-Justices on the Republic's Supreme Court. Therefore,

Hemphill presided in district court as a trial judge and served as a member of the Supreme Court. Little is known of Hemphill's short term as a district judge, except for an oft-recorded incident that happened in San Antonio on March 19, 1840. Comanche chiefs had taken hostage a number of Texans. In response the military invited the chiefs to exchange the hostages for supplies and selected the council house as the location for the exchange. Negotiations took place with Hemphill as a mere bystander. When the chiefs only produced one hostage, however, the military decided to hold the chiefs in exchange for the remaining hostages. Violence quickly erupted, and Hemphill found himself in the midst of it.

The official report, registered by Colonel McLeod as recorded in David McWhirter's *The Legal 100,* stated: "John Hemphill . . . assailed in the council house by a chief and slightly wounded, felt reluctantly compelled (as he remarked to the writer afterwards) to disembowel his assailant with his bowie knife, but declared that he did so under a sense of duty, while he had no personal acquaintance with nor personal ill-will towards his antagonist." The episode sheds light on the nature of the dangerous and unsettled Texas territory. In the aftermath of the event, Hemphill was among the party that returned the sole remitted hostage, a young girl, to her family near Gonzales, Texas.

Became Chief Justice

On December 5, 1840, the Texas Congress elected Hemphill as Chief Justice. The first candidate, James Collingsworth, was elected in 1836, but died before the court ever convened. At the congressional session, Thomas J. Rusk was selected to replace Collingsworth, but he only served for a brief time before resigning in late 1840. As a result, Hemphill, who retained his place on the bench for eighteen years, is often considered the first chief justice of Texas. Hemphill's bid for the position was not unopposed; also on the ballot was James Webb, a former Attorney General. In a joint vote of Congress, the two candidates split the Senate with seven votes each, but Hemphill received twenty-one votes in the House of Representatives to Webb's nineteen. A false rumor circulating about Webb may have aided his defeat, but Hemphill, whose dignity was beyond reproach, was not associated with any plot to upend his opponent.

Despite his important position as Chief Justice, records indicate that Hemphill did not receive a regular salary. In at least two memorandums to Congress, Hemphill requested payment for his services and noted that he had exhausted his personal funds and even incurred debts in order to sustain the functions of the Supreme Court. In such a correspondence with Congress, Hemphill asked that he be paid his salary as district judge from March 20 to December 5, 1840, in the amount of $2,125 and as Chief Justice from December 5 to January 3, 1842, in the amount of $3,250.

Hemphill had not been fulfilling his new duties long before being interrupted by an eruption in the volatile relationship between Texas and Mexico. Mexico, still refusing to concede to Texas's independence and fearing the Republic's growing relationship with the United States, invaded in 1842. General Vasquez moved Mexican troops into the Republic and overtook San Antonio, causing a general panic in nearby Austin. The Congress was moved to Washington-on-the-Brazos and activity came to a near halt. Court records show that the Supreme Court did not convene between January 1942 and June 1843. During this extended break, Hemphill joined General Somervell's expedition to the Rio Grande to counter the Mexican attack, serving as Adjunct General. Upon arriving at the Texas-Mexico border, the mission was abandoned as it was decided the company lacked sufficient numbers to stage an invasion across the river.

In 1843 and 1844 Hemphill was encouraged to run for the presidency; however, both times he declined due to poor health. In 1845 Hemphill served as the Washington county delegate to the annexation convention, which convened on July 4. Hemphill, a strong proponent of Texas statehood, was appointed chair of the Judiciary Committee. On July 11 he presented the convention with a draft of the judiciary section of the new constitution. His plan, which called for the Supreme Court to consist of three judges appointed by the government and confirmed by the senate, was adopted with little debate, although he did fail to stop the passage of an amendment that allowed for jury trials in equity cases, a measure he opposed. Once Texas became a state, Hemphill was appointed by the Governor Lubbock as Chief Justice of the State Supreme Court and confirmed by unanimous vote in the Senate. Abner S. Lipscomb and Royall T. Wheeler were appointed to the two remaining seats.

The John Marshall of Texas

Hemphill has been called the John Marshall of Texas because, like U.S. Chief Justice Marshall, Hemphill was instrumental in laying the foundation for the judiciary system in its infancy. As James P. Hart noted in his essay "John Hemphill—Chief Justice of Texas:" "Living conditions in Texas generally and particularly in Austin were primitive; there was constant danger from Indian raids and Mexican invasions. Access to texts and decisions of other courts was limited, even in situations where helpful precedents might be expected to exist. In such an atmosphere and under such handicaps, it is truly remarkable that Hemphill and his colleagues turned out opinions whose general excellence has probably never been equaled by any other court in Texas history." Hemphill considered Spanish civil law to be superior to the common law standards adopted by Texas. As both a republic and a state, Texas adhered to common law in most matters, except issues of property, in which case Spanish property laws prevailed. Hemphill consistently referred to Spanish law in his opinions, drew on its precedents, and often made his comments in Spanish.

As a proponent of civil law, Hemphill, who never married, was a strong advocate for women's property rights. Hart reprints a portion of Hemphill's opinion in *Wood v. Wheeler,* brought before the Supreme Court in 1851: "Husband and wife are not one under our laws. The existence of a wife is not merged in that of her husband. Most certainly is this true, so far as the rights of property are concerned; they are distinct persons as to their estates. . . . They are co-equals in life; and at death the survivor, whether husband or wife, remains head of the family." Hemphill's opinions formed much of the common property system of Texas, which allowed married women to own property in their own names and gave a half-interest to wives in all property purchased as a married couple. Hemphill also continually advanced Spanish civil law principles in matters of debt, expanding the homestead exemption so that families were protected from forced sale of their property to settle a debt. He further liberalized the provision by applying it to all persons, not just heads of families and Texas citizens.

Final Years: Secession

Hemphill served as Chief Justice for eighteen years until he resigned at the end of 1847 when the Texas legislature selected him to replace Sam Houston in the U.S. Senate. He served in the Senate from 1859 to 1861. In that year he joined thirteen other Senators who met on January 6 to call for the secession of the Southern states from the Union. Expelled from the Senate in July for his support of secession, he traveled to Montgomery, Alabama, to serve as a Texas delegate to the Confederate constitutional convention where he helped formulate the judicial foundation for the Confederacy. During the second half of 1861, he turned down an offer to become a Confederate district judge for Texas, was elected as a member of the Confederate Congress, and lost a race for the Confederate Senate. He was fulfilling his duties in the Confederate Congress, which met in Richmond, Virginia, when he contracted pneumonia. He died on January 4, 1862; he was buried on February 10 in Austin at the Texas State Cemetery.

Books

Garraty, John A., and Mark C. Carnes, eds. *American National Biography.* Oxford University Press, 1999.

Jacob, Kathryn Allamong, and Bruce A. Ragsdale, eds., *Biographical Dictionary of the United States Congress, 1774–1989,* Joint Committee on Printing, 1989.

Lewis, William Draper. *Great American Lawyers,* The John C. Winston Company, 1908

McWhirter, Darien A. *The Legal 100: A Ranking of the Individuals Who Have Most Influenced the Law,* Carol Publishing Group, 1998.

Periodicals

Hart, James P. "John Hemphill—Chief Justice of Texas." *Southwestern Law Journal* 3 (fall 1949): pp. 395-415.

Online

"Hemphill, John." The Handbook of Texas Online. Available from http://www.tsha.utexas.edu/handbook/online/articles/view/HH/fhe13.html.

"Hemphill, John." Hemphill County Texas. Available from http://www.rootsweb.com/~txhemphi.

"John Hemphill." State Cemetery of Texas, Austin. Available from http://www.cemetery.state.tx.us/pub/user_form.asp?step=1&pers_id=59. □

Donald Ainslie Henderson

Donald Henderson (born 1928) spearheaded the drive to eradicate smallpox, the only disease ever to have been wiped out. He is the head of the Office of Public Health Preparedness, a position responsible for protecting the public from bioterrorism.

Henderson Wiped Out Smallpox

Donald Ainslie Henderson, known as D.A., was born in Lakewood, Ohio, in 1928 to David and Grace Henderson. He received his bachelor of arts degree from Oberlin College in 1950. In 1951, he married Nana Irene Bragg. The couple have three children. Henderson received his medical degree from the University of Rochester in 1954 and was an intern and resident at the Mary Imogene Bassett Hospital in Cooperstown, New York. From 1955 to 1966 he also worked for the Center for Disease Control.

Henderson ran the World Health Organization's smallpox eradication program from 1966 to 1977. During the 20th century, at least 300 million people died of smallpox. As late as 1960, about five million people a year died of the disease. The eradication of smallpox has been called "perhaps the greatest medical feat of all time." "An ancient, contagious and particularly hideous disease, smallpox kills a third of those infected with it, and Dr. Henderson is one of the few doctors in this country today to have actually seen a case," noted Sheryl Gay Stolberg in an article in the *New York Times,* dated November 18, 2001. "The World Health Organization's smallpox eradication program, which Dr. Henderson ran from 1966 to 1977, was, he said, the effort of countless public health workers who toiled under grueling conditions, often living in villages without electricity and running water, in nations torn apart by war. They operated under the principle of 'ring vaccination,' containing outbreaks by vaccinating every patient infected, and everyone around those patients, moving outward in concentric circles until the virus stopped spreading."

Smallpox experts believe the eradication effort, carried out with the former Soviet Union during the Cold War, succeeded because of Henderson's determination. When the health minister of Ethiopia would not cooperate with him, Henderson made his way into the country and got to know the personal physician of the country's emperor, Haile Selassie. When Henderson suspected the Russians were giving him an inferior smallpox vaccine, he traveled to Moscow—violating orders from his superiors, who were worried about a diplomatic nightmare—and demanded a better vaccine.

After finishing his work with the World Health Organization, Henderson served as dean of the Johns Hopkins School of Public Health from 1977 to 1990. He then worked for the administration of President George Bush, serving as science adviser to the White House from 1991 to 1993, as associate director of the Office of Science and Technology Policy. Henderson worked for the Department of Health and Human Services (HHS) from 1993 to 1995 as deputy assistant secretary of HHS for health and science. He left in 1995 because he felt he was being underutilized and returned to the Johns Hopkins School of Public Health as a professor. Because of his fears about bioterrorism, in 1997, Henderson founded and became director of the Johns Hopkins University Center for Civilian Biodefense Studies, a research institution.

Destructionists Versus Preservationists

Since smallpox was officially declared eradicated worldwide in 1980, a debate has raged among epidemiologists and others as to whether or not the two official stocks of the smallpox virus kept in freezers at the U.S. Centers for Disease Control and Prevention (CDC) in Atlanta, Georgia, and at the State Research Center of Virology and Biotechnology in Novosibirsk, Siberia, should be destroyed or maintained for future study. Henderson firmly believes that the virus should be destroyed, fearing that it could escape, but others want it preserved in order to develop better treatments, should smallpox ever be used as a weapon. Although officially only the U.S. and Russian smallpox stocks are known to exist, strong evidence indicates that Iraq, North Korea, and Russia are probably concealing the smallpox virus for possible military use.

Henderson has argued that the United States should be stockpiling the smallpox vaccine for use in case of biological warfare attacks. "Its potential for devastation today is far greater than at any previous time," Henderson and 14 other experts noted in the June 9, 1999, issue of *The Journal of the American Medical Association.* "In a now highly susceptible, mobile population, smallpox would be able to spread widely and rapidly throughout this country and the world."

Henderson has been harshly criticized for his stance on the destruction of the official smallpox stocks. Wendy Orent, in her 1999 article, "The Smallpox Wars: Biowarfare vs. Public Health," published in *The American Prospect,* writes of Henderson, "He now insists that he never cared much about destruction before 1994 or 1995, when he first learned about smallpox weaponization and proliferation. Henderson hopes, through destruction, to 'raise the moral high bar' and inspire anyone growing smallpox as a weapon to destroy their stocks too. He insists that not until we destroy our stocks can the possession of illegal supplies be a crime against humanity. He hopes, by the force of his gigantic will, to force the world to yield to his increasingly irrational demand, a demand that remains the official position of the U.S. government."

On January 17, 2002, the World Health Organization, acting on fears of bioterrorism, reversed its order for the destruction of all smallpox virus stocks and recommended that the stocks be kept for research purposes, in the hope of creating new vaccines or treatments. There had been a deadline of 2002 for the destruction of the virus.

"We Should Be Prepared"

In a recent simulation of a smallpox outbreak in three American cities, scientists learned that after three months, the smallpox virus would have spread to 25 states and 15 countries, wiping out one million people. In an interview with CNN correspondents, Henderson noted, "There were some who said this is an extreme example of what might happen in a worst-case scenario. I wish I could say that, but I can't."

In a January 2001 interview with "Health Insider," on WebMD Live, Henderson expressed his concern over the possibility of bioterrorist attacks. "I believe that the risk is far greater than has ever been present in history. . . . As we look to the future, we see that many of the factors, which now make bioterrorism more likely, are only going to intensify. And thus, our concern is that we should be prepared. There are those who say that because we have not had major attacks of bioterrorism, that we need not be worried for the future. My only reply is that until 1941, no one had ever bombed Pearl Harbor. I'm afraid there will be a first time, and I'm afraid the time that will occur is in the not-too-distant future."

The possibility of a smallpox outbreak received more attention after the September 11, 2001, terrorist attacks on New York City and Washington, D.C. The events made people consider the possibility that a bioterrorist attack could happen. People worried about someone releasing smallpox, anthrax, or pneumonic plague in a city using crop-dusters or other means. "There is a possibility, but we still believe this is an unlikely possibility," explained Henderson. "The risk that this is going to happen is small, but it's there. It's not zero," he said in an interview with CNN.

Government Work Resumed

On November 1, 2001, Tommy G. Thompson, the secretary of HHS, named Henderson the head of the new Office of Public Health Preparedness. The appointment came at a time when the government faced criticism for its lack of coordination in the anthrax attacks perpetrated by mail, which killed four people and infected more than a dozen. Henderson's responsibilities include analyzing information as it comes to HHS' bioterrorism war room and helping coordinate multiple government agencies in responding to public health threats. Henderson must bring these agencies together and create alliances with law enforcement and intelligence authorities.

According to the *New York Times,* Henderson "said he was committed to remaining with the government only as long as it took to create a bioterrorism preparedness program that others might carry out. Asked how long that might be, he replied by saying that he had promised the World Health Organization he would stay in Geneva for 18 months. He stayed 11 years. More than anything, Dr. Henderson said, he would like to figure out a way to persuade the countries of the world to come together to condemn the use of germs as weapons. Of smallpox, he said, 'We've got to put the genie back in the bottle.'"

It is ironic, that the man who dedicated most of his career to wiping out disease in the wild, will spend the final years of his working life trying to protect people from intentional exposure to disease. "I find this unfortunate that we really have to spend as much time and effort as we are trying to combat diseases in which man is responsible for spreading it," Henderson told interviewer Susan Dentzer on the *MacNeil/Lehrer News Hour's* "Health Spotlight." "There's so much in the way of problems out there, tuberculosis and AIDS and malaria, that I really regard this as a very unhappy kind of interlude in my life to have to revert to, to this; but I think the problem is so important that as a citizen I just can't walk away from it."

"A Real American Hero"

Henderson is a husky, white-haired man with a deep, rough voice and a friendly smile. He has little patience for foolishness and red-tape. His is a strong, confident personality, and he is used to being obeyed. Although Henderson has received many awards and honorary degrees, he has not yet won the Nobel Prize, although many people feel that he should. In November 2001, when Henderson appeared in front of a U.S. House of Representative's committee, Representative Billy Tauzin, a Republican from Louisiana, introduced Henderson as "a real American hero." The legislators gave Henderson a standing ovation.

Periodicals

New York Times, October 8, 2001; November 18, 2001.
Science,, October 19, 2001, p. 498.
Time, March 29, 1999, p. 168.

Online

"Battling Bioterrorism," *Online NewsHour,* http://www.pbs.org/ newshour (January 19, 2002).
"The Dangers of Smallpox and Anthrax," *WebMD Health,* http://my.webmd.com (January 19, 2002).
"Fears of Anthrax Addressed," *CBS News,* http://www.cbsnews .com (January 19, 2002).
"Smallpox, Anthrax: What Could Happen," *CNN,* http://www .CNN.com (January 19, 2002). □

Robert Henri

A revolution in American art circles was led by Robert Henri (1865-1929), instigator of what was referred to as "The Eight" and the "revolutionary black gang." Henri, along with John Sloan, William Glackens, George Luks, Everett Shinn, James Preston, Edward Davis, and Charles Redfield, held academic and officially sanctioned art in contempt. They complained that it was cloistered, effete, monotonous, and "fenced in with tasseled ropes and weighed down with bronze plates."

T hese young artistic rebels believed that American art should be public in the broadest sense of the word and have relevance to the people, not just to art experts. According to Henri, American artists had too long been under the sway of the standards and subject matter of European high art. Henri and The Eight challenged the enshrining of European aesthetics. Following in the footsteps of novelists such as Nathaniel Hawthorne and Herman Melville, and the essayist Henry David Thoreau, who celebrated what they called "an American spirit," Henri turned his artistic vision to native themes. By doing so, he insisted that the unique qualities of America should shape its artists and its art.

Henri was born Robert Henry Cozad on June 25, 1865 in Nebraska. He studied art at the Pennsylvania Academy of Fine Arts. Henri became fascinated by the realism of his teacher, Thomas Eakins, who counseled his students to study their own country and to "portray its types." To the dismay of the academy, Eakins insisted that his students paint from nude models rather than from plaster molds. Eakins's rebelliousness against the decorum of academic art cost him his job but won the admiration of Henri, who continued his studies with Eakins's gifted student, Thomas Anshutz. In 1888 Henri left for Paris and enrolled in the bastion of classicism, the Ecole des Beaux-Arts, for two years. While in Paris the radical Henri found Post-Impressionism, the European challenge to academic art, uninteresting.

The Eight

When Henri returned to Philadelphia in 1891, a friend introduced him to two newspaper illustrators, William Glackens and John Sloan. They, along with other renegade artists, made Henri's studio at 806 Walnut Street in downtown Philadelphia a gathering place. At these meetings the group discussed music, literature, art, and, most of all, the stifling confines of the academy. Unlike more institutional gatherings of artists, such as those of Philadelphia's Tile Club or the Art Club, The Eight's meetings were run in the spirit of a European café—spontaneous and casual discussions. As newspaper artists, Sloan, Glackens, Luks, and Shinn illustrated the city's disasters in quick sketches. Henri found their perspective refreshingly honest. He encouraged them to paint in oil, rather than in charcoal, and to see urban America as a worthy subject for serious art. As a result, The Eight became known for their psychological portraiture, their eye for detail, their sympathy with humanity, and their use of a drab, realistic urban palette.

Returned to Paris

In 1898 Henri married and went to Paris for his honeymoon. His compositions from this trip were a series of broadly painted figures that stood in contrast to simple silhouettes, and scenes in which shadow and light figured prominently. While these paintings were rejected by the progressive Salon des Indépendants, the French government purchased one of them, *Snow* in 1899. When he returned to the United States, Henri and his wife settled in New York City, a place he felt was more hospitable to his artistic vision than was Philadelphia. Henri took a job as an instructor at the New York School of Art, or the Chase School. Soon many of his friends joined him. While teaching in New York City, he continued to think about and challenge the place of art in the modern world. Henri believed that art should be realistic. He filled his canvases with unglamorous models and urban action scenes. At the same time, Henri believed that the camera freed artists from the obligation to paint realistically. Artists, he felt, should not paint for details but concentrate on the subjective underpinnings of the scene, such as the expression of the model and the feelings that the scene invoked.

Gained a Reputation

In the 1900s The Eight were known as the New York Realists. Many critics found their work to be joyless and unhealthy; others found it a compelling counterpart to the exposé journalism of the muckrakers and the social realism of novelists such as Theodore Dreiser and Frank Norris. Despite their distance from academic art, the conservative National Academy of Design had accepted all of them as members by 1905. Two years later, the National Academy of Design appointed Henri to judge its prestigious spring exhibition. His friends' excitement at finally having one of their own officiate such an exhibit was soon crushed when Henri discovered that he had no meaningful say in the evaluation process. The jury gave two of his own paintings a "number two" rating, meaning they were not to be hung on eye level, but either above or below. Henri was furious and quickly withdrew his canvases from the show.

"Apostles of Ugliness"

The group met shortly after Henri's resignation and decided to produce an alternative and cooperative exhibition to be financed by the artists themselves. William Macbeth offered them space in his gallery. Henri, Shinn, Luks, Davies, Lawson, and Maurice Prendergast participated in the show. A newspaper announcing the show referred to the artists as "the apostles of ugliness." The show opened in February 1908 and was a success, selling seven canvases. Critics denounced the show as unfit for civilized viewing. "Is it fine art," one critic asked, "to exhibit our sores?" Henri was singled out for his "streak of coarseness." Despite such criticism, The Eight had made a mark. They had created an alternative to the one-horse art town that New York City had been. Now, at least, those artists whom museums refused to exhibit had a place to display their work.

Ash Can School

In 1909 Henri established his own art school on upper Broadway in New York City, and many of his students followed him there from the New York School of Art, including George Bellows and Edward Hopper. Henri inspired another generation of modern painters, including Stanton Macdonald-Wright, Patrick Henry Bruce, and Stuart Davis. He continued to train his students in his philosophy of freedom of expression. He read from Walt Whitman's *Leaves of Grass*. Henri and his students took to wandering the streets looking for subjects and turned their sights on the city's new immigrants. They filled their canvases with scenes of Coney Island, Union Square, and the Bowery. Henri painted the rivers in and around New York City and painted them in bleakest winter. For Henri, the New York skyline, with its looming buildings and steel bridges, symbolized the energy of the city. Others labeled the creators of these works the "Ash Can School" for their gritty imagery.

Galvanized by another wave of rejections from the New York art establishment, Henri set out to organize a second group show of independent artists. He timed this show to coincide with the academy's spring exhibition in 1910. When the independents' show opened on West Thirty-fifth Street, Henri's portrait of his wife, which the academy had rejected, hung in the place of honor. The show was large, with more than two hundred canvases, displayed alphabetically by artist. Within an hour, one thousand people had crowded into the gallery, while another fifteen hundred waited outside. A riot squad eventually came to manage the disorderly crowd. Critics continued to see Henri and the show's other artists as vulgar and coarse. But others viewed The Eight's "revolt" as a success, claiming that it injected a healthy vitality into American art.

Later Life

In his later years Henri continued to teach and to rebel against the boundaries between official and nonofficial art. He wrote a book, *The Art Spirit* in 1923. He continued to inspire students by demanding innovation in subject matter. Henri died in New York City on July 12, 1929.

Books

Homer, William Innes and Violet Organ. *Robert Henri and His Circle,* Hacker, 1988.
Rose, Barbara. *American Art Since 1900,* Praeger, 1975. □

Hildegard of Bingen

Through her studies and writings, twelfth-century Benedictine abbess Hildegard of Bingen (1098-1179) helped German scholars to emerge from the Dark Ages by presenting a revisioning of the cosmos and the interrelationship between man and his environment.

erman scientist, philosopher, theologian, and composer Hildegard of Bingen devoted half her life to sharing, through her writing, both the insight gained through her visionary experiences and her joy in the Christian faith. Many centuries later, historians still study her texts, and the over 70 chants and hymns she composed continue to be performed and recorded. An influential abbess, Hildegard was considered by historians to be among the most important scientists of her age and perhaps the most significant woman scientist in Medieval Europe. Her written works, which focus on natural history, medicine, and cosmology—a theory about the natural order of the universe—received renewed critical interest in the late twentieth century following a reevaluation of the previously overlooked contributions of female scholarship. In addition to the republication of her many books and letters, a recording of Hildegard's medieval-styled chants and hymns topped the classical music charts in 1998.

Visionary Child Destined to Serve God

Hildegard was born at her parents' home on the banks of the Nahe River in Bermersheim, Germany, some time during the summer of 1098. Her parents, believed to bear the Christian names Hiltebert and Mechthild, were most likely members of the local nobility. At the birth of their tenth daughter, they decided to follow the custom then practiced of giving their tenth child over to the service of God when she reached a suitable age. A sickly young girl destined to live a cloistered life rather than marriage, Hildegard was given little in the way of education or other training. Along with a series of physical infirmities, she experienced momentary experiences of a brilliant light. To young Hildegard, such experiences seemed normal, as they had been a part of her childhood since she could remember. However, when she admitted them to her nurse, the reaction of the older woman at such "visions" convinced Hildegard to keep such things to herself in future.

In 1106 Hildegard's parents made good on their commitment to tithe their daughter to the Church. The sickly, eight-year-old girl was delivered into the care of Jutta von Spanheim, a relative who served as abbess of a cloistered community of nuns associated with the Benedictine monastery at Disibodenberg. While Jutta intended to provide the young Hildegard with a religious education, the child's frequent inability to either rise from her bed or focus her sight on things around her prevented more than a rudimentary education. However, the abbess was able to instill in Hildegard a knowledge and love of music, the Latin Psalms, and the Holy Scriptures.

Hildegard took her vows and became a Benedictine nun during her teen years. Her infirmities lessened after she gained adulthood, and she was able to fulfill her desire for knowledge, her interests ranging from natural history and German folk medicine to the ancient Greek cosmologies that were by now reaching the convents and monasteries of Germany in Latin translation. Unlike her illnesses, her visions continued, and even intensified after she reached puberty. However, Hildegard admitted them to only a few people, including Abbess Jutta and Volmar, a Disobodenberg monk who served as her mentor.

In 1136 Jutta passed away, leaving the 38-year-old Hildegard as abbess of the Disobodenberg community of women religious. Five years later, Hildegard experienced a vision of great intensity, which she later described as "a fiery light [that] flashed from the open vault of heaven. It permeated my brain and enflamed my heart and the entire breast not like a burning, but alike a warming flame, as the sun warms everything its rays touch. And suddenly I was given insight into the meaning of Scripture." Compelled by her faith to record what she had learned through 16 of her visions, and with the aid and encouragement of Volmar, Hildegard began what would be her first book, *Liber Scivias,* in 1141. In this work, destined to become widely read, she presents her unique cosmology by explaining the workings of the physical universe using a spiritual allegory based on Greek tradition. The earth, Hildegard maintained, was a sphere composed of the four elements—wind, fire, air, and water. Surrounded by layers of air and water, it was encased in an egg-shaped universe with an external "shell." A *purus aether* contained stars, the moon, and other planets, which were immobile. An inner "fire" or energy source generated thunderous lightening and hail, while an outer fire fueled the sun. Winds within this contained universe caused movements of clouds and resulted in seasonal changes on earth.

Writings Viewed as Voice of God

The "vision" that provided the impetus for *Scivias* was not unique to the book's author. Such mystical experiences were regularly reported throughout the Middle Ages and have been attributed by forensic archaeologists and secular historians to physical disorders such as epilepsy or severe migraine headaches. Also during this period, the Catholic Church provided the only environment in which studious activity could flourish; without the approval of the Roman Catholic Church new ideas were often met with charges of heresy that did not bode well for their originator. For this reason, religious numbered among the preeminent scientists, historians, theologians, and authors of the 12th century. Because insight and intellectual ability were fully integrated with religious faith, they were seen as gifts from God. Therefore, linking new scholarship or scientific discoveries to a "vision" implied a direct communication from God, thus earning more easy acceptance in a society still emerging from an age of superstition, fear, and widespread ignorance. For women, this stamp of approval from God was particularly important, and in Hildegard's case her visions perhaps accounted for the spread of her ideas over those of other scholarly female religious of the age.

Received Papal Approval

Through the efforts of Volmar, the first sections of Hildegard's yet-unfinished *Scivias* were sent to the archbishop of Mainz. At the Council of Trier in 1147, the archbishop presented it to reforming Pope Eugenius III (1145-1153), who declared the abbess's prophecies to be authentic. Compelled by the pope to continue her work, Hildegard completed outlining her cosmology and also added to *Scivias* 14 liturgical songs and a morality play unusual for its day in that it was sung rather than recited. Composed in Latin as was all scholarship of the day, *Scivias* was recorded on a wax tablet—either by Hildegard herself or by Volmar—and then transcribed by Volmar onto parchment, with the inclusion of detailed illustrations likely the work of Volmar's assistants. While the text reflects its author's lack of literary sophistication and her rudimentary knowledge of Latin grammar, it is compelling in its imagery.

The approval of the Catholic Church caused interest in Hildegard's writings to spread across Europe, where she became known as the "Sibil of the Rhine." Hundreds of Catholic faithful undertook pilgrimages to Disobodenberg to visit with the abbess, and soon Hildegard's celebrity status began to interfere with her scholarship and writing. In 1148, claiming her decision the result of a vision from God, she decided to break with the monastery at Disibodenberg. Using her political influence to override the monk's opposition, in 1150 Hildegard founded the Benedictine convent of Mount St. Rupert, located near Bingen, Germany. Accompanying the abbess were over a dozen young novices and her devoted friend Volmar, who continued to serve as her secretary and scribe. At Mount St. Rupert she established a community that catered to aristocrats among the faithful, and an air of theatricality permeated the convent on feast days, when nuns dressed in flowing white robes, golden crowns atop their heads.

Due to Hildegard's growing celebrity, her move to Mount St. Rupert, and her need to review her work to be sure that it not be perceived in any way to be heretical, *Scivias* required over a decade to complete. In addition to presenting her view of the cosmos, it also contains Hildegard's ideas regarding the science of biology, among them the belief that, like plants, humans generated from seeds and inherited characteristics of their parents. As familiarity with her wide-ranging studies spread among scholars, Hildegard's study of the folk medicine of her country made her known among the common folk as a healer with miraculous powers. Beginning in 1155, when she was in her late fifties, she began to travel around Europe, preaching pacifism, promoting the Catholic faith, and spreading her ideas about science and medicine. A conservative Catholic who opposed the new religious orders that proliferated in the wake of the reforms of Pope Gregory, she also used her notoriety to encourage religious zealots to persecute sects she believed were heretical. She began to engage in an extensive correspondence with political leaders and church officials, answering requests for advice and giving prophesies. She also founded a second convent at Eibingen, Germany.

Authored Works on Nature, Medicine

Scivias was the first of many works Hildegard composed during her lifetime. An encyclopedic work on natural history, her *Physica* (*Liber Simplicis Medicinae*) contains detailed descriptions of numerous plants, animals, and geological formations existing in the abbess's native Europe, along with their German and Latin names. She categorizes her nine healing systems as Plants, Elements, Trees, Stones, Fish, Birds, Animals, Reptiles, and Metals, each group containing medicinal components. This work also includes information and medical applications for the many plants known by Hildegard to have healing powers, making the *Physica* useful to physicians advising poorer patients on the manufacture of simple home remedies. After its widespread publication during the Renaissance, Hildegard's *Physica* became a popular medical school text, making its author the first German medical writer to gain renown.

The abbess's visionary *Scivias* was followed by *Liber Vitae Meritorum,* a book of subsequent visions that Hildegard began in 1158 and finished in 1162. Her *Liber Divinorum Operum Simplicis Hominis,* finished in 1170 when its author was 64 years of age, reconciles the cosmology of *Scivias* with the notion of concentric spheres that shaped more the contemporary scientific theories of her age. In *Liber Divinorum* she focuses in detail on the relationship between the larger cosmos and the parallel, integrated "microcosm" of the human body, describing the manner in which the heavenly bodies influence the state of health of man. In the corner of several pages Hildegard is pictured receiving visions from God, a reminder to readers of the stamp of heavenly approval on her ideas. Her final book, *Causae et curae,* is a medical compendium that describes the causal relationship between the movement of the universe and the many diseases of the human body and provides medicinal cures. The importance of boiling drinking water figured prominently in her remedies. Like *Physica,* Hildegard's *Causae et curae* remained an influential work into the 16th century.

Truly a Renaissance woman, Hildegard of Bingen died in 1179 at the age of 81, and her biography was begun the following year by Benedictine monks Theodor and Godefrid, who had worked under the famed abbess at Mount St. Rupert. She quickly became known as St. Hildegard despite the fact that, while she was added to the Roman Catholic Martyrology and investigated for sainthood, she was never canonized by the Catholic Church.

Books

Bowie, Fiona, editor, *Hildegard of Bingen: Mystical Writings,* Crossroads Press, 1990.

Crane, Renate, *Hildegard: Prophet of the Cosmic Christ,* Crossroad Publishing Co., 1997.

Flanigan, Sabina, *Hildegard of Bingen, 1098-1179: A Visionary Life,* Routledge, 1998.

King-Lezneier, Anne H., *Hildegard of Bingen: An Integrated Vision,* Liturgical Press, 2001.

Maddocks, Fiona, *Hildegard of Bingen: The Woman of Her Age,* Doubleday, 2001.

Periodicals

Commonweal, May 19, 1995, Lawrence Cunningham, review of *The Letters of Hildegard of Bingen,* p. 40.

Washington Post, April 4, 1999.

World & I, January 1998.

Online

"Saint Hildegard," *Catholic Encyclopedia,* http://www .newadvent.org (October 30, 2001). □

Chester Bomar Himes

His reputation rests largely on his detective novels, which in their own right rank with the best noir fiction, but Chester Himes (1909-1984) was hardly a

man to be pigeonholed. In his lifetime he published 17 novels, more than 60 short stories, and 2 volumes of autobiography in which he detailed the pain of being an African American writer in the twentieth century.

Named for his maternal grandfather, Chester Bomar Himes was born on July 29, 1909, in Jefferson City, Missouri, the youngest son of Joseph Sandy and Estelle Bomar Himes. Himes's father was head of the mechanical department at Lincoln Institute, where he taught blacksmithing and wheelwrighting; his mother was formerly on the faculty of Georgia State College, teaching English composition and music. The Himes family led a nomadic life during Himes's early years. In 1914 they moved to Cleveland following his father's resignation from Lincoln Institute. Their stay there was brief as Himes's father accepted a position on the faculty of Alcorn College in Lorman, Mississippi. Tension between Himes's parents— attributed to his father's humble status and his mother's attempts at social climbing—soon caused a riff. Estelle Himes accepted an offer to teach in South Carolina and she took Chester and his middle brother, Joseph, Jr. However, less than a month later Estelle relocated again, this time to Augusta, Georgia. She taught music at the Haines Normal and Industrial School, which both her sons attended.

At the end of the school year the family was reunited, with the exception of the eldest son, Edward, who left home to attend Atlanta University and eventually made his way to New York. Himes's father took a position at the Branch Normal School in Pine Bluff, Arkansas, while his mother taught in local public schools. In June 1923 an accident during a chemistry demonstration on gunpowder left Joseph, Jr. blind, and Chester, who was forbidden to take part in the demonstration because of misbehavior, was despondent over his brother's injury. The family moved to St. Louis shortly thereafter, but by 1925 they were back in Cleveland.

In 1926 Himes graduated from Glenville High School in Cleveland. He planned on attending Ohio State University, and in order to earn money he worked as a busboy at the Wade Park Manor Hotel. While on the job Himes was seriously injured after he fell down an elevator shaft. The hotel was found liable and Himes was awarded a monthly disability payment. He enrolled at Ohio State but left in 1927 because of poor grades and bad health. Himes thereupon returned to Cleveland and began working as a bellhop in the Gilsey Hotel. Attracted by the seamier side of Cleveland, he began carrying a gun and hanging out at a bar and gambling club called Bunch Boy's, where he dealt blackjack. Himes soon found himself in trouble with the law. His first arrest, for passing bad checks, ended with a two-year suspended sentence, plus a five-year parole. His second arrest was far more serious: the armed robbery of an elderly couple. In December 1928 Himes was sentenced to 20 to 25 years' hard labor. He served time in the Ohio State Penitentiary from December 27, 1928. until September 21, 1934, when he was transferred to a work farm; he was paroled into his mother's custody on April 1, 1936.

In *The Quality of Hurt,* the first volume of his autobiography, Himes wrote, "I grew to manhood in the Ohio State Penitentiary. I was nineteen years old when I went in and twenty-six years old when I came out. I became a man dependent on no one but myself. I learned all the behavior patterns necessary for survival. . . . I survived, I suppose, because I knew how to gamble." Himes admitted that his explosive rage also served as a shield in prison, as did his education. It was in prison that Himes began to write, and his first stories naturally dealt with crime and criminals. "Crazy in the Stir," "To What Red Hell" (based on an infamous prison fire at the Ohio State Penitentiary), "The Visiting Hour," "Every Opportunity," "The Night's for Crying," "Strictly Business," and other stories appeared in various newspapers and magazines, including *Coronet* and *Esquire.* This early success bolstered Himes's confidence, and upon his release he began working on a prison novel, originally titled *Black Sheep.* On August 13, 1937, he married Jean Lucinda Johnson, whom he had lived with before his incarceration.

The Great Depression came upon the United States during Himes's prison term and, ironically, Himes was spared its harshest years. The Works Project Administration (WPA) was one of the New Deal programs designed to kick-start the economy, and in 1937 he went to work for the WPA, at first as a laborer and then a research assistant for the Cleveland Public Library. By 1938 Himes was working for the WPA's Federal Writers' Project, assigned to write a history of the state of Ohio and later a guide to Cleveland. In

retrospect Himes considered this one of the happier periods in his life, both personally and professionally. Himes was even writing a column (though unsigned) for the *Cleveland Daily News* titled, "This Cleveland." In March 1940 he successfully petitioned Ohio Governor Harold Burton for termination of his parole and restoration of his citizenship. Himes afterward joined the Democratic Party.

In 1941, after his term in the Federal Writers' project had expired and he could not find work in Cleveland, Himes decided to head to California. Before doing so, however, he went to work as a butler on Malabar Farm, located in the countryside southwest of Cleveland. Malabar was owned by the writer Louis Bromfield, who at the time was at the height of his popularity. Bromfield, a Pulitzer Prize winner who also wrote Hollywood screenplays, read Himes's *Black Sheep* and promised to help get it published.

Himes spent most of World War II working in the war industry in Los Angeles and California. During this time he published stories and essays in such black-run magazines as *Crisis* and *Opportunity.* By 1944 Himes was working on another novel and was awarded a Rosewald fellowship to complete it. That year he moved to New York City. He completed the 1945 novel, *If He Hollers Let Him Go,* a semi-autobiographical tale of the absurd and rage-filled life of a young, educated African American man who eventually lands a job in the shipyards. After the novel's publication Himes returned to California and began working on a new novel. When he had finished it Himes moved back to New York City. His second novel, *Lonely Crusade,* was published in 1947. The following year Himes spent two months at the famed Yaddo Writer's Colony in Saratoga Springs, New York. It seemed his career was finally on its way. However his home life suffered and by 1950 Himes and his wife had separated for good.

In 1952 Himes was again running out of money when he managed to finally sell his prison novel, now retitled *Cast the First Stone.* Unfortunately this was such an over edited version of the manuscript that it amounted almost to censorship. Even Himes's choice of a new title, *Yesterday Will Make You Cry,* was changed. It was not until 1998 that the novel was finally published in its entirety, along with Himes's preferred title. Also in 1952 Himes met a young woman who worked as an executive at the International Institute of Education; Himes's violent and often destructive affair with Vandi Haygood eventually became the basis for his 1955 novel *The Primitive* (also titled *The End of a Primitive.*). By the time that book came out, though, Himes was no longer living in the United States. In 1953 he immigrated to France already the refuge for such prominent African American writers as Richard Wright and James Baldwin. In 1954 Himes published *The Third Generation;* later that year he moved to Mallorca, a Spanish island also known as Majorca.

1956 was the real turning point in Himes's career. Marcel Duhamel, who had translated *If He Hollers Let Him Go* into French, became the editor of Gallimard publishing house's "La Sârie Noir" and persuaded Himes to write detective fiction. Since Himes's earliest published work had dealt with crime and his subsequent novels had both noirish and absurdist touches, this was not so unusual a request. Himes decided to give it a try and what resulted was a long series featuring literature's first two African American detectives, Coffin Ed and Gravedigger Jones, who were patterned after characters in a story Himes had written while in prison. The series became known as the "Harlem Cycle."

The "Harlem Cycle" and many of Himes' other novels are a mixture of elements, their violence and absurdity at times seemingly at odds with each other, while at other times serving as perfect counterpoints. As Himes himself wrote in *My Life of Absurdity*, "It never occurred to me that I was writing absurdity. Realism and absurdity are so similar in the lives of American blacks one cannot tell the difference."

The first novel in the series, published in 1957, was titled *La Reine des pommes (For Love of Imabelle)*. The novel, which won the Grand Prix in 1958 as the best detective novel of the year, introduces Coffin Ed Johnson and Gravedigger Jones. When it was finally published in the United States it was heavily re-edited, but years later was restored under the title *A Rage in Harlem*. By the time *For Love of Imabelle* was published Himes had already finished the next two books in the series, *The Crazy Kill (Couchâ dans le pain)* and *The Real Cool Killers (Il pleut des coups durs)*, both published in 1959.

Himes' next novel, *Dare Dare*, was also published in France in 1959, but did not reach its American audiences, under the title *Run Man Run*, until 1966. It is unique among the "Harlem" novels in that it does not feature Coffin Ed and Gravedigger Jones. In 1960 Himes published two more "Harlem Cycle" novels: *All Shot Up* and *The Big Gold Dream*. The early 1960s proved to be the peak of Himes' career, though not his fame. Ever the gypsy, Himes traveled widely about Europe and back and forth to the United States. He also became more deeply involved with Lesley Packard, whom he married in 1965. In 1961 he finished another novel in the "Harlem Cycle," *The Heat's On*, which, like *Run Man Run*, wasn't published in the United States until 1966. That same year, Himes also took a break from the "Harlem Cycle" with the publication of *Pinktoes*.

In 1962 Himes returned to the United States to do a film documentary about Harlem for France-Soir. The next year he published *Une Affair de viol*, published in the United States in 1984 as *A Case of Rape*. Himes suffered a stroke while in Mexico later that year, prompting his return to France. In 1965 he published *Cotton Comes to Harlem*. The best-known novel in the "Harlem Cycle," it was made into a 1970 film directed by Ossie Davis and starring Godfrey Cambridge and Raymond St. Jacques. Over the next few years Himes continued his hectic pace of travel. He and his wife moved to southern France and from there went to Paris, London, Barcelona, Sweden, and Egypt. In 1968 the couple moved to Spain and the following year built a house in Moraira. In 1969 Himes published what was to be the final volume of the "Harlem Cycle," *Blind Man with a Pistol*.

In 1972, after publishing *The Quality of Hurt*, the first volume of his autobiography, Himes went to New York, where he was recognized by the Carnegie Endowment for International Peace. In 1973 *Black on Black* was published;

it is an anthology of Himes' selected shorter works. In 1974 *The Heat's On* was filmed as *Come Back Charleston Blue*, again starring Cambridge and St. Jacques. Himes published the second volume of his autobiography, *My Life of Absurdity*, in 1976. Seven years later *Plan B* was published, though Himes himself was too ill to finish it. Featuring Coffin Ed and Gravedigger Jones, *Plan B* is a novel of African American revolution begun in the early 1970s but scrapped when Himes decided to devote his energy to his autobiography. Himes died on November 12, 1984.

Books

Himes, Chester, *My Life of Absurdity: The Autobiography of Chester Himes, Vol. II*, Doubleday, 1976.
Himes, Chester, *The Quality of Hurt: The Autobiography of Chester Himes, Vol. I*, Doubleday, 1972.
Muller, Gilbert H., *Chester Himes*, Twayne Publishers, 1989.
Sallis, James, *Chester Himes, a Life*, Walker & Company, 2000.

Periodicals

Cleveland Plain Dealer, February 1, 1998.
New Yorker, June 4, 2001.
New York Times, November 14, 1984.
St. Louis Post-Dispatch, August 20, 2000.
Times-Picayune (New Orleans, LA), April 15, 2001.

Online

"Chester Himes (1909-1984)," http://www.kirjasto.sci.fi/chimes.htm (November 7, 2001).
"Chester Himes Books: The Coffin and Gravedigger Mysteries," *Giveadamn Chester Himes*, http://www.math.buffalo.edu/~sww/HIMES/himes-coffingravedigger.htm (November 7, 2001). □

Helen Sawyer Hogg

Helen Sawyer Hogg (1905-1993) was one of the few women working as a professional astronomer during the first half of the 20th century. Making a career out of studying the variable stars of global star clusters outlining the Milky Way Galaxy, Hogg photographed over 2,000 stars and published more than 200 papers. Although she was an American who studied at Harvard, she lived most of her life in Canada and spent most of her professional career working at the Dunlap Observatory in Toronto. Not only did Hogg have a strong reputation in academics, but she was also popular among the general public due to a weekly newspaper column she wrote to explain astronomical phenomena to lay people.

Early Education

Helen Battles Sawyer Hogg was born on August 1, 1905 in Lowell, Massachusetts. Her father, Edward Everett Sawyer, was a banker and her mother, Carrie Myra (Sprague) Sawyer, was a teacher. As a child her parents strongly encouraged her to explore nature, including the stars. At the age of five she was allowed outdoors in the evening to witness the 1910 appearance of Halley's Comet. In a 1985 interview for the *Graduate,* the University of Toronto alumni magazine, Hogg recollected, "I don't remember much about the experience, but I can still visualize the thing with its lovely tail." She would become one of the few people to witness the comet twice when she saw it reappear again in 1986.

Hogg attended Lowell public schools as a child and then went to Mount Holyoke College to study chemistry in 1922. She changed her major, however, after a total eclipse of the sun on January 24, 1925. Hogg's astronomy professor, Anne Young, took her class to Connecticut to view the event, which proved to be a turning point in Hogg's academic career. A year later Hogg had the opportunity to meet astronomer Annie Cannon of the Harvard College Observatory. Cannon arranged for Hogg to attend graduate school at Harvard and work with Harlow Shapley, a renowned astronomer who specialized in global star clusters. Hogg graduated magna cum laude from Mount Holyoke in 1926 and then left for the Harvard Observatory.

Studied Global Star Clusters

Hogg was the first student of Shapley's to study global star clusters and she soon became an expert in the field. There are about 130 global clusters surrounding the Milky Way Galaxy. These clusters were the first stellar formations and each contains thousands of stars. Hogg specialized in the study of variable stars which change in size, temperature, and brightness. Information from such stars allow astronomers to calculate stellar distances which can then be used to estimate the size of the galaxy. Shapley's work in this area showed that the Milky Way was larger than previously thought and than the sun was not the center of the galaxy, which was a controversial assertion at that time.

Hogg graduated with a master's degree in 1928 and a doctorate in 1931 from Radcliffe College, since at that time Harvard did not award graduate degrees in science to women. She began teaching astronomy before she finished her graduate work. In 1927 Hogg worked as a lecturer at Smith College in Northampton, Massachusetts. and in 1930 she returned to her alma mater, Mount Holyoke, as a teacher.

In 1930 Hogg married Frank Hogg, a fellow astronomy student at Harvard who specialized in stellar spectrophotometry. Frank Hogg was from Ontario, Canada, and once they completed their graduate work the couple moved to Canada. While Frank Hogg obtained a research position at the Dominion Astrophysical Observatory in Victoria, British Columbia, Helen Hogg was not offered a position at the observatory despite her qualifications. One reason for this was that, during the Depression, it was not considered acceptable for a woman to be employed at a government service if her husband was already employed there. Fortunately, Hogg was able to pursue her research by working as a volunteer at the observatory. While women were discouraged from working in the observatory at night since the technical staff were all male, Hogg accompanied her husband while he worked and therefore gained access to the telescope and other equipment. At that time the telescope at the Dominion Observatory was the second largest in the world at 72 inches. While the Hoggs were in Victoria they had an infant daughter, Sarah, who often slept in the observatory while her parents worked.

In 1935 Frank Hogg took a job at the David Dunlap Observatory at the University of Toronto, which had a new telescope two inches larger than the one in Victoria. Helen Hogg continued to work for free until she was offered a position as a research assistant in 1936. As Hogg's professional career grew, so too did her family. In 1936 she gave birth to son David and in 1937 James was born. Hogg continued her professional activities even as she raised her three children.

Recognized as an Accomplished Astronomer

Hogg's work was painstaking and required much patience. Tracking a single star's cycle could take hundreds of days and if something interfered with the observations, such as clouds or a scheduling conflict, the astronomer had to wait a year to continue following the cycle. Hogg was able to incorporate her husband's knowledge of stellar spectrophotometry into her own work and produce extended time-exposure photographs of global clusters. This technique allowed her to discover 142 new variable stars. In 1939 Hogg published the first complete catalog of 1,116 variable stars.

During World War II Hogg was given increased responsibilities at the Dunlap Observatory since many men from the facility were called into military service. From 1940 to 1941 she was the acting chairperson of the Astronomy Department at Mount Holyoke and in 1941 she began teaching at the University of Toronto. In 1946 her husband became director of the observatory. In 1950 Hogg was awarded the prestigious Annie J. Cannon award from the American Astronomical Society for outstanding research by a woman astronomer.

On January 1, 1951, Frank Hogg died suddenly. Although Helen Hogg was left to care for their three children, she continued to forge her own career in astronomy. Her next major career move came in 1955-1956 when she became the program director of astronomy with the U.S. National Science Foundation. Then in 1957 she became full professor at the University of Toronto, a position which she held until 1976.

Introduced Astronomy to Lay People

In addition to her academic duties, Hogg took over a weekly column in the *Toronto Star* called "The Stars" that her husband had been writing until his death. Hogg used this forum to explain astronomical phenomenon to lay people. For example, in a 1975 article she explained the meaning of "a blue moon," which she said was most likely caused by certain types of dust particles that are slightly larger than a wavelength of light. These particles filter red light, but allow blue light to pass through, thereby creating the illusion of a blue moon. Hogg continued to write the popular column until 1981. Her effectiveness in writing for lay people led to her 1976 book *The Stars Belong to Everyone: How to Enjoy Astronomy.* In the foreword to the book she wrote, "Very little time is required to see and enjoy the beauties of the sky; once you come to know them, they never lose their appeal." For almost 30 years she also taught basic astronomy to non-science students.

Hogg retired from teaching in 1976 but continued to go to the observatory daily. During her long career she had taken thousands of pictures of global clusters and had published hundreds of scientific articles. As Christine Clement and Peter Broughton wrote in the *Royal Astronomical Society of Canada Journal,* Hogg's "knowledge of the sky was phenomenal. Even on cloudy nights when she was scheduled to observe at the David Dunlap Observatory, she always watched for breaks in the clouds just in case one of her 'clusters' might appear. She never missed an opportunity." Even when she was no longer able to climb the stairs to the telescope, Hogg continued to analyze and write about her photographs. She updated her first catalog of variable stars twice, in 1955 and 1973, and was working on another edition at the time of her death. In 1985 Hogg married F. E. L. Priestley, professor emeritus of English at the University of Toronto. Her passion for astronomy affected her new husband, too. He published two articles in the *Royal Astronomical Society of Canada Journal* in 1986 and 1987. However, her second marriage did not last long, for Priestley died in 1988.

Service and Legacy

Hogg was very humble about her career in astronomy. In 1985 she told the University of Toronto *Graduate,* "I don't think I've made that many earth-shaking discoveries. It's just a case of working and accumulating a lot of information in one area." Her colleagues, however, properly recognized her work. Throughout her lifetime Hogg received numerous professional awards for her contributions to astronomy. Aside from the prestigious Cannon Prize, Hogg also received the Rittenhouse Medal from the Rittenhouse Astronomical Society and the Service Award Medal from the Royal Astronomical Society of Canada, as well as six honorary degrees. She also served as a member as well as the president of many professional societies, including the Royal Astronomical Society of Canada. She also made many contributions as a pioneering woman in the field. She was the first woman president of the Royal Canadian Institute, the first woman president of the physical sciences section of the Royal Society of Canada, one of the first two women to serve as director of Bell Canada, and the founding president of the Canadian Astronomical Society. Just before her death she taped an interview for the University of Toronto to encourage young women to pursue careers in science. Hogg was also awarded honorary lifetime memberships to the Ontario Field Naturalists, the Royal Canadian Institute, the University Women's Club of Toronto, and Science North, Sudbury.

Hogg died of a heart attack in Richmond Hill, Ontario, on January 28, 1993, at the age of 87. Her contributions to astronomy have been recognized by the scientific community in many ways. In 1984 small planet 2917 which orbits between Jupiter and Mars was named Sawyer Hogg. In 1985 the Helen Sawyer Hogg lectureship was established by the Canadian Astronomical Society and the Royal Astronomical Society of Canada. Four years later the observatory a the National Museum of Science and Technology was named in her honor. In 1992 the University of Toronto named its telescope in Chile after Hogg. Her son David also pursued a career in astronomy, serving as a radio astronomer at the National Radio Astronomy Observatory and a life member of the Royal Astronomical Society of Canada.

Books

Jarrell, Richard A., *The Cold Light of Dawn: A History of Canadian Astronomy,* University of Toronto Press, 1988.

Hogg, Helen Sawyer, *The Stars Belong to Everyone: How to Enjoy Astronomy,* Doubleday Canada Unlimited, 1976.

Periodicals

Royal Astronomical Society of Canada Journal, December 1993.

Toronto Star, December 3, 1985; October 1, 1989; June 20, 1992; January 29, 1993; February 7, 1993; October 24, 1993; June 9, 1996.

Online

"Helen Sawyer Hogg: A Gift of Stars," http://www.sdsc.edu/ScienceWomen/hogg.html (October 22, 2001).

"Path of Heroes: Helen Sawyer Hogg," http://www.pch.gc.ca/poh-sdh-2000/english/routeeight/r8-hero4.html (October 22, 2001).

University of Toronto Astronomy Department Web site, http://www.astro.utoronto.ca/ (November 2, 2001). □

Buddy Holly

One of rock 'n' roll's founding fathers, Buddy Holly (1936-1959) recorded a highly influential body of work before his untimely death. Holly's unique mix of pop melodicism, aggressive rhythmic drive, and imaginative arrangement ideas directly inspired the Beatles, the Rolling Stones, and numerous other bands in the coming decades.

At age 22, a fatal plane crash made Buddy Holly into an instant rock 'n' roll legend. His string of hit records—including "That'll Be the Day," "Peggy Sue," "Oh Boy!," and "Rave On"—had made him a celebrity in America and beyond. What proved to be remarkable about Holly was that his stature increased with time, rather than fading as was typical with pop music idols. His distinctive mix of rock 'n' roll, country, and R & B served to inspire a generation of younger artists and remained vital for decades to come. In terms of both his creative output and his stage persona, Holly helped to broaden the range of possibilities within the rock 'n' roll idiom.

Holly was born Charles Hardin Holley in Lubbock, Texas on September 7, 1936. The youngest of three children, he was nicknamed "Buddy" by his mother, Ella Drake Holley. His father, Larry Holley, worked at various times as a cook, carpenter, tailor, and clothing salesman. Holly showed an early interest in music, winning a local talent contest at age five. By age 11, he had taken piano lessons and was beginning to learn guitar. During his high school years, he performed regularly on a Lubbock radio station, first with Jack Neal, then with Bob Montgomery as a partner. Eventually, a group evolved that included Holly and Montgomery on guitar and Don Guess on acoustic bass. The combo—known as Buddy and Bob and, later, the Rhythm Playboys—played country music, although Holly was beginning to take an interest in R & B and blues as well. In January of 1955 Holly saw Elvis Presley perform in Lubbock, inspiring him to play rock 'n' roll. By the time he graduated high school that same year, he was already a popular performer on the local dance and club scene.

Recording Session with Producer Owen Bradley

Playing the country/rock hybrid dubbed "rockabilly," Holly and his group opened shows for Presley, Bill Haley, and other notable acts on tour in late 1955. After meeting talent scout Eddie Crandall, he signed a recording contract with Decca Records as a solo artist and, with Sonny Curtis replacing Montgomery on guitar, went to Nashville on January 26, 1956, to record four songs. Producing these sessions was Owen Bradley, later famous as the man behind the hits of Patsy Cline. After further touring on the country-music circuit, he recorded several more tunes, including "That'll Be the Day," a song co-written by Holly and newly recruited drummer Jerry Allison. None of the songs recorded for Decca attracted much attention, and he was released from his contract.

Undaunted, Holly took his band—now including rhythm guitarist Niki Sullivan and re-named the Crickets—to the Clovis, New Mexico, studio of producer Norman Petty, known for his work with rockabilly artist Buddy Knox. In February 1957 the Crickets recorded new versions of "That'll Be the Day," "Maybe Baby," and several other tunes. Petty was impressed by the young musician's talent and attitude. "I was amazed at the intensity and honesty and sincerity of [Buddy's] whole approach to music," Petty later told author Philip Norman in an interview for *Rave On: The Biography of Buddy Holly*, ". . . . to see someone so honest and so completely himself was super-refreshing. He wasn't the world's most handsome guy, he didn't have the world's most beautiful voice, but he was himself."

The songs recorded at Petty's studio were turned down by Roulette, Columbia, RCA, and Atlantic Records before Holly placed them with Coral/Brunswick. Ironically, the label was a subsidiary of Decca, the same company that had dropped Holly the previous year. Because Decca owned the rights to the earlier recording of "That'll Be the Day," Brunswick credited the song to the Crickets upon its release in May 1957. The song was a slow-building hit, finally hitting the top of the U.S. singles charts on September 23. Holly and the Crickets spent the intervening months touring the country in package shows with other acts. They became one of the first white acts to perform at Harlem's famous Apollo Theater. Appearances on such television programs as *American Bandstand* and *The Ed Sullivan Show* further increased their visibility. The band's first album, *The Chirping Crickets,* was released by Brunswick in November 1957. "That'll Be the Day" became a major hit in Britain as well, encouraging the Crickets to tour there in March 1958.

Began His Climb up the Charts

Further singles followed, some credited to Holly, others to the Crickets. "Peggy Sue," perhaps Holly's most recognizable song, reached number three on the U.S. singles chart in January of 1958. The song's rumbling beat and stark, clear-toned guitar playing were unique for the time, as were Holly's idiosyncratic, hiccup-accented vocals. "Oh Boy," "Maybe Baby," and "Rave On" continued his success into the spring and summer of that year. These and other Holly records represented major innovations in the still-fledgling rock 'n' roll genre. His use of multi-track recording techniques and reliance on largely self-written material were widely imitated. Rather than conforming to the rock 'n' roll sex symbol image popularized by Presley, the gangling, bespectacled Holly set a different standard for pop music stardom. The instrumental line-up of the Crickets—two guitars, bass, and drums—became the prototype of countless rock bands who followed a few years later.

Compared to such flamboyant rock 'n' roll peers as Little Richard and Jerry Lee Lewis, Holly led a conservative lifestyle. Playful and exuberant on stage, he was shy and introverted when not performing and was prone to taking long solitary drives in the Texas desert. His exterior meekness disguised an inner self-confidence and drive which grew as his success increased. The summer and fall of 1958 brought considerable changes in his life. On August 15, he married Maria Elena Santiago, a publishing company receptionist Holly had met in New York two months earlier. That October he parted company with producer/manager Petty and split with the Crickets as well. His career was heading in new directions: that fall he produced the first recording by a then-unknown Waylon Jennings and began experimenting with string section backup on his own recordings. In November 1958 he recorded four songs with the Dick Jacobs Orchestra—including the Paul Anka-composed "It Doesn't Matter Anymore" and Holly's own "True Love Ways"—that found him moving away from frenetic rock 'n' roll and toward more polished pop balladry.

Tragedy in Iowa

In January 1959, Holly made what would prove to be his last recordings at his apartment in New York City's Greenwich Village. That same month, he embarked on a "Winter Dance Party" tour with a newly formed backup group which included guitarist and former Cricket Tommy Allsup, drummer Carl Bunch, and bassist Waylon Jennings. The tour, which also included such acts as J.P "Big Bopper" Richardson, Richie Valens, and Dion and the Belmonts, stopped in Clear Lake, Iowa, on February 2. Tired of traveling in his poorly heated tour bus, Holly chartered a small Beechcraft Bonanza plane to travel to the next concert stop in Moorhead, Minnesota. The plane, carrying Richardson and Valens along with Holly, took off at one a.m. in severe winter weather. It crashed a few minutes later not far from the airfield, killing all on board.

News of Holly's death at age 22 sparked a genuine sense of loss in America, Great Britain, and elsewhere. The tragedy helped to make "It Doesn't Matter Anymore" a posthumous hit, the first of many to follow. In May of 1959 Coral Records released *The Buddy Holly Story*, a retrospective album that stayed on the charts for three years and became the label's biggest-selling release. Old Holly tunes revived or discovered included "Midnight Shift," "Peggy Sue Got Married," "True Love Ways," and "Learning the Game." Former producer Petty acquired the rights to a number of Holly's recordings and released them with over dubbed additional musicians. Holly's recordings remained in print and sold well, particularly in Great Britain where the "best of" collection *20 Golden Greats* topped the charts in 1978.

The following decades demonstrated Holly's continued influence on popular music. Both the Beatles and the Rolling Stones performed and recorded his songs at the start of their careers. Such rock artists as Bob Dylan, Elton John, and Bruce Springsteen acknowledged their creative debt to Holly in interviews. Singer/songwriter Don McLean's 1971 hit "American Pie" mourned his death as "the day the music died." Linda Ronstadt, the Knack, and Blondie were among the pop/rock artists who revived his tunes in the 1970s. In 1975 Paul McCartney purchased Holly's entire song catalogue and, a year later, commemorated the late singer's 40th birthday by launching "Buddy Holly Week" in Great Britain. Recognition continued into the 1980s, when Holly became one of the Rock and Roll Hall of Fame's original inductees. Such tribute albums as 1989's *Everyday Is a Holly Day* and 1996's *Notfadeaway: Remembering Buddy Holly* featured new interpretations of his material. Holly's life was brought to the screen in the 1978 film *The Buddy Holly Story*, which earned lead actor Gary Busey an Academy Award nomination.

Over 40 years after Holly's death, his recordings continued to rank among the most significant in modern popular music. What course his work might have taken had he lived remains one of the great unanswered questions in rock 'n' roll history. Beyond such speculation, Holly's music continues to be played and enjoyed, and his presence missed.

Books

All Music Guide, edited by Michael Elewine, Vladimir Bogdanov, Chris Woodstra, and Stephen Thomas Erlewine, Miller Freeman Books, 1997.
Contemporary Musicians, Volume 1, Gale, 1989.

Goldrosen, John, *The Buddy Holly Story,* Quick Fox, 1979.

Laing, Dave, *Buddy Holly,* Collier Books, 1972.

Norman, Philip, *Rave On: The Biography of Buddy Holly,* Simon & Schuster, 1996. □

Basil Hume

The archbishop of Westminster from 1976 to his death, Cardinal Basil Hume (1923-1999) sought to increase tolerance and understanding between the Roman Catholic Church and other faiths.

As archbishop during the last quarter of the twentieth-century, Cardinal Basil Hume presided over one of the most turbulent periods of Catholicism in British history since the Protestant Reformation led by Martin Luther all but abolished the practice of Catholicism in England in the 16th century. From his office, Hume dealt with such issues as the declining in the number of practicing British Catholics, as well as abortion, female priests, birth control, homosexuality, the continued violence in Northern Ireland, the plight of the homeless, and married clergy. During his tenure as leader of the Catholic Church in the United Kingdom, Hume displayed a dislike for dogmatic observance of Vatican pronouncements. Rather than actively protest, however, Hume chose a more diplomatic approach, encouraging tolerance, diversity, and a liberal understanding of the Roman Catholic faith rather than rigid adherence. Among the views he held in conflict with Rome were the acceptance of homosexuals into the Church, the ordination of female priests, and the abandonment of the vows of chastity required of Catholic clergy. While advocating reform within the Church, however, he also supported the tenets of modernism enumerated by the Second Vatican Council of the 1960s that freed priests to celebrate the Catholic Mass in their native languages rather than in Latin. He also upheld the Church's refusal to recognize homosexual marriages. Hume was instrumental also in opening dialogues between British Catholics and British of other faiths. His diplomacy especially was noted when he worked with Pope John Paul II to allow married Anglican clergy unhappy with the Church of England's decision to ordain female priests to become Roman Catholic priests. Hume's efforts to modernize the Catholic Church were appreciated by many, although he also had his detractors. Citing Hume's quiet dissent against the Vatican as a factor weakening the Catholic Church in England, the cardinal's detractors pointed to the dramatically falling numbers of professed practicing Catholics in England as evidence of the failure of his more relaxed approach and proof that its members appreciate the structure of the traditional Church.

From Birth to the Benedictines to Westminster

Hume was born George Haliburton Hume in 1923. His father was a Protestant heart surgeon from Scotland, and his mother was a Roman Catholic from France. The couple met in France, where Hume's father was stationed during World War I. Raised as a Catholic by his mother, Hume decided to become a monk when he was 11 years old. Two years later he took the name Basil upon entering the Order of St. Benedict, and, in 1945, took the vows of a monk. At age 18 Hume was ordained a Roman Catholic priest. From the early 1950s to 1963, he coached secondary school rugby and was head of the modern languages department at Benedictine-run Ampleforth College. In 1963 he was named abbot of the monastery.

In 1976 Hume was named by the Vatican to replace Cardinal Heenan as archbishop of Westminster, traditionally the highest Catholic office held in the United Kingdom. The announcement surprised many, as an Irish clergyman traditionally occupied the post. In 1976 Hume was elevated to cardinal. He served on several Vatican-appointed committees, including as president of the Bishops's Conference of England and Wales, as chairman of the Benedictine Ecumenical Commission, and as president of the Council of European Episcopal Conferences. When he attempted to resign in the 1990s, Pope John Paul II refused his resignation, and Hume carried out the duties of his office until his death in 1999 from cancer two weeks after receiving the Order of Merit from Queen Elizabeth II. Called a "personal gift of the queen," the distinction is limited to only 26 living people, and represented the first instance of a Catholic receiving the honor.

Viewed as England's Spiritual Leader

Hume was perceived as the man largely responsible for creating an active spiritual dialogue with the Anglican Church, the most influential church in England. His popularity endeared him to Catholics and Anglicans alike, and through his efforts Hume was able to create a truly ecumenical conversation among all faiths, Jews and other Protestant faiths included. In his first act as archbishop of Westminster, Hume led Benedictine monks in singing Vespers at the Anglican Westminster Abbey for the first time since the Protestant Reformation. Among the many homilies he delivered as part of the Catholic Common Ground initiative was one titled "One in Christ: Unity and Diversity in the Church Today." He also urged acceptance of non-Catholic Christians who wished to partake of such Catholic sacraments as the Eucharist, reconciliation, and the anointing of the sick. These efforts caused Hume to be considered the spiritual leader of England despite the fact that the official Church of England is the Anglican Church.

Through Hume's efforts, the Catholic Church gained acceptance as a native church for the first time since Henry VIII established the Anglican church as a means to secure personal ends. The Penal Laws put in place during Henry's reign, which were repealed in the early 1960s, had continued to inspire prejudicial behavior against British Catholics through the 1970s. Hume's stance did much to end such prejudice. For his many supporters, however, Hume also had his detractors. Such staunch Roman Catholics as Auberon Waugh considered Hume a "profoundly silly man," while Free Presbyterian minister Reverend Neil Ross echoed traditional Reformation attitudes in declaring that the only destination for a man answering to the Vatican in Rome is hell.

Hume supported an open debate over the policies of the Catholic Church, telling the *National Catholic Reporter:* "I ask myself whether it is even sensible to stifle debate in the church. . . . I am constantly being urged to suppress this group or that, drive out of the church this lot or that. I do not believe this is right. I believe that as a bishop I have to try to lead people from where they are to where they never dreamt they might go." On matters of sexuality, he often demurred by explaining that he had no direct experience with the subject. He famously put off a television host's questions about a priest's vow of celibacy when asked how Hume would react if a physically attractive woman were to enter the room. Hume responded that he was married to the Church, then asked the married host how he'd respond under similar circumstances. On homosexuality, Hume wrote a paper in 1993 urging homosexuals against feeling "a sense of guilt and . . . think[ing] of themselves as unpleasing to God. On the contrary, they are precious to God." He also interceded on behalf of social and economic injustice, arguing for the release of reputed Irish Republican Army terrorists imprisoned on circumstantial evidence; persuading the Thai government to release a British woman suspected of drug smuggling; and visiting Ethiopia during the 1985 famine and lobbying European nations to send increased assistance. In 1986 he joined Pope John Paul II at a gathering of world religious leaders at Assisi to pray for

world peace. In his later years, he concerned himself with such issues as human rights, homelessness, and nuclear disarmament. He also organized seminars on business and moral standards in the former European communist-bloc nations, the arms race, and debt-relief for impoverished third-world countries.

Books

Cross, F. L., and E. A. Livingstone, editors, *The Oxford Dictionary of the Christian Church,* Oxford University Press, 1997.
New Catholic Encyclopedia: The Wojtyla Years, Catholic University of America, 2000.

Periodicals

Christian Century, July 10, 1999.
Daily Telegraph (London, England), June 22, 1999; June 26, 1999; July 14-21, 1999.
Financial Times, June 19, 1999.
Guardian, June 21, 1999.
Independent, January 20, 2000.
Irish Times, July 3, 1999; August 4, 1999.
National Catholic Reporter, July 2, 1999; July 16, 1999.
New Statesman & Society, September 20, 1996.
New York Times, June 18, 1999.
Publishers Weekly, February 21, 2000; November 27, 2000; August 13, 2001.
Spectator, July 3, 1999. □

John Marcellus Huston

As the most important member of a Hollywood family dynasty whose professional roots were planted in vaudeville, John Huston (1906-1987) left an indelible mark on American cinema as a director, writer, and actor.

The son of actor Walter Huston and Rhea Gore Huston, John Huston was born in Nevada, Missouri, on August 5, 1906. He was named for his maternal grandfather. At age four Huston's parents separated; they divorced in 1912. His father, who had temporarily quit vaudeville to take various jobs as an electrical engineer, decided to return to his true calling and left for New York. John and his mother moved to Dallas. In 1916 Huston was diagnosed as having an enlarged heart and Bright's disease, or nephritis, a sometimes fatal kidney disease. For the next two years Huston and his mother (who had remarried) traveled around the United States to get the opinions of various doctors. He was a sickly child. After they moved to Phoenix, they decided that a recommended cure of a strict diet and sweat baths was harmful. Once back on a normal regimen, he regained his health.

At age 13, living in southern California, Huston and a friend were arrested for juvenile delinquency after setting fire to a condemned building. Huston was sent to a detention home. After his release his mother enrolled him in the San Diego Army and Military Academy, where he stayed for six months before returning to public school in Los Angeles.

He went to Lincoln Heights High School because of its boxing program. He eventually compiled a 23-2 amateur record as a lightweight. A magazine article on futurism got him interested in art, and he enrolled first in the Smith Art School and later the Art Students League. In 1924 Huston moved to New York, where his father's guidance provided a new direction for his creative passion.

Acted with his Father

By 1924 vaudeville veteran Walter Huston had scored his first successes in the legitimate theater. That year John Huston had a small role in *The Easy Mark,* a play that starred his father. Huston acted in two other plays in 1924, Sherwood Anderson's *The Triumph of the Egg* and *Ruint.*

Acting soon took a backseat to creative writing. Huston's first published piece, in 1929, was a short story, "Fool." It was published by H.L. Mencken in his *American Mercury* magazine, which paid Huston $200. Other stories soon followed.

In 1929, Huston eloped with Dorothy Harvey. That year also marked Huston's film acting debut, in the short *Two Americans* for Paramount Pictures. *Two Americans* also starred Huston's father. In 1930 his puppet play, *Frankie and Johnny,* went over well in New York and was nearly produced for the legitimate stage, starring Fanny Brice.

Early Hollywood Years

For Huston the 1930s marked his transition from the theater to film and from acting to screenwriting. During the decade he acted in only one play—*The Lonely Man* in 1937—and no films. Except for a few cameo appearances, Huston would not act again in films until the 1960s. After the success of *Frankie and Johnny,* Huston began working as a scriptwriter for Universal Studios, contributing to three films in 1932: *A House Divided, Law and Order* (both of which starred his father), and *Murders in the Rue Morgue.* Huston wrote much of the dialogue for these pictures.

As his professional life was on the upswing, his personal life took a turn for the worse. Living the fast life, he began neglecting Dorothy, who descended into alcoholism as his infidelities became more apparent. During the first half of 1933, Huston was arrested twice for drunk driving and in September of that year his car struck and killed a woman. He was cleared by a grand jury when the evidence proved that he had a green light when he hit the woman, but Universal let him go. He and his wife divorced. Huston went to Great Britain and worked on two films for Gaumont-British.

Huston married Lesley Black in 1937 and returned to Hollywood to work as a scriptwriter for Warner Brothers on the film *Jezebel.* In 1939, loaned out to Goldwyn-United Artists, he worked (though without being credited) on the script for *Wuthering Heights.* He also earned his first Academy Award nomination for his screenplay for *Dr. Erhlich's Magic Bullet.*

In 1940, Huston directed his father in the play *A Passenger to Bali.* In his autobiography, *An Open Book,* Huston assessed his first directorial effort as "an honorable failure, even though it closed after only a few performances."

Succeeded as a Director

After the play closed, Huston went back to Warner Brothers and received his second Academy Award nomination for the screenplay for *Sergeant York.* He also collaborated with W.R. Burnett on the screenplay of Burnett's novel, *High Sierra.* The film was the turning point in the careers of Huston and actor Humphrey Bogart, who was the fifth choice to play the role of Roy Earle, the film's protagonist. The success of *High Sierra* convinced Warner Brothers to allow Huston to direct his first film, *The Maltese Falcon.*

Released in 1941, *The Maltese Falcon* made Bogart into a star, and Walter Huston had a small part in the film. John Huston got another Oscar nomination. From then on Huston was primarily a director, though he also wrote screenplays for films he did not direct, notably *The Killers* and *The Stranger,* both released in 1946.

During World War II, Huston was commissioned as a lieutenant in the Army Signal Corps. His military service involved making documentary films about the military in the Aleutians and in Italy. His final documentary for the Signal Corps, *Let There Be Light,* narrated by Walter Huston, was about the treatment of "psychoneurotic" combat veterans. The film was made in 1946 but was suppressed by the Army for more than 30 years. Also in 1946 Huston divorced

Lesley Black and married actress Evelyn Keyes; they divorced in 1950. After the war, Huston returned to the theater, directing Jean-Paul Sartre's play *No Exit* on Broadway. Huston wanted to film *No Exit,* but nothing ever came of it.

In 1948 Huston returned to film directing in Hollywood, making another classic, *The Treasure of the Sierra Madre.* Huston wrote the screenplay and also made a brief appearance in the film, which again starred Bogart and Walter Huston. John Huston won Academy Awards for best director and best screenplay and Walter Huston won for best supporting actor. While filming the movie Huston took in a thirteen-year-old Mexican boy, Pablo Albarran, and adopted him. In later years the two became estranged and lost contact. In addition to Pablo, Huston had four other children: Tony, Anjelica, Danny, and Allegra.

By this time Huston was an admired film director with a unique method of working. Peter Flint, writing in the *New York Times* after Huston's death, noted that Huston "edited cerebrally so that financial backers would have trouble trying to cut scenes. He made brilliantly evocative use of color . . . closely supervised all stages of production" and always worked within his budget. In *Open Book* Huston discussed his preferred method of shooting scenes in sequence. "Even more important is the sense of storytelling—the cadence and rhythm that's in the director's subconscious. Jumping back and forth in time is interruptive." Besides *The Treasure of the Sierra Madre,* Huston also directed and co-wrote (with Richard Brooks) *Key Largo* in 1948. In the early 1950s Huston had another success with *The African Queen,* which he directed and co-wrote with James Agee.

Opposed Red-Baiting

In the late 1940s and early 1950s U.S. Senator Joseph McCarthy initiated the "Red Scare," and the effect on the film and television industries was the infamous blacklist. In late 1947 Huston, along with writer Philip Dunne and director William Wyler, formed the Committee for the First Amendment (CFA), trying to counter the influence of McCarthy's House Un-American Activities Committee (HUAC). But when Hollywood producers went along with the blacklist, the CFA was doomed. In 1950, Huston, along with Wyler and director John Ford, successfully opposed an attempt to have Joseph L. Mankiewicz removed as president of the Screen Directors Guild after Mankiewicz refused to take a loyalty oath.

The day after his divorce from Evelyn Keyes, Huston married Enrica (Ricky) Soma, a ballerina. In 1953 the financial success of *Moulin Rouge* allowed Huston to immigrate to Ireland, which remained his permanent residence until 1978; Huston became an Irish citizen in 1964. By then he had separated from Ricky Soma; she died in an auto crash in 1969. In 1972 he married Celeste Shane and divorced her in 1975.

The variety of Huston's directorial output never abated. In the 1950s he directed such films as *Moby Dick* (1956) and the war movie, *Heaven Knows Mr. Allison* (1957). Films he directed in the 1960s included *The Misfits* (1961), *The List of Adrian Messenger* (1963), *The Night of the*

Iguana (1964), *The Bible* (1966), and *Reflections in a Golden Eye* (1967). Among Huston's films from the 1970s were *The Kremlin Letter* (1970), *The Life and Times of Judge Roy Bean* (1972), and *The Man Who Would Be King* (1975). Also during that decade Huston managed to balance his directing responsibilities with numerous acting roles. Though some of his appearances were in his own films, his best-known role was playing the manipulative Noah Cross in *Chinatown,* directed by Roman Polanski.

Final Years

In the 1980s Huston's output, though diminished due to illness, remained as varied as ever. His movies included *Wise Blood* (1980), *Annie* (1982), *Under the Volcano* (1984), *Prizzi's Honor* (1985), and *The Dead* (1987). *Prizzi's Honor* costarred Huston's eldest daughter, Anjelica, who received an Academy Award for best supporting actress. The film received four Golden Globe Awards including best director. *The Dead* was released posthumously.

Huston's first serious brush with death occurred in 1977 when an aneurysm required emergency surgery and an abdominal blockage forced a second operation. In his later years Huston suffered from emphysema, which was the cause of his death on August 28, 1987, in Middletown, Rhode Island. By then Huston was an icon in the film community. Just three months before his death he testified (on videotape) before a congressional committee in opposition to the colorization of black-and-white films. In 1980 he was honored by the Film Society of Lincoln Center; in 1983 came the American Film Institute's Life Achievement Award. He was honored at the 1984 Cannes Film Festival "for the entirety of his work and his extraordinary contribution to the cinema," and in 1985 he was given the D.W. Griffith Career Achievement Award.

Books

Ceplair, Larry and Steven Englund, *The Inquisition in Hollywood: Politics in the Film Community, 1930-1960,* Anchor Press/ Doubleday, 1980.
Grobel, Lawrence, *The Hustons,* Charles Scribner's Sons, 1989.
Huston, John, *An Open Book,* Alfred A Knopf, 1980.

Periodicals

Los Angeles Times, February 13, 1985; June 4, 1987; August 29, 1987; August 29, 1987.
Newsweek, May 19, 1980.
New York Times, January 16, 1981; March 5, 1983; May 24, 1984; May 13, 1987; August 29, 1987; September 6, 1987.
Toronto Star, December 19, 1985.

Online

"John Marcellus Huston," *Internet Movie Data Base,* http://us .imdb.com/Name?Huston%2C + John (October 21, 2001). □

Ida Henrietta Hyde

A pioneering neurophysiologist and supporter of allowing women to pursue studies in the sciences

despite a prevailing gender bias, Dr. Ida Henrietta Hyde (1857-1945) was the first woman to earn a Ph.D. in science at Heidelberg University in Germany. She pursued original zoological research on animal cardiac movement, circulation, respiration, and nervous systems. In addition to laboratory work, teaching, and scholarly writing, Hyde assisted other women locate scholarships, education, and jobs suited to their talents and professional aspirations.

Born in Davenport, Iowa, on September 8, 1857, Henrietta Hyde was one of four children born to Chicago businesswoman Babette Loewenthal and Meyer Heidenheimer, a merchant. The Heidenheimers altered their surname to Hyde after emigrating from Germany. Her mother supported the family, who lost both residence and business in the great Chicago Fire of 1870.

Advancement by Slow Degrees

In her teens, Hyde apprenticed at hat-making at an urban clothing factory and toiled at the trade for seven years. She longed to study at the Athenaeum, a Chicago Museum, and spent her work-day lunch breaks reading a discarded biology book she retrieved from a packing crate. Intrigued by science, she walked several miles to work and saved her unspent car fare to pay college tuition for night classes at the University of Illinois. At her brother's graduation from the university, she met female student role models and longed to be a part of academic life and to increase her knowledge of living things.

Against her family's wishes, Hyde took entrance exams at the University of Illinois. After her brother became ill, she temporarily shelved her plans for higher education and tended him at home. In 1881, on limited savings, she enrolled at the university for one year to study natural history, the basis for a teaching job. While instructing seven- and eight-year-olds for seven years in Chicago public schools, she compiled a system-wide science curriculum.

Prepared for a Career in Laboratory Research

Discontent in the classroom, Hyde completed a B.S. degree in pre-medicine at Cornell University in three years and initiated graduate study at Bryn Mawr College in Pennsylvania under Dr. Jacques Loeb, an expert on physiochemical processes in animals. During the summer, as the first female researcher at Woods Hole Marine Laboratory Corporation, a scholarly consortium operated in Massachusetts by the U.S. Fish Commission, Hyde analyzed octopus embryos, jellyfish development, and the respiration of grasshoppers, horseshoe crabs, skates, amphibians, and mammals. In 1892, as an official Woods Hole investigator, she lectured on the anatomy and embryology of *Scyphomedusae,* the class of sea animals comprised of jellyfish and other gelatinous organisms.

Hyde's work in zoology impressed a colleague, Professor Goette. Her findings regarding the neurophysiology of vertebrates and invertebrates ended a longstanding scholarly dispute between Goette and a colleague named Klaus who taught in Vienna. Goette extended to Hyde an invitation to conduct further research at the University of Strassburg, France. She paid her tuition with a fellowship she received from the Association of Collegiate Alumnae, later known as the American Association of University Women.

A Challenge to Academic Gender Bias

Hyde's laboratory work was so advanced and thorough that Professor Goette offered her reports to the academic committee in lieu of a doctoral dissertation. Because the university was governed by a heavy-handed Prussian sexism, the academic staff rejected her petition to take final exams and, solely on the basis of gender, refused to grant her a doctorate in physiology. With a stipend from the Association of Collegiate Alumnae, Hyde transferred to the University of Heidelberg, where a more liberal staff objectively evaluated her achievements and admitted her as a doctoral candidate.

Despite being enrolled in the biology Ph.D. program, Hyde faced a new obstacle in the person of physiologist Dr. Wilhelm Kuhne, a noted researcher who coined the word "enzyme." Kuhne refused to seat her in lectures and labs, which had been limited to males since the Middle Ages. For six semesters, she studied independent of the classroom and of hands-on laboratory projects by poring over his assistants' notes and lab sketches. After a four-hour oral examination by Kuhne's academic committee, she earned the professor's respect and proved her worthiness for a Ph.D. However, instead of the *summa cum laude* degree she qualified for, Kuhne conferred a doctorate *multa cum laude superavit*—Latin for "She overcame with much praise." Kuhne concocted the belittling phrase to acknowledge her brilliance, yet reserve the highest honors for male students only.

On Kuhne's recommendation, Hyde earned a postdoctoral position at the Heidelberg-supported research program at the Naples Marine Biological Laboratory, where she studied the nature and function of salivary glands. To ease the lives of subsequent female staff members, Hyde arranged for a permanent visiting professorship for women. After more research at the University of Berne, Switzerland, she obtained a fellowship to Radcliffe College of Harvard University and became the first female researcher at Harvard Medical School. Her laboratory findings resulted in an article, "The Effect of Distention of the Ventricle on the Flow of Blood through the Walls of the Heart," which she published in 1898 in the first issue of the *American Journal of Physiology.*

A Rigorous, Eventful Career

At age 41, Hyde joined the staff at the University of Kansas under the counsel of Chancellor Francis H. Snow, who admired her accomplishments and chose her to strengthen the physiology program at the university's medical school. As an associate professor, she taught undergraduates and developed new curriculum. Simultaneously, she wrote articles on cell study for the University of Kansas

Science Bulletin and issued two textbooks, *Outlines of Experimental Physiology* (1905) and *Laboratory Outlines of Physiology* (1910), the latter widely adopted as an undergraduate research manual.

Hyde, who never found fulfillment in teaching, sought outside projects that could benefit from her knowledge of living organisms and possibly lead to scientific breakthroughs. She analyzed the effect of oxygen deprivation on grasshopper brains, studied the effects of music on human listeners' blood pressure, and published findings on the breathing, heart action, and blood flow in skates. Her extensive laboratory findings resulted in numerous articles on developing embryos and on the microtechniques of cell study. For her incisive writings contributing to the knowledge of cell and organ function, in 1902 Hyde was named the first female member of the American Physiological Society.

Even after the University of Kansas promoted Hyde to full professor and appointed her to chair its newly created physiology department, sexism continued to dominate academia. She earned a lower salary than male professors having comparable rank, achievements, and duties. The University's board of regents denied her funding for compiling and publishing a laboratory guide for student use. Undeterred, Hyde continued to press for full participation for women in all phases of school life. Among her pro-woman innovations at the university was the addition of restroom facilities to the science building for female faculty and students.

Hyde refused to let gender bias diminish her enthusiasm or intrude on her personal principles and educational methods. She instructed classes on hygiene, public health, human reproduction, and sexually transmitted disease, intimate subjects generally avoided by polite society. To avoid shocking any students with a direct discussion of human sexuality, she read lines of poetry referring to human and animal reproduction. In lieu of anatomical charts of male and female, during lectures referencing such matters she pointed to the organs of nude Greek and Roman statues.

Later Career

Hyde did some of her most satisfying work late in her career. At age 55 she completed the remaining requirements for a medical degree at Chicago's Rush Medical College. To educate Kansans on promiscuous sex and disease, she carried classroom lessons on gonorrhea and syphilis to factory women. To prevent crippling and death from spinal meningitis and tuberculosis, she teamed with medical doctors to examine school children. For her volunteerism and promotion of state health in women and children, in 1918, Governor Arthur Capper named Hyde chair of the Kansas Women's Committee on Health, Sanitation, and National Defense. During World War I President Woodrow Wilson selected her to chair the U.S. Women's Commission on Health and Sanitation.

In 1920, the year American women gained the right to vote, Hyde retired from teaching. She continued her involvement in both academic pursuits and the attainment of rights for female scientists. On return to Heidelberg, she studied the effects of radiation on human tissue, the syndrome that killed Nobel Price-winning physicist Marie Curie. Hyde also funded scholarships at Cornell University and established the Ida H. Hyde Scholarship for the Biological Sciences at the University of Kansas, which funds educational opportunities for female researchers in biological, chemical, or physical research. One of the university's first endowments, it set a standard for supporting females in pursuit of higher education. With $25,000 of her own money, she later endowed the Ida H. Hyde Woman's International Fellowship of the American Association of University Women. In June 1938, she criticized 19th-century gender discrimination in "Before Women Were Human Beings: Adventures of an American in German Universities in the '90s," a darkly humorous autobiographical article about her experiences at Heidelberg University that appeared in the *Journal of the American Association of University Women.*

On August 22, 1945, Hyde died from cerebral hemorrhage at her home in Berkeley, California; she was 88 years old. History has since lauded her for developing a micro-electrode powerful enough to stimulate tissue chemically or electronically and small enough to inject or remove tissue from a cell. This multi-use device, which records the electrical activity within cells, has since revolutionized the study of contractile nerve tissue.

Books

American Women in Science, ABC-CLIO, 1994.
Book of Women's Firsts, Random House, 1992.
Larousse Dictionary of Women, Larousse, 1996.
Notable American Women: The Modern Period, Harvard University Press, 1980.
Notable Women in the Life Sciences: A Biographical Dictionary, Greenwood Press, 1996.
Notable Women Scientists, Gale, 2000.
Women of Science: Righting the Record, Indiana University Press, 1990.

Periodicals

American Physiological Society Bulletin, 1981.
Creative Woman Quarterly, Spring 1978.
Journal of the American Association of University Women, June 1938.
Physiologist, December 1981.

Online

"Ida Hyde Scholarship," http://kuhttp.cc.ku.edu/cwis/units/biol/bhawk00/hyde.html (December 23, 2001).
"Women in Science and Engineering," http://ublib.buffalo.edu/libra . . . /units/sel/exhibits/women.html (December 23, 2001). □

I

Tadashi Imai

Tadashi Imai (1912-1991) was one of Japan's most prolific and controversial 20th-century film directors. He infused his staunch left-wing political views into almost all his films, sometimes succeeding in combining masterful art with social criticism, but at other times crafting didactic films that succeeded only as propaganda.

The son of a priest, Tadashi Imai was born in Tokyo in 1912. He rebelled against authority from a young age, showing a disdain for traditional religion, culture, and social structure. During the time Imai was a teen, dissent from the official ideology was considered a capital crime in Japan, so the young man's political views were highly dangerous. At the Imperial University in Tokyo in the early 1930s, Imai became heavily involved in leftist political causes. Although arrested twice for his role in protests, he was released both times.

In 1934 Imai began writing screenplays as a vehicle for expressing his strong political beliefs, and the first became the 1939 feature film *Numazu Heigakkô ("The Numazu Military Academy")*, released in 1939, a scathing although amateurish profile of one of Japan's most prestigious military training grounds.

Despite his left-wing political views, Imai became a staunch supporter of Japanese imperial power during World War II. His films released during that period were little more than wartime propaganda in support of Emperor Hirohito's regime. After the war, however, Imai gradually returned to making topical films that displayed a more and more overt Marxist bent. His immediate post-war films, few of which garnered any substantial international audience, included political thrillers such as 1946's *Minshu no Teki ("Enemy of the People")*, the intriguing 1947 film *24 Hours of a Secret Life,* starring Setsuko Hara, and *Aoi Sanmyaku ("The Green Mountains")*, released in 1949.

While most Japanese directors were making safe, noncontroversial historical dramas or contemporary light comedies and romances, Imai continually ventured into socially volatile territory during Japan's long years of recovery from losing the war. While his *Mata Au Hi Made ("Until We Meet Again")*, released in 1950, enjoyed limited exposure abroad, films such as *Dokkoi Ikiteru* (1950), *Himeyuri No To* (1953), and *Susureba Koso* (1954) did not receive much attention outside Japan.

Achieved International Notoriety

Imai's films sometimes drew on the works of modern writers trying to break through Japan's postwar cultural and social malaise. *Nigorie* (1954) is a three-part film based on the short stories of Ichiyo Higuchi. Here Imai casts a penetrating gaze on the difficulties faced by three young Japanese women: one is cruelly abused in an arranged marriage; another is a prostitute thwarted in her efforts to gain respectable employment; and yet another is a young servant whose rich employers make her life hellish.

In the mid-1950s, Imai directed *Koko Ni Izumi Ari* and then *Mahiru No Ankoku,* the second film which first gained him significant attention in the United States under the titles *Darkness at Midnight, Darkness at Noon* or *Darkness at Midday.* A crime thriller and courtroom drama, the film concerns a young loner who confesses to the grisly murder of an older married couple and then fingers two men as accomplices. Their cases are railroaded through the legal

255

system and are all found guilty before the full truth about the murder is known.

By the mid-1950s Imai had gained a reputation as a filmmaker who championed the working classes. His 1957 film, *Kome* ("The Rice People") is a typical example of his focus and became a controversial but acclaimed entry at the Cannes Film Festival. In the film a group of struggling rice farmers attempt to fend off government bureaucrats and predatory corporate interests. A group of young rebels among them refuse to follow their ancestors as rice growers, instead making their living by fishing and stealing from other farmers.

Imai continued to direct films at a prodigious rate in the late 1950s. *Jun'ai Monogatari* ("The Story of a Pure Love") and *Yoru no Tsuzani*—released to English-speaking audiences under the titles *The Adulteress, The Adulterous Wife*, or *Night Drum*—each dealt with the intersecting problems of romantic relationships and social conventions. Filmed in 1957, *Jun'ai Monogatari* was a big success at the 1958 Berlin Film Festival. It concerns a young couple who are battling against a society that stymies their love. The young woman is a victim of the U.S. bombing of Hiroshima in 1945. She has anemia and is slowly dying, and her condition is worsened by the repeated beatings she has to endure in a reformatory. Set in 18th-century Japan, *Yoru no Tsuzani* depicts a man who neglects his wife and is frequently gone from home. When in desperation the wife turns to another man for comfort, she becomes a social outcast. The law demands that both the adulterous wife and her lover be executed. The woman's husband, realizing his own neglect is to blame, attempts to persuade the authorities not to carry out their responsibilities.

In 1959 Imai released *Kiku To Isamu* ("Kiko and Isamu"), a film about two young boys growing up in poverty. Both boys are subject to prejudice and discrimination because their fathers were black American GI's stationed in Japan as part of the postwar American occupation. Imai is unsparing in his depiction of Japanese racism.

Continued Wide-Ranging Examination of Japanese Society

Imai's prolific pace slowed a bit in the 1960s. He made a samurai film titled *Bushido Zankoku Monogatari* that was distributed to English-speaking audiences as *Oath of Obedience, Cruel Tales of Bushido* and *Cruel Story of the Samurai's Way*. Some critics hailed the film as a masterpiece, making it perhaps Imai's best-known work. He followed with *Echigo Tsutsuishi Oyashirazu* in 1964 and *Adauchi* ("Revenge") the following year, neither of which received wide distribution outside Japan. Later in the decade he returned to prominence with three films of uneven quality. 1967's *Satogashi Ga Kowareru Toki* ("When the Cookie Crumbles") was based on a novel by Aiyako Sono about a Japanese actress whose life resembles that of Marilyn Monroe. *Fushin No Taki* ("The Time of Reckoning") transforms a screwball-comedy plot into a sober study of a successful businessman with serious relationship problems involving three women: his wife of ten years who announces she is pregnant by another man; a mistress who wants to have a

baby with him; and an ex-lover who claims he fathered her son.

In 1969, Imai's *Hashi no Nai Kawa* ("The River without a Bridge") returned to his favorite subject: the plight of the working classes. In the movie, newly freed peasant laborers battle bias as they try to win their freedom and equality in modern Japan. Imai makes the plot into a farcical black comedy that ends up with a class struggle over a prize flag won in a friendly local competition that turns serious.

After two unremarkable films in the early 1970s—*Aa Koe Naki Tomo* (1972) and *Kaigun Tokubetsu Shonen Hei* (1973)—Imai made the biographical film *Takiji Kobayashi* in 1974. The title character is a Japanese writer whose life was tragic. Raised in poverty in the Japanese countryside, he fell in love with a prostitute who would not marry him and instead married a woman he did not love. Kobayashi's writings betrayed his leftist views, and the Imperial authorities arrest him and tortured him to death in 1933. His works were banned until after the war and only later was his greatness acknowledged. In making this film Imai returned to the struggles of his own youth, and the film gained considerable acclaim worldwide as one of the director's most potent and effective efforts.

Continuing to alternate between overtly political films and others that focused on personal relationships, Imai made *Yoba* and *Ani Imouto* ("Older Sister, Younger Brother") in 1976. *Ani Imouto* is the story of a loving but tempestuous sibling relationship as a brother becomes upset when his sister becomes pregnant and beats up her lover. In 1980's *Kosodate Gokko* ("The Proper Way"), Imai sent a surprising message of protest against modern liberal education with a story about a childless couple who take care of the rebellious daughter of a pompous academician. They straighten her out by using old-fashioned teaching methods.

One of Imai's most powerful films was released in 1982. *Himeyuri no To* (literally, "Himeyuri Lily Tower") takes the point of view of a group of Japanese nurse trainees working in Okinawa during World War II. They cheerily tend to their duties caring for the wounded in between potent scenes of brutality by both the U.S. and Japanese armed forces during their decisive battle. Imai condemns both sides in his saga about the U.S. invasion of Okinawa. The film was a huge box-office hit in Japan but didn't translate well for American audiences.

Final Efforts

After having made films for nearly half a century, Imai tried something new as he approached age 70: an animated featured released as *Yuki the Snow Fairy*. Set in feudal Japan, the film focuses on Yuki, an adolescent goddess whose task is to clean up the Earth, both by ridding it of oppressive authorities and by covering it with a blanket of snow. She tames a wild stallion and stirs up a peasant revolt. The animation is whimsical but the message is a bit heavy handed. Now in his late 70s, Imai directed his final and most significant films, *Senso to Seishin* ("War and Youth"). In a prologue, a contemporary Japanese schoolgirl (played by actress Yuki Kudo) tries to discover facts about the war from her father, whose memories are too painful for him to share. Then she learns about her mute aunt's dead child, who was lost during the Allied firebombing of Tokyo in 1945. The film then shifts to tell the story of the aunt (also played by Kudo), and how she loses her husband and child in the chaos of the air raids. Imai used donations from air raid survivors to underwrite the film so he could make and distribute it without the control of major studios, thus capping his career with a thought-provoking, powerful film made completely independently. A few months after its international release, Imai died in Toyko.

Online

"Tadashi Imai," *All-Movie Guide,* http://www.allmovie.com/ (February 23, 2002).
"Tadashi Imai," *Internet Movie Database,* http://us.imdb.com/ (February 23, 2002). □

John Irving

One of a few modern best-selling writers who also has literary stature, John Irving (born 1942) rose to prominence in 1979 with his fourth novel, *The World According to Garp.* His novels have combined 19th century traditions with modern-day melodrama, sex, and random violence. In 2000, his screenplay adaptation of *The Cider House Rules* won an Academy Award.

Beginnings in Academic Life and Wrestling

Born John Wallace Blunt, Jr., in Exeter, New Hampshire, Irving grew up in academia. His mother, Frances, and father, an Army Air Force pilot, divorced before Irving was born and at age six Irving's mother remarried. Her new husband adopted Irving, giving him the name he is known by today. Absent parents played major roles in Irving's later novels, but in real life Irving grew up satisfied to have his stepfather and never met his biological father. His stepfather, Colin, taught history at the exclusive Phillips Exeter Academy. Irving enjoyed the rights of a faculty child, gaining automatic entry into Exeter, despite his poor grades. It was years before anyone realized he suffered from undiagnosed dyslexia.

During his time at Exeter, Irving took up wrestling, and it became a lifelong pursuit that spilled over into his novels. Beyond being an integral part of his novels, Irving credited wrestling with preparing him for life. Comparing writing and wrestling, Irving explained to Joan Smith of the on-line publication *Salon,* "I think what success I've had is more a testimony to my stamina, to my ability to work hard and work long than it is to any talent I would consider God-given or natural." Irving said that he loved wrestling because it was the first thing he was good at. He has often spoken of his first coach, Ted Seabrooke, as a major influence on his life.

After graduating from Exeter in 1961, Irving followed his interest in wrestling to the University of Pittsburgh. The following year, Irving transferred to New Hampshire and won a grant to study in Europe in 1963-64. He chose the University of Vienna Institute of European Studies because it seemed an exotic atmosphere, a place where he found a sense of anonymity and learned to "pay attention." Austria was central to Irving's first five novels.

In August 1964, Irving married photographer Shyla Leary whom he had met in Cambridge. He re-enrolled in the University of New Hampshire (where he had briefly studied earlier) in 1965. His first son, Colin, was born the same year Irving received a B.A. degree cum laude. Irving would point to the importance of becoming a father and how it later shaped his view of the world as a dangerous place. He told *People's* Kim Hubbard, "I think the anxiety of being a parent—that's really been my sense of myself." While at New Hampshire, Irving had two short stories published—"A Winter Branch" in a 1965 issue of *Redbook* and "Weary Kingdom" in a 1968 *Boston Review.*

Now fully focused on writing, Irving moved his family to Iowa so he could attend the prestigious University of Iowa Writer's Workshop. Once there, he studied with Vance Bourjaily and Kurt Vonnegut. *Setting Free the Bears,* published in 1968, was well reviewed but sold modestly. It was the first of several books in which bears would play a key role.

After earning his M.F.A. in 1967, Irving had a university writing career that spanned ten years. It included grants from Rockefeller Foundation in 1972, the National Endowment for the Arts fellowship in 1974, and the Guggenheim in 1976. Over the coming years, Irving would teach at Windham College in Putney, Vermont; Mount Holyoke College in Massachusetts; the Writer's Workshop in Iowa; and Bread Loaf Writers' Conference in Middlebury, Vermont. He helped make ends meet by coaching wrestling.

Following the release of *Bears,* Irving lived in Putney, Vermont, and in Vienna. His second son, Brendan, was born in 1971 and Irving wrote his second novel, *The Water-Method Man,* in 1972. He admitted to Marcus Griel in a December 13, 1979, *Rolling Stone* interview that he had "wanted to write a book, if I could, with a happy ending, because I didn't feel I had a happy ending in me, and I wanted to get one. I wanted to write a book that was absolutely comic." In her book *John Irving,* Carol Harter declared that this second novel was an enormous improvement over his first. She praised Irving's strong characters, fine control of tone, successful manipulation of point of view, and dramatic shifts in time sequence. She was not alone in her critical praise, but Irving enjoyed little reward in the way of sales. He worked as a writer-in-residence at the University of Iowa from 1972 to 1975.

Irving patterned his third novel, *The 158-Pound Marriage,* on Ford Maddox Ford's *The Good Soldier* and John Hawkes's *The Blood Oranges* and in the process grew more comfortable with first person narration. But some critics consider it one of his weaker novels. The *Los Angeles Times's* Michael Harris wrote in 1994, "In retrospect [*The 158-Pound Marriage*] seems the thinnest and meanest of his books. Its wife-swapping American academics lack seriousness, and Irving lets his contempt for them show."

Literary Acclaim Achieved

Despite his past critical acclaim, no one could have predicted the meteoritic rise Irving would experience when his fourth novel, *The World According to Garp,* was released in 1978. Irving became an immediate sensation and was able to leave academia and become a full-time writer. *Garp* was a family saga of the admirable hero T. S. Garp, a writer and father, and the illegitimate son of a nurse turned radical feminist. The novel was a complex interweaving of several life stories, filled with the steadying influence of the New England coastline. Its plot featured such surprises as a pro-football player-turned transvestite family friend, along with several catastrophic events. The novel was wildly popular and in 1980 was awarded the American Book Award for best paperback novel of 1979.

Irving's first marriage ended in 1981, as his career continued to soar. His next book, *The Hotel New Hampshire,* shared the reach of *Garp,* following the life arcs of a family full of quirky characters, while maintaining a comic-satiric tone.

After *Hotel,* Irving wrote some less convoluted novels. *The Cider House Rules,* published in 1985, was almost entirely a birth to death narrative. But *Cider House* stood out from his earlier novels in another way—it was a polemic, taking on the issue of abortion, filled with detailed descriptions of abortion and the depressing reality of unwanted pregnancies. "[It] not only imitates the form of a Victorian novel, it may *be* the most Victorian novel of our times," said Harris of the *Los Angeles Times. A Prayer for Owen Meany,* published in 1989, was called Irving's "second breakthrough," by Harris. The novel followed the lifespan of Owen Meany, a Christ-like figure, against the backdrop of the Vietnam War. Some critics considered it his best novel.

In answer to questions about how autobiographical his novels were, Irving dismissed the notion, "I can invent more interesting characters than most people I know," he stated at a question-and-answer session at New York's 92nd Street Y in 2001. "In the world of writing about writers, personal experience is, in my view, always overestimated, and the imagination is almost always devalued." On other occasions, however, Irving also acknowledged the autobiographical themes present in his novels of absent parents and lost children, and that his grandmother was the model for Harriet Wheelwright in *A Prayer for Owen Meany.*

Books Became Films

At the same time Irving became a best-selling author, his celebrity-status increased because of films based on his novels. His unusual characters and event-filled novels attracted attention as potential screenplays. *The World According to Garp* was made into a film of the same name starring Robin Williams in 1982. In 1984 *The Hotel New Hampshire* followed. One project, *Simon Birch,* was a failed attempt at adapting *Owen Meany,* and lost Irving's endorsement. Irving finally got the chance to adapt one of his novels to screen with *The Cider House Rules.* In 1999, he documented his turn to scriptwriting and the 13-year struggle he undertook to bring *Cider House* to the screen in *My Movie Business: A Memoir.*

Irving remarried in 1987. His second wife, Janet Turnbull, was a publisher at Bantam-Seal books when she met him and, after their marriage, became his literary agent and first editor. In 1991, their son Everett was born.

Critics sometimes pointed to Irving's writing as pandering to his audience. "I've read about myself that I am not to be taken seriously because I am a shameless entertainer, a crowd pleaser," he told Richard Bernstein of the *New York Times.* "You bet. I am. My feeling is I'm not going to get you to believe anything if I can't get you to finish the book. I have a very simple formula, which is that you've got to be more interested on page 320 than on page 32." Irving cited Dickens, George Eliot, Gunter Grass, Robertson Davies, Gabriel Garcia Marquez, and Salman Rushdie as his models. He believed in diligent rewriting and again pointed to the value of his wrestling discipline, saying that writing was one-eighth talent and seven-eighths discipline.

Believing strongly in his role as a storyteller, Irving described his approach to writing. "There's a procedure I go through when I write," he told *People's* Hubbard. "I always try to think: Okay, this is what you think is coming. But what would be worse?" And in another interview with *New York Times's* Bernstein he stated, "It is my deliberate decision to create someone who is capable of moving you and then hurting him. It's an honorable 199th-century technique." With his later novels, *A Son of the Circus, A Widow for One Year,* and *The Fourth Hand* Irving continued a remarkable career and his novels enjoyed wide appeal.

Although widely recognized for his successful career in the United States, Irving benefited significantly from his international appeal. "More than half of my audience is in translation," Irving told *Salon's* Smith. "'A Son of the Circus,' my last novel, sold as many hardcover copies in France as it sold in the U.S. . . . So my biggest market is not English language and it hasn't been in the United States for years."

In the acknowledgements for *The Fourth Hand,* Irving wrote: "Every novel I've written has begun with a 'What if . . .'" The seed for *Hand* came from his wife, Janet, asking a question as they watched a news story about the first hand transplant in the United States, "What if the donor's widow demands visitation rights with the hand?" Irving worked feverishly and over the next 48 hours developed the entire storyline and title overnight. In one way, this was typical for Irving, because he always knew where his books would end before starting them, then he worked back to the beginning. "At the point where I actually write that first sentence," he told *New York Times's* Mel Gussow, "I'm really ready to go until I drop. I'm remembering the story." *The Fourth Hand* was shorter than most of Irving's novels and was the first that didn't trace its character from childhood and span generations.

Irving's work on *The Fourth Hand* drew him away from research he was doing for a novel called *Until I Find You,* set in the world of tattoo artists and church organists. In 2001, plans were announced for Irving and director Lasse Hallstrom (*The Cider House Rules*) to adapt *The Fourth Hand* for the screen. George Clooney was mentioned as a possible lead.

Irving maintains a strong relationship with all three of his sons. He divides his time between a rustic, hilltop home in southern Vermont overlooking the Green Mountains, a Toronto apartment, and an Ontario cottage on Georgian Bay. His routine includes sitting down eight hours each day to write and taking time out to practice wrestling. He writes his first drafts in longhand and then continues on one of many of his Selectric typewriters. Despite a prolific career, Irving seemed to be at another peak in 2001, busy on both a screenplay and a new novel. "It's funny to be 59 and busier than I was 20 years ago," he told *New York Times's* Gussow. " . . . I have never filled the day and the night so much with writing."

Books

Harter, Carol C. and Thompson, James R., *John Irving,* Twayne, 1986.
John Irving, edited by Harold Bloom, Chelsea House, 2001.

Periodicals

Los Angeles Times, September 4, 1994.
Maclean's, July 23, 2001.
Mother Jones, May/June 1997.
New York Times, April 25, 1989; April 28, 1998; August 1, 2001.
People, July 30, 2001.

Publishers Weekly, October 25, 1999.
Variety, April 23, 2001.

Online

Contemporary Novelists, reproduced in *Biography Resource Center,* http://galenet.galegroup.com/servlet/BioRC (November 9, 2001).
Joan Smith, "The Salon Interview: John Irving," http://www.salon.com/march97/interview970303.html (October 26, 2001).
"John Irving/Author Biography," http://www.randomhouse.com/atrandom/johnirving/author.html (November 13, 2001). □

James Benson Irwin

In 1971, during the U.S. Apollo 15 space mission, James Irwin (1930-1991) became the eighth person to walk on the moon. During the first-ever use of the lunar roving vehicle, or "moon buggy," he and mission commander David Scott found a four-billion-year-old rock. Irwin experienced the lunar mission as a religious awakening and later founded an evangelical Christian religious organization.

James Irwin was born and grew up in Pittsburgh, Pennsylvania. His father worked as a steamfitter at the Carnegie Museums, running the power plant. "Some of my earliest memories are of waiting for Dad in this tremendous place," Irwin wrote in his autobiography *To Rule the Night.* His lifelong fascination with flying machines began before second grade when a neighbor gave him a model plane. His interest grew when his father would take him to a nearby airport to watch planes take off and land.

When Irwin was eleven years old, the family moved to Florida, but his father could not find work, and he was forced to return to Pittsburgh and his old job. "I took over the role of the man in the house," Irwin said in his book. "It was a very maturing experience for me." When was in the sixth grade, Irwin felt drawn to go inside a Baptist church; he became a convert and remained religious through the rest of his life.

Irwin spent his junior high and high school years in Salt Lake City. After graduation, he entered the United States Naval Academy in Annapolis, Maryland. Upon graduating from the academy in 1951, Irwin, who was still interested in becoming a pilot, jumped at the chance to join the U.S. Air Force. He finally learned to fly at an airbase in Hondo, Texas. The base had not seen service since World War II and had been used as a chicken farm. "They still had chicken wire up," Irwin wrote in his book, "and there were feathers and droppings all over the place. It was the most primitive living I had seen."

Irwin learned so quickly that he soon found the T-6 training planes not enough of a challenge. He earned his Air Force pilot wings with thoughts of leaving the service and

top-secret mission to test what was to be the highest flying, fastest plane ever built.

Just when it appeared that his career was finally going to take off, a student pilot he was training crashed the plane they were flying. They both survived, but Irwin suffered compound fractures, amnesia, and nearly lost a leg. He was grounded for many months, and became so discouraged that he began to study to become a lawyer.

Irwin was back in the air by 1962, however, and gunning for the astronaut corps. In 1963, he applied to be an astronaut but was turned down. Also that year, he and his wife had a son, James, followed by another daughter, Jan, in 1964. Later they adopted a fifth child, Joe. In 1964, Irwin tried again for the astronaut corps, and he was again turned down.

In 1966, the year he turned 36, the age limit for astronaut candidates, he was finally accepted in the astronaut program. He was put in charge of the testing program for the lunar landing module that was being built. "This entire experiment was in many ways the most rewarding experience I ever had," he recalled in his book. "In a personal way, it was almost more rewarding than the trip to the moon."

After a year and a half of training, Irwin, David Scott, and Alfred Worden were assigned to fly Apollo 15. The launch and the three-day journey to the moon went without a hitch. On July 30, 1971, Irwin piloted Apollo 15's lunar module, *Falcon,* touching down in a plain near the moon's Apennine mountain range.

After a good night's sleep, Irwin and Scott ventured outside. For the first time in history, they deployed a four-wheeled lunar roving vehicle, or "moon buggy," and it took them farther from their ship than any previous lunar astronauts had ventured. Aside from a brief scare when the vehicle slid away from them as they worked beside it on a steep slope, the machine did its job well. It helped the astronauts make one of the most exciting discoveries of the Apollo program—a rock, more than four billion years old, that the media dubbed the Genesis Rock. The mission also set an endurance record for time spent on the moon.

During his 67 hours on the moon, 19 of which were spent outside the ship in three separate excursions, Irwin experienced a religious reawakening, saying he felt the presence and power of God in a new way. He retired from NASA in 1972 and founded the High Flight Foundation, an interdenominational religious organization based in Colorado Springs, Colorado. "Before the flight, I was really not a religious man," Irwin explained in his autobiography. "I believed in God, but I really had nothing to share. But when I came back from the moon, I felt so strongly that I had something that I wanted to share with others, that I established High Flight, in order to tell all men everywhere that God is alive, not only on earth but also on the moon."

In the early 1980s, Irwin mounted annual expeditions to Mount Ararat in Turkey in search of Noah's Ark. In 1982, he made it to the mountaintop but fell and was injured. The next year, he flew a plane over the summit to look for remains of the ark, but he never found any. Irwin had a

going to work for an airline. However, when he was assigned to a base in Yuma, Arizona, he encountered his first P-51 fighter plane. "Those 51s were the hottest planes I had ever seen in my life," he later wrote. "From that point on, I found myself living to fly."

During this time, he married a Catholic woman named Mary Etta despite the objections of his family. Soon, their religious differences led to a divorce.

Seriously committed to flying, Irwin decided to become a test pilot. To do that he would have to attend graduate school, so he entered the University of Michigan in Ann Arbor. He also applied to the test pilot school at Edwards Air Force Base in California and was accepted. But a new rule preventing Air Force personnel from attending two schools at once caused him to be assigned instead to Dayton, Ohio, where he helped to design missiles. He kept up his flight status by becoming a flight instructor. Irwin got a master's degree in aeronautical and instrumentation engineering in 1957. He married his second wife, a model named Mary Ellen Monroe. They soon had a baby girl named Joy.

By this time, the National Aeronautics and Space Administration (NASA) had started sending people into space, and Irwin wanted to be an astronaut. But NASA was accepting only test pilots. Finally, in 1960, Irwin was admitted into the test pilot school at Edwards. While he was training at Edwards, his second child was born, a girl named Jill. After graduating from pilot school, Irwin decided to stay on at Edwards as a test pilot. He was immediately assigned to a

history of heart problems and succumbed to a heart attack on August 8, 1991. He was the first of the moon walkers to die.

Books

Chaikin, Andrew, *A Man on the Moon: The Voyages of the Apollo Astronauts,* Penguin Books, 1994.

Irwin, James and William A. Emerson, Jr., *To Rule the Night* A. J. Holman Company, 1973.

Periodicals

Houston Chronicle, August 10, 1991.
New York Times, August 10, 1991.
Sunday Telegraph (Sydney, Australia), December 21, 1997.

Online

"Apollo 15 Crew Information," *Apollo Lunar Surface Journal,* http://www.hq.nasa.gov/office/pao/History/alsj/a15/a15 .crew.html (November 15, 2001).

"Astronaut Bio: James Irwin.," Web site of the Lyndon B. Johnson Space Center, http://www.jsc.nasa.gov/Bios/htmlbios/irwin-jb.html (November 15, 2001).

"James Irwin," *Astronaut Hall of Fame,* http://www.astronauts .org/astronauts/irwin.htm (November 13, 2001). □

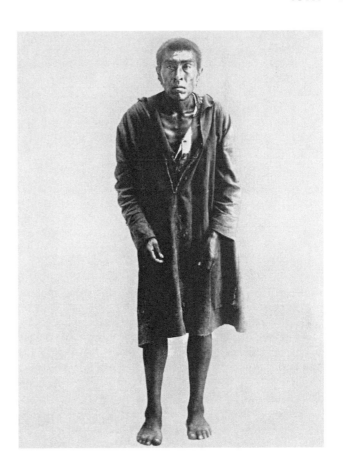

Ishi

Ishi (c.1860-1916), considered the last aboriginal Native American in the United States, left his native homeland in 1911 when he walked into a settlement near Oroville, California. He lived for the next five years at the University of California at San Francisco's anthropology museum, where he was the subject of intense interest by the public and the academy. Ishi died in 1916; in 2000, Native American activists successfully petitioned the Smithsonian Institute to return Ishi's remains for a traditional Indian burial in California.

n August of 2000, the already fascinating story of an aboriginal American known only as Ishi added another chapter. The last surviving member of the Yahi tribe of the Yana Indians, Ishi was regarded as the last aboriginal Indian to survive in North America when he wandered into Oroville, California, on August 29, 1911. The middle-aged Ishi was regarded as both a public curiosity from the Stone Age as well as the source of vital anthropological data on Native American life prior to European settlement. By all accounts an outgoing yet dignified man, Ishi lived in a museum at the University of California at San Francisco for five years, where he was avidly studied by linguist Thomas T. Waterman and anthropologist Alfred L. Kroeber.

In 1916 Ishi died of tuberculosis. Against his own wish to be cremated immediately upon his death, an autopsy was performed on Ishi and his brain was sent to the Smithsonian Institute for storage. Although officials at the Smithsonian

later denied having Ishi's brain, Native American activists began a campaign in the 1990s for the return of the final Yahi's remains so that they could be given a traditional Yahi burial. Citing the 1990 Native American Graves Protection and Repatriation Act, which stipulated that any Native American remains in federally funded collections must be returned to their descendants, the activists were finally successful in forcing the Smithsonian to turn over Ishi's brain to the Redding Rancheria and Pit River Tribes, the closest surviving descendants of Ishi's Yahi tribe. Together with the rest of Ishi's remains, which had been cremated and buried in Colma, California, the two Indian groups finally buried Ishi in his ancestral home land around Deer Creek Canyon in north-central California in August of 2000.

The Demise of the Yana Indians

Ishi's sudden appearance in Oroville in 1911 stunned the area's residents, who had assumed that members of the Yahi tribe had long since died off. As the southernmost branch of four main tribes of the Yana Indians, who resided around the Sacramento River Valley in north-central California, the Yahi inhabited the area around Mill Creek and Deer Creek just south of Mount Lassen, about 100 miles north of the present-day state capital of Sacramento. In the early 1800s, possibly as many as 3,000 Yana Indians lived in the Sacramento River Valley; however, their lives were upturned with the California Gold Rush of 1849, when thousands of prospectors streamed into northern California in search of fortune. The Yahi had already clashed with previous settlers to the Valley and had a reputation as fierce and stealthy fighters when challenged. Thus, the rough-and-ready '49ers, as the prospectors and their families were called, were determined to exterminate the tribe as they settled the area. In addition to epidemics of previously unknown diseases such as measles, smallpox, and tuberculosis, the brutal warfare waged between the two troops reduced the Yana population by about 95 percent by the 1890s.

Ishi was probably born around 1860, at a time when the Yahi faced the last of their battles with settlers around the Sacramento River Valley. His father was killed in one of the last attacks around 1865; after another confrontation in 1870, an estimated 20 surviving Yahi withdrew into the wilderness. By 1880 the Yana's home land was largely settled by white landowners, although stretches of forbidding territory in the foothills of the Cascade Mountains remained largely unexplored. Instead of driving off the settlers with violence, the Yahi instead inhabited the rocky territory, which effectively hid them from view. Surviving by hunting and fishing in their traditional manner, they added to their stock of food and clothing by occasionally raiding a settler's cabin for supplies. One such occurrence happened when Ishi and the other Yahi made a raiding party on a cabin on Dry Creek in April of 1885. The owner of the cabin encountered a group of four Indians leaving with some of his family's old clothes and let them leave with the items without interfering. Later that year, the settler found two Yana baskets left in his cabin, perhaps a sign of thanks for his generosity.

By 1894 only about five Yahi tribe members were left, including Ishi, his mother, a female relative that Ishi identified as his sister, and an elderly man. These survivors established a small encampment with two dwellings at the confluence of Deer Creek and Sulfur Creek in a clearing well hidden from any intrusions. Indeed, it was well over a decade before any outsiders came across the camp, although the Yahi themselves were spotted at times over the years. In 1908 engineers for the Oro Light & Power Company undertook a land survey of the area in preparation for building a dam there. On November 8, 1908, two surveyors returning to their camp after a day of work unexpectedly encountered Ishi as he was fishing in Deer Creek. Ishi immediately scampered off, and most of the other surveyors refused to believe that an Indian would still be living in the area. The next day the company's guide decided to investigate; as he proceeded up Deer Creek, he was almost hit by an arrowhead launched by an unknown shooter. Returning with the rest of the engineering company, the men soon found the Yahi encampment, which had just been abandoned except for one old woman who could not walk. Some of the men took a few items they found in the camp as souvenirs, and they left the old woman alone. Troubled by his conscience, the guide returned to the camp again the next day to see if the old woman could be helped; when he reached the camp, she had disappeared.

The Last of the Yahi

Ishi himself eventually described the arrival of the surveying party that led to the final dissolution of the Yahi tribe.

With their camp about to be discovered by the engineers, Ishi ran in one direction while his sister accompanied the elderly man in the other direction, leaving Ishi's elderly mother behind. After the engineers left, Ishi returned to take his mother away; she died a short time later, although Ishi was vague about the details. He never saw his sister and the old man again; because they never appeared at any of the group's common meeting areas, he assumed that they had fallen into Deer Creek and drowned or met some other fatal encounter. With the loss of his tribe, Ishi entered a period of mourning and burned off his hair. He remained alone in the wilderness for the better part of three years.

Close to starvation and exhaustion, Ishi finally decided to surrender himself to the settlers that had largely destroyed his people's existence. On August 29, 1911, he walked to a slaughterhouse near Oroville, California, and gave himself up to the men who worked there. The Butte County sheriff was quickly summoned; not knowing what to do with the Indian, he took Ishi to the county jail for his own safety. News of the appearance of an aboriginal Yahi Indian, years after the tribe was assumed to have been decimated, immediately made headlines around the state. One person who took particular notice of the stories was University of California linguistics professor Thomas T. Waterman, who traveled to Oroville as soon as he heard the reports.

Waterman's arrival in Oroville was fortuitous, as he was one of the foremost authorities on the Yana Indians. Taking a list of Yana words with him, Waterman attempted to communicate with Ishi without success, until he pointed to the wooden frame of Ishi's bed and said the Yahi word for wood. Gradually, the two discovered a few words that were mutually intelligible, and the arrival of a northern Yana Indian, who knew a few more words of Yahi, helped Ishi become more outgoing. Although the language barrier made it difficult to reveal much of his life history at first, Waterman recognized that Ishi was indeed the last surviving member of the Yahi tribe. Even his actual name was surrounded in mystery; in accordance with Yahi custom, Ishi never spoke his own name or revealed it to any outsider; instead, he took the name "Ishi," meaning "man" in the Yahi language, and he was known by the epithet for the rest of his life.

Final Home in Anthropological Museum

From September 1911 until his death in 1916, Ishi made his home on the grounds of the University of California at San Francisco. He lived in a room in the university's anthropological museum and performed a few janitorial tasks in exchange for a modest stipend. Under the guidance of Professor Alfred L. Kroeber, Ishi learned a few hundred words of English and adapted many habits from his new surroundings. Ishi immediately started to wear long pants and dress shirts, although he took to wearing shoes only after living at the museum for several months. He patronized the school's cafeteria and enjoyed eating most of the new foods he encountered to the extent that he became somewhat overweight. Although he avoided the company of women in accordance with the social mores he had learned as a Yahi, Ishi was regarded as an outgoing and even-tempered person who quickly charmed anyone he met.

Although a genuine friendship likely evolved between Ishi and his academic mentors, professors Waterman and Kroeber also viewed Ishi as an invaluable source of information on Native American ways that had been obliterated by white settlement. As such, the men exhaustively studied Ishi's language, beliefs, and material culture. Ishi was also put on display at the museum and attracted thousands of people who watched him make bow-and-arrow sets, arrowheads, and traditional Yahi dwellings. More recent academics have criticize Ishi's objectification as a museum attraction, although most agreed that such intrusions into Ishi's life were not out of line with practices of the period. Indeed, during his time at the museum, Ishi gladly shared information about the Yahi, even though he was hesitant to discuss the painful loss of his family. In the spring of 1914, Ishi returned to his ancestral home land one last time on an expedition arranged by the university. There he showed his companions a range of hunting and fishing skills, and his academic colleagues were glad to take advantage of the opportunity to record Ishi's activities for posterity.

Became a Symbol of Indian Rights

Like many Native Americans entering a foreign society, Ishi was plagued by recurring illnesses, particularly colds. In the winter of 1915, his illness deepened into tuberculosis. By the time the correct diagnosis was made, Ishi had weakened considerably and he died at the university on March 25, 1916. It was estimated that he was in his mid-fifties.

Prior to his death, Ishi expressed an adamant opposition to being autopsied; he had witnessed surgeries at the university's medical school and remained skeptical of Western medicine. With Kroeber absent at the time of his death, however, Ishi's brain was removed and preserved. Although upset with this action, Kroeber sent the brain to the Smithsonian Institute in Washington, D.C., where it sat, undisturbed, for several decades. With the passage of the 1990 Native American Graves Protection and Repatriation Act, however, several Native American groups began to press for a full inventory of Indian artifacts and remains in federally funded collections, and requested that, per the act, any such objects be returned to their rightful tribes. In 1997 the case of Ishi became a *cause celebre* when several California tribes publicized the Smithsonian's refusal to admit that they possessed Ishi's remains.

The following year, the institute acknowledged that it still had Ishi's brain and entered discussions to decide which tribes were the closest legitimate descendants to the extinct Yahis. In August 2000, the Smithsonian turned over Ishi's brain to two groups of northern California Indians, the Redding Rancheria and Pit River tribes. The two groups collected the rest of Ishi's cremated remains, which had been buried in the city of Colma, California, and made a final burial in Deer Creek Canyon. Eighty-five years after his death, Ishi was finally laid to rest in accordance with his own wishes. Although Ishi's final burial was a fitting conclusion to his own story, the repatriation of other Native American remains and artifacts continued to be a contentious topic. A decade after its passage, most museums subject to the 1990 Native American Graves Protection and Repatriation Act had yet to comply with its mandate.

Books

Heizer, Robert F., and Theodora Kroeber, editors, *Ishi the Last Yahi: A Documentary History,* University of California Press, 1979.
Kroeber, Theodora, *Ishi in Two Worlds: A Biography of the Last Wild Indian in North America,* University of California Press, 1962.

Periodicals

AP Worldstream, August 28, 2000.
Indian Country Review, August 18, 2000.
Science News, January 8, 2000.
U.S. News & World Report, August 21, 2000.
Wild West, October, 2000. □

Juzo Itami

One of Japan's few filmmakers to achieve success both at home and abroad, Juzo Itami (1933-1997) made clever, farcical satires about the rituals of everyday Japanese life. Starting his career as a director at age 50, he directed ten popular films before committing suicide at age 64.

Mansaku Itami was a renowned director of Japanese samurai movies during the 1930s. Forsaking the grand, costumed epics of the genre, he made films that took a satirical look at his country's samurai culture. One of Mansaku's sons, born Ikeuchi Yoshihiro in 1933, followed in his father's footsteps and became known in the world of film under the name Juzo Itami.

For a long time, Juzo Itami resisted the impulse to follow in his famous father's footsteps. As a young man, he spent some time as a professional boxer and worked as a manager for musical groups. Eventually he turned to writing, publishing essays on a wide range of subjects and translating works of American authors such as William Styron. This initial literary bent was shared by Itami's brother, Itami Kenzaburo Oe, who became a Nobel Prize laureate in literature. Itami slowly made the transition from printed page to celluloid by becoming the host of a television talk show.

One of several interests, cinema held a natural attraction for Itami. He began acting in films in 1960 with a role in Yasuzo Masumura's *Nise Daigakusei* ("A False Student"). In 1961 he appeared under the name Ichizo Atami in a joint American-Japanese production of the Pearl Buck novel *The Big Wave*. Later roles included parts in the American movies *55 Days at Peking* (where he was listed in the credits as Ichizo Itami) in 1963 and *Lord Jim*. He also appeared in Japanese films that got wide distribution worldwide, such as the Japanese-French confection *Private Collections* in 1979

and *Kazoku Geimu* ("The Family Game") and *Sasameyuki* (released to English-speaking audiences as *The Makioka Sisters* or *Fine Snow*) in 1983. His last role as an actor was in *Suito Homu* ("Sweet Home") in 1989.

It was not until Itami was 50 that he turned to writing and directing his own films. His first screenwriting/directorial effort came in 1984 with *Ososhiki* ("The Funeral"), an instant box-office hit in Japan. The film was a black comedy mocking the way modern Japanese culture short-circuits traditional burial rites for the sake of expediency and profit. To mourn the death of an old patriarch who operated a whorehouse, his movie-star daughter (Nobuko Miyamoto) and her actor husband must leave a movie set and spend three days at an elaborate wake. Miyamoto, Itami's wife, would go on to star in all his films.

In directing *Ososhiki* and the films that followed—most of which Itami also wrote—he used a disarming lightheartedness and an incisive, subtle wit to dissect some of the foibles of contemporary Japanese culture. Until Itami's films became popular, Japanese audiences were more interested in Hollywood movies or animation. However, Itami quickly gained favor by breaking through the cultural taboo against poking fun at the rituals of everyday Japanese life.

Inventing the Noodle Western

Itami's second directorial effort, *Tampopo*, is a light and intoxicating satire about the Japanese affection for eating noodles. Its heroine is a young woman named Tampopo

whose ambition is to make the perfect noodle. A cowboy-style truck driver gives her pointers on how to popularize her restaurant. While making fun of the Japanese obsession for cooking and eating in ritualized fashion, it also presented the perverse and romantic possibilities of food. *Tampopo* (also released as *Dandelion*) became a hit on the U.S. art-house circuit and sent plenty of Americans scurrying off to Japanese restaurants to sample noodle dishes. Dubbed the first "noodle Western," the film serves up a delightful stew of movie genres, from so-called spaghetti western to screwball comedy to French New Wave to the films of surrealist Luis Buauel. Episodic and unconventionally structured, the film indulges in puns, edgy humor, and wry mockery of Japan's materialistic 1980s culture. Characters who represent many distinct cultures all share an obsession with food and use food as a way to thumb their noses at the autocratic, hierarchical Japanese social structure. Critic Jonathan Crow of *All Movie Guide* called *Tampopo* "a wildly inventive, fantastically entertaining movie by a film master at the peak of his powers."

Itami's next film, *A Taxing Woman,* was also an international hit following its release in 1987. In it the director casts a wry eye on the Japanese penchant for tax evasion. The film's protagonist works for the national revenue collection service. She relentlessly tracks down people who cheat on their income taxes, including a millionaire with mob connections who falls in love with her. The film is both an offbeat romantic comedy and a satire of the ambivalent Japanese attitude toward authority.

The following year, Itami wrote and directed a sequel, *A Taxing Woman's Return.* In this comedy, Miyamoto's character exposes a group of people pretending to be members of a religious organization in order to avoid paying their taxes. She discovers the group is really a front for a corrupt land developer. The film takes potshots at many Japanese institutions, including business, education, and gender relations.

Took Bolder Jabs

Itami's first three films were very popular in Japan and also made substantial amounts of money abroad, a rare combination for a Japanese filmmaker. In his subsequent films Itami retained his sense of humor but more sharply honed his deadly satire, and his movies contained increasing doses of violence and pointed social commentary. In *Ageman* (*Tales of a Golden Geisha*), Itami turned his attention to the contemporary plight of traditional Japanese geisha girls. Miyamoto stars as Nayoko, a so-called "golden geisha" who brings good luck to whatever wealthy man contracts for her services. The plot involves several men bidding for her attentions. Finally, a man who really loves her buys her contract. While this film casts Itami's customary intense glare on Japanese customs, it has a happy ending and a fairly light touch.

Much more serious, though just as funny, was Itami's next film, *Minbo; or, The Gentle Art of Japanese Extortion,* released in 1992. It is a scathing satire about the Japanese mobsters known as *yakuza*, depicting these men not as the latter-day samurai they pretended to be but as grunting, cowardly petty crooks who travel in packs and lack the guts to back up their verbal threats. Miyamoto stars as a courageous attorney who goes after the mob and defeats them; in the process Itami virtually instructs his audience on how to defeat these extortionists.

The objects of Itami's ridicule in *Minbo* did not take such jabs lightly. A group of five yakuza attacked the filmmaker within days after the film first opened in Tokyo. They slashed Itami's face with knives, leaving him with a deep scar on his cheek, which he wore from that day forward as something of a badge of honor.

Scandal, Death, and Honor

In 1995, Itami directed *Shizukana Seikatsu* (*A Quiet Life*), based on a novel by his brother, Itami Kenzaburo Oe. More melodramatic than most of Itami's later films, *A Quiet Life* centers on a young musician who has a severe mental disability. His father is a novelist and his sister is sheltered and devoted. A patient swim instructor seems a godsend for the young man and a possible mate for his sister until he is found to have a darker side.

Toward the end of his career, Itami's films began exploring mortality. He rejected modern attitudes toward dying in hospitals and showed reverence for traditional Japanese deaths at home and surrounded by family members. *The Last Dance* is an almost chillingly prophetic black comedy whose protagonist is an aging, drunken film director and actor who is making a movie about a married couple stricken with cancer. He is having an affair with his on-screen co-star. Eventually, the director learns that he has stomach cancer and that his doctors, true to Japanese convention, have concealed it from him. His wife finds out about the affair and prepares to leave him, but they reconcile when she learns he is fatally ill. The director considers suicide but eventually returns home to die in the comfort of his family.

One of Itami's most successful films was 1996's *The Supermarket Woman*. In this movie, the proprietor of a family-owned grocery store finds himself being squeezed out by a more modern competitor. A recently widowed suburban housewife awakens him from his stupor by pointing out how poorly he has managed his business. *The Supermarket Woman*, directed as a farce, with food fights and a chase through a darkened store, is another of many Itami films in which actress Miyamoto plays a strong-willed, effective protagonist who turns around a difficult situation.

Itami's final film, *Marutai no Onna*, released in 1997, focuses on a religious cult much like Aum Shinrikyo, the apocalyptic group that released nerve gas in the Tokyo subway in 1995 killing a dozen people and sending thousands more to hospitals. A veteran stage actress named Hiwako (Miyamoto) witnesses a murder; the victim is an attorney investigating the cult. When the cult learns she will testify against them, Hiwako too becomes a target. Her opponents discover she is having an affair and they enlist tabloid newspapers to expose it and ruin her career.

In December 1997 Itami died after he leaped from the rooftop of the eight-story Tokyo condominium where he had his office and home. He had learned that the weekly Japanese pictorial news magazine *Flash* was planning to publish an article suggesting that he was having an affair with a 26-year-old woman. Itami left notes angrily denying the affair. He wrote that his death would prove he was innocent of the charges, adding, "I can find no other means to prove there was nothing." *Flash* publisher Kenji Kaneto issued a statement saying: "It is quite regrettable that the movie world has lost a great talent. But I firmly believe that the content of the article is correct."

Instead of a funeral, the family held a memorial service that stretched over many days and included a screening all of Itami's films. At the director's own request, the service did not include elaborate floral arrangements or cash gifts. Meanwhile, Itami's sensational death shocked Japan. During his short directorial career, he had become the reigning ambassador of Japanese cinema, a prolific producer of popular movies and a first-class celebrity. The circumstances of his death seemed to shed new light on several of his films, in particular *The Last Dance* and *Marutai no Onna*, both of which concern the effect of the discovery of a romantic affair on an entertainment celebrity. These films, together with *Minbo no Onna*, also make palpable the threat of a gifted artist's violent death at the hands of his opponents or himself. For all his efforts to expose the hypocrisy of Japanese customs, Itami in the end seemed to be stymied by some of the very values he skewered so wittily on film.

Periodicals

Entertainment Weekly, November 24, 1995.
Far Eastern Economic Review, October 21, 1993.
New York Times, December 22, 1997.
Variety, August 18, 1997.

Online

"Juzo Itami," *All-Movie Guide,* http://www.allmovie.com/ (February 23, 2002).
"Juzo Itami," *Internet Movie Database,* http://us.imdb.com/ (February 23, 2002). □

J

Dan Jacobson

Author Dan Jacobson (born 1929) used his experiences as a child growing up in South Africa to mold his writings about human nature.

Dan Jacobson was born March 7, 1929, in Johannesburg, South Africa, where his parents' families had come to avoid the persecution of Jews in their European homelands. His father, Hymann Michael Jacobson, was born in Iluxt, Latvia, in 1885. His mother, Liebe (Melamed) Jacobson, was born in Kelme, Lithuania, in 1896. Jacobson had two older brothers, Israel Joshua and Hirsch Jacob, and a younger sister, Aviva. His mother's family immigrated to South Africa in 1919, after the death of his grandfather. His grandfather, Heshel Melamed, was a rabbi, and refused to leave Lithuania after traveling to the United States and finding that many Jews were not following their religion. Jacobson later wrote about his travels back to Lithuania to find out more information about his grandfather.

Learned about Prejudice

When Dan was four, the family moved from Johannesburg to Kimberley, which was then under British control. The city had once been a huge diamond mining center, but the mines had closed and the town was in decline. However, the De Beers Consolidated Mines Company continued to have great power. He attended a public school and learned English. During his childhood, he became aware of the ways that different people were treated based on their race, religion, economic status, and social status. In his autobiography *Time and Again,* he refers to the many classes of people in his community: "The Africans lived either in rooms in the back yards of their employers' houses or in sprawling, dusty, tatterdemalion 'locations'; the Cape Coloureds (people of mixed blood) lived in their parts of town; the whites in theirs. Interspersed among these groups were smaller communities: Indians and Chinese among the non-whites, Jews and Greeks among the whites. As for the major division among the whites themselves, that between English-speaking and Afrikaans-speaking, or Briton and Boer. . . . All these peoples met in the streets, they did business with one another, but just about every aspect of their social life was severely segregated. To sit together in the same room with anyone of a darker skin than their own was a moral impossibility for most whites." He later recalled that many of his Jewish friends and acquaintances sympathized with the blacks in South Africa. He began to observe the ways that the government, churches, and the newspapers justified the ill treatment of blacks.

At the age of 11, an event occurred that affected Jacobson for the rest of his life. After helping a boy rescue his book bag from a filthy trash bin, he went to school unaware that he had gotten dirt on the back of his legs. When his teacher mentioned the dirt in front of the class, several of the boys made fun of him and led the class in ignoring him for six to eight weeks. He was stunned at the mob mentality, seeing how a few leaders of the class could control the actions of the entire group. Paul Gready writes in *Research in African Literatures:* "A childhood experience of bullying and ostracism was something from which Jacobson was 'never to wholly recover.'"

Identified as a Jew

The Jewish community in Kimberley was a strong one. More Lithuanian Jews traveled to South Africa in the early

20th century than to any other country except the United States. Many were hoping to follow in the footsteps of Sammy Marks, a Lithuanian who had made his fortune in the diamond mines. The Jewish community grew even closer together in the 1930s as Nazism rose, and they felt connected to Jews around the world.

Jacobson's parents were not particularly religious, but his father insisted that the children attend synagogue and Hebrew lessons, because, as Jacobson later wrote, "To have done less, especially as the Nazi madness swept across Europe, would have seemed to him spineless, even treacherous." Jacobson attended, but usually under protest.

Jacobson attended Boys' High School in Kimberley and graduated at the age of 16. He went on to the University of Witwatersrand in Johannesburg, where he graduated at the top of his class with a bachelor's degree in English Literature. Following his graduation in 1948, he worked as a laborer in an Israeli kibbutz for about a year. Then he got a job as a teacher at a Jewish school in London. In less than a year, he was asked to leave, according to his autobiography, because he did not know enough about Orthodox Judaism.

Became a Writer

He returned to Johannesburg in 1951 and worked for the South African Jewish Board of Deputies as a public relations assistant and then as a journalist for *Press Digest.* In 1952 he returned to Kimberley to work as a correspondence secretary on his father's cattle farm. During this period he became determined to be a writer. His first literary success

occurred with a short story entitled "The Box," which was published in *Commentary.* It was followed by other short stories in *Harpers Bazaar,* the *New Yorker,* and other magazines.

In February 1954, he married Margaret Pye, whom he had met while working in London. She was a teacher and children's writer from Rhodesia and had a son named Julian. They set up residence in London, where they brought up three additional children, Simon Orde, Matthew Lindsay, and Jessica Liebe.

His first novel, *The Trap,* was released in 1955, followed by *A Dance in the Sun* in 1956. Both books drawn upon his childhood experiences. Together the two books earned him a yearlong creative writing fellowship at Stanford University in California. During his time at Stanford, he completed his third novel, *The Price of Diamonds,* which was also set in South Africa but was a lighthearted comedy-mystery with a moral message. All three books dealt with prejudice and racism.

He returned to England in 1957, determined to seek greater depth in his writing. In 1959, he received the John Llewelyn Rhys Award for fiction for his collection of short stories, *A Long Way from London.* In 1960, *The Evidence of Love* was published. It dealt with the racism involved in a romantic relationship between a black man and a white woman who were put in prison for getting married. In 1964, he received the W. Somerset Maugham award for his first collection of essays, *Time of Arrival.* One of his short stories, "The Zulu and the Zeide," was adapted into a musical and produced on Broadway in 1965. In 1966, he published *The Beginners,* a longer, in-depth novel following the lives of a Jewish family after their emigration to South Africa. It was a great literary success.

Over the next two decades, he continued to write while holding various teaching positions. In 1965-66, he was visiting professor at Syracuse University in New York. *A Dance in the Sun,* his second novel, was produced as the play *Day of the Lion* in Cleveland in 1968. He was a Visiting Fellow at the State University of New York at Buffalo in the summer of 1971. In 1974, he became vice chair of the Literature Panel of the Arts Council of Great Britain. In 1981, he was a Fellow at the Humanities Research Centre at Australian National University. He also took a position at the University of London as a lecturer; from 1979 to 1987 he was a reader in English. In 1988, he became a professor of English, a position he would hold until his retirement in 1994.

A Change in Focus

Jacobson's first five novels all focused on South Africa. His writing focus then shifted to moral and ethical issues involving all of humanity. Although he had no interest in learning the Bible as a child, he developed a strong interest in the Old Testament as an adult. In *The Rape of Tamar,* he retells the story of the rape of Tamar by her half-brother Amnon, the brother of Absolom. The book was adapted into a play called *Yonadeb,* after the narrative character in the book, and was produced in London in 1985.

In *The Story of Stories: The Chosen People and its God,* he provided a study of the Bible. His goal was to have a textual analysis as a narrative. The book was criticized by many Jews, probably because he refers to God as "an imaginative creation."

Themes that continued to reveal themselves in his works included race relations, class consciousness, human nature, universal traits, group mentality, corruption, betrayal, guilt, power, and social morality. In an article that he wrote for *Commentary* in 2000, entitled "My Jewish Childhood," Jacobson said: "It is always going to be difficult to get socially and racially diverse people to live harmoniously together within a single polity."

In 1985, his autobiography, *Time and Again: Autobiographical Essays,* was published. Each of the 13 chapters tells of an event in his life that shaped his way of thinking about the human race. The book won the J.R. Ackerly Prize for autobiography.

The God-Fearer, published in 1992, is a story of persecution. Jews are in the majority and oppress a group called the "Christers." In a *Washington Post* article, Anne Roiphe observed: "By making the majority Jewish, Jacobson makes it clear that power is the source of oppression: not that the power is German or Christian, but that it has the weight of numbers. . . . The horror of the story lies not in gruesome details or heated prose, but in the calm truth of what we call normal behavior when we try to save our skin at any cost."

In the middle 1990s, Jacobson turned to nonfiction. In 1994 he published *The Electronic Elephant: A South African Journey* about his travels back to South Africa to observe the changes in the land and the culture since his childhood. In 1998, *Heshel's Kingdom* provided a moving story of his travels to Lithuania to learn more about the life of his grandfather. He started with his grandfather's identity document, spectacles, an address book, an old photograph, and the memories of relatives. Sadly, he found no trace of his grandfather, and, indeed, not even the cemetery he was buried in remained. He did find that in 1941, within six weeks' time, the Nazis essentially wiped out the Lithuanian Jewish community, killing 210,000.

Although retired from the University of London, Jacobson continues to write. *A Mouthful of Glass* was published in 2000.

Books

The International Who's Who, Europa Publications Limited, 2001.
Jacobson, Dan, *Time and Again: Autobiography,* The Atlantic Monthly Press, 1985.

Periodicals

Commentary, November 2000.
Daily Mail and Guardian, July 20, 1998.
Judaism, Winter 2001.
Research in African Literatures, Winter 1994.
Washington Post, December 26, 1993.

Online

"Dan Jacobson," *Gale Literary Databases,* http://www.galenet .com (January 21, 2002).

"Dan Jacobson," *Harry Ranson Humanities Research Center,* http://www.hrc.utexas.edu (January 21, 2002). □

William Johnson

William Johnson (1771-1834) served on the U.S. Supreme Court from 1804 until his death in 1834. He melded federalists and states' rights views in his opinions. His most important contribution was his insistence on freedom of judicial expression in the form of dissenting opinions.

Family Life

William Johnson was born on December 27, 1771, near Charleston, South Carolina in St. James Goose Creek Parish, one of two sons born to William and Sarah (Nightingale) Johnson. His father had relocated to South Carolina from New York in the early 1760s and became a hero of the Revolutionary War. When the British captured Charleston, Johnson's father was placed in detention in Florida and the family was evicted from their home. Several months later Johnson's father was released, and the family was reunited in Philadelphia and returned to Charleston together.

Johnson attended grammar school in Charleston, and in 1790 he graduated first in his class from Princeton University. He returned to Charleston to study law under Charles Cotesworth Pinckney, a close adviser to President George Washington. Johnson was admitted to the bar in 1793. On March 20, 1794, he married Sarah Bennett, the sister of Thomas Bennett, who would later become governor of South Carolina. The couple had eight children but only two lived to adulthood. They later adopted two children from St. Domingue who had fled the island during a slave revolt.

Became State Legislator, Judge

Under the laws of the time, Johnson was eligible to run for political office due to his property holdings, which included several slaves. In 1794 Johnson was elected to the South Carolina House of Representatives as a member of Thomas Jefferson's Republican Party. He served three two-year terms, and in 1798, the last year of his tenure in the lower assembly, he was elected as Speaker of the House.

In 1798 he chose not to seek reelection to the House of Representatives so that he could accept an appointment to the Court of Common Pleas, the state's highest court. For the next six years Johnson gained valuable experience addressing many important issues of the time, most notably the relationship between the states and the infant federal government.

Named to Supreme Court

In 1804 Johnson was tapped as President Jefferson's first Supreme Court nominee. At issue for Jefferson was Republican control of the judiciary. His predecessor, President John Adams, had appointed John Marshall, a staunch Federalist, as chief justice. Marshall took strong control of the court, insisting on unanimous decisions. Prior to Marshall's appointment, nearly twenty percent of the court's decisions contained dissenting opinions; after his appointment, no dissenting opinions had been rendered. Jefferson saw Johnson's independent nature and strong personality as a means to exert a brake on Marshall's dominance. Jefferson nominated Johnson on March 22, 1804. Two days later Johnson received Senate confirmation by a voice vote. On May 7, 1804, at 33 years of age, he took the oath of office.

As Jefferson hoped, Johnson provided an independent voice on the court. Although it was several years before he ventured to issue a dissenting opinion, from early on he struggled to overcome Marshall's insistence that the court present a unified front to the public. Although Johnson was successful in easing the iron grip Marshall held over the court, his opinions were often in line with Marshall's, which sometimes earned him the wrath of the president.

Judicial Impact

Johnson's first judiciary controversy of note occurred in 1808 in the case *Gilchrist v. Collector of Charleston.* Under the executive orders of President Jefferson's Embargo Act, the collector of the Port of Charleston refused sailing clear-ance to vessels in port. Jefferson had issued the orders to withhold trade to France and Great Britain, which were at war with each other and regularly raiding U.S. ships. When Adam Gilchrist, owner of a grounded ship, petitioned Johnson in circuit court, Johnson reportedly boarded the ship himself and issued sailing orders. His opinion upon granting the mandamus stated that the executive instructions had no legal basis, namely, Congress had not authorized the detention of ships, and the president held no executive right to enforce such acts that infringed on personal liberties.

Jefferson was dismayed at this apparent betrayal by his appointee. The Federalists, on the other hand, were overjoyed with Johnson's reproach of the president and made sure the incident was highly publicized. The president turned the matter over to the U.S. Attorney General, Caesar A. Rodney, who rebuffed Johnson's actions, stating that Johnson acted outside the Constitution when he ordered the ship to sail. Although Johnson initially defended his actions, in a separate Supreme Court decision in 1813 he conceded that he had acted outside his jurisdiction. Nonetheless, Johnson's actions were instrumental in cementing the Supreme Court's role as a protector of individual rights and establishing the connection between legislative action and presidential powers. As a result, Congress passed legislation that clearly delineated the president's right to order such detentions.

Another important decision came in 1812 when Johnson issued the court's opinion rejecting common law federal crimes. Up to that time, federal courts had ruled on criminal cases over which they had not been given legislative authority, which was limited by Congress to such offenses as treason and counterfeiting. The matter became political when a federal grand jury indicted several newspaper editors in Connecticut for seditious libel against President Jefferson. Whereas the Federalists believed that the federal government held inherent powers of self-defense that allowed it to prosecute cases without explicit criminal statutes, Jeffersonians viewed the practice of trying common law crimes in federal courts as an abuse of power. When the seditious libel case came before the Supreme Court as *U.S. v. Hudson and Goodwin,* Johnson issued the court's majority opinion, which refused to extend federal jurisdiction to include criminal cases. According to James W. Ely, Jr. in *Historic U.S. Court Cases,* "Although the case before the Court concerned prosecution of seditious libel, Johnson addressed the broader issue of whether the federal courts could exercise any non-statutory criminal jurisdictions. . . . [His] opinion was grounded on federalism and strict construction of legislation. Stressing the limited nature of the federal government, Johnson declared that federal power was 'made up of concessions from the several States' and that the states reserved all powers not expressly delegated." As he often did in opinions, Johnson relied on both Federalist and Republican principles, pleasing and displeasing each party.

Justice Joseph Story, the most prominent figure on the bench next to Marshall, vehemently disagreed with Johnson's common law opinion. He wrote a sharply worded dissent and disregarded Johnson's majority decision in his own rulings. Johnson butted heads with Story again over extending the jurisdiction of the admiralty into inland waterways. Johnson, who believed in limiting the powers of the government at sea, was also unsympathetic to extending corporate power. Although he concurred with the constitutionality of maintaining a federal bank, he denied the bank's right to sue in federal court.

Johnson, a firm believer in states' rights, was opposed to the federal government superseding its power; however, at the same time, he was a staunch defender of the union, especially in matters of trade and commerce. Because he did not fit easily into any camp, he incurred the wrath of both parties. The Federalists bemoaned Johnson's close reading of legislative authority, and the Jeffersonians, with whom he aligned himself politically, complained of his restrictive interpretation of executive power and his commitment to states' rights.

Resentment in the South

Johnson was viewed with growing ambivalence in his home state. His pro-union sentiment did not play well in South Carolina at a time when anti-federalism was strong. Resentment grew in 1823 after Johnson invalidated the South Carolina Negro Seaman Act in circuit court in the case *Elkison v. Deliesseline.* According to the act, all free black seamen who docked in a South Carolina port were required to be jailed during the time their ships were in port. Johnson ruled that such an ordinance violated the federal government's power over commerce and greatly weakened the state of the union. Despite the ruling, South Carolina continued the practice of incarcerating black sailors, and Johnson defended his opinion in a series of letters, written under the pen name Philonimus, which were printed in the Charleston newspapers. Though Johnson was against the abolition of slavery, he did abhor the inhumane treatment of slaves and further alienated his home state by denouncing South Carolina for withholding the rights of due process to slave rebel Denmark Vesey.

Johnson provoked the anger of South Carolinians again when he rebuked the state's efforts to nullify the Tariff of 1828. According to vice president John C. Calhoun, who vehemently opposed the tariff in an anonymous letter, the Constitution was not supreme law, but rather a contractual agreement among sovereign states. States therefore had the right to nullify or reject any federal requirements they believed to be unconstitutional. Johnson, who saw nullification as a serious threat to the stability of the union, once again voiced his opinions in the South Carolina newspapers, first under the pseudonym Hamilton and later in a signed eight-point statement that rejected nullification. Johnson became so unpopular in his home state that he moved to Pennsylvania in 1834.

The First Great Dissenter

Johnson's opinions were sometimes very sound and forthright; however, other times he tended to lack clarity, often basing his opinions on abstract political or natural law theories. He was in many ways overshadowed by Marshall. Johnson did play an important role in reinstating the standard practice of submitting dissenting opinions. Prior to Marshall's reign, each Supreme Court Justice offered a separate, or seriatim, opinion. Over the course of his 29 years as a Supreme Court Justice, Johnson wrote 112 majority opinions, 21 concurrences, 34 dissents, and five seriatim opinions for a total of 172. Only Justices Marshall and Story rendered more opinions.

In his 1953 article on Johnson in *The William and Mary Quarterly,* Donald Morgan noted that Johnson "set up a record of separate utterance unparalleled in the early Court. . . . As elsewhere, Johnson's approach to opinion procedure was experimental. Besides expressing his views alone and agitating for seriatim opinions, he even introduced views held privately in an opinion rendered for the majority. The outcome of his ventures in strategy is clear: it was the establishment of that procedure for rendering the decrees of the Supreme Court which most harmoniously reconciled authoritativeness with intellectual freedom—the single statement for the majority combined with separate utterances by independents." Thus, Johnson is often referred to as "the first great Dissenter."

Not always completely comfortable with his roll as instigator on the court, Johnson found himself distracted by outside interests, including land speculation and writing. He published a two-volume biography of Revolutionary War hero Nathaniel Greene in 1822 and the *Eulogy of Thomas Jefferson* in 1826. He was also a member of the American Philosophical Society, and he contributed frequently to its meetings and publications. Although Johnson's independent temperament made him prickly with those who did not share his opinions, Johnson was also known as a man of sincerity, modesty, and warmheartedness. He died unexpectedly on August 4, 1834, in New York City, due to post-surgical complications after jaw surgery.

Books

Biskupic, Joan, and Elder Witt, *Guide to the U.S. Supreme Court, 3rd edition,* Congressional Quarterly, Inc., 1997.

Chase, Harold, Samuel Krislov, Keith O. Boyum, and Jerry N. Clark, *Biographical Dictionary of the Federal Judiciary,* Gale, 1976.

Garraty, John A., and Mark C. Carnes, *American National Biography,* Oxford University Press, 1999.

Hall, Kermit L., ed., *The Oxford Companion to the Supreme Court of the United States,* Oxford University Press, 1992.

Johnson, John W., *Historic U.S. Court Cases, 1690-1990: An Encyclopedia,* Garland Publishing, 1992.

Mauro, Tony, *Illustrated Great Decisions of the Supreme Court,* CQ Press, 2000.

Roller, David C., and Robert W. Twyman, *The Encyclopedia of Southern History,* Louisiana State University Press, 1979.

Witt, Elder, *Congressional Quarterly's Guide to the U.S. Supreme Court, 2nd ed.,* Congressional Quarterly, Inc., 1990.

Periodicals

The William and Mary Quarterly, January 1953. □

K

Garrison Keillor

Garrison Keillor (born 1942), host of public radio's popular *A Prairie Home Companion* and author of the best-selling *Lake Wobegon Days,* has made a career of telling stories about the fictional Minnesota town of Lake Wobegon and the lives of its residents. Keillor has become an American icon, and his show is heard by nearly three million U.S. listeners each week on over 500 public radio stations. It is also heard overseas on America One and the Armed Forces Networks in Europe and the Far East.

Author and radio personality Garrison Keillor writes about God's Frozen People, the Scandinavian settlers of the American Midwest, a quirky cast of characters united only by their religious faith and distrust of worldliness. After decades on the air, Keillor's *A Prairie Home Companion* became a cultural guidepost; a cottage industry has grown around him, including a store in Minnesota's Mall of America devoted to his fictional hometown. The television program *The Simpsons* "once did dead-on parody of a Keillor monologue," explained Bill Virgin in the *Seattle Post-Intelligencer,* adding that "the term 'Lake Wobegon effect' was coined for school test results that showed that all the students were, like those in Keillor's fictional town, 'above average.'"

Had Conservative Religious Upbringing

Keillor was born Gary Edward Keillor in Anoka, Minnesota, on August 7, 1942. His paternal ancestors came from Yorkshire, England, around 1770; his maternal grandfather left Scotland in 1906. The third of six children, Keillor was raised in a conservative religious household. His family belonged to the Plymouth Brethren sect, which frowned upon activities such as drinking, dancing, and singing. Television was banned in the Keillor home. "[W]e were not allowed to go to movies because they glorified worldliness," Keillor told *Associated Press* reporter Jeff Baenen. " People drank in movies. They drank like fish. They smoked cigarettes. They danced. And we did not do those things." Radio, however, was allowed because "I don't think people smoked as much on radio."

Despite the strictures in his home, Keillor harbored lofty literary ambitions from a young age. At age 11 he started a newspaper called *The Sunnyvale Star.* In junior high, he submitted poems to the school paper under the pseudonym "Garrison Edwards," which he considered more grandiose than his given name Gary. He also developed a taste for the erudite *New Yorker,* which he discovered at the public library. "'My people weren't much for literature,'" Jay Nordlinger quoted Keillor as saying in the *National Review,* "so for him the magazine was 'a fabulous sight, an immense, glittering ocean liner off the coast of Minnesota.'" Adopting as his life dream to work at the *New Yorker,* Keillor graduated from Anoka High School in 1960 and received his B.A. in English from the University of Minnesota in 1966. In college he worked at the *Minnesota Daily* and at the University radio station, KUOM, two extracurricular activities that ultimately helped his career.

After college, Keillor embarked on a month-long job hunt among magazines and publishing houses on the East Coast. He had interviews at the *Atlantic Monthly* in Boston and at the *New Yorker* and *Sports Illustrated* in New York. Keillor told *Atlantic Unbound* interviewer Katie Bolick that the trip convinced him, ironically, that where he really

wanted to work was in the Midwest. "If I had really wanted to get a job in New York, or course, I would have simply moved there and taken any job I could get and hoped for something better eventually," Keillor explained. "But I didn't: I was engaged to marry a girl who didn't want to move to New York, and I could see that New York is a tough place to be poor in, and then, too, I thought of myself as a Midwestern writer. The people I wanted to write for were back in Minnesota. So I went home."

Landed Job in Public Radio

In 1969 Keillor landed a job at Minnesota Public Radio that evolved into a career. At the same time, he took writing stints, and while researching an article for the Grand Ole Opry in Nashville, developed the idea for a radio show with musical guests and commercials for imaginary products. In the summer of 1974, he hosted the first broadcast of *A Prairie Home Companion,* which takes its name from a cemetery at Macalester College in St. Paul, Minnesota. In 1978 the show moved to its present broadcast site at the World (now Fitzgerald) Theater in Saint Paul and two years later began national broadcasts. In 1996 the show began broadcasting live over the Internet and direct to worldwide satellite. From its humble beginnings at a college auditorium, the show has played in well-known venues such as Radio City Music Hall, the Hollywood Bowl, and the Fox in Atlanta.

A Prairie Home Companion is a serial about the fictional town of Lake Wobegon and its inhabitants. Keillor described Lake Wobegon, population 942, as "the town that time forgot and decades cannot improve." The show celebrates small-town values in what *Washington Post* reporter David Segal described as "a seamless and enchanting two-hour variety program of homilies, comedy and music." The show consists of various segments, including news, comedy sketches, and fake commercials for sponsors like Ralph's Pretty Good Grocery Store ("Remember, if you can't find it at Ralph's, you can probably get along without it"). But the centerpiece of each show is always a 20-minute monologue, done by Keillor himself. "For me, the monologue was the favorite thing I had done in radio," Keillor told *New York Times* reviewer Mervyn Rothstein. "It was based on writing, but in the end it was radio, it was standing up and leaning forward into the dark and talking, letting words come out of you."

In 1985 Keillor married second wife Ulla Skärved, who had been a Danish exchange student at Anoka High and whom he met again at his 25th high school reunion. By 1987 Keillor quit *A Prairie Home Companion*—from "sheer exhaustion," he explained on the show's Web site—and moved to Denmark. However, within two years he had returned to the United States and started a new radio show in New York City. The show, *American Radio Company of the Air,* first broadcast in 1989 from the Majestic Theater in Brooklyn. It strongly resembled *A Prairie Home Companion*; so strongly in fact that in 1993 Keillor decided to revive the show back home to St. Paul.

Pursued Parallel Track as a Writer

Alongside his work as a radio personality, Keillor carried on a parallel life as a writer. After sending stories to the *New Yorker* for several years, he had his first story accepted for publication in 1969 and went on to become a regular contributor at his favorite magazine. In the early years writing for the *New Yorker* he lived with his wife and son Jason on a farm near Freeport, Minnesota, and would send two or three stories to his editor each month. But everything changed in 1992 when Tina Brown became editor of the magazine, replacing the legendary William Shawn. She introduced big changes to the magazine, which including phasing out a lot of the old writers. Keillor was one of the casualties of the new order, an event he recalls bitterly. "The New Yorker used to be a writers' magazine and it was very important to me," he told *Irish Times* contributor Frank McNally. "But under Tina Brown's editorship, it's been transformed into a magazine . . . driven by gossip. It's not a writer's magazine any more—it's all about 'buzz' now."

After his tenure at the *New Yorker* ended, Keillor started writing novels and in 1985 published the best-selling *Lake Wobegon Days.* Drawing on the same material he used for his radio show, Keillor spins tales of family life, school days, and growing up in the fictional small town of Lake Wobegon. Many of the stories describe the town's history and social conventions. It was the beginning of a literary phenomenon, as the book spawned a number of sequels and spin-offs.

In 1998 he published *Wobegon Boy,* a novel about John Tollefson, a radio manager stuck in a mid-life crisis.

While some reviewers have compared Keillor to American humorists like Mark Twain and Will Rogers, *National Review* critic E. V. Kontorovich compared the author to Thomas Jefferson, noting that both rely on common-sense morality. "The antidote to self-absorption, self-pity, and other manifestations of the 12-step society can be found among the unpretentious Norwegian townsmen," asserted Kontorovich. "The reader will smile for as long as it takes him to read three hundred pages."

In 1998, at the age of 55, Keillor had a daughter Maia, with his third wife, violinist Jenny Lind Nilsson. Keillor's first son, Jason Keillor, from his marriage to Mary C. Guntzel, grew up to work as stage manager on his father's radio show.

While most of his works center upon Lake Wobegon, Keillor dabbled in politics with 1999's *Me: By Jimmy "Big Boy" Valente as Told to Garrison Keillor,* a satirical spoof about then-newly elected Minnesota governor and former wrestler Jesse Ventura. That same year he was awarded a National Humanities medal and was honored at a White House dinner hosted by President Bill Clinton. Explaining the selection of recipients, William R. Ferris, chairman of the National Endowment for the Humanities, said "They are gifted people with extraordinary powers of creativity and vision, and their work in preserving, interpreting and expanding the nation's cultural heritage."

In 2001 Keillor published *Lake Wobegon Summer 1956,* a quasi-autobiographical coming-of-age tale. The novel's humor arises from the conflict between the protagonist's strict religious upbringing and his pent-up desires. *New York Times* reviewer Malcolm Jones found it only mildly amusing. "The same qualities that endear the show to us—its easygoing, deliberate corniness and amateurishness," wrote Jones, "suddenly seem merely cute, annoying and sometimes just plain trite on the page."

In July of 2001 Keillor underwent heart surgery at the Mayo Clinic in Rochester, Minnesota. He made a full recovery and continued to broadcast his show and write. His books include story collections, novels, and children's books. In addition, he penned an occasional essay for *Time* and an advice column for the online magazine *Salon* and taught a writing class at the University of Minnesota. Keillor has considers his double-track existence satisfying both personally and socially. "Writing is pure entrepreneurship and a great way of life," he noted on the *Prairie Home Companion* Web site. "And then, if you do a radio show every Saturday, you have a built-in social life. So it's a pretty good deal."

Books

Contemporary Popular Writers, St. James Press, 1997.

Periodicals

Irish Times, March 7, 1998.
National Review, December 8, 1997; April 19, 1999.
New York Times, August 20, 1985; August 26, 2001.
Seattle Post-Intelligencer, October 7, 1999.
Washington Post, July 9, 2001; July 15, 2001.

Online

Baenen, Jeff, "Garrison Keillor Spins More Tales from Lake Wobegon," *Prime Time Online,* http://www.rny.com/pubs/pt/pt9801/leisure/keillor.html (November 13, 2001).
Bolick, Katie, "It's Just Work," *Atlantic Unbound,* http://www.theatlantic.com/ (October 8, 1997).
Minnesota Author Biographies Project, http://people.nmhs.org/authors/biog (November 12, 2001).
A Prairie Home Companion Web site, http://www.phc.mpr.org/ (November 13, 2001). □

Patrick Kelly

Patrick Kelly (c. 1954-1990) began designing and sewing clothing when he was a teenager in Mississippi. Although he had some formal fashion training, many of his skills were self-taught. While in his twenties Kelly moved to Paris, started his own design company, and quickly established himself as a reputable designer. He clothes were colorful, fun, and unusual and often had a Southern influence. Large, bright, plastic buttons were his trademark. Kelly was the first American to be allowed into the elite Parisian fashion designer's organization called Chambre Syndicale.

Started Career at an Early Age

Patrick Kelly was born in Vicksburg, Mississippi, on September 24 around 1954. Kelly kept the exact year of his birth a secret. As he stated in a 1986 *Time* magazine article, "I never tell my age because I hope I'll always be the new kid on the block." He came from a working-class African American family. His mother had a master's degree and worked as a home economics teacher. His father worked as a fishmonger, insurance agent, and cab driver. At some point in his childhood his father left home and he was raised primarily by his mother and grandmother, who worked as a cook for an upper-class white family. His keen interest in fashion showed even as a child. His earliest recollection of this passion was when he was about six years old. One day his grandmother brought home a fashion magazine and Kelly noticed that there were not pictures of African American women in it. His grandmother explained that designers did not have time for African American women and Kelly was determined to change this.

Kelly taught himself to sew and began his career as a designer at an early age. While still in junior high Kelly began to design and sew party dresses for girls in the neighborhood. Later in high school he began designing department store windows and drawing sketches for newspaper advertisements. After he graduated from high school in 1972 Kelly attended Jackson State University on a scholarship and studied art history and African American history. He only stayed there for two years when he decided to leave

Mississippi to escape the oppressive racial tensions and to pursue a serious career in fashion.

Kelly moved to Atlanta and got a job sorting clothing for AMVETS, an American veterans' organization. To work his way into the fashion industry Kelly also volunteered to decorate windows for an Yves Saint Laurent boutique called Rive Gauche. These humble beginnings helped Kelly build his fashion career. From the job at AMVETS Kelly had access to a large collection of clothes, some of which carried designer labels. Kelly would redesign the old clothes and sell them on the streets along with some of his original creations. Soon he also began to collect a regular salary for working at the Saint Laurent boutique and this job also gave him some exposure in the fashion industry. Eventually Kelly set up his own vintage clothing store in Atlanta. He also worked as an instructor at the Barbizon Modeling School, where he became friends with several fashion models. One model, Pat Cleveland, convinced him that he should move to New York City if he wanted to really get noticed by the fashion industry.

Moved to Fashion Capital

Kelly followed his friend's advice, moved to New York, and enrolled in the prestigious Parsons School of Design. He struggled financially, however. He was not able to find a steady job and he supported himself with sporadic work, including a part-time job working at Baskin Robbins. He also earned money by selling his own dresses to models. Then his friend Pat Cleveland suggested that he move again,

this time to Paris. Kelly laughed at the idea because he knew he could not afford the trip. However, when a one-way ticket to Paris was mailed to Kelly anonymously in 1979, he seized the opportunity and moved to the fashion capital of the world. Looking back on this important move, Kelly told *Time* magazine in 1986, "I can't say I wouldn't have made it in New York because I didn't stay to find out."

Kelly had much better luck in Paris than he did in New York. He was quickly hired as a costume designer for a nightclub called Le Palace. He continued to sell his own creations on the street and even sold homemade fried chicken dinners to make ends meet. He shared a tiny apartment with a model and made dresses with one Singer sewing machine. His hard work and perseverance paid off for him. People began to recognize Kelly's designs and soon there they were in demand. In 1984 an exclusive Paris boutique called Victoire hired Kelly and gave him a workshop and a showroom. Only a year later Kelly went into business for himself. He and his friend, photographer Bjorn Amelan, joined together to create Patrick Kelly Paris. Soon they were making outfits for Benetton and an upscale Right Bank boutique.

Kelly quickly established his reputation as a designer and his business blossomed. In 1987 he was interviewed by Gloria Steinem for NBC's *Today Show*. Steinem then introduced Kelly to Linda Wachner, the chief executive officer of Warnaco, an apparel manufacturer. Kelly signed a five million dollar contract to create a line of clothing for Warnaco, which gave him international recognition. Soon afterwards he also signed two licensing deals with Vogue Patterns and Streamline Industries for his famous big buttons. After making these deals Kelly's business revenue increased from less than one million dollars a year to more than seven million dollars a year.

Created a Fun Fashion Style with a Southern Touch

Kelly's popularity stemmed from his fun, colorful, and exotic style. As the *Washington Post* described him in 1988, "Patrick Kelly has a witty way with fashion." Kelly's earliest influence was his grandmother. Since she had limited resources, she would replace lost buttons on his clothing with whatever she could find and she would often add her own touch to spruce up the clothing a bit. Large, colorful buttons later became a trademark of Kelly's designs, but his creativity did not stop there. He decorated dresses with colorful bows, embroidered lips and hearts, and even billiard balls. In 1986 *Time* magazine described his clothes as "fitted, funny, and a little goofy."

Price was an important factor for Kelly's designs and he stressed the importance of differentiating between cheap and affordable. *Contemporary Fashion* described Kelly's designs as "unpretentious yet sexy, affordable while glamorous." He strove for the latter in order to distinguish himself from other Parisian designers whose clothes came with a hefty price tag. In a 1986 *Time* magazine article Kelly declared, "I'm the hero of people who just don't want to spend a lot of money on clothes."

Kelly's designs also carried a Southern flavor. He was proud of his heritage and his upbringing as an African American child in Mississippi was reflected in his work. For example, he was known for his watermelon brooches, dresses decorated with gardenias, and polka-dotted bandannas. He also made Billie Holliday and Michael Jackson earrings and used Josephine Baker memorabilia to decorate his showroom. Kelly's use of African American culture in his art even generated some controversy. He created lapel pins featuring black babydoll faces that some thought were offensive to African Americans. Kelly defended the image as a part of Black history. In fact he had a collection of over 6,000 Black dolls from various eras of American history that he hoped to house in a museum. Nonetheless, the pins were more popular in Europe than America because some Americans were afraid the image would be misinterpreted. In an interview with *Essence* magazine, Kelly noted his surprise regarding the controversy. He said, "Recently somebody Black told me they were harassed about wearing the Black baby-doll pin. And I thought, you can wear a machine gun or a camouflage war outfit and people think it's so chic, but you put a little Back baby pin on and people attack you." These pins became a trademark for Kelly and he gave them away to everyone he met. It was estimated that he gave away 800-1,000 pins a month.

Kelly's carefree style and southern heritage were apparent in his own image as well. He was most often seen dressed in a pair of oversized denim overalls. He often sported a baseball cap and his favorite means of transportation was a skateboard. He had a fun-loving and extroverted personality. For example, he would start his fashion shows by entering the stage dressed in his overalls and spray-painting a large read heart on the backdrop of the runway. Parisians loved Kelly's persona as much as they loved his designs. Despite his humble beginnings and simple personal style, Kelly was a sharp businessman and a skilled marketer. He understood the importance of publicity in the fashion industry.

Died at the Height of His Career

Kelly's designs never became a household name, but his clientele included many famous people, such as Bette Davis, Grace Jones, Jessye Norman, Isabella Rossellini, and Jane Seymour. In 1988 Kelly was voted in as a member of the Chambre Syndicale, an elite organization of designers based in Paris. Kelly was the first American to join the ranks of famous designers such as Saint Laurent, Lagerfeld, and Lacroix. One privilege of being a member of this elite group was the opportunity to have a show at the Louvre Palace. True to Kelly's fun style, his first show was a spoof on the Mona Lisa.

Unfortunately, Kelly's career ended soon after he became famous. Kelly died on January 1, 1990. While the official cause of death was listed as bone marrow disease, many suspect he died of acquired immunodeficiency syndrome (AIDS) like several other young prominent figures in the fashion industry who had died in the 1980s, including Perry Ellis, Willi Smith, Isaia Rankin, and Angel Estrada. By the early 1990s the fashion industry had suffered huge losses, both personal and financial, due to the epidemic. A 1990 article in *Time* magazine declared that "The industry's creative energy is being dissipated—and diminished—by AIDS."

Kelly's rather sudden death left a lot of unfinished business. He was negotiating licenses for his designs for furs, sunglasses, and jewelry. He was also looking for a museum to house his large, unique Black doll collection. There was even talk of making an autobiographical movie.

Despite his untimely death, Kelly left his mark on the fashion world. In his obituary *The Independent* declared, "Kelly belonged to that rare group of designers who knew how to wield the cutting scissors and sew a seam. Both proved invaluable when in 1979 he arrived in Paris with nothing but that unflagging good humour." Kelly has also inspired a new generation of designers, including Sharon "Magic" Jordan and Patrick Robinson. Kelly's designs are also on display at the Black Fashion Museum in Washington, D.C. and a special exhibit at the Los Angeles County Museum of Art called "A Century of Fashion, 1900-2000."

Books

Contemporary Fashion, St. James Press, 1995.

Periodicals

Ebony, February 2000.
Essence, May 1989; December 1996.
Independent, January 11, 1990.
Newsweek, June 27, 1988; October 31, 1988; July 13, 1992.
Seattle Times, January 17, 1990.
Time, November 10, 1986; April 3, 1989; April 9, 1990.
U.S. News and World Report, January 15, 1990.
Washington Post, September 25, 1988.

Online

"Black Fashion Museum in Washington, D.C.," http://www.anyiams.com/Fashion_museum.html (November 1, 2001).
"LACMA: A Century of Fashion," http://www.lacma.org/info/press/centFashion.html" (November 1, 2001). □

Walt Kelly

Walt Kelly (1913-1973) was the creator of the popular and acclaimed comic strip "Pogo," whose memorable characters and potent political satire set a new standard for topical humor and complexity. The work of Kelly influenced the creators of *Bone*, "Calvin and Hobbes," "Liberty Meadows," "Mutts," and hundreds of other comic strips and books.

Walter Crawford Kelly was born on August 25, 1913, in Philadelphia, Pennsylvania. While he was still a child, Kelly's family moved to Bridgeport, Connecticut. Kelly's father worked in a munitions plant but dabbled in painting and drawing. He ex-

posed Kelly to art and art technique. In high school, Kelly drew illustrations and cartoons for the school paper and yearbook and illustrated a biography of Bridgeport native P.T. Barnum for the local newspaper.

Kelly graduated from high school in 1930. That same year he met Helen DeLacy at a choir practice. For the next five years, Kelly pursued DeLacy, who was a few years older than him. DeLacy took a job as a Girl Scout executive in southern California in 1935, hoping to leave Kelly behind. But Kelly left his job at General Electric in Bridgeport and moved to Los Angeles, not only to be near DeLacy, but also to work for Walt Disney Studios. There, he finally won her over and they eventually married.

The Disney Years

At Disney, Kelly started as a story man and sketch artist on *Pinocchio* and then became an assistant animator. In addition to working on short subjects, Kelly animated sequences in *Fantasia* and *Dumbo*. But Kelly had problems at the studio, according to his long-time friend, Disney animator Ward Kimball. Most of the creative staff dressed in casual clothes, but Kelly always worked in a three-piece suit, starched collar and bow tie. And his highly personal drawing style made it hard for him to copy model sheets that others designed. Scenes Kelly drew were too distinct, spoiling the seamlessness of the animation. "When Kelly worked with other people, he would always manage to change the drawing of the character a little," Kimball told interviewers Thomas Andrae and Geoffrey Blum in 1988. "Maybe, in

hindsight, we should have made our drawings look like his. He drew very funny Mickeys."

Kelly grew tired of trying to suppress his style. He was more of a writer than an animator and wanted to do his own work and be his own boss. A strike by animators at Disney in 1941 was a turning point for Kelly. Although he agreed with the strikers, mainly in-betweeners and assistants, he had friends in supervisory positions as well, and he did not want to be forced to choose between the two camps. The strike provided the impetus for Kelly to leave Disney. He took a leave of absence, claiming that his sister was ill, and moved back to Connecticut.

Pogo

After months of commuting to New York City looking for freelance work, Kelly took advantage of a contact Disney provided him at Western Printing and Lithographing Company, a magazine and children's book printer that produced Disney and Dell comics. Kelly began writing comic books for Western. In late 1942, his first original comic story, "Albert Takes the Cake," appeared in the inaugural issue of *Animal Comics*. It was the first appearance of the character that would make Kelly famous, Pogo Possum. Pogo and other residents, including Albert the Alligator and a small boy named Bumbazine, lived in and around a swamp Kelly imagined somewhere in the southern United States. Pogo and Bumbazine were both thoughtful, intelligent characters that provided contrast to the antics of others, and Kelly soon realized they were redundant. Bumbazine soon left the stories, which continued to run in *Animal Comics,* and human beings would never again appear in Kelly's swamp.

Health problems kept Kelly from military service during World War II. Instead, he illustrated dictionaries and guidebooks for the U. S. Army. He also continued drawing for Dell comic titles such as *Our Gang* and *Raggedy Ann and Andy.*

Animal Comics ended its run in 1947. In June 1948, just as Kelly was about to attempt a career as a political cartoonist, a new opportunity came his way. The independent liberal newspaper *PM* changed owners. The new owners changed the name to the *New York Star* and hired Kelly as art director and general illustrator. Kelly provided spot drawings, decorative borders, and even the daily "ears" that accompanied the one-word weather forecasts on the masthead. He also became the paper's political cartoonist. Comics historian R. C. Harvey called Kelly's political cartoons "entirely competent, journeyman efforts" but "scarcely brilliant." They were only a foretaste of what was to come.

Pogo Meets the Papers

In September 1948, Kelly decided to start his own comic strip at the *Star,* using the swamp creatures from his earlier story but making the strip more sophisticated. Kelly indulged his love of language with stronger Southern accents, more colorful word choices, malapropisms, and plenty of puns. But the *Star* folded in January 1949.

Kelly shopped the strip around to a number of syndicates, and Post-Hall agreed to give it a try. *Pogo* debuted nationally on May 16, 1949. Kelly reused some of the material from the *Star* strips with revisions. Over the next year, *Pogo* grew in circulation, while Kelly's style matured greatly.

Kelly and his wife had three children, Kathy, Carolyn, and Peter, but in 1951 their marriage ended. He soon married his second wife, Stephanie, who may have been the model for Pogo's love interest, Mam'selle Hepzibah, a cute skunk with a French accent. They would also have three children, Andrew, John, and Stephen.

Pogo Meets the Real World

In 1952, Kelly began to hit his stride with *Pogo*. The possum threw his hat into the ring for the U.S. presidential election. He became the candidate of many college students, and the slogan "I Go Pogo" appeared on posters and lapel pins. Pogo would run for president in every election through 1972 and again in 1988. Also in 1952, the first caricature of an identifiable public figure appeared in *Pogo*, a bullying backwoods wildcat named Simple J. Malarkey, who bore more than a passing resemblance to U.S. Senator Joseph R. McCarthy of Wisconsin.

McCarthy was becoming famous and powerful by investigating the U.S. Army and searching for Communists in the U.S. State Department. He used misinformation and bullying to manipulate the media and Senate witnesses to support his claims. These were tactics that Kelly despised, and he made Malarkey look evil and dangerous. Some newspapers complained that the comics pages were not the place for politics. Some editors moved the strip to the editorial page, others dropped it all together, and a few demanded that Kelly stop drawing caricatures of McCarthy. Kelly responded by putting Malarkey's head in a sack. That only made Malarkey more ominous, since the sack resembled the hoods worn by Klansmen or executioners.

The rest of the 1950s was *Pogo*'s heyday. Kelly reviewed books, wrote articles and nonsense verse, illustrated books, drew magazine covers, delivered hundreds of lectures, and wrote and sang some of the strip's many songs in the record *Songs of the Pogo*. Kelly's peers elected him president of the National Cartoonists Society.

Still a Political Cartoonist

Though an unapologetic liberal, Kelly was never afraid to poke fun at any politician. In 1968, *Pogo* strips featured characters based on Democratic presidential candidates Bobby Kennedy and Eugene McCarthy. The 1970s brought even more acidic caricatures of U.S. Vice President Spiro Agnew and FBI Director J. Edgar Hoover. Once again, some newspapers dropped *Pogo* and others moved it off the comics page. This time, Kelly provided replacement "bunny strips," non-political gags often featuring cute rabbits.

Kelly's strips championed the underdog, the powerless, and the threatened. In the late 1960s, his attention turned to the environment, and he provided the world with an unforgettable slogan. As Pogo looked upon a large pile of trash that was cluttering the swamp, he said: "We have met the enemy, and he is us." This was a paraphrase of a famous dispatch announcing the victory at the battle of Lake Erie during the War of 1812: "We have met the enemy, and they are ours." Kelly's version became a household catch phrase.

Ventured into TV

By the 1960s, Kelly's heart disease, diabetes, smoking, drinking, and hard work began to catch up with him. His wife, Stephanie, was diagnosed with cancer. His assistants, George Ward and Henry Shikuma, began to take over more of the art chores on *Pogo,* and Kelly cut back on some of his outside interests. In the late 1960s, Kelly began to toy with the idea of animating his characters. Legendary cartoon director Chuck Jones, famous for his Bugs Bunny and Daffy Duck cartoons in the 1950s, teamed up with Kelly to produce a half-hour television cartoon, *The Pogo Special Birthday Special.* Selby Daley of MGM Studios, who had also worked for Disney in the 1930s, became Kelly's assistant on the production.

The Pogo Special Birthday Special aired in May 1969, and although it was a ratings success, it disappointed fans of the comic strip. Most disappointed was Kelly. The characters—although they were speaking Kelly's words, and in some cases, even using his voice—were drawn in a style that unmistakably belonged to Jones, not Kelly. After his wife died in early 1970, Kelly decided that he wanted to see his characters animated correctly, and he began to work with Selby Daley on a new television special, *We Have Met the Enemy and He Is Us.*

In October 1972, Kelly had his left leg amputated above the knee due to diabetes. He and Daley were married in the intensive care ward a half-hour before Kelly was wheeled into surgery. The two lived in New York City for the next year. In the fall of 1973, Kelly and Selby traveled to Hollywood to work on *We Have Met the Enemy and He Is Us.* Though under doctor's orders not to drink alcohol, Kelly had one or two drinks. He lapsed into a coma. He died in the Motion Picture and Television Hospital in Woodland Hills, California, on October 18, 1973. The film, though completed by Daley, was never broadcast.

After Kelly's death, Daley and Kelly's son Stephen, with the help of several assistants, continued the strip for a few years. In 1989, the Walt Kelly Estate authorized a new version, titled *Walt Kelly's Pogo.* The strip was written by Larry Doyle and drawn by Neal Sternecky. After Doyle left the strip in 1991, Sternecky went solo with it until 1992, when Kelly's children Pete and Carolyn took over. It only lasted one more year.

Kelly's Legacy

All other attempts at *Pogo* strips paled in comparison to Kelly's originals. Simon and Schuster, for years the publisher of *Pogo* in book form, kept many of the 30-plus titles in print long past Kelly's death and the strip's disappearance from the newspapers. Early editions of the books are prized by collectors and command large sums of money. Another publisher is currently taking on the daunting task of reprinting the entire run of *Pogo* daily strips in multiple volumes, each with remarks by R. C. Harvey.

Pogo broke the ground for comic strips that followed, especially those that wanted to say something about the world. Garry Trudeau's *Doonesbury* and Berke Breathed's *Bloom County* both featured political commentary. Bill Watterson's *Calvin and Hobbes* borrowed a lot of *Pogo's* sense of whimsy and humanity.

Jeff Smith, creator of *Bone,* a fantasy comic book that is published around the world, wrote: "Whenever I get to thinking I've got this whole cartooning gig down cold, I just pull out a *Pogo* book and see how much better it can be."

Books

Kelly, Mrs. Walt and Bill Crouch, *Outrageously Pogo,* Simon and Schuster, 1985.
Kelly, Mrs. Walt and Bill Crouch, *Phi Beta Pogo,* Simon and Schuster, 1989.
Kelly, Mrs. Walt and Bill Crouch, *Pluperfect Pogo,* Simon and Schuster, 1987.
Kelly, Walt, *Pogo,* Volume 1, Fantagraphics Books, 1992.
Levin, Martin, ed., *Five Boyhoods,* Doubleday, 1962. □

Henry Kingsley

Henry Kingsley (1830-1876), the younger brother of famed novelist Charles Kingsley, showed signs of brilliance in his early works, but the majority of the twenty novels he published were either panned or simply ignored. *The Recollections of Geoffrey Hamlyn* (1859) received considerable attention in Australia, and critics concur that his best work is *Ravenshoe* (1862). Following a brief period of marginal fame in the early 1860s, the remainder of Kingsley's life was marked by literary failure and poverty.

Fun and Folly

Henry Kingsley was born on January 2, 1830, at Barnack in the Northamptonshire countryside of England. The youngest child, he was the fifth son born to Reverend Charles and Mary (Lucas) Kingsley. Two of his brothers achieved significant fame during their life times, Charles as a novelist and George as a traveler and scientist. Soon after Kingsley's birth, before his first birthday, the family moved to Clovelly, Devonshire. When Kingsley was six years old, his father became the rector at St. Luke's Church in Chelsea. Both Devonshire and Chelsea later figured prominently into Kingsley's novels. Most of his childhood was spent in London, where he investigated his literary interests in his father's well-stocked library and local bookstalls.

Kingsley's formal education began in 1844 at King's College School. Six years later, in 1850, he matriculated at Worcester College, Oxford. Kingsley's time at Oxford was marked by a near total disregard for his studies and a clear commitment to folly and fun. Kingsley's taste for pleasure and athletic prowess made him considerably popular

among his peers. He once won a wager with friend Sir Edwin Arnold by running a mile, rowing a mile, and trotting a mile within fifteen minutes. Yet like his interest in strenuous sports, Kingsley's behavior often verged on overindulgence, including smoking and drinking. He and Arnold also formed a short-lived secret society, called the Fez Club, which was based on misogyny (hatred of women) and a commitment to celibacy.

Australia

After three wasted years Kingsley suddenly, and much to his parents' disappointment, left Oxford without obtaining a degree to pursue adventure and fortune in Australia, which was at the peak of its gold rush. Having accrued significant debt due to his lavish spending, Kingsley was surprised by an unexpected inheritance of three hundred pounds from a great aunt. This money allowed him to settle his accounts and purchase passage to Australia. Whatever Kingsley expected or hoped to find in the wild outback, any visions of wealth or glory were quickly replaced by a harsh reality of uncertainty and deprivation. The naïve twenty-three-year-old Kingsley soon discovered that the glowing letters of introduction he had brought along were absolutely without value. For the next five years, with no contact with his family, he moved from job to job.

After laboring fruitlessly in the gold mines, Kingsley was employed by the Sydney Mounted Police for a time. He then moved on to work briefly as a farmer worker and stock driver. After another stint in the gold mines, Kingsley found himself panhandling for food and lodging to sustain his merger existence. Then, as suddenly as he left his family, he returned to them in 1958. Fearing that his parents may have died without his knowledge, Kingsley was pleased to find his mother and father living in Eversley, Hampshire, where his brother Charles was serving as the curate. His parents, overjoyed to see their prodigal son, welcomed him back into the family. Encouraged by Charles, who had in his younger brother's absence established himself as a well-known novelist, Kingsley decided to make a serious attempt at writing.

Early Success

Kingsley's first attempt as a fiction writer produced one of his best works. *The Recollections of Geoffrey Hamlyn,* published in 1859 by Alexander Macmillan upon George's recommendation, became something of a literary and popular success. The three-volume novel starts the reader off in England, but in volume two moves to the landscape of Australia. Drawing on his personal experiences, Kingsley painted a splendidly romance picture of the rugged, heroic life of Australian settlers. Although critics remarked that his plot was marked by unnecessary and annoying digressions, Kingsley displayed his ability to create a sensational, dramatic scene, offering readers the adventures of an Australian brushfire, a kangaroo hunt, a child lost in the brush, and encounters with aborigines. Well received in England, *Geoffrey Hamlyn* became a national phenomenon in Australia, even being called the greatest Australian novel of all time.

Kingsley followed the success of *Geoffrey Hamlyn* with the publication in 1862 of his second novel, *Ravenshoe,* considered by literary critics to be his best work. The complex plot of the novel revolves around the life of Charles Ravenshoe. In line to inherit the family estate, Charles meets an incredible list of obstacles that force him from boyhood into manhood. The plot is set in motion when Densil Ravenshoe agrees to allow his wife to raise George in the Protestant faith. In turn, the Roman Catholic family priest, fearing a loss of influence and position, attempts to disavow George's claim as rightful heir. "Not only is the plot complex," noted William H. Scheuerle in his introduction to *Ravenshoe,* "but it is melodramatic and a little silly, turning around a duality of Kingsley's favorite devices: infants switched at birth, and children falsely declared to be illegitimate until a secret marriage certificate establishes their legitimacy. Disappearances and minor but related mysteries compound the complications, and overhanging and influencing all is a religious turbulence that initiates much subterfuge."

The early 1860s were probably the happiest time in Kingsley's life. He was living with his mother after his father's death in 1862 and enjoying mostly positive reviews of his writing. In 1863, he published his third novel, *Austin Elliott,* which follows the life of its title character in the aftermath of a duel. On July 19, 1864, Kingsley married his second cousin, Sarah Maria Kingsley Haselwood, a twenty-two-year-old penniless ex-governess who also brought the responsibility of her mother's welfare to the marriage. The couple moved into a charming cottage, called Hillside House, in Wargrave, Berkshire, and at first led a pleasant life, frequently entertaining literary guests, such as famed authors Adolph Huxley, George Meredith, and Lewis Carroll. However, no longer under his mother's financial umbrella, Kingsley soon found himself in financial trouble. His wife's ongoing health problems, including multiple miscarriages, added to his burden. Before long, Kingsley was complaining to family and friends that he had no money at all.

Financial Hardships

Under pressure to produce royalty moneys, Kingsley began a speedy pace of writing. First appearing in monthly installments in *MacMillan's Magazine* from November 1863 to April 1865, and later published in 1865 as a three-volume set, Kingsley's *The Hillyars and the Burtons* received barely a passing glance from critics and the public alike. Although the novel is set in Australia, it failed to garner the hearts of Australian readers as *Geoffrey Hamlyn* had. Whereas *Geoffrey Hamlyn* was the tale of aristocratic British settlers attempting to reap rewards from the land, *The Hillyars and the Burtons* follows the lives of hardworking immigrants who pursue success in Australia through thriftiness and hard work.

The novel suffered from a confused plot, a fault in Kingsley's writing that would come to denote the decline of his literary works. Yet, as a writer of romance, Kingsley showed glances of talent in the midst of his disintegrating story line. "One boy-dream he found had faded away," Kingsley wrote near the end of his novel, "in the rude

daylight of frost, hunger and failure; the dream of Emma Burton. She is but as a figure in a dream to him now. The man Erne thinks of the love which the child Erne had to her, as a boy's fancy, beautiful enough, but childish, romantic, and purged him from him in those horrible trenches. Do you like the Child Erne or Man Erne the best? It is not for me to decide, but I think I will choose the child."

Writing out of financial necessity seldom brings forth fountains of literary brilliance, and in Kingsley's case, seemed to have caused what imperfect talent he had to begin with to disintegrate completely. Over the next four years he published four more works: *Leighton Court* (1866), *Silcote of Silcotes* (1867), *Mademoiselle Mathilde* (1868), and *Stretton* (1869). Each received poor reviews and was wholly ignored by the reading public. Desperate to relieve himself of his financial difficulties and beaten down by the successive failures of his writing, Kingsley moved to Edinburgh in 1869 to become the editor of the *Daily Review,* a newspaper run by the Free Church Party, a coalition that seceded from the Church of Scotland over political and civil, rather than religious, grounds. By all accounts, Kingsley was a poor fit for his new post. Along with his predisposition to support the Church of England, his life as a novelist hardly equipped him with the skills to meet constant deadlines, attend to details, and oversee administrative functions.

War Correspondent

In August 1870, with the onset of the Franco-Prussian War, Kingsley abandoned his editor's desk to become a reporter in the battlefields. He was present at the battle of Sedan, which took place on September 1, 1870, and marked the defeat of the French army and the surrender of Napoleon. The brutality and inhumanity of the war scenes that spread before him captured Kingsley's creative spirit again, and he wrote with distinction of the horrors he encountered. Scheuerle offered an example of Kingsley's war correspondence: "The night was profoundly dark, but there were innumerable stars over head as I sat down to look over the battlefield of that morning towards Metz. . . . There was no movement of any kind; now and then some wandering wind, coming from the battlefield, would whisper in the rye-grass about my head, like the whispers of the dead men who lay heaped below. Knowing what had happened below that morning, the matter became somewhat too solemn, and so I rose and left the night winds to whistle round that desolate down by themselves."

Literary Decline

After two months, Kingsley, recovering from malaria, returned to his editorship in Edinburgh. However, before the end of 1870 he stepped down from the job at the request of the owners who were dissatisfied with his level of service. Kingsley and his wife moved to London, and Kingsley renewed his writing career by rapidly producing several more works. By the end of 1872, he had published three novels, an allegory, and a story for boys—each with the same lack of success. In 1872 he attempted to regain his place in the literary world with *Oakshott Castle, Being the Memoirs of an Eccentric Nobleman,* but the three-volume work was so disjointed that critics were too confused to offer much specific criticism, except to conclude that it was one of the worst novels ever published. *Oakshott Castle* is so stunningly disorganized and incoherent that it has made literary historians wonder at the cause of Kingsley's seemingly complete loss of literary conception. Alcoholism, mental imbalance, and poor health have been theorized, but remain pure conjecture.

Kingsley, who had been reduced to pleading for funds from his famous brother Charles, finally found a respite from poverty in 1873 when he received an inheritance upon his mother's death. With the money, Kingsley and his wife moved to Kentish Town, an outlying area of London. The following year, upon receiving the news that he was dying from cancer of the tongue and throat, caused by excessive smoking, Kingsley moved to Cuckfield, a quaint country village in Sussex. In the two years before his death, Kingsley continued to write, producing four more novels, along with a series of literary essays. He died on May 24, 1876, having never regained a modicum of his early success.

Books

Drabble, Margaret, ed. *The Oxford Companion to English Literature.* Rev. ed. Oxford: Oxford University Press, 1998.

Kirkpatrick, D. L., ed. *Reference Guide to English Literature.* 2nd ed. Chicago: St. James Press, 1991.

Kramer, Leonie. Introduction to *The Hillyars and the Burtons,* by Henry Kingsley. Sydney: Sydney University Press, 1972.

Nadel, Ira B., and William E. Fredeman, eds. *Dictionary of Literary Biography, Volume 21: Victorian Novelists Before 1885.* Detroit: The Gale Group, 1983.

Scheuerle, William H., ed. Introduction to *Ravenshoe,* by Henry Kingsley. Lincoln: University of Nebraska Press, 1967.

Sutherland, John. *The Stanford Companion to Victorian Fiction.* Stanford: Stanford University Press, 1989.

Sanders, Lloyd C., ed. *Celebrities of the Century: A Dictionary of Men and Women of the Nineteenth Century.* London: Cassell and Company, 1887. Reprint, Ann Arbor: Gryphon Books, 1971.

Stephen, Sir Leslie, and Sir Sidney Lee. *The Dictionary of National Biography.* Oxford: Oxford University Press, 1973.

Vinson, James, ed. *Great Writers of the English Language: Novelists and Prose Writers.* New York: St. Martin's Press, 1979.

Wilde, William H., Joy Hooton, and Barry Andrews. *The Oxford Companion to Australian Literature.* 2nd ed. Melbourne: Oxford University Press, 1994. □

Sophia Vasilevna Kovalevsky

Sophia Kovalevsky (1850-1891) was the first woman to earn a Ph.D. in mathematics, despite the fact that Russia, her native country, and many other European universities at that time did not allow women. Kovalevsky was inspired by the nihilist movement in Russia, which emphasized the power of education and the equality of women. Kovalevsky was also an accomplished writer and a strong proponent of higher education for women.

Family Life

Sophia Korvin-Krukovsky was born on January 15, 1850, in Moscow to Vasily Vasilevich Korvin-Krukovsky, a general in the artillery garrison of the Russian army, and Elizabeth Fedrovna. She was the second child born to the couple; her sister, Anna, was six years older. Five years after her birth, her brother, Fedor, was born. Sophia was raised primarily by a serf nurse named Praskovia. As a child she was nicknamed "Little Sparrow" because she was small and energetic.

When Sophia was eight years old her father, then 59, resigned his commission in the army and moved the family to his country estate in Palibino. At this time he also hired a Polish tutor, Iosif Ignatevich Matevich, and an English governess, Margarita Frantsevna Smith, to supervise his children. In her memoir, Kovalevsky portrays herself as a sad and lonely child who felt unloved. Her sister garnered much attention for being the oldest and her brother was the pride of his parents because he was the only son. However, she eventually developed a special bond with her father and became his favorite child when her intellectual potential became apparent.

Sophia was also close to her father's older brother, Petr Vasilevich Korvin-Krukovsky. He was a well-read man who shared with his niece his political views and knowledge on various subjects, including mathematics. Her introduction to advanced mathematics came as an accident. When the

Korvin-Krukovsky family moved to Palibino, they redecorated their home. When they ran out of wallpaper for the nursery, her father used sheets of old school notes instead. The notes were on differential integral analysis and were her first encounter with calculus.

Early Education

Sophia struggled against social conventions to get a proper education as a child. Though it was then believed that very young children should not be taught to read, she sat in on her sister's lessons and practiced reading by herself. When her governess limited the number and types of books she was allowed, she sneaked into her father's study to read from his collection. Her formal education was the responsibility of the family tutor, Malevich. He taught her a broad range of subjects from age the time she was 8 until she was 17. She excelled in mathematics. When her father realized this, he instructed her to focus on other subjects. She followed his orders during her tutoring time, but continued to read math books alone at night.

Sophia was allowed to continue her formal mathematics training after she impressed a neighbor with her skills. The neighbor was Nikolai Nikanorovich Tyrtov, a professor of physics at the St. Petersburg Naval Academy. He brought the Korvin-Krukovsky family a copy of a beginning physics textbook as a gift, and she immediately began to read it. She had difficulty understanding it at first because it contained trigonometry, and Malevich was unable to explain the advanced math to her. Through perseverance Sophia figured out the mathematical formulae by herself and finished the book. Tyrtov was impressed by her ability to explain how she figured out the trigonometry. Tyrtov was a strong proponent of higher education for women, and he eventually persuaded the general to allow his daughter to pursue an education in mathematics.

When Sophia was 18, her family moved to St. Petersburg in order to get a better education for her and her brother. Her father hired Alexander Nikolayevich Strannoliubsky, a highly accomplished teacher, as a math tutor. Her remarkable mathematical abilities persuaded Strannoliubsky to become actively involved in promoting women's education in Russia. Eventually he encouraged her to pursue a broader university education. However, Russian universities were closed to women and unmarried women were not allowed to travel abroad, even to study, unless accompanied by a chaperone.

Nihilist Influences

While Sophia was pursuing her scientific interests, her older sister was developing her literary talents and political views, both of which later influenced Sophia's life. Anna began writing as a pastime but eventually secretly published two short stories without her father's permission in a literary journal edited by Fedor and Mikhail Dostoevsky. This led to a brief courtship between Anna and the famous novelist Fedor Dostoevsky, whom Sophia was also very fond of. Anna also became involved in the nihilist movement in Russia. As Koblitz explained in *A Convergence of Lives,* a nihilist "basically denoted a person who questioned just about everything in traditional tsarist Russia, had great faith in the natural sciences and the power of education, strongly believed in the equality of women, and desired to be of use to the common people in some capacity." Anna's political views influenced her sister, who saw this movement as a means to pursue her education. The sisters decided that the only way to further their education would be for one of them to marry so they could both travel abroad. They planned a "fictitious marriage" whereby a man would agree to the marriage ceremony, but would then let the woman pursue her own life. This was not an unusual arrangement at the time since it was the only way to free a woman from her parents' authority.

The sisters decided that Anna should partake in the fictitious marriage since she was older. However, when the intended husband, nihilist Vladimir Onufrievich Kovalevsky, a publisher of political and scientific works, met the sisters, he was more interested in Sophia because of her intellectual achievements. The couple married in September 1868 and settled in St. Petersburg. Sophia Kovalevsky continued her math lessons with Strannoliubsky but also sat in on classes at the Medical-Surgical Academy. There she befriended a woman who had started her own gynecological practice, and Kovalevsky briefly entertained the idea of a career in medicine. However, she soon realized that mathematics was her true passion.

Pursuit of Higher Education

In order for Kovalevsky to pursue a formal education in mathematics, the newlyweds first moved to Vienna. Kovalevsky was allowed to study physics there, but she could not find a math professor to work with her, so the couple moved to Heidelberg. There, Kovalevsky was allowed to take math courses as well as a variety of other subjects, and her husband studied geology and paleontology. During this time the couple traveled extensively and had social contacts with the leading intellectuals of that time, including Charles Darwin, Thomas Huxley, George Elliot, and Herbert Spencer.

The Kovalevskys soon left Heidelberg to pursue their separate educations. Vladimir moved to Vienna, while Sophia went to Berlin to study with the world-renowned mathematician, Karl Theodore Weierstrass. Weierstrass was reluctant to take Kovalevsky as a student and gave her a test with difficult math problems before agreeing to work with her. He was so impressed by her performance on his test that he tried to get her admitted to the university. He was not successful, so Weierstrass tutored her privately for the next four years. At first he did not consider the possibility of preparing her for a doctorate because he did not believe that married women needed a career. However, when he learned the truth about Kovalevsky's marriage, he changed his mind.

Kovalevsky worked on three doctoral theses under Weierstrass's guidance and applied to the University of Gottingen, which allowed foreigners to obtain degrees in abstentia. Her first paper, and most significant contribution to mathematics, was on the theory of partial differential equations. It was published in *Crulle's Journal,* which was a major accomplishment for a young academic. Her second paper, in theoretical astronomy, was about the form of Saturn's rings, and the third paper explained how to reduce certain integrals to less complicated forms. Her papers were accepted at Gottingen and were so remarkable that she was excused from taking the final oral examination. She received her Ph.D. in mathematics, summa cum laude, in August 1874. Kovalevsky was the first woman to obtain a doctorate in this field.

Two years earlier Vladimir Kovalevsky completed his dissertation in paleontology from Jena University in Germany. In 1874 Kovalevsky and her husband reunited and returned to Russia in search of academic positions. Neither was successful, so Vladimir got involved with some business ventures and Sophia began writing for a newspaper as a theater critic and became a public supporter of women's higher education. As Kovalevsky explained in *A Russian Childhood*, "Various circumstances existed in Russia which distracted me from serious scientific work: society itself, and those conditions under which one had to live." The couple's marriage became stronger and they decided to have a child together. In October 1878 their daughter, Sophia Vladimirovna, was born. For the next two years Kovalevsky concentrated on her new family instead of mathematics.

International Recognition

In 1880 a colleague of the Kovalevskys invited Sophia to present a paper at the Sixth Congress of Natural Scientists in Petersburg. Since Kovalevsky had not done any mathematical work in six years, she presented one of her dissertations from Gottingen. The response was very positive, and colleagues persuaded Kovalevsky to return to academia. She traveled to Berlin and Paris to reunite with Weierstrass and conduct research on the refraction of light in crystals. During this time her husband's financial enterprises failed. Vladimir had been suffering from depression, and when his next job opportunity also fell through he committed suicide.

Kovalevsky was devastated by her husband's death. In 1883 a colleague offered Kovalevsky a teaching position at Stockholm University. After only a year, she was appointed to full professor and published her research on light refraction. In 1885 Kovalevsky was appointed chair of mechanics. Throughout her life Kovalevsky was also very interested in literature and now she decided to pursue it more seriously. She co-authored a play called *A Struggle for Happiness* with Anne Charlotte Leffler. The play was not well received, but Kovalevsky did not give up writing. She wrote some novels, radical political books such as *A Nihilist Girl,* and her memoirs.

Mathematics remained her main passion. In 1888 she won the prestigious Prix Bordin competition sponsored by the French Academy of Science. Her brilliant career was cut short, however, when she died on February 10, 1891, of pneumonia at age 41. Kovalevsky's legacy lies not only in her accomplishments as a mathematician, but also in the recognition and respect that she brought women in academia and her efforts to support women pursuing a higher education.

Books

Cooke, Roger, *The Mathematics of Sonya Kovalevskaya,* Springer-Verlag, 1984.

Kennedy, Don H., *Little Sparrow: A Portrait of Sophia Kovalevsky,* Ohio University Press, 1983.

Koblitz, Ann Hubner, *A Convergence of Lives. Sofia Kovalevskaia: Scientist, Writer, Revolutionary,* Rutgers University Press, 1993.

Kochina, Pelageya, *Love and Mathematics: Sofya Kovalevskaya,* Mir Publishers, 1985.

Kovalevskaya, Sofya, *A Russian Childhood,* Springer-Verlag, 1978.

Leffler, Ana Carlotta, *Sonia Kovalevaky,* MacMillan and Co., 1895.

Periodicals

Natural History, June 1996.

Online

"Engines of Our Ingenuity No. 225: Sonya Kovalevsky," *University of Houston,* http://www.uh.edu/engines/epi225.html (January 11, 2002).

"The Queen of PDE's,"*Women in Math,* http://www.mathnews.uwaterloo.ca/Bestof/WomenInMath6904.html (January 11, 2002).

"Sofia Vasilevna Kovalevskaia (1850-1891)," *American University,* http://www.american.edu/academic.depts/cas/mathstat/skday01/BIO-SK.html (January 11, 2002).

"Sofia Vasilevna Kovalevskaya,"*University of St. Andrews,* http://www-groups.dcs.st-andrews.ac.uk/~history/Miscellaneous/Kovalevskaya/biog.html (January 11, 2002).

"Sonya Kovalevsky," *Bellevue Community College,* http://www.scidiv.bcc.ctc.edu/Math/Kovalevsky.html (January 11, 2002).

"Sophia Kovalevskaya," *Agnes Scott College,* http://www.agnesscott.edu/lriddle/women/kova.html (January 10, 2002). □

Stanley Kunitz

At the age of 95, Stanley Kunitz (born 1905) became the oldest person ever to serve as Poet Laureate of the United States. One of the finest American poets of the Twentieth Century, Kunitz produced only 12 books in more than 70 years, but the quality of his work remained consistent. Kunitz has earned many awards, including the Pulitzer Prize, National Book Award, and Bollingen Prize in Poetry.

Haunted by his Father's Death

Stanley Jasspon Kunitz was born in Worcester, Massachusetts, on July 29, 1905. He was raised in a Lithuanian Jewish household in a working-class community, the son of Solomon Kunitz, a dressmaker, and Yetta Helen (Jasspon) Kunitz. His father killed himself

shortly before Stanley was born "by drinking carbolic acid in a park," according to *People* magazine's William Plummer. Kunitz spent a lonely childhood. Birthdays were not celebrated in his house and his father's death was a taboo topic. Nevertheless, the tragic event visited Kunitz in his dreams, and later, as an adult, he grappled with the loss in his poems. The poem "End of Summer" evokes the event: "Bolt upright in my bed that night/ I saw my father flying;/ the wind was walking on my neck,/ the windowpanes were crying." In a later volume, *The Testing Tree: Poems,* published in 1971, Kunitz "ruthlessly prods wounds," according to Stanley Moss of the *Nation.* "His primordial curse is the suicide of his father before his birth. The poems take us into the sacred woods and houses of his 66 years, illuminate the images that have haunted him."

Despite his depressing home life, Kunitz excelled at school. He was class valedictorian at Worcester Classical High School and won a scholarship to Harvard University, where he studied under the famous philosopher Alfred North Whitehead and rubbed shoulders with the future head of the Manhattan Project, J. Robert Oppenheimer. In 1926, Kunitz graduated summa cum laude with a degree in English and enrolled in a doctoral degree program. He wanted to teach at Harvard, but anti-Semitic attitudes in the Ivy League proved to be an obstacle, and he dropped out after completing the requirements for his master's degree.

Kunitz took a newspaper job at *The Worcester Telegram.* The highlight of his journalism career was covering the 1921 trial of Nicola Sacco and Bartolomeo Vanzetti,

Italian anarchists convicted of robbing and killing a Boston shoe factory paymaster and his guard. After the trial ended, Kunitz went to New York seeking a publisher for Vanzetti's letters. Though he failed to interest any editors in the project, he wound up staying in the city.

Early Success as Poet

Eventually, he moved to a farmhouse in Connecticut, where he wrote poetry and edited reference books for the H.W. Wilson publishing house. He was editor of the *Wilson Library Bulletin* and co-editor of *Twentieth Century Authors.* Around this time, his poems started appearing in some of the most prestigious literary magazines in the United States, including the *Dial, New Republic, Poetry,* and *Commonweal.*

In 1930, at the age of 25, Kunitz published his first book of poems, *Intellectual Things.* Kunitz's early poems reflect an opaque style influenced by English metaphysical poets John Donne and George Herbert. He later adopted a simpler style, more accessible to readers. His next book of verse, *Passport to the War: A Selection of Poems,* published fourteen years later, likewise garnered critical praise. The poems in this volume reflected Kunitz's attempt to work out his anger on the page. "I had to address the trauma of my childhood and resolve it," he later told Plummer.

In 1959, Kunitz won the Pulitzer Prize for his third book *Selected Poems, 1928-1958.* His next book, *The Testing Tree: Poems,* published in 1971, marked a significant departure from his earlier work. Poet Robert Lowell compared the two books in the *New York Times Book Review* by saying that the two volumes "are landmarks of the old and new style. The smoke has blown off. The old Delphic voice has learned to speak 'words that cats and dogs can understand.'"

Other volumes by Kunitz include *The Terrible Threshold: Selected Poems, 1940-70* and *The Wellfleet Whale and Companion Poems,* which appeared in 1983. The lengthy title poem of the latter volume recalled the beaching and death of a whale near his Provincetown, Massachusetts, home. Marie Henault in the *Dictionary of Literary Biography* called it "an austere and ambitious philosophic poem. . . . Its first-person-plural speaker gives the poem an elevated tone that allows the whale to become 'like a god in exile/ . . . delivered to the mercy of time. . . .'"

Expressed Political Views

Kunitz maintained a status as a conscientious objector during World War II, but he was drafted anyway and served in the U.S. Army from 1943 to 1945. He was not forced to fight on the front lines but was assigned the task of cleaning bathrooms. Eventually, he rose to the rank of sergeant, but Kunitz never forgot his early humiliation. It took 20 years, but Kunitz finally got his revenge on the military. In 1965, he and fellow poet Lowell organized a Vietnam War protest that turned the White House Arts Festival into what Kunitz proudly termed "a passionate fiasco."

Kunitz's anti-government attitudes seeped into his poetry. From 1974 to 1976, Kunitz served as a poetry consultant in the Library of Congress's Poetry Office. His poem

"The Lincoln Relics," which he wrote during those years, reflects his disdain for the U.S. government: "Mr. President/ In this Imperial City,/ awash in gossip and power,/ where marble eats marble/ and your office has been defiled,/ I saw piranhas darting/ between the rose-veined columns, avid to strip the flesh/ from the Republic's bones./ Has no one told you/ how the slow blood leaks/ from your secret wound?"

Kunitz believes the poet's role is to "demonstrate the power of the solitary conscience," as he told *Washington Post* staff writer Elizabeth Kastor. "It's a terrible power to entrust to people who are not spiritually great, that's all there is to it," Kunitz said of government officials. "You see it in the callousness, self-aggrandizement, insensitivity to the plight of the poor. In the general level of ethical conduct, the state has become an abomination."

Teaching Work

In 1945, Kunitz won a prestigious Guggenheim fellowship, and a year later took his first teaching post at Bennington College in Vermont. During the 1950s and 1960s, he taught at several other institutions, including the New School for Social Research in New York, Brandeis University, the University of Washington, and Columbia University. From his early brush with anti-Semitism at Harvard, he went on to teach at Ivy League schools such as Columbia, Yale, and Princeton. But rather than settling on one campus, Kunitz preferred to do short-term stints. He thought that accepting a long-term commitment would stifle his creativity. "I never accepted tenure," he explained in an interview in the *Boston Globe,* "because I recognized that it would be fatal for me to be a professor who wrote poetry rather than a poet who had a job in the academy."

Through his writing and teaching, Kunitz amassed a group of proteges and friends that reads like a *Who's Who* of Twentieth Century poetry. His closest friends included Lowell and Theodore Roethke. Allen Ginsberg solicited Kunitz's comments before publishing "Howl," the Beat poem that defined a generation. Kunitz taught or advised well-known poets such as Carolyn Kizer, James Wright, Louise Gluck, and Robert Hass.

Kunitz's mentoring extended to the visual arts. He interacted with painters Robert Motherwell and Mark Rothko and married artist Elise Asher on June 21, 1958. Each had one daughter from a previous marriage. The couple divided time between New York and Provincetown, where Kunitz ran Fine Arts Work Center, a colony for young poets and artists he founded in 1968.

In 2000, Kunitz was appointed to be the tenth Poet Laureate of the United States, the highest literary honor in America. In explaining the selection, Librarian of Congress James Billington said Kunitz "continues to be a mentor and model for several generations of poets, and he brings uniquely to the office of poet laureate a full lifetime of commitment to poetry." Literary critics applauded the choice. "What sets Kunitz apart from most people," observed Henry Taylor in the *Washington Post,* "is his level of emotional intensity that historically has been difficult to maintain as one ages." The job requires recipients to give a reading at the start of their tenure, deliver an essay at the end, and help organize the library's literary programs. "It's a wonderful selection," *Atlantic* poetry editor Peter Davison told the *Boston Globe.* "Stanley is going to hold the office as a symbol of dedication to a life in poetry."

Despite his lofty achievements, Kunitz always maintained a solid grounding. Gardening became a lifelong passion for Kunitz and provided inspiration for his poetry. He tried his hand at farming twice in his life, first in Connecticut, then in Pennsylvania. The success of his 2,000 square-foot garden in the front yard of his Provincetown home is one of his proudest achievements.

Kunitz explained his fascination with nature to *Contemporary Authors:* "One of my feelings about working the land is that I am celebrating a ritual of death and resurrection. Every spring I feel that. I am never closer to the miraculous than when I am grubbing in the soil." Indeed, he told the *Boston Globe* that gardening refreshed his spirit and prepared him for writing: "To conquer a piece of earth," Kunitz said, "an area of earth, and make it as beautiful as one can dream of it being: That is art, too. A man cannot be separated from the earth. I come out of the garden every day feeling, oh, inspired in a way that one needs in order to convert the daily-ness of the life into something greater than that little life itself."

Books

Henault, Marie, *Stanley Kunitz,* Twayne, 1980.
Newsmakers, Issue 2, The Gale Group, 2001.

Periodicals

Boston Globe, August 27, 2000.
Nation, September 20, 1971.
New York Times Book Review, March 21, 1971.
People, October 30, 2000, p. 159.
Washington Post, May 12, 1987; July 29, 2000; October 1, 2000; June 21, 2001.

Online

Contemporary Authors Online, The Gale Group, 2001. ☐

L

Kenesaw Mountain Landis

As major league baseball's first commissioner, Judge Kenesaw Mountain Landis (1866-1944) cleaned up a sport that had been almost fatally corrupted by ties to organized gambling. Ruling with an autocratic hand, Landis saved baseball from squabbling owners and miscreant players and presided over the sport's ascendancy into American's undisputed national pastime during the era between the two World Wars.

A Self-Promoter

During the U.S. Civil War, Abraham H. Landis was a surgeon with the 35th Ohio Volunteer Infantry Regiment. On General William Sherman's famous march through Georgia in 1864, Landis nearly lost a leg to a Confederate cannonball at the Battle of Kennesaw Mountain. Two years later, he insisted on naming the sixth of his seven children after that battle, though he misspelled the mountain's name, dropping one ''n.''

Many of his friends called Kenesaw Mountain Landis by the nickname Kennie. His older brothers and sisters called him ''the Squire'' for his pompous manner, even at a young age. The family moved to Logansport, Indiana, when Kennie was eight. There he learned to play baseball around the same time as the first professional baseball league, the National League, was forming. He was skilled at baseball but bedeviled by mathematics, and he dropped out of high school before graduation.

As a teenager, Landis played first base for the semipro Goosetown, Indiana, team, and at the age of 17 became its manager. Though only a wiry 5 foot 7 inches, he was offered a professional contract but turned it down because he said he wanted to play ''merely for sport and the love of the game.'' Yet he did not lack competitive drive, winning many medals in bicycle races at county fairs. On one occasion, displaying his unique gift from self-promotion, he pinned 20 store-bought medals on his chest and showed up in a strange town for a big race. Intimidated, his rivals were defeated.

After working various odd jobs as a handyman, an errand boy, a clerk in a general store, and a newspaper hawker, Landis caught on as a court reporter in South Bend, Indiana. He loved the showmanship of the world of law and quickly gained influential friends. In 1886 he became the aide to Indiana's Secretary of State. The following year he was admitted to the state bar, and in 1891 he graduated from Union College of Law in Chicago. Early in his law school days, he was denied admission to a fraternity because he looked like a country bumpkin. Outraged, he organized the other non-fraternity students and they took over the school government.

Even though he had been a high school dropout, Landis proved to be a genius at advancing himself. His rapid rise continued in 1893 when his father's former commanding officer, Walter Greshman, became U.S. Secretary of State and made Landis his personal secretary. President Grover Cleveland was so impressed with his work that he offered him a post as minister to Venezuela, but Landis declined, instead moving back to Chicago in 1895 to practice law and marry a young socialite, Winifred Reed.

Landis became an ardent Chicago Cubs fan and sometimes asked for postponements of court hearings so he could

285

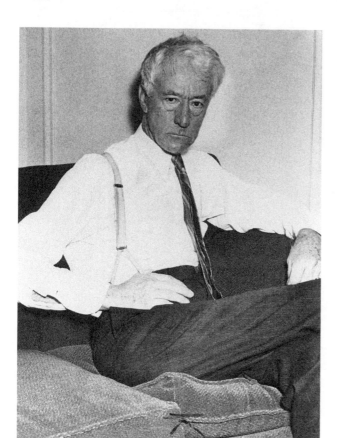

attend a crucial game. He said baseball was a great game and "remarkable for its cleanness" in an era where other sports had an unsavory relationship with gamblers.

Trust-busting Judge

Two of Landis's brothers were elected to the U.S. Congress and Landis was approached to run, but declined. In 1905, President Theodore Roosevelt appointed Landis to a newly created federal judgeship, the District Court of Northern Illinois, in Chicago. Landis was a flamboyant judge who engaged in frequent theatrical flourishes, jumping out of his chair and pointing fingers at recalcitrant witnesses. His procedures often were unorthodox and autocratic; for instance, he would hold suspects without warrants and order people to appear before him without subpoenas.

Landis became famous in 1907 when he summoned the nation's wealthiest man, John D. Rockefeller, to testify in an antitrust case against his own company, Standard Oil. After Rockefeller's evasive testimony, Landis slapped a $29.2 million fine on Standard Oil for colluding with railroads to fix prices. His decision was later overturned on appeal. Citing many cases where his decisions were eventually overturned, critics denounced Landis as a judge who played to the crowds. "His career typifies the heights to which dramatic talent may carry a man in America if only he has the foresight not to go on the stage," wrote sportswriter Heywood Broun.

In 1915, Landis presided over an antitrust suit by the upstart Federal League against baseball's two established major leagues, challenged organized baseball's reserve clause, which gave the American and National leagues lifetime rights to a player's services. He delayed his decision for 11 months, and the frustrated Federal League owners finally agreed to a buyout before Landis rendered a verdict.

During World War I, Landis was an ardent patriot. He issued several harsh verdicts to alleged seditionists, fining members of the International Workers of the World a total of $2.3 million for draft evasion and sentencing them to up to 20 years in prison. The sentences later were commuted. In another famous trial, Landis, who had said German Americans' hearts were "reeking with disloyalty," gave radical German Austrian émigré Victor Berger and five other socialists twenty-year sentences for conspiracy, saying later he wished he could have had them "lined up against a wall and shot." The Supreme Court later reversed that decision.

Cleaned Up Baseball

In 1919, at the behest of a ring of mobsters, members of the Chicago White Sox conspired to throw the World Series to the underdog Cincinnati Reds. The affair was covered up but suspicions grew about a fix. The owners, who had run the sport for decades with a weak governing commission, realized they needed a strong leader to dispel debilitating doubts about the game's integrity. On November 12, 1920, 14 owners showed up in Landis's courtroom, hats in hand. The judge told them to be quiet while his court was in session, demonstrating to them that he would not be cowed. That same day, he took the new job of baseball commissioner for $50,000 a year after getting a contract which specified that he could not be fired, fined, or criticized in public by the owners, his ostensible employers. He stayed on as judge for a year, then quit when he was accused of a conflict of interest.

Landis's first important act as commissioner was to banish forever eight members of the 1919 Series fixers, the so-called Chicago "Black" Sox, even though they had been acquitted of all criminal charges in connection with the conspiracy. The banished included the great "Shoeless" Joe Jackson, who was little more than a patsy in the fix and had played his hardest during the games. Landis said the eight "will be and remain outlaws." Because of Landis's ruling, Jackson has never been admitted to baseball's Hall of Fame, though many baseball experts and fans feel he should be exonerated.

Landis's cleanup of baseball, which had become corrupted by its association with gamblers, was harsh but uneven. In his first five years as commissioner, he banned seven other players for life and suspended 38 others. Most of those punished had merely been approached by gamblers and had failed to disclose their conversations. Others did even less. Landis banned pitcher Ray Fisher for life when he took a job as a coach at the University of Michigan while still under contract to the Cincinnati Reds. He banned New York Giants outfielder Benny Kauff after Kauff was acquitted on auto-theft charges.

Landis was unafraid to tackle even the game's biggest star, Babe Ruth. In 1921 Landis suspended Ruth and New York Yankees teammate Bob Meusel for 40 games for violating a rarely invoked rule against post-season barnstorming, a common practice in those days. But he reinstated Ty Cobb and Tris Speaker, two future Hall of Famers, who had been suspended by American League President Ban Johnson for allegedly throwing games during the 1919 season, even though there was written evidence they were involved in a fix.

Owners who had thought Landis would be their lackey proved sadly mistaken. He ordered owners with financial interests in racetracks to quit any involvement with horse racing or anything related to gambling. He turned down singer Bing Crosby's bid to buy the Pittsburgh Pirates because he owned racehorses. He slammed owners for stockpiling deserving players in their expanding minor league "farm" systems. In 1930 he declared St. Louis Browns player Fred Bennett a free agent, claiming owner Fred Ball had unfairly stymied his career. Ball took Landis to federal court and lost. By the end of the 1930s, Landis had freed almost 200 players under similar circumstances. He often nixed player trades that he figured were not in the best interests of baseball's competitiveness. "He was always on the side of the ballplayer," said manager Leo Durocher. "He had no use for the owners at all."

Landis frequently clashed with Ban Johnson, who had been the most powerful figure in the game for many years. Eventually, he told the owners that either he would go or Johnson would go. It was Johnson who resigned.

The Judge

Along with Ruth and the "lively" ball, which transformed the game into a crowd-pleasing spectacle with more home runs, Landis was largely responsible for redeeming the tarnished reputation of the sport and turning baseball into the nation's undisputed national pastime during the years between the two world wars. With his shock of long white hair and his imperious manner, Landis was a frail-looking, scowling, patrician figure. Autocratic and stern, Landis projected an image of rectitude even while unleashing a vituperative storm of profanity, and he issued frequent lectures against anyone who would besmirch the sport. Baseball historian Harold Seymour described him as a "scowling, white-haired, hawk-visaged curmudgeon who affected battered hats, used salty language, chewed tobacco, and poked listeners in the ribs with a stiff right finger."

Landis frequently attended games and was the sport's unflagging ambassador. He selected announcers for the World Series and watched every inning of every game from his box. In the 1934 World Series, when angry fans in Detroit showered St. Louis outfielder Ducky Medwick with produce during a lopsided game, Landis ordered the Cardinals to remove Medwick to avoid a forfeit. They complied.

Few people dared defy Landis, who as commissioner was known simply as "the Judge." His office in downtown Chicago had a single word stenciled on the door: BASEBALL. He was the game's one-man judge and jury. His centralized authority was a stark contrast to the lackadaisical way the game had been run prior to his install-

ment. Critics said too much decision-making power had been invested in one man.

Landis's obstinate views on race thwarted all attempts to integrate baseball under his watch. He repeatedly upheld the sport's unwritten ban against African American players. When the Pittsburgh Pirates sought to sign legendary Negro League star Josh Gibson to a contract in 1943, Landis stopped them. "The colored ballplayers have their own league," he said. "Let them stay in their own league." Owner Bill Veeck claimed Landis prevented him from buying the Philadelphia Phillies because Veeck had told him he planned to integrate the team, but some historians doubt Veeck's account.

Two days before the start of the 1944 World Series, Landis was hospitalized for his chronic respiratory problems. In mid-November, the owners again renewed Landis's contract for seven years, but it was mainly an act of tribute. Landis died on November 25, 1944, at the age of 78. He had decreed there would be no funeral, so he was cremated and buried modestly in Chicago. Two weeks later he was inducted into the Hall of Fame in Cooperstown, New York. His plaque reads: "His Integrity and Leadership Established Baseball in the Respect, Esteem and Affection of the American People."

Never again did baseball's owners invest a commissioner with such sweeping powers. Subsequent baseball commissioners often kowtowed to the owners and rarely interfered in trades and sales of teams. Never again would one man wield such supreme authority over the sport.

Books

Alexander, Charles C., *Ty Cobb,* Oxford University Press, 1984.
Asinof, Eliot, *Eight Men Out,* Holt, Rinehart and Winston, 1963.
Seymour, Harold, *Baseball: The Golden Age,* Oxford University Press, 1971.

Periodicals

Smithsonian, October 2000, p. 120.
Sports Illustrated, July 19, 1993, p. 76. □

Alfred Mossman Landon

Kansas Governor Alfred M. Landon (1887-1987) was the Republican nominee opposing Franklin D. Roosevelt in the U.S. presidential election of 1936. Running against popular New Deal policies, Landon lost to Roosevelt by the largest electoral vote margin of any candidate since 1820. After his defeat, he continued to speak out on issues as a Republican Party elder statesman.

Republican presidential candidate Alfred M. Landon holds the dubious distinction of being one of the great losers in American political history. Buried in the Democratic landslide of 1936, he managed to carry only

two states against Franklin D. Roosevelt, a distinction unmatched until Democrat George McGovern's loss to Richard M. Nixon in 1972. The magnitude of Landon's defeat obscured his praiseworthy record as a two-term governor of Kansas. A moderate, reasonable leader who believed in orderly political change, Landon was never comfortable in championing old-fashioned Republican conservatism, as he was obliged to do in his campaign against Roosevelt. Though he never held another elected office after his years as governor, he remained a respected figure within the Republican Party for the remainder of his life.

Landon was born September 9, 1887, in West Middlesex, Pennsylvania, the son of John Manuel and Anne Mossman Landon. His father was an oil prospector and promoter whose work led the Landon family to move, first to Marietta, Ohio, and then, in 1904, to Independence, Kansas. At his father's urging, Landon attended the law school of the University of Kansas. He distinguished himself in student government and earned the nickname ''The Fox'' for his political skills. Rather than pursue a legal career, Landon took a job as a bookkeeper at an Independence bank after graduation. Still restless, he followed his father into the oil business, investing in various ventures until he launched his own firm in 1912. His drive and resourcefulness at scouting and developing oil fields eventually earned him a comfortable fortune.

Landon and his father shared an interest in politics. Together, they attended the 1912 Progressive (''Bull

Moose'') Party convention of 1912 that nominated former President Theodore Roosevelt. Landon worked hard for the Bull Moose campaign in Kansas, establishing enduring ties with such influential figures as editor William Allen White. In 1915 he married Margaret Fleming, who died less than two years later while giving birth to their daughter, Margaret Anne. That same year, America's entry into World War I prompted Landon to enlist in the Army, where he received a commission in the chemical warfare corps. He was still in training when the Armistice was declared.

Began Lifetime Career as Civil Servant

In 1922 Landon took a hiatus from the oil business and served as Kansas Governor Henry Allen's private secretary for six weeks. His interest in politics reinvigorated, he ran for the post of local Republican county committeeman and gradually rose in the party ranks. He was identified with the liberal, reform-minded wing of the party, but worked for harmony with the conservative Old Guard faction as well. Still, he was willing to break with the Republicans at times, such as when he supported William Allen White's 1924 independent candidacy for the Kansas governorship in protest against the Ku Klux Klan-backed major party nominees.

Landon's natural friendliness and ready smile made him a popular figure in political circles. He was elected Republican state chairman in 1928 and that same year managed Clyde Reed's successful gubernatorial campaign. Democrat Harry H. Woodring won the job two years later, prompting Landon to seek the Republican nomination to oppose him in 1932. He went on to beat Woodring by a small margin, becoming the only Republican west of the Mississippi to be elected governor that year. Taking office in the midst of the Great Depression, Landon worked to fulfill his campaign pledge to cut government spending and promote moderately progressive policies. He lowered tax rates, promoted utility regulation, passed a moratorium on mortgage foreclosures, and sponsored laws to shore up the state's troubled banking system. Perhaps his most notable achievement was supporting recovery programs while keeping the state budget balanced. Landon proved to be a popular governor and became the only Republican state chief executive to be re-elected in 1934.

Republican national leaders saw Landon as a promising candidate to oppose Franklin D. Roosevelt's re-election bid in 1936. Few members of the party had the stature or voter appeal to seriously contest the popular president, and Landon's folksy image and common-sense political stands made him an early favorite for the nomination. After expressing disbelief that anyone saw him as presidential material, he pursued the nomination in earnest, tapping Kansas national committeeman John D. M. Hamilton as his campaign manager. His candidacy was officially launched at the 1935 American Legion Convention. Among his early supporters was powerful newspaper mogul William Randolph Hearst, whose publications hailed Landon as the ''Horse and Buggy Governor'' and the ''Kansas Coolidge.''

Philosophical Differences with "Grand Old Party"

The comparison with former president Calvin Coolidge rankled Landon; rather than a rigidly pro-business conservative, he saw himself as a sensible, fiscally prudent liberal. In fact, he had supported many of the goals of Roosevelt's New Deal, including business regulation, unemployment insurance, and agricultural support programs. He did feel that the New Deal's programs were poorly executed, showing "too much of the slap-dash, jazzy method." Instead of condemning them completely, he favored eliminating the waste and inefficiency in specific programs. Unlike the Republican Old Guard, Landon didn't seek a return to the unfettered capitalism of an earlier era. "I do not believe the Jeffersonian theory that the best government is the one that governs the least can be applied today," he told a Kansas audience. "I think that as civilization becomes more complex, government power must increase." Such statements put him at odds with his party's conservatives, as did his support for the League of Nations and the World Court that were set up to deal with international issues following World War I.

Though he declined to officially contest any of the 1936 presidential primaries, Landon had his name entered in the Massachusetts and New Jersey contests, both of which he won. His main Republican rivals included Senator William E. Borah of Idaho, newspaper publisher Colonel Frank Knox, and Senator Arthur Vandenberg of Michigan. By the time the Republican National Convention opened in Cleveland on June 9, Landon's nomination was all but assured. He was chosen on the first ballot, with Knox selected as his running mate. The party emerged from the convention with an almost divine sense of mission. As one Kansas delegate put it, "God has His hand on Alf Landon's shoulder."

At the start of the campaign, Landon was reluctant to criticize Roosevelt harshly. He kept his distance from conservatives like ex-President Herbert Hoover and avoided a wholesale denunciation of the New Deal. Others supporting the Republican ticket were far more brutal in their attacks. John D. M. Hamilton and Frank Knox, among others, lambasted Roosevelt as a revolutionary out to destroy the U.S. Constitution. Hearst's newspapers asserted that the Soviet Union had ordered American communists to back Roosevelt. Commentators in the press noted the dissonance between Landon's moderation and the bitter rhetoric of his backers.

Political Race Proved Unwinnable

An awkward, halting public speaker, Landon found it hard to compete with Roosevelt as a campaigner. As the race entered its final months, his message grew more strident. In a Los Angeles speech, he accused the New Deal of being "obsessed with the idea that it had a mandate to control America business, American agriculture, and American life." In Baltimore, he declared that "business as we know it is to disappear" if Roosevelt won re-election. The Democrats leveled charges of their own, portraying Landon as a tool of the reactionary ultra-rich who would dismantle the New Deal if elected. In the final days of the campaign, the Republican National Committee circulated the charge that Roosevelt's Social Security Act would cut wages and force workers to wear identification tags around their necks.

In October the highly regarded *Liberty Digest* straw poll predicted a Landon victory. The results on election day proved to be far different: the incumbent Roosevelt carried 46 states (worth 523 electoral votes), leaving only Maine and Vermont (8 electoral votes) in his opponent's column. Roosevelt also overwhelmed Landon in the popular vote, garnering 27,757,333 to the Kansan's 16,684,231. Landon took the defeat philosophically, remarking to a friend: "I don't think that it would have made any difference what kind of a campaign I made as far as stopping this avalanche is concerned. That is one consolation you get out of a good licking."

Political Legacy Extended to Next Generation

After completing his second term as governor, Landon retired from public life. He returned to private business and settled down to home life with his second wife, Theo Cobb. Interested in world affairs, he supported the United States against Nazi Germany and, after World War II, endorsed President Harry S Truman's Marshall Plan for the reconstruction of Europe. Landon played a key role in nominating Wendell Willkie for president at the 1940 Republican National Convention. In the 1960s he supported Lyndon B. Johnson's Medicare program and other of Johnson's Great Society initiatives. In a 1962 interview, Landon labeled himself a "practical progressive, which means that the Republican Party or any political party has got to recognize the problems of a growing and complex civilization. And I don't think the Republican Party is really wide awake to that."

Surviving most of his political peers, Landon lived to see his daughter Nancy Landon Kassebaum elected to the U.S. senate in 1978. Ronald and Nancy Reagan were among the visitors who helped him celebrate his 100th birthday. On October 12, 1987, Landon died peacefully at his Topeka home, having put his political wins and losses far behind him. Kansas Senator Robert Dole was among those who eulogized Landon, hailing him as "a legendary Republican who taught generations of politicians what integrity and leadership were all about."

Books

McCoy, Donald R., *Landon of Kansas,* University of Nebraska Press, 1966.

Palmer, Frederick, *This Man Landon,* Dodd, Mead & Company, 1936.

Schlesinger, Arthur M., Jr., *The Age of Roosevelt, Volume III: The Politics of Upheaval,* Houghton Mifflin, 1960.

Stone, Irving, *They Also Ran,* Doubleday & Company, 1966.

Thornton, Willis, *The Life of Alfred M. Landon,* Grosset & Dunlap, 1936.

Periodicals

New York Times, September 7, 1982; October 13, 1987. □

Tom Landry

Legendary football coach Tom Landry (1924-2000) was the founding coach of the Dallas Cowboys who brought the team from a winless first season into a dominating force in the National Football League (NFL). Over 29 seasons, Landry guided the Cowboys to 20 consecutive winning seasons, 19 NFL playoff appearances, 13 division titles, five Super Bowl appearances, and two Super Bowl victories. His overall record was 271-180-6. "From the late 1960s through the 1970s and into the 1980s," contended *Washington Post* staff writer Bart Barnes, "the Cowboys under Landry were a perennial power in the NFL, with a mystique that transcended the sports community and Texas."

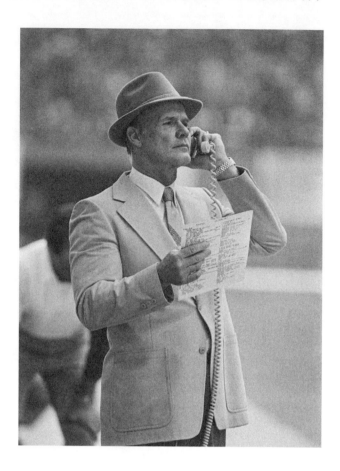

andry also helped restore the image of Dallas, dubbed the City of Hate after the 1963 assassination of President John F. Kennedy, into a city known for its winning all-American football team. The coach's strong work ethic and Christian belief fueled the success of his team and earned the Cowboys the nickname "America's Team." Landry is the third-winningest coach in NFL history, behind Don Shula and George Halas. Yet the coach is equally well known for his style. Standing on the sidelines with folded arms and a stoic expression, Landry wore his signature fedora hat, sports coat, and tie to games. A bronze statue, unveiled in October 2001, captured this pose and is displayed outside the Dallas Cowboy's home stadium in Texas. Landry remains a national icon of control and loyalty.

Excelled in Classroom and Football Field

Tom Landry was born Thomas Wade Landry in Mission, Texas, on September 11, 1924. He was the son of Ron Landry, who worked as an auto mechanic, served as the town's fire chief, and supervised Sunday school at First Methodist Church in Mission, Texas. At Mission High School, Landry was an A-student, president of his class, and a member of the National Honor Society. He also excelled on the football field, playing all-regional fullback on a team that outscored its opponents 322-0 during his senior year. A devout Christian, Landry took part in the Fellowship of Christian Athletes.

Landry served in the Army Air Forces in World War II, participating in 30 B-17 combat missions over Europe and even surviving a crash landing. In 1945 Landry was discharged as a first lieutenant and enrolled in the University of Texas, where he resumed playing fullback and some quarterback and defensive back for the Longhorns football team. During his junior year he made the all-Southwestern Conference second team, and in his senior year, he served as co-captain. In 1948, Texas won the Sugar Bowl, and in 1949 his team won the Orange Bowl. In 1949, Landry graduated with a degree in business administration from the University

of Texas and later earned a degree in mechanical engineering from the University of Houston.

Began Career in New York

Landry began his professional football career playing cornerback for the New York Yankees in the All-American Football Conference. After the 1949 season, the team merged with the New York Giants, where he continued to play cornerback for the next six seasons, making the All-Pro defensive team in 1954. When Jim Lee Howell became head coach of the Giants, Landry became a player-coach under him for the 1954 season. He left the field permanently as a player in 1955 when he took a position as the team's defensive coordinator. From 1956 to 1959, he worked as assistant coach alongside offensive coordinator Vince Lombardi, who later rose to fame as coach the Green Bay Packers.

During his time with the Giants, Landry developed his famous 4-3 defense that became the NFL standard, later evolving that into the Flex. The strategy replaced the "umbrella defense—a six-man line with a roving line-backer—with a four-man line and three linebackers." Landry said "My industrial engineering degree shaped my coaching," reported Keith Whitmire in the *Chicago Tribune.* "The whole coordinated defense, the Flex defense came out of that idea, of putting everybody together with certain responsibilities. It was a very technical approach to football." In Landry's four years as defensive coach, the

Giants earned a record of 33-14-1, with two Eastern Conference division titles and one NFL championship, in 1956.

Headed to Dallas

Landry left New York in 1960 to take a job as head coach of the Dallas Cowboys expansion team. A Dallas group headed by owner Clint Murchison Jr. and General manager Tex Schramm recruited Landry for the top job, signing him on for 5 years at $34,000 a season. Landry ran an insurance business in Dallas during the off-season and the offer gave him a chance to move closer to home.

In his first season as head coach, Landry failed to win a single game. The team posted a 0-11-1 record. Landry offset the team's lack of talent with an innovative offensive strategy that called for multiple formations based on the strengths and weaknesses of his own players and those of his opponents. A 1968 NFL press release described Landry's offense as using "10 or 11 formations a game, with up to six variations of each. This is several times as much offense as the NFL average . . . the Landry defense, on the other hand, is a one-formation machine. It is as complex as a computer, and its individual parts are coordinated like the works of a clock." "He was renowned in the NFL for his ability to think ahead," noted *Washington Post* staff writer Bart Barnes. "not just for the next down but to the next series of downs."

Despite a sub-par record, Landry had won the confidence of Cowboys owner Clint Murchison. In 1964, Murchison signed Landry for an additional 10 years as head coach of the Cowboys. This marked an unprecedented show of support for a coach with only a 13-38-3 record. But the gamble paid off. By 1965, the team won as many games as they lost. And in 1966, the Cowboys made the playoffs for the first time after posting a 10-3-1 season. That year Landry was named the NFL's Coach of the Year. In 1967 the team won the Eastern Division title. After the 1970 season, the Cowboys advanced to the Super Bowl for the first time, but lost the championship game to the Baltimore Colts. The Cowboys eventually made it to the Super Bowl five times, winning in 1972 and 1978 and losing in 1971, 1976, and 1979. Throughout his career, Landry earned a record of 250-162-6 in the regular season and 20-16 in the playoffs.

Achieved Celebrity Status

In the 1970s, the team gained national popularity and was dubbed "America's Team." Football became the most-watched professional sport in the United States. Super Bowl VI, in which the Tom Landry's Dallas Cowboys beat Don Shula's Miami Dolphins 24-3, marked a turning point for the team. They shed forever their image as lovable losers and became a dominating force in the NFL. "The title validated Landry's status and the Cowboys' claim as one of the league's elite teams," wrote David Moore in the *Chicago Tribune*. "It forever altered the perception of the franchise."

Landry and his players became national celebrities. Moore recounted the defining events of the Dallas Cowboy's celebrity era. In 1975, the Dirty Dozen referred to the 12 rookies who made the team. The 50-yard Hail Mary pass from Roger Staubach to Drew Pearson climaxed a 17-14

playoff victory over Minnesota later that season. Troubled running back Duane Thomas called Landry "a plastic man, no man at all."

The Dallas Cowboy's cheerleading squad had a certain cachet. Former Cowboys wide receiver Pete Gent wrote a best-selling novel, *North Dallas Forty* based on his time with the team. The book, which was made into a movie starring Nick Nolte, portrayed the organization in a negative light, characterizing the owners as more concerned with the bottom line than with the welfare of the players.

Landry also revolutionized the college draft system by introducing the computer to organize the annual selection process. The coach became an iconic figure, known for wearing a fedora hat and pacing the sidelines with a stoic expression. Admirers saw a caring, warm, and devoutly religious man. But his aloofness also drew criticism. Landry was called "plastic man" and "computer face," and even referred to cynically as Pope Landry I by some of his players. Moreover, Peter Golenbock in the *Wall Street Journal* suggested that Landry also exhibited racist tendencies. His black players, especially Bob Hayes, Duane Thomas, and Thomas Henderson, "felt they never got the same respect or recognition from either the coach or the city as his favorite white players: Bobby Lilly, Lee Roy Jordan, and Roger Staubach," according to Golenbock.

Became Corporate Symbol

In 1983, Landry appeared in a national commercial for the American Express corporation. By that time, the Cowboys-Redskins rivalry had become legendary. The advertisement showed Landry walking into a tavern filled with large men in burgundy and gold Redskins football uniforms. Golenbock asserted that Landry became a symbol of corporate America. "His national fame grew around the same time this country was enjoying dizzying economic growth. His coaching philosophy centered on sacrifice for the good of the organization and working like a dog for victory at the cost of everything else. Corporate workers were expected to do the same."

By the early 1980s, the Cowboys had begun to fade. The owner sold them to a consortium, and they never seemed to regain strength. Landry's last season with the team was 1988. In 1989, the Cowboy's new owner Jerry Jones fired long-time coach Tom Landry and longtime general manager Tex Schramm. At his firing, he shed public tears, according to *Time* magazine, which "shocked an America that saw him as the faultlessly tailored, taciturn but brilliant sideline tactician." "The great irony was that in the end Coach Landry became a victim of the same corporate culture he had championed," contended Golenbock.

After his coaching career ended, Landry and his son became partners in an investment firm, and he also served as a goodwill ambassador for the Fellowship of Christian Athletes. He was elected to the Pro Football Hall of Fame in 1990 and was inducted into the Dallas Cowboys Ring of Honor in 1993.

In May 1999, Landry began undergoing treatment for acute myelogenous leukemia and died at Baylor University Medical Center in Texas the following February at age 75.

He married Alicia Wiggs, whom he met in college, in 1949, and she survives him along with their children, Tom Landry, Jr. and Kitty Phillips. The couple also had another daughter, Lisa Childress, who died of liver cancer in 1995.

The city of Dallas commemorated Landry by renaming one of its main highways. In addition, it commissioned a nine-foot-two bronze likeness of the coach. On October 15, 2001, the statue was unveiled at halftime of the game between the Dallas Cowboys and the Washington Redskins. It shows the coach on the sidelines wearing his trademark fedora and carrying a game plan placard from a 1983 game against the New York Giants. The statue stands on a star-shaped pedestal at Texas Stadium.

Landry explained his coaching philosophy this way: "The players are basically in my hands—whether they start, whether they play, what they do," according to Whitmire in the *Chicago Tribune.* "That's an awesome responsibility when you come down to it. Therefore, my feeling is you must have some distance from the players in order for them to do the things they have to do. Once you get close to a player, you give them an out."

Books

Newsmakers, Gale Group, 2000.

Periodicals

Associated Press, October 16, 2001; October 30, 2001.
Chicago Tribune, February 13, 2000; February 20, 2000, p. C3.
Dallas Morning News, October 11, 2001.
Los Angeles Times, February 13, 2000.
New York Times, February 14, 2000.
Time, February 21, 2000.
Wall Street Journal, February 16, 2000.
Washington Post, February 13, 2000. □

Marie Paulze Lavoisier

A century before Marie Curie made a place for women in theoretical science, editor, translator, and illustrator Marie Paulze Lavoisier (1758-1836), wife and research partner of chemist Antoine Laurent Lavoisier, surrounded herself with laboratory work. As assistant and colleague of her husband, she became one of chemistry's first female researchers. In addition, she cultivated the arts and welcomed the era's intellectuals to her Paris salon for stimulating conversation.

Born Marie-Anne Pierrette Paulze in 1758, she enjoyed a comfortable lifestyle in Paris, France, as the beautiful, intellectually curious daughter of scholar and nobleman Jacques Paulze, wealthy nephew of the Abb, Terray. In 1771, after her mother's death, she left a convent school to become her father's hostess. On her own, she studied chemistry and languages. To avoid an arranged marriage at age 14 to Count d'Amerval, a family friend and unscrupulous fortune-hunter who was 36 years her senior, she agreed to wed 28-year-old Antoine Laurent Lavoisier, a frequent guest at the Paulze house. Her husband, who held a law degree, was a respected geologist and chemist and a member of the French Academy of Science. After his mother made him independently wealthy with a handsome inheritance, he was able to pursue his love of theoretical chemistry and initiate a chemical revolution based on logic and mathematical principles.

The Lavoisiers shared much in common, including the scientific laboratory on the upper floor of the house in Paris that they received as a wedding present. They enjoyed board games and discussions of astronomy, chemistry, and geology. He educated her in the use of balances, burning lenses, and reduction vessels and taught her German and Latin, the language of the scientific community. She took an interest in his refutation of the claims of mesmerists, perusals of hot-air balloons, the causes of contagious disease in cities, and refinements to the metric system. To help her husband at his investigation of the physical nature of fire and heat, she taught herself English and introduced him to American and British articles she translated into French. She also took art lessons from French painter Jacques-Louis David and began illustrating Antoine's articles.

Wife and Lab Partner

Although the marriage produced no children, Marie Lavoisier contented herself by regulating the couple's daily work with a research schedule. As a team, they established modern chemistry by separating its scientific aspects from alchemy and by evolving an updated scientific glossary. They coined the term "oxygen," identified it as an elemental gas, described the oxidation process that changes iron to rust, and analyzed the products of normal human respiration as water and carbon dioxide. In spring 1774, the couple experimented on the calcination of tin and lead in sealed containers and confirmed that the increase in the weight of calcinated metals derived from a combination with air. The results of their meticulous project disproved earlier theories of combustion, which maintained that the element phlogiston was essential to combustion. Most important to science, Antoine formulated the law of conservation of matter, which established that there is no gain or loss of weight in the elements of a chemical reaction, a theory that bound chemistry to physical and mathematical laws.

During these experiments, Marie Lavoisier made notes and compiled research records. For Antoine's scientific papers and monographs, she translated text into Latin and appended commentaries. After conferring with English physicist Joseph Priestley in October 1774, who visited their home and discussed his own laboratory findings, the Lavoisiers examined residue from burning. Subsequently, they disproved the faulty theories of German chemist Georg Ernst Stahl and others about phlogiston. In celebration, Marie burned their erroneous texts to symbolize their worthlessness.

Established the Lavoisier Name for Scientific Discoveries

Credit for the advance to chemistry did not reward the Lavoisiers. On April 1775, Antoine read to the French Academy his groundbreaking treatise, "On the Nature of the Principle Which Combines with Metals during Their Calcination and Increases Their Weight," which he published in 1778. Antoine obtained a government post with the gunpowder commission, which offered the Lavoisiers a home and laboratory at the Royal Arsenal, which remained their home and workplace from 1775 to 1792. In 1777, Antoine lobbied Gustaf III, the king of Sweden, for the Nobel prize in theoretical chemistry and recreated the Lavoisiers' lab experiments with gases and balloons. Nonetheless, Antoine lost out to Priestley and Carl Wilhelm Scheele, both of whom claimed to have discovered oxygen before the experimentations of the Lavoisiers.

Marie Lavoisier obviously weathered the loss of renown for the breakthrough in chemistry that she and Antoine accomplished together. In 1783, they publicized their newly formulated theories of fire, combustion, and oxygen and popularized the scientific law that, in any chemical change, "Nothing is gained, nothing is lost." In 1788, Marie Lavoisier translated the writings of Henry Cavendish and Joseph Priestley and Irish chemist Richard Kirwan's "Essai sur le Phlogistique" [An Essay on Phlogiston] and "De la force des Acides, & de la proportion des Substances qui composens les Sels neutres" [Strength of Acids and the Proportion of Ingredients in Neutral Salts]. Along with her comments and Antoine's section-by-section rebuttal,

Kirwin's article on Phlogiston appeared in *Annales de Chimie* [Annals of Chemistry] in 1792.

Scientific Studies, Writings, and Drawings

Looking to the future of science, Marie Lavoisier welcomed scientists to a salon held in her home. Of these occasions, agriculturist and writer Arthur Young, author of *Travels in France During the Year 1787, 1788, and 1789,* noted, "Madame Lavoisier, a lively, sensible, scientific lady, had prepared a déjeuné Anglois of tea and coffee, but her conversation on Mr. Kirwan's 'Essay on Phlogiston,' which she is translating from the English, and on other subjects, which a woman of understanding that works with her husband in his laboratory knows how to adorn, was the best repast." Young remarked on her vigor and drive and on her knowledge of prevailing chemical theory, which she obtained from international sources.

For her husband's classic summation, *Traité Élémentaire de Chimie* [Treatise on the Elements of Chemistry] (1789), the first modern chemistry textbook, she provided original sketches, watercolors, and 13 precise copperplate illustrations to accompany an improved system of scientific nomenclature, which replaced such imprecise phrases as butter of arsenic or sugar of lead. The Lavoisier chemistry text established new definition of "element" and a summation of the 23 elements science had identified up to that time. For each experiment, she engraved schematic drawings equipment and outcomes and labeled parts alphabetically to explain the function of each mechanical element. To mark the sketches that were ready for printing, she initialed them and wrote "Bonne" [good] and signed the completed plates "Paulze Lavoisier sculpsit" [(Mme.) Paulze Lavoisier engraved (it).]

Revolution and Widowhood

During the Reign of Terror that followed the French Revolution, the Lavoisiers were forced out of their home and lab in 1792 after authorities booted Antoine off the gunpowder commission. A year later, revolutionaries halted the work of scientific academies. Presented with an arrest warrant on November 24, 1793, Lavoisier attempted to escape extremists, but they apprehended and tried him at a Jacobin tribunal on charges of immuring Parisians by building a wall around his home and of watering soldiers' tobacco, a muddled reference to experiments on methods of retaining moisture in the leaves.

Marie Lavoisier was orphaned and widowed on May 8, 1794, after members of the Republic guillotined her father and husband for treason. An old enemy, revolutionary Jean-Paul Marat, who bore a grudge against Antoine for rejecting him for membership in the Academy of Sciences, blamed the two men and 26 alleged confederates for enriching themselves at the public's expense through the Ferme-Générale, a private tax collection company. In the face of Marat's persecutions based on ridiculous accusations that their wall cut off air supply to Paris, Marie fled France and served 65 days in the Bastille, the infamous Paris prison.

Penniless after the confiscation of her land, she came into the care of a former servant.

Life without Antoine

Fortunately for science, within the year, the Republic restored Marie Lavoisier's estate and the confiscated scientific library, which she intended to keep in print. She edited her husband's beginnings on chapters one, two, and four of a projected eight-volume *Mémoires de Chimie* [Memoirs of Chemistry]. She and a colleague edited the notes in 1796, but parted company after a disagreement. Alone, Marie published the work in two volumes along with her original introduction. In 1805, she issued free copies to French scientists.

That same year, Marie Lavoisier spurned the repeated proposals of chemical magnate Pierre Samuel Dupont de Nemours and gave her attention to a long-time visitor to her salon, expatriate inventor Benjamin Thompson, Count Rumford, the American-Bavarian military adviser, founder of the Royal Institution of Great Britain, and designer of a kitchen range. After four years of friendship, she married Thompson, but chose to retain Antoine's surname. While they traveled Europe, their stormy, mismatched union produced none of the contentment and challenge of her 18 years with Antoine. She is reported to have ruined his flower collection with boiling water after quarreling over his seizure of her money and domination of her activities. Four years later, Rumford and Lavoisier divorced.

Madame Lavoisier gave up scientific experimentation and for a quarter century devoted herself to business and philanthropy until her death in 1836. She left neither diary nor autobiography to clarify her role in Antoine's laboratory experiments or to establish her contribution to chemistry. Remaining of her personal life are a self-portrait that she executed in her teens, her portrait of American scientist and statesman Benjamin Franklin, and an oil painting by Jacques-Louis David showing a neat, sensibly dressed young woman with a cascade of soft curls. In the scenario, she leans companionably on her husband's shoulder before a table spread with their experiments.

Modern biography is at a loss to determine whether Marie Lavoisier was a true scientist overlooked by 19th-century gender discrimination or merely the secretary, translator, and publisher of her husband's remarkable discoveries. In 2000, scientists Carl Djerassi and Roald Hoffman, a Nobel-Prize winner in chemistry, reprised the partnerships of the famed Lavoisiers in a witty history play, *Oxygen,* published the following year. The text comments on the selection of Nobel committee's selection of scientists to honor, the influence of translation method on scientific research, childlessness, and the position of women in science, which was historically overlooked when the female researcher partnered with her mate.

Books

Creations of Fire: Chemistry's Lively History from Alchemy to the Atomic Age, Perseus Books, 1995.
Great Thinkers of the Western World, HarperCollins, 1992.
The Hutchinson Encyclopedia of Biography, ed. by C. S. Nicholls, 1996.
Imaging a Career in Science: The Iconography of Antoine Laurent Lavoisier, Science History Publications, 2001.
Lavoisier, Chemist, Biologist, Economist, University of Pennsylvania, 1996.
Notable Women Scientists, Gale Group, 2000.
Oxygen, John Wiley & Sons, 2001.
Women's World, ed. by Irene Franck and David Brownstone, HarperPerennial, 1995.
World of Scientific Discovery, 2nd ed. Gale Group, 1999.

Periodicals

Ambix, 1989.
American Scientist, January-February 1996; January-February 2002.
Bulletin for the History of Chemistry, No. 24, 1999.
Chemical Educator, Vol. 3, Issue 5, 1998.
Chemistry and Industry, July 24, 2000; September 3, 2001.
Chymia, 1953.
Education in Chemistry, November 1985.
Journal of Chemical Education, 1975.
Natural History, December 1998.

Online

"The Age of Revolution," http://teachers.springisd.org/johnp/wch20scientificrevolution.html (January 16, 2002).
"Antoine Laurent de Lavoisier," http://histoirechimie.multimania.com/Lien/LAVOISIER.htm (January 16, 2002).
Biography Resource Center, http://galenet.galegroup.com/servlet/BioRC (January 16, 2002).
"The Man Huntington Loved to Hate," http://www.lihistory.com/4/hs412a.htm (January 16, 2002).
"Women in Science," http://www1.umn.edu/ships/gender/giese.htm (January 16, 2002). □

Charles Lee

British-born General Charles Lee (1731-1782) joined the forces of George Washington's Continental Army in 1775. His capture by British troops a year later and his retreat during the Battle of Monmouth, which led to a court-martial and removal from the army, prompted historians to question both his military ability and his allegiance to his adopted country.

One of the most puzzling and ambiguous characters in American military history, Charles Lee served as third in command in the Continental Army during the American Revolution. Captured only a year into the war while staying at a New Jersey tavern and imprisoned for 18 months, he later compromised an attack by General George Washington's army by retreating during the Battle of Monmouth in 1778. Haunted by growing disapproval due to his outspoken criticism of Washington, Lee was court-martialed and subsequently suspended from the army.

No Fixed Allegiance

Of Irish heritage, Lee was born in Dernhall, Cheshire, England, on January 25, 1731. His father, a former colonel in the British Army, encouraged his son's interest in the military and enrolled Lee in a Swiss military school in 1744. An ensign from the age of 14, Lee was sent to the American colonies during the French and Indian War and in 1755 served in British General Edward Braddock's 44th Regiment. This regiment contained several officers who would go on to shape history, among them George Washington, Horatio Gates, and Thomas Gage. Unlike his colleagues, Lee flouted convention with his unkempt appearance and his coarse demeanor, although he was known to quote from Latin scholars when the occasion suited him. Known for his bouts of drunkenness and vulgar language, Lee was rarely seen without his train of dogs. He said dogs, unlike men, were faithful. In 1756, while in northern New York, he was adopted into a Mohawk tribe, entered what he considered a non-binding union with the daughter of Seneca tribal leader White Thunder, and was given the name Ounewaterika, or "Boiling Water," referring to his quickness to anger.

His life with the Mohawks was brief. In July 1758 Lee was back under British command and serving in the 44th Regiment under General Abercromby during the unsuccessful British attack on Fort Ticonderoga. Wounded during battle, he was sent to Long Island to recover. He disagreed with his surgeon on proper treatment of his wounds and whipped the doctor, who later tried to kill him. Lee's brash, impetuous nature frequently got him into trouble.

In 1759, Lee and the 44th Regiment fought French forces at Fort Niagara. He served under General Amherst during the siege and capture of Montreal on September 8, 1760. Spending the winter in England, he was promoted to the rank of major in the 103rd Regiment. On August 10, 1761, he became a major in the 103rd Regiment of the British Army. The following spring, he was a lieutenant colonel when he accompanied an expeditionary force to Portugal under Major General John Burgoyne.

With Great Britain once again at peace, Lee saw no future as an officer on half-pay in the British Army. Lee traveled to Warsaw in March 1765 and gained the confidence of Poland's King Stanislaus. However, a trip to Turkey caused him to rethink this career move. After becoming snowbound in the Balkans and then surviving a deadly earthquake in Constantinople in May 1776, Lee returned to the relative safety of England. He spent the next two years penning sarcastic essays critical of the British crown and lived off his gambling winnings. When civil war broke out in Poland he returned to aid King Stanislaus and was commissioned a general in the Polish army. During a campaign in Turkey in late 1769 Lee became ill and was sent to the Mediterranean to recover. During 1771 he alternated between England and France, but he was discontented with the political situation in both nations.

Joined American Cause

Excited by the growing spirit of the Enlightenment, Lee desired to fight on behalf of liberty, and he enlisted in the cause of the American patriots after returning to the American colonies in 1773. Making a home in current-day West Virginia, he attacked efforts at reconciliation between colonists and the British crown in the pamphlet *Strictures on a Pamphlet, entitled "A Friendly address to All Reasonable Americans."* His enthusiastic support of the colonial cause gained him the admiration of Richard Henry Lee, Patrick Henry, and Samuel and John Adams. His military experience made him a valuable asset to the newly formed Continental Army. In December 1774, Lee traveled to Mount Vernon and Washington's side. After war broke out in 1775, he renounced his commission in the British Army. Artemas Ward was named first major general and Lee became second major general in Washington's Continental Army, a commission Lee accepted on June 17, 1775.

A month later, Lee accompanied Washington to Cambridge, Massachusetts, and fought during the siege of Boston under General Ward. The following March, the Continental Congress ordered Lee south to fight British troops in Virginia and North Carolina as head of the army's Southern department. On June 4, 1776, Lee arrived in Charleston and assumed command of the South Carolina troops, making his headquarters in nearby Williamsburg. Unenthusiastic about the post, he anticipated a retreat. Colonel William Moultrie had other ideas, and repulsed the British naval force from his position at Fort Sullivan on Sullivan's Island. While Lee and Moultrie both received commendations for their actions, Moultrie was considered primarily responsible for the victory.

Captured by the British

In September 1776, after the British withdrawal from the southern colonies, Lee was ordered to return to the main army, now stationed in New York and New Jersey. He expressed reluctance to rejoin Washington after learning that threatening maneuvers by British General Howe had forced a colonial retreat. He believed he would be more effective and gain more notoriety as head of a "rogue" unit that engaged the British using guerilla tactics. However, Lee eventually followed orders and headed into New Jersey. On December 12, 1776, he took quarter at White's Tavern in Basking Ridge, two miles from where his 4,000-member detachment encamped, and the following day sent a terse letter to General Horatio Gates, referring to Washington by noting that "a certain great man is most damnably deficient. He has thrown me into a situation where I have my choice of difficulties."

Camped less than four miles away, British troops led by Lieutenant General Cornwallis discovered Lee's whereabouts. Soon after writing his letter to Gates, Lee was captured by Colonel Harcourt. General Lee was "hurried off in triumph," Continental Army Captain James Wilkinson later recalled in his memoirs, "bareheaded, in his slippers and blanket coat, his collar open, and his shirt very much soiled from several days' use."

Lee was taken to New York and imprisoned. An order to return him to England for trial as a deserter was rescinded by British General Howe, who knew of Lee's resignation. Washington attempted to secure Lee's release through a prisoner exchange, but he had no captives of similar rank with which to bargain, and Lee remained in British custody for almost 18 months. During this time Lee appears to have wavered in his allegiance to his adopted country. In 1858 a document titled "Mr. Lee's Plan, 29th March 1777" was discovered; it advised Howe on a way to defeat the Continental Army. While some historians have argued that Lee's plan was an attempt to mislead the British commander, in the light of his later activities his loyalty remains in question.

After Burgoyne's defeat at the Battle of Saratoga, Lee was exchanged for recently captured Major General Richard Prescott and released in April 1778. After a quick trip to Congress to complain about his lack of promotion during his capture, Lee traveled to Valley Forge and by late May had rejoined his command.

The Battle of Monmouth

Throughout his involvement in the Revolutionary War, Lee earned a reputation as a loose cannon, a recalcitrant officer resentful of taking orders from Washington, whom he believed to be of lesser ability. His actions in June 1778 during the Monmouth campaign cemented this reputation and led to the end of his military career.

Washington was determined to attack the British during their retreat from Philadelphia to New York, and he overtook General Henry Clinton and his 11,000 British regulars near New Freehold, New Jersey, near Monmouth Court House. The Battle of Monmouth provided Washington with the chance for a much-needed victory. While generals Nathanael Greene, Wayne, and the Marquis de Lafayette urged a full assault, Lee argued against such an approach. Put in command of the main flank supporting the advance force led by General Wayne, he was suddenly confronted by more soldiers than he had anticipated. Informed by a scout of an area to his rear that would be easily defended, Lee began to retreat, forcing Wayne to fall back. Washington quickly reformed the regiments of Greene, Stirling, and Wayne into a second formation that successfully stalled the British until dark, while General von Steuben assumed command of Lee's forces.

Washington's words to Lee on the battlefield were not recorded, but they were severe enough that Lee immediately demanded an apology. Two days later he sent the commander-in-chief a critical letter that angered Washington. Further correspondence between the two men resulted in Lee's request for a court of inquiry so that he could prove his case. On July 4 Lee's court martial began, with General Stirling presiding, and on August 12 he was found guilty of disrespect to his commanding officer, disobedience, and leading a disorderly and unauthorized retreat. His punishment, one year's suspension, was eventually sanctioned by Congress on January 10, 1780, although colonial leaders expressed regret at the loss of a commanding officer during wartime. As Eric Ethier reported in *American History,* when Lee heard the decision of Congress to approve his suspension, he pointed to one of his dogs and said, "Oh, that I was that animal, that I might not call man my brother."

Lee sent repeated letters to congressmen, members of the military, and the press attacking the character of Washington and complaining of mistreatment by the Continental Congress. After reading Lee's defamatory "Vindication," published in the *Pennsylvania Packet* on December 3, 1778, Colonel John Laurens challenged Lee to a duel over his slanderous remarks about Washington's character. In the duel, Lee was wounded and could not fight a second duel requested by General Wayne.

In July 1779 Lee returned to his home in Virginia, remaining there for two years before moving to Philadelphia. He died of pneumonia in a tavern on October 2, 1782. Up to the time of his death he continued to express animosity toward Washington as a "puffed up charlatan." In Lee's last will and testament he asked that he not be buried in a churchyard. "I have kept so much bad company when living," he wrote, "that I do not choose to continue it when dead." Despite these wishes, Lee was buried at the cemetery at Christ Church, Philadelphia. Though he had been unpopular only months before, his funeral was attended by Washington, members of the Continental Congress and the assembly of Pennsylvania, the minister of France, and other officers of distinction.

Books

Commager, Henry Steele, and Richard B. Morris, editors, *The Spirit of 'Seventy-Six: The Story of the American Revolution as Told by Participants,* Bonanza, 1983.
Dictionary of American Biography, American Council of Learned Societies, 1928-1936.
Langguth, A. J., *Patriots: The Men Who Started the American Revolution,* Simon & Schuster, 1988.

Sparks, Jared, *Lives of Charles Lee and Joseph Reed*, Little, Brown, 1846.

Stryker, William Scudder, *The Battle of Monmouth*, Houghton, 1896.

Wilkinson, James, *Memoirs of My Own Times*, A. Small, 1816.

Periodicals

American History, October 1999. □

Jack Lemmon

For more than four decades, whether working in comedy or tragedy, actor Jack Lemmon (1925-2001) epitomized the joys and travails of Americans in the latter half of the 20th century. Noted as one of the most versatile U.S. film actors of his generation, Lemmon gave numerous memorable performances in theater, film, and television, greatly influencing a later generation of actors.

Actor Jack Lemmon was born in the Boston suburb of Newton, Massachusetts, on February 8, 1925—legend has it that he was actually born in the hospital elevator. The son of a successful businessman, Lemmon grew up under the expectation that he would follow his father into the bakery business. He was educated at Andover Academy and by the time he graduated from Harvard University he was thoroughly bitten by the acting bug, having acted in summer stock and in some of Harvard's Hasty Pudding productions. In a 1990 interview in the *Independent* Mark Steyn quoted Lemmon's account of how he broke the news of his aspiration to be an actor to his father after graduating from Harvard University in 1947: "'Pop, can you lend me 300 bucks so I can go to New York and see if I can get in the theatre?' He said, 'Eugh—acting. Do you really love it?' I said I did, and he said, 'Okay, good. Because when the day comes that I don't find romance in a loaf of bread, I'll quit.' Boy, that came in handy during the terrible dry periods. Then I remembered, well, I do love it, like he loved what he did." Lemmon's initial show business job in New York involved playing piano in the Old Knickerbocker Music Hall on Second Avenue as an accompanist to the silent films of Charlie Chaplin and Buster Keaton. He also performed in skits there and tended bar, among other tasks. During his early years in the business he continued doing summer stock.

Made Break into New Medium of Television

In late 1949 Lemmon appeared in a television series, *That Wonderful Guy,* along with Cynthia Stone, whom he later married. The series was canceled after 17 weeks, but Lemmon soon landed a job as master of ceremonies on a talent show named *Toni Twin Time,* where he received mixed reviews as an MC. When the show was canceled he and Stone found work on an improvisation show called *The*

Ad Libbers. After that show was canceled Lemmon and Stone were paired once again, this time in a continuing 15-minute segment in which they played a young married couple. For the two, art mirrored life, as they had married on May 7, 1952. In 1952 Lemmon and Stone were cast in yet another situation comedy, *Heaven for Betsy,* which was panned by the critics.

By the early 1950s Lemmon, who now worked regularly in television, landed a part in the Broadway revival of *Room Service,* a hit play from the 1930s. Lemmon's Broadway debut was not so fortunate; this time around. *Room Service* closed after 18 performances, leaving Lemmon undaunted by the show's generally poor reviews. For one thing, he received valuable experience and exposure; for another, Hollywood literally beckoned him. He signed a seven-year nonexclusive contract with Columbia Pictures that required him to do two films a year, with a studio option for a third. Unfortunately, as his career moved forward his marriage with Stone steadily declined.

Lemmon's first film for Columbia was *It Should Happen to You,* which starred Academy Award-winner Judy Holliday and was directed by George Cukor. In it Lemmon plays a struggling documentary filmmaker. The film was successful and Lemmon caught the attention of the critics. In his second film, *Phfft,* he was again paired with Holliday. By this time he had reconciled with Stone, and the couple now relocated to California. In 1954 their son Christopher was born. Lemmon next had a small role in *My Sister Eileen,* but it was his fourth film that marked his entrance into the Hollywood pantheon.

First Academy Award

Lemmon's real breakthrough in movies came when legendary director John Ford literally handed him the role of Ensign Pulver in the film *Mister Roberts*. Based on the successful play, the film starred veteran actors Henry Fonda, James Cagney, William Powell, and Ward Bond, but it was Lemmon's performance as the laundry and morale officer Pulver that truly shone. This performance earned Lemmon an Academy Award for best supporting actor in 1955 and proved to the film world that he was a talent to be reckoned with. Unfortunately his increasing work schedule and his growing fame as a result of *Mister Roberts* took their toll on Lemmon's marriage. Soon after receiving the best supporting actor award, he received a divorce summons from his wife.

During the late 1950s Lemmon continued working in television as well as film and became friends with comedian Ernie Kovacs, a comic genius until his 1962 death in an automobile accident. The two worked together on two films, *Operation Mad Ball* and *It Happened to Jane*, the latter co-starring Doris Day. Lemmon's friendship with Kovacs was so close that in his *Lemmon*, biographer Don Widener quoted director Richard Quine as noting: "If Ernie had lived, the Lemmon-Matthau team might well have been Lemmon-Kovacs. They reminded me of a sophisticated Laurel and Hardy."

In 1959 Lemmon was paired with Tony Curtis in *Some Like It Hot*. Under the brilliant direction of Billy Wilder Lemmon gave one of the greatest performances of his career opposite Marilyn Monroe by playing Jerry/Daphne, a Depression-era musician on the run from Chicago gangsters who hides out in an all-female band touring Florida. The next year Lemmon starred in *The Apartment*, also directed by Wilder. Lemmon's performance as C. C. Baxter, an up-and-coming corporate man who allows his superiors to use his apartment for liaisons, is perhaps his truest personification of the "everyman" for which he was best known.

Three things happened in 1962 that altered Lemmon's life and career. Kovacs died in an automobile accident, thus ending a flourishing professional partnership and close friendship; in August Lemmon married actress Felicia Farr, with whom he would have a daughter, Courtney, in 1966; and he starred with Lee Remick in the independent film, *Days of Wine and Roses*. As good as Lemmon's film work had been up to that time—he had won an additional two Academy Award nominations for his performances in *Some Like It Hot* and *The Apartment*—Lemmon stunned critics and audiences alike with his performance as the alcoholic Joe Clay in *Days of Wine and Roses*. The breakout performance earned him his fourth Academy Award nomination.

Over the next few years Lemmon returned to light comedy, with many of the roles shoring up his Everyman persona. He also acted in such high-farce films as *The Great Race*, until the mid-1960s when his career took another fateful turn. In 1966 he was teamed up for the first time with

Walter Matthau in *The Fortune Cookie*, a Wilder-directed comedy about a photographer who, at the instigation of an unscrupulous lawyer, fakes the seriousness of an injury in order to defraud an insurance company. Two years later Lemmon and Matthau were cast as Felix and Oscar in *The Odd Couple*, their best-known film together. The two enjoyed a 34-year friendship until Matthau's death in 2000, working together on 11 films, most of which were produced in the 1990s.

Earned Second Academy Award

In the 1970s the middle-aged Lemmon took on greater challenges, promoting his recognizable Everyman persona even as he discarded the youthful innocence that he had up to then played as counterpoint. In 1971 he tried his hand at directing and the result was *Kotch*, starring Matthau and with a cameo appearance by Lemmon. In 1973 came the role that brought Lemmon his second Academy Award, this time for best actor. As Harry Stoner in *Save the Tiger*, he played a businessman suffering through a mid-life crisis who must now weigh his ethics against his struggling business. Lemmon returned to television work in 1976, in a remake of *The Entertainer* reprising the role of second-rate entertainer Archie Rice formerly performed by Sir Laurence Olivier. While some criticized Lemmon for remaking the film, it was Olivier himself who had suggested he take on the part. Lemmon also starred in one of the decade's better disaster movies, *Airport '77*. He closed out the decade with another stunning performance, as the tormented but scrupulous Jack Godell in the controversial film *The China Syndrome*. The performance earned Lemmon his sixth Academy Award nomination, a Golden Globe nomination, a BAFTA (the British film award), the best actor award at the Cannes Film Festival, and a David (Italian film award) for best foreign actor, the last which he shared with fellow actor Dustin Hoffman.

The 1980s saw no letdown in the quality of Lemmon's work. He followed his turn in *The China Syndrome* with *Tribute*, in which he played the shallow agent Scotty Templeton, who discovers he is dying. The performance earned him another Academy Award nomination. as well as consideration for a Golden Globe Award. In 1982 Lemmon turned in yet another stunning performance in *Missing*, directed by controversial filmaker Costa-Gavras. In the film Lemmon plays a father whose son has gone missing as a result of the CIA-sponsored 1973 coup that overthrew Chilean President Salvador Allende. The film sparked lawsuits and official rebuttals but nevertheless became a turning point in the American public's perception of the coup. For his performance Lemmon received his eighth and final Academy Award nomination. He was also nominated for a BAFTA Award and a Golden Globe Award and received the award for best actor at the Cannes Film Festival.

During the 1980s Lemmon became increasingly involved in television work. He appeared in tributes to Frank Capra, Billy Wilder, Harold Lloyd, and even himself, but more important were the dramatic roles he took on. During the decade he appeared in the television films *Long Day's Journey into Night* (1987) and *The Murder of Mary Phagan*

(1988). Yet Lemmon's film career was far from over. During the 1990s he appeared in Robert Altman's *The Player* (1992) and *Short Cuts* (1993) and also did a noteworthy job in David Mamet's *Glengarry Glen Ross,* (1992) which Roger Ebert, writing in the *Chicago Sun-Times,* described as Lemmon's ''version of *Death of a Salesman.*''

Lemmon was remarkably busy during the 1990s. At the beginning of the decade he appeared in yet another political drama, *JFK,* and also starred in a number of comedies, particularly reviving his partnership with Matthau. The pair made five movies together during the decade, including *Grumpy Old Men, Grumpier Old Men,* and *The Odd Couple II,* all of which enjoyed fair commercial success but mixed critical reviews. Lemmon's television work included remakes of *12 Angry Men* and *Inherit the Wind,* both of which earned him Emmy and Golden Globe nominations. He won the Golden Globe for his performance as Henry Drummond, the Clarence Darrow-like defense attorney in the latter. Lemmon's last important role came in the 1999 television film *Tuesdays with Morrie,* for which he won an Emmy award. He died from cancer on June 27, 2001.

Books

Widener, Don, *Lemmon,* Macmillan, 1975.

Periodicals

Boston Globe, April 23, 1995.
Chicago Sun-Times, June 29, 2001.
Independent (London, England), February 21, 1990.
Los Angeles Times, December 9, 1996; January 24, 2000; June 30, 2001; September 11, 2001.
San Francisco Chronicle, November 30, 2000. □

Jacques Loeb

From an early age German physiologist Jacques Loeb (1859-1924) was interested in the question of whether or not free will existed. Rather than pursue his interests via a philosophical approach, Loeb used science to address his question. Using biological experiments on a wide range of specimens, including dogs, caterpillars, and marine animals, Loeb concluded that there was not free will. He believed that all animals, including people, operated mechanistically, as a result of physical and chemical reactions to stimuli. He took this position a step further by arguing that, once scientists understood the mechanics of biology, they could ultimately control development.

Born in Mayen, Germany, in 1859, Jacques Loeb, born Isaak Loeb, was the first of two sons born to Benedict and Barbara Isay Loeb. His father worked as an importer, but was very interested in science, literature, and collecting books. He was especially interested in 18th century French humanists and he exposed his children to these ideas. In 1873 Loeb's mother passed away from pneumonia and his father died three years later of tuberculosis. At the age of 16 Loeb went to Berlin to work in his uncle's bank. However, he soon became bored with this line of work so he decided to continue his education at the Askanische Gymnasium, a school for Berlin's Jewish elite that taught Latin, Greek, German literature, math, physics, and philosophy. There Loeb was exposed to the writings of philosophers such as Spinoza, Kant, Nietzche, and Schopenhauer. Even at this young age, he showed a great interest in the issues of instincts and free will.

In 1880 Loeb enrolled in the University of Berlin and also changed his name from Isaak to Jacques. This change to a French name symbolized both his secularization and his disapproval of the German Nationalism that was gaining in strength as a result of the Franco-Prussian War. At this time Loeb also decided to pursue a career in medicine rather than continue his classical training in philosophy. After one semester in Berlin Loeb transferred to the University of Munich and then to the University of Strasbourg. He became involved in a research project with Friedrick Goltz on the localization of brain functions, which he found fascinating. This experience convinced him to pursue physiology as a career. In 1884 Loeb received his medical degree from Strasbourg and he passed the government medical exams in 1885. He then returned to Berlin to study the effects of brain lesions at the Agricultural College.

Began Research on Animal Tropisms

In 1886 Loeb began working as an assistant for Adolf Fick, a physiology professor at Wurzburg, and befriended Julius von Sachs, a famous botanist. Von Sachs was researching plant tropism: the ability of plants to respond to external stimuli, such as light or gravity, like simple machines. Loeb saw this approach as a way to answer his philosophical questions about free will and viewed animal tropism as a way to see if free will could be controlled. If he could show that "lower" animals were affected by external stimuli just like plants, then he would prove that animals had no free will.

Loeb's first experiment in animal tropisms involved caterpillars' reaction to light. When caterpillars hatch from cocoons they climb to the tips of branches for food. It was believed that caterpillars had an instinct for where to find food. Loeb, however, had a more mechanistic hypothesis. He believe that the caterpillars had no such instinct and were simply responding to the external stimulus of light. His experiments proved his theory correct. Caterpillars were given the choice of light or food and they chose light even though they starved to death. Loeb worked feverishly on this idea for two years until he published his first paper on animal tropisms. This was the beginning of a lifelong pursuit to show how life could be manipulated by science if the ruling mechanisms were known. As Loeb wrote in *The Mechanistic Conception of Life,* "Our wishes and hopes, disappointments and sufferings have their source in instincts which are comparable to the light instinct of the heliotropic animals."

In 1888 Loeb returned to the University of Strasbourg to work as an assistant in Goltz's physiological institute. His main responsibility was teaching and he worked with several students on psychophysiological problems. However, political and financial problems led Loeb to leave Strasbourg after only a year, and from 1889 to 1990 he spent his summers in Zurich where his brother was attending medical school. In the winters he worked at the Naples biological station, where he studied the depth migrations of pelagic invertebrates and regeneration in marine animals in an effort to learn how to control development. Philip J. Pauly, in *Controlling Life,* explained Loeb's broad range of experimental interests: "In contrast to most physiologists, he was interested not only in functions of adult vertebrates, but also invertebrates and embryos; he was concerned not only with routine functions but with behavior, development, and ultimately . . . evolution. Loeb's program was not applied science. It was a refocusing of biological inquiry itself around what Loeb conceived as the activity of the engineer."

In the spring of 1890 Loeb met his future wife while visiting physiology Professor Justus Gaule in Zurich. Anne Leonard was a young American who had just earned her Ph.D. in philology from the University of Zurich. The couple married in October of 1890 and had three children together: the eldest child, Leonard, became a physicist, Robert became a teaching physician, and daughter Anne attended Barnard College prior to her marriage.

Developed Mechanistic Conception of Biology

Between 1889 and 1991 Loeb developed his views on biological engineering. He was greatly influenced by physicist Ernst Mach, who believed that sensation, perception, and behavior were physical, rather than mental or emotional, reactions. In particular, Loeb moved from the narrow perception of biological change exhibited by his work on animal tropisms to a more radical view of the nature of biology and the scientist's ability to manipulate it. According to Charles Rasmussen and Rich Tillman in *Jacques Loeb: His Science and Social Activism and Their Philosophical Foundations,* "This prominent scientist was not only a major influence on Loeb's mechanistic and engineering notions for a biology of behavior, his influence reinforced and shaped Loeb's belief in the importance of social issues in his life as a practicing scientist; in this regard, the influence of Mach can be traced through the remainder of Loeb's life."

Continued Academic Career in America

Once married, Loeb searched for an academic job which would offer his family more financial stability. He was increasingly unhappy with the political situation in Germany, so the young couple moved to America. Loeb was offered a teaching job at Bryn Mawr College in Pennsylvania. Although he enjoyed his new position, the research facilities were not suitable to his needs. In January 1892 he was asked to join the new University of Chicago. He stayed at this university for the next ten years, eventually becoming head of the physiology department, and he spent his summers teaching physiology at Woods Hole, Massachusetts.

Loeb extended his work on free will to see if it was possible to control the entire developmental process. To this end, he conducted experiments in parthenogenesis, reproduction without fertilization. He subjected eggs to both chemical and physical stimuli and discovered several methods by which an egg could develop without sperm fertilization. Loeb's work on artificial parthenogenesis gained him fame in both the scientific community and the popular press and established him as a major figure in biology. Though Loeb never won the Nobel Prize for science or medicine, he was nominated for the prestigious award in 1901. As Philip J. Pauly explained in *Controlling Life: Jacques Loeb and the Engineering Ideal in Biology,* "In the period from 1890 to 1915 Loeb was the major public advocate of what can be termed 'the engineering standpoint.' . . . By the turn of the century he had come to symbolize both the appeal and the temptation of open-ended experimentation among biologists in America, and he became the center of scientific and popular controversies over the place of manipulation in the life sciences."

Loeb spent the winter of 1898-1899 in Pacific Grove, California, where he planned to work on marine research. During this visit he wrote *Comparative Physiology of the Brain and Comparative Psychology* in German and his wife translated it to English. This book, a tribute to Mach, summarized Loeb's career in neurophysiological and behavioral research. It also introduced to new areas that Loeb was interested in, particularly colloidal substances (molecular structures such as proteins) and reflexes. Loeb was impressed with the California climate and liked the possibility of doing marine research all year round. In 1902 he accepted a position at the University of California and a laboratory was built for him in Pacific Grove. The only drawback to working in California was that Loeb was isolated from his professional colleagues. He did not like to travel so he attended few professional meetings. As a result of this isolation, Loeb decided to accept a position as head of experimental biology at the Rockefeller Institute for Medical Research in 1910, which allowed him to dedicate all of his time to research. There he pursued his research on animal tropisms as well as bioelectrical phenomena, regeneration, and the properties of proteins. In the same year he was also elected to the National Academy of Sciences. In 1912 Loeb published a collection of his essays in a volume titled *The Mechanistic Conception of Life*. In 1918 he started the *Journal of General Physiology* with Winthrop J.V. Osterhout, as well as a series of *Monographs on Experimental Biology*.

Legacy

While on vacation in Bermuda, Loeb suffered from angina and died on February 11, 1924. His ashes were brought to Woods Hole and a memorial was placed there at the Marine Biological Institute, as well as at the Rockefeller Institute for Medical Research. Throughout his prolific career, Loeb published over 400 scientific works. His engineering approach to science impacted other scientists in many fields, including behaviorism, genetics, biochemistry, and physiology. Loeb was a hard worker who was passionate about science and its role in society. As Osterhout wrote in *The Journal of General Physiology: Jacques Loeb Memorial Volume*, "He had a passionate love of truth and what appeared to him to be true had to be so expressed that all could feel the inspiration and see the beauty of what he saw." In *Controlling Life*, Philip J. Pauly stated that "Loeb was important primarily as a model, both of what it meant to be a scientist, and of a particular approach to biological research."

Books

The Journal of General Physiology: Jacques Loeb Memorial Volume, edited by W. J. Crozier, John H. Northrop, and W.J.V. Osterhout, The Rockefeller Institute for Medical Research, 1928.

Loeb, Jacques, *The Mechanistic Conception of Life,* University of Chicago Press, 1912.

Pauly, Philip J., *Controlling Life: Jacques Loeb and the Engineering Ideal in Biology,* Oxford University Press, 1987.

Rasmussen, Charles, and Rick Tillman, *Jacques Loeb: His Science and Social Activism and Their Philosophical Foundations,* American Philosophical Society, 1998.

Periodicals

Science, September 8, 2000.
Scientific America, September 2000.

Online

"Jacques Loeb Papers, 1906-1924," http://www.rockefeller.edu/archive.ctr/ru_jl.html (January 17, 2002).

"Jacques Loeb's Influence on Korzybski," http://www.kcmetro.cc.mo.us/pennvalley/biology/lewis/loeb.html (January 17, 2002).

Wozniak, Robert H., "Jacques Loeb, Comparative Physiology of the Brain, and Comparative Psychology," http://www.brynmawr.edu/Acads/Psych/rwozniak/loeb.html (January 17, 2002). □

James Longstreet

General James Longstreet (1821-1904) fought on the side of the Confederacy in almost every major battle of the U.S. Civil War. In addition to commanding one of the most noted offensives of the war at Chickamauga, he led troops at both First and Second Manassas and Gettysburg and stood beside Confederate general Robert E. Lee to the assignation at Appomattox Courthouse that brought an end to the war in the spring of 1865.

Despite the fact that he was highly respected by Robert E. Lee and one of the most noted commanders of the Confederate Army, General James Longstreet has been the subject of controversy since the U.S. Civil War. A highly respected soldier whose courage and thoughtfulness gained the respect of all under him, Longstreet fought in the Battle of Bull Run (First Manassas), Sharpesburg, Fredericksburg, Gettysburg, Chickamauga, and on the lengthy Wilderness Campaign and commanded the Confederate First Corps from its creation in 1862 to Lee's surrender at Appomattox Courthouse in early April 1865. Although Longstreet's military record shows him to be a soldier as valiant as fellow Confederates Lee and Stonewall Jackson, his later criticism of Lee's maneuvers during the battle of Gettysburg was viewed as traitorous by southerners still loyal to Lee after the war. The blame for the heavy losses suffered at Gettysburg was placed squarely upon Longstreet's shoulders, and he was excluded from Confederate circles—even military reunions—through his death in 1904.

No Patience with Bookish Pursuits

The second surviving son of James and Mary Ann (Dent) Longstreet, James Longstreet was born January 8, 1821, at his paternal grandmother's home in Edgefield District, South Carolina. His family was of Dutch descent—the family name had originally been Langestraet—and his grandfather, William Longstreet, moved the family south from its original home in New Jersey in the 1780s. His father was a farmer, and James Junior was raised on the family's cotton plantation in the northeastern Georgia town of Piedmont. On his mother's side, which hailed from Maryland, Longstreet was related to Supreme Court Chief Justice

friends who he would retain throughout his adult life: one of these was a young man named Ulysses S. Grant, who was in the class behind Longstreet. At the time he graduated from West Point as part of the class of 1842, he ranked 54th in a class of 56, 16 of whom would go on to be Civil War generals.

Following graduation, Longstreet was commissioned a brevet second lieutenant with the U.S. Fourth Infantry, then stationed outside of St. Louis, Missouri. While stationed there, he fell in love with Mary Louisa Garland, the daughter of his regiment's commander; the couple honored her parent's request that they wait until Mary was older and were married in Lynchburg, Virginia, on March 8, 1848. Meanwhile, the ambitious Longstreet undertook tours of duty in Louisiana and Florida before traveling to Texas to join General Zachary Taylor's Eighth Infantry. During the border dispute that escalated into the Mexican War in May of 1846, 25-year-old Longstreet fought at the Battle of Cherubusco under General Winfield Scott, and a severe wound to the leg at Chapultepec prevented him from joining the U.S. troops as they marched into Mexico City on September 14, 1847, to end the war. He remained in Mexico at an army hospital until the end of the year, then returned to his regiment.

Gained Experience in Mexican War

Longstreet continued his career in the U.S. Army for over a decade, serving in Texas, Kansas, and New Mexico, and moved up the ranks through a promotion to major in the paymaster's department in July of 1858. Meanwhile, the political climate between the northern states and Longstreet's native south deteriorated, issues of states' rights, slavery, and economics creating a divide that politics could not mend. When Alabama seceded from the Union in January of 1861, Longstreet, like many other officers with ties to the south, felt the pull of his allegiance to his home in Georgia. He resigned his commission in the U.S. Army in May and joined the forces of the Confederacy as a lieutenant colonel. He traveled to the Confederate capitol at Richmond, Virginia, was appointed brigadier-general in June, and was sent to Manassas Junction, Virginia, to head a brigade of Virginia infantry.

The battle at Manassas, which became known as Bull Run, was the first major fight between north and south. Longstreet and his men participated in fighting on the 18th of July and stood as reserve troops during the actual battle at Bull Run, which occurred three days later. Although a Confederate victory, the battle revealed the bloody nature the war would take. During the fall and winter of 1861, while both sides regrouped, Longstreet was promoted to major-general and wintered with his division in Centreville, Virginia. Despite the lull in the war, the winter would hold tragedy for the Longstreets when the younger three of their four children died within a week of one another during an outbreak of scarlet fever. Longstreet, his wife, and their surviving son, 13-year-old Garland, were devastated.

After Longstreet returned to his command at Centreville, the Confederate Army was ordered to stop a move by Union troops toward Richmond. He showed himself to be a competent leader at skirmishes at Yorkton and Wil-

John Marshall. Dubbed "Pete" by his family, Longstreet spent the first nine years engaged in farm work or outdoor activities with his older siblings William and Anna, as well as the four younger sisters he accumulated between 1822 and 1829. His father owned slaves and through the combined efforts of their toil and the family's work the Longstreet farm was prosperous. Young James's early education was one gained through hard work and time spent out of doors, and Longstreet developed physical strength, independence of mind, and a strong work ethic. While he dreamed of a military career, his parents recognized that entrance into West Point Military Academy would require preliminary academic training. On October 7, 1830, young Longstreet was removed from the rural life he loved and sent to the Augusta, Georgia, home of his uncle, noted attorney Augustus B. Longstreet, where he enrolled at the prestigious Richmond County Academy.

Three years after moving to Augusta, Longstreet suffered a family tragedy when his father died in a local cholera epidemic while on a visit. In June of 1838 seventeen-year-old Longstreet was admitted to West Point Academy in New York, an appointment obtained through the efforts of his uncle, Augustus. While a cadet at West Point, his interests continued to remain athletic rather than intellectual—he later wrote that he "had more interest in the school of the soldier, horsemanship, sword exercise, and the outside game of foot-ball than in the academic courses"—and he consistently ranked in the bottom third of his class. A sociable young man, Longstreet retained the family nickname "Old Pete" among his fellow cadets, and he gained several

liamsburg in early May of 1862. At the Battle of Seven Pines, on May 31, Longstreet led the Confederate attack, a move that proved costly when he confused his orders. Fortunately, he learned from this mistake, and when General Robert E. Lee was appointed commander of the Army of Northern Virginia by Confederate president Jefferson Davis, Longstreet quickly proved his competency to the new commander, willing Lee's confidence during the Seven Days' Battles near Richmond in late June. In mid-August of 1862 Lee reengaged Union forces at the battle of Second Manassas. A Union victory under Major-General John Pope seemed foregone when, on August 29, Longstreet and his men arrived to support Lee's battered troops and sent five divisions in to storm a two-mile-long section of the Union flank. One of the bloodiest battles of the war, Second Manassas resulted in 25,000 casualties and proved a victory for the south.

Became Lee's "Old Warhorse"

At Sharpesburg, Maryland, on September 15, 1862, Longstreet watched, with General Lee and 18,000 Confederate troops, as 95,000 Union soldiers under General George B. McClellan marched before them. The following morning the armies engaged at the battle of Antietam; that afternoon Lee's valiant effort to make a northern push into Maryland cost him one fourth of his army. As the tide of battle turned against the Confederate ranks, Longstreet boosted moral among the scattered troops by ordering his personal staff to begin rapid fire of unused cannon into the Union line. This move inflicted casualties upon Federal troops sufficient to stop their advance. The Battle of Antietam, which casualties totaled 10,318 Confederate and 12,401 Union, was considered a technical victory for the South due to its battle against superior odds, but the course of the war was radically altered in its aftermath. On September 22, 1862, President Abraham Lincoln issued the Emancipation Proclamation. From this point on the war no longer turned on issues of states' rights or economics; it became a war against the enslavement of African Americans and as such, the north claimed the moral high ground.

His performance at Antietam earned Longstreet the epithet "old warhorse" from General Lee, who promoted him to lieutenant-general on October 11, 1862, and gave him command of the First Corps of Virginia. Another officer equally rewarded was Thomas "Stonewall" Jackson, who became leader of the Second Corps. Relied upon by Lee due to his methodical nature and thoroughness, Longstreet remained a trusted advisor and Lee followed his counsel in many battles. A believer in tactical defense, Longstreet saw greater chance of victory in preserving the lives of his men and resisting the temptation to make heroic assaults on the enemy. Rather, he counseled Lee that a series of counterstrikes against Union offensives were the best chance of winning the war.

Turning back to the south, Lee marched his troops toward Virginia, pursued by General Ambrose Burnside, who had succeeded McClellan. Three months and 75 miles into this withdrawal, on December 13, the two armies collided in the small Virginia town of Fredericksburg. Lee, with Longstreet at his left flank and Jackson at his right, led 75,000 men against Burnside's 120,000. As wave upon wave of Union troops were ordered by General George Sumner to advance upon his 40,000 troops positioned on the high ground to the west of town, Longstreet recalled that the men downed by his firepower were like "the steady dripping of rain from the eaves of a house." Despite the tragic death of Jackson—shot accidentally by one of his own men during the night of May 2—Fredericksburg was a Confederate victory, Union losses numbering 12,600 compared to Lee's 5,300. Most of the Confederate casualties were "missing" men who abandoned their post in order to return to their families for Christmas.

The Tide Turned at Gettysburg

A Confederate victory at Chancellorsville in May of 1863 continued to build the south's confidence in their new general. Determined to give a show of Confederate strength, Lee marched north with Generals Longstreet, Richard S. Ewell, and A. P. Hill, and 70,000 troops. Lee's aim was to invade southern Pennsylvania, attack Philadelphia, and force Union General Ulysses S. Grant to defend the District of Columbia. Under Lee were Generals Longstreet, Richard S. Ewell, and A. P. Hill. On July 1, 1863, Hill's advance corps were spotted by a Union picket as they marched toward the small rural town of Gettysburg, Pennsylvania. With little intelligence as to the size or location of the opposing army, both Union troops under General George Meade and Lee's Confederates were in the process of resupplying and reorganizing their forces in anticipation of a major conflict. The clash of advance troops that occurred at Gettysburg ignited this conflict and brought about the longest three days of the war.

On July 1, the first day of battle, the Confederate army claimed victory, as Union casualties outnumbered Confederate, and Lee was left with 35,000 men compared to Meade's 25,000. The second day of battle opened with an attack by Lee on the union right flank, a decision Longstreet strongly argued against in favor of taking a defensive position on Seminary Ridge and repulsing Meade's advance. Longstreet believed that an offensive posture should only be adopted when an attack was planned in advance, and victory was probable. Both Longstreet, who opposed the Union's southern flank, and Ewell, equally uncomfortable with Lee's plan and directed by Lee to oppose the Union north, stalled their attacks until the afternoon. According to his chief of staff, Longstreet neglected to send scouts out to study the ground of the proposed battle—a move a prudent general would undertake—and this negligence on his part was later used as evidence of his contravention of Lee's orders. During the hours Longstreet postponed his attack, Union General Daniel Sickle made the probably misguided decision to move his troops from the high ground at Little Round Top and cross the orchard below. At 4:00 in the afternoon, Longstreet ordered his First Corps northeast from Warfield Ridge, attacking Sickle's men in the Peach Orchard in an effort to occupy the strategic advantage at Little Round Top. The battle raged for three hours, Sickle's troops strengthened by reserves led by General Gouverneur K. Warren. At the close of July 2, Longstreet's effort had failed and Union troops retained control of Little Round Top.

That evening Longstreet met with Lee, Ewell, and Hill. In the belief that the Union army was weakened, Lee was determined to stage a frontal assault, and he ordered Longstreet to command this action. In vain, the "old warhorse" attempted to convince Lee that the Union forces were far from vanquished; as he later wrote, "when the [second day's] battle was over, General Lee pronounced it a success . . . but we had accomplished little toward victorious results." Longstreet also realized—as did others—that Lee's proposed attack—across an open field surrounded by Union troops occupying the high ground—spelled disaster. Longstreet proved to be correct. The following morning Meade, anticipating Lee's attack, reinforced his center, and after an unsuccessful seven-hour effort by Ewell to gain the high ground at Culp's Hill, the Confederates pulled back. Two hours later, at 1:00 in the afternoon, after once again failing to dissuade Lee, Longstreet supervised a 140-cannon bombardment of the Union left flank. This barrage was answered by 110 Union guns, making it the largest artillery battle in U.S. history. After an hour Meade ordered a cease fire, leading Lee to believe the Union batteries had been demolished. When the smoke cleared at three in the afternoon, Lee ordered Longstreet to advance on the Union center, an order Longstreet transferred to his friend, Major General George E. Pickett. Horrified, Longstreet and Pickett watched as a line of well-shielded Union forces armed with highly accurate rifled muskets fired on their 13,000 Confederate troops marching in formation toward Cemetery Ridge. Over 6,500 of Longstreet's men marched to their death, fell wounded on the field of battle, or were captured.

After the Turning Point of the War

A devastating defeat for the Confederacy, the Battle of Gettysburg cost the south 3,903 dead, 18,735 wounded, and 5,425 missing; the Union army suffered 3,155 dead, 14,529 wounded, and 5,365 missing. These casualties forced the south into a defensive war and energized the Union into beginning its push south into northwest Georgia. Longstreet and the First Corps were sent by rail to the aid of General Braxton Bragg, who with his ill-kempt force had been holding defensive positions near Lafayette, Georgia, since late December 1862. Union forces collided with Bragg at Chickamauga Creek on Saturday, September 19, 1863, and fought on for hours in confusion. By Sunday morning, when Longstreet and his 12,000 men arrived, he was given an additional 11,000 troops and ordered into the fray. Cognizant of his men's fatigue following their all-night march, Longstreet postponed his assault until 11:00, then ordered five divisions to attack the Union front line. His attack severely weakened the Union array and forced the opposing troops into a large-scale retreat toward Chattanooga. Longstreet's decision to delay his attack resulted in one of the strongest offensive battles of the war; he continued on the offensive for the duration of the Chickamauga conflict, halting the Union advance southward and contributing to what became a costly victory for the South.

In the days following Chickamauga, Longstreet urged General Bragg to pursue the withdrawing Union force and destroy it, but Bragg resisted, thereby losing the south's momentum. Longstreet was so angered that he formally requested President Davis to order Bragg's dismissal, noting: "I am convinced that nothing but the hand of God can help as long as we have our present commander." His efforts proved unsuccessful, and Bragg remained in command. While the Union Army remained entrenched in Chattanooga, Bragg and his generals surrounded the city and awaited the north's surrender. Camped on Lookout Mountain, Longstreet and his men waylaid all shipments of food and supplies into Chattanooga except a meager flow from the north. The arrival of Generals Grant, George Sherman, and Joseph Hooker in late October would spark the battle at nearby Brown's Ferry that broke the Confederate blockade of the starving Union forces in Chattanooga. However, Longstreet would not be there to participate; before the battle at Brown's Ferry he was ordered to Knoxville to engage in an unsuccessful effort to seize that city from Union General Ambrose Burnside. On the 25th of September the Confederate forces at Chickamauga fell to Union advances. Union General George Sherman now began his move south, creating the path of devastation through Atlanta into Savannah that became known as "Sherman's march to the Sea." A Union victory appeared imminent.

Longstreet and his men wintered in eastern Tennessee and joined Lee in Virginia in late April of 1864. In May of 1864 Longstreet helped Lee repulse efforts by Grant to breech the Confederate lines near Chancellorsville, part of a prolonged battle that became known as the Wilderness Campaign. Wounded by a bullet that passed through his throat and into his shoulder, Longstreet was forced to leave his post until October. Meanwhile, stalemates at battles at North Harbor and Cold Harbor continued to draw on Confederate strength. When Longstreet rejoined his command, Lee was defending the Confederate capitol of Richmond against Grant at nearby Petersburg; the battle deteriorated into trench warfare after Union troops finally breached Richmond's fortifications on April 3, 1865. The Army of the Confederacy was now in retreat. On Sunday, April 9, 1865, Longstreet accompanied a tired and beaten Robert E. Lee to Appomattox, West Virginia. There, in the town's small courthouse, the war between the states was brought to a close, the cost the death of over 620,000 Americans.

Became Scapegoat for Lee's Defenders

After the war, Longstreet planned to move his family to Texas, where he had served prior to the Civil War, but ultimately moved to New Orleans where he worked in insurance and became a cotton factor. Grant's election to the presidency in 1869 provided him with a new opportunity: the position of surveyor of customs in New Orleans, Louisiana, for a salary of $6,000 per year. Longstreet accepted and joined the Republican Party of longtime friend Grant, his loyalty to the administration eventually earning him federal appointments as postmaster of Gainesville, minister to Turkey, U.S. marshal, and U.S. commissioner of railroads. He and his wife made their home in Gainesville, where they remained until Mary Longstreet died in December 1889, at the age of sixty-two.

Although the war was over, the battle lines between the republican north and the south were still very much in evidence, and Longstreet's party affiliation—and his surprising conversion to Roman Catholicism—branded him a traitor in the Protestant south. Although continuing to retain Lee's friendship until the general's death in 1870, many southerners—even those who had once hailed him as a military hero—now cast dispersions on his military record and blamed him for the disaster at Gettysburg. In defense of his criticism of Lee's tactical offensive at the Battle of Gettysburg, which Longstreet maintained resulted in the death of thousands of Confederate troops during Pickett's Charge, the former general published *From Manassas to Appomattox: Memoirs of the Civil War in America* in 1896. His position was further defended by his second wife, Helen Dorch Longstreet, who married him on September 8, 1897, when she was thirty-four. Helen continued to defend her husband even after his death from pneumonia on January 2, 1904, publishing *Lee and Longstreet at High Tide: Gettysburg in the Light of the Official Record.* Through the twentieth century a battle of the books raged as supporters of Robert E. Lee attempted to rest the blame for Gettysburg squarely on the shoulders of Longstreet, and revisionist historians attempted to reevaluate Lee's record as a general after his aura as the leader of the "Lost Cause" began to fade.

Books

Conrad, Bryan, *James Longstreet: Lee's War Horse,* University of North Carolina Press, 1986.

Dinard, R. L, and Albert A. Nofi, editors, *Longstreet: The Man, the Soldier, the Controversy,* Da Capo Press, 1998.

Longstreet, James, *From Manassas to Appomattox: Memoirs of the Civil War in America,* edited by Jeffry D. Wert, Da Capo Press, 1992.

Piston, William Garrett, *Lee's Tarnished Lieutenant,* University of Georgia Press, 1990.

Wert, Jeffry D., *General James Longstreet: The Confederacy's Most Controversial Soldier,* Fireside Books, 1994.

Periodicals

American History, March 1998, p. 16. □

Sidney Lumet

Filmmaker Sidney Lumet (born 1924) has made some of America's most memorable movies, including *Serpico, Dog Day Afternoon,* and *Network.* His films have received more than 50 Academy Award nominations. Often called "an actor's director," Lumet is known for the superior performances he draws from his actors.

Sidney Lumet's films often deal with social themes, such as the police, law, or Jewish life. Most of his films are shot in New York City and are often rough and emotional. Lumet treats the camera as an actor, making sure that the camerawork relates to what is happening dramatically. His vast technical knowledge allows him to use the tools of camera, lighting, and set design in a subtle yet distinctive style that is all his own.

A Child of the Theater

Lumet was born on June 25, 1924, in Philadelphia, Pennsylvania. His parents were actor Baruch Lumet and dancer Eugenia Wermus Lumet, both performers in Yiddish theater. Eugenia Lumet passed away when her son was a child. Lumet began his acting career at age four at the Yiddish Art Theater in New York City. He played many roles on radio and on Broadway, where he first performed in 1935. Lumet appeared in his only film role at the age of 15 in *One Third of a Nation,* in 1939. World War II interrupted Lumet's acting career; he spent three years in the U.S. army, including stints in Burma and India, where he served as a radio repairman. He often got into fights with his fellow servicemen, many of whom were from the South.

From Actor to Director

Lumet studied acting with Sanford Meisner, a famous acting teacher. In 1947 Lumet founded an off-Broadway theater troupe that included Yul Brynner and Eli Wallach, taught acting, and directed plays. In 1950 he joined the

Columbia Broadcasting System (CBS) and became a respected director of live television programs, including a crime series called *Danger* and a program titled *You Are There*. New York City was the heart of television production during the Golden Age of television of the 1950s, and many talented writers, actors, and directors lived and worked there. At the time, television was a medium that allowed intimate direction, much like the theater. Many television directors, like Lumet, progressed to films, often focusing on complex social and psychological themes and retaining a style derived from their informal origins in television.

Lumet creates "message pictures," movies that tackle social problems, and has been viewed as among the most perceptive and unsentimental directors of this genre. His films often feature actors who studied "Method" acting, characterized by an earthy, introspective style. And along with cinematographer Boris Kaufman, Lumet creates the appearance of spontaneity, an improvisational look achieved by shooting much of his work on location.

Lumet's work falls into several categories: the message picture; adaptations of plays and novels; large, showy pictures; films about families; tense melodramas; and New York-based black comedies. According to Gerald Mast and Bruce Kawin in their *A Short History of the Movies*, "Lumet's sensitivity to actors and to the rhythms of the city have made him America's longest-lived descendant of the 1950s Neorealist tradition and its urgent commitment to ethical responsibility. . . . Beneath the social conflicts of Lumet's best films lies the conviction that love and reason will eventually prevail in human affairs, that law and justice will eventually be served—or not."

In 1957 Lumet directed his first film, *Twelve Angry Men*, a courtroom drama that was based on a TV play. The film received the Golden Bear Award at the Berlin Film Festival and was nominated for Academy awards for best picture, best director, and best screenplay adaptation. In this film Lumet used a theme that would reappear later in his work: the motif of the enclosed space. *Twelve Angry Men* was filmed almost entirely in a single room, and in his book *Making Movies*, the director described the feeling he was trying to create. "One of the most important dramatic elements for me was the sense of entrapment those men must have felt in that room. . . . As the picture unfolded, I wanted the room to seem smaller and smaller. . . . The sense of increasing claustrophobia did a lot to raise the tension of the last part of the movie."

Theatrical Adaptations

Harkening back to his roots in the theater, Lumet proceeded to direct three films that were adapted from plays. In 1960 he made *The Fugitive Kind,* based on the play *Orpheus Descending* by Tennessee Williams and starring Marlon Brando. The theme, according to Lumet, was "the struggle to preserve what is sensitive and vulnerable both in ourselves and in the world." Next came *A View from a Bridge,* an adaptation of a play by Arthur Miller. *Long Day's Journey into Night,* based on the Eugene O'Neill play, starred Katharine Hepburn and Jason Robards in a tale of a family's downward spiral into tragedy. In 1965 Lumet made

the film *The Pawnbroker,* a powerful work about a Holocaust survivor haunted by his past and trapped in a lonely present that starred Rod Steiger. In this film, Lumet once again used the theme of the enclosed space, showing the main character caught in his own prison of pain.

From Slump to Apex

After *The Pawnbroker* Lumet's career entered a slump. He made a number of films in the second half of the 1960s, but not until 1971 did he have another hit with *The Anderson Tapes,* starring Sean Connery in a crime caper, followed by *The Offense,* a film about police brutality. Lumet's next work, *Serpico,* about police corruption, marked the beginning of the most respected period of his career. Lumet described the film as "a portrait of a real rebel with a cause." In 1974 he made *Murder on the Orient Express,* based on the Agatha Christie mystery, for which Ingrid Bergman won an Academy award. In this period piece, Lumet noted, "The object was to thrust the audience into a world it never knew—to create a feeling of how glamorous things used to be. . . . Richness was the order of the day. . . . No detail was spared in creating a glamorous look."

Dog Day Afternoon, which received Academy Award nominations for best picture and best director, is a dark comedy about a bank robbery. The film, made in 1975, was based on actual events involving a bisexual man who wanted to rob a bank to finance his male lover's sex-change operation. Film critic Pauline Kael called the film "one of the best 'New York' movies ever made." Regarding *Dog Day Afternoon,* Lumet explained that because the material was so shocking, he felt his first obligation was to indicate to the audience that these events really happened. To do so, Lumet shot the entire beginning section with a hidden camera, filming ordinary people on the streets of New York.

In 1976 Lumet made *Network,* a satire about television. The film received ten Academy Award nominations and won four, including best actor, best actress, best original screenplay, and best supporting actress. Lumet also walked away with a Golden Globe and two Los Angeles Film Critics Association awards for *Network.* In a 1995 interview with Rick Schultz, the director asserted that television has anesthetized the American consciousness and blurred the line between reality and fiction.

In 1981 Lumet won the New York Film Critics Circle Award for best director for *Prince of the City,* a three-hour film about police corruption. He also receive an Oscar nomination for the screenplay, which he co-wrote. The theme of this work, Lumet noted in his book, is that "When we try to control everything, everything winds up controlling us. Nothing is what it seems." Lumet's *The Verdict,* a courtroom drama starring Paul Newman, was nominated for best picture and best director in 1982. The 1980s also saw release of Lumet's *Deathtrap, Daniel, Garbo Talks, Power, The Morning After, Running on Empty,* and *Family Business. Running on Empty,* about a family on the run from the FBI, won awards for two actors, and the screenplay won a Golden Globe.

In the 1990s Lumet directed *Q&A, A Stranger among Us, Guilty as Sin, Night Falls on Manhattan, Critical Care,* and *Gloria.* In 2000 Lumet directed *The Beautiful Mrs. Seidenmann,* the story of a blonde-haired, blue-eyed Jewish woman who attempts to use her Nordic looks to escape the concentration camps during World War II. Reflecting on the director's body of work as a whole, film critic Leonard Maltin noted that "Lumet's films are generally intelligent and marked by a clean, unobtrusive directing style, but his signature is the caliber of the performance he elicits from his actors who speak of him—and his theater-based rehearsal process—in the most glowing terms."

A Return to Television

For the 2000-2001 television season, the A&E Network featured *100 Centre Street,* a series created by Lumet, who also directed and served as executive producer as well as writing several episodes. The series concerns prosecutors, defense attorneys, and accused criminals as their lives unfold in the night court of the city of New York. The show broke new ground in high-definition video as one of the first major TV series to use Sony's 24P technology.

A Messy Personal Life

Lumet has been married four times. His first marriage, to Rita Gam, a television actress, ended in divorce. His second wife was Gloria Vanderbilt, the heiress who made a name for herself as a very successful designer. Married on August 27, 1956, the couple remained together for seven years. When Vanderbilt ended the union, Lumet attempted suicide by taking an overdose of pills. He telephoned Gail Jones, the daughter of singer Lena Horne, to tell her what he had done, and she called the police. Lumet and Jones, a journalist and author, were married from 1963 until 1978

and have two daughters, Amy and Jenny, both actors. After his third marriage ended in divorce, Lumet married Mary Gimbel in 1980.

Aram Saroyan, in *Trio: Oona Chaplin, Carol Matthau, Gloria Vanderbilt. Portraits of an Intimate Friendship,* described Lumet's personality as crisp and kinetic. "He really seemed to be, quite naturally, the Hollywood idea of the 'director'," noted Saroyan, "—always hugging everybody and calling them 'baby' and 'sweetheart.' And yet there was something genuinely sweet and generous in the way he did it."

Books

Cunningham, Frank R., *Sidney Lumet: Film and Literary Vision,* University Press of Kentucky, 2001.
Lumet, Sidney, *Making Movies,* Knopf, 1995.
Maltin, Leonard, *Leonard Maltin's Movie Encyclopedia,* Signet, 1994.
Mast, Gerald, and Bruce F. Kawin, *A Short History of the Movies,* Allyn & Bacon, 2000.
Matthau, Carol, *Among the Porcupines: A Memoir,* Turtle Bay Books, 1992.
Saroyan, Aram, *Trio: Oona Chaplin, Carol Matthau, Gloria Vanderbilt. Portraits of an Intimate Friendship,* Linden Press, 1985.

Periodicals

People Weekly, June 10, 1985.

Online

Mr. Showbiz, http://www.mrshowbiz.go.com/ (October 25, 2001). □

Madhva

The founder of the Madhvism sect of Hinduism, Madhva (c. 1197-c. 1276) stressed the importance of *bhakti,* or devotion, in the worship of his *Dvaita,* or dualist, interpretation of the Vedanta, the philosophy of Hinduism as expressed in the Hindu scriptures, the Veda.

Believed to be the incarnation of the Hindu god Vayu, Madhva is believed by his followers to have performed many miracles. Regarding the Samkara branch of Hinduism to be a facsimile of Buddhism, Madhva developed his own theology based on his interpretations of the Upanishads, the last section of the Veda, in which he stressed his pluralistic view of the separate realms of the world, the human soul, and Vishnu (God). Madhva developed his theology from the Vedanta, a philosophy that stresses the search for ultimate meaning. Madhva's theories differ, however, from other such Vedantic faiths as Samkara. Similar to the Christian and Muslim faiths, Madhva preached predestination and the existence of an eternal heaven and hell. He believed as well that eternal salvation is possible through the continuous practice of bhakti, but is not guaranteed. Some religious scholars note the many similarities between the stories of Madhva and Biblical New Testament accounts of the life of Jesus Christ.

Developed New Hindu Sect

Experts disagree on the approximate date of Madhva's birth; some believe it was 1197 while others place the date as late as 1238. As an infant, Madhva was named Vasudeva. His father, Madhyageha Bhatta—also called Madhya Geha—and mother, Vedavati, were Tulu Brahmins who lived in the Indian city of Rajatapitha, located near the modern city of Udipi. Credited with tremendous physical power, Madhva earned the nicknamed Bhima, after the Hindu deity who also dedicated himself to refuting the tenets of Samkara. Stories of Madhva performing miraculous feats are numerous, including stilling ocean waves so that he might bathe undisturbed; diving to the ocean floor to retrieve an image of Krishna from a capsized boat; and unconsciously building a dam in a single day while in a meditative trance. As an adult, he received Samkara religious instruction from Achyutapreksa, also known as Achyutaprakashacharya, and was initiated under the name Purnabodha, or Purnaprajna. He continued his Vendantic studies at the Anantesvara monastery in Udipi, where he adopted his penname Ananda Tirtha, also transliterated Anandatirtha.

Madhva traveled through southern India, developing a contrary view of the monism—a belief that all existence consists of one element—expressed by the Samkara. His preaching of dualism led him to several debates with religious leaders in the area, and he ultimately raised the anger of the head monk of the Samkara-based Sringeri monastery in Anantapura, in modern-day Trivandrum. Fearing for his life, Madhva removed himself to Ramesvara for four months before returning to Udipi. The result of the heated debate, however, was a lasting enmity between Madhva's followers and the Sringeri monks. After several years spent researching and writing on the *Vedanta Sutras,* Madhva embarked on a tour of northern India. Upon reaching Hardwar, he disappeared into the Himalayan mountains, where his followers believe he encountered Vyasa, the supernatural being credited with convincing Madhva to publish his Vedantic interpretation. When he returned to Hardwar, he declared the invalidity of the Samkara monistic system of belief and initiated the conversion of his teacher Achyutapreksa. The Sringeri monks vehemently opposed the new sect and confiscated Madhva's library. A local prince intervened, however, and the library was returned. He traveled again to northern India; there, his followers believe, he resides with Vyasa and awaits his return to the human world. He composed many commentaries before his death, many of them interpretations of the *Vedanta Sutras,* the *Bhagavad-Gita,* and the *Mahabharata.*

Madhvacharis

Among the principal teachings of Madhva was that Vishnu is the brahman of the Upanishads. Vishnu always is accompanied by his son, Vayu, who is considered the savior of humankind. Followers of Madhva call themselves Sad-Vaisnavas; they harbor the dualistic belief that the spirit of Vishnu is independent from human life and further believe in five separate distinctions. The first is a difference between the Godhead and the human soul; the second a difference between the Godhead and physical matter; the third a difference between the human soul and physical matter; the fourth a difference between individual souls; and the fifth a difference between various types of matter. Existence came into being, wrote Madhva, not as an order of creation from Vishnu, but as a gradual evolution from pre-existing matter that responds to the will of Vishnu. In addition, the existence of Vishnu cannot be proven, but only learned through the study of the Hindu sacred texts. He acknowledged that reality was not grounded in appearance but only through objective experience, foreshadowing the theories of 19th-century German philosopher Immanuel Kant. Bhakti, the dedicated display of devotion to Vishnu, is the only hope of humans for eternal salvation, according to Madhva. Study of the sacred texts is one step toward this salvation, because it readies the mind to receive divine grace.

Many scholars note that Madhva's theology owes much to Christian beliefs. In fact, a group of Nestorian Christians resided in Kalyanpur, near Madhva's childhood home, and their presence generally is regarded as the earliest encroachment of Christianity upon the Indian continent. Many of the stories told about Madhva, for example, closely resemble the stories of the Christian Son of God, Jesus Christ. For example, Madhva's birth was foretold by a messenger who declared that a kingdom of heaven was imminent, resembling the Christian story of the visitation of Jesus' mother Mary by the Archangel Michael, who informed her of her pregnancy. Another story relates how a five-year-old Madhva disappeared for three days before his parents found him teaching religious scholars, a story that is often told about a 12-year-old Jesus. Like Jesus, Madhva is said to have also performed such miracles as walking on water and multiplying food for his disciples. Madhva's stay in the Himalayas is similar to the story of Jesus' 40-day fast in the desert. The greatest similarity to Christianity, however, is the concept of bhakti as imperative for eternal salvation. Salvation itself is only possible through the acceptance of Vayu as the son of Vishnu, resembling the central precept of Christianity of salvation granted through the belief that Jesus Christ is the Son of God.

Devotion to Vayu is displayed by Madhva's followers by the branding of symbols representing Vishnu on the shoulders and chests and expressed by naming one's sons after one of the many names of Vishnu. Followers are also expected to perform bhakti in words, thoughts, and deeds. The sect also encourages frequent fasting and sacrifices of symbolic lambs made from rice meal. The sect is centered in Udipi in a monastery believed to be built by Madhva. Two other monasteries exist in Madhyatala and Subrahmanya in the Mangalor district of India.

Books

Dictionary of Comparative Religion, Charles Scribner's Sons, 1970.

Hastings, James, editor, *Encyclopedia of Religion and Ethics,* Charles Scribner's Sons, 1958.

Online

Nidamboor, Rajgopal, "Meditations on Madhva," *Mythos and Logos,* http://www.mythosandlogos.com/Madhva.html (February 7, 2002).

Sivandanda, Sri Swami, "Madhva," http://www.sivanandadlshq.org/saints/madhva.htm (February 7, 2002). □

Miriam Makeba

Legendary South African singer and activist Miriam Makeba (born 1932) rose to international fame during the 1960s, attracting a wide following through concert appearances and recordings. Although capable of great vocal versatility in a variety of languages and settings, including jazz and blues, Makeba became best-known for singing in her native dialect, distinguishable by explosive, clicking sounds formed with the epiglottis in the back of the throat.

Forced into exile from her native country in 1960, Makeba used her stature to speak out against apartheid—the institutionalized practice of political, economic, and social oppression along racial lines. Such efforts earned her the title "Mama Africa," as she became an enduring symbol in the fight for equality. In 1991, following the 1990 prison release of Nelson Mandela, Makeba triumphantly returned to South Africa, settling in the city of Johannesburg. Since then, she has served as a spiritual mother and inspiration to numerous South African musicians and remains committed to social change within the country. South Africa, despite the dissolution of the apartheid regime and the creation of a new democracy, continues to face racial tensions, economic hardships, a high rate of crime, and a rising AIDS epidemic, all of which count among Makeba's primary concerns. In 1995, she founded her own charitable organization designed to help protect the women and young girls of her homeland.

"We have a beautiful country. We are a beautiful people. We are a forgiving people," Makeba told *Interview*

magazine in May of 2001. "We've had a past of being oppressed and maimed, but when we gained our independence in 1994, our president then, Nelson Mandela, and even our president now, Thabo Mbeki, told us yes, we went through this, but we must try to forgive. We may never forget and we must not forget—but we must forgive. So please, world—you out there in the world—forgive us."

Raised within an Oppressive Society

Zensi Miriam Makeba, born on March 4, 1932, came into a world that offered few opportunities. The South African government, amid worldwide condemnation for its inhumanity, denied non-white citizens the most basic of human rights, including the right to vote and own land, as well as laws restricting where blacks could live, eat, work, or travel. Such a policy of white supremacy through racial segregation—which became official law in 1948 under Prime Minister Daniel Malan—prevailed for decades, regardless of the fact that blacks (or Africans) outnumbered whites in South Africa at a ratio of four-to-one.

Makeba's father, a schoolteacher and member of the Xhosa tribe, could only choose between two places for his family to live: either a rural tribal reservation where the soil remained uncultivated or a regulated township near a city. He opted for the latter and, after securing government permission, moved to Prospect Township. Located near Johannesburg, Prospect, Makeba's birthplace, was one of many segregated shantytowns surrounding the city. Typically, the cheaply-built homes on the crowded reservations had no

electricity or running water, and children had little room outdoors to play. Africans were permitted to work in Johannesburg, where they arrived on designated buses each day, but the law required them to leave in the evenings by a certain time. In order to help make ends meet, Makeba's mother, a Swazi, took a job as a domestic worker at a white household in Johannesburg. She supplemented her income by illegally selling home-brewed beer. Eventually, she was charged for the offense and spent six months in jail. Makeba, then just 18 days old, went with her.

Inclined to Sing

Because free public education ceased to exist for black children, when Makeba reached school age, she attended Kilnerton Training Institute, a Methodist school for African children in the South African administrative capital of Pretoria, located a short distance from Johannesburg. Here she received limited musical training through participation in the school choir, where her vocal talents were readily recognized, as well as the opportunity to perform in public. At the age of 13, Makeba gave her first solo performance before King George VI of England during his visit to South Africa.

Music had always played an important role in Makeba's life. Early on, she listened to and picked up the traditional songs of the Xhosa and Zulu dialects. And beyond the music of her native people, characterized by clicks unknown in any other language, she discovered other music from listening to the radio and phonograph records. She particularly loved American jazz recordings, especially those of singer Ella Fitzgerald. "Anyone who sings," Makeba once said, as quoted by Louise Crane in *Ms. Africa: Profiles of Modern African Women*, "makes music, as long as it's good to my ear."

Makeba spent eight years at Kilnerton, then took work with her mother performing servants' chores in white homes. An early marriage around age 17 resulted in the birth of a daughter named Bongi, but her husband died when Makeba was just 19 years old. Thus, with a baby to support, she continued to work as a domestic and sang at weddings, funerals, and other events in her spare time. These amateur showings led to contact with a professional group of eleven men called the Black Manhattan Brothers, who asked Makeba to join as their female vocalist in 1954. She remained with the ensemble until 1957, during which time Makeba performed throughout South Africa, Rhodesia (now Zimbabwe), and the Belgian Congo (now Zaire), and in 1956 recorded her signature song, "Pata Pata," which would eventually become a major American hit in 1967.

After breaking with the Black Manhattan Brothers, Makeba formed an all-female group called the Skylarks in 1958. The following year, she toured for 18 months with a musical extravaganza, African Jazz and Variety, and began performing solo engagements. These personal appearances, coupled with a series of popular recordings, established Makeba throughout her native land. Thereafter, Makeba further enhanced her reputation playing the female lead of Joyce, the owner of an illegal African drinking place called a "shebeen," in the jazz opera *King Kong*. Based on the tragic account of an African prize fighter jailed for a crime of passion, the production, which premiered on February 2, 1959, toured South Africa for eight months with surprising success, despite the humiliating restrictions levied because of apartheid.

King Kong was forced to play before separate black and white audiences, and performances for Africans were usually given under difficult circumstances. For instance, special transportation arrangements for African audiences had to be made, shows for blacks were restricted to small halls with inadequate acoustics, and the production was banned altogether in all-white Pretoria. Nevertheless, in the legislative capital city of Cape Town, whites lined up at dawn to reserve seats to the always sold-out shows. In the end, audiences of both races fell in love with and cheered the voice of the young star, Miriam Makeba, who transformed songs first introduced in King Kong, such as "Back of the Moon," into best-selling records.

International Fame

Prior to her role in King Kong, Makeba had already begun to attract international attention by playing the female lead and singing two songs in the 1958 film Come Back, Africa, an antiapartheid, semi-documentary produced and directed by independent American filmmaker Lionel Rogosin. Banned for obvious reasons in South Africa, the film was shot on location in Sofiatown, a reservation outside Johannesburg that was being demolished for a new, all-white suburb. Although Rogosin convinced authorities his intention was to simply document the ethnic music and folkways of African people, his real aim was to provide evidence to the world about the injustices of the South African government. Smuggled out of the country, Come Back, Africa debuted outside of competition at the 1959 Venice Film Festival and, when shown commercially thereafter, received critical praises for its dramatic impact.

Makeba, who had applied for a legal passport around 1957 to travel abroad, attended the Venice Film Festival. At the time married to Sonny Pillay, a ballad singer of Indian descent who Makeba both married and divorced in 1959, and concerned for her small child in South Africa, she initially intended to return home directly from Venice. But from the moment of her arrival, several American entertainers—namely Steve Allen—were so captivated by Makeba that they were determined to bring the young singer to the United States. Thus, from Venice, Makeba traveled first to London, England, where she met vocalist Harry Belafonte at a screening for Come Back, Africa. Judging her a revolutionary talent, he offered to act as Makeba's chief sponsor and mentor.

Next, she arrived in America for an appearance on Allen's national television show. After the program, airing on November 30, 1959, Max Gordon, owner of New York City's Village Vanguard nightclub, booked the singer for four weeks on the recommendation of Belafonte. The already accomplished performer coached Makeba on her stage poise and hired an arranger, clothing designer, and musicians in preparation for her club debut. On opening night, February 2, 1960, Makeba delighted the audience

sprinkled heavily with other entertainers. "Alternating between sensuous and explosive styles," according to a Look magazine review, "she interpreted both dialect tunes and jazz standards with a finesse that heralded the appearance of a new star."

Throughout the early-1960s, she continued to draw enthusiastic crowds, embarking upon several national as well as international tours with Belafonte, who allowed Makeba to share the bill with him. The pair also collaborated on a record, winning a Grammy Award for An Evening with Belafonte/Makeba in 1965. Over the years, Belafonte and Makeba continued to reunite periodically, releasing in 1972 the album Miriam Makeba and Harry Belafonte. Makeba later made a special guest appearance for the Harry Belafonte Tribute at Madison Square Garden in 1997.

As a solo artist, Makeba recorded such popular albums as Miriam Makeba (1958) and The Voice of Africa (1964). Her eclectic repertoire included English ballads, Portuguese fados, Brazilian bossa novas, Hebrew and Yiddish melodies, Haitian chants, and other folk and popular styles from around the world. However, American audiences were most taken by the songs of Makeba's native heritage, particularly "Qonqonthwane," or "The Click Song," a Xhosan wedding tune, and "Mbube," also known as "Wimoweh," a Zulu lion-hunting song.

Forced Into Exile

Fortunately, Makeba quickly achieved international stardom, for when she attempted to return to South Africa in 1960 to attend her mother's funeral, she learned that the apartheid government had banned her from returning to the country. She also endured personal turmoil during the 1960s, including another failed marriage to trumpeter Hugh Masekela (the couple married in 1964 and divorced in 1966), as well as a serious threat to her health when she battled cervical cancer through radical surgery.

After South Africa revoked Makeba's citizenship, she was initially reluctant to speak too much about her political views, fearing the safety of family members who remained near Johannesburg. But increasingly, she became more vocal. During an exile spanning over three decades, Makeba was issued passports from nine different countries and often referred to herself a "citizen of the world." On two occasions, in 1964 and 1975, she addressed the General Assembly of the United Nations on the horrors of apartheid and in 1968 won the Dag Hammerskjold Peace Prize.

Also in 1968, Makeba married controversial black activist Stokely Carmichael (later known as Kwame Toure), a union that negatively impacted her career in America. Possibly fearing that Makeba's earnings would aid Carmichael, promoters cancelled concerts, and RCA dropped Makeba from her record contract. Ultimately, Carmichael's "black power" activism led to his exclusion from the mainstream in the U.S., and the couple fled to Guinea, West Africa. After their divorce in 1978, Makeba remained in Guinea for several years, continued to perform in Europe and parts of Africa, and served as Guinean ambassador to the United Nations. While an honorary citizen of Guinea, Makeba suffered another tragic loss when, in 1985, daughter Bongi died giving birth to a stillborn child.

According to Makeba, music and religious faith helped her overcome life's misfortunes, and she remained an active and respected musician throughout her life. In 1975, Makeba recorded the acclaimed album *A Promise,* and during 1987 and 1988, she joined Paul Simon and South Africa's Ladysmith Black Mambazo for the legendary Graceland world tour. Then, recording her first American set in two decades, she released a tribal collection entitled *Sangoma* in 1988, followed by an album of both traditional and standard compositions, *Welela,* in 1989. During the 1990s and beyond, her works included *Eyes on Tomorrow,* a commercial blend of jazz, blues, and pop released in 1991, and the Grammy-nominated *Homeland,* an album of both South African roots and American blues-pop released in 2000.

Makeba published her autobiography, *Makeba: My Story,* in 1987. It was subsequently translated and published in German, French, Dutch, Italian, Spanish, and Japanese, a testament to Makeba's musical and social influence on people not only in South Africa and the U.S., but throughout the world. "I'm always in Europe, and in Africa there are maybe five countries that I haven't been to," said Makeba in a *Down Beat* interview with Aaron Cohen. "When they say I'm in the 'World' category, I say, 'Actually, I am a world category.'"

Books

Almanac of Famous People, Gale Research, 1998.
Crane, Louise, *Ms. Africa: Profiles of Modern African Women,* J.B. Lippincott, 1973.
Contemporary Musicians, Volume 8, Gale Research, 1992.
Makeba, Miriam with James Hall, *Makeba: My Story,* New American Library, 1987.
Newsmakers, Issue 4, Gale Research, 1989.

Periodicals

Billboard, May 22, 1993; April 15, 2000.
Down Beat, April 2001.
Interview, May 2001.
Jet, April 18, 1994.
Time, May 1, 2000.
UNESCO Courier, July 2000. □

Biddy Mason

Biddy Mason (1818-1891) was a southern slave who become free after she moved with her masters to California. She built a career in Los Angeles as a nurse and a midwife, bought a piece of property, and used her business skills to become one of the wealthiest black women in the United States after the Civil War, as well as a notable philanthropist.

Lived as a Slave

Bridget Mason, known to everyone as "Biddy," was born into slavery on August 15, 1818. Her place of birth was probably Hancock County, Georgia, though some historians cite it as Mississippi. She was of mixed African American and Native American descent, but the names of her parents are unknown. As a slave child, she was separated from her parents and sold several times, working on plantations in Georgia, Mississippi, and South Carolina. She spent much of her childhood working on John Smithson's plantation in South Carolina, where she assisted the house servants and midwives. In 1836 Smithson gave the 18-year-old Mason, two other female house servants, and a blacksmith to his cousins, Robert Marion Smith and Rebecca (Crosby) Smith, as a wedding present.

Mason was forbidden to learn to read or write, but she learned many practical skills, including medicine and midwifery. These skills made her a valuable asset to the Smiths on their plantation in Logtown, Mississippi. Mason took care of Rebecca Smith, who was often ill, and helped with the deliveries of the Smiths' six children. She also worked outdoors in the cotton fields and cared for livestock.

While working for the Smiths in Mississippi, Mason had three daughters. The first, Ellen, was born on October 15, 1838. The second, Ann, was born in 1844, and Harriet was born four years later. Robert Smith was probably the father of all three. The children added to Smith's wealth because they could provide additional slave labor.

Around 1844, Smith became a member of the Church of Jesus Christ of Latter Day Saints, the Mormon religion. On March 10, 1848, Smith and a group of Mississippi Mormons left Fulton, Mississippi, for the Salt Lake area in present-day Utah, where Mormon leaders had established a center for their faith. The group consisted of 56 whites and 34 slaves, including Mason and her three daughters, the youngest only an infant. They followed the Overland Trail through Tennessee, Kentucky, Missouri, Iowa, Nebraska, and Wyoming. The trip covered over 2,000 miles and took about seven months. Mason, her children, and the other slaves walked behind the wagons and the livestock. The slaves cooked, cleaned, and tended the livestock. Mason was responsible for setting up camp each evening and packing up the next morning. Several children were born to slaves and white women during the trip, and Mason helped deliver them.

When a group of Mormon pioneers left for San Bernardino, California, to establish a new settlement, Smith decided to join them. Mason and the other slaves again walked behind the wagons, most of them not knowing they were walking to potential freedom.

Gained Freedom

In 1849 California drafted a constitution forbidding slavery, and in September 1850 joined the Union as a free state. Slave owners who had arrived before 1850 could keep their slaves as indentured servants. Smith and his slaves arrived in 1851. Smith probably did not know that California was a free state when he made the trip.

In San Bernardino, several free blacks told Mason how she could try to become free. They included Charles and Elizabeth Rowan, who had come with her from Utah, and Charles Owens and Manuel Pepper. Owens was courting Mason's 17-year-old daughter Ellen, and Pepper wanted to marry the daughter of Mason's friend, Hannah, another of Smith's slaves.

By 1855 anti-slavery sentiment was growing stronger in California. Smith decided to move his family and his slaves to Texas, a state that allowed slavery. He planned to settle there or sell his slaves and make a profit. Smith's journey was delayed because Hannah was about to give birth to another of Smith's children. The group camped in the Santa Monica Mountains and awaited the child's birth.

Meanwhile, Elizabeth Rowan and Robert Owens, the father of Charles Owens and a successful businessman, persuaded the county sheriff to prevent Smith from taking his slaves out of the state. The sheriffs kept the Smith slaves in the county jail for their protection until their legal status could be determined. Rowan and Owens filed a petition claiming that Smith was holding his slaves illegally in a free state. Smith claimed they were not slaves but members of his family. Los Angeles County District Judge Benjamin Hayes granted the petition and set the Smith slaves free on January 21, 1856.

Nurse, Midwife, Property Owner

Robert Owens invited Mason and her family to live with him in Los Angeles. His son and her daughter soon married. Mason began to work as a midwife and nurse for Dr. John Strother Griffin. She quickly gained a reputation, becoming well known for her herbal remedies. Mason delivered babies for families of various races and social classes. She earned $2.50 a day, a good wage for an African American woman at that time. She also often gave her services to those unable to pay. After working as a midwife for ten years, Mason had saved $250. On November 28, 1866, Mason bought two lots bounded by Spring, Fort, Third, and Fourth Streets on the outskirts of the city. She was one of the first African American women to buy property in the United States.

Mason initially used the land for gardening and built some small wooden houses to rent for additional income. She continued to rent accommodations for the next 18 years. Mason finally moved to her own land in 1884, when she was 66. She sold part of her land for $1,500 and built a commercial building on another part. Mason rented out storerooms on the ground floor and lived with her family on the second floor. Her neighborhood developed quickly, and by the early 1890s the main financial district of Los Angeles was one block from Mason's property. Due to her shrewd investments, Mason was the wealthiest African American woman in Los Angeles by the late 1800s.

Community Impact and Legacy

Mason devoted much of her time and energy to religious and community works. She opened her homestead to needy people, and lines of people seeking her assistance often formed on Spring Street. She also donated money and land to schools, day care centers, grocery stores, and churches, and she visited jail inmates regularly. Mason did much to help working African American families establish themselves in Los Angeles. In 1872, she and her son-in-law, Charles Owen, formed the Los Angeles branch of the First African Methodist Episcopal Church. According to Dolores Hayden's article in *California History*, Mason's great-granddaughter Gladys Owens Smith quoted Mason as saying, "If you hold your hand closed, nothing good can come in. The open hand is blessed, for it gives in abundance, even as it receives."

Despite her prosperity, Mason was buried in an unmarked grave in Evergreen Cemetery in the Boyle Heights neighborhood of Los Angeles. A tombstone was laid at the site nearly one hundred years later on March 27, 1988, by Mayor Tom Bradley, the first African American mayor of Los Angeles, and several thousand members of the First African Methodist Episcopal church. A year later, November 16, 1989, was declared "Biddy Mason Day" in Los Angeles. The next day, a new mixed-use building called the Broadway Spring Center was opened on the spot where Mason's homestead once stood. The site included an 8-by-81-foot memorial wall dedicated to Mason that included a collage of Mason's original frame house at the site.

Books

Beasley, Delilah L., *The Negro Trail Blazers of California,* G.K. Hall and Co., 1998.

Hayden, Dolores, *Urban Landscapes as Public History,* MIT Press, 1995.

Hine, Darlene Clark, ed., *Black Women in America: An Historical Encyclopedia,* Carlson Publishing, 1993.

Massey, Sara R., ed., *Black Cowboys of Texas,* Texas A & M University Press, 2000.

Pinkney, Andrea Davis, *Let It Shine: Stories of Black Women Freedom Fighters,* Harcourt, 2000.

Smith, Jessie Carney, ed., *Notable Black American Women, Book 1,* Gale Research, 1992.

Periodicals

California History, Fall 1989.

Cobblestone, February 1999.

Denver Rocky Mountain News, February 8, 1996.

Los Angeles Times, March 28, 1988; November 17, 1989; July 31, 1991.

New York Times, December 7, 1989.

Online

"Angelinos of Ebony Hue," *Black History Month, USC Libraries,* http://www.usc.edu/isd/locations/ssh/doheny/ref/BHH/Exhibit/biddy_mason_1.html (October 27, 2001).

"Bridget 'Biddy' Mason," *Distinguished Women of Past and Present,* http://www.distinguishedwomen.com/biographies/mason-b.html (October 27, 2001). □

Walter Matthau

For half a century Walter Matthau (1920-2000) delighted theater, television, and movie audiences with his portrayals of a huge variety of characters. Although known best for his comedy, Matthau could play any kind of role from romantic lead to grouchy slob to Supreme Court justice. Matthau was memorable as an actor because his face, posture, and voice were always his own, yet he had the ability to create a completely believable character.

O ff-screen, Matthau battled chronic gambling and health problems caused by smoking and an unhealthy diet. He loved to joke, and interviewers often had difficulty knowing what to believe when he spoke of his past. Friends and family adored him. His son Charlie, according to *People Weekly,* wrote in a Father's Day card, "You are a giant. The most loyal and patient husband, and as a father, a volcanic and infinite explosion of unconditional love, universal wisdom and a supernova of everything that is right and good in this world. Apart from that, however, I'm not very pleased with you!" On reading it, Matthau broke down and cried and then never mentioned it again.

Rough Beginnings

Walter Matthau was born on October 1, 1920, in New York City. According to his son, Charlie Matthau, speaking on "Larry King Live," on July 14, 2000, his real last name was spelled Matthow. Walter Matuschanskayasky, which he claimed was his real name, was made up to run in the credits of *Earthquake* (1974), so Matthau could get even for being tricked into a much larger part in the movie than he had wanted.

Matthau's Lithuanian seamstress mother, Rose, raised him alone in the mostly Jewish Lower East Side of New York. His father Milton, a former peddler from Kiev, Ukraine, became an electrician and then a process server. He abandoned Matthau and his older brother, Henry, when Matthau was a three-year-old. According to an article in *People Weekly,* Matthau ran a card game on the roof of his building when he was six years old. He sold refreshments at local Yiddish theaters and broke into acting when, at age 11, he got a small part in *The Dishwasher.* He played bit parts in Yiddish musical comedies while still selling refreshments during the intervals. He was paid 50 cents for each of his occasional parts. "I was shaped by the whole experience of the Depression," he stated in an interview with *The San Francisco Examiner* in 1996. "The humiliation of the competition in the theater, the humiliation of poverty." The Lower East Side "was a nightmare—a dreadful, horrible, stinking nightmare," he recalled in an interview with *The New York Times* in 1971. After graduating from Seward Park High School, Matthau held government positions as a forester in Montana, a gym instructor for the Works Progress Administration, and a boxing coach for policemen.

From Bombs to Broadway

In 1942, Matthau enlisted in the United States Army Air Force as radio cryptographer in a heavy bomber unit of the U.S. Army Air Corps in Europe. He served as a radio operator and gunner in England, France, Holland, Belgium, and Germany and won six battle stars. He spent three years in the service.

After leaving the army, he took some journalism courses at Columbia University and studied acting on the G.I. Bill at New York's New School for Social Research. He met actor Tony Curtis when they studied acting together in the late 1940s. Work in summer stock led to small parts on Broadway and television shows. Matthau's first role on Broadway was as an understudy for the part of an 83-year-old English bishop in *Anne of the Thousand Days.* By 1948 Matthau played regularly on Broadway. He made his first film appearance in 1955 in *The Kentuckian,* as a villain. Through the rest of the 1950s, he played bad guys and drunks in a variety of modest movies, including the Elvis Presley movie *King Creole* (1958) and a Western, *Ride a Crooked Trail* (1958).

Hello, Hollywood

David Ansen described Matthau's physique in a *Newsweek* article. "He was a cross between W. C. Fields and a bloodhound, poured into a stooped, 6-foot-3 frame. No Hollywood leading man has ever looked or sounded or shuffled like Walter Matthau: out of that craggy sourpuss face, with its seen-it-all eyes, came a growl of withering disdain that could stop any outburst of innocence in its tracks."

Matthau had a serious gambling habit. In the 1950s, he owed several hundred thousand dollars in gambling debts. His luck changed in 1955 when he got a part in the hit Broadway show *Will Success Spoil Rock Hunter?* He fell in love with a fellow cast member, actress Carol Marcus, the former wife of the writer William Saroyan. At the time, Matthau was married to Grace Johnson, whom he had wed in 1948 and with whom he had two children, David and Jenny. Matthau and Johnson divorced in 1958. He married Marcus in 1959, and the two had one son, Charlie. In her book *Among the Porcupines* Carol Matthau wrote of her husband, "To the outside world, he is casual, a man's man, funny, rude. . . . In actuality, he is the most passionate man I have ever known. He is the most tender, the most romantic, the most sensual."

Carol Matthau co-starred with her husband in *Gangster Story* (1960), which he directed and described as one of the worst movies ever made. He played a ship's doctor in *Ensign Pulver* (1964), a professor in *Fail-Safe* (1964), and a private detective in *Mirage* (1965). His part as the ambulance-chasing lawyer opposite his friend, actor Jack Lemmon, in *The Fortune Cookie* (1966) earned him his only Academy Award, for best supporting actor. Director Billie Wilder tailored the role of shyster lawyer "Whiplash Willie" for Matthau after seeing him play sportswriter slob Oscar

Madison on Broadway in *The Odd Couple.* Matthau's true calling was comedy, although he disliked being labeled a comic actor. Describing his work habits, his wife noted, "I don't know of anyone who works that hard and yet seems never to work at all. He insists on maintaining his relaxed manner when he is working, in order to make the rest of the players feel more comfortable. That, too, is acting. It is not Walter. Walter is not a relaxed man."

Matthau recreated his Tony Award-winning Broadway role, which playwright Neil Simon created for him, in the movie version of *The Odd Couple* (1968). "Every actor looks all his life for a part that will combine his talents with his personality," Matthau said in an interview with *Time* in 1971. "*The Odd Couple* was mine. That was the plutonium I needed. It all started happening after that."

In the 1970s, Matthau appeared in *A New Leaf* (1971), *Pete 'n' Tillie* (1972), and *The Front Page* (1974) and received Oscar nominations for *Kotch* (1971) and *The Sunshine Boys* (1975). Besides comedic roles, Matthau could successfully play a romantic leading man, a bank-robber hero, or even a horse trainer. Neil Simon praised him as "the greatest instinctive actor" he'd ever seen.

Although he worked throughout the 1980s, his films from this period were not memorable. In May 1993, Matthau was honored with a Lifetime's Achievement Award by America's National Association of Theatre Owners. The 1993 hit movie *Grumpy Old Men* (in which he starred once again with Lemmon) rejuvenated his career. Charlie Matthau, a filmmaker, directed his father in 1995's *The Grass Harp.* In his last film, *Hanging Up,* Matthau gave a powerful performance as a dying screenwriter. Charlie appeared in his father's last film as the younger version of his father's character. Matthau has appeared in a number of TV movies, including the Emmy-winning *The Incident* (1990) and *Mrs. Lambert Remembers Love* (1991), in which he was directed by his son.

Matthau described his versatility as an actor in a 1994 interview with Karen Duffy for *Interview.* "I could play a cop, I could play a crook, I could play a lawyer, I could play a dentist, I could play an art critic—I could play the guy next door. I am the guy next door. I could play Catholic, Jewish, Protestant. As a matter of fact, when I did *The Odd Couple,* I would do it a different way each night. On Monday I'd be Jewish, Tuesday Italian, Wednesday Irish-German—and I would mix them up. I did that to amuse myself, and it always worked." Describing how he did 20 takes of a scene in movie in which he had to cry, Matthau noted, "I wasn't thinking of the sadness, of my mother dying, of my child being run over by a car. I just did it! You gotta just do it, and it either comes or it doesn't. Because if you start thinking about it, it's too late."

Matthau believed that his true talent was performing in theater, rather than in films. "That's where I was good—on the stage," he said in an interview in 1996. "In the movies . . . passable. But on the stage I could move with freedom and ease. And I had something: presence. On screen, all the power is in the hands of the director or the editor."

Plagued by Ill Health

Matthau suffered his first heart attack in 1966, which caused him to quit smoking. It occurred during the filming of *The Fortune Cookie.* Production of the film had to stop for three months while he recuperated. Ten years later he underwent quadruple bypass surgery. He had cancer three times. He spent two weeks in the hospital with pneumonia in May 1999, but made a full recovery. Matthau refused to be depressed about his health. "Even just rolling by in a stretcher, he would say 'Hi!' to the person rolling by in the other direction," says Delia Ephron, in an article in *People Weekly.* "He was in the hospital on a respirator for 24 or 26 weeks, and who walks out of a hospital after that? But he did. You knew he just loved every minute of every day."

Even with his poor health, Matthau did not intend to retire. In a 1995 interview with *People Weekly* he stated, "Some people retire and go fishing. If I retired, I'd go acting." Matthau died of a heart attack on July 1, 2000, at the age of 79.

A Simple Burial

"He wanted as little fuss made about it as possible, a simple burial in a plain pine casket," Charlie Matthau stated to an Associated Press reporter after his father's death. About 50 family members and close friends attended the service, where Matthau was buried according to Jewish law. He was laid to rest at Pierce Brothers Westwood Village Memorial Park in Los Angeles. Noted his wife, "It was impossible not to love him."

Books

Matthau, Carol, *Among the Porcupines,* Turtle Bay Books, 1992.

Saroyan, Aram, *Trio: Oona Chaplin, Carol Matthau, Gloria Vanderbilt. Portraits of an Intimate Friendship,* Linden Press, 1985.

Periodicals

Entertainment Weekly, January 5, 2001.
"Genius," *Interview,* December 1994.
Newsweek, July 10, 2000.
People Weekly, January 16, 1995; July 17, 2000.

Online

"Actor Walter Matthau dies at 79," *CNN,* http://www.cnn.com (October 29, 2001).
"Walter Matthau," *Mr. Showbiz,* http://mrshowbiz.go.com (October 29, 2001). □

Reinhold Messner

Reinhold Messner (born 1944) is the first people ever to climb all 14 of the world's mountain peaks over 8,000 meters high. He has written over 30 books on his adventures, and his minimalist techniques have revolutionized Himalayan mountain climbing.

Internationally known mountain climber Reinhold Messner was born in the Tyrolean Alps in 1944, the second child in a family of eight brothers and one sister. He began climbing at a very early age, ascending his first mountain at the age of four with his father.

In 1970, when he was 25, Messner climbed his first 8,000-meter peak, Nanga Parbat in the Himalayas. Tragedy struck during the climb when Messner's brother Gunther was killed in an avalanche. Although Messner searched extensively for his brother, losing six toes to frostbite in the process, he never found him. Despite his great loss, he continued to climb, next summiting Manaslu in central Nepal.

For Messner these early climbs were only the beginning of an incredible achievement—eventually, he would become the first person to climb all 14 of the world's peaks over 8,000 meters (26,246 feet). Above this altitude, the air is so thin that most people would die, or at best only live for a few hours, without supplemental oxygen.

Messner's Innovations

Although Messner has become famous for climbing without the supplemental oxygen needed for the human brain to function properly at extreme elevations, his decision to climb this way was not the result of a deliberate decision. In 1972 he began dreaming of becoming the first person to climb the southwest face of Everest, but was beaten to it by another climber. Because this achievement was taken, Messner decided to become the first person to climb Everest without oxygen. Paul Deegan commented in *Geographical,* "In an instant . . . this brilliant mountaineer took the game of climbing one-upmanship to a new dimension. By doing so he would change the face of high-altitude climbing forever."

Messner was responsible for other innovations in Himalayan climbing. Prior to his climbing career, mountaineers traditionally spent a great deal of time ascending, moving in stages from one camp to another and resting in between to allow their bodies to become used to the decreased levels of oxygen available at higher altitudes. Messner realized that this slow acclimatization progress was not necessary if the climber spent a relatively short time at high altitudes. In addition, traditional climbs required a great deal of assistance, employing local people to help them carry the large amounts of gear and food they needed. Messner reasoned that if climbers moved quickly and lightly, they would not need so much assistance.

In 1975 Messner applied his ideas to a climb of the northwest face of Gasherbrum I, an 8,068-meter peak in Pakistan. He planned to become accustomed to the altitude at 5,500 meters and then go up to the summit and back in a mere three or four days. Messner and his climbing partner, Peter Habeler, trained intensively for the climb, dieting, long-distance running, and weight training. His resting pulse rate, which indicates the efficiency and strength of an endurance athlete's heart, dropped to an impressive low of 42. With the strength and endurance gained through their rigorous training, the two men were able to climb an amazing 1,000 meters in under an hour. They also defied climbing tradition by ascending near each other, but not roped together, as most climbers were. This freedom also sped their ascent, and they reached the summit in three days, the fastest climb ever of a Himalayan summit via a new route.

In *Outside,* Jon Krakauer quoted American climber Tom Hornbein's comment that Messner's Garsherbrum climb "was a quantum leap. Like Copernicus, Messner had conceived a whole new way of seeing his world. He transformed mountaineering as we know it."

Messner and Habeler were criticized by many for their techniques. Some climbers considered them foolhardy, risking brain damage and death from the severe oxygen restriction. Despite this, they continued with their minimalist methods, forcing some exercise physiologists to reconsider their theories about human limitations at high altitudes. Surprisingly, although Messner has been found to have a very strong physique, his respiratory ability is similar to that of "an above-average marathon runner," according to Jamie Murphy in *Time,* meaning that although he is genetically gifted, he is not unlike thousands of other athletes. What sets him apart, Murphy noted, is his drive to succeed.

Summited Everest without Oxygen

In 1978 Messner and Habeler climbed Mount Everest, the highest mountain in the world, without supplemental oxygen. They began their first attempt on April 21, but two days later Habeler became violently ill from food poisoning. Messner set off with two local men the next morning, but they were overtaken by a violent storm with temperatures of 40 degrees below zero and 125-mph winds for two days. Exhausted, Messner turned back and managed to return to base camp, where Habeler had by now recovered. Habeler was considering using oxygen, but Messner said he would not use it and in addition would not climb with anyone who did, because he wanted to set a record for climbing as high as possible without it. Habeler gave in, and on May 6 they set out again. They ascended in stages, moving to Camp II at 7,200 meters, then to the mountain's South Col at 7,986 meters. They were beginning to experience the effects of oxygen deprivation: headache, double vision, and an inability to sleep because the need to gasp for air kept them awake.

On May 8 the men began preparing for their final ascent. The air was so thin that they could not speak; they used hand signals to communicate in order to save breath. Getting dressed took them two hours, and it took them four hours to ascend to Camp V at 8,500 meters. Despite threatening weather, they moved on to the South Summit, 260 meters higher. They were so oxygen-deprived that every few steps they had to lie down to breathe and regain some strength. Sometime between one and two in the afternoon, they finally reached the summit.

Habeler later was quoted in *Outthere.com* as writing that Messner's "face was contorted in a grimace, his mouth wide open while he gasped panting for air . . . His face was almost without human traits. Our physical reserves were exhausted. We were so utterly spent that we scarcely had the strength to go ten paces in one go." Messner later recalled that when he stood on the summit, he felt like "nothing more than a single narrow gasping lung, floating over the mists and the summits."

Challenged More Peaks

In 1979 Messner climbed K2, the second-highest mountain in the world, and in 1980 he became the first person to make a solo climb of Everest. Kangchenjunga was next, followed by Gasherbrum II, and Broad Peak. Climbing these three mountains in one season, he told Murphy, made Messner think "it was easy, or at least it was possible, for one human being to climb all the highest mountains in the world . . . in a lifetime." In 1985 he climbed Annapurna and Dhaulagiri.

Each new mountain presented a new challenge for Messner, despite his previous successes. He attempted to climb Makalu three times, eventually telling a *Time* interviewer, "You could do twenty to twenty-five steps, and you had to stop for a while and breathe deeply ten to twenty times." In 1986 he and partner Hans Kammerlander climbed Lhotse, making Messner the first person ever to climb all 14 8,000-meter peaks.

An *Economist* contributor commented that many climbers have since speculated that Messner's obsessive drive to conquer all the high peaks in the world was "a penance for [brother] Gunther's death," but also noted that Messner denied this. However, the contributor added, "That tragic climb undoubtedly taught him about the thin line that exists between success and failure, life and death, on the mountains—and so prepared him mentally for the remaining thirteen ascents.''

Following his achievement, Messner became the third person to climb the highest mountain on each of the seven continents on earth. Turning away from mountains, he traveled across Greenland, made a trip across the Antarctic, and skied across the frozen Arctic Ocean to the North Pole. He also found time to write over 30 books about his exploits.

Encounters with the *Yeti*

Messner excited controversy in 1999 with the publication of his book *My Quest for the Yeti.* In it, he described his encounters with the legendary *yeti,* or ''abominable snowman'' of the Himalayas; he believes this creature is actually a rare kind of bear. He spent 15 years researching the book by traveling throughout the Himalayas, and before he saw one of the creatures for himself he considered stories about their existence to be nonsense. However, in 1986, he encountered one at night. As Messner told Ted Chamberlain in *National Geographic Adventure,* he did not immediately think it was a *yeti.* ''I was only looking and thinking, What's that? But I couldn't see colors or faces. I could only see a shadow because it was very late.''

The next morning he found footprints in the snow that resembled those taken by earlier adventurers who claimed they were the tracks of a *yeti.* The footprints appeared to be those of a two-legged animal, but Messner later learned that a certain species of Tibetan brown bear walks in snow by putting its back feet into the holes left by its front feet, so that its track looks like that left by an animal walking upright. Like most bears, it rears up on its hind legs when it meets people, as a gesture of curiosity or threat, which Messner believed led to the legendary descriptions of an animal that stands upright. When asked why the regions local people did not identify the yeti as a bear, Messner contended that the bear is a nocturnal animal, very dangerous and frightening, and the local people stay inside at night and thus rarely see it. He told Chamberlain, ''In their stomachs, a few of them know this is a bear. They call it a bear with human abilities.'' Messner has approached within 20 meters of a sleeping Tibetan bear, with a local who identified it as a *yeti.*

Messner's Legacy

Messner makes his home in a medieval castle in northern Italy. A member of the European parliament, he explained to Paul Deegan in *Geographical* that ''MEPs have no real power, only the possibility to give guidance to the commission and the council of ministers.'' He has used his position in the realm of politics to speak out on behalf of Tibet, which endured invasion and repression by the Chinese government beginning in the 1940s. Messner's climbing techniques inspired mountaineers worldwide. According to Murphy in *Time,* Everest climber Chris Bonington noted of Messner: ''There is a wall called 'impossible' that the great mass of people in any field face. Then one person who's got a kind of extra imaginative drive jumps that wall. That's Reinhold Messner.'' Messner had a different view, telling *Genovagando,* ''I'm a fellow living a

normal life. My mountain climbing has always been a way to put myself to the test. I've always gone where I met danger and effort to test my skill. Making even little progresses is my dream. And it's a dream that keeps me awake.''

Periodicals

Economist, June 25, 1994.
Geographical, December 2000.
Outside, October 1997.
Time, October 27, 1986.
Vietnam Investment Review, May 7, 2001.

Online

''Everest without Oxygen,'' *Outthere.com,* http://www.outthere .co.za/ (November 9, 2001).
''First without Oxygen,'' *Public Broadcasting System Web site,* http://www.pbs.org/ (November 9, 2001).
''Interview to Reinhold Messner,'' *Genovagando,* http://www .ulisse.it/ospiti/genovagando/ (November 9, 2001).
''Reinhold Messner: Climbing Legend, Yeti Hunter,'' *National Geographic Adventure,* http://nationalgeographic.com/ adventure/ (November 9, 2001).
''Reinhold Messner: The World's Greatest Living Mountaineer,'' *OSB,* http://www.osb2000.com/ (November 9, 2001). □

Edgar Dean Mitchell

Edgar Dean Mitchell (born 1930) became the sixth person to walk on the surface of the moon during the third manned moon mission, *Apollo 14.* With him on the surface was Alan B. Shepard, who had made history in 1961 as the first American in space. The two landed on the moon aboard *Apollo 14*'s lunar module *Antares* in February 1971, while crewmate Stuart A. Roosa orbited the moon aboard the mission's command module *Kitty Hawk.*

Born in Hereford, Texas, on September 17, 1930, Edgar Dean Mitchell grew up in the southwest, attending elementary school in Roswell, New Mexico, a town that would later become famous for its UFO sightings. His father was a rancher, his mother a fundamentalist Baptist. Mitchell learned to fly an airplane when he was just 13 years old, even before attending high school in Artesia, New Mexico. Artesia, where he spent his teenage years, was the city he thereafter considered his hometown.

After high school Mitchell went on to the Carnegie Institute of Technology, graduating in 1952 with a bachelor of science degree in industrial management. Next, he attended the U.S. Naval Postgraduate School, from which he graduated in 1961 with another B.S., this one in aeronautical engineering. He completed his academic career in 1964 when he received a doctorate of science degree in aeronautics/astronautics from the Massachusetts Institute of Technology.

Began Military Career

Mitchell joined the U.S. Navy in 1952 and went through basic training at the San Diego Recruit Depot. He was commissioned as an ensign after graduating from the Officers Candidate School in Newport, Rhode Island. After completing flight training at Hutchinson, Kansas, in 1954, he joined Patrol Squadron 29 and was sent to Okinawa, Japan. In 1957 Mitchell was assigned to Heavy Attack Squadron Two operating on the aircraft carriers USS *Bon Homme Richard* and USS *Ticonderoga.* Afterwards, he became a test pilot for Air Development Squadron Five, which he served until 1959. Between 1964 and 1965 he was part of the Navy's Manned Orbiting Laboratory program as head of the project management division. When this program stalled, he left it to join the astronaut corps.

Mitchell had to follow a long, hard career path in order to become an astronaut. As he recalled to Eric M. Jones for the online *Apollo Lunar Surface Journal,* "I'd applied at every opportunity from 1958 on. But my jet hours weren't enough, since I'd started out in props. . . . Building up my jet hours . . . and then getting my test pilot credentials . . . took me until I was 36. It took me damn near nine years to get all the qualifications . . . in order to be selected."

Made the Cut to Astronaut

Selected as one of the National Aeronautics and Space Administration's (NASA's) fifth group of astronauts in 1966, Mitchell joined Project "Apollo," America's manned moon landing program. He worked on the Apollo 9 mission as a member of the astronaut support crew while the mission test-flew the lunar module designed to land astronauts on the moon in low Earth orbit. He then became backup lunar module pilot for the Apollo 10 mission, a dress-rehearsal for the first moon landing in which astronauts Gene Cernan and Tom Stafford descended to within 50,000 feet of the lunar surface.

A member of the lunar module design team, Mitchell was an expert on lunar module systems. In 1970, when *Apollo 13* suffered an onboard explosion that ruined the mission and nearly killed its crew, he was called on as an advisor in the effort that got the astronauts home safely. As he later told Jones, "During the Apollo 13 experience, where Fred and Jim had to bring their lunar module back as a lifeboat, I spent the five days of that emergency in the lunar module simulator, creating the procedures they had to use. And radioing them up to them in space."

Joined Alan Shepard for a Trip to the Moon

Mitchell got his chance to go to the moon himself in 1971. His ship was *Apollo 14,* and along for his ride were Alan B. Shepard, commander, and Stuart A. Roosa, command module pilot. Mitchell and Shepard were to land on the moon in *Apollo 14*'s lunar module *Antares,* while Roosa orbited the moon aboard the ship's command module *Kitty Hawk.* The mission, Mitchell's only trip into space, was the second trip for Shepard, who had previous been aboard the one-man Mercury capsule, *Freedom 7.* That flight had lasted just 15 minutes, not even reaching Earth orbit, and Shepard was eager to return to space. Unfortunately fate intervened in the form of an inner ear disorder known as Meniere's syndrome, which affected Shepard's balance and took him off active flight status. However, he wasted no time in becoming one of two astronauts in charge of crew selection at NASA, and after an experimental surgical procedure cured his affliction, he got himself assigned to the *Apollo 14* crew.

Two major glitches marred an otherwise perfect flight. On the way out to the moon, just two hours after leaving Earth's orbit, the command module failed to dock to the lunar module. This was an essential procedure, and a landing could not be accomplished without it. Four attempts failed to engage the docking mechanism, and the two spacecrafts simply bounced off each other without connecting. Just when it seemed the mission might be lost, controllers in Houston radioed up a plan that might work: use the command module's thrusters to hold the two spacecraft together while Shepard threw a switch to retract a docking probe. The plan worked.

During his first sleep period in space, and every other sleep period during the mission, Mitchell conducted a secret procedure of his own. Long interested in the untapped potential of the human mind, he had arranged an extra sensory perception (ESP) experiment with collaborators on Earth. According to plan, Mitchell waited until 45 minutes past the start of sleep time on the ship and then concentrated on a series of symbols and shapes printed on a clipboard.

Four men on Earth tried to "receive" in their minds the shapes that Mitchell concentrated on.

The second major glitch of the mission occurred as *Antares* headed down from lunar orbit to the moon's surface. At 30,000 feet, the landing radar refused to engage as it was supposed to. As Mitchell later told Jones, "When it didn't come in by 30 thousand, we got alarmed. And at 20 thousand feet, that's when we were frantically trying to get it to come in because, at 10 thousand feet, there was automatic (meaning 'mandatory') abort without landing radar." If the landing radar did not come on, mission rules stated that the astronauts would have to abort the mission and return to lunar orbit without ever setting foot on the moon. Fortunately, all it took was simply turning the radar off and then on again to get it to engage, and the mission proceeded as planned.

On February 5, 1971, Mitchell and Shepard touched down to a feather-light landing in the highlands of the moon's Fra Mauro region. The mission set a record for longest time spent on the surface (33 hours), longest time spend on the moon outside of a spacecraft (more than 9 hours in two excursions), and the most lunar sample material returned from Earth (some 100 pounds). The mission also marked the first use of a color television camera for transmitting video back to Earth.

Continued to Promote Space Exploration

After serving as backup lunar module pilot for the Apollo 16 mission, Mitchell retired from NASA in 1972. He founded the Institute of Noetic Sciences in 1973 to "expand knowledge of the nature and potentials of the mind and spirit, and to apply that knowledge to advance health and well-being for humanity and our planet," according to the institute's Web site. From 1974 to 1978 he headed the Edgar Mitchell Corporation, based in Palm Beach, Florida, and later became head of Mitchell Communications. In 1996 Mitchell published a book about the consciousness-expanding aspects of his moon voyage titled *The Way of the Explorer.*

Books

Chaikin, Andrew, *A Man on the Moon: The Voyages of the Apollo Astronauts,* Penguin, 1994.

Online

Apollo Lunar Surface Journal, http://www.hq.nasa.gov/office/pao/History/ (November 14, 2001).
Astronaut Hall of Fame Web site, http://www.astronauts.org/ (November 13, 2001).
Institute of Noetic Sciences Web site, http://www.noetic.org/ (November 14, 2001).
Lyndon B. Johnson Space Center Web site, http://www.jsc.nasa.gov/ (November 13, 2001). □

Ashley Montagu

Anthropologist and educator Ashley Montagu (1905-1999) focused on human bio-social evolution and maintained throughout his long career that cultural phenomena are not genetically predetermined. In more than 50 books published for both an academic and general readership, Montagu broadened understanding of human social evolution. His topics ranged from human aggression and the use of profanity to infant nurturing, the importance of touch, and the nature of human love.

Montagu committed himself to popularizing the findings of modern science in the hopes of improving civil society and the quality of life. He brought his message to the public not only in books, but also in college classrooms, lecture halls, articles appearing in periodicals ranging from the *Washington Post* to *Ladies' Home Journal,* and appearances on popular television talk shows.

Took Aristocratic Name

The son of Jewish tailor Charles Ehrenberg and his wife, Mary Plot Ehrenberg, Montagu was born Israel Ehrenberg on June 28, 1905. He was raised in London's working class East End neighborhood. It is not known why he decided to change his name, but it may have been due to prejudice against East End Jews in those days. The young boy's decision to take the aristocratic name Ashley Montagu distanced him from his father's Polish and his mother's Russian ethnic roots.

By age ten Montagu was a keen observer of human behavior, and he closely studied the linguistic differences between his Cockney neighbors and the more educated university students who rented rooms in his parents' home. Anatomy was another interest—one that would continue throughout Montagu's life—and in 1917 he made an unannounced visit to British anatomist Sir Arthur Keith, hoping Keith would help him identify a skull Montagu found. Keith was so impressed that he invited the 12-year-old to visit him at the Museum of the Royal College of Surgeons and continue his study of anatomy.

Many adults encouraged young Montagu's intelligence and curiosity, and he read philosophers such as John Stuart Mill, Thomas Henry Huxley, and Friedrich Nietzsche at a relatively young age. His interests included biology, psychology, and anthropology. When he was 15, Montagu won a literary contest and chose as his prize a book titled *Introduction to Social Psychology*. His early interest in the relationship between environment and behavior foreshadowed Montagu's long career in the social sciences.

Published Works on Race

After completing his secondary education in London, in 1922 Montagu enrolled at the University of London and spent the next three years studying anthropology. Witnessing the British government's harsh treatment of striking workers during a general labor strike in 1926 prompted the idealistic 21-year-old to leave England. In late 1927 he arrived in New York City and took several classes at Columbia University. He was quoted in a *Los Angeles Times* obituary as once commenting: "I was brought up as a stuffed shirt Englishman. I wasn't very human. What America did for me was humanize me, democratize me." Traveling to Italy in 1928, he took classes in ethnography and anthropology at the University of Florence, broadening his knowledge and developing the framework for his compelling arguments against biologically determined concepts of race. In 1931, while working as an assistant professor of anthropology at New York University, Montagu married Marjorie Peakes; the couple would have two daughters, Audrey and Barbara, and a son, Geoffrey. In 1934, Montagu resumed his studies at Columbia and earned his Ph.D. there in 1936 under noted professors Franz Boaz and Ruth Benedict. He became a naturalized U.S. citizen in 1940.

In 1937 Montagu published his first book, *Coming into Being among the Australian Aborigines,* which was based on his dissertation. As a newly graduated Ph.D., he left New York University and joined the staff of Hahnemann Medical College in Philadelphia in 1938. While at Hahnemann, he published a number of papers on the topic of race. With the rise of Nazism and anti-Semitism and the persistence of American racial segregation, Montagu decided that his ideas would be valuable to the public, and he condensed them in the seminal 1942 work *Man's Most Dangerous*

Myth: The Fallacy of Race. In it, he challenged the then largely accepted notion that characteristics based on race were a biological construct. He argued that since humans in all parts of the world developed in hunter-gatherer societies, the challenges they faced in order to survive were similar and their mental capacities equivalent. Given similar genetic traits, differences in the development of human cultures in different parts of the globe must have been caused by external conditions, such as geography, climate, and the availability of natural resources, he argued.

Man's Most Dangerous Myth was highly influential, and Montagu's argument revolutionized the perception of race. In 1949 he was asked to serve on a United Nations Educational, Scientific, and Cultural Organization (UNESCO) task force and became the principal author of that committee's "Statement on Race." Montagu was not, however, an ardent UN backer. He once commented: "Most of the United Nations is really a forum for the exhibition of national prejudices on a hitherto unprecedented scale. . . . It's a colossal disaster. What it reflects, of course, is the dehumanization of human beings as human beings." *Man's Most Dangerous Myth* was revised several times, including in the 1990s to incorporate Montagu's thoughts on ethnic cleansing in Bosnia and several African nations and the debate over IQ testing, affirmative action, and race. Considered a classic, the book remained in print 60 years after it was first published. Others expanded on Montagu's ideas in the 1975 book *Race and IQ,* a collection of essays edited by Montagu.

On Love and Gender

Montagu became involved in many projects that brought scientific findings to mass audiences. Involved in drafting the bill creating the National Science Foundation in 1946, he also wrote, directed, and produced the documentary film *One World, or None.* In 1948, Montagu organized an archaeological dig in Kent, England. Leaving Hahnemann Medical College in 1949, he became professor of anthropology at Rutgers University and chair of the department.

In addition to teaching, Montagu continued to spark discussion with a number of books on sociology. One topic that fascinated him was the role of love in the formation of personality. For Montagu, the benefits of encouraging a caring, committed love for others far outweighed those of organized religion. 1950's *On Being Human* and 1955's *The Direction of Human Development: Biological and Social Bases* are among books Montagu wrote about the scientific basis and social manifestations of love. In a 1981 interview for *Contemporary Authors,* he commented: " . . . in our modern societies, especially in America, . . . we have a great deal of talk about love, but it's love of an unloving kind, an absence of the real love behind the show of love, which literally means that children and others are being unloved to death."

While at Rutgers, Montague wrote perhaps his most famous work: 1953's *The Natural Superiority of Women.* First serialized in the mainstream *Saturday Evening Post,* the essay takes a somewhat humorous tone in discussing men, who possess "the bruited advantages of larger size and muscular power" that in a modern society of desk workers has led some of them to become psychopaths, drug abusers, and barroom brawlers. Examining each sex from an anthropological perspective, Montagu concluded that women are superior because their genetic "bag of tricks" has enabled them to survive both as individuals and in a group during the evolution from a hunter-gatherer to a technological society. For its time, *The Natural Superiority of Women* was a radical work: Montagu suggested that women should receive equal pay for doing equal work. However, it angered feminists, who took umbrage at Montagu's views that women should stay home to raise their children rather than leaving the home to work.

Broadened Public Presence

Montagu's decision to leave Rutgers in 1955 was guided by his continued success as an author. At 50, he wanted to devote more attention to writing. He continued to teach, however, as a visiting professor at universities such as Harvard and Princeton. Montagu increased his involvement in the public sector by serving as the director of the New Jersey Committee on Physical Growth and Development from 1951 to 1957, as chairman of the Anisfield-Wolf Award Committee on Race Relations, and as an advisory consultant to the International Childbirth Education Association and the Peace Research Institute. He continued to attract acclaim and detractors with outspoken criticism of prominent theorists whose works he considered harmful to society.

In his later career, Montagu broadened his sociological scope to include anatomy, heredity, marriage, sex, and even the history of cursing, drawing on current scientific research to support his humanist position. He encouraged modern mothers to return to breast-feeding in 1971's *Touching: The Human Significance of the Skin*. That same year, his book *The Elephant Man: A Study in Human Dignity* inspired the Tony Award-winning play and a later motion picture with its compelling history of a horribly disfigured man in Victorian England.

Montagu's 1976 work, *The Nature of Human Aggression,* presents the argument that, unlike animals, humans are without instincts and therefore possess no aggressive instincts. In contrast to the position of such ethnologists as Konrad Lorenz, he maintained that all human behavior is learned behavior; while man has the potential for aggressive action, Montagu argued, he has an equal potential for a non-aggressive response.

After retiring from the academic world, Montagu continued to write, revising his earlier books as new scientific studies provided additional insights and reflecting on his own life and career. In his 1981 book, *Growing Young,* he encouraged readers to cultivate the qualities of curiosity, imagination, and the desire to learn, all inborn traits suppressed in adulthood due to time constraints and stress. Montagu remained a strong advocate of play and spent his free time in book collecting and vegetable gardening at his home in Princeton, New Jersey. Stricken with heart disease while working on completing his memoirs, Montagu was

hospitalized in March 1999 and died on November 26, 1999, in Princeton, at age ninety-four.

Periodicals

American Anthropologist, October 1951; February 1969; October 1969.
American Journal of Sociology, January 1952.
Christian Science Monitor, June 20, 1968.
Commonweal, August 4, 1950.
Los Angeles Times, November 28, 1999.
National Review, November 28, 1967.
New York Times, November 29, 1999.
Psychology Today, August 1977.
Skeptical Inquirer, January 2000.

Online

Contemporary Authors Online, http://www.galenet.com/ (October 30, 2001). □

Montezuma I

Montezuma I (1397-1469), who ruled the Aztecs from 1440 to 1469, is best known for his expansion of the empire and for his building projects, including the dike across Lake Texcoco and the temple to the god Huitzilopochtli. He declared that war was the main task of the Aztecs in order to ensure a constant supply of sacrificial victims for Huitzilopochtli, who demanded many victims a year. Montezuma's pattern of conquering an enemy and demanding tribute became the norm for all future Aztec conquests.

Montezuma I, also known as Motecuhzoma Ilhuicamina ("'The Angry Lord, Archer of the Skies") was the grandson of the first leader of Tenochtitlan ("Cactus Rock"). The great city-state of the Aztecs, Tenochtitlan was the great city-state of the Aztecs. It was located on an island in Lake Texcoco in the Valley of Mexico. Tenochtitlan was the forerunner of Mexico City, the capital of modern Mexico. Montezuma's father, Huitzilhuitl ("Hummingbird Feather"), had many children; Montezuma was born about 1397, the son of a princess of Cuernavaca named Miahuaxihuitl.

After Huitzilhuitl died, Montezuma's warrior brother Chimalpopoca ruled for ten years, then was assassinated. During Chimalpopoca's reign, another brother, Tlacaelel, joined Montezuma in gaining the support of a group of young, militant nobles. This group chose Itzcoatl ("Serpent of Knives") as the next leader of the Aztecs. Itzcoatl, brother of Huitzilhuitl, enlarged the area controlled by the Aztecs, with his nephews, Tlacaelel and Montezuma as generals of the army.

Upon Itzcoatl's death in 1440, Montezuma was picked to take over the reins of command. Unlike the previous leaders, who held the title "Speaker," he was called "Great Speaker," because he spoke for not only the Aztecs, but also

for the tribes who paid tribute to them. Montezuma's coronation was a vast ceremony, with the sacrifice of many prisoners. Seated on a basketwork throne, Hungry Coyote, the Lord of Texcoco, placed the fire crown, a turquoise diadem, on the head of his friend Montezuma.

Montezuma was a wise ruler and a modest man. He lived in a simple, clean palace and had only a few wives. A great deal of his time was passed in conversation with sage friends, as well as with his half-brother, Tlacaelel, who acted as the "serpent woman" or chief military and political adviser to several Aztec rulers. Montezuma consulted Tlacaelel about every matter, and Tlacaelel told him that it was Montezuma's duty to constantly seek advantage for his household, court, and domains and to enlarge his empire at every opportunity. Tlacaelel sat next to Montezuma in court and was the only person allowed to be treated as the king's equal.

Satisfied the Sun God

Montezuma solidified the triple alliance between Tenochtitlan, Texcoco, and Tlacopan with a formula for dividing the spoils of war. The booty was split into five parts; one part went to Tlacopan and the remainder was shared by the other two groups. Encouraged by Tlacaelel, Montezuma also began construction of a new temple to Huitzilopochtli, originally the hummingbird god but now worshiped as the god of battle, the lord of creation, and the all-powerful Sun god. The temple of Huitzilopochtli, also known as the templo mayor, great temple, or great pyramid, had more

than one hundred steps. Over a period of two years during Montezuma's reign, thousands of slaves and workers constructed this edifice, even during times of famine. They used canoes to transport the stone and wood to the sacred area. The temple was inaugurated in 1455 following the Aztec victory over the Huaxtecs, who served as the temple's first sacrificial victims.

Montezuma ordered all subject people to provide workers and material for the building of the new temple. Although he hesitated to force the fierce and numerous Chalca tribe to contribute, Tlacaelel insisted. The Chalcas were stubborn opponents who killed a great many Aztecs, including three brothers of Montezuma and Tlacaelel. The two tribes battled periodically for 20 years, at first with Montezuma in command of the Aztec army. This was a new concept, invented by Tlacaelel who maintained that the ruler should begin his rule by leading his subjects in battle and wetting his feet with the blood of sacrificed victims. Montezuma was a successful warrior and sacrificed the first group of Chalca victims to the Sun god in Tenochtitlan.

Huitzilopochtli required a continual supply of sacrificial victims, whose blood and body parts fed the god to ensure the daily journey of the sun across the sky. The ceremony required four priests to hold the victim, while the king lifted an obsidian knife above his head, brought it down on the victim's body, reached in to grab the heart, pulled it out, and held the beating heart up, sprinkling the blood in the direction of the sun. The king then placed the heart in the mouth of the statue of Huitzilopochtli. Montezuma and Tlacaelel took turns killing the first few victims, after which the chief priests took over. Up to 20,000 victims were sacrificed to Huitzilopochtli and other Aztec deities every year.

Ensured a Food and Water Supply

The Valley of Mexico where the Aztecs ruled contained about one million people during Montezuma's reign. "This Aztec heartland included not only Tenochtitlan, but at least nine provincial centers and a large number of smaller settlements, the largest and densest population concentration in the entire history of pre-Hispanic American. The only way to feed everyone was by efficient, government-controlled agriculture," explained Brian Fagan in The Aztecs. Montezuma employed inspectors to make sure that every bit of land was planted and that extra food was sent to the capital.

In 1449 Lake Texcoco flooded the city of Tenochtitlan. Rain and hail ruined the harvests and famine struck the Valley of Mexico. Montezuma asked his cousin Nezahualcoyotl, ruler of Texcoco, for help. Nezahualcoyotl directed the construction of a nine-mile-long dike that would help control the water level and also lessen the saltiness of the water so it could be used for farming. The immense project took almost ten years and tens of thousands of workers to complete. After the dike was finished, Montezuma requested that Nezahualcoyotl direct the construction of a three-mile-long aqueduct to bring more drinking water to the city.

In the first half of the 1450s many disasters struck the Aztecs. Grasshoppers and frost destroyed two harvests. Snow and rain caused terrible flooding one year; and the next two years saw an extended drought. People had no food, and some even sold their children to distant tribes for corn. Famine led to rebelliousness among the tribes paying tribute to the Aztecs. Montezuma and Tlacaelel met with the provincial puppet rulers of these tribes and arranged for phony wars, called "Flower Wars," in which the chieftains told the Aztecs the size and location of their armies, guaranteeing an Aztec win.

In 1455 the Aztec calendar's 52-year cycle ended and the calendar began again, an occasion marked by fasting and making new fire. Also at this time, the famine ended because of abundant harvests. Worried about future famines, Montezuma decided to ensure a reliable food supply by conquest and the collection of tribute. In 1458 he and his army attacked and conquered the province of Panuco, thus extending the Aztec empire to the sea. In 1461 the army conquered the lands of the Totonacs to the south, along with the people of Coatzocoalcos, and four years later Montezuma defeated the Chalca. His last war, against the Tepeaca in 1466, solidified a course of military expansion that determined Aztec policies until the Spanish arrived in 1519.

During Montezuma's rule, an old garden in Huaxtepec was rediscovered. Montezuma hired an overseer named Pinotetl to renovate the garden's stone fountains, as well as the area's irrigation system. While Pinotetl worked, Montezuma sent requests to the Lord of Cuetlaxtla for vanilla orchids, cacao trees, and other valuable plants, as well as for gardeners who would know how to replant and care for them. The replantings were successful, giving Montezuma great joy, for which he thanked the gods.

Montezuma's Sumptuary Laws

During Montezuma's reign rules of conduct were established that drew lines between various levels of Aztec society and singled out those of high birth or bravery in battle. Dress and forms of salutation were ritualized, as embellished clothing was reserved for various noble classes and lower classes were prohibited from donning cotton cloth, wearing sandals, or owning clothes that extended below the knee. Only noblemen could reside in homes of more than one story or use fine glazed ceramic eating vessels. Montezuma himself wore the finest jewels and finely woven cotton clothing and donned a headdress with bright feathers. His laws legislated all forms of behavior, from adultery to drunkenness to more criminal activities, with slavery a typical punishment.

Montezuma died in 1469 and was succeeded by his 19-year-old cousin Axayacatl. Axayacatl was the father of Montezuma II, the ruler of the Aztecs at the time of the Spanish invasion and conquest. More than five centuries later, in 1978, excavations began in Mexico City at the site of the great temple. Nearby were found funerary urns made of clay and obsidian and inscribed with the year of Montezuma's death. Archaeologists surmised that these may be the funereal urns of the great Aztec ruler himself.

Books

Fagan, Brian, *The Aztecs,* W. H. Freeman and Company, 1984.

Kandell, Jonathan, *La Capital: The Biography of Mexico City,* Random House, 1988.

Thomas, Hugh, *Conquest: Montezuma, Cortes, and the Fall of Old Mexico,* Simon & Schuster, 1993.

Townsend, Richard F., *The Aztecs,* Thames & Hudson, 2000.

Periodicals

Papers from the Institute of Archaeology, Volume 4, 1993.

Online

Museo del Templo Mayor Web site, http://archaeology.la.asu .edu/ (January 26, 2002). □

Gustave Moreau

French artist Gustave Moreau (1826-1898) is known for his strange and mystical works, often portraying scenes from mythology or religion. Although admired in his time, his works fell out of favor until the 1960s, when there was a revival of interest. Moreau instructed Henri Matisse and Georges Rouault, two famous French artists.

Received Artistic Encouragement

Gustave Moreau was born in Paris on April 6, 1826. His father, Louis-Jean Marie Moreau, born in 1790, was a successful architect for the city of Paris and the Ministry of the Interior. He was head of construction for the Place de la Concorde and a number of other buildings. The artist's mother, Adele Pauline Desmoutier, born in 1802, was the daughter of a chateau owner and former mayor of Douai. Like her husband, she had a comfortable, upper-middle-class childhood. Gustave Moreau had a younger sister, Camille, who died when he was 14 years old.

Moreau attended boarding school, the College Rollin, beginning at age 11 but left when his sister died. At the school, he won an award for draftsmanship. After he left school, his parents educated him at home, where they had a large library of books that Moreau read eagerly, including works on mythology. Moreau also studied Roman architecture, the Middle Ages, the Renaissance, the artistic themes of the Middle East and Far East, Shakespeare, and the Bible. In 1841, Moreau's mother, aunt, and uncle took him on a trip to Italy, where they visited Turin, Milan, Parma, Pisa, Florence, and Genoa. Moreau's sketchbook from this trip still exists and is kept in the Moreau Museum in Paris.

Moreau knew he wanted to be an artist and his parents supported him in his goal. In the mid-1840s, his parents showed his work to a painter, Pierre-Joseph Dedreux-Dorcy, who also encouraged him. Around 1844, Moreau began to study art with the neoclassical painter and art instructor Francois-Edouard Picot, who gave his student a solid technical foundation for his work. While studying with Picot, Moreau painted studies of nudes, copied Old Masters, and made oil sketches and large paintings.

With Picot, a follower of the artist Jean-Auguste-Dominique Ingres, Moreau got ready for the difficult entrance examinations for the Ecole des Beaux-Arts, a famous art school in Paris. Anyone who hoped to make a living as an artist in France at that time was expected to attend that school. Moreau gained admission on his first try, and he began studying there in October 1846.

Left the Academy

Serious art students were expected to compete each year for the prestigious Prix de Rome, which was awarded by the Academie des Beaux-Arts and was the highest honor a French art student could win. The award included a four-year scholarship at the Villa Medici in Rome. Moreau entered the competition twice, in 1848 and 1849, losing both times.

Moreau left the academy and struck out on his own, using his father's connections to win several government commissions. He entered the seasonal salons, gaining acceptance at some, failing at others. The government commissioned a work and placed it in a museum in Dijon. Another entry went to a museum in Bourg-en-Bresse. One of these government commissions was the first work Moreau ever exhibited, a Pieta, which was shown in the Salon of 1852 and received favorable reviews from art critics. The annual salons were the official place of exhibition for French artists, run by the Academy of Fine Arts.

In the early 1850s, Moreau met the Romantic painters Eugene Delacroix and Theodore Chasseriau, who greatly influenced his style of painting. From them, Moreau learned to love exotic romanticism, dramatic lighting, and bright colors. Moreau moved next door to Chasseriau and became interested in the latest fashions, often visiting Paris's literary and artistic salons. In 1854, Louis Moreau bought a house on the rue de La Rochefoucauld, number 14, which became the family home, Moreau's studio, and eventually the Gustave Moreau Museum.

Moreau Returned to Italy

Chasseriau's death in 1856, at the age of 37, greatly upset Moreau. Unhappy with his work and saddened by his friend's death, Moreau went to Italy in 1857 to study the methods and work of Renaissance artists and the architectural remains and artifacts of ancient Greece and Rome. He traveled throughout the country, going to Rome, Florence, Siena, Pisa, Milan, Venice, Naples, and Pompeii. Italy's art deeply affected his work. "The trip also exposed him to the influence of Byzantine enamels, early mosaics, and Persian and Indian miniatures, all of which would play a significant role in the evolution of his individual style and in the jewel-like effect of his technique," noted Bennett Schiff in the *Smithsonian*. "At the Villa Medici in Rome, Moreau met Edgar Degas and traveled around the country with him for a while. They became fast friends, but over time, as their styles diverged, the friendship cooled."

After returning to Paris from Italy in 1859, Moreau met Alexandrine Dureux and they became romantically involved. They never lived together, but he paid her rent on a nearby apartment. Moreau painted for a number of years without exhibiting his work, but during this time he developed his unique style. The colors he used reflected the Romantic style, but his figures were static. He spent many hours studying Persian, Indian, and Japanese prints and from them took motifs, which he used to create his own vision of myths and religions.

Back in the Public Eye

In the Salon of 1864, Moreau exhibited his painting *Oedipus and the Sphinx,* the work that launched him into prominence. To Moreau, the work represented man facing the eternal mystery with moral strength and self-confidence. "Outstanding examples of psychological and physical detachment can be seen in one after another of Moreau's paintings," wrote Schiff. "In *Oedipus and the Sphinx* (1864), for instance, the winged creature—half nude female, half lion, an incubus clawed into Oedipus' breast—does not seem to inflict pain at all. Instead, the grotesque creature and its placid victim appear to be dreamily engrossed in each other, although Oedipus is soon to answer the Sphinx's riddle and she, or it, is to fall dead to the ground, finally, having already shredded any number of hapless voyagers unable to answer the riddle. Their bits and pieces are, in Moreau's superbly rendered canvas, strewn about the foreground." Finally, Moreau had achieved formal recognition of his talent. From then on, he helped re-energize the tradition of history painting, giving epic tales poetic imagination, exoticism, and wonder.

In the Salon of 1865, Moreau exhibited *Young Man and Death* and *Jason and Medea.* In 1866, he showed *Orpheus* and *Diomedes Devoured by his Horses.* He exhibited each year in the Salon through 1869, when his works were criticized in the press. After that he sold a few paintings to admirers but rarely left his studio.

In 1876, he began to exhibit in the Salon again, showing three of his most famous paintings: *Hercules and the Hydra, Salome Dancing Before Herod,* and *The Apparition.* He last exhibited in the Salon in 1880, showing *Galatea* and *Helen.*

Moreau was devoted to Alexandrine Dureux for 31 years, until her death in 1890 at age 54. After her death, Moreau's style altered. "His brushwork became looser and more expressive; his pigment grew thicker, more impastoed; and his forms became increasingly abstract," Schiff wrote. "The overriding effect of these later paintings was to evoke an emotional response through the use of color, line and form. Some even view his later nonfigurative works as heralds of Abstract Expressionism. Certainly his art inspired a generation of Symbolist painters, poets and writers and had a marked impact on other artists, including the Surrealists and the radical group known as the Fauves."

Taught Painting

In 1888, Moreau was elected to the Academie des Beaux-Arts. At age 65, he became a professor in charge of a studio at the Ecole des Beaux-Arts. He was considered the last great teacher there. He taught Georges Rouault, Henri Matisse, and others, developing their natural talents and encouraging them to use color imaginatively.

In 1895, Moreau remodeled his house into a four-story building to create a museum for his works. He died of stomach cancer in Paris on April 18, 1898. Moreau left to the state his home and its contents, about 1,200 paintings and watercolors and roughly 10,000 drawings. Moreau sold about 500 works while alive, and these are in other collections and museums.

From about 1914 until 1960, art historians lost interest in Moreau, viewing him as an eccentric, although he was always considered a great teacher. In 1961, a large retrospective of Moreau was held in Paris at the Louvre, which led to more exhibitions in the 1960s. In 1974, the Los Angeles County Museum of Art held an exhibition and so did the Zurich Kunsthaus in 1986. In 1998 and 1999, an exhibition of his works appeared in Paris, Chicago, and New York. "Exactly where Moreau fits in, and his real place in art history, is as difficult to determine in 1999, however, as it was in 1899," wrote Laura Morowitz in *The Art Bulletin*. "Perhaps our only safe judgment is to agree with the critic Theophile Gautier, writing a century and a half ago, that ' . . . his work stands in singular isolation, and whether it pleases or not, one has to reckon with it.'"

Books

Kaplan, Julius, *The Art of Gustave Moreau: Theory, Style, and Content,* UMI Research Press, 1982.

Kaplan, Julius, *Gustave Moreau,* Los Angeles County Museum of Art, 1974.

Mathieu, Pierre-Louis, *Gustave Moreau, with a catalogue of the finished paintings, watercolors and drawings,* New York Graphic Society, 1976.

Periodicals

The Art Bulletin, June 2000.
Smithsonian, August 1999. □

Willard Motley

An African American author who wrote predominantly about white characters, Willard Motley (1909-1965) gained recognition with the 1947 release of his critically acclaimed first novel *Knock Down Any Door*. His realistic, detailed depictions of life in slums, prisons, and reform schools earned him comparisons to other naturalist authors such as Theodore Dreiser. Despite the fact that two of his novels were made into films, Motley never surpassed the success of his first novel.

B orn into a middle-class, Roman Catholic, African American family in 1909 (some sources cite the year of his birth as 1912), Motley enjoyed some early advantages. His family lived in Englewood, a white neighborhood on the south side of Chicago. Living as the only black family in an all white neighborhood meant Motley's family was not considered a threat, and unlike most blacks of that time Motley had few hostile interactions with whites. He grew up believing his grandparents were his parents and his mother, Florence (Flossie), was his sister. Florence moved to New York and left Motley to be raised by his grandparents. Despite this, Motley had a steady family life, full of strong role models. His grandfather, Archibald Motley, Sr., worked as a Pullman porter on a train running between New York City and Chicago and his grandmother, Mary (Mae), was a housewife who imbued him with a strong social consciousness. His uncle, Archibald J. Motley, Jr, whom he thought of as a brother, was a famous painter. Seeing the success of his uncle in the arts led the way for Motley to pursue a career in writing.

At age 13, Motley's writing career took off when the *Chicago Defender* published a short story he had submitted. As a result, Motley began writing a weekly column in the children's section of the newspaper called "Bud Says." He took the pen name of "Bud Billiken" and had his own byline and photograph. For the next two years, he wrote on topics ranging from pure entertainment to social issues such as poverty. In high school, Motley wrote for the school newspaper and worked on the yearbook as well as participating in several sports. When he graduated in 1929, he knew he wanted to attend University of Wisconsin and become a writer, but the coming of the Great Depression put an end to that dream.

With few options available, Motley continued living with his parents and volunteered as an assistant football coach for his high school. Unable to get work, he decided it was time he began to travel and gather material for his writing. In July of 1930, Motley bicycled from Chicago to New York, living the life of a hobo. The next nine years were to become a tangle of travel and writing, winning Motley little monetary reward or recognition. He took several automobile trips to California and the West, living a simple life as he worked as a migrant laborer, cook, photographer, radio scriptwriter, and newspaper editor, among other jobs. It was also during this time that he served a month-long jail sentence in Wyoming for vagrancy. In the midst of his travels, he focused on writing short stories and submitted them to many popular magazines and newspapers. All were rejected. Though he had some success getting travel articles published in the late 1930s, he began losing the support of his family, who felt he was too much of a dreamer. His grandmother Mae remained supportive, but Motley realized he needed to stay in Chicago and move out from his grandparents' home.

Began Living in Reality of Future Novel Subjects

His new home was a far cry from the middle-class surroundings he had grown up in. He took a slum apartment in the Maxwell Street neighborhood. It was ethnically diverse and downtrodden, full of the type of characters that would inhabit his future novels. Motley began spending time at Hull House, the famous settlement house founded by Jane Addams in 1889 which had become an intellectual center for young artists. In 1939, he helped William P. Schenk and Alexander Saxton establish *Hull-House Magazine,* a journal affiliated with the organization. Under Schenk and Saxton's tutelage, Motley became schooled in the literature that he had missed at college. As Motley's works of short fiction were published in the magazine his writing style seemed to take shape. His writing was ultra-realistic and centered on tough social issues surrounding poverty. In 1940, he contributed to the Works Progress Administration Federal Writers' Project along with authors such as Richard Wright, Margaret Walker, Nelson Algren, and Arna Bontemps.

During this time, Motley began writing his first novel, *Knock On Any Door.* The story dealt with Nick Romano, an altar-boy turned murderer. The son of Italian immigrants, Nick is shaped by a life of poverty. His family had been forced to move into a poor Denver neighborhood when Nick's father lost his store during the Depression. There, he commits his first petty crime at age 14. Seven short years later Nick is executed in the electric chair for the murder of a policeman. Motley blames Nick's destruction on his environment. He tells wrenching details of life in the slum and the brutalization Nick experienced within the penal system. Motley makes it clear that each place led Nick one step closer to his ultimate fate. Although Nick's family moves to Chicago after Nick is released from reform school, he has forever been changed by his experience in the school. He begins committing robberies as part of a youth gang and ends up killing a policeman. Motley finished writing the book and submitted it to Harper's in 1943, only to have it rejected. The following year, Macmillan gave Motley a contract and asked for extensive revisions. Motley won a Newberry Library and a Rosenwald Foundation grant in 1946, which allowed him to re-write and finish the novel. With the release of the novel in 1947, Motley enjoyed immediate popular success. The novel sold 47,000 copies during its first three weeks in print, becoming popularized in a King Features comic-strip and in a 1949 movie version starring Humphrey Bogart.

Critics hailed Motley's first novel as a superior "naturalist" novel and compared it favorably to Richard Wright's *Native Son.* Black critics recognized its success as a "raceless novel" and applauded it for showcasing the talents of an African American novelist at telling a nonracial story. This praise came despite Motley's outward refusal to identify with the struggles unique to African Americans. He was fond of saying, "My race is the human race."

Although Motley had little interest in racial issues, he remained true to his interest in social issues in his second novel, *We Fished All Night.* Critics found little to like in the novel, calling it a great disappointment and describing it as weak, unfocused, and confused. The novel follows three men who return to Chicago after World War II and are forever changed as a result of the war. The novel addresses political corruption, labor issues, and the myth that America is a "melting pot." Motley traveled to Mexico soon after the release of his second novel. In 1952 he bought a house outside of Mexico City and made a new home with his adopted sons, Sergio and Raul, as he began writing his next novel.

Motley's third novel, *Let No Man Write My Epitaph,* was a return to the characters of *Knock On Any Door* and was his third and final novel set in Chicago. N. Jill Weyant wrote in the Summer 1977 *Black American Literature Forum* that "the decision to write a sequel to *Knock* was dictated in large part by Motley's desperate financial situation in 1952 . . . Frankly, *Epitaph* was written to make money, and Motley's poverty may help account for *Epitaph's* tone, which is noticeably more bitter than in the other novels . . . " Whatever the reason for writing *Epitaph* reviews were generally weak and criticized the novel for lacking authenticity or focus. While Motley's first novel won him praise and his second criticism, his third re-kindled interest in Motley to some extent. Columbia Pictures simplified the story and made it into a movie. The novel follows the life of Nick Romano, Jr., a son born to Nellie Watkins, a waitress who we find out is pregnant by Nick, Sr. at the end of *Knock On Any Door.* Although Nick, Jr. is raised in a tough neighborhood, his mother takes care to see him succeed. In addition to his mother, a whole assortment of oddball characters offer him support. Still, over time Nick's mother becomes a drug addict and Nick must learn to survive without her. Motley included several black characters in his novel and showed more racial awareness than in his previous novels.

On March 4, 1965, Motley died in Mexico City from intestinal gangrene. He was buried in nearby Cuernavaca. He had finished the first draft of his final novel just two weeks before his death. *Let Noon Be Fair* was published one year later, in 1966. With *Let Noon Be Fair* Motley delved into the issue of exploitation of Mexicans by the United States. The novel followed the decline of a small fishing village from its first inhabitants through its invasion by American tourists. "At the urging of his new publisher, Putnam," Robert E. Fleming wrote in *Dictionary of Literary Biography,* "Motley emphasized the sexual exploitation of the Mexican people in an attempt to commercialize the book . . ." Since Motley had only just finished the first draft of the novel before his death, he did not participate in the final editing of the book. Fleming described the reviews of *Let Noon Be Fair* as "uniformly negative." *The Diaries of Willard Motley* published in 1979, was another posthumous publication. It included Motley's diary entries from age 16 to 34 and was considered a valuable tool for understanding how Motley incorporated real-life experiences into his writing.

As Clarence Major stated in *The Dark and Feeling,* Motley was "A kind of ghost among Negro writers . . ." Fleming summarized his career in this way: "His literary reputation, which had been so high after the publication of his first novel, suffered from two factors—the decline of interest in naturalistic fiction and the rise of African-American authors who addressed black life more directly than he did." Still, Fleming writes: "Motley is likely to retain his place in literary history as one of the best practitioners of the 'raceless novel' movement of the 1940s and 1950s. . . ."

Books

Notable Black American Men, edited by Jessie Carney Smith, Gale Research, 1999.
Dictionary of Literary Biography, volume 143: American Novelists Since World War II. Third Series, edited by James R. Giles and Wanda H. Giles, The Gale Group, 1994.
Twentieth-Century American Literature, edited by Harold Bloom, Chelsea House Publishers, 1987.

Online

"Willard (Francis) Motley," *Contemporary Authors Online,* Gale Literary Databases (January 9, 2002).
Mark A. Williams, "The Willard Motley Collection," http://libws66.lib.niu.edu/rbsc/2wm2.html (January 17, 2002). □

Dhan Gopal Mukerji

Dhan Gopal Mukerji (1890-1936) wrote numerous books and stories for children, most of which describe the animal life of India and Hindu lore and beliefs. Mukerji is also known for his autobiography *Caste and Outcast,* which tells of life in India and

America. He is considered the first Asian Indian writer of significance in the United States.

Dhan Gopal Mukerji was born on July 6, 1890, in a jungle village near Calcutta, India, and was the son of Kissori and Bhuban (Goswami) Mukerji. His family were members of the Brahmin priest class and for centuries had been in charge of the temple in their village. Brahmins are members of the highest caste in India and follow Vedanta, the system of Hindu philosophy that seeks to transcend the limitations of self-identity and become one with Brahman, the essential divine reality of the universe. At the age of 14, Mukerji entered the Brahmin priesthood, as had many previous family members. Before beginning his priestly work, he traveled for two years as a beggar. "You cannot be a priest if you do not know how people live," he stated in his autobiography *Caste and Outcast,* "and the best way to find out about people is to beg from them. So there is a law of the priesthood that before officiating in the temple, you must go begging from door to door. But at 14, to be turned loose in the world—even after forswearing it, makes one feel rather forlorn."

Sought a Broader, Secular Education

Soon after returning home and beginning his priestly duties, Mukerji decided to give up his family's traditional occupation and go to school. "I went to the Christian school, and studied the New Testament carefully," he noted in *Caste and Outcast.* "It was hardly a year before I gave up being a priest, because I realized that I was not in my right place. This may seem very strange to a Westerner after all I had experienced, but to a Hindu it was not strange. A Brahmin boy often fulfills the duties of a priest for a time, but if he finds it is not his vocation he is expected to resign and to seek the Lord in other ways. We think the end is holiness, not a profession."

In 1908 Mukerji studied at the University of Calcutta. He then relocated to Japan, where he went to the University of Tokyo in 1909. A year later the 19-year-old Mukerji moved to the United States and attended the University of California, Berkeley from 1910 to 1913. He earned his graduate degree from Stanford University in 1914, then taught for a short time at Stanford as a lecturer in the field of comparative literature.

Over the next few years Mukerji published plays and collections of poetry. He wrote, with Mary Carolyn Davies, *Chintamini: A Symbolic Drama* (1914), adapted from a play by Girish C. Ghose; the play *Layla-Majnu* (1916); the poetry collections *Rajani: Songs of the Night* (1916) and *Sandhya: Songs of Twilight* (1917); and the play *The Judgment of India* (1922). In 1918 he married Ethel Ray Dugan, an American teacher, and the couple had a son, Dhan Gopal II.

Returned to India and Entered Political Realm

Following World War I, Mukerji returned to India, where he dedicated himself to promoting greater awareness of his country's many different cultures. Politically he was a member of the Indian independence movement. He wrote his first book, *Kari, the Elephant,* for children in 1922. Promoting the notion that people should live in harmony with nature, the story is set in the jungle Mukerji grew up in. The author vividly describes the jungle's wildlife, something he did in many of his other works, as well as linking together incidents from his own early childhood. Mukerji published his autobiography, *Caste and Outcast,* in 1923, in which he describes his adult life in India and as an immigrant in the United States.

In the 1920s and 1930s Mukerji published a number of works about India and Hinduism, including *My Brother's Face* (1924), the novel *The Secret Listeners of the East* (1926), *A Son of Mother India Answers,* (1928), and *The Path of Prayer* (1934). In 1923 he released his second children's book, *Jungle Beasts and Men,* a series of short stories that give a realistic view of the jungle and its inhabitants. His *Hari, the Jungle Lad,* published in 1924, is about a young Indian boy who goes with his father on hunting expeditions and encounters wild buffalo, a panther, and other jungle creatures.

Awarded Newbery Medal

In 1927 Mukerji published his most famous book, *Gay-Neck: The Story of a Pigeon,* which won the 1928 Newbery Medal. In an interview in *Newbery Medal Books: 1922-1955,* Mukerji explained that much of the book "is a record of my experience with about forty pigeons and their leader. . . . I had to go beyond my experiences, and had to draw upon those of the trainers of army pigeons. Anyway, the message implicit in the book is that man and the winged animals are brothers." Calling *Gay-Neck* "the heartwarming and sometimes almost heartbreaking story of the training and care of a carrier pigeon," Elizabeth Seeger noted in her review for *Horn Book* that "Gay-Neck is truly a carrier pigeon, a bearer of messages, and his messages are words of courage and love." Mukherje closes *Gay-Neck* by saying: "No labor would be in vain if it could heal a single soul of [fear and hate]. . . . Whatever we think and feel will colour what we say or do. He who fears, even unconsciously, or has his least little dream tainted with hate, will inevitably, sooner or later, translate those two qualities into his action. Therefore, my brothers, live courage, breathe courage and give courage. Think and feel love so that you will be able to pour out of yourselves peace and serenity as naturally as a flower gives forth fragrance. Peace be unto all."

In 1928 Mukerji published *Ghond, the Hunter,* a sequel to *Gay-Neck,* in which the lad meets up with a tiger, cobra, python, and other animals. In his introduction to *Bunny, Hound, and Clown,* Mukherje called *Ghond, the Hunter* "the most valuable juvenile book that I have written. . . . In it I have sought to render the inmost things of Hindu life into English."

Mukerji continued to write children's books for the rest of his career, publishing *Hindu Fables for Little Children,* a collection of ten stories with jungle creatures as the main characters, and *The Chief of the Herd,* about elephants, in 1929. Three years later he published *The Master Monkey,* about the Hindu monkey god Hanuman. *Fierce-Face: The Story of a Tiger,* published in 1936, was Mukerji's last work for children.

One of Mukerji's stories that best demonstrates the beauty and simplicity of his imagery is *A Greedy Bee.* In it, a bee named Lobhi becomes trapped in a lotus flower because of its greediness for nectar but escapes when the flower opens up in the moonlight. "Lotus upon lotus lay with their heads drooping into the water, save a few white ones. These had opened their hearts to the moon, who poured into them her silence. Every flower seemed to drink it in with the eagerness of a thirsty bee. Now Lobhi realized to whom she owed her life. Had not the moon risen in time and had not the lotus opened its heart to the moon's light, our little bee would have been dead by now. . . . Though a lot of the most excellent nectar still lay in the flower, Lobhi . . . said to her friends, 'I have learned the lesson of my life. I will not be greedy any more!'"

An Untimely End

Following a six-month nervous breakdown, Mukerji committed suicide by hanging himself in his New York City apartment in July of 1936. While his work was ignored by critics for several years, a new edition of *Caste and Outcast* appeared in 2002 in response to renewed academic interest.

Books

Hutner, Gordon, editor, *Immigrant Voices: Twenty-four Narratives on Becoming an American,* Signet, 1999.

Mukerji, Dhan Gopal, *Caste and Outcast,* Dutton, 1923.
Mukerji, Dhan Gopal, *Gay-Neck: The Story of a Pigeon,* Dutton, 1927.

Periodicals

Child Life, June 2000.

Online

Meghdutam.com, http://www.meghdutam.com/ (January 31, 2002). □

F. W. Murnau

Next to Fritz Lang and G. W. Pabst, motion picture director F. W. Murnau (1888-1931) was one of just three directors responsible for revolutionizing German silent cinema during the 1920s.

Born Friedrich Wilhelm Plumpe, F. W. Murnau was the son of Heinrich Plumpe, a textile manufacturer, and Plumpe's second wife, Otilie. Born in Bielefeld, Westphalia, Germany, on December 28, 1888, he adopted the stage name "Murnau" as a young man, both as an attempt to hide his theatrical ambitions from his unsupportive father and as homage to the famed artists' colony south of Munich. The town of Murnau provided a creative haven for some of the expressionist period's most notable figures, including Wassily Kandinsky, Franz Marc, and others associated with the Blaue Reiter ("Blue Rider") movement of 1911-1914.

In 1892 the Plumpe family moved to Kassel, where young Murnau attended secondary school. During this period he frequented local museums, an activity that helped to nurture his growing fascination with the fine arts. A precocious youngster said to have been reading the works of Schopenhauer, Nietzsche, Shakespeare, and Ibsen at age 12, Murnau was already staging miniature plays in his family's Kassel villa. Though he failed to win his father's support in this area, his mother and two elder stepsisters were instrumental in encouraging him to pursue his creative interests.

In 1907, after completing his schooling in Kassel, Murnau left for the University of Berlin to study philology. Although he had originally intended to become a teacher, his aspirations changed when he met the expressionist poet Hans Ehrenbaun-Degele, with whom he developed an intense friendship. The two men left Berlin for the University of Heidelberg, where Murnau expanded his studies to include not only literature and linguistics, but art history as well.

The War Years

From 1909 to 1913 Murnau was active in Heidelberg's student theatre community. During this period he caught the attention of renowned impresario Max Reinhardt, who invited him to return to Berlin to join his Deutsches Theatre company. Reinhardt, who owned and operated theatres in Austria and Germany, served as a mentor to a number of important Austrian and German film figures of the period, many of which later earned fame in Hollywood.

In 1914, at the beginning of World War I in Europe, Murnau put his acting career temporarily on hold to volunteer in the German military. He saw active duty both as a company commander in East Prussia where he served on the Eastern Front and as a combat pilot in the Luftwaffe where he flew combat missions over France. He survived eight plane crashes without serious injury, as well as a 1917 internment in neutral Switzerland during which he wrote the script for his first film and staged a play. At the close of the war Murnau returned to Berlin and moved into a house belonging to longtime friend Ehrenbaun-Degele, who had tragically been killed in battle.

Early Films

In 1919 Murnau co-founded the small, independent studio Murnau-Veidt Filmgesellchatt with Conrad Veidt, a German actor best known for his leading role in the silent-film classic *The Cabinet of Dr. Caligari.* This same year, Murnau made his first film, *Der Knabe in Blau* ("The Boy in Blue"). Released in 1921 under the title *Der Todessmaragd,* the film was patterned after Oscar Wilde's story about a 1770 Thomas Gainsborough painting. As was the case for most early silent films, *Der Knabe in Blau* was shot on silver nitrate, the highly flammable medium responsible for the eventual decay or non-existence of most silent-era works. No original prints of *Der Knabe in Blau,* or of Murnau's second film, *Satanas* (1920, starring Veidt), are believed to exist today.

Murnau's earliest surviving film, 1920's *Der Gang in die Nacht* ("Journey into the Night") is a tragedy based around a love triangle. Through it can be seen the director's early creative vision, particularly his interest in combining the then-highly influential styles of *Kammerspielfilm* (literally, "chamber play" or "instinct" film) and expressionism. Kammerspielfilm, founded by Austrian screenwriter Carl Mayer, dealt with intimate, fatalistic stories about everyday people. Highly cinematic and with few intertitles—the between-scene "dialogue" used in most silent films—Kammerspielfilm was a stark, minimalist genre that required few characters to tell its stories. Expressionism, the primary influence among early German filmmakers, became influential in painting and poetr y around 1910 and was translated to film during World War I, when the German government funded its own film industry as a means of combating foreign competition. Murnau's *The Cabinet of Dr. Caligari* was the first expressionist film to be produced; as such, it contains most of the elements that would define the genre, as well as Murnau's work in the years to come. Co-written by Carl Mayer, *Caligari* appears as a painting brought to life: distorted, abstract, and heavily stylized and with extreme contrast between light and dark in the same scenes. There are elements of the fantastic, as well as a seeming obsession with the grotesque, the gothic, the psychologically unhealthy, and the absurd.

Shadow of the Vampire

Almost universally considered a masterpiece of expressionist theatre, the 1922 film *Nosferatu* provided Murnau with his first artistic breakthrough in Germany. Subtitled *Ein Symphonie des Grauens* ("A Symphony of Horror"), *Nosferatu* was an unauthorized adaptation—as well as the earliest surviving screen rendering—of British author Bram Stoker's 1897 novel *Dracula*—hence the different title, as well as screenwriter Henrik Galeen's intentional changing of all settings and character names. (Despite Galeen's and Murnau's efforts, Stoker's widow sued *Nosferatu's* production company, Pana-Film, for copyright infringement and in the process nearly crushed the film.) Murnau's version of the age-old vampire tale—indeed, the legend dates back to the 1100s—was just as much a reflection of the horror that befell Germany in the post-World War I era as it was of Stoker's novel.

From 1920 to 1922 the ghost of the Great War hung over Germany, and many soldiers that returned to the country were left crippled or horribly disfigured. The radical Spartacist League, a socialist group opposed to the war from the outset, led several uprisings in Berlin and Munich before being crushed in a bloody response from the republic. Postwar inflation was bleeding the German economy dry, and a Spanish flu epidemic and famine ravaged the country's citizens, ultimately killing more civilians than had the war itself. As Thomas Elsaesser note in *Sight & Sound,* "the cholera whose origins *Nosferatu* is supposed to record is doubled by several successive disasters befalling a defeated Germany, during which public opinion only too readily

blamed the victors of Versailles for not coming to the country's aid. Instead, the French, adding insult and humiliation to injury and penury, insisted on the prompt payment of war reparations and annexed the Rhineland, setting off a chain of events that gave the nationalist right its first electoral successes among the working class."

Beyond reflecting a period of cultural unease, *Nosferatu* provided the dramatic template for every big-screen vampire that followed, from Bela Lugosi's 1931 portrayal of Dracula to Klaus Kinski's 1979 reprisal of the original Murnau character created by actor Max Schreck. Viewed from a modern perspective, Murnau's film is no longer horrifying in the traditional sense, yet it remains effective for its dark, minimalist approach, as well as its dramatic tension and uncomfortably believable tone. Film critic Roger Ebert, looking back on *Nosferatu* in his *Chicago Sun-Times* column, wrote, "It knows none of the later tricks of the trade, like sudden threats that pop in from the side of the screen. But *Nosferatu* remains effective: It doesn't scare us, but it haunts us. It shows not that vampires can jump out of shadows, but that evil can grow there, nourished on death."

A Misunderstood Genius

In part because of the financial distress surrounding the Stoker lawsuit, the already troubled Pana-Films was unable to distribute *Nosferatu* widely, leaving the film for later audiences to discover. However, the visual breakthroughs Murnau and cinematographer Fritz Arno Wagner achieved with *Nosferatu*—the almost dreamlike use of sharp angles, shadows, negatives, and superimposed images—set the stage for 1924's expressionist masterpiece *The Last Laugh,* the film that put Murnau's name on the lips of Hollywood moguls like William Fox. *The Last Laugh* uses cinematographer Karl Freund's flowing, subjective camera angle to depict—from the protagonist's viewpoint—the emotional pain of a man who has found his life suddenly devoid of meaning. Thanks largely to his work with Freund in *The Last Laugh,* Murnau is widely credited as being among the fathers of *mise-en-scène,* the art of telling the story by moving and blocking the action within the frame itself.

Murnau remained in Germany long enough to adapt Moliere's *Tartuffe* (1925) and Goethe's *Faust* (1926) to the screen; in 1927, having been offered a four-year contract in Hollywood, he left his native country for the United States. *Sunrise* was Murnau's American debut and his first project for Hollywood's Fox Film Corporation, as well as Fox's most expensive film project to date. Subtitled *A Song of Two Humans, Sunrise* was the first feature film to be released with a synchronized soundtrack-on-film: a Movietone musical score by Austrian composer Hugo Riesenfeld. Unfortunately for all involved, the film suffered from poor timing. Appearing just days before the opening of Warner Brothers famous "talkie" debut *The Jazz Singer* and overshadowed by the Warner project's publicity, *Sunrise* was a box-office failure that came to be recognized among film connoisseurs as one of the 100 greatest motion pictures ever made only decades later. Released in the first year of the Academy Awards, Murnau's vivid, impressionistic love story received four nominations and won awards in three of those categories. *Sunrise's* fluid, "moving camera" perspective also influenced numerous American films to come, including Orson Welles's 1941 classic *Citizen Kane.*

Tabu and a Legacy's End

Whatever acclaim Murnau received upon *Sunrise*'s release was overshadowed, in Fox's eyes, by the film's commercial failure. *Sunrise* simply did not recoup its production costs, and as a result, Fox cut back on Murnau's budget for future projects. After making the now-forgotten *Four Devils* (1929) and *City Girl* (1930) for the studio, Murnau severed his contract and began collaborating with documentary filmmaker Robert Joseph Flaherty on the film *Tabu.* Filmed entirely in Tahiti, *Tabu* was the ambitious, fairytale-like story of Matahi and Reri, two indigenous young lovers doomed to fate by tribal constraints. Although Flaherty, like Murnau, was an iconoclastic figure who found himself out of place amid the glitz and glamour of Hollywood, the two directors also found themselves at odds with each other throughout the duration of the project; although Tabu was labeled "a Murnau-Flaherty Production," Flaherty withdrew from the film before its completion.

On March 11, 1931, Murnau and his chauffeur were killed while driving on California's Pacific Coast Highway. *Tabu* was just one week from its premiere, and Murnau, age 42 at the time of his death, was considering a new contract with the more artist-friendly Paramount Studios. Though Murnau left behind a rich film legacy that endures today, his life also became the subject of intense, often wildly inaccurate, artistic interpretation.

Books

Collier, Jo Leslie, *From Wagner to Murnau: The Transposition of Romanticism from Stage to Screen,* UMI Research Press, 1988.

Eisner, Lotte H., *Murnau,* 1964, translated into English, University of California Press, 1973.

Shepard, Jim, *Nosferatu,* Alfred A. Knopf, 1998.

Periodicals

Sight & Sound, February 2001.

Online

"A Bloody Disgrace," *Guardian Unlimited,* http://film.guardian .co.uk/ (January 26, 2001).

Ebert, Roger, "Nosferatu," *Chicago Sun Times,* http://www .suntimes.com/ebert/ebert_reviews/ (January 1999). □

Pervez Musharraf

In October 1999 General Pervez Musharraf (born 1943) came to power in Pakistan when he seized control of the government in a bloodless military coup. His pretext was that he sought to stabilize the nation, but Musharraf not only heightened the level of distrust from Pakistan's long-time antagonist,

India, he also succeeded in alienating the Islamic fundamentalists within his own country. Much of the latter was due to the unforeseen actions by terrorists against the United States, and the subsequent response which involved Musharraf's aligning Pakistan with the international coalition against the Al-Qaida terrorist organization and Afghanistan's ruling Taliban.

Education and Early Career

Musharraf was born on August 11, 1943, in Delhi, India, when it was still under British sovereignty. Following independence from Great Britain and the creation of the state of Pakistan, the Musharraf family moved to Karachi. Musharraf's father was a diplomat and the family spent seven years, from 1949 to 1956, in Turkey. Musharraf became fluent in Turkish, but his education also included attending Saint Patrick's High School in Karachi and Lahore's Forman Christian College. Musharraf entered the Pakistan Military Academy in 1961 and in 1964 received a commission to an artillery regiment in which he served during a 1965 conflict. During that conflict Musharraf was awarded the Imtiazi Sanad for gallantry. Afterward Musharraf volunteered for a commando outfit and also saw action in the 1971 conflict as a company commander.

Musharraf was promoted to major general in 1991 and lieutenant general in 1995. He also attended the Command and Staff College at Quetta, the National Defense College, and the Royal College of Defense Studies in Great Britain. Musharraf later held appointments at both the Command and Staff College and the National Defense College. He was eventually named director of general military operations at general headquarters.

The real turning point in Musharraf's career came in October 1998 when he was promoted to general and named the army's chief of staff by Prime Minister Nawaz Sharif. This placed him near the center of power in Pakistan. Musharraf replaced General Jehangir Karmat, who had advocated civilian power-sharing with the military in the form of a joint national security council, which upset the prime minister. As if to reassure Sharif, Musharraf a few weeks after his appointment reiterated that the army would "remain apolitical." Six months later he was named chairman of Pakistan's joint chiefs of staff; in another six months he would lead the coup that toppled Sharif from power. All of this came amid one of Pakistan's most serious difficulties with India—the contention of the border region of Kashmir. In July 1999 Musharraf admitted that India's allegations that Pakistani soldiers had crossed into the Indian section of Kashmir to fight alongside Islamic rebels were true. Crime and corruption also plagued Pakistan. Just a week before the coup Musharraf was quoted in *The Hindu* as declaring, "The law and order situation is bad. It should improve. It will improve."

The Coup

Musharraf's career took a dramatic turn when, on a visit to Sri Lanka on October 12, 1999, he was abruptly fired by Prime Minister Sharif. However the move backfired and the army, in support of General Musharraf, arrested Sharif and other government officials in what was essentially a bloodless coup. Musharraf became Chief Executive of Pakistan and quickly consolidated his power—an action he would repeat more than once. Within days of the coup he subverted Pakistan's constitution by dismissing parliament and imposing martial law. Musharraf also claimed the airliner carrying him and more than 200 others from Colombo (the capital of Sri Lanka) to Karachi had been denied permission to land on orders from Sharif. The landing was eventually made with only seven minutes' worth of fuel left. The deposed prime minister was charged with hijacking, kidnapping, attempted murder, and treason and became the center of a highly publicized trial.

Meanwhile the conflict with India loomed large, and to cool it down Musharraf ordered troop withdrawal from the border. However in late December 1999 he decided that Kashmir would be given top priority in diplomatic discussions with India. On a visit to the region he declared: "Pakistan is Kashmir and Kashmir is Pakistan." By the end of the month he had also revived the idea of a National Security Council and named four civilians to the seven-member body, as well as three civilians to his cabinet. He also set up the National Accountability Bureau to investigate corruption. Under its auspices former Prime Minister Sharif's fa-

ther, son, and brothers were all charged with corruption and arrested.

In December Musharraf revealed a new plan for reviving Pakistan's weak economy. The economic plan included a sales tax similar to a value added tax as well as a farm tax. He also moved to close loopholes regarding foreign currency accounts that were seen as money-laundering schemes. Still, the issue of Kashmir remained of primary concern. In January 2000, in a rare interview with an Indian newspaper, *The Hindu,* Musharraf declared that the Indian government "(has) to trust me and that whatever I am saying, I mean, and they have to come along." But he also admitted: "(W)e need to accept Kashmir as a problem and start a dialogue and simultaneously let us discuss everything else. I am open to discussion on every other thing." Musharraf, however, would make a complete turnaround on this position in a May 2000 press conference.

Consolidated His Power

In March 2000 Musharraf deflected attention from the opening of former Prime Minister Sharif's trial when he replaced six judges of Pakistan's Supreme Court, including Chief Justice Saeed uz Zaman Siddiqi, for refusing to swear allegiance to his government. The trial itself took many strange twists and turns. Initially, Sharif's lawyers resigned after he was barred from testifying in open court, and when he did testify he claimed he was being framed by the military. Then in March another of his lawyers was murdered by a gunman. Sharif was eventually found guilty and sentenced to life in prison.

United States President Bill Clinton also made a quick trip to Pakistan in March 2000, adding the country to his itinerary. Clinton urged a return to democracy and a quick settlement of the Kashmir conflict, which seemed to signal a changing attitude toward one of the U.S.'s staunchest Cold War allies. Musharraf was undaunted by Clinton's remarks. The next day he was off on his own trip to strengthen economic ties with Southeast Asia. In April 2000, as part of a human rights pledge, Musharraf condemned the Pakistani practice of "honor killing" in which a woman is murdered for "shaming" her family by seeking a divorce or otherwise choosing her spouse. Among the other problems he sought to tackle were the effects of drought and frequent sectarian clashes.

Musharraf was not without his critics in the Islamic fundamentalist community as well as the small business community, which protested the general sales tax. Possibly to assuage their fear and anger he announced he would accede to a Supreme Court decision that he step down after three years and allow democratic elections to be held. Still, in June 2000 the two groups joined forces to protest the sales tax. In July he made further concessions to the fundamentalists when he decreed the revival of the Islamic provisions of Pakistan's suspended constitution. In a BBC World Service interview in August 2000 Musharraf declared Pakistan's continued support for Afghanistan's ruling Taliban. "The Taliban administration represents the majority Pashtun population in Afghanistan and it is in our interest to support them," he said.

In September 2000 Musharraf again took steps to strengthen his position when he reshuffled senior Army advisers. The move was made four days before Musharraf flew to New York City to attend the Millenium Conference sponsored by the United Nations Assembly. Then in October 2000, almost a year to the day he took over the government, Musharraf promised that federal and provincial elections would take place before the end of the 2002. The next month while on a trip to Moscow Musharraf admitted not knowing the extent of Pakistan's nuclear force. He also declared neutrality regarding Osama bin Laden, suspected of masterminding attacks on U.S. embassies in Africa. In November Musharraf sought further to legitimize his position by amending the Provisional Constitutional Order to have the Chief Executive assume all acts that were previously the responsibility of the Prime Minister. In December 2000 he surprised everyone by releasing former Prime Minister Sharif, who immediately went into exile.

On January 1, 2001, local elections were held in 18 of Pakistan's 106 administrative areas. The first elections since the coup, they were nonetheless criticized by the voters themselves because of the military's involvement and the banning of political parties. Indeed, in March political leaders from the coalition Alliance for Restoration of Democracy were detained just prior to an anti-military rule rally. Later that month Musharraf announced he planned to extend his three-year term as Army Chief of Staff beyond October 2001. However, under the law Musharraf's term could only be extended by the president. Musharraf solved that problem in June 2001 by appointing himself Pakistan's president and head of state.

Despite Musharraf's machinations, many of Pakistan's problems remained, not least of which was the military tension with India. In July 2001 Musharraf traveled to India to hold talks with Indian Prime Minister Atal Behari Vajpayee over the disputed Kashmir region. The talks failed to produce an agreement, or even a joint declaration. Nonetheless Musharraf invited Vajpayee to Islamabad for a future round of negotiations. Musharraf next turned his attention to two other problems: the U.S. sanctions against Pakistan and terrorism. In August 2001 he began making his case to have the sanctions (imposed against Pakistan and India as a result of their 1998 nuclear weapons tests) lifted. He also vowed to get tough against terrorism—though at the time he was referring to Pakistan's own domestic violence. He again vowed to hold elections before the third anniversary of the coup, in October 2002.

Aligned Pakistan with the International Coalition

Following the September 11, 2001, terrorist attacks on the World Trade Center in New York City and on the Pentagon in Washington, D.C., Musharraf early on gave Pakistan's support to the anti-terrorist cause. He was quoted by Tyler Marshall in a *Los Angeles Times* article as saying, "Pakistan has been extending cooperation to international efforts to combat terrorism in the past and will continue to do so." Musharraf then had to make his case with his people, and while he was successful in convincing the army

of his decision the clerics and other fundamentalists, who were already opposed to him, were a different story, especially after bin Laden was identified as the primary culprit.

In the beginning Musharraf hoped to assuage the clerics and others by brokering a deal with the Taliban to hand over bin Laden, thus avoiding military action. But that ploy was doomed to failure. Nine days after the attack Musharraf appeared on Pakistani television to explain his decision to assist the United States. He quoted the Koran and cited Islamic tradition for political compromise as his argument. The speech was largely ineffective as far as the (minority) fundamentalists were concerned and during the ensuing weeks numerous anti-U.S. and anti-Musharraf demonstrations were held, many peaceful though some ended in violence.

In the first, tense week of October 2001 Musharraf admitted defeat in brokering a deal with the Taliban. On the positive side Canadian sanctions against Pakistan were eased. Furthermore, upon reviewing the U.S. evidence against bin Laden the Pakistani government declared there was enough proof to indict him. On October 6, 2001, British Prime Minister Tony Blair met with Musharraf in Islamabad. Blair promised economic and humanitarian aid to Pakistan. Perceiving that his position was no longer as secure as it had been only that summer, Musharraf removed from the military and the intelligence services those men who had assisted the Taliban militia. As the bombs rained down upon Afghanistan Musharraf turned toward India, hoping to renew talks over the Kashmir. He was rebuffed. To make matters worse for Musharraf Pakistani border troops fought with Taliban forces two days after the bombing began. The fighting and Musharraf's agreeing to let U.S. forces use two airfields near the Afghanistan border led to more widespread protests, which he vowed to crack down on. Indeed Musharraf seemed to dig in against his domestic opponents. In a mid-October meeting with U.S. Secretary of State Colin Powell he "pledged his indefinite support," as reported by Jack Kelley in *USA Today*. By the end of October Musharraf took further steps to halt the growing wave of protests, especially the use of mosque loudspeakers to incite antigovernment protests.

At the beginning of November 2001, as Pakistani fundamentalists were urging the army to overthrow Musharraf the call was echoed by none other than Osama bin Laden himself in a statement sent to the al-Jazeera, the BBC, and CNN. To allay Western fears Musharraf responded by arresting an opposition leader; he also declared that Pakistan's nuclear facilities were under secure control. Also in November he closed Pakistan's borders with Afghanistan, thus cutting off approximately 300,000 refugees seeking asylum. At the end of the first month of the bombing Musharraf traveled to Britain to again meet with Blair and then to New York to meet with President George W. Bush. The meeting with the U.S. president fell short of Musharraf's expectations of having the sanctions lifted, though his unswerving support for the coalition brought U.S. aid and debt restructuring that totaled more than $1 billion.

For his part, Musharraf warned that an alternative government must be ready to replace the Taliban in order to prevent anarchy in Afghanistan. He also went on record as doubting that bin Laden possessed nuclear or chemical weapons. In the aftermath of the fall of Kabul Musharraf voiced his dissatisfaction with the Northern Alliance (ethnic minorities in Afghanistan who opposed the Taliban), called for the demilitarization of the Afghan capital, and proposed the creation of a UN peacekeeping force made up of troops from Moslem countries. All three propositions were intended to forestall the setting up of a government hostile to Pakistan, which in the past had been one of three nations to recognize the legitimacy of the Taliban. Musharraf also increased border security to prevent fleeing Taliban and Al-Qaida members from crossing into Pakistan.

Periodicals

Boston Globe, November 14, 1999; November 1, 2001; November 11, 2001.

Financial Times, October 19, 1999; July 17, 2000; March 9, 2001; March 26, 2001; August 15, 2001; September 15, 2001; November 15, 2001.

Gazette (Montreal), February 2, 2000; May 26, 2000; July 13, 2000.

Guardian (London), March 9, 2000; April 7, 2000; November 14, 2001.

Hindu, October 30, 1998; October 6, 1999; December 28, 1999; January 17, 2000; March 28, 2000; May 4, 2000; May 27, 2000; September 3, 2000; November 2, 2000; November 18, 2000; August 3, 2001.

Houston Chronicle, October 26, 1999; October 5, 2001.

Independent (London), October 16, 1999; January 27, 2000; July 17, 2001; November 8, 2001.

Los Angeles Times, October 14, 1999; September 13, 2001; October 6, 2001.

New York Times, October 13, 1999; October 15, 1999; December 9, 1999; March 9, 2000; March 11, 2000; January 1, 2001; March 22, 2001; June 21, 2001; October 9, 2001.

Ottawa Citizen, October 2, 2001; November 2, 2001.

St. Louis Post-Dispatch, October 10, 2001.

San Francisco Chronicle, February 29, 2000.

Seattle Times, September 20, 2001; October 11, 2001.

Statesman, November 23, 1999.

Times (London), June 21, 2000; August 3, 2000.

Toronto Star, July 17, 1999; November 3, 2001.

USA Today, October 11, 2001; October 17, 2001.

Washington Post, October 19, 1999; March 27, 2000; April 22, 2000; December 11, 2000; September 17, 2001.

Online

"Profile: General Pervez Musharraf," http://www.pak.gov.pk/public/chief/ce_profile.htm (November 7, 2001). □

N

John Forbes Nash, Jr.

Awarded a Nobel Prize in Economics in 1994 for his pioneering work in game theory, John Nash (born 1928) distinguished himself as one of the foremost mathematical researchers and theorists of the twentieth century.

Game theory was the subject of Nash's doctoral dissertation at Princeton University. Expanding upon the initial game theory of John von Neumann and Oskar Morgenstern, published in their *The Theory of Games and Economic Behavior,* Nash developed what became known as "Nash's equilibrium" to explain how two or more competitors can arrive at a mutually beneficial yet non-cooperative business arrangement. In 1951, he developed the theory that manifolds—objects containing various forms and components—can be described accurately using algebraic equations. He later developed what became known as the Nash-Moser theorem, which explained how it was possible to embed a manifold in a Euclidean space by employing differential calculus instead of algebra and geometry. Nash's subsequent career was diminished by severe mental illness, which was documented in Sylvia Nasar's biography of Nash, *A Beautiful Mind,* and the film of the same name directed by Ron Howard.

Early Interest in Math

Nash was born on June 13, 1928, in Bluefield, West Virginia, and raised by his parents, John Nash, Sr., an electrical engineer for the Appalachian Power Company, and Margaret Nash, a teacher who retired after her marriage and placed a high value on the education of her two children. As a young man he seemed disinclined to study but displayed a passion for electronics and chemistry experiments that he conducted in his bedroom.

When he was a young teenager, Nash read a book by E. T. Bell, *Men of Mathematics,* to which Nash attributed his eventual passion for number theory. While attending high school and concurrent classes at Bluefield College, Nash collaborated with his father on a paper titled "Sag and Tension Calculations for Cable and Wire Spans Using Catenary Formulas," which was published in a 1945 edition of *Electrical Engineering.* Nash also entered the George Westinghouse competition, winning one of ten nationally awarded full scholarships, which he used to enroll in the Carnegie Institute of Technology in Pittsburgh.

Mixed Success in Education

Initially aspiring to become an engineer like his father, Nash changed his major to chemistry after performing poorly in mechanical drawing. After he also had trouble with a physical chemistry class, he was convinced by his calculus instructor John Synge to major in mathematics. In 1948, Nash was awarded the John S. Kennedy Fellowship at Princeton University.

At Princeton, Nash was in close proximity to the Institute of Advanced Study, which attracted such notable mathematicians as Albert Einstein, Kurt Godel, Karl Oppenheimer, Hermann Weyl, and John von Neumann. According to Sylvia Nasar, "Princeton in 1948 was to mathematicians what Paris once was to painters and novelists, Vienna to psychoanalysts and architects, and ancient Athens to philosophers and playwrights." In 1949, Nash was awarded an Atomic Energy Commission fellowship to continue his doctoral studies at Princeton. The school's faculty

and students admired Nash for his obvious intellect, but his academic career remained undistinguished.

While at Princeton, Nash invented two board games. The first, called "Nash" or "John," was a two-person, zero-sum game, meaning that one player's advantage must result in a proportional disadvantage for the opponent. Unlike other zero-sum games such as chess and tic-tac-toe, however, a tie or draw was impossible in Nash's game. The game had been invented independently from Nash and eventually was marketed in the 1950s as Hex. Nash also collaborated with several students to create the game "So Long, Sucker," a multiple-player game that rewarded the player most skilled at deception.

Battled Mental Illness

After graduating from Princeton, Nash taught mathematics at the Massachusetts Institute of Technology in Cambridge. He had a son with Eleanor Stier before marrying Alicia Larde in 1957, with whom he also fathered a son. Along with teaching at MIT, Nash worked at the RAND Corporation think tank in Santa Monica, California. Nash was fired in 1954 after being arrested for indecent exposure in a public restroom during a Santa Monica police sting against homosexuals. Nasar wrote: "The biggest shock to Nash may not have been the arrest itself, but the subsequent expulsion from RAND." In 1957, he divided his time between the Institute for Advanced Study and the Courant Institute of Mathematical Sciences at New York University.

In early 1959, Nash began exhibiting symptoms of paranoid schizophrenia. After losing his ability to teach and do research, he underwent insulin coma therapy during several stays in psychiatric hospitals, including one where he shared a room with poet Robert Lowell. When not institutionalized, he made several trips to Europe, where he attempted to establish a world government and resign his United States citizenship because he was convinced he was a political prisoner. He also declared himself the emperor of Antarctica and tried to establish a defense fund for what he believed was an impending extra-terrestrial attack.

In 1962, Alicia Nash filed for divorce, and Nash lived with his widowed mother until her death in 1969. He then moved back into the house he shared with Alicia Nash. For the next 15 years, Nash spent much of his time wandering freely on the Princeton campus. In the late 1980s, however, he showed signs of remission from mental illness. He accepted the Nobel Prize for economics in 1994 and spent much of the 1990s attending to his second son's schizophrenia. He and Alicia Nash eventually remarried.

Developed Game Theory

While at RAND, Nash participated in developing new technologies, theories, and strategies for the United States military through a private nonprofit organization that employed many of the nation's most prominent intellectuals. One of the strategies that RAND was beginning to explore for modern warfare was game theory, which expressed itself in such Cold War strategies as mutual deterrence and the arms race. Whereas John von Neumann and Oskar Morgenstern had conceived of game theory as a zero-sum relationship between non-cooperating competitors, Nash argued that some competitors could benefit from an adversarial relationship by seeking an equilibrium point that would either minimize negative repercussions or maximize positive outcomes. Jeremy Bernstein, writing in *Commentary,* noted: "Part of Nash's contribution was to allow one to relax the assumptions of von Neumann's theorem; the game does not have to be zero-sum or involve only two players. . . . What he showed was that in a very wide range of such 'games,' there must be at least one such strategy leading to equilibrium, and if there are several, one must decide among them." Assuming that all competitors behave in a rational manner, Nash hypothesized that each party would apply its dominant strategy to yield mutually beneficial results.

In 1950, Nash submitted his equilibrium theory as his Princeton doctoral thesis. It has since become widely used in military and economic strategies, as well as in biology. According to animal behaviorist Peter Hammerstein, quoted by Robert Pool in *Science,* "The Nash equilibrium turns out to be terribly important in biology. . . . Such concepts are proving vital in analyzing a range of biological data, from sex ratios to animals' decisions about whether to fight each other for territory or food." The theory earned him the Nobel Prize, shared with fellow game theorists John Harsanyi and Reinhard Selten.

Following his work in game theory, Nash focused on, among other things, manifolds. According to Nasar: "In one dimension, a manifold may be a straight line, in two dimensions a plane, or the surface of a cube, a balloon, or a doughnut." Although the object remains the same, it appears different when viewed from different perspectives. Because of their mutability, manifolds seemingly defied accurate depictions until Nash employed polynomial algebraic equations to describe them in 1950 and 1951.

In September 1951, beginning his tenure at MIT, Nash combined his work with manifolds with an interest in fluid dynamics. Nash applied the results of this research to his next mathematical theory, which asserted that it is possible to embed a Riemannian manifold in a Euclidean space. An eighteenth-century German mathematician, G.F.B. Riemann theorized that previous Euclidean notions of geography were inaccurate, due to the curvature of the earth's surface, therefore making all parallel lines subject to intersection and the sums of any triangle's angles unequal to 180 degrees. Rather than employ geometry or algebra to solve the problem, Nash developed a new method of applying 19th-century differential calculus. Jurgen Moser later applied the breakthrough to celestial mechanics, resulting in its eventual name: the Nash-Moser theorem.

Books

Nasar, Sylvia, *A Beautiful Mind: The Life of Mathematical Genius and Nobel Laureate John Nash,* Simon & Schuster, 1998.

Periodicals

Commentary, August 1998.
Forbes, July 3, 1995.
Science, October 21, 1994.
Time, October 24, 1994.
Washington Post, December 18, 2001. ☐

Youssou N'Dour

Senegalese singer, songwriter, and bandleader Youssou N'Dour (born 1959) is a leading proponent of World Music, combining traditional music from his homeland with Western popular culture, Cuban rhythms, and contemporary instrumentation.

N'Dour is among the most popular practitioners of a Senegalese form of music called mbalax, which features the heavy rhythms normally associated with the indigenous mbung mbung drum, kora harp, and balafon xylophone instead being performed by electric guitars and keyboards. Mbalax also employs the traditional Senegalese vocal methods of tassou and bakou; which, respectively, resemble Western rap and rhythm-and-blues vocal techniques. N'Dour helped pioneer mbalax in the 1970s with tremendous success in his homeland and brought the music to international popularity in the 1980s when he toured Europe and the United States as a solo performer and with such Western musical artists as Peter Gabriel, Paul Simon, Sting, and Bruce Springsteen. His efforts to introduce mbalax music to international audiences is assisted by a stunning vocal ability that has been put to good effect on N'Dour's own recordings and on popular recordings by such artists as Gabriel and Harry Belafonte.

Cultural Influences

Born in Dakar, N'Dour was immersed in Senegal's cross-pollination of indigenous music with European traditions. Frequented by Portuguese explorers and French colonialists since the seventeenth-century because of its central location on the continent and its Atlantic Ocean coastline, Senegal became the base for French operations on the African continent in the nineteenth century. As a result, Dakar became a center of commerce that attracted different Central African cultures as well. For example, N'Dour's father was from the Serer culture, and his mother was from a culture known as the Tukulor. However, N'Dour has stressed that he is a Wolof, a national Senegalese culture arising from a language originated in Dakar, which embraces many of Senegal's varied traditional and popular cultural forms.

N'dour was the eldest of eight children. His father was a garage mechanic and his mother was a well-known traditional praise singer or griot. Griots inherit their historical songs and stories from a griot family member of the previous generation and then teach it to the griot of the following generation. Senegalese griots perform at religious ceremonies and family celebrations, combining the distinct vocal phrasings of the Wolof and other Senegalese languages with the singing style of Central African Islamic traditions. After her marriage, however, a female griot violated local customs, and she abandoned public performances.

N'Dour's voice filled the void left by his mother. He began singing at religious ceremonies such as traditional circumcisions, and word of his talent spread until he received an invitation to join the local band Diamono. When he was sixteen, he became one of the chief vocalists for Dakar's most popular band, the Star Band. Formed by Ibra Kasse, the Star Band achieved its popularity by adapting Cuban and Latin American songs into Wolof.

In 1977, N'Dour formed Etoile de Dakar, featuring many of the younger musicians from the Star Band. The music performed by Etoile de Dakar was a polyglot of griot and Wolof regionalism, Senegalese nationalism, Third World rhythms, and urban teenage bravado. Tremendously successful, Etoile de Dakar ended when co-founders El Hadji Faye and Badou Ndiaye left the band. N'Dour rebounded by forming Super Etoile de Dakar and rose to prominence as Senegal's most revered performer.

Much of the music performed by Super Etoile de Dakar displays the influence of N'Dour's adherence to the Mourides belief system. Mourides, one of several Senegalese Islamic groups, adhere to the teachings of Cheikh Ahmadou Bamba, a nineteenth-century teacher of the Koran who encouraged his followers to spend their lives preparing for salvation in the afterlife rather than resorting to violence against economic, cultural, and military oppression perpetrated by their enemies. This salvation is attained by following the instructions of Mourides holy men, called marabouts. N'Dour's songs frequently contain spiritual messages that encourage listeners to obey the instructions of Mourides's marabouts.

While sometimes spiritual, mbalax music also is a highly energetic music that marries Cuban and Latin American styles, and, as John Cho explained: "Melismatic upper-register vocals of Islamic muezzins with the accompanying Arabic modalities were introduced, resulting in a fresh harmonic mix." Mbalax features such percussive instruments as sabars (bass drums), djembes (drums with goatskin heads), and tamas, also known as talking drums. Cho noted: "The rapid-fire dialog between the singer and the tama player is often the climax of a song.... Mbalax also spawned its own high-stepping, high-energy dance called the ventilateur, which raised a ruckus among the pious because of the provocative manner in which the women hiked their boubous and flashed their forbidden legs."

International Stardom

The emigration of African audiences to European capitals created a ready-made audience for N'Dour outside Senegal. N'Dour adapted his music to accommodate French, Fulani, Serer, and English languages for the European tours Super Etoile de Dakar conducted in the early 1980s to fulfill the demands of Africans living in London and Paris. The tours provided international exposure for N'Dour's voice and mbalax music, leading to several fortuitous events.

Performing in London in 1984, Super Etoile de Dakar was seen by former Genesis frontman and successful solo artist Peter Gabriel. Gabriel's interest in World Music was evidenced on his third solo album, released in 1981, which featured African polyrhythms on the song "Games without Frontiers" and a song about slain South African leader Stephen Biko. Gabriel's positive impression of Super Etoile de Dakar's London performance inspired him to travel to Senegal, where he convinced N'Dour to contribute vocals to the song "In Your Eyes" on the English performer's *So* release. Gabriel also contracted Super Etoile de Dakar as the support act on his world tour. The song, "In Your Eyes," became a huge success for Gabriel after its inclusion on the soundtrack for a pivotal romantic scene in the Cameron Crowe film *Say Anything,* exposing N'Dour's voice and singing style to international audiences.

Another musical celebrity seeking to reinvigorate his creative impetus was American singer and songwriter Paul Simon. Simon immersed himself in the various musics of Africa while writing and recording the songs for his album *Graceland.* Among the artists Simon collaborated with on the album and subsequent tour were Hugh Masekela, Miriam Makeba, Ladysmith Black Mambazo, and N'Dour. *Graceland* was the most successful album of new material in Simon's solo career, furthering international recognition for N'Dour.

Human Rights Advocate

The exposure granted N'Dour and Super Etoiles de Dakar led to an invitation to participate in a 1986 worldwide tour of international artists commemorating South African political prisoner Nelson Mandela's release after twenty-five years. That same year, he wrote and recorded the song "Nelson Mandela." In 1988, he headlined the Amnesty International tour with Sting, Bruce Springsteen, Peter Gabriel, and Tracy Chapman. "Sometimes I feel like a missionary," he told a BBC reporter. "I have a mission to develop something, to bring people together, bring things together, to make things happen at home." In 1990, he contributed a song to the video music project *Viva Mandela* and performed at a concert in Mandela's honor at London's Wembley Arena.

N'Dour's financial success has enabled him to assist his Senegalese countrypeople. His ownership of a newspaper, a recording studio, a record label, a nightclub, and a radio station allows him to provide employment opportunities. "All these things happening now—my studio, my label, my club, or my radio station—is happening because I'm already a musician," he told the BBC. "My newspaper is not my newspaper. It's just a kind of help, to solve the employment problem and to give the journalists the chance to do what they really want to do."

N'Dour's humanitarian concerns led to his naming as goodwill ambassador for the United Nations Children's Fund (UNICEF) in the 1990s. In 2000, he was named Goodwill Ambassador of the United Nations Food and Organisation.

International Recording Star

Although N'Dour was an established recording star in Senegal, it was not until the late 1980s that he began releasing music on an international label. Released in 1989, *The Lion,* features the collaborative single "Shaking the Tree" with Peter Gabriel. *The Set,* released in 1991, furthered N'Dour's reputation as an artist with international appeal. Brian Cullman noted: "If any third-world performer has a real shot at the sort of universal popularity last enjoyed by Bob Marley, it's Youssou, a singer with a voice so extraordinary that the history of Africa seems locked inside it."

N'Dour received two Grammy Award nominations and sales of more than six-hundred-thousand for his 1994 album, *The Guide,* which includes guests Branford Marsalis and Neneh Cherry. His recording of "Seven Seconds," a duet with Cherry, sold more than one million copies and was named the number one song of 1994 at the MTV Awards Europe. In 1998, he wrote the official anthem of the soccer World Cup finals, "France '98," which he also performed with Belgian singer Axelle Red.

N'Dour took a hiatus from recording for five years before releasing *Joko: From Village to Town* in 2000. The album contains song collaborations with Sting and Peter Gabriel as well as several songs co-produced by Wyclef Jean that introduce American hip-hop elements to N'Dour's mbalax. "I try to bring things out in the modern way and in the urban way and musically I create a lot of connections," N'Dour said.

Books

Broughton, Simon, Mark Ellingham, and Richard Trillo, editors, *The Rough Guide: World Music, Volume I: Africa, Europe and the Middle East,* Rough Guides Ltd, 1999.
Romanowski, Patricia and Holly George-Warren, editors, *The New Encyclopedia of Rock & Roll,* Rolling Stone Press, 1995.

Online

Cho, John, "Senegal: Baobabs, Boubous, and Mbalax," *Roots World,* 1996, http://www.rootsworld.com/rw/feature/cho_mbalax.html.
McLane, Daisann, "Youssou N'Dour Eyes Open," *Rolling Stone,* No. 638, http://www.rollingstone.com/recordings/.
"Youssou N'Dour," *African Music Encyclopedia,* http://www.africanmusic.org/artists/youssou.html.
"Youssou N'Dour," *Leigh Bailey Artists of Woodstock,* http://www.woodstock.com/html/biow0045.
"Youssou N'Dour: Africa's Music Missionary," *BBC Homepage,* May 24, 2000, http://news.bbc.co.uk/hi/english/world/africa/newsid_761000/761088.stm. □

John Shaw Neilson

John Shaw Neilson (1872-1942) was an Australian poet whose work was notable for its originality, spiritual questioning, and emphasis on nature.

Early Religious Conflicts

John Shaw Neilson was born in Penola, Australia, in 1872, to an impoverished bush family. He was the first child of seven, and his family called him Jock. Because he had a speech impediment, his family kept him out of school, but he received some education at home. His father, a farmer, and his uncle wrote poetry and encouraged him to read and write. Neilson read the work of English Romantic authors, as well as some of the Victorians and was familiar with songs from England, Ireland, Scotland, and America, as well as the ballads of the Australian bush.

Because he did not go to school, Neilson had plenty of time to experience the freedom and beauty of the Australian bush country. In *Jock: A Life Story of John Shaw Neilson,* Cliff Hanna wrote that Neilson spent his days wandering through the landscape around Penola, taking in "the green pastures, trees, swamps, animals and birds [that were] his schoolmates."

However, Neilson's enjoyment of nature was blunted by his family's strict religious beliefs. From his mother, a Presbyterian who emphasized sin, guilt, and damnation, Nelson gained an acutely religious sensibility, as well as a lifelong religious conflict. Though the bush tormented his family with droughts, floods, plagues, and fires, Neilson was fascinated with its beauty, wildlife, and freedom. His mother, who was generally warm-hearted and loving, told him that the bush was a place of the devil, innately corrupt, and that loving nature too much would lead him to hell. In addition, her religious beliefs stressed suffering and divine punishment, and anything that was pleasurable was suspect. On Sundays, farm work was strictly forbidden. This meant that the cattle, left unmilked, bellowed all day in pain. As Hanna wrote in *The Folly of Spring: A Study of John Shaw Neilson's Poetry,* "Divine vengeance hung over the house like a thundercloud. Not even death offered escape. There must have been many discussions on predestination, and on who would be among the Elect. Satan was an almost palpable presence."

Neilson was disturbed by these ideas and in his late teens became obsessed with the nature of God, and how God, as a perfect being, could be so separate from imperfect nature and humanity. These questions inspired his poetry; he began publishing in the early 1890s in the local newspaper at Nhill in Victoria and in the *Australian,* a Melbourne newspaper. His first poem to attract wider attention, "The Tales We Never Hear," won a contest sponsored by the Australian Natives Association in 1893. The poem considered the conflict between God's will and people's will. Although Neilson believed that people did have free will, he did not see how a just and good God could allow sin, or why humans, who were supposedly created in God's image, were doomed to decay and death.

Throughout his life, Neilson would ponder God's inaccessibility. As Hanna observed: "The bush is normally a paradise for a child to explore; [Neilson] roamed it as a criminal desperate for atonement. . . . the bush, with its beauty, power and wisdom, became Satan's device to trap unwary little boys. The mind must always be on guard against the treacherous desires of the body; emotions must be treated with the utmost caution since the body is a temple of sin. Love, unless exalted through thoughts of God, is debased and ultimately lecherous.''

As a result, Neilson kept a tight rein on his emotions and distrusted physical pleasures, although he always retained a fascination with nature. In ''The Gentle Water Bird,'' he contrasts the frowning, terrible view of God with a beautiful, regal bird he saw in the bush. According to Hanna, he later said of the bird, ''It seemed so confident and happy, without any fear. It wasn't frightened about God like me.'' Neilson also noted that in the bush, death was not a punishment, but a necessary part of the cycle of life and renewal of nature. In addition, he often used the sun as a symbol of enlightenment and the divine. His use of nature imagery to express religious concepts was not a complete rejection of his family's Presbyterianism, ''but a development of it,'' according to Hanna.

Life of Hard Labor

Neilson's father eventually went bankrupt, and the family moved to Minimay in Victoria, but his fortune did not improve. A series of crop failures, debts, and foreclosures forced the family to move from place to place and to suffer grinding poverty. Two of Neilson's sisters died of malnutrition. Neilson quit school in 1886 at age 13 after receiving only three years of education. To help his family survive, he took a series of hundreds of rural jobs, traveling throughout most of western Victoria as well as parts of New South Wales in search of work. He worked in harvesting, cattle driving, fencing, picking fruit, clearing, making roads, shearing sheep, working in quarries, and cutting wood. He often suffered painful injuries and walked hundreds of miles to places where he had heard there was work.

During this time, he rebelled strongly against his family's religious ideas, but at a great cost to his health: he suffered two nervous breakdowns and developed poor eyesight for which no physical cause could be found. Hanna speculated that his eye trouble, which prevented him from reading, was a rebellion against reading the Bible. When he was suffering from it, he had to ask other farm laborers, who often were not very sympathetic to his aims, to help him by writing down verses he had composed while working. This ability to compose poetry while engaged in backbreaking labor may seem startling, but according to Clement Semmler in *Quadrant,* it was ''a refuge from the harsh reality of his daily life as well as his mother's relentless religious teaching.''

Neilson felt guilty for rejecting his mother's religious dogma, and he felt conflict about that for his entire life. However, he continued to use his own system of dividing God into two images: one of thunder, darkness, and punishment, and one of kindness and light. These two images were inherently in conflict with each other, and they appear repeatedly in his poetry.

Neilson's baby brother Neil died in 1889, and when his mother died in 1897, Neilson experienced a period of nervous illness that lasted for eighteen months and that re-

turned later in his life. He believed he had inherited this from his mother's side of the family, and he may have been right; his brother William was mentally ill, and his sister Maggie, who was strongly religious and who idolized their mother, was always on the edge of nervous collapse. Maggie died in 1903, and another sister, Jessie, died in 1907. The stress of the deaths, as well as his work exposure to dust and heat, exacerbated his eye problems, and by 1905 it was extremely painful to him to read or write. He could not afford to visit a doctor, so he went to a local practitioner who put curry pellets in his eyes, which nearly blinded him for a year.

He experienced another setback when millions of mice swarmed over Australia, eating everything they could find. The mice ate his notebooks, which contained most of his poems and correspondence. Despite his health problems and the mouse plague, during these years he began to write more poetry, fueled by the success of ''The Tales We Never Hear.'' He printed copies of his poems and sold them from door to door in Nhill. By 1897, he had published 18 poems, which along with over 30 other unpublished pieces, are now considered his juvenilia.

Literary Success

Neilson sent his poems to A.G. Stephens, editor of the *Bulletin* and the *Bookfellow.* Stephens often published his work but with heavy editorial changes. Stephens helped Neilson publish his first collection of poems, *Heart of Spring* (1919), as well as Neilson's next books, *Ballad and Lyrical Poems* (1923) and *New Poems* (1927). After his third collection was published, Stephens declared that he was ''the first and finest of Australian poets, past and present,'' according to Hanna.

In 1926, Neilson met Mary Gilmore, who admired his poems and had corresponded with him for many years. He traveled to Sydney, his hands rough and scarred from working in a quarry, and met many well-regarded Australian writers, as well as Stephens, for the first time. In 1928, another admirer, Frank Wilmot, gave Neilson a job as a messenger at Melbourne's County Roads Board. Exhausted from years of hard labor, he gratefully accepted. After taking this job, he wrote very little. From this time until 1934, he worked on his *Collected Verse* (1934). James Devaney, a poet and novelist, helped him with this work as well as with a collection of poems, *Beauty Imposes* (1938).

Neilson enjoyed his new life in the city. He attended political rallies, the theater, and cricket matches, and he became a founding member of a literary society, the Bread and Cheese Club, in 1938. He died after a heart attack in 1942.

According to Ken Goodwin in *A History of Australian Literature,* Neilson's poems have been compared to ''the unaffected directness'' of William Blake, William Barnes, and John Clare. In addition, Neilson's critics have compared Neilson's vision to Blake's, Goodwin wrote, ''for there is something of the possessed mystic at times in Neilson. The circular movement of his poems, the way in which they dwell on a few related images and then return to the original cause of inspiration, strengthens this impression.''

Goodwin noted that critic A.R. Chisholm believed that though Neilson's work was "timeless," with no clearly marked phases of development, it is possible to see a progression from "innocence to experience and disillusion" in Neilson's poetry. In his earlier work, written until about 1910, he emphasizes the purity of childhood and youth and a God of light. From 1910 through 1911, he wrote about the physical aspects of love; as Goodwin wrote, "Woman, rather than spring, youth, or the colour green, now seems to permeate the universe." In his later works, such as "The Orange Tree," he examined a young girl's experience of love, suggesting that her spiritual awakening may be the result of love.

World War I, fought from 1914 through 1918, as well as the Great Depression of the 1930s, were events which disillusioned many, including Neilson; this disillusionment was apparent in his later poetry.

Hanna summed up Neilson's work: "The originality and the intellectual integrity of Neilson's poetic world stand in stark contrast to much Australian writing, which has been burdened down by foreign traditions." Perhaps, Hanna speculated, this originality came partly from Neilson's lack of formal education, rough life in the bush, and his eye problems, which prevented him from reading other writers or critical works. "As a poet he went his own way: nature, and the search for a proper Deity determined what was acceptable, and not literary fashion or established views." In *Preoccupations in Australian Poetry,* Judith Wright wrote, "The more we read of his poetry—even though at first, knowing that it was written in our own century, we may reject it as childish or naive—the more its special note, the particular clarity of its inner truth, rings clear and unmistakable."

Books

Goodwin, Ken, *A History of Australian Literature,* St. Martin's Press, 1986.

Hanna, Cliff, *The Folly of Spring,* University of Queensland Press, 1990.

Hanna, Cliff, *Jock: A Life Story of John Shaw Neilson,* University of Queensland Press, 1999.

Pierre, Peter, editor, *Oxford Literary Guide to Australia,* Oxford University Press, 1993.

Wright, Judith, *Preoccupations in Australian Poetry,* Oxford University Press, 1965.

Periodicals

Australian Literary Studies, May 2000.

Quadrant, April 2000. □

O

Carroll O'Connor

Five-time Emmy award-winning actor Carroll O'Connor (1924-2001) was best known for playing Archie Bunker, the big-hearted bigot on the groundbreaking 1970s television comedy *All in the Family.*

Early Years

Carroll O'Connor was born in the Bronx, New York, on August 2, 1924. He was the eldest of three sons of a lawyer and schoolteacher raised in an Irish Catholic household. The O'Connors weathered the years of the Great Depression in comfort, living in their single-family home in Forest Hills, Queens, at the time a wealthy neighborhood. His father was a successful attorney and his two brothers became doctors.

O'Connor was a poor student who later attributed his lackluster academic performance to being pushed ahead a year in school. In his memoirs, he described how he skipped kindergarten and entered first grade at the age of five: "Thereafter I became impossible to teach and nobody was comfortable with me." In 1941 O'Connor enrolled at Wake Forest University in North Carolina, but dropped out when the United States entered World War II. He volunteered for the Naval Air Corps but was rejected because of his low grades and bad teeth. Instead, he entered the less-selective United States Merchant Marine Academy and became a midshipman. He eventually joined the National Maritime Union and sailed the North Atlantic, Caribbean, and Mediterranean as a merchant seaman during the late stages of the war.

Discovered Acting

After the war, O'Connor spent a few years uncertain what he wanted to do with his life. In 1946, he left the merchant marines, returned to his mother's house in Queens, and worked for an Irish newspaper run by his family. At the time, his father was serving a prison sentence for a fraud conviction in the Sing-Sing penitentiary in upstate New York. O'Connor considered a career in journalism and in 1948 returned to Wake Forest. He also took courses at Montana State University, where he met his future wife Nancy Fields. He married her in 1951. In 1950 he went to Dublin, Ireland, with his brother, Hugh, and enrolled at University College, Dublin, where he studied Irish history and English literature. O'Connor finished his undergraduate studies at the National University of Ireland, earning a bachelor's degree in 1952.

In the 1950s, O'Connor performed in various plays throughout Europe. Using the stage name George Roberts, O'Connor appeared in productions at Dublin's Gate Theater and in productions of Shakespeare's plays at the Edinburgh Festival in Scotland and in Cork, Limerick, and Galway in Ireland.

In 1954, O'Connor returned to New York and struggled to find acting work. For several years, he worked as a substitute teacher in the New York public school system while he earned his master's degree in education. His break came in the late 1950s when his wife noticed a casting call for a stage production of James Joyce's *Ulysses*. That audition eventually landed him another role, as a Hollywood boss in the off-Broadway production of the Clifford Odets play *Big Knife*.

In 1960 O'Connor landed the role of a prosecutor in *The Sacco-Vanzetti Story* for the Armstrong Circle Theater. He earned a reputation as a reliable character actor and

started getting movie roles. Over his career, O'Connor appeared in more than 30 films, including *A Fever in the Blood* (1961), *Lad: A Dog* (1961), *Lonely are the Brave* (1962), and *Cleopatra* (1963).

Debuted as Archie Bunker

All in the Family, an American sitcom that ran from 1971 to 1979, was adapted from the British show *Till Death Do Us Part,* a serial on BBC. Producer Norman Lear loosely based the character of Archie Bunker on his own father. Bunker's family included his scatterbrained wife Edith, played by Jean Stapleton; their daughter Gloria, played by Sally Struthers; and her liberal and outspoken husband Mike "Meathead" Stivic, played by Rob Reiner.

O'Connor was living in Rome when he received an offer to play Archie Bunker. He was so convinced it would fail that he demanded a round-trip ticket from the producers so he could return to Italy. O'Connor disliked the pilot script, but agreed to play Archie after it was rewritten. The show had some difficulty getting on the air because of its subject matter. ABC rejected it, but CBS broadcast *All in the Family* for the first time on January 12, 1971.

All in the Family marked a departure from earlier American television shows. Before, the "television landscape . . . had been largely filled with innocuous characters and . . . generally steered clear of sensitive topics," noted Brian Lowry in the *Los Angeles Times.* Americans never saw couples sleeping in the same bed or heard a toilet flush on television before *All in the Family.* The show talked about

topics hitherto taboo on American TV: gender, race, religion, and sex. Though critics initially panned *All in the Family,* it eventually became one of television's most popular sitcoms, ranking number one for five years and spinning off three successful shows—*Archie Bunker's Place, Maude,* and *The Jeffersons.*

Part of the show's success was due to its timing. "Coming out of the 1960s civil rights movement and with Vietnam continuing to jar the country," wrote Allan Johnson in the *Chicago Tribune,* "it got Americans thinking and talking about race, sexism and social status in the country." The character of Archie Bunker personified the emotions that millions of Americans were experiencing: "the character wasn't just a narrow-minded bigot, he was a confused, sometimes scared middle-aged man who was coming to grips with his place in a world that was changing too fast," explained Johnson.

Archie was a political conservative who thought the Democratic Party was a front for Communism and admired Republican President Richard Nixon. Frustrated by his dead-end job and unfulfilling life, Archie reacted with fear toward his bosses and with antagonism toward women and blacks. His distrust extended to anyone who was not a white Anglo-Saxon Protestant. He insulted Jews, Roman Catholics, blacks, Hispanics, and other ethnic groups. But while using racial slurs broke down a barrier in television broadcasting, it also drew criticism. Whitney Young, Jr., head of the Urban League, found nothing funny about Archie's racial epithets, calling them "gratuitous insults." "In the role of Archie, O'Connor tapped into angst, anger and unthinking prejudice that buffeted the U.S. in the Vietnam-war ear," a CNN obituary noted. "He admitted his character was both loved and hated, but said he just played Archie as truthfully as he knew how."

At its height, the show drew 50 million weekly television viewers. The show became a national icon and Archie Bunker a household name. O'Connor won four Emmy Awards for his performances. The furniture from the show's living room set was installed in the Smithsonian museum in Washington, DC. Eventually the other actors decided to leave the show, and *All in the Family* morphed into *Archie Bunker's Place,* with O'Connor playing a co-owner of a bar. That show, which ran from 1979 to 1983, never garnered the same popularity or critical acclaim as its predecessor.

Broke Color Barriers

After the Archie Bunker role had run its course, O'Connor wrote or acted in several unsuccessful productions. His first Broadway flop was *Brothers* (1983), which he directed and in which he played a father with four sons. He then wrote and produced a television movie called *Brass* and played the lead character, a chief of detectives for the New York police.

In 1984 he was in *Home Front,* a play about a father, mother, and daughter terrorized by a son who is a Vietnam vet. It closed after 13 performances. In 1995 O'Connor's play, *A Certain Labor Day,* opened in San Francisco with O'Connor in a starring role. The *San Francisco Chronicle* called it a "heartfelt bungle of a new play" and nothing more than a "transformation of O'Connor's most enduring creation, television's Archie Bunker." The review embittered O'Connor and reinforced his dislike of the press.

In 1988, O'Connor finally landed a role on another hit television series. He played Sheriff Bill Gillespie in the drama series *In the Heat of the Night.* The show, which ran for six seasons, was based on the 1967 Oscar-winning film. O'Connor also served as executive producer and head writer for the series. He directed several episodes and his adopted son, Hugh, played a police officer.

The show was remarkable for its controversial subject matter. *In the Heat of the Night* featured a romantic relationship between a white man and a black woman. Gillespie had an affair with a black city councilwoman, and the two married in the final episode of the series. This was groundbreaking material for television, and O'Connor won awards from the NAACP for his role on the drama. He also earned his fifth Emmy Award.

Shattered by Son's Suicide

In 1995, O'Connor's son, Hugh, committed suicide after a long battle with cocaine addiction. The event inspired O'Connor to start a crusade against the man who sold the drugs to Hugh. He called Harry Perzigian "a partner in murder" and a "sleazeball." Perzigian filed a defamation lawsuit against the actor. In 1997, a California jury threw out the case. In an interview on CNN's *Larry King Live* soon after the verdict, O'Connor said he would never be able to put his son's death behind him. "I can't forget it. There isn't a day that I don't think of him and want him back and miss him, and I'll feel that way until I'm not here anymore," he said. O'Connor became an advocate against drug abuse and appeared in several television anti-drug commercials.

O'Connor suffered from poor health in his final years. He lost a toe to complications from diabetes and underwent gall bladder surgery. He also had a coronary artery bypass operation in 1989. His last project was the role of Minnie Driver's grandfather in the movie *Return to Me* in 2000.

Despite his well-rounded repertoire, O'Connor will be remembered for his indelible role as Archie Bunker. O'Connor said in a 1994 interview that the character of Archie "wasn't even close" to who he was as a person. Still, the actor conceded, "I'll never play a better part than Archie. He was the best character, the most fulfilling character, and I never thought it was going to develop that way. There's no role that can top that."

Books

Contemporary Theatre, Film and Television, Volume 27, Gale Group, 2000.
O'Connor, Carroll, *I Think I'm Outta Here,* Simon & Schuster, 1998.

Periodicals

Chicago Tribune, June 22, 2001.
Los Angeles Times, June 22, 2001.
New York Times, June 22, 2001.
Washington Post, June 22, 2001. □

John Joseph O'Connor

John O'Connor (1920-2000) is recognized as one of the most important American representatives of 20th-century Roman Catholicism.

As a Roman Catholic leader, Cardinal John O'Connor was his generation's most outspoken and unwavering supporter of the Vatican's policies and procedures. He tirelessly defended Pope John Paul II's positions against abortion, homosexual marriages, capital punishment, divorce, contraception, and sex education. He also worked to help financially disadvantaged families, supported labor unions, spread the moral message of the Catholic Church by opposing specific art installations and performances, questioned the need for unchecked military spending and nuclear armaments, fought against racism, and advocated maximum employment and minimum wages. His tenure as cardinal and archbishop of New York occurred during the 1980s, a time when tremendous religious, cultural, and political upheavals arose between conservative and liberal attitudes. O'Connor remained conservatively steadfast behind the dictums of the Church and is credited with reinvigorating the faith in America by engaging in the most controversial social and political dialogues of the era. When asked why he became involved in social issues not normally regarded part of the Church's domain, O'Connor replied: "I am a priest. About 900,000 individuals in New York City live in substandard conditions, including overcrowding, with all the attendant evils of that kind of life. I would be failing, as a priest, if all I did was to say Mass and carry out the customary religious duties of my office."

Recognized His Vocation

Born in Philadelphia on January 15, 1920, O'Connor was the fourth of five children born to Thomas and Dorothy O'Connor, both practicing Catholics. Thomas O'Connor was a skilled painter who was adept at applying gold-leaf to auditorium and church ceilings. In addition, he was also a staunch defender of unions, often citing the writings of popes Leo XIII and Pius XI to support his beliefs. When O'Connor was still a young boy, his mother suffered blindness for a year. When her sight returned a year later, O'Connor recalled that "She attributed her cure to St. Rita of Cascia, and afterward she made a novena at St. Rita's Shrine every year, having to take two trolleys and a bus to get there." O'Connor credited his mother's infirmity with elevating his consciousness to assist the disabled. He also displayed an interest in helping mentally handicapped children when he was only ten years old.

O'Connor attended public school in Philadelphia before entering West Catholic High School for Boys. The school was operated by the Members of the Brothers of the Christian Schools, who were dedicated to assisting the financially disadvantaged with educational opportunities. In 1936 O'Connor enrolled at St. Charles Borromeo Seminary in Philadelphia and was ordained a priest nine years later.

A Navy Chaplain

O'Connor's first seven years as a priest were spent as an assistant pastor in a Philadelphia parish. During this period, he taught high school and night school courses, hosted two Catholic radio programs each week, and worked with mentally retarded children. In 1952 he left Philadelphia to begin a 27-year tenure as a Navy chaplain, his new vocation taken in response to a request from Cardinal Francis Spellman, the military vicar of the American Catholic Church, for additional military clergy. He became a full lieutenant in 1955 and served for five years in Washington, D.C. as an assistant for moral leadership to the chief of chaplains. He was chaplain on a guided-missile cruiser before accepting an assignment as chaplain of the Naval Postgraduate School in Monterey, California. In 1964 O'Connor was sent to Vietnam for combat duty with the Third Marine Division.

While serving in Vietnam, O'Connor published *A Chaplain Looks at Vietnam,* in which he attempts to justify American military involvement in the Vietnam conflict. He later repudiated the claims of the book to biographer Nat Hentoff: "That's a bad book, you know. . . . It was a very limited view of what was going on. I regret having published it." In his 1981 book *In Defense of Life,* O'Connor maintained that he was responding to his perception that many other writers of the same era were biased in favor of the North Vietnamese. Despite his changing perception of the value of the war effort he aided, O'Connor received a Legion of Merit award for his service in Vietnam, earning the praise of his commanding general, Lewis Walt: "It is my

opinion that no single individual in this command contributed more to the morale of the individual Marine here in Vietnam than Father O'Connor, who spent the majority of his time in the field with the men."

After Vietnam, O'Connor earned master's degrees in advanced ethics and clinical psychology at the Catholic University of America before earning a doctorate in political science from Georgetown University. In 1972 he became the first Catholic senior chaplain at the Naval Academy at Annapolis. Three years later he became chief of Navy chaplains and was promoted to the rank of rear admiral. By 1979 O'Connor intended to retire to a priesthood in a small parish. Instead, he was made a bishop by Pope John Paul II and installed as a military vicariate, a civilian position in which he still supervised military chaplains.

Attended National Conference of Catholic Bishops

In 1981 O'Connor was one of five men named to the National Conference of Catholic Bishops and charged with the task of drafting a pastoral letter on the American Catholic Church's position on the building and use of nuclear warheads. As the only member of the committee with a military background, his views were interpreted as hawkish, especially when he unsuccessfully attempted to change the word "halt" to "curb" in text covering the testing, building, and use of nuclear armaments. The bishops eventually issued a document condemning the use of nuclear weapons and stressing that nuclear capabilities were acceptable only as deterrents—and even then only if total disarmament was the eventual goal. The pastoral letter resulted in a meeting with Pope John Paul II. Shortly thereafter, the pope named O'Connor bishop of Scranton, New Jersey. When Cardinal Cooke, archbishop of New York, died in 1984, O'Connor was installed as his successor and in 1985 was elevated to cardinal.

Engaged in Abortion, Homosexuality Controversies

Almost immediately after becoming a bishop in the late 1970s, O'Connor became an outspoken opponent of abortion. His support of the Church's stance on abortion led him to pronounce in the mid-1980s that the willful and legal termination of pregnancy was "precisely the same" as the Holocaust perpetrated by the Nazi Party in Germany during the 1940s in which six million Jews were exterminated. The quote angered many Jewish listeners and abortion rights advocates who felt that the comparison was unjustified. Undeterred by such criticism, O'Connor continued to state his views on the abortion issue, declaring at one point that he did not understand how a Catholic would, in good conscience, be able to vote for a political candidate supporting abortion. His position rankled supporters of New York Governor Mario Cuomo and vice presidential candidate and New York congressional representative Geraldine Ferraro, both of whom were both Italian American Catholics who supported abortion rights. In the instance of Cuomo, O'Connor refused to deny rumors in the press that he might excommunicate the governor; in the instance of Ferraro, he issued a statement that she had "misrepresented Catholic teaching on abortion." In addition to being vehemently opposed to abortion, O'Connor was equally opposed to violence against those who either provided or received the procedure.

Throughout his tenure as cardinal, O'Connor also earned notoriety among many liberals for his opposition to the legalization of homosexual unions. Still, he was the first archbishop to meet with homosexual activists to hear them voice their concerns. He also visited and ministered both homosexual and heterosexual patients afflicted with Acquired Immune Deficiency Syndrome (AIDS). Continuing to publicly support the Vatican's position denying homosexual unions, O'Connor refused to support homosexual participation in New York City's annual St. Patrick's Day Parade. He also sparred legally with New York Mayor Ed Koch, who had issued an executive order banning discrimination against homosexuals by employers receiving city funds. Since the Catholic Church provided city services, O'Connor objected to the order on the grounds that the city did not possess the right to mandate hiring practices overseen by the Catholic Church. O'Connor won the battle but lost a later fight against a similar bill that exempted religious institutions.

Because of his outspokenness, O'Connor was targeted by gay rights groups who led several demonstrations against him. Masses officiated by O'Connor were interrupted more than once by gay rights protestors who chained themselves to pews and disrupted services. In one case, a gay pride parade was deliberately routed in front of St. Patrick's Cathedral. O'Connor urged the congregation: "Please do not believe for a moment that you would be defending the Church or advancing Church teachings by expressions of hatred."

Was Honored with Congressional Gold Medal

Before O'Connor's death from brain cancer in 2000, President Bill Clinton signed legislation awarding the cardinal the Congressional Gold Medal. In part, Clinton's statement read: "For more than fifty years, Cardinal O'Connor has served the Catholic Church and our nation with consistency and commitment. . . . Whether it was the soldier on the battlefield or the patient dying of AIDS, Cardinal O'Connor has ministered with a gentle spirit and a loving heart. Through it all, he has stood strong as an advocate for the poor, a champion for workers and an inspiration for millions." O'Connor died on May 3, 2000.

Books

Golway, Terry, *Full of Grace: An Oral Biography of John Cardinal O'Connor,* Simon & Schuster, 2001.
Hentoff, Nat, *John Cardinal O'Connor: At the Storm Center of a Changing American Catholic Church,* Charles Scribner's Sons, 1988.

Periodicals

New Republic, March 18, 1985; May 22, 2000.
New York Times, May 4, 2000. □

P

Grace Paley

The American writer Grace Paley (born 1922) is best known for her three collections of short stories, *The Little Disturbances of Man* (1959), *Enormous Changes at the Last Minute* (1974), and *Later the Same Day* (1985). As long as she has been a writer, Paley has also been an activist, supporting various anti-war, anti-nuclear, and feminist movements. In her writing, however, she does not push a political agenda and prefers instead to chronicle the everyday lives of men and women.

Studied Poetry First

Born in the Bronx, New York, Paley was the youngest child of Russian-Jewish immigrant parents. She grew up in a socialist, intellectual household amid a babble of three languages—Yiddish, Russian, and English. As a writer of fiction, Paley would pick up on the music of all three tongues, celebrating their rhythms and idioms.

From an early age, she wrote poetry, and at age 17 she took a course with the British poet W. H. Auden. "When I wrote poetry I was very keenly aware of being influenced," Paley told the online literary magazine *Salon*. "When I was young, I wrote a lot like Auden. It's kind of comical, because after all, I didn't have a British accent. . . . I had no sense of my own language yet."

As a student Paley attended Hunter College and New York University. She married early, in 1942, and settled with her husband in Greenwich Village, where they raised two children (the marriage would eventually end in divorce). In this community of artists, intellectuals, and bohemians, Paley became involved in leftist politics. She frequented anti-war and anti-nuclear demonstrations, and she became engaged in local issues (opposing, for example, the city's proposed plan to build a road through Washington Square).

Wrote First Short Stories

As a young mother in the mid-1950s, Paley made her initial forays into writing fiction. The urge to tell stories had begun to grow in her, but the responsibilities of motherhood called. Falling ill one day, she arranged for her children to attend an after-school program while she convalesced. Paley was not too ill to sit at a typewriter, however, and the extra hours of quiet and solitude were all she needed to begin writing fiction. Thus was born her first short story, "Goodbye and Good Luck."

Paley then wrote two more stories, "The Contest" and "A Woman, Young and Old." She submitted them to editors, but like most beginning writers without connections in the field, she often received them back with form rejection slips. She did eventually publish her first three stories in little-known journals.

These stories would eventually launch Paley's career. In "Two Ears, Three Lucks," an introductory essay that begins her *Collected Stories* (1994), she describes her big break: the ex-husband of a friend offered to read her work. A couple of weeks later, Paley recalled, "He asked if I could write seven more stories like the three he'd read. He said he'd publish the book. Doubleday would publish them. He was Ken McCormick, an editor who could say that and it would happen."

And happen it did. Doubleday published Paley's first collection of short stories, *The Little Disturbances of Man,* in 1959. The ten quirky tales, most of them in the first-person voices of women, garnered rave reviews. The *New York Times* called her "a newcomer possessed of an all-too-infrequent literary virtue," but the stories did not attract a mass audience. Rather, they appealed to a narrow literary readership, gaining a kind of cult following. The book remained in print until 1965, but its reputation survived. Meanwhile, Paley continued to publish new stories in the *New Yorker,* the *Atlantic Monthly,* and other reputable magazines. Her readership continued to grow.

Paley's stories explored the everyday lives of her contemporaries, focusing most attentively on the lives of women. The dreams and goals of her female characters—independent, strong-minded, and often idealistic—propelled these narratives forward. She was perhaps the first writer to explore, with gritty realism, the lives and experiences of divorced mothers. Some critics point to her early stories as the beginnings of a feminist literature, written years before the women's movement of the 1970s.

If feminism entered Paley's stories, it did so only indirectly. She strove to capture in her fiction not political discourse but the rhythms of daily life. The spoken word and the power of dialogue fascinated her, and she reveled in the music of her characters' voices, the inflected, lively urban vernacular that she liked to describe as "a mixture of literary and neighborhood sound."

Only three years after it had gone out of print, a reprint of *Little Disturbances* appeared in 1968. It was with this edition, many critics note, that Paley reached a wide enough audience to establish a place for herself in contemporary American literature.

Became an Outspoken Activist

During the 1960s and 1970s, Paley entered the spotlight not only as a writer but also as an activist. She later classified herself as a "somewhat combative pacifist and cooperative anarchist," a label that stuck, repeated often by writers of articles and books about Paley. Her pacifism led her to help found the Greenwich Village Peace Center in 1961, and when the Vietnam War broke out, she became even more active. Vehemently opposed to the war, Paley spent time in jail for her anti-war activities. She also visited Hanoi as a member of a peace delegation.

While Paley the activist drew press coverage, Paley the writer was not forgotten. Those who had read *Little Disturbances* awaited another book, but it was long in coming. Her involvement with anti-war activism took time away from her writing. She later recalled to the 1997 graduating class of Williams College, "I remember I was writing stories, and a lot of stuff was coming up at the time during Vietnam, and my mind simply went away from what I was doing, and that was all there was to it. I had to wait a couple of months until I could really wander off into that space."

Enormous Changes at the Last Minute, her second collection of stories, appeared 15 years after her first, in 1974. The reviews were mixed. Many critics said her new book did not have the dazzling power of her debut collection, and some suggested that Paley's activist involvement had somehow marred her literary pursuits.

"It was ridiculous," Paley told the *New York Times* a few years later. "I mean, in Europe, for a writer not to be political is peculiar, and in this country for a writer to be political is considered some sort of aberration, or time waste. I'm not writing a history of famous people. I am interested in a history of everyday life."

Meanwhile, Paley continued pursuing her activist passions. In the late 1970s she turned her attention to the anti-nuclear movement. Participating in a protest on the White House lawn in February 1979, she carried a banner that read "No Nuclear Weapons—No Nuclear Power—U.S. or U.S.S.R" and distributed leaflets with a similar message. She and two other writers were arrested and fined.

When she was not writing or protesting, Paley was teaching. Like most authors, she needed a source of income to supplement earnings from the occasional publication. Though her original motivation to teach was financial, Paley grew to enjoy the work and even to gain inspiration from it.

As a teacher of creative writing at Sarah Lawrence, a women's college in Bronxville, New York, Paley encouraged her students to develop their own particular voices, culled from both family life and literary tradition. "What I'm trying to do," she told the *New York Times* in 1978, "is to remind students they have two ears. One is the ear that listens to their ordinary life, their family and the street they live on, and the other is the tradition of English literature.''

Published Third Short Story Collection

The 1980s brought accolades for Paley, who was elected to the Academy of American Arts and Letters (1980) and was named New York's first state author (1986-88). It also brought the publication of her third collection of stories, *Later the Same Day* (1985). Critics received the new book with respectful, enthusiastic appraisals. ''It's been worth the wait,'' said a *New York Times* reviewer, who called it ''another collection of remarkable stories.''

Many readers mused that Faith, a character who recurred in several stories in Paley's collections, must be an autobiographical rendering of the author. Like Paley, Faith had two children and eventually went through a divorce. But Paley claimed the similarities between her life and her character's ended there. ''[I]t's as if [Faith] were one of my friends,'' she told Andrea Stephens of the *New York Times.* ''I didn't bring up my kids alone; I married a second time. I was always interested in the lives of women and in the idea of a woman alone bringing up two boys.'' (Paley, unlike Faith, had one son and one daughter.)

The 1990s was an unusually prolific decade for Paley, who had previously published so rarely. *Long Walks and Intimate Talks,* a compilation of fiction and poetry, came out in 1991. This book, with illustrations by the artist Vera B. Williams, did not attract as much attention as the three previous collections, but it did gain some praise in critical circles. *New and Collected Poems* came out the following year to mixed reviews. Comparing Paley's poetry to her prose, most critics seemed to prefer the latter.

It was as a fiction writer, and not as a poet, that Paley would be most remembered. Indeed, she had already secured a place for herself in the canon of American fiction, and her works graced the syllabuses of many contemporary American Literature courses. In the late twentieth and early twenty-first centuries, women's studies and ''political correctness'' were hot topics on college campuses, and many professors included Paley among examples of women writers or Jewish American writers. Some readers felt such categorization was too limiting or pigeon-holing. Paley, on the other hand, did not mind. ''I feel that everything I am enhances the word 'writer,''' she told the *Berkshire Eagle.* ''It doesn't modify it. I feel being Jewish has been very important to my writing, being a woman has been extremely important to my writing—all those things that I am have made me what I am and what I write about and how I write. . . . But I think they should start calling them 'male writers.' That would solve the whole problem. Nobody would feel bad, except the men.''

In a career milestone, Farrar, Straus and Giroux published *The Collected Stories* (1994), which included all of the short stories from Paley's first three books. For younger readers unfamiliar with Paley's early work, the book provided a chance to see her fiction in a broader context. The poet Robert Pinksy, reviewing the collection in the *New York Times,* called the stories ''delicious.'' When *Collected Stories* came out, the 71-year-old writer had finished teach-

ing regularly, although she gave lectures and led workshops on occasion. Living in Vermont with her second husband, the writer Robert Nichols, Paley continued writing, though she would never produce the novel that many of her fans expected. (''I tried,'' she told Laurel Graeber of the *New York Times.* ''It didn't come out so good. So why should I?'')

It was the short story that Paley had mastered as an art form, and devoted readers hope for more tales of Faith and other characters in the coming years. Late in her life, she remains one of America's most esteemed authors.

Books

Paley, Grace, *The Collected Stories,* Farrar, Straus and Giroux, 1994.

Periodicals

Berkshire Eagle, June 19, 1997.
New York Times, April 19, 1959; April 30, 1978; April 14, 1985; April 24, 1994.

Online

''Featured Author: Grace Paley,'' *NYTimes.com,* http://www.nytimes.com/books/98/04/19/specials/paley.html. (October 30, 2001).
''Grace Paley,'' http://www.bedfordstmartins.com/litlinks/fiction/paley.htm (October 29, 2001).
''Grace Paley: New York State Author, 1986-1988,'' http://www.albany.edu/writers-inst/paley.html (October 30, 2001).
''Writing with Both Ears,'' *Salon,* http://www.salon.com/11/departments/litchat1.html. (October 29, 2001). □

Christabel Harriette Pankhurst

Christabel Pankhurst (1880-1958) was an English feminist activist. With her mother Emmeline, she was a co-founder of the Women's Social and Political Union and devised strategies for its increasingly militant campaign for votes for women.

Pankhurst was born in 1880, the daughter of feminist activist Emmeline Pankhurst and lawyer Richard Marsden Pankhurst. In *Women in World History,* Nancy Ellen Rupprecht wrote, ''Adored by both her parents, she was almost a textbook illustration of the first child born to a middle-class family. In childhood as well as adulthood, she was beautiful, intelligent, graceful, confident, charming, and charismatic.'' She was very close to her mother, and they had a special bond that was not shared by any of her siblings. She was also loved by her father; according to Roger Fulford in the *Dictionary of National Biography,* he named her Christabel after a line by Coleridge: ''The lovely lady, Christabel/ Whom her father loves so well.''

Her family was educated and progressive, but not wealthy. Early in her childhood, her family moved to London, and her father practiced law there and in Manchester;

her mother opened a shop where she sold silks, pottery, lampshades, and other fancy items.

Educated at home, Pankhurst learned to read early, later attending school in Manchester before moving to Geneva to study French while staying in the home of a family friend. When her father died in 1898, she returned to Manchester to help her mother raise her siblings. She also became her mother's assistant when Emmeline became the Registrar of Births and Deaths in Manchester. At the time, it was considered somewhat shameful to be poor, and according to Fulford, "They comforted themselves with the knowledge that they were poor because they were idealists: they preferred causes to comfort."

Encouraged by her progressive family, she joined the Manchester Women's Trade Union Council, which worked to promote women's causes. In 1901 she became a member of the executive committee of the North of England Society for Women's Suffrage. Her compelling speaking style, smooth voice, and intelligent argument led her to become a valued speaker about women's emancipation. According to Rupprecht, she later wrote, "Here, then, was an aim in life for me—the liberation of politically fettered womanhood."

With her mother, in 1903 she founded the Women's Social and Political Union (WSPU), a more radical offshoot of the British Labour Party. She also followed her father's example by studying law at Victoria University; in 1905 she won a prize for International Law, and in 1906 she won first-class honors in the LL.B. exam. She was not allowed to practice law, however, because she was a woman. That

same year, she moved to London to continue her political activities on behalf of the WSPU. When she and fellow activist Annie Kenney resisted arrest after interrupting a Liberal Party meeting with speeches about women's suffrage, they were arrested. The police treated them roughly and Pankhurst spat at one of them because her arms were restrained; this event became the first feminist protest to be covered by a newspaper. According to Rupprecht, Pankhurst later wrote, "Where peaceful means had failed, one act of militancy succeeded and never again was the cause ignored by that or any other newspaper."

Following this publicity success, she became increasingly militant in her quest for votes for women. She justified her militancy with legal arguments, saying that because force is justified when one is acting in self-defense, it is justified for women who are acting in defense of their rights as citizens. Because of her defiant stance and personal charisma, the newspapers nicknamed her "Queen Christabel," and she became one of the first British celebrities who was not from royal or theatrical backgrounds. Although some suffrage workers complained that her arrogant demeanor detracted from the legitimacy of their cause, most found her compelling. Rupprecht noted that Annie Kenney said, "If the world were on one side and Christabel Pankhurst on the other, I would walk straight over to Christabel Pankhurst." Activist Grace Roe said, "I would follow her anywhere."

Pankhurst decided to limit the efforts of the WSPU solely to the cause of obtaining votes for women and to aim her recruitment efforts at middle- and upper-class women. Her sister, Sylvia Pankhurst, was opposed to both of these tactics; she believed they were turning the WPSU into an elitist group that ignored the many other issues that working-class women had to face. Pankhurst argued that wealthier women had the power to change things for all women, and that suffrage was such an important issue that it should not be diluted by other causes. In addition, she noted, if women got the vote, it would give them the ability to change all the other issues.

However, the WPSU did attack the traditional sexual oppression of women, because Pankhurst believed it was the basis for British culture's refusal to allow women to vote. According to Rupprecht, she wrote, "The inferiority of women is a hideous lie which has been enforced by law and woven into the British constitution." She also spoke out against cultural values that held that the actions of sexually active woman should be viewed as prostitution, while those of a sexually active man should be applauded or, at the worst, simply overlooked. Espousing a chaste lifestyle for men and women, she summed up her cause by saying "Votes for women, chastity for men!"

After a demonstration in 1910 in which protesters were beaten, maimed, and in two cases killed, WSPU protests became more violent. Pankhurst and her supporters viewed themselves as fighting in a civil war against the patriarchal British system. So many WSPU leaders were arrested as a result of this increased militancy that Christabel had to flee to Paris in disguise in order not to be imprisoned. While in France, however, she lost touch with what was really going on in Britain and became increasingly dogmatic and visionary rather than practical. While in Paris, she joined the lesbian feminist circle of Princess Edmond de Polignac.

When World War I began in 1914, she was convinced that the suffrage cause was almost won and returned to England to turn the WSPU into a patriotic group that would rescue women from their own patriarchy. She believed that if the British government took her up on this offer to help, it would have to give the vote to women; if it did not, she warned, she and her group would resume their militant action as soon as the war was over. In 1918, the British Representation of the People Act allowed women over 30 and men over 25 to vote. This inequality of age was made equal in 1928.

Once women gained voting rights, Pankhurst was free to work for other causes. She ran for Parliament as a coalition candidate for Smethwick, an industrial area. She was defeated by a tight margin, winning 8,614 votes, the most of any woman who ran in the election, which incidentally was the first English election that women were allowed to participate in. She was galled by the fact that Nancy Astor, who had won far fewer votes and who had done nothing for the cause of women, nevertheless won a seat in Parliament because of her personal and social connections. Pankhurst ran for election to Parliament again but did not win. Soon after, she retired from politics.

In 1919, the Parliament passed the Sex Disqualification Act in 1919, which would allow Pankhurst and other female lawyers to practice law, but she was no longer interested in this career. Instead, she began writing *The Confessions of Christabel,* a series of articles on the WSPU published in the *Weekly Dispatch.* Confession #1 explained that she had never married because of her "personal unending unyieldingness as a leader." Another confession was an attack on journalists who claimed that it was not the WSPU that had gained votes for women, but the effect of women's work during the war, which had changed attitudes toward women.

In 1921, she placed advertisements in various newspapers, asking for "non-personal employment." She received many offers, including some from film companies, but found none interesting. In the same year, she visited her mother in Canada and the United States, where she became interested in Second Adventism, a religious movement that proclaimed the Second Coming of Christ. Between 1922 and 1926 she published three Second Adventist books, *The Lord Cometh!, Pressing Problems of the Closing Age,* and *The World's Unrest of Visions of the Dawn.* The books, which expressed her shift toward political conservatism as well as her belief that the end of the world was near, were quite popular in religious circles in both Britain and the United States, and when she gave a series of lectures at Knox Presbyterian Church in Toronto, Ontario, huge crowds gathered to hear her.

In 1926, at the urging of Emmeline Pankhurst, she went to the French Riviera, where together they opened a tea shop, but it soon failed, and they returned to England together. In 1928, Emmeline died; it was a great loss for Christabel, and she spent the next two years in deep grief.

By 1930 she was feeling better enough to adopt a daughter, Betty, and then resumed preaching the Second Adventist gospel in Britain, as well as supporting candidates for the Conservative Party. She was still a compelling and popular speaker, and she was able to fill the 10,000-seat Royal Albert Hall to overflowing several times when speaking on the Second Coming.

In 1936 she was proclaimed a Dame Commander of the British Empire, an honor she was proud of for the rest of her life. In 1940 she moved to the United States, where her daughter Betty had previously emigrated. She settled in Santa Monica, California, where, Rupprecht reported, she was viewed as "a strange combination of former suffragist revolutionary, evangelical Christian and almost stereotypically proper 'English lady' who always was in demand as a lecturer. During World War II her popularity on the religious speaking circuit increased, and when television became widespread, she was a frequent guest on California public affairs broadcasts.

Pankhurst's financial security in later life was assured when an aged British widow, Olivia Durand-Deacon, was brutally murdered and her body dissolved in an acid bath by her male companion. For unknown reasons, she had bequeathed the sum of 250 pounds per year to Pankhurst.

Although Pankhurst was involved in a car accident not long after this, she survived her serious injuries and completely recovered. Thus, her housekeeper was shocked on February 13, 1958, to find her dead, sitting upright in a straight-backed chair with no indication of how she had died. With the exception of the automobile accident, she had never been sick and was never ill before her death.

Of her career as a feminist, Fulford noted, "Christabel Pankhurst, at a time when women were still excluded from whole regions of the national life, made forcibly plain to all the world that this exclusion could no longer be maintained." According to Marina Warner in *Time,* at the start of her activist career, she said, "We are driven to this. We are determined to go on with this agitation. It is our duty to make this world a better place for women."

Books

Commaire, Anne, and Deborah Klezner, *Women in World History,* Volume 12, Yorkin Publishers, 2001.

Raven, Susan, and Alison Weir, *Women of Achievement,* Harmony Books, 1981.

Williams, E. T., and Helen M. Palmer, editors, *Dictionary of National Biography, 1951-1960,* Oxford University Press, 1971.

Periodicals

Time, June 14, 1999, p. 176. □

Mary Engle Pennington

Mary Engle Pennington (1872-1952), a chemist and bacteriologist, was a pioneer in the advancement of

the preservation of perishable foods during the first half of the 20th century.

Mary Engle Pennington was born on October 8, 1872, in Nashville, Tennessee, the elder of two daughters born to Henry and Sarah B. (Molony) Pennington. A few years after her birth, Pennington's family moved to Philadelphia, Pennsylvania, to be closer to her mother's relatives, a well-to-do Quaker family. Her father established a successful business in label manufacturing, and the family lived in a three-story red brick house near the University of Pennsylvania. Her parents were very supportive of their daughters and encouraged them to pursue their interests. As a youngster, Pennington learned to garden, a hobby she shared with her father and maintained throughout her life.

Pennington also enjoyed reading and spent considerable time at the public library. When she was 12 years old, she came across a book on medical chemistry that sparked her interest, and she spent the summer studying the chapter on nitrogen and oxygen. "Suddenly, one day," Pennington told the New Yorker in 1941, "I realized, lickity hoop, that although I couldn't touch, taste, or smell them they really existed. It was a milestone." Unfortunately, in the late 19th century, girls were discouraged from studying science. When she approached the headmistress at the all-girl boarding school she attended and demanded that she receive instruction in chemistry, Pennington was flatly denied—

such pursuits by women were considered wholly inappropriate and decidedly unladylike.

Studied Chemistry and Biology

When Pennington returned from school in 1890, her desire to study chemistry was unabated. Refusing to concede to the social standards of the time, the 18-year-old woman went to the dean of the University of Pennsylvania and asked that she be admitted to the school of science. The dean was impressed and agreed, and Pennington became a student of the university's Towne Scientific School, where she studied chemistry, biology, and hygiene. Two years later she completed the requirements necessary for a bachelor's degree; however, the board of trustees, who disapproved of a woman's presence at the university, refused to grant her a diploma. Instead, she was given a certificate of proficiency in biology.

Because she did not hold a bachelor's degree, Pennington was ineligible for graduate studies. This technicality was circumvented with the support of the faculty who invoked a seldom-used university statute that allowed special students to be enrolled in graduate studies in extraordinary cases. Thus, Pennington became a doctoral student in the university's electrochemical school and studied under Edgar Fahs Smith. She was awarded a Ph.D. in 1895; her dissertation was a study of the derivatives of the elements columbium and tantalum. After spending an additional two years at the University of Pennsylvania studying chemical botany, Pennington accepted a one-year fellowship at Yale University, where she studied physiological chemistry, teaming with Russell Chittenden to examine the effect colored light had on plant growth.

A Bacteriological Chemist

In 1898 Pennington returned to Philadelphia and accepted a position as an instructor in physiological chemistry at Women's Medical College, a position she retained until 1906. At the same time she began making plans to open her own business. Securing commitments from some 400 local doctors, each of whom agreed to give her at least $50 in business annually, Pennington partnered with university colleague Elizabeth Atkinson and opened the doors to the Philadelphia Clinical Laboratory in 1901. The laboratory, which conducted bacteriological and chemical analyses, was quite successful, and Pennington began to develop a reputation for her work.

In 1904 she was asked to head the bacteriological laboratory for the Philadelphia Department of Health and Charities. There Pennington focused the energies of her small staff on the problem of unsafe milk. Carefully examining all phases of milk production, she established basic standards for the industry that were adopted first statewide and eventually throughout the country. She also studied the preservation of milk at low temperatures. During this time, Pennington's persuasive abilities came to light. With no laws to enforce safe handling or storage, she nonetheless convinced local ice cream vendors who sold their good from carts mainly to children to adopt more sanitary measures by showing the vendors microscopic slides of the bacteria growth on their equipment. Convinced, vendors agreed to disinfect their pots and utensils by boiling them.

Created Standards in Food Safety and Handling

At the turn of the 20th century, refrigerated foods were highly suspect among the public. As cities grew, the demand for foods transported over longer distances and stored for longer periods of time also increased. However, there existed no standards for safe food handling or storage. As a result, many refrigerated or frozen products that entered the market were not safe. Hundreds died and thousands more became ill every year after consuming spoiled foods. Of special concern were eggs, milk, poultry, and fish. Along with the safety issues, the public complained that preserved perishables were poor in quality and taste, arriving either dried out or moldy. Pennington entered the field of refrigeration in 1905 when Dr. Harvey W. Wiley, a family friend and chief of the U.S. Department of Agriculture's Bureau of Chemistry, asked her to join his staff and study the effects of refrigeration on behavior of perishable foods.

The passage of the landmark Pure Food and Drug Act in 1906 was the beginning of government regulation of food safety. However, no standards existed and the terms "safe" and "unsafe" lacked scientific definition, thereby rendering the new law unenforceable. As a result the Bureau of Chemistry decided to establish the Food Research Laboratory, which would conduct research that would provide scientific standards for food safety, particularly for milk, poultry, eggs, and fish. The data collected would be used both as evidence in the prosecution of food dealers who failed to comply with the act and as a resource for those in the industry who desired to implement reforms to avoid coming under the scrutiny of the government.

Chief of the Food Research Laboratory

Wiley believed Pennington was the perfect person to head up the new laboratory. However, she remained skeptical that the government would award the position of chief of the Food Research Laboratory to a woman. Wiley nonetheless convinced her at least to take the Civil Service examination required for the position. Unbeknownst to Pennington, Wiley submitted her exam under the name M. E. Pennington, a fact that later infuriated Pennington when she found out. She scored highest on the exam and was offered the job. Upon her acceptance, the Civil Service discovered that M. E. Pennington was in fact Ms. Pennington and the offer was revoked. However, Wiley stepped in on her behalf and convinced the Civil Service to hire Pennington despite her gender.

Wishing to remain outside the fray of Washington politics, Pennington set up her office in the same building that housed the Philadelphia Clinical Laboratory and then got busy with her assignment. She studied every stage through which chicken passes on the way to the consumer, including the slaughterhouse and packinghouse, during transport from the wholesaler to the retailer, and the storage conditions provided by the retailer. Pennington believed that in order for cold-stored poultry to arrive safely on the con-

sumer's supper table, each step of the process must provide a properly refrigerated and hygienic environment. She also examined the poultry carefully to discover the signs of deterioration. She took note of visual changes in color and texture and performed chemical and microscopic examinations to detect other changes, such as fat acidity. Her research led her to establish that poultry could be safely stored and retain a high quality of flavor for up to one year at a temperature of zero degrees Fahrenheit.

Through her hands-on research in slaughtering chickens, Pennington established that piercing the chicken's brain with a small knife and cutting the jugular veins from the inside was more effective than the traditional block-and-axe method because, for reasons unknown, piercing the chickens made them easier to pluck, thus causing less damage to the chickens before transporting them. The process also left the chickens intact, which lessened the chance of bacterial growth. Along with changing the basic strategy for slaughtering poultry, she also transformed the transportation system. Chickens were normally packed in barrels of chipped ice to be shipped. However, by the time they arrived, the chickens were often waterlogged, floating in tepid water. Pennington devised a way to extract the heat from the slaughtered chickens so that they could then be dry-packed in boxes and transported in refrigerated train cars.

During her tenure with the Food Research Laboratory, Pennington instituted basic standards for the sanitary handling of eggs. She encouraged farmers to collect eggs, which are highly perishable, more frequently in warm weather and is credited with the invention of the modern egg crate, which she designed to protect the eggs in transport. In 1911 the H. J. Keith Egg Company sued the U.S. Department of Agriculture (USDA) for libel after the USDA seized over 400 cans of liquid eggs declared to be dangerously decomposed. Cracked, oversized, or otherwise scarred eggs were commonly shipped to egg-breaking plants where they were frozen, canned, or dried and then sold to bakers and confectioners. The unsanitary practices of the egg-breakers led to high levels of bacteria in the product. Because no legal or scientific standards existed to back the government's claims, the USDA called upon Pennington to investigate. Once again, she started from the very beginning, at the farms that produced the eggs, and followed the eggs into the egg-breaking plants and through the transportation system.

Due to flaws in the legal wording of the Pure Food Act, the USDA lost its court battle against H. J. Keith. However, Pennington won over the egg-breaking industry using her natural gift of persuasion and scientific logic. She convinced three plants to adopt her methods of sanitization and refrigeration, arguing that such ventures would earn the public's trust. When those plants were overwhelmed with orders, other egg-breakers followed suit. According to Lisa Mae Robinson in *Agricultural History*, Pennington relied on "personal persuasion of individual plant owners and warehousemen to improve conditions and encourage stricter standards. She encouraged these people to see that their livelihood depended on consumer confidence in their products and that such confidence could only be won by turning out a superior product."

Along with substantially affecting the poultry and egg industries, Pennington also reformed the methods of processing fresh fish. She created a standardized system for scaling, skinning, quick-freezing, and dry-packing the fish immediately after they were caught.

Advancements in Refrigeration

During World War I Pennington served as a consultant for the Perishable Products Division of the U.S. Food Administration. The government had 40,000 refrigerated train cars available for transporting perishables. Research conducted by Pennington revealed that only 3,000 of those cars had proper air circulation and refrigeration. After taking some 500 train trips, during which Pennington studied the effects of extreme heat and cold on a variety of perishables, she established the important link between humidity and food preservation. According to Ethlie Ann Vare and Greg Ptacek in *Mothers of Invention,* "Pennington didn't actually invent refrigeration, but she made it workable. Like the atmosphere outside, air within a refrigerated locker would lose its ability to hold moisture as it approached freezing temperature. The result was dried-out food; yet, when humidity was increased, the food became moldy." By monitoring humidity levels, along with attending to proper insulation and air circulation, the quality of refrigerated foods could be greatly enhanced. Pennington was awarded a Notable Service Medal in 1919 for her contribution to the war effort.

Became Independent Consultant

In 1919 Pennington left the Food Research Laboratory and moved to New York to run the research department of the American Balsa Company, a manufacturer of insulation. Three years later she opened a business as a consultant to food storage and shipping companies. Highly successful, by 1936 she had moved her office to the prestigious Woolworth Building. She studied frozen foods and developed improvements for commercial and home refrigeration systems. She even managed to convince several major universities to incorporate courses on household refrigeration. With no textbooks to be had, Pennington then created 13 pamphlets, with such catchy titles as "Journeys with Refrigerated Foods" and "The Romance of Ice," to be used in the classroom.

Pennington never married and was a lifelong active member of the Society of Friends. She wrote numerous articles and technical papers during her career and co-authored *Eggs* (1933). She also held two patents with A. B. Davis for insulating material. During the final years of her life, she enjoyed knitting, sewing, and gardening on the terrace of her Riverside Drive penthouse, which she shared with a Persian cat named Bonny. Her kitchen was completely electric, uncommon at the time, and she proudly ate frozen, refrigerated, and canned products as part of her everyday diet. Pennington, who never retired from her consulting business, died of a heart attack on December 27, 1952. She was buried in Philadelphia.

Books

Garraty, John A., and Mark C. Carnes, editors, *American National Biography,* Oxford University Press, 1999.

McGrath, Kimberly A., editor, *World of Invention,* 2nd edition, Gale, 1999.

McMurray, Emily, J., editor, *Notable 20th-Century Scientists,* Gale, 1995.

Shearer, Benjamin F., and Barbara S. Shearer, editors, *Notable Women in the Physical Sciences: A Biographical Dictionary,* Greenwood Press, 1997.

Vare, Ethlie Ann, and Greg Ptacek, *Mothers of Invention. From the Bra to the Bomb: Forgotten Women and Their Unforgettable Ideas,* Morrow, 1987.

Zierdt-Warshaw, Linda, Alan Winkler, and Leonard Bernstein. *American Women in Technology: An Encyclopedia,* ABC-CLIO, 2000.

Periodicals

Agricultural History, Spring 1990.
New Yorker, September 6, 1941. □

William Pinkney

U.S. senator and statesman William Pinkney (1764-1822) was notable for his support of the Missouri Compromise, a piece of legislation designed to restrict the advance of slavery that was passed by Congress in 1820.

William Pinkney began his career as an attorney but quickly entered the realm of politics as a congressman in his home state of Maryland. His talent for public speaking attracted the attention of presidents from Washington to Madison, gaining Pinkney promotion to U.S. diplomat and his ultimate election as a U.S. senator. Among his most noteworthy accomplishments in the political arena was his skill in negotiating the Missouri Compromise of 1819, although this was eclipsed in the mind of legal scholars by his defense of such landmark cases as *McCulloch vs. Maryland.* He appeared before the U.S. Supreme Court over seventy times before his death in 1822 and was the acknowledged leader of the U.S. bar throughout his career.

The Son of British Sympathizers

Pinkney was born in Annapolis, Maryland, on March 17, 1764. His father, born in England and still loyal to the English crown, incurred the wrath of many of his colonial neighbors after the colonies declared independence in 1776. During the Revolutionary War he, like many other loyalists, had his lands confiscated. Thirteen-year-old Pinkney, who had by now begun his studies at the King Williams School in Annapolis, left school due to his family's newfound poverty and began what would become a lifelong course of independent study and learning. A few years later Pinkney sought out the tutelage of a Baltimore physician and began the study of medicine. While debating medical

Began Dual Career as Attorney and Statesman

While representing his region in the legislative realm, Pinkney retained his law practice and became known for his unrestrained oratory and his obvious delight in gaining the spotlight. Considered almost snobbish by some contemporaries, Pinkney's manner of dress was considered almost foppish in his delight with fashion and rich textiles, and this characteristic became more extreme as he aged. In his later years Pinkney, who insisted on the best in food and spirit, resorted to a corset to present a more slender figure and used cosmetics to accentuate his features. Despite his vanity, he presented a striking figure, and in 1796 President George Washington appointed Pinkney as joint commissioner, along with fellow attorney Christopher Gore, to London, where the United States wished to argue its right to claim international maritime losses under the Jay Treaty. Although the work of the two men ultimately proved unsuccessful in promoting American interests, Pinkney spent his free time immersing himself in the classics, in British law, and in the study of history and literature. He also began what proved to be a lifelong interest in dictionaries and lexicons.

Upon his return home eight years later in 1804, Pinkney was heralded for an unrelated victory in successfully defending the state of Maryland in its efforts to regain monies held by a British Bank. His victory in this court action, begun by Chase several years before, proved a book to the reestablishment of Pinkney's private law practice, now located in Baltimore. In December of 1805 he was appointed Maryland's attorney-general, but after six months he resigned this post to return to private practice.

Pinkney's study of British law and his involvement in litigation surrounding the Jay Treaty made him something of an expert in defending American maritime interests. When British Admiralty courts began to exact punishment on the former colonies by condemning and confiscating the cargoes of certain U.S. ships under an invalid article of war, Pinkney authored a legal strategy against this action and submitted it to Congress. His *Memorial of the Merchants of Baltimore, on the Violation of Our Neutral Rights* resulted in his appointment by President Thomas Jefferson to act as an emissary to the English Parliament. Together with then foreign minister James Monroe, Pinkney debated both the matter of war reparations and the legality of the impressment—the coercive or forced enlistment—of American sailors by the English Navy. While Pinkney and Monroe managed to gain a signed agreement from Parliament, it failed to include three conditions stipulated by Jefferson, and it was never even submitted to Congress for ratification.

Tired of Diplomacy, Returned to Law

During this stay in England in the company of Monroe, Pinkney gained the political connections and experience necessary to assume his fellow commissioner's post as U.S. Minister to England after Monroe was transferred to Madrid, Spain, in October of 1807. Frustrated by an obstinate Parliament still resentful over the loss of its former colonies, by the British Admiralty's authorization of attacks upon neutral

matters with his fellow medical students in 1782, Pinkney was overheard by attorney Samuel Chase, a former delegate to the Continental Congress who would be appointed to the U.S. Supreme Court in 1796. Chase was impressed by the eighteen-year-old Pinkney's arguments and oratory and decided to offer the young man the chance to train as an attorney. Pinkney joined Chase in February of 1783 and was called to the Bar of the state of Maryland in 1786.

Setting up a private law practice in Hartford County, Maryland, Pinkney quickly gained a high profile due to his ambition, his intellect, and the striking appearance he presented in public. Constantly seeking the public eye, he easily fell into the political realm and in the spring of 1788 was elected to the state of Maryland's convention to ratify the U.S. Constitution. Despite the opposition of both Pinkney and his mentor Chase, the Constitution was approved. Despite his unpopular stance at the convention, Pinkney won a seat to the U.S. House of Representatives and served his constituents there beginning in 1788; a term in the Second Congress was cut short by questions regarding Pinkney's right to represent a constituency wherein he had no established residence and he resigned after only a few months. In 1789, a year after becoming a member of Congress, Pinkney married Ann Maria Rodgers, with whom he would have ten children.

U.S. ships during England's war with French emperor Napoleon, and the active opposition of pro-British constituents at home, Pinkney ended negotiations, resigned his post, and returned home four years later, in February of 1811. Despite the fact that Pinkney's skills as a diplomat did not match his acumen as an attorney, the tensions between the United States and England were undoubtedly incapable of being diminished by the efforts of a single man; they erupted a year later in the War of 1812.

Upon his return home, Pinkney was recognized for what he did best; he was appointed attorney-general to President James Madison. After war broke out, the thirty-eight-year-old statesman left his post to become a major in the Maryland militia. His decision to do so was prompted as much by Congress's request that he relocate his home to Washington, D.C. as it was by enthusiasm for the battlefield. Wounded at the battle of Bladensburg shortly after enlisting in 1814, he returned to civilian life, and his work before the Maryland Supreme Court quickly found him back in politics. Serving in Congress briefly from March of 1815 to the following spring, he once again retired to pursue U.S. diplomatic interests, this time as U.S. Minister Plenipotentiary to Russia. Eastern Europe proved a less entertaining prospect than had London, and Pinkney quickly handled the business at hand—recalling all Russian diplomats in the United States following the arrest by a Russian consul named Kosloff, broaching the possibility of a commercial treaty with Russia, and establishing more amicable relations with that country. He quickly returned to the United States and the practice of law. Pinkney was elected to the U.S. Senate in December of 1819 to fill a vacancy resulting from the death of Senator Alexander Contee Hanson and retained his position in Congress until his death three years later in 1822.

Preserved the Stability of a Fragile Union

During Pinkney's three years as a senator he made his most significant contribution to U.S. history. By the early nineteenth century slavery had already begun to loom as an issue that threatened to divide the country along regional lines, and it was revisited repeatedly as new regions made application for statehood. The application for statehood made by the Missouri territory in 1819 threatened to disrupt the balance between slave states and free states. Pinkney, eloquently representing the interest of the slave-holding states, helped to draft what became known as the Missouri Compromise, which allowed Missouri's admission as a slave state to be balanced by Maine's admission as a free state and made the concession to the north of prohibiting slavery in the sections of the Louisiana Purchase that would later become Kansas and Nebraska. While the Missouri Compromise helped to maintain a tenuous union among the states until the mid-1850s, the Supreme Court's 1857 ruling in the case of the runaway slave Dred Scott overturned this ruling by claiming that the Missouri Compromise unfairly deprived citizens of their property—in this case the slave Scott—and was unconstitutional. This ruling was one of the many factors precipitating the U.S. Civil War only three years later.

Despite his dedication to serving his country, Pinkney's true love remained the law, which provided a showcase for his intellect and his many skills as a speaker. His arguments made before the U.S. Supreme court during the final two decades of his thirty-six years as a practicing attorney remain some of the most respected in U.S. legal history. Among the seventy-two cases he argued before the Supreme Court are many landmarks, the most notable being *McCulloch vs. Maryland* and *Cohens vs. Virginia*. Brought before the court in 1819, *McCulloch vs. Maryland* concerned the distribution of power between the states and the federal government and specifically involved the right of the federal government to incorporate a bank and the individual states' rights to tax that bank's branches. James McCulloch, a cashier at the Baltimore branch of the government's Second Bank of the United States, refused to pay the state-levied tax. When the right to tax a federal institution was upheld by the Maryland court, McCulloch appealed to the U.S. Supreme Court. Pinkney's eloquent argument in defense of the plaintiff impressed the Court, which sided with the plaintiff while also rendering a controversial decision that dramatically broadened the powers of the federal government. Argued before Chief Justice John Marshall in 1821, a year before Pinkney's death, *Cohens vs. Virginia* was an attempt to overturn Marshall's ruling in *McCulloch*. While Pinkney's clients won, the underlying attempt failed.

After Pinkney's death in 1822 he was widely eulogized as the most talented attorney of his time. Supreme Court Chief Justices Marshall and Roger Brooke Taney cited his abilities, Taney noting in his *Memoir* that "I have heard almost all the great advocates of the United States, both of the past and present generation, but I have seen none equal to Pinkney." Unfortunately for those who would follow after him, Pinkney never drafted his speeches on paper, but memorized them. His death was a fitting end to his dramatic life: while making final arguments against opposing counsel Daniel Webster in the case of *Richard vs. Williams,* he collapsed on the floor of the U.S. Supreme Court and was carried home to survive only two more days. Following his death on February 25, 1822, at the age of fifty-seven, Pinkney was laid to rest in the Congressional Cemetery; his portrait now hangs in the National Portrait Gallery.

Books

Johnson, Allen, and Dumas Malone, editors, *Dicitonary of American Biography,* Charles Scribner's Sons, 1929.

Tyler, Samuel, editor, *Momoir of Roger Brooke Taney,* 1876.

Van Doren, Charles, editor, *Webster's American Biographies,* G. & C. Merriam Company, 1979.

Wheaton, Henry, *Some Account of the Life, Writings, and Speeches of William Pinkney,* E. J. Coale, 1826.

Online

Shapiro, Steven M., "William Pinkney: The Supreme Court's Greatest Advocate," *Appellate.Net,* http://www.appellate.net (July, 1999). □

Martín Alonso Pinzón

Spanish navigator and explorer Martín Alonso Pinzón (1441-1493) captained the *Pinta* during Genoese explorer Christopher Columbus's first voyage to the New World in 1492.

In 1492 when Christopher Columbus set out aboard the *Santa Maria* on the voyage that made him known for centuries afterward as the man who discovered the New World, he was accompanied by Martín Alonso Pinzón, a former explorer in his own right, who captained the *Pinta*. An accomplished navigator and seaman, Pinzón was ruled by ambitions shared by many such men, including Columbus: the thirst for wealth, glory, and the approval of royalty. While for some such ambitions led to glory, such was not the case for Pinzón. Due to what Columbus described as frequent disobedience and Pinzón's abandonment of the small squadron in search of personal glory, he became known as the man who thwarted the Italian's efforts and died in relative disgrace. Often unmentioned in history texts is Pinzón's role as financial backer of Columbus's voyage— he was the co-owner of both the *Niña* and the *Pinta*—and the factor this played in his actions during the journey.

Destined for a Seafaring Life

Pinzón was born in 1441 in Palos de Moguer, a seaport town in the Spanish province of Andalusia. He was the eldest son of a wealthy family of seafarers and shipowners, and he became a strong, capable sailor and skillful pilot himself. In the prime of his career, under Cousin, a navigator from Dieppe, Pinzón sailed to the eastern coast of Africa. There he and his crew followed that continent to the southwest, where they discovered the mouth of a large river. He also sailed in the Mediterranean and had traveled the Atlantic to the Canary Islands.

In the mid-1470s Italian explorer Cristóbal Colón formulated a plan to reach India and the Orient by sailing around the circumference of the earth in the opposite direction. However, he needed funding for what would likely be a costly and uncertain voyage. After the Italian, French, and English crown refused to back him, Colón, or Columbus, as he is most widely known, traveled west across the Pyrenees to Spain, and, after much convincing, in April of 1492 gained the patronage of King Ferdinand of Aragon and Queen Isabella of Castile. With expenses totaling more than Ferdinand and Isabella were willing to bestow, Columbus solicited additional backers, one of which was 51-year-old Pinzón, who fronted part of the money needed to purchase supplies for the voyage as well as a part-interest in both the *Niña* and the *Pinta*.

Several years before meeting Columbus, Pinzón had retired from active life as a sailor, and set up shop as a shipbuilder. According to some sources, he became acquainted with Columbus through Franciscan Father Juan Perez, prior of the convent of La Rábida. Other historians argue that, while in Rome years before, Pinzón learned about a country named Vineland, and realized that there were land masses that had yet to be discovered. Curious, he examined charts in the possession of the Vatican that were drawn up by Norman explorers years earlier. Whatever his initial reason or motive, Pinzón became an enthusiastic backer of the voyage and when asked by Queen Isabella's advisors for his opinion regarding the proposed voyage he expressed confidence in Columbus. He also paid the Italian the sum of one-eighth of the anticipated expenses of the trip. In addition, it was through his efforts that a crew of men with skills and temperament suitable for such an arduous voyage was secured.

Set Sail for China and the Indies

On August 3, 1492, Columbus set sail from Palos, Spain; his squadron of three ships contained 120 men. Columbus commanded the flagship, the *Santa Maria,* while in the smaller *Pinta*, Pinzón captained his crew of 26 men. Pinzón's younger brother Vicente Yanez Pinzón served as commander of the 24-man crew of the *Niña,* while yet another brother, Francisco Martin Pinzón, worked under Martín as pilot or first mate. The largest of the three ships, the cumbersome *Santa Maria* was a full-rigged ship that weighed about 100 tons and measured approximately 100 feet from stem to stern. Forty crewmen served aboard the *Santa Maria,* which covered a distance of approximately 150 miles in a day.

The *Niña* and the *Pinta* were caravels: lighter, faster, and more maneuverable that the squadron flagship. The *Pinta* was a three-masted, square rigger 70 feet in length, with a mast rising 26 feet in the air and a draft—the depth of water a loaded ship requires in order to float—of less than eight feet. Together with its two companion ships, the *Pinta* made for the Canary Islands but, three days out of Palos, dropped its rudder and was forced to limp along with a makeshift device until the 15th, when Pinzón arrived at the Canary Islands to do the necessary repairs.

On September 6, the squadron again weighed anchor and set their course due west. By mid-September Pinzón was actively encouraging Columbus to turn to the north, a move he decided was prudent based upon the rough maps they were sailing by. In the ship's log for September 18, 1492, Columbus describes the captain of the *Pinta* as "very resourceful, but his independence disturbs me somewhat." Pinzón had sailed some distance ahead of Columbus for the greater part of two days—"I trust that this tendency to strike out on his own does not continue, for we can ill afford to become separated this far from home."

Land Ho!

Under Columbus's orders, the three ships maintained a course westward, but on October 7 Pinzón convinced the commander to alter their direction to southwest, where he remained convinced they would find land. The mood aboard all three ships was dour; as Columbus noted in his log as early as September 24, "the more God shows the men manifest signs that we are near land, the more their impatience and inconstancy increases." Fearful of losing his life at the hands of a crew loyal to Pinzón and his brothers, Columbus expressed his concern in the ship's log: "I know that Martín Alonso cannot be trusted. . . . he wants the rewards and honors of this enterprise for himself. . . . But I am fully aware that I must use him, for his support is too great among the men." On the night of October 11 land was sighted and at first light the squadron had its first view of the "Indies:" it had reached the Bahamas. Columbus and his crew rowed to the nearest of several land masses, probably Watling's Island although it has yet to be agreed upon by historians. Before a group of native Taino (a branch of the Arawak), who had never before seen such curious folk as these Europeans, Columbus claimed the island for the king and queen of Spain and named this island San Salvador. Expeditions to the surrounding islands of the Bahamas during the next few weeks resulted in the discovery of Cuba, which Columbus named Juana in honor of the Spanish princess.

On November 21, 1492, Pinzón abandoned his squadron and sailed off on his own from San Salvador. "I think he believes that an Indian I had placed on the *Pinta* could lead him to much gold," wrote Columbus in his log that night, "so he departed without waiting and without the excuse of bad weather." Making for an island called Babeque (Great Inagua), Pinzón hoped to find gold or valuable spices, but was disappointed to find no such things upon landing. Meanwhile, Columbus reached la Isla Espanola (Hispaniola; now Haiti) on December 5. Columbus believed this land to be "Cipango" (Japan), based on the map he and Pinzón both carried during the voyage. If this was indeed Cipango, he reasoned, then China lay only slightly further to the west! But where?

Finding no riches on Babeque, Pinzón turned as well toward la Isla Española, landing there at Puerto Blanco, a distance away from his captain. After finding some gold inland, he and his men returned, having received word that tragedy had befallen the squadron. On Christmas Eve 1492, during Pinzón's temporary desertion of Columbus, the *Santa Maria* had been driven ashore by rough seas and sank on a coral bed two miles off the coast of Isla Espanola. With the *Pinta* currently at large, Columbus did not have sufficient room aboard ship to house the 39 men now stranded. Using the planking and other objects salvaged from the ship, his men built a rustic fort at La Navidad (now Caracol Bay) and the *Niña* became the new flagship. Following Pinzón's return with the *Pinta,* he came aboard the *Niña* to apologize. "He gave many reasons for his departure but they are all false," wrote an angry Columbus. "Pinzón acted with greed and arrogance . . . and I do not know why he has been so disloyal and untrustworthy toward me on this voyage." On la Isla Espanola Pinzón is reported to have captured four men and two young girls, perhaps with the intention of enslaving them. On January 16, with the squadron now turned for Spain and home, Pinzón was requested by Columbus to clothe the six captured Haitians and return them to their island home; as the admiral reasoned, "honor and favor must be shown to the people, since there is so much gold on this island and such good lands and so much spice." Pinzón would later excuse his absence near Haiti as a result of bad weather.

Difficult Homecoming Fraught with Contention

Passing through the Antilles during the trip home to Spain, Pinzón once again abandoned Columbus, although the reasons for this remain unclear. As the two ships sailed off the coast of the Azores in mid-February, a storm hit, lasting for several days. Whether Pinzón became lost in the storm or intentionally deserted in an attempt to beat Columbus in bringing news of the discovery to Ferdinand and Isabella is not known. In either case, he returned to Spain by a separate course and arrived at the northwestern port of Bayone in early March. Perhaps believing Columbus to have perished at sea, or attempting to gain an audience in advance of the Italian, Pinzón immediately sent a letter to King Ferdinand describing the discovery of the new world. Not waiting for a reply, he continued on to Palos, which he reached on March 15, 1493. Ironically, he was only a few hours behind Columbus, who had arrived in Spain after just avoiding imprisonment at the hands of the king of Portugal. Because Columbus had already informed the king about the discovery of the Indies, Ferdinand refused Pinzón an audience in favor of one with Columbus. Despite extreme fatigue, the elderly Pinzón planned to set out immediately for Madrid to make a fresh attempt to see the king, but was met by a messenger who forbade him to appear at court.

Columbus was received by Ferdinand and Isabella with great honor on March 15, 1493. Some historians believe that had Pinzón been present to tell his side of the story of the discovery of the New World, Columbus's star may not have shined so brightly. His tendency toward embellishment, as well as his antagonisms toward many men he formerly held as friends, suggest that he may have portrayed his fellow captain unfairly in the pages of his logbooks. Columbus made four more voyages to the New World, reaching Dominica and the coast of South America before retiring in 1504. He died a year later and was buried in a monastery in Seville, although his remains were eventually reintered in Santa Dominga, Hispaniola, before being returning to Spain in 1899.

For Pinzón there was no such future. Exhausted, angry, and disheartened after his return voyage, he is also reported to have also suffered from syphilis. He died at his birthplace, Palos de Moguer days after his return in late March of 1493. His younger brother Vicente Yáñez Pinzón became famous for exploring the coasts of Brazil and Central America from 1500 to 1509 and was appointed governor of Puerto Rico in 1505. The *Pinta* too went on to make several Atlantic crossings and was commanded by Vicente Pinzón while serving as the flagship for the discovery of the Amazon river. In July of 1500, the ship was caught in a hurricane and went down in the vicinity of the Turks and Caicos Islands.

In the early 1920s British historian William Giles Nash argued that a man named Alonso Sanchez was the true discoverer of the New World and that it was only through the support of Martín Alonso Pinzón that Columbus was able to follow in Sanchez's path and claim the status as discover of the Americas.

Books

Columbus, Christopher, *The Log of Christopher Columbus,* translated by Robert H. Fuson, International Marine Publishing, 1987.

Fernández-Armesto, Felipe, *Columbus,* Oxford University Press, 1991.

Frye, John, *Los otros: Columbus and the Three Who Made His Enterprise of the Indies Succeed,* E. Mellen Press, 1992.

Marchena Colombo, Jos, *Martín Alonso Pinzón,* Imprenta Editorial de la Gavidia (Seville, Spain), 1942.

Morison, Samuel Eliot, *The European Discovery of America: The Southern Voyages,* Oxford University Press, 1974.

Nash, William Giles, *America, The True History of Its Discovery,* G. Richards (London, England), 1924.

Taviani, Paolo Emilio, *Columbus: The Great Adventure: His Life, His Times, and His Voyages,* translated by Luciano F. Farina and Marc A. Beckwith, Orion, 1991. □

Vicente Yáñez Pinzón

Spanish navigator Vicente Yáñez Pinzón (1463-1514) captained the ship *Niña* during Italian explorer Christopher Columbus's first expedition to the New World in 1492 and went on to participate in the exploration of Brazil, becoming that nation's first governor.

When 15th-century Genoese-born explorer Christopher Columbus embarked upon the voyage that would change the course of world history, he traveled with a crew of what he considered foreigners. Funded by the king of Spain rather than Italy, he headed what was essentially a Spanish expedition. From the helm of the flagship *Santa Maria,* Columbus benefited from the navigational skills of the brothers Pinzón in captaining the two remaining ships in his small squadron. Martín Alonso Pinzón, destined to become a thorn in Columbus's side during the voyage, was in charge of the *Pinta* while the less volatile Vicente Yáñez Pinzón captained the *Niña.* While Martín died, dishonored, shortly after his return from the New World, Vicente went on to distinguish himself as an explorer in his own right in subsequent years and is credited with the discovery of the Brazilian mainland and being the first European to sail up the mouth of the Amazon River.

Grew Up in Sight of the Sea

Pinzón was born in 1443 in the Spanish seaport town of Palos de Muguer. Raised in comfortable circumstances, he was one of a long line of seafarers and shipowners, and as a child he spent many hours on the sea. Hearing tales of faroff lands and the wonders—and wealth—they contained from men who, like his much older brother Martín, had explored Africa and the Mediterranean, Vicente caught the spirit of adventure that characterized the age of exploration. He also became skilled in navigation and developed into a talented captain.

The spring of 1492 found the 30-year-old Pinzón at work in the family shipbuilding trade when he was approached by his brother Martín, 20 years his senior, with a proposition. An Italian explorer named Cristóbal Colón had just been granted funding from King Ferdinand V and Queen Isabella of Spain and was planning a voyage to India and the Orient by a very novel means: he planned to sail around the circumference of the earth in the opposite direction and had several rudimentary maps to guide him. Martín had already provided the Italian with much-needed additional funding; now he was helping him secure a competent crew. Would Vicente be interested?

Set Sail for China and Fabled West Indies

Vicente, of course, quickly became an enthusiastic participant in Columbus's expedition, and when the squadron of three ships set sail from Palos, Spain, on August 3, 1492, he was among the estimated 120 men on board. Columbus commanded the flagship *Santa Maria,* while Vicente took charge of the *Niña* and its crew of 24. In the *Pinta* was Martín Alonso Pinzón, who counted among his 26 men yet another Pinzón, his first mate and youngest brother Francisco Martín Pinzón. The largest of the three ships, the cumbersome *Santa Maria* was a full-rigged ship that weighed in at over 100 tons and measured approximately 100 feet from stem to stern. Slow due to her size and large crew, she could cover only 150 miles per day under the best of sailing conditions. The *Niña* and the *Pinta* were caravels; smaller and lighter than the *Santa Maria,* they were also far more maneuverable and capable of maintaining greater speeds. The four-masted *Niña* was 67 feet long, her 21-foot mast the shortest in Columbus's small fleet, and her shallow draft allowed her to anchor close to shore and maneuver in less than seven feet of water. The only ship of the three to carry arms, the *Niña* was outfitted with ten breech-loading *bombardas* or swivel guns.

After weeks of sailing, land was sighted on October 11th, and the next day Columbus, the Pinzóns, and the rest of the crew set foot in the New World, believed to be India but which was later determined to be an island in the Bahamas, probably Watling's Island. Columbus and his men explored several islands in the region, including Cuba and Haiti (Hispaniola), and in front of curious groups of native Arawaks claimed each piece of land they set foot on as the property of Ferdinand and Isabella of Spain. Cuba was named Juana in honor of the Spanish princess.

On November 21, 1492, Vicente's brother Martín rashly abandoned his squadron, a controversial move that ultimately destroyed his reputation and which left the *Niña* and *Santa Maria* anchored off the coast of San Salvador. A month later, on December 24, the *Santa Maria* ran aground on a coral reef two miles off the Haitian coast, where it quickly capsized and filled with water. With the *Pinta*'s whereabouts unknown—Martín by then had done some exploring on his own and was anchored much further up the coast of Haiti—Vicente Pinzón prudently refused to allow the 39 crewmembers of the damaged ship to come aboard the *Niña* and thereby compromise her seaworthiness. Columbus became captain of the *Niña* and ordered that planks be salvaged from the first known shipwreck in the New World and a shelter be constructed on shore for those crewmen now without shelter. Leaving these men well-provisioned at this new fort, named La Navidad, he ordered that the *Niña* set sail for home. In the nick of time Martín returned with the *Pinta,* arriving on January 6, and ten days later the squadron set sail for Spain. After a difficult voyage the *Niña* made a safer return, and on March 15, 1493, Columbus was received by Ferdinand and Isabella with great pomp and ceremony. Vicente Pinzón was also recognized for performing his duty as captain of his craft, although Martín was disgraced and died, probably of syphilis, shortly after reaching Spain.

Discovered Brazil and the Amazon River

Although loyal to Columbus as his commanding officer throughout the course of the voyage, Vicente Pinzón resented what he considered to be the captain's unfair treatment of his brother. He continued to maintain, as did many others, that Martín Alonso Pinzón was due equal credit for the discovery of the New World. After several attempts to embark on a second voyage westward were canceled by bad weather, Pinzón joined mapmaker Juan de la Costa in obtaining the concession needed from the Spanish crown to make a second trip to Cuba in the spring of 1499. It is reported that on this voyage the two men circumnavigated Cuba, thereby negating Columbus's contention that Cuba was part of a large mainland rather than an island. Upon his return to Spain, Pinzón sought the backing of a wealthy patron and in December 1499 was outfitted and ready to set sail again from Palos as captain of his brother's former ship, the trusty *Pinta.* Under Pinzón was a squadron of four caravels, including the flagship *Pinta* manned by a crew of 75, all of whom signed on with the promise of a share of any riches found. The squadron sailed to the Caribbean and arrived without incident within four weeks. Reaching the coast of Brazil and landing at Cabo Santa Maria de la Consolacion, near what is now Pernambuco, on January 26, 1500, Pinzón and his crew followed the Brazilian coast northward, eventually reaching the mouth of the Orinoco river in what would eventually become Venezuela. During this part of his voyage he became the first European to enter the Amazon, which he mistook for the Ganges of India due to the inaccuracy of his map. Encountering groups of native Arawaks, Pinzón accomplished what his late brother had wished to do on Columbus's first voyage: he acquired a great quantity of gold, as well as emeralds and pearls, through trades. By July, with his four ships fully laden, Pinzón and his men decided to turn northward and begin their return trip to Spain. During a stop off the coast of Haiti he encountered Columbus, now on his third voyage, whose efforts to colonize the area were proving problematic due to the animosity developing between the Arawaks and the European interlopers. In late July of 1500 Pinzón's good luck finally ran out, as the *Pinta* was lost, caught in a hurricane while anchored near the Turks and Caicos Islands. She sank, fully loaded with gold and jewels, along with another ship, the *Frailia.* Suffering the loss of many men and now with only two somewhat battered ships remaining,

Pinzón limped back to Palos, arriving there in October. Two years later, during a subsequent voyage, he made an effort to salvage the cargo of the two vessels lost on this expedition, but no record remains regarding the success or failure of this attempt. Instead, he reported of success in trade, as he anchored in the Gulf of Paria and traded with the native tribes for gold and other valuables. Turning southeast toward the South American continent, Pinzón made the return trip to Spain via Santo Domingo where in July of 1504 he encountered a distraught Columbus, now on what would be the Italian's final voyage.

Received Numerous Honors from Spanish Crown

On April 24, 1505, in honor of his success on behalf of Spain, Pinzón was appointed governor of Brazil by Ferdinand and Isabella. Despite this honor, no record survives of the navigator actually taking over his duties. Instead, Pinzón continued to return to the sea. In a voyage of discovery begun in 1506 he traced Columbus's route through Central America, this time due to the urging of the Spanish king who was eager to find new trade routes to the Orient. Two years later, in 1508 he was jointly commissioned with Juan de Solis to set sail for South America. Jointly in command of the *Isabeleta* and the larger *Magdalena,* their movements at sea would be the will of de Solis, while Pinzón had command on land. The two men's search for an interoceanic strait through South America proved fruitless and they returned within the year, each blaming the other for the lack of success. This trip would be Pinzón's final voyage. He died several years later, in 1514, at his family's home in Palos, at the age of fifty one. Remembered as one of the most skillful navigators of his age, he remained respected by both his crew and his king, thereby restoring honor to the family name.

Several years after his death, Pinzón's renown prompted Holy Roman Emperor and king of Spain Charles V (1500-1558) to honor him by presenting the Pinzón family with their own coat of arms. The name Pinzón remained well known in the New World, as sons of Vicente and his brothers served as navigators for later Spanish, Portuguese, French, and English governments. Some Pinzóns acquired sizeable land grants in Spanish-controlled Cuba, Texas, Mexico, and Florida, and one branch was known to have settled the Commonwealth of Virginia after migrating from Spain to England during the 16th century.

Books

Columbus, Christopher, *The Log of Christopher Columbus,* translated by Robert H. Fuson, International Marine Publishing, 1987.

Fernández-Armesto, Felipe, *Columbus,* Oxford University Press, 1991.

Frye, John, *Los otros: Columbus and the Three Who Made His Enterprise of the Indies Succeed,* E. Mellen Press, 1992.

Morison, Samuel Eliot, *The European Discovery of America: The Southern Voyages,* Oxford University Press, 1974.

Taviani, Paolo Emilio, *Columbus: The Great Adventure: His Life, His Times, and His Voyages,* translated by Luciano F. Farina and Marc A. Beckwith, Orion, 1991. □

R

Jean-Pierre Rampal

One of the greatest flutists of all time, Jean-Pierre Rampal (1922-2000) introduced the flute as a solo instrument to audiences around the world, drawing audiences comparable to those attracted by piano and violin virtuosos. His technical genius and artistic brilliance won for his instrument a popularity even greater than it had enjoyed during the Baroque period. For much of his career, Rampal averaged 120 concerts a year.

Jean-Pierre Louis Rampal was born on January 7, 1922, in the southern French port city of Marseilles. Son of Joseph (a flute professor and performer) and Andree Roggero Rampal, he was not drawn to music early, despite his father's career in music. Throughout his childhood, he dreamed instead of a career in medicine and only reluctantly did he take up the flute at age 13 when his father—equally reluctantly—began giving him lessons. His father only consented to teach his son when he needed additional students to fill out his class at the Marseilles Conservatory. The senior Rampal and his wife both wanted their son to find a life outside music, which they considered an unreliable means of support. Despite his lack of enthusiasm about the flute and music in general, young Rampal showed a natural talent for the instrument and advanced rapidly. He played second chair flute in the Classical Concert Orchestra of Marseilles and made his professional solo debut at the Salle Mazenod in Marseilles when he was only 16. Although he was well received in his premiere recital, the audience calling for several encores, Rampal remained fixated on a life in medicine, preferably as a surgeon. After graduating from Marseilles' Lycee Thiers (the equivalent of high school) with a degree in letters and philosophy in 1939, Rampal began his studies toward a pre-medical degree at the University of Marseilles.

Of his father's influence, Rampal wrote in his autobiography, "I worshipped my father and wanted to be like him. In his wisdom, he permitted me to develop my own style. I often played pieces too difficult for me, and my father was sometimes angry. I played everything in the music library and was so excited. I was really walking like a giant. . . . My father taught me how to nurture my musical talent and also how to lead my life. He said to walk out on the stage knowing that you are the best, and when you are finished and walk off the stage, always know that there is someone better. My father's influence, encouragement, and example have stayed with me all my life."

War Brought Change in Plans

Under the Nazi occupation of France, Rampal faced mandatory service in the German military but managed to avoid it—at least for a time—by joining the Chantiers de Jeunesse, which he later described as a kind of "Boy Scout army without arms." He received permission from the group to audition at the Paris Conservatory and was selected for admission after the first round of auditions. Rampal asked that his admission to the conservatory be deferred for a year. Shortly thereafter, however, he learned that his unit was going to be sent to Germany for forced labor only days after his scheduled return to Marseilles. Desperate to remain in France, Rampal went into hiding. With the help of his extended family, he managed to elude German authorities for a year until he could enter the Paris Conservatory. He felt certain he would be safe once he began classes there, be-

Flute's Popularity Soared

Not since the Baroque period, which stretched from roughly 1600 to about 1750, had the flute found such favor with the general public as it did in the years following World War II. In an interview with David Wright of the *New York Times,* Rampal himself offered this explanation for the ascendancy of Baroque-style music—and with it, the flute—after the war: "With all this bad mess we had in Europe during the war, people were looking for something quieter, more structured, more well balanced than Romantic music." As for the specific appeal of the flute, Rampal told the *Chicago Tribune:* "For me, the flute is really the sound of humanity, the sound of man flowing, completely free from his body almost without an intermediary.... Playing the flute is not as direct as singing, but it's nearly the same."

During a rehearsal for a 1946 performance of Mozart's "Concerto for Flute and Harp" at the spa in Vichy, Rampal was introduced to Francoise-Anne Bacqueyrisse, the 17-year-old daughter of harpist Odette le Dentu, with whom he was to play. In his autobiography, Rampal admitted that about a week after meeting Francoise, he told her: "If I weren't engaged already, I'd ask you to marry me," to which she replied: "If I weren't engaged as well, I might have accepted." Prior commitments notwithstanding, Rampal and Francoise were married on June 7, 1947. Like her mother, Francoise was a harpist, but she abandoned her musical career to manage the Rampal household. For his part, Rampal deeply valued his wife's support and insight. Of Francoise, he wrote: "She is my severest critic, but she believed in me from the beginning. . . . She has inspired my work and my life. It was the best thing I ever did when I married her." Rampal and Francoise had two children, Isabelle and Jean-Jacques, both of whom grew up to become amateur musicians.

From the earliest years of his career, Rampal recorded extensively. Strong record sales in the 1950s earned him two Grand Prix du Disque awards, while his concert appearances across Europe and Asia won for him the Oscar du Premier Virtuose Français in 1956. In 1958 he made his U.S. debut with a performance at the Library of Congress in Washington, D.C. Writing in the *Washington Star,* critic Day Thorpe observed: "Although I have heard many great flute players, the magic of Rampal still seems to be unique. In his hands, the flute is three or four music makers—dark and ominous, bright and pastoral, gay and salty, amorous and limpid. The virtuosity of the technique in rapid passages simply cannot be indicated in words."

Toured the World

Once he'd made his debut in the United States, he toured the country frequently, making appearances with the leading symphony orchestras of Boston, Chicago, Cincinnati, Dallas, Detroit, Indianapolis, Houston, Los Angeles, Minneapolis, New York, San Diego, and San Francisco. In addition to his solo performances on the flute, Rampal occasionally conducted the orchestras with which he appeared. He appeared in all the world's major musical venues, including London's Royal Albert Hall, Carnegie Hall and Avery Fisher Hall in New York City, the Holly-

cause the school's director, Claude Delvincourt, had earned a reputation for sheltering illegal students in the past. In 1944, after only five months of study, Rampal won first prize in the conservatory's annual flute competition.

Suddenly Rampal discarded his plans for a life in medicine. "I decided to be a flute player," he later explained in *Instrumentalist.* "Up until I was 21 I had thought my future was to be a surgeon, no doubt about it. But then I changed my mind. . . . Suddenly I just knew that I would be unable to do anything but music. . . . I was excited but also upset, because I didn't want to disappoint my parents by leaving medical studies. Finally I did it." Upon graduation from the conservatory, Rampal won a job with the prestigious orchestra of the Paris Opera, rapidly working his way to the chair of principal flutist. After the liberation of Paris in 1945 he was invited by French National Radio to perform Jacques Ibert's "Concerto for Flute" in a national broadcast that helped to launch Rampal's concert career. It was during the latter half of the 1940s that Rampal developed the musical relationships that were to play a significant role in his life for decades. He engaged pianist Robert Veyron-Lacroix as his accompanist, a collaboration that continued for 35 years. In 1946 Rampal founded the French Wind Quintet, a group that remained active until the early 1960s. Two years later he organized the Paris Baroque Ensemble, which lasted until the late 1970s.

wood Bowl in Los Angeles, Paris's Theatre de Champs-Elysees, and the Kennedy Center in Washington, as well as smaller halls on four continents.

Rampal's ventures into music other than the classics sometimes brought criticism from musical purists, but it widened the flutist's audience. In the very early 1970s, collaborating with harpist Lily Laskine, he released an album of Japanese folk songs that was eventually named record of the year in Japan. Even more successful was Rampal's collaboration with French jazz artist Claude Bolling. Their album together—the *Bolling Suite* album—was enormously successful in the mid-1970s and gave Rampal a much higher profile with the general public. In the wake of this commercial success, Rampal was invited to appear on Jim Henson's *Muppet Show,* where he performed ''Ease on down the Road'' from *The Wiz* with Miss Piggy. Other musical forms explored by Rampal included English folk songs and the music of India. A number of France's best-known 20th-century composers wrote works specifically for him. These included Jean Françaix, André Jolivet, Jean Martinon, Francois Poulenc, and Pierre Boulez. In the early 1990s he debuted the ''Flute Concerto'' of Krzsztof Penderecki.

Rampal appeared on the Sony label from the 1970s until the end of his life, recording almost every major work for the flute. Among his better-known recordings were the flute concertos and sonatas of Johann Sebastian Bach and the flute concertos and quartets of Wolfgang Amadeus Mozart, as well as the flute compositions of Franz Joseph Hadyn, Antonio Vivaldi, Georg Philipp Telemann, and such lesser-known composers as Johann Kuhnau, Boccherini, Giuliani, and Carulli. In 1982 Rampal's longtime accompanist Robert Veryron-Lacroix retired because of ill health and was replaced by American pianist John Steele Ritter. In his appearances around the world, Rampal played one of his two trademark 14-carat gold flutes—not an affectation or a gimmick but a simple preference for the sound produced by instruments crafted from the precious metal.

When he was not touring the world, Rampal and his wife shared a home on the Avenue Mozart in Paris, where their child and their families visited them often. The end came suddenly for Rampal, who died in Paris of heart failure on May 20, 2000. One of the first to note Rampal's passing was French President Jacques Chirac, who was quoted in the *Washington Times* as saying that ''his flute . . . spoke to the heart. A light in the musical world has just flickered out.'' Issac Stern, who had collaborated extensively with Rampal, was quoted in the same article as recalling: ''Working with him was pure pleasure, sheer joy, exuberance. He was one of the great musicians of our time, who really changed the world's perception of the flute as a solo instrument.'' Fellow flutist and musical commentator Eugenia Zukerman observed: ''He played with such a rich palette of color in a way that few people had done before and no one since. He had an ability to imbue sound with texture and clarity and emotional content. He was a dazzling virtuoso, but more than anything he was a supreme poet.''

Books

Contemporary Musicians, Gale, 1991.

Newsmakers, Gale, 1989.
Rampal, Jean-Pierre, *Music, My Love,* Random House, 1989.

Periodicals

American Record Guide, July 1, 2001.
Minneapolis Star Tribune, May 21, 2000.
U.S. News & World Report, June 5, 2000.
Washington Times, May 21, 2000.

Online

Sony Classical Web site, http://www.sonyclassical.com/ (January 31, 2002).
Jean-Pierre Rampal Web site, http://www.mindspring.com/~fsimone/ (January 21, 2002). □

Nicholas Ray

American-born film director Nicholas Ray (1911-1979) rose to prominence in the 1950s with such films as *Johnny Guitar, They Live by Night,* and his best-known work, *Rebel Without a Cause,* which transformed leading man James Dean into an American icon. He often portrayed the sensitive, troubled outsider, a heroic figure thwarted by life and love in a dysfunctional postwar society. Although he directed more than 20 feature films between 1948 and his death in 1979, Ray's most critically acclaimed works were made between 1952 and 1955.

Trained in Theater

Ray was born Raymond Nicholas Kienzle on August 7, 1911, in the Wisconsin town of Galesville, near La Crosse. Suspended from high school on several occasions, he nonetheless showed himself to be a gifted and intelligent teen and was accepted to the University of Chicago in 1930, the same year he married a young woman named Jean Evans.

Reconfiguring his name as Nicholas Ray, he attended college for less than a year. An interest in visual design prompted him to spend several months under the wing of noted architect and arts supporter Frank Lloyd Wright; a move to New York in 1932 drew him into the left-wing theater community. Involved in Elia Kazan's Theater of Action from 1935 to 1937, he made his acting debut on the New York stage before transferring to director John Houseman's Phoenix Theatre troupe. Ray gained technical experience in a production by Joseph Losey for the Depression-era Federal Theater Project. In 1942, following the start of World War II, Ray became involved in radio when Houseman found him a job as program director for the Office of War Information. He also continued his work with theatre and directed his first play in 1943.

Ray's work in New York provided him with the connections into film, and by 1944 he was living in Hollywood. His first movie job was as an assistant on Kazan's *A Tree Grows in Brooklyn.* Assisting on several other films and in early television, Ray also directed a play on Broadway. Houseman gave him the chance to direct his first solo film, and Ray signed a contract with RKO Studios. Ray's *They Live by Night* was based on the novel *Thieves Like Us* by Edward Anderson and released in Great Britain as *The Twisted Road.* Filmed in grainy black and white, it is an outlaw film infused with sympathy for its main characters, a bank robber duo played by Farley Granger and Cathy O'Donnell. The criminal lovers flee across the rural Midwest, the law hot on their trail, and desperately grasp for fleeting moments of peace as their destiny spirals out of control. In a review of the film for the *Chicago Tribune,* Michael Wilmington noted that *They Live by Night* is "permeated with a sweetness and vulnerability unusual for any crime movie."

Days with RKO

Ray's directorial debut was not a success at the box office. His next production for RKO was the 1949 murder mystery *A Woman's Secret,* which starred noir actress Gloria Grahame. During the film Ray, who had divorced his first wife, married his leading lady. Grahame divorced her own husband and married Ray later that same day. The couple survived four tumultuous years of marriage—years made more difficult because of Ray's lifelong battle with alcoholism—before divorcing in 1952. Ray would marry twice more, to dancer Betty Schwab and finally to Susan Ray, with whom he would have four children. In 1961 Grahame married Ray's oldest son, Anthony Ray.

In 1949 Ray was hired to direct popular actor Humphrey Bogart in *Knock on Any Door,* a drama about an attorney hired to defend a juvenile delinquent played by John Derek. Bogart and Grahame starred in Ray's next movie, *In a Lonely Place,* a 1950 noir film that focuses on a successful screenwriter charged with murder. Through Bogart's troubled, violent protagonist, Ray showed the ill effects of nonconformity, as the screenwriter, by nature a loner, found himself branded as an outsider by the police, by colleagues, and even by former friends.

The theme of *In a Lonely Place,* which Ray explored again in later works such as *On Dangerous Ground* and *Johnny Guitar,* reflected Ray's attitude about the McCarthyism of the 1940s and 1950s. While RKO owner Howard Hughes sheltered his stable of directors from the blacklist sparked by Senator Joseph P. McCarthy's efforts to purge the nation of what he believed was a Communist menace, Ray watched the destruction of the careers of many talented Hollywood actors and directors, including his former mentor Elia Kazan.

In appreciation for Hughes's protection, Ray directed several films for RKO in quick succession: *Born to Be Bad,* about two ruthless women who stop at nothing to win a battle over a man; the John Wayne vehicle *The Flying Leathernecks* (1951); the highly praised 1951 noir *On Dangerous Ground* starring Robert Ryan and Ida Lupino as a troubled young outcast and the woman who shelters him; and *The Lusty Men,* a western about the competing affections of rodeo riders Robert Mitchum and Arthur Kennedy for the beautiful Susan Hayward. After all this work for RKO, Ray decided to leave the studio in 1953, a year after *The Lusty Men* was released.

Championed the Outsider

Out from under Hughes's thumb, Ray found himself free to expand on his developing noir vision. The result was 1954's *Johnny Guitar,* a stylish western produced by Republic Pictures that starred Sterling Hayden. With its somewhat stiff, stylized approach, subversive sexual undercurrents, and quasi-melodramatic story line, *Johnny Guitar* also introduced the symbolic use of color that characterized many subsequent Ray films. Even more so than *In a Lonely Place,* the film is considered to be a strong cinematic statement condemning the injustices of the McCarthy-era witch hunts.

The quality of Ray's films during the mid- to late 1950s—particularly those made after the release of *Johnny Guitar*—prompted critics to reexamine his early work, and he gained cult status in the United States and also in Europe, especially among Jean-Luc Godard and other France New Wave directors and critics. Well-known actors continued to appear in his films. His 1955 father-and-son drama *Run for Cover* featured young John Derek alongside veteran actor James Cagney. While considered a good film, *Run for Cover* would be quickly eclipsed by the notoriety surrounding Ray's next film.

Rebel Without a Cause

Ray's eye for color, movement, and setting that was so apparent to audiences of *Johnny Guitar*—and which would become even more pronounced in 1958's *Party Girl*—meshed seamlessly with the director's fascination with the psychology of loneliness in his landmark film *Rebel Without a Cause*. Released in 1955 and shot in vivid color in a wide-screen format, the film starred James Dean, Natalie Wood, and Sal Mineo, three of the most popular young actors of the era. As portrayed by the leather-jacketed Dean, protagonist Jim Stark enters adulthood in suburban Los Angeles, the little guidance he receives from his distant father supplemented by his supportive but equally estranged and futureless friends. Stark is the epitome of teenage rebellion, and the movie culminates in classic 1950s fashion: in a deadly game of chicken behind the wheel of a souped-up hot-rod. Dean's tragically similar death a month before the film's release helped transform Ray's motion picture into an immediate classic. *Rebel Without a Cause* earned three Academy Award nominations, including one for Ray's screenplay.

Rebel Without a Cause was, for Ray, an impossible act to follow, but he continued on undaunted, filming *Bigger than Life* (1956), *Bitter Victory* (1957), and other motion pictures of less renown. For several years he worked in Europe but returned to the United States to film the garish 1958 gangland flick *Party Girl,* his last Hollywood film. Ray returned to Europe after making 1959's *The Savage Innocents* and tackled the life of Jesus in the popular 1961 epic drama *King of Kings*. Although his stature in the United States was diminished, European critics continued to praise Ray's work.

Ill Health Ended Career

Ray returned to the epic format of *King of Kings* for 1963's *55 Days at Peking*. A story about the 1900 Boxer Rebellion in China, the big-budget film was shot in Madrid, where noted opera designers Veniero Colasani and John Moore created the city of Peking in the suburb of Las Matas. The Oscar-nominated score by Dimitri Tiomkin was equally lavish.

The pressure of directing the epic took its toll on the 52-year-old director. Although he made a brief appearance in the film as a wheelchair-bound foreign ambassador, Ray suffered a heart attack and left the set before the film was completed, leaving director Andrew Marton to shoot the battle scenes. Many critics panned *55 Days at Peking* as confusing, and Ray realized his mainstream career was at an end. He remained in Europe, where he was still well known, until an offer to shoot a documentary drew him back into the United States. The documentary was never completed, and financial circumstances forced Ray to remain in the United States.

During the 1970s Ray taught courses on film at the State University of New York at Binghamton, worked with students on film productions, and cooperated with German director Wim Wenders in the making of a 1974 documentary, *I'm a Stranger Here Myself*. The title was taken from a line in *Johnny Guitar*. In 1977, Ray was diagnosed with lung cancer. As the illness took its toll, he managed small acting roles in films such as Wenders's *Der Amerikanische Freund* and Milos Forman's 1979 production *Hair*. *Guardian* reviewer Derek Malcolm described Ray as "a tragic, neglected figure surrounded by obsequious young acolytes." Wenders, a tremendous fan of Ray, made a documentary about him, *Lightning over Water (Nick's Movie),* that contained interviews with the director in his last days. It was released in 1980, a year after Ray's death. Containing lectures, interviews, and other writings, Ray's autobiography, *I Was Interrupted: Nicholas Ray on Making Movies,* was edited by his widow Susan Ray and released in 1993.

Books

International Dictionary of Films and Filmmakers, 3rd edition, Volume 2: Directors, St. James Press, 1996.
Kreidl, John Francis, *Nicholas Ray,* Twayne, 1977.
Ray, Nicholas, *I Was Interrupted: Nicholas Ray on Making Movies,* University of California Press, 1993.

Periodicals

Cahiers du cinema, no. 66, 1956; November, 1958; January, 1962; January, 1985.
Chicago Tribune, May 29, 1998.
Film Comment, September/October 1973.
Film Quarterly, Fall 1974.
Guardian (London, England), March 25, 1999.
New York Times, June 18, 1979.
Sight and Sound, Autumn 1973; no. 4, 1979; spring, 1981; Autumn, 1986. □

Jean Renoir

French-born Jean Renoir (1894-1979) directed two of the twentieth century's most critically acclaimed films, *La Grande Illusion* and *La Regle du jeu (Rules of the Game),* and is credited with inspiring the subsequent film noir and French New Wave cinematic movements.

The son of Impressionist painter Pierre Auguste Renoir, Jean Renoir today seems predestined to become one of film's most visually compelling directors. While mastering such signature visual styles as deep focus for the respective mise-en-scenes of his body of work, Renoir's reputation is for his films that depict "life as a tissue of disappointments," in which the boundaries of human comedy and tragedy seamlessly overlap. Rather than offer subjective moral observations of his characters, however, Renoir held firmly to the dictum that "Everyone has their reasons," which freed him from exploring character motivations and the inevitable long-term results of their actions. Instead, his films force the viewer to witness the actions of his actors—most of whom display both positive and negative qualities—in relation to the situations in which he places them. He underscores this dramatic element by allowing the audience to acknowledge that they are observing

the characters' actions from a camera's perspective, framing the action so that the characters may freely walk off camera. The combination of the actions of Renoir's characters freed from motivations and consequences, and his technique of filming them so that the audience is conscious of the camera's presence is acknowledged by critics as a profound method to display the complexities of humanity as being neither completely good nor completely evil, prompting Jay Carr to note: "The films of Jean Renoir never land heavy on the eye or the spirit. There are no conquering heroes in them. Identifying profoundly with uncertainty and frailty, Renoir became the poet of chaos theory. He humanized it long before existentialism and physics got their hands on it." Renoir's career as a filmmaker is commonly divided into several groups: His silent pictures which display the cinematic influences of directors Erich von Stroheim and Charlie Chaplin and featuring Renoir's first wife; his early sound pictures in which he adapted plays and novels; his films of political engagement, communism, and pacifism made just before the outbreak of World War II; his films made during his tenure in Hollywood; and his films made following his return to Europe that celebrate European history.

Born into an Artist's Family

As the son and model of an enormously successful and wealthy painter, Renoir enjoyed a childhood surrounded by art and artists. His father's success and exacting critical standards, however, intimidated Renoir, and he sought to distance himself from his father's artistic milieu. He attended several schools, including the College de Sainte-

Croix, Neuilly-sur-Seine, 1902; Ecole Sainte-Marie de Monceau, 1903; and the University of Aix-en-Provence, where he earned a degree in mathematics and philosophy in 1913.

Seeking to distance himself from his father's fame at the onset of World War I, Renoir enlisted in the French cavalry in 1914. He nearly lost a leg in battle, however, and transferred to the French Flying Corps in 1916. His pilot duties included aerial photographing of German troop movements. After aggravating his leg injury during a particularly bad landing of his aircraft, Renoir was sent back to Paris to work behind the lines as a full lieutenant until 1918. While he recuperated, he entertained himself by attending the Parisian movie houses. After the war, he expressed his intent to become a ceramic artist.

An Undistinguished Silent Film Director

Following the war, Renoir married Andree (Dedee) Madeleine Heuchling, who adopted the stage and screen name Catherine Hessling when her husband began making films. Renoir explained his decision to become a filmmaker: "I set foot in the world of the cinema only in order to make my wife a star, intending, once this was done to return to my pottery studio. I did not foresee that once I had been caught in the machinery I should never be able to escape. If anyone had told me that I was to devote all my money and all my energies to the making of films I should have been amazed."

Renoir financed his first films by selling paintings by his father. For these films, he served as producer, screenwriter, financier, and actor. In 1924, Renoir directed *La Fille de l'eau,* a melodrama starring Hessling. Unable to obtain distribution for the film and nearly bankrupt as a result, Renoir resigned himself to running a ceramic gallery and studio. His retirement from film was premature, however, as evidenced by the inclusion of a surreal dream sequence from *La Fille de l'eau* in a revue of film excerpts compiled by Jean Tedesco. The overwhelmingly positive audience reaction convinced Renoir to continue his vocation, and he soon adapted Emile Zola's novel *Nana* and Hans Christian Anderson's *The Little Match Girl.* He also accepted assignments to direct *Marquitta* for the Artistes Reunis production company; the slapstick war comedy *Tire au flanc;* and two films for Henry Dupuy-Mazuel, *Le Tournoi* and *La Bled.* The latter film was shot on location in Algeria.

Primarily influenced by the films of D. W. Griffith, Charlie Chaplin, and Erich von Stroheim, Renoir's first films were "more interesting for their technical innovations and visual inventiveness," according to Martin O'Shaughnessy. In several of these films, he pioneered the use of the camera as a narrative device with a limited frame of reference and objective point of view. By allowing characters to move freely outside of the camera frame, Renoir displayed the limitations of the cinematic narrative, making the audience aware that it is incumbent upon them to engage their intellect while viewing the film. The films are noted also for their use of outdoor-location photography, an element that became an essential component of many of Renoir's subsequent sound films.

First Sound Pictures

Renoir's first sound films are noted for his development of mobile panning and tracking shots in which the camera follows the movements of the characters. In these films, he adapted his screenplays from such sources as popular theater and fiction. In order to secure financing, however, he needed to convince possible monetary backers that he could make films economically by writing and directing *On purge bebe,* an adaptation of an Ernest Feydeau play concerning a constipated baby and the adults who accidentally ingest the baby's laxative. The film's success afforded Renoir the opportunity to direct *La Chienne,* a comedy about an adulterous relationship between a married banker and a prostitute that leads to murder. Based on a novel by Georges de la Fouchardiere, the film generally is considered Renoir's first important work.

His next film, *Boudo Saved from Drowning,* based on a play by Rene Fauchois, is a lampoon of bourgeoisie life, concerning a bum who alters the life of a middle-class family and narrowly escapes marriage. This successful comedy was followed by adaptations of Gustave Flaubert's *Madame Bovary* and Georges Simenon's *La Nuit du carrefour,* the first film appearance of Simenon's most famous character, Inspector Magritte.

Politically Engaged Films

The political climate in Europe during the 1930s inevitably impacted the remainder of Renoir's films of the decade. The Spanish Civil War, the rise of Fascism in Italy, the increasingly vocal Socialist and Communist parties in France, and a firsthand experience of Nazism in Germany—where he witnessed Nazi soldiers force a Jewish woman to lick the ground—caused Renoir to confront contemporary issues in *Toni, Le Crime de Monsieur Lange,* and *La Vie est a nous.* The latter film was a Socialist collaborative effort between directors Jean-Paul Le Chanois and Jacques Becker that combines drama and documentary. He also attempted to create cinematic representations of his father's paintings in *A Day in the Country,* which was not edited and released until after World War II because he had to leave the film in order to fulfill a contractual obligation to direct *Les Bas-Fonds.* Renoir claimed that he never completed *A Day in the Country,* but critics consider it to subtly convey Renoir's pantheistic tendencies, genius as a visual artist, and political sensibilities.

Critics generally acknowledge Renoir's next film, *La Grande Illusion,* as a masterpiece of war cinema. Starring Erich von Stroheim as the commandant of a prison-camp, the film presents a powerful pacifist argument. *Rules of the Game,* however, is considered Renoir's cinematic triumph, a film that displays how the venality of human nature can create situations where violence and war can erupt. Each of the characters is presented in a sympathetic way, prompting Jay Carr to note: "Subtle, prismatic, acute, infinitely embracing, *Rules of the Game* is one of the century's undisputed masterworks. Renoir thought he was reworking Beaumarchais and de Musset, but *Rules of the Game*—right down to its figure of the little poacher bringing mischievous nature indoors—seems kin to Shakespeare's *Midsummer Night's Dream.* It is a sublime comedy of the mutability of human feelings that manages, without ever becoming sentimental, to turn into a celebration of humankind.''

Hollywood and Later Films

Renoir left France for America in 1940. He arrived in Hollywood, where he made several films that he—and many critics—consider among his weakest due to the restrictive effects of the Hollywood studio system on a director accustomed to working independently. Among the films he made in America are *Swamp Water, This Land Is Mine, The Southerner, The Diary of a Chambermaid,* and *The Woman on the Beach.* Of these films, *The Southerner,* on which he worked with uncredited writer William Faulkner, is considered his best Hollywood film. James Agee, in a June 9, 1945, review, wrote: "When a good man gets a real chance in Hollywood it is not only news; the least one can do is salute those who, aware of the gamble, gave him the money and the chance and protected him in it. So, with pleasure, I salute David Loew and Robert Hakim, thanks to whom Jean Renoir has made *The Southerner,* his own adaptation of George Sessions Perry's *Hold Autumn in Your Hand.* . . . Though its people are exceedingly poor, this is not a political or social 'exposure' of the tenant system, nor does it pay any attention to class or racial friction. It tries simply to be a poetic, realistic chronicle of a farm year's hope, work, need, anxiety, pride, love, disaster, and reward—a chronicle chiefly of soil, seasons, and weather, the only other dramatic conflict being furnished by a pathologically unkind neighbor.''

Renoir's next film was an adaptation of Rummer Godden's novel, *The River,* which he filmed on location in India. The film was beset by illness, bad weather, and cost overruns. While agreeing that his use of color photography is visually compelling, most critics negatively dismissed the film. For the remainder of his career, Renoir made films in France that drew attention largely due to his growing reputation as the director of *La Grande Illusion* and *Rules of the Game.* These films never came close to matching the artistic successes of his previous work, but served as tutorials for the French New Wave cinema movement of the 1950s and 1960s, as well as laying the groundwork for the moral ambiguity displayed in American film noir films of the 1940s and 1950s. Although he never worked with a Hollywood studio, Renoir became an American citizen and lived in California for the remainder of his life.

Books

Agee, James, *Agee on Film: Criticism and Comment on the Movies,* Modern Library: The Movies, Random House, Inc., 2000.

Bergan, Ronald, *Jean Renoir: Projections of Paradise,* The Overlook Press, 1992.

Huffhines, Kathy Schulz, editor, *Foreign Affairs: The National Society of Film Critics' Video Guide to Foreign Films,* Mercury House Incorporated, 1991.

O'Shaughnessy, Martin, *Jean Renoir,* Manchester University Press, 2000.

Sarris, Andrew, editor, *The St. James Film Directors Encyclopedia,* Visible Ink Press, 1998.

Video Hound's Golden Movie Retriever, Visible Ink Press, 1994.

Online

"Jean Renoir," *Contemporary Authors Online,* The Gale Group, 2000.

"Jean Renoir" *Film Reference,* http:www.filmref.com/directors/dirpages/renoir.html.

"Jean Renoir, Director" *French Culture,* http://www.frenchculture.org/cinema/festival/renoir. □

Judith Arlene Resnik

The astronaut Judith A. Resnik (1949-1986) became the second American woman in space in 1984, on the maiden flight of the orbiter *Discovery*. She logged 145 hours in space on that mission, at what should have been the beginning of a promising career. But on January 28, 1986, only seconds after liftoff during her second mission, Resnik died in the tragic explosion of the space shuttle *Challenger*. Six other astronauts perished with her, nine miles above the Atlantic Ocean, leaving a country shocked and mourning.

The daughter of Russian Jewish immigrants, Judith A. Resnik was born (on April 5, 1949) and raised in an affluent neighborhood of Akron, Ohio. Her parents were Marvin Resnik, an optometrist, and Sarah Resnik. She had one brother, Charles, who was four years younger.

Resnik attended Firestone High School in Akron, where she was a diligent student who excelled in mathematics and played classical piano. The valedictorian of Firestone's class of 1966, Resnik was described by friends as popular and meticulous, rolling her hair in orange-juice cans to straighten her curls and attaining perfect scores on her college entrance exams. "She seemed more focused than most of the teenagers I knew," high-school music teacher Pat Pace told the *New York Times*. Raised in a Jewish household, Resnik attended Hebrew school and was bas mitzvahed in a local synagogue. As an adult she did not practice Judaism and disliked any reference to her as "the first Jewish astronaut."

In 1966 Resnik entered Carnegie Tech (now called Carnegie Mellon University) in Pittsburgh, where she planned to major in math. "I was good at math, so I decided to become a math major," she told the *Cleveland Plain Dealer* in 1984. "After a year, math stopped being numbers, which I liked, and started being concepts, which I didn't. So I looked around for the most mathematics-oriented major I could switch to, and that was electrical engineering." As a freshman at Carnegie Tech, Resnik met Michael Oldak, another electrical engineering major, who became her boyfriend. She studied so hard in college that friends teasingly referred to Oldak as "Judy's only extravagance."

The couple married in 1970, the same year Resnik entered a graduate program in electrical engineering at the University of Pennsylvania. When Oldak started law school

at Georgetown in 1971, she attended the University of Maryland as a doctoral candidate. While working toward her degree, Resnik held several jobs. She and Oldak worked together for RCA, designing radar circuits, and Resnik later worked for the National Institutes of Health in Bethesda, Maryland, as a biomedical engineer. By 1977 Resnik was finishing up her Ph.D. in electrical engineering, but on the home front her marriage was ending, in part because Oldak wanted children, but Resnik chose to focus intensely on her career. She and Oldak separated in 1975 and divorced two years later, remaining friends.

Headed for the Stars

Not long after her divorce, Resnik spotted an advertisement for NASA's astronaut program. The then-all-male program, influenced by the affirmative-action movement, was looking for women and minorities with "the right stuff" to become astronauts. NASA was also looking for scientists, or "mission specialists," to conduct experiments in space. On a lark, Resnik decided to apply.

Resnik was not your typical astronaut applicant. Unlike her future coworkers, she did not grow up with dreams of walking on the moon; her decision to apply for the job was the result of a spur-of-the-moment urge, not a lifelong desire. She competed with some 8,000 military and civilian applicants, 1,000 of which were women. Although she did not think NASA would select her, she told friends she was going to fill out the application because she had nothing to lose. "She was looking for a purpose in her life," her father told the *New York Times.* In preparation for her NASA interview, Resnik began a program of exercise and reading. She was particularly anxious about passing the notoriously rigorous physical examination. While NASA considered her application, she also started a new job, relocating to California to work as a systems engineer for the Xerox Corporation.

To her amazement, Resnik found out in January 1978 that she had been selected by NASA to become an astronaut. Her background in electrical engineering had made her a primary candidate for the mission specialists needed to conduct scientific experiments in space. Along with Resnik, five other women were also accepted. The newcomers commenced their one-year training and evaluation period in August 1978, periodically flying from NASA's Houston, Texas, base to Washington, D.C. to log hours in modified flight training. "She was so imbued with the philosophy that space was a coming frontier," her father told the *Washington Post.* "She was the hardest-working astronaut at Johnson Space Center, and they knew it because they always asked her to do more. . . . If I wanted to get her, I'd call her at Johnson Space Center."

By 1979 Resnik had completed the training and evaluation period and had become a mission specialist eligible for assignments on space shuttle flight crews. Her work on the ground included the development of experiment software for astronaut-scientists and the creation of a remote manipulator system, an exterior mechanical arm astronauts could use to perform operations outside the spacecraft.

Spent Seven Days in Space

Of the six new female astronauts, one was destined to become the first American woman in space, but the honor did not go to Resnik. Sally Ride took the title in a 1983 mission of the space shuttle *Challenger.* Resnik was second on the list, and she was promised a role in a mission planned for the following year. On June 26, 1984, Resnik boarded the orbiter *Discovery,* geared up in her spacesuit and ready for her first flight. But it was not to be. Four seconds before liftoff, a fuel valve malfunctioned, and the launch was aborted. Two months later, on August 30, she boarded *Discovery* once again, and this time the orbiter launched without a hitch. Resnik was to spend a week in space as a mission specialist on the *Discovery*'s maiden voyage. Accompanying her were spacecraft commander Hank Hartsfield, pilot Mike Coats, payload specialist Charlie Walker, and fellow mission specialists Steve Hawley and Mike Mullane.

During the mission, Resnik had the job of operating the remote manipulator system she had helped to design. With this exterior mechanical arm, she successfully positioned multimillion-dollar satellites and removed dangerous ice particles from the surface of the *Discovery,* earning her crew the nickname "Icebusters." Other goals of the mission carried out by Resnik and her crewmates were to activate a solar cell wing experiment, to deploy three satellites, and to operate a series of scientific and photographic experiments. Several of these experiments involved using an IMAX motion picture camera.

Watching video images beamed back to Earth from the *Discovery,* viewers could spot Resnik by the dark, curly halo of hair floating up around her in zero gravity. She was serious about her responsibilities, but she could also be playful, holding up a sign that said "Hi Dad!" to the video monitor. The spacecraft completed 36 orbits of Earth during its week-long mission, touching down at Edwards Air Force Base in California on September 5, 1984.

Perished in a Star-crossed Launch

Resnik, who had now passed from a rookie to an experienced astronaut, busily prepared for her second mission, which was to take place a year and a half later. This time she would ride in the space shuttle *Challenger.* Shuttle missions had become fairly routine for NASA, which had completed 24 of them without a hitch. In late January 1986, the launch of the *Challenger* was scheduled to occur any day, but inclement weather and mechanical problems caused several delays. Finally, on the unseasonably cold morning of January 28, in Cape Canaveral, Florida, the launch was set to take place. At 8:35 a.m., Resnik boarded the *Challenger* with her crewmates: Francis "Dick" Scobee, the commander; Michael J. Smith, the pilot; Gregory B. Jarvis, a Hughes Aircraft engineer; Christa McAuliffe, a teacher and the first "private citizen" to accompany a shuttle mission; and two other mission specialists, Ellison Onizuka and Robert McNair. On this mission, Resnik would again have the job of operating the spacecraft's exterior arm. One of her tasks would be the deployment of a satellite designed to study Halley's Comet, which was then approaching Earth.

Among those watching the space shuttle launch were Resnik's father as well as a childhood friend and her family. "Roger, go with throttle up," commander Scobee radioed to mission control. At 11:38 a.m. the *Challenger* roared off the launch pad and into the sky. But after only 73 seconds it became clear that something had gone terribly wrong. The shuttle had carved an arc into the sky, but then suddenly it blossomed into an orange fireball. "Obviously a major malfunction," came an announcement from the public affairs officer. After a long pause the officer added, "We have a report from the flight dynamics officer that the vehicle has exploded."

Throughout the country Americans watched in horror as television stations aired the *Challenger* explosion footage over and over. Debris rained down into the Atlantic Ocean, and it required seven months for recovery teams to retrieve the wreckage. Forty days after the accident, they recovered the crew compartment and discovered that some of the astronauts had been alive during the spacecraft's three- to four-minute plunge into the sea.

Investigations after the explosion revealed that a faulty O-ring seal on the solid rocket fuel booster had led to the demise of the $1.2 billion space shuttle. The O-ring—a $900 synthetic rubber band—had been an object of some concern to engineers because it was vulnerable to changes in temperature. When the *Challenger* launched it was 36 degrees Fahrenheit, cold enough to weaken the O-ring's seal. The decision to go ahead with the launch on such a cold morning had proven fatal for the seven astronauts.

After the tragedy, the U.S. government settled with the victims' families, but less was done for the families of the two unmarried astronauts, Resnik and McNair. Resnik and McNair's families sued the manufacturer of the O-ring, Morton Thiokol, and each family settled for more than $2 million. Resnik's family donated part of the money to the Challenger Center for Space Science in Houston and created scholarship funds in Resnik's name at her former high school and three universities.

Resnik was 36 years old when she perished in the *Challenger* explosion. The unidentified remains of all seven astronauts lie in a memorial in Arlington National Cemetery in Virginia, not far from a famed memorial to an unknown soldier.

Periodicals

Cleveland Plain Dealer, January 28, 1996.
Columbus Dispatch, January 28, 1996.
Life, February 1, 1996.
Los Angeles Times, February 18, 1988.
New York Times, February 9, 1986.
Washington Post, February 2, 1986.

Online

National Aeronautic and Space Administration Web site, http://www.christa.org/ (November 2, 2001). □

Mordecai Richler

One of Canada's most accomplished writers, Mordecai Richler (1931-2001) produced screenplays, novels, children's literature, and essays. At the time of his death, he was acknowledged as Canada's leading curmudgeon for his witty insights on topics such as the Canadian personality and the foibles of Quebec separatism.

Mordecai Richler was a prominent figure on the Canadian literary landscape for more than 40 years after the 1959 publication of his breakthrough novel, *The Apprenticeship of Duddy Kravitz.* Richler was much more than just a popular novelist, however; as a prolific contributor to magazines, movies, and children's literature, Richler probably reached a broader audience than any contemporary Canadian writer. His blunt words on Canadian political affairs also made Richler a household name throughout the country, particularly for his unsparing criticism of the ongoing battles over Quebec sovereignty. His description of the conflict as "Canada's longest running *opera bouffe,* a far from life-and-death struggle over the size of English lettering and outdoor commercial signs in Montreal," in a 1999 Stanley Knowles Lecture at the University of Waterloo was just a sampling of Richler's disdain for the separatist forces in his native province.

St. Urbain Street Childhood

Richler's grandfather, a rabbinical scholar, emigrated to Montreal in 1904 from Galicia, a region then part of the Austro-Hungarian Empire and today split between Poland and the Ukraine. Establishing a scrapyard, the elder Richler gradually built the concern into a successful business that employed some of his fourteen children. Moses Isaac Richler, the eldest of the Richler sons, followed his father into the family business; however, unlike his younger brother, Solly, he was never made a full partner. Moses Richler's failure to achieve as much as his siblings was later explored in the writings of his son, Mordecai Richler, who was born on January 27, 1931.

A family of devout Orthodox Jews, the Richlers lived in the Jewish enclave in Montreal centered around St. Urbain Street; at one time, three generations of the family lived across the street from one another. Richler later immortalized the area in his novel *St. Urbain's Horseman* as a lively, nurturing place despite the economic hardships that many of the residents faced. At home, however, the young Richler was witness to his parents' increasingly unhappy marriage, which he attributed to his father's passive nature. In 1943, his mother, Lily Richler, had the marriage annulled on the grounds that she had been an underage bride and had married without her parents' consent; although Richler and his older brother were then adolescents, the annulment was granted.

Richler was encouraged in his religious studies at a Jewish parochial school; his parents hoped that he might become a rabbi. After entering Baron Byng High School, however, Richler began to develop a more secular identity. Even though Richler's Jewish roots remained central to his identity for the rest of his life, he abandoned most of the Orthodox practices that he had been taught. His greatest rebellion, however, occurred when he abandoned his course work at Sir George Williams College (today known as Concordia University) after his second year. Richler was uninspired by his studies and longed to break free of his provincial life and pursue a career as a writer.

Expatriate Writer

In 1949, after a brief stint on the staff of the Montreal *Herald,* Richler began traveling in Europe and eventually spent an extended time in Paris, where he published his first piece of fiction, "Shades of Darkness (Three Impressions)" in the literary magazine *Points.* Encouraged by this early success, Richler also worked on the manuscript for a novel, *The Acrobats,* about a wandering Canadian idealist inspired by the International Brigades of the Spanish Civil War.

With his pockets empty, Richler returned to Montreal in 1951 while his first manuscript made the rounds of several European publishing houses. He worked as both a salesman and as a radio editor for the Canadian Broadcasting Corporation while he revised *The Acrobats* following its conditional acceptance by a British publisher. In 1954, the book finally was published. It received fairly good reviews, but sold only about 900 copies in its first few years in print in Canada. As Richler recalled in his debut essay in 1958 (reprinted in commemoration of his death in 2001) in *Maclean's,* a Canadian news magazine, "My last royalty statement from New York cost me a good deal of sleep. It covered the last six months in 1956, and in that period two copies of *The Acrobats* had been sold. One domestic and the other Orient. For nights, I was kept awake thinking, 'Who in the hell do I know in the Orient? Would it be possible to trace the buyer? Shouldn't we correspond? Or did he, perhaps, buy the book in error?'"

Richler returned to Europe to take up life as an expatriate writer in London. An early marriage ended in divorce, but his second marriage in 1960, to onetime couture fashion model Florence Wood, lasted until his death; they had three sons and two daughters.

After two more novels that received fairly positive critical notices, yet disappointing sales figures—*Son of a Smaller Hero* in 1955 and *A Choice of Enemies* in 1957—Richler published a breakthrough work, *The Apprenticeship of Duddy Kravitz,* in 1959. Set in Montreal, the novel explored the rise of an ambitious young Jewish man determined to be successful; praised by critics, the book eventually became part of the modern canon of Canadian literature. Richler also established his reputation as a screenwriter for television and film during this period; perhaps his best-known early contribution was his uncredited work on the classic British film on class conflict, *Room at the Top* and his acknowledged work on its sequel, *Life at the Top.*

Demonstrating his versatility as a novelist, Richler published two works of humorous fiction, *The Incomparable*

Atuk (distributed in the United States as *Stick Your Neck Out*) in 1963 and *Cocksure* in 1968. Both works used fish-out-of-water protagonists to illuminate larger observations about contemporary society, particularly the pretensions of the academic and artistic elites. Together with a collection of essays, *Hunting Tigers Under Glass, Cocksure* received the Governor General's Award in 1968, one of the highest honors bestowed by the Canadian government. Richler continued his string of successes with the 1971 publication of *St. Urbain's Horsemen,* which again received the Governor General's Award. A novel that included more autobiographical elements than any of his other fictional works, *St. Urbain's Horsemen* followed the life of an expatriate Canadian living in London as he made sense of his life in middle age.

Canada's Leading Curmudgeon

In 1972, Richler returned to Montreal with his family. He remained a resident of the city—which he claimed was the most culturally sophisticated in Canada—for the rest of his life. Over the next decade, his output as a writer remained as varied as ever. In addition to various projects for television, Richler wrote the screenplay for the movie adaptation of *The Apprenticeship of Duddy Kravitz,* which earned him an Academy Award nomination in 1975. That year, Richler also published a novel for children, *Jacob Two-Two Meets the Hooded Fang,* about the travails of a young boy who had to repeat everything he said twice for adults to understand him. The novel won the first Ruth Schwartz Children's Book Award in 1976.

In 1980, Richler reemerged as a novelist with the publication of *Joshua Then and Now.* Another work that incorporated some autobiographical elements, the novel explored the life of a Jewish-Canadian writer coming to terms with the past; the book was made into a film in 1985, with Richler as screenwriter. In 1990, Richler touched off controversy when he published *Solomon Gursky Was Here,* a novel inspired by the real-life history of Canada's Bronfman family. The country's wealthiest family, the Bronfmans made their fortune from their Seagram's Whiskey business and later built a wide-ranging entertainment empire including large holdings in Universal Studios and Time-Warner; one member of the family, Edgar Bronfman, also served as the head of the Jewish World Congress. Richler's last novel, *Barney's Version,* appeared in 1998.

Although he enjoyed uninterrupted success after *The Apprenticeship of Duddy Kravitz,* Richler became far better known as a humorist and social commentator in the last decade of his career. In addition to his regular essays in *Maclean's,* Richler published humorous and nostalgic pieces in magazines and journals ranging from *Playboy* to *Atlantic* to the *New York Times Book Review.* A lengthy piece he published in the *New Yorker,* however, gained Richler the most attention with its examination of the attempts to restrict the use of the English language in public places in Quebec. Richler eventually published an entire book devoted to the subject of Quebec separatism, *Oh Canada! Oh Quebec! Requiem for a Divided Country,* in 1992. Richler's defiance of Quebec separatist demands made him a reviled figure in some quarters, and death threats were made against him after the book was published. Richler fought the separatists with satire and humor. As he told an audience at the University of Waterloo in 1999, "I manned the barricades, so to speak, for the legal right to munch unilingually labeled kosher matzos in Quebec for more than sixty days a year. I also protested the right of a pet shop parrot to be unilingually English. As a consequence, nice people still stop me on the street and thank me for taking a stand. It's embarrassing, for my stand, such as it is, hardly qualifies me as a latter-day Spartacus or Tom Paine or Rosa Luxemburg."

In declining health for some time, perhaps due to his favored pastimes of drinking malt whiskey and smoking, Richler had his kidney removed in a 1998 operation. A recurrence of cancer led to more treatment, but Richler died on July 3, 2001. He was one of the most respected literary figures in Canada by the time of his death.

Colleagues and friends memorialized Richler as a writer who was not overawed by his own success. His readers mourned the loss of one of the first internationally renowned Canadian writers. Indeed, Richler's ability to describe the Canadian perspective was one of his greatest contributions to the country's culture. Speaking at the University of Waterloo in 1999, he said: "One of our most attractive qualities, I think, is that we are a self-deprecating people. Had Babe Ruth, for instance, been born a Canadian rather than an American, he would not be celebrated as the Sultan of Swat, the man who hit 714 home runs. Instead he would be deprecated as that notorious flunk who struck out 1330 times."

Books

Richler, Mordecai, *Home Sweet Home: My Canadian Album,* Alfred A. Knopf, 1984.
Richler, Mordecai, *Oh Canada! Oh Quebec! Requiem for a Divided Country,* Alfred A. Knopf, 1992.

Periodicals

Maclean's, July 16, 2001.
Toronto Star, July 5, 2001.

Online

"The Apprenticeship of Mordecai Richler," *CBC News,* http://www.cbc.ca/news/indepth/richler/ (October 24, 2001).
"Canadian Conundrums," *University of Waterloo,* http://www.arts.uwaterloo.ca/ECON/needhdata/richler.html (October 24, 2001).
"Mordecai Richler," *Internet Movie Database,* http://us.imdb.com/Name?Richler, + Mordecai (October 24, 2001).
"Mordecai Richler Biocritical Essay," *University of Calgary Library,* http://www.ucalgary.ca/library/SpecColl/richlerbioc.htm (October 24, 2001). □

John Rollin Ridge

John Rollin Ridge (1827-1867) was born into one of the ruling families of the Cherokee Tribe during a period of great division. Under pressure to cede their lands in the southeastern United States and relocate to the Indian Territory in the West, the Ridge family signed the Treaty of New Echota in 1835, which completed a removal agreement with the United States government over the objections of many Cherokees. In 1839 John Rollin Ridge's father and grandfather were murdered in revenge for their support of removal; not long afterwards, Ridge himself was forced to flee to California to escape his family's enemies. Working primarily as a newspaper editor, Ridge also published perhaps the first novel set in California, *The Life and Adventures of Joaquín Murieta, the Celebrated California Bandit,* in 1854. A longtime slave holder, Ridge was the political leader of California's anti-abolitionist movement before the Civil War and a leader of the Copperheads, pro-slavery Democrats, during the conflict. In declining health after the Civil War, Ridge died in Grass Lake, California, in 1867; his widow, the former Elizabeth Wilson, published a collection of his poetry after his death.

The saga of the Ridge Family is one of the best known in Native American history. John Rollin Ridge's grandfather, Major Ridge—often called "The Ridge"—was born in 1771 in present-day Tennessee, an area then inhabited by the Cherokee Tribe. The Ridge earned a fearsome reputation as a skilled fighter against white settlers in the 1780s while he was still a teenager. Around 1792, Ridge married Susanna Wicket, and the couple built a sizable farm along the lines of their white settler neighbors. In 1813, Ridge fought on the side of the American government against the Creek Nation, which demonstrated how his loyalty had shifted. Returning to his farm—now more of a plantation, complete with slaves—Ridge and his wife raised their four surviving children, including John Ridge, born about 1800.

Believing that acculturation into white society was the best hope for the survival of the Cherokee people, the Ridge children received the best education that the frontier setting could provide. John Ridge was taught by a series of missionary workers at schools in Georgia before attending the American Board of Commissioners for Foreign Missions (ABCFM) school in Cornwall, Connecticut. There he met Sarah Bird Northrup, the daughter of a nurse who was caring for him during a brief illness. The two married in 1824 and Northrup returned with him to Georgia. In addition to working as a lawyer, John Ridge became a major landholder in his own right: His farm covered 419 acres and was manned by eighteen slaves. Added to The Ridge's 280-acre farm, eight-room manor, trading post, and ferry service, the Ridge family was the wealthiest and most influential among the Cherokees.

Like his parents, John Ridge emphasized the importance of formal education and acculturation in raising his children, including John Rollin Ridge, born on March 19, 1827. The Ridge children attended a school built by their parents and staffed by a missionary teacher trained at the ABCFM. During John Rollin Ridge's childhood, however, the Cherokees came under increasing pressure to cede their lands to white settlers and move to the Indian Territory, comprising much of present-day Oklahoma. Despite their belief that acculturation into white society was the best course for the Cherokees, the Ridge Family eventually perceived that they had to leave their land. The 1828 election of Andrew Jackson to the presidency brought the issue to a head; although The Ridge had fought with Jackson's troops against the Creeks in 1813, Jackson was resolute on the policy of Indian Removal, as the plan to relocate tribes to the Indian Territory was called. In addition to the federal government, the state of Georgia also increased pressure for removal. In 1830 Georgia passed legislation to nullify the Cherokee's sovereignty and followed it with a series of measures to force them to sell their lands. The discovery of gold in the region also brought numerous fortune-hunters into the lands where the Cherokees had farmed since the late 1700s.

The Trail of Tears

With the Ridges leading the Treaty Party of the Cherokees, the Treaty of New Echota was signed with the federal government on December 29, 1835. It provided the Cherokee Tribe with 13.8 million acres for settlement in the Indian Territory as well as a payment of $4.5 million and an annuity payment to support a school. While the Ridges insisted that they had negotiated the best possible deal, many Cherokees were outraged at the prospect of removal to the West. To make matters worse, the journey to the Indian Territory was poorly planned; many Cherokees died during the treks of 1836 through 1839, which became known as "The Trail of Tears." By the time the removal of the Cherokee had been completed, the Ridge family's leadership was under attack by a hostile faction who accused them of profiting from their people's misery.

On June 22, 1839, the Ridges' rivals got their revenge. Dragging John Ridge out of his home, a band of his fellow Cherokees brutally murdered him while his family watched. Later, Major Ridge was also attacked and killed. Fleeing to Fayetteville, Arkansas, the surviving family members pled with the federal government to guarantee their safety and restore their losses, as their homes were looted after the killings. At the age of twelve, then, John Rollin Ridge's life was changed forever. Not only was the economic security of his family diminished, but his very safety as the future leader of the Ridge family was in doubt as well.

Despite the tragedy, John Rollin Ridge continued his family's tradition of educational attainment. After studying in Fayetteville, Ridge entered the Great Barrington Academy, named after its site in Massachusetts, in 1843. After two years in the East, Ridge returned to Fayetteville to study the law. In 1847, the twenty year-old married Elizabeth Wilson, a native of Fayetteville, and the couple settled on a farm nearby. Their only child, Alice, was born in 1848. With his inheritance, which included ownership of two slaves, Ridge retained a measure of prosperity, even if it paled to the Ridges' fortune in the past.

Tensions within the Cherokee Tribe resurfaced again in 1849, when John Rollin Ridge entered into a dispute with a neighbor whom he accused of stealing and injuring his horse. During the argument, Ridge claimed that he had been threatened and had shot the man in self-defense. Soon rumors were circulating that the neighbor, who was part of the anti-Ridge faction of the Cherokees, had set up the event in order to have an excuse to kill Ridge. Whatever the exact circumstances, Ridge decided not to risk a trial and decided to flee to California. Encouraged by news of gold strikes there, Ridge took out mortgages on his two slaves to finance the trip and departed with his brother and one slave in April 1850.

Gold Rush Years

After an arduous trip that exhausted most of his resources, Ridge realized that the tales of prosperity in California were greatly exaggerated. After one full day of mining that brought him only fifty cents worth of gold dust, it was obvious to Ridge that prospecting would not provide enough money to bring his wife and daughter out west. Instead, Ridge turned to writing to make a living; as a spokesman for the Ridge Family, he had already been published in a number of newspapers. In California, his topics typically included stories about prospecting in addition to covering Native American topics. While his essays on California's tribes exhibited many of the biases of the day—including the belief that they were primitive and possibly doomed to extinction unless they acculturated into white society—Ridge often took a more sympathetic point of view than other observers, for example, in calling for measures to protect Native Americans from exploitation and violence by white settlers.

Published *The Life and Adventures of Joaquín Murieta, the Celebrated California Bandit*

While working for several different newspapers during his career in California, Ridge was successful enough to reunite his family by 1854. That same year, Ridge published his only novel, *The Life and Adventures of Joaquín Murieta, the Celebrated California Bandit*. The story was a fictionalized account based on the lives of a group of bandits operating in central California; according to various reports, there were between two and five men who used the name Murieta, although Ridge condensed them into one figure for his novel. While the exploits of Murieta were melodramatic, the larger theme of the novel demonstrated a greater sensitivity to the ethnic tensions that dominated Californian society at the time. In the wake of the recent war with Mexico, which concluded in 1848, and pervasive discrimination against Mexicans and other Spanish-speaking residents, white settlers in California attempted to pass legislation to limit their rights, including the right to prospect for gold. Although such a law was passed in the state, it was later rescinded; however, tensions remained at a boiling point throughout the state. In one incident that Ridge included in his book, a group of whites accused Murieta of stealing and beat him in front of his wife, who was also attacked. In response, Murieta became a bandit, raiding the homes of white and Asian settlers throughout California. Eventually, officials killed at least two men who were thought to be operating under Murieta's name, but not before he became a folk hero to many beleaguered Spanish-speaking residents.

Political Controversies

The publication of the ninety-page novel *The Life and Adventures of Joaquín Murieta, the Celebrated California Bandit* was an immediate success; unfortunately, it was often republished in plagiarized editions, and Ridge's hoped-for economic gain never materialized. Instead, he worked as a Yuba County Deputy Clerk and as a part-time police officer in addition to publishing his work in several newspapers. In 1856 Ridge joined the staff of the *Californian American*, a newspaper affiliated with the Know-Nothing Party. A racist and nativist organization, the Know-Nothings advocated strict limits on immigration to the United States and espoused a deep anti-Catholic resentment. Although the California branch of the Know-Nothing Party was more moderate on some issues, it nevertheless represented one extreme end of the political spectrum.

Throughout 1857 and 1858, Ridge worked for a number of other newspapers in northern California; with the decline of the Know-Nothing Party, he now supported the pro-slavery faction of the Democratic Party. Although he believed that the Union should be preserved, Ridge was also adamant that the existing rights of slave holders not be infringed. After the Civil War broke out, Ridge continued to support the efforts of negotiators to bring the war to an end without abolishing slavery. In May 1861 Ridge became the editor of the San Francisco *Evening Journal* and often wrote essays against President Lincoln and the *Emancipation Proclamation*. As the war continued in the Union's favor, however, Ridge was increasingly criticized for his attacks on Lincoln and the Union's cause.

At the conclusion of the war, Ridge stepped into controversy for his role as a negotiator on behalf of the Cherokees, who had once again split ranks over the war. While some slaveholding Cherokees sided with the Confederacy, others supported the Union's effort. In securing a position as the agent for all the Cherokees east of the Mississippi River, John Rollin Ridge was once again accused of profiting from the division among his tribe. As he approached his fortieth birthday, however, Ridge was increasingly in poor health and suffered diminished mental capacity. In the last weeks of his life he was largely incoherent. Ridge died in his home at Grass Lake, California, on October 5, 1867. After his death, his wife published a collection of his poetry; however, he remains best known as the author of perhaps the first Californian novel and as a somewhat tragic figure in the history of the Cherokee people.

Books

Gibson, Arrell Morgan, *The American Indian: Prehistory to the Present,* D.C. Heath and Company, 1980.

Parins, James W., *John Rollin Ridge: His Life and Works,* University of Nebraska Press, 1991.

Sellers, Charles, *The Market Revolution: Jacksonian America, 1815-1846,* Oxford University Press, 1991.

Wilkins, Thurman, *Cherokee Tragedy: The Ridge Family and the Decimation of a People,* University of Oklahoma Press, 1986.

Periodicals

ATQ, September 1994, p 173.

MELUS, Summer 1991, p. 61.

Online

"John Rollin Ridge: A Biographical Sketch," *University of Arkansas-Little Rock American Native Press Association Web Site,* http://anpa.ualr.edu/DTP/JRR/JRR_Bio.htm (January 9, 2002). □

Jason Robards

Jason Robards (1922-2000) was one of the most distinguished American actors of the twentieth century, making his mark in both theater and film. The son of an actor, Robards first made a name for himself in the late 1950s with impressive performances in the

plays of Eugene O'Neill. He went on to win two Academy Awards for best supporting actor and a Tony Award for best actor, one of eight Tony Awards for which he was nominated.

Robards was born in Chicago on July 26, 1922, son of Jason Nelson, an actor, and Hope Maxine (Glanville) Robards. When he was only 5, his parents divorced, and young Robards moved with his father and brother to Los Angeles. Growing up he showed little interest in following in his father's footsteps, focusing instead on a possible career in sports. He was a star athlete at Hollywood High School, playing baseball, basketball, football, and track. Academically, he was a B+ student whose favorite subjects were civics, drama, French, and Spanish. He graduated in 1939.

Shortly after graduating from Hollywood High, Robards enlisted in the U.S. Navy and was trained as a radio operator. Stationed at Pearl Harbor on the Hawaiian island of Oahu, he narrowly survived the Japanese attack on December 7, 1941. For most of World War II, he served in the Pacific Theater, seeing action in a total of 13 sea battles, and was later awarded the Navy Cross. It was during his years in the Navy that Robards first began to show an interest in the theater, borrowing the plays of Eugene O'Neill from the ship's library and toying with the idea of a career as an actor.

Bitten by the Acting Bug

After his discharge from the Navy in 1946, Robards returned home and confided to his father his growing interest in acting. The senior Robards urged his son to attend the American Academy of Dramatic Arts (AADA) in New York, which he himself had attended and now recommended to his son as an excellent place to learn the actor's craft. Although Robards's stay at AADA lasted only eight months, it was at the academy that he first met actress Colleen Dewhurst, who would play opposite him in a number of O'Neill plays in years to come. His first professional appearance was as the rear end of a cow in the Children's World Theatre production of *Jack and the Beanstalk,* hardly the most auspicious start to an acting career. Next up, Robards won a walk-on role in a D'Oyly Carte production of *The Mikado* on Broadway. A year later he enjoyed somewhat more substantive roles in the D'Oyly Carte productions of *Iolanthe* and *The Yeoman of the Guard.*

Things began to look up a bit for Robards in the early 1950s. In 1951 he landed a job as an understudy and assistant stage manager for the Broadway production of *Stalag 17.* After its Broadway run, Robards joined the national touring company of the play. His first big break, however, came in 1953 when director Jose Quintero cast him in the leading role in Victor Wolfson's *American Gothic,* which opened off Broadway at the Circle in the Square. That experience helped to pave the way for the role that would first win the actor broad recognition and critical acclaim. When director Quintero was casting his upcoming production of O'Neill's *The Iceman Cometh* early in 1956, he remembered Robards from their prior collaboration and cast him in the relatively minor role of Jimmy the Priest. As the production began to come together, Quintero continued to search for just the right actor to play Hickey, the lead role. Robards pleaded with Quintero to give him a stab at the part. Hickey, as written by O'Neill, is a short, rotund figure in his 50s, which could hardly have been more different than the tall, lean Robards, who was then 34. Despite his initial misgivings, Quintero allowed the actor to read for the part and was so impressed at Robards's ability to transform himself into O'Neill's tragic hero that he quickly signed him for the part.

Won Best Actor Award

Thus began for Robards and Quintero a successful partnership in the interpretation of O'Neill's work. Playwright O'Neill, who had died in November 1953, had requested that one of his plays—*A Long Day's Journey into Night*—not be produced until 25 years after his death. So impressed with Robards' interpretation of Hickey was O'Neill's widow that she gave Quintero and Robards the green light to bring *Long Day's Journey* to Broadway only three years after O'Neill's death. The play, written by O'Neill between 1939 and 1941, is autobiographical in theme, painting a painful portrait of the tortured relationships within the Tyrone family. Its Broadway debut in the fall of 1956 won for O'Neill a posthumous Pulitzer Prize, his third for drama, and for Robards the 1957 New York Drama Critics Award for best actor.

New York Times theater critic Brooks Atkinson said that with Quintero's production of *Long Day's Journey into Night,* "the American theater acquires size and stature." Of Robards' contribution, Atkinson wrote: "As the evil brother, Jason Robards Jr., who played Hickey in *The Iceman Cometh,* gives another remarkable performance that has tremendous force and truth in the last act." Even more effusive in his praise of Robards was Walter Kerr, critic for the *New York Herald-Tribune:* "Mr. Robards lurches into the final scene with his hands, his mouth, and his mind wildly out of control, cracks himself in two as he pours out every tasteless truth that is in him, and subsides at last into the boozy sleep of the damned. The passage is magnificent."

After his stunning success in two back-to-back O'Neill vehicles, Robards sought to prove to the world—and perhaps to himself as well—that he could act convincingly in works by other playwrights. He followed up with his successful run as Jamie Tyrone in *Long Day's Journey* with two Shakespearean roles in the summer of 1958. He first played Hotspur in *Henry IV, Part I* at the Stratford Shakespeare Festival in Stratford, Ontario, after which he took the role of Polixenes in *The Winter's Tale.* Returning to contemporary drama in the fall of 1958, he opened on Broadway opposite Rosemary Harris in Budd Schulberg's and Harvey Breit's *The Disenchanted,* a thinly disguised tale of F. Scott Fitzgerald. Robards played the role of Manley Halliday (the Fitzgerald character) so convincingly that he picked up the Tony Award in 1959 as best actor. Joining Robards in the cast of *The Disenchanted* was his father, making his first appearance on Broadway since 1922, the year of his actor son's birth.

Made His Film Debut

In 1959 Robards returned briefly to Shakespeare, playing the title role in a production of *Macbeth* at the Metropolitan Boston Arts Center in Cambridge, Massachusetts. More importantly, 1959 saw the actor's film debut in *The Journey,* released by MGM. Then it was back to Broadway where he won critical praise for his roles as Julian Berniers in *Toys in the Attic* in 1960, William Baker in *Big Fish, Little Fish* in 1961, and Murray Burns in *A Thousand Clowns* in 1962.

After a two-year absence, Robards returned to the screen in 1961 in two roles, playing Julius Penrose in *By Love Possessed* and Dick Diver in *Tender Is the Night.* In 1962 Robards recreated his role as Jamie Tyrone in the film version of *A Long Day's Journey into Night,* starring with Katharine Hepburn, Ralph Richardson, and Dean Stockwell. The critics were duly impressed, and it seemed certain that Robards had carved a niche for himself in Hollywood. In 1964, Robards played George S. Kaufman in the film version of Moss Hart's *Act One,* which he followed with in 1965 with a reprisal of his role as Murray Burns in the motion picture version of *A Thousand Clowns.* He also managed to stay active on Broadway, appearing in 1964 and 1965 in four different roles: Quentin in Arthur Miller's *After the Fall,* Seymour Rosenthal in *But for Whom Charlie,* Erie Smith in *Hughie,* and Vicar of St. Peter's in *The Devils.*

While Robards' career continued to flourish, his personal life was quite another matter. For much of his adult life he was plagued with debilitating bouts of depression, some of which he later suggested may have had its roots in the breakup of his family when he was only 5 years old. Although he lived with his father and stepmother after his parents' divorce, he saw his mother frequently but spent much of his early life hoping that the family could be reunited. Even more damaging than the depression was Robards's struggle with alcohol. He remained a heavy drinker until 1972 when he was almost killed in an alcohol-related automobile accident. No less complicated was Robards's love life. In all he was married four times. He married Eleanor Pitman in 1948. The couple had three children—Jason III, Sarah Louise, and David—before divorcing in 1952. In 1959 Robards married Rachel Taylor. They had no children and divorced in 1961, shortly after which he married Lauren Bacall, with whom he had a son, Sam. Robards and Bacall split in 1969. The following year he married Lois O'Connor, with whom he remained until his death in 2000. They had two children, Shannon and Jake.

Work in Films Increased

Robards remained active in the theater for most of his life, but the late 1960s brought a sharp increase in his work in film. In 1966 he appeared in *Any Wednesday* and *A Big Hand for the Little Lady.* The following year he played Al Capone in *The St. Valentine's Day Massacre,* Doc Holliday in *Hour of the Gun,* and Nelson Downes in *Divorce American Style.* Between 1968 and 1976 he appeared in 16 films, but the best was yet to come for Robards. His portrayal of *Washington Post* editor Ben Bradlee in 1976's *All the President's Men* won for Robards an Academy Award as best supporting actor. He repeated that feat only a year later when he picked up the Oscar for his portrayal of Dashiell Hammett in *Julia.*

On the stage, the 1970s brought a return to the plays of Eugene O'Neill for Robards. In 1973 he portrayed James Tyrone Jr. in *A Moon for the Misbegotten* at the Eisenhower Theatre in Washington, D.C., and the Morosco in New York City. The following year he took the play to Los Angeles, appearing at the Ahmanson Theatre. In 1975, he played Erie Smith in O'Neill's *Hughie* at the Zellerbach Theatre in Los Angeles and at the Lake Forest Theatre in Illinois in 1976. In 1975 Robards also played the role of James Tyrone Sr. in *A Long Day's Journey into Night* at the Eisenhower and the following year at the Brooklyn Academy of Music. The actor next portrayed Cornelius Melody in *A Touch of the Poet* at the Helen Hayes Theatre in New York City. He wrapped up the decade with an appearance in *O'Neill and Carlotta,* a drama about the tortured relationship between Eugene O'Neill and his third and last wife, Carlotta Monterey.

In addition to his many appearances on stage and in film, Robards found time for an amazing amount of work in television. He appeared in more than 20 made-for-TV movies, including four—*The House without a Christmas Tree, The Thanksgiving Treasure, The Easter Promise,* and *Addie and the King of Hearts*—in which he played the same character, James Mills. He either appeared in or lent his voice to ten miniseries, including *The Atlanta Child Mur-*

ders, *The Long Hot Summer, An Inconvenient Woman,* and *Heidi.* In the mid- to late 1950s, Robards also appeared in a number of television dramas, including productions that appeared on *Studio One, Playhouse 90, Armstrong Circle Theatre,* and *Philco Television Playhouse.*

Robards remained active in film until just before his death in 2000. Ironically, his final film, released in 1999, was *Magnolia,* in which he portrayed Earl Patridge, bedridden and dying of cancer, with which the actor himself was then waging a losing battle. Although *Magnolia* was not a major commercial success, Robards' work in the film was widely praised by critics.

Books

Contemporary Theatre, Film and Television, Gale Group, 2000.
International Dictionary of Theatre, Volume 3: Actors, Directors, and Designers, St. James Press, 1996.
Newsmakers, Gale Group, 2001.

Periodicals

New York Herald Tribune, November 8, 1956.
New York Times, November 8, 1956.

Online

''Biographies: Jason Robards,'' Videoflicks.com, http://www .videoflicks.com/biographies/A101/1013198.htm (January 21, 2002).
''Jason Robards Jr.,'' Jason Robards, JAT Entertainment Group, http://www.jatentertainment.com/robards/index.htm (January 21, 2002). □

Sir John Ross

British explorer Sir John Ross (1777-1856) joined the Royal Navy at the age of nine and spent much of the rest of his life at sea. In the early nineteenth century, he made three expeditions to the Arctic, looking for the Northwest Passage, exploring King William Island and the Boothia Peninsula, and searching for the lost expedition of Sir John Franklin.

Ross was the fifth son of Andrew Ross and his wife, Elizabeth. He was born in Balsarroch, Wigtonshire in Scotland on June 24, 1777. While still a boy, he joined the crew of a ship called the *Pearl* and spent the next three years in the Mediterranean. In 1790 he sailed on the *Impregnable,* whose captain, Sir Thomas Byard, advised him to join the merchant marine. He did so and became an apprentice to Byard for four years, sailing to the West Indies and the Baltic. After that he sailed on a number of ships as midshipman or mate and in 1805 became a lieutenant. In 1809 he was made a Swedish knight for a brief period of service to the Swedish admiral.

Explored the Northwest Passage

Ross was a good navigator, skilled at surveying land, and the inventor of a new type of sextant known as the Royal William. A sextant is an instrument that measures angular distances and is often used by navigators to determine latitude and longitude. He was also a believer in phrenology, a popular pseudoscience of the time that deduced a person's character from the shape of the skull.

In 1812 he was promoted to a naval commander and took the helm of a series of ships in the Baltic, North Sea, and the White Sea. In January 1818 he was appointed commander of the ship *Isabella,* which joined with the ship *Alexander,* commanded by Lieutenant Edward Parry, to explore the Northwest Passage through Davis Strait.

In *The Arctic Grail,* Pierre Barton wrote, ''This stocky, red-haired Scot . . . seemed the best choice for an Arctic adventure. Not yet forty-three, he had three decades of sea experience. He was undeniably brave, having been wounded no fewer than thirteen times in battle—'scarred from head to foot' in the words of a future polar explorer, Elisha Kane.''

The two ships were merely refitted transports not specially built for the rigors of the Arctic. By mid-June they were in the Davis Strait between Baffin Island and Greenland, where the amazing extent and grandiosity of the world of ice astonished them. According to Barton, Ross wrote in his journal, ''It is hardly possible to imagine anything more exquisite . . . by night as by day they glitter with a vividness of colour beyond the power of art to represent.''

In early July, on the coast of Greenland, they met a group of native people who had never seen outsiders; even John Sacheuse, their native interpreter, had never heard of these people and could barely understand their dialect. These people had never seen boats or trees, and so they were baffled when Parry, trying to show peaceful intentions, sent out an officer carrying a flag with an olive branch on it. Ross, who was more practical, put up a flag on a pole and tied a bag of presents to it. The natives understood that as a gesture of peace. Communications were severely limited, and the Europeans, underestimating these seemingly naive people, never thought to learn some of their techniques for surviving in such difficult terrain.

The expedition eventually reached the top of Baffin Bay, where no Europeans had been for two centuries. Ross then sailed west to the southern tip of what is now known as Ellesmere Island, then went south, looking for a channel that might enter into the fabled Northwest Passage. At the end of August he found a long inlet that led to the west. This had been named Lancaster Sound, but no one knew whether it led to the Pacific Ocean.

"Discovered" Croker Mountains

After sailing thirty miles into the sound, Ross became convinced that it was a dead end. In fact, he thought he saw a mountain range in the distance, blocking all passage. He was the only one who saw the mountains, but he turned his ship around and headed back the way he had come with no explanation to Parry, who was enraged by his actions. Ross named the imaginary range the Croker Mountains and returned to England, claiming the range blocked the Northwest Passage. He was promoted to post rank in recognition of his discovery, and in 1819 he published his book, *A Voyage of Discovery, Made Under the Orders of the Admiralty, in His Majesty's Ships Isabella and Alexander, for the Purpose of Exploring Baffin's Bay and Inquiring into the Probability of a North-West Passage*, about the trip. In it, he claimed that in addition to the mountains, the passage had been completely choked by ice. This was a lie; Parry and others had not seen any ice. Barton noted, "It was almost as if the doughty seaman didn't believe in the existence of the North West Passage and had seized on the first opportunity to confirm that opinion"—whether it was true or not. Some members of the admiralty doubted the reality of the Croker Mountains, and they dispatched another expedition, under Parry's command, to verify Ross's claims. Meanwhile, the existence or nonexistence of the mountains became a public controversy, which was not put to rest until Parry returned in October 1820 with the news that Ross had been wrong.

Another Voyage

Ross became a laughingstock and was deeply embarrassed. In some quarters, according to Barton, anyone who was excessively vain was said to be suffering from "Rossism." Anxious to clear his name and prove that he was still a good sailor, navigator, and observer despite the mistake, Ross asked for another commission, but did not get one until 1829, when he was given command of a small vessel. A friend named Felix Booth, who was the distiller and sheriff of London, sponsored a new Arctic voyage and contributed 7,000 pounds. Ross put up 3,000 pounds of his own money.

Once in the Arctic, Ross sailed through Lancaster Sound and then searched for a passage south from Prince Regent Inlet, but was stopped by ice and trapped until the summer of 1830. In that summer, he made a few miles south, but once again became stuck in the ice until May 1832, when he and his men abandoned the ship and spent a fourth winter on Fury Beach, in a hut built from the remnants of a wrecked ship named the *Fury*, previously under Parry's command; they survived on provisions left by Parry.

The greatest hazards of this voyage were the boredom and depression endured by the men during the long immobile periods. Parry knew that these could easily lead to friction, fights, and mutiny, and made sure that his ships had music, sports, and other entertainment. Ross was not as lighthearted. William Light, a steward on the expedition, published his reminiscence of the voyage, and, according to Barton, summed up Ross as "a haughty, unsociable, and almost hermit-like officer who treated his men with iron authority but little compassion and kept to his cabin, sustaining himself on his sponsor's gin." He was the oldest man on the ship and came from a different era. In addition, his stubborn insistence that he was always right led to difficulty when he was wrong. However, his nephew, James Clark Ross, who was a member of the crew, was far more energetic and enthusiastic and actually made most of the expedition's notable discoveries.

Boredom was alleviated by the native people, who visited the Europeans in the winter. The sailors taught them to play leapfrog and soccer and in return learned how to survive through the winter. However, Ross continued to view them as barbarians and, once he had pumped them for information about the geography of the surrounding land and water, refused to allow them on the ship, even though they were unfailingly generous with their homes and personal possessions.

During this difficult voyage, Ross and his men were able to map the peninsula now known as Boothia, as well as the Gulf of Boothia. In addition, James Clark Ross was able to map the precise location of the magnetic North Pole.

In the summer of 1833 they were able to reach Ross's old ship, the *Isabella*, in Lancaster Sound, and they returned to England in October. As a result of his achievements, Ross was knighted in 1834 and received gold medals from the Geographical Societies of London and Paris. In 1835 he published a book about the expedition, *Narrative of a Second Voyage in Search of a North-West Passage, and of a Residence in the Arctic Regions During the Years 1829-1833, with Appendix*.

The Controversy Over Franklin

Ross served as consul to Stockholm from 1839 to 1846. In 1845 another expedition was preparing to leave for the Arctic, under the command of Sir John Franklin, and Ross's advice was snubbed. In addition, Sir John Barrow, another explorer, wrote a bitter attack on Ross, and the community of Arctic explorers, including Ross's nephew, sided with

Barrow. Ross replied by writing a vitriolic pamphlet defending himself, and when Franklin's expedition did not return at the planned time, Ross urged the admiralty to send out a rescue ship with him in command. The admiralty, as well as the other explorers, replied that it was too early to send out a rescue expedition. Ross was probably too old to be captain of such an expedition, but he attributed the rejection to Barrow's influence.

Ross wrote another pamphlet presenting his theories about why the admiralty had refused to allow a rescue expedition, but his arguments were marred by his obvious personal anger toward Barrow and some members of the admiralty. By 1849, he had gathered enough money from Felix Booth, the Hudson's Bay Company, and other donations to finance a small ship, the *Felix,* which he sailed to Lancaster Sound. In the end, however, it turned out that no one had seen Franklin or any of his men after 1845; no one knows how they died, and their bodies were never found.

Ross died in London on August 30, 1856. During his life he had married twice, and he had one son, who was a civil servant in the East India Company. His nephew, James Clark Ross, became a famed and much more successful explorer of the Antarctic.

Books

Barton, Pierre, *Arctic Grail,* Viking, 1988.
Dictionary of National Biography, Earliest Times to 1900, edited by Sir Leslie Stephen and Sir Sidney Lee, Oxford University Press, 1949-1950.
Langnas, I. A., *Dictionary of Discoveries,* Philosophical Library, 1959.
Ruby, Robert, *Unknown Shore,* Henry Holt & Co., 2001.
Wright, Noel, *Quest for Franklin,* Heinemann, 1959. □

Vera Cooper Rubin

Although her ideas on the nature of the universe were at first largely discounted, astronomer Vera Cooper Rubin (born 1928) has gained recognition for her research leading to the discovery of "dark matter."

V era Cooper Rubin's measurement of the speed of spinning galaxies suggests that science has only scratched the surface of the true nature of the heavens. Dark matter is believed to make up 90 percent of the universe. It is material that is thought to exert gravitational force on stars to keep them spinning inside their galaxies.

Watched the Stars

Rubin was born on July 23, 1928, in Philadelphia, Pennsylvania. At age 10, she was already fascinated by the stars. From her home in Washington, D.C., she searched the skies and watched the constellations until late at night. Despite warnings from her mother not to overdo her star

gazing, Rubin continued to pursue her passion in the night skies. At age 14 she built her first telescope with the help of her father. Her early fascination for astronomy followed her into adulthood; now she scans the stars with some of the world's largest and most powerful telescopes.

Even though a high school physics teacher warned Rubin away from science, and an admissions officer at Swarthmore College in Pennsylvania advised her to major in something more suitable than astronomy, Rubin went her own way. She was determined to investigate the universe's secrets for herself. She earned her bachelor's degree in astronomy at Vassar College in 1948 and went on to earn a master's degree from Cornell University in 1951. At Cornell she studied quantum mechanics with Hans Bethe, who later won a Nobel Prize for his research on fusion reactions in the sun, and attended lectures on quantum electrodynamics given by Richard Feynman, who later won a Nobel Prize for his research on particle interactions. Rubin's thesis challenged the big bang theory which postulates that the universe is expanding out from an original central explosion of matter. Instead, she argued, the galaxies themselves are actually rotating around a central point, not just expanding out from it. "My first paper got an enormous amount of publicity, almost all negative," Rubin told *Discover.* "But, at least, from then on, astronomers knew who I was."

Rubin, then a young woman of only 22 years, had no intention of stirring up controversy with her work. But her findings were unorthodox and continued to be so. In 1954, while working toward a doctorate from Georgetown University at night, Rubin completed research that showed galaxies were not evenly spaced throughout the universe. This was another controversial finding, since the big bang theory suggested that galaxies were evenly distributed. For years Rubin carefully measured the speed of spiral galaxies. She found that they spin so fast that their stars ought to spin away from them, rather than stay in orbit. Perhaps, she thought, galaxies remain intact due to gravitational forces exerted by matter that human technology cannot detect: so-called "dark matter."

Astronomers knew that the universe was expanding because of the shift toward red exhibited by light waves emanating from distance galaxies. This red shift indicates movement away from Earth at speeds so high that astronomers found it hard to believe that stars within these galaxies were not actually spinning out of them. (Blue light, on the other hand, would indicate a movement toward Earth.) An accepted explanation for star movement within galaxies was that, much like planets in orbit around the sun, stars on the edge of a galaxy moved more slowly than those closer in. Prior to Rubin's discovery that stars on the edge of a galaxy moved just as quickly as others, many astronomers believed that the laws of physics dictated that stars would behave more like planets. Rubin's research changed all that.

Discovered "Dark Matter"

The gravitational pull of large bodies such as the Sun lessens as distance increases; therefore, if stars on the edge of a galaxy were moving just as swiftly as the rest of the stars in their galaxy, what was keeping them from spinning away?

The answer seemed to be another gravitational force, a cosmic force that was at work although not visible through a telescope.

In the 1970s, while other astronomers pursued quasars (blue specks of light thought to be the birthing place of galaxies), Rubin and her colleague W. Kent Ford investigated galactic movement. They looked into the possibility that galaxies did not just expand in a predictable manner toward a region called the Great Attractor, but rather moved on their own. The idea was not received well, so Rubin turned her attention to the rotation of spiral galaxies. After she discovered that the Andromeda Galaxy was actually moving at a fast rate but that stars were not spiraling away from it, she went on to investigate other galaxies. She found that, far from being the exception to the rule, Andromeda was behaving much the same as other galaxies. Stars on the edge of the galaxy moved with the same speed as those on the interior. Some kind of matter must be exerting a force on those stars to keep them from out of the galaxy.

Rubin began to hypothesize that the mass of the galaxy was spread out rather than concentrated in one central spot. If the velocities of clouds farther out from the "central bulge" of a galaxy were not less than the velocities of clouds closer in, as Keplerian motion predicts, then all mass in the galaxy must not be at its center. Could it be that there were heavenly bodies generating mass as yet unknown to astronomers?

Although Rubin's work was not easily accepted in the 1970s, she was not the first astronomer to notice galaxies were moving too fast to stay together. In the 1930s astronomers Fritz Zwicky and Sinclair Smith had realized that galaxies were speeding along at higher rates than expected, and they wondered if some kind of matter was keeping galaxies together through gravitational pull. Their idea about "missing mass" influencing galactic movement seemed to agree with Rubin's findings.

It took some time, but after studying more than 200 galaxies, Rubin and her colleagues documented enough data to convince other astronomers that the universe was virtually 90 percent undiscovered matter. Thanks to Rubin's efforts, the possible existence of dark matter became scientifically accepted.

"So important is this dark matter to our understanding of the size, shape, and ultimate fate of the universe that the search for it will very likely dominate astronomy for the next few decades," Rubin wrote in an article published in the *Scientific American.* The findings from Rubin's research opened new vistas for exploration. "With over ninety percent of the matter in the universe still to play with, even the sky will not be the limit," she explained to *Discover.*

The possible existence of dark matter set the scientific world agog with curiosity. Some astronomers, such as Rubin, believe the dark matter was ordinary in make-up—just defunct stars or planets—but others believe it was an entirely different substance, made of particles that weighed 100 times more than visible matter. While the truth of the matter as yet remains a mystery, Rubin's research gained considerable respect within the scientific community. For all the attention her work received, Rubin remained more interested in the work itself. "Fame is fleeting," she told *Discover.* "My numbers mean more to me than my name. If astronomers are still using my data years from now, that's my greatest compliment."

Shared Passion for Astronomy with Others

Years before she asked for a job at the Department of Terrestrial Magnetism (DTM) at the Carnegie Institution of Washington in 1965, Rubin already had an interest in DTM. After she became a staff member there, she enjoyed the freedom to pursue her interests without the pressure to publish. The family-like atmosphere at DTM included daily staff lunches and scientific discussions. It was the right place for Rubin to thrive. David Burstein, who worked with Rubin from 1977 to 1979, noted that she always found personal satisfaction in her work that had nothing to do with money or publicity.

As Rubin changed modern understanding of the universe, she shared her vision with the younger generation through teaching. From 1954 to 1955 she served as an instructor of mathematics and physics at Montgomery County Junior College. From 1955 to 1965 she was a research associate astronomer at Georgetown University and from 1959 to 1965 was a lecturer then assistant professor of astronomy at Georgetown University. Even after she accepted a research position, Rubin taught astronomy courses at her children's high school and served on an advisory board for an inner-city youth science program. She also worked with the National Academy's Committee on Human Rights.

Despite her years of teaching, it was not until 1963 that Rubin began to feel like an astronomer. She worked at the University of California at San Diego with Margaret and Geoffrey Burbidge, who had done notable research indicating that chemical elements are made in stars. Rubin felt she was finally working with people who were interested in what she had to say and that her ideas had credibility. Rubin became a professional observer at Kitt Peak in Arizona before she settled on her career at DTM and was the first woman allowed to observe at Palomar Observatory.

Personal

Rubin is married to Robert Rubin, whom she met while he was a fellow graduate student at Cornell University majoring in physical chemistry. Robert chauffeured Rubin, who does not drive, back and forth to class while she was working on her Ph.D. At the time, Rubin's parents helped her take care of her first two children. All four of her children have since earned doctorates in scientific fields. David (born 1950) has a Ph.D. in geology, Judy (born 1952) has a Ph.D. in cosmic-ray physics, Karl (born 1956) has a Ph.D. in mathematics, and Allan (born 1960) has a Ph.D. in geology.

Because of her struggles to gain credibility as a woman astronomer, Rubin continued to encourage young girls to pursue their dreams of investigating the universe. She wrote a children's book titled *My Grandmother Is an Astronomer* in the hopes that other children will experience some of the joy she feels watching the night skies.

Periodicals

Discover, October 1990.
Scientific American, March 1998.

Online

Biography.com, http://search.biography.com/ (October 15, 2001).
''Vera Rubin and Dark Matter,'' *CWP at Physics, UCLA,* http://www.physics.ucla.edu/~cwp/ (October 15, 2001).
''Vera Rubin's Dark Universe,'' *Lake Afton Public Observatory Web site,* http://web.physics.twsu.edu/lapo/ (October 15, 2001). □

S

Allan Rex Sandage

Astronomer Allan Rex Sandage (born 1926) took it as his life's work to find out how old and how large the universe is. His work led him to conclude the universe is 15 billion to 20 billion years old. Sandage is credited with the discovery of quasars, small blue cosmic objects that may be places where stars are born.

Became a Stargazer

Born on June 18, 1926, Sandage was an only child. His father was a business professor at Miami (Ohio) University and his mother was the daughter of the president of a Church of Jesus Christ of Latter Day Saints (Mormon) school. On quiet Ohio nights, Sandage enjoyed watching the stars through a friend's telescope. Soon he was keeping an eye on the skies day and night. As a teenager, he kept a record of sunspots he observed over a period of four years. Young Sandage read writings by British astronomer and mathematician Arthur Stanley Eddington and *The Realm of the Nebulae* (1936) by Edwin P. Hubble.

After studying physics and philosophy at Miami University, Sandage served in the U.S. Navy as an electronics specialist during World War II. After the war, he earned a bachelor's degree in physics from the University of Illinois in 1948 and a Ph.D. from the California Institute of Technology in 1953.

While still a student, Sandage worked at the Palomar Observatory with astronomers Hubble and Walter Baade,

trying to discover the secrets of the universe through the world's largest telescope at that time. Sandage later used the 100-inch Hooker telescope on Mount Wilson and the 200-inch Hale telescope on Mount Palomar to uncover mysteries such as the evolution of stars.

Measured the Universe

In 1952, Sandage joined Carnegie Observatories, where he became involved in investigating the origins of the universe. During his first year, he equated the luminosity of the globular clusters M92 and M3 to the luminosity of the sun. He found that stars in those globular clusters were as much as 12 billion years old.

In September 1953, Hubble died of a heart attack. Sandage continued the painstaking work that Hubble had begun. He found that gathering data and eliminating errors were daunting tasks. Still, after much analysis, he found that Hubble's original estimates of the universe's age were more conservative than the data seemed to indicate. Sandage's results in 1958 seemed to show that the universe was 7 to 13 billion years old, much greater than Hubble had thought. By 1975, Sandage began to think the universe was even more ancient, perhaps 15 or 20 billion years old.

To determine the age of a star, Sandage looked at a classic color-magnitude diagram. He plotted the brightness of stars against their colors or temperatures. How bright a star is depends on its age, mass, and chemical makeup. Sandage looked at the relationships between stars that belong to younger clusters and stars that belong to older clusters to find clues to stellar evolution.

Working with Gustav Tammann, of the University of Basel, Switzerland, and Dr. Abijit Saha, of Kitt Peak National Observatory, Sandage found that the universe is expanding at a speed of about 55 kilometers/second/

megaparsec. This speed indicates that the universe is about 14 billion years old. Some stars have since been calculated to be about 15 billion years old, which bolsters Sandage's theory.

As an observational cosmologist, Sandage built on the work Hubble began in the 1920s and 1930s. Before long, Sandage was known as Mr. Cosmology, or the SuperHubble. Hubble-Sandage variable stars take their name from the energetic astronomer and his mentor.

Discovered Quasars

In 1964, Sandage and his colleague Thomas Matthews discovered sources of concentrated radio energy in distant space. They called them quasars, short for quasi stellar radio sources. The center of a quasar is thought to be a black hole that sucks in gases and other materials that form the discus shape associated with quasars. Quasars are very bright, probably about 1,000 times brighter than the Milky Way Galaxy. They are thought to be the most distant objects in the universe: in 1968 Maarten Schmidt found that they are located on the edge of the known universe.

Wrote on Religion

Unlike some scientists who see religion and science as opposed, Sandage believes they are complementary. In an article he wrote for *Truth Journal*, Sandage said science should take religion seriously and religion should respect science. "Science makes explicit the quite incredible natural order, the interconnections at many levels between the laws of physics, the chemical reactions in the biological processes of life, etc.," he wrote. "But science can answer only a fixed type of question. It is concerned with the *what, when,* and *how.* It does not, and indeed cannot, answer within its method (powerful as that method is), *why.*"

Defended Theories

Observational cosmologists disagree on how to measure distances between Earth and the stars. Critics have often attacked Sandage's premise that the universe is always expanding, and others have questioned his findings. But time proved Sandage's measurements to have validity, even if they were not accepted at first by all his peers.

When Sandage and Tammann found that some scientists were selecting stars and galaxies that were too bright to represent "standard candles"—a measurement scientists use to determine distances between Earth and celestial objects—Sandage found new ways to take measurements. While critics ignored Sandage's findings, he and his team looked into Type 1A supernovas to correlate galactic rotational velocities with brightness.

Sandage's skirmishes with his colleagues and critics over the expansion rate of the universe were so heated at times that they were sometimes called the "Hubble Wars." Despite all the controversy over his work, Sandage was always regarded as one of the top observational cosmologists in the world.

Sandage's book *Lonely Hearts of the Cosmos,* was published in 1991. In retirement, Sandage lives in Pasadena, California, with his wife, Mary Lois. They have two sons, David and John.

Periodicals

Astronomy, December 1997.
Current Biography Yearbook, January 1999.

Online

"Allan Rex Sandage," *The Bruce Medalists,* http://www.phys-astro.sonoma.edu/BruceMedalists/Sandage/index.html (October 15, 2001).
"Allan Sandage," *Carnegie Observatories,* http://www.ociw.edu/research/sandage.html (October 15, 2001).
"Discovery of Quasars," *Stellar,* http://www.stellar.co.nz/tl19.html (October 15, 2001).
"Sandage, Allan R.," *Biography.com,* http://search.biography.com/print_record.pl?id=19167 (October 15, 2001).
"Sandage, Allan R.," *Zoom Astronomy,* http://www.allaboutspace.com/subjects/astronomy/glossary/indexs.shtml (October 15, 2001).
"A Scientist Reflects on Religious Belief," *Origins: Truth Journal,* http://www.origins.org/truth/1truth15.html (October 15, 2001).
"2000 Cosmology Prize Recipient: Allan R. Sandage," *Peter Gruber Foundation,* http://www.petergruberfoundation.org/sandage.htm (October 15, 2001). □

Jack Schmitt

Harrison "Jack" Schmitt (born 1935), a geologist, was the first professional scientist to walk on the moon. In December 1972, he and Gene Cernan spent three days on the moon's surface, logging a record 301 hours on the surface and collecting a record 249 pounds of lunar material.

America's First Scientist-Astronaut

Born in Santa Rita, New Mexico, on July 3, 1935, Jack Schmitt received a bachelor's degree in science from the California Institute of Technology (Cal Tech) in 1957. He then traveled to Oslo, Norway, on a Fulbright Scholarship. He studied at the University of Oslo in 1957 and 1958 and worked with the Norwegian Geological Survey. Schmitt received his Ph.D. in geology from Harvard University in 1964.

After finishing his studies, Schmitt worked for the United States Geological Survey in New Mexico and Montana. He spent two summers in Alaska doing fieldwork. After that, he worked on photo and telescopic surveys of the moon for the U.S. Geological Survey's Astrogeology Center in Flagstaff, Arizona. While there, he helped teach geology to astronauts bound for the moon. On regular field trips,

Schmitt and other geologists taught the astronauts how to recognize rocks and geological formations they might find on the moon.

In June 1965, the National Aeronautics and Space Administration (NASA) selected Schmitt as the first of its scientist-astronauts. Alone among the astronauts in the Apollo program, Schmitt had no background as a pilot. He first had to learn to fly aircraft before he could progress to spacecraft training. After a 53-week flight training course at Williams Air Force Base in Arizona, Schmitt was certified by the Air Force as a jet pilot in 1965. He was also certified as a helicopter pilot by the U.S. Navy in 1967. He was an active participant in the space program during this time, helping to design the science mission to the moon and select landing sites and participating in the development of the field equipment used on the moon to sample rocks and other lunar material.

Chance of a Lifetime

Schmitt was named mission scientist for Apollo 11, the first flight to land people on the moon. He also trained as backup lunar module pilot for Apollo 15, the first flight to make use of a lunar rover, or "moon buggy."

Because he was not a career pilot, Schmitt initially felt that his chances for a moon landing "were very, very small, almost nonexistent," as he told EXN.ca, the Discovery Channel's Canadian web site. "It wasn't until really 1970, five years later, that I began to think that there was a possibility I might have a chance to go to the moon." In August 1971 Schmitt learned that he would walk on the moon. As he told EXN.ca, "That was when NASA finally made a decision to put a scientist on the last crew, and unfortunately to bump Joe Engle, who was the lunar module pilot on the backup crew for Apollo 14 that normally would have cycled into that mission."

Originally named for the Apollo 18 crew, Schmitt was reassigned to Apollo 17 after budget cuts and a dwindling public interest in manned moon flights led to the cancellation of all the moon missions scheduled to follow Apollo 17.

"A Geologist's Paradise"

On December 7, 1972, Schmitt took the geologist's ultimate field trip. After a three-day flight to the moon, Schmitt and mission commander Gene Cernan descended to the lunar surface aboard their lunar module *Challenger*, while the third crew member, Ron Evans, orbited the moon in the command module *America*. Schmitt and Cernan landed in a valley called Taurus-Littrow for a three-day stay on the moon. They stayed on the surface longer (301 hours, 51 minutes), spent more time out of their spacecraft (22 hours, 4 minutes), and returned more samples of lunar material (115 kilograms, or 249 pounds) than any previous lunar mission.

In an article titled "A Field Trip to the Moon," and published on the Internet, Schmitt wrote about seeing the moon after touchdown: "My first view out of the right-hand window, looking northwest across the Valley of Taurus-Littrow at mountains 2000 meters high, encompassed only part of a truly breathtaking vista and geologist's paradise.

Only later, when I could walk a few tens of meters away from the Challenger, did the full and still unexpected impact of the awe inspiring setting hit me: a brilliant sun, brighter than any desert sun, fully illuminated valley walls rising against a blacker than black sky, with our beautiful, blue and white marbled Earth hanging over the southwestern mountains."

In the same article, Schmitt described the lunar module to be "one of the more serviceable and comfortable camps in my experience as a field geologist.... Although two large, empty spacesuits made things cramped, sleeping in one-sixth G provided better rest than on Earth—just enough gravity to feel the hammock beneath you but not enough pressure to cause you to toss and turn. The freeze dried, dehydrated, and irradiated foods tasted fine, certainly better than some food prepared by geological field assistants in Alaskan field camps I have known. Possibly most important, there were no black flies or mosquitoes."

The most significant discovery Schmitt and Cernan made on the moon's surface was an unusual orange volcanic glass. The material was made up of microscopic glass beads formed in an ancient volcanic eruption as hot gasses thrown out of the moon's interior cooled into tiny spheres and fell back to the moon's surface. The Apollo 17 astronauts returned to Earth safely on December 19, 1972, and Schmitt was the last human being to walk on the moon in the twentieth century.

Served as U.S. senator

Schmitt stayed at NASA to manage the agency's Energy Program Office until 1975, then entered politics. In 1977, he became a United States senator representing New Mexico. He served on several Senate committees, including the Commerce, Science and Transportation Committee; the Banking, Housing and Urban Affairs Committee; and the Select Committee on Ethics. He also served as chairman of the Subcommittee on Science, Technology, and Space.

After his single six-year term as senator, Schmitt remained in the public eye, teaching, lecturing, consulting, and writing on lunar exploration, space policy, and geology. He became an adjunct professor of engineering at the University of Wisconsin, teaching a course called "Resources from Space." He has advised or served as a board member of the Independent Strategic Assessment Group of the U.S. Air Force Phillips Laboratory, the Orbital Sciences Corporation, the Draper Laboratory, the National Space Society, and the Lovelace Institutes, a biomedical research organization for which he served as chief executive officer in 1996.

Schmitt continued to be a strong advocate for the exploration and eventual settlement of space, lecturing extensively on the use of the moon as a natural resource and a source of non-polluting, non-toxic nuclear power. As he told EXN.com, " . . . Most important is the light isotope of helium that has been implanted in the lunar soils [by solar wind], called Helium 3. That is ideal fuel for fusion power. It is non-radioactive to begin with. It does not produce radioactivity in its purest form. It provides highly efficient power, twice as efficient as other types of power plants that we now use here on earth."

Schmitt predicts that, once power generation using nuclear fusion is perfected, Helium 3 from the moon would be worth "about $3 billion a metric ton" in today's dollars, allowing a lunar colony to be profitable. Schmitt told the University of Wisconsin publication Wisconsin Engineer, "The government will not sponsor the next major space program; the money will have to come from a private investor."

Books

Chaikin, Andrew, A Man on the Moon: The Voyages of the Apollo Astronauts, Penguin Books, 1994.

Online

"Apollo 17 Crew Information," Apollo Lunar Surface Journal, http://www.hq.nasa.gov/office/pao/History/alsj/a17/a17 .crew.html (October 29, 2001).
"Ask an Astronaut: Archives: Apollo 17 Crew," National Space Society, http://www.ari.net/nss/askastro/Apollo17/schmitbio .html (October 29, 2001).
"Astronaut Bio: Harrison Schmitt," Lyndon B. Johnson Space Center, http://www.jsc.nasa.gov/er/seh/schmitt.htm (October 29, 2001).
"Faculty Profile—Professor Harrison Schmitt," Wisconsin Engineer, http://www.cae.wisc.edu/~wiscengr/issues/feb98/ faculty.html (October 29, 2001).
"A Field Trip to the Moon," NEEP533 Syllabus, http://silver.neep .wisc.edu/~neep533/FALL2001/neep533/FILES/trip.html (October 29, 2001).
"Harrison Schmitt," Astronaut Hall of Fame, http://www .astronauts.org/astronauts/schmitt.htm (October 29, 2001).
"Harrison Schmitt," EXN.ca, http://www.exn.ca/Stories/1999/ 07/07/54.asp □

Menachem Mendel Schneerson

One of the most influential and prolific figures in 20th century Judaism, Rabbi Menachem Mendel Schneerson (1902-1994) expanded the Chabad Lubavitch from a small Jewish sect to a large, powerful religious movement.

Menachem Mendel Schneerson was the seventh rabbi of the Lubavitcher Hassidim. Descended from a rabbinical dynasty, the prolific Jewish leader guided his people through turbulent and triumphant times. His innovative efforts to reach out to Jews worldwide were essential in expanding the Chabad Lubavitch to a notable movement with more than 200,000 followers. Chabad Lubavitch is a sect of Hassidism, an Orthodox mystical form of Judaism. Founded in the 18th century by Rabbi Schneur Zalman, the movement originated in the Russian town of Lubavitch. The leader of the Lubavitchers is

a rabbi known as the Rebbe, a person believed to possess a unique soul with experiential knowledge of the divine. Schneerson was such an influential leader that after his death in 1994 many followers expected him to return to life and thereby prove he was the true Messiah.

Matured in Difficult Times

Menachem Mendel Schneerson was born to an illustrious Jewish family on April 18, 1902, in Nikolaev, a town in Ukrainian Russia. His father, Rabbi Levi Schneerson, was a great Torah scholar and respected Kabbalist. His mother, Rebbetzin Chanah, came from a prestigious rabbinical family. Menachem Mendel was named for his paternal great-grandfather, the third Lubavitcher Rebbe. At the age of five, Schneerson moved with his parents to the city of Yekatrinislav, where his father became the chief rabbi.

Under Czarist rule, Russian Jews were often subjected to pogroms and persecution simply for practicing their religion. Many were so strongly devoted to their faith and traditions that they refused to abandon them. Witnessing the persecution and commitment of his people at such an early age would influence Schneerson's views, goals, and teachings as an adult.

During his childhood, Schneerson was recognized by teachers as a Torah prodigy. He quickly outgrew formal Jewish schooling and was taught by private tutors. However, his knowledge soon surpassed that of the tutors. By the time Schneerson was in his teens he was corresponding with several noted Torah scholars.

At the same time, the social and political climate in Russia worsened. In 1917, as the Communists took control, their "Yevsekzia" (Jewish Section) embarked on a brutal attack against Judaism, shutting down schools and synagogues. The government imprisoned and sometimes executed Jewish leaders. At great personal risk, Rabbi Yosef Yitzchak Schneersohn, the sixth Lubavitcher Rebbe, established underground schools and provided money and kosher food to the struggling Jewish population. In 1923, Menachem Mendel Schneerson met Rabbi Yosef Yitzchak for the first time and joined him in his critical mission. Five years later, he married the rabbi's daughter, Chaya Mushka.

Shortly after the wedding, Schneerson and his new bride moved to Berlin, where he enrolled in the University of Berlin, studying mathematics, philosophy, and the Torah. When the Nazis came to power in 1933, the couple relocated to Paris. There, Schneerson continued his education, attending the Sorbonne and an engineering college until 1938. Following the Nazi invasion of Paris, the couple moved to the French cities of Vichy and then Nice.

Became Leader of Movement

In June 1941, Schneerson and his wife moved to New York to join her father, who had moved there the previous year. In New York, Schneerson resumed working with Yitzchak to establish the Lubavitcher movement in America and abroad. Schneerson was appointed head of the movement's educational arm, its social service organization, and its publishing house.

On January 28, 1950, the sixth Lubavitcher Rebbe died. Although he was the obvious choice for successor, Schneerson was initially reluctant to take the position, but he was committed to his father-in-law's vision for the movement's expansion—"to reach out to every Jew no matter how geographically or spiritually distant from his people." On January 17, 1951, Menachem Mendel Schneerson became the seventh Chabad Lubavitcher Rebbe.

Schneerson was determined to expand the Lubavitcher movement. He instituted a new and revolutionary approach to spreading Judaism and the Torah's message called *Shelichut. Shelichut* is a legal term in the Torah, referring to the appointment of an emissary to act in the place of another person. The Rebbe appointed thousands of *schluchim* (emissaries) to aid in recruiting converts.

In 1953, Schneerson founded the Lubavitcher Women's Organization to train women as community leaders. Schneerson addressed his teachings to both men and women, believing women had an important role in Jewish society.

Outreach was the crucial element in the growth of the Lubavitch and in Schneerson's growing popularity in the Jewish community. While Schneerson continued to inspire and educate practicing Hassidim, he also extended himself to disenfranchised Jews throughout the world. In a warm and non-judgmental manner, he welcomed people of all backgrounds to the movement.

Innovative Outreach

In the early 1960s, when many authority figures ignored or condemned rebellious youth, Schneerson reached out to them, developing Chabad Houses throughout the world where young people could study and congregate. New temples and synagogues soon sprouted up in remote areas around the globe.

In 1974, Schneerson tried a new form of outreach. Vans known as Mitzvah Tanks rolled through Manhattan. Religious melodies would blast from a loudspeaker on top of the vehicle. Adherents would approach people on sidewalks and ask them if they were Jewish. Men were invited to board the van and recite a short prayer to perform a mitzvah, or commandment. Women, who were not allowed to do a mitzvah, would receive a small kit for lighting Sabbath candles. Everyone would receive free literature. Before Schneerson's "mitzvah campaign," performing a mitzvah was always a private act in the home or synagogue.

Technology played a large role in Schneerson's outreach. In 1960, Schneerson began using radio to teach the Torah. In the 1970s Schneerson's talks were broadcast via telephone to major Chabad centers around the world. By the 1980s, they were delivered on cable television. As computer technology was introduced, the Chabad Lubavitch established a presence on the worldwide web.

Schneerson's influence continued to grow. His teachings were visibly noticeable in Crown Heights, a section of Brooklyn where the movement was centered. When Schneerson emphasized the Jewish commandment about having children, families in the Crown Heights Hassidic community doubled in size.

Schneerson's impact was also felt in Jewish communities throughout the world, especially in Israel. In 1967, the Israeli government launched a preemptive strike against its Arab neighbors. Schneerson spoke strongly and confidently about the Israeli victory, though he preached that spiritual strength was more important than military strength. Schneerson was an important factor in Israeli elections, a voice of confidence in Israel's security, and an advisor to many of the country's major political leaders. Pictures of the Rebbe were common in Israel, everywhere from army outposts to food stands on the street.

Time of Redemption

In 1978, Schneerson suffered a massive heart attack. Against his doctor's advice, he resumed working within a few weeks. Schneerson's work revolved around making the world ready for its impending time of redemption. He strongly believed that everyone has the power and responsibility to fulfill his or her spiritual potential and that each individual can bring the world closer to the time of the Messiah. He encouraged people of all faiths to practice good deeds.

In 1986, Schneerson started one of his most famous efforts to cultivate kindness and giving. Every Sunday, thousands of people would receive a single dollar bill and a blessing from the Rebbe. In this way, Schneerson hoped to encourage others to do charitable work.

As time passed, Schneerson amplified his message about what he believed was the impending arrival of the Messiah. At the close of his public address on April 11, 1991, the Rebbe stated: "I have done my part. Now it is in your hands." Shortly thereafter, Schneerson suffered a debilitating stroke, which left him unable to speak.

On June 12, 1994, the seventh Lubavitcher Rebbe died in Brooklyn. Schneerson had no children and named no successors, and that prompted many in the Hassidic community to speculate whether Schneerson was the Messiah. A year later, Schneerson was recognized for his achievements in education by being awarded the Congressional Medal of Honor. After his death, his teachings continued to remain influential throughout the world.

Books

Dalfin, Chaim, *The Seven Chabad Lubavitcher Rebbes*, Jason Aronson, 1998.
Deutsch, Shaul Shimon, *Larger than Life: The Life and Times of the Lubavitcher Rebbe Rabbi Menachem Mendel Schneerson*, Chasidic Historical Productions, 1995.
Jacobson, Simon, *Toward a Meaningful Life: The Wisdom of the Rebbe Menachem Mendel Schneerson*, William Morrow & Company, 1995.

Periodicals

The Christian Century, June 29, 1994; January 4, 1995.
National Review, November 30, 1992.
New Republic, June 27, 1994.
Publishers Weekly, July, 10, 1995; September 11, 1995.
U.S. News & World Report, December 26, 1994.

Online

"The Chabad Lubavitch of Cyberspace," *The Rebbe,* http://www.Chabad.org (December 2, 2001).
"The Rebbe," *The Rebbe,* http://www.TheRebbe.org (December 1, 2001). □

William Howard Schuman

American composer William Howard Schuman (1910-1992) was celebrated for his propulsive and energetic music, a body of work built upon the foundations of both traditional and modern techniques. His early compositions, largely conservative and deliberate, evoked the themes of American folk and straight-ahead jazz, while his later works departed somewhat from key signatures, though without sacrificing a melodic and lyrical quality.

Over the course of his career, composer William Schuman wrote ten symphonies, five ballet scores, four string quartets, concertos for various instruments, band pieces, and several works for voice, most notably the opera *The Mighty Casey.* Sharing his musical knowledge and organizational skills with others, he taught

operas, or listening occasionally to the recordings of Enrico Caruso and Efrem Zimbalist on the phonograph or pianola. During his grade-school days, Schuman did take lessons in violin and even performed a few times in public. But for the most part, he found learning the instrument a slow and painstaking process. Sports were Schuman's foremost passion, and he was particularly drawn to baseball. A true team participant, he played every fielding position, caught, pitched, and hit.

As a student at the Speyer Experimental Junior High School, a school for gifted children, Schuman excelled at sports and was seen more as a class prankster than a serious student. Slowly, however, he began to display signs of sensitivity. Favoring English over mathematics and science, Schuman harbored a secret love for poetry he kept from his sports-minded friends. Some of his favorites included Keats, Shelley, and other romantic writers, as well as modern poets such as Carl Sandburg, Robert Frost, and Walt Whitman. In 1925 he was selected, along with other school boys from New York, by the French government to spend a summer in France, his first trip abroad.

From Speyer, Schuman graduated to George Washington High School, where he experienced a new sense of independence. Although he continued to prefer baseball to music and literature, Schuman decided to form a jazz band he called Billy Schuman and his Alamo Society Orchestra, serving not only as the group's founder and manager, but also as its fiddler, banjo player, solo vocalist, and any other part needed. He could play just about any instrument he picked up, including the clarinet and piano. Still unschooled in writing scores and arranging, he taught each member their parts note for note. The Alamo Society Orchestra enjoyed a moderate amount of success playing local dances, weddings, bar mitzvahs, and the like. Meanwhile, Schuman took up the contrabass in his high school's orchestra, and at one competition for area high school ensembles he played the *Oberon Overture* with 19 different orchestras because contrabass players were so few.

During summers off from school, Schuman continued to explore his musical potential. At age 16, while at a camp in Maine that he had attended annually for several years, Schuman wrote his first piece of music, a tango titled "Fate." Additionally, he wrote music to lyrics for friend and fellow camper Edward B. Marks, Jr., the son of a well-known music publisher. Over the years, Schuman and Marks collaborated in writing and performing shows at camp, eventually co-authoring a musical comedy called *It's up to Pa,* from which two songs were later published. He also collaborated with another childhood friend, Frank Loesser, who later became a successful songwriter. In the case of Loesser's first-published song, "In Love with a Memory of You," Schuman composed the music, while Loesser penned the words.

Despite an obvious preoccupation with music, Schuman, upon graduating from high school in February of 1928, immediately entered New York University's School of Commerce to prepare himself for a career in business or possibly advertising. He worked for a time at Paramount Advertising Agency as a copywriter, took a job as a sales-

at Sarah Lawrence College from 1935 through 1945, served as president at New York's prestigious Juilliard School of Music from 1945 through 1961, and served as president of the Lincoln Center for the Performing Arts from 1962 until 1969. Schuman, the recipient of numerous awards and honorary degrees, won two Pulitzer prizes for his musical achievements, one in 1943 for the secular cantata "A Free Song" and the other in 1985 for his overall contributions to the art.

The son of Samuel Schuman, a businessman, and Rachel "Ray" (Heilbrunn) Schuman, William Howard Schuman—named after President William Howard Taft—was born in New York City on April 4, 1910, and grew up in a household that typified American life in the early decades of the 20th century. His parents, both born in New York City and of German Jewish descent, shared with many Americans a sense of idealism about their country, a pragmatic outlook on life, and a respect for the value of education. According to Schuman, his father probably never expected him to pursue anything but a practical career. Nonetheless, the elder Schuman, an open-minded man, never stood in the way of his son's ultimate artistic goals.

Followed Typical Boyhood Interests

Unlike many accomplished composers, Schuman never pursued music in earnest during his formative years. In fact, music played a relatively minor role in the Schumans's lives, aside from a ritual every Sunday evening when the family gathered around the piano singing light

man for a lithographer, and joined and quit a university social fraternity. Throughout these years, Schuman was drawn to popular music and the area near Manhattan's Times Square known as Tin Pan Alley more than ever. While pursuing his business interests, Schuman continued to write tunes for Marks and Loesser and performed in night clubs.

A New Discovery

On April 4, 1940, Schuman witnessed an event that would forever alter the direction of his life. That night, after much persuasion from his mother and sister, he saw Arturo Toscanini conduct the New York Philharmonic Orchestra. Schuman had previously resisted attending classical concerts, convinced they would bore him. But to his amazement, he was immediately captivated and realized at that moment he wanted to compose serious music. Schuman abruptly quit his business courses to seek formal musical study at the Malkin Conservatory of Music. Here, he studied harmony with Max Persin, who, in addition to introducing the aspiring composer to the classics, encouraged Schuman not to abandon his interest in popular music. Along the way, Schuman decided that he, too, wanted to teach, and in 1933, he enrolled at the Columbia University Teachers College, earning a bachelor's degree in 1935. Columbia University subsequently awarded Schuman a master's degree in music in 1937.

Schuman spent the summer of 1935 in Salzburg, Austria, working on his first symphony and studying conducting. Upon his return that autumn, he joined the faculty of Sarah Lawrence College in Bronxville, New York, where he taught music appreciation, harmony, and choral singing and conducted a student chorus that became masterful enough to perform with the Boston Symphony Orchestra at Carnegie Hall under Serge Koussevitsky. During his tenure at Sarah Lawrence, from 1935 until 1945, Schuman instituted a new approach to teaching by supplementing general arts instruction with courses in history and theory. Aside from learning the creative process, Schuman intended to provide students with a knowledge about art that would enrich their lives beyond graduation.

All the while, Schuman found time to further his own composing endeavors. Following years of composition study with Roy Harris, he won a contest with his second symphony in 1938, while his "Symphony No. 3" won the New York Music Critics' Circle Award in 1942. His "Symphony No. 4," completed in 1941, debuted with the Cleveland Symphony Orchestra in January of 1942. In April of that year, Eugene Ormandy and the Philadelphia Symphony presented it in both Philadelphia and New York. Another significant achievement arrived in 1943 when Schuman won the first Pulitzer Prize ever awarded in music for his "secular cantata" for chorus and orchestra titled "A Free Song."

Despite such successes, it was Schuman's "Symphony No. 5"—also known as the "Symphony for Strings"—that solidified the composer's public acceptance. Commissioned by the Koussevitzky Music Foundation and premiering on November 12, 1943, the work received numerous hearings. Compared to his third symphony, regarded for its grandeur and expansiveness, the tight, concise "Symphony No. 5" demonstrated Schuman's ability to appeal to the masses. Representative of his early affirmative and dynamic style, it remained his most popular work. After hearing the composer's latest work, Antony Tudor commissioned Schuman to write a score for his new ballet, "Undertow," which premiered in April of 1945 and remained in the repertoire of the American Ballet Theater for years thereafter.

Back at Sarah Lawrence, Schuman, since the early 1940s, had grown somewhat restless in his teaching position. Increasingly, the school forced him to take on private students, leaving him less time to focus on his own composing. Therefore, when asked to join music publisher G. Scribner as director of publications, he accepted the offer in June of 1945. With Scribner in a position that yielded him greater earnings and more time to explore composing opportunities, Schuman promoted such renowned figures as Samuel Barber, Leonard Bernstein, and Roger Sessions. However, three days after assuming his full-time directorial duties, Schuman left in order to accept another invitation, to serve as the new president of the famous Juilliard School of Music. Before taking on the role, though, Schuman, identifying several of the school's problems, met with the school board to ensure that he would be given sufficient latitude in which to implement certain changes.

Impacted Music Education in the United States

Under Schuman's leadership, Juilliard was essentially transformed into a 20th-century institution. His first area of business was to unify the joint, yet decidedly unequal, wings of the conservative graduate school and the school's Institute of Musical Art as a single entity. Next, he founded the Juilliard String Quartet, an ensemble that soon became one of the school's most famous representatives. Other important implementations included the creation of a bachelor of science program, the revival of Juilliard's opera program, the addition of contemporary music to the school's curriculum, and the introduction of a program of academic studies to produce enlightened, well-rounded musicians. "If the student truly absorbs the concept of free inquiry in the field of music," reasoned Schuman in the *Juilliard Report,* "unimpeded by blind adherence to doctrine and tradition, he will bring something of this approach not only to other fields of knowledge but to the conduct of his daily life."

While an administrator at Juilliard, Schuman continued to compose. His most recognized work of the late-1940s included ballet scores for modern dance pioneer Martha Graham: her masterpiece "Night Journey" (1947) as well as "Judith" (1949). In 1953 Schuman completed his first opera, "The Mighty Casey," wherein he ably extolled his love for baseball in a style that married operatic conventions with music-hall lightness. That same year, on August 18, also saw the premiere of "Voyage," Schuman's most ambitious piano work. In 1955, for the first time in history, the government of the United States commissioned a musical work, and Schuman responded to the request—from a State

Department commission for the U.S. National Committee for UNESCO—with "Credendum," an orchestral work that showed his growing rhythmic sophistication paired with the affirmative tone of his earlier compositions.

In 1962 Schuman became president of the Lincoln Center for the Performing Arts, for which the Juilliard School had acted as a constituent. Fittingly, the New York Philharmonic Symphony opened its 1962-1963 season at Philharmonic Hall of Lincoln Center with Schuman's recently completed "Symphony No. 8." During his tenure at the Lincoln Center, lasting until 1969, Schuman encouraged commissions and performances of American music, established a chamber music society and a film society, emphasized services to the urban community, and organized a summer series of special events. Following his resignation, he continued to serve on the boards of several distinguished organizations, among them the Metropolitan Opera Association, the Koussevitzy Music Foundation, the Walter W. Naumburg Foundation, and the Composers Forum. He was a fellow of the National Institute of Arts and Letters and an honorary member of the Royal Academy of Music in London, England.

In his later years, Schuman returned to his love of poetry, particularly Whitman, and vocal music, evidenced by works such as "Declaration Chorale" (1971), "Time to the Old" (1971), and "Perceptions" (1982). He also composed his second and last opera, "A Question of Taste" (1989). Following hip surgery, on February 15, 1992, Schuman died in New York City. He was survived by his wife, Frances Prince, whom he married in 1936, and the couple's two children, Anthony William and Andrea Frances Weiss.

Schuman will forever be remembered for his significant contributions to music education, his promotion of the arts in America, and his unique style as a composer. "If there is more of one ingredient than another in the rich mixture of William Schuman's music it is the strong-flavored energy that generates a constant boil of movement," concluded biographers Flora Rheta Schreiber and Vincent Persichetti. "There is motion stirred by boldness and intensity, movement that pushes forward resourcefully and seriously, and beneath even the quietest pages a restless current that will eventually surface in a rush."

Books

Contemporary Musicians, Gale, 1993.
Rouse, Christopher, *William Schuman, Documentary,* Theodore Presser Co., 1980.
Schreiber, Flora Rheta, and Vincent Persichetti, *William Schuman,* G. Schirmer, 1954.

Periodicals

New York Times, March 8, 1992. □

George C. Scott

George C. Scott (1927-1999) was one of the finest and most versatile stage, television, and film actors of the last half of the twentieth century, best known for his Oscar-winning performance as American General George Patton.

In an acting career that spanned five decades, Scott displayed a natural ability to capture the contradictory characteristics of intense inner anger and external composure. His performances in such films as *Anatomy of a Murder, The Hustler, Dr. Strangelove, Patton,* and *The Hospital* earned him a reputation for understated yet powerful performances. Scott's range and professionalism attracted many of American cinema's most acclaimed directors, including Stanley Kubrick, Stanley Kramer, Robert Rossen, John Huston, Otto Preminger, William Friedkin, Peter Medak, Stanley Donen, and Paul Schrader. Featuring rugged facial characteristics, including a nose frequently broken in bar fights, and a gruff voice, Scott was a prodigious drinker until the early 1980s. Scott was remembered for his rejection of the Academy Award he won for *Patton* in 1971 and of television's Emmy Award for his performance in Arthur Miller's *The Price.* He considered actors competing for awards "demeaning."

Struggled to Find Career

Scott was born in Wise, Virginia, a small, coal mining community in the Appalachian Mountains, on October 18, 1927. His paternal grandfather was a miner and his father worked as a mining surveyor. His mother wrote poetry and appeared on local radio stations; she died when Scott was young. His father took a job at a General Motors plant in the Detroit area when Scott was eight, moving the family to Michigan, where they lived first in Pontiac and then in Redford.

When he was old enough to enlist, Scott quit high school and joined the Marines for four years. Shortly after he enlisted, World War II ended and Scott spent much of his time assigned to Arlington National Cemetery in Virginia. Scott later said this job prompted him to start drinking regularly to help him cope with his daily contact with grieving family members and the corpses of soldiers.

Intent on becoming a writer, Scott used the G.I. Bill to enroll at the University of Missouri at Columbia and began studying journalism. His writing bent leaned more to creative writing than journalism, and he spent much of his time crafting short stories and submitting them to magazines. None were accepted, and Scott turned to the theater for creative expression. He tried out for the university's production of Terrence Rattigan's *The Winslow Boy* and earned the part of Sir Robert Morton. Scott was immediately bitten by the acting bug. "It was like tumblers falling in a lock," he later recalled. "I knew what a good safe-cracker felt like." He appeared in several more productions at the University of Missouri and a play at the all-female Stephens University, where he also taught a course in Western literature.

At Stephens, he met his first wife, Carolyn Hughes, and they had a daughter. Scott also fathered an illegitimate child with another Stephens student. He and his wife sought acting work in Ohio, Detroit, and Canada, but with little success. He divorced his wife and returned to Stephens hoping to resume teaching, but his divorce and illegitimate child caused the school to refuse to hire him. He worked one year in construction before auditioning for a semi-professional repertory theater in 1954.

Success on Stage and Screen

By 1956, Scott had married actress Pamela Reed and moved to New York City. He appeared in roles on such 1950s television programs as *Hallmark Hall of Fame, Kraft Theatre, Omnibus,* and *Playhouse 90.* In 1957, he won the title role in William Shakespeare's *Richard III* in Joseph Papp's New York Shakespeare Festival. His performance earned him a critical appraisal as "the meanest Richard III ever seen by human eyes," as well as an Obie Award. In 1958, he made his first Broadway appearance in *Comes a Day.*

In 1959, Scott was offered a supporting role as the drunk preacher Dr. George Grubb in the Gary Cooper western film *The Hanging Tree.* His next film role earned him a reputation as an actor's actor. Playing a hotshot big-city prosecuting attorney in *Anatomy of a Murder,* Scott was the nemesis of James Stewart's small-town defense attorney.

Directed by Otto Preminger and featuring a musical score composed and performed by Duke Ellington, the film earned Scott his first Academy Award nomination.

Following *Anatomy of a Murder,* Scott returned to New York, divorced Reed, and married actress Colleen Dewhurst. In 1961, he returned to film with a critically heralded performance as promoter Bert Gordon in Robert Rossen's adaptation of the Walter Tevis novel about pool players, *The Hustler.* Writing about Scott's performance in the film, Michael Sragow said: "Scott brought something novel to the screen: an electric wariness. No actor was better at portraying the point where thought and instinct fuse—and he did it best in *The Hustler* (racking up another supporting-actor nomination). If you saw it as a teenager, his image embodied everything murky and menacing in city life. He was the nightmare image of the man in the back room. . . . Studying the play of the game, Scott's craggy face oozes alertness from its pores, and his trim, energetic body (Scott grew massive later on) keeps him from seeming sedentary." Once again, Scott was nominated for a Best Supporting Actor Academy Award. Although Scott refused the nomination, his name remained on the ballot.

Before returning to Hollywood, Scott won another Obie Award for Eugene O'Neill's *Desire under the Elms.* Scott made his debut as a Hollywood leading man in John Huston's 1963 film *The List of Adrian Messenger.* During the 1963-64 television season, Scott starred in the weekly series *East Side, West Side* with Cicely Tyson.

Kubrick, Abraham, and Patton

In 1964, Scott appeared as General Buck Turgidson in Stanley Kubrick's satire of the Cold War, *Dr. Strangelove,* a role that allowed him to portray comically the anger that he usually repressed on screen. A parody of an insensitive military commander, Turgidson is an Air Force general who orders a nuclear strike against the Soviet Union, speaking such outrageous lines as "I don't say we wouldn't get our hair mussed, but I do say no more than ten to twenty million people killed."

His next big role was quite different. Starring as Abraham opposite Ava Gardner in the 1966 film *The Bible,* Scott's personal and professional life collided. Becoming romantically obsessed with Gardner, Scott allowed his marriage to Dewhurst to disintegrate while he pursued Gardner and accelerated his alcohol intake. He and Dewhurst divorced. Then he was fired from *How to Steal a Million* when he arrived on the film's set five hours late. His next film projects were *The Flim-Flam Man* in 1967 and *Petulia* with Julie Christie in 1968. He remarried Dewhurst but divorced her again five years later, marrying actress Trish Van Devere.

The film role for which he became best known was as the cantankerous but brilliant World War II military figure General George Patton in the 1970 film *Patton.* The film was given the Academy Award for Best Picture of 1970 and Scott was nominated and won the Academy Award, Golden Globe Award, and National Society of Film Critics Award for Best Actor. Dismissing the awards as a "self-serving meat parade," Scott stayed home to watch a hockey game rather than attend the Oscar ceremonies. Scott reprised his characterization of Patton in 1986 for a television drama *The Last Days of Patton*. He also refused his 1971 Emmy Award for his performance in Arthur Miller's *The Price.*

Stating that he loved acting more than stardom, Scott continued to act in both films and television. He portrayed a doctor disgusted with the political and financial aspects of the medical profession in *The Hospital*. The performance earned him another Academy Award nomination. His other notable films of the 1970s include *They Might Be Giants, Islands in the Stream, Movie Movie, Hardcore,* and *The Changeling*. While he continued to make films until his death, his best work in his later career came in television films such as *A Christmas Carol, The Murders in the Rue Morgue, The Last Days of Patton, 12 Angry Men,* and *Inherit the Wind*. For the last, he won an Emmy Award and Golden Globe Award. Scott died on September 22, 1999, in Westlake Village, California.

Books

Video Hound's Golden Movie Retriever, Visible Ink Press, 1994.

Online

"The Films of George C. Scott," *Images Journal,* http://www .imagesjournal.com/issue04/features/georgecscott5.htm

"George C. Scott," *Internet Movie Database,* http://us.imdb .com/Bio?Scott,+George+C

"George C. Scott," *The Sunday-Times of London,* September 24, 1999, http://www.sunday-times.co.uk/news/pages/tim/99/ 09/24/timobiobi02004.html?1996766.

"Piper Laurie Remembers George C. Scott," *Salon.com,* September 30, 1999, http://www.salon.com □

Thomas Alexander Scott

A respected railroad man of his generation, Thomas Alexander Scott (1823-1881) was instrumental in the expansion of Pennsylvania Railroad, though he failed to realize his vision of a true transcontinental railroad. Scott also played a significant role in the use of rail travel for the Union war effort during the Civil War.

Scott was born on December 28, 1823, in Fort Loudon, Pennsylvania (some sources say London, Franklin County, Pennsylvania). He was the seventh child born to Thomas Scott and had four younger siblings. His mother was Rebecca Douglas Scott. Scott's father ran a tavern, Tom Scott's Tavern, which was located in Franklin County on a turnpike between Philadelphia and Pittsburgh. It served as a stop for stagecoaches. Scott's father also ran a stage line.

Work was an important component of Scott's life from an early age. While receiving some education in country schools during the winter, he worked on the farm during the rest of the year. His father died when Scott was rather young

(sources vary about Scott's exact age, noting he was 10, 12, or 16). His first jobs were working in general stores, in locales such as Waynesboro and Bridgeport, when he lived with different siblings. Among Scott's positions was handyman. Though his education was limited, Scott became well-read because he continually educated himself through books.

In about 1840, Scott took a position as a clerk in a state office in Columbia, Pennsylvania. It was run by his brother-in-law, Major James Patton, and collected tolls on roads and canals. He spent about six years there through 1847. Scott then spent about three years as chief clerk of the Philadelphia toll collector. Scott also spent a year working for Leech and Company, a transporting firm. During this time in his professional life, Scott gained much experience in business practices that would help him in his career in railroads.

Began Working for Pennsylvania Railroad

In 1850, Scott was hired by the Pennsylvania Railroad as a station agent in Duncansville. It was a fortuitous time to enter the railroad business. Railways were expanding throughout the country, and many new lines were being built. Those with solid decision-making ability, like Scott, could move quickly up the company ladder because of the need for numerous managers. Scott himself was promoted regularly throughout the 1850s.

Scott was elevated to the position of general-superintendent of the mountain district of Altoona, headquartered at Duncansville, in 1852. He was named the general agent at the Pennsylvania Railroad's Pittsburgh office in 1853. By 1855, Scott was promoted to third assistant superintendent and was based in Pittsburgh for the company's western division. Among Scott's employees was Andrew Carnegie, whom Scott came to mentor after hiring him as his personal telegraph operator and later his assistant. Scott taught him much about railroads and business methods, and Carnegie went on to become one of America's leading businessmen in the late nineteenth century.

By the second half of the 1850s, Scott was given the position of general superintendent of the whole of the Pennsylvania Railroad line. In 1859, Scott was again promoted to first vice president in charge of all operations, advising J. Edgar Thompson, the company's president. The company continued to expand and Scott played a key role in it. Scott's move up the company ladder was temporarily halted, however, by the beginning of the Civil War.

Played Key Roles in Civil War

When the Civil War broke out in the early 1860s, Scott served his country and his company in numerous capacities. One of the first ways was in an advisory role to the newly elected president, Abraham Lincoln, in 1861. He told the president that to avoid potential assassination attempts, Lincoln should not take the published route into Washington. Instead, Scott believed, Lincoln should enter the city on the sly, using the rail. Lincoln took his advice.

From 1861 to 1862, Scott served as an assistant secretary of war and was in charge of supervising all government railways and transportation lines. Among his duties related to this position, Scott controlled all railways and telegraphs related to the Union government. Scott also organized railroad resources to allow communications between Annapolis and Washington. In addition, Scott initiated a new railway line that ran between Washington and Philadelphia. This allowed the government to transport men and supplies between Harrisburg and Annapolis. But railways were not Scott's only focus. He also organized the use of rivers in the northwest and west for the army.

Scott was also an officer in the Union Army and served on the staff of Governor Andrew G. Curtin. He advised the general and others on how to use railway in the war. Scott also accomplished a first in modern warfare. In 1863, he organized and oversaw a large-scale movement by rail of an entire army. Scott supervised the movement of 13,000 men, their supplies, and their horses from Nashville to Chattanooga, Tennessee. Scott planned other such troop movements as well. In 1863, Scott also served as the assistant quartermaster general for General Hooker's staff. As an unnamed author wrote in the *Journal of Commerce,* "Mr. Scott's logistical efforts are credited with keeping the Union Army well supplied and on the move throughout the struggle."

Named President of Pennsylvania Company

When the Civil War ended, Scott returned to the Pennsylvania Railroad as president of the western division with goals of continued expansion at the fore. Scott also contin-

ued his rise through the ranks of the company. In 1870, he was named president of the Pennsylvania Company. This was a newly created subsidiary of the Pennsylvania Railroad which was to consolidate and operate all the company's lines (owned or leased) west of Pittsburgh. It was part of an aggressive campaign to expand the railroad west. Newly built lines in the east and Midwest came under Pennsylvania's control by lease or stock ownership.

As part of this strategy of expansion as well as for his own personal gain, Scott played key roles in other railroad operations. He had interests in railroads such as the Southern Railway Security Company and the Atlantic and Pacific Railroad. From 1871 until 1872, Scott served as president of the Union Pacific Railroad. Scott's tenure ended when he sold his part to Jay Gould, who was trying to build his own transcontinental railway system centered around the Erie Railroad. Scott shared this goal and was soon put in a position to realize it.

Promoted to Head of Pennsylvania Railroad

In 1874, the head of the Pennsylvania Railroad, J. Edgar Thompson, died. Upon his death, Scott was named president in his place. When Scott took over, he was in charge of the world's largest railroad that was under one management. Because the Pennsylvania Railroad was already well run and ordered, Scott had the freedom to pursue his ultimate goal: a transcontinental railroad that stretched from the Atlantic Ocean (in Pennsylvania) to the Pacific Ocean (in California) via St. Louis. This railroad was to be called the Texas and Pacific Railroad. Scott was its founder and also served as president while remaining at the helm of the Pennsylvania.

Faced Numerous Challenges

Scott's focus at Pennsylvania Railroad continued to be strengthening the company's position and consolidation. He worked to reduce floating debt. Scott revised operating methods to be more economically efficient and improve coordination between parts of the company to reduce costs. Despite Scott's best efforts, earnings at the railroad continued to fall. The company had to tighten its belt by limiting improvements to those that were necessary, except for replacing all the iron rails with stronger steel.

On another front Scott also failed. His dream of a transcontinental railroad with the Texas and Pacific—and the related California and Texas Railroad Construction Company which was to build it—was not fully realized. The final terminus for this railroad was just past El Paso in west Texas. Scott's difficulties in the matter were not of his own making, though. Neither his companies nor any railroad looking to expand in the west could get land grants from the Federal government after the scandal surrounding Credit Mobilier. There were also widespread economic problems because of the financial panic and the economic depression that followed in 1873. While his construction company had problems for several years, a financial reorganization in 1875 solved many of the money flow problems.

In 1877, Scott had to deal with a difficult situation related to the Pennsylvania Railroad. From July 19 to 22 of that year, the great Pittsburgh riot occurred, then spread west to St. Louis when it could not be dispersed by sheriffs or the local militia. It was initially caused by a trainmen's strike that came to engage other workers and the unemployed as well. The strike began in response to Scott and the Pennsylvania Railroad's decision to reduce wages by ten percent and double the amount of cars per train, which meant that fewer trainmen would be used. Scott made this decision as part of a cost reduction move. The riot resulted in the death of many and $5 million in property damage in Pittsburgh alone.

On June 1, 1880, Scott retired from Pennsylvania Railroad. His retirement was prompted by two circumstances. One was his failure to complete his transcontinental railroad, leaving his tenure at the top of his profession incomplete. Scott also had serious health problems. In 1878, Scott suffered a stroke. While he was able to continue working at first, the effects of the stroke began to make working impossible within months.

Before his death a short time after his retirement, Scott sold the Texas and Pacific Railroad to his old competitor, Jay Gould. Despite the ups and downs of the deal, Scott did not lose any money. Scott was not always so successful in his business dealings. In addition to his work with railroads, Scott was something of a venture capitalist on his own. He invested in the oil boom in Pennsylvania and California (the latter failed) as well as agricultural land development, primarily in California.

Scott died on May 21, 1881, at his home, named "Woodburn," which was located near Darby, Pennsylvania. It was believed by some that he worked himself to death. He was survived by his second wife, Anna Dike Riddle, and four children, two from his first marriage to Anna Margaret Mullison and two from his second. As George H. Burgess and Miles C. Kennedy wrote in *Centennial History of the Pennsylvania Railroad Company,* "From all existing accounts, Thomas Scott was a man of truly extraordinary charm. In an age when democracy and democratic manners were little known to business executives, Scott was affable, friendly and unassuming. . . . Add to this a keen intelligence, even temper, boundless energy, and inexhaustible patience, it is clear that he would have gone far in any field." Scott was inducted into the Railroad Hall of Fame in 1992.

Books

Burgess, George, and Miles C. Kennedy, *Centennial History of the Pennsylvania Railroad Company,* The Pennsylvania Railroad Company, 1949.

Garraty, John A., and Jerome L. Sternstein, eds., *Encyclopedia of American Biography,* HarperCollins, 1996.

Ingham, John N., *Biographical Dictionary of American Business Leaders: N-U,* Greenwood Press, 1983.

Johnson, Rossiter, ed., *The Twentieth Century Biographical Dictionary of Notable Americans,* The Biographical Society, 1904.

Kamm, Samuel Richey, *The Civil War Career of Thomas A. Scott,* University of Pennsylvania, 1940.

Lamar, Howard R., ed., *The New Encyclopedia of the American West,* Yale University Press, 1998.

Malone, Dumas, ed., *Dictionary of American Biography,* Charles Scribner's Sons, 1963.

Periodicals

Journal of Commerce, January 7, 1992. □

Eric Sevareid

Joining CBS Radio as a protege of noted journalist Edward R. Morrow, Eric Sevareid (1912-1992) was the last U.S. correspondent to broadcast from Paris, France, before that country fell to the Nazi invasion in June 1940, near the start of World War II. He went on to a long career as a radio and television news broadcaster, writer, and commentator.

Journalist Eric Sevareid understood the average American, and Americans learned about the Spanish Civil War, World War II, the Korean conflict, and the Vietnam War through his reporting. A self-proclaimed sentimental lover of the English language, he was given to drawn-out discussions rife with sophisticated vocabulary. Asked by veteran journalist Edward R. Murrow to join young reporters such as William L. Shirer, Charles Collingwood, Howard K. Smith, and Daniel Schorr on the popular Columbia Broadcast System (CBS) Radio news program in 1939, Sevareid became known and trusted by millions of listeners for whom CBS News was their source for news about World War II and the Cold War that followed. Sevareid and "Murrow's Boys," as these young journalists were dubbed, remained at the top of their field until radio news was overshadowed by the rise of television in the 1950s. Sevareid continued his long career in television news. Even into the 1990s, Sevareid continued to appear on special reports on American news shows.

Early Interest in Press

Sevareid was born on November 26, 1912, in Velva, North Dakota. His parents, Alfred and Clare (Hougen) Sevareid, like many of the wheat farmers and other inhabitants of the area, were of Norwegian descent. Alfred Sevareid was college educated and a bank president. Clare, who had a love of classical music and the plays of William Shakespeare, devoted herself to raising Eric and his two brothers and sister. Young Eric's interest in the press was evident as early as age six, when he hung around the offices of his father's friend Bill Francis, editor of the *Velva Journal.* In 1925, when Eric was 13, he and his family left drought-ridden Velva after Arnold Sevareid's bank failed. The Sevareids moved first to Minot before settling in a middle-class neighborhood in Minneapolis, Minnesota.

After graduating from Minneapolis Central High School in 1930 with experience as editor of the school paper, Sevareid and close friend Walter Port began a 2,250-mile

wilderness canoe trip north to Canada's Hudson Bay. The *Minneapolis Star* sponsored the two young men on their adventure. In his 1946 autobiography, *Not So Wild a Dream,* Sevareid wrote: "I knew instinctively that if I gave up, no matter what the justification, it would become easier forever afterwards to justify compromise with any achievement." Sevareid transformed this trip into the book *Canoeing with the Cree,* published in 1935.

Began Career in Journalism

Sevareid started with the *Minneapolis Journal* as a copy boy and within two months was promoted to reporter. Working full time for the *Journal* during his freshman year, he enrolled in night classes in economics and political science at the University of Minnesota. In the fall of 1932 he became a full-time student, supporting himself with articles for the rival *Star* and becoming involved in a number of liberal clubs and causes. He graduated in 1935 with a degree in political science. The previous fall, he had eloped with Lois Finger, the sister of a college teacher. She completed her law degree around the time the couple had their public wedding in May 1935.

Sevareid returned to the *Journal* as a reporter, but in 1937 the paper fired him because of his independent stance on several social issues. Sevareid and his wife moved to Europe in the fall of 1937. On their trip they had dinner with a friend of a friend, an American news correspondent stationed in London named Edward R. Murrow. Once in Paris, Eric was determined to continue his education. He edited

the Paris edition of the *New York Herald Tribune* while studying at the Alliance Française and doing coursework at the London School of Economics.

In Paris, Sevareid came into his own. Dropping his first name of Arnold and using his middle name professionally, he got a job as night editor at the Paris branch of United Press International. Then a phone call changed the course of his career. In August 1939, with war on the horizon, Murrow telephoned from London and asked Sevareid to join his team of news correspondents. Impressed by the 27-year-old reporter's spare yet refined journalistic style, Murrow took Sevareid under his wing at CBS. As a European correspondent for what was becoming the most popular radio news network in the United States, Sevareid transfixed Americans with his on-the-spot reports on the progress of the French Army and Air Force in central Europe.

On the Front Lines

Living in France with his wife and their newborn twins Michael and Peter on the eve of the Nazi occupation, Sevareid was the last U.S. reporter to make a live broadcast from the vicinity of Paris before that city fell to Germany. Sending Lois and his children back to safety in New York City, Sevareid moved on to Tours and Bordeaux, and he was the first reporter to break the story of France's capitulation to the Germans.

Relocating to London, he joined Murrow and the rest of the CBS news team in reporting on the Nazi bombing campaign during the Battle of Britain. The imagery he included in his reports struck at the heart of America and conveyed the tragedy of war. In a broadcast made in London near the close of the war, Sevareid noted: "Only the soldier really lives the war. The journalist does not. He may share the soldier's outward life and dangers, but he cannot share his inner life because the same moral compulsion does not bear on him. War happens inside a man. It can never be communicated. A million martyred lives leave an empty place at only one family table. That is why, at bottom, people can let wars happen. And that is why nations survive them and carry on."

Sevareid soon returned to the United States. One of his first actions was to register for the draft. "When you've seen the homes of civilians destroyed, hospitals bombed and helpless women and children killed in the streets and in air raid shelters," Sevareid noted in an interview with the U.S. press upon his return, "you have a new idea of what's important." Though a seasoned combat reporter, Sevareid was put on a less dangerous assignment, covering the war effort from Washington, but in 1943 he was assigned to cover the Chinese-Burma-India theater. He and 19 others were forced to bail out of a damaged aircraft just before it crashed behind Japanese lines in the jungles of Burma. Discovered by a tribe of headhunters, the group emerged from the jungle a month later and Sevareid went on to cover the war in Asia. In January 1944 he moved to Italy, France, Germany, and into parts of eastern Europe before the war ended. He covered the United Nations peace conference in the spring of 1945.

Assigned to Washington, D.C. in a variety of capacities for CBS radio following World War II, Sevareid covered the 1948, 1952, and 1956 presidential elections and in 1949 received the first of three George Foster Peabody Awards for his role as chief Washington correspondent.

Television Brought New Challenges

The arrival of television in the 1950s signaled a new era in news reporting, and although Sevareid continued to view himself as a writer—he published articles in a number of news magazines and was the author of a weekly newspaper column—he quickly became a media celebrity. He was featured in Murrow's 1951 documentary *See It Now.* In 1961 he narrated *Great Britain: Blood, Sweat, and Tears plus Twenty Years* for CBS. In 1961 he moved to New York and a year later he divorced his wife, Lois. In February 1963 he married Cuban singer Belén Marshall. They had a daughter, Cristina, before divorcing 11 years later.

During the early 1960s Sevareid was a common sight on CBS, as moderator of the programs *Town Meeting of the World, Years of Crisis,* and *Where We Stand* and covering both political parties' national conventions in 1964. In November 1964, he left New York and returned to Washington, where he became a national correspondent and commentator for CBS. Watergate, a political scandal that rocked the United States during the presidential campaign of 1972 and culminated in the resignation of President Richard M. Nixon two years later, prompted a harsh reaction from Sevareid, who commented in a broadcast on May 1, 1974: "These are men whose minds are irrevocably fixed in the 'We or They' view of life and politics. . . . They are not interested in destroying their opponent's arguments, but in destroying their opponents, personally. . . ."

In 1977 Sevareid was forced to retire from CBS because of the network's mandatory retirement policy. However, he remained at CBS as a consultant and continued to appear on special news programming throughout the next 15 years. He married for the third time in 1979 to television producer Suzanne St. Pierre. On December 7, 1991, he made his final appearance on the CBS program *Remember Pearl Harbor?* On July 9, 1992, Sevareid died of stomach cancer in Washington.

The author of several books and numerous articles, Sevareid received many acknowledgments of his contribution to American journalism, among them awards from the Overseas Press Club and the New York Newspaper Guild, which honored him with their Page One Award for an article he wrote on statesman Adlai E. Stevenson two days before Stevenson's death in July 1965. To those Americans who recalled his many broadcasts, Sevareid was considered one of the best radio war correspondents of all time; to students of mass media he was respected as a consummate journalist, as well as one of the groundbreaking reporters in television commentary.

Books

Gates, Gary Paul, *Air Time: The Inside Story of CBS News,* Harper & Row, 1978.
McKerns, Joseph P., editor, *Biographical Dictionary of American Journalism,* Greenwood Press, 1987.
Newsmakers, Gale, 1993.
Schroth, Raymond A., *The American Journey of Eric Sevareid,* Steerforth Press, 1995.
Sevareid, Eric, *Not So Wild a Dream,* 1946.
Sevareid, Eric, *This Is Eric Sevareid,* McGraw Hill, 1967.

Periodicals

New York Post, November 21, 1965. □

Ravi Shankar

Perhaps the best known Indian musician, sitar player and composer Ravi Shankar (born 1920) is credited more than any other individual with introducing Indian musical traditions to the West and expanding those traditions to incorporate Western classical, popular music, and minimalist musical forms.

Already an established musician and composer in his homeland during the 1940s, Shankar gained international attention in the 1950s with his collaborations with violinist Yehudi Menuhin and, in the 1960s and 1970s, with his featured performances at the 1967 Monterey Pop Festival, the 1969 Woodstock Festival, and the 1971 Concert for Bangladesh. His friendship with guitarist, songwriter, and producer George Harrison of the Beatles, which began in 1966, resulted in the introduction of traditional Indian instrumentation on several Beatles recordings. Harrison repaid the favor by lending his guitar playing and production to Shankar's albums *Shankar Family & Friends* and *Festival of India.* These recordings and his close association with the Beatles raised the Western youth culture's interest in Indian music. Shankar is also credited with influencing the jazz recordings of John and Alice Coltrane and the minimalist compositions of Phillip Glass, with whom Shankar collaborated on *Passages.* He has also composed music for flautist Jean Pierre Rampal, Japanese musician Hosan Yamamoto, and jazz musicians Bud Schank, John Handy, and Buddy Rich.

Early Years in Bengal and Paris

Born Robindra Shankar in West Bengal on April 7, 1920, Shankar was the youngest of four sons who survived childhood born to the Brahmin family of Pandit Shyam Shankar, a Sanskrit, Vedic, and philosophy scholar. The elder Shankar also served as a diwan, or legal minister serving the Maharaja (king) of Jhalawar in Rajasthan. The close relationship of Shankar's mother with the Maharani (queen) granted him access to private royal musical events, which exposed him to many of India's most famous performers of the day.

By the time he was ten, Shankar's older brother, Uday Shankar, established himself as a professional dancer in Europe with Anna Pavlova. After forming his own Indian

dance company in Paris, Uday invited his mother and brothers to join him in 1930. The troupe toured throughout Europe, introducing the Shankars to European culture. Ravi Shankar became an accomplished dancer and contemplated making dance his profession. When virtuoso Indian musician Ustad Allauddin Khan joined the troupe for one year in 1935, however, Shankar's interest in becoming a musician was renewed.

Khan, called "Baba" by Shankar, began giving him sitar and voice lessons but became annoyed that the lessons seemed secondary to dancing. "Sometimes, he would become upset and grow angry when I was learning, because, although I was a good student, he felt that dance was uppermost in my thoughts," Shankar later noted. "It angered and hurt him that I should be 'wasting my musical talent' and living in glitter and luxury. Baba insisted that this was no way to learn music from him, not in these surroundings, and he swore I would never go through the discipline and master the technique of the sitar."

Shankar quit dancing in 1938 and returned to India to finish his Brahmin initiation, determined to master the sitar. After spending two months abstaining from worldly comforts and eating specially prepared foods, he traveled to Maihar in central India to seek more lessons from Khan. Khan conducted his school like an ashram, requiring his pupils to approach their instrument as a spiritual exercise and to honor him as their guru. Khan and Shankar became very close during the seven years that Shankar studied in Maihar. Shankar married Khan's daughter, Annapurna, in

1941, and they had a son, Shubho, in 1942. Khan's son, Ali Akbar Khan, became a world-renowned musician and a frequent collaborator and touring partner with Shankar.

National and International Fame

After completing his training with Khan, Shankar moved to Bombay, where he joined the Indian People's Theatre Association. He composed the music for the ballet *India Immortal* in 1945, and, in 1946, soundtrack music for the films *Dharti Ke Lal* and *Neecha Nagar* and wrote new music for India's national song "Sara Jahan Se Accha." In 1947, he celebrated India's independence by adapting the works of Nehru for the ballet *Discovery of India.*

In 1949, Shankar moved to Delhi to accept the director of music post at All-India Radio. He organized and composed music for Vadya Vrinda, the National Orchestra, which is credited with expanding the possibilities of Indian orchestral music. He also composed film scores for Satyajit Ray's acclaimed *Apu* trilogy.

In 1954, Shankar toured the Union of Soviet Socialist Republics with the first Indian Cultural Delegation. He conducted a solo tour of Europe and America in 1956. After releasing two acclaimed albums, *Ravi Shankar Plays Three Classical Ragas* and *India's Master Musician,* in 1957, he toured Japan as leader of a cultural delegation and played at the UNESCO Music Festival in Paris in 1958.

Influenced Western Music

Recognition for Shankar's music increased in the 1960s, and he began seeking ways to integrate Indian music with Western musical forms. In 1962, he released the jazz-influenced album *Improvisations* with Bud Shank. He also instructed horn player Don Ellis and jazz saxophonist John Coltrane in Indian music, leading to Coltrane's modal experimentation on several groundbreaking jazz albums of the 1960s. Shankar also contributed his composition *Rich a la Rakha* to jazz drummer Buddy Rich and tabla player Alla Rakha.

In 1966, Shankar met and became friends with George Harrison, the guitarist of the Beatles. Harrison's interest in Eastern religions had led him to Indian music. Harrison, in turn, introduced the band's producer, George Martin, and the other Beatles to Indian music. The Beatles first employed a sitar accompaniment on the song "Norwegian Wood." Soon, other rock groups such as the Butterfield Blues Band and the Byrds were displaying Indian influences. Shankar's appearances at both the Monterey Pop and Woodstock festivals increased his popularity among Western youth. But Woodstock's audience mistakenly applauded him for tuning his instrument, and, with the exception of the Concert for Bangladesh, Shankar refused to perform at other pop music festivals. "After I went to Woodstock and one or two others, I thought maybe I should not go anymore," he noted, adding, "It sort of hurts me to see people all stoned and doing silly things, things I couldn't imagine. And our music needs a bit of respect like any serious music—Bach, Mozart—so when I found that it was not possible, I thought it was better to keep away."

In 1971, Shankar won a Grammy Award for Best Album for the *Concert for Bangladesh* soundtrack, the same year he debuted his *Concerto for Sitar* with the London Symphony Orchestra, featuring Andre Previn and Shankar as soloists. In 1981, he performed a similar feat with conductor Zubin Mehta and the New York Philharmonic Orchestra.

In 1974, Shankar toured the United States with Harrison. Ben Fong Torres reviewed a Seattle performance of Shankar's "Dispute and Violence:" "A sometimes loose, sometimes tight fusion of various forms of Eastern and Western music—folk, classical and spiritual Indian; rock, jazz and even big-band swing. . . . Shankar at the podium, arms flailing, index fingers dipping and pointing, took it all to a victorious, symphonic, last-stomp halt."

Harrison produced two of Shankar's albums in the first half of the 1970s and described his friend as "the godfather of world music." In 1978, Shankar collaborated with Japanese shakahachi player Hozan Yamamoto and koko player Susumii Miyashita on the album *East Greets East*. In 1982, he was named Artistic Director of the Asian Olympics held in Delhi and was nominated with George Fenton for an Academy Award for Best Original Score for the Richard Attenborough film *Gandhi*. He also served a six-year term from 1986 to 1992 in India's parliamentary upper chamber, the Rajya Sabha. His past experience as a dancer benefited him when he performed at the Kremlin in Moscow in the late 1980s, employing Bolshoi dancers alongside traditional Indian and contemporary electronic instrumentation. The recording of this performance, *Ravi Shankar inside the Kremlin,* is considered to be one of his best releases.

In 1989, he toured Europe and India with Zubin Mehta and the European Youth Orchestra. Shankar also composed and performed in a musical theater piece, *Ghanashyam,* in Britain in 1989 and India in 1991, and collaborated with Phillip Glass on *Passages* in 1990. Even into the new millenium, he continued to write, perform, and tour.

Books

Fong-Torres, Ben, editor, *What's That Sound?,* Rolling Stone Press, Anchor Press/Doubleday, 1976.

Online

"Pandit Ravi Shankar," *David Philipson's Home Page,* http://music.calarts.edu/~bansuri/ravi_shankar.html.

"Pandit Ravi Shankar," *Top-Biography.com,* http:www.top-biography.com/9138-Pandit%20Ravi%20Shankar/.

"Ravi Shankar," *EyeNeer.com,* http://www.eyeneer.com/Labels/Angel/Ravi.html.

"Ravi Shankar," *AllMusic.com,* http://allmusic.com/cg/amg.dll.

"Ravi Shankar," *Suite101.com,* http://www.Suite101.com/article.cfm/Indian_music_musicians/36834.

"Sitar Guru," *The New Statesmen,* April 24, 2000, http://www.findarticles.com/cf_0/m0FQP/4483_129/62213858/p2/article.jhtml?term=. □

Elisabetta Sirani

A short-lived Baroque virtuoso painter, Elisabetta Sirani (1638-1665) of Bologna, Italy, was one of the first successful female artists in an era that denied academy training to women. Educated in voice, harp, poetry, classical literature, and the Bible, she drew on a wealth of influences for subjects. In a brief career, she etched 14 plates and turned out an astonishing collection of oil paintings of allegorical and dramatic art from historical, scriptural, and mythological subjects.

E lisabetta, Barbara, and Anna Maria Sirani were the three artistic daughters of painter and art teacher Giovanni (or Gian) Andrea Sirani, a follower of renowned Bolognese religious etcher-painter Guido Reni. Elisabetta was born on January 8, 1638. A beauty known for modesty and hard work, she studied classic models from antiquity and perused the best canvases and statuary of 16th- and 17th-century Italian painters from her home town as well as Florence and Rome. Unlike men apprenticed in art, she made no formal study of male nudes.

The Artist in Training

Sirani was fortunate in acquiring a mentor, the collector, biographer, and art historian Count Carlo Cesare Malvasia. He recognized her promise and affirmed in *Vite di Pittori Bolognesi* [Lives of Bolognese Painters] that her work was "of supreme quality." He advised Giovanni Sirani to encourage her in the arts beyond the usual attainments of Renaissance girls.

Under skilled instructors, Elisabetta developed a distinctive style. From Reni, an imitator of Raphael, she learned narrative organization and lyricism while serving as her teacher's studio assistant. From studying with her father, she developed a taste for dark, rich jewel tones, the dominant palette in Italian fashions and residential decor. By her mid-teens, she soon outpaced his talent and earned her own commissions from admirers and seekers of vigorous, creative talent.

A Teenage Professional Artist

Sirani's father never intended for Elisabetta to earn a living painting and engraving. After he lost flexibility in his hands from gout in 1655, however, he set his 17-year-old successor to support the family from her earnings. Historians surmise that he not only influenced her to paint quickly, he also discouraged suitors to keep his golden goose unmarried, working at her easel and earning profits from her admired canvases. She apparently kept none of her earnings for herself.

Locals doubted Elisabetta Sirani's skills and assumed that she had help in completing oil paintings at such a fast pace. To prove them wrong, she arranged an exhibition of work in progress at the Sirani studio and invited European artists and the public to observe her methods. According to one anecdote, when the Grand Duke Cosimo III de' Medici visited her workplace in 1664 to watch her paint his uncle, Prince Leopold de' Medici of Tuscany, Cosimo commissioned a Madonna for himself. Sirani filled the order immediately so that it could dry before he left for home.

Artist of Narrative Dramas

Sirani flourished at historic and religious scenarios and, by age 17, completed over 190 drawings. One of her most dramatic works is the unmasked figure of Melpomene, the Greek tragic muse, who inspired creators of drama, art, poetry, and music. Pale-hued and cool against a backdrop of fringed drapes, she sits turbaned and pensive at a table among the tools of her trade, including quill pen, ink pot, books, and the flesh-toned mask worn by the stage performer.

Sirani flourished at biblical representations of the temptress Dahlia, mistress and betrayer of Samson with scissors in hand; a penitent Mary Magdalene set against a gloomy cave with her guileless young face uplifted and one hand drawing auburn tresses over her breast as though concealing a sinful heart from a slender crucifix and skull; and many views of the Virgin and Child. Sirani's other period works include a sly Cleopatra dropping herbs into a bowl, Berenice clipping a strand of hair, Cain killing his brother Abel, Michael overcoming Satan, "The Madonna of the Rose" (ca. 1660), a jubilant cherub lifting bow and purple banner to the skies, and "St. Jerome in the Wilderness" (1650; a narrative depiction of the translator of the Vulgate Bible). Well received for its grace, the undated "Holy Family with St. Elizabeth and St. John the Baptist" groups the Virgin Mary and her maternal aunt Elizabeth in conversation over active a nursing infant Jesus and his toddler cousin John while Joseph turns his back and sets about his carpentry plans. The scene implies that women recognize the most important work, while men absorb themselves with temporal affairs.

Captured the Lives of Women

Like her Bolognese forerunner, painter Lavinia Fontana, Sirani tended to focus on bold, outstanding female subjects. From classic mythology, she chose the rape of Europa, which she produced on oversized four-by-five foot canvas. In 1664, Sirani painted a languorous pose featuring Galatea, Pygmalion's ivory statue whom the goddess Aphrodite brought to life, selecting a pearl from the salver held out by a cherub. One of Sirani's most admired scriptural scenarios is Judith, the majestic heroine of the apocrypha who murdered the drunken Assyrian overlord Holofernes and beheaded him with his own sword. In the painting, Sirani presents Judith in jeweled turban triumphantly extracting the gory head by the hair from a sack with a firm two-handed grip. While three onlookers gaze down by torchlight at the results of her deed, Judith looks confidently ahead, fearless in the exacting of justice against a feared despoiler and threat to the Jews. Contributing to the bold act is a wisp of a moon, horns turned upward as though reflecting the power of Astarte, goddess of war and sexuality.

From Roman history, in 1664, Sirani painted "Portia, Wounding Her Thigh," a mini-drama in which the noble daughter of Cato and wife of Marcus Brutus contemplates stabbing herself with a knife to prove that she can keep quiet during the conspirators' plot to assassinate Julius Caesar. The elegiac pose pictures the anguished wife with cool flesh exposed for the deed. Anachronistically, Sirani costumes her in the deep wine and gold tones common to formal Renaissance dress and emphasizes jewelry, billowing sleeves, brocaded wrap, jeweled scabbard, and pearl-entwined hairstyle over the knife, a minuscule blade that is mostly concealed in Portia's clenched hand. In the background, Sirani reduces in size and importance the four men in debate of their murderous scheme. The scenario parallels the quiet desperation of women whose lives account for little against the grand actions of males.

Renowned for chiaroscuro, the play of light figures against a dark backdrop, Sirani avoided stark outlines and applied pen and wash to soften edges, a method that enhanced her wild-eyed figure of St. Madeleine. The artist's brushwork was a flurry of rapid daubs, evidenced in images of women as victims of society and self. One bare-breasted figure pictures a female painter, whom some identify as Sirani. Art historians detect notes of masochism in her self-image, suggesting some resentment against a daily life filled with painting, but leaving little time for friends and relaxation.

Sirani's self-portrait, completed around age 22, features a plain, yet appealing woman, paintbrush in hand, with large oval eyes sizing up her subject. Disarmingly rosy-toned and feminine in high-busted blue gown, full white sleeves, dusky pink drapings, pearls, and brooches, she seems overdressed and out of place with palette clasped in her left thumb and daubs of paint ready for application to her canvas. She duplicated the pose and detailing for "The Allegory of Painting," which placed a rapt artist concentrating on completing her canvas.

The Unfortunate Death of a Great Talent

In the spring of 1665, Sirani grew depressed and underweight. An undiagnosed stomach ailment triggered her collapse. She forced herself back to work through the summer and died on August 25 at age 27. The city of Bologna honored her with a lavish public funeral. Her body was displayed on a catafalque symbolizing the Temple of Fame. An effigy depicted Elisabetta at work with her brushes. At the church of San Domenico in Bologna, her family interred her alongside Guido Reni, who had instilled in her a love of elegance, lyricism, and artistic invention. Malvasia, her mentor, penned an ornate, celebratory biography that called her "the glory of the female sex, the gem of Italy, the sun of Europe."

Andrea Sirani blamed Elisabetta's maid for the unexplained illness and death and charged her with poisoning the girl's meals. After a court acquitted, but exiled, the accused, the authorities grew suspicious of Elisabetta's death. They exhumed her remains and discovered that she died from a perforated stomach, perhaps from the combined effects of overwork, exhaustion, and gastric ulcers.

Sirani's Contributions to Religious Art

Elisabetta Sirani's oil paintings earned the praise of her contemporaries, including royal collectors who displayed her canvases in palaces and public halls. In addition to arranging a painting school for women, to a doubting world, she left proof of the female artist's competence—a collection of studies and drawings, 14 etchings, and 170 paintings. For one commission, she executed for the Church of the Certosini in Bologna "The Baptism of Christ." In 1658, she produced a nave adornment for the Church of San Girolamo, an achievement that increased her fame.

One outstanding mother-and-babe pose, the tender "Virgin and Child" (1663), Sirani painted for Paolo Poggi. The scene, set against a dark backdrop, displays the babe tossing a rose garland onto the head of his mother. The smiling pose placing face by face depicts a sweet and intimate relationship. Crucial to contrast are the Virgin Mary's finely worked headdress and Semitic skin tones against the swaddling clothes and innocent pink of Jesus' face and arms. In 1994, the United States Postal Service honored the painting, making it the first historical work by a female artist printed on a Christmas stamp. The image adorned over 1.1 billion stamps. In August 2000, Sirani's works were exhibited at Christ Church, Oxford, in a showing of drawings of the Old Masters.

Books

Bolognese Drawings of the XVII & XVIII Centuries in the Collection of Her Majesty the Queen at Windsor Castle, Phaidon, 1955.
The Bulfinch Guide to Art History, Bulfinch Press, 1996.
The Concise Oxford Dictionary of Art & Artists, ed. by Ian Chilvers, Oxford University Press, 1996.
Dictionary of Art, Grove, 1998.
Dictionary of Art & Artists, ed. by Linda Murray and Peter Murray, Penguin, 1976.
Macmillan Dictionary of Women's Biography, ed. by Jennifer S. Uglow, Macmillan, 1999.
Outrageous Women of the Renaissance, John Wiley & Sons, 1999.
The Oxford Guide to Classical Mythology in the Arts, 1300-1990s, Oxford University Press, 1993.
The Penguin Biographical Dictionary of Women, Market House Books, 1998.
Seeing Ourselves: Women's Self-Portraits, by Frances Borzello, Harry N. Abrams, 1998.
Women, Art and Society, by Whitney Chadwick, Thames and Hudson, 1997.
Women Artists, 1550-1950, ed. by Ann S. Harris, Alfred A. Knopf, 1977.
Women Artists: An Illustrated History, ed. by Nancy G. Heller, Abbeyville Publishing Group, 1987.
Women in Art, ed. Edith Krull, Cassell UK, 1990.
Women's World, ed. by Irene Franck and David Brownstone, HarperPerennial, 1995.

Periodicals

Christian Science Monitor, October 5, 1989.
Criticism, Winter 1996.
History Today, August 2000.
Monkeyshines on Art & Great Artists, 1996.
School Arts, September 1995.

Online

"Elisabetta Sirani," http://www.artloop.com/artist/Elisabetta_Sirani/artist1070.html
"Elisabetta Sirani," http://www.bluffton.edu/womenartists/ch3(16-17c)/sirani.html
"Elisabetta Sirani," http://www.giovanetto.com/burghley/sirani.html
"Elisabetta Sirani," http://www.hyperhistory.com/online_n2/people_n2/women_n2/sirani.html.
"Elisabetta Sirani," http://www.mystudios.com/women/pqrst/sirani.html
"Elisabetta Sirani," http://www.nmwa.org/legacy/bios/bsirani.htm
"Women Artists," http://www.csupomona.edu/~plin/women/17_18century.html
"Women Printmakers, 1540-1940," http://www.antiquecc.com/articles/960504.html. □

George Cooper Stevens

George Stevens (1904-1975) is highly regarded for the diverse number of films he directed, his work ranging from romance and comedies to Westerns and historical epics. Nominated for five Academy awards for best director, he won twice, for the dramas *A Place in the Sun* and *Giant*.

George Cooper Stevens is noted for allowing the actors in his films to improvise on the set, sometimes causing scenes to be shot dozens of times. His movies feature many of the most noted actors from the 1930s to 1960s, including Katherine Hepburn, Cary Grant, Spencer Tracy, Joel McCrea, Irene Dunne, Ginger Rogers, Jean Arthur, James Stewart, Fred Astaire, and Carole Lombard. While most of these films were romantic comedies, it was for dramas that he received his greatest kudos; as James Harvey noted in *Romantic Comedy in Hollywood:* "Probably his most serious liability as a comic filmmaker is his apparent lack of any anarchic or subversive or even dissident impulse. He has the temperament of a solid citizen, and he tends to temper and meliorate whatever is harsh or abrasive or unsettling in the familiar people and plots." While not as admired as other directors of his generation, such as Alfred Hitchcock, Howard Hawks, George Cukor, John Ford, and William Wyler, Stevens is credited with investing his films with subtle social messages; and several of his films—*Gunga Din, Woman of the Year, A Place in the Sun, Shane,* and *Giant*—are considered Hollywood classics by critics.

Began Directing Two-Reel Comedies

Stevens was born on December 18, 1904, in Oakland, California. He began acting and working as a stage manager for his father's theatrical company before moving to Hollywood in 1921 and finding work as a cameraperson. In 1927 he began directing two-reel comedies for Hal Roach and directed many silent films by comedians Stan Laurel and

might have delivered a really original, really native comedy, and the types are set up to carry this comedy are not bad in conception; they are spoiled in the execution. Stevens has a free, pretty feeling for business . . . for special colorations of talk . . . , and for gratuitous satire. . . . Yet the film as a whole is a tired souffl,, for unfortunately Stevens doesn't know where to stop.

Post-War Films and Activities

During World War II Stevens traveled to Europe as a U.S. Army Signal Corps head of Special Motion Pictures Unit assigned to the 6th Army and was among those film-makers who photographed the grounds and interiors of Nazi Germany's concentration camps. When he returned to the United States, he expressed a wish to make a film nostalgic for simpler times. That film was *I Remember Mama,* about which Agee wrote that Stevens "developed while he was away at war, like a few other talented picture-makers. . . . In *Mama* . . . he felt no timidity about tackling a script that lacked action and a strong plot. He concentrated, with confidence and resourcefulness, on character, mood and abundant detail, and on the continuous invention of satisfying and expressive things to look at." Stevens chose to shoot many different versions of the same scenes, sometimes taking ten days to film one scene, in order to compose montage sequences comprised of varied camera angles. The result was a film costing more than three million dollars, an outrageous sum for 1948, and a tremendous critical and public success that never recouped its production expenses.

Among his other postwar projects was the short-lived Liberty Studios, which Stevens set up with directors Frank Capra and William Wyler and which produced only one film, Capra's classic *It's a Wonderful Life.* Stevens also served as president of the Academy of Motion Picture Arts and Sciences and briefly became embroiled in the blacklisting scandals perpetrated by Senator Joseph McCarthy's Un-American Activities Committee and the effort to route out suspected communists during the height of the cold war. Stevens was responsible for preventing screenwriter Dalton Trumbo from receiving an Academy Award for his screenplay *The Brave One* because the blacklisted writer had deceived the Academy by using the pseudonym Robert Rich.

An American Trilogy

Of the films Stevens released in the 1950s, *A Place in the Sun, Shane,* and *Giant* have collectively been considered his "American Trilogy," for it is through these films he attempts to critique elements of American culture and society. Based on Theodore Dreiser's novel *An American Tragedy, A Place in the Sun* concerns the attempt of a young middle-class male (Montgomery Clift) to marry into society (represented by Elizabeth Taylor). His aspirations are thwarted, however, when he impregnates a woman from his own class (Shelley Winters). *Shane,* listed as one of the American Film Institute's Top 100 American Films, stars Alan Ladd as a former gunslinger who is forced to defend homesteaders from ruthless land-grabbers. According to Stanley J. Solomon in *Beyond Formula: American Film*

Oliver Hardy. In the early 1930s he became one of RKO Studios' most important directors after he directed Katherine Hepburn her 1935 comedy *Alice Adams.* The following year he worked with dancers Fred Astaire and Ginger Rogers on a film featuring songs by Jerome Kern, *Swing Time.* In 1938 Stevens directed James Stewart and Ginger Rogers in *Vivacious Lady* and was expected to direct the Marx Brothers comedy *Room Service.* When fellow director Howard Hawks was fired from the production of *Gunga Din* for budget overruns, however, Stevens was hired to replace him.

Starring Cary Grant and Douglas Fairbanks, Jr., *Gunga Din* is an adaptation of a Rudyard Kipling poem about British soldiers fighting on the Indian frontier. It is remembered mostly by film historians for the difficulties Stevens encountered during filming. For example, he and the film's writers improvised much of the movie since a script was never finalized. Stevens later recalled that the battle scenes were the greatest problem. Some scenes required 1,500 extras, hundreds of mules and horses, and a few elephants.

Stevens followed his action picture with two romantic melodramas, *Vigil in the Night* and *Penny Serenade,* before releasing two of his most respected comedies, *Woman of the Year,* featuring the first cinematic pairing of Hepburn and Spencer Tracy, and *The More the Merrier.* Critic James Agee assessed Stevens's abilities as a comedic director in *The More the Merrier* by noting in *Agee on Film* that the film is "partly nice and partly disappointing. The chiseling, cringing sex and claustrophobia of war-torn Washington

Genres, "*Shane* was evidently conceived in terms of an interpretation of the Western genre film as an allegorical battleground between good and evil. . . . But Stevens chose to heighten the symbolic import of the genre's typical iconography (costume, language, manners, and rituals) by setting his film in an immense, open environment, dominated by the snowcapped mountains of Wyoming in the distance. By continually locating the immediate scene within a vast, calm, rigidly endurable locale, Stevens deliberately and recurringly directs our attention to the genre's mythic dimensions, in regard to the lonely hero, the isolated community, the natural conflict between people and the terrain, and the violent power struggle between the land-grabbing local tyrant and the individual homestead farmers over who will control the territory." In filming *Giant,* Stevens earned his second Academy Award for his adaptation of Edna Ferber's novel about the beginnings of the Texas oil boom and the instant wealth it provided. At the heart of the story, however, is a love triangle between characters portrayed by Elizabeth Taylor, Rock Hudson, and James Dean in his third and final film.

Directed Three Final Films

Before he retired in the early 1970s, Stevens directed three more films, *The Diary of Anne Frank, The Greatest Story Ever Told,* and *The Only Game in Town.* While his casting of Millie Perkins in the title role in the first film drew negative criticism, *Anne Frank* co-star Shelley Winters won an Academy award for best supporting actress, and Stevens won another Academy award nomination. In *The Greatest Story Ever Told,* he attempted to create an epic film about the life of Jesus Christ, starring Max von Sydow, Charlton Heston, Sidney Poitier, and John Wayne. The film's detractors were numerous and included James Harvey, who wrote that "Even when he embarks on a mad and ludicrous enterprise like *The Greatest Story Ever Told,* the result, though elephantine, turns out to be impersonal, perfectly without religious feeling of any kind, and in its way rather modest: a life of Jesus drawn not only from Scripture but from a *Reader's Digest* rewrite of them." Stevens's final film, *The Only Game in Town,* starred Warren Beatty. Reputedly angered that 20th Century-Fox didn't promote the film effectively, Stevens opted to retire following its release. He died on March 9, 1975, in Paris.

Books

Agee, James, *Agee on Film: Criticism and Comment on the Movies,* Random House, 2000.

Behlmer, Rudy, *America's Favorite Movies: Behind the Scenes,* Frederick Ungar, 1982.

Harvey, James, *Romantic Comedy in Hollywood,* Alfred A. Knopf, 1987.

Sarris, Andrew, editor, *St. James Guide to Film Directors,* Visible Ink Press, 1998.

Silvester, Christopher, editor, *The Grove Book of Hollywood,* Grove Press, 1998.

Solomon, Stanley J., *Beyond Formula: American Film Genres,* Harcourt Brace Jovanovich, 1976.

Online

Reel Classics, http://www.reelclassics.com/ (February 21, 2002).
□

Thomas Sully

Portrait artist Thomas Sully (1783-1872) reflected the manners and demeanor of great people of his day. A naturalized American citizen, he preserved for posterity the nation's politicians, military heroes, inventors, actors, and aristocrats as well as European nobles and the queen of England. In the decades preceding the invention of photography, his prolific output of portraits and historic scenes became a storehouse of details from the past.

Born in Horncastle in Lincolnshire, England, on June 8 (some sources say June 19), 1783, to actors Sarah Chester and Matthew Sully, Thomas Sully emigrated to America with his parents and eight siblings at age nine and lived in Charleston, South Carolina. In 1795, his father arranged for his training for a career in business at an insurance office. The broker urged Sully's father to allow the boy to pursue art, his first love. He received coaching from school friend Charles Fraser, who became Charleston's most famous miniaturist, and from an elder brother, Lawrence Sully, who also painted miniatures.

Beginnings of Career

Sully quickly ended formal lessons with his first art teacher, his brother-in-law, Monsieur Belzons, and settled in Richmond, and then in Norfolk, Virginia, to live with his brother Lawrence's family and to study his studio work. According to Sully's logbook, which he maintained throughout a 75-year career, he painted his first miniature on May 10, 1801. After mastering the basics, he began working in oils on large canvases the next year.

After Lawrence's death in 1803, Thomas Sully married his widow, Sarah Annis Sully. With earnings from a growing list of clients, he supported her three children plus nine of their own. Content with a large, energetic family, he settled in New York and advanced his career by painting city notables. After six-and-a-half years, according to his precise calculations, he had produced 70 portraits and earned $3,203.

Advice from the Masters

Business slowed during an economic recession resulting from a trade embargo, forcing Sully to lower his rates to $30 per portrait. An encounter with painter Gilbert Stuart, a fashionable artist famed for his three portraits of George Washington, buoyed Sully's hopes and provided sensible advice. Relocated to Philadelphia, he found the city that suited him for life. To improve his methods, he studied briefly with Stuart and in June 1809 traveled to England to

His family well provided for, Sully relaxed into a steady rhythm of painting famous subjects, including the Marquis de Lafayette. At the accession of the 18-year-old Queen Victoria in 1837, Sully returned to England to execute his masterwork, a full-length painting of her commissioned by Philadelphia's Society of the Sons of Saint George. On this journey, he depended on his daughter Blanche for companionship and assistance. At Buckingham Palace, he posed her in royal robe and crown to take the queen's place after he completed the bust. The task was tedious and fraught with palace protocol, but the effort immortalized Sully's work and influenced three generations of painters and coin sculptors.

Back in Philadelphia in 1838, Sully received the accolades due a master artist. Into advanced age he added to his logbook, which numbered his life's work at 2,631 paintings and miniatures. A year after his death on November 5, 1872, in Philadelphia, his heirs published posthumously *Hints to Young Painters and the Process of Portrait-Painting as Practiced by the Late Thomas Sully* (1873). Its explanation of artistic works from the colonial and federal periods retained for history the inside information on color selection, lighting, and technique. His likenesses of 500 historic figures, including Daniel Boone, Benjamin Franklin, and U.S. presidents Thomas Jefferson, James Monroe, and Andrew Jackson, are national treasures. In 2000, the Metropolitan Museum of Art in New York City presented a retrospective of his drawings and canvases.

Books

Almanac of Famous People, Gale Research, 1998.
Benet's Reader's Encyclopedia, 1987.
Chilvers, Ian, editor, *The Concise Oxford Dictionary of Art & Artists,* Oxford University Press, 1996.
Columbia Encyclopedia, 2000.
Dictionary of American Biography Base Set, American Council of Learned Societies, 1928-1936.
Merriam-Webster's Biographical Dictionary, 1995.
Murray, Linda and Peter Murray, *A Dictionary of Art & Artists,* Penguin, 1976.

Periodicals

Magazine Antiques, July 1983; September 2000.
New York Times, October 27, 2000.
Time International, September 25, 2000.
Virginian-Pilot and The Ledger-Star, March 28, 1999.
Washington Times, January 28, 2001.

Online

Biography Resource Center, http://galenet.galegroup.com/servlet/BioRC. □

observe art at major museums. He repaid the friends who had advanced him cash for the journey with copies of great art by European masters.

Experiences in England focused Sully's attention on a need for improvement in modeling the human form. Following a study of osteology and anatomy, he advanced to historical pieces. To ready him for the shift, he observed the era's foremost artists, including Benjamin West, narrative painter for King George III. Europe's artistic giant of his day, Sir Thomas Lawrence, taught Sully how to produce flowing, glossy brush strokes for the elegant, romantic poses that earned him the nickname "the Lawrence of America." Lawrence introduced Sully to the family of Fanny Kemble, who was then a year old. In adulthood, the famed Shakespearean actress became one of his favorite subjects. She posed for him 13 times.

Achieved His Best Work

Returning to Philadelphia in 1810, Sully began painting narrative scenes, including one based on a play by Friedrich Schiller and another drawn from William Shakespeare's *Richard III.* He joined his peers in the Pennsylvania Academy of Art, which was founded in 1805. As his prospects rose, he painted perhaps his most famous historical narrative, the massive *Washington Crossing the Delaware* (1819). The North Carolina legislature, which had commissioned the scene, rejected it because it was oversized. Sully managed to sell it to a frame maker at the cut-rate price of $500.

Joan Sutherland

Joan Sutherland (born 1926) is widely considered one of the best opera singers of her time, a soprano who specialized in the bel canto repertoire. Known for her lovely voice, excellent range, and command-

ing stage presence, Sutherland was dubbed "La Stupenda" by Italian critics.

Sutherland was born on November 7, 1926, in Sydney, Australia, to William and Muriel (Alston) Sutherland. Her father, a Scottish immigrant and tailor, died of a heart attack on Sutherland's sixth birthday. Joan and her elder sister Barbara were raised by their mother, an amateur singer and music teacher, and members of her family.

Early Musical Education

While attending St. Catherine's Girls' School in Waverly, Sutherland received her first education in music, primarily piano, from her mother. Muriel Sutherland had been taught in the bel canto tradition which her daughter would later help revive interest in. However, her mother would not allow her to be trained vocally until after the age of 18. One of the most important lessons Sutherland's mother taught her was the importance of breathing correctly. Despite a promising future in music, after leaving school at 16, Sutherland took a secretarial course and worked as a secretary at Sydney University as she trained for her singing career.

In 1946 when Sutherland was 19 years old, she won a two-year scholarship for vocal training with John and Aida Dickens in Sydney in 1946. The couple helped Sutherland develop the upper range of her voice, which would prove important in her development as an opera singer. In 1947, Sutherland made her concert debut in Sydney as Dido in

Dido and Aeneas. That same year, she met fellow music student Richard Bonynge, a pianist and her future husband, who would play a significant role in Sutherland's opera career.

Continued Education in London

Sutherland's future was determined by several important singing competition wins. In 1949, she won the *Sun Aria* competition and the 1950 Mobil Quest, among other singing competitions. Her successes allowed her to attend the Royal College of Music in London on scholarship in the early 1950s. With her mother, Sutherland moved to London and studied with Clive Carey at the prestigious institution. Sutherland also received some training at London's Opera School.

Sutherland made her debut with Royal Opera at Covent Garden in 1952, as the First Lady of *The Magic Flute.* She appeared as part of the company of the Royal Opera, which made its home at Covent Garden a number of years, essentially serving as its leading soprano. Among her early appearances were roles in *Aida* (1954) and *Rigoletto.* Sutherland first drew significant critical attention when she created the role of Jennifer in Michael Tippett's *The Midsummer Marriage* in 1955. Though Sutherland was not altogether pleased with her performance, by this time, her basic characteristics as a vocalist were there. Being a member of company allowed Sutherland to learn solid technique, which played into her vocal agility and purity.

Learned Bel Canto Repertoire

In 1954, Sutherland and Bonynge were married. He had come to London in 1950 to study. The couple had become reacquainted and married when Sutherland's mother made a trip back to Australia. The couple later had one son, Adam. Bonynge and Sutherland also formed a musical partnership. He helped her learn how to reach higher notes in her flexible range as a lyric-coloratura soprano. It was through Bonynge's influence and tutelage that Sutherland learned the bel canto repertoire.

At this time, the bel canto repertoire was relatively unfashionable. Bel canto (Italian for "beautiful singing") operas were primarily of the Italian romantic variety of the 18th and 19th centuries. Such operas featured roles that often used the kind of high range that Sutherland had successfully developed. Sutherland and Bonynge had been influenced by Maria Callas, who had first revived the bel canto repertoire. The couple attended many of her rehearsals and performances at Covent Garden, and Sutherland modeled her vocal stylings on Callas. Sutherland performed in such bel canto operas by Vincenzo Bellini, Geatano Donzietti, Gioacchino Rossi, and others. Sutherland appeared in a 1952 production of Bellini's *Norma* as Clothide with Callas as the Druid priestess

Sutherland had wanted to do more Wagner, as was regularly put on at Covent Garden, but Bonynge talked her out of it. He believed such heavy works did not suit her voice and vocal strengths. Though Sutherland did perform some Wagner and similar works, Sutherland later believed that she would not have had such a long career if she had focused on such operas. Because of her and her husband's enthusiastic embrace of works in the bel canto repertoire, the genre was revived. By the 1960s, Bonynge began conducting her productions and the pair eventually came as a package. This subjected the couple to criticism over the years.

Received International Acclaim

In 1959, Sutherland cemented her reputation as a superior coloratura soprano in her acclaimed turn as Lucia in Donizetti's *Lucia di Lammermoor* at Covent Garden. With her husband, Sutherland studied the source material for the opera, a novel by Sir Walter Scott. She grew to love this role, which she would play over 100 times, though her interpretation of Lucia would change as she matured.

The 1959 production was directed by Italian director Franco Zeffirelli who gave Sutherland some acting training. Sutherland herself was more concerned with her vocals and stage presence than acting. As she told Susan Heller Anderson of the *New York Times*, "If you want to see a wonderful actress, you go to see a straight play.... You can't be as emotionally involved when you sing as when you're acting. There are many singing actresses who do the sort of roles that don't demand the vocal techniques of bel canto."

Despite a brief setback when Sutherland had to have an operation on her sinuses, she made her first of many appearances in the United States, as Alcina in *Alcina* in Dallas, Texas, in 1960. Though her voice continued to evolve, her range and tone were especially noted. In 1961, Sutherland made her debut at New York City's Metropolitan Opera, again as Lucia in *Lucia*. That same year, Sutherland had a triumphant appearance at Milan's famous La Scala. It was here that she was given the honored nickname of "La Stupenda." This was arguably the best appearance on stage in her career.

From the early 1960s to the end of her career, Sutherland regularly appeared in the major opera houses in the United States and Europe, as well as other countries in the world. But she did not forget her roots in Australia. She brought her own opera company there between 1965 and 1974. Sutherland then regularly appeared with Sydney's Australian Opera because Bonynge served as music director there between the mid-1970s to the mid-1980s. Though the couple's legal residence was in Montreaux, Switzerland— where they lived since 1964 and could exist relatively anonymously—she still lived in Sydney for a number of months during the year. Sutherland often played roles that she had done well before in works like *Lucia di Lammermoor, La Traviata,* and *The Tales of Hoffmann.*

Sutherland continued to challenge herself as an artist, even late in her career. In the 1970s, she took on more dramatic soprano roles in operas like *Maria Stuarda* and *Lucrezia Borgia* by Donizietti and Leonora in *Il trovatore.* Though Sutherland's voice and its flexibility remained strong points throughout her stage life, critics had often criticized her poor diction, a common problem for coloratura sopranos. Sutherland addressed this issue with some success by the early 1980s. Even as Sutherland entered her sixties, she was able to take on new roles because of her

dedication and skill, even though learning new roles was hard for her because of a relatively poor memory. As her range changed with age, however, she did had to have some parts rewritten in a lower key.

Retired from Opera Stage

By the late 1980s, Sutherland had decided that she would retire in the early 1990s. On October 2, 1990, she made her last appearance in an opera, singing Margaret de Valois in a Sydney production of *Les Huguenots.* Her last song was an operatic version of "Home Sweet Home." Over the course of her career, she had sung in 48 operas and had recorded 60 albums.

After retirement, Sutherland has remained active in a number of arenas both related and not related to opera. She is involved in the opera world by acting as a judge in major singing competitions like the Queen Elisabeth in Brussels, Belgium. She also taught, often with her husband, some master classes, though she did not like the limited possibilities of the format.

Made Screen and Literary Debuts

Though Sutherland's acting was often a weak point for many critics, she tried her hand at film acting in a 1994 release. It was not the first time that she was offered a role in a movie. When Sutherland was in Italy in 1959, Federico Fellini wanted to cast her in his film *La Dolce Vita,* without even knowing who she was. She was advised against it by Zeffirelli and Anita Ekberg took on the role. Sutherland later regretted her decision. After a year of convincing by Anthony Buckley, Sutherland agreed to play the unglamorous role of Mother Rudd in *On our Selection,* a film based on an Australian play based on sketches by Steele Rudd. Sutherland was still eager to learn during the production and improve herself as an actress, though she did not prepare for the role.

Three years later, Sutherland published her autobiography, *The Autobiography of Joan Sutherland: A Prima Donna's Progress.* Sutherland wrote the book herself instead of working with ghost writer, beginning soon after her retirement. Though critics chided her for not revealing more of herself and found the book hard to read because it was bogged down in details, Sutherland hoped to show aspiring opera singers how to train properly and what it takes to have a long career. As she told Chris Pasles of the *Los Angeles Times* of her own experiences in opera, "I've had a wonderful career. It outran everything I expected...."

Books

Arnold, John, and Deidre Morris, editors, *Monash Biographical Dictionary of 20th Century Australia,* Reed Reference Publishing, 1994.
Atkinson, Ann, *The Dictionary of Famous Australians,* Allen & Unwin, 1992.
Greenfield, Edward, *Joan Sutherland,* Drake Publishers, Inc., 1973.
Guinn, John and Les Stone, editors, *The St. James Opera Encyclopedia,* Visible Ink, 1997.
Kuhn, Laura, *Baker's Dictionary of Opera,* Schirmer Books, 2000.

Kuhn, Laura, compiler, *Baker's Student Encyclopedia of Music,*
    Vol. 3, Schirmer Books, 1999.

Periodicals

The Advertiser, November 1, 1997.
Associated Press, March 8, 1998.
The Australian, October 25, 1997.
Daily Telegraph, January 16, 1996; October 9, 1997.
Los Angeles Times, February 11, 1989; June 19, 1990.
New York Times, October 31, 1982; November 10, 1996; January 22, 1998.
Opera News, September 1994; June 1995; October 1995; February 28, 1998; March 28, 1998; November 1998.
Time, January 14, 1991.
Toronto Star, October 3, 1990. □

Gustavus Franklin Swift

Gustavus Swift (1839-1903) headed a large American corporation that revolutionized the meatpacking industry by using refrigerated railroad cars, strict cost controls at his plants, and "vertical integration." His practices helped overcome consumer mistrust of processed meat and inspired the vast, mechanized meatpacking businesses depicted in Upton Sinclair's infamous 1906 novel *The Jungle.*

Chicago-based meatpacker Swift and Company earned its fortune by organizing the large-scale slaughter and processing of cattle in the Midwest and shipping its products to East Coast population centers via refrigerated railroad cars. Gustavus Swift, the company's founder, battled public distrust for meat processed hundreds of miles away and found many profitable uses for byproducts of the slaughterhouse. Swift, a pioneer of the "vertical integration" concept, was obsessed with controlling costs at his plants and offices.

Yankee Butcher

Swift was born on June 24, 1839, near Sandwich, on Massachusetts's Cape Cod Bay. He was one of 12 children and was educated at a local school, which he left at age 14. He joined his older brother, Noble, in the butcher's shop he ran but was unhappy with the lack of prospects for advancement. At 16, he decided to move to Boston, but his father loaned him $25 as an inducement to stay. Swift used $19 of it to buy a heifer from a local farmer, slaughtered it, and sold the beef door to door. He made a $10 profit and from then on went weekly to the local cattle market in the town of Brighton. Around 1859 he opened his own butcher shop in Eastham and hired another brother to run it while he set up a second shop in Barnstable. By this time Swift had wed Annie Higgins; they would have nine children.

Swift soon opened other shops in Clinton and Freetown, Massachusetts. He recognized certain principles of retail psychology that helped make his stores a success. His butcher shops were clean, and he tried to display his wares attractively on large white marble trays. He displayed the cuts he needed to sell first and offered smaller cuts, which seemed to induce shoppers to buy more.

Swift expanded his operations rapidly. He began a meat wagon business and soon became a wholesale cattle dealer. In 1872, he entered into a partnership with James A. Hathaway, a Boston meat dealer. He took the business westward, to Albany and Buffalo, New York, and finally to Chicago in 1875.

Conceived Refrigerated Car

Chicago was the center of the cattle trade in the United States. It was a railroad hub serving all regions of the country and was close to the Great Plains. Its South Side rail yards were the site of the famous Chicago Stockyards, where cattle were penned before shipment elsewhere. Some of the breeds still roamed the plains freely, descendants of European stock brought over by the Spanish in the 1500s.

As the cattle buyer in his partnership, Swift came to realize that shipping live cattle from Chicago to the country's most populous markets along the Atlantic seaboard was an inefficient strategy. The cattle had to be fed along the way, some died in transit, and—since the railroads charged per pound—huge freight charges added tremendously to the cost of doing business. Smith also worried about the expenses involved in waste, since many parts of the slaughtered animal were unusable. A 1,000-pound steer might yield 600 pounds of beef, but the rest was a loss for the company, since someone had to be paid to cart it away.

Swift believed that butchering cattle and shipping dressed beef was a far more profitable idea. He tried it with one carload in the winter of 1877, and it was a success. Still, railroad-car refrigeration technology was inadequate for the rest of year, and even in the winter months proved problematic: a shipment might freeze in one city, then thaw in another. Hathaway, Swift's Boston partner, was wary of the idea and exited the partnership with a $30,000 buyout. Swift used some of that money to hire an engineer to perfect a refrigeration car that used circulating fresh air cooled by ice and established his meatpacking business in Chicago. He approached the McMillens, a wealthy railroad-car family in Detroit, to become his partners, and they agreed to build the first refrigerated cars. Swift made arrangements with the holders of various patents on the parts used for the refrigerated cars and created his own design. He contracted ice harvesters in Wisconsin to produce enough ice for the cars and established icing stations along the railroad routes heading east.

Battled Railroad Cartel

The meatpackers in Chicago, who made pork and mutton products, at first paid little attention to Swift's dressed-beef enterprise. Swift was viewed as a Yankee who did not know the business. His real opponents were much more formidable. For one, consumers in Eastern cities did not trust that meat slaughtered elsewhere, perhaps a week before, was safe. Local butchers warned of dire consequences. The railroads also opposed Swift, for they preferred the larger freight revenues from shipping live cattle. Forming a cartel against Swift, they began charging exorbitantly high prices for dressed meat.

Swift was ingenious in conquering these obstacles. He mounted large-scale advertising campaigns to win public confidence and made advantageous partnerships with local butchers. For transport, he negotiated with the Grand Trunk Railway, whose line ran through Michigan and Canada and had never made much profit shipping cattle. Its owners gave Swift a more favorable rate, and Swift and Company was officially incorporated in 1885.

From the start, Swift's South Side plant was a model of time-saving production principles. Upton Sinclair described its efficiency with contempt in the muckraking novel from 1906, *The Jungle,* detailing the work of the men who butchered steer for the fictitious Durham Company, modeled after Swift & Company: "They worked with furious intensity, literally upon the run—at a pace with which there is nothing to be compared except a football game. It was all highly specialized labor, each man having his task to do; generally this would consist of only two or three specific cuts, and he would pass down the line of fifteen or twenty carcasses, making these cuts upon each."

Model of Cost-Effectiveness

Swift's company grew phenomenally. Profits rose because of Swift's belief that cleanliness reduced spoilage and losses. He hired engineers and chemists to find uses for the byproducts of cattle slaughter. Sinclair's description of the Durham plant aptly detailed the progress Swift made in

reducing waste: "No tiniest particle of organic matter was wasted in Durham's. Out of the horns of the cattle they made combs, buttons, hairpins, and imitation ivory; out of the shinbones and other big bones they cut knife and toothbrush handles, and mouthpieces for pipes; out of the hoofs they cut hairpins and buttons, before they made the rest into glue. From such things as feet, knuckles, hide clippings, and sinews came such strange and unlikely products as gelatin, isinglass, and phosphorus, bone black, shoe blacking, and bone oil. They had curled-hair works for the cattle tails, and a 'wool pullery' for the sheepskins; they made pepsin from the stomachs of the pigs, and albumen from the blood, and violin strings from the ill-smelling entrails. When there was nothing else to be done with a thing, they first put it into a tank and got out of it all the tallow and grease, and then they made it into fertilizer.'"

Swift was also an innovator in automating his plant. An overhead trolley carried cattle carcasses to the various processing stations on the floor. The system reportedly gave carmaker Henry Ford the idea for the first automobile assembly line. Swift's was one of first companies in modern business history to boast complete "vertical integration:" it had departments for purchasing, production, shipping, sales, and marketing.

The company established plants in other cattle towns, such as St. Louis, Kansas City, and St. Joseph, Missouri; Omaha, Nebraska; St. Paul, Minnesota; and Fort Worth, Texas. Then Swift moved on to international territory. He captured the British market, and he exported beef via refrigerated compartments on ships to distributing houses he established in Tokyo, Osaka, Shanghai, Hong Kong, Manila, Singapore, and Honolulu. He expanded into pork and mutton products as well, and at the start of the twentieth century the company he had founded just 15 years earlier was worth $25 million.

Swift was known as a tough taskmaster who regularly inspected plants and tyrannized employees when he found evidence of waste—even pencil stubs in office wastebaskets. He wrote his business correspondence on half sheets of paper. He sometimes inspected "Bubbly Creek," the fetid stream into which the slaughterhouses dumped their chemicals and unusable byproducts, making sure that nothing of value—such as a piece of animal fat that could be used to make soap—was leaving his plant. He once hired an efficiency expert to make suggestions at the office headquarters but then fired him as a fraud. The man protested on grounds of breach of contract, and Swift agreed to keep him, but sent him to squeegee blood into the drains at the slaughterhouse.

Became Philanthropist

Swift and his family lived near the Stockyards until 1898, when they moved to a home on Ellis Avenue in Chicago's affluent Kenwood area, adjacent to Hyde Park. The area was also home to the University of Chicago, one of the local institutions that benefited from Swift's philanthropy. He was a trustee of the university for many years. In 1895, he donated money for a building in memory of his daughter, Annie May Swift, that eventually became Northwestern University's School of Speech. He was also a bene-factor of St. James Methodist Episcopal Church.

Swift and his rivals, who owned the Morris and Armour plants, were known as Chicago's meatpacking barons, and public opinion eventually turned against what was called the "Beef Trust." In 1902, the company came under federal scrutiny as the first of the anti-trust prosecutions brought by the U.S. Attorney General on orders from President Theodore Roosevelt. The firms of Swift, Armour, Morris, and three others were indicted for price fixing and other business conspiracies. In response, Swift, Armour, and Morris merged into the National Packing Company; others soon joined, and their hold on the beef industry remained strong.

Swift died on March 29, 1903, in Chicago, Illinois, after an operation caused internal bleeding. Management of the company remained in family hands, for Swift was fond of asserting "I can raise better men than I can hire." In 1905, in another anti-trust case, *Swift & Co. v. the United States,* the U.S. Supreme Court ruled against Swift's company and its practices. Government legislation—such as the Pure Food and Drug Act of 1906, the Meat Inspection Act, and the Packers and Stockyards Act of 1921—soon regulated the meat industry. In the 1980s, Swift's company fell victim to the leveraged buyouts of the era but survived as Armour Swift-Eckrich, owned by ConAgra.

Books

Dictionary of American Biography Base Set, American Council of Learned Societies, 1928-1936.
Sinclair, Upton, *The Jungle,* New American Library, 1906.
Swift, Louis F., in collaboration with Arthur Van Vlissinggen Jr., *The Yankee of the Yards: The Biography of Gustavus Franklin Swift,* A. W. Shaw, 1927.

Online

DISCovering U.S. History, http://galenet.galegroup.com, 1997.
□

T

Jacques Tati

Jacques Tati (1908-1982), born Jacques Tatischeff, is recognized internationally as one of the twentieth-century film's most innovative and perceptive comic directors and actors.

Tati's film personas—Francois the Postman in *Jour de fete* and the popular Monsieur Hulot in *Les Vacances de Monsieur Hulot, Mon Oncle, Playtime,* and *Traffic*—helped reveal the inherent humor of humanity attempting to exist in an increasingly mechanized society and drew positive comparisons to the silent film comedians Charlie Chaplin, Buster Keaton, and Harold Lloyd. As co-writer, star, and director of these films, he sought to depict the foibles of society as it became more dependent upon as well as more confused by technology. While hugely successful with popular filmgoers, these films are also recognized by film critics for Tati's revolutionary method of conveying humor through overlapping audio effects and mise-en-scenes in which several comedic acts occur at once, which sometimes required more than one viewing to witness every action. Several subsequent directors, most notably Robert Altman, have employed this style successfully for their own films. While Tati only produced five films in a career spanning more twenty-five years, he is admired for developing a brand of humor that ennobles humanity while poking gentle fun at it, conveying that humor in a way that entertains and challenges audiences and advancing the film-comedy genre. Critic Dave Kehr, in his review of *Les Vacances de Monsieur Hulot,* asserted that, without the films of Tati, "There would be no Jean-Luc Godard, no Jean-Marie Straub, no Marguerite Duras—no modern cinema.

With his 1953 film, Jacques Tati drove the first decisive wedge between cinema and classical narration.'' In these films, the only recognizable actor is Tati as either Francois or Hulot, in order to keep audiences from focusing on the celebrity onscreen and concentrated on the situations and actions. Tati also composed his scenes to include several activities at the same time, which he captured with one stable camera that captured everything. He rarely employed close-ups or reaction shots, believing that audiences did not need such devices to find the scene's humor.

From Rugby to Film

Tati's father was an art framer and restorer who was disappointed that his son did not enter the family business. After attending the Lycee de St.-Germain-en-Laye, Tati was a rugby player for the Racing Club de Paris from 1925 to 1930. In the 1930s, he worked as a pantomimist and impressionist and toured European music halls and circuses. Much of his act consisted of pantomimes of famous athletes of the era. Several of these routines were filmed, including *Oscar, champion de tennis* and *On demande une brute* in 1934 and 1935.

In 1939, Tati enlisted in the French Army. Following World War I, he was a supporting actor in two films by Claude Autant-Lara, *Sylvie et le fantome* and *Le Diable au corps.* In 1947, he made the short film *L'Ecole des facteurs,* which he expanded into the 1949 feature film *Jour de fete,* a comedy film in which Tati portrays the French postman Francois. Francois becomes obsessed with attempts to make his post office operations more efficient after observing an American postal training film. Tati employs this premise to lampoon the impersonality of technology. While much of the film's humor is physical, Tati consciously avoids slapstick by staging much of the action behind objects

placed in the camera's foreground, forcing audiences to imagine the full thrust of the gags they are visually denied. *Jour de fete* is, for many critics, similar thematically to Chaplin's *Modern Times;* both directors seem to believe that civilized humanity is lost in the rushing onslaught of its own technology.

Mr. Hulot

Following the release of *Jour de fete,* Tati spent four years making the internationally successful *Les Vacances de Monsieur Hulot (Mr. Hulot's Holiday),* which introduces the character he portrays in all his subsequent films. Hulot is a tall, thin pipe-smoking man, who is presented as an objective, innocent observer of the pratfalls of the characters he encounters. Hulot is as much a straight man as a source of humor.

The English-language version of *Les Vacances de Monsieur Hulot* begins with a warning: "Don't look for a plot, for a holiday is meant purely for fun." The film does not feature a plot in the traditional sense of a novel or short story, but presents recurring themes, episodes, and characters that bear more of a resemblance to poetic structure. The film is also noted for Tati's use of wide-angle cinematic framing, in which a motionless camera captures the action without following the actors or cutting to close ups that emphasize the jokes and actors' reactions.

In 1958, Tati released *Mon Oncle,* a sequel to *Les Vacances de Monsieur Hulot.* In this film, Monsieur Hulot receives much less screen time as the uncle who conspires with his nephew to thwart the encroaching modernism of household appliances. Tati's first color film was also an international success, despite the fact that he had relegated Monsieur Hulot to a supporting character. During the 1950s, Tati was approached by American television with an offer to produce a series of fifteen-minute short films featuring Monsieur Hulot, which he turned down.

Increasingly annoyed by audiences' association of Tati with his creation Monsieur Hulot, Tati only employed the character briefly in his next film, *Playtime.* The film took Tati more than nine years to film, largely because he insisted on constructing large, elaborate, futuristic sets that were both expensive and time consuming. An epic film, originally clocking in more than two-and-a-half hours, *Playtime* was shot using seventy millimeter film and stereophonic sound for enhanced visuals and audio. In order to finance the film, Tati sold the rights to his previous films and eventually went bankrupt when the film failed at the box office upon its release in 1967. He tried to recoup his loss by shortening the film by more than forty-five minutes; it was shortened again to ninety-three minutes upon its release as a thirty-five-minute monaural film in the United States. Reducing the length and width of the film, however, rendered much of the visual humor unintelligible. The film revolves around Monsieur Hulot's attempt to arrive at a job interview in a modernistic city that is confusing and impersonal.

In *Playtime* Tati once again refused to allow the camera to isolate the humor. Instead he used long shots to create what Kehr called: "Long-shot tableaux that leave the viewer free to wander through the frame, picking up the gags that may be occurring in the foreground, the background, or off to one side. The film returns an innocence of vision to the spectator; no value judgments or hierarchies of interest have been made for us. We are given a clear field, left to respond freely to an environment that has not been polluted with prejudices." While the film was unpopular with film audiences, other directors borrowed freely from Tati's style, including Robert Altman, who used a similar style in his film, *M*A*S*H.*

While some critics believe Tati's last theatrical film *Traffic,* released in 1971, marked a creative retreat by Tati in order to recover the financial losses of *Playtime,* others compliment the film as an inspired revisiting of Monsieur Hulot's battle against technology. Tati abandoned the futuristic settings of *Playtime* for a more contemporary setting of Monsieur Hulot's automobile and the roadways he travels on his way to the Paris Auto Show. The films, however, bear thematic resemblances in their handling of modern progress and human isolation. While *Playtime* is set in an ultramodern city constructed of glass, steel, and concrete behind which humans lose contact with one another, *Traffic* is set inside the cars of the individual characters who also have cut themselves off inadvertently from each other. The more relaxed visual style of *Traffic* marked a return to the style of Tati's earlier films. His last film, *Parade,* is a one-hour film made for Swiss television. Tati died in 1982 of a pulmonary embolism in Paris.

Books

Lyon, Christopher, *The International Dictionary of Films and Filmmakers,* St. James Press, Chicago, 1984.

Sarris, Andrew, editor, *The St. James Film Directors Encyclopedia,* Visible Ink Press, 1998.

Wilhelm, Elliot, editor, *VideoHound's World Cinema: The Adventurer's Guide to Movie Watching,* Visible Ink Press, 1999.

VideoHound's Golden Movie Retriever, Visible Ink Press, 1994.

Online

''Jacques Tati,'' *Contemporary Authors Online,* The Gale Group, 2000. □

V

Roger Vadim

French-born film director Roger Vadim (1928-2000) broke ground in the 1950s by pushing the boundaries of mainstream European art films to include more sensuality. Vadim became more renowned for the female actors he cast in his lushly photographed films than for his technical and artistic achievements, but he is credited with being one of the early instigators of the French New Wave.

Vadim's first film, *And God Created Woman,* released in 1955, caused a scandal. It featured Vadim's first wife, Brigitte Bardot, partially nude and sexually engaged with three different men. The film's subject matter, titillating use of sexuality, and the beauty of stars Bardot, Curt Jurgens, Christian Marquand, and Jean-Louis Trintignant assured the film's success internationally. *And God Created Woman* established the French "art film" as a 1950s euphemism for movies featuring nude scenes. After his divorce from Bardot, Vadim continued to employ Bardot in several films that never matched the notoriety of *And God Created Woman,* and he also made films prominently displaying other leading ladies, including second wife Annette Stroyberg, lover Catherine Deneuve, third wife Jane Fonda, Angie Dickinson, Jeanne Moreau, Susan Sarandon, and Rebecca DeMornay. While Vadim never again achieved the notoriety he received for his first film, some critics regarded him as a progenitor of the themes and styles used by such French New Wave directors as Francois Truffaut and Jean-Luc Godard. He was also critically commended for his lush photography, which he used to convey the beauty of the human form as well as natural, historic, and futuristic settings.

Son of a Diplomat

Vadim was born on January 26, 1928, in Paris. He was the son of Igor Plemiannikov, a Russian diplomat. His mother, Marie-Antoinette Plemiannikov, was a photographer. Vadim used his middle name professionally and dropped the surname Plemiannikov. He was nine years old when he witnessed his father's death from a heart attack, an event that reduced his family to poverty. During World War II, his mother took a job as manager of a hostel in the French Alps. Vadim wrote in his autobiography, *Memoirs of the Devil,* that the hostel was a haven for Jews and other exiles from France and Germany, and that he helped these fugitives get through the mountains into neutral Switzerland. The family returned to Paris after the Allied forces liberated the city.

In Paris, Vadim attended the Theatre Sarah Bernhardt, where he met film director Marc Allegret. Allegret introduced Vadim to filmmakers and writers including Jean Cocteau, Jean Genet, and Andre Gide. Allegret also introduced him to sixteen-year-old ingenue Brigitte Bardot, who would appear in several of Allegret's films before attaining international stardom with Vadim. Bardot and Vadim married in 1952.

International Scandal and Success

After several years as a minor actor and unsuccessful screenwriter, Vadim secured financing for his own film, which would feature his young wife. In 1955, he released *And God Created Woman,* starring Bardot as a woman who marries in order to escape life in an orphanage. She does not love her new husband, however, and seduces his younger

413

brother. The film became known for two scenes that spotlight the sensuality of Bardot. The first is the film's opening sequence in which Bardot lounges nude on the beach of Saint-Tropez, and the second is a barefoot dance she performs on a table top. Though she did not appear completely nude, Bardot's sensuality and her character's sexual freedom incited critical debates about art and pornography. The arguments created a tremendous amount of free publicity for the film, and it became an international success.

The film also brought charges that Vadim was a Svengali intent on exploiting the physical charms of his young bride. Vadim responded: "I did not invent Brigitte Bardot. I simply helped her to blossom, to learn her craft, while remaining true to herself. I was able to shield her from the ossification of ready-made rules which in films, as in other professions, often destroy the most original talents by bringing them into line." In fact, Vadim's direction emphasizes Bardot's natural attractiveness, rather than relying on ornate hairstyles, makeup, studio lighting, or fashionable apparel; this naturalism was later adopted by Godard and other French New Wave directors.

New Leading Ladies

Vadim made two more films with Bardot in the 1950s, *No Sun in Venice* (also known as *When the Devil Drives*) and *The Night Heaven Fell*. While both films managed to display Bardot in various stages of undress and included provocative sex scenes, neither achieved the success of

their first film together. By the time he released *The Night Heaven Fell,* his marriage to Bardot had ended in divorce.

Vadim cast his second wife, Annette Stroyberg, in a modern adaptation of Choderlos de Laclo's 1782 novel *Dangerous Liaisons,* which also featured racy scenes. Vadim faced legal proceedings initiated by France's Society of Authors, who claimed he had taken undue liberties with the story. His defense attorney, future French President Francois Mitterrand, read letters written by de Laclo that warned future generations to beware censors. Vadim's victory in court and the scandal surrounding the film failed to garner it any public or critical success at the time. However, when it was reissued in 1987 to coincide with a remake directed by Stephen Frears, some critics conceded that Vadim's version merited a positive reconsideration.

Stroyberg also appeared in Vadim's adaptation of Sheridan LeFanu's classic vampire story *Carmilla,* which he entitled *Blood and Roses.* While lauding the film's photography by legendary cinematographer Claude Renoir, many critics and audiences were confused by the story. After Vadim and Stroyberg divorced, Vadim teamed up again with Bardot for *Please Not Now!* and *Love on a Pillow.* Their stories were similar and both were financially successful, although neither film was nearly as popular as *And God Created Woman.*

Vadim once again found himself the center of controversy after the release of *Vice and Virtue.* The 1963 film featured another of his paramours, Catherine Deneuve, and concerned a Parisian bordello during the Nazi occupation. Opening night audiences booed the film. According to Vadim, "The French were still very sensitive about the Nazi occupation and they didn't appreciate the liberties I had taken with history. Associations of former Resistance fighters tried to have the film banned. I had to wait two years for *Vice and Virtue* to open in art theaters in New York and San Francisco before I received good reviews."

Jane Fonda

Vadim fathered a child with Deneuve and the two were engaged to be married. His next wife, however, was American actress Jane Fonda. Fonda appeared in Vadim's adaptation of Arthur Schnitzler's play *La Ronde* and his modern adaptation of Emile Zola's novel, *La Curee,* (also known as *The Game is Over*). Although the first film features a screenplay by Jean Anouilh, it suffered in comparison to Max Ophuls's 1951 classic rendering of the same material. In *La Curee,* Fonda's character, like Bardot's in *And God Created Woman,* marries a man to escape her immediate surroundings, in this case, a convent. Following her marriage of convenience, she finds love with her husband's son by his first marriage. Learning of the infidelity, her husband tries to drive her into madness.

Of the films Fonda and Vadim collaborated on, none achieved more notoriety than *Barbarella.* Based on the French science fiction comic strip by Jean-Claude Forest, it was adapted by Terry Southern, who also scripted Stanley Kubrick's classic antiwar film *Dr. Strangelove. Barbarella* eventually became a cult classic for its refusal to take itself seriously—and for the various sexual situations and states of undress in which Fonda's heroine finds herself. Fonda also starred in a sequence directed by Vadim for the film *Spirits of the Dead,* a triptych of Edgar Allen Poe stories, which also featured sequences directed by Federico Fellini and Louis Malle. Fonda and her brother Peter are cast as incestuous siblings. After divorcing Vadim, Fonda eventually denounced their film collaborations, saying they were exploitative.

Hollywood

Before his divorce from Fonda, Vadim had relocated to Hollywood. He remained there to direct Rock Hudson as a homicidal high school counselor in 1971's *Pretty Maids All in a Row* and reunited with Bardot for *Ms. Don Juan* (also known as *If Don Juan Were a Woman*), in which she plays the seductive counterpart to the infamous womanizer.

Vadim spent the remainder of the 1970s writing literary works, including two volumes of memoirs, *Memoirs of the Devil* and *Bardot Deneuve Fonda.* He returned to film in 1981 with *Night Games,* in which a young married woman who was the victim of a childhood rape attempts to conquer her sexual fears by engaging in sexual fantasizing. Vadim's final film was a remake of his first, *And God Created Woman.* Starring Rebecca De Mornay in the role created by Bardot, the 1988 version tells the story of a wrongly imprisoned female who promises her inheritance to a prison worker in exchange for a marriage that will expedite her parole. Once released, however, she focuses her energies on becoming a rock-and-roll star rather than a wife. While finding much to recommend the film, Roger Ebert wrote: "Is this a movie worth seeing? Sort of. You have to put the plot on hold, overlook the contrivances of the last half hour and find a way to admire how De Mornay plays the big scene, even while despising the scene itself. If you can do that, you'll find good work here—even by Vadim, who may have been as trapped by the plot as everyone else."

Books

Lyon, Christopher, *The International Dictionary of Films and Filmmakers,* St. James Press, 1984.

Vadim, Roger, *Bardot Deneuve Fonda: My Life with the Three Most Beautiful Women in the World,* Simon and Schuster, 1986.

VideoHound's Golden Movie Retriever, Visible Ink Press, Gale Research, 1994.

Wilhelm, Elliot, editor, *VideoHound's World Cinema: The Adventurer's Guide to Movie Watching,* Visible Ink Press, 1999.

Online

"Review of *And God Created Woman,*" *Chicago Sun Times,* http://www.suntimes.com/ebert/ebert_reviews/1988/03/282266.html.

"Roger Vadim," *Contemporary Authors Online,* http://galenet.galegroup.com/servlet/BioRC, 2002. □

Ritchie Valens

In a recording career that spanned less than two years and produced only one album released during his lifetime, Ritchie Valens (1941-1959), born Richard Steven Valenzuela, has had an enduring influence on rock 'n roll music despite the fact that he died before his eighteenth birthday in a plane crash that also claimed the lives of rockers Buddy Holly and J. P. Richardson (The Big Bopper). Valens's music is admired for his gritty proto-punk, garage-rock guitar style, lack of sentimentality, and embracement of his Hispanic heritage, which are apparent in his most successful hit single "La Bamba."

With the concurrent deaths of Holly and Valens, it has been argued that the evolution of the rock 'n roll genre stalled until the Beatles (a band whose name was inspired by the name of Holly's band, the Crickets) took up where the two American performers left off. Valens, inspired by Holly and Eddie Cochran to write and play guitar on his own compositions, displayed a tremendous degree of potential as a songwriter, guitarist, and showman as evidenced by the performances captured on his two studio albums, *Ritchie Valens* (1959) and *Ritchie* (1959), and a live recording, *Ritchie Valens in Concert at Pacoima Junior High* (1960). These recordings inspired such later guitarists and songwriters as diverse as The Ramones's Johnny Ramone, Led Zeppelin's Jimmy Page, and Los Lobos's David Hidalgo and Cesar Rosas. Such was Valens's influence on Los Lobos that the band re-recorded two of his biggest hits for the soundtrack of the Valens's biographic motion picture *La Bamba* (1987), which revitalized interest in Valens's life and music.

Born in East Los Angeles

Valens was raised in the Los Angeles suburb of Pacoima, the son of Joseph "Steve" Valenzuela, who worked at times as a tree surgeon, miner, and horse trainer. Valens's mother, Concepcion "Connie" Valenzuela, worked in a munitions plant and had one son, Robert, from a previous marriage. The parents separated when Valens was three years old, and the young man spent much of his time with his father who introduced his son to blues, flamenco, and other traditional Mexican music and taught his son how to play guitar. The heavy ethnicity of the Los Angeles area also exposed him to the rhythm and blues music of such acts as the Drifters, the Penguins, Bo Diddley (Elias McDaniel), and, perhaps most importantly, Little Richard, as well as the rock 'n roll music of Holly, Cochran, Jerry Lee Lewis, and Elvis Presley.

When Joseph Valenzuela died of diabetes-related complications, Valens lived for a while with his uncle, Henry Felix, in Santa Monica, California, before moving back to stay with his mother, step-brother and two younger stepsisters in Pacoima. He continued to pursue his musical interests, studying guitar and listening to recordings by Chuck Berry, Richard, Presley, and others, while learning traditional Mexican songs from his relatives. He practiced and entertained his friends at Pacoima Junior High during lunch hours, refining the guitar skills and vocal prowess that led to an invitation to join The Silhouettes.

The Silhouettes

When he was sixteen years old, Valens accepted The Silhouettes's invitation to join the band as guitarist and singer. The racially integrated group included African American and Japanese American musicians who played local high-school dances, church social functions, and neighborhood parties. Other members of the band included vibes player Gil Rocha, who was twenty-one years old and often credited with instilling a sense of professionalism within the band. Valens shared vocal responsibilities with female vocalists Emma Franco and Phyllis Romano. His tenure with The Silhouettes is credited with assisting him overcome stage fright and shyness and led him to be nicknamed "The Little Richard of Pacoima" for one of his chief stylistic influences. His stage demeanor, however, was reportedly far more reserved than Little Richard's. Other writers claim that Valens's exhibited more of a Bo Diddley "shave-and-a-haircut-two-bits" rhythmic influence, but in either instance, it is clear that Valens was pioneering the use of rhythmic guitar as a lead rock 'n roll instrument, a style that is also used to good effect by guitarists Pete Townshend, Robbie Robertson, and Johnny Ramone as well as hundreds of guitarists in lesser-known garage and punk bands.

Bob Keane and Del-Fi Records

In May 1958, Valens auditioned for Bob Keane, the owner of Del-Fi Records. Recording at Gold Star Studios in Los Angeles, Valens cut his first single, "Come On, Let's Go." Although it is recognized by contemporary critics as a classic rock 'n roll song, it failed to chart in the top-40 upon its release.

Valens's second recording session yielded a two-sided hit single, "Donna" and "La Bamba." The first song was written by Valens for his high-school girlfriend and was rush-released after Los Angeles's most popular radio station, KFWB, broadcast a test-pressing of the song to overwhelming positive response. A softly sung guitar ballad with simple lyrics and guitar-chord changes, "Donna" inspired a whole generation of feminine-named songs from Neil Sedaka's "Oh, Carol!" to Randy and the Rainbows "Denise."

Rock critic Lester Bangs summed up the appeal of "Donna" in this way: "Valens sang with an unassuming sincerity that made him more truly touching than any other artist from his era. 'Donna' is one of the classic teen love ballads, one of the few which reaches through layers of maudlin sentiment to give you the true and unmistakable sensation of what it must have been like to be a teenager in that strange decade." Bangs continued: "The agonizing sense of frustration which is so crucial to adolescent life is never very far from his lyrics, and in his best songs, like 'Donna' and 'Come On Let's Go,' it is right up front, just as it is in Eddie Cochran's classic 'Summertime Blues.'" "Donna" entered the pop-music charts on December 29, 1958, and became a number 2 hit with fourteen weeks on the *Billboard* American charts; it climbed to number 20 in Great Britain.

The single's flipside, however, may have contributed significantly to the success of "Donna." "La Bamba" was a huapango—a traditional Mexican folksong of celebration that is often sung at wedding receptions. Reputedly taught to Valens by his cousin, Dickie Cota, "La Bamba" is the song that became most closely associated with the singer, guitarist, and songwriter. While it rose to only Number 22 on the *Billboard* American charts, the song combines a flamenco-influenced lead guitar riff to a more visceral garage-band rhythm, resulting in one of rock 'n roll's seminal records of the 1950s.

All three singles were collected on the album *Ritchie Valens,* which was released February 12, 1959, slightly more than one week after Valens's death. In October 1959, however, Del-Fi Records released a second album of Valens's recordings, *Ritchie,* which yielded no hit singles but remains essential to fans of 1950s rock, proto-punk, and garage rock. Del-Fi also released *Ritchie Valens in Concert at Pacoima Junior High,* which included live concert versions of "Come On, Let's Go," and "Donna" and cover versions of Eddie Cochran's "Summertime Blues" and the Mexican folksong "Malaguena." Reviewing the record, Bangs wrote: "Richie Valens was a quiet, underrated yet enormously influential member of that handful of folk visionaries who almost single-handedly created rock and roll in the Fifties. . . . It is a dignified, sincere memorial and a beautiful document out of the Fifties, but it is also a great rock and roll recording in its own right, because Richie Valens himself was a great artist." Numerous repackages of Valens's music have been released since his death.

Played with the Big Boys

Capitalizing on the success of "Donna," the upcoming release of his first album, and the forthcoming release of "La Bamba" as a single in its own right, Valens was asked to appear on Dick Clark's *American Bandstand* and Alan Freed's *Christmas Show* in New York in December 1958. He also filmed an appearance in the 1959-released film, *Go, Johnny, Go,* in which he appears with Freed alongside performances by Cochran and Jackie Wilson.

In January 1959, Valens joined Buddy Holly and the Crickets, the Big Bopper, and Dion and the Belmonts on a package-concert tour organized by Clark, called "The Winter Dance Party." Such package shows were popular during the 1950s and 1960s and typically featured two shows every evening that allowed each act fifteen minutes to one-half hour to perform their hits. After a performance on February 2, 1959, several of the performers elected to fly in a plane chartered by Holly rather than ride on the tour bus with a broken heater in sub-zero temperatures. Valens earned a seat on the plane by winning a coin toss with Crickets guitarist Tommy Allsop and was killed along with Holly, the Big Bopper, and the twenty-one-year-old pilot when the plane crashed in a cornfield.

Enduring Popularity

Since his death in 1959, Valens's music and life have enjoyed renewed interest through the song "American Pie" by Don McLean, which presents the fatal plane crash as an allegory for lost innocence, and through the heavily fictionalized film biography *La Bamba,* featuring actor Lou Diamond Phillips as Valens. The film's title track, performed by the band Los Lobos, became a number one hit single the same year. Valens's name also appeared in music news when Led Zeppelin songwriter and guitarist Jimmy Page was sued for plagiarizing Valens's "Ooh! My Head" for the British band's song "Boogie with Stu." Page, who acknowledged Valens as "my first guitar hero," settled the suit for an undisclosed sum in 1978.

Books

Nugent, Stephen and Charlie Gillett, *Rock Almanac: Top Twenty American and British Singles and Albums of the '50s, '60s, and '70s,* Anchor Books, 1978.

Online

"The Real Story of Ritchie Valens," *The Rockabilly Hall of Fame,* http://www.rockabillyhall.com/RitchieValens.html.

"Ritchie Valens," *Ritchie Valens,* http:www/ritchievalens.net/bio/rvbio.html.

"Ritchie Valens," *The Rock'n'Roll Hall of Fame,* http://www.rockhall.com/hof/inductee.asp?id+1145.

"Ritchie Valens," (review by Lester Bangs), *Rolling Stone,* http://www.rollingstone/recordings/r. □

Hartmann von Aue

Hartmann von Aue (c. 1160-c. 1205) was a medieval German literary figure who wrote epic poems in the *minnesang* tradition. The Minnesinger were court poets who lived and worked inside the great castles of princes and other nobles and whose work paid homage to the concept of "minne," or love. Their predecessors were the Provençal troubadours of the eleventh century, and von Aue's work shared attributes of both these and the Arthurian legends popular at the time.

Of Swabian Origins

Little is known of von Aue's life, save for the fact that he lived and worked in the later decades of the twelfth century and was alive during the first years of the 1200s. The Middle High German language of his verse has Alemannic traces, which points to his origins near the region that became Swabia and the state of Baden-Württemberg in southern Germany. He was also referred to later in the Middle Ages in one source as "from the land of Swabians." Scholars believe that one of von Aue's ancestors may have married unwisely, which drastically reduced the family's economic circumstances. In one of his works, he refers to himself as a *dienstman,* or servant, for the minnesinger were part of the ministeriale class at court. They were its functionaries, administrators, and servants, and were not free to leave.

In illustrated volumes of Minnesang from the period, one depicts von Aue with a coat of arms that has been linked to the Zähringer family in Swabia, and the surname "Aue" was also present in the region. He possessed knowledge of French, which showed that he spent time in France at some point in his life, and of Latin, hinting that he received some education, probably at a cloister or a cathedral school. He wrote in one of his works that he was a *rîter* (knight) who could also read and write, and from this scholars infer that this combination of talents was uncommon. Other clues that place von Aue in the service of the Zähringer court were that family's links to the patrons of French writer Chrétien de Troyes, whose *Erec et Enide* (c. 1165) was the basis for von Aue's *Erec* some 15 years later.

The Troubadour Tradition

Like Chrétien's work, von Aue was strongly influenced by the ideals of chivalry and courtly love. This marked a new era in European literature, for prior to this epic works usually centered around overtly religious themes. Scholars believe *Die Klage* ("The Complaint") to be von Aue's first work. It is a narrative poem in rhymed couplets and shares similarities with some French works of the era. Its verse relates a conflict between the body and the heart in the form of an allegorical dialogue. It mentions *krûtzouber von Kärlingen,* a magical root from France, as a part of a formula that can create the ideal man. To become such, one requires *milte* (generosity), *zuht* (appropriate behavior), *diemut* (modesty), *triuwe* (loyalty), *staete* (constancy), *kiuscheit* (purity), and *gewislîchiu manheit* (dependable manhood) to be present in a heart absent of hate.

Von Aue's first adaptation of an Arthurian work was *Erec*. Scholars date it to at least the year 1180, for it contains a reference to Connelant, or Ikonium, and it was known that Emperor Friedrich I, called Barbarossa, made diplomatic contact with this kingdom around 1179. The Arthurian legends originated in Celtic Britain, and provided the basis for other epic works, such as the *Gereint and Enid,* from Wales, and the Norse *Erexsaga*. Von Aue may have consulted these in writing his own. It begins at the court of King Arthur, with the announcement of a contest involving the hunt for an elusive white stag. Erec, a knight, does not take part in the hunt, but instead accompanies the Queen and one of her attendants. They meet an unknown knight, a lady, and a dwarf servant who whips the Queen's attendant and then Erec. He vows to avenge the slight, and follows the trio to a thriving town near a castle. He meets Koralus, a impoverished count, who offers Erec hospitality and introduces him to his daughter, Enite.

Adventures and Romance

Erec learns that the knight he seeks is called Iders, and the townspeople have assembled for a beauty contest. Iders's lady has been its winner twice before, but captured the title through Iders's intimidating tactics. If she wins a third time, the contest will conclude forever, and she will receive a sparrow hawk. Koralus lends Erec armor and weapons in order to beat Iders, and in return for this help, Erec promises to wed Enite. At the contest, the lady moves to take the sparrow hawk, but Erec declares Enite most beautiful in realm instead. He and Iders battle, and Erec is victorious. The dwarf is duly thrashed, a wedding at Arthur's court takes place, and Erec and Enite return to Erec's land. This concludes the first part.

In the second part of *Erec,* the knight is so enamored with his new bride that he neglects all other duties. He is unaware of the loss of honor until Enite one day utters words of regret when she thinks Erec is asleep. Ashamed, Erec vows to change his ways, and they leave the castle and set off on a series of adventures. They ride through a forest, where robber knights try to kidnap her. Then Enite believes Erec has died battling fierce giants. She is captured by a devious count, but refuses to marry him. Erec rescues Enite after her weeping has roused him from his deathlike state. Erec's final battle of the story is with Mabonagrin, who has been isolated from Arthur's court and resides in a garden surrounded by stakes, on which are impaled the heads of those he has defeated. Erec wins this battle, and both knights return to the court. Erec tells Mabonagrin, "Bî den liuten ist sô guot" ("It is so good to be with other people").

Wrote More Spiritual Work

Scholars assume that von Aue's next work was *Gregorius,* and date it to about 1187. Its tale begins with an orphaned brother and sister, whose parents had been rulers of Aquitaine. The songs of the "minne" influence the brother negatively, and he begins to desire his sister. They commit incest, and both are guilt-stricken. He atones by joining a Crusade to the Holy Land, but remains lovesick and dies. His sister became pregnant, and the new ruler of Aquitaine as well. She places the infant in a boat with some gold marks and an ivory tablet attesting to its noble lineage but sinful origin. The tablet instructs the child to atone for its parents' wrongdoing. The princess is courted by a powerful neighbor, but refuses to marry him. He attacks her and the kingdom and takes all but the capital city. Meanwhile, the infant is discovered and raised by fishermen. The local abbot names him Gregorius. He accidentally learns of his tragic origins as a young man and flees to become a knight. As such, he helps free Aquitaine's besieged city and receives the princess's hand in marriage. Neither realize that they are mother and son, but she discovers the ivory tablet after another act of incest has recurred, and both resolve to atone once again for their sin.

Gregorious instructs a fisherman to take him out to sea and chain him to a rock. The key is then tossed into the ocean. He lives on nothing but water for 17 years. Church officials in Rome learn of this and believe him to be extraordinarily holy. Legates from Rome arrive with an invitation to become the new pope. The legates visit the fisherman, who serves them fish; inside its stomach is the key once tossed into the sea. Gregorious accepts the offer, and his mother—the princess—comes to ask forgiveness for her sin from him. "From the lowest depths of sinfulness, Gregorius is raised by God's grace to the position of God's highest earthly servant," wrote Will Hasty in a *Dictionary of Literary Biography* essay. Hasty notes that *Gregorious,* with its absolution of a sin that was involuntarily committed, "seems to be characterized by a religiosity that more closely corresponds to the values and customs of the lay nobility than to the practices of the church."

May Have Chronicled Ancestor's Fall

Der arme Heinrich ("Poor Heinrich"), which scholars date to the year 1191, is perhaps von Aue's best known work, even earning praise from eighteenth-century German Romantic writer Johann Wolfgang von Goethe. The theme of this epic poem can be linked to the medieval myth that leprosy could be cured by blood from human sacrifice and from the belief that the severely disfiguring disease was a form of divine punishment, God's retribution for rotten soul. Its hero, Heinrich von Aue, is a wealthy and powerful noble who contracts leprosy. He is told that the sacrifice of a young maiden, willing to die for him, will cure him. He gives his riches to the poor and the church, and moves in with a peasant family. To their eight-year-old daughter he gives many gifts and even calls her his bride. A period of three years pass, and she learns that his illness can be cured by sacrifice and resolves to be his savior. She and Heinrich journey to a doctor, who explains that he must extract her still-beating heart from her body. Heinrich hears the doctor sharpening his blade and cries out to spare her. He asserts that he will accept his illness as God's will. She objects vehemently, and the experience shatters her health. They journey home, and both are restored to health along the way. Heinrich returns to a position of nobility, even richer than before, and marries the girl. Such a match between a noble and a peasant could bring financial ruin, and scholars believe that von Aue's ancestor may have entered into an disadvantageous match, which reduced the family's fortunes and caused their descent into the ministeriale class.

The Exemplary *Iwein*

It is thought believe that von Aue may have taken up arms and joined the Crusade organized by Holy Roman Emperor Henry VI in 1197. His next work, *Iwein,* dates from about 1203, and is considered by scholars as the zenith of his literary talents. "Nowhere is his simple elegance of style and aesthetic conception more evident than in *Iwein,*" opined Hasty. A large number of surviving manuscripts from the Middle Ages attest to its popularity at the time, and the story was also reproduced in tapestries and frescoes. The work opens at the court of Arthur, where Iwein and his cousin Kalogreant serve as knights. Kalogreant relates a story that he once met a wild man, who instructs him to journey to the land of a fountain. He battles with Ascalon, a watchman at a bridge, and is unhorsed. The knights at Arthur's court vow to avenge him. Iwein arrives first, fights Ascalon, but becomes trapped in the land of his foes. He is helped by a servant, Lunete, who gives him a magic ring, and in time marries the lady of the castle, Laudine.

In the second part of *Iwein,* the hero leaves the land, but Laudine states that she will wait only one year for him. Iwein and another knight, Gawein, embark on a series of adventures. He forgets his promise to Laudine, and Lunete arrives to take back the ring. He realizes that he has lost his love and his lands, and he succumbs to madness. He strips his clothes and runs to live in forest as a wild man.

In 1210, *Tristan,* a work by Gottfried von Strassburg, mentions von Aue as still living. Another German poet, Heinrich von dem Türlin, wrote *Krone* some time between 1215 and 1220, and paid homage to the late von Aue. "Besides the elegant clarity of his style, Hartmann's individual mark on German courtly literature may well be the social concern of his works," noted Hasty in the *Dictionary of Literary Biography* essay. "Even those works addressing religious questions deal with one's obligations to others, with conflicts that can result from such obligations, and with false and legitimate solutions to these conflicts."

Books

Dictionary of Literary Biography, Volume 138: *German Writers and Works of the High Middle Ages: 1170-1280,* edited by James Hardin and Will Hasty, Gale, 1994.

Periodicals

Medium Aevum, Fall 1995, p. 189. □

Lawrence Welk

The music performed by Lawrence Welk (1903-1992) and his Champagne Music Makers alternately has been admired and reviled for the bandleader's insistence on inoffensive subject matter emphasizing American patriotism and traditional Christian values and arrangements emphasizing melody over improvisation and technical skill.

Lawrence Welk had been performing music professionally for more than 35 years before garnering national exposure as host of his own television program in 1951. Four years later, Welk's local Los Angeles program was picked up by the American Broadcasting Company (ABC), bringing his particular brand of music into millions of American homes twice a week for 15 years. The network subsequently canceled the show when executives determined that Welk's program was not attracting a younger demographic viewing audience coveted by advertisers. Welk rebounded with a syndicated program following the same format as his network telecasts and recognized even greater financial success. Reruns of the popular series continued to be broadcast weekly on Public Broadcasting as late as 2000, a testimony to the enduring appetite of a large portion of the American television-viewing public for wholesome entertainment.

Born in a Sod Shack

Welk was the sixth of eight children born to German immigrants Ludwig and Christina Welk. The Welks arrived in the United States after an exile in Russia and, after a long trip by ox-drawn cart, settled on a land claim in Emmons County, North Dakota, in 1893. Welk was born on March 11, 1903, in Strasburg, North Dakota. The family lived in a wood-sided sod home and earned their livelihood through farming. The Welk family spoke only German, schooling their children in a parochial school staffed by German-speaking nuns.

Welk's education was cut short when he suffered acute appendicitis when he was ten years old. The prolonged recovery from the resulting appendectomy and subsequent peritonitis allowed Welk to abandon school and focus on farm work, fur trapping, and teaching himself to play his father's accordion. The elder Welk earned extra money by performing at local barn dances, and his son soon followed in his footsteps. As Welk recalled in his autobiography *Wunnerful, Wunnerful,* "My earliest clear memory is crawling toward my father who was holding his accordion. I can still recall the wonder and delight I felt when he let me press my fingers on the keys and squeeze out a few wavering notes." When he was 17 years old, Welk made a deal with his father that committed him to continue working on the family farm until his 21st birthday in exchange for a $400 accordion. In addition, Welk promised to give his parents all the monies earned with his new instrument.

A Long Musical Internship

In 1924 Welk left home with three dollars pinned to the inside of a new jacket, his accordion, a thick German accent, and an extremely limited grasp of the English language. He toured with such bands as the Jazzy Junior Five, Lincoln Bould's Chicago Band, and George T. Kelly's Peerless Entertainers. Welk recalled that Kelly "taught me all he knew about show business, traveling, booking, and how to get along with all kinds of people." After leaving the

Peerless Entertainers, Welk formed a quartet with drummer Johnny Higgins, saxophonist Howard Keiser, and pianist Art Beal. This lineup became known as the Lawrence Welk Novelty Orchestra and, later, the Hotsy Totsy Boys and the Honolulu Fruit Gum Orchestra.

In 1927 the band decided to relocate to New Orleans to escape the early and harsh winters of North Dakota. The band never made it farther than Yankton, North Dakota, however. The quartet auditioned for local radio station WNAX, and the success of the audition's live broadcast netted them a contract for a regular radio program featuring the orchestra's music and commercials for hog tonic and other agricultural products.

The band was able to parlay its radio success with live performances and appearances throughout the Midwest, necessitating the purchase of a tour bus for the expanding entourage. While in Yankton, Welk met and courted Fern Renner, a nurse working in Yankton's Sacred Heart Hospital. The pair married in 1931 in Sioux City, Iowa. By the mid-1930s, Welk moved the orchestra's base of operations to Omaha, Nebraska.

Champagne Music

In 1938 the orchestra garnered major performance exposure for a concert at the St. Paul Hotel in Pittsburgh, Pennsylvania, where, according to a legend perpetuated by Welk, the group's music earned the descriptive "Champagne Music" from a listener who pronounced that the orchestra's music was "effervescent, like champagne."

From that time forward, the band was billed as The Champagne Music of Lawrence Welk. During the 1940s, Welk and his band performed as the house orchestra at the Trianon Ballroom in Chicago, Illinois. After a successful decade in Chicago, Welk moved what he called his "musical family" to Southern California, where a 1951 late-night appearance on television station KTLA became the springboard for his later national fame.

Found Television and Chart Success

Response to his band's first televised performance in 1951 led to Welk's increasing popularity among southern Californians. In 1955 ABC debuted *The Dodge Dancing Party,* which was renamed *The Plymouth Show Starring Lawrence Welk* in 1958 and *The Lawrence Welk Show* in 1962. The show's mixture of instrumental music, songs performed by a variety of staff singers, and dance numbers was so successful that Welk's program was soon broadcast twice weekly.

Throughout the program's network run, Welk ignored contemporary trends in the music industry while assisting the launch of several careers, including surf guitarist Dick Dale, jazz musician Pete Fountain, country singer Lynn Anderson, and the Lennon Sisters singing act. While other variety shows such as *The Ed Sullivan Show* featured performances by Elvis Presley, the Animals, the Rolling Stones, and the Beatles, the music selected for Welk's program relied heavily on traditional Tin Pan Alley and Big Band standards that endorsed Middle American values, patriotism, and morality. Such was his adherence to this approach that one of Welk's "Champagne Ladies," Alice Lon, reportedly was fired after displaying too much knee to the television viewing audience while singing a song perched atop a desk.

In fact, Welk was known as a very rigid taskmaster, requiring that the members of his musical ensemble rehearse constantly and follow what he perceived to be virtuous lives. He also abjured musical arrangements that he deemed "too fussy" or complicated favoring instead music that emphasized a song's melody more than its rhythm. "Our fans told us with cheers and applause and requests that they liked 'our' music, music with a heart, a beat, music you could remember and hum, that brought back memories." Welk also commented, "I'm not a creative kind of musical director in the sense that I come up with something entirely fresh and unusual. I think my usefulness lies in evaluating somebody else's ideas and adapting them."

The songs performed on his program were introduced in Welk's trademark accent and vocal mannerisms, which betrayed his inability to pronounce the letter "D" and his difficulty with certain English pronunciations. Several of his trademark phrases—"Wunnerful, Wunnerful" and "Ah, One-uh an-uh Two-uh"—became part of the national lexicon. Welk's program also served as an effective promotional device for the hundreds of albums his 45-piece orchestra recorded during the 1950s and 1960s. While most of these recordings were remakes of compositions from other writers, Welk scored a number-one hit in 1961 with a harpsichord instrumental titled "Calcutta" and another moderate hit with "Baby Elephant Walk."

Became Pioneer in Syndication

Welk's refusal to allow most rock 'n' roll and pop songs on his program and his insistence that his performers dress modestly and groom themselves according to Eisenhower-era standards resulted in Welk's program becoming a source for ridicule by many comics as the epitome of "square" conservatism. The truth, however, was that ratings for Welk's program remained consistently high. Despite this fact, the ABC network cancelled the program in 1971 in an effort to attract more youthful audiences, reasoning that more advertising revenue could be generated from a younger demographic.

Tremendously wealthy from real estate transactions and music publishing (he owned all the publishing for the songs of Jerome Kern), Welk considered retiring. Don Fedderson, Welk's producer, however, suggested that Welk continue to produce the program independently of ABC and offer it to stations to broadcast prior to their network prime-time schedule. Fedderson suggested offering the program free to any station desiring to broadcast it in exchange for reserving five minutes of national advertising that Welk's producer would solicit. The results were dramatic: When the *Lawrence Welk Show* debuted as a syndicated program in September 1971, it appeared on more than 200 stations, more than ABC's total number of affiliates at the time.

Welk continued to produce new programs for syndication until his semi-retirement in 1982. New programs edited from his 11 years of syndicated programs and 16 years of network television continued to be broadcast on Public Broadcasting stations since 1987. Following his death on March 17, 1992, in Santa Monica, California, from pneumonia, Welk's heirs opened the Lawrence Welk Theatre and Resort in Branson, Missouri, where many of the television program's stars performed.

Books

Knopper, Steve, editor, *MusicHound Lounge: The Essential Album Guide to Martini Music and Easy Listening,* Visible Ink Press, 1998.

Welk, Lawrence, with Bernice McGeehan, *Ah-One, Ah-Two: Life with My Musical Family,* G. K. Hall, 1975.

Welk, Lawrence, with Bernice McGeehan, *Wunnerful, Wunnerful!,* The Welk Group, 1971.

Periodicals

Forum (Fargo, North Dakota), May 16, 1999.

Online

AllMusic.com, http://www.allmusic.com/ (February 21, 2002).

The German American Corner, http://www.germanheritage .com/ (February 21, 2002).

"Lawrence Welk," *Horatio Alger Association of Distinguished Members,* http://www.horatioalger.com/ (February 21, 2002).

"Lawrence Welk," *Red Hot Jazz,* http://www.redhotjazz.com/ (February 21, 2002).

"Lawrence Welk: Post-Modernist," *Jeffrey Zeldman Presents,* http:www.zeldman.com/ (1995-2001). □

Edward Bennett Williams

Edward Bennett Williams (1920-1988) was one of the best known and most successful trial lawyers in Washington in his day. Well connected politically, he had access to every president from John Kennedy through Ronald Reagan. A sports fan, Williams was part owner of the Washington Redskins football team and the Baltimore Orioles baseball club.

As a defense attorney, Williams represented some of the most colorful and controversial figures of the mid to late twentieth century. His clients included singer Frank Sinatra, fugitive financier Robert Vesco, Soviet spy Igor Melekh, Teamsters boss Jimmy Hoffa, reputed Mafioso Frank Costello, U.S. Senator Joseph McCarthy, and the Reverend Sun-Young Moon, founder of the Unification Church. According to biographer Evan Thomas, author of *The Man to See: Edward Bennett Williams—Legendary Trial Lawyer, Ultimate Insider,* Williams wasn't content to be just a great lawyer: "He wanted power, and he wanted to be seen as a force for larger ends than the narrow representation of his clients. He was, at least in the beginning, an effective crusader for individual freedom."

Quick Rise as Lawyer

The only child of Joseph Barnard Williams, a department store detective, and Mary Bennett Williams, a homemaker, he was born in Hartford, Connecticut, on May 31, 1920. Shortly after the beginning of the Great Depression in the early 1930s, Joseph Williams's father lost his job and was often out of work during the lean years that followed. To help the family make ends meet, young Williams worked after school. A good student at Bulkeley High School in Hartford, he won an academic scholarship to Holy Cross College in Worcester, Massachusetts, where he distinguished himself as a first-rate debater. In 1941, he graduated from Holy Cross summa cum laude.

When Japan attacked Pearl Harbor in December 1941, thrusting the United States into World War II, Williams joined the U.S. Army Air Forces but was discharged after sustaining a back injury in training. After his brief stint in the military, Williams began studying for his law degree at Georgetown University in Washington, D.C. He graduated in 1944 and was admitted to the District of Columbia Bar in 1945. That same year he joined the prestigious Washington law firm of Hogan and Hartson. On May 3, 1946, Williams married Dorothy Adair Guider, with whom he had three children.

By the end of the 1940s Williams left Hogan and Hartson to open his own law office. He specialized in cases dealing with civil liberties and first came to prominence in the early 1950s when he represented U.S. Senator Joseph R.

McCarthy of Wisconsin in censure proceedings. A number of McCarthy's fellow senators had charged him with abusing his power as chairman of a subcommittee investigating Communist Party infiltration into the federal government and military. Williams skillfully negotiated an agreement with senators to dismiss the censure charge and substitute for it a much milder punishment. However, the deal fell apart when McCarthy suggested in a speech that those senators arrayed against him were "unwitting handmaidens" of the Communist Party.

Tangled with Buckley

Years later, conservative commentator William F. Buckley, publisher of the *National Review*, recalled his stormy relationship with Williams over the years. In the summer of 1954, Buckley was first approached by the attorney, who pleaded for his help in clearing the name of McCarthy, a man he characterized as "a great and important American," Buckley recalled. The publisher recommended that Williams seek the assistance of L. Brent Bozell, Buckley's brother-in-law, in his defense of McCarthy. But Bozell had written the McCarthy speech that sabotaged the deal negotiated by Williams. Buckley's next encounter with Williams came when the Washington attorney agreed to defend Representative Adam Clayton Powell Jr. of New York on charges of income tax evasion that were first brought to light in an expose by Buckley. The relationship between Buckley and Williams deteriorated even further when the *National Review* panned *One Man's Freedom,* a book by Williams about civil liberties. Not long after, Wil-

liams, in a speech at Yale, referred to Buckley as "an Ivy League George Rockwell." Buckley threatened to sue for libel, and Williams eventually retracted the statement. In the end, although their politics put them poles apart, an uneasy truce was struck between Williams and Buckley.

Although his defense of McCarthy first brought Williams to national attention, he was equally comfortable representing the Communists and fellow travelers that the senator from Wisconsin was trying to track down. As biographer Thomas observed, "Williams would defend anyone, he liked to say, as long as the client gave him total control of the case and paid up front. He would represent Mafia dons and pornographers for enormous fees. He would also represent priests, judges, and attractive women in distress for little or nothing." After his defense of McCarthy, Williams was called a fascist by those who abhorred the Wisconsin senator and his witch-hunt. At the same time, others branded him a Communist sympathizer because of his representation of several people accused by the House Un-American Activities Committee. Williams's willingness to represent almost anyone brought him criticism throughout his career. His own views were expressed in *One Man's Freedom,* published in 1992. In it, he wrote: "The lawyer is neither expected nor qualified to make a moral judgement on the person seeking his help."

Williams suffered a personal tragedy in 1959 when his wife, Dorothy, died. In June 1960 he married Agnes Anne Neill. The couple had four children.

Defended Hoffa

In the early 1960s, Williams took on another notorious client, Teamsters union boss Jimmy Hoffa. Indicted on charges that he had taken kickbacks from a Detroit trucking company, Hoffa escaped conviction because the jury deadlocked. However, the Justice Department, led by Attorney General Robert F. Kennedy, was not through with Hoffa, who eventually was sent to prison in 1967. Williams felt strongly that the strategy the government employed against Hoffa was fundamentally unfair.

Another of his more notorious clients was Frank Costello, alleged by the government to be a key figure in organized crime. Costello, facing charges of tax evasion and possible deportation, reportedly was reluctant to retain Williams because of the attorney's defense of McCarthy. Costello was convicted of tax evasion but with the help of Williams managed to avoid deportation.

An attorney of uncommon skill, Williams was most at home in the courtroom, where he won his greatest victories. He also was fascinated by the political intrigues of Washington and forged strong alliances with many of the most influential politicians in the nation's capital. Although he was a lifelong Democrat, Williams counseled Republicans and Democrats alike. In 1974 he was elected national treasurer of the Democratic Party, a post he held until 1977. So highly regarded was Williams that in the early 1970s General Alexander Haig, a close adviser to Richard Nixon, urged the president to retain Williams to provide legal advice during the Watergate affair. Nixon, however, rejected Haig's suggestion, mostly because Williams was a Democrat. Williams had been closely identified with the Kennedy family and the *Washington Post,* two of Nixon's biggest enemies.

In 1967, Williams abandoned the solo practice he had opened in 1949 and founded the law firm of Williams and Connolly. In the years that followed, the firm was widely recognized as one of the most successful criminal law practices in the country. Many prominent Republicans hired him. For John Connally, secretary of the Treasury under Nixon, Williams won an acquittal on charges of bribery in connection with the approval of federal price supports for milk production. Williams also represented former CIA Director Richard Helms, accused of lying to a congressional committee.

"Back on the Front Page"

It was Williams' representation of Connally that put the attorney "back on the front page," according to biographer Evan Thomas. When Connally ran afoul of the law in the mid-1970s, it had been nearly 15 years—since Williams had kept Powell out of jail in 1960—that Williams had taken a high-profile case. Williams jumped at the opportunity to defend Connally. His handling of the case, according to Thomas, provided a "how-to guide for the defense of politicians accused of corruption."

According to Thomas's account, Williams celebrated his win in the Connally case by getting drunk at the post-trial victory party, held in the Watergate apartment of Robert Strauss, chairman of the Democratic Party. President Gerald Ford called to congratulate Williams, and so did Richard Nixon. "I wish you were my lawyer," Nixon told Williams, according to Thomas. "It's too bad you represent the *Post.*" The disgraced former president, then living in exile on the West Coast, invited Williams to come visit him in San Clemente. A few weeks later Williams said that if he had been Nixon's lawyer during the Watergate scandal, he would have urged the president to burn the Oval Office tapes on the White House lawn.

Outside the courtroom, one of Williams's greatest passions was sports. He was part owner of both the Washington Redskins football franchise and the Baltimore Orioles baseball club. Williams was overjoyed in 1983 when both teams captured the ultimate prize in their respective sports, the Redskins winning in the Super Bowl and the Orioles taking the World Series.

Williams died at Georgetown University Hospital in Washington on August 13, 1988, after a lengthy battle with colon cancer. Buckley wrote in *National Review:* "He was larger than life, always something of a mystery to his associates. He worked every day, including Sundays, and yet he was simultaneously everywhere, owner of athletic teams, hotels, counselor to the mighty, Democratic official with less than jerky-left positions (an improvement over his book). A year ago I had a call. Would I telephone the president and urge him to name Ed Williams as head of the CIA to succeed Bill Casey? I was able to do so with enthusiasm: but was told that Ed was sick. We had been hearing this for years, except this time, he died. We mourn the death of a big man, all-American."

Books

Contemporary Authors Online, Gale Group, 1999.
Newsmakers, Gale Research, 1988.
Scribner Encyclopedia of American Lives, Volume 2: 1986-1990, Charles Scribner's Sons, 1999.

Periodicals

National Review, September 16, 1988.
Washington Monthly, October 1991. □

William Wyler

Whether directing motion pictures depicting heart-stopping chariot races in *Ben Hur* or heart-rendering depictions of military servicemen attempting to return to post-war normalcy in *The Best Years of Our Lives,* William Wyler (1902-1981) is recognized by critics as among the 20th century's best American film directors and is among several directors credited with raising the level of American film from popular entertainment to art.

Wyler is noted for the consistently high quality of his films, which focused on a wide range of themes, settings, and subject matter. While most Hollywood film directors of his era are associated with a specific genre—film noir, screwball comedies, Westerns, historical dramas, social dramas, or war films—Wyler's body of work features critically acclaimed films in many areas. He is considered to be the first American director to select his own projects, often commissioning scripts several years before attempting to make them and then spending at least two weeks rehearsing actors and camera operators before beginning filming. The resulting films proved to be among the most popular and critically admired films of Hollywood's Golden Era into the 1960s because of their intricately choreographed and tasteful camera work. Wyler captured some of the best performances of the time, including those of actors such as Bette Davis, Gary Cooper, Laurence Olivier, Merle Oberon, John Barrymore, Henry Fonda, Barbra Streisand, Charlton Heston, Humphrey Bogart, Audrey Hepburn, Walter Huston, Kirk Douglas, and Greer Garson. All told, 14 actors received Academy Award nominations in Wyler films, which remains a Hollywood record. Many of these performances resulted from the director's notorious insistence on numerous shots of the same scene until he was satisfied with the actor's presentation. Wyler was nominated for 12 Academy awards for best direction, more than any other director, and actually won three times, a feat bested only by John Ford, who won four times.

Germany, France, and Hollywood

Wyler was born in Mulhouse, Alsace, Germany, on July 1, 1902, to Jewish parents and studied in Germany,

sics of American cinema due to Wyler's deft handling of literary themes in a cinematic context. *Mrs. Miniver,* in particular, is widely admired for its contribution to the morale of the Allied efforts in World War II through its depiction of an English family struggling to survive the travails of war.

During the 1930s and 1940s, film historians note that Wyler expanded his repertoire of camera movements among other directorial techniques to subtly underscore the literary nature of his films while continuing to elicit some of American cinema's best performances. Among the most noted qualities of his films is that he encouraged his actors to convey the realism of their characters, rather than expose themselves as Hollywood stars simply playing a role. Wyler enhanced this approach by determining the best camera angles with which to capture his actors' performances.

Wyler spent part of the World War II years directing documentaries. He traveled to Europe in late 1942 and joined B17 bombing raids in France and German. He put these experiences and the footage he shot into the films *The Memphis Belle* and *The Fighting Lady.*

Enjoyed Numerous Postwar Successes

Wyler's first film after returning from World War II often is considered his best, earning him his second Academy Award. Starring Frederic March, Myrna Loy, Teresa Wright, Dana Andrews, and a non-actor named Harold Russell, *The Best Years of Our Lives* prompted film critic James Agee to write in *Agee on Film:* "Wyler has always seemed to me an exceedingly sincere and good director; he now seems one of the few great ones. He has come back from the war with a style of great purity, directness, and warmth, about as cleanly devoid of mannerism, haste, superfluous motion, aesthetic or emotional over-reaching, as any I know; and I felt complete confidence, as I watched this work, that he could have handled any degree to which this material might have been matured as well as or even better that the job he was given to do." Agee continued to compliment Wyler's direction of Russell, who had actually lost both hands in World War II: "His direction of the nonprofessional, Harold Russell, is just an exciting proof, on the side, of the marvels a really good artist can perform in collaboration with a really good non-actor; much more of the time it was his job to get new and better things out of professionals than they had ever shown before."

Wyler formed Liberty Films with directors Frank Capra and George Stevens after World War II. The studio produced only one film, Capra's classic *It's a Wonderful Life.* In 1949 actor Olivia de Havilland won an Academy Award for her performance in Wyler's *The Heiress,* an adaptation of Henry James's novel *Washington Square* that featured a musical score by composer Aaron Copeland as well as what many critics consider to be among the best performances of actor Montgomery Clift. In 1951, Wyler adapted Sidney Kingsley's Broadway play *Detective Story* to film, starring Kirk Douglas and Eleanor Parker. The following year, he adapted Theodore Dreiser's novel *Sister Carrie* as the Laurence Olivier and Jennifer Jones vehicle *Carrie.*

Switzerland, and France. His early interest in American culture was gratified when he met a distant relative, Carl Laemmle, in Paris. The president of Universal Pictures in the United States, Laemmle invited Wyler to work as a publicist for the company's New York office in 1920. In 1921 Wyler moved to Hollywood, eventually landing work as an assistant director. In 1924 he directed the two-reel Western *Crook Buster,* before directing his first feature-length film, *Lazy Lightning* in 1925.

With the advent of sound, Wyler became one of Universal's top directors of "talkies," beginning with 1929's *Love Trap.* He continued his string of popular films for Universal with 1930's *Hell's Heroes* and the 1933 John Barrymore film, *Counsellor-at-Law.* In 1935, he employed a script from Preston Sturges for *The Good Fairy,* starring his first wife Margaret Sullavan.

Worked with Producer Samuel Goldwyn

In 1936 Wyler signed a contract with producer Samuel Goldwyn. The pair's relationship resulted in a ten-year run of critical and financially successful dramas, including three films scripted by playwright Lillian Hellman: 1936's *These Three,* 1937's *Dead End,* and 1941's *The Little Foxes;* an adaptation of Sinclair Lewis's novel of a disintegrating marriage titled *Dodsworth;* a 1936 collaboration with Howard Hawk's on the adaptation of Edna Ferber's novel *Come and Get It;* 1938's *Jezebel;* 1940's *The Westerner* and *The Letter;* and the 1942 film that won him his first Academy Award, *Mrs. Miniver.* Each of these films is acknowledged as clas-

In 1947 Wyler assisted in the founding of the Committee for the First Amendment in response to Congress's House Un-American Activities Committee investigation of suspected communists in Hollywood. In 1953 he used a script written by blacklisted writer Dalton Trumbo to film *Roman Holiday,* starring Gregory Peck and marking the starr ing debut of Audrey Hepburn, who won an Academy award for best actress. In 1955 Wyler adapted Joseph Hayes's novel and play *The Desperate Hours* for a film noir reuniting him with his *Dead End* star Humphrey Bogart. In 1956, he adapted Jessamyn West's novel about Quakers during the U.S. Civil War, *Friendly Persuasion,* into a film that reunited him with his *The Westerner* star, Gary Cooper. He employed Peck and Charlton Heston for his next film, *The Big Country,* which resulted in an Academy award for best supporting actor for folksinger Burl Ives.

Won Third Academy Award

In 1959 Wyler released his epic *Ben Hur,* which some film sources claim as one of the greatest films of all time. In addition to the film's epic sweep and incredibly detailed sets and action sequences, the film succeeds as a character study of a Palestinian Jew during the time of Jesus Christ and the Roman occupation of the Holy Land. The film netted Wyler his third Academy award and went on to win an unprecedented 11 Academy awards, including best actor for Charlton Heston.

Wyler directed several more films before retiring in 1970. Of these, *The Collector,* an adaptation of the John Fowles novel, and 1968's *Funny Girl,* which earned Barbra Streisand an Academy award for best actress, are considered the best. In 1965 Wyler received the Irving G. Thalberg Award for Career Achievement from the Academy of Motion Picture Arts and Sciences. After his retirement, he was presented with the American Film Institute Life Achievement Award. During his long, fruitful career, Wyler's films received nine best director nominations and 36 best actor or best actress nominations. He died on July 28, 1981, in Beverly Hills, California.

Books

Agee, James, *Agee on Film: Criticism and Comment on the Movies,* Random House, 2000.
Sarris, Andrew, editor, *The St. James Guide to Film Directors,* St. James Press, 1998.

Online

Internet Movie Database, http://us.imdb.com/ (February 28, 2002).
Reel Classics, http://www.reelclassics.com/ (February 28, 2002).
"William Wyler," *American Masters,* http://www.pbs.org/wnet/americanmasters/ (February 28, 2002). □

Y

Loretta Young

Few actors have enjoyed the professional longevity of the stunning Loretta Young (1913-2000) and even fewer in three media—motion pictures, radio theatre, and television. Her remarkable career, begun as a child extra during the Silent Era of motion pictures, extended through the Golden Age of Hollywood. She attained star status on film as well as on the radio, even though she had no theater or dramatic school instruction. Young ended her film career to become a pioneer of the Golden Age of Television. She was the first actor to win both an Academy Award and an Emmy. Except for absences for serious illness and the births of her children, she was continuously before the cameras from age 12 through the early 1960s, making more than 250 film performances and appearing on more than 300 television programs.

Child Standout

Loretta Young was named Gretchen by her parents when she was born on January 6, 1913, in Salt Lake City, Utah. Her parents were Earl Young, a railroad auditor, and Gladys Royal Young. She joined sisters Polly Ann and Betty Jane (who became the actress Sally Blane); a brother Jack came along later. One day in 1916, Earl left for work and did not come back. Gladys packed up her children and moved to Hollywood, where she opened a boarding house to support her family.

Gladys's brother-in-law, Ernest Traxler, lived nearby. An assistant director for Famous Players-Lasky, he persuaded Gladys to let her older girls become movie extras. When Gretchen turned four, she too started earning money as an extra. Her first role was as a fairy in *The Primrose Ring.* Mae Murray, the picture's star, liked the little girl and asked Gladys if she could come live with her. Gladys consented when "Maetsie" agreed to take Gretchen's cousin Carleen Traxler, too, and allow them to return home whenever they wanted. The two girls lived with Maetsie and her husband for over a year. Jack also went to live with another family; he never returned permanently. When Young was 10, her mother married George Belzer. The union produced daughter, Georgiana, in 1925. The couple would later remain friends after their divorce.

Young's mother was a devout Catholic who saw to her daughters' educations by sending them to parochial schools, including the Ramona Convent boarding school and Catholic Girls' High School, and by inviting priests for dinner. Young developed a strong faith and moral convictions from which she never wavered, although it might be said she strayed. As a student, Young would get days off from school whenever the studio needed her as an extra. Often her classroom was a corner of the studio stage and her teacher a tutor. With determination and help from others, she managed her academic problems in reading and spelling. She would eventually discover her learning disability was dyslexia.

On movie sets, Young gained attention by doing things a little differently. If the children were supposed to sit, she stood. If they were supposed to move left, she moved right.

This attention garnered her juvenile bit parts when she was 11, a studio contract when she was 12, and starring adult roles when she was 14. Young got her first adult part after asking a telephone caller if she could substitute for her sister Polly, who was unavailable, at a casting call. Colleen Moore, the star of *Naughty But Nice,* in which Young appeared, noticed her uniqueness and talked the studio into giving her a screen test. The studio officials did not like the name Gretchen, though. Moore had a favorite doll named Lauritia and suggested that as a name. Thinking the name too European, it was decided Loretta was a better choice. Young read about her new name in the newspapers. The studio also saw another problem with the girl—her protruding front teeth. Fortunately, Mrs. Young found out about their plan to remove the teeth and replace them with ones going inward. Young would eventually have her bite corrected with braces and retainers.

Movie Star

Naughty But Nice led to a contract and the stardom Young had wanted nearly all her life. In the prologue to *The Things I Had to Learn,* Helen Ferguson wrote: "By the time [Loretta] was six, she had decided to be a star. In her lexicon, decision and determination have always been synonymous and at fourteen, as the tightrope walker in *Laugh, Clown, Laugh,* starring Lon Chaney, her sixty-five inches of reedy gracefulness encased in padding and symmetrical created by the wardrobe department, to provide the curves which nature had not yet provided—she did become a star." Joel Morella and Edward Z. Epstein related in *Loretta*

Young: An Extraordinary Life that: "the problem of her thinness . . . had been solved by the wardrobe department. 'I had the most divine figure that ever walked in front of a camera, courtesy of the studio,' recalled the adult Miss Young. 'It was all pads-false hips, false front, false behind.'" But the role identified her with star quality. By 1929 she was making a half dozen pictures a year and bringing in $250 per week, when the average family made $50 a month.

Despite her screen presence, some at First National studio did not want to try Young in the "talkies" because they thought her voice was too low. They acquiesced when studio president Al Rockett said he would sign her personally if the studio did not. Young appeared in First National's first sound motion picture, *The Squall.* Because there were no soundstages then, it was filmed at night when there was not as much noise around. Unlike many silent movie stars, she did have a voice suitable for a soundtrack. In fact, the American Institute of Voice Teachers recognized hers as the "finest female speaking voice on the 'talking pictures' screen" three years running. Apparently the smoking habit that she started at age 9 and continued for more than 50 years did not make her voice harsh.

For 13 years, Young worked under yearly option deals. After that a studio offered her a five-year, $2 million contract. To the dismay of everyone she knew, she turned the deal down. Young remarked in *The Things I Had to Learn:* "Well, I didn't work at all for nine months! But, after that there were studios where I could get the parts I wanted on a free-lance basis and, eventually at the salary Myron [Selznick, her agent] was brave enough to demand." In 1947 she was sent a script that would showcase her acting abilities. Thinking she could not do a convincing Swedish accent, she at first declined playing "Katie" in *The Farmer's Daughter.* Once she accepted the part, she worked with Ruth Roberts, who had coached the Swedish accent out of Ingrid Bergman, to cultivate one. Young's performance was awarded the Academy Award for Best Actress in a Leading Role. The film was the seventy-fourth of her adult career.

Young was nominated for a second Oscar for her role as a nun in *Come to the Stable.* It was while working on this movie that she placed her first "swear box," which would become a fixture on subsequent projects. Profanity on movie sets was always common, but Young thought blasphemy on the set of *Come to the Stable* was intolerable. She established a fine of 25 cents for anyone using blasphemous language. Young made nearly 100 motion pictures before retiring from the big screen in 1953. Her last picture was *It Happens Every Thursday* with John Forsythe.

Romantic Involvements

Like many actresses, Young fell in love with the leading men she played against. In 1929 she was opposite Grant Withers in *Second Floor Mystery.* The rising 25-year-old matinee idol was considered a catch, even though he was a drinker who had already been married and divorced. Two weeks past her seventeenth birthday, Young eloped with Withers aboard a charter airplane to Yuma, Arizona. Her mother, with whom she was close, disapproved of the marriage and stopped speaking to her. Nine months later, ironically while working together on the movie *Too Young to Marry,* Young was granted a civil divorce.

Having successfully gone from an ingénue to a leading lady, Young started receiving "star treatment" in 1931 that would continue for decades. She appeared as the subject of a story or cover photo nearly every month that year, although she gave few personal interviews. It is estimated she posed for more than 125,000 photographs during her career, but never in the gauzy drapes that made the model look undressed. Joan Wester Anderson pointed out in *Forever Young* that "the gossip columnists were usually benevolent where Loretta was concerned. She was easy to like because she genuinely enjoyed people, and she had a fragile, vulnerable quality that inspired protectiveness in others." Not that Young did not provide plenty to gossip about. She dated Howard Hughes until tiring of his jealousy. After working with Spencer Tracy on *Man's Castle,* Tracy became her escort. He was 13 years older than she, married, and had two children. Months passed before Young realized she was "the other woman" and that Tracy would not divorce because of his Catholicism. She broke off their relationship.

Young's next paramour leading man was Clark Gable. He, too, was married. On location at Mount Baker in Bellingham, Washington, a romance blossomed between the two while waiting for the weather to clear so shooting could be done on their movie, *Call of the Wild.* In the spring of 1935, Young and her mother visited Europe, then quietly slipped back home. Once the media found out she was home, her family explained she was in bed with an "internal condition." Her "condition" was daughter Judy, who was born on November 6. Fearing retribution from the studio because of the morality clause in her contract, as well as a major scandal (unwed motherhood was a disgrace at the time), Young cared for Judy for a few months then secreted her at an orphanage with which she was involved. The following year, Young announced she was adopting two girls, Judy and Jane, but supposedly before she could adopt Jane, the girl's mother wanted her back. It was not until Judy wrote a book that her parentage was revealed. Not long after adopting Judy, Young became engaged to businessman William Buckner. The engagement was broken after he was found guilty of fraud.

Radio Theatre

Radio theatre was favorite family entertainment before television sets became affordable. Every week the Lux Theatre of the Air, under Cecil B. DeMille's direction, in front of a live audience and with a full orchestra, presented condensed versions of old and current movies to an estimated 50 million listeners. Young made a record number of star performances on the program. She also made appearances on other radio broadcasts, including the Hallmark Hall of Fame, and was a regular on the Family Theatre of the Air, a radio program focusing on moral problems begun by Father Peyton in 1947.

Young was dating Jimmy Stewart when she met her second husband. The head of the radio department of the Young & Rubicam advertising agency, Thomas H. A. Lewis

had recently put together the Screen Guild Theatre radio show. The show's performers donated their salaries to the Motion Picture Relief Fund to build a hospital and retirement home. He asked Young to accept a part. Lewis initiated their first "date" when he took Young to Sunday mass so she would make the rehearsal he had called. They married July 31, 1940, and honeymooned in Mexico. On their second honeymoon, they toured the USS Arizona in Hawaii two months before it was bombed. During the war, Lewis enlisted and developed shows and arranged troop entertainment. Young visited hospitals and induction centers and talked to servicemen. She also appeared on many patriotic radio programs. The couple had two sons, Christopher Paul, born in 1944, and Peter Charles, born in 1945. The studio, not wanting to delay production again so soon, fired Young when she became pregnant the second time and refused to have an abortion. She did only two movies a year after her marriage. The couple divorced in 1969, long after Lewis had convinced Young to sign papers giving him half of her assets, even those she had earned before their marriage.

Trademark Entrance

The early 1950s saw many radio and motion picture actors moving to television; Young wanted to be one of them. In 1953 she retired from motion pictures and developed a television pilot that Proctor & Gamble snatched up. "It was a new medium, and we all felt like pioneers," Anderson quoted Young. Titled *Letters to Loretta,* Young's weekly show began with her reading a fan letter at her dressing table, which posed a question answered by a presentation. Though ratings were adequate, they were not great, "and some critics were not kind, labeling 'Letters' 'treacle' and 'a disappointment,'" said Anderson. Thirteen weeks into the program, the show was renamed *The Loretta Young Show* and the format changed. The show now started with Young making her trademark entrance—twirling into her television studio living room in a lovely gown to introduce the evening's story. As she stated in *The Things I Had to Learn:* "My entrance on *The Loretta Young Show* meant much more to me than any actress's entrance I'd ever made. Every time I opened that door I was a hostess greeting very welcome guests." Young acted in 165 teleplays for *The Loretta Young Show,* playing the lead in many, and hosted 300 programs. In 1955 she became the first actor to receive both an Oscar and an Emmy when she was awarded an Emmy for best actress, an award she would win twice more. The show itself became television's most awarded anthology program. Also in 1955, friends filled in 18 weeks for Young while she recovered from a life-threatening infection. None used "her living room door;" all ended the show with "Goodnight, Loretta."

Morella and Epstein noted that "Loretta's shows had moral themes, but never overtly religious ones." Yet Proctor & Gamble cancelled their contract in 1958, saying the content was "too religious." The same year she was named television's most important female personality. Two other sponsors soon picked up the program, which ran another two years. Young never allowed the show's focus changed to compete with melodramas. *The New Loretta Young*

Show cast Young in the recurring role of a widowed mother of seven children and lasted just one season.

In 1959 NBC bought 176 installments of *The Loretta Young Show.* Always fashion conscious, Young stipulated in the contract that her trademark entrance would be cut out from the reruns shown in the United States and in foreign markets. On a visit home to England, Young's housekeeper was excited to see her employer on TV twirling into the room. Young was concerned that being seen in outdated fashions, hairstyles, and makeup would ruin her reputation. In 1972, after five years of litigation, she was awarded $559,000 from NBC. In 1970 Young had successfully defended her reputation by suing to have clips that used her face and dialogue as double entendre removed from the motion picture *Myra Breckinridge.*

Retirement

After retiring from acting, Young, who had always devoted much time to Catholic charities, continued to support favorite causes, including a home for unwed mothers and a children's foundation. She also engaged in business ventures, including bridal salons, fashion and self-improvement courses, and a line of cosmetics. In 1961 she published her philosophy of life in a book titled *The Things I Had to Learn.* During 1966 she answered teens' questions in a column she wrote for the Catholic News Service. Filmex (the Los Angeles International Film Exposition) honored Young as the subject of a film retrospective in 1981. In 1983 she was elected to the Fashion Hall of Fame. That award added to the numerous others she had been given by the Boy Scouts, Girl Scouts, teachers' associations, milliners, magazines, broadcasters, and other organizations.

Young eventually returned to television for selected projects. She acted in the pilot *Dark Mansions* in 1985, which never sold. Her performance in 1987's *Christmas Eve* garnered her a Golden Globe award for best actress in a television movie. At 76, she performed her last role with Brian Keith in the made-for-TV movie *Lady in a Corner.*

In 1993 Young married Jean Louis. An award-winning fashion designer, Louis had designed many of her dresses and was the widower of her good friend. He died in 1997. Young retained her beauty throughout her life. Referring to a photo of Young in the 1998 Hollywood issue of *Vanity Fair* magazine, Liz Smith wrote: "At 85, described simply as 'The Face,' she was the most beautiful woman in the entire magazine!" Young died of ovarian cancer in 2000. As Smith noted, Young was "the last mega-star leading lady who presided over the end of the Silent Era and the Golden Age of Hollywood as well as the Golden Age of Television."

Books

Anderson, Joan Wester, *Forever Young: The Life, Loves and Enduring Faith of a Hollywood Legend,* Thomas Moore Publishing, 2000.

Morella, Joe, and Edward Z. Epstein, *Loretta Young: An Extraordinary Life,* Delacorte Press, 1986.

Young, Loretta, as told to Helen Ferguson, *The Things I Had to Learn,* Bobbs-Merrill, 1961.

Online

"Biography for Loretta Young," http://us.imdb.com/Bio?Loretta + Young (October 16, 2001).

Liz Smith Columns, http://www.geocities.com/Hollywood/set/1478/lizsmith.html (November 15, 2001).

"Loretta Young, Epitome of Hollywood Glamour, Dies of Ovarian Cancer at 87," http://www.cnn.com/2000/SHOWBIZ/News/08/12/loretta.young.obit/ (October 16, 2001).

"Loretta Young Show," http://www.geocities.com/Hollywood/set/1478/introduction.html (October 16, 2001). □

Z

Muhammad Zahir Shah

Muhammad Zahir Shah (born 1914), last in the 226-year dynasty of Pashtun monarchs to rule Afghanistan, emerged in the fall of 2001 as a symbol of unity for his country as its hard-line Taliban rulers were dislodged from power. In December 2001 Zahir Shah gave his blessing to Hamid Karzai, a fellow Pashtun selected as an interim leader for the troubled country.

The son of King Nadir Shah of Afghanistan, Muhammad Zahir Shah was born on October 15, 1914, in the capital city of Kabul. Educated in both his native country and France, he was thrust suddenly into power at the age of 19, only hours after his father was assassinated. On November 8, 1933, he replaced his father on the throne of the Durani dynasty, first established in 1747 by Ahmad Shah. The young monarch adopted the title *Mutawakkil Ala'llah, Pairaw-I Din-I Matin-I slam* ("Confident in God, Follower of the Firm Religion of Islam"). For nearly three-quarters of his years on the throne, however, he was the country's ruler in little more than name, as two of his uncles—Muhammad Hashim and Shah Mahmud Ghazi—effectively ran the government. The elder of the two, Muhammad Hashim, had been prime minister under King Nadir Shah, and he remained in that post until 1946, when he was succeeded by his younger brother, Shah Mahmud.

In the years immediately following the assassination of Nadir Shah, Hashim, who was described by insiders as a statesman of high personal integrity and impressive administrative ability, focused on two main objectives: building up the nation's army and developing Afghanistan's economy. To accomplish these goals, Hashim needed to attract foreign aid, but he desperately wanted to avoid any political entanglements with either Great Britain or the Soviet Union. Instead he turned to Germany, which had both an interest in the Afghan project and the technical expertise needed to get the job done. Limited amounts of foreign aid were also accepted from Italy and Japan. As a result of Hashim's powers of persuasion, Germany by the beginning of the 1940s had become Afghanistan's principal foreign partner.

As the winds ushering in World War II began to blow across Afghanistan, King Zahir Shah on August 17, 1940, issued a declaration of his country's neutrality in the conflict. This proved easier said than done, however. The presence in Afghanistan of large numbers of nondiplomatic German personnel was more than Britain and the Soviet Union could tolerate. The Allies demanded that the Afghan government eject all nondiplomatic personnel from the Axis countries. Although it bristled at the Allies' demand, in the end Afghanistan complied, having already seen British and Soviet forces invade neighboring Iran when that country ignored a similar demand. Although Afghanistan did cave on the issue of expelling nondiplomatic Axis personnel, a *loya jirga,* or grand assembly called by the king, upheld Zahir Shah's policy of neutrality.

Not long after the end of World War II, Hashim was replaced as prime minister by his younger brother, Shah Mahmud, who ushered in a period of upheaval in Afghanistan's internal and external politics. Shah Mahmud presided over the initial phase of the Helmand Valley Project, a joint venture between the Afghan government and an American company. The project was launched to harness the irrigation and hydroelectric potential of the Helmand River. More significantly, Shah Mahmud was in office during the resolu-

Allowed Tacit Consent for Political Parties

The 1964 constitution also provided for the formation of political parties, but the king never ratified that provision. Although not legally permitted, political parties were formed; their members kept in touch with one another through party-affiliated newspapers and periodicals. All members of the Afghan parliament were officially elected as independents, yet they all brought with them to the legislature the sharply differing philosophies of the political parties with which they were unofficially affiliated. The result was a parliament that was virtually paralyzed by political infighting.

Using foreign assistance flowing in from a number of the world's industrial countries, particularly the United States and the Soviet Union, Zahir Shah spearheaded a series of projects to help develop Afghanistan's infrastructure. However, most of the projects, which focused on irrigation and highway construction, were limited to the area in and around Kabul. Exacerbating the country's problems, particularly outside Kabul, was the drought of the early 1970s, which in time led to widespread famine and growing unrest in the countryside, particularly among some of the tribal factions along the Afghan border with Pakistan. On the plus side, one of the major accomplishments of the king's reign was his success in maintaining the country's neutrality in the increasingly divisive world of international politics.

In July of 1973 Zahir Shah traveled to England for surgery on an eye he had injured in a volleyball game. Once the surgery was complete, he continued on to Italy. As he and his family relaxed on the island of Ischia, not far from Naples, Muhammad Daoud, ousted as prime minister in 1963, staged a bloodless coup, and Afghanistan was declared a republic under Daoud's presidency. Daoud warned Zahir Shah not to attempt to return to Kabul, a warning the king apparently took seriously for he remained outside Afghanistan through the 2002 war against terrorism waged by the United States and formally abdicated on August 24, 1973. Daoud's days as the country's leader were numbered; he died in a 1978 coup that brought to power a communist government. The following year the Soviet Union, which bordered Afghanistan to the north, invaded the country and installed yet another communist government, sparking a ten-year war between Soviet forces and the *mujaheddin,* a rag-tag army of anti-Communist guerilla fighters. The United States supplied extensive military assistance to the mujaheddin to enable them to continue their struggle against the Soviets. Unfortunately the Soviet withdrawal from Afghanistan in 1989 brought no lasting peace, for the country was soon torn apart by factional fighting. In the latter half of the 1990s the fundamentalist Taliban secured control of most of the country and imposed an oppressive rule. The Taliban's sponsorship of terrorist training camps run by terrorist leader Osama bin Laden eventually brought them into conflict with the United States, which ironically had been closely allied with many in the Taliban during their struggle with the Soviets.

tion of international border issues between Afghanistan and the newly formed country of Pakistan.

In 1953 Zahir Shah's cousin, Muhammad Daoud, succeeded Shah Mahmud as prime minister. The younger members of the royal family, Daoud among them, had successfully agitated against the dominance of the king's uncles, eventually winning access to the seat of power for Daoud. Although he was western educated and was expected by many observers to push for a more open political system, Daoud proved to possess a more authoritarian bent than most anticipated. Although Daoud did little to open up Afghanistan politically, he did take steps to modernize the country, including providing continued support for the Helmand Valley Project, designed to transform life in the southwestern corner of Afghanistan. He also moved to emancipate Afghan women, allowing the wives of his ministers to appear unveiled in public for the 40th anniversary celebration of national independence, and managed to exert a degree of control over the region's tribes. However, Daoud's foreign policy resulted in an unhealthy dependence on the Soviet Union as Afghanistan's principal trade and transit link with the outside world, and he was forced from office in 1963 by the king. Zahir Shah eventually wrested total control of the government from his relatives under the constitution of 1964, which established a constitutional monarchy and barred royal relatives from all high-level government offices. The new constitution also established a two-house parliament, free elections, and freedom of the press and gave women the right to vote.

During the years of turbulence in his homeland, Zahir Shah lived quietly in a villa outside Rome. Every time another government fell in Kabul, the aging king was inevitably mentioned as a possible interim ruler until a permanent new government could be established. It all came to naught, however, for events within Afghanistan always seemed to overtake the best intentions of Afghan exiles and others who hoped to see a return to stability in that country. Zahir Shah remained a potent symbol for those desiring the restoration of the monarchy, however, and in 1991 was stabbed three times by an unknown assailant in a suspected political assassination attempt. Although he remained outside Afghanistan, Zahir Shah remained connected to developments in his country. In 1993 he called upon the United Nations to allow the convocation of a *loya jirga* to select a new president to replace Professor Burnahuddin Rabbani, whose 1992 election the former king alleged was tainted by corruption and should be declared invalid.

In the wake of the September 11, 2001, attack on the United States and the beginning of the U.S. war on international terrorism, Zahir Shah called for another *loya jirga* to select an alternative to the government of the Taliban, accused of sheltering the Al Qaeda terrorist network of Osama bin Laden. In November 2001, after the liberation of Kabul, Zahir Shah called on the United States to end its bombing campaign in Afghanistan. He also urged all factions in Afghanistan "to safeguard life, property, and also be vigilant in preventing foreign designs from inflicting more harm on our people." The king threw his support behind Hamid Karzai, who was to lead Afghanistan until a grand national assembly could be convened in 2002 to select a transitional government to rule the country in the 18 months leading up to new national elections.

In January of 2002, Zahir Shah called up the government of Karzai, who like the king is an ethnic Pashtun, to guarantee women's rights. He noted that under the country's 1964 Constitution women enjoyed full rights, most of which had been revoked under the harsh rule of the Taliban. In an interview with the London-based *Asharq al-Awsat* newspaper, Zahir Shah said: "I firmly believe that every effort must be exerted to guarantee (women's) rights. Their active participation is a vital part of rebuilding our country." According to Reuters, the former monarch also said the new Afghan government needed "to find job opportunities to enable men and women to access resources. A whole generation has been deprived of their basic rights in education and health care."

Zahir Shah fathered seven children in all, five of whom survive. Although he was fourth in the line of succession, Prince Mir Wais was groomed as his father's heir. Like his father, Mir Wais lived near Rome, and served as his father's closest adviser. Whatever role Zahir Shah and his family might play in the political future of their troubled homeland, the former king remained intensely concerned with Afghanistan's future and was prepared to work to ensure his country's future political stability.

Periodicals

Associated Press, October 8, 2001; November 14, 2001; January 28, 2002.
Time International, November 18, 1991.

Online

"Hamid Karzai No Stranger to Leadership," *CNN.com,* http://cnn.worldnews.com/ (February 3, 2002).
"Mohammed Zahir Shah," *Biography Resource Center Online,* http://galenet.galegroup.com/ (January 20, 2002).
"Mohammad Zahir Shah: King of Afghanistan from 1933-1973," *Afghan-Info.com,* http://www.afghan-info.com/ (February 3, 2002). □

Pinchas Zukerman

One of the premier musicians to emerge in the second half of the twentieth century, Pinchas Zukerman (born 1948) was not only a brilliant instrumentalist on the violin and viola but a chamber musician and conductor as well. In 1998, nearly thirty years after its founding, Zukerman was named music director of Canada's National Arts Centre Orchestra.

Early Teachers

Zukerman was born on July 16, 1948, in Tel Aviv, Israel, son of Yehuda (Juhda), a professional violinist, and Miriam (Lieberman-Skotchilas) Zukerman. His parents survived the Nazi concentration camps and moved from Poland to Israel in 1947. It was a musical family, and when Pinchas was only five, he began to study music with his father. He first learned to play the recorder and clarinet and later the violin, his father's instrument. At age eight, Zukerman began studies at the Academy of Music in Tel Aviv with Ilona Feher, a noted violinist who had immigrated to Israel from Hungary.

While visiting Israel in 1961, Spanish-born cellist Pablo Casals and Russian-born violin virtuoso Isaac Stern heard Zukerman play. So impressed was Stern that he helped to guide the teenager's musical education. In 1962, with the support of Stern and the Helen Rubenstein and America-Israel Cultural foundations, Zukerman came to New York to study at the Juilliard School with Ivan Galanian. Galanian, born in Iran in 1903 and educated in Russia and France, was one of the best-known violin teachers of the 20th century. With Galanian, Zukerman first studied violin and later the viola. While studying at Juilliard, Zukerman lived with the parents of pianist Eugene Isotomin and rounded out his education by attending both the Professional Children's School and the High School for Performing Arts.

Zukerman's studies with Galanian did not always go smoothly. The prodigy bristled under Galanian's tutelage, resisting his teacher's insistence that he maintain a rigorous practice schedule and concentrate on the basics. He later

admitted to an interviewer that he often skipped school and roamed the New York streets. Disappointed by Zukerman's attitude, Stern, his mentor, told him to take his studies more seriously or risk being sent back to Israel. The young musician buckled down.

Performed and Conducted

In 1967 Zukerman shared with Kyung Wha Chung of Korea first prize in the 25th annual Leventritt International Competition. On the strength of his Leventritt win and the added exposure he received when he replaced Stern, who had fallen ill, in a series of concerts, Zukerman's solo career was launched. In an interview with David Hawley of the *St. Paul Pioneer Press,* he later said of his student days: "I knew I had something in me, something on the violin I had to say. And I knew that eventually I was going to say it. With the guidance of these people [Stern and Galanian] it luckily worked out." In 1968 Zukerman married Eugenia Rich. The couple had two daughters, Natalia and Arianna, but later divorced.

Although his studies at Juilliard focused on instrumental instruction, Zukerman was exposed to the fundamentals of conducting as well. He first became seriously interested in conducting in the late 1960s when he played with the English Chamber Orchestra, which was conducted by Daniel Barenboim, a fellow Israeli. As the lead violinist, or concertmaster, of the orchestra, Zukerman was given an opportunity to conduct selected works by Bach and Vivaldi, from the first violinist's chair, a tradition that developed

before the emergence of the modern-day conductor. In 1974 he made his official conducting debut with the English Chamber Orchestra. In the years that followed he served as a guest conductor with some of the premier symphony orchestras of the United States, including the New York Philharmonic, the National Symphony, Boston Symphony, and Los Angeles Philharmonic.

In 1980 Zukerman took over as musical director of the St. Paul Chamber Orchestra, a position he held for seven seasons. During his stay in St. Paul, he was credited with increasing the number of musicians, tripling attendance at local concerts, and leading the drive for the construction of the Ordway Theatre, the permanent home of the orchestra. Under his direction, the orchestra made eight albums on major labels and toured extensively throughout the United States and South America. Although his focus at St. Paul was on conducting, he did not abandon his solo career, performing occasionally and conducting from the concertmaster's chair. While in St. Paul, Zukerman married actress Tuesday Weld in 1985. They later divorced. His decision to leave St. Paul in 1987 was motivated largely by his growing dislike for the administrative side of his responsibilities as music director.

Back to Solo Career

Although Zukerman again focused on his solo career after leaving St. Paul, he continued to direct frequently. For several years, he limited his conducting career to seasonal events. He served as music director of the Baltimore Symphony Orchestra Summer MusicFest, conductor of London's South Bank Festival, and conductor of the Dallas Symphony's International Summer Music Festival, each for three years. He also was named principal guest conductor of the Dallas Symphony for two years.

Throughout the late 1980s and into the 1990s, Zukerman appeared as a solo performer with some of the world's finest orchestras. He also collaborated frequently with some of the music world's best-known musicians, sharing the stage with such notables as Stern, violinist Itzhak Perlman, cellist Ralph Kirshbaum, pianist Yefim Bronfman, pianist Marc Neikrug, cellist Jacqueline Du Pre, flautist Jean-Pierre Rampal, and the Guarneri and Cleveland string quartets.

Zukerman recorded extensively, and his discography grew to more than 100 titles by 2002. He won two Grammy Awards for his recordings—Best Chamber Music Performance in 1980 and Best Classical Performance by an Instrumental Soloist without Orchestra in 1981. Through 2001, he had been nominated for a total of 21 Grammy Awards. Zukerman joined cellist Ralph Kirshbaum and pianist John Browning to record the Brahms Double and Beethoven Triple Concertos with Christoph Eschenbach conducting the London Symphony Orchestra, released in 1998 on BMG Classics/RCA Victor Red Seal. Other recordings for BMG included the complete violin/piano and viola/piano repertoire of Beethoven, Brahms, Mozart, and Schumann, performed with pianist Marc Neikrug. Decca released a recording of Schubert's Piano Trios performed by pianist Vladimir Ashkenazy, cellist Lynn Harrell, and Zukerman.

Zukerman's earlier recordings were on the Angel, CBS, Deutsche Grammophon, London, and Phillips labels.

In the late 1990s, Zukerman returned to conducting. In April 1998, he was named music director of the National Arts Centre Orchestra of Canada. Based in the Canadian capital of Ottawa, the orchestra was founded in 1969 as the resident orchestra of the newly completed National Arts Centre. His association with the orchestra stretched back to 1976, when he first appeared with the group as a soloist. In 1990 he led the orchestra on a successful tour of Europe.

Young Artists Program

As the beneficiary of the mentoring of Stern, Casals, and other great musicians, Zukerman devoted a good deal of time and energy to sharing his expertise with promising young musicians. A year after taking over as music director of the National Arts Centre Orchestra, he founded the orchestra's Young Artists Program, a summer training program for talented young classical musicians. The program began in the summer of 1999 with only 12 violin and viola students and expanded to 33 within two years. In June 2001, he launched an annual two-week training course for young would-be conductors, and he hoped eventually to begin a program for promising young opera singers. When it was first launched, the Young Artists Program was open only to musicians from Canada, but Zukerman opened it to promising young performers from around the world. "The first couple of years, it was confined to the village," he told *Maclean's* in 2001. "Now, it's Canadians-plus. People have finally come to the realization that we are a global institution."

In July 2001, *Maclean's* profiled Zukerman's work with 13-year-old Canadian violin prodigy Caitlin Tully, the youngest student in his 2001 Young Artists Program. Zukerman first heard Tully at a master class he was giving in Vancouver, her hometown. The following year Tully came to Ottawa for her first summer in the Young Artists Program. "Just being there with that sound, just hearing him play, opens up new ideas," she told the Canadian magazine.

Although his position in Ottawa kept him extremely busy, Zukerman also found time to serve as music director of the Ilona Feher Music Center in Holon, Israel, which he founded, and as chairman of the Pinchas Zukerman Performance Program at the Manhattan School of Music in New York City. He was also artist in residence of the Milwaukee Symphony Orchestra.

Books

Complete Marquis Who's Who, Marquis Who's Who, 2001.
Contemporary Musicians, Gale Research, 1990.

Periodicals

Maclean's, July 30, 2001.

Online

"About Pinchas Zukerman," *Pittsburgh Symphony,* http://www.pittsburghsymphony.org/ (January 28, 2002).
"Pinchas Zukerman: Biography," *Kirschbaum Demler & Associates Inc.,* http://www.skassoc.com/BioZukerman.htm (January 22, 2002). □

HOW TO USE THE *SUPPLEMENT* INDEX

The *Encyclopedia of World Biography Supplement* Index is designed to serve several purposes. First, it is a cumulative listing of biographies included in the entire second edition of *EWB* and its supplements (volumes 1-22). Second, it locates information on specific topics mentioned in volume 22 of the encyclopedia—persons, places, events, organizations, institutions, ideas, titles of works, inventions, as well as artistic schools, styles, and movements. Third, it classifies the subjects of *Supplement* articles according to shared characteristics. Vocational categories are the most numerous—for example, artists, authors, military leaders, philosophers, scientists, statesmen. Other groupings bring together disparate people who share a common characteristic.

The structure of the *Supplement* Index is quite simple. The biographical entries are cumulative and often provide enough information to meet immediate reference needs. Thus, people mentioned in the *Supplement* Index are identified and their life dates, when known, are given. Because this is an index to a *biographical* encyclopedia, every reference includes the *name* of the article to which the reader is directed as well as the volume and page numbers. Below are a few points that will make the *Supplement* Index easy to use.

Typography. All main entries are set in boldface type. Entries that are also the titles of articles in *EWB* are set entirely in capitals; other main entries are set in initial capitals and lowercase letters. Where a main entry is followed by a great many references, these are organized by subentries in alphabetical sequence. In certain cases—for example, the names of countries for which there are many references—a special class of subentries, set in small capitals and preceded by boldface dots, is used to mark significant divisions.

Alphabetization. The Index is alphabetized word by word. For example, all entries beginning with *New* as a separate word (*New Jersey, New York*) come before *Newark*. Commas in inverted entries are treated as full

stops (*Berlin; Berlin, Congress of; Berlin, University of; Berlin Academy of Sciences*). Other commas are ignored in filing. When words are identical, persons come first and subsequent entries are alphabetized by their parenthetical qualifiers (such as *book, city, painting*).

Titled persons may be alphabetized by family name or by title. The more familiar form is used—for example, *Disraeli, Benjamin* rather than *Beaconsfield, Earl of.* Cross-references are provided from alternative forms and spellings of names. Identical names of the same nationality are filed chronologically.

Titles of books, plays, poems, paintings, and other works of art beginning with an article are filed on the following word (*Bard, The*). Titles beginning with a preposition are filed on the preposition (*In Autumn*). In subentries, however, prepositions are ignored; thus *influenced by* would precede the subentry *in* literature.

Literary characters are filed on the last name. Acronyms, such as UNESCO, are treated as single words. Abbreviations, such as *Mr., Mrs.,* and *St.,* are alphabetized as though they were spelled out.

Occupational categories are alphabetical by national qualifier. Thus, *Authors, Scottish* comes before *Authors, Spanish,* and the reader interested in Spanish poets will find the subentry *poets* under *Authors, Spanish.*

Cross-references. The term *see* is used in references throughout the *Supplement* Index. The *see* references appear both as main entries and as subentries They most often direct the reader from an alternative name spelling or form to the main entry listing.

This introduction to the *Supplement* Index is necessarily brief. The reader will soon find, however, that the *Supplement* Index provides ready reference to both highly specific subjects and broad areas of information contained in volume 22 and a cumulative listing of those included in the entire set.

INDEX

A

AALTO, HUGO ALVAR HENRIK (born 1898), Finnish architect, designer, and town planner **1** 1-2

AARON, HENRY LOUIS (Hank; born 1934), American baseball player **1** 2-3

ABBA ARIKA (circa 175-circa 247), Babylonian rabbi **1** 3-4

ABBADO, CLAUDIO (born 1933), Italian conductor **22** 1-3

ABBAS I (1571-1629), Safavid shah of Persia 1588-1629 **1** 4-6

ABBAS, FERHAT (born 1899), Algerian statesman **1** 6-7

ABBOTT, BERENICE (1898-1991), American artist and photographer **1** 7-9

ABBOTT, GRACE (1878-1939), American social worker and agency administrator **1** 9-10

ABBOTT, LYMAN (1835-1922), American Congregationalist clergyman, author, and editor **1** 10-11

ABBOUD, EL FERIK IBRAHIM (1900-1983), Sudanese general, prime minister, 1958-1964 **1** 11-12

Abby (literary character)
Welk, Lawrence **22** 420-422

ABD AL-MALIK (646-705), Umayyad caliph 685-705 **1** 12-13

ABD AL-MUMIN (circa 1094-1163), Almohad caliph 1133-63 **1** 13

ABD AL-RAHMAN I (731-788), Umayyad emir in Spain 756-88 **1** 13-14

ABD AL-RAHMAN III (891-961), Umayyad caliph of Spain **1** 14

ABD EL-KADIR (1807-1883), Algerian political and religious leader **1** 15

ABD EL-KRIM EL-KHATABI, MOHAMED BEN (circa 1882-1963), Moroccan Berber leader **1** 15-16

ABDUH IBN HASAN KHAYR ALLAH, MUHAMMAD (1849-1905), Egyptian nationalist and theologian **1** 16-17

ABDUL RAHMAN, TUNKU (1903-1990), Former prime minister of Malaysia **18** 340-341

ABDUL-BAHA (Abbas Effendi; 1844-1921), Persian leader of the Baha'i Muslim sect **22** 3-5

ABDUL-HAMID II (1842-1918), Ottoman sultan 1876-1909 **1** 17-18

ABDULLAH II (Abdullah bin al Hussein II; born 1962), king of Jordan **22** 5-7

'ABDULLAH AL-SALIM AL-SABAH, SHAYKH (1895-1965), Amir of Kuwait (1950-1965) **1** 18-19

ABDULLAH IBN HUSEIN (1882-1951), king of Jordan 1949-1951, of Transjordan 1946-49 **1** 19-20
Abdullah II **22** 5-7

ABDULLAH IBN YASIN (died 1059), North African founder of the Almoravid movement **1** 20

ABDULLAH, MOHAMMAD (Lion of Kashmir; 1905-1982), Indian political leader who worked for an independent Kashmir **22** 7-9

ABE, KOBO (born Kimifusa Abe; also transliterated as Abe Kobo; 1924-1993), Japanese writer, theater director, photographer **1** 20-22

ABEL, IORWITH WILBER (1908-1987), United States labor organizer **1** 22-23

ABEL, NIELS (1802-1829), Norwegian mathematician **20** 1-2

ABELARD, PETER (1079-1142), French philosopher and theologian **1** 23-25

ABERCROMBY, RALPH (1734-1801), British military leader **20** 2-4

ABERDEEN, 4TH EARL OF (George Hamilton Gordon; 1784-1860), British statesman, prime minister 1852-55 **1** 25-26

ABERHART, WILLIAM (1878-1943), Canadian statesman and educator **1** 26-27

ABERNATHY, RALPH DAVID (born 1926), United States minister and civil rights leader **1** 27-28

ABIOLA, MOSHOOD (1937-1998), Nigerian politician, philanthropist, and businessman **19** 1-3

Abolitionists, American
African Americans
Craft, Ellen **22** 125-127
moral suasion
Einhorn, David Rubin **22** 164-166

ABRAHAMS, ISRAEL (1858-1925), British scholar **1** 29

ABRAMOVITZ, MAX (born 1908), American architect **18** 1-3

ABRAMS, CREIGHTON W. (1914-1974), United States Army commander in World War II and Vietnam **1** 29-31

ABRAVANEL, ISAAC BEN JUDAH (1437-1508), Jewish philosopher and statesman **1** 31

ABU BAKR (circa 573-634), Moslem leader, first caliph of Islam **1** 31-32

ABU MUSA (born Said Musa Maragha circa 1930), a leader of the Palestinian Liberation Organization **1** 32-33

ABU NUWAS (al-Hasan ibn-Hani; circa 756-813), Arab poet **1** 33-34

ABU-L-ALA AL-MAARRI (973-1058), Arab poet and philosopher **1** 32

ABZUG, BELLA STAVISKY (1920-1998), lawyer, politician, and congresswoman **1** 34-35

Accordion (musical instrument)
Welk, Lawrence **22** 420-422

437

ANDRADA E SILVA, JOSÉ BONIFÁCIO DE (1763-1838), Brazilian-born statesman and scientist **1** 221-222

ANDRÁSSY, COUNT JULIUS (1823-1890), Hungarian statesman, prime minister 1867-1871 **1** 222-223

ANDREA DEL CASTAGNO (1421-1457), Italian painter **1** 223-224

ANDREA DEL SARTO (1486-1530), Italian painter **1** 224-225

ANDREA PISANO (circa 1290/95-1348), Italian sculptor and architect **1** 225-226

ANDRÉE, SALOMON AUGUST (1854-1897), Swedish engineer and Arctic balloonist **1** 226

ANDREESSEN, MARC (born 1972), American computer programmer who developed Netscape Navigator **19** 3-5

ANDREOTTI, GIULIO (born 1919), leader of Italy's Christian Democratic party **1** 226-228

ANDRETTI, MARIO (born 1940), Italian/American race car driver **1** 228-230

ANDREW, JOHN ALBION (1818-1867), American politician **1** 230-231

ANDREWS, CHARLES McLEAN (1863-1943), American historian **1** 231

ANDREWS, FANNIE FERN PHILLIPS (1867-1950), American educator, reformer, pacifist **1** 231-232

ANDREWS, ROY CHAPMAN (1884-1960), American naturalist and explorer **1** 232-233

ANDROPOV, IURY VLADIMIROVICH (1914-1984), head of the Soviet secret police and ruler of the Soviet Union (1982-1984) **1** 233-234

ANDROS, SIR EDMUND (1637-1714), English colonial governor in America **1** 234-235

ANDRUS, ETHEL (1884-1976), American educator and founder of the American Association of Retired Persons **19** 5-7

ANGELICO, FRA (circa 1400-1455), Italian painter **1** 235-236

ANGELL, JAMES ROWLAND (1869-1949), psychologist and leader in higher education **1** 236-237

ANGELOU, MAYA (Marguerite Johnson; born 1928), American author, poet, playwright, stage and screen performer, and director **1** 238-239

ANGUISSOLA, SOFONISBA (Sofonisba Anguisciola; c. 1535-1625), Italian artist **22** 22-24

ANNA IVANOVNA (1693-1740), empress of Russia 1730-1740 **1** 240-241

ANNAN, KOFI (born 1938), Ghanaian secretary-general of the United Nations **18** 19-21

ANNE (1665-1714), queen of England 1702-1714 and of Great Britain 1707-1714 **1** 241-242

ANNING, MARY (1799-1847), British fossil collector **20** 14-16

ANOKYE, OKOMFO (Kwame Frimpon Anokye; flourished late 17th century), Ashanti priest and statesman **1** 242-243

ANOUILH, JEAN (1910-1987), French playwright **1** 243-244

ANSELM OF CANTERBURY, ST. (1033-1109), Italian archbishop and theologian **1** 244-245

Antarctic exploration
United States
Boyd, Louise Arner **22** 73-74

ANTHONY, ST. (circa 250-356), Egyptian hermit and monastic founder **1** 246-248

ANTHONY, SUSAN BROWNELL (1820-1906), American leader of suffrage movement **1** 246-248

ANTHONY OF PADUA, SAINT (Fernando de Boullion; 1195-1231), Portuguese theologian and priest **21** 7-9

Anthropological linguistics
see Linguistics

Anthropology (social science)
Native Americans
Ishi **22** 261-263
social
Montagu, Ashley **22** 320-322

ANTIGONUS I (382-301 B.C.), king of Macedon 306-301 B.C. **1** 248-249

ANTIOCHUS III (241-187 B.C.), king of Syria 223-187 B.C. **1** 249-250

ANTIOCHUS IV (circa 215-163 B.C.), king of Syria 175-163 B.C. **1** 250

ANTISTHENES (circa 450-360 B.C.), Greek philosopher **1** 250-251

ANTONELLO DA MESSINA (circa 1430-1479), Italian painter **1** 251-252

ANTONIONI, MICHELANGELO (born 1912), Italian film director **1** 252-253

ANTONY, MARK (circa 82-30 B.C.), Roman politician and general **1** 253-254

ANZA, JUAN BAUTISTA DE (1735-1788), Spanish explorer **1** 254-255

AOUN, MICHEL (born 1935), Christian Lebanese military leader and prime minister **1** 255-257

Apartheid (South Africa)
opponents
Brink, Andre Philippus **22** 80-83
Makeba, Miriam **22** 309-312

APELLES (flourished after 350 B.C.), Greek painter **1** 257

APESS, WILLIAM (1798-1839), Native American religious leader, author, and activist **20** 16-18

APGAR, VIRGINIA (1909-1974), American medical educator, researcher **1** 257-259

APITHY, SOUROU MIGAN (1913-1989), Dahomean political leader **1** 259-260

APOLLINAIRE, GUILLAUME (1880-1918), French lyric poet **1** 260

Apollo program (United States)
Bean, Alan **22** 48-50
Cernan, Gene **22** 100-102
Conrad, Pete **22** 114-116
Irwin, James Benson **22** 259-261
Mitchell, Edgar Dean **22** 318-320
Schmitt, Jack **22** 385-386

APOLLODORUS (flourished circa 408 B.C.), Greek painter **1** 261

APOLLONIUS OF PERGA (flourished 210 B.C.), Greek mathematician **1** 261-262

APPELFELD, AHARON (born 1932), Israeli who wrote about anti-Semitism and the Holocaust **1** 262-263

APPERT, NICOLAS (1749-1941), French chef and inventor of canning of foods **20** 18-19

APPIA, ADOLPHE (1862-1928), Swiss stage director **1** 263-264

APPLEGATE, JESSE (1811-1888), American surveyor, pioneer, and rancher **1** 264-265

APPLETON, SIR EDWARD VICTOR (1892-1965), British pioneer in radio physics **1** 265-266

APPLETON, NATHAN (1779-1861), American merchant and manufacturer **1** 266-267

APULEIUS, LUCIUS (c. 124-170), Roman author, philosopher, and orator **20** 19-21

AQUINO, BENIGNO ("Nino"; 1933-1983), Filipino activist murdered upon his return from exile **1** 267-268

AQUINO, CORAZON COJOANGCO (born 1933), first woman president of the Republic of the Philippines **1** 268-270

B

BEARD, MARY RITTER (1876-1958), American author and activist **2** 85-86

BEARDEN, ROMARE HOWARD (1914-1988), African American painter-collagist **2** 86-88

BEARDSLEY, AUBREY VINCENT (1872-1898), English illustrator **2** 88-89

BEATLES, THE (1957-1971), British rock and roll band **2** 89-92

BEATRIX, WILHELMINA VON AMSBERG, QUEEN (born 1938), queen of Netherlands (1980-) **2** 92-93

BEAUCHAMPS, PIERRE (1636-1705), French dancer and choreographer **21** 27-29

BEAUFORT, MARGARET (1443-1509), queen dowager of England **20** 29-31

BEAUJOYEULX, BALTHASAR DE (Balthasar de Beaujoyeux; Baldassare de Belgiojoso; 1535-1587), Italian choreographer and composer **21** 29-30

BEAUMARCHAIS, PIERRE AUGUST CARON DE (1732-1799), French playwright **2** 93-94

BEAUMONT, FRANCIS (1584/1585-1616), English playwright **2** 95

BEAUMONT, WILLIAM (1785-1853), American surgeon **2** 95-96

BEAUREGARD, PIERRE GUSTAVE TOUTANT (1818-1893), Confederate general **2** 96-97

BECARRIA, MARCHESE DI (1738-1794), Italian jurist and economist **2** 97-98

BECHET, SIDNEY (1897-1959), American jazz musician **22** 50-52

BECHTEL, STEPHEN DAVISON (1900-1989), American construction engineer and business executive **2** 98-99

BECK, LUDWIG AUGUST THEODOR (1880-1944), German general **2** 99-100

BECKER, CARL LOTUS (1873-1945), American historian **2** 100-101

BECKET, ST. THOMAS (1128?-1170), English prelate **2** 101-102

BECKETT, SAMUEL (1906-1989), Irish novelist, playwright, and poet **2** 102-104

BECKMANN, MAX (1884-1950), German painter **2** 104-105

BECKNELL, WILLIAM (circa 1797-1865), American soldier and politician **2** 105-106

BECKWOURTH, JIM (James P. Beckwourth; c. 1800-1866), African American fur trapper and explorer **2** 106-107

BÉCQUER, GUSTAVO ADOLFO DOMINGUEZ (1836-1870), Spanish lyric poet **2** 107-108

BECQUEREL, ANTOINE HENRI (1852-1908), French physicist **2** 108-109

BEDE, ST. (672/673-735), English theologian **2** 109-110

BEDELL SMITH, WALTER (1895-1961), U.S. Army general, ambassador, and CIA director **18** 30-33

BEEBE, WILLIAM (1877-1962), American naturalist, oceanographer, and ornithologist **22** 52-54

BEECHER, CATHARINE (1800-1878), American author and educator **2** 110-112

BEECHER, HENRY WARD (1813-1887), American Congregationalist clergyman **2** 112-113

BEECHER, LYMAN (1775-1863), Presbyterian clergyman **2** 113

BEERBOHM, MAX (Henry Maximilian Beerbohm; 1872-1956), English author and critic **19** 16-18

BEETHOVEN, LUDWIG VAN (1770-1827), German composer **2** 114-117

BEGAY, HARRISON (born 1917), Native American artist **2** 117-118

BEGIN, MENACHEM (1913-1992), Israel's first non-Socialist prime minister (1977-1983) **2** 118-120

BEHAIM, MARTIN (Martinus de Bohemia; 1459?-1507), German cartographer **21** 30-32

BEHN, APHRA (1640?-1689), British author **18** 33-34

BEHRENS, HILDEGARD (born 1937), German soprano **2** 120-121

BEHRENS, PETER (1868-1940), German architect, painter, and designer **2** 121-122

BEHRING, EMIL ADOLPH VON (1854-1917), German hygienist and physician **2** 122-123

BEHZAD (died circa 1530), Persian painter **2** 123

BEISSEL, JOHANN CONRAD (1690-1768), German-American pietist **2** 123-124

BELAFONTE, HARRY (Harold George Belafonte, Jr.; born 1927), African American singer and actor **20** 31-32

BELASCO, DAVID (1853-1931), American playwright and director-producer **2** 124-125

BELAÚNDE TERRY, FERNANDO (born 1912), president of Peru (1963-1968, 1980-1985) **2** 125-126

BELGRANO, MANUEL (1770-1820), Argentine general and politician **2** 126-127

BELINSKY, GRIGORIEVICH (1811-1848), Russian literary critic **2** 128

BELISARIUS (circa 506-565), Byzantine general **2** 128-129

BELL, ALEXANDER GRAHAM (1847-1922), Scottish-born American inventor **2** 129-131

BELL, ANDREW (1753-1832), Scottish educator **2** 131-132

BELL, DANIEL (Bolotsky; born 1919), American sociologist **2** 132-133

BELL, GERTRUDE (1868-1926), British archaeologist, traveler, and advisor on the Middle East **22** 54-55

BELL BURNELL, SUSAN JOCELYN (born 1943), English radio astronomer **2** 133-134

BELLAMY, EDWARD (1850-1898), American novelist, propagandist, and reformer **2** 134-135

BELLARMINE, ST. ROBERT (1542-1621), Italian theologian and cardinal **2** 135-136

BELLECOURT, CLYDE (born 1939), Native American activist **2** 136-137

BELLINI, GIOVANNI (circa 1435-1516), Itlalian painter **2** 137-138

BELLINI, VINCENZO (1801-1835), Italian composer **2** 138-139

BELLO, ALHAJI SIR AHMADU (1909-1966), Nigerian politician **2** 139-140

BELLO Y LÓPEZ, ANDRÉS (1781-1865), Venezuelan humanist **2** 140-141

BELLOC, JOSEPH HILAIRE PIERRE (1870-1953), French-born English author and historian **2** 141

BELLOW, SAUL (born 1915), American novelist and Nobel Prize winner **2** 141-143

BELLOWS, GEORGE WESLEY (1882-1925), American painter **2** 143

BELLOWS, HENRY WHITNEY (1814-1882), American Unitarian minister **2** 143-144

BELMONT, AUGUST (1816-1890), German-American banker, diplomat, and horse racer **22** 56-57

Belmont Stakes (thoroughbred racing) Belmont, August **22** 56-57

BEMBO, PIETRO (1470-1547), Italian humanist, poet, and historian **2** 144-145

BEN AND JERRY ice cream company founders **18** 35-37

BEN BADIS, ABD AL-HAMID (1889-1940), leader of the Islamic Reform Movement in Algeria between the two world wars **2** 147-148

BEN BELLA, AHMED (born 1918), first president of the Algerian Republic **2** 148-149

Ben Hur (film)
Wyler, William **22** 424-426

BENDIX, VINCENT (1881-1945), American inventor, engineer, and industrialist **19** 18-20

BEN-GURION, DAVID (born 1886), Russian-born Israeli statesman **2** 160-161

BEN-HAIM, PAUL (Frankenburger; 1897-1984), Israeli composer **2** 161-162

BEN YEHUDA, ELIEZER (1858-1922), Hebrew lexicographer and editor **2** 181-182

BENALCÁZAR, SEBASTIÁN DE (died 1551), Spanish conquistador **2** 145-146

BENAVENTE Y MARTINEZ, JACINTO (1866-1954), Spanish dramatist **2** 146-147

BENCHLEY, ROBERT (1889-1945), American humorist **2** 150-151

BENDA, JULIEN (1867-1956), French cultural critic and novelist **2** 151-152

BENEDICT XV (Giacomo della Chiesa; 1854-1922), pope, 1914-1922 **2** 153-154

BENEDICT, RUTH FULTON (1887-1948), American cultural anthropologist **2** 154-155

BENEDICT, ST. (circa 480-547), Italian founder of the Benedictines **2** 154-155

Benedictines (religious order)
scholarship
Hildegard of Bingen **22** 240-242

BENEŠ, EDWARD (1884-1948), Czechoslovak president 1935-1938 and 1940-1948 **2** 155-157

BENÉT, STEPHEN VINCENT (1898-1943), American poet and novelist **2** 157-158

BENETTON, Italian family (Luciano, Giuliana, Gilberto, Carlo and Mauro) who organized a world-wide chain of colorful knitwear stores **2** 158-159

BENEZET, ANTHONY (1713-1784), American philanthropist and educator **2** 159-160

BENJAMIN, ASHER (1773-1845), American architect **2** 162-163

BENJAMIN, JUDAH PHILIP (1811-1884), American statesman **2** 163-164

BENJAMIN, WALTER (1892-1940), German philosopher and literary critic **20** 32-34

BENN, GOTTFRIED (1886-1956), German author **2** 164

BENN, TONY (Anthony Neil Wedgewood Benn; born 1925), British Labour party politician **2** 164-166

BENNETT, ALAN (born 1934), British playwright **2** 166-167

BENNETT, ENOCH ARNOLD (1867-1931), English novelist and dramatist **2** 167-168

BENNETT, JAMES GORDON (1795-1872), Scottish-born American journalist and publisher **2** 168-169

BENNETT, JAMES GORDON, JR. (1841-1918), American newspaper owner and editor **2** 169-170

BENNETT, JOHN COLEMAN (1902-1995), American theologian **2** 170-171

BENNETT, RICHARD BEDFORD (1870-1947), Canadian statesman, prime minister 1930-1935 **2** 171-172

BENNETT, RICHARD RODNEY (born 1936), English composer **2** 172

BENNETT, ROBERT RUSSELL (1894-1981), American arranger, composer, and conductor **21** 32-34

BENNETT, WILLIAM JOHN (born 1943), American teacher and scholar and secretary of the Department of Education (1985-1988) **2** 172-174

BENNY, JACK (Benjamin Kubelsky; 1894-1974), American comedian and a star of radio, television, and stage **2** 174-176

BENTHAM, JEREMY (1748-1832), English philosopher, political theorist, and jurist **2** 176-178
Hart, Herbert Lionel Adolphus **22** 218-219

BENTLEY, ARTHUR F. (1870-1957), American philosopher and political scientist **2** 178

BENTON, SEN. THOMAS HART (1782-1858), American statesman **2** 178-179

BENTON, THOMAS HART (1889-1975), American regionalist painter **2** 178-179

BENTSEN, LLOYD MILLARD (born 1921), senior United States senator from Texas and Democratic vice-presidential candidate in 1988 **2** 180-181

BENZ, CARL (1844-1929), German inventor **2** 182-183

BERCHTOLD, COUNT LEOPOLD VON (1863-1942), Austro-Hungarian statesman **2** 183-184

BERDYAEV, NICHOLAS ALEXANDROVICH (1874-1948), Russian philosopher **2** 184-185

BERELSON, BERNARD (1912-1979), American behavioral scientist **2** 185-186

BERENSON, BERNARD (1865-1959), American art critic and historian **20** 34-35

BERG, ALBAN (1885-1935), Austrian composer **2** 186-187

BERG, PAUL (born 1926), American chemist **2** 187-189

BERGER, VICTOR LOUIS (1860-1929), American politician **2** 189-190

BERGMAN, (ERNST) INGMAR (born 1918); Swedish film and stage director **2** 190-191

BERGMAN, INGRID (1917-1982), Swedish actress **20** 35-37

BERGSON, HENRI (1859-1941), French philosopher **2** 191-192

BERIA, LAVRENTY PAVLOVICH (1899-1953), Soviet secret-police chief and politician **2** 192-193

Beriberi (medicine)
Funk, Casimir **22** 187-189

BERING, VITUS (1681-1741), Danish navigator in Russian employ **2** 193-194

BERIO, LUCIANO (born 1925), Italian composer **2** 194-195

BERISHA, SALI (born 1944), president of the Republic of Albania (1992-) **2** 195-197

BERKELEY, BUSBY (William Berkeley Enos; 1895-1976), American filmmaker **20** 38-39

BERKELEY, GEORGE (1685-1753), Anglo-Irish philosopher and Anglican bishop **2** 197-198

BERKELEY, SIR WILLIAM (1606-1677), English royal governor of Virginia **2** 198-199

BERLE, ADOLF AUGUSTUS, JR. (1895-1971), American educator **2** 199-200

BLAKE, WILLIAM (1757-1827), English poet, engraver, and painter **2** 316-318

BLAKELOCK, RALPH ALBERT (1847-1919), American painter **2** 318

BLANC, LOUIS (1811-1882), French journalist, historian, and politician **2** 318-319

BLANC, MEL (1908-1989), American creator of and voice of cartoon characters **2** 319-320

BLANCHARD, FELIX ("Doc" Blanchard; born 1924), American football player and military pilot **21** 43-45

BLANCHE OF CASTILE (1188-1252), French queen **21** 45-47

BLANCO, ANTONIO GUZMÁN (1829-1899), Venezuelan politician, three-times president **2** 320-321

BLANDIANA, ANA (born Otilia-Valeria Coman, 1942), Romanian poet **2** 321-322

BLANDING, SARAH GIBSON (1898-1985), American educator **2** 322-323

BLANKERS-KOEN, FANNY (Francina Elsja Blankers-Koen; born 1918), Dutch track and field athlete **20** 50-52

BLANQUI, LOUIS AUGUSTE (1805-1881), French revolutionary **2** 323-324

BLAVATSKY, HELENA PETROVNA (Helena Hahn; 1831-1891), Russian theosophist **22** 67-69

BLEDSOE, ALBERT TAYLOR (1809-1877), American lawyer, educator, and Confederate apologist **2** 324-325

BLEULER, EUGEN (1857-1939), Swiss psychiatrist **2** 325

BLIGH, WILLIAM (1754-1817), English naval officer and colonial governor **2** 325-326

BLOCH, ERNEST (1880-1959), Swiss-born American composer and teacher **2** 326-327

BLOCH, ERNST (1885-1977), German humanistic interpreter of Marxist thought **2** 327-328

BLOCH, FELIX (1905-1983), Swiss/American physicist **2** 328-330

BLOCH, KONRAD (born 1912), American biochemist **2** 330-332

BLOCH, MARC (1886-1944), French historian **2** 332-333

BLOCK, HERBERT (Herblock; 1909-2001), American newspaper cartoonist **2** 333-334

BLOK, ALEKSANDR ALEKSANDROVICH (1880-1921), Russian poet **2** 335

Blood (human)
banks
Gallo, Robert Charles **22** 191-193

BLOOM, ALLAN DAVID (1930-1992), American political philosopher, professor, and author **2** 335-337

BLOOMER, AMELIA JENKS (1818-1894), American reformer and suffrage advocate **2** 337

BLOOMFIELD, LEONARD (1887-1949), American linguist **2** 338

BLOOR, ELLA REEVE ("Mother Bloor"; 1862-1951), American labor organizer and social activist **2** 338-340

BLÜCHER, GEBHARD LEBERECHT VON (Prince of Wahlstatt; 1742-1819), Prussian field marshal **2** 340-341

BLUFORD, GUION STEWART, JR. (born 1942), African American aerospace engineer, pilot, and astronaut **2** 341-343

BLUM, LÉON (1872-1950), French statesman **2** 343-344

BLUME, JUDY (born Judy Sussman; b. 1938), American fiction author **2** 344-345

BLUMENTHAL, WERNER MICHAEL (born 1926), American businessman and treasury secretary **2** 345-346

BLY, NELLIE (born Elizabeth Cochrane Seaman; 1864-1922), American journalist and reformer **2** 346-348

BLYDEN, EDWARD WILMOT (1832-1912), Liberian statesman **2** 348-349

BOAS, FRANZ (1858-1942), German-born American anthropologist **2** 349-351
anthropological linguistics
Deloria, Ella Clara **22** 136-138

BOCCACCIO, GIOVANNI (1313-1375), Italian author **2** 351-353

BOCCIONI, UMBERTO (1882-1916), Italian artist **2** 353-354

BÖCKLIN, ARNOLD (1827-1901), Swiss painter **2** 354-355

BODE, BOYD HENRY (1873-1953), American philosopher and educator **2** 355-356

BODIN, JEAN (1529/30-1596), French political philosopher **2** 356-357

BOEHME, JACOB (1575-1624), German mystic **2** 357

BOEING, WILLIAM EDWARD (1881-1956), American businessman **2** 357-358

BOERHAAVE, HERMANN (1668-1738), Dutch physician and chemist **2** 358-359

BOESAK, ALLAN AUBREY (born 1945), opponent of apartheid in South Africa and founder of the United Democratic Front **2** 359-360

BOETHIUS, ANICIUS MANLIUS SEVERINUS (480?-524/525), Roman logician and theologian **2** 360-361

BOFF, LEONARDO (Leonardo Genezio Darci Boff; born 1938), Brazilian priest **22** 69-71

BOFFRAND, GABRIEL GERMAIN (1667-1754), French architect and decorator **2** 361

BOFILL, RICARDO (born 1939), post-modern Spanish architect **2** 362-363

BOGART, HUMPHREY (1899-1957), American stage and screen actor **2** 363-364

BOHEMUND I (of Tarantò; circa 1055-1111), Norman Crusader **2** 364

BOHLEN, CHARLES (CHIP) EUSTIS (1904-1973), United States ambassador to the Soviet Union, interpreter, and presidential adviser **2** 364-366

BÖHM-BAWERK, EUGEN VON (1851-1914), Austrian economist **2** 366

BOHR, NIELS HENRIK DAVID (1885-1962), Danish physicist **2** 366-368

BOIARDO, MATTEO MARIA (Conte di Scandiano; 1440/41-1494), Italian poet **2** 369

BOILEAU-DESPRÉAUX, NICHOLAS (1636?-1711), French critic and writer **2** 369-371

BOK, DEREK CURTIS (born 1930), dean of the Harvard Law School and president of Harvard University **2** 371-372

BOK, EDWARD WILLIAM (1863-1930), American editor and publisher **22** 71-73

BOK, SISSELA ANN (born 1934), American moral philosopher **2** 372-374

BOLEYN, ANNE (1504?-1536), second wife of Henry VIII **18** 47-49

BOLINGBROKE, VISCOUNT (Henry St. John; 1678-1751), English statesman **2** 374-375

BOLÍVAR, SIMÓN (1783-1830), South American general and statesman **2** 375-377

BOLKIAH, HASSANAL (Muda Hassanal Bolkiah Mu'izzaddin Waddaulah; born 1946), Sultan of Brunei **18** 49-51

BOUDINOT, ELIAS (Buck Watie; Galagina; 1803-1839), Cherokee leader and author **21** 52-54

BOUGAINVILLE, LOUIS ANTOINE DE (1729-1811), French soldier and explorer **2** 443-444

BOULANGER, NADIA (1887-1979), French pianist and music teacher **20** 56-58

BOULEZ, PIERRE (born 1925), French composer, conductor, and teacher **2** 444-445

BOUMEDIENE, HOUARI (born 1932), Algerian revolutionary, military leader, and president **2** 445-446

BOURASSA, JOSEPH-HENRI-NAPOLEON (1868-1952), French-Canadian nationalist and editor **2** 446-447

BOURASSA, ROBERT (born 1933), premier of the province of Quebec (1970-1976 and 1985-) **2** 447-449

BOURDELLE, EMILE-ANTOINE (1861-1929), French sculptor **2** 449-450

BOURGEOIS, LÉON (1851-1925), French premier 1895-1896 **2** 450-451

BOURGEOIS, LOUISE (born 1911), American sculptor **2** 451-452

BOURGEOYS, BLESSED MARGUERITE (1620-1700), French educator and religious founder **2** 452-453

BOURGUIBA, HABIB (1903-2000), Tunisian statesman **2** 453-455

BOURKE-WHITE, MARGARET (1904-1971), American photographer and photojournalist **2** 455-456

BOURNE, RANDOLPH SILLIMAN (1886-1918), American pacifist and cultural critic **2** 456-457

BOUTROS-GHALI, BOUTROS (born 1922), Egyptian diplomat and sixth secretary-general of the United Nations (1991-) **2** 457-458

BOUTS, DIRK (1415/20-1475), Dutch painter **2** 458-459

BOWDITCH, HENRY INGERSOLL (1808-1892), American physician **2** 459-460

BOWDITCH, NATHANIEL (1773-1838), American navigator and mathematician **2** 460-461

BOWDOIN, JAMES (1726-1790), American merchant and politician **2** 461-462

BOWEN, ELIZABETH (1899-1973), British novelist **2** 462-463

BOWERS, CLAUDE GERNADE (1878-1958), American journalist, historian, and diplomat **2** 463

BOWIE, DAVID (David Robert Jones; born 1947), English singer, songwriter, and actor **18** 58-60

BOWLES, PAUL (1910-1999), American author, musical composer, and translator **19** 31-34

BOWLES, SAMUEL (1826-1878), American newspaper publisher **2** 464

BOWMAN, ISAIAH (1878-1950), American geographer **2** 464-465

BOXER, BARBARA (born 1940), U.S. Senator from California **2** 465-468

Boxers
see Athletes, American—boxers

Boycott
see Labor unions

BOYD, LOUISE ARNER (1887-1972), American explorer **22** 73-74

BOYER, JEAN PIERRE (1776-1850), Haitian president 1818-1845 **2** 468-469

BOYLE, ROBERT (1627-1691), British chemist and physicist **2** 469-471

BOYLSTON, ZABDIEL (1679-1766), American physician **2** 471

BOZEMAN, JOHN M. (1837-1867), American pioneer **2** 471-472

BRACKENRIDGE, HUGH HENRY (1749-1816), American lawyer and writer **2** 472-473

BRACTON, HENRY (Henry of Bratton; c. 1210-1268), English jurist **21** 54-55

BRADBURY, RAY (born 1920), American fantasy and science fiction writer **2** 473-474

BRADDOCK, EDWARD (1695-1755), British commander in North America **2** 474-475

BRADFORD, WILLIAM (1590-1657), leader of Plymouth Colony **2** 475-476

BRADFORD, WILLIAM (1663-1752), American printer **2** 476-477

BRADFORD, WILLIAM (1722-1791), American journalist **2** 477

BRADLAUGH, CHARLES (1833-1891), English freethinker and political agitator **2** 478

BRADLEY, ED (born 1941), African American broadcast journalist **2** 478-481

BRADLEY, FRANCIS HERBERT (1846-1924), English philosopher **2** 481-482

BRADLEY, JAMES (1693-1762), English astronomer **2** 482-483

BRADLEY, JOSEPH P. (1813-1892), American Supreme Court justice **22** 74-77

BRADLEY, MARION ZIMMER (born 1930), American author **18** 60-62

BRADLEY, OMAR NELSON (1893-1981), American general **2** 483-484

BRADLEY, TOM (1917-1998), first African American mayor of Los Angeles **2** 484-485

BRADMAN, SIR DONALD GEORGE (born 1908), Australian cricketer **2** 485-486

BRADSTREET, ANNE DUDLEY (circa 1612-1672), English-born American poet **2** 486-487

BRADY, MATHEW B. (circa 1823-1896), American photographer **2** 487-488

BRAGG, SIR WILLIAM HENRY (1862-1942), English physicist **2** 488-489

BRAHE, TYCHO (1546-1601), Danish astronomer **2** 489-490

BRAHMS, JOHANNES (1833-1897), German composer **2** 490-492

BRAILLE, LOUIS (1809-1852), French teacher and creator of braille system **2** 492-493

BRAMAH, JOSEPH (Joe Bremmer; 1749-1814), English engineer and inventor **20** 58-59

BRAMANTE, DONATO (1444-1514), Italian architect and painter **2** 493-494

BRANCUSI, CONSTANTIN (1876-1957), Romanian sculptor in France **2** 494-496

BRANDEIS, LOUIS DEMBITZ (1856-1941), American jurist **2** 496-497

BRANDO, MARLON (born 1924), American actor **2** 497-499

BRANDT, WILLY (Herbert Frahm Brandt; 1913-1992), German statesman, chancellor of West Germany **2** 499-500

BRANSON, RICHARD (born 1950), British entrepreneur **19** 34-36

BRANT, JOSEPH (1742-1807), Mohawk Indian chief **2** 500-501

BRANT, MARY (1736-1796), Native American who guided the Iroquois to a British alliance **2** 501-503

BRANT, SEBASTIAN (1457-1521), German author **2** 503-504

BRAQUE, GEORGES (1882-1967), French painter **2** 504-505

BRATTAIN, WALTER H. (1902-1987), American physicist and co-inventor of the transistor **2** 505-507

BRAUDEL, FERNAND (1902-1985), leading exponent of the *Annales* school of history **2** 507-508

BRAUN, FERDINAND (1850-1918), German recipient of the Nobel Prize in Physics for work on wireless telegraphy **2** 508-509

BRAY, JOHN RANDOLPH (1879-1978), American animator and cartoonist **21** 55-57

BRAZZA, PIERRE PAUL FRANÇOIS CAMILLE SAVORGNAN DE (1852-1905), Italian-born French explorer **2** 509-510

BREASTED, JAMES HENRY (1865-1935), American Egyptologist and archeologist **2** 510-511

BRÉBEUF, JEAN DE (1593-1649), French Jesuit missionary **2** 511-512

BRECHT, BERTOLT (1898-1956), German playwright **2** 512-514

BRECKINRIDGE, JOHN CABELL (1821-1875), American statesman and military leader **22** 77-79

BRENDAN, SAINT (Brenainn; Brandon; Brendan of Clonfert; c. 486-c. 578), Irish Abbott and explorer **22** 79-80

BRENNAN, WILLIAM J., JR. (born 1906), United States Supreme Court justice **2** 514-515

BRENTANO, CLEMENS (1778-1842), German poet and novelist **2** 515-516

BRENTANO, FRANZ CLEMENS (1838-1917), German philosopher **2** 516-517

BRESHKOVSKY, CATHERINE (1844-1934), Russian revolutionary **2** 517-519

BRETON, ANDRÉ (1896-1966), French author **2** 519-520

BREUER, MARCEL (1902-1981), Hungarian-born American architect **2** 520-521

BREUIL, HENRI EDOUARD PROSPER (1877-1961), French archeologist **2** 521-522

BREWSTER, KINGMAN, JR. (1919-1988), president of Yale University (1963-1977) **2** 522-523

BREWSTER, WILLIAM (circa 1566-1644), English-born Pilgrim leader **2** 523-524

BREYER, STEPHEN (born 1938), U.S. Supreme Court justice **2** 524-527

BREZHNEV, LEONID ILICH (1906-1982), general secretary of the

Communist party of the Union of Soviet Socialist Republics (1964-1982) and president of the Union of Soviet Socialist Republics (1977-1982) **2** 527-528

BRIAN BORU (940?-1014), Irish king **18** 62-64

BRIAND, ARISTIDE (1862-1932), French statesman **2** 528-529

BRICE, FANNY (1891-1951), vaudeville, Broadway, film, and radio singer and comedienne **3** 1-2

BRIDGER, JAMES (1804-1881), American fur trader and scout **3** 2-3

BRIDGES, HARRY A.R. (1901-1990), radical American labor leader **3** 3-5

BRIDGMAN, PERCY WILLIAMS (1882-1961), American physicist **3** 5-6

BRIGHT, JOHN (1811-1889), English politician **3** 6-7

BRIGHT, RICHARD (1789-1858), English physician **3** 7-8

BRIGHTMAN, EDGAR SHEFFIELD (1884-1953), philosopher of religion and exponent of American Personalism **3** 8-9

BRINK, ANDRE PHILIPPUS (born 1935), South African author **22** 80-83

BRISBANE, ALBERT (1809-1890), American social theorist **3** 9

BRISTOW, BENJAMIN HELM (1832-1896), American lawyer and Federal official **3** 9-10

British Broadcasting Corporation
Davis, Colin Rex **22** 131-133

British Columbia (province, Canada)
Bulwer-Lytton, Edward **22** 87-88

British India
see India (British rule)

BRITTEN, BENJAMIN (1913-1976), English composer **3** 10-11

BROAD, CHARLIE DUNBAR (1887-1971), English philosopher **3** 12

BROCK, SIR ISAAC (1769-1812), British general **3** 12-13

BRODSKY, JOSEPH (Iosif Alexandrovich Brodsky, 1940-1996), Russian-born Nobel Prize winner and fifth United States poet laureate **3** 13-15

BRONTË, CHARLOTTE (1816-1855), English novelist **3** 17-18

BRONTË, EMILY (1818-1848), English novelist **3** 18-19

BRONZINO (1503-1572), Italian painter **3** 19

BROOK, PETER (born 1925), world-renowned theater director **3** 19-21

BROOKE, ALAN FRANCIS (Viscount Alanbrooke; 1883-1963), Irish military leader **20** 59-61

BROOKE, SIR JAMES (1803-1868), British governor in Borneo **3** 21-22

BROOKE, RUPERT (1887-1915), English poet **3** 22-23

BROOKNER, ANITA (born 1928), British art historian and novelist **3** 23-24

BROOKS, GWENDOLYN (born 1917), first African American author to receive the Pulitzer Prize for Literature **3** 24-26

BROOKS, PHILLIPS (1835-1893), American Episcopalian bishop **3** 26

BROTHERS, JOYCE (Joyce Diane Bauer; born 1927), American psychologist who pioneered radio phone-in questions for professional psychological advice **3** 26-28

BROUDY, HARRY SAMUEL (born 1905), American philosopher, teacher, and author **3** 28-29

BROUGHAM, HENRY PETER (Baron Brougham and Vaux; 1778-1868), Scottish jurist **22** 83-85

BROUWER, ADRIAEN (1605/06-1638), Flemish painter **3** 29-30

BROWDER, EARL RUSSELL (1891-1973), American Communist leader **3** 30-31

BROWN, ALEXANDER (1764-1834), American merchant and banker **3** 31-32

BROWN, BENJAMIN GRATZ (1826-1885), American politician **3** 32-33

BROWN, CHARLES BROCKDEN (1771-1810), American novelist **3** 33

BROWN, CHARLOTTE EUGENIA HAWKINS (born Lottie Hawkins; 1882-1961), African American educator and humanitarian **3** 34

BROWN, GEORGE (1818-1880), Canadian politician **3** 35-36

BROWN, HELEN GURLEY (born 1922), American author and editor **3** 36-37

BROWN, JAMES (born 1928), African American singer **3** 37-39

BROWN, JOHN (1800-1859), American abolitionist **3** 39-41

BROWN, JOSEPH EMERSON (1821-1894), American lawyer and politician **3** 41-42

BROWN, LES (Leslie Calvin Brown; born 1945), American motivational speaker, author, and television host **19** 36-39

BUKHARIN, NIKOLAI IVANOVICH (1858-1938), Russian politician **3** 112-113

BUKOWSKI, CHARLES (1920-1994), American writer and poet **3** 113-115

BULATOVIC, MOMIR (born 1956), president of Montenegro (1990-1992) and of the new Federal Republic of Yugoslavia (1992-) **3** 115-116

BULFINCH, CHARLES (1763-1844), American colonial architect **3** 116-117

BULGAKOV, MIKHAIL AFANASIEVICH (1891-1940), Russian novelist and playwright **3** 117

BULGANIN, NIKOLAI (1885-1975), chairman of the Soviet Council of Ministers (1955-1958) **3** 118-119

BULOSAN, CARLOS (1911-1956), American author and poet **21** 59-61

BULTMANN, RUDOLF KARL (1884-1976), German theologian **3** 119-120

BULWER-LYTTON, EDWARD (1st Baron Lytton of Knebworth; 1803-1873), English novelist **22** 87-88

BUNAU-VARILLA, PHILIPPE JEAN (1859-1940), French engineer and soldier **3** 120-121

BUNCHE, RALPH JOHNSON (1904-1971), African American diplomat **3** 121-122

BUNDY, McGEORGE (born 1919), national security adviser to two presidents **3** 122-124

BUNIN, IVAN ALEKSEEVICH (1870-1953), Russian poet and novelist **3** 124

BUNSEN, ROBERT WILHELM (1811-1899), German chemist and physicist **3** 124-125

BUNSHAFT, GORDON (1909-1990), American architect **3** 125-127

BUÑUEL, LUIS (1900-1983), Spanish film director **3** 127-128

BUNYAN, JOHN (1628-1688), English author and Baptist preacher **3** 128-129

BURBANK, LUTHER (1849-1926), American plant breeder **3** 129-131

BURCHFIELD, CHARLES (1893-1967), American painter **3** 131-132

BURCKHARDT, JACOB CHRISTOPH (1818-1897), Swiss historian **3** 132-133

BURCKHARDT, JOHANN LUDWIG (1784-1817), Swiss-born explorer **3** 133

BURGER, WARREN E. (1907-1986), Chief Justice of the United States Supreme Court (1969-1986) **3** 133-136

BURGESS, ANTHONY (John Anthony Burgess Wilson; 1917-1993), English author **3** 136-137

BURGOYNE, JOHN (1723-1792), British general and statesman **3** 137-138

BURKE, EDMUND (1729-1797), British statesman, political theorist, and philosopher **3** 138-141

BURKE, KENNETH (born 1897), American literary theorist and critic **3** 141-142

BURKE, ROBERT O'HARA (1820-1861), Irish-born Australian policeman and explorer **3** 142-143

BURKE, SELMA (1900-1995), African American sculptor **3** 143-144

BURLINGAME, ANSON (1820-1870), American diplomat **3** 144-145

BURNE-JONES, SIR EDWARD COLEY (1833-1898), English painter and designer **3** 145-146

BURNET, SIR FRANK MACFARLANE (1899-1985), Australian virologist **3** 146-147

BURNET, GILBERT (1643-1715), British bishop and historian **3** 147

BURNETT, FRANCES HODGSON (Frances Eliza Hodgson Burnett; 1849-1924), English-born American author **18** 64-67

BURNETT, LEO (1891-1971), American advertising executive **19** 45-47

BURNEY, FRANCES "FANNY" (1752-1840), English novelist and diarist **3** 147-148

BURNHAM, DANIEL HUDSON (1846-1912), American architect and city planner **3** 148-149

BURNHAM, FORBES (1923-1985), leader of the independence movement in British Guiana and Guyana's first prime minister **3** 149-151

BURNS, ANTHONY (1834-1862), African American slave **3** 151

BURNS, ARTHUR (1904-1987), American economic statesman **3** 151-153

BURNS, GEORGE (born Nathan Birnbaum; 1896-1996), American comedian and actor **3** 153-155 Allen, Gracie **22** 18-20

BURNS, KEN (Kenneth Lauren Burns; born 1953), American documentary filmmaker **20** 63-65

BURNS, ROBERT (1759-1796), Scottish poet **3** 155-156

BURR, AARON (1756-1836), American politician, vice president 1801-1805 **3** 156-159

BURRI, ALBERTO (1915-1995), Italian painter **3** 159-160

BURRITT, ELIHU (1810-1879), American pacifist, author, and linguist **3** 160

BURROUGHS, EDGAR RICE (1875-1950), American author **18** 67-68

BURROUGHS, JOHN (1837-1921), American naturalist and essayist **3** 160-161

BURROUGHS, WILLIAM S. (1914-1997), American writer **3** 162-163

BURTON, RICHARD (Richard Jenkins; 1925-1984), British actor **3** 163-164

BURTON, SIR RICHARD FRANCIS (1821-1890), English explorer, author, and diplomat **3** 164-166

BURTON, ROBERT (1577-1640), English author and clergyman **3** 166-167

BUSCH, ADOLPHUS (1839-1913), American brewer and businessman **19** 47-49

BUSH, GEORGE (George Herbert Walker Bush; born 1924), United States vice president (1981-1989) and president (1989-1993) **3** 167-169

BUSH, GEORGE WALKER (born 1946), United States president (2001-) **21** 61-64

BUSH, VANNEVAR (1890-1974), American scientist and engineer **3** 169-171

BUSHNELL, DAVID (1742-1824), American inventor **21** 64-65

BUSHNELL, HORACE (1802-1876), American Congregational clergyman **3** 171-172

BUSIA, KOFI ABREFA (1914-1978), Ghanaian premier and sociologist **3** 172-173

Business and industrial leaders, American
automobile industry
Couzens, James **22** 121-125
Haynes, Elwood **22** 231-234
bankers (19th century)
Belmont, August **22** 56-57
bankers (20th century)
Eccles, Marriner Stoddard **22** 160-162
food and beverage industry
Pennington, Mary Engle **22** 352-355
Swift, Gustavus Franklin **22** 407-409
metals industry
Haynes, Elwood **22** 231-234
printing industry
Harper, James **22** 213-216
railroad industry (builders)

CALLAGHAN, LEONARD JAMES (born 1912), Labor member of the British Parliament and prime minister, 1976-1979 **3** 230-231

CALLAHAN, DANIEL (born 1930), American philosopher who focused on biomedical ethics **3** 231-233

CALLAHAN, HARRY (1912-1999), American photographer **20** 67-69

CALLAS, MARIA (Cecilia Sophia Anna Maria Kalogeropoulos; 1923-1977), American opera soprano **18** 73-75

CALLEJAS ROMERO, RAFAEL LEONARDO (born 1943), president of Honduras (1990-) **3** 233-234

CALLENDER, CLIVE ORVILLE (born 1936), African American surgeon **18** 75-77

CALLES, PLUTARCO ELÍAS (1877-1945), Mexican revolutionary leader **3** 234-235

CALLIMACHUS (circa 310-240 B.C.), Greek poet **3** 235-236

CALLOWAY, CAB (1907-1994) American singer, songwriter, and bandleader **3** 236-238

CALVERT, CHARLES (3rd Baron Baltimore; 1637-1715), English proprietor of colonial Maryland **3** 238

CALVERT, GEORGE (1st Baron Baltimore; circa 1580-1632), English statesman, founder of Maryland colony **3** 238-239

CALVIN, JOHN (1509-1564), French Protestant reformer **3** 239-242

CALVIN, MELVIN (1911-1986), American chemist **3** 242-243

CALVINO, ITALO (1923-1985), Italian author **3** 243-244

CAMDESSUS, MICHEL (born 1933), French civil servant and managing director of the International Monetary Fund **3** 244-246

CAMERON, JULIA MARGARET (1815-1879), British photographer **20** 69-71

CAMERON, SIMON (1799-1889), American politician **3** 246-247

CAMOËNS, LUIS VAZ DE (1524-1580), Portuguese poet **3** 247-249

CAMPANELLA, ROY (1921-1993), American baseball player **19** 55-57

CAMPANELLA, TOMMASO (Giovanni Domenico Campanella; 1568-1639), Italian philosopher, political theorist, and poet **3** 249

CAMPBELL, ALEXANDER (1788-1866), Irish-born American clergyman **3** 249-250

CAMPBELL, AVRIL PHAEDRA DOUGLAS (KIM) (born 1947), Canada's first woman prime minister **3** 250-252

CAMPBELL, BEN NIGHTHORSE (born 1933), Native American United States senator from Colorado **3** 252-253

CAMPBELL, COLIN (Baron Clyde; 1792-1863), English army officer **20** 71-73

CAMPBELL, JOSEPH (1904-1987), American editor and popularizer of comparative mythology **3** 253-255

CAMPIN, ROBERT (circa 1375/80-1444), Flemish painter **3** 255

CAMPOS, ROBERTO OLIVEIRA (1917-2001), Brazilian economist and diplomat **18** 77-79

CAMUS, ALBERT (1913-1960), French novelist, essayist, and playwright **3** 255-257

Canadian literature
children's books
Richler, Mordecai **22** 371-373
political commentary
Richler, Mordecai **22** 371-373

CANALETTO (1697-1768), Italian painter **3** 257-258

Cancer research
Folkman, Judah **22** 176-179
Gallo, Robert Charles **22** 191-193

CANISIUS, ST. PETER (1521-1597), Dutch Jesuit **3** 258

CANNING, GEORGE (1770-1827), English orator and statesman **3** 258-260

CANNON, ANNIE JUMP (1863-1941), American astronomer **3** 260-261

CANNON, JOSEPH GURNEY (1836-1926), American politican **3** 261-262

CANOT, THEODORE (1804-1860), French-Italian adventurer and slave trader **3** 262-263

CANOVA, ANTONIO (1757-1822), Italian sculptor **3** 263-264

CANTOR, EDDIE (Isador Iskowitz; 1892-1964), American singer and comedian **3** 264-265

CANTOR, GEORG FERDINAND LUDWIG PHILIPP (1845-1918), German mathematician **3** 265-266

CANUTE I THE GREAT (c. 995-1035), Viking king of England and Denmark **3** 266-269

CANUTT, YAKIMA (Enos Edward Canutt; 1896-1986), American rodeo performer, actor, stuntman, and film director **21** 71-72

CAPA, ROBERT (Endre Friedmann; 1913-1954), Hungarian-American war photographer and photojournalist **3** 269-271

ČAPEK, KAREL (1890-1938), Czech novelist, playwright, and essayist **3** 271-272

CAPETILLO, LUISA (1879-1922), Puerto Rican labor leader and activist **20** 73-74

CAPONE, AL (Alphonso Caponi, a.k.a. "Scarface;" 1899-1947), American gangster **3** 272-273

CAPOTE, TRUMAN (born Truman Streckfus Persons; 1924-1984), American author **3** 273-275

CAPP, AL (Alfred Gerald Capp; 1909-1979), American cartoonist and satirist **3** 275-276

CAPRA, FRANK (1897-1991), American film director **3** 276-278

CAPRIATI, JENNIFER (born 1976), American tennis player **3** 278-281

CAPTAIN JACK (Kientpoos; circa 1837-1873), American tribal leader **21** 72-74

CARACALLA (188-217), Roman emperor **3** 281-282

CARAVAGGIO (1573-1610), Italian painter **3** 282-284

CARAWAY, HATTIE WYATT (1878-1950), first woman elected to the United States Senate in her own right **3** 284-285

CARDANO, GERONIMO (1501-1576), Italian mathematician, astronomer, and physician **3** 285-286

CARDENAL, ERNESTO (born 1925), Nicaraguan priest, poet, and revolutionary **19** 57-59

CÁRDENAS, LÁZARO (1895-1970), Mexican revolutionary president 1934-1940 **3** 286-287

CÁRDENAS SOLORZANO, CUAUHTÉMOC (born 1934), Mexican politician **3** 287-288

CARDIN, PIERRE (born 1922), French fashion designer **18** 79-81

CARDOSO, FERNANDO HENRIQUE (born 1931), sociologist and president of Brazil **18** 81-83

CARDOZO, BENJAMIN NATHAN (1870-1938), American jurist and legal philosopher **3** 288-290

CARDUCCI, GIOSUÈ (1835-1907), Italian poet **3** 290-291

CAREW, ROD (born 1945), Panamanian baseball player **3** 291-292

CAREY, GEORGE LEONARD (born 1935), archbishop of Canterbury **3** 293-294

CAREY, HENRY CHARLES (1793-1879), American writer on economics **3** 294-295

CAREY, PETER (born 1943), Australian author **3** 295-297

CAREY, WILLIAM (1761-1834), English Baptist missionary **3** 297

CAREY THOMAS, MARTHA (1857-1935), American educator **3** 297-298

CARÍAS ANDINO, TIBURCIO (1876-1969), Honduran dictator (1932-1949) **3** 298-299

CARISSIMI, GIACOMO (1605-1674), Italian composer **3** 299-300

CARLETON, GUY (1st Baron Dorchester; 1724-1808), British general and statesman **3** 300-301

CARLIN, GEORGE (born 1937), American comedian **3** 301-303

CARLSON, CHESTER F. (1906-1968), American inventor of the process of xerography **3** 303-304

CARLYLE, THOMAS (1795-1881), Scottish essayist and historian **3** 304-305

CARMICHAEL, STOKELY (1941-1998), African American civil rights activist **3** 305-308

CARNAP, RUDOLF (1891-1970), German-American philosopher **3** 308-309

CARNEADES (circa 213-circa 128 B.C.), Greek philosopher **3** 309

CARNEGIE, ANDREW (1835-1919), American industrialist and philanthropist **3** 309-312
influenced by
Scott, Thomas Alexander **22** 393-395

CARNEGIE, HATTIE (born Henrietta Kanengeiser; 1889-1956), American fashion designer **3** 313

CARNOT, LAZARE NICOLAS MARGUERITE (1753-1823), French engineer, general, and statesman **3** 313-314

CARNOT, NICHOLAS LÉONARD SADI (1796-1832), French physicist **3** 315

CARO, ANTHONY (born 1924), English sculptor **3** 316

CARO, JOSEPH BEN EPHRAIM (1488-1575), Jewish Talmudic scholar **3** 316-317

CAROTHERS, WALLACE HUME (1896-1937), American chemist **3** 317-318

CARPEAUX, JEAN BAPTISTE (1827-1875), French sculptor and painter **3** 318-319

CARR, EMILY (1871-1945), Canadian painter and writer **3** 319

CARR, EMMA PERRY (1880-1972), American chemist and educator **22** 89-91

CARR-SAUNDERS, SIR ALEXANDER MORRIS (1886-1966), English demographer and sociologist **3** 333-334

CARRANZA, VENUSTIANO (1859-1920), Mexican revolutionary, president 1914-1920 **3** 321-322

CARREL, ALEXIS (1873-1944), French-American surgeon **3** 322-323

CARRERA, JOSÉ MIGUEL (1785-1821), Chilean revolutionary **3** 323-324

CARRERA, JOSÉ RAFAEL (1814-1865), Guatemalan statesman, president 1851-1865 **3** 324-325

CARRERAS, JOSE MARIA (born 1946), Spanish opera singer **22** 91-93

CARRIER, WILLS (1876-1950), American inventer who was the "father of air conditioning" **3** 325-326

CARRINGTON, BARON (born 1919), British politician and secretary-general of the North Atlantic Treaty Organization (1984-1988) **3** 326-327

CARROLL, ANNA ELLA (1815-1893), American political writer and presidential aide **3** 327-331

CARROLL, JOHN (1735-1815), American Catholic bishop **3** 331-332

CARROLL, LEWIS (pseudonym of Charles Lutwidge Dodgson; 1832-1898), English cleric and author **3** 332-333

CARSON, BEN (born 1951), African American surgeon **18** 83-85

CARSON, CHRISTOPHER "KIT" (1809-1868), American frontiersman **3** 334-335

CARSON, JOHNNY (born 1925), American television host and comedian **3** 335-337

CARSON, RACHEL LOUISE (1907-1964), American biologist and author **3** 337-338

CARTER, ELLIOTT COOK, JR. (born 1908), American composer **3** 338-339

CARTER, HOWARD (1874-1939), English archaeologist and artist **20** 74-76

CARTER, JAMES EARL ("Jimmy" Carter; born 1924), United States president (1977-1981) **3** 339-342

CARTIER, SIR GEORGE-ÉTIENNE (1814-1873), Canadian statesman **3** 342-343

CARTIER, JACQUES (1491-1557), French explorer and navigator **3** 343-344

CARTIER-BRESSON, HENRI (born 1908), French photographer and painter **19** 59-61

Cartography (science)
Hayden, Ferdinand Vandiveer **22** 227-229

CARTWRIGHT, ALEXANDER (1820-1898), baseball pioneer **21** 74-77

CARTWRIGHT, PETER (1785-1872), American Methodist preacher **3** 344-345

CARUSO, ENRICO (1873-1921), Italian operatic tenor **3** 345

CARVER, GEORGE WASHINGTON (1864-1943), African American agricultural chemist **3** 346-347

CARVER, JONATHAN (1710-1780), American explorer and writer **3** 347-348

CASALS, PABLO (born Pau Carlos Salvador Casals y Defill; 1876-1973), Spanish cellist, conductor, and composer **3** 348-350

CASANOVA, GIACOMO JACOPO GIROLAMO, CHEVALIER DE SEINGLAT (1725-1798), Italian adventurer **3** 350-351

CASE, STEVE (born 1958), American businessman **19** 61-64

CASEMENT, ROGER (1864-1916), Irish diplomat and nationalist **20** 76-78

CASEY, WILLIAM J. (1913-1987), American director of the Central Intelligence Agency (CIA) **3** 351-353

CASH, JOHNNY (born 1932), American singer and songwriter **3** 353-355

CASH, W. J. (Joseph Wilbur Cash; 1900-1914), American journalist and author **22** 93-95

CASS, LEWIS (1782-1866), American statesman **3** 355-356

CASSATT, MARY (1845-1926), American painter **3** 356-357

CASSAVETES, JOHN (1929-1989), American filmmaker **22** 96-98

CASSIODORUS, FLAVIUS MAGNUS AURELIUS, SENATOR (circa 480-circa

CHAMPLAIN, SAMUEL DE (circa 1570-1635), French geographer and explorer **3** 419-421

CHAMPOLLION, JEAN FRANÇOIS (1790-1832), French Egyptologist **3** 421

CHANCELLOR, RICHARD (died 1556), English navigator **3** 422

CHANDLER, ALFRED DU PONT, JR. (born 1918), American historian of American business **3** 422-423

CHANDLER, RAYMOND, JR. (1888-1959), American author of crime fiction **3** 423-425

CHANDLER, ZACHARIAH (1813-1879), American politician **3** 425-426

CHANDRAGUPTA MAURYA (died circa 298 B.C.), emperor of India 322?-298 **3** 426

CHANDRASEKHAR, SUBRAHMANYAN (1910-1995), Indian-born American physicist **3** 426-429

CHANEL, COCO (born Gabrielle Chanel; 1882-1971), French fashion designer **3** 429

CHANEY, LON (Alonzo Chaney; 1883-1930), American actor **19** 68-70

CHANG CHIEN (1853-1926), Chinese industrialist and social reformer **3** 429-430

CHANG CHIH-TUNG (1837-1909), Chinese official and reformer **3** 430-431

CHANG CHÜ-CHENG (1525-1582), Chinese statesman **3** 431-432

CHANG CHÜEH (died 184), Chinese religious and revolutionary leader **3** 432-433

CHANG HSÜEH-CH'ENG (1738-1801), Chinese scholar and historian **3** 433

CHANG PO-GO (died 846), Korean adventurer and merchant prince **3** 433-434

CHANG TSO-LIN (1873-1928), Chinese warlord **3** 434-435

CHANNING, EDWARD (1856-1931), American historian **3** 435

CHANNING, WILLIAM ELLERY (1780-1842), Unitarian minister and theologian **3** 435-436

CHAO MENG-FU (1254-1322), Chinese painter **3** 436-437

CHAPIN, F(RANCIS) STUART (1888-1974), American sociologist **3** 437-438

CHAPLIN, CHARLES SPENCER (1889-1977), American film actor, director, and writer **3** 438-440

CHAPMAN, GEORGE (1559/60-1634), English poet, dramatist, and translator **3** 440-441

CHAPMAN, JOHN (Johnny Appleseed; c. 1775-1847), American horticulturist and missionary **21** 77-78

CHAPMAN, SYDNEY (1888-1970), English geophysicist **3** 441

CHARCOT, JEAN MARTIN (1825-1893), French psychiatrist **3** 442

CHARDIN, JEAN BAPTISTE SIMÉON (1699-1779), French painter **3** 442-443

CHARGAFF, ERWIN (born 1905), American biochemist who worked with DNA **3** 444-445

CHARLEMAGNE (742-814), king of the Franks, 768-814, and emperor of the West, 800-814 **3** 445-447

CHARLES (born 1948), Prince of Wales and heir apparent to the British throne **3** 448-450

CHARLES I (1600-1649), king of England 1625-1649 **3** 450-452

CHARLES II (1630-1685), king of England, Scotland, and Ireland 1660-1685 **3** 452-454

CHARLES II (1661-1700), king of Spain 1665-1700 **3** 454

CHARLES III (1716-1788), king of Spain 1759-1788 **3** 454-455

CHARLES IV (1316-1378), Holy Roman emperor 1346-1378 **3** 455-456

CHARLES IV (1748-1819), king of Spain 1788-1808 **3** 456-457

CHARLES V (1337-1380), king of France 1364-1380 **3** 459-460

CHARLES V (1500-1558), Holy Roman emperor 1519-1556 **3** 457-459

CHARLES VI (1368-1422), king of France 1380-1422 **3** 460-461

CHARLES VII (1403-1461), king of France 1422-1461 **3** 461-462

CHARLES VIII (1470-1498), king of France 1483-1498 **3** 462-463

CHARLES X (1757-1836), king of France 1824-1830 **3** 463-464

CHARLES XII (1682-1718), king of Sweden 1697-1718 **3** 464-466

CHARLES XIV JOHN (1763-1844), king of Sweden 1818-1844 **2** 205-206

CHARLES, RAY (Robinson; born 1932), American jazz musician—singer, pianist, and composer **3** 469-470

CHARLES ALBERT (1798-1849), king of Sardinia 1831-1849 **3** 466

CHARLES EDWARD LOUIS PHILIP CASIMIR STUART (1720-1788), Scottish claimant to English and Scottish thrones **3** 466-467

CHARLES THE BOLD (1433-1477), duke of Burgundy 1467-1477 **3** 467-469

CHARNISAY, CHARLES DE MENOU (Seigneur d'Aulnay; circa 1604-1650), French governor of Acadia **3** 470-471

CHARONTON, ENGUERRAND (circa 1410/15-after 1466), French painter **3** 471

CHARPENTIER, MARC ANTOINE (1634-1704), French composer **3** 471-472

CHARRON, PIERRE (1541-1603), French philosopher and theologian **3** 472

CHASE, PHILANDER (1775-1852), American Episcopalian bishop and missionary **3** 472-473

CHASE, SALMON PORTLAND (1808-1873), American statesman and jurist **3** 473-475

CHASE, SAMUEL (1741-1811), American politician and jurist **3** 475-476

CHASE, WILLIAM MERRITT (1849-1916), American painter **3** 476-477

CHATEAUBRIAND, VICOMTE DE (1768-1848), French author **3** 477-479

CHATELET, GABRIELLE-EMILIE MARQUISE DU (1706-1749), French physicist and chemist **22** 102-103

CHATICHAI CHOONHAVAN (1922-1998), prime minister of Thailand (1988-1990) **3** 479-480

CHATTERJI, BANKIMCHANDRA (1838-1894), Bengali novelist **3** 480-481

CHATTERTON, THOMAS (1752-1770), English poet **3** 481-482

CHAUCER, GEOFFREY (circa 1345-1400), English poet **3** 482-485

CHAUNCY, CHARLES (1705-1787), American Calvinist clergyman and theologian **3** 485-486

CHÁVEZ, CARLOS (1899-1978), Mexican conductor and composer **3** 486

CHAVEZ, CESAR (1927-1993), American labor leader **3** 486-487

CHÁVEZ, DENNIS (1888-1962), Hispanic American politician **3** 488-489

CHAVEZ, LINDA (born 1947), Hispanic American civil rights activists **3** 489-491

CHAVIS, BENJAMIN (born 1948), African American religious leader, civil

CRUMB, GEORGE (born 1929), American composer and teacher **4** 326-328

CRUZ, OSWALDO GONÇALVES (1872-1917), Brazilian microbiologist and epidemiologist **4** 328-329

CUAUHTEMOC (circa 1496-1525), Aztec ruler **4** 329

CUBBERLEY, ELLWOOD PATTERSON (1868-1941), American educator and university dean **4** 329-331

CUDWORTH, RALPH (1617-1688), English philosopher and theologian **4** 331

CUFFE, PAUL (1759-1817), African American ship captain and merchant **4** 331-332

CUGOANO, OTTOBAH (circa 1757-after 1803), African abolitionist in England **4** 332-333

CUKOR, GEORGE (1899-1983), American film director **19** 82-84

CULLEN, COUNTEE (1903-1946), African American poet **4** 333-334

CULLEN, MAURICE GALBRAITH (1866-1934), Canadian painter **4** 334

CULLEN, PAUL (1803-1879), Irish cardinal **20** 100-103

Cultural evolution
see Evolution, cultural

CUMMINGS, EDWARD ESTLIN (1894-1962), American poet **4** 334-336

CUNHA, EUCLIDES RODRIGUES PIMENTA DA (1866-1909), Brazilian writer **4** 336-337

CUNNINGHAM, GLENN (1909-1988), American track and field athlete **21** 96-99

CUNNINGHAM, IMOGEN (1883-1976), American photographer **19** 84-86

CUNNINGHAM, MERCE (born 1919), American dancer and choreographer **4** 337-338

CUOMO, MARIO MATTHEW (born 1932), Democratic New York state governor **4** 338-339

CURIE, ÈVE (Eve Curie Labouisse; born 1904), French musician, author and diplomat **18** 109-111

CURIE, MARIE SKLODOWSKA (1867-1934), Polish-born French physicist **4** 339-341

CURIE, PIERRE (1859-1906), French physicist **4** 341-344

CURLEY, JAMES MICHAEL (1874-1958), American politician **4** 344-345

CURRIE, SIR ARTHUR WILLIAM (1875-1933), Canadian general **4** 345

CURRIER AND IVES (1857-1907), American lithographic firm **4** 345-346

CURRY, JABEZ LAMAR MONROE (1815-1903), American politician **4** 346-347

CURTIN, ANDREW GREGG (1815-1894), American politician **4** 347-348

CURTIN, JOHN JOSEPH (1885-1945), Australian statesman, prime minister **4** 348-349

CURTIS, BENJAMIN ROBBINS (1809-1874), American jurist, United States Supreme Court justice **4** 349

CURTIS, CHARLES BRENT (1860-1936), American vice president (1929-1932) and legislator **21** 99-100

CURTIS, GEORGE WILLIAM (1824-1892), American writer and reformer **4** 349-350

CURTISS, GLENN HAMMOND (1878-1930), American aviation pioneer **4** 350-351

CURZON, GEORGE NATHANIEL (1st Marquess Curzon of Kedleston; 1859-1925), English statesman **4** 351-352

CUSA, NICHOLAS OF (1401-1464), German prelate and humanist **4** 352-353

CUSHING, HARVEY WILLIAMS (1869-1939), American neurosurgeon **4** 353-354

CUSHMAN, CHARLOTTE (1816-1876), American actress **4** 354-355

CUSTER, GEORGE ARMSTRONG (1839-1876), American general **4** 355-356

CUTLER, MANASSEH (1742-1823), American clergyman, scientist, and politician **4** 356-357

CUVIER, BARON GEORGES LÉOPOLD (1769-1832), French zoologist and biologist **4** 357-359

CUVILLIÉS, FRANÇOIS (1695-1768), Flemish architect and designer **4** 359-360

CUYP, AELBERT (1620-1691), Dutch painter **4** 360-361

CYNEWULF (8th or 9th century), Anglo-Saxon poet **20** 103-104

CYPRIANUS, THASCIUS CAECILIANUS (died 258), Roman bishop of Carthage **4** 361-362

CYRIL (OF ALEXANDRIA), ST. (died 444), Egyptian bishop, Doctor of the Church **4** 362

CYRIL, ST. (827-869), Apostle to the Slavs **4** 362

CYRUS THE GREAT (ruled 550-530 B.C.), founder of the Persian Empire **4** 363-364

D

DA PONTE, LORENZO (Emanuele Conegliano; 1749-1838), Italian librettist and poet **20** 105-106

DAGUERRE, LOUIS JACQUES MANDÉ (1787-1851), French painter and stage designer **4** 365-366

DAHL, ROALD (1916-1990), Welsh-born English author **4** 366-367

DAIGO II (1288-1339), Japanese emperor **4** 367-368

DAIMLER, GOTTLIEB (1834-1900), German mechanical engineer **4** 368

DALADIER, ÉDOUARD (1884-1970), French statesman **4** 369

DALAI LAMA (Lhamo Thondup; born 1935), 14th in a line of Buddhist spiritual and temporal leaders of Tibet **4** 369-371

DALE, SIR HENRY HALLETT (1875-1968), English pharmacologist and neurophysiologist **4** 371-373

DALEY, RICHARD J. (1902-1976), Democratic mayor of Chicago (1955-1976) **4** 373-375

DALHOUSIE, 1ST MARQUESS OF (James Andrew Broun Ramsay; 1812-1860), British statesman **4** 375-376

DALI, SALVADOR (1904-1989), Spanish painter **4** 376-377

DALLAPICCOLA, LUIGI (1904-1975), Italian composer **4** 377-378

DALTON, JOHN (1766-1844), English chemist **4** 378-379

DALY, MARCUS (1841-1900), American miner and politician **4** 379-380

DALY, MARY (born 1928), American feminist theoretician and philosopher **4** 380-381

DALZEL, ARCHIBALD (or Dalziel; 1740-1811), Scottish slave trader **4** 381-382

DAM, CARL PETER HENRIK (1895-1976), Danish biochemist **4** 382-383

DAMIEN, FATHER (1840-1889), Belgian missionary **4** 383

DAMPIER, WILLIAM (1652-1715), English privateer, author, and explorer **4** 384

DOBELL, SIR WILLIAM (1899-1970), Australian artist **5** 34-35

DOBZHANSKY, THEODOSIUS (1900-1975), Russian-American biologist who studied natural selection **5** 35-37

Dr. Strange Love (film)
Scott, George Campbell**22** 391-393

DOCTOROW, EDGAR LAURENCE (born 1931), American author **19** 89-91

Doctors of the Church
see Religious leaders, Christian—Doctors

DODGE, GRACE HOADLEY (1856-1914), American feminist, philanthropist, and social worker **5** 37-38

DODGE, GRENVILLE MELLEN (1831-1916), American army officer and civil engineer **22** 142-145

DODGE, JOHN FRANCIS (1864-1920) AND HORACE ELGIN (1868-1920), American automobile manufacturers **18** 121-123

DOE, SAMUEL KANYON (1951-1990), Liberian statesman **5** 38-39

DOENITZ, KARL (1891-1980), German naval officer **20** 116-117

DOI TAKAKO (born 1928), chairperson of the Japan Socialist party **5** 39-41

DOLE, ELIZABETH HANFORD (born 1936), American lawyer, politician, and first female United States secretary of transportation **5** 41-43

DOLE, ROBERT J. (born 1923), Republican Senator **5** 43-46

DOLE, SANFORD BALLARD (1844-1926), American statesman **5** 46

DOLLFUSS, ENGELBERT (1892-1934), Austrian statesman **5** 47

DÖLLINGER, JOSEF IGNAZ VON (1799-1890), German historian and theologian **5** 47-48

DOMAGK, GERHARD JOHANNES PAUL (1895-1964), German bacteriologist **5** 48-50

DOMINGO, PLACIDO (born 1941), Spanish-born lyric-dramatic tenor **5** 50-51
Carreras, Jose Maria **22** 91-93

DOMINIC, ST. (circa 1170-1221), Spanish Dominican founder **5** 51-52

DOMINO, FATS (Antoine Domino, Jr.; born 1928), African American singer, pianist, and composer **22** 145-147

DOMITIAN (Titus Flavius Domitianus Augustus; 51-96), Roman emperor 81-96 **5** 52-53

DONATELLO (Donato di Niccolò Bardi; 1386-1466), Italian sculptor **5** 55-56

DONATUS (died circa 355), schismatic bishop of Carthage **5** 56-57

DONG, PHAM VAN (born 1906), premier first of the Democratic Republic of Vietnam (DRV) and after 1976 of the Socialist Republic of Vietnam (SRV) **5** 57-59

DONIZETTI, GAETANA (1797-1848), Italian opera composer **5** 59-60

DONLEAVY, JAMES PATRICK (born 1926), Irish author and playwright **19** 91-93

DONNE, JOHN (1572-1631), English metaphysical poet **5** 60-61

DONNELLY, IGNATIUS (1831-1901), American politician and author **5** 62

DONNER, GEORG RAPHAEL (1693-1741), Austrian sculptor **5** 63

DONOSO, JOSÉ (1924-1996), Chilean writer **5** 63-65

DONOVAN, WILLIAM JOSEPH (1883-1959), American lawyer and public servant **22** 147-149

DOOLITTLE, HILDA (1886-1961), American poet and novelist **5** 65-66

DOOLITTLE, JAMES HAROLD (1896-1993), American transcontinental pilot **5** 66-68

DORIA, ANDREA (1466-1560), Italian admiral and politician **18** 123-125

DORR, RHETA CHILDE (1868-1948), American journalist **5** 68-69

DORSEY, JIMMY (James Dorsey; 1904-1957), American musician and bandleader **19** 93-95

DORSEY, THOMAS ANDREW (1900-1993), African American gospel singer and composer **22** 149-151

DOS PASSOS, RODERIGO (1896-1970), American novelist **5** 69-71

DOS SANTOS, JOSÉ EDUARDO (born 1942), leader of the Popular Movement for the Liberation of Angola and president of Angola **5** 71-72

DOS SANTOS, MARCELINO (born 1929), Mozambican nationalist insurgent, statesman, and intellectual **5** 72-74

DOSTOEVSKY, FYODOR (1821-1881), Russian novelist **5** 74-77

DOUGLAS, DONALD WILLS (1892-1981), American aeronautical engineer **5** 77

DOUGLAS, GAVIN (circa 1475-1522), Scottish poet, prelate, and courtier **5** 77-78

DOUGLAS, SIR JAMES (1286?-1330), Scottish patriot **5** 80-82

DOUGLAS, MARY TEW (born 1921), British anthropologist and social thinker **5** 79-80

DOUGLAS, STEPHEN ARNOLD (1813-1861), American politician **5** 80-82

DOUGLAS, THOMAS CLEMENT (1904-1986), Canadian clergyman and politician, premier of Saskatchewan (1944-1961), and member of Parliament (1962-1979) **5** 82-83

DOUGLAS, WILLIAM ORVILLE (1898-1980), American jurist **5** 83-85

DOUGLAS-HOME, ALEC (Alexander Frederick Home; 1903-1995), Scottish politician **20** 117-119

DOUGLASS, FREDERICK (circa 1817-1895), African American leader and abolitionist **5** 85-86

DOUHET, GIULIO (1869-1930), Italian military leader **22** 151-152

DOVE, ARTHUR GARFIELD (1880-1946), American painter **5** 86-87

DOVE, RITA FRANCES (born 1952), United States poet laureate **5** 87-89

DOW, CHARLES (1851-1902), American journalist **19** 95-97

DOW, NEAL (1804-1897), American temperance reformer **5** 89-90

DOWLAND, JOHN (1562-1626), British composer and lutenist **5** 90

DOWNING, ANDREW JACKSON (1815-1852), American horticulturist and landscape architect **5** 90-91

DOYLE, SIR ARTHUR CONAN (1859-1930), British author **5** 91-92

Dracula; film (book)
Murnau, F.W. **22** 330-332

DRAGO, LUIS MARÍA (1859-1921), Argentine international jurist and diplomat **5** 92-93

DRAKE, DANIEL (1785-1852), American physician **5** 93-94

DRAKE, EDWIN (1819-1880), American oil well driller and speculator **21** 108-110

DRAKE, SIR FRANCIS (circa 1541-1596), English navigator **5** 94-96

DRAPER, JOHN WILLIAM (1811-1882), Anglo-American scientist and historian **5** 96-97

DRAYTON, MICHAEL (1563-1631), English poet **5** 97-98

DREISER, (HERMAN) THEODORE (1871-1945), American novelist **5** 98-100

DREW, CHARLES RICHARD (1904-1950), African American surgeon **5** 100-101

DREW, DANIEL (1797-1879), American stock manipulator **5** 101-102

DREXEL, KATHERINE (1858-1955), founded a Catholic order, the Sisters of the Blessed Sacrament **5** 102-103

DREXLER, KIM ERIC (born 1955), American scientist and author **20** 119-121

DREYER, CARL THEODOR (1889-1968), Danish film director **22** 152-155

DREYFUS, ALFRED (1859-1935), French army officer **5** 103-105

DRIESCH, HANS ADOLF EDUARD (1867-1941), German biologist and philosopher **5** 105

DRUCKER, PETER (born 1909), American author and business consultant **21** 110-112

DRUSUS, MARCUS LIVIUS (circa 124-91 B.C.), Roman statesman **5** 105-106

DRYDEN, JOHN (1631-1700), English poet, critic, and dramatist **5** 106-107

DRYSDALE, SIR GEORGE RUSSELL (1912-1981), Australian painter **5** 107-109

DUANE, WILLIAM (1760-1835), American journalist **5** 109

DUARTE, JOSÉ NAPOLEÓN (1926-1990), civilian reformer elected president of El Salvador in 1984 **5** 109-111

DUBČEK, ALEXANDER (1921-1992), Czechoslovak politician **5** 112-113

DUBE, JOHN LANGALIBALELE (1870-1949), South African writer and Zulu propagandist **5** 113

DU BELLAY, JOACHIM (circa 1522-1560), French poet **5** 113-114

DUBINSKY, DAVID (1892-1982), American trade union official **5** 114-115

DUBNOV, SIMON (1860-1941), Jewish historian, journalist, and political activist **5** 115-116

DU BOIS, WILLIAM EDWARD BURGHARDT (1868-1963), African American educator, pan-Africanist, and protest leader **5** 116-118

DU BOIS-REYMOND, EMIL (1818-1896), German physiologist **5** 118-119

DUBOS, RENÉ JULES (1901-1982), French-born American microbiologist **5** 119

DUBUFFET, JEAN PHILLIPE ARTHUR (born 1901), French painter **5** 119-120

DUCCIO DI BUONINSEGNA (1255/60-1318/19), Italian painter **5** 121-122

DUCHAMP, MARCEL (1887-1968), French painter **5** 122-123

DUCHAMP-VILLON, RAYMOND (1876-1918), French sculptor **5** 123

DUDLEY, BARBARA (born 1947), American director of Greenpeace **5** 123-124

DUDLEY, THOMAS (1576-1653), American colonial governor and Puritan leader **5** 124-125

Due process of law
see Constitution of the United States—14th Amendment

DUFAY, GUILLAUME (circa 1400-1474), Netherlandish composer **5** 125-126

DUFF, ALEXANDER (1806-1878), Scottish Presbyterian missionary **5** 126-127

DUGAN, ALAN (born 1923), American poet **5** 127-128

DUGDALE, RICHARD LOUIS (1841-1883), English-born American sociologist **5** 128-129

DUHEM, PIERRE MAURICE MARIE (1861-1916), French physicist, chemist, and historian of science **5** 129

DUKAKIS, MICHAEL (born 1933), American governor of Massachusetts **5** 130-133

DUKE, JAMES BUCHANAN (1856-1925), American industrialist and philanthropist **5** 133-134

DULL KNIFE (born Morning Star; c. 1810-1883), Northern Cheyenne tribal leader **5** 135-136

DULLES, JOHN FOSTER (1888-1959), American statesman and diplomat **5** 134-135

DUMAS, ALEXANDRE (1803-1870), French playwright and novelist **5** 136-138

DUMAS, JEAN BAPTISTE ANDRÉ (1800-1884), French Chemist **5** 138-139

DU MAURIER, DAPHNE (Lady Browning; 1907-1989), English author **18** 125-127

DUNANT, JEAN HENRI (1828-1910), Swiss philanthropist **5** 139-141

DUNBAR, PAUL LAURENCE (1872-1906), African American poet and novelist **5** 141-142

DUNBAR, WILLIAM (circa 1460-circa 1520), Scottish poet and courtier **5** 142-143

DUNBAR, WILLIAM (1749-1810), Scottish-born American scientist and planter **5** 143-144

DUNCAN, ISADORA (1878-1927), American dancer **5** 144-145

DUNHAM, KATHERINE (born 1910), African American dancer, choreographer, and anthropologist **5** 145-146

DUNMORE, 4TH EARL OF (John Murray; 1732-1809), British colonial governor **5** 147

DUNNE, FINLEY PETER (1867-1936), American journalist **5** 147-148

DUNNING, WILLIAM ARCHIBALD (1857-1922), American historian **5** 148-149

DUNS SCOTUS, JOHN (1265/66-1308), Scottish philosopher and theologian **5** 149-150

DUNSTABLE, JOHN (circa 1390-1453), English composer **5** 150-151

DUNSTAN, ST. (circa 909-988), English monk and archbishop **5** 151-152

DUNSTER, HENRY (circa 1609-1659), English-born American clergyman **5** 152-153

DUONG VAN MINH (born 1916), Vietnamese general and politician **18** 285-287

DUPLEIX, MARQUIS (Joseph François; 1697-1763), French colonial administrator **5** 153

DU PONT, ÉLEUTHÈRE IRÉNÉE (1771-1834), French-born American manufacturer **5** 154

DU PONT, PIERRE SAMUEL (1870-1954), American industrialist **5** 154-155

DU PONT DE NEMOURS, PIERRE SAMUEL (1739-1817), French political economist **5** 155-156

DURAND, ASHER BROWN (1796-1886), American painter and engraver **5** 156-157

DURANT, THOMAS CLARK (1820-1885), American railroad executive **5** 157-158

DURANT, WILLIAM CRAPO (1861-1947), American industrialist **5** 158

G

GADAMER, HANS-GEORG (born 1900), German philosopher, classicist, and interpretation theorist **6** 162-163

GADDAFI, MUAMMAR AL- (born 1942), head of the revolution that set up the Libyan Republic in 1969 **6** 163-165

GADSDEN, JAMES (1788-1858), American soldier and diplomat **6** 165-166

GAGARIN, YURI ALEXEIVICH (1934-1968), Russian cosmonaut **6** 166-167

GAGE, MATILDA JOSLYN (1826-1898), American reformer and suffragist **6** 167-169

GAGE, THOMAS (1719/20-1787), English general **6** 169-170

GAGNÉ, ROBERT MILLS (born 1916), American educator **6** 170

GAINSBOROUGH, THOMAS (1727-1788), English painter **6** 170-172

GAISERIC (died 477), king of the Vandals 428-477 **6** 172

GAITÁN, JORGE ELIÉCER (1898-1948), Colombian politician **6** 172-173

GAITSKELL, HUGH (1906-1963), British chancellor of the exchequer (1950-1951) and leader of the Labour Party (1955-1963) **6** 173-174

GALBRAITH, JOHN KENNETH (born 1908), economist and scholar of the American Institutionalist school **6** 174-177

GALDÓS, BENITO PÉREZ (1843-1920), Spanish novelist and dramatist **6** 177-178

GALEN (130-200), Greek physician **6** 178-180

GALILEO GALILEI (1564-1642), Italian astronomer and physicist **6** 180-183

GALLATIN, ALBERT (1761-1849), Swiss-born American statesman, banker, and diplomat **6** 183-184

GALLAUDET, THOMAS HOPKINS (1787-1851), American educator **6** 185

GALLEGOS FREIRE, RÓMULO (1884-1969), Venezuelan novelist, president 1948 **6** 185-186

GALLO, ROBERT CHARLES (born 1937), American virologist **22** 191-193

GALLOWAY, JOSEPH (circa 1731-1803), American politician **6** 186-187

GALLUP, GEORGE (1901-1984), pioneer in the field of public opinion polling and a proponent of educational reform **6** 187-189

GALSWORTHY, JOHN (1867-1933), English novelist and playwright **6** 189-190

GALT, SIR ALEXANDER TILLOCH (1817-1893), Canadian politician **6** 190-191

GALT, JOHN (1779-1839), Scottish novelist **18** 156-158

GALTIERI, LEOPOLDO FORTUNATO (born 1926), president of Argentina (1981-1982) **6** 191-193

GALTON, SIR FRANCIS (1822-1911), English scientist, biometrician, and explorer **6** 193-194

GALVANI, LUIGI (1737-1798), Italian physiologist **6** 194-195

GÁLVEZ, BERNARDO DE (1746-1786), Spanish colonial administrator **6** 195-196

GÁLVEZ, JOSÉ DE (1720-1787), Spanish statesman in Mexico **6** 196

GALWAY, JAMES (born 1939), Irish flutist **18** 158-160

GAMA, VASCO DA (circa 1460-1524), Portuguese navigator **6** 196-198

GAMBETTA, LÉON (1838-1882), French premier 1881-1882 **6** 198-199

Games, theory of (math) Nash, John Forbes, Jr. **22** 336-338

GAMOW, GEORGE (1904-1968), Russian-American nuclear physicist, astrophysicist, biologist, and author of books popularizing science **6** 199-200

GANDHI, INDIRA PRIYADARSHINI (1917-1984), Indian political leader **6** 200-201

GANDHI, MOHANDAS KARAMCHAND (1869-1948), Indian political and religious leader **6** 201-204

GANDHI, RAJIV (1944-1991), Indian member of Parliament and prime minister **6** 204-205

GARBO, GRETA (1905-1990), Swedish-born American film star **6** 205-207

GARCIA, CARLOS P. (1896-1971), Philippine statesman, president 1957-61 **6** 207-208

GARCIA, JERRY (Jerome John Garcia; 1942-1995), American musician **21** 150-152

GARCÍA MÁRQUEZ, GABRIEL (born 1928), Colombian author **6** 208-209

GARCÍA MORENO, GABRIEL (1821-1875), Ecuadorian politician, president 1861-1865 and 1869-1875 **6** 209-210

GARCILASO DE LA VEGA, INCA (1539-1616), Peruvian chronicler **6** 210-211

GARDINER, SAMUEL RAWSON (1829-1902), English historian **6** 211

GARDNER, ERLE STANLEY (1889-1970), American mystery writer **22** 193-195

GARDNER, ISABELLA STEWART (1840-1924), American art patron and socialite **21** 152-155

GARDNER, JOHN W. (born 1912), American educator, public official, and political reformer **6** 211-213

GARFIELD, JAMES ABRAM (1831-1881), American general, president 1881 **6** 213-214

GARIBALDI, GIUSEPPE (1807-1882), Italian patriot **6** 215-217

GARLAND, HANNIBAL HAMLIN (1860-1940), American author **6** 217-218

GARLAND, JUDY (1922-1969), super star of films, musicals, and concert stage **6** 218-219

GARNEAU, FRANÇOIS-XAVIER (1809-1866), French-Canadian historian **6** 219-220

GARNER, JOHN NANCE ("Cactus Jack" Garner; 1868-1967), American vice president (1933-1941) **21** 155-157

GARNIER, FRANCIS (Marie Joseph François Garnier; 1839-1873), French naval officer **6** 220-221

GARNIER, JEAN LOUIS CHARLES (1825-1898), French architect **6** 221-222

GARRETT, JOHN WORK (1820-1884), American railroad magnate **6** 225

GARRETT, THOMAS (1789-1871), American abolitionist **6** 225-226

GARRETT (ANDERSON), ELIZABETH (1836-1917), English physician and women's rights advocate **6** 222-225

GARRISON, WILLIAM LLOYD (1805-1879), American editor and abolitionist **6** 226-228

GARVEY, MARCUS MOSIAH (1887-1940), Jamaican leader and African nationalist **6** 228-229

GARY, ELBERT HENRY (1846-1927), American lawyer and industrialist **6** 229-230

GASCA, PEDRO DE LA (circa 1496-1567), Spanish priest and statesman **6** 230-231

GASKELL, ELIZABETH (1810-1865), English novelist **6** 231-232

GATES, WILLIAM HENRY, III ("Bill"; born 1955), computer software company co-founder and executive **6** 232-234

GOODMAN, ELLEN HOLTZ (born 1941), American journalist **6** 438-439

GOODNIGHT, CHARLES (1836-1926), American cattleman **6** 439

GOODPASTER, ANDREW JACKSON (born 1915), American Army officer active in organizing NATO forces in Europe and adviser to three presidents **6** 439-441

GOODYEAR, CHARLES (1800-1860), American inventor **6** 441

GORBACHEV, MIKHAIL SERGEEVICH (born 1931), former president of the Union of Soviet Socialist Republics. **6** 441-444

GORBACHEV, RAISA MAXIMOVNA (née Titorenko; 1932-1999), first lady of the Soviet Union **6** 444-446

GORDEEVA, EKATERINA (born 1971), Russian ice skater and author **18** 164-166

GORDIMER, NADINE (born 1923), South African author of short stories and novels **6** 446-447

GORDON, AARON DAVID (1856-1922), Russian-born Palestinian Zionist **6** 447-448

GORDON, CHARLES GEORGE (1833-1885), English soldier and adventurer **6** 448-449

GORDON, JOHN BROWN (1832-1904), American businessman and politician **6** 449-450

GORDON, PAMELA (born 1955), Bermudan politician **18** 166-167

GORDY, BERRY, JR. (born 1929), founder of the Motown Sound **6** 450-451

GORE, ALBERT, JR. (born 1948), Democratic U.S. representative, senator, and 45th vice president of the United States **6** 452-453

GORGAS, JOSIAH (1818-1883), American soldier and educator **6** 453-454

GORGAS, WILLIAM CRAWFORD (1854-1920), American general and sanitarian **6** 454-455

GORGES, SIR FERDINANDO (1568-1647), English colonizer and soldier **6** 455-456

GORGIAS (circa 480-circa 376 B.C.), Greek sophist philosopher and rhetorician **6** 456

GÖRING, HERMANN WILHELM (1893-1946), German politician and air force commander **6** 457-458

GORKY, ARSHILE (1905-1948), American painter **6** 458

GORKY, MAXIM (1868-1936), Russian author **6** 458-460

GORRIE, JOHN (1803-1855), American physician and inventor **21** 172-174

GORTON, SAMUELL (circa 1592-1677), English colonizer **6** 460

GOSHIRAKAWA (1127-1192), Japanese emperor **6** 460-461

GOSHO, HEINOSUKE (1902-1981), Japanese filmmaker **22** 199-200

Gospels
see Bible—New Testament

GOTTFRIED VON STRASSBURG (circa 1165-circa 1215), German poet and romancer **6** 461-462

GOTTLIEB, ADOLPH (1903-1974), American Abstract Expressionist painter **6** 462-463

GOTTSCHALK, LOUIS MOREAU (1829-1869), American composer **6** 463-464

GOTTWALD, KLEMENT (1896-1953), first Communist president of Czechoslovakia (1948-1953) **6** 464-466

GOUDIMEL, CLAUDE (circa 1514-1572), French composer **6** 466

GOUJON, JEAN (circa 1510-1568), French sculptor **6** 466-467

GOULART, JOÃO (1918-1976), Brazilian statesman **6** 467-469

GOULD, GLENN (1932-1982), Canadian musician **6** 469-470

GOULD, JAY (1836-1892), American financier and railroad builder **6** 470-472

GOULD, STEPHEN JAY (born 1941), American paleontologist **6** 472-473

GOUNOD, CHARLES FRANÇOIS (1818-1893), French composer **6** 473-474

GOURLAY, ROBERT (1778-1863), British reformer in Canada **6** 474

GOURMONT, REMY DE (1858-1915), French author, critic, and essayist **6** 475

GOWER, JOHN (circa 1330-1408), English poet **6** 475-476

GOYA Y LUCIENTES, FRANCISCO DE PAULA JOSÉ DE (1746-1828), Spanish painter and printmaker **6** 476-478

GOYEN, JAN VAN (1596-1656), Dutch painter **6** 478-479

GRACCHUS, GAIUS SEMPRONIUS (ca. 154-121 B.C.) member of a Roman plebeian family referred to as the Gracchi; flourished 3rd-2nd century B.C. **6** 479-480

GRACCHUS, TIBERIUS SEMPRONIUS (ca. 163-133 B.C.) member of a Roman plebeian family referred to as the Gracchi; flourished 3rd-2nd century B.C. **6** 479-480

GRACE, WILLIAM RUSSELL (1832-1904), Irish-born American entrepreneur and politician **6** 480-481

GRACIÁN Y MORALES, BALTASAR JERÓNIMO (1601-1658), Spanish writer **6** 481-482

GRADY, HENRY WOODFIN (1850-1889), American editor and orator **6** 482-483

GRAETZ, HEINRICH HIRSCH (1817-1891), German historian and biblical exegete **6** 483

GRAHAM, KATHARINE MEYER (1917-2001), publisher who managed *The Washington Post* **6** 483-485

GRAHAM, MARTHA (1894-1991), American dancer and choreographer **6** 485-486

GRAHAM, OTTO (born 1921), American football player and coach **21** 174-176

GRAHAM, SYLVESTER (1794-1851), American reformer and temperance minister **6** 486-487

GRAHAM, WILLIAM FRANKLIN, JR. ("Billy"; born 1918), American evangelist **6** 487-488

GRAMSCI, ANTONIO (1891-1937), Italian writer and Communist leader **6** 488-489

GRANADOS, ENRIQUE (1867-1916), Spanish composer and pianist **6** 489-490

Grand Illusion, la (film)
Renoir, Jean **22** 366-369

GRANGE, RED (Harold Edward Grange; 1903-1991), American football player **19** 128-130

GRANT, CARY (born Archibald Alexander Leach; 1904-1986), English actor **6** 490-492

GRANT, ULYSSES SIMPSON (1822-1885), American general, president 1869-1877 **6** 492-494
Cabinet
    Longstreet, James **22** 301-305

GRANVILLE, EVELYN BOYD (born 1924), African American mathematician **6** 494-496

GRASS, GÜNTER (born 1927), German novelist, playwright, and poet **6** 496-497

GROMYKO, ANDREI ANDREEVICH (1909-1988), minister of foreign affairs and president of the Union of Soviet Socialist Republic (1985-1988) **7** 9-11

GROOMS, RED (born 1937), American artist **7** 11-12

GROOTE, GERARD (1340-1384), Dutch evangelical preacher **7** 12-13

GROPIUS, WALTER (1883-1969), German-American architect, educator, and designer **7** 13-14

GROS, BARON (Antoine Jean Gros; 1771-1835), French romantic painter **7** 14-15

GROSS, SAMUEL DAVID (1805-1884), American surgeon, author, and educator **21** 183-185

GROSSETESTE, ROBERT (1175-1253), English bishop and statesman **7** 15

GROSSINGER, JENNIE (1892-1972), American hotel executive and philanthropist **7** 15-17

GROSZ, GEORGE (1893-1959), German-American painter and graphic artist **7** 17-18

GROTIUS, HUGO (1583-1645), Dutch jurist, statesman, and historian **7** 18-19

GROTOWSKI, JERZY (born 1933), founder of the experimental Laboratory Theatre in Wroclaw, Poland **7** 19-20

GROVE, ANDREW (András Gróf; born 1936), American businessman **18** 171-174

GROVE, FREDERICK PHILIP (circa 1871-1948), Canadian novelist and essayist **7** 20-21

GROVES, LESLIE (1896-1970), military director of the Manhattan Project (atom bomb) during World War II **7** 21-22

GRÜNEWALD, MATTHIAS (circa 1475-1528), German painter **7** 23-24

GUARDI, FRANCESCO (1712-1793), Italian painter **7** 24-25

GUARINI, GUARINO (1624-1683), Italian architect, priest, and philosopher **7** 25-26

GUCCIONE, BOB, JR. (born ca. 1956), American publisher **7** 26

GUDERIAN, HEINZ (1888-1953), German military leader **20** 163-165

GÜEMES, MARTÍN (1785-1821), Argentine independence fighter **7** 26-27

GUERCINO (Giovanni Francesco Barbieri; 1591-1666), Italian painter **7** 27

GUERICKE, OTTO VON (1602-1686), German physicist **7** 27-28

GUERIN, VERONICA (1959-1996), Irish investigative reporter and journalist **18** 174-176

GUERRERO, VICENTE (1783-1831), Mexican independence fighter, president 1829 **7** 28-30

GUEVARA, ERNESTO ("Che"; 1924-1967) Argentine revolutionary and guerrilla theoretician **7** 30-31

GUEYE, LAMINE (1891-1968), Senegalese statesman **7** 31

GUGGENHEIM, DANIEL (1856-1930), American industrialist and philanthropist **21** 185-187

GUGGENHEIM, MEYER (1828-1905), Swiss-born American industrialist **7** 31-32

GUICCIARDINI, FRANCESCO (1483-1540), Italian historian and statesman **7** 32-33

GUIDO D'AREZZO (circa 995-circa 1050), Italian music theorist **7** 33

GUILLAUME DE LORRIS (circa 1210-1237), French poet **7** 33-34

GUILLÉN, NICOLÁS (born 1902), Cuban author **7** 34-35

GUILLÉN Y ALVAREZ, JORGE (1893-1984), Spanish poet **7** 35-36

GUINIZZELLI, GUIDO (1230/40-1276), Italian poet **7** 36-37

GUINNESS, ALEC (born 1914), British actor of the stage, films, and television **7** 37-38

GÜIRÁLDEZ, RICARDO (1886-1927), Argentine poet and novelist **7** 38-39

GUISCARD, ROBERT (1016-1085), Norman adventurer **7** 39-40

GUISEWITE, CATHY (born 1950), American cartoonist and author **18** 176-177

GUIZOT, FRANÇOIS PIERRE GUILLAUME (1787-1874), French statesman and historian **7** 40-41

GUMPLOWICZ, LUDWIG (1838-1909), Polish-Austrian sociologist and political theorist **7** 41

GUNN, THOM (born 1929), English poet **18** 177-178

GÜNTHER, IGNAZ (1725-1775), German sculptor **7** 41-42

GUSTAVUS I (Gustavus Eriksson; 1496-1560), king of Sweden 1523-1560 **7** 42-43

GUSTAVUS II (Gustavus Adolphus; 1594-1632), king of Sweden 1611-1632 **7** 43-45

GUSTAVUS III (1746-1792), king of Sweden 1771-1792 **7** 45-46

GUSTON, PHILIP (1913-1980), American painter and a key member of the New York School **7** 47-48

GUTENBERG, JOHANN (circa 1398-1468), German inventor and printer **7** 48-49

GUTHRIE, EDWIN RAY (1886-1959), American psychologist **7** 49-50

GUTHRIE, TYRONE (1900-1971), English theater director **7** 50-51

GUTHRIE, WOODROW WILSON ("Woody"; 1912-1967), writer and performer of folk songs **7** 51-52

GUTIÉRRÉZ, GUSTAVO (born 1928), Peruvian who was the father of liberation theology **7** 52-53

GUY DE CHAULIAC (circa 1295-1368), French surgeon **7** 54

H

HABASH, GEORGE (born 1926), founder of the Arab Nationalists' Movement (1952) and of the Popular Front for the Liberation of Palestine (PFLP; 1967) **7** 55-56

HABER, FRITZ (1868-1934), German chemist **7** 56-58

HABERMAS, JÜRGEN (born 1929), German philosopher and sociologist **7** 58-60

HABIBIE, BACHARUDDIN JUSUF (born 1936), president of Indonesia **19** 134-136

HADRIAN (76-138), Roman emperor 117-138 **7** 60-61

HAECKEL, ERNST HEINRICH PHILIPP AUGUST (1834-1919), German biologist and natural philosopher **7** 61-62

HAFIZ, SHAMS AL-DIN (circa 1320-1390), Persian mystical poet and Koranic exegete **7** 63

HAGEN, UTA THYRA (born 1919), American actress **18** 179-180

HAGEN, WALTER (1892-1969), American golfer **21** 188-190

HAGUE, FRANK (1876-1956), American politician **7** 63-64

HAHN, OTTO (1879-1968), German chemist **7** 64-65

HAHNEMANN, SAMUEL (Christian Friedrich Samuel Hahnemann; 1755-1843), German physician and chemist **21** 190-193

HAIDAR ALI (1721/22-1782), Indian prince, ruler of Mysore 1759-1782 **7** 65-66

HAIG, ALEXANDER M., JR. (born 1924), American military leader, diplomat, secretary of state, and presidential adviser **7** 66-67

HAIG, DOUGLAS (1st Earl Haig; 1861-1928), British field marshal **7** 67-68

Haiku (haikai; literary form) Akutagawa, Ryunosuke **22** 13-14

HAILE SELASSIE (1892-1975), emperor of Ethiopia **7** 68-70

HAKLUYT, RICHARD (1552/53-1616), English geographer and author **7** 70

HALBERSTAM, DAVID (born 1934), American journalist, author and social historian **18** 180-183

HALDANE, JOHN BURDON SANDERSON (1892-1964), English biologist **7** 70-71

HALE, CLARA (nee Clara McBride; 1905-1992), American humanitarian and social reformer **20** 166-168

HALE, EDWARD EVERETT (1822-1909), American Unitarian minister and author **7** 71-72

HALE, GEORGE ELLERY (1868-1938), American astronomer **7** 72-74

HALE, SARAH JOSEPHA (née Buell; 1788-1879), American editor **7** 74-75

HALES, STEPHEN (1677-1761), English scientist and clergyman **7** 75

HALÉVY, ÉLIE (1870-1937), French philosopher and historian **7** 76

HALEY, ALEX (1921-1992), African American journalist and author **7** 76-78

HALEY, MARGARET A. (1861-1939), American educator and labor activist **7** 78-79

HALFFTER, CHRISTÓBAL (born 1930), Spanish composer **7** 79-80

HALIBURTON, THOMAS CHANDLER (1796-1865), Canadian judge and author **7** 80

HALIDE EDIP ADIVAR (1884-1964), Turkish woman writer, scholar, and public figure **7** 80-82

HALIFAX, 1ST EARL OF (Edward Frederick Lindley Wood; 1881-1959), English statesman **7** 82-83

HALL, ASAPH (1829-1907), American astronomer **7** 83-84

HALL, DONALD (born 1928), New England memoirist, short story writer, essayist, dramatist, critic, and anthologist as well as poet **7** 84-85

HALL, EDWARD MARSHALL (1858-1927), British attorney **22** 204-205

HALL, GRANVILLE STANLEY (1844-1924), American psychologist and educator **7** 85-86

HALL, RADCLYFFE (Marguerite Radclyffe Hall; 1880-1943), British author **20** 168-170

HALLAJ, AL-HUSAYN IBN MANSUR AL (857-922), Persian Moslem mystic and martyr **7** 86-87

HALLAM, LEWIS, SR. AND JR. (Lewis Sr. ca. 1705-55; Lewis Jr. 1740-1808), American actors and theatrical managers **7** 87

HALLECK, HENRY WAGER (1815-1872), American military strategist **22** 205-207

HALLER, ALBRECHT VON (1708-1777), Swiss physician **7** 87-88

HALLEY, EDMUND (1656-1742), English astronomer **7** 88-89

HALS, FRANS (1581/85-1666), Dutch painter **7** 89-91

HALSEY, WILLIAM FREDERICK (1882-1959), American admiral **7** 91-92

HALSTED, WILLIAM STEWART (1852-1922), American surgeon **22** 207-209

HAMANN, JOHANN GEORG (1730-1788), German philosopher **7** 92

HAMER, FANNIE LOU (born Townsend; 1917-1977), American civil rights activist **7** 93-94

HAMILCAR BARCA (circa 285-229/228 B.C.), Carthaginian general and statesman **7** 94-95

HAMILTON, ALEXANDER (1755-1804), American statesman **7** 95-98

HAMILTON, ALICE (1869-1970), American physician **7** 98-99

HAMILTON, EDITH (1867-1963), American educator and author **22** 209-211

HAMILTON, SIR WILLIAM ROWAN (1805-1865), Irish mathematical physicist **7** 99-100

HAMMARSKJÖLD, DAG (1905-1961), Swedish diplomat **7** 100-101

HAMM-BRÜCHER, HILDEGARD (born 1921), Free Democratic Party's candidate for the German presidency in 1994 **7** 101-103

HAMMER, ARMAND (1898-1990), American entrepreneur and art collector **7** 103-104

HAMMERSTEIN, OSCAR CLENDENNING II (1895-1960), lyricist and librettist of the American theater **7** 104-106

HAMMETT, (SAMUEL) DASHIELL (1894-1961), American author **7** 106-108

HAMMOND, JAMES HENRY (1807-1864), American statesman **7** 108-109

HAMMOND, JOHN LAWRENCE LE BRETON (1872-1952), English historian **7** 108-109

HAMMOND, LUCY BARBARA (1873-1961), English historian **7** 109

HAMMURABI (1792-1750 B.C.), king of Babylonia **7** 109-110

HAMPDEN, JOHN (1594-1643), English statesman **7** 110-111

HAMPTON, LIONEL (born 1908), African American jazz musician **22** 211-213

HAMPTON, WADE (circa 1751-1835), American planter **7** 111-112

HAMPTON, WADE III (1818-1902), American statesman and Confederate general **7** 112

HAMSUN, KNUT (1859-1952), Norwegian novelist **7** 113-114

HAN FEI TZU (circa 280-233 B.C.), Chinese statesman and philosopher **7** 124-125

HAN WU-TI (157-87 B.C.), Chinese emperor **7** 136

HAN YÜ (768-824), Chinese author **7** 136-137

HANAFI, HASSAN (born 1935), Egyptian philosopher **7** 114

HANCOCK, JOHN (1737-1793), American statesman **7** 114-116

HAND, BILLINGS LEARNED (1872-1961), American jurist **7** 116

HANDEL, GEORGE FREDERICK (1685-1759), German-born English composer and organist **7** 116-119

HANDKE, PETER (born 1942), Austrian playwright, novelist, screenwriter, essayist, and poet **7** 119-121

HANDLIN, OSCAR (born 1915), American historian **7** 121-122

HANDSOME LAKE (a.k.a. Hadawa' Ko; ca. 1735-1815), Seneca spiritual leader **7** 122-123

HECHT, BEN (1894-1964), American journalist, playwright, and Hollywood scriptwriter **7** 248-250

HECKER, ISAAC THOMAS (1819-1888), American Catholic religious founder **7** 250-251

HECKLER, MARGARET MARY O'SHAUGHNESSY (born 1931), American attorney, congressional representative, secretary of health and human services, and ambassador **7** 251-252

HEDIN, SVEN ANDERS (1865-1952), Swedish explorer and geographer **7** 252-253

HEFNER, HUGH (born 1926), founder and publisher of Playboy magazine **7** 253-254

HEGEL, GEORG WILHELM FRIEDRICH (1770-1831), German philosopher and educator **7** 254-256

HEIDEGGER, MARTIN (1889-1976), German philosopher **7** 257-258

HEIDENSTAM, CARL GUSTAF VERNER VON (1859-1940), Swedish author **7** 258-259

HEIFETZ, JASCHA (1901-1987), American violinist **20** 170-172

HEINE, HEINRICH (1797-1856), German poet and essayist **7** 259-260

HEINRICH, ANTHONY PHILIP (1781-1861), American composer **7** 261

HEINZ, HENRY JOHN (H.J. Heinz; 1844-1919), American businessman **19** 136-138

HEISENBERG, WERNER KARL (born 1901), German physicist **7** 261-263

Heliocentric theory (astronomy)
see Universe, systems of—heliocentric

HELLER, JOSEPH (1923-1999), American author **7** 263-265

HELLER, WALTER (1915-1987), chairman of the Council of Economic Advisors (1961-1964) and chief spokesman of the "New Economics" **7** 265-266

HELLMAN, LILLIAN FLORENCE (born 1905), American playwright **7** 267-268

HELMHOLTZ, HERMANN LUDWIG FERDINAND VON (1821-1894), German physicist and physiologist **7** 268-269

HELMONT, JAN BAPTISTA VAN (1579-1644), Flemish chemist and physician **7** 269-271

HELMS, JESSE (born 1921), United States Senator from North Carolina **7** 271-272

HELPER, HINTON ROWAN (1829-1909), American author and railroad promoter **7** 272-273

HELVÉTIUS, CLAUDE ADRIEN (1715-1771), French philosopher **7** 273-274

HEMINGWAY, ERNEST MILLER (1898-1961), American novelist and journalist **7** 274-277

HÉMON, LOUIS (1880-1913), French-Canadian novelist **7** 277

HEMPHILL, JOHN (1803-1862), American jurist and statesman **22** 234-236

HENDERSON, ARTHUR (1863-1935), British statesman **7** 277-278

HENDERSON, DONALD AINSLIE (D.A.; born 1928), American public health official **22** 236-238

HENDERSON, RICHARD (1735-1785), American jurist and land speculator **7** 278-279

HENDRIX, JIMI (born Johnny Allen Hendrix; 1942-1970), African american guitarist, singer, and composer **7** 279-283

HENG SAMRIN (born 1934), Cambodian Communist leader who became president of the People's Republic of Kampuchea (PRK) in 1979 **7** 283-285

HENIE, SONJA (1912-1969), Norwegian figure skater **20** 172-173

HENRI, ROBERT (Robert Henry Cozad; 1865-1929), American painter **22** 238-240

HENRY I (876-936), king of Germany 919-936 **7** 285-286

HENRY I (1068-1135), king of England 1100-1135 **7** 286-287

HENRY II (1133-1189), king of England 1154-1189 **7** 287-289

HENRY III (1017-1056), Holy Roman emperor and king of Germany 1039-1056 **7** 290

HENRY III (1207-1272), king of England 1216-1272 **7** 290-292

HENRY IV (1050-1106), Holy Roman emperor and king of Germany 1056-1106 **7** 292

HENRY IV (1367-1413), king of England 1399-1413 **7** 292-293

HENRY IV (1553-1610), king of France 1589-1610 **7** 293-295

HENRY V (1081-1125), Holy Roman emperor and king of Germany 1106-1125 **7** 295-296

HENRY V (1387-1422), king of England 1413-1422 **7** 296-297

HENRY VI (1421-1471), king of England 1422-61 and 1470-1471 **7** 298-299

HENRY VII (1274-1313), Holy Roman emperor and king of Germany 1308-1313 **7** 299-300

HENRY VII (1457-1509), king of England 1485-1509 **7** 300-302

HENRY VIII (1491-1547), king of England 1509-1547 **7** 302-305

HENRY, AARON (born 1922), African American civil rights activist **7** 306-307

HENRY, JOSEPH (1797-1878), American physicist and electrical experimenter **7** 307-308

HENRY, MARGUERITE (Margurite Breithaupt; 1902-1997), American author **19** 138-140

HENRY, O. (pseudonym of William Sydney Porter; 1862-1910), American short-story writer **7** 308-309

HENRY, PATRICK (1736-1799), American orator and revolutionary **7** 309-311

HENRY THE NAVIGATOR (1394-1460), Portuguese prince **7** 305-306

HENSON, JIM (James Maury Henson, 1936-1990), American puppeteer, screenwriter, and producer **19** 140-142

HENSON, JOSIAH (1789-1883), African American preacher and former slave **7** 311-312

HENSON, MATTHEW A. (1866-1955), African American Arctic explorer **7** 312-314

HENZE, HANS WERNER (born 1926), German composer **7** 314

HEPBURN, AUDREY (born Edda Van Heemstra Hepburn-Ruston; 1929-1993), Swiss actress and humanitarian **7** 314-316

HEPBURN, KATHARINE (born 1907), American actress on the stage and on the screen **7** 316-317

HEPPLEWHITE, GEORGE (died 1786), English furniture designer **7** 317-318

HEPWORTH, BARBARA (1903-1975), English sculptor **7** 318-319

HERACLIDES OF PONTUS (circa 388-310 B.C.), Greek philosopher **7** 319-320

HERACLITUS (flourished 500 B.C.), Greek philosopher **7** 320

HERACLIUS (circa 575-641), Byzantine emperor 610-641 **7** 320-321

HOWE, GEOFFREY (Richard Edward; born 1926), British foreign secretary 7 531-532

HOWE, GORDIE (born 1928), Canadian hockey player 7 532-534

HOWE, JOSEPH (1804-1873), Canadian journalist, reformer, and politician 7 534-535

HOWE, JULIA WARD (1819-1910), American author and reformer 7 535-536

HOWE, RICHARD (Earl Howe; 1726-1799), English admiral 7 536-537

HOWE, SAMUEL GRIDLEY (1801-1876), American physician and reformer 7 537

HOWE, WILLIAM (5th Viscount Howe; 1729-1814), British general 7 538-539

HOWELLS, WILLIAM DEAN (1837-1920), American writer 7 539-541

HOWELLS, WILLIAM WHITE (born 1908), American anthropologist 7 541-542

HOXHA, ENVER (1908-1985), leader of the Communist Party of Albania from its formation in 1941 until his death 8 1-3

HOYLE, EDMOND (1672-1769), English authority on card games 21 206-208

HOYLE, FRED (born 1915), English astronomer and author 18 200-202

HRDLIČKA, ALEŠ (1869-1943), American physical anthropologist 8 3-4

HSIA KUEI (flourished 1190-1225), Chinese painter 8 4-5

HSIEH LING-YÜN (385-433), duke of K'ang-lo, Chinese poet 8 5-6

HSÜAN TSANG (circa 602-664), Chinese Buddhist in India 8 6-7

HSÜAN-TSUNG, T'ANG (685-762), Chinese emperor 8 7-8

HSÜN-TZU (Hsün Ch'ing; circa 312-circa 235 B.C.), Chinese philosopher 8 8

HU SHIH (1891-1962), Chinese philosopher 8 63-65

HUANG CH'AO (died 884), Chinese rebel leader 8 8-9

HUANG TSUNG-HSI (1610-1695), Chinese scholar and philosopher 8 9-10

HUBBARD, L. RON (1911-1986), American author and founder of Scientology 18 202-204

HUBBLE, EDWIN POWELL (1889-1953), American astronomer 8 10-11
Sandage, Allan Rex 22 383-384

HUBLEY, JOHN (1914-1977), American animator and filmmaker 21 208-210

HUCH, RICARDA (1864-1947), German novelist, poet, and historian 8 11-12

HUDSON, HENRY (flourished 1607-1611), English navigator 8 12-13

HUERTA, DOLORES (born 1930), Hispanic American labor activist 18 204-207

HUERTA, VICTORIANO (1854-1916), Mexican general and politician 8 13-14

HUGGINS, SIR WILLIAM (1824-1910), English astronomer 8 14-15

HUGHES, CHARLES EVANS (1862-1948), American jurist and statesman 8 15-16

HUGHES, HOWARD ROBARD (1905-1976), flamboyant American entrepreneur 8 16-17

HUGHES, JOHN JOSEPH (1797-1864), Irish-American Catholic archbishop 8 17-18

HUGHES, LANGSTON (1902-1967), African American author 8 18-19

HUGHES, RICHARD (1900-1976), English author 19 158-160

HUGHES, TED (1930-1998), English poet laureate 8 19-21

HUGHES, WILLIAM MORRIS (1864-1952), Australian prime minister 1915-1923 8 21-22

HUGO, VICOMTE VICTOR MARIE (1802-1885), French author 8 22-25

HUI-TSUNG (1082-1135), Chinese emperor and artist 8 25

HUI-YÜAN (334-416), Chinese Buddhist monk 8 25-26

HUIZINGA, JOHAN (1872-1945), Dutch historian 8 26-27

HULAGU KHAN (Hüle'ü; circa 1216-1265), Mongol ruler in Persia 8 27-28

HULL, BOBBY (Robert Marvin Hull; born 1939), Canadian hockey player 20 181-183

HULL, CLARK LEONARD (1884-1952), American psychologist 8 28

HULL, CORDELL (1871-1955), American statesman 8 28-29

HULL, WILLIAM (1753-1825), American military commander 8 29-30

Human rights
activists for
Agaoglu, Adalet 22 11-13

HUMAYUN (1508-1556), Mogul emperor 1530-1556 20 183-185

HUMBOLDT, BARON FRIEDRICH HEINRICH ALEXANDER VON (1769-1859), German naturalist and explorer 8 30-31

HUMBOLDT, BARON WILHELM VON (1767-1835), German statesman and philologist 8 31

HUME, BASIL CARDINAL (George Haliburton Hume; 1923-1999), English clergyman and theologian 22 249-250

HUME, DAVID (1711-1776), Scottish philosopher 8 31-34

HUMPHREY, HUBERT HORATIO, JR. (1911-1978), mayor of Minneapolis, U.S. senator from Minnesota, and vice-president of the U.S. 8 34-36

HUN SEN (born 1951), Cambodian prime minister 8 39-42

HUNDERTWASSER, FRIEDENSREICH (Friedrich Stowasser; 1928-2000), Austrian-born visionary painter and spiritualist 8 36-37

HUNG HSIU-CH'ÜAN (1814-1864), Chinese religious leader, founder of Taiping sect 8 37-38

HUNG-WU (1328-1398), Chinese Ming emperor 1368-98 8 38-39

HUNT, H. L. (1889-1974), American entrepreneur 8 42-44

HUNT, RICHARD MORRIS (1827-1895), American architect 8 44

HUNT, WALTER (1796-1859), American inventor 21 210-212

HUNT, WILLIAM HOLMAN (1827-1910), English painter 8 44-45

HUNTER, FLOYD (born 1912), American social worker and administrator, community worker, professor, and author 8 45-46

HUNTER, MADELINE CHEEK (1916-1994), American educator 8 47-48

HUNTER, WILLIAM (1718-1783), Scottish anatomist 8 48-49

HUNTINGTON, COLLIS POTTER (1821-1900), American railroad builder 8 49

HUNTLEY AND BRINKLEY (1956-1970), American journalists and radio and television news team 8 49-51

HUNYADI, JOHN (1385-1456), Hungarian military leader, regent 1446-1452 8 51-52

HURD, DOUGLAS (born 1930), English Conservative Party politician and foreign secretary **8** 52-55

HURSTON, ZORA NEALE (1903-1960), African American folklorist and novelist **8** 55-56

HUS, JAN (a.k.a. John Hus; ca.1369-1415), Bohemian religious reformer **8** 56-59

HUSÁK, GUSTÁV (born 1913), president of the Czechoslovak Socialist Republic (1975-1987) **8** 59-61

HUSAYN, TAHA (1889-1973), Egyptian author, educator, and statesman **8** 61-62

HUSAYNI, AL-HAJJ AMIN AL- (1895-1974), Moslem scholar/leader and mufti of Jerusalem (1922-1948) **8** 62-63

HUSEIN IBN ALI (circa 1854-1931), Arab nationalist, king of Hejaz 1916-1924 **8** 63

HUSSEIN IBN TALAL (1935-1999), king of the Hashemite Kingdom of Jordan (1953-80s) **8** 65-67

HUSSEINI, FAISAL (1940-2001), Palestinian political leader **19** 160-162

HUSSERL, EDMUND (1859-1938), German philosopher **8** 67-68

HUSTON, JOHN MARCELLUS (1906-1987), American film director, scriptwriter, and actor **22** 250-252

HUTCHINS, ROBERT MAYNARD (1899-1977), American educator **8** 68-69
Adler, Mortimer Jerome **22** 9-11

HUTCHINSON, ANNE MARBURY (1591-1643), English-born American religious leader **8** 69-71

HUTCHINSON, THOMAS (1711-1780), American colonial governor **8** 71-72

HUTTEN, ULRICH VON (1488-1523), German humanist **8** 72-73

HUTTON, JAMES (1726-1797), Scottish geologist **8** 73-74

HUXLEY, ALDOUS LEONARD (1894-1963), English novelist and essayist **8** 74-75

HUXLEY, JULIAN (1887-1975), English biologist and author **8** 75-77

HUXLEY, THOMAS HENRY (1825-1895), English biologist **8** 77-79

HUYGENS, CHRISTIAAN (1629-1695), Dutch mathematician, astronomer, and physicist **8** 79-81

HUYSMANS, JORIS KARL (1848-1907), French novelist **8** 81-82

HYDE, DOUGLAS (1860-1949), Irish author, president 1938-45 **8** 82-83

HYDE, IDA HENRIETTA (1857-1945), American physiologist and educator **22** 252-254

HYMAN, LIBBIE HENRIETTA (1888-1969), American zoologist **8** 83-84

HYPATIA OF ALEXANDRIA (370-415), Greek mathematician and philosopher **8** 85

I

IACOCCA, LIDO (LEE) ANTHONY (born 1924), American automobile magnate **8** 86-88

IBÁÑEZ DEL CAMPO, CARLOS (1877-1960), Chilean general and president **8** 88

ÍBARRURI GÓMEZ, DOLORES (1895-1989), voice of the Republican cause in the Spanish Civil War **8** 88-90

IBERVILLE, SIEUR D' (Pierre le Moyne; 1661-1706), Canadian soldier, naval captain, and adventurer **8** 90-91

IBN AL-ARABI, MUHYI AL-DIN (1165-1240), Spanish-born Moslem poet, philosopher, and mystic **8** 91

IBN BATTUTA, MUHAMMAD (1304-1368/69), Moslem traveler and author **8** 91-92

IBN GABIROL, SOLOMON BEN JUDAH (circa 1021-circa 1058), Spanish Hebrew poet and philosopher **8** 92

IBN HAZM, ABU MUHAMMAD ALI (994-1064), Spanish-born Arab theologian and jurist **8** 93

IBN KHALDUN, ABD AL-RAHMAN IBN MUHAMMAD (1332-1406), Arab historian, philosopher, and statesman **8** 93-94

IBN SAUD, ABD AL-AZIZ (1880-1953), Arab politician, founder of Saudi Arabia **8** 94-95

IBN TASHUFIN, YUSUF (died 1106), North African Almoravid ruler **8** 95-96

IBN TUFAYL, ABU BAKR MUHAMMAD (circa 1110-1185), Spanish Moslem philosopher and physician **8** 96

IBN TUMART, MUHAMMAD (circa 1080-1130), North African Islamic theologian **8** 96-97

IBRAHIM PASHA (1789-1848), Turkish military and administrative leader **8** 97-98

IBSEN, HENRIK (1828-1906), Norwegian playwright **8** 98-100

ICKES, HAROLD LECLAIRE (1874-1952), American statesman **8** 100-101

ICTINUS (flourished 2nd half of 5th century B.C.), Greek architect **8** 101

IDRIS I (1889-1983), king of Libya 1950-69 **8** 102

IDRISI, MUHAMMAD IBN MUHAMMAD AL- (1100-1165?), Arab geographer **8** 102-103

IGLESIAS, ENRIQUE V. (born 1930), Uruguayan economist, banker, and public official **8** 106-107

IGNATIUS OF ANTIOCH, SAINT (died circa 115), Early Christian bishop and theologian **8** 107-108

IGNATIUS OF LOYOLA, SAINT (1491-1556), Spanish soldier, founder of Jesuits **8** 108-109

IKEDA, DAISAKU (born 1928), Japanese Buddhist writer and religious leader **8** 109-110

IKHNATON (ruled 1379-1362 B.C.), pharaoh of Egypt **8** 110-111

ILIESCU, ION (born 1930), president of Romania (1990-) **8** 111-112

ILITCH, MIKE (born 1929), American businessman **19** 163-165

ILLICH, IVAN (born 1926), theologian, educator, and social critic **8** 112-114

IMAI, TADASHI (1912-1991), Japanese film director **22** 255-257

IMAM, ALHADJI ABUBAKAR (1911-1981), Nigerian writer and teacher **8** 114-115

IMAOKA, SHINICHIRO (1881-1988), progressive and liberal religious leader in Japan **8** 115

IMHOTEP (ca. 3000 B.C. - ca. 2950 B.C.), Egyptian vizier, architect, priest, astronomer, and magician-physician **8** 116-117

In the Heat of the Night
O'Connor, Carroll **22** 343-345

INCE, THOMAS (1882-1924), American film producer and director **21** 213-215

India, Republic of (nation, southern Asia)
• Circa 1600-1947 (BRITISH)
  and Kashmir
    Abdullah, Mohammad **22** 7-9
  nationalism
    Bai, Lakshmi **22** 41-42
• SINCE 1947 (REPUBLIC)
  and Kashmir
    Abdullah, Mohammad **22** 7-9

Indian literature (Asia)
  drama and poetry
    Mukerji, Dhan Gopal **22** 328-330
  fiction

L

LIBBY, WILLARD FRANK (1908-1980), American chemist **9** 397-398

Liberation theology
Boff, Leonardo **22** 69-71

Libraries
medical
Billings, John Shaw **22** 57-60

Library of Congress (United States)
Hayden, Robert Earl **22** 229-231

LICHTENSTEIN, ROY (1923-1997), American painter, sculptor, and printmaker **9** 398-399

LIE, TRYGVE HALVDAN (1896-1968), Norwegian statesman and UN secretary general **9** 400-401

LIEBER, FRANCIS (circa 1798-1872), German American political scientist **9** 401-402

LIEBERMANN, MAX (1847-1935), German painter **9** 402-403

LIEBIG, BARON JUSTUS VON (1803-1873), German chemist **9** 403-404

LIGACHEV, YEGOR KUZ'MICH (born 1920), member of the Central Committee of the Communist Party of the Soviet Union (1966-1990) **9** 404-406

LIGETI, GYÖRGY (born 1923), Austrian composer **9** 406-407

LIGHTNER, CANDY (born 1946), American activist and founder of Mothers Against Drunk Driving **19** 201-203

LILBURNE, JOHN (1615-1657), English political activist and pamphleteer **9** 409-410

LILIENTHAL, DAVID ELI (1899-1981), American public administrator **9** 410-411

LILIENTHAL, OTTO (1848-1896), Prussian design engineer **21** 260-262

LILIUOKALANI, LYDIA KAMAKAEHA (1838-1917), queen of the Hawaiian Islands **9** 411-412

LIMBOURG BROTHERS (flourished circa 1399-1416), Netherlandish illuminators **9** 412-413

LIN, MAYA YING (born 1959), American architect **9** 413-415

LIN PIAO (1907-1971), Chinese Communist military and political leader **9** 429-430

LIN TSE-HSÜ (1785-1850), Chinese official **9** 431-432

LINCOLN, ABRAHAM (1809-1865), American statesman, president 1861-1865 **9** 415-418
advisers
Scott, Thomas Alexander **22** 393-395

LINCOLN, BENJAMIN (1733-1810), American military officer **9** 418-419

Lincoln Center (New York City)
Schuman, William Howard **22** 388-391

LIND, JAKOV (Heinz "Henry" Landwirth; born 1927), Austrian autobiographer, short-story writer, novelist, and playwright **9** 419-420

LINDBERGH, ANNE MORROW (born 1906), American author and aviator **9** 420-421

LINDBERGH, CHARLES AUGUSTUS (1902-1974), American aviator **9** 421-423

LINDSAY, JOHN VLIET (born 1921), U.S. congressman (1959-1965) and mayor of New York (1966-1973) **9** 423-424

LINDSAY, VACHEL (1879-1931), American folk poet **9** 424-425

LINDSEY, BENJAMIN BARR (1869-1943), American jurist and reformer **9** 425-426

Linguistics (science)
Deloria, Ella Clara **22** 136-138

LINH, NGUYEN VAN (1915-1998), secretary-general of the Vietnamese Communist Party (1986-1991) **9** 426-427

LINNAEUS, CARL (Carl von Linné; 1707-1778), Swedish naturalist **9** 427-429

LINTON, RALPH (1893-1953), American anthropologist **9** 431

LIPCHITZ, JACQUES (1891-1973), Lithuanian-born American sculptor **9** 432-433

LIPPI, FRA FILIPPO (circa 1406-1469), Italian painter **9** 439

LIPPMANN, WALTER (1889-1974), American journalist **9** 439-440

LIPPOLD, RICHARD (born 1915), American Constructivist sculptor **9** 440-442

LIST, GEORG FRIEDRICH (1789-1846), German economist **9** 443-444

LISTER, JOSEPH (1st Baron Lister of Lyme Regis; 1827-1912), English surgeon **9** 444-445

LISZT, FRANZ (1811-1886), Hungarian composer **9** 445-447

Literature for children
Canada
Richler, Mordecai **22** 371-373
India
Mukerji, Dhan Gopal **22** 328-330
United States
Cleary, Beverly **22** 110-112

Lithography (printing process)
Baskin, Leonard **22** 43-46

Little Big Man (film)
George, Dan **22** 196-198

LITTLE, ROYAL (born 1896), American textile tycoon **9** 449-451

LITTLE RICHARD (Richard Penniman; born 1932), American rock 'n' roll musician **9** 447-449

LITTLE WOLF (1818?-1904), Cheyenne chief **18** 255-257

LITVINOV, MAXIM MAXIMOVICH (1876-1951), Soviet diplomat **9** 451-452

LIU HSIEH (circa 465-522), Chinese literary critic **9** 452-453

LIU PANG (Han Kao-tsu or Liu Chi; 256 B.C.-195 B.C.), Chinese emperor **9** 453

LIU SHAO-CH'I (born 1900), Chinese Communist party leader **9** 453-455

LIU TSUNG-YÜAN (773-819), Chinese poet and prose writer **9** 455-456

LIUZZO, VIOLA (1925-1965), American civil rights activist **19** 203-205

LIVERPOOL, 2ND EARL OF (Robert Barks Jenkinson; 1770-1828), English statesman, prime minister 1812-1827 **9** 456-457

LIVIA (ca. 58 B.C. - 29 A.D.), Roman empress, wife of Augustus **9** 457-460

LIVINGSTON, EDWARD (1764-1836), American jurist and statesman **9** 460-461

LIVINGSTON, ROBERT (1654-1728), American colonial politician **9** 461-462

LIVINGSTON, ROBERT R. (1746-1813), American jurist and diplomat **9** 462-463

LIVINGSTONE, DAVID (1813-1873), Scottish missionary and explorer in Africa **9** 463-465

LIVY (Titus Livius; circa 64 B.C.-circa 12 A.D.), Roman historian **9** 465-467

LLERAS CAMARGO, ALBERTO (1906-1990), Colombian statesman, twice president **9** 467

LLEWELYN AP GRUFFYDD (died 1282), Prince of Wales **9** 468

MADERO, FRANCISCO INDALECIO (1873-1913), Mexican politician, president 1911-13 **10** 118-119

MADHVA (Vasudeva; Madhwa; Anande Tirtha; Purna Prajna; c. 1199-c. 1276), Indian theologian and philosopher **22** 308-309

MADISON, DOLLY (wife of James Madison, born Dorothea Payne; 1768-1849), American First Lady **10** 119-121

MADISON, JAMES (1751-1836), American statesman, president 1809-1817 **10** 121-123

MADONNA (Madonna Louise Veronica Ciccone, born 1958), American singer and actress **10** 123-125

MAETERLINCK, COUNT MAURICE (1863-1949), Belgian poet, dramatist, and essayist **10** 125-126

MAGELLAN, FERDINAND (1480-1521), Portuguese explorer **10** 126-127

MAGNASCO, ALESSANDRO (1667-1749), Italian painter **10** 127-128

MAGRITTE, RENÉ (1890-1967), Surrealist painter **10** 128-130

MAGSAYSAY, RAMON (1907-1957), Philippine statesman, president 1953-1957 **10** 130-131

MAHAL, HAZRAT (Iftikarun-nisa; 1820?-1879), Indian revolutionary **18** 271-273

MAHAN, ALFRED THAYER (1840-1914), American naval historian and strategist **10** 131-132

MAHARISHI MAHESH YOGI (born 1911?), Indian guru and founder of the Transcendental Meditation movement **10** 132-133

MAHATHIR MOHAMAD (born 1925), prime minister of Malaysia **10** 134-135

MAHDI, THE (Mohammed Ahmed; circa 1844-1885), Islamic reformer and Sudanese military leader **10** 137-138

MAHENDRA, KING (Bir Bikram Shah Dev; 1920-1972), ninth Shah dynasty ruler of Nepal (1955-1972) **10** 138-139

MAHERERO, SAMUEL (ca. 1854-1923), Supreme Chief of the Herero naion in southwest Africa **10** 139-142

MAHFUZ, NAJIB (born 1912), Egyptian novelist **10** 142-144

MAHLER, GUSTAV (1860-1911), Bohemian-born composer and conductor **10** 144-145

MAHMUD II (1785-1839), Ottoman sultan 1808-1839 **10** 145-147

MAHMUD OF GHAZNI (971-1030); Ghaznavid sultan in Afghanistan **10** 147

MAHONE, WILLIAM (1826-1895), American politician and Confederate general **10** 147-148

MAILER, NORMAN KINGSLEY (born 1923), American author, producer, and director **10** 148-150

MAILLOL, ARISTIDE (1861-1944), French sculptor **10** 150-151

MAIMONIDES (1135-1204), Jewish philosopher **10** 151-152

MAINE, SIR HENRY JAMES SUMNER (1822-1888), English legal historian and historical anthropologist **10** 152

MAISONEUVE, SIEUR DE (Paul de Chomedey; 1612-1676), French explorer and colonizer in Canada **10** 153

MAISTRE, JOSEPH DE (1753-1821), French political philosopher **10** 153-154

MAITLAND, FREDERIC WILLIAM (1850-1906), English historian, lawyer, and legal scholar **10** 154-155

MAJOR, JOHN (born 1943), British prime minister **10** 155-157

MAKARIOS III (Michael Christodoulou Mouskos; 1913-1977), archbishop and ethnarch of the Orthodox Church of Cyprus and first president of the Republic of Cyprus (1959-1977) **10** 157-158

MAKEBA, MIRIAM (Zensi Miriam Makeba; born 1932), South African singer and activist **22** 309-312

MAKEMIE, FRANCIS (1658-1708), Irish-born Presbyterian missionary **10** 158-159

MAKI, FUMIHIKO (born 1928), Japanese architect **10** 159-161

MAKIBI, KIBI-NO (693-775), Japanese courtier and statesman **10** 161

MÄKONNEN ENDALKAČÄW (1892-1963), Ethiopian writer and official **10** 161-162

MALAMUD, BERNARD (1914-1986), American novelist and short-story writer **10** 162-163

MALAN, DANIEL FRANCOIS (1874-1959), South African pastor, journalist, and prime minister 1948-1954 **10** 163-164

MALCOLM III (died 1093), king of Scotland 1058-1093 **10** 164-165

MALCOLM X (1925-1965), African American civil rights leader **10** 165-166

MALEBRANCHE, NICOLAS (1638-1715), French philosopher and theologian **10** 166-167

MALENKOV, GEORGY MAKSIMILIANOVICH (1902-1988), head of the Soviet government and leader of its Communist Party (1953) **10** 168

MALEVICH, KASIMIR (1878-1935), Russian painter **10** 168-169

MALHERBE, FRANÇOIS DE (1555-1628), French poet **10** 169-170

MALINOWSKI, KASPAR BRONISLAW (1884-1942), Austrian-born British social anthropologist **10** 170-171

MALIPIERO, GIAN FRANCESCO (1882-1973), Italian composer **10** 171

MALKAM KHAN, MIRZA (1831-1908), Persian diplomat **10** 172

MALLARMÉ, STÉPHANE (1842-1898), French poet **10** 172-173

MALLE, LOUIS (1932-1995), French film director and producer **18** 273-275

MALLON, MARY (Typhoid Mary; 1869-1938), Irish woman who unwittingly infected many with typhoid fever **21** 266-268

MALLORY, GEORGE (1886-1924), English mountain climber **21** 268-271

MALONE, DUMAS (1892-1986), American historian and editor **10** 174-175

MALORY, SIR THOMAS (flourished 15th century), English author **10** 175-176

MALPIGHI, MARCELLO (1628-1694), Italian anatomist **10** 176-178

MALRAUX, ANDRÉ (1901-1976), French novelist, essayist, and politician **10** 178-180

Maltese Falcon, The (film; book) Huston, John Marcellus **22** 250-252

MALTHUS, THOMAS ROBERT (1766-1834), English economist **10** 180-181

MAMET, DAVID ALAN (born 1947), American author **10** 181-182

MAMUN, ABDALLAH AL- (786-833), Abbasid caliph **10** 183

MANASSEH BEN ISRAEL (1604-1657), Dutch rabbi and theologian **10** 183-184

MANCINI, HENRY (Enrico Mancini; 1924-1994), American composer, pianist, and film music scorer **18** 275-276

MENZIES, WILLIAM CAMERON (1896-1957), American film director, producer, and set designer **21** 291-293

MERCATOR, GERHARDUS (1512-1594), Flemish cartographer **10** 511-512

MEREDITH, GEORGE (1828-1909), English novelist and poet **10** 512-513

MEREDITH, JAMES H. (born 1933), African American civil rights activist and politician **10** 514-515

MEREZHKOVSKY, DMITRY SERGEYEVICH (1865-1941), Russian writer and literary critic **10** 515-516

MERGENTHALER, OTTMAR (1854-1899), German-American inventor of the Linotype **10** 516-517

MERIAN, MARIA SIBYLLA (1647-1717), German artist and entomologist **20** 268-269

MERICI, ANGELA (St. Angela; 1474-1530), Italian nun and educator **21** 293-295

MÉRIMÉE, PROSPER (1803-1870), French author **10** 517

MERLEAU-PONTY, MAURICE (1908-1961), French philosopher **10** 518

MERMAN, ETHEL (Ethel Agnes Zimmermann; 1909-1984), American singer and actress **21** 295-297

MERRIAM, CHARLES EDWARD (1874-1953), American political scientist **10** 518-519

MERRILL, CHARLES E. (1885-1956), founder of the world's largest brokerage firm **10** 519-520

MERRILL, JAMES (1926-1995), American novelist, poet, and playwright **10** 521-522

MERTON, ROBERT K. (born 1910), American sociologist and educator **10** 522-523

MERTON, THOMAS (1915-1968), Roman Catholic writer, social critic, and spiritual guide **10** 523-525

MERULO, CLAUDIO (1533-1604), Italian composer, organist, and teacher **10** 525-526

MESMER, FRANZ ANTON (1734-1815), German physician **10** 526-527

MESSALI HADJ (1898-1974), founder of the Algerian nationalist movement **10** 527-528

MESSIAEN, OLIVIER (1908-1992), French composer and teacher **10** 528-529

MESSNER, REINHOLD (born 1944), Italian mountain climber and author **22** 316-318

METACOM (King Philip; 1640-1676), Wampanoag cheiftain **10** 529-531

METCALFE, CHARLES THEOPHILUS (1st Baron Metcalfe; 1785-1846), British colonial administrator **10** 531-532

METCHNIKOFF, ÉLIE (1845-1916), Russian physiologist and bacteriologist **10** 532-533

METHODIUS, SAINT (825-885), Greek missionary and bishop **4** 362-363

METTERNICH, KLEMENS VON (1773-1859), Austrian politician and diplomat **10** 533-536

MEYERBEER, GIACOMO (1791-1864), German composer **10** 536-537

MEYERHOF, OTTO FRITZ (1884-1951), German biochemist **10** 537-539

MEYERHOLD, VSEVOLOD EMILIEVICH (1874-1942?), Russian director **10** 539

MFUME, KWEISI (born Frizzell Gray; born 1948), African American civil rights activist and congressman **10** 539-542

MI FEI (1051-1107), Chinese painter, calligrapher, and critic **11** 12-13

MICAH (flourished 8th century B.C.), prophet of ancient Israel **10** 542-543

MICHAEL VIII (Palaeologus; 1224/25-1282), Byzantine emperor 1259-1282 **11** 1-2

MICHELANGELO BUONARROTI (1475-1564), Italian sculptor, painter, and architect **11** 2-5

MICHELET, JULES (1798-1874), French historian **11** 5-6

MICHELOZZO (circa 1396-1472), Italian architect and sculptor **11** 6-7

MICHELSON, ALBERT ABRAHAM (1852-1931), American physicist **11** 7-8

MICHENER, JAMES (1907-1997), American author **19** 245-247

Michigan (state; United States) Cooley, Thomas McIntyre **22** 116-119

Middle East
peace promoters
Abdul-Baha **22** 3-5
political division of after World War I
Bell, Gertrude **22** 54-55

MIDDLETON, THOMAS (1580-1627), English playwright **11** 8-9

MIDGELY, MARY BURTON (born 1919), British philosopher who focused on the
philosophy of human motivation and ethics **11** 9-10

MIES VAN DER ROHE, LUDWIG (1886-1969), German-born American architect **11** 10-12

Mihna
see Islam—Mihna

MIKAN, GEORGE (born 1924), American basketball player **21** 297-299

MIKULSKI, BARBARA (born 1936), United States senator from Maryland **11** 13-15

MILÁN, LUIS (circa 1500-after 1561), Spanish composer **11** 15-16

MILES, NELSON APPLETON (1839-1925), American general **11** 16-17

MILHAUD, DARIUS (born 1892), French composer and teacher **11** 17-18

Military leaders, American
• ARMY AND AIR FORCE
Army generals (18th century)
Lee, Charles **22** 294-297
Army generals (19th century; Confederate)
Breckinridge, John Cabell **22** 77-79
Longstreet, James **22** 301-305
Army generals (19th century; Union)
Dodge, Grenville Mellen **22** 142-145
Halleck, Henry Wager **22** 205-207

Military leaders, Aztec
Montezuma I **22** 322-324

Military leaders, British
• ARMY
colonels
Fuller, John Frederick Charles **22** 185-186
• NAVY
admirals
Fisher, John Arbuthnot **22** 171-173

Military leaders, Italian
Douhet, Giulio **22** 151-152

Military leaders, Pakistani
Musharraf, Pervez **22** 332-335

Military strategy
techniques
Douhet, Giulio **22** 151-152
Fisher, John Arbuthnot **22** 171-173
treatises
Halleck, Henry Wager **22** 205-207

MILIUKOV, PAVEL NIKOLAYEVICH (1859-1943), Russian historian and statesman **11** 18-19

MILK, HARVEY BERNARD (1930-1978), American politician and gay rights activist **11** 19-21

MILKEN, MICHAEL (born 1946), American businessman **19** 247-249

MILL, JAMES (1773-1836), Scottish philosopher and historian **11** 21

MILL, JOHN STUART (1806-1873), English philosopher and economist **11** 21-23
Hart, Herbert Lionel Adolphus **22** 218-219

MILLAIS, SIR JOHN EVERETT (1829-1896), English painter **11** 23-24

MILLAY, EDNA ST. VINCENT (1892-1950), American lyric poet **11** 24-25

MILLER, ARTHUR (born 1915), American playwright, novelist, and film writer **11** 25-26

MILLER, GLENN (Alton Glenn Miller; 1904-1944), American musician **19** 250-251

MILLER, HENRY (born 1891), American author **11** 26-27

MILLER, JOAQUIN (1837-1913), American writer **11** 27-28

MILLER, PERRY (1905-1963), American historian **11** 28-29

MILLER, SAMUEL FREEMAN (1816-1890), American jurist **11** 29-30

MILLER, WILLIAM (1782-1849), American clergyman **11** 30-31

MILLET, JEAN FRANÇOIS (1814-1875), French painter **11** 31

MILLET, KATE (born 1934), American feminist author and sculptor **11** 31

MILLIKAN, ROBERT ANDREWS (1868-1953), American physicist **11** 33-35

MILLS, BILLY (Makata Taka Hela; born 1938), Native American runner and businessman **19** 251-253

MILLS, C. WRIGHT (1916-1962), American sociologist and political polemicist **11** 35-36

MILLS, ROBERT (1781-1855), American architect **11** 36-37

MILNE, ALAN ALEXANDER (A.A. Milne; 1882-1956), British author **19** 253-254

MILNE, DAVID BROWN (1882-1953), Canadian painter and etcher **11** 37-38

MILNER, ALFRED (1st Viscount Milner; 1854-1925), British statesman **11** 38-39

MILOSEVIC, SLOBODAN (born 1941), president of Serbia **11** 39-40

MILOSZ, CZESLAW (born 1911), Nobel Prize winning Polish author and poet **11** 40-42

MILTIADES (circa 549-488 B.C.), Athenian military strategist and statesman **11** 42-43

MILTON, JOHN (1608-1674), English poet and controversialist **11** 43-46

MIN (1851-1895), Korean queen **11** 46-47

Mind of the South, The (book)
Cash, W. J. **22** 93-95

MINDON MIN (ruled 1852-1878), Burmese king **11** 47

MINDSZENTY, CARDINAL JÓZSEF (1892-1975), Roman Catholic primate of Hungary **11** 47-49

MINK, PATSY TAKEMOTO (born 1927), Asian American congresswoman **18** 287-289

MINTZ, BEATRICE (born 1921), American embryologist **11** 49-50

MINUIT, PETER (1580-1638), Dutch colonizer **11** 50

MIRABEAU, COMTE DE (Honoré Gabriel Victor de Riqueti; 1749-1791), French statesman and author **11** 51-52

MIRANDA, FRANCISCO DE (1750-1816), Latin American patriot **11** 52-53

MIRÓ, JOAN (1893-1983), Spanish painter **11** 53-54

MISHIMA, YUKIO (1925-1970), Japanese novelist and playwright **11** 54-55

Missouri Compromise (United States; 1820)
provisions
Pinkney, William **22** 355-357

MISTRAL, GABRIELA (1889-1957), Chilean poet and educator **11** 55-56

MITCHELL, BILLY (1879-1936), American military officer and aviator **20** 269-272

MITCHELL, EDGAR DEAN (born 1930), American astronaut **22** 318-320

MITCHELL, GEORGE JOHN (born 1933), Maine Democrat and majority leader in the United States Senate **11** 56-58

MITCHELL, JOHN (1870-1919), American labor leader **11** 58-59

MITCHELL, MARGARET (Munnerlyn; 1900-1949), American author of Gone With the Wind **11** 59-60

MITCHELL, MARIA (1818-1889), American astronomer and educator **11** 61

MITCHELL, WESLEY CLAIR (1874-1948), American economist **11** 61-62

MITRE, BARTOLOMÉ (1821-1906), Argentine historian and statesman, president 1862-1868 **11** 62-63

MITTERRAND, FRANÇOIS (born 1916), French politician and statesman and president (1981-1990) **11** 63-66

MIZRAHI, ISAAC (born 1961), American designer **11** 66-67

MLADIC, RATKO (born 1943), Bosnian Serb military leader **11** 68-69

MOBUTU SESE SEKO (Joseph Désiré Mobuto; 1930-1997), Congolese president **11** 69-71

MODEL, LISETTE (nee Lisette Seyberg; 1906?-1983), American photographer and educator **19** 254-256

MODERSOHN-BECKER, PAULA (1876-1907), German painter **11** 71-72

MODIGLIANI, AMEDEO (1884-1920), Italian painter and sculptor **11** 72-73

MOFFETT, WILLIAM ADGER (1869-1933), American naval officer **21** 299-301

MOFOLO, THOMAS (1876-1948), Lesothoan author **11** 74

MOGILA, PETER (1596/1597-1646), Russian Orthodox churchman and theologian **11** 74-75

Mogul empire
see India—1000-1600

MOHAMMAD REZA SHAH PAHLAVI (1919-1980), king of Iran **11** 75-76

MOHAMMED (circa 570-632), founder of Islam **11** 76-78

MOHAMMED V (Mohammed Ben Youssef; 1911-1961), king of Morocco **11** 79-81

MOHAMMED ALI (1769-1849), Ottoman pasha of Egypt 1805-1848 **11** 81-82

MOHOLY-NAGY, LÁSZLÓ (1895-1946), Hungarian painter and designer **11** 82-83

MOI, DANIFI ARAP (born Daniel Toroitich arap Moi; born 1924), president of Kenya **11** 83-86

Molecular biology
see Biology, molecular

MOLIÈRE (1622-1673), French dramatist **11** 86-88

MOLINARI, SUSAN K. (born 1958), American newscaster **18** 289-291

MOLINOS, MIGUEL DE (1628-1696), Spanish priest **11** 88-89

MOLOTOV, VYACHESLAV MIKHAILOVICH (1890-1986), Soviet statesman **11** 89-90

MOLTKE, COUNT HELMUTH KARL BERNARD VON (1800-1891), Prussian military leader **11** 90-91

PALACKÝ, FRANTIŠEK (1798-1876), Czech historian and statesman **12** 69-70

PALAMAS, KOSTES (1859-1943), Greek poet **12** 70

Paleontology (science)
evolution controversy
Edinger, Tilly **22** 163-164

PALESTRINA, GIOVANNI PIERLUIGI DA (circa 1525-94), Italian composer **12** 70-72

PALEY, GRACE (born 1922), American author and activist **22** 348-350

PALEY, WILLIAM (1743-1805), English theologian and moral philosopher **12** 72

PALEY, WILLIAM S. (1901-1990), founder and chairman of the Columbia Broadcasting System **12** 72-75

PALLADIO, ANDREA (1508-1580), Italian architect **12** 75-77

PALMA, RICARDO (1833-1919), Peruvian poet, essayist, and short-story writer **12** 77

PALMER, ALEXANDER MITCHELL (1872-1936), American politician and jurist **12** 77-78

PALMER, ARNOLD DANIEL (born 1929), American golfer **12** 78-80

PALMER, NATHANIEL BROWN (1799-1877), American sea captain **12** 80-81

PALMERSTON, 3D VISCOUNT (Henry John Temple; 1784-1865), English prime minister 1855-65 **12** 81-83

PAN KU (32-92), Chinese historian and man of letters **12** 86-87

PANDIT, VIJAYA LAKSHMI (1900-1990), Indian diplomat and politician **12** 83-84

PANETTA, LEON E. (born 1938), Democratic congressman from California and chief of staff to President Clinton **12** 84-85

PANKHURST, CHRISTABEL HARRIETTE (1880-1958), English reformer and suffragette **22** 350-352

PANKHURST, EMMELINE (1858-1928), English reformer **12** 85-86
Pankhurst, Christabel Harriette **22** 350-352

Pankhurst, Sylvia (1882-1960), English reformer
Pankhurst, Christabel Harriette **22** 350-352

PANNENBERG, WOLFHART (born 1928), German Protestant theologian **12** 87-88

PAPANDREOU, ANDREAS (1919-1996), Greek scholar and statesman and prime minister **12** 88-91

PAPINEAU, LOUIS-JOSEPH (1786-1871), French-Canadian radical political leader **12** 91

PARACELSUS, PHILIPPUS AUREOLUS (1493-1541), Swiss physician and alchemist **12** 91-93

PARBO, ARVI (born 1926), Australian industrial giant **12** 93-94

PARÉ, AMBROISE (1510-1590), French military surgeon **12** 94-95

PARETO, VILFREDO (1848-1923), Italian sociologist, political theorist, and economist **12** 95-96

Paris, School of (art)
see French art—School of Paris

PARIZEAU, JACQUES (born 1930), Canadian politician and premier of Quebec **12** 96-99

PARK, CHUNG HEE (1917-1979), Korean soldier and statesman **12** 99-102

PARK, MAUD WOOD (1871-1955), suffragist and first president of the League of Women Voters **12** 102

PARK, ROBERT E. (1864-1944), American sociologist **12** 102-104

PARK, WILLIAM HALLOCK (1863-1939), American physician **12** 104-105

PARKER, CHARLES CHRISTOPHER, JR. (Charlie Parker; 1920-55), American jazz musician **12** 105-106

PARKER, DOROTHY ROTHSCHILD (1893-1967), American writer **12** 106

PARKER, ELY SAMUEL (Ha-sa-no-an-da; 1828-1895), Native American tribal leader **12** 106-108

PARKER, HORATIO WILLIAM (1863-1919), American composer **12** 109

PARKER, QUANAH (c. 1845-1911), Native American religious leader **12** 109-112

PARKER, THEODORE (1810-1860), American Unitarian clergyman **12** 112-113

PARKES, ALEXANDER (1813-1890), British metallurgist and inventor of plastic **21** 334-336

PARKES, SIR HENRY (1815-1896), Australian statesman **12** 113

PARKMAN, FRANCIS (1823-1893), American historian **12** 113-115

PARKS, GORDON (born 1912), American photographer, composer, and filmmaker **19** 275-277

PARKS, ROSA LEE MCCAULEY (born 1913), American civil rights leader **12** 115-116

PARMENIDES (flourished 475 B.C.), Greek philosopher **12** 116-117

PARMIGIANINO (1503-1540), Italian painter **12** 117

PARNELL, CHARLES STEWART (1846-1891), Irish nationalist leader **12** 117-119

Parochial schools (United States)
see Education (United States)

PARRINGTON, VERNON LOUIS (1871-1929), American historian **12** 119-120

PARSONS, SIR CHARLES ALGERNON (1854-1931), British engineer **12** 120-121

PARSONS, FRANK (1854-1908), American educator and reformer **12** 121-122

PARSONS, LOUELLA (Louella Oetlinger; 1881-1972), American gossip columnist **21** 336-338

PARSONS, TALCOTT (1902-1979), American sociologist **12** 122

PASCAL, BLAISE (1623-1662), French scientist and philosopher **12** 122-124

PASHA, ENVER (1881-1922), Turkish soldier and Young Turk leader **5** 290-291

PASHA, TEWFIK (1852-1892), khedive of Egypt 1879-92 **15** 157-158

PASTERNAK, BORIS LEONIDOVICH (1890-1960), Russian poet, novelist, and translator **12** 124-125

PASTEUR, LOUIS (1822-1895), French chemist and biologist **12** 125-127

PATCHEN, KENNETH (1911-1972), American experimental poet and novelist **12** 128-129

PATEL, VALLABHBHAI (1875-1950), Indian political leader **12** 129-130

PATER, WALTER HORATIO (1839-1894), English author **12** 130-131

PATERSON, ANDREW BARTON (1864-1941), Australian folk poet **12** 131-132

PATERSON, WILLIAM (1745-1806), American jurist **12** 132-133

PATIÑO, SIMÓN ITURRI (1862-1947), Bolivian industrialist and entrepreneur **12** 133-134

PATON, ALAN STEWART (1903-1988), South African writer and liberal leader **12** 134-135

PATRICK, JENNIE R. (born 1949), African American chemical engineer **12** 136-137

PATRICK, RUTH (born 1907), American limnologist **12** 137-138

PATRICK, ST. (died circa 460), British missionary bishop to Ireland **12** 135-136

PATTEN, SIMON NELSON (1852-1922), American economist **12** 138-139

PATTERSON, FREDERICK DOUGLAS (1901-1988), African American educator **12** 139-140

Patton (film)
Scott, George Campbell**22** 391-393

PATTON, GEORGE SMITH, JR. (1885-1945), American Army officer **12** 140-141

PAUL I (1754-1801), Russian czar 1796-1801 **12** 143-144

PAUL III (Alessandro Farnese; 1468-1549), pope 1534-49 **12** 144-145

PAUL IV (Giampietro Carafa; 1476-1559), pope 1555-59 **12** 145-146

PAUL VI (Giovanni Battista Montini; 1897-1978), pope **12** 146-148

PAUL, ALICE (1885-1977), American feminist and women's rights activist **19** 277-280

PAUL, ST. (died 66/67), Christian theologian and Apostle **12** 141-143

PAULI, WOLFGANG ERNST (1900-1958), Austrian theoretical physicist **12** 149

PAULING, LINUS CARL (born 1901), American chemist **12** 150-152

PAVAROTTI, LUCIANO (born 1935), Italian tenor **12** 152-154
Carreras, Jose Maria **22** 91-93

PAVESE, CESARE (1908-1950), Italian novelist, poet, and critic **12** 154-155

PAVLOV, IVAN PETROVICH (1849-1936), Russian physiologist **12** 155-157

PAVLOVA, ANNA (1881-1931), Russian ballet dancer **12** 157-159

PAYNE, JOHN HOWARD (1791-1852), American actor, playwright, and songwriter **12** 159

PAYNE-GAPOSCHKIN, CECILIA (1900-1979), American astronomer **12** 159-161

PAYTON, WALTER (1954-1999), American football player **20** 294-296

PAZ, OCTAVIO (1914-1998), Mexican diplomat, critic, editor, translator, poet, and essayist **12** 161-162

PAZ ESTENSSORO, VICTOR (1907-2001), Bolivian statesman and reformer **12** 163-164

PAZ ZAMORA, JAIME (born 1939), president of Bolivia (1989-) **12** 165-167

PÁZMÁNY, PÉTER (1570-1637), Hungarian archbishop **12** 164-165

PEABODY, ELIZABETH PALMER (1804-1894), American educator and author **12** 167-168

PEABODY, GEORGE (1795-1869), American merchant, financier, and philanthropist **12** 168

PEACOCK, THOMAS LOVE (1785-1866), English novelist and satirist **12** 169

PEALE, CHARLES WILLSON (1741-1827), American painter and scientist **12** 169-171

PEALE, NORMAN VINCENT (1898-1993), American religious leader who blended psychotherapy and religion **12** 171-172

PEALE, REMBRANDT (1778-1860), American painter **12** 172-173

PEARSE, PATRICK HENRY (1879-1916), Irish poet, educator, and revolutionary **12** 173-174

PEARSON, LESTER BOWLES (1897-1972), Canadian statesman and diplomat, prime minister **12** 174-175

PEARY, ROBERT EDWIN (1856-1920), American explorer **12** 175-176

PECHSTEIN, HERMANN MAX (1881-1955), German Expressionist painter and graphic artist **12** 176-177

PECK, ROBERT NEWTON (born 1928), American author of children's literature **12** 177-178

PECKINPAH, SAM (1925-1984), American film director **21** 338-340

PEDRARIAS (Pedro Arias de Ávila; circa 1440-1531), Spanish conqueror and colonial governor **12** 179

PEDRO I (1798-1834), emperor of Brazil and king of Portugal **12** 179-180

PEDRO II (1825-1891), emperor of Brazil 1831-89 **12** 180-181

PEEL, SIR ROBERT (1788-1850), English statesman, prime minister 1834-35 and 1841-46 **12** 181-183

PÉGUY, CHARLES PIERRE (1873-1914), French poet **12** 183-184

PEI, I. M. (Ieoh Ming Pei; born 1917), Chinese-American architect **12** 184-187

PEIRCE, BENJAMIN (1809-1880), American mathematician **21** 340-342

PEIRCE, CHARLES SANDERS (1839-1914), American scientist and philosopher **12** 187-188

PEIXOTO, FLORIANO (1839-1895), Brazilian marshal, president 1891-94 **12** 188-189

PELAGIUS (died circa 430), British theologian **12** 189-190

PELE (Edson Arantes Do Nascimento Pele; born 1940), Brazilian soccer player **12** 190-191

PELLI, CESAR (born 1926), Hispanic American architect and educator **12** 191-192

PELTIER, LEONARD (born 1944), Native American activist **12** 193-195

PENDERECKI, KRZYSZTOF (born 1933), Polish composer **12** 195-197

PENDLETON, EDMUND (1721-1803), American political leader **12** 197-198

PENDLETON, GEORGE HUNT (1825-1889), American politician **12** 198

PENFIELD, WILDER GRAVES (1891-1976), Canadian neurosurgeon **12** 198-200

PENN, WILLIAM (1644-1718), English Quaker, founder of Pennsylvania **12** 200-202

PENNEY, J. C. (James Cash Penney; 1875-1971), American chain store executive and philanthropist **12** 202-203

PENNINGTON, MARY ENGLE (1872-1952), American chemist **22** 352-355

Pennsylvania Railroad (United States)
Scott, Thomas Alexander **22** 393-395

PENROSE, BOIES (1860-1921), American senator and political boss **12** 203-204

PENROSE, ROGER (born 1931), British mathematician and physicist **12** 204-205

PENSKE, ROGER (born 1937), American businessman and race car team owner **19** 280-282

Pentagon (building, United States)
bin Laden, Osama **22** 60-62

PEP, WILLIE (William Guiglermo Papaleo; born 1922), American boxer **21** 342-344

PEPPER, CLAUDE DENSON (1900-1989), Florida attorney, state

PHILIP II (Philip Augustus; 1165-1223), king of France 1180-1223 **12** 268-269

PHILIP II (1527-1598), king of Spain 1556-1598 **12** 271-273
court
Anguissola, Sofonisba **22** 22-24

PHILIP III (1578-1621), king of Spain 1598-1621 **12** 273-274

PHILIP IV (the Fair; 1268-1314), king of France 1285-1314 **12** 274

PHILIP IV (1605-1665), king of Spain 1621-65 **12** 275

PHILIP V (1683-1746), king of Spain 1700-46 **12** 276-277

PHILIP VI (1293-1350), king of France 1328-50 **12** 277-278

PHILIP THE GOOD (1396-1467), duke of Burgundy 1419-67 **12** 278-279

PHILLIP, ARTHUR (1738-1814), English governor of New South Wales **12** 279-280

PHILLIPS, DAVID GRAHAM (1867-1911), American journalist and novelist **12** 280-281

PHILLIPS, WENDELL (1811-1884), American abolitionist and social reformer **12** 281-282

Philosophers, American
20th century
Adler, Mortimer Jerome **22** 9-11

Philosophers, Indian (Asia)
Madhva **22** 308-309

Philosophers, Turkish
Al-Farabi **22** 14-16

Philosophy
and law
Hart, Herbert Lionel Adolphus **22** 218-219
and literature
Adler, Mortimer Jerome **22** 9-11
ethics
Austin, John **22** 33-35
theosophy
Blavatsky, Helena Petrovna **22** 67-69

PHIPS, SIR WILLIAM (1650/51-95), American shipbuilder and colonial governor **12** 283

PHOTIUS (circa 820-891), Byzantine patriarch **12** 283-284

PHYFE, DUNCAN (1768-1854), American cabinetmaker **12** 284-285

Physiology (science)
mechanistic theory of
Loeb, Jacques **22** 299-301
of nervous system
Hyde, Ida Henrietta **22** 252-254

PIAF, EDITH (Edith Giovanna Gassion; 1915-63), French music hall/cabaret singer **12** 285-287

PIAGET, JEAN (1896-1980), Swiss psychologist and educator **12** 287-288

PIANKHI (ruled circa 741-circa 712 B.C.), Nubian king **12** 288-289

Piano (musical instrument)
Ashkenazy, Vladimir **22** 24-26
Domino, Fats **22** 145-147

PIANO, RENZO (born 1937), Italian architect, lecturer, and designer **12** 289-291

PICABIA, FRANCIS (1879-1953), French artist, writer, and bon vivant **12** 291-292

PICASSO, PABLO (1881-1973), Spanish painter, sculptor, and graphic artist **12** 292-295

PICASSO, PALOMA (born 1949), Spanish fashion designer **12** 295-297

PICCARD, AUGUSTE (1884-1962), Swiss scientist **12** 297-298

PICCARD, JACQUES ERNEST JEAN (born 1922), Swiss explorer, scientist, oceanographer, and engineer **18** 320-322

PICKENS, THOMAS BOONE JR. (T. Boone Pickens; born 1928), American businessman **19** 284-286

PICKERING, EDWARD CHARLES (1846-1919), American astronomer **12** 298
Fleming, Williamina **22** 175-176

PICKERING, TIMOTHY (1745-1829), American Revolutionary soldier and statesman **12** 298-299

PICKETT, BILL (1870-1932), American rodeo cowboy **19** 286-288

PICKFORD, MARY (Gladys Louise Smith; 1893-1979), Canadian-American actress, screenwriter, and film producer **19** 288-290

PICO DELLA MIRANDOLA, CONTE GIOVANNI (1463-1494), Italian philosopher and humanist **12** 299-300

PIERCE, FRANKLIN (1804-1869), American statesman, president 1853-57 **12** 300-301

PIERCE, JOHN ROBINSON (born 1910), American electronics engineer and author **21** 349-351

PIERO DELLA FRANCESCA (circa 1415/20-92), Italian painter **12** 301-302

PIGOU, ARTHUR CECIL (1877-1959), English economist **12** 302

PIKE, ZEBULON (1779-1813), American soldier and explorer **12** 302-304

PILLSBURY, CHARLES ALFRED (1842-1899), American businessman **12** 304

PILON, GERMAIN (circa 1535-90), French sculptor **12** 305

PILSUDSKI, JOSEPH (1867-1935), Polish general, president 1918-21 **12** 305-306

PINCHBACK, PINCKNEY BENTON STEWART (1837-1921), African American politician **12** 306-308

PINCHOT, GIFFORD (1865-1946), American conservationist and public official **12** 308-309

PINCKNEY, CHARLES (1757-1824), American politician and diplomat **12** 309-310

PINCKNEY, CHARLES COTESWORTH (1745-1825), American statesman **12** 310

PINCUS, GREGORY GOODWIN (1903-1967), American biologist **12** 310-312

PINDAR (552/518-438 B.C.), Greek lyric poet **12** 312-313

PINEL, PHILIPPE (1745-1826), French physician **12** 313-314

PINERO, ARTHUR WING (1855-1934), English playwright **18** 322-324

PINKERTON, ALLEN (1819-1884), American detective **12** 314-315

PINKHAM, LYDIA ESTES (1819-1883), American patent medicine manufacturer **21** 351-353

PINKNEY, WILLIAM (1764-1822), American attorney, diplomat, and statesman **22** 355-357

PINOCHET UGARTE, AUGUSTO (born 1915), Chilean military leader and dictator **12** 315-317

PINTER, HAROLD (born 1930), English playwright **12** 317-318

PINTO, ISAAC (1720-1791), Jewish merchant and scholar **12** 318

PINZÓN, MARTIN ALONSO (1440?-1493), Spanish navigator **22** 358-360
Pinzón, Vicente Yáñez **22** 360-361

PINZÓN, VICENTE YÁÑEZ (1460?-1524?), Spanish navigator **22** 360-361
Pinzón, Martin Alonso **22** 358-360

PIO, PADRE (Francesco Forgione; 1887-1968), Italian priest **20** 297-299

PIPPIN, HORACE (1888-1946), African American painter **12** 318-319

PIRANDELLO, LUIGI (1867-1936), Italian playwright novelist, and critic **12** 319-321

SENDAK, MAURICE (born 1928),
American author, artist, and illustrator
19 329-331

SENECA THE YOUNGER, LUCIUS
ANNAEUS (circa 4 B.C.-A.D. 65),
Roman philosopher 14 103-105

Sengalese music
N'Dour, Youssou 22 338-340

SENFL, LUDWIG (circa 1486-circa
1543), Swiss-born German composer
14 105-106

SENGHOR, LÉOPOLD SÉDAR (born
1906), Senegalese poet, philosopher,
and statesman 14 106-107

SENNACHERIB (ruled 705-681 B.C.),
king of Assyria 14 108

SENNETT, MACK (1884-1960), American
film producer and director 14 108-109

SEQUOYAH (circa 1770-1843),
American Cherokee Indian scholar 14
110-111

Sergeant York (film)
Huston, John Marcellus 22 250-252

Serpico (film)
Lumet, Sidney 22 305-307

SERRA, JUNIPERO (Miguel José Serra;
1713-84), Spanish Franciscan
missionary, founder of California
missions 14 111-112

SERRANO ELÍAS, JORGE ANTONIO
(born 1945), president of Guatemala
(1991-1993) 14 112-113

SERTÜRNER, FRIEDRICH (Friedrich
Wilhelm Adam Ferdinand Sertürner;
1783-1841), Prussian pharmacist 21
379-381

SERVAN-SCHREIBER, JEAN-JACQUES
(born 1924), French journalist and
writer on public affairs 14 113-115

SERVETUS, MICHAEL (circa 1511-53),
Spanish religious philosopher 14
115-116

SESSHU, TOYA (1420-1506), Japanese
painter and Zen priest 14 116-117

SESSIONS, ROGER HUNTINGTON
(1896-1985), American composer 14
117-118

SETON, ELIZABETH ANN BAYLEY
(1774-1821), American Catholic leader
14 118-119

SETON, ERNEST THOMPSON (1860-
1946), Canadian author and co-
founder of the Boy Scouts of America
14 119-120

SETTIGNANO, DESIDERIO DA (1428/
31-1464), Italian sculptor 4 509

SEURAT, GEORGES PIERRE (1859-1891),
French painter 14 120-122

SEVAREID, ERIC (Arnold Eric Sevareid
1912-1992), American broadcast
journalist and author 22 395-397

SEVERINI, GINO (1883-1966), Italian
painter 14 122

SEVERUS, LUCIUS SEPTIMIUS (146-
211), Roman emperor 193-211 14
109-110

SEVIER, JOHN (1745-1815), American
frontiersman, soldier, and politician 14
122-123

SEWALL, SAMUEL (1652-1730),
American jurist and diarist 14 123-124

SEWARD, WILLIAM HENRY (1801-
1872), American statesman 14
124-125

SEXTON, ANNE (Anne Gray Harvey;
1928-74), American ''confessional''
poet 14 125-126

SEYMOUR, HORATIO (1810-1886),
American politician 14 126-127

SEYMOUR, JANE (1509-1537), third wife
and queen consort of Henry VIII of
England 18 367-368

SFORZA, LODOVICO (1452-1508), duke
of Milan 14 127-128

SHABAKA (ruled circa 712-circa 696
B.C.), Nubian king, pharaoh of Egypt
14 130

SHABAZZ, BETTY (1936-1997), African
American educator, activist, and health
administrator 14 130-132

SHACKLETON, SIR ERNEST HENRY
(1874-1922), British explorer 14
132-133

SHAFFER, PETER LEVIN (born 1926),
English/American playwright 14
133-135

SHAFTESBURY, 1ST EARL OF (Anthony
Ashley Cooper; 1621-83), English
statesman 14 135-136

SHAFTESBURY, 3D EARL OF (Anthony
Ashley Cooper; 1671-1713), English
moral philosopher 14 136-137

SHAFTESBURY, 7TH EARL OF (Anthony
Ashley Cooper; 1801-85), English
social reformer 14 137-138

SHAH JAHAN (1592-1666), Mogul
emperor of India 1628-58 14 138-139

SHAHN, BEN (1898-1969), American
painter, graphic artist, and
photographer 14 139-140

SHAHPUR II (310-379), king of Persia
14 140-141

SHAKA (circa 1787-1828), African Zulu
military monarch 14 141-142

SHAKESPEARE, WILLIAM (1564-1616),
English playwright, poet, and actor 14
142-145

SHALIKASHVILI, JOHN MALCHASE
DAVID (born 1936), chairman of the
U.S. Joint Chiefs of Staff 14 145-147

SHAMIR, YITZCHAK (Yizernitsky; born
1914), Israeli prime minister and
leader of the Likud Party 14 147-149

SHAMMAI (flourished 1st century B.C.),
Jewish sage 14 149

SHANG YANG (circa 390-338 B.C.),
Chinese statesman and political
philosopher 14 149-150

SHANKARA (Shankaracharya; circa 788-
820), Indian philosopher and reformer
14 150-151

SHANKAR, RAVI (Robindra Shankar;
born 1920), Indian musician 22
397-399

SHANKER, ALBERT (1928-1977),
American education leader 14
151-153

SHANNON, CLAUDE ELWOOD (born
1916), American mathematician 14
153-154

SHAPEY, RALPH (born 1921), American
composer, conductor, and teacher 14
154-155

SHAPLEY, HARLOW (1885-1972),
American astronomer 14 155-156
Hogg, Helen Battles Sawyer 22
244-247

SHARIATI, ALI (1933-1977), ''Ideologue
of the Iranian Revolution'' 14 156-157

SHARIF, NAWAZ (Niam Nawaz Sharif;
born 1949), Pakistani prime minister
19 331-333

SHARON, ARIEL (Arik; born 1928),
Israeli politician and defense minister
14 157-159

SHARPTON, AL (born 1954), African
American civil rights leader and
minister 14 159-162

SHAW, ANNA HOWARD (1847-1919),
American suffragist leader, reformer,
and women's rights activist 14
162-163

SHAW, GEORGE BERNARD (1856-
1950), British playwright, critic, and
pamphleteer 14 163-164

SHAW, LEMUEL (1781-1861), American
jurist 14 164-165

SHAW, MARY (born 1943), American
computer science professor 14
165-167

SWEELINCK, JAN PIETERSZOON (1562-1621), Dutch composer, organist, and teacher 15 50-51

SWIFT, GUSTAVUS FRANKLIN (1839-1903), American businessman 22 407-409

SWIFT, JONATHAN (1667-1745), English-Irish poet, political writer, and clergyman 15 51-54

SWINBURNE, ALGERNON CHARLES (1837-1909), English poet, dramatist, and critic 15 54-55

SWITZER, MARY E. (1900-1971), American champion of rehabilitation 15 55-56

SWOPE, GERARD (1872-1957), president of General Electric 15 56-58

SYDENHAM, BARON (Charles Edward Poulett Thomson; 1799-1841), English merchant and politician 15 59-60

SYDENHAM, THOMAS (1624-1689), English physician 15 59-60

SYED AHMED KHAN (1817-1898), Moslem religious leader, educationalist, and politician 15 60

SYLVIS, WILLIAM (1828-1869), American labor leader 15 60-61

SYNGE, EDMUND JOHN MILLINGTON (1871-1909), Irish dramatist 15 61-62

SZENT-GYÖRGYI, ALBERT VON (1893-1986), Hungarian-American biochemist 15 62-64

SZILARD, LEO (1898-1964), Hungarian-born nuclear physicist 15 64-66

SZOLD, HENRIETTA (1860-1945), American Jewish leader 15 66-67

SZYMANOWSKI, KAROL (1882-1937), Polish composer 15 67-68

T

TABARI, MUHAMMAD IBN JARIR AL- (839-923), Moslem historian and religious scholar 15 69-70

TABOR, HORACE AUSTIN WARNER (1830-1899), American mining magnate and politician 15 70

TACITUS (56/57-circa 125), Roman orator and historian 15 70-72

TAEUBER-ARP, SOPHIE (1889-1943), Swiss-born painter, designer, and dancer 15 73-74

TAEWON'GUN, HŬNGSON (1820-1898), Korean imperial regent 15 74-75

TAFAWA BALEWA, SIR ABUBAKAR (1912-1966), Nigerian statesman, prime minister 1957-1966 15 75

TAFT, LORADO (1860-1936), American sculptor 15 75-76

TAFT, ROBERT ALPHONSO (1889-1953), American senator 15 76-78

TAFT, WILLIAM HOWARD (1857-1930), American statesman, president 1909-1913 15 78-81

TAGORE, RABINDRANATH (1861-1941), Bengali poet, philosopher, social reformer, and dramatist 12 529-531

TAHARQA (reigned circa 688-circa 663 B.C.), Nubian pharaoh of Egypt 15 81-82

TAINE, HIPPOLYTE ADOLPHE (1828-1893), French critic and historian 15 82-83

T'AI-TSUNG, T'ANG (600-649), Chinese emperor 15 83-84

TAKAHASHI, KOREKIYO (1854-1936), Japanese statesman 15 84-85

TAL, JOSEF (Josef Gruenthal; born 1910), Israeli composer, pianist, and professor of music 15 85-86

TALBERT, MARY MORRIS BURNETT (1866-1923), American educator, feminist, civil rights activist, and lecturer 15 86-88

TALLCHIEF, MARIA (born 1925), Native American prima ballerina 15 88-89

TALLEYRAND, CHARLES MAURICE DE (Duc de Tallyrand-Périgord; 1754-1838), French statesman 15 89-90

TALLIS, THOMAS (circa 1505-85), English composer and organist 15 91

TALON, JEAN (1626-1694), French intendant of New France 15 91-92

TAMBO, OLIVER REGINALD (1917-1993), serves as acting president of the African National Congress 15 92-94

TAMERLANE (1336-1405), Turko-Mongol conqueror 15 94-95

TAN, AMY (born 1952), American author 15 95-96

TANAKA, KAKUEI (1918-1993), prime minister of Japan (1972-1974) 15 96-98

TANEY, ROGER BROOKE (1777-1864), American political leader, chief justice of U.S. Supreme Court 15 98-99

TANGE, KENZO (born 1913), Japanese architect and city planner 15 99-101

TANGUY, YVES (1900-1955), French painter 15 101

TANIZAKI, JUNICHIRO (1886-1965), Japanese novelist, essayist, and playwright 15 101-102

TANNER, HENRY OSSAWA (1859-1937), African American painter 15 102-103

T'AO CH'IEN (365-427), Chinese poet 15 104-105

TAO-AN (312-385), Chinese Buddhist monk 15 103-104

TAO-HSÜAN (596-667), Chinese Buddhist monk 15 105

TAPPAN BROTHERS (19th century), American merchants and reformers 15 105-106

TAQI KHAN AMIR-E KABIR, MIRZA (circa 1806-52), Iranian statesman 15 106-107

TARBELL, IDA MINERVA (1857-1944), American journalist 15 107-108

TARDE, JEAN GABRIEL (1843-1904), French philosopher and sociologist 15 108-109

TARKINGTON, NEWTON BOOTH (1869-1946), American author 15 109

TARLETON, SIR BANASTRE (1754-1833), English soldier; fought in American Revolution 15 110

TARSKI, ALFRED (1902-1983), Polish-American mathematician and logician 15 110-111

TARTAGLIA, NICCOLO (1500-1557), Italian mathematician 15 111-112

TARTINI, GIUSEPPE (1692-1770), Italian violinist, composer, and theorist 15 112-113

TASMAN, ABEL JANSZOON (circa 1603-59), Dutch navigator 15 113-114

TASSO, TORQUATO (1544-1595), Italian poet 15 114-116

TATE, ALLEN (1899-1979), American poet, critic and editor 15 116

TATLIN, VLADIMIR EVGRAFOVICH (1885-1953), Russian avant garde artist 15 117-118

TATI, JACQUES (Jacques Tatischeff; 1908-1982), French actor and director 22 410-412

TAUSSIG, HELEN BROOKE (1898-1986), American physician 15 118-120

TAWNEY, RICHARD HENRY (1880-1962), British economic historian and social philosopher 15 120-121

TAYLOR, BROOK (1685-1731), English mathematician 15 121-122

VON STROHEIM, ERICH (Erich Oswald Stroheim; 1885-1957), Austrian actor and director **21** 418-420

VONDEL, JOOST VAN DEN (1587-1679), Dutch poet and dramatist **16** 19-20

VONNEGUT, KURT, JR. (born 1922), American author **16** 25-27

VORSTER, BALTHAZAR JOHANNES (1915-1983), South African political leader **16** 30-32

VOS SAVANT, MARILYN (born 1946), American columnist and consultant **16** 32-33

VUILLARD, JEAN ÉDOUARD (1868-1940), French painter **16** 36

VYSHINSKY, ANDREI (1883-1954), state prosecutor in Stalin's purge trials and head of the U.S.S.R.'s foreign ministry (1949-1953) **16** 36-37

W

WAALS, JOHANNES DIDERIK VAN DER (1837-1923), Dutch physicist **15** 417-418

WADE, BENJAMIN FRANKLIN (1800-1878), American lawyer and politician **16** 38-39

WAGNER, HONUS (Johannes Peter Wagner; 1874-1955), American baseball player **20** 393-395

WAGNER, OTTO (1841-1918), Austrian architect and teacher **16** 39-40

WAGNER, RICHARD (1813-1883), German operatic composer **16** 40-43

WAGNER, ROBERT F. (1910-1991), New York City Tammany Hall mayor (1954-1965) **16** 44-45

WAGNER, ROBERT FERDINAND (1877-1953), American lawyer and legislator **16** 43

WAINWRIGHT, JONATHAN MAYHEW (1883-1953), American general **16** 45-46

WAITE, MORRISON REMICK (1816-1888), American jurist, chief justice of U.S. Supreme Court 1874-88 **16** 46

WAITE, TERRY (born 1939), official of the Church of England and hostage in Lebanon **16** 47-48

WAKEFIELD, EDWARD GIBBON (1796-1862), British colonial reformer and promoter **16** 48-49

WAKSMAN, SELMAN ABRAHAM (1888-1973), American microbiologist **16** 49-50

WALCOTT, DEREK ALTON (born 1930), West Indian poet and dramatist **16** 50-51

WALD, GEORGE (born 1906), American biochemist interested in vision **16** 51-53

WALD, LILLIAN (1867-1940), American social worker and reformer **16** 53-54

WALDEMAR IV (Wlademar Atterdag; 1320-1375), King of Denmark, 1340-1375 **20** 395-397

WALDHEIM, KURT (born 1918), Austrian statesman and president **16** 54-55

WALDO, PETER (flourished 1170-84), French religious leader **16** 55-56

WALDSEEMÜLLER, MARTIN (circa 1470-circa 1518), German geographer and cartographer **16** 56

WALESA, LECH (born 1943), Polish Solidarity leader and former president **16** 57-59

WALKER, ALICE MALSENIOR (born 1944), African American novelist, poet, and short story writer **16** 59-61

WALKER, MADAME C. J. (Sarah Breedlove; 1867-1919), African American entrepreneur **16** 61-62

WALKER, DAVID (1785-1830), African American pamphleteer and activist **16** 62-63

WALKER, JOSEPH REDDEFORD (1798-1876), American fur trader **16** 63-64

WALKER, LEROY TASHREAU (born 1918), U.S. sports official, university chancellor, educator, and track coach **16** 64-65

WALKER, MAGGIE LENA (1867-1934), American entrepreneur and civic leader **16** 65-66

WALKER, MARGARET (born 1915), American novelist, poet, scholar, and teacher **16** 67

WALKER, ROBERT JOHN (1801-1869), American politician **16** 67-68

WALKER, WILLIAM (1824-1860), American adventurer and filibuster **16** 68-69

WALLACE, ALFRED RUSSEL (1823-1913), English naturalist and traveler **16** 69-70

WALLACE, DeWITT (1889-1981), American publisher and founder of *Reader's Digest* **16** 70-71

WALLACE, GEORGE CORLEY (1919-1998), American political leader **16** 71-72

WALLACE, HENRY (1836-1916), American agricultural publicist and editor **16** 73

WALLACE, HENRY AGARD (1888-1965), American statesman, vice-president 1940-44 **16** 73-74

WALLACE, LEWIS (1827-1905), American general and author **16** 74-75

WALLACE, SIR WILLIAM (circa 1270-1305), Scottish soldier **16** 75-76

WALLACE-JOHNSON, ISAAC THEOPHILUS AKUNNA (1895-1965), West African political leader and pan-Africanist **16** 76-77

WALLAS, GRAHAM (1858-1932), English sociologist and political scientist **16** 77-78

WALLENBERG, RAOUL (1912-?), Swedish diplomat **16** 78-80

WALLENSTEIN, ALBRECHT WENZEL EUSEBIUS VON (1583-1634), Bohemian soldier of fortune **16** 80-81

WALLER, THOMAS WRIGHT (Fats; 1904-43), American jazz singer, pianist, organist, bandleader, and composer **16** 81-82

WALPOLE, ROBERT (1st Earl of Oxford; 1676-1745), English statesman **16** 82-84

WALRAS, MARIE ESPRIT LÉON (1834-1910), French economist **16** 84-85

WALSH, STELLA (Stanislawa Walasiewiczowna; 1911-1980), Polish American athlete **19** 404-406

WALSH, THOMAS JAMES (1859-1933), American statesman **16** 85-86

WALTER, JOHANN (1496-1570), German composer **16** 86

WALTERS, BARBARA (born 1931), American network newscast anchor **16** 86-88

WALTON, ERNEST (1903-1995), Irish physicist **16** 88-90

WALTON, IZAAK (1593-1683), English writer and biographer **16** 90-91

WALTON, SAM MOORE (1918-1992), American businessman who co-founded Wal-Mart **16** 91-92

WALTON, SIR WILLIAM TURNER (1902-1983), English composer **16** 91-92

WANG, AN (1920-1990), Chinese-American inventor, electronics expert, and businessman **16** 93-95

WANG AN-SHIH (1021-1086), Chinese reformer, poet, and scholar **16** 95-97